DTT	dithiothreitol	HCFA	Health Care Financing Administration
EACA	epsilon aminocaproic acid		
EBAA	Eye Bank Association of America	Hct	hematocrit
EBV	Epstein-Barr virus	HCV	hepatitis C virus
ECMO	extracorporeal membrane oxygenation	HDN	hemolytic disease of the newborn
		HDV	hepatitis D virus
EDTA	ethylenediaminetetraacetic acid	HES	hydroxyethyl starch
EIA	enzyme immunoassay	HEV	hepatitis E virus
ELAT	enzyme-linked antiglobulin test	HPC	hematopoietic progenitor cell
ELBW	extremely low-birthweight	HIV	human immunodeficiency virus
ELISA	enzyme-linked immunosorbent assay	HTLA	high-titer, low avidity
		HTLV-I	human T-cell lymphotropic virus type I
EPO	erythropoietin		
ESR	erythrocyte sedimentation rate	HTR	hemolytic transfusion reaction
FDA	Food and Drug Administration	HUS	hemolytic uremic syndrome
FFP	Fresh Frozen Plasma	IAT	indirect antiglobulin test
FMH	fetomaternal hemorrhage	Ig	immunoglobulin
FNH	febrile nonhemolytic	IHA	immune hemolytic anemia
FTA-ABS	fluorescent treponemal antibody absorption test	IL-1α	interleukin 1 alpha
		IL-1ß	interleukin 1 beta
5-FU	5-fluorouracil	IL-2	interleukin 2
G-CSF	granulocyte colony-stimulating factors	IPT	intraperitoneal route
		IS	immediate spin
GalNAc	N-acetylgalactosamine	ISBT	International Society of Blood Transfusion
GM-CSF	granulocyte macrophage colony-stimulating factors		
		ITP	idiopathic thrombocytopenic purpura
GMP	good manufacturing practice		
Gp	glycoprotein	IUT	intrauterine transfusion
GPA	glycophorin A	IVIG	intravenous immunoglobulin
GPB	glycophorin B	IVT	intravascular approach
GPC	glycophorin C	JCAHO	Joint Commission on Accreditation of Healthcare Organizations
GPD	glycophorin D		
GVHD	graft-vs-host disease	L/S	lecithin to sphingomyelin
Gy	Gray	LDH	lactate dehydrogenase
HAM	HTLV-associated myelopathy	LDL	low-density lipoproteins
HAV	hepatitis A virus	LISS	low ionic strength saline
HAZMAT	hazardous material	LTC-IC	long-term culture-initiating cells
Hb	hemoglobin	MAC	membrane attack complex
HBc	hepatitis B core antigen	2-ME	2-mercaptoethanol
HBIG	hepatitis B immunoglobulin	MF	mixed field
HBsAg	hepatitis B surface antigen	MHC	major histocompatibility complex
HBV	hepatitis B virus	MIRL	membrane inhibitor of reactive lysis
4-HC	4-hydroperoxycyclophosphamide	MLC	mixed lymphocyte (leukocyte) culture

MLR	mixed lymphocyte (leukocyte) reaction
MoAb	monoclonal antibody
mRNA	messenger ribonucleic acid
MSBOS	maximum surgical blood order schedule
MSDS	material safety data sheets
NAIT	neonatal alloimmune thrombocytopenia
NAT	nucleic acid test(ing)
NATP	neonatal alloimmune thrombocytopenic purpura
NCCLS	National Committee for Clinical Laboratory Standards
NIH	National Institutes of Health
NK	natural killer
NMDP	National Marrow Donor Program
NRC	Nuclear Regulatory Commission
NT	not tested
OSHA	Occupational Safety and Health Administration
p	probability
PBPC	peripheral blood progenitor cell
PBS	phosphate-buffered saline
PCH	paroxysmal cold hemoglobinuria
PCR	polymerase chain reaction
PEG	polyethylene glycol
PHA	phytohemagglutinin
PI	paternity index
PPE	personal protective equipment
PPF	plasma protein fraction
PT	prothrombin time or proficiency test
PTP	posttransfusion purpura
PUBS	percutaneous umbilical blood sampling
PVC	polyvinyl chloride
QA	quality assessment or quality assurance
QC	quality control
QSE	quality system essential

RBCs	Red Blood Cells (blood donor unit)
RCA	regulators of complement activation
RES	reticuloendothelial system
RFLP	restriction fragment length polymorphism
Rh	Rhesus factor
RhIG	Rh Immune Globulin
RIBA	recombinant immunoblot assay
RNA	ribonucleic acid
RPGN	rapidly progressive glomerulonephritis
RPR	rapid plasma reagin (serologic test for syphilis)
RR	repeatedly reactive or relative risk
RT	room temperature
SBO	standard blood order
SCF	stem cell factor
SGP	sialoglycoprotein
SOP	standard operating procedure
SPA	staphylococcal protein A
SSO	sequence-specific oligonucleotide
STS	serologic test for syphilis
TA	transfusion-associated
TCR	T-cell receptor
TPE	therapeutic plasma exchange
TRALI	transfusion-related acute lung injury
tRNA	transfer ribonucleic acid
TNF-α	tumor necrosis factor alpha
TTP	thrombotic thrombocytopenic purpura
UNOS	United Network of Organ Sharing
VLBW	very low-birthweight
VNTR	variable numbers of tandem repeats
vWD	von Willebrand's disease
vWF	von Willebrand factor
WAIHA	warm autoimmune hemolytic anemia
WB	Whole Blood or Western blot
XM	crossmatch

TECHNICAL MANUAL

13TH EDITION

aaBB AMERICAN ASSOCIATION OF BLOOD BANKS

To purchase additional copies of this book, please call our sales department at (301)215-6499 or fax orders to (301)907-6895. AABB sales representatives are available from 8:30 am to 5:00 pm, ET, Monday through Friday, for telephone access. For other book services, including chapter reprints and large quantity sales, ask for the Senior Sales Associate.

Visit the American Association of Blood Banks Web site on the Internet at www.aabb.org or e-mail our sales department at sales@aabb.org.

Mention of specific products or equipment by contributors to this AABB publication does not represent an endorsement of such products by the AABB nor does it necessarily indicate a preference for those products over other similar competitive products. Any forms and/or procedures in this book are examples. AABB does not imply or guarantee that the materials meet federal, state, or other applicable requirements. It is incumbent on the reader who intends to use any information, forms, policies, or procedures contained in this publication to evaluate such materials for use in light of particular circumstances associated with their institution.

Efforts are made to have publications of the AABB consistent in regard to acceptable practices. However, for several reasons, they may not be. First, as new developments in the practice of blood banking occur, changes may be recommended to the *Standards for Blood Banks and Transfusion Services*. It is not possible, however, to revise each publication at the time such a change is adopted. Thus, it is essential that the most recent edition of the *Standards* be consulted as a reference in regard to current acceptable practices. Second, the views expressed in this publication represent the opinions of authors. The publication of this book does not constitute an endorsement by the AABB of any view expressed herein, and the AABB expressly disclaims any liability arising from any inaccuracy or misstatement.

13TH EDITION

TECHNICAL MANUAL

aa BB AMERICAN ASSOCIATION OF BLOOD BANKS

8101 GLENBROOK ROAD   BETHESDA, MARYLAND 20814

American Association of Blood Banks
8101 Glenbrook Road
Bethesda, Maryland 20814-2749

ISBN No. 1-56395-115-0
Printed in the United States

 Text paper meets EPA guidelines for minimum recovered material content (50% recycled fiber, including 10% postconsumer waste).

Technical Manual Committee

Virginia Vengelen-Tyler, MBA, MT(ASCP)SBB, CQA(ASQ)
Chair and Editor

Mark E. Brecher, MD
Suzanne H. Butch, MT(ASCP)SBB
Alana R. Calhoun, MT(ASCP)SBB
Eberhard Walter Fiebig, MD
Lawrence Tim Goodnough, MD
Linda Hahn, MPM, MT(ASCP)SBB
Daniel J. Ladd, MD
Linda McKenna, MT(ASCP)
Hans J. Peters, MD
Steven R. Pierce, SBB(ASCP)
Patricia Pisciotto, MD
Ann Rearden, MD
Susan F. South, MAOM, MT(ASCP)SBB
Jill R. Storry, MS, FIBMS

Liaisons

Mary Gustafson, MT(ASCP)SBB
Food and Drug Administration

Michael Fitzpatrick, PhD, MT(ASCP)
Department of Defense

Acknowledgments

The Technical Manual Committee extends special thanks to those volunteers who reviewed the manuscripts and made other contributions:

Maureen E. Ahler, MT(ASCP)

Mae E. Allen, PhD, MT(ASCP)

Robert W. Allen, PhD

James P. AuBuchon, MD

Harvey J. Alter, MD

Peter J. Bianchine, MD

Celso Bianco, MD

Peggy Brown, PhD, MT(ASCP)SBB

Michael P. Busch, MD, PhD

Ann Church, MT(ASCP)SBB

Judy Ellen Ciaraldi, MT(ASCP)SBB

Gail Coghlan, RT, BSc

Martha Rae Combs, BS, MT(ASCP)SBB

Gilliam Conley, SBB(ASCP)

Brian Curtis, MS, MT(ASCP)SBB

Geoff Daniels, PhD

Phillip J. DeChristopher, MD, PhD

Nicole DeLong, MS, MT(ASCP)SBB

Marian Dynis, RN

Michelle Evans, DrPH

Minoru Fukuda, PhD

George Garratty, PhD, FIBMS, FRCPath

Frankie Gibbs, MT(ASCP)SBB

Gary A. Gochman, MD

Brenda J. Grossman, MD

Emmanuel Hackel, PhD

N. Rebecca Haley, MD, MT(ASCP)SBB

Teresa Harris, BA, MT(ASCP)SBB

Nora V. Hirschler, MD

Sallie Holliman, MT(ASCP)SBB

Leslie Holness, MD

Janet Ishimoto, MT(ASCP)SBB

Susan T. Johnson, MT(ASCP)SBB

W. John Judd, FIBMS, MIBiol

Sherwin V. Kevy, MD

Donna Killian, RT(CLST)

Mary Kowalski, MT(ASCP)SBB

Margot Kruskall, MD

C. Lee Landman, MT

Lauralynn K. Lebeck, PhD, MS, MT(ASCP)SBB

Judy Levitt, MT(ASCP)SBB

Jeanne V. Linden, MD

Naomi L.C. Luban, MD

Ricki A. Miller, BS, MT(ASCP)SBB

Kenneth Moise, Jr., MD

Terri G. Monk, MD

Joanne Moore, MT(ASCP)SBB

Gary Moroff, PhD

Tania Motschman, MS, MT(ASCP)SBB, CQA(ASQ)

Marilyn Moulds, BS, MT(ASCP)SBB

Scott Murphy, MD

Sandra Nance, MS, MT(ASCP)SBB

Paul M. Ness, MD

Steve Noga, MD

Helen Owen, RN

Sharon Phelan, MD

Alvara Pineda, MD

Betsy Poindexter

Mark A. Popovsky, MD

Thomas H. Price, MD

Marion E. Reid, PhD, FIBMS

Heather Russell, MBA, MT(ASCP)SBB, CQA(ASQ)

Christina M. Santos, MT(ASCP)SBB

Susan B. Schoultz, BS, MT(ASCP)SH

Arell Shapiro, MD

Sue Shirey, MS, MT(ASCP)SBB

Don Siegel, MD, PhD

Toby Simon, MD

Leigh C. Sims, BS, MT(ASCP)

James Smith, MD, PhD

Louise Smith, MPA, MT(ASCP)SBB

Janice Davis-Sproul, MAS, MT(ASCP)SBB

Margaret J. Stoe, MT(ASCP)SBB

Patricia Tippett, PhD

Darrell Triulzi, MD

Phyllis Walker, MS, MT(ASCP)SBB

Robert Weinstein, MD

Frances Widmann, MD

Judith E. Woll, MD

Wylen Won, MT(ASCP)SBB

Roslyn Yomtovian, MD

Monica Yu, MT(ASCP)SBB

Teresa Zelinski, PhD

The staff of the Transplantation and Transfusion Service, McClendon Clinical Laboratories, UNC Hospitals

Introduction

The 13th edition of the *Technical Manual* and the 19th edition of the *Standards for Blood Banks and Transfusion Services* have been coordinated in their release dates. Change, which has become a fact of life, is very evident in both of the above documents. Foremost among the changes is the emphasis on quality in all aspects of transfusion and transplantation medicine. Perhaps this is best reflected in the changes to Chapter 1, Quality Systems. This chapter introduces the book with a description of the 10 Quality System Essentials (QSEs) that make up Section A in the newest series of standards published by the American Association of Blood Banks. Implementation processes or examples of the QSEs are apparent in most of the chapters of this book.

Comments from readers led to the inclusion of an appendix in Chapter 1 describing suggested quality control testing intervals. This is an updated version of the table found in the 6th edition of the AABB *Accreditation Requirements Manual*, published in 1995. Additional comments from readers resulted in the extensive updating of Chapter 2, Facilities and Safety. Readers will find new material on blood-borne pathogens, biohazardous waste management, and chemical safety, including valuable tables on incidental spill responses, classifications of chemicals, and how to work safely with chemicals in various categories. Appendices include web site addresses for the safety resources, and extensive information on personal protective equipment.

The reorganization of the blood components chapter has resulted in two separate chapters. Chapter 7 now covers the laboratory aspect of donor testing and labeling and Chapter 8 covers the processes of preparing, storing, shipping, and transporting these blood components. Chapter 8 also includes helpful appendices on quality control monitors and required and suggested component quality control.

A new chapter on platelet and granulocyte antigens and antibodies is included in this edition. Chapter 16 covers the biochemical structure and serologic testing of platelet and granulocyte antigens and antibodies. Some adverse consequences of transfusion, such as platelet refractoriness and platelet alloimmunization, are a few of the other topics covered in this chapter.

Additional updates to each chapter are too numerous to list. A few highlights include discussions on the administrative aspects of pretransfusion testing in Chapter 18; a discussion on new technologies and processes for collection and transplantation of hematopoietic progenitor cells in Chapter 25; an expanded table on the categories and management of adverse transfusion reactions in Chapter 27; and an update on hepatitis viruses and new and emerging tests for transfusion-transmitted viruses in Chapter 28. The methods sections were reorganized by consolidating many of the serologic methods.

The previous edition of the *Technical Manual* introduced a CD-ROM of the *Technical Manual* and the *Standards for Blood Banks and Transfusion Services,* editions 1-17. The new CD-ROM keeps the 12th edition of the *Technical Manual* with its links to the 17th edition of *Standards*, as well as all editions of *Standards for Blood Banks and Transfusion Services*, now through edition 19. Added to the new CD-ROM is the 13th edition of the *Technical Manual*, with its links to the 19th edition of *Standards*.

Finally, I would like to thank the members of the Technical Manual Committee for their dedication and hard work in collecting the data and implementing the changes in this edition. I would also like to thank all the liaisons to other committees who have offered numerous helpful suggestions, to the readers who have submitted comments and suggestions, and to the expert reviewers who are listed in this book. Special thanks go to the associate editors, Patricia Pisciotto, MD; Mark Brecher, MD; and Steven Pierce, SBB(ASCP). In addition to working on their assigned chapters, they helped review the completed sections for continuity and accuracy. Additional thanks go to Mark Brecher, MD, for his added reviews and expert directions on many issues of this manual. And last but certainly not least, I am grateful to the staff of the American Association of Blood Banks for their work on the many administrative functions involved in the publication of this book. Special thanks go to Laurie Munk, staff liaison to the Committee and AABB Director of Publications, for her tenacity in moving the book forward over the 3 years of development and for her skills and knowledge of the editorial process.

Virginia Vengelen-Tyler,
MBA, MT(ASCP)SBB, CQA(ASQ)
Committee Chair and Editor

Contents

Blood Donation and Collection

Immunologic and Genetic Principles

Blood Groups

Serologic Principles and Transfusion Medicine

Clinical Considerations in Transfusion Practice

Methods

Appendices

1

Quality Systems

QUALITY, IN ALL ASPECTS OF CARE and services, is the primary goal of blood centers and transfusion services. Many discrete activities, such as quality control of reagents, staff competence, laboratory proficiency testing programs, procedures for equipment maintenance, and documentation of error and accident investigations, are standard practice. Thus, for many organizations the foundations for a quality system have been in place for some time. Use of quality and operational systems guided by a quality program is changing the approach to quality issues from detection to prevention.

Quality programs encompass quality control (QC), quality assurance (QA), and quality improvement into a broad-based program that ensures application of quality principles throughout the operational areas of an organization.

The following regulatory agencies have established requirements for quality assurance:

- Health Care Financing Administration (HCFA). The CLIA '88 regulation (published as 42 CFR 493) requires laboratories to establish and follow a quality assurance program.[1]

- Food and Drug Administration. In addition to the blood product requirements in 21 CFR 606,[2] the requirements in 21 CFR 211.22[3] describe an independent quality control or quality assurance unit that has responsibility for the overall quality of the finished product and the authority to control processes that may affect this product.

The following accrediting agencies also have requirements for quality assurance:

■ American Association of Blood Banks
■ Joint Commission on the Accreditation of Healthcare Organizations (JCAHO)
■ College of American Pathologists (CAP)

Business and industry have used the International Organization of Standardization (ISO) standards to describe the elements of a quality system.

The AABB Quality System Essentials (QSEs)[4] were developed to be consistent with ISO standards and the FDA *Guidelines for Quality Assurance in Blood Establishments*.[5] The AABB QSEs are compatible with the ISO 9000 series of standards, and implementation of the AABB QSEs is a good starting point for any facility interested in acquiring ISO certification. Table 1-1 shows a comparison of AABB QSEs and ISO 9000 requirements.[4,6] The QSEs include the following:

1. Organization
2. Personnel
3. Equipment
4. Supplier issues
5. Process control, final inspection, and handling
6. Documents and records
7. Incidents, errors, and accidents
8. Assessments: internal and external
9. Process improvement
10. Facilities and safety

The remainder of this chapter discusses the 10 AABB QSEs and provides important information facilities should consider when developing their quality systems.

Organization

The first QSE relates to facility management, which must be organized in a manner that promotes the implementation of an effective quality management system. The structure of the organization must be defined to clearly identify the responsibilities for the provision of blood, blood components, products, and services. This structure must also clearly define the relationship of the position(s) responsible for key quality functions to the rest of the organization.

Management must demonstrate active support of the goals, objectives, and policies of the quality function. The quality function should be overseen by a designated person who reports to management; the quality system shall address all matters related to compliance with federal, state, and local regulations and AABB standards identified by the organization to facilitate its operations. The quality function has the authority to recommend corrective action when appropriate and initiate corrective action as appropriate.[5]

Each facility can define its structure in any format that suits its operations. Organizational trees or charts that show the relationships, including operational individuals responsible for quality function, are helpful. The facility's mission or vision statement must show support of its quality functions, and there should be active participation by management in the review and approval of quality and technical policies, processes, and procedures.

The person designated to oversee the quality function has the responsibility to coordinate, monitor, and facilitate quality assurance activities.[5] Depending on the size and scope of the organization, the designated QA person may work within a department (eg, laboratory or transfusion service), may have responsibilities covering several areas, or may be part of an organization-wide unit. Individuals acting as the designated QA person should not have final oversight of work they have performed (21 CFR 211.194).

QA functions could include the following[5]:

■ Review and approval of the operational units' standard operating procedures (SOPs) and training plans and/or development of the procedures.

■ Review and approval of validation and revalidation plans and results.

Table 1-1. Comparison of the AABB Quality System Essentials and the ISO 9000 Categories*

AABB Quality System Essentials	ISO 9000/9001
1. Organization	4.1 Management responsibility 4.2 Quality system
2. Personnel	4.18 Training
3. Equipment	4.11 Inspection, measuring and test equipment
4. Supplier issues	4.3 Contract review 4.6 Purchasing 4.7 Customer-supplied product
5. Process control, final inspection, and handling	4.4 Design control 4.8 Production identification and traceability 4.9 Process control 4.10 Inspection and testing 4.12 Inspection and test status 4.15 Handling, storage, packaging 4.20 Statistical techniques
6. Documents and records	4.5 Document and data control 4.16 Control of quality records
7. Incidents, errors, and accidents	4.13 Control of nonconforming product
8. Assessments: internal and external	4.17 Internal quality audits
9. Process improvement	4.14 Corrective and preventive action
10. Facilities and safety	[4.9(b) Process control, inferred] 4.19 Servicing

* This comparison is only one way of looking at the two systems.

- Review and approval of document control and record-keeping systems.
- Approval of lot release, ie, the review of all operations or manufacturing records and the decision whether to distribute, quarantine, or discard blood and blood components.
- Audit of operational functions.
- Review and approval of reports of adverse reactions, errors and accidents, deviations, and customer complaints.
- Participation in a material review board, ie, an interdisciplinary group of management staff with authority to review deviations in supplies received or in the blood manufacturing process and to determine suitability for use or distribution based on a documented decision-making process.
- Review and approval of corrective action plans.
- Development of criteria for evaluating systems and identifying trends so that changes can be made before a situation worsens and products are affected.
- Surveillance of problems, eg, error reports, Form FDA 483 observations, customer complaints, and the effectiveness of corrective actions implemented to solve these problems.
- Preparation of yearly reports of findings, and corrective and preventive actions.

- Review and approval of suppliers.
- Review and approval of product specifications, ie, requirements to be met by the products used in the manufacturing, distribution, or transfusion of blood and blood components.

Policies, processes, and procedures must exist to define the roles and responsibilities of all staff in the development and maintenance of these QA goals. Policies should define quality processes (ie, the QSE or ISO elements) as they transcend departments or work areas, define responsible people, and provide a documentation system to maintain and retrieve records.

Personnel

This QSE addresses personnel management. Each blood bank, transfusion service, or donor center must have a process in place to hire qualified personnel who have appropriate education, training, and experience to ensure competent performance of assigned duties.[7(p2)] The facility's requirements must be compatible with the established CLIA '88 personnel qualifications and training requirements for laboratory staff.[3]

Job descriptions should exist for all personnel involved in any aspect of the quality functions of the transfusion service or donor center. Effective job descriptions will clearly define the qualifications for the job and the responsibilities and reporting relationships of the position. The selection process for personnel should be based on the applicant's qualifications for a particular position as determined by licensure, education, or training qualifications.

Once a person is hired, there must be a well-defined program that introduces the new employee to the position. This orientation program could include facility-specific requirements, and an introduction to facility programs for safety, blood-borne pathogens, facility security, cGMP training, etc. The job-related portion of the orientation program should cover the technical aspects of the job. All aspects of training must be documented to identify the areas covered and the joint approval of the training by the facility trainer and the employee. At this point the employee must be given the opportunity to ask questions and seek additional help or clarification on processes. The ultimate result of this orientation is to deem new employees competent to work independently to perform the duties and responsibilities defined in their job descriptions. Time frames need to be established to accomplish this goal, and the employee and the facility trainer should mutually agree upon the determination of competency.

The facility must have regularly scheduled competency evaluations of staff involved in the transfusion service or donor center to ensure that their skills are maintained.[3] Facility competency assessments must be compatible with CLIA '88 requirements, which state that employees must be assessed 6 months after hire and annually thereafter [42 CFR Part 493.1451(b)(9)]. A formal plan that includes acceptable performance standards and remedial measures is one way to ensure appropriate and consistent competency assessments.

Competency programs should include but are not limited to: written evaluations, direct observation of test procedures, review of work records or reports, computer records and/or QC/QA records, testing of unknown samples, and evaluation of the employee's problem-solving skills. Competency must also be assessed 6 months after new procedures or tests are introduced into the work area, and annually thereafter.[3] Documentation of all aspects of employee training and competence is required.[7(p2)]

The responsible QA person should assist in the development, review, and approval of training programs, including the criteria for retraining.[5] The QA officer also monitors the effectiveness of the training program and competency evaluations, reviews proficiency testing results, and makes recommendations for changes as needed.

Equipment

Validation, calibration, and preventive maintenance must be established for all equipment, instruments, and measuring devices used in the provision of blood, blood components, and services.[7(p2-3)] Schedules for equipment monitoring, calibration, and maintenance help to ensure that performance is according to the specifications defined by the facility. The diversity and complexity of blood bank equipment and computer systems require well-developed validation and implementation plans, procedures, and monitoring to ensure optimal and consistent performance.

Installation of new critical equipment must be clearly defined in policies and operating procedures. These policies and procedures should include the installation, calibration, and validation requirements of new equipment. After installation, there must be documentation of any problems and the follow-up actions taken. Recalibration and revalidation may need to occur if repairs are made that affect the critical operating functions of the equipment or measuring devices.

The transfusion service or blood center must keep a list of all critical equipment, or develop a like system, that identifies all critical equipment and measuring devices. This list could also be used as a control function for scheduling preventive maintenance and calibrations or planning quality control.[3] All records of maintenance, repairs, or calibrations must be kept and reviewed periodically. These records will assist the facility in reviewing the functionality of the equipment, allow for better control to manage defective equipment, and can serve as a gauge of when equipment or measuring devices need to be replaced.[2,3,8]

Supplier Issues

Products used in the collection, testing, processing, holding, and distribution of blood that have the potential to affect the quality of blood should be purchased from suppliers who can meet the facility's requirements.[7(p3)] The process for determining supplier issues focuses on three elements: supplier qualifications; contract review; and receipt, inspection, and testing of incoming supplies.

Supplier Qualification

A list must exist of suppliers of critical materials or services. In order to be in control of the quality of suppliers' products or services, the facility must have clearly defined functional requirements or expectations for its suppliers that are shared with staff and the supplier. Based on these expectations and requirements, the facility can document a supplier's ability or inability to meet these expectations. Documented failures of suppliers to meet these expectations should result in immediate action to correct the problem. These actions should include notification of the supplier, the QA officer, and management if applicable. Further action may involve quarantine or replacement of supplies until all quality issues are resolved.

Careful review of the documentation of the supplier's qualifications will alert management to trends in the supplier's qualifications and should result in early detection of supplier problems. Tracking the supplier's ability to meet expectations over time also gives the facility valuable information about the stability of the supplier and their commitment to quality.

Agreement Review

Agreements or changes to agreements should be reviewed to ensure that all parties' expectations are defined and in agreement.[7(p3),8] Transfusion services and donor centers should be able to review contracts, and make suggestions to management to ensure that all critical aspects of the materials and services are clearly covered. Examples of issues that could be addressed in a contract include: a definition of the responsible party during shipping of the product; the responsibility of the supplier to promptly notify the facility when changes have been made to the materials or services that could affect the safety of blood, blood components, or patients; and the responsibility of the supplier to notify the facility when knowledge that a product may not be considered safe is discovered, such as during look-back procedures. Continued surveillance of the materials and services, as discussed above, is critical. The greater the potential risk to the safety of the blood supply or patients, the more emphasis should be placed on evaluation and qualification of supplies and services.

Receipt, Inspection, and Testing of Incoming Supplies

Prior to acceptance and use, incoming supplies and critical materials must be inspected and tested (if necessary) to ensure that they are satisfactory for their intended use.[2,7(p3)] It is essential that supplies used in the collection, preservation, testing, and storage of blood and blood components meet or exceed FDA regulations.

Documentation of receipt of supplies should allow the facility to trace the product from the time it assumes control of it. Policies and procedures should define acceptance of incoming critical supplies, blood, and blood components in terms of packaging, shipping, labeling, and storage requirements. Materials not meeting the acceptance requirements must be quarantined until further action is determined. Corrective actions could result in the return or destruction of products. Tracking receipt and inspection records will give the facility a method of determining how the supplier ships and packages critical materials.

Facility policies, processes and procedures should define which materials and products require testing before the materials are allowed to be added to the facility's supplies. Generally, reagents used in critical procedures such as ABO, Rh, and infectious disease marker testing, must be checked prior to their use in patient or donor testing. These tests will give a measure of assurance that shipping and storage of the reagents did not adversely affect their potency or purity.

The QA function plays a major role in approving supplier specifications and criteria for accepting supplies or services and also has input into supplier contracts.

Process Control, Final Inspection, and Handling

This QSE is perhaps the most encompassing of the QSEs as they relate to the functions of the laboratory. Full compliance with this QSE allows the laboratory and/or facility to be in control of its operating processes. This QSE can be divided into three parts: process control; final inspection and testing; and handling, storage, distribution, and transport.

Process Control

Each facility must have a method in place to ensure that process steps are accomplished as expected and are performed in a manner consistent with defined procedures.[7(p4)] Table 1-2 lists elements that constitute sound process control. See the section on SOPs under Documents and Records for more information on formatting and content of SOPs.

Policies, processes, and procedures must exist for all critical functions in the facility. Processes and procedures must be validated, and the policies, processes, or procedures reviewed by the QA person, technical management (medical director of transfusion services or donor center), and upper management, if applicable. Annual review must be documented, and changes made to policies, processes, or procedures must be documented, validated, and reviewed. Additional information on policies, processes, and procedures can be found in the Documents and Records section.

Validation

Validation can be defined as establishing documented evidence that provides a high degree of assurance that a specific process consistently produces a product that meets its predetermined specifications and quality attributes.[5] The importance of proper validation procedures cannot be overstated.

The Validation Plan. One of the most critical areas for validation is the validation plan. The plan may consist of prospective validation (most often used for new or revised processes) or retrospective validation (used for processes in use before the validation requirement). It is suggested that an organization develop a template for a validation plan. Development of a validation plan is best accomplished after obtaining an adequate understanding of the system. Although no single format for a validation plan is required by regulation, the following elements are common to most:

- System description
- Purpose/objectives
- Risk assessment
- Responsibilities
- Validation procedures
- Acceptance criteria
- Approval signatures
- Required supporting documentation
- Implementation time line

Validation of new processes that include equipment should include installation qualification, operational qualification, and product qualification. Installation qualification focuses on the capability of the equipment to operate within the established limits and specifications supplied by the manufacturer. Operational qualification demonstrates that in all cases the process will produce the desired result or defines the process limits. Product qualification provides assurance that the process results in acceptable measurable or quantifiable specifications attributed to the product.

Once the validation plan is approved, staff most experienced in the process usually perform validation activities. Should the validation process not result in the expected outcome, corrective actions must be documented. The responsible QA person should have final review and approval of the validation plan, results, and corrective actions, and determine whether new or modified processes and equipment can be implemented. When there are significant changes to a process, such as a change of equipment, revised SOP, or change of supplies or reagents, the need for revalidation must be evaluated.

Computer System Validation. The FDA issued a draft guideline for computer system validation in 1993.[9] This guideline defined a

Table 1-2. Elements of a Sound Process Control System

- Development and use of standard operating procedures.
- Processes to control change to policies, processes, or procedures.
- Processes for acceptance testing for new/revised software involved in blood bank procedures.
- Process validation for new policies, processes, or procedures.
- Monitoring and control of production processes.
- Participation in proficiency testing appropriate for each testing system in place.
- Establishment of quality control schedules and monitoring of quality control policies, processes, and procedures.
- Processes to determine supplier qualifications and product specifications are maintained.
- Processes to control nonconforming blood and blood components and products.

computer system to include: "hardware, software, peripheral devices, personnel, and documentation." Thus, validation plans for computer systems in blood banking must include all of the areas referenced above. Computer systems may be custom-developed, vendor-developed, or a hybrid. The development of a validation plan specific to computers depends on the type of system to be used. The AABB publication on validation, cited in the Suggested Reading section, provides an excellent resource for computer validation plans. Testing performed by the vendor or supplier of computer software is not a substitute for computer validation by the user.

Blood and Blood Components Label Control

Controls should be in place for each stage of the labeling process to ensure that only suitable units are available for labeling, that the blood is maintained at the appropriate temperature during the labeling process, and that the correct labels are applied. Before blood can be made available for distribution, the completely labeled unit should be reviewed for accuracy, including a review of appropriate manufacturing records. A second process must verify that records and labels are complete and correct [21 CFR 606.100(c), 211.194(a)]. Facility SOPs should specify which records must be reviewed before labeling. These may include records from donor's medical history and phlebotomy, testing and component preparation, storage, and applicable QC.

In the transfusion service, label controls should be used when products are aliquoted, pooled, or otherwise require a labeling change. When feasible, the labeling of the final container should be verified by a second process. The verification process should verify the product name, ABO group and Rh type, and product expiration date. The QA function may include:

- Auditing or monitoring the audits of the labeling process.
- Ensuring the reconciliation of any discrepancies before unit labeling.

- Ensuring the adherence of labeling procedures to applicable regulations.

In the near future, labeling will take on a new look. The blood banking community is changing from CODABAR to ISBT 128. The ISBT 128 barcode is a variant of the CODE 128 symbology. The International Council for Commonality in Blood Banking Automation (ICCBBA) is charged with maintaining and disseminating the ISBT 128 specifications. The new barcode symbology will provide for a worldwide standard to identify each blood component with a unique identifier and a less error-prone barcode system. The ISBT 128 barcode will have a new unit identification number that incorporates the facility's registration number, year of collection and sequential number; a new ABO-Rh structure that allows inclusion of phenotype information, type of donation, additional information such as Biohazard, Emergency, etc; and a product code structure that allows such designations as research, therapeutic, volunteer, etc. The advent of ISBT 128 will require blood centers and transfusion services to evaluate their computer systems and consider the need for new scanners, new barcode label verification, on-demand label printing, and new or upgraded software. ISBT 128 will ensure that more donor/processing information is available while providing better quality and safety in blood component labeling.[10-12]

Proficiency Testing

Proficiency testing (PT) is one of several means for determining that test methods (including supplies and equipment used in those test methods) are working as expected and that test outcomes are meeting predetermined standards. Controlling the PT process by having clear SOPs ensures that all staff who perform the procedures, using both routine and backup test methods, will have a consistent process to follow. SOPs should cover how to handle PT samples from receipt through testing and how to report the results. The review process for the summary evaluation should include how to perform and document corrective action when applicable. The responsible QA person reviews and monitors PT results, periodically evaluates the proficiency program, and approves corrective action plans taken when PT results are unacceptable. CLIA '88 requires in 42 CFR 493.1213 that test performance be verified for each analyte.[3] Blood centers and transfusion services are required to participate in an HCFA-approved proficiency testing program.[7(p4)] In addition, CLIA '88 defines consequences for failed proficiency testing.[3]

Quality Control

Quality control procedures are an essential component of the QA program; QC results are used to determine if specific critical practices are performed within the established range of acceptability. Quality control of equipment and methods used for collecting, testing, modifying, or otherwise affecting blood for transfusion is essential. Performance characteristics and acceptable ranges should be readily available so that unacceptable variations or results can be promptly detected and appropriately handled. QC results must be documented concurrently with performance.[1,2] Records of QC testing must include identification of staff, identification of reagent (including lot number, expiration dates, etc), testing date and/or time, testing results, interpretation, and reviews. Corrective action for unacceptable QC results should also be carefully documented and reviewed. Quality control testing frequency should be determined by each facility in accordance with the appropriate CLIA '88, FDA, AABB, and state requirements. (See Appendix 1-1 and Methods Section 7 for specific QC procedures and suggested QC testing frequencies.)

Statistical records may be used to summarize one or more processes during a defined time and are useful for evaluating service demands, production, adequacy of personnel, inventory control, and other variables. In ensuring that manufacturing systems perform as expected and yield quality products, QA programs use statistical records to identify problems. Early detection of trends makes it possible to develop corrective actions before blood products or patient safety are adversely affected. Evaluation summaries provide information useful in correcting individual or group performance problems and ensuring adequacy of test methods and equipment.

Identification and Traceability

Donor centers must be able to trace any unit of blood or component from its source (the donor or the collecting facility) to its final disposition (transfused, shipped, discarded).[7(p5)] This is especially important when investigating adverse events and tracking look-back records. Records must be organized in a manner whereby donors are positively identified with each of their donations and with every component prepared from each donation.

Transfusion services must maintain records of ABO and Rh testing performed in the past 12 months and records of any difficulties encountered in determining blood type. The records must include the report of clinically significant unexpected antibodies, and severe reactions to transfusions during the past 5 years must be readily available. Facility personnel must be able to produce, within a reasonable time, legible hard copy of the record, if requested during an inspection or for other needs.

The FDA requires that component preparation records be kept for at least 10 years or for 6 months after product expiration. For frozen red cells, this means that records must be retained for 10 years and 6 months. Records must be kept indefinitely when there is no dating period for the component, such as recovered plasma.[13,14] (See Appendices 1-2 to 1-9 for specific retention requirements.)

Final Inspection and Testing

Final inspection and testing must ensure that the finished blood and blood component, product, or service is acceptable prior to distribution or issue.[7(p5)] In a donor center this would mean that blood or blood components are released only after the review of records of preparation, testing, and acceptability of the blood or blood components. Also, QC records should be reviewed prior to the release of blood and blood components. In the transfusion service, there must be a process to ensure that blood or blood components released for transfusion have been reviewed and that product QC records are checked prior to final release.

Handling, Storage, Distribution, and Transport

There must be a process that ensures proper handling, packaging, and transport of blood and blood components. SOPs must document critical storage temperatures for the various blood components, and how these temperatures are controlled. SOPs and QC methods must exist for shipping blood and blood components in the facility's transport containers. Records detailing the complete history of the blood or blood component must be carefully maintained during this process. Returned blood or blood components must be documented to include storage temperatures, dates and times received, and inspections upon return. In the transfusion service, when blood or blood components are returned, acceptable times for the units to be out of controlled temperature storage must be defined. Inspections of the units must be part of the return process, to ensure the integrity of the blood container.

Documents and Records

Documents

The Documents and Records QSE sets the groundwork for many of the processes in the Process Control QSE. To be in compliance with this essential, facilities must have a process to ensure that documents (policies, process descriptions, and procedures) are identified, approved, implemented, and retained.[7(p5)] Forms must be designed to effectively capture outcomes. These forms must also be controlled, and the records (completed forms) must be stored and archived in a defined manner consistent with local, state, and federal regulations. It is necessary to ensure that when critical records are generated they are reviewed for completeness and accuracy, approved, maintained in usable condition, retained for specified periods, and organized for traceability and retrievability. The facility's record and document management system can be manual and/or automated.

Achieving control of the documents system requires a well-defined structure. The structure should be capable of linking policies, process descriptions, procedures, forms, and records together in an organized and workable system.

Developing documents within an organization should be based on reasonable methods that will satisfy regulations and allow for usable documents that provide staff and others a clear idea of how the objectives of the documents are accomplished. Although there are many ways to develop and maintain documents, the approach embraced by the National Committee for Clinical Laboratory Standards (NCCLS) and the AABB is based on the ISO 9001 model.[6,15-17]

Level I Documents

Document control based on the ISO 9001 model is best described as the pyramid shown in Fig 1-1. The first level of the pyramid, Level I, could consist of the facility's quality policy manual or quality program. This document is time-independent and describes the facility's policies that conform to federal, state, and local regulations. It states the facility's quality policy or mission statement and is usually written by managers from top-level management and the quality department. This document may be brief, but should include the facility's policies with regard to the 10 QSEs, and could reference other more detailed documents for additional information. A quality program document could include the quality policy, organization chart (including the quality functions within that organization), statement of authority and responsibility, a distribution list of controlled copies, a list of the facility's quality system essentials, and procedures and forms indexes.

Level II Documents

Level II documents describe the overall processes within the organization such as contract review, design control, and preventive actions. These documents define how to perform activities at the departmental level and may include

several departments. Level II documents are usually written by department supervisors, and should define what, when, where, who, and how the policies are to be managed. These process documents should provide the reader with an idea of the flow of information from area to area, department to department, etc, as well as the responsibilities of each area or department in the process.

Level III Documents

Level III documents are known as standard operating procedures. These documents are used by persons expected to perform job tasks and are step-by-step directions on how to perform those tasks. The SOPs should be detailed

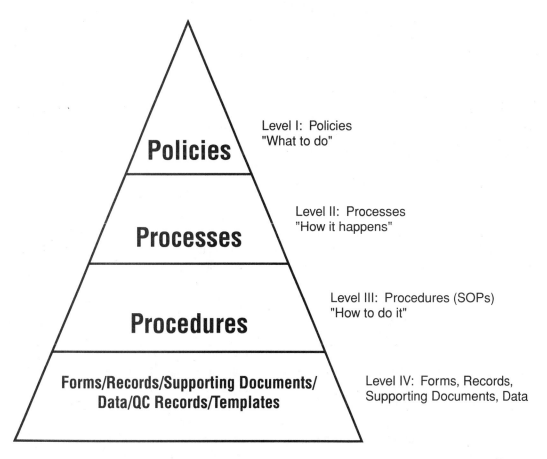

Level I: Policies
"What to do"

Level II: Processes
"How it happens"

Level III: Procedures (SOPs)
"How to do it"

Level IV: Forms, Records,
Supporting Documents, Data

Policies

Processes

Procedures

**Forms/Records/Supporting Documents/
Data/QC Records/Templates**

Figure 1-1. Documentation hierarchy—representing the levels of documents in an organization.[15]

enough to provide the information needed to perform the task, but not so detailed as to make it difficult to find the directions for the task. Procedures should be in a standardized format to assist staff and management in their control and implementation.[7(p6)] Also, procedures must be written for QA, QC, clerical, and operations functions. Relevant procedures must be available to staff at each site where the procedures are performed.[7(p6),8] NCCLS offers detailed instructions on how to write Level I, II, III, and IV documents.[16]

Level IV Documents

Level IV documents are blank (not filled in) forms or formats, templates, blueprints, schematics, data sheets, etc. They can be paper or electronic. These documents specify the data requirements called for in the various SOPs and processes. Forms are completed to become records.

The Process for Document Development

Each facility must have a process that defines its approach to developing and maintaining documents. This Level II process (sometimes called the "SOP for SOPs") should define the chosen structure for SOPs; the process of review and approval of new documents by quality assurance and management; review of revisions to these documents; annual review; review and approval of changes to documents; control of document distribution; control of obsolete documents; and the process for archiving, protecting, and retrieving obsolete documents. There must be a description of the process of how to change procedures and how to document and track changes as well as to review and validate those changes when needed. The review process needs to define who reviews, how the review is documented, and how often the review is performed.

Because supplies and reagents must be used in a manner consistent with the manufacturer's directions (21 CFR 606.65), incorporat-

ing the directions supplied by the manufacturers of the reagents and equipment in use into the SOPs is advisable. However, incorporation of manufacturer's directions requires the user to be vigilant to changes in the package inserts and make concurrent changes to SOPs. The user who believes changes in the manufacturer's directions would be appropriate, should encourage the manufacturer to make changes in the labeling. The user who has unsuccessfully encouraged a manufacturer to alter its instructions may request a variance to the requirements of 21 CFR 606.65(e) under 21 CFR 640.120. However, the user should understand that the FDA would be hesitant to approve a use not intended by the original manufacturer and possibly not supported by the manufacturer in future updates. To be successful, the application and accompanying documentation must present a compelling, well-supported case.

Inclusion of current blood and component labels in SOP manuals is acceptable. CLIA '88 and most other blood bank regulations and standards suggest that SOPs include examples of forms used to record test results and interpretations. Procedures for the review, maintenance, and disposition of these records must also be available. Written and/or pictorial descriptions of how to read, score, and record all test results and interpretations, when applicable, are helpful. Directions for managing possible problems should be included, as well as the limits placed on an individual's independent judgment and criteria for consulting a supervisor.

Before implementation, procedures should be validated, ie, tested for accuracy and completeness, and evaluated for their conformance to regulations and for their potential impact on other systems. Procedures are to be reviewed and approved by the QA unit and management before their implementation.

There must be a master copy of each policy, process description, and procedure; an index of all current policies, process descriptions, and procedures; and an archive of obsolete SOPs.[5] The number of policies and procedures in circulation (working copies) should be controlled to ensure that none is overlooked when changes are implemented. It is essential to include the date a policy, process, or procedure was written and dates of implementation and revision.

Procedure Review and Revision

After publication of each new edition of AABB *Standards for Blood Banks and Transfusion Services*[7] or upon receipt of any change in federal, state, or local requirements, relevant SOPs should be examined for conformance with the new requirements. There must be review and approval of new or changed documents before their issue.[7(p6)]

When procedures are added to or replaced in the manual, the new instructions must be marked with the effective date. Retired documents (SOPs, forms, etc) must be retained as defined by existing and applicable standards and regulations. Regulatory agencies require appropriate demonstrable control of SOPs (no unauthorized, antiquated, or inconsistent SOPs in use); however, those in charge are free to delegate such responsibilities. 21 CFR 211.100 requires SOPs to be drafted, reviewed, and approved by the appropriate organizational units and reviewed and approved by the quality control unit.[2]

Records

Requirements for Level IV document control are similar to those for Level II and III documents. Even though Level IV documents are blank forms, they must be reviewed to determine if they will capture the needed information and that they comply with regulations. There must be a mechanism to control these forms, track their distribution, control changes made to them, and validate their use.

When forms are used for data entry or recording of test results, the forms become records. Each facility must define how to complete its forms and the content for each form. SOPs must also define the processes of how to review, time factors for the review, and how to store and archive reports. The SOPs must also describe how long records must be kept, how they are kept, and how they are archived. (See Appendices 1-2 to 1-9 for some details on record-keeping requirements.) Obsolete computer software necessary to reconstruct or trace records must also be archived appropriately.

Electronic media such as magnetic tapes, optical disks, or on-line computer data storage are widely used for archiving documents. Microfiche records can be stored for years. The potential also exists to use optical character-reading devices to archive written records onto electronic media.

Confidentiality of blood bank records, as all medical information, must be addressed. Organizations should establish policies and procedures to maintain the security and confidentiality of records.[7(p80)] An appropriately maintained computer access security system that will restrict unauthorized use must be described. This system may include levels of security defined by job responsibility and administered by the use of security codes and passwords.

If records are electronically maintained, adequate backup must exist in case of electronic system failure. Records must also be easily retrieved for reference or review. It should be noted that "easily retrieved" has various definitions depending on the organization requesting retrieval.

If it is necessary to alter or correct any record, a common practice is to indicate the date and the person responsible for the change and evidence of review by a person responsible for critical SOPs. The original recording must not be obliterated in written records; it may be circled or crossed out, but it should remain legible. Computer records should permit tracking of both original and corrected data to include the date and the user identification of the person making the change. There must be a process for controlling changes.[7(p5)] A method for referencing changes to records, linked to the original records, and a system for reviewing changes for completeness and accuracy are essential. Audit trails for changed data in computerized systems are required by the FDA. The information may be maintained manually or electronically.

The following are issues that might be considered when planning record storage:

- Storage of records in a manner that protects them from damage and from accidental or unauthorized destruction or modification.
- Degree of accessibility of records in proportion to frequency of their use.
- Method and location of record storage related to the volume of records and the amount of available storage space.
- Availability of a properly functioning viewer for microfilmed or microfiched records.
- Documentation that microfilmed or microfiched records legitimately replace original documents that may be stored elsewhere or destroyed.
- Retention of original copies of color-coded records, which lose meaning in black-and-white reproduction.

Considerations for computer-maintained records include:

- A method of verifying accuracy of data entry.
- Prevention of unintended deletion of data or access by unauthorized persons.
- Adequate protection against inadvertent data loss (eg, when a storage device is full).
- Validated safeguards to ensure that a record can be edited by only one person at a time.
- Security and access of confidential data.

A backup disk or tape should be maintained in the event of unexpected loss of information from the storage medium. It would be wise to store magnetic media used to back up or archive computer records and databases off-site

under appropriate conditions, in accordance with the manufacturer's recommendations and instructions. An archival copy of the computer operating system and applications software should be stored in the same manner.

Alternative systems must exist to ensure information access in the event that computerized data are not available. The backup system(s) for computer downtime should be defined, with validation documentation to show that the backup system works properly. It would be prudent to periodically check processes to ensure that the backup systems remain effective.

To relate pertinent personnel to the recorded data, a record with inclusive dates of employment and signatures and identifying initials or identification codes, of personnel authorized to sign, initial, or review reports and records must be maintained. This list should include full-time and part-time personnel, including phlebotomists, transfusionists, volunteers, and medical and contract personnel, if appropriate. Magnetically coded employee badges and other computer-related identifying methods are generally accepted in lieu of written signatures.

Incidents, Errors, and Accidents

The Incidents, Errors, and Accidents QSE offers staff and managers a process to document, review, and improve processes. This QSE requires a facility to have a process in place to capture and assess incidents, errors, and accidents (occurrences). Policies, processes, and procedures should define how to classify, prioritize, and analyze these occurrences.

Once an occurrence has been identified, it should be classified in such a manner that allows the facility to determine the severity of the situation. More investigation should add data to further classify the occurrence and determine if additional investigation must occur. The process for classifying occurrences must include parameters on how to determine if the occurrences are reportable to the FDA, and then how to proceed with the FDA report if needed.

Once occurrences have been identified, the facility should determine if the occurrence is a one-time event. If so, the facility must assess the severity of the occurrence and if there is a potential of it happening again. If the occurrence has happened with increased frequency, that occurrence must be reviewed to determine the root cause and action taken to correct the trend toward noncompliance. cGMP regulations require an investigation and documentation of the results of occurrences if a specific event could adversely affect patient's safety or the purity, potency, safety, or effectiveness of blood or a blood component.[1-3]

Facilities should track occurrences and look for trends. If a particular process or procedure is involved in more than two or three occurrences in a short period, that process should be further investigated. This investigation could involve setting up a Continuous Quality Improvement (CQI) team, brainstorming, developing a cause-and-effect diagram or run chart, or using any number of other quality tools to determine the root cause of the occurrence. If the root cause can be determined, controlled corrective action should be taken and monitored. The amount of monitoring and length of time to monitor processes will depend on the frequency of the occurrence and the critical aspects of the occurrences.

Included in the process for reporting occurrences must be a process to report occurrences of when and how blood components and critical materials fail to meet established requirements. This should include failures of blood or blood components at the time of incoming inspection, while held in inventory, or at the time of distribution or issue. Occurrences must also be reported if computer systems are not functioning properly. There must be a mechanism to report medical adverse events to the FDA (21 CFR 803).

Other occurrence reporting in the transfusion service could involve reports of patients experiencing adverse effects as the result of transfusion. Suspected cases of transfusion-associated diseases must be evaluated and confirmed cases must be reported to the blood collecting facility. FDA requirements for look-back regarding human immunodeficiency virus (HIV) have been defined in 21 CFR Parts 610.46 and 610.47. The requirements apply to collection and transfusion facilities that are not subject to HCFA regulations. HCFA has identical look-back requirements for transfusion services [42 CFR 482.27(c)]. Additional FDA memoranda address recommendations for other transfusion-transmitted diseases and should be referred to when developing look-back procedures.

Fatalities related to blood collection or transfusion must be reported promptly to the Director, Center for Biologics Evaluation and Research (CBER), Office of Compliance and Biologics Quality, Attn: Fatality Program Manager (HFM-650), 1401 Rockville Pike, Rockville, MD 20852-1448. A report should be made by telephone (301-827-6220) or e-mail (fatalities2@cber.fda.gov) within one working day and a written report should be submitted within 7 days [21 CFR 606.170(b)]. The report should include a description of any new procedures implemented to avoid recurrence.

All licensed facilities must report errors and accidents that affect the safety, purity, potency, or identity of blood and blood components to the FDA.[1,2] JCAHO requires transfusion services must also report hemolytic transfusion reactions that are the result of ABO-incompatible blood or blood component transfusions.[18]

Assessments: Internal and External

This QSE defines how facilities monitor, assess, and evaluate their processes. The AABB *Accreditation Information Manual* (*AIM*) defines assessments as "a systematic, independent evaluation that is performed at defined intervals and at sufficient frequency to determine whether activities and the results of the activities comply with requirements and procedures, that the procedures are implemented effectively, and that the procedures are suitable to achieve defined objectives."[8] The *AIM* defines audit as "systematic inspection or evaluation to determine whether approved policies and procedures are being properly implemented."[8]

To comply with this QSE, there should be a process to manage internal and external assessments. External assessments include inspections, surveys, some audits, etc, performed by facilities not affiliated with the organization, such as the FDA, the AABB, or the CAP. Facilities must have policies and procedures that define how to manage external assessments; how to greet the assessors or inspectors; and who is responsible for the assessors or inspectors during the time they are in the facility. A clear delineation of the responsibilities of all staff members is essential. Clear descriptions of what information can be given and in what form that information can be given to external assessors or inspectors will help the facility through the assessment or inspection process.

Transfusion services and donor centers must also define a process for internal assessments. The process and procedures must outline a plan and schedule for these assessments. The details of who performs the assessments and how they are performed should be addressed. In addition to a schedule for the assessments, there must be a process for responding to the issues raised as a result of the assessment, including review processes and time frames. In order to make the best use of these assessments there must be a process to track and analyze problems to identify opportunities for improvement.[7(p7),8]

Blood usage review committees in the hospital setting are an example of internal audits.

A transfusion audit is a defined review of policies and practices to ensure safe and appropriate transfusions and is based on measurable, predetermined performance criteria. Guidelines are available from the AABB for both adult and pediatric utilization review.[19-21]

Criteria for transfusion audits may be explicit or implicit or a combination of both. Explicit criteria are easily measured and specified in advance, such as laboratory data used for initial screening of blood requests and transfusions. Implicit criteria are less easily measured and involve individual judgment, such as medical history and clinical assessment, and are characteristically used in final audit reviews.

Peer review of transfusion practices, required by the AABB, is also required by the JCAHO[18] for hospital accreditation, by the CFR[3] for hospitals to qualify for Medicare reimbursement, and by some states for Medicaid reimbursement.

Transfusion services should investigate enough of a sampling of cases (5% of the number of cases occurring within a defined time frame or 30 cases, whichever is larger). The audit should assess the facility's effectiveness in:

- Evaluating usage of all categories of blood and products.
- Reviewing all confirmed transfusion reactions.
- Developing and approving policies and procedures for distribution, handling, use, and administration of blood products.
- Monitoring blood ordering practices.
- Ensuring that the institution's transfusion service adequately meets patient's needs.
- Informing patients and physicians in a timely and confidential manner when look-back is required for possible HIV transmission.

Currently, JCAHO incorporates the above requirements into performance improvement standards, stated as follows[18]:

1. There must be a planned, systematic, organization-wide approach to design, measure, assess, and improve process performance and blood usage review.
2. New processes must be designed effectively.
3. Data must be systematically collected. The data should be collected to measure existing processes and improvement initiatives. The data must be collected on important processes or outcomes related to the organization's functions and mission including at least:
   a. patient preparation
   b. handling specimens
   c. communication processes
   d. utilization management
   e. needs, expectations, and satisfaction of patients and other customers
   f. staff's views regarding performance and improvement opportunities
   g. data from risk management and quality control activities
4. There must be a systematic process to assess collected data in order to determine:
   a. compliance with specifications
   b. level of performance and stability of existing processes
   c. priorities for improvement
   d. actions to improve performance
   e. whether changes result in improvement
5. The organization must systematically improve its performance by improving processes.

One important aspect of transfusion safety is monitoring the blood administration process, ie, following a unit of blood as it is issued for transfusion and observing the transfusion procedure.[22] Another aspect of transfusion safety is the review of transfusion reactions and transfusion-transmitted diseases. The committee may monitor policies and practices for notifying recipients of recalled products (look-back notification) and donors of abnormal test results.

Other audits important in transfusion practice include review of policies for informed consent, for release of directed donor units, or for outpatient and home transfusion. Additional audits should include where appropriate: therapeutic apheresis, procurement and storage of hematopoietic progenitor cells, perioperative autologous blood collection, procurement and storage of tissue, and evaluation of evolving technologies and products such as solvent/detergent-treated plasma, growth factors, and cytokines.

Internal assessments may include routine, scheduled system checks (also called quality indicators), audits, and other findings initiated by the facility. Audits by the QA unit should be conducted periodically according to a predetermined schedule, to assess the effectiveness of the quality system and current programs. Although a focused audit may be required from time to time to address a specific problem area, QA audits usually focus on systems. The results of the audit should be documented and submitted to responsible management personnel for review.

Quality assessment plans that include an outline of major systems found in a blood center or transfusion service are available. The *Accreditation Information Manual* gives examples of implementation that can be used as the basis for developing assessments and audits.[8]

Process Improvement

For all internal audits and assessments, whether performed by the blood usage review committee or QA units, the course of action to take when inappropriate practice is identified must be determined in advance. (See Appendix 1-10 for examples of blood utilization measurements.) In the event of blood usage review committee audits, these actions should be discussed with the hospital's administration and legal office, be shared with the medical staff, and be outlined in the medical staff bylaws, as appropriate. Other focused audits, internal to laboratories or departments, should also have defined actions to be taken when appropriate. Before conducting the audits, the department or laboratory management must agree upon these actions. Corrective action policies are subject to the institution's confidentiality rules. The following concepts should be considered:

- Corrective action should be educational and not punitive; the goal is to improve transfusion practice. Educational materials should be sent to the involved physician(s) and patient care units as deemed necessary.
- Actions should be completed in a timely fashion.
- Reports can either include the patient's name and the name of the involved physician(s) or patient care units, or can be generated as anonymous statistical summaries.
- A letter or other written notice of variance in practice should be sent to some or all of the following persons or bodies: the responsible physician(s), the department chair, the chief of professional services, the hospital's risk management office, the hospital's credentials committee or the patient care unit supervisor, manager, or director.
- The involved physician(s) (in the blood usage review audit), patient caregivers (in the transfusion practice audit), or laboratory supervisor (in an internal department audit) should be encouraged to respond to or meet with the committee or department chair to clarify or discuss actions deemed inappropriate.

Most quality programs and systems have activities to promote ongoing process improvement. Follow-up of findings from external assessments, reviews, and inspections, as well as occurrence reporting provide mechanisms for continued improvement. Review of internal assessments (audits) and customer complaints also provides opportunities for improvement.

A summary of error and accident records provides an overview of operations and may identify processes and procedures that need clarification and personnel who need retraining. Summaries also contain information useful for internal audits. Strict adherence to the facility's SOP manual and uniform notation among staff are critical if useful data are to be obtained with a minimum of effort.

Analysis of data from internal and external assessments is best done with statistical tools. Statistical tools and their applications may be found in publications from the American Society for Quality as well as specific AABB publications.[17] Typical tools used to analyze data are the Pareto chart, run charts, and control charts.

A yearly report prepared by the QA unit (and possibly tied to the budget planning period) systemizes evaluation of a blood center's or transfusion service's total operation. FDA requirements should be taken into consideration when compiling data and information for yearly reports. The report should be prepared according to a formal plan that includes information from and analysis of error and accident reports, adverse reaction reports (including transfusion-transmitted diseases), fatalities, product returns or recalls, QC records, and proficiency test results. The yearly report should also describe corrective and preventive actions already taken, with an analysis of their effectiveness and proposals for additional actions that may be needed.

Facilities and Safety

Multiple federal, state, and local agencies (see Chapter 2 for a list of these agencies) have regulations addressed in this QSE. To comply with this QSE, the facility must provide a safe workplace with adequate environmental controls and emergency procedures for the safety of the employees, donors, patients, and all other inhabitants or visitors.[7(p8)] Procedures must be in place that cover:

- Disaster preparedness
- Chemical safety
- Biologic safety (blood-borne pathogens)
- General safety
- Radiation safety, if applicable

The cGMP regulations include requirements for:

- Adequate space and ventilation
- Sanitation and trash disposal
- Equipment for controlling air quality and pressure, humidity, and temperature
- Water systems
- Toilet and hand-washing facilities

An evaluation of the physical structure and limitations of a facility are necessary prior to implementation of procedures or equipment to ensure maximum efficiency and safety. Chapter 2 addresses safety more completely.

Summary

Any facility that operates under the 10 QSEs described in this chapter should be in control of its processes, able to direct itself toward high quality products and services, and able to perform in a cost-efficient manner. Having the ability to identify processes that need improvement, being able to improve those processes, and monitoring the improvement process give the facility strength and leadership in today's competitive environment. As the facility continues toward its mission, these QSEs can and should be applied to all its processes.

References

1. Code of federal regulations. Title 21 CFR Parts 600-799. Washington, DC: US Government Printing Office, 1998 (revised annually).
2. Code of federal regulations. Title 21 CFR Parts 200-299. Washington, DC: US Government Printing Office, 1998 (revised annually).
3. Code of federal regulations. Title 42 CFR Parts 493 to end. Washington, DC: US Government Printing Office, 1998 (revised annually).
4. Quality program implementation. Association Bulletin 97-4. Bethesda, MD: American Association of Blood Banks, 1997.
5. Food and Drug Administration. Guideline for quality assurance in blood establishments. Docket #91N-0450. July 1995. Rockville, MD: CBER Office of Communication, Training, and Manufacturer's Assistance, 1995.
6. Schlickman JJ. ISO 9000 quality management system design. Milwaukee, WI: ASQ Quality Press, 1998:3-20;69-80.
7. Menitove J, ed. Standards for blood banks and transfusion services. 19th ed. Bethesda, MD: American Association of Blood Banks, 1999.
8. Sazama K, ed. Accreditation information manual. 2nd ed. Bethesda, MD: American Association of Blood Banks, 1998.
9. Food and Drug Administration. Draft guideline for the validation of blood establishment computer systems. Docket #93N-0394. September 28, 1993. Rockville, MD: CBER Office of Communication, Training, and Manufacturer's Assistance, 1993.
10. Food and Drug Administration. Memorandum: United States industry consensus standard for the labeling of blood and blood components using ISBT 128 (draft). November 27, 1998. Rockville, MD: CBER Office of Communication, Training, and Manufacturers Assistance, 1998.
11. ISBT Code 128 implementation plan. Bethesda, MD: American Association of Blood Banks, 1998.
12. Steane EA, ed. United States industry consensus standard for the uniform labeling of blood and blood components using ISBT 128. Durham, NC: International Council for Commonality in Blood Banking Automation, 1997.
13. Food and Drug Administration. Guidance for Industry: Current good manufacturing practice for blood and blood components: (1) Quarantine and disposition of units from prior collections from donors with repeatedly reactive screening tests for antibody to hepatitis C virus (anti-HCV); (2) Supplemental testing, and the notification of consignees and blood recipients of donor test results for anti-HCV. September 23, 1998. Rockville, MD: CBER Office of Communication, Training, and Manufacturers Assistance, 1998.
14. Code of federal regulations. Title 21 CFR Part 606.160(d). Washington, DC: US Government Printing Office, 1998 (revised annually).
15. Ziebell LW. Process control. In: Ziebell LW, Kavemeier K, eds. Quality control: A component of process control in blood banking and transfusion medicine. Bethesda, MD: AABB Press, 1999 (in press).
16. A quality system model for health care; proposed guideline. GP26-P. Vol. 18 No. 10. Wayne, PA: National Committee for Clinical Laboratory Standards, 1998.
17. Anderson TD. Tools for statistical process control. In: Ziebell LW, Kavemeier K, eds. Quality control: A component of process control in blood banking and transfusion medicine. Bethesda, MD: AABB Press, 1999 (in press).

18. Comprehensive accreditation manual for hospitals: The office handbook. Oakbrook Terrace, IL: Joint Commission on the Accreditation of Healthcare Organizations, 1998.

19. Shulman IA, Lohr K, Derdiarian AK, et al. Monitoring transfusionist practices: A strategy for improving transfusion safety. Transfusion 1994; 34:11-15.

20. Stehling L, Luban NLC, Anderson KC, et al. Guidelines for blood utilization review. Transfusion 1994; 34: 438-48.

21. Strauss RG, Blanchette VS, Hume H. National acceptability of American Association of Blood Banks Hemotherapy Committee guidelines for auditing pediatric transfusion practices. Transfusion 1993;33:168-71.

22. Wallas CH, Muller VH, eds. The hospital transfusion committee. Arlington, VA: American Association of Blood Banks, 1982.

Suggested Reading

Berte LM. Managing quality in hospital transfusion medicine. Lab Med 1994;25:118-23.

Bozzo P. Implementing quality assurance. Chicago: American Society of Clinical Pathologists, 1991.

Clark G. Continuous quality improvement. Chicago: American Society of Clinical Pathologists, 1992.

FDA workshop for licensing blood establishments. Bethesda, MD: American Association of Blood Banks, 1995.

Food and Drug Administration. Guideline on general principles of process validation. May 1987. Rockville, MD: CBER Office of Communication, Training, and Manufacturer's Assistance, 1987.

Guidelines for preparing standard operating procedures for blood bank computer systems. Arlington, VA: American Association of Blood Banks, 1991.

Holliman S, ed. Supplies, suppliers and contract review. Bethesda, MD: American Association of Blood Banks, 1997.

Holliman SM, ed. Validation in blood establishments and transfusion services. Bethesda, MD: AABB Press, 1996.

Maffei L, ed. Evaluation of new equipment and systems. Bethesda, MD: American Association of Blood Banks, 1997.

McCurdy K, Gregory K. Blood bank regulations A to Z. 2nd ed. Bethesda, MD: AABB Press, 1999.

McCurdy K, Wilkinson S, ed. CLIA and transfusion medicine: A guide to total compliance. Bethesda, MD: AABB Press, 1996.

Rhamy J, ed. Error management: A central part of process improvement. Bethesda, MD: AABB Press, 1999 (in press).

Russell H, Wallhermafechtel M, eds. AABB quality program: An introduction. Bethesda, MD: American Association of Blood Banks, 1997.

Russell JP, ed. The quality audit handbook. Milwaukee, WI: ASQ Quality Press, 1997.

Umiker W. The customer-oriented laboratory. Chicago: American Society of Clinical Pathologists, 1991.

Validation guidelines. Microprocessor-controlled test instruments. Association Bulletin 93-2. Bethesda, MD: American Association of Blood Banks, 1993.

Appendix 1-1. Quality Control Testing Intervals*

Equipment/Reagents/Tests	Frequency
I. Refrigerators/Freezers/Platelet Incubators	
A. Refrigerators	
1. Recorder	Daily
2. Manual temperature	Daily
3. Alarm system board (if applicable)	Daily
4. Temperature charts (review daily)	Weekly
5. Alarm activation	Quarterly
B. Freezers	
1. Recorder	Daily
2. Manual temperature	Daily
3. Alarm system board (if applicable)	Daily
4. Temperature charts (review daily)	Weekly
5. Alarm activation	Quarterly
C. Platelet incubators	
1. Recorder	Daily
2. Manual temperature	Daily
3. Temperature charts (review daily)	Weekly
4. Alarm activation	Quarterly
D. Ambient platelet storage area	Every 4 hours
II. Laboratory Equipment	
A. Centrifuge/cell washers	
1. Tube fill level (serologic)	Daily
2. Saline fill volume	Weekly
3. Speed	Quarterly
4. Timer	Quarterly
5. Function	Yearly
6. Temperature of refrigerated centrifuge (record daily)	Monthly
7. Volume of antihuman globulin dispensed by cell washer	Monthly
B. Heating blocks/Waterbaths	
1. Temperature	Day of use
2. Quadrant/area checks	Periodically
C. View boxes (temperature)	Day of use
D. Component thawing devices	Day of use
E. pH meters	Day of use
F. Blood irradiators	
1. Calibration	Yearly
2. Turntable	Yearly
3. Timer	Monthly/quarterly
4. Source decay	Dependent on source type

(cont'd)

Appendix 1-1. Quality Control Testing Intervals* (cont'd)

Equipment/Reagents/Tests	Frequency
5. Leak test	Biannually
6. Dose delivery verification	
a. Cesium-137	Yearly
b. Cobalt-60	Biannually
G. Thermometers (vs NIST-certified)	Yearly
H. Timers/clocks	Yearly
I. Pipette recalibration	Yearly
J. Sterile connecting device	
1. Weld check	Each use
2. Function	Yearly
K. Blood warmers	
1. Effluent temperature	Quarterly
2. Heater temperature	Quarterly
3. Alarm activation	Quarterly
III. Blood Collection Equipment	
A. Whole blood equipment	
1. Agitators	Day of use
2. Balances/scales	Day of use
3. Gram weight (vs NIST-certified)	Yearly
B. Microhematocrit centrifuge calibration	Yearly
Centrifuge timer check	Quarterly
C. Cell counters/hemoglobinometers	Day of use
D. Blood pressure cuffs	Periodically
E. Apheresis equipment	
1. Checklist requirements	As specified by manufacturer
2. Photopheresis	Monthly
IV. Reagents	
A. Red cells	Day of use
B. Antisera	Day of use
C. Antiglobulin serum	Day of use
V. Blood Products and Components	
A. RBCs	
Hematocrit <80%	Monthly
B. Cryoprecipitated AHF	
$\geq$ 80 IU/unit in 100% of units tested	Monthly
$\geq$ 150 mg fibrinogen in 100% of units tested	Monthly
C. Platelets	
$\geq 5.5 \times 10^{10}$ platelets in 75% of units tested	Monthly
$\geq$ pH 6.2 at max. storage in 100% of units tested	Monthly

Appendix 1-1. Quality Control Testing Intervals* (cont'd)

Equipment/Reagents/Tests	Frequency
D. Platelets, Pheresis	
$\geq 3 \times 10^{11}$ platelets in 75% of units tested	Monthly
$\geq$ pH 6.2 at max. storage in 100% of units tested	Monthly
E. Granulocytes, Pheresis	
$\geq 1.0 \times 10^{10}$ in 75% of units tested	Monthly
F. Whole Blood, Leukocytes Reduced[†]	
Residual leukocyte count of $<5 \times 10^6$ in each container tested *and* retain a minimum of 85% of original Whole Blood component	Monthly/test at least 1% of components produced or four, whichever is more
G. Red Blood Cells, Leukocytes Reduced[†]	
Residual leukocyte count of $<5 \times 10^6$ in each red cell container tested *and* retain a minimum of 85% of original red cells in the component	Monthly/test at least 1% of components produced or four, whichever is more
H. Platelets, Leukocytes Reduced[†]	
Residual leukocyte count of $<8.3 \times 10^5$ is 85% in each container tested *and* retain a minimum of 85% of original platelets in the component	Monthly/test at least 1% of components produced or four, whichever is more
I. Platelets, Pheresis, Leukocytes Reduced[†]	
(applies to components prepared by cytapheresis without secondary processing as well as components reduced by filtration)	Monthly/test at least 1% of components produced or four, whichever is more
Residual leukocyte count of $<5 \times 10^6$ in each container tested *and* retain a minimum of 85% of original platelets in the component	
VI. Miscellaneous	
A. Copper sulfate specific gravity	Day of use
B. Shipping containers for blood transport (usually at temperature extremes)	Biannually

*Sazama K, ed. Accreditation requirements manual. 6th ed. Bethesda, MD: American Association of Blood Banks, 1995.
†Food and Drug Administration. Memorandum: Recommendations and licensure requirements for leukocyte-reduced blood products. (May 29, 1996). Rockville, MD: CBER Office of Communication, Training, and Manufacturers Assistance, 1996.

Appendix 1-2. Minimum Record Requirements (Patients)

Laboratory Tests

- Patient's first and last name and patient identification number, or two unique identifiers, and collection date
- Phlebotomist's identification
- Testing date
- The test performed, results observed, and final interpretation
- Results and interpretation of ABO and Rh testing, including control for autoagglutinins and weak D testing, if performed
- Results and interpretation of tests for unexpected antibodies
- Difficulty in blood grouping, clinically significant unexpected antibodies, and serious adverse effects of transfusion

Compatibility Tests

- Patient's ABO and Rh type
- Identification numbers for the patient and for donor unit(s)
- ABO and Rh types of donor unit(s)
- Testing date
- Results and interpretation of compatibility tests
- Component being tested or prepared

Transfusion Requests

- Patient's first and last name
- Patient's identification number
- Requesting physician's identification

Issue for Transfusion

- Time and date of issue or reissue
- Donor unit number of blood or component, or lot number of product

- Pool number and unit number for each component in the pool
- Comparison of the patient's current ABO and Rh types with results of previous tests performed in preceding 12 months
- Review of the patient's prior records for difficulty in determining ABO or Rh types, presence of clinically significant unexpected antibodies and severe reactions to transfusions recorded during the past 5 years

Transfusion

- A signed statement that the information on the container label and the compatibility record has been matched with the wristband or other identification of intended recipient, item by item
- Documentation of vital signs
- Transfusionist's identification and date/time of transfusion

Emergency Issue of Blood

- Label or tie-tag must clearly identify those required tests that have not been completed
- A statement of the requesting physician indicating that the clinical situation is sufficiently urgent to require release of blood before completion of testing
- Depending on local procedures, the requesting physician's statement concerning the abbreviated testing before issuing the transfusion - OR -
- The compatibility label must clearly state that tests routinely performed in that facility have not been completed
- All other record requirements apply as usual

Appendix 1-3. Minimum Record Requirements (Donors and Processing of Donor Units)

General Collection Information

- Donor unit number
- Donor's first and last name and middle initial
- Donor's address and phone number
- Donor's date of birth
- Donor's social security number or other equivalent unique permanent identifier that will ensure accurate maintenance of donor deferral registries
- Date of donation
- Date of last donation
- Record of physical examination (temperature, blood pressure, pulse, hemoglobin or hematocrit, arm examination)
- Identification of the examiner
- Documentation that the donor weighs at least 110 pounds or that a low-volume unit was collected
- Medical history with answers recorded as "yes" or "no" for each question, with any pertinent explanation
- Identification of the interviewer
- Record of whether the donor was accepted
- Record of whether the phlebotomy was satisfactory or unsatisfactory
- If the donor is deferred, state the reason, with notation about temporary, indefinite, or permanent deferral
- Informed consent:
  - Consent to have blood drawn and tested
  - An opportunity to exclude use for transfusion (if applicable)
  - A statement that AIDS information educational material is understood and an accurate medical history has been given
  - Permission for the blood bank to use blood as it deems fit if unsuitable for transfusion and signature of the donor
- Identification of the phlebotomist
- Record of any donor reaction; symptoms, treatment, condition of the donor upon release; and notation about whether the donor can be accepted again
  - Identification of person attending the donor
  - Time released
  - Notation if the donor refuses treatment or advice
- Documentation of postdonation information reports
  - Identity of the source of the information (eg, from the donor, competent health-care professional)

- Documentation of evaluation, investigation, and follow-up on these reports[1]
- The name of the manufacturer and lot number of the container/anticoagulant

Special Collections Information

- Donors under age 17: Written permission from a parent or guardian if it is required by state law. (Minors who are in the military or legally married are generally exempt from this requirement.)
- Autologous Donations:
  - Written consent of the patient's physician, the blood bank physician, and the patient (or, if indicated, the patient's parent or guardian)
  - Physician examination of the donor and certification of good health if the donation interval is less than 8 weeks. (The physician's written order requesting autologous collections is an acceptable alternative.)
  - Permission from the receiving transfusion service and a written statement from the attending physician indicating it is acceptable to ship units: confirmed positive for hepatitis B surface antigen, confirmed positive for antibodies to human immunodeficiency virus, type 1 (anti-HIV-1) and/or anti-HIV-2 (or repeatedly reactive and confirmation is not yet available), repeatedly reactive for HIV-1 antigen. However, a US Supreme Court decision makes it illegal to offer autologous blood services without offering those services to individuals protected under the Americans with Disabilities Act.[2]
  - Documentation that the attending physician has been notified if the units are positive for antibodies to hepatitis C virus, repeat reactive for antibodies to hepatitis B core antigen, or confirmed positive for syphilis
  - Documentation of destruction of blood not released
- Apheresis (Cytapheresis and Plasmapheresis): The following record-keeping requirements are in addition to those that apply to Whole Blood donation.
  - The name of the manufacturer and the lot numbers and volumes of all solutions, software, and drugs used
  - The results of laboratory tests that qualify the donor, time the procedure begins and ends, the volume of blood processed, the volume of each component harvested, the estimated blood cell loss, and any adverse events

(cont'd)

Appendix 1-3. Minimum Record Requirements (Donors and Processing of Donor Units) (cont'd)

- Description of the procedure and informed consent
- For apheresis donors who are given medications or are immunized, there must be a separate informed consent as well as complete information on the drug or antigen source; the schedule, dosage, and route of administration; adverse events; and response (eg, antibody titer) to the stimulating agent as measured by laboratory tests
- All initial and periodic physical examinations by a physician, including medical history interviews
- The physician's acceptance or rejection of the donor, based on the accumulated laboratory data
- Therapeutic apheresis/Hematopoietic progenitor cells:
  - Physician's order
  - Patient identification
  - Diagnosis
  - Type of procedure performed
  - Method used
  - Extracorporeal blood volume
  - Nature and volume of component removed
  - Nature and volume of replacement fluids
  - Any occurrence of adverse events
  - Medication administered
  - Informed consent
- Therapeutic phlebotomy:
  - A record that the patient's physician has ordered phlebotomy
  - Volume of blood drawn
  - Final disposition of unit
  - If transfusion components are prepared, the records of these procedures must include all information required for blood donors as well as the name of the disease

Tests on Donor Blood Samples

- Donor unit number
- Reagents used, manufacturer, lot number, expiration date, control values and calculations if applicable, and evidence that reagents have been subjected to performance checks
- Results and interpretation of ABO and Rh testing, including the test for weak D if indicated
- Results of tests for expected antibodies in the ABO system
- Results of positive and negative controls run with the donor samples
- Results and interpretations of tests for the detection of unexpected antibodies, if indicated, including use of IgG-coated control cells if used

- Results and interpretation of serologic test for syphilis
- Results and interpretation of screening and confirmatory or supplemental tests for all infectious disease markers and surrogate tests
  - Relevant calculations to define control and positive results. (The record of these calculations may be kept separately from the results of donor samples but must be readily associated with specific sample records.)
  - Record of incubation times and temperature
  - Record of reason for invalidating a test result, details of the investigation, records of supervisory review, outcome of the investigation, and, if indicated, any corrective action taken. (These records should be completed before any donor samples are retested.[3])
- Results and interpretation of tests that are performed by outside testing laboratories, with the name and location of the testing laboratory on the record

Component Preparation

- Donor unit number
- Date and, if appropriate, time drawn, and documentation of method used (manual or automated)
- Name and volume of anticoagulant
- Name of component
- Date and time each component was prepared. (If the preparation involves multiple steps such as separation, freezing, and thawing, the time each step was taken must be documented.)
- Date and time of component expiration
- Volume of component, except for Cryoprecipitated AHF and Red Blood Cells (RBCs) prepared in a routine manner from Whole Blood
- When recovered plasma is pooled for further manufacture, records must indicate the donor unit number and the identification of the collecting facility for each unit in the pool
- Pooled component labels must have:
  - Name of the pooled component
  - Final volume of the pooled component
  - Name of the facility preparing the pooled component
  - Unique numeric or alphanumeric identification
  - Number of units in the pool
  - ABO and Rh type of units in the pool

Appendix 1-3. Minimum Record Requirements (Donors and Processing of Donor Units) (cont'd)

Labeling and Lot Release

- Documentation that ensures current, accurate donor deferral registries have been checked and necessary action has been taken to prevent distribution of unsuitable products
- Documentation that verifies all records of test results are reviewed for completeness and accuracy prior to labeling
- Identity of each component in quarantine to prevent unsuitable units from being released
- Prior to release, documentation that the completely labeled product has been examined for correct labeling. (This examination must be verified by a second process.[4])

Disposition of Blood and Components

- Documentation and confirmation that all components from a unit have been quarantined, as indicated; documentation of appropriate release from quarantine
- When destruction is necessary, the identification of each of the components destroyed, the reason for destruction, date and method of destruction
- When units are shipped, the shipping facility must record the following information:
  - Name and address of receiving facility
  - Date and time of shipment
  - A list of each donor unit number, blood group and expiration date
  - Name of each blood component
  - Results of final inspection of Whole Blood and components
  - Name of person filling order
  - Periodic tests documenting that shipping containers maintain an acceptable storage temperature range

Blood and Components Received from Other Facilities

- Name and address of shipping facility. It is not necessary to record the address with each unit if this information is readily available.
- Name of blood component
- Donor unit number assigned by collecting facility
- Accession or inventory number, if any, assigned by receiving facility
- ABO and Rh type
- Component expiration date and time, if indicated

- Date component was received
- For blood that is received already crossmatched, the name and identification number of the intended recipient and interpretation of results of compatibility tests
- Results and interpretation of tests done by the receiving facility

Storage and Inspection of Blood Components

- Central monitor listing every 4 hours of temperatures, refrigerator identification, date, and time; or continuous monitoring chart for each piece of equipment being monitored; or manual recording of time, temperatures, and staff identification every 4 hours for each piece of equipment being monitored
- Explanation of abnormal temperatures and action taken, and initials of personnel
- If components are stored in an open storage area, the ambient temperature must be recorded at least every 4 hours
- Records of periodic testing of alarm systems and backup power supply; comparisons of central monitor readings with a calibrated reference thermometer
- Preissue inspections, date performed, unit number, and description of any abnormalities detected; for reissued Whole Blood or components, a record that proper temperature has been maintained, that container and closure are intact and that inspection for abnormal color or appearance is satisfactory
- Notation of quarantine of unsatisfactory units, record of any tests performed, and final disposition of each unit

Irradiated Blood and Blood Components[5]

- Identity of the source and strength, duration, and level/dose of irradiation
- Total dose of irradiation. If a product is irradiated more than once, document the steps taken, individual irradiation dose, and the total (additive) irradiation dose
- Temperature and length of time out of controlled storage
- Identification of the operator and the date and time of irradiation
- Site of irradiation if the facility irradiating is different than the collecting facility

(cont'd)

Appendix 1-3. Minimum Record Requirements (Donors and Processing of Donor Units) (cont'd)

- Quality control of the irradiating device, including calibration and monitoring of dose delivered to the center of the container (corrected for air-liquid differences), turntable check, length of time required to deliver the radiation, and records of calibration studies conducted annually and after repairs
- Personnel training, including safety procedures and radiation monitoring

- Written agreement if product irradiation is to be performed in a different facility (eg, hospital radiation therapy department) which specifies that the irradiation of blood products are under the control of the blood establishment, and permits review of training and audit by the blood establishment
- Monitoring personnel exposure to radiation

1. Food and Drug Administration. Memorandum: Guidance regarding post donation information reports. December 10, 1993. Rockville, MD: CBER Office of Communication, Training, and Manufacturer's Assistance, 1993.
2. Pub. Law No. 101-336, 104 Stat. 327 (1990) codified at 42 U.S.C. §12101-12213.
3. Food and Drug Administration. Memorandum: Recommendations for the invalidation of test results when using licensed viral marker assays to screen donors. January 3, 1994. Rockville, MD: CBER Office of Communication, Training, and Manufacturer's Assistance, 1994.
4. Food and Drug Administration. Current good manufacturing practice in manufacturing, processing, packing, or holding of drugs; revision of certain labeling controls. Final rule. Fed Regist 1993;58:147.
5. Food and Drug Administration. Memorandum: Recommendations regarding license amendments and procedures for gamma irradiation of blood products. July 22, 1993. Rockville, MD: CBER Office of Communication, Training, and Manufacturer's Assistance, 1993.

Appendix 1-4. Minimum Record Requirements (Computer Systems)*

System Documentation

- Instruction manuals (eg, user's manual, operations manual, training manual, and a program maintenance manual if the user will be maintaining the software)
- Hardware configuration diagrams and system flowcharts; descriptions that define the interactions between software modules (including interfaces)
- Installation requirements and instructions, including environmental specifications
- User's requirements
- Detailed description of system's intended functions
- Description of test data base
- Location and the means of access to the source code
- Documentation of in-house programming methodology, program development, and system modifications
- Records demonstrating that the system met its predetermined specifications and requirements prior to implementation

Training and Procedures

- Training and continuing competency of personnel
- SOPs that reflect current standards, integrate computer functions into operations, and clearly explain system use
- Policies and procedures for system maintenance and operation; maintenance schedules (including preventive maintenance); backup; hardware and software change control; validation and monitoring of data integrity; periodic audits

Change Control

- System name
- Version, release or model number
- Modules affected
- Description of change and reason for the change; all changes explained both in complete technical detail and in language understood by users
- Person authorizing the change
- Person making the change
- Date and time of change
- Records documenting that procedures for hardware and software change controls are being followed

Validation

- Validation protocol that describes functions to be tested and test cases with expected results and actual results
- Records of acceptance testing to demonstrate that the intended functions performed as expected; records of testing of integrated hardware, software, and peripheral devices
- Log of problems and corrective actions taken
- Summary of validation review and approval for implementation

Audit Trail

- Identification number of donor, sample or unit
- Original value
- New value
- Originator identification, person, or device that created the record
- Modifier identification, person, or device that changed the record
- Date and time of change
- Authorization signature

---

* Food and Drug Administration. Draft: Guideline for the validation of blood establishment computer systems. October 28, 1993. Rockville, MD: CBER Office of Communication, Training, and Manufacturer's Assistance, 1993.

Appendix 1-5. Minimum Record Requirements (Automatic, Mechanical, or Electronic Equipment)[1]

- Name and identification of equipment (including software version number), inclusive dates of use, links to other equipment
- Installation qualification, process validation and revalidation
- Schedule of cleaning, preventive maintenance, quality control, calibration, and recalibration, and the results of such activities
- Problem log:
  - Down time
  - Problem descriptions
  - Error/alarm messages
  - Corrective actions (eg, hardware upgrades, repairs)
  - Results of any diagnostic tests performed
  - Analysis for trends
  - Staff and reviewer initials and dates

- Documentation of change to implement new blood typing equipment, including written approval from CBER when licensed facilities plan to deviate from the manufacturer's instructions. Records to include:
  - Calibration
  - Validation
  - Parallel testing (minimum of 500 samples over 3 days under representative conditions)
  - Complete history of instrument during pre-implementation phase
  - Discrepancies
  - NTD (no type determined) rate $\leq 6\%$
  - Lot numbers and manufacturer of all reagents used[2]

1. Food and Drug Administration. Guideline for quality assurance in blood establishments. July 11, 1995. Rockville, MD: CBER Office of Communication, Training, and Manufacturer's Assistance, 1995.
2. Food and Drug Administration. Memorandum: Changes in equipment for processing blood donor samples. July 21, 1992. Rockville, MD: CBER Office of Communication, Training, and Manufacturer's Assistance, 1992.

Appendix 1-6. Minimum Record Requirements (Quality Assessment and Quality Control)

- Dated and signed or initialed temperature recording charts for each refrigerator and freezer or central monitor record, temperature records of refrigerated centrifuges, heat-regulated devices (ie, blood warmers, incubators)
- Record of quality control tests performed on reagents for infectious disease marker tests, antihuman globulin, blood typing serum and reagent red blood cells as specified by the procedures manual
- Results of tests to evaluate the performance of other reagents (eg, copper sulfate) and equipment
- Results of equipment calibration, validation of equipment software (see also Appendix 1-4) and equipment maintenance logs
- Record of quality control tests of components prepared
- Record of periodic checks on sterile technique if components are prepared in an open system, unless an equivalent method has been approved by the FDA
- Record of sterilization of supplies and reagents prepared within the facility, including date, time interval, temperature, and mode; records of biological indicator tests to determine the effectiveness of sterilization
- Record of disposition of rejected supplies or reagents used in collection, processing, and compatibility testing of blood and blood components
- Record of supplies and reagents used, including manufacturer, lot numbers, date received, inclusive dates in use, and expiration date

- Record of employee participation in job-related education or training with inclusive dates, subjects, and evaluation, if appropriate; documentation of staff qualifications and annual competency review
- Records of proficiency testing. The Health Care Financing Administration has proficiency testing requirements for blood banks and transfusion service laboratories.* It is recommended, therefore, that the following documentation be available:
  - Sources of samples and expected answers
  - Frequency and number of tests related to each laboratory category
  - Identity of personnel performing the proficiency testing assays and relevance to their work assignments
  - System by which responsibility for proficiency testing assays is rotated or other assurance that the competence of all employees is ensured
  - Dates of testing and evaluation of performance
  - Corrective action, if necessary, and monitoring to ensure effectiveness of corrective action, if indicated
  - Training and retraining of personnel when indicated
  - Notification of state or federal agency, if required
  - Records of parallel studies performed

---

* Code of federal regulations. Title 42 CFR Part 493.801. Washington, DC: US Government Printing Office, 1998 (revised annually).

Appendix 1-7. Minimum Record Requirements (Occupational Safety and Health)[*]

- Medical record for each employee with occupational exposure, which includes
  - Name and social security number of the employee
  - Hepatitis B vaccination status and dates
  - Results of testing and examinations
  - Health-care professional's written opinion
  - Information provided to the employee
- OSHA No. 200, "The Log and Summary of Occupational Injuries and Illnesses," used to classify and record illnesses and injuries
- OSHA No. 101, "The Supplementary Record of Occupational Injuries and Illnesses," used to expand information in the log, such as how an incident happened, what part of the body was affected
- Training records will include
  - Dates of training session
  - Summary of training session
  - Names and qualifications of person conducting training
  - Names and job titles of all persons attending the training

---

[*] Code of federal regulations. Title 29 CFR Part 1904. Washington, DC: US Government Printing Office, 1998 (revised annually).

Appendix 1-8. Minimum Record Requirements (Errors and Accidents, Adverse Events, and Complaints)

- A description of the error or accident, including whether all components involved were completely tracked
- The name of the blood component(s) or product(s) involved
- The donor unit number(s) of the blood component(s) or lot numbers of the blood product(s) implicated and the manufacturer (ie, collecting or processing facility if not the same as reporting facility)
- The date of discovery
- The date of occurrence
- Whether or not the blood component or product was transfused
- Whether or not the patient's physician was made aware of the error or accident, if the blood or blood component was transfused
- An explanation of how the error or accident occurred
- The actions taken to prevent a recurrence of the error or accident
- The name of the manufacturer, lot number, and expiration date of the product if defective reagents or supplies were implicated
- Identity of the individual responsible for the error
- A copy of the notification of appropriate authorities, when applicable. All licensed establishments are required to notify the FDA of errors or accidents in the manufacture of products that may affect the safety, purity or potency of any biological product (21 CFR 600.14). The FDA has requested voluntary notification of these errors or accidents by unlicensed, registered facilities.* The FDA has identified the following examples as reportable events if components or products are released for distribution:

  - Units repeatedly reactive for viral marker testing
  - Units from donors for whom test results were improperly interpreted due to testing errors related to improper use of equipment or failure to strictly follow the reagent manufacturer's directions for use
  - Units from donors who are (or should have been) either temporarily or permanently deferred due to medical history or a history of repeatedly reactive results for viral marker tests
  - Units released prior to completion of all tests
  - Incorrectly labeled blood components (eg, ABO, expiration date)
  - Microbial contamination of blood components when the contamination is attributed to an error in manufacturing

---

* Food and Drug Administration. Memorandum: Responsibilities of blood establishments related to errors and accidents in the manufacture of blood and blood components. March 20, 1991. Rockville, MD: CBER Office of Communication, Training, and Manufacturer's Assistance, 1991.

Appendix 1-9. Record Retention

Indefinite Retention

- Donors' identifying information (including address), medical history, physical examination, consent, and interpretations of tests for disease markers, including deferral status, for each donation, including apheresis
- For patients, difficulty in blood typing, clinically significant antibodies, and adverse reactions to transfusion and special requirements for transfusion
- Blood and components received from outside sources, including numeric or alphanumeric identification of blood unit, and identification of the collecting facility; however, the information from an intermediate facility may be used if the intermediate facility retains the unit number and identification of the collecting facility
- Information to identify facilities that carry out any part of the preparation of blood components and the function performed
- Final disposition of each unit of blood or component and, if issued by the facility for transfusion, the identity of the recipient.
- Notification to donors of permanent deferral
- Records of prospective donors who have been indefinitely deferred for the protection of the potential recipient or placed on surveillance
- Look-back notifications to transfusing facilities
- Records documenting the quarantine, consignee notification, testing, and disposition of products required under proposed 21 CFR 610.46 (a)(b); notification records should include: identity of all persons who gave and received the notification, the dates and times of notification, the types and unit numbers of all blood and blood components that are the subject of the notification, the dates that the donor tested repeatedly reactive, the dates and results of more specific testing, and other information regarding the notification event[1]
- Notification to recipients of potential exposure to disease transmissible by blood
- Names, signatures, initials or identification codes, and inclusive dates of employment of those authorized to sign or initial or review reports and records
- Records shall be created and maintained to ensure tracking of prior collections, appropriate component quarantine, consignee notification, and disposition of components identified as potentially infectious based on subsequent testing
- Transfusion history, including unique identification of components received

Minimum of 5 Years or Longer as Required by Law [See Also 21 CFR 600.12(b)]

- Records of patient ABO and Rh type determined in the past 12 months must be immediately available in order to compare with the interpretations of current tests to detect possible error.
- Donors' ABO and Rh types, and difficulty in determining patient or donor ABO and Rh types
- Severe adverse reactions to donation or transfusion
- Donor apheresis clinical records and patients' therapeutic procedures, including outpatient transfusion
- Compatibility test interpretation
- Blood component inspection during storage and prior to issue
- Superseded procedures (including labels, instruction circulars, and product inserts), equipment and computer manuals, and publications with inclusive dates of use
- Obsolete source code, computer system documentation, and validation documentation must be retained for 5 years after software is no longer in use; actual results of validation testing must be retained for 5 years
- Storage temperatures, control testing, and proficiency testing surveys and any resulting corrective actions taken
- Documentation of staff qualifications, training, and competency
- Retain OSHA No. 200 and OSHA No. 101 forms for 5 years[2]
- Retain specified medical records for duration of employment plus 30 years[2]

Temporary Retention

- AABB *Standards for Blood Banks and Transfusion Services*[3] requires temporary retention of records of prospective blood donors who have been temporarily deferred for the protection of the potential recipient, for the required deferral period, including interpretations of prescreening or qualifying tests

---

1. Food and Drug Administration. Current manufacturing practices for blood and blood components; notification of consignees receiving blood and blood components at increased risk for transmitting HIV infection. Proposed rule. Fed Regist 1993;58:34962.
2. Code of federal regulations. Title 29 CFR Parts 1904, 1910.1030. Washington, DC: US Government Printing Office, 1998 (revised annually).
3. Menitove JE, ed. Standards for blood banks and transfusion services. 19th ed. Bethesda, MD: American Association of Blood Banks, 1999:82-5.

Appendix 1-10. Examples of Blood Utilization Measurement*

A blood usage review committee should consider the following areas of practice and develop specific measurements for monitoring blood transfusion processes. Some measurements provide data for several processes.

Ordering of appropriate blood components

1. Preanalytical errors. Errors in specimen collection, verbal orders, transfusion orders.
2. Units transfused. Figures for Whole Blood; Red Blood Cells, including liquid-stored, washed, leukocyte-reduced, deglycerolized, and reconstituted with plasma; Platelets, including random-donor and plateletpheresis concentrates; Plasma, including Fresh Frozen Plasma, cryoprecipitate-removed, 24-hour, and other variants; Cryoprecipitated AHF; coagulation factor concentrates; RhIG. Use of autologous and directed donor collections. Analyze by service or by prescriber.
3. Patients transfused. Total number of patients receiving each of the components or products listed in item 2.
4. Units transfused per patient transfused. Average number of units of each component or product given to patients receiving that component. May be useful to analyze by diagnosis or surgical/medical procedure.
5. Special components prepared and transfused. Number and relative percent of leukocyte-reduced, irradiated, cytomegalovirus-negative units; aliquots prepared and transfused; outpatient and home transfusions.
6. Units returned unused. Number and percent of units issued and later returned unused. Analyze by ward, by clinical service, or by prescriber.
7. Crossmatch-to-transfusion (C:T) ratio. Number of units crossmatched divided by the number of units transfused. Analysis could be by institutional total, by emergency vs routine requests, or by specific departments, clinical services, surgical procedures, or prescribers, as needed. Although no longer required by JCAHO, these data can still provide helpful information.
8. Transfusion guidelines. Are guidelines current, appropriate for the patient population being treated, and readily available to physicians? Is there a surgical blood order schedule or type and screen protocol? Are they current and appropriate?

Distribution, handling, and dispensing of blood components

1. Turnaround time. Interval between the time a transfusion request is received and time the unit is available for transfusion and/or is transported to the patient's bedside. May analyze by emergency, routine, or operative requests.
2. Emergency requests. Number and percent may be analyzed by department, service, prescriber, and diagnosis. Distribution of requests by day, week, shift, or hour may be revealing. C:T ratios can give an indication of appropriateness.
3. Uncrossmatched units. Number and percent of units issued uncrossmatched or with abbreviated pretransfusion testing. May analyze by department, service, or prescriber.
4. Age distribution of units. Age of inventory units and crossmatched units by ABO and Rh type, age of units when received from the supplier, age at the time of transfusion, age when returned to the supplier. May be analyzed by statistical methods and/or frequency histograms.
5. Surgical cancellations due to unavailability of blood. Number and percent of cases delayed due to unavailability of blood; number of hours or days of delay, analyzed by surgical procedure and by cause (eg, antibody problem in an individual patient, general shortage, or shortage of particular ABO or Rh type).
6. Significant type switches due to unavailability of blood. Number of Rh-negative patients given Rh-positive RBCs or platelets; transfusions with ABO-incompatible plasma.
7. Outdate rate. Total number of units outdated (expired unused) divided by the number of units received; should be monitored for all blood components and derivatives. Analysis by ABO and Rh type may prove informative.
8. Wastage rates. Number of units wasted due to breakage, improper preparation, improper handling or storage; units prepared and held for a patient but not used; number of units that failed to meet inspection requirements.
9. Adequacy of service from the blood supplier. Number of orders placed that could be filled as requested; average time between the order and receipt of emergency delivery; number of orders associated with an error such as improper unit received or units improperly shipped.
10. Compatibility testing requirements. Adequacy, currency, and appropriateness of policies and procedures.

(cont'd)

Appendix 1-10. Examples of Blood Utilization Measurement* (cont'd)

11. Quality control policies and procedures. Number of records of temperature, equipment, component preparation or testing that are incomplete or have deviations.

Administration of blood and blood components

1. Blood issue/delivery errors. Number of wrong units issued; number of units delivered to wrong patient-care area or improperly transported.
2. Blood administration policies and procedures. Availability of copies of current policies and procedures and of current *Circular of Information for the Use of Human Blood and Blood Components.*
3. Blood administration audits. Summary of on-site performance reviews, to include number of deviations by category (eg, identification of patient and donor unit, documentation and completeness of medical record). May include audit for documentation of transfusion order or informed consent.
4. Transfusion equipment devices. Review of quality control documentation for equipment, including blood warmers, infusion pumps, special filters or administration sets; documentation in the medical record that devices were used; number of situations where use was inappropriate.
5. Special transfusion situations. Review of compliance with policies for out-of-hospital transfusions and perioperative and postoperative collection of autologous blood.

Monitoring transfusion results

1. Compliance with transfusion guidelines. Number of inappropriate transfusions, as determined by the blood usage review committee; analysis of reasons for inappropriate transfusion.
2. Transfusion reactions. Number and percent of reported transfusion reactions; turnaround time for complete investigation; documentation of transfusion service and committee review; documentation in the medical record. May review medical record audits to ensure proper reporting.
3. Transfusion-transmitted disease. Number of cases by agent; turnaround time of investigation; completeness of review and recording.
4. Look-back/case investigations. Number of cases by agent; turnaround time of investigation; completeness of case-finding, notification, review, and recording.
5. Annual review of policies and procedures. Adequacy, currency, and appropriateness of policies and procedures for detection and reporting of adverse effects of transfusion.

Management data that may prove useful when assessing transfusion services

1. Workload and productivity. Evaluation of activities and efficiency of the laboratory; may be analyzed by day of week and by shift. Hours worked per unit transfused or patient transfused may be more valuable as an efficiency measure than data obtained from traditional productivity calculations.
2. Error reports. Number of errors dealing with laboratory processes (eg, labeling, preparation, testing, issue); procedural errors in blood administration; errors and recalls by blood supplier(s).
3. Staff training and competency. Documentation of training and continuing competency of laboratory and nursing staff to perform transfusion-related procedures and policies.

---

* Comprehensive accreditation manual for hospitals: The office handbook. Oakbrook Terrace, IL: Joint Commission on the Accreditation of Healthcare Organizations, 1998.

Facilities and Safety

2

SAFETY AND THE OPERATION OF A facility are integral parts of every blood bank and transfusion service process, and all employees of an organization have a responsibility for providing continual maintenance and improvement. There must be defined processes, training, and competency programs in accordance with regulations for emergency and disaster preparedness, chemical hygiene, blood-borne pathogens, and radiation safety when applicable. A full discussion of facilities and safety is beyond the scope of this chapter, which introduces only general elements. The references and Appendix 2-1 may be used to obtain more information.

General Safety Principles

Regulations

The American Association of Blood Banks (AABB) requires accredited blood banks and transfusion services to have in operation a program to minimize risks to the health and safety of donors, patients, volunteers, and employees from biological, chemical, and radiological hazards.[1] The College of American Pathologists (CAP) and the National Committee for Clinical Laboratory Standards (NCCLS) also require safety programs and offer more specific guidelines for clinical laboratory safety.[2,3] In addition, the Joint Commission on the Accreditation of Healthcare Organizations (JCAHO) supports facility-wide safety programs.[4]

The safety requirements mentioned in this chapter are based on the published regulations and recommendations from the following agencies: Occupational Safety and Health Administration (OSHA), the Food and Drug Administration (FDA), the Centers for Disease Control and Prevention (CDC), the Environmental Protection Agency (EPA), the National Fire Protection Agency (NFPA), the Nuclear Regulatory Commission (NRC), the Department of Transportation (DOT), the United States Postal Service (USPS), and the International Air Transportation Association (IATA).

Safety Programs

Good safety practices start with a written facility safety program. This program defines which regulatory requirements apply and how they will be met and maintained. In general, institutions are required to:

- Provide a hazard-free workplace.
- Evaluate all procedures for potential exposure risks.
- Evaluate each employment position for potential exposure risks.
- Identify hazardous areas or materials with appropriate labels and signs.
- Educate staff, document training, and monitor compliance.
- Apply Standard Precautions (includes Universal and Blood and Body Fluid Precautions) to the handling of blood, body fluids, and tissues.
- Dispose of hazardous waste appropriately.
- Report incidents and accidents and provide treatment and follow-up.
- Provide ongoing review of safety policies, procedures, operations, and equipment.
- Develop facility policies for disaster preparedness and response.

Safety programs should consider the needs of all persons affected by the work environment. Most obvious is the safety of technical staff, but potential risks for blood donors, ancillary personnel, volunteers, visitors, housekeeping staff, maintenance workers, and repair staff must also be evaluated and appropriate

provisions applied if these individuals cannot be excluded from risk areas.

The safety program, with its policies, guidelines, and supporting regulatory documents, should be detailed in a safety manual and made available to all personnel at risk. This manual, along with operational procedures manuals, should be reviewed at least annually and updated as technology evolves and new information becomes available. Work sites and safety equipment also should be inspected regularly to ensure compliance and response readiness. Checklists are helpful in documenting these audits and assessing safety preparedness. Sources[2,3,5,6] exist for checklist items and essential key elements for safety and environmental management audits.

NCCLS recommends that laboratories appoint a safety officer who can provide general guidance and expertise.[3] This individual might develop the safety program, oversee orientation and training, perform safety audits, survey work sites, recommend changes, and serve on or direct the activities of safety committees, but he or she is usually not directly responsible for safety. It is also recommended that facilities using hazardous chemicals and radioactive materials appoint a chemical hygiene officer and radiation safety officer to oversee chemical and radiation protection programs.[7,8] A general safety officer with sufficient expertise may fill these roles, or separate officers may be appointed and program oversight given to a safety committee.

Those responsible for safety must be concerned with protecting the environment, as well as staff. Every effort should be made to establish facility-wide programs to reduce solid wastes including nonhazardous and especially hazardous wastes (ie, biohazardous, chemical, and radiation wastes). A hazardous waste reduction program instituted at the point of use of the material achieves several goals. It reduces the institutional risk for occupational exposures to hazardous agents and "cradle to grave" liability for disposal, as well as enhances compliance with environmental mandates to reduce pollution generated from daily operations of the laboratory. These mandates require a facility to minimize pollution of the environment via the three R's (reduce, reuse, and recycle).[9] This is especially important in dealing with mixed hazardous waste, which is typical of the waste generated by blood bank activities.

Physical Workplace

Design

Proper design of facilities and organization of work can reduce or eliminate many potential hazards. State and local building codes should be consulted in design planning stages for architectural safety standards regarding space, furnishings, and storage. The nationally accepted specifications for ventilation are published by the American Society for Heating, Refrigeration, and Air Conditioning Engineers, Inc.

Laboratories must be designed with adequate electrical power and conveniently located outlets. The National Electric Code is routinely used as a national guideline for the design of essential electrical distribution systems with modifications approved by the local "building" authority having jurisdiction.

Staff handling biohazardous materials must have ready access to hand-washing stations. Specific workplace requirements for biological, chemical, radiation, and fire safety are discussed in the sections below.

Housekeeping

The workplace should be kept clean and free of clutter. Work surfaces should be regularly cleaned and disinfected. Trash should not be allowed to accumulate and exits must not be blocked or obstructed in any way. Receptacles and disposal guidelines for nonhazardous solid waste vs biohazardous, chemical, and radiation waste should be clearly delineated. Housekeeping responsibilities, methods, and schedules should be defined for every work area. Written

procedures, initial training and continuing education of personnel, and ongoing monitoring of housekeeping effectiveness are essential to safe operations.

Restricted Areas

Hazardous areas should be clearly and uniformly identified with warning signs in accordance with OSHA and NCR standards so that personnel entering them are aware of existing biologic, chemical, or radiation dangers.[3,8,10-12] Staff not normally assigned to these areas should receive adequate training to avoid endangering themselves when they enter.

"High risk" areas include chemical fume hoods, biological safety cabinets, and storage areas for volatile chemicals or radioisotopes. Technical work areas are considered "moderate risk" and are restricted to laboratory personnel. Administrative and clerical areas are considered to be "low risk" and are not restricted.

Whenever possible, functions not requiring special precautions should be separated from those performed in restricted areas. Every effort should be made to prevent the contamination of designated "clean" areas and common equipment. Work area phones can be equipped with speakers to eliminate the need to pick up the receiver and computer keyboards and telephones can be covered with plastic and should be cleaned on a regular basis and when visibly soiled. Employees should remove their personal protective barriers such as gloves and aprons and wash their hands when leaving a "contaminated" area.

Concerns for safety dictate that there be no casual visitors in areas where blood and other biohazards may be encountered.[13-14] Children, especially, should not be allowed in areas where they could be exposed to hazards and should be closely supervised in those areas where their presence is permitted. Facilities should consider establishing specific safety guidelines for visitors with business in restricted areas and documenting that this information was received and understood.

Mobile Sites

Mobile blood collection operations can present special problems. An individual trained in safety principles should make an advance visit to the collection site to ensure that hazards are minimized. All mobile personnel should be trained to recognize unsafe conditions and understand infection control policies and procedures, but responsibility for site safety should be assigned to a senior-level employee.

Hand-washing access is essential at all collection sites. Carpeted or difficult-to-clean surfaces can be protected with an absorbent overlay with waterproof backing if blood spills might occur. Portable screens and ropes are helpful in directing traffic flow to maintain safe work areas. Food service areas should be physically separated from areas for blood collection and storage. Blood-contaminated waste must be either returned to a central location for disposal or packaged and decontaminated using thermal (autoclave, incinerator) or chemical disinfectant in accordance with local regulations for medical wastes. Trained staff must perform this decontamination with particular attention paid to postcollection cleanup of mobile sites.

Safety Training

Who Needs Training and When

The mandate for employee training programs is based on good general practice as well as OSHA requirements.[10-11,15] All persons working with hazardous materials must be trained to protect themselves appropriately before beginning work. Supervisors or their designees are responsible for documenting employee's understanding of and ability to apply safety precautions before independent work is permitted. Safety training must precede even temporary work assignments if significant differences in potential hazards exist. Staff who do not demonstrate the requisite understanding and skills must undergo retraining, and staff with no prior experience in handling human pathogens must

be progressively instructed in the handling of infectious agents after they demonstrate competence in each area.

OSHA also requires[15] periodic training (at least annually) for all employees whose tasks carry risk of infectious exposure. The frequency with which training is provided or updated will depend on changes made in work environments and on acquisition of new information about hazards.

Training programs must be tailored to the target group, both in level and content. General background knowledge of biohazards, understanding of control procedures, or previous work experience cannot meet the requirement for specific training, although assessment of such knowledge is a first step in planning program content. Volunteer employees require at least as much safety training as paid staff performing similar functions. Indeed, they may require more frequent training because their more limited experience can make them less aware of hazards.

Specific training programs may be tailored for the needs of housekeeping personnel or other personnel at risk of exposure, prior to job assignment. In these situations, job tasks with increased risk (eg, working in an area where infectious units are quarantined) should be clearly distinguished from tasks that require basic safety training. Periodic (at least annual) updates on safety training are particularly important for this group.

Topics to Cover

Work safety training programs should ensure that all personnel:

■   Have access to a copy of pertinent regulatory texts and an explanation of the contents.

■   Understand the employer's exposure control plan and know how to obtain a copy of the written plan.

■   Understand how hepatitis and human immunodeficiency virus (HIV) are transmitted and how often; know the symptoms and consequences of hepatitis B virus (HBV) and HIV infection and are offered vaccination against HBV.

■ Recognize tasks that pose infectious risk and distinguish them from other duties.

■ Know what protective clothing and equipment are appropriate for the procedures they will perform.

■ Know and understand the limitations of protective clothing and equipment, (eg, different types of gloves are recommended based on the permeability of the hazardous material to be used). Employers and staff who use protective equipment should be forewarned against a false sense of security.

■ Know where protective clothing and equipment are kept, how to use them properly and how to remove, handle, decontaminate, and dispose of contaminated material.

■ Are familiar with and understand all requirements for work practices and protective equipment specified in standard operating procedures (SOPs) for the tasks they perform, including the meaning of signs and labels.

■ Know the appropriate actions to take and persons to contact if exposed to blood or other biological, chemical, or radiological hazards.

■ Know the corrective actions to take in the event of spills or personal exposure to fluids, tissues, and contaminated sharps, the appropriate reporting procedures and the medical monitoring recommended when parenteral exposure may have occurred.

■ Know their right of access to medical treatment and medical records.

Assessing Competence and Compliance

Assessing competence of staff with all safety training is no different than assessing their competence with regard to technical issues. Staff must be provided the appropriate training to meet the expectations of their particular jobs, and the staff must demonstrate an understanding of the safety regulations as they apply to their jobs. Periodic retraining or additional training must be documented, to ensure that all personnel are provided with appropriate safety training.

Supervisory personnel must monitor safety practices in their areas of responsibility. Continuing attention to safety issues should be addressed in routine staff meetings and training sessions. Periodic audits performed by a safety professional may help increase safety awareness.

Internal assessments or audits should review error /accident or occurrence reports relating to safety issues and, when appropriate, root-cause analysis should be used to find opportunities for improvement. This analysis may result in the detection of equipment flaws or workflow problems that may result in unsafe practices. Any changes that are instituted as a result of process improvement should be validated prior to implementation, and should be tracked to ensure resolution of problems or improvement of safety in the workplace. Continual monitoring of the problem area will be helpful in assessing the impact of the change, and may lead to further changes or processes for improvement.

Personal Protective Equipment

OSHA requires that hazards be controlled by engineering means whenever possible. Where hazards cannot be eliminated, OSHA requires employers to provide appropriate personal protective equipment (PPE) and clothing, and to clean, launder, or dispose of PPE at no cost to their employees.[11]

Standard PPE and clothing include uniforms, laboratory coats, gloves, face shields, masks, safety goggles, biologic safety cabinets and fume hoods, hand-washing facilities, eyewashes, and emergency showers. Indications for their use as well as concerns about latex allergy are discussed in depth in Appendix 2-2.

Facilities should consider the need for establishing guidelines on the use of appropriate shoes and hair coverings and on wearing jewelry in laboratory areas.

Hepatitis Prophylaxis

All employees routinely exposed to blood must be offered hepatitis B vaccine if they do not already have HBV-protective antibodies. OSHA requires that the vaccine be offered at no cost to the employee, and if the employee refuses the vaccine, that the refusal be documented.[10-11,15]

Accidents and Injuries

Injury Reports

When an injury occurs, as much information as possible should be documented, including:

- Name and address of the injured person.
- Time of the accident (hour, day, month, year).
- Specific place where the accident occurred.
- Details of the injured person's activities at the time of injury.
- Nature of injury (bruise, laceration, burn, etc).
- Part of the body injured (head, arm, leg, etc).
- Nature of the known or potential agent, in cases of exposure to pathogenic organisms or other hazardous materials.
- Nature of medical attention or first aid applied in the workplace.
- Date the injured person stopped work.
- Date the injured person returned to work.
- Estimated cost of damage to property or to equipment.
- Injured person's statement of the events leading to the accident.
- Statements from witnesses.
- Cause of the accident.
- Corrective action taken or recommendations for corrective action.

In addition, the supervisor should complete any accident reports and investigation forms required by the institution's insurer and worker's compensation agencies. Medical reports for individual employees should be preserved for the duration of employment plus 30 years, with few exceptions.

OSHA requires health service employers with 11 or more workers to maintain records of occupational injuries and illnesses.[16] Initial documentation must be completed within 6 days of the incident. All logs, summaries, and supplemental records must be preserved for at least 5 years beyond the calendar year of occurrence. Employers must report fatalities and injuries resulting in the hospitalization of three or more employees to OSHA within 8 hours of the accident.

Medical Follow-up

When requested by a worker who has sustained known or suspected blood exposure, monitoring for HBV and HIV antibodies must be provided free of charge along with appropriate counseling. Informed consent is required for this voluntary testing; rejection of offered testing must be documented. The usual schedule would include immediate tests on the worker and on the source of the potentially infectious material, with follow-up of the worker at intervals after exposure.[10-11,17] All aspects of accident follow-up should be appropriately documented.

The CDC has published recommendations for both pre- and postexposure prophylaxis if the contaminating material is HBV-positive or if this information is unknown.[17] Hepatitis B Immune Globulin is usually given concurrently with hepatitis B vaccine in cases of penetrating injuries. When administered in accordance with the manufacturer's directions, both products are very safe and carry no risk for infection with HBV and HIV. Because postexposure prophylaxis for HIV is continually evolving, policies for this are generally determined by the facility medical director and based on Public Health Service recommendations and current standards of practice.

Blood-Borne Pathogen Safety

Standard Precautions

Standard Precautions described by the CDC in 1996, incorporate Universal Precautions and Blood and Body Fluid Precautions together. Standard Precautions and the OSHA document for prevention of occupational exposure to blood-borne pathogens[10-11] apply to blood, body fluids, and tissues from *all* patients regardless of diagnosis. The precautions are intended for all routine practices, as parenteral or mucous membrane exposures to blood from persons with nonreactive diagnostic test results may transmit infection.

Standard Precautions constitute a safe approach to preventing adverse occupational exposures to body fluids because employees have a single standard, and errors in assessing patient's status will not endanger employee's safety. The Standard Precautions do acknowledge a difference between hospital patients and healthy donors, in whom the prevalence of infectious disease markers is significantly lower. Some blood centers classify donor phlebotomy as a low-risk task and modify the precautions taken.

The US Department of Health and Human Services has published safety recommendations for laboratories where individuals are at risk of exposure to infectious agents. The recommendations for four levels of biosafety were based on the potential hazards for specific infectious agents and the laboratory activity performed.[13]

Biosafety Level 1

Work that involves agents of no known or of minimal potential hazard to laboratory personnel and the environment is classified as Biosafety Level 1 (BSL 1). Work is usually conducted on open surfaces and no containment equipment is needed.

Biosafety Level 2

Work that involves agents of moderate potential hazard to personnel and the environment, usu-ally from contact-associated exposure is classified as Biosafety Level 2. Personnel wear laboratory coats and gloves as indicated; access to work areas is limited; and containment equipment should be used for procedures likely to create aerosols. All work with human blood requires minimal precautions outlined for BSL 2 precautions. Work at BSL 2, typical of blood banking activities, can be performed safely on a laboratory counter if workers follow means that reduce the risk of direct contact with blood (eg, gloves, pipette aids, and disinfectants).

Biosafety Level 3

Biosafety Level 3 includes work that involves indigenous or exotic agents that may cause serious or potentially lethal disease as a result of exposure to aerosols (eg, *Mycobacterium tuberculosis*) or by other routes that, should infection occur, would result in grave consequences to the host (eg, HIV). BSL 3 recommends a combination of work practices, safety equipment, and facility design features that contain biohazardous aerosols and minimize the risk of surface contamination to a higher degree than the recommendations for work at BSL 2.

Biosafety Level 4

Work that involves dangerous or exotic agents that pose high individual risk of life-threatening disease from aerosols (eg, agents of hemorrhagic fevers, filoviruses) is classified as Biosafety Level 4. BSL 4 is not applicable to routine blood bank-related activities.

Special Precautions

Several factors need to be considered when assessing the risk of blood exposures among laboratory personnel. Some factors include the number of specimens processed, inappropriate behaviors, flawed laboratory techniques, and malfunctioning equipment.[18] BSL 2 precautions that are applicable to the laboratory setting are summarized in Appendix 2-3. Should certain procedures be considered higher risk (eg, higher than BSL 2 risks), the laboratory director may wish to institute BSL 3 practices. Work typical of blood banking operations may benefit from using the higher level of work practices and containment equipment without making costly changes to the structure of the facility. All changes in procedures should be fine tuned based on the risk assessment of work performed in the laboratory and when new procedures are introduced to staff. When there is doubt whether an activity is BSL 2 or BSL 3, the safety precautions for BSL 3 should be followed.

Procedures used in the donation of blood should also be assessed for risks of biohazardous exposures and risks inherent in working with a donor or patient. Some procedures are more likely to cause injury than others, such as using lancets for finger puncture, handling capillary tubes, crushing vials for arm cleaning, handling any unsheathed needle, cleaning scissors, and giving cardiopulmonary resuscitation (CPR).

In areas where Source Plasma is collected for plasma production or such as vaccine production, it may be necessary to collect blood from donors known to pose a high risk of infectivity. The FDA provides the following recommendations[19]:

- The consent document makes it clear that blood collection and processing staff will be aware of positive test results and that the component will have special biohazard labeling.

- The phlebotomy is performed away from normal donor operations, either at a separate time or in a separate area.

- The phlebotomy area and all equipment used are cleaned and disinfected after each procedure.

- Personnel wear protective gowns, gloves, masks, and eye shields throughout all aspects of the procedure.

- Only closed, disposable collection systems with integrally attached satellite containers are used.

- The blood or components are stored separately from other blood components, in double overwraps that are sealed at all times.

- Labeling, packaging, and shipping conditions comply with applicable CDC and DOT regulations for biohazardous materials. (See Method 1.1 for shipping specimens.)

- All disposable materials used are promptly autoclaved or incinerated under the supervision of trained staff.

- Employers must offer HBV vaccination free of charge to all employees who are exposed to blood or other potentially infectious materials as part of their job duties.

Always consult the most recent FDA regulations and guidelines for changes or additions to these procedures.

Decontamination

Surfaces and all reusable equipment contaminated with blood require daily cleaning and decontamination. Obvious spills should be cleaned up immediately; routine wipe-downs should occur at the end of each shift or on a regular basis that provides equivalent safety.

Choice of Disinfectants

The EPA maintains a list of chemical products that have been shown to be effective antimicrobial disinfectants.[20] (See web site www.epa.gov for a current list.) Before selecting a product, workers should consider several factors. Among them are the type of material or surface to be treated, the hazardous properties of the chemical such as corrosiveness, and the level of disinfection required. After selecting a product, procedures need to be written to ensure effective and consistent cleaning and treatment of work surfaces. Some factors to consider for effective decontamination include the contact time, the type of microorganisms, the presence of organic matter, and the concentration of the chemical agent. Workers should review the basic information on decontamination and follow the manufacturer's instructions.[21]

Workers in the blood bank should select products based on their need to clean surfaces on biomedical equipment and counters. Lipid-containing viruses such as HIV and HBV, the most likely infectious agents found in blood banks, are susceptible to all categories of disinfectants recommended for cleaning environmental surfaces.[21]

Blood Spills

Every facility handling blood should prepare for spills in advance. Cleanup is easier when preparation includes the following elements:
- Design work areas so that cleanup is relatively simple.
- Prepare a spill cart that contains all necessary supplies and equipment, and instructions for their use. Place the cart near areas where spills are anticipated.
- Assign responsibility for cart maintenance, spill handling, record-keeping, and review of significant incidents.
- Train all potentially involved personnel in cleanup and reporting of significant incidents.
- When blood spills occur, the following steps should be taken:
- Contain the spill if possible.
- Evacuate the area for 30 minutes if an aerosol has been created and post warnings to keep the area clear. Remove clothing if it is contaminated. If the spill occurs in the centrifuge, turn the power off immediately and leave the cover closed for 30 minutes. The use of overwraps helps prevent aerosols and helps contain the spill.
- Wear appropriate protective clothing and gloves. If sharp objects are involved, gloves must be puncture-resistant, and a broom or other instrument should be used during cleanup to avoid injury.

- Clean with detergent.
- Flood the area with disinfectant and use it as described in the manufacturer's instructions.
- Wipe up residual disinfectant if necessary.
- Dispose of all materials safely in accordance with biohazard guidelines. All blood-contaminated items must be autoclaved or incinerated.

Biohazardous Waste Management

A goal of waste management should be to reduce to a minimum the volume of hazardous material. Noninfectious waste should always be separated from infectious waste. Changes in techniques or materials, which reduce the volume of infectious waste or render it less hazardous, should be carefully considered and employees should be encouraged to identify safer alternatives wherever possible.

The facility's biosafety program must address the disposition of waste contaminated with blood or body fluids. The safety officer should design a program that adequately protects staff and the general public and that meets federal, state, and local regulatory requirements.[7]

Hazardous Waste Definitions

Laboratory staff or other technically knowledgeable personnel are responsible for identifying the kinds of waste that require special handling and disposal.[22,23]

Hazardous waste, which may or may not be infectious, is defined as waste that because of its quantity; concentration; or physical, chemical, or infectious characteristics may pose a substantial or potential threat to human health or the environment. Hazardous waste can be biological, chemical, or radioactive in nature.

Infectious waste includes disposable equipment, articles, or substances that may harbor or transmit pathogenic organisms or their toxins.

Medical waste includes but is not limited to infectious waste. It is any waste (solid, semisolid, or liquid) generated in the diagnosis, treatment, or immunization of human beings or animals in related research, production, or testing of biologics.

In addition, the EPA lists the following as infectious waste that may be found in the laboratory[22]: isolation wastes, cultures and stocks of etiologic agents, bulk blood and blood products, pathologic wastes, microbiology laboratory waste, other wastes from surgery and autopsy, contaminated laboratory wastes, sharps, dialysis unit wastes, discarded biologics, and contaminated equipment. In general, these items should either be incinerated or decontaminated prior to disposal in a sanitary landfill. Bulk blood, suctioned fluids, excretions, and secretions may be carefully poured down a drain connected to a sanitary sewer. Sanitary sewers may also be used to dispose of other potentially infectious wastes that can be ground and flushed into the sewer. Always check state and local health departments about laws and regulations on disposal of biological waste into the sewer.

Laboratories should clearly define the hazardous vs nonhazardous waste generated in specific areas. For example, in the blood bank all items obviously contaminated with liquid, semiliquid, or dried ("caked-on") blood are biohazardous. Used gloves, used swabs, plastic pipettes with excess liquid removed, or gauze contaminated with "drops" of blood that subsequently dry such that the item is stained but not soaked or caked may be considered nonhazardous.

Guidelines for Biohazardous Waste Disposal

Employee training is essential; untrained personnel should not handle or dispose of biohazardous waste, even if it is packaged. The following disposal guidelines are recommended[4]:

- Identify biohazardous waste consistently; red seamless plastic bags or containers carrying the biohazard symbol are recommended.

- Double-bag waste or place in a protective container, to avoid breakage and leakage during storage or transport.

- Discard sharps (eg, needles, broken glass, glass slides, wafers from sterile connecting devices) in rigid, puncture-proof, leakproof containers.

- Put liquids only in leakproof unbreakable containers.

- Do not compact waste materials.

Areas in which infectious material is stored must be secured to reduce accident risk. Never place infectious waste in the public trash collection system. Most facilities hire private carriers to decontaminate and dispose of infectious or hazardous waste. Contracts with these companies should include disclosure of the risks of handling the waste by the facility, and an acknowledgment by the carrier that all federal, state, and local laws for biohazardous (medical) waste transport, treatment, and disposal are known and followed.

Treating Infectious or Medical Waste

In 1997 the EPA published the final rule for standards of performance for new stationary sources and emission guidelines for existing sources.[24] This document should be read in full by all facilities incinerating hazardous waste. In this regulation, a hospital/medical/infectious waste incinerator (HMIWI) is any device that combusts any amount of hospital waste or medical/infectious waste. Medical/infectious waste includes but is not limited to: human blood and blood products (liquid waste human blood, products of blood, items saturated or dripping with human blood), sharps and broken or unbroken glassware that were in contact with infectious agents.

The new regulations set guidelines for emissions from incinerators and sets timelines for the facility to control certain designated pollutants from the HMIWI. This regulation includes guidelines for operator training and sets qualification guidelines for operators, inspection guidelines, and compliance and performance testing and monitoring guidelines. Each facility coming under this regulation must test and determine the emissions of specific pollutants, and work toward reducing those emissions based on the size and quantity of materials incinerated.

Decontamination of biohazardous waste by autoclaving is another common method for decontamination/inactivation of blood samples and blood products. The following elements are considered in determining processing time for autoclaving:

- Size of load being autoclaved.
- Type of packaging of item(s) being autoclaved.
- Density of items being autoclaved.
- Number of items in single autoclave load.
- Placement of items in the autoclave, to allow for steam penetration. It is useful to place a biological indicator in the center of loads that vary in size and contents to evaluate optimal steam penetration times. The EPA provides detailed information about choosing and operating equipment.[22]

Longer treatment times are needed for sterilization, but decontamination requires a minimum of 1 hour. A general rule is to process 1 hour for every 10 pounds of waste being processed. Usually decontaminated laboratory wastes can be disposed of as nonhazardous solid wastes. Staff should check with the local solid waste authority to ensure that the facility is in compliance with the regulations for their area. Waste containing broken glass or other sharp items should be disposed of in a method consistent with policies for the disposal of other sharp or potential dangerous materials.

Storage, Transportation, and Shipment of Hazardous Materials

Storage Recommendations

Hazardous materials must be segregated and areas for different types of storage must be clearly demarcated. Blood must be protected from unnecessary exposure to other materials and vice versa. If transfusion products cannot be stored in a separate refrigerator from reagents, specimens, and unrelated materials, areas within the refrigerator must be clearly labeled and extra care must be taken to reduce the likelihood of spills and other accidents. Storage areas must be kept clean and orderly; food or drink is never allowed where biohazardous materials are stored.

Open containers should be prohibited during storage and transportation. Containers and their lids or seals should be designed to prevent spills or leakage in all reasonably anticipated conditions. Containers should be able to safely store the maximum anticipated volume and should be easy to clean. Surfaces should be kept clean and dry at all times.

Controlled Transport Recommendations

Local surface transport of blood specimens, components, and biohazardous materials from one facility (or part thereof) to another may be made by a local approved courier service. The safe transport of these materials requires they be packaged in such a way that the possibility of leakage or other release from the package under normal conditions of transport does not occur. The following practices should be observed[25]:

- Package specimens or materials in watertight and leakproof containers.
- Package specimens within a container so that they will not leak and will remain in an upright position.
- Secure all transport containers with tight-fitting covers.
- Secure containers in the transport vehicle.
- Label the containers with the contents of the container.
- Accompany the containers with identifying forms of the contents of the containers.

- Maintain a spill kit equipped with enough absorbent material and chloride disinfectant to clean up the contents of the container in the transport vehicle. A leakproof waste disposal container and heavy-duty gloves should also be in the vehicle.
- Ensure that a person trained in transporting hazardous material accompanies the transport of the materials.
- Ensure that all state and local regulations are followed.

Shipping Recommendations

Three federal agencies specify packaging and shipping requirements for biological material: the PHS, USPS, and DOT.[26] In addition, the IATA, which adopts the international recommendations of the United Nations on packing and shipping such materials, helps regulate the transport of dangerous goods by air.

Because all these regulations are similar and most carriers follow the shipping guidelines set forth in the IATA Dangerous Goods Regulations,[27] this document can offer general shipping advice for all hazardous materials. Facilities should also consult their specific local carriers for additional requirements.

Dangerous Goods Classifications. IATA classifies hazards into nine categories: explosives, gases, flammable liquids, flammable solids, oxidizing substances and organic peroxides, toxic and infectious substances, radioactive materials, and miscellaneous dangerous goods. The infectious category includes:

- Infectious substances: microbiologic agents or their toxins that cause, or may cause, disease; also called etiologic agents.
- Biological products: products that are prepared and shipped in compliance with the provisions of 9 CFR 102, 9 CFR 103, 9 CFR 104, 21 CFR 312, or 21 CFR 600-680.
- Diagnostic specimens: human or animal material (including excreta, secreta,

blood/components, body fluids, tissue) being shipped for the purpose of diagnosis.
- Genetically modified organisms.
- Clinical and medical waste.

Blood Bank Applications. Although the USPS regulates some biological products such as live poliovirus vaccine, the PHS, DOT and IATA take the position that biological products and diagnostic specimens are exempt from regulation unless they contain or are reasonably believed to contain an infectious substance.[27]

Units of blood that meet disease testing requirements and unscreened blood from healthy donors meeting all FDA donor suitability criteria may be shipped without hazard restrictions.

Specimens with a low probability of disease being shipped for routine screening or initial diagnosis purposes are packaged as diagnostic samples (IATA packing instruction 650), but specimens from individuals known, or thought likely, to have disease are shipped as infectious substances (IATA packing instruction 602).[22]

Packaging Guidelines. See Method 1.1 for detailed shipping instructions for diagnostic and infectious specimens. The goal is to package biological materials so that leakage does not occur.

Primary containers should be leakproof and securely closed, with screw caps reinforced with adhesive tape. The primary container should be placed in a watertight secondary container, such as a sealed plastic bag. Absorbent material capable of absorbing the entire liquid contents in the package is placed between the primary and secondary containers. The outer packaging should have adequate strength for its intended use and capacity and be labeled in accordance with current regulations. "Wet" ice, if included as a coolant, is placed in sealed plastic bags to prevent leakage.

Training Guidelines. The DOT requires anyone who packages infectious or toxic materials for shipment to be trained every 2 years.

Dry Ice

Solid carbon dioxide or "dry ice" is classified as a hazardous material (HAZMAT), because it can cause burns on contact and it gives off CO_2 gas as it volatilizes. Dry ice should be handled in a well-ventilated area; its gas can cause lightheadedness and, in extreme cases, asphyxiation.

Adequate ventilation is also required during transit. If dry ice is kept in a tightly sealed shipping container, the gas could rupture the packaging. Procedures for packing blood products with dry ice must include instructions for sealing the shipping container in a manner that allows the gas to escape. Insulated gloves should be worn when handling dry ice; eye protection should be worn when breaking up chunks of solid ice or when breaking apart ice pellets.

Labels. Packages with dry ice must be labeled with the following information[27] (see also Method 1.1):

- The diamond-shaped Class 9 symbol for miscellaneous hazardous materials.
- The words "Dry Ice" or "Carbon Dioxide, Solid."
- "UN 1845," the United Nations hazardous material category for dry ice (if shipped out of the country).
- The weight of the dry ice, if it is more than 5 pounds.

Training. HAZMAT training requirements are found in 49 CFR 172.704.[28] Training for staff who come in contact with dry ice should include information on:

- Potential hazards associated with dry ice.
- Personal protective equipment to use when handling or chipping dry ice.
- Procedures for packing, sealing, and labeling boxes containing dry ice.
- Procedures for handling boxes containing dry ice.
- Special considerations in operating a vehicle used to transport boxes containing dry ice.

Chemical Safety

OSHA mandates that facilities with laboratories using hazardous chemicals develop a formal, written, and employee-accessible Chemical Hygiene Plan (CHP) that conforms to recommendations published by the National Research Council.[7] The facility's CHP must comply with current federal, state, and local regulations, and must be capable of protecting laboratory personnel and other support staff from potential adverse health effects associated with exposure to hazardous chemicals.[7,12] The CHP should outline procedures, equipment, personal protective equipment, and work practices that are capable of protecting employees from hazardous chemicals used in the facility. This plan must also provide assurance to the employees and to management that equipment and protective devices are functioning properly and that criteria to determine implementation and maintenance of all aspects of the plan are in control. Employees must be informed of all chemical hazards in the workplace and be trained how to recognize chemical hazards, how to protect themselves when working with these chemicals, and where to find information on particular hazardous chemicals. Safety audits and annual reviews are important control steps that help maintain continual safety practices and ensure that the CHP is up to date.

The Hazard Communication program[12] is meant to complement the CHP. This program is meant to "ensure that the hazards of all chemicals produced or imported are evaluated, and that information concerning their hazards is transmitted to employers and employees."[12] Facilities are required to have a comprehensive hazard communication program that includes labeling hazardous chemicals, when and how to post warning labels for chemicals, managing material safety data sheets (MSDS) for hazardous chemicals in the facilities, and employee training. The development of a comprehensive education and training program regarding hazards of chemicals and protective measures is an integral part of this program.

General Principles

Chemical safety is an essential part of a facility's overall safety program. One of the most productive preventive measures a facility can take to reduce hazardous chemical exposure is to evaluate the use of alternative nonhazardous chemicals whenever possible. A review of ordering practices of hazardous chemicals can also result in the purchase of smaller quantities of hazardous chemicals, thus reducing the risk of storing excess chemicals and later dealing with the disposal of these chemicals.

A major problem in any facility in establishing a CHP is a clear definition of what constitutes hazardous chemicals. Generally, hazardous chemicals are those chemicals that have been shown to pose a significant risk (acute or chronic health effects may occur) if an employee is exposed to that chemical. The chemicals considered to be health hazards are grouped into the following categories:

- Carcinogens: ability to induce a malignant tumor.
- Toxic or highly toxic: causing serious biological effects following inhalation, ingestion, or skin contact with relatively small amounts.
- Reproductive toxins: chemicals that affect reproductive capabilities, including chromosomal damages and effects on fetuses.
- Irritants: causing irritations (edemia, burning, etc) to skin or mucous membranes upon contact.
- Corrosive: causing destruction of human tissue at the site of contact.
- Hepatotoxins, nephrotoxins, neurotoxins, agents that act on the hematopoietic systems, and agents that damage the lungs, skin, eyes, or mucous membranes: self-explanatory.

Other chemical hazards affecting safety are physical hazards. These include chemicals or substances that are:

- Combustible or flammable: ability to burn (includes combustible and flammable liquids, solids, aerosols, and gases). Tables 2-1 and 2-2 address allowable container sizes.
- Compressed gas: a gas or mixture of gases in a container under pressure.
- Explosive: unstable or reactive chemicals that undergo violent chemical change at normal temperatures and pressure.
- Unstable (reactive): chemicals that could be self-reactive under conditions of shocks, pressure, or temperature.
- Water-reactive: chemicals that react with water to release a gas that is either flammable or presents a health hazard.

Specific guidelines for facilities determining what constitutes a hazardous material are the responsibility of the chemical hygiene officer, who "is qualified by training or experience to provide technical guidance in the development and implementation of the provisions of the Chemical Hygiene Plan."[7] This person/persons is accountable for monitoring and documenting accidents and initiating process change as needed.

Guidelines for laboratory areas in which hazardous chemicals are used or stored must be established. Physical facilities, especially ventilation, must be adequate for the nature and volume of work conducted. Chemicals must be stored according to chemical compatibility (eg, corrosives, flammables, oxidizers, etc) and in minimal volumes. Bulk chemicals should be kept outside work areas. NFPA standards provide guidelines for proper storage.[3,29]

Hazard Communication

Employers must prepare a comprehensive hazard communication program for all areas using hazardous chemicals. The program must provide information about container labeling, warnings, MSDS, and employee training.

Table 2-1. Maximum Allowable Container Size—Flammable Liquids

Container	Class of Liquid*		
	IA	IB	IC
Glass or approved plastic	1 pt or 500 mL	1 qt or L	1 gal
Safety cans: NFPA, JCAHO	1 gal	2 gal	2 gal
OSHA	2 gal	5 gal	5 gal

*Class IA = FP <73 F, BP <100 F
 Class IB = FP <73 F, BP ≥100 F
 Class IC = FP 73-100 F, BP >100 F
FP = Flash point (temperature at which the vapors will support a flash fire across the liquid surface)
BP = Boiling point

Safety materials made available to employees should include:

- The federal standards for occupational exposure to hazardous chemicals in laboratories.
- The federal hazard communication standard.
- The facility's written CHP.
- The facility's written program for hazard communication.
- Work areas where hazardous chemicals are located.
- Required list of hazardous chemicals and their MSDS. (It is the responsibility of the facility to determine which chemicals may present a hazard to employees. This determination should be based on the quantity of chemical used; the physical properties, potency, and toxicity of the chemical; the manner in which the chemical is used; and the means available to control the release of, or exposure to, the chemical.)

Hazardous Chemical Labeling and Signs

The Hazard Communication Standard requires manufacturers or producers of chemicals and hazardous materials to provide the user with basic information about the hazards of these materials. This hazardous information is provided by the manufacturer in the form of product labeling and by providing MSDS for hazardous chemicals. In turn, employers are required to provide employees who are expected to work with these hazardous materials information about the hazards of the materials, how to read the labeling, how to interpret symbols and signs on the labels, and how to read and use the MSDS.

Table 2-2. Maximum Allowable Container Size-Combustible Liquids

Container	Class of Liquid*	
	II	III
Glass or approved plastic	1 gal	1 gal
Safety cans: NFPA, JCAHO	2 gal	2 gal
OSHA	2 gal	5 gal

*Class II = FP 100-140 F
 Class III = FP ≥140 F
FP = Flash point (temperature at which the vapors will support a flash fire across the liquid surface)

At a minimum, hazardous container labels must include the name of the chemical, the name and address of the manufacturer, hazard warnings, labels, signs, placards, and other forms of warning to provide visual reminders of specific hazards. The MSDS may be referred to on the label for additional information. Labels applied by the manufacturer must remain on containers. The user may add dates of receipt and expiration and storage requirements.

If chemicals are removed from their original container, the secondary container must be labeled to indicate the chemical, its concentration if applicable, date of preparation, and appropriate hazard warnings. The contents of the secondary container must be traceable back to the original source. Portable containers used for temporary storage need not be labeled if the person performing the transfer intends them for immediate use.

Signs meeting OSHA requirements must be posted in areas where hazardous chemicals are used. Decisions on where to post warning signs are based on the manufacturer's recommendations on the chemical hazards, the quantity of the chemical in the room or laboratory, and the potency and toxicity of the chemical.

Material Safety Data Sheets

The MSDS identifies the physical and chemical properties of a hazardous chemical (eg, flash point, vapor pressure), its physical and health hazards (eg, potential for fire, explosion, signs and symptoms of exposure), and precautions for safe handling and use. Specific instructions in an individual MSDS take precedence over generic information in the HAZMAT program. Appendices 2-4 and 2-5 provide useful information on chemical hazards and Appendix 2-6 gives an example of information on an MSDS.

Although the MSDS will provide the employee with information concerning the hazardous properties of a chemical, employees should be aware of some shortcomings of the MSDS. Trace amounts of chemicals may not be listed on the MSDS, and disposal of that material as nonhazardous solid waste rather than as chemical wastes could result in violations of EPA, state, or local regulations. For example, some laboratory products (stains and cleaners) may contain trace quantities of mercury that meet the threshold for chemical waste and must be collected and disposed of accordingly. In some cases, the employer or safety officer may find it necessary to contact a manufacturer for additional proprietary information or may need to contact other sources to identify what are permitted options for hazardous waste disposal.

Hazardous Communication Training

Initial training for all employees who will be working with, or who may be potentially exposed to, hazardous chemicals must occur before the employees begin their initial assignment. This training must also occur whenever a new hazardous chemical is introduced into the workplace. In addition to this introductory training, an annual training program must be provided to employees.

Specific Chemical Categories

Table 2-3 lists specific chemicals and suggestions on how to work with them safely.

Managing Chemical Spills

The time to prepare for a chemical spill is not after a spill has occurred. A comprehensive employee training program should provide the employee with all tools necessary to act responsibly at the time of a chemical spill. The employee should know response procedures, be able to identify the severity of a chemical spill, know the basic physical characteristics of the chemicals or be able to quickly look up these characteristics, and know where the phone numbers of emergency response groups are posted or kept. The employee should be able to assess the spill, stop the spill, confine the spill, clean up the spill, and follow up on the report of the spill. The employee must know when to ask for assistance, when to isolate the area, and where to find cleanup materials.

There are three types of chemical spills:

■ Small or Incidental Releases: These spills are limited in quantity and toxicity and pose no exposure risk to the employees or the working environment under all circumstances. Waste from the cleanup may be classified as hazardous and must be disposed of in the proper fashion. Table 2-4 describes appropriate responses to incidental spills.

■ Incidental Release with Considerations: The circumstances of this spill may require an emergency response. This spill may pose an exposure risk to the employees or the environment depending upon the circumstances. The response to this spill requires specialized training to recognize the hazard potential and to react responsibly.

■ Emergency Response: The response to this spill depends on the nature and quantity of the substance involved in the spill. The location and size of the room, the ventilation in the room, and the possible public exposure or release to the environment of hazardous and/or toxic substances will all contribute to the definition of an emergency response.

With any incidental spill of a hazardous chemical, but especially with a carcinogenic agent, it is essential to refer to the MSDS and contact a designated supervisor or designee trained to handle these spills and hazardous waste disposal.[3] Facility environmental health and safety personnel also can offer assistance.

Spill cleanup kits tailored to the specific hazards present should be available in each area. These spill carts may contain rubber gloves and aprons, shoe covers, goggles, suitable aspirators, general absorbents, neutralizing agents, broom, dust pan, appropriate trash bags or cans for waste disposal, and cleanup directions. Some chemical absorbents such as vermiculite can be used for cleanup of a number of chemicals and thus may be easier for the employee to use in spill situations.

An employee involved in a chemical spill must notify the employer of any exposure to hazardous chemicals, and the employer must assess the extent of the employee's exposure. After an exposure, the employee must be given an opportunity for medical consultation, which could lead to determining the need for a medical examination.

All spills should be investigated to determine the root cause of the accident, if applicable. Appropriate changes in procedures, storage, training, etc recognized as the root cause should be explored, validated, and implemented as soon as possible. Table 2-5 addresses hazardous chemical spills.

Another source of a workplace hazard is the unexpected release of hazardous vapors into the environment. In the air contaminants standard[30] for toxic and hazardous substances, OSHA has set limits for exposure to hazardous vapors. The limits are determined by the manufacturers and are listed on the MSDS. See Table 2-6 for a listing of the limits of exposure.

Chemical Waste Disposal

Most laboratory chemical waste is considered hazardous and is regulated by the EPA through the Resource Conservation and Recovery Act.[7] This regulation specifies that hazardous waste can only be legally disposed of at an EPA-approved disposal facility. Disposal of chemical waste into a sanitary sewer is regulated by the Clean Water Act and most states have strict regulations concerning disposal of chemicals in the water system. These and applicable state regulations should be consulted regularly.

The easiest and most economic method of hazardous waste disposal is to limit the amount of hazardous chemicals in the laboratory. As mentioned previously, make it a point to review the possibilities of using alternative nonhazardous chemicals and to reduce the

Table 2-3. Specific Chemical Categories and How to Work Safely with These Chemicals

Chemical Category	Hazard	Precautions	Special Treatment
Acids, alkalis, and corrosive compounds	Irritation Severe burns Tissue damage	During transport, protect large containers with plastic or rubber bucket carriers During pouring, wear eye protection and chemical-resistant-rated gloves and gowns as recommended Always ADD ACID TO WATER, never water to acid When working with large jugs, have one hand on the neck and the other at the base, and position away from the face	Store concentrated acids in acid safety cabinets Limit volumes of concentrated acids to 1 liter Post cautions for materials in the area Report changes in appearance (perchloric acid may be explosive if it becomes yellowish or brown) to chemical safety officer
Acrylamide	Neurotoxic Cancer-causing agent adsorbed through the skin	Wear chemically rated gloves Wash hands immediately after exposure	Store in chemical cabinet
Compressed gases	Explosive	Label as to contents Leave valve safety covers on until use Open valves slowly for use Label empty tanks	Transport using hand trucks or dollies Store in well-ventilated separate rooms Oxygen should not be stored close to combustible gas or solvents Check connections for leaks with soapy water

Liquid nitrogen	Freeze injury Severe burns to skin or eyes	Use heavy insulated gloves and goggles when working with liquid nitrogen	The tanks should be securely supported to avoid being tipped over The final container of liquid nitrogen (freezing unit) must be securely supported to avoid tipping over
Flammable solvents	Classified according to flash point —see MSDS Classified according to volatility (see Tables 2-1 and 2-2)	Use extreme caution when handling Post NO SMOKING signs in working area Have a fire extinguisher and solvent cleanup kit in the room Pour volatile solvents under suitable hood Use eye protection when pouring and chemical-resistant neoprene gloves No flame or other source of possible ignition should be in or near areas where flammable solvents are being poured Label as FLAMMABLE	Make every attempt to replace hazardous materials with less hazardous materials Store containers larger than 1 gallon in flammable solvent storage room or in fire safety cabinet Ground metal containers by connecting the can to a water pipe or ground connection; if recipient container is also metal, it should be electrically connected to the delivery container while pouring

Table 2-4. Incidental Spill Response*

Solution	Substances Covered	Health Hazards	Physical Hazards	Equipment		Control Materials
				PPE		
Acids	Acetic Hydrochloric Nitric Perchloric Sulfuric Photographic chemicals containing acids	Severe irritant if inhaled Contact causes burns to skin and eyes	Corrosive Fire or contact with metal may produce irritating or poisonous gas Nitric, perchloric and sulfuric acids are water-reactive oxidizers	Acid-resistant gloves; apron and coveralls; goggles and face shield; acid-resistant foot covers		Acid neutralizers/absorbent Absorbent boom Leakproof containers Absorbent pillow Mat (cover drain) Shovel or paddle
Bases and caustics	Potassium hydroxide Sodium hydroxide Photographic chemicals containing base	Corrosive Fire may produce irritating or poisonous gas	Gloves; impervious apron or coveralls	Goggles or face shield; impervious foot covers		Base control/neutralizer Absorbent pillow Absorbent Absorbent boom Drain mat Leakproof container Shovel/paddle
Chlorine	Bleach Sodium hypochlorite	Inhalation can cause respiratory irritation Liquid contact can produce irritation of the eyes or skin Toxicity due to alkalinity, possible chlorine gas generation, and oxidant properties	Gloves (double set 4H underglove and butyl or nitrile overgloves); impervious apron or coveralls	Goggles or face shield Impervious foot covers (neoprene boots for emergency response releases) Self-contained breathing apparatus (emergency response releases)		Chlorine control powder Absorbent pillow Absorbent Absorbent boom Drain mat Vapor barrier Leakproof container Shovel/paddle
Cryogenic gases	Carbon dioxide Nitrous oxide	Contact with liquid nitrogen can produce frostbite Asphyxiation–displaces oxygen	Anesthetic effects (nitrous oxide)	Full face shield or goggles; neoprene boots; gloves (leather to protect from the cold)		Hand truck (to transport cylinder outdoors if necessary) Soap solution (to check for leaks) Putty (to stop minor pipe and line leaks)

Liquid nitrogen

Category	Examples	Hazards	PPE	Spill response equipment
Flammable gases	Acetylene Oxygen gases Butane Propane	Simple asphyxiate (displaces air) Anesthetic potential Extreme fire and explosion hazard Release can create an oxygen-deficient atmosphere	Face shield and goggles; neoprene boots; double set of gloves; coveralls with hood and feet	Hand truck (to transport cylinder outdoors if needed) Soap solution (to check for leaks)
Flammable liquids	Acetone Zylene Methyl alcohol Toluene Ethyl alcohol Other alcohols	Extreme flammability Liquid evaporates to form flammable vapors Vapors harmful if inhaled (central nervous system depressants) Harmful via skin absorption	Gloves (double 4H underglove and butyl or nitrile overglove); impervious apron or coveralls; goggles; or face shield; impervious foot covers	Absorbent Absorbent boom Absorbent pillow Shovel or paddle (nonmetal, nonsparking) Drain mat Leakproof containers/drum
Formaldehyde and glutaraldehyde	4% formaldehyde 37% formaldehyde 10% formalin 2% glutaraldehyde	Keep away from heat, sparks, and flame (37% formaldehyde) Harmful if inhaled or absorbed through skin Irritation to skin, eyes, and respiratory tract Formaldelyde is a suspected human carcinogen	Gloves (double set 4H underglove and butyl or nitrile overglove); impervious apron or coveralls; goggles; impervious foot covers	Aldehyde neutralizer/absorbent Absorbent boom Absorbent pillow Shovel or pallet (nonsparking) Drain mat Leakproof container
Mercury	Cantor tubes Thermometers Barometers Sphygmoma-nometers Mercuric chloride	Avoid evaporation of mercury from tiny globules by quick and thorough cleaning Mercury and mercury vapors are rapidly absorbed by membranes of respiratory tract, GI tract, and skin Short-term exposure may cause erosion of respiratory/GI tracts, nausea, vomiting, bloody diarrhea, shock, headache, metallic taste Inhalation of high concentrations can cause pneumonitis, chest pain, dyspnea, coughing stomatitis, gingivitis, and salivation	Gloves (double set 4H underglove and butyl or nitrile overglove); impervious apron or coveralls; goggles; impervious foot covers	Mercury spill kit Scoop Aspirator Hazardous waste containers (leakproof containers/drum) Mercury indicator powder Absorbent Spatula Disposable towels Sponge with amalgam Vapor suppressor

*This list of physical and health hazards is not intended as a substitute for the specific MSDS information. In the case of a spill or if any questions arise, always refer to the chemical-specific MSDS for more complete information.

GI=gastrointestinal; MSDS=material safety data sheet; PPE=personal protective equipment.

Table 2-5. Managing Hazardous Chemical Spills

Actions	Acids, Bases, Caustics, Chlorine, Formaldehyde/Gluteraldehyde and Flammable Liquids	Cryogenic or Flammable Gases	Mercury
De-energize	For 37% formaldehyde, de-energize and remove all sources of ignition within 10 feet of spilled hazardous material For flammable liquids, remove all sources of ignition	Remove all sources of heat and ignition within 50 feet for flammable gases Remove all sources of heat and ignition for nitrous oxide release	NA
Isolate, evacuate, and secure the area	Isolate the spill area, evacuate everyone from the area surrounding the spill except those responsible for the spill cleanup	Isolate release area Evacuate everyone from the area surrounding leak except those responsible for the cleanup Secure area	Isolate spill area Evacuate immediate area within 10 feet of spill for small spills (thermometer) Evacuate entire room if spill occurs in small room Evacuate area within 20 feet of spill for larger spills Secure area
Have the appropriate PPE	See Table 2-4 for recommended PPE	See Table 2-4	See Table 2-4 for appropriate PPE
Contain the spill	Stop the source of spill if possible	Assess the scene; consider the circumstances of the release (quantity, location, ventilation) If circumstances indicate it is an emergency response release, make appropriate notifications; if release is determined to be incidental, contact supplier for assistance	Stop the source of spill if possible
Confine the spill	Confine spill to initial spill area using appropriate control equipment and material For flammable liquids, dike off all drains	Follow supplier's suggestions or request outside assistance	Use appropriate materials to confine the spill (see Table 2-4) Expel mercury from aspirator bulb into leakproof container, if applicable

Neutralize the spill	Apply appropriate control materials to neutralize the chemical—see Table 2-4	NA	Use mercury spill kit if needed
Spill area cleanup	Scoop up solidified material, booms, pillows, and any other materials Put used materials into a leakproof container Label container with name of hazardous material Wipe up residual material Wipe spill area surface three times with detergent solution Rinse areas with clean water Collect supplies used (goggles, shovels, etc) and remove gross contamination; place into separate container for equipment to be washed and decontaminated	Follow supplier's suggestions or request outside assistance	Scoop up mercury paste after neutralization and collect it in designated container Use sponge and detergent to wipe and clean spill surface three times to remove absorbent Collect all contaminated disposal equipment and put into hazardous waste container Collect supplies and remove gross contamination; place into separate container for equipment that will be thoroughly washed and decontaminated
Disposal	Material that was neutralized, dispose of as solid waste Follow facility procedures for disposal For flammable liquids, check with facility safety officer for appropriate waste determination	The manufacture or supplier will instruct facility on disposal if there is any	Label with appropriate hazardous waste label and DOT diamond label
Report	Follow appropriate spill documentation and reporting procedures Investigate the spill, perform root cause analysis if needed. Act on opportunities for improving safety	Follow appropriate spill documentation and reporting procedures Investigate the spill, perform root cause analysis if needed Act on opportunities for improving safety	Follow appropriate spill documentation and reporting procedures Investigate the spill, perform root cause analysis if needed Act on opportunities for improving safety

DOT=Department of Transportation; NA=not applicable; PPE=personal protective equipment.

Table 2-6. Regulatory Limits for Exposure to Toxic and Hazardous Vapors[30]

Limit	Definition
Permissible exposure limit	The maximum concentration of vapors in parts per million (ppm) that an employee may be exposed to in an 8-hour day/40-hour work week
Short-term exposure limit	The maximum allowable concentration of vapors that an employee may be exposed to in a 15-minute period, with maximum of four exposures per day allowed with at least 1 hour between each
Ceiling limit	The maximum concentration of vapors that may not be exceeded instantaneously at any time

volume of chemicals stored by ordering only the amount of chemicals needed.

Facilities should check with state and local health departments for current regulations on storing and disposing of a particular multi-hazardous waste before creating that waste. If the multihazardous waste cannot be avoided, minimize volumes generated.

In some states, copper sulfate contaminated with blood is considered a multihazardous waste. The disposal of this waste poses several problems with transportation from draw sites to a central facility to disposal of the final containers. State and local health departments must be involved in the review of transportation and disposal practices where this is an issue, and procedures must be developed in accordance with their regulations.

Radiation Safety

Radiation can be defined as energy, in the form of waves or particles, emitted and propagated through space or a material medium. Gamma rays are electromagnetic radiation, while alpha rays and beta rays are examples of particulate radiation. The presence of radiation in the blood bank either from radioisotopes used in laboratory testing or from self-contained blood irradiators requires additional precautions and training.[3,31]

Biological Effects of Radiation

Any harm to tissue begins with the absorption of radiation energy and subsequent disruption of chemical bonds. Molecules and atoms become ionized and/or excited by absorbing this energy. The "direct action" path leads to radiolysis or formation of free radicals that in turn alter the structure and function of molecules in the cell.

Molecular alterations can cause chromosomal or cellular changes, depending upon the amount and type of radiation energy adsorbed. Cellular changes can manifest as a visible somatic effect, eg, erythema. Chromosomal changes may manifest as leukemia or other cancers, or possibly as germ cell defects that are transmitted to future generations. The low levels of ionizing radiation (<1 Gy) likely to be associated with exposure of blood bank personnel should not pose any detrimental risk.[32-35]

The type of radiation influences biologic damage, the part of the body exposed, the total absorbed dose, and the dose rate. The total absorbed dose is the cumulative amount of radiation absorbed in the tissue. The greater the dose, the greater the biologic damage. Exposure can be acute or chronic.

Radiation Measurement Units

The measurement unit quantifying the amount of energy absorbed per unit mass of tissue is the *rad* (radiation absorbed dose). The common unit for measuring dose is the *Gray* (Gy); 1 Gy equals 100 rads.

Dose equivalency measurements are more useful than simple energy measurements because they take into account the different biologic effects of different types of radiation. For example, exposure to a given amount of alpha particles is far more damaging than exposure to an equivalent amount of gamma rays. The common unit of measurement for dose equivalency is the *rem* (rad equivalent man).

Exposure Limits

The Nuclear Regulatory Commission (NRC) sets standards for protection against radiation hazards arising from licensed activities, including dose limits.[8] These limits, or maximum permissible dose equivalents, are a measure of the radiation risk over time and serve as standards for exposure. The occupational total effective-dose-equivalent limit is 5 rem/year. The shallow dose equivalent (skin) is 50 rem/year, the extremity dose equivalent limit is 50 rem/year, and the eye dose equivalent limit is 15 rem/year.[32-35] Dose limits to an embryo/fetus must not exceed 0.5 rem during the pregnancy.[32-33,36]

Employers are expected not only to maintain radiation exposure below allowable limits, but also to keep exposure levels as far below these limits as can reasonably be achieved. Short-term limits may be advisable in some laboratory areas, such as 2 mrem/hour or 100 mrem/week.

General Regulatory Requirements

The NRC controls use of radioactive materials by establishing licensure requirements. States may also have requirements for inspection and/or licensure. The type of license for using radioisotopes or irradiators will depend on the scope and magnitude of the use of radioactivity. Facilities should contact the NRC and appropriate state agencies for license requirements and application as soon as such activities are proposed.

NRC-licensed establishments must have a qualified radiation safety officer who is responsible for personnel protection requirements and for proper disposal and handling of radioactive materials. Specific radiation safety policies and procedures should address dose limits, employee training, warning signs and labels, shipping and handling guidelines, radiation monitoring, and exposure management. Emergency procedures must be clearly defined and readily available to staff.

Radiation Training

Personnel who handle radioactive materials or work with blood irradiators must be given radiation safety training before beginning work and annually thereafter. This training should cover an explanation of the presence and potential hazards of radioactive materials found in the employee's specific work area, general health protection issues, emergency procedures, and radiation warning signs and labels in use. Instruction in the following is also suggested:

- NRC regulations and license conditions.
- Instruction in observing license conditions and regulations and in reporting violations or conditions of unnecessary exposure.
- Precautions to minimize exposure.
- Interpretation of results of monitoring devices.
- Instructions for pregnant workers.
- Employees' rights during inspections.
- Documentation and record-keeping requirements.

Radiation Monitoring

Monitoring is essential for early detection and prevention of problems due to radiation exposure. It is used to evaluate the environment, work practices, and procedures, and to comply with regulations and NRC licensing requirements. Monitoring is accomplished with the use of dosimeters, survey meters, and wipe tests.[3]

Film or thermoluminescent badges and/or rings measure personnel radiation doses. The need for dosimeters depends on the amount and type of radioactive materials in use; the facility radiation safety officer will determine individual dosimeter needs. Film badges must be changed at least quarterly, protected from high temperature and humidity, and stored at work away from sources of radiation.

Survey meters are sensitive to low levels of gamma radiation and provide a quantitative assessment of radiation hazard. They can be used to monitor storage areas for radioactive materials or wastes, testing areas during or after completion of a procedure, and packages or containers of radioactive materials. Survey meters must be calibrated periodically by an authorized NRC licensee.

Laboratory work surfaces should be checked regularly for surface contamination with a wipe test. In the wipe test, a moistened absorbent material (the wipe) is passed over the surface and then counted for radiation. Kits are available for this purpose. In most clinical laboratories, exposure levels of radiation are well below the limits set by federal and state regulations.

Radiation Safety in Laboratory Testing

Laboratory Practices

In addition to requiring general laboratory safety principles about PPE and universal precautions, radiation safety can be improved with the following:

1. Minimize time of exposure by working as efficiently as possible.
2. Maximize distance from the source of the radiation by staying as far from the source as possible.
3. Maximize shielding by wearing lead aprons, if needed, or by using a self-shielded irradiator. These requirements are usually stipulated in the license conditions.
4. Use good housekeeping practices to minimize spread of radioactivity to uncontrolled areas.

Radioactive Spills

Radioactive contamination, or a "spill," is the dispersal of radioactive material into or onto areas where it is not intended, for example the floor, work areas, equipment or onto personnel clothing or skin. The NRC regulations state that gamma or beta radioactive contamination cannot exceed 2200 dpm/100 cm^2 in the posted (restricted) area or 220 dpm/100 cm^2 in an unrestricted area such as corridors; for alpha emitters these values are 220 dpm/100 cm^2 and 22 dpm/100 cm^2, respectively.[32-33]

1. Notify the radiation safety officer if skin contamination occurs, if large amounts of radioactivity (>1 liter) are spilled, if large areas are contaminated (<10 sq ft), and if contamination occurs in unrestricted areas such as public access corridors.
2. Clear the area, tape it off, and monitor it.
3. Use soap and water or a solution approved for cleaning up radioactive spills to wash the area after blotting the spill with paper towels.
4. Discard the gloves and paper towels in a plastic bag. Before the bag is discarded into the "hot locker," label it with date and name of radioactive material.
5. Remove any clothing or apparatus that becomes contaminated, place in a properly labeled plastic bag, and store in the hot locker.
6. Wash contaminated skin surfaces several times and take readings. The radiation safety officer should be notified of any skin contamination so that skin dose may be properly determined.

Radioactive Waste Disposal

Policies for the disposal of radioactive waste, whether liquid or solid, should be established with input from the radiation safety officer and the disposal contractor, if an approved company is used.

Liquid radioactive waste may be collected into large sturdy bottles labeled with an appropriate radiation waste tag. The rules for separation by chemical compatibility apply. Bottles must be carefully stored to protect against spillage or breakage. Metal carrying containers are recommended for transport. Dry or solid waste may be sealed in a plastic bag and tagged as radiation waste. Radiation waste must never be discharged into the drain system.

Self-Contained Blood Irradiators

Although self-contained blood irradiators present little risk to laboratory staff and film badges are not required for routine operation, blood establishments with irradiation programs must be licensed by the NRC.[31]

The manufacturer of the blood irradiator usually accepts responsibility for radiation safety requirements during transportation, installation, and validation of the unit as part of the purchase contract. The radiation safety officer can help oversee the installation and validation processes and confirm that appropriate training, monitoring systems, SOPs, and maintenance protocols are in place prior to use. They must reflect the manufacturer's recommendations. Suspected malfunctions must be reported immediately.

Blood irradiators should be located in secure areas with limited access so that only trained individuals have access. Fire protection for the unit must also be considered. Automatic fire detection and control systems should be readily available in the immediate area.

Blood products that have been irradiated are not radioactive and pose no threat to staff or the general public.

Protection from Physical Hazards

Fire Safety

Fire prevention is a combination of facility design based on the Life Safety Code, NFPA guidelines, and good fire safe work practices. The Life Safety Code includes both active and passive fire protection systems (eg, alarms, smoke detectors, sprinklers, egress lights and corridors, and fire-rated barriers). Laboratories storing large volumes of flammable chemicals are usually built with 2-hour fire separation walls, or with 1-hour separation if there is an automatic fire extinguishing system.[3] Secondary exits may be required for areas larger than 1000 square feet; consult local safety authority having jurisdiction such as the local fire marshal and the NFPA. Fire detection and alarm systems should be provided in accordance with federal, state, and local regulations.

All fire equipment should be inspected on a regular basis to ensure good working order. Fire hoses and extinguishers should be made readily available and staff should be trained to use them properly. Fire safety training is recommended at the start of employment and at least annually thereafter. Training should emphasize prevention and an employee's awareness of the work environment, including established safety rules on the use and storage of flammable chemicals and compressed gases and the use and maintenance of electrical equipment and circuits. Training should include how to recognize and report unsafe conditions, how to report fires, the locations of the nearest alarm, and fire containment equipment and their use, evacuation policies and routes. Annual fire drills are required of all staff on all shifts by the JCAHO and the CAP. Staff participation and understanding should be documented. Personnel should be trained to immediately "stop, drop, and roll" in the event of a clothing fire.

Disaster Preparedness

Blood banks and transfusion services should establish action guidelines for uncommon dangers, such as floods, hurricanes, tornadoes, earthquakes, acts of terrorism, and kidnapping, to ensure the safety of their patients, visitors, workers, and the blood supply. Such disasters may involve the facility alone, the surrounding community, or both and can be categorized by severity level: minor impact on normal operations; moderate substantial reduction in operations; or severe, prolonged loss of operations.

Employees should be trained in the facility's disaster response policies which may address communication, evacuation, and safety/protection issues, as well as administration's expectations of staff. Typically, the first person who becomes aware of the disaster takes immediate action and notifies a supervisor, who then implements the initial response steps and contacts the facility's disaster coordinator. During the disaster, staff must be prepared to make modifications as necessary; every disaster is a unique occurrence. Once the disaster is under control and recovery is under way, actions should be evaluated and modifications made to the disaster plan as needed. However, the single most effective protection a facility has against unexpected danger is the awareness that safety-minded employees have for their surroundings.

References

1. Menitove JE, ed. Standards for blood banks and transfusion services. 19th ed. Bethesda, MD: American Association of Blood Banks, 1999:8.
2. Inspection checklist: General laboratory. Chicago, IL: College of American Pathologists, 1996:45-56.
3. National Committee for Clinical Laboratory Standards. Clinical laboratory safety; approved guideline. NCCLS document GP17-A. Wayne, PA: NCCLS, 1996.
4. Accreditation manual for hospitals. Chicago, IL: Joint Commission on Accreditation of Healthcare Organizations, 1996.
5. Quality program. Vols 1 and 2. Bethesda, MD: American Association of Blood Banks, 1994.
6. Wagner KD, ed. Environmental management in healthcare facilities. Philadelphia: WB Saunders, 1998.
7. Occupational Safety and Health Administration. Occupational exposure to hazardous chemicals in laboratories. Title 29 CFR Part 1910.1450. Fed Regist 1990; 55:3300-35.
8. Code of federal regulations. Title 10 CFR Part 20. Washington, DC: US Government Printing Office, 1998 (revised annually).
9. Treatment methods and waste forms for long-term storage and ultimate disposal of radioactive biological materials. US Department of Energy, 1992.
10. Garner JS, Hospital Infection Control Practices Advisory Committee. Guideline for isolation precautions in hospitals. Infect Control Hosp Epidemiol 1996;17:53-80.
11. Occupational Safety and Health Administration. Occupational exposure to blood-borne pathogens, final rule. Title 29 CFR Part 1910.1030. Fed Regist 1991;56(235): 64175-82.
12. Occupational Safety and Health Administration. Hazard communication standard. Title 29 CFR Part 1910.1200. Fed Regist 1994;59:65947.
13. Richmond JY, McKinney RW, eds. Biosafety microbiological and biomedical laboratories. HHS Publication No. (CDC) 93-8395. Washington, DC: US Government Printing Office, 1993.
14. Code of federal regulations. Title 21 CFR Part 600. Washington, DC: US Government Printing Office, 1998 (revised annually).
15. Occupational Safety and Health Administration. OSHA Instruction CPL2-2.44b. Enforcement procedures for occupational exposure to hepatitis B virus (HBV) and human immunodeficiency virus (HIV). Washington, DC: US Government Printing Office, 1990.
16. Code of federal regulations. Title 29 CFR Part 1904.2. Washington, DC: US Government Printing Office, 1998 (revised annually).
17. Centers for Disease Control. Recommendations of the Immunization Practices Advisory Committee. MMWR 1990;39:1-26.
18. Evans MR, Henderson DK, Bennett JE. Potential for laboratory exposures to biohazardous agents found in blood. Am J Public Health 1990;80:4;423-7.
19. Food and Drug Administration. Memorandum: Guideline for collection of blood products from donors with positive tests for infectious disease markers ("high risk" donors). October 26, 1989. Rockville, MD: CBER Office of Communication, Training, and Manufacturer's Assistance, 1989.
20. Environmental Protection Agency. Registered hospital disinfectants and sterilants (TS767C). Washington, DC: Antimicrobial Program Branch, 1992.
21. Vesley D, Lauer JL. Decontamination, sterilization, disinfection and antisepsis. In: Fleming DO, Richardson JH, Tulis JJ, Vesley D, eds. Laboratory safety, principles and practices. 2nd ed. Washington, DC: American Society for Microbiology Press, 1995:219-37.
22. Environmental Protection Agency. EPA guide for infectious waste management. EPA/530-SW-86-014. NTIS #PB86-199130. Washington, DC: National Technical Information Service, 1986.

23. National Committee for Clinical Laboratory Standards. Clinical laboratory waste management. Approved Standard Doc GP5-A. Villanova, PA: NCCLS, 1993.

24. Code of federal regulations. Title 40 CFR Part 60. Standards of performance for new stationary sources and emission guidelines for existing sources: Hospital/medical/infectious waste incinerators. Washington, DC: US Government Printing Office, 1998 (revised annually).

25. World Health Organization. Guidelines for the safe transport of infectious substances and diagnostic specimens. Geneva, Switzerland: World Health Organization, 1997.

26. McVicar JW, Suen J. Packing and shipping biologic materials. In: Fleming DO, Richardson JH, Tulis JJ, Vesley D, eds. Laboratory safety, principles and practices. 2nd ed. Washington, DC: American Society for Microbiology Press, 1995:239-46.

27. International Air Transportation Association. Dangerous goods regulations. Montreal: IATA, 1996.

28. Code of federal regulations. Title 49 CFR Part 171-3. Washington, DC: US Government Printing Office, 1998 (revised annually) .

29. Lisella FS, Thomasston SW. Chemical safety in the microbiology laboratory. In: Fleming DO, Richardson JH, Tulis JJ, Vesley D, eds. Laboratory safety, principles and practices. 2nd ed. Washington, DC: American Society for Microbiology Press, 1995:247-54.

30. Code of federal regulations. Title 29 CFR Part 1910.1000. Air contaminants: Toxic and hazardous substances. Washington, DC: US Government Printing Office, 1998 (revised annually).

31. Cook SS. Selection and installation of self-contained irradiators. In: Butch S, Tiehen A, eds. Blood irradiation: A user's guide. Bethesda, MD: AABB Press, 1996:19-40.

32. Beir V. Health effects of exposure to low levels of ionizing radiation. Washington, DC: National Academy Press, 1990:1-8.

33. Regulatory Guide 8.29: Instruction concerning risks from occupational radiation exposure. Washington, DC: Nuclear Regulatory Commission,1996.

34. NCRP Report No. 115: Risk estimates for radiation protection: Recommendations of the National Council on Radiation Protection and Measurements. Bethesda, MD: National Council on Radiation Protection and Measurements, 1993.

35. NCRP Report No. 105: Radiation protection for medical and allied health personnel: Recommendations of the National Council on Radiation Protection and Measurements. Bethesda, MD: National Council on Radiation Protection and Measurements, 1989.

36. NRC Regulatory Guide 8.13: Instruction concerning prenatal radiation exposure. Washington, DC: Nuclear Regulatory Commission, 1987.

Suggested Readings

CDC Office of Biosafety. Radiation safety manual. Atlanta, GA: Centers for Disease Control, 1992.

Disaster plan development procedure manual. In: Developing a disaster plan. Bethesda, MD: American Association of Blood Banks, 1998.

Handbook of compressed gases. 3rd ed. Compressed gas association. New York: Chapman and Hall, 1990.

Heinsohn PA, Jacobs RR, Concoby BA, eds. Biosafety reference manual. 2nd ed. Fairfax, VA: American Industrial Hygiene Association Biosafety Committee, 1995.

International Civil Aviation Organization. Technical instructions for the safe transport of dangerous goods by air. Montreal: ICAO, 1995-1996. (Available from American Label Mark, 5724 N. Pulaski Road, Chicago, IL 60646.)

Liberman DF, ed. Biohazards management handbook. 2nd ed. New York: Marcel Dekker, Inc, 1995.

NIH guide to waste disposal. Http://www.nih.gov/od/ods/wastecal/chem/chemwn.html.

Prudent practices for handling hazardous chemicals in laboratories. Washington, DC: National Academy Press, 1981.

Risk management and safety procedure manual. In: Developing a disaster plan. Bethesda, MD: American Association of Blood Banks, 1998.

United States Postal Service. Domestic mail manual. Nonmailable matter-articles and substances; special mailing rules; disease germs and biological products (Issue 44, September 20, 1992). Washington, DC: USPS, 1992. (Available from USPS Eastern Area Supply Center, Route 206 VA Supply Center, Sommerville, NJ 08877.)

Appendix 2-1. Resources for Safety Information

Centers for Disease Control and Prevention
Health and Biosafety Branch, MS F-OS
1600 Clifton Road, NE
Atlanta, GA 30333
(404) 639-3311
Fax (404) 639-2294
www.cdc.gov

Department of Agriculture
Animal and Plant Health Inspection Services
Federal Building, Room 756
6505 Bellcrest Road
Hyattsville, MD 20782
(301) 436-7830
Fax (301) 436-8226
www.usda.gov

Department of Transportation
Office of Hazardous Materials Standards
Research and Special Programs Administration
400 7th Street, SW
Washington, DC 20590
(202) 366-0656
www.dot.gov

Environmental Protection Agency
Office of Solid Waste
Mail Code OS 332
401 M Street, SW
Washington, DC 20460
(202) 260-4610
www.epa.gov

Food and Drug Administration
Division of Blood Applications
HFM-370
Center for Biologics Evaluation and Research
1401 Rockville Pike
Rockville, MD 20852-1448
(301) 827-3524
www.fda.gov

International Air Transportation Association
200 Peel Street
Montreal, Quebec
Canada H3A 2R4
(514) 844-6311
www.iata.gov

International Civil Aviation Organization
100 Sherbrook Street W
Montreal, Quebec
Canada H3A 2R2
(514) 285-8219
www.icao.int

National Committee for Clinical Laboratory
  Standards
Suite 1400, 940 West Valley Road
Wayne, PA 19087
(610) 688-0100
Fax (610) 688-0700
www.nccls.org

National Fire Protection Association
1 Batterymarch Park
P.O. Box 9101
Quincy,MA 02269-9101
(800) 593-6372
www.nfpa.org

National Institute for Occupational Safety and Health
Robert A. Taft Laboratory, C13
4676 Columbia Parkway
Cincinnati, OH 45226
(800) 356-4674
www.hin.gov/niosh/homepage.html

National Institutes of Health
Division of Safety
Building 13, Room 3K04
Bethesda, MD 20892
(301) 496-2346
www.nih.gov

Nuclear Regulatory Commission
475 Allandale Road
King of Prussia, PA 19406
(610) 337-5000
www.nrc.gov

Occupational Safety and Health Administration
Office of Information
Room N-3647
200 Constitution Avenue, NW
Washington, DC 20210
(202) 219-8148
(202) 219-7075 (Standards)
www.osha.gov

US Postal Service
Headquarters, Room 9301
475 L'Enfant Plaza, SW
Washington, DC 20260
(202) 268-2000
www.usps.gov

Appendix 2-2. Personal Protective Equipment

Uniforms and Laboratory Coats

Closed laboratory coats or full aprons over long-sleeved uniforms or gowns should be worn when personnel are exposed to blood, corrosive chemicals, or carcinogens. The material of required coverings should be appropriate for the type and amount of hazard exposure. Plastic disposable aprons may be worn over cotton coats when there is a high probability of large spills or splashing of blood and body fluids; nitrile rubber aprons may be preferred when pouring caustic chemicals.

Protective coverings should be removed before leaving the work area and should be discarded or stored away from heat sources and clean clothing. Contaminated clothing should be removed promptly, placed in a suitable container and laundered or discarded as potentially infectious. Home laundering of garments worn in Biosafety Level 2 areas (see below) is not permitted because unpredictable methods of transportation and handling can spread contamination, and home laundering techniques may not be effective.[1]

Gloves

Gloves or equivalent barriers should be used whenever tasks are likely to involve exposure to hazardous materials. Latex or vinyl gloves are adequate for handling most blood specimens and chemicals (see latex allergy issues below).

Types of Gloves

Glove type varies with the task:

- Sterile gloves: for procedures involving contact with normally sterile areas of the body.
- Examination gloves: for procedures involving contact with mucous membranes, unless otherwise indicated, and for other patient care or diagnostic procedures that do not require the use of sterile gloves.
- Rubber utility gloves: for housekeeping chores involving potential blood contact, for instrument cleaning and decontamination procedures, for handling concentrated acids and

organic solvents. Utility gloves may be decontaminated and reused but should be discarded if they show signs of deterioration (peeling, cracks, discoloration) or if they develop punctures or tears.
- Insulated gloves: for handling hot or frozen material.

Indications for Use

The following guidelines should be used to determine when gloves are necessary[1]:

- For donor phlebotomy when the health-care worker has cuts, scratches, or other breaks in his or her skin.
- For phlebotomy when hand contamination with blood may occur, eg, with an uncooperative patient. For phlebotomy of autologous donors or patients (eg, therapeutic apheresis procedures, intraoperative red cell collection).
- For finger and/or heel sticks by persons who are receiving training in phlebotomy.
- When handling "open" blood containers or specimens.
- When collecting or handling blood or specimens from patients or from donors known to be infected with a blood-borne pathogen.
- When examining mucous membranes or open skin lesions.
- When handling corrosive chemicals and radioactive materials.
- When cleaning up spills or handling waste materials.
- When likelihood of exposure cannot be assessed because of lack of experience with a procedure or situation.

The Occupational Safety and Health Administration (OSHA) does not require routine use of gloves by phlebotomists working with healthy prescreened donors or the changing of unsoiled gloves between donors if gloves are worn.[1,2] Experience has shown that the phlebotomy process is low risk because donors have low rates of infectious disease markers. Also, exposure to blood is rare during routine phlebotomy, and

(cont'd)

Appendix 2-2. Personal Protective Equipment (cont'd)

other alternatives can be utilized to provide barrier protection, such as using a folded gauze pad to control any blood flow when the needle is removed from the donor's arm.

The employer whose policies and procedures do not require routine gloving should periodically reevaluate the potential need for gloves. Employees should never be discouraged from using gloves, and gloves should always be available.

Guidelines on Use

Guidelines for the safe use of gloves include the following[3,4]:

- Securely bandage or cover open skin lesions on hands and arms before putting on gloves.
- Change gloves immediately if they are torn, punctured, or contaminated; after handling high-risk samples; or after performing a physical examination, eg, on an apheresis donor.
- Remove gloves by keeping their outside surfaces in contact only with outside and by turning the glove inside out while taking it off.
- Use gloves only where needed and avoid touching clean surfaces such as telephones, door knobs, or computer terminals with gloves.
- Change gloves between patient contacts. Unsoiled gloves need not be changed between donors.
- Wash hands with soap or other suitable disinfectant after removing gloves.
- Do not wash or disinfect surgical or examination gloves for reuse. Washing with surfactants may cause "wicking" (ie, the enhanced penetration of liquids through undetected holes in the glove). Disinfecting agents may cause deterioration of gloves.
- Use only water-based hand lotions with gloves, if needed; oil-based products cause minute cracks in latex.

Latex Allergy Issues

Adverse reactions associated with latex and/or powdered gloves include contact dermatitis, allergic dermatitis, urticaria, and anaphylaxis. These reactions pose a sufficiently significant health risk that the Food and Drug Administration has issued a Medical Glove Powder Report[4] and has enacted legislation[5] that requires medical devices containing natural rubber latex to be labeled with "Caution: This product contains natural rubber latex, which may cause allergic reactions." Devices containing dry natural rubber that contact humans must be labeled with: "Caution: This product contains dry natural rubber." When the packaging of medical devices contains natural rubber latex or dry natural rubber, similar warning labels are required so that staff who might contact natural rubber particles while opening the package are alerted.

The National Institute for Occupational Safety and Health has also issued an alert on preventing allergic reactions to natural rubber latex in the workplace.[6] They offer the following recommendations:

- Provide workers with nonlatex gloves to use when there is little potential for contact with infectious material.
- If latex gloves are used, provide reduced protein, powder-free gloves. (Note: This is not a requirement, but a recommendation to reduce exposure.)
- Use good housekeeping practices to remove latex-containing dust from the workplace.
- Use work practices that reduce the chance of reaction, such as hand washing and avoiding oil-based hand lotions.
- Provide workers with education programs and training material about latex allergy.
- Periodically screen high-risk workers for latex allergy symptoms.
- Evaluate current prevention strategies.
- If symptoms of latex allergy develop, avoid direct contact with latex and consult a physician about allergy precautions.

Face Shields, Masks, and Safety Goggles

Where there is a risk of blood or chemical splashes, the eyes and the mucous membranes of the mouth and nose should be protected.[7] Permanent shields, fixed as

Appendix 2-2. Personal Protective Equipment (cont'd)

a part of equipment or bench design, are preferred, eg, splash barriers attached to tubing sealers or centrifuge cabinets. All barriers should be cleaned and disinfected on a regular schedule.

Safety glasses alone provide impact protection from projectiles but do not adequately protect eyes from biohazardous or chemical splashes. Full-face shields or masks and safety goggles are recommended when permanent shields cannot be used. Many designs are commercially available; eliciting staff input on comfort and selection can improve compliance on use.

Masks should be worn whenever there is danger from inhalation. Simple, disposable dust masks are adequate for handling dry chemicals, but respirators with organic vapor filters are preferred for areas where noxious fumes are produced, eg, for cleaning up spills of noxious materials. Respirators should be fitted to their specific wearers and checked annually.

Biological Safety Cabinets/Fume Hoods

Biological safety cabinets (BSCs) are containment devices that facilitate safe manipulation of infectious materials and reduce the risk to personnel and the laboratory environment. A vertical laminar flow cabinet is an example of a BSC that protects both the worker and the material handled. BSCs are not required for Universal Precautions, but centrifugation of open blood samples or manipulation of units known to be positive for hepatitis B surface antigen or human immunodeficiency virus are examples of blood bank procedures for which a BSC could be useful.

Recommendations from the Centers for Disease Control and Prevention (CDC) and National Institutes of Health for effective use of biological safety cabinets are[8]:

■ Keep the laboratory meticulously clean. Minimize storage of boxes and supplies, particularly near the BSC.

■ Wash hands thoroughly before and after working in a BSC. Wear a clean laboratory coat and gloves while working in a BSC to increase safety and help reduce contamination of research materials.

■ Understand how the cabinet works. The effectiveness of the BSC is a function of directional airflow inward and downward, through a high-efficiency filter. Efficacy is reduced by anything that disrupts the airflow pattern, eg, rapidly moving arms in and out of the BSC, rapid movements behind the employee using the BSC, downdrafts from ventilation systems, or open laboratory doors. Performance should be certified annually.

■ Plan the work to be done in the BSC to provide maximal protection for the worker, the material, and any coworkers.

■ Follow manufacturer's instructions for using the BSC.

These guidelines are equally appropriate for fume hoods, which are recommended for use with organic solvents, volatile liquids, and dry chemicals with a significant inhalation hazard.[3] Although constructed with safety glass, most fume hood sashes are not designed as safety shields. Additional information can be obtained by visiting the CDC web site, www.cdc.gov/od/ohs/biosafty/bsc.

Hand Washing

Frequent effective hand washing is the first line of defense in infection control. Blood-borne pathogens generally do not penetrate intact skin, so immediate removal reduces the likelihood of transfer to a mucous membrane or broken skin area or of transmission to others. Thorough washing of hands (and arms) also reduces the risks from exposure to hazardous chemicals and radioactive materials.

Hands should always be washed before leaving a restricted work area, before using a biosafety cabinet, between medical examinations, immediately after becoming soiled with blood or hazardous materials, after removing gloves, and after using the toilet. Washing hands thoroughly before touching contact lenses or applying cosmetics is essential.

Hand wipes (waterless hand cleaners) have been developed that claim to provide suitable antiseptic cleansing for health-care workers. These are useful for

(cont'd)

Appendix 2-2. Personal Protective Equipment (cont'd)

mobile donor collections or in areas where water is not readily available for cleanup purposes. Because there is no listing or registration of acceptable hand wipe products similar to the one the Environmental Protection Agency maintains for surface disinfectants, consumers should request data from the manufacturer to support advertising claims.

Eye Washes

Laboratory areas that contain hazardous chemicals must be equipped with eye wash stations.[3] Procedures and indications for use must be posted and routine function checks must be performed. Testing eye wash fountains weekly helps ensure proper function and flushes out the stagnant water. Portable eye wash systems also should be routinely monitored to ensure the purity of their contents.

Employees should be trained in the proper use of eye wash devices, although prevention, through consistent and appropriate use of safety glasses or shields, is preferred. If a splash occurs, the employee should be directed to keep the eyelids open and use the eye wash according to procedures, or go to the nearest sink and direct a steady, tepid stream of water into the eyes. Solutions other than water should be used only upon a physician's direction.

After adequate flushing (many facilities recommend 15 minutes), follow-up medical care should be sought, especially if pain or redness develops. Whether eye washing is effective in preventing infection has not been demonstrated but it is considered desirable when accidents occur.

Emergency Showers

Emergency showers should be available to areas where caustic, corrosive, flammable, or combustible chemicals are used.[3] Like eyewash stations, they should be periodically tested for function and flushed. Associated floors drains should be checked to ensure that drain traps remain filled with water.

1. Occupational Safety and Health Administration. Occupational exposure to blood-borne pathogens, final rule. Title 29 CFR Part 1910.1030. Fed Regist 1991;56(235): 64175-82.
2. Occupational Safety and Health Administration. OSHA Instruction CPL2-2.44b. Enforcement procedures for occupational exposure to hepatitis B virus (HBV) and human immunodeficiency virus (HIV). Washington, DC: US Government Printing Office, 1990.
3. National Committee for Clinical Laboratory Standards. Clinical laboratory safety; approved guideline. NCCLS document GP17-A. Wayne, PA: NCCLS, 1996.
4. Food and Drug Administration. Center for Devices and Radiological Health. Medical glove powder report, September 1997, http//www.fda.gov/cdrh/glvpwd.html.
5. Food and Drug Administration. Federal Register: Natural rubber-containing medical devices; user labeling. Fed Regist 1997;62:51021-30.
6. National Institute for Occupational Safety and Health. NIOSH Alert: Preventing allergic reactions to natural rubber latex in the workplace, June 1997, DHHS (NIOSH) Publication No. 97-135, http://www.cdc.gov/niosh/latexalt.html.
7. Inspection checklist: General laboratory. Chicago, IL: College of American Pathologists, 1996:45-56.
8. Richmond JY. Safe practices and procedures for working with human specimens in biomedical research laboratories. J Clin Immunoassay 1988;11:115-9.

Appendix 2-3. Biosafety Level 2 Precautions

Biosafety Level 2 precautions as applied in the blood establishment setting include at least the following[1,2]:

- High-risk activities are appropriately segregated from lower risk activities and the boundaries are clearly defined.

- Bench tops are covered with absorbent paper and are decontaminated daily with a hospital disinfectant approved by the Environmental Protection Agency.

- Laboratory rooms have closable doors and sinks. An air system with no recirculation is preferred, but not required.

- Workers are required to perform procedures that create aerosols (eg, opening evacuated tubes, centrifuging, mixing, or sonicating) within a biologic safety cabinet or equivalent, or to wear masks and goggles in addition to gloves and gowns during such procedures. (Note: Open tubes of blood should not be centrifuged. If whole units of blood or plasma are centrifuged, overwrapping is recommended to contain leaks.)

- Gowns and gloves are used routinely and in accordance with general safety guidelines. Face shields or their equivalent are used where there is a risk from splashing.

- Mouth pipetting is prohibited.

- No eating, drinking, smoking, application of cosmetics, or manipulation of contact lenses occurs in the work area. All food and drink are stored outside the restricted area, and laboratory glassware is never used for food or drink. Personnel are instructed to avoid touching their face, ears, mouth, eyes, or nose with their hands or other objects, such as pencils and telephones.

- Needles and syringes are used and disposed of in a safe manner. Needles are never bent, broken, sheared, replaced in sheath, or detached from syringe before being placed in puncture-proof, leakproof containers for controlled disposal. Procedures are designed to minimize exposure to sharp objects.

- All blood specimens are placed in well-constructed containers with secure lids to prevent leaking during transport. Blood is packaged for shipment in accordance with regulatory agency requirements for etiologic agents or clinical specimens, as appropriate.

- Infectious waste is not compacted and is decontaminated before its disposal in leakproof containers. Proper packaging includes double, seamless, tear-resistant, orange or red bags enclosed in protective cartons. Both the carton and the bag inside display the biohazard symbol. Throughout delivery to an incinerator or autoclave, waste is handled only by suitably trained persons. If a waste management contractor is used, the agreement should clearly define respective responsibilities of the staff and the contractor.

- Equipment to be repaired or submitted for preventive maintenance, if potentially contaminated with blood, must be decontaminated before its release to a repair technician.

- Accidental exposure to suspected or actual hazardous material is reported to the laboratory director or responsible person immediately.

---

1. National Committee for Clinical Laboratory Standards. Clinical laboratory safety; approved guideline. NCCLS document GP17-A. Wayne, PA: NCCLS, 1996.
2. Fleming DO. Laboratory biosafety practices. In: Fleming DO, Richardson JH, Tulis JJ, Vesley D, eds. Laboratory safety, principles and practices. 2nd ed. Washington, DC: American Society for Microbiology Press, 1995:203-18.

Appendix 2-4. Sample Hazardous Chemical Data Sheet

The following information should be a part of the procedures for use of hazardous chemicals.

FACILITY
IDENTIFICATION   : _____

LAB NAME   : _____

ROOM NUMBER   : _____

NAME OF CHEMICAL   : _____

SYNONYMS   : _____

CHEMICAL ABSTRACT   : _____
NO. (CASE #)

COMMON NAME   : _____

PRIMARY HAZARD   Carcinogen: ___ Reproductive toxin: _____
                        High acute toxicity: _____
                        Other health hazard: _____
                        Safety hazard: _____
                        MSDS or other reference available: _____
                        Is prior approval required for use of the chemical; if so,
                        by whom? _____

GENERAL AND SPECIAL PRECAUTIONS:

   SIGNS REQUIRED (Warning signs indicating presence of hazardous chemicals/ operations):

   _____

   STORAGE (Secondary containment, temperature-sensitive, incompatibilities, water-reactive,
   etc):_____

   SPECIAL CONTROLS AND LOCATION (Fume hood, glove box, etc): _____

   _____

   SPECIAL EQUIPMENT AND LOCATION (Vacuum line filter, liquid or other traps, special
   shielding): _____

   PERSONAL PROTECTIVE EQUIPMENT (Glove type, eye protection, special clothing, etc):

   _____

EMERGENCY PROCEDURES:

   Spill or release: _____
   Fire: _____
   Decontamination procedures: _____

DISPOSAL PROCEDURES:

   _____

   _____

Appendix 2-5. Sample List of Hazardous Chemicals in the Blood Bank

Chemical	Hazard
Ammonium chloride	Irritant
Bromelain	Irritant, sensitizer
Calcium chloride	Irritant
Carbon dioxide, frozen (dry ice)	Corrosive
Carbonyl iron powder	Oxidizer
Chloroform	Toxic, suspected carcinogen
Chloroquine	Irritant, corrosive
Chromium-111 chloride hexahydrate	Toxic, irritant, sensitizer
Citric acid	Irritant
Copper sulfate (cupric sulfate)	Toxic, irritant
Dichloromethane	Toxic, irritant
Digitonin	Toxic
Dry ice (carbon dioxide, frozen)	Corrosive
Ethidium bromide	Carcinogen, irritant
Ethylenediaminetetraacetic acid (EDTA)	Irritant
Ethyl ether	Highly flammable and explosive, toxic, irritant
Ficin (powder)	Irritant, sensitizer
34.9% Formaldehyde solution	Suspected carcinogen, combustible, toxic
Glycerol	Irritant
Hydrochloric acid	Highly toxic, corrosive
Imidazole	Irritant
Isopropyl (rubbing) alcohol	Flammable, irritant
Liquid nitrogen	Corrosive
Lyphogel	Corrosive
2-Mercaptoethanol	Toxic, stench
Mercury	Toxic
Mineral oil	Irritant, carcinogen, combusitible
Papain	Irritant, sensitizer
Polybrene	Toxic
Potassium hydroxide	Corrosive, toxic
Saponin	Irritant
Sodium azide	Toxic, irritant, explosive when heated
Sodium ethylmercurithiosalicylate (thimerosal)	Highly toxic, irritant
Sodium hydrosulfite	Toxic, irritant
Sodium hydroxide	Corrosive, toxic
Sodium hypochlorite (bleach)	Corrosive
Sodium phosphate	Irritant, hygroscopic
Sulfosalicylic acid	Toxic, corrosive
Trichloroacetic acid (TCA)	Corrosive, toxic
Trypsin	Irritant, sensitizer
Xylene	Highly flammable, toxic, irritant

Appendix 2-6. Sample Material Safety Data Sheet Form

Identify: (used on label and chemical list)

Section I.

Manufacturer's name: _____   Emergency telephone number _____

Address (number, street, city, state zip)   Information telephone number _____

_____   Date prepared: _____

_____   Signature of preparer: _____

Section II. Hazardous Ingredients/Identity Information

Hazardous components (specific chemical)	OSHA PEL	ACGIH TLV	Other limits Recommended	% (Optional)

Section III. Physical/Chemical Characteristics

Boiling point _____   Specific gravity (H_2O-1) _____

Vapor pressure (mmHg) _____   Melting point _____

Vapor density (air-1) _____   Evaporation range (butyl acetate-1) _____

Solubility in water _____   Appearance/odor _____

Section IV. Fire and Explosion Hazard Data

Flash point (method used)   Flammable limits   LEL   UEL

Section V. Reactivity Data

Stability (unstable/stable)   Conditions to avoid

Incompatibility (materials to avoid)

Hazardous decomposition of by-products

Hazardous polymerization (may occur/will not occur)   Conditions to avoid

Appendix 2-6. Sample Material Safety Data Sheet Form (cont'd)

Section VI. Health Hazard Data

Route(s) of entry (inhalation/skin/ingestion): _____

Health hazards (acute and chronic): _____

Carcinogenicity (NTP/IARC monographs/OSHA-regulated): _____

Signs and symptoms of exposure: _____

Medical conditions generally aggravated by exposure: _____

Emergency and first aid procedures: _____

Section VII. Precautions for Safe Handling and Use

Steps to be taken in case material is released or spilled: _____

Waste disposal method: _____

Precautions to be taken in handling and storing: _____

Other precautions: _____

Section VIII. Control Measures

Respiratory protection (specify type)   Ventilation (local exhaust/general mechanical/other)

_____   _____

Protective clothing/equipment   Work/hygienic practices
(gloves/eyewear/other)

_____   _____

Note: This sample MSDS identifies the key categories of information that need to be included in an MSDS. Blank spaces are not permitted. If any item is not applicable or no information is available, the space must be marked to indicate that.

Blood Utilization Management

THE GOAL OF BLOOD UTILIZATION management is to ensure effective use of blood resources. It includes the policies and practices related to inventory management and blood usage review. Although regional blood centers and transfusion services approach utilization management from different perspectives, they share the common goal of providing appropriate, high-quality blood products with minimum waste. This chapter reviews the elements of utilization management, emphasizing the primary user (the transfusion service), to promote understanding between collecting and transfusing facilities and to improve blood utilization.

Determining Inventory Levels

The ideal inventory level provides adequate supplies of blood for routine and emergency situations, without outdating. Both surpluses and shortages of blood products lead to inefficient use of resources for the donor center and the transfusion service. During a shortage, a donor center must import blood from outside the local area. If there is a large surplus of blood the donor center may not be able to find another blood center in need of the product before it outdates.

In a transfusion service with low transfusion activity, a large inventory carries a higher potential for outdating. Conversely, the smaller the inventory, the greater the likelihood of blood shortages and emergency deliveries from the blood supplier.

Forecasting is an attempt to determine future blood product use from data collected about past usage. The optimal number of units to keep in inventory can be estimated using mathematical formulae, computer simulations, or empirical calculations. Forecasting product needs has been studied extensively in management literature. With the moving average method, the total number of units used in each period (such as a day or week) is added to the total use and the total use is divided by the number of periods (days or weeks) used. As new data are added, old data are deleted. This method tends to level off variation from period to period. Management texts on inventory management should be reviewed for specific information on the use of complex techniques such as exponential smoothing. The accuracy of the estimate is increased when the ideal inventory is estimated with two statistical techniques. Two less complicated methods of estimating ideal inventory are described below.

Average Weekly Use Estimate

This method gives an estimate of the average weekly blood usage of each ABO group and Rh type.
1. Collect weekly blood and product usage data over a 6-month period.
2. Record usage by ABO group and Rh type for each week.
3. Disregard the single highest usage for each type to correct for unusual week-to-week variation (eg, a large volume used for an emergency).
4. Total the number of units of each ABO group and Rh type, omitting the highest week in each column.
5. Divide each total by 25 (total number of weeks minus the highest week), as shown in Table 3-1. This gives an estimate of the average weekly blood usage of each ABO group and Rh type.

Average Daily Use Estimate

Facilities with more transfusion activity may calculate daily blood usage.

1. Determine the total use over several months.
2. Divide the total use by the number of days in the period covered.
3. Determine the percentage of each of the blood types used during one or more representative months.
4. Multiply the average blood use per day by the percentage of blood use by type.
5. Determine the minimum inventory level by multiplying the daily use by the number of days of blood supply required to be on hand (this may be 3, 5, or 7 days depending on the delivery schedule from the blood supplier) and add an "emergency" level of units.

A transfusion service may find the average daily use more helpful when blood shipments are made once or more per day. When inventory is replenished weekly, the empirical method may prove more satisfactory.

Ideal Inventory Levels

Desirable inventory levels depend on many factors. Logistic considerations include the amount of storage space for temperature-monitored products, local weather, traffic problems, and distance from the blood supplier. Other practical considerations include blood bank staffing and workload patterns, as well as prior agreements related to hospital services such as transplant surgery or support of a level one trauma center.

Inventory levels should be evaluated periodically and adjusted if needed. Important indicators of performance include, but are not limited to, outdate rates, the frequency of emergency blood shipments, the frequency of switching from ABO-specific to ABO-compatible blood, and delays in scheduling elective surgery. Such data should be reviewed on an ongoing basis as part of the quality assurance program. Inventory levels should be reevaluated periodically and whenever a

Table 3-1. Whole Blood and Red Blood Cells Transfused by Week and by Blood Group (Small Hospital Example)

Week	O+	A+	B+	AB+	O-	A-	B-	AB-
1	4	2	-	-	2	-	-	-
2	-	6	6	-	-	2	-	-
3	10	-	-	-	2	-	1	-
4	-	2	-	-	4	2	1	-
5	4	2	-	-	9	-	-	-
6	-	5	2	-	-	-	-	-
7	1	13	-	-	1	2	2	-
8	20	9	-	-	5	2	-	-
9	2	12	2	-	-	-	-	-
10	-	8	-	-	-	-	1	-
11	-	-	-	-	-	2	1	-
12	4	3	2	-	1	-	-	-
13	2	4	-	-	2	-	-	-
14	2	9	3	-	-	2	2	-
15	7	-	-	-	1	-	-	-
16	3	2	-	-	-	-	-	-
17	-	2	1	2	1	2	1	-
18	11	1	1	2	1	1	1	-
19	3	3	4	-	2	-	1	-
20	3	3	4	-	-	1	1	-
21	2	1	-	-	2	1	-	-
22	4	-	1	-	-	-	-	-
23	2	5	1	-	-	1	2	-
24	4	-	1	-	-	2	-	-
25	9	4	1	-	6	8	-	-
26	5	-	-	-	4	-	2	-
Total used	102	96	29	4	43	28	16	0
Highest week (subtract)	20	13	6	2	9	8	2	0
Subtotal	82	83	23	2	34	20	14	0
Divided by 25 = average weekly blood usage	3.3	3.3	0.9	0	1.4	0.8	0.6	0

significant change is planned or observed. Adding more beds, performing new surgical procedures, or changing practices in oncology, transplantation, neonatology, or cardiac surgery will affect blood usage and should trigger a reevaluation of optimal inventory levels.

Factors That Affect Outdating

Little has been published on the average outdate rate for transfusion services or donor centers. The College of American Pathologists has surveyed blood product utilization in participating transfusion services in its Q-Probe series of quality assurance monitors. In the 1989 Q-Probe on Blood Utilization, the red cell outdate rate was less than 5.0% for 95% of the participating institutions.[1] The autologous red cell expiration rates were 52.0% or less for three-fourths of the participants. The median autologous outdate rate was 34.4%. Of note, 5% reported autologous expiration rates between 71.5% and 96.2%. In the 1991 survey, the median outdate rate for allogeneic red cell units remained at 0.8%.[2] Eighty percent of the participants reported allogeneic red cell outdate rates below 5.0% and plasma and platelet product expiration rates less than 17%. Autologous blood expiration rates ranged from less than 3.0% in the top 10% of participants to greater than 69.0% in the bottom 10% of participants.

The outdate rate is affected by many factors other than inventory level. These include the factors described below.

Size of the Hospital and Services Provided

Acute care or teaching facilities and active trauma centers often put stress on blood inventories. Large amounts of blood may be ordered for trauma emergencies or complicated surgery, but not all the ordered units may be used. If not carefully managed, such ordering practices can inflate the inventory and lead to outdating.

Remaining Shelf Life

The shorter the shelf life of a unit at entry into inventory, the more likely it is to expire unused. This varies, of course, with daily usage patterns.

Transfusion services providing blood for acute-care hospitals with large surgical services or active emergency rooms often receive and use units nearing expiration because they transfuse large volumes of blood daily. Blood centers may transfer short-dated units to "sure users" rather than allow the units to expire unused at smaller transfusion services. While this practice can reduce overall blood waste in a community, it may adversely affect the expiration statistics of the receiving facility.

Shipping Distance and Frequency

Transfusion services that are a great distance from the supplier or that receive infrequent shipments must maintain enough blood to cover their usual use and most emergencies. The larger the inventory compared to the amount of blood actually used, the greater the outdate rate. Reciprocal agreements with nearby institutions to transfer units in acute emergencies can help reduce inventory size. Programs to issue fresher stock to smaller or more distant transfusion services with rotation of the unused stock (with at least 2 weeks remaining before expiration) to larger transfusion services have proved to reduce outdating while maintaining higher inventory levels at outlying institutions.

Ordering Policies

Transfusion services should establish both minimum and ideal inventory levels. Establishment of maximum inventory levels may assist staff in determining when to arrange for return or transfer of indate products to avoid outdating. Both transfusion services and donor centers should establish record-keeping systems that allow personnel to determine the number of units ordered and the number of units actually received or shipped. The responsibility for ordering may be centralized and orders should be based on established policies for minimal and maximal levels.

Standing orders can simplify inventory planning for both transfusion services and blood centers. Blood centers may send a predetermined number of units on a regular schedule or may keep the transfusion service inventory at established levels by replacing all units reported as transfused.

Donor center policies are often set to optimize inventory levels and encourage resource-sharing. However, policies that penalize transfusion services that return unneeded inventory to the donor center for redistribution may contribute to increased outdating.

Issuing Policies

Good inventory management demands distribution and transfusion of the oldest blood first and this requires clearly written policies on blood storage and blood selection. Technologists generally find it easier to select, crossmatch, and issue the oldest units first when inventories are arranged by expiration date.

Policies on blood selection must be flexible, to allow use of fresher blood when indicated (eg, for infants). Generally, however, oldest units are crossmatched for patients most likely to need transfusion. The crossmatching of older units for more than one patient (ie, "double crossmatching") can help ensure blood use, but it requires careful monitoring so that additional units are prepared, if needed, after a "double-set" unit is issued.

Autologous and Directed Donor Policies

AABB *Standards for Blood Banks and Transfusion Services*[3(p75)] does not allow crossover of autologous units to allogeneic inventory. The crossover of directed donor units is controversial.[4] Therefore, autologous and directed donor units not given to the intended patient may expire. If autologous and directed units are included in the total number of expired units, they will contribute to a facility's outdate rate.[5]

Improving Transfusion Service Blood Ordering Practices

Available shelf life decreases each time a unit is held or crossmatched for a patient who does not use it. When house staff order more blood than needed it is unavailable for other patients, which may increase the outdate rate. Providing crossmatch guidelines such as type and screen (T/S) policies, maximum surgical blood order schedules (MSBOS),[6] and monitoring crossmatch-to-transfusion (C:T) ratios may be helpful. A C:T ratio greater than 2.0 usually indicates excessive crossmatch requests. In the CAP Q-Probe studies, the median C:T ratio for participants fell from 1.95 in 1988 to 1.91 in 1990.[2] In some situations, it may be useful to determine C:T ratios by physician or by service to identify areas with the highest ratio.

Some institutions define those procedures that do not normally use blood in a "type and screen" guideline. Both the T/S guideline and the MSBOS use data about past surgical blood use to recommend a T/S order or a maximum number of units that may be ordered initially for common elective surgical procedures. With the MSBOS, physicians may always order fewer units than the maximum. Some institutions have modified the MSBOS concept into a "standard" blood order (SBO) system for surgical procedures.[7]

Ordering guidelines such as those in Table 3-2 are derived by reviewing a facility's actual blood use over a suitable period. Data for each surgical procedure could include the number of patients for whom blood was requested, number of patients who received blood, number of units crossmatched, number of units transfused, the average number of units transfused per patient crossmatched, and the C:T ratio.

Conclusions can then be drawn about the likelihood of transfusion and probable blood use for each surgical procedure. A type and screen order is a recommended SBO for proce-

Table 3-2. Example of a Maximum Surgical Blood Order Schedule

Procedure	Units*
General Surgery	
Breast biopsy	T/S
Colon resection	2
Exploratory laparotomy	2
Gastrectomy	2
Hernia repair	T/S
Laryngectomy	2
Mastectomy, radical	T/S
Pancreatectomy	4
Splenectomy	2
Thyroidectomy	T/S
Cardiac-Thoracic	
Aneurism resection	6
Coronary artery bypass graft, adults	4
Coronary artery bypass graft, children	2
Lobectomy	2
Lung biopsy	T/S
Vascular	
Aortic bypass with graft	4
Endarterectomy	T/S
Femoral-popliteal bypass with graft	4
Orthopedics	
Arthroscopy	T/S
Laminectomy	T/S
Spinal fusion	3
Total hip replacement	3
Total knee replacement	2
OB-GYN	
Abdomino-perineal repair	T/S
Cesarean section	T/S
D & C	T/S
Hysterectomy, abdominal	T/S
Hysterectomy, radical	2
Labor/delivery, uncomplicated	(Hold)
Urology	
Bladder, transurethral resection	T/S
Nephrectomy, radical	3
Prostatectomy, perineal	2
Prostatectomy, transurethral	T/S
Renal transplant	2

*Numbers may vary with institutional practice.

dures that require less than 0.5 unit of blood per patient per procedure. An SBO often represents the average number of units transfused for each procedure, while the MSBOS often defines the number of units needed to meet the needs of 80-90% of patients undergoing a specific procedure.[7]

An institution's guidelines must reflect local patterns of surgical practice and patient population. These may be compared to published guidelines to ensure that local practice does not markedly deviate from generally accepted standards of care. (Transfusion audits are discussed in Chapter 1.) Once the SBO, T/S, MSBOS, or other schedule is accepted, inventory levels often can be reduced. Ordering guidelines should be periodically reviewed to keep pace with changing methods and practices. A change in the C:T ratio might signal a significant modification in clinical practice.

The SBO, T/S, or MSBOS system is intended for typical circumstances. Surgeons or anesthesiologists may individualize specific requests and override the system to accommodate special needs. The transfusion service must give special consideration to patients with a positive antibody screen. The antibody should be identified and, if it is clinically significant, an appropriate number of antigen-negative units should be identified (eg, two, if the original order was a type and screen).

Transfusion Service Procedures

Clearly written policies and procedures plus adequate training are needed so that transfusion service personnel understand the demands of inventory management. Storage of all products must comply with AABB *Standards*,[3(pp41-46)] and equipment must be clean, well-maintained, and properly monitored. Both manual systems (eg, cards or lists) or computer systems are acceptable for tracking inventory.

Routine vs Emergency Orders

Transfusion services should establish procedures that define ideal stocking levels for each blood type and critical levels at which emergency orders are indicated. Transfusion service staff should have institutional policies identifying the following:

- *Who* is responsible for placing orders?
- *When* and how are orders to be placed (by phone or facsimile)?
- *How* are orders documented?

The addresses and phone numbers of approved blood suppliers and any needed courier or cab services should be immediately available. Transfusion services need to establish guidelines for handling blood shortages and unexpected emergencies. Equally important is specifying the actions to take if transfusion requests cannot immediately be met.

Transfusion services should develop policies defining the following:

- When ABO-compatible units may be given instead of ABO-identical.
- When Rh-positive units may be given to Rh-negative recipients.
- When units crossmatched for a surgical procedure may be released before the standard interval.
- If units may be crossmatched for more than one patient at a time.
- What resources are available for transfer of inventory.
- Mechanisms to notify physicians of critical blood shortages.
- When cancellation of elective procedures should be considered.
- Methods to notify staff and patients of surgery cancellations.

Inventory Counts and Inspection

On-hand units may be counted once or several times a day to determine ordering needs; computerized facilities may prefer to take inventory electronically. Individual units must be visually inspected for signs of contamination or atypical appearance before issue or shipping. Units that do not meet inspection criteria must be quarantined for further evaluation.

An organizational format for storage should be established and followed. Unprocessed or incompletely processed units, autologous units, and unsuitable units must be clearly separated (quarantined) from routine stock. Most institutions organize their blood inventory by status (quarantined, retype unconfirmed, retype confirmed, available, crossmatched, etc), by product, by ABO group and Rh type and, within these categories, by expiration date. Attention to detail in placing blood into storage is necessary because a placement error could be critical if a quarantined unit is issued or a group O Rh-positive unit, incorrectly placed among group O Rh-negative units, is issued without careful checking in an emergency situation.

Inventory Issues for Blood Centers

Blood centers collect most of the allogeneic units in the United States. Collection goals are set by evaluating both local blood use and the donor base. Depending on community needs and geographic location, blood centers may be net importers of blood, net exporters, or self-sustaining.

Blood centers characteristically have trained personnel dedicated to managing the community's blood supply, recruiting donors to maintain a continuous supply, and distributing the inventory in an equitable manner among community transfusion services. How much control the blood center maintains after distribution depends on its relationship as a supplier to its customer transfusion services.

Reimbursement and Control

There are a number of contractual arrangements that influence the perceived ownership of the blood supply. The two most common arrangements are consignment and direct reimbursement. When a blood center supplies a transfusion service under a *consignment arrangement*, blood remains under the control of the blood center until it is transfused; the transfusion service pays the processing fee only if the unit is transfused. With this arrangement, remote transfusion services can be stocked with units having a long shelf life. As they near their expiration, unused units can be returned to the blood center for full credit and redistributed to closer, large-volume transfusion service users. This reduces total regional outdating and the blood center usually absorbs the cost of outdated blood.

Transfusion services having a *direct reimbursement arrangement* with the supplier are billed for units delivered and accepted into inventory. Typically, the blood center has little control over the blood after delivery and the transfusion service absorbs the expense of outdated units.

Cooperation between transfusion services and blood suppliers can help ensure that blood resources are not wasted.

Institutional Communication Issues

Whatever the inventory control arrangement, blood suppliers need clearly defined ordering and distribution policies that are understood by their own staff as well as their transfusion service customers. The blood center distribution staff needs to know how orders are filled and prioritized within the community. Potentially ambiguous terms should be defined; the term STAT, for example, is better expressed as a time frame (ie, within 1 hour) than left to individual interpretation. If orders cannot be filled as requested, it is desirable to explain what corrective actions the blood center is taking. Good communication reduces misunderstandings and increases customer satisfaction.

To overcome anticipated seasonal shortages, blood centers and transfusion services that draw donors can work together to develop recruitment plans well in advance. When possible, large draws can be scheduled shortly before holiday periods. Using blood additives that increase red-cell shelf life to 42 days adds flexibility to donor drive scheduling and helps to decrease the outdate rate.

During acute shortages, blood centers and transfusion services can request blood products from other blood centers, either directly or through national or multicenter organizations. It is common practice to share excess inventory, and blood exchange programs simplify the communication routes. For a small transaction fee, the National Blood Exchange (NBE) of the AABB will serve as an intermediary, matching institutions with shortages to those with excesses. The phone number of the NBE is (301) 907-6551. The NBE's e-mail address is nbe@aabb.org.

Finally, blood centers depend on the media—television, radio, and newspapers—to make the public aware of the community's blood needs. Appeals are more effective when associated with a specific community need; their effect is lost if they are overused.

Special Product Concerns

Platelets

Few articles address management of platelet inventory. Optimal levels are difficult to determine because demand is episodic and the shelf life is short. Often, the effective shelf life is 3 days because, of the allowable 5 days after phlebotomy, day 1 may be taken for testing and day 2 for shipment. Planning is further complicated by requests for special products, such as leukocyte-reduced, crossmatched, HLA-matched, or cytomegalovirus (CMV) seronegative platelets.

Platelet inventory management requires good communication and cooperation among transfusion services and blood centers. Information about patients' diagnoses and expected transfusion schedules helps the blood center plan how many platelets to prepare and which donors to recruit for plateletpheresis.

Transfusion services with low platelet use usually order platelets only when they receive a specific request. If the transfusion service staff follows daily platelet counts and special transfusion requirements of known platelet users, they can often anticipate needs and place orders in advance. Transfusion services with high use may find it helpful to maintain platelets in inventory. Transfusion services should define selection and transfusion guidelines for ABO group, Rh type, irradiated, CMV serologic testing, and leukocyte reduction of platelet products. The formulas described in the beginning of the chapter may be used to estimate ideal inventory ranges.

Platelet usage often increases the day after a holiday because elective procedures and oncology transfusions will have been postponed. Planning ahead to stock Platelets, Pheresis helps ease postholiday demand.

Red Blood Cells, Frozen

Frozen storage is ideal for extending the shelf life of units with rare or uncommon phenotypes and may be helpful in autologous transfusion programs. Facilities may routinely freeze excess units from inventory, group A and O units from donors with unexpected antibodies, or selected units rejuvenated at the time of outdating.

Although Red Blood Cells, Frozen may be stored for routine transfusion up to 10 years, the cost/benefit analysis of frozen blood programs indicates high costs with fewer benefits. It is expensive to prepare and store Red Blood Cells, Frozen, and the length of time needed to thaw and deglycerolize a unit limits its use in urgent situations. The 24-hour expiration imposed on units deglycerolized in an open system adds to the likelihood that these units will expire unless inventories are carefully monitored. In light of changing requirements for infectious disease testing, it is prudent to freeze serum or plasma aliquots from donors of all frozen units, for use if new tests are implemented. However, test method requirements such as the age of the specimen may preclude the use of these specimens for infectious disease testing.

Frozen Plasma Products

Because Fresh Frozen Plasma (FFP) and Cryoprecipitated Antihemophilic Factor (AHF) can be stored up to 1 year if stored at −18 C or colder and plasma may be stored for up to 7 years if stored at −65 C or colder, these inventories are easier to manage. Optimal inventory levels are determined by assessing statistics on patient population and usage patterns. Production goals and schedules can then be established. Most centers find it best to maintain consistent production levels throughout the year, to achieve evenly distributed expiration dates.

Some facilities preferentially freeze plasma from group AB and A donors because these units will be ABO-compatible with most potential recipients. Plasma can be collected by apheresis to increase general stock and provide for special needs.

Cryoprecipitated AHF is a labor-intensive product to prepare and supplies cannot easily be increased to meet large acute needs. It is prudent to maintain inventories at close-to-maximum levels.

Autologous and Directed Units

If autologous and directed donor units constitute an increasing fraction of inventory, their management becomes a significant and controversial issue both for the intended recipients and for institutions.[4] An extended discussion of autologous blood collection and transfusion can be found in Chapter 5.

Autologous and directed units should be stored in separate designated areas within the blood refrigerator. Such units are often arranged alphabetically by the intended recipi-

ent's last name. Available units must be clearly identified and monitored to ensure issue in the proper sequence. Autologous blood should always be used first, followed by directed donor blood and, finally, allogeneic units from general stock. Policies about the reservation period for directed donor units and possible release to other recipients should be established at both the transfusion service and donor center and should be made known to laboratory staff, to potential recipients, and to their physicians.

Special Inventories

Donor centers and transfusion services are faced with increased demands for CMV-seronegative, leukocyte-reduced, and irradiated blood products. The appropriate use of these products is discussed in Chapter 21. Depending on how and when they were prepared, these products may have shortened expiration dates.

If demand and inventory levels are very high, a transfusion service may need to keep separate inventories of these products to make them easier to locate and monitor. These special units can be rotated into general stock as they near their outdate because they can be given safely to others.

References

1. Q-Probes: Blood utilization data analysis and critique (89-08A). Northfield, IL: College of American Pathologists, 1990.
2. Q-Probes: Blood utilization data analysis and critique (91-07A). Northfield, IL: College of American Pathologists, 1992.
3. Menitove J, ed. Standards for blood banks and transfusion services. 19th ed. Bethesda, MD: American Association of Blood Banks, 1999.
4. Whyte G, Coghlan P. Comparative safety of units donated by autologous, designated and allogeneic (homologous) donors. Transfus Med 1996;6(2):209-11.
5. Yawn DH. Autologous blood transfusion programs. In: Rock G, Seghatchian MJ, eds. Quality assurance in transfusion medicine. Volume I: Conceptual, serological and microbiological aspects. Boca Raton, FL: CRC Press, 1992:135-56.

6. Friedman BA, Oberman HA, Chadwick AR, et al. The maximum surgical blood order schedule and surgical blood use in the United States. Transfusion 1976;16:380-7.

7. Devine P, Linden JV, Hoffstadter L, et al. Blood donor-, apheresis-, and transfusion-related activities: Results of the 1991 American Association of Blood Banks Institutional Membership Questionnaire. Transfusion 1993;33:779-82.

Suggested Reading

Duffield J. Blood inventory management. In: Administrative manual, Volume IV. Bethesda, MD: American Association of Blood Banks, 1993:113-34.

Fuller MJ, Holland PV. Comprehensive reimbursement model: An alternative to fee for service reimbursement by blood centers. Transfus Med Rev 1997;11:38-43.

4

Donor Selection and Blood Collection

BLOOD CENTERS AND TRANSFUSION services depend on voluntary donors to provide the blood necessary to meet the needs of the patients they serve. To attract volunteer donors initially and to encourage their continued participation, it is essential that conditions surrounding blood donation be as pleasant, safe, and convenient as possible. For the protection of the recipient, donors are questioned about their medical history and are given a mini-physical examination to help blood center staff determine whether they are suitable donors. The phlebotomy is conducted carefully to minimize any potential donor reactions, or potential contamination of the unit.

Blood Donation Process

The donor area should be attractive, accessible, and open at hours convenient for donors, and must be well lighted, comfortably ventilated, and clean. Personnel should be friendly, understanding, professional, and well trained.

Each blood bank must have a manual detailing its standard operating procedures (SOPs). The SOP manual must indicate actual practices and cover all phases of activity in the donor area. The procedures must meet the requirements of the most recent edition of the AABB *Standards for Blood Banks and Transfusion Services*[1] for AABB accreditation. The manual must reflect current local, state, and federal regulations pertaining to blood bank operation and must be reviewed at least annually by an authorized person. The medical director must approve changes in procedures that relate to the safety of patients and donors.

For laboratories to be accredited by the College of American Pathologists (CAP) Commission on Laboratory Accreditation, the SOP manual should include documentation of annual review by the blood bank director or the designee. Chapter 1 contains more detailed information on SOPs and SOP manuals.

Registration

The information obtained from the donor during registration must fully identify the donor and link the donor to existing donor records. Some facilities require a photographic identification. Current information must be obtained and recorded for each donation; single-use or multiple-donation forms may be used. Donation records must be kept indefinitely, and must make it possible to notify the donor of any information that needs to be conveyed.[1] The following information should be included:

1. Date and time of donation.
2. Name: Last, first (and middle initial if available).
3. Address: Residence and/or business.
4. Telephone: Residence and/or business.
5. Gender.
6. Age and/or date of birth. Blood donors must be at least 17 years of age except that:
    a. Those who are considered minors under applicable law may be accepted only if written consent to donate blood has been obtained in accordance with the law. Because laws vary among jurisdictions, local legal opinion must be obtained and a copy of the applicable law be readily available.
    b. *Standards* does not set an upper age limit for donation; thus, elderly prospective donors may be accepted at the discretion of the blood bank physician. Many blood centers safely involve their senior citizen population in the donation process.[2]

c. The decision to accept these donors may be made on a case-by-case basis, or the SOP manual may include general policy statements.

    c. While *Standards* sets no age limit for autologous blood collection, each patient must be evaluated by the blood bank physician or designee to determine if collecting blood will be safe.

7. A record of reasons for previous deferrals, if any. Persons who have been placed on indefinite deferral or surveillance must be identified before any unit drawn from them is made available for release. Ideally, a donor deferral registry should be available to identify ineligible donors before blood is drawn. If such a registry is not available, there must be a procedure to review prior donation records and/or deferral registries before the labeling process is completed.[3] Under certain circumstances, such as on a bloodmobile location, it may not be possible to defer a donor on the basis of computer records before the unit is collected. There must be a system to prevent the issue of blood or components from donors who, upon later testing or review of records, are judged to be ineligible.

The following information may also be useful:

1. Additional identification such as social security or driver's license number or any other name used by the donor on a previous donation. These data are required for information retrieval in some computerized systems. Other names used by a donor are particularly important to ensure that the appropriate donor file is accessed or that a deferral status is accurate.
2. Name of patient or group to be acknowledged or credited when such a system is used. Even if the donor is deferred, the record may be useful to those concerned with donor recruitment or credit accounts.

3. Race. This information can be particularly useful when blood of a specific phenotype is needed for patients who have unexpected antibodies. Care should be taken to be sure that minority populations understand the medical importance and scientific applications of this information.[4,5]

4. Unique characteristics of the donor. Certain information about the donor may enable the blood bank to make optimal use of the donation. For example, blood from donors who are seronegative for cytomegalovirus (CMV), or who are group O, Rh negative, is often designated for neonatal patients. The blood center may specify that blood from these individuals be drawn routinely into collection bags suitable for pediatric transfusion. Individuals known to have clinically significant antibodies may be identified so that their blood can be processed into components that contain only minimal amounts of plasma.

5. A record of special communications to a donor, special drawing of blood samples for studies, etc.

6. If the donation is directed to a specific patient, information about when and where the intended recipient will be hospitalized should be obtained. The intended recipient's date of birth, social security number, or other identifiers may be required by the transfusion service. If the donor is a blood relative of the intended recipient, the cellular components must be irradiated.[1(p68)] Such relationship between donor and the intended recipient must appear in the donor drawing record to ensure irradiation of all cellular components.

Information Provided to the Prospective Donor

All donors must be given educational materials informing them of the clinical signs and symptoms associated with HIV infection and AIDS, of high-risk activities for HIV transmission, and of the importance of refraining from donating blood if they have engaged in these activities or experienced the signs or symptoms. Before donating, the prospective donor must document that they have read the material and have been given the opportunity to ask questions about the information. This information must include a list of activities defined by the Food and Drug Administration (FDA) that increase the risk of exposure to HIV. A description of HIV-associated clinical signs and symptoms, including the following, should be provided[6]:

1. Unexplained weight loss, greater than 10 lbs.

2. Night sweats.

3. Blue or purple spots typical of Kaposi's sarcoma on or under the skin or on mucous membranes.

4. Swollen lymph nodes lasting more than 1 month.

5. Persistent white spots or unusual blemishes in the mouth.

6. Temperature greater than 100.5 F for more than 10 days.

7. Persistent cough and shortness of breath.

8. Persistent diarrhea.

It is useful to provide the donor with information about the tests to be done on his/her blood, the agencies to be notified of abnormal results, and the existence of registries of ineligible donors. The donor must also be informed if his/her blood is to be tested with an investigational new drug test such as nucleic acid amplification tests. The possibility that testing may fail to identify infective individuals in an early seronegative stage of infection should also be included.[7] The same educational material can also be used to warn the prospective donor of possible reactions and provide suggestions for postphlebotomy care.

It is very important to present this information in a way that the donor will understand it.[6] Provisions should be made for the hearing- or vision-impaired or for donors not fluent in English (eg, interpreters). In some locations it may be necessary to have brochures in more than one language. It is also helpful to provide more detailed information for first-time donors. Information about alternative sites or other mechanisms to obtain HIV tests should be available to all prospective donors. Prospective donors must be informed about regulations or local SOPs that require notification to government agencies of the donor's infectious disease status. The requirement to report positive test results may differ from state to state; these may include HIV, syphilis, and hepatitis testing. Prospective donors must also be informed[1(p20)] if there are routine circumstances in which some tests for disease markers are not to be performed. The donor should be told that he/she will be notified when abnormal test results are recorded and the donor has been placed on a deferral status.

Donor Selection

The suitability of donors must be determined by a qualified physician. The responsibility may be delegated to a designee working under his/her direction after appropriate training.[8] The donor screening process is one of the most important steps in protecting the safety of the blood supply. The process is intended to identify elements of the medical history and behavior or events that put a person at risk for transmissible disease. It is, therefore, imperative that proper guidelines and procedures be followed to make the donor screening process effective.

Donors must understand the information that is presented to them in order to make an informed decision to donate their blood. Effective communication is vital for conveying important information and eliminating unsuitable donors from the donor pool. Of equal importance is the training of blood bank staff. Screening can only be effective if the staff members are proficient in their jobs and understand thoroughly the technical information

required to perform the job. Good interpersonal and public relations skills are essential for job competency. Because blood bank staff are in constant contact with donors, knowledgeable personnel and effective communication contribute to positive public perception and to the success of donor screening programs.

Donor selection is based on a medical history and a limited physical examination done on the day of donation to determine whether giving blood will harm the donor or transfusion of the unit will harm a recipient.[1(p10,12),10] The medical history questions may be asked by a qualified interviewer or donors may complete their own record, which must then be reviewed with the donor and initialed by a trained knowledgeable staff member of the donor service. Direct questions pertaining to risk behavior associated with HIV infections should be presented to potential donors orally.

The interview and physical examination should be performed in a manner that ensures adequate auditory and visual privacy, allays apprehensions, and provides time for any necessary discussion or explanation. Answers to questions must be recorded "yes" or "no." Details explaining answers that require further investigation should be noted. Results of observations made at the time of physical examination and of tests must be recorded.

Medical History

While the medical history is obtained, some very specific questions are necessary to ensure that, to the greatest extent possible, it is safe for the donor to donate and for the blood to be transfused. Properly trained staff should question prospective donors about risk behaviors and indicate whether satisfactory responses are received. The interviewer should evaluate all responses to determine suitability for donation and document the decision. To be sure that all the appropriate questions are asked and that donors are given a consistent message, use of the most recent FDA-approved uniform donor history questionnaire is recommended. (See Appendix 4-1.) One area of the medical history—medications and drugs taken by the donor—often requires further investigation. New prescription drugs and over-the-counter medications enter the marketplace daily, and donors may report use of a drug not specifically noted in the facility's SOP manual. While there is consensus on those drugs that are always or never a cause for deferral, many drugs fall into a category over which disagreement exists. Appendix 4-2 lists drugs that many blood centers do consider acceptable without approval from a blood center physician. The Armed Services Blood Program Office makes its drug deferral list available to the public on its web site, http://www.tricare.osd.mil/asbpohme.html.

Deferring or rejecting potential donors often leaves those persons with negative feelings about themselves as well as the system. Donors who are deferred should be given a full explanation of the reason and be informed whether or when they can return to donate. Donor deferral rates should be monitored closely by the blood bank physician to ensure they are within a reasonable range.

Confidential Unit Exclusion

If an opportunity for confidential unit exclusion (CUE) is offered, it should be provided by a suitably trained person in a setting that ensures strict confidentiality and privacy in which to make the decision. All donors must be given the opportunity to indicate confidentially whether their blood is or is not suitable for transfusion to others. CUE may be accomplished by having a detachable "ballot" as part of the educational material given to the donor. At the time of drawing, the phlebotomist can attach a bar-coded number to the "ballot" and ask the donor to mark the appropriate response. The "ballots" are deposited in a box when the donor leaves the donor room. Another method is to provide the donor with a sheet having a bar-coded *yes* or *no* sticker. The donor chooses the desired sticker and places it on the blood bag or donor card. If the bar-coded response is placed directly on the unit (an ideal location is the area to be covered by the ABO label), the unit of Whole Blood may be scanned and discarded before any further processing is carried out. It may not always be possible to discard the unit before tubes are sent for processing. In these cases, there must be a procedure to ensure that only those units of blood or component with an acceptable CUE designation ("yes" or "okay") are made available for shipping.

Alternatively, the donor may be given instructions to the effect that he or she may call the blood bank within a short period of time after the donation and ask that the unit collected not be used. A mechanism should exist to allow retrieval of the unit without obtaining the donor's identity.

If an opportunity is provided for the donor to indicate that blood collected should not be used for transfusion, the donor should be informed that the blood will be subjected to testing and that there will be notification of any positive results. Counseling or referral must be provided for positive HIV antibody test results, or if any other medically significant abnormalities have been detected.

Because CUE procedures do not preclude donation, an alternate method to augment self-exclusion may be used. A private interview conducted by a trained, competent health-care professional may include an oral presentation of the option for self-exclusion, along with AIDS-related educational material and the offer of an opportunity for self-deferral before the phlebotomy starts.[8]

Physical Examination

The following variables must be evaluated for each donor. Exceptions to routinely acceptable findings must be approved by the blood bank physician. For special donor categories, the medical director may provide policies and procedures to guide decisions. Other donors may require individual evaluation.

1. General appearance: If the donor looks ill, appears to be under the influence of drugs or alcohol, or is excessively nervous, it is best to defer the donation. If possible, this should be done in a way that does not antagonize the donor and, if appropriate, encourages donation at a future time.

2. Weight: Donors weighing 50 kg (110 lb) or more ordinarily may donate a maximum of 525 mL, but not more than 15% of the donor's estimated blood volume, including samples drawn for processing. For donors weighing less than 50 kg (110 lb), as little as 300 mL may be drawn without reducing the amount of anticoagulant in the 450-mL primary bag. Units containing 300-405 mL of blood must be labeled as "Low Volume Unit: _____ mL." These units should not be used to prepare Platelets or plasma components. If it is necessary to draw less than 300 mL, the amount of anticoagulant must be reduced proportionately, by expressing the excess into an integrally attached satellite bag and sealing the tubing. The formula in Table 4-1 may be used to determine the amount of anticoagulant to remove. The volume of blood drawn must be measured carefully and accurately.

3. Temperature: The donor's temperature must not exceed 37.5 C (99.5 F) if measured orally, or its equivalent if measured by another method. Lower than normal temperatures are usually of no significance in healthy individuals; however, they should be repeated for confirmation. Caution: If a glass thermometer is used, it should not be in the donor's mouth during puncture to obtain blood for hematocrit or hemoglobin determination. The use of thermometer covers is advised. Use of electronic thermometers is encouraged.

4. Pulse: The pulse rate should be counted for at least 15 seconds. It should exhibit no rhythmic irregularity, and the frequency should be between 50 and 100 beats per minute. If a prospective donor is a known athlete with high exercise tolerance, a pulse rate below 50 may be noted and should be acceptable. A blood bank physician should evaluate marked abnormalities of pulse and recommend acceptance, deferral, or referral for additional evaluation.

5. Blood pressure: The blood pressure should be no higher than 180 mm Hg systolic and 100 mm Hg diastolic. Prospective donors whose blood pressure is above these values should not be drawn without individual evaluation by a qualified physician. It may be helpful to define upper and lower limits in the SOPs, as lower blood pressures may likewise be a reason for exclusion.

6. Hemoglobin or packed cell volume (hematocrit): Before donation, the hemoglobin or hematocrit must be determined from a sample of blood obtained by fingerstick, earlobe puncture, or venipuncture. Although this screening test is intended to prevent collection of

Table 4-1. Calculations for Drawing Donors Weighing Less Than 50 kg (110 lb)

A. Volume to draw* = (Donor's weight in kg/50) × 450 mL

B. Amount of anticoagulant[†] needed = (A/100) × 14

C. Amount of anticoagulant to remove from collection bag = 63 mL − B

*Approximately 12% of total blood volume.
[†]CPD or CPDA-1 solutions for which desired anticoagulant:blood ratio is 1.4:10.

blood from a donor with anemia, it does not ensure that the donor has an adequate store of iron. Table 4-2 gives the lower limits for accepting allogeneic and autologous donors. Individuals with unusually high hemoglobin or hematocrit levels may need to be evaluated by a physician because elevated levels may reflect pulmonary, hematologic, or other abnormalities. Methods to evaluate oxygen-carrying capacity include specific gravity determined by copper sulfate (see Method 6.1), spectrophotometric measurement of hemoglobin or determination of the hematocrit, or by alternate accepted methods to rule out erroneous results that may lead to rejection of a donor.

7. Skin lesions: The skin at the site of venipuncture must be free of lesions. Both arms must be examined for signs of repeated parenteral entry, especially multiple needle puncture marks and/or sclerotic veins as seen with drug use. Such evidence is reason for indefinite exclusion of a prospective donor. Mild skin disorders or the rash of poison ivy should not be cause for deferral unless unusually extensive and/or present in the antecubital area. Prospective donors who have taken Accutane within the 30 days prior to donation or Soriatane within the

3 years prior to donation, or those who have ever been treated with Tegison, must be deferred.[1(p14)] (Note: These drugs are usually taken for acne or psoriasis. Although Tegison is no longer on the market, because the deferral is indefinite, all donors who have taken Tegison in the past must be deferred.) Individuals with boils, purulent wounds, or severe skin infections anywhere on the body should be deferred, as should anyone with purplish-red or hemorrhagic nodules or indurated plaques suggestive of Kaposi's sarcoma.

The record of the physical examination and the medical history must identify and contain the examiner's initials or signature. Any reasons for deferral must be recorded and explained to the donor. A mechanism must exist to notify the donor of clinically significant abnormal findings in the physical examination, medical history, or postdonation laboratory testing. Abnormalities found before donation may be explained verbally by qualified personnel. Test results obtained after donation that preclude further donation may be reported by telephone or letter. Donors should be asked to report any illness developing within a few days after donation and, especially, to report a positive HIV test or the occurrence of hepatitis or AIDS that develops within 12 months after donation.

Table 4-2. Minimum Levels of Hemoglobin and Hematocrit for Accepting a Blood Donor

Type of Donor	Test Method	Minimal Acceptable Value[1]
Allogeneic	Hemoglobin	12.5 g/dL
	Hematocrit	38%
	Copper sulfate	1.053 sp gr
Autologous	Hemoglobin	11 g/dL
	Hematocrit	33%
	Copper sulfate	1.049 sp gr

Informed Consent

Written informed consent that allows blood bank personnel to collect and use blood from the prospective donor is required.[1(p19)] The consent form is part of the donor record and must be completed before donation. The procedure must be explained in terms that donors can understand, and there must be an opportunity for the prospective donor to ask questions. The signed donor card or consent form should also indicate that the donor has read and understood the information about infectious diseases transmissible by transfusion and has given accurate and truthful answers to the medical history questions. Wording equivalent in meaning to the following is suggested:

"I have read and understand the information provided to me regarding the spread of the AIDS virus (HIV) by blood and plasma. If I am potentially at risk for spreading the virus known to cause AIDS, I agree not to donate blood or plasma for transfusion to another person or for further manufacture. I understand that my blood will be tested for HIV and other disease markers. If this testing indicates that I should no longer donate blood or plasma because of the risk of transmitting the AIDS virus, my name will be entered on a list of permanently deferred donors. I understand that I will be notified of a positive laboratory test result(s). If, instead, the results of the testing are not clearly negative or positive, my blood will not be used and my name may be placed on a deferral list without my being informed until the results are further clarified."

Special Donor Categories

Exceptions to the usual eligibility requirements may be made for special donor categories:

1. Autologous donors: The indications for collection and variations from usual donor procedures are discussed in Chapter 5.

2. Hemapheresis: Special requirements and recommendations for cytapheresis donors or for donors in a plasmapheresis program are detailed in Chapter 6.

3. Recipient-specific "designated" donations: Under certain circumstances, it may be important to use blood or components from a specific donor for a specific patient. Examples include the patient with an antibody to a high-incidence antigen or a combination of antibodies that makes it difficult to find compatible blood; the infant with neonatal thrombocytopenia whose mother can provide platelets; the patient awaiting a kidney transplant from a living donor; or the multitransfused patient whose family members can provide components.

    The repeated use of a single donor to supply components needed for a single patient is allowed, provided it is requested by the patient's physician and approved by the blood bank physician. The donor must meet all the usual requirements for donation, except that the frequency of donation can be as often as every 3 days, as long as the predonation hemoglobin level meets or exceeds the minimum value for routine allogeneic blood donation.

    The blood must be processed according to AABB *Standards*.[1] Special tags identifying the donor unit number and the intended recipient must be affixed to the blood or component bag, and all such units must be segregated from the normal inventory. A protocol for handling such units must be included in the SOP manual.

4. Directed donors: The public's AIDS-related concern about the safety of transfusion has generated demands from potential recipients to choose the donors to be used for their transfusions. Several states have laws establishing this as an ac-

ceptable procedure that must be offered by a donor service in nonemergency situations, if requested by a potential blood recipient or ordered by a physician. Despite logistical and philosophical problems associated with these "directed" donations, most blood centers and hospitals provide this service. The selection and testing of directed donors should be the same as for other allogeneic donors, although special exemptions to the 56-day waiting period between donations may be made. Federal regulations state that a person may serve as a source of Whole Blood more than once in 8 weeks only if at the time of donation the donor is examined and certified by a physician to be in good health.[9] To avoid misunderstandings, it is important to establish SOPs that define the time interval required between collection of the blood and its availability to the recipient; the policy about determining ABO type before collection; and the policy for releasing units for use to other patients.

Collection of Blood

Blood is to be collected only by trained personnel working under the direction of a qualified licensed physician. Blood collection must be by aseptic methods, using a sterile closed system. If more than one skin puncture is needed, a new container and donor set must be used for each additional venipuncture unless the SOP allows the use of an FDA-approved device to attach a new needle while preserving sterility. The phlebotomist must sign or initial the donor record, even if the phlebotomy did not result in the collection of a full unit.

Materials and Instruments

Many items used for phlebotomy are available in sterile, single-use, disposable form. Commercially sterilized items will have an expira-

tion date listed on the package. If the package leaks or gets wet, the contents must not be used. Items such as gauze, cotton balls, applicators, forceps, and forceps holders may be sterilized adequately by steam under pressure for at least 30 minutes at 121.5 C, by dry heat for at least 2 hours at 170 C, or by gas sterilization. Containers of bulk-sterilized items should be labeled and dated as to when they were sterilized and when opened. Unopened sterilized containers may be stored for up to 3 weeks if the container closure ensures sterility of the contents. Open containers may be used for 1 week if the contents are removed using aseptic technique and lids are replaced.

Blood Containers

Blood must be collected into an FDA-approved container that is pyrogen-free and sterile and contains sufficient anticoagulant for the quantity of blood to be collected. The container label must state the type and amount of anticoagulant, and the approximate amount of blood collected.

Blood bags may be supplied in packages containing more than one bag. The manufacturer's directions should be followed for the length of time unused bags may be stored in packages that have been opened.

Identification

Identification is essential in each step from donor registration to final disposition of each component. A numeric or alphanumeric system must be used that identifies, and relates to, the source donor, the donor record, the specimens used for testing, the collection container, and all components prepared from the unit. Extreme caution is necessary to avoid any mix-up or duplication of numbers. All cards and labels should be checked for printing errors prior to use and if duplicate numbers are found, they must be removed and may be investigated as to the reason for the duplication (ie, supplier error, etc). A record must be kept of all voided numbers.

Before beginning the collection, the phlebotomist should:

1. Identify the donor record, at least by name, with the donor and ask the donor to state or spell his/her name.
2. Attach identically numbered labels to the donor record, blood collection container, attached satellite bags, and tubes for donor blood samples. Attaching the numbers at the donor chair, rather than during the examination procedures, helps reduce the likelihood of identification errors.
3. Be sure that the processing tubes are correctly numbered and that they accompany the container during the collection of blood. Tubes may be attached in any convenient manner to the primary bag or integral tubing.
4. Recheck all numbers.

Preparing Venipuncture Site

Blood should be drawn from a large firm vein in an area (usually the antecubital space) that is free of skin lesions. Both arms must be inspected. A tourniquet or a blood pressure cuff inflated to 40-60 mm Hg makes the veins more prominent. Having the donor open and close the hand a few times is also helpful. Once the vein is selected, the pressure device should be released before the skin site is prepared.

There is no way to make the venipuncture site completely aseptic, but surgical cleanliness can be achieved to provide maximal assurance of an uncontaminated unit. Several acceptable procedures exist. (See Method 6.2.) Occasionally, donors may be sensitive to iodine. The SOP manual may provide an alternative method. (See Method 6.2.) After the skin has been prepared, it must not be touched again to repalpate the vein. The entire site preparation must be repeated if the cleansed skin is touched.

Phlebotomy and Collection of Samples

A technique for drawing a donor unit and collecting samples for testing appears in Method

6.3. The unit should be collected from a single venipuncture after the pressure device has again been inflated. During collection the blood should be mixed with the anticoagulant. The amount of blood collected should be monitored carefully so the total, including samples, does not exceed 10.5 mL per kilogram per donation. When the appropriate amount has been collected, segments and specimen tubes must be filled. The needle and any blood-contaminated waste must be disposed of safely in accordance with universal precaution guidelines. The needle must not be recapped unless a safety recapping device is used. Disposal of the uncapped needle must be in a puncture-proof container. After collection, there must be verification that the identifiers on the unit, the donor history, and the tubes are the same. Gloves must be available for use during phlebotomy and must be worn by phlebotomists when collecting autologous blood and when individuals are in training.

Care of the Donor After Phlebotomy

After removing the needle from the vein, the phlebotomist should:

1. Apply firm pressure with sterile gauze over the point of entry of the needle into vein. (The donor may be instructed to continue application of pressure for several minutes.) Check arm and apply bandage only after all bleeding stops.
2. Have donor remain reclining on bed or in donor chair for a few minutes under close observation by staff.
3. Allow the donor to sit up under observation when his/her condition appears satisfactory and follow the donor to the observation/refreshment area. Staff should monitor donors in this area. The period of observation and provision of refreshment should be specified in the SOP manual.
4. Give the donor instructions about post-phlebotomy care. The medical director may wish to include some or all of the fol-

lowing recommendations or instructions:

a. Eat and drink something before leaving the donor site.

b. Do not leave until released by a staff member.

c. Drink more fluids than usual in the next 4 hours.

d. Avoid consuming alcohol until something has been eaten.

e. Do not smoke for 30 minutes.

f. If there is bleeding from the phlebotomy site, raise arm and apply pressure to the site.

g. If fainting or dizziness occurs, either lie down or sit with the head between the knees.

h. If any symptoms persist, either telephone or return to the blood bank or see a doctor.

i. Resume all normal activities if asymptomatic. Donors who work in certain occupations (eg, construction workers, operators of machinery) or persons working at heights should be cautioned that dizziness or faintness may occur if they return to work immediately after giving blood.

j. Remove bandage after a few hours.

k. Maintain high fluid intake for several days to restore blood volume.

5. Thank the donor for an important contribution and encourage repeat donation after the proper interval. All personnel on duty throughout the donor area, volunteer or paid, should be friendly and qualified to observe for signs of a reaction such as lack of concentration, pallor, rapid breathing, or excessive perspiration. Donor room personnel should be competent to interpret instructions, answer questions, and accept responsibility for releasing the donor in good condition.

6. Note on the donor record any adverse reactions that occurred; if the donor leaves the area before being released, note this on the record.

Adverse Donor Reactions

Most donors tolerate giving blood very well, but adverse reactions occur occasionally. Personnel must be trained to recognize adverse reactions and to provide initial treatment.

Donor room personnel are required to have had training in cardiopulmonary resuscitation (CPR). Special equipment to handle emergency situations must be available.

Syncope (fainting or vasovagal syndrome) may be caused by the sight of blood, by watching others give blood, or by individual or group excitement; it may also happen for unexplained reasons. Whether caused by psychologic factors or by neurophysiologic response to blood donation, the symptoms may include weakness, sweating, dizziness, pallor, loss of consciousness, convulsions, and involuntary passage of feces or urine. On occasion, the skin feels cold and blood pressure falls. Sometimes the systolic levels fall as low as 50 mm Hg or cannot be heard with the stethoscope. The pulse rate often slows significantly. This can be useful in distinguishing between vasovagal attack and cardiogenic or hypovolemic shock, in which cases the pulse rate rises. This distinction, although characteristic, is far from absolute.

Deep breathing or hyperventilation may cause the anxious or excited donor to lose excessive amounts of CO_2. This may cause generalized sensations of suffocation or anxiety, or localized problems such as tingling or twitching.

The blood bank physician must provide written instructions for handling donor reactions, including a procedure for obtaining emergency medical help. Sample instructions might be as follows:

1. General.

    a. Remove the tourniquet and withdraw the needle from the arm if signs of reaction occur during the phlebotomy.

b. If possible, remove any donor who experiences an adverse reaction to an area where he/she can be attended in privacy.

c. Apply the measures suggested below and, if they do not lead to rapid recovery, call the blood bank physician or the physician designated for such purposes.

2. Fainting.

a. Apply cold compresses to the donor's forehead or the back of the neck.

b. Administer aromatic spirits of ammonia by inhalation if donor does not respond to initial measures. Test the ammonia on yourself before passing it under the donor's nose, as it may be too strong or too weak. Strong ammonia may injure the nasal membranes; weak ammonia is not effective. The donor should respond by coughing, which elevates the blood pressure.

c. Place the donor on his/her back with legs raised above level of the head.

d. Loosen tight clothing.

e. Be sure the donor has an adequate airway.

f. Monitor blood pressure, pulse, and respiration periodically until the donor recovers.

Note: Some donors who experience prolonged hypotension may respond to an infusion of normal saline. The decision to initiate such therapy should be made by the blood bank physician either on a case-by-case basis or in a policy stated in the facility's SOP manual.

3. Nausea and vomiting.

a. Make the donor as comfortable as possible.

b. Instruct the donor who is nauseated to breathe slowly and deeply.

c. Apply cold compresses to the donor's forehead and/or back of neck.

d. Turn donor's head to the side.

e. Provide a suitable receptacle if the donor vomits and have cleansing tissues or a damp towel ready. Be sure the donor's head is turned to the side because of the danger of aspiration.

f. After vomiting has ended, give the donor some water to rinse out his/her mouth.

4. Twitching or muscular spasms. Extremely nervous donors may hyperventilate, causing faint muscular twitching or tetanic spasm of their hands or face. Donor room personnel should watch closely for these symptoms during and immediately after the phlebotomy.

a. Divert the donor's attention by engaging in conversation, to interrupt the hyperventilation pattern.

b. Have the donor rebreathe into a paper bag if he/she is symptomatic. **Do not give oxygen.**

5. Hematoma during or after phlebotomy.

a. Remove the tourniquet and the needle from the donor's arm.

b. Place three or four sterile gauze squares over the venipuncture site and apply firm digital pressure for 7-10 minutes with the donor's arm held above the heart level. An alternative is to apply a tight bandage, which should be removed after 7-10 minutes to allow inspection.

c. Apply ice to the area for 5 minutes, if desired.

d. Should an arterial puncture be suspected, immediately withdraw needle and apply firm pressure for 10 minutes. Apply pressure dressing afterwards. Check for the presence of a radial pulse. If pulse is not palpable or is weak, call a blood bank physician.

6. Convulsions.
   a. Call for help immediately. Prevent the donor from injuring him/herself. During severe seizures, some people exhibit great muscular power and are difficult to restrain. If possible, hold the donor on the chair or bed; if not possible, place the donor on the floor. Try to prevent injury to the donor and to yourself.
   b. Be sure the donor has an adequate airway. Jaws should be separated by a padded device *after* convulsion has passed.
   c. Notify the blood bank physician.
7. Serious cardiac difficulties.
   a. Call for medical aid and/or an emergency care unit immediately.
   b. If the donor is in cardiac arrest, begin CPR immediately and continue it until help arrives.
8. The nature and treatment of all reactions should be recorded on the donor record or a special incident report form. This should include a notation of whether the donor should be accepted for future donations.

The medical director should decide what emergency supplies and drugs should be in the donor area. The distance to the nearest emergency room or emergency care unit heavily influences decisions about necessary supplies and drugs. Most blood banks maintain some or all of the following:

1. Emesis basin or equivalent.
2. Towels.
3. Oropharyngeal airway, plastic or hard rubber.
4. Oxygen and mask.
5. Emergency drugs: Drugs are seldom required to treat a donor's reaction. If the blood bank physician wishes to have any drugs available, the kind and amount to be kept on hand must be specified in writing. In addition, the medical director must provide written policies stating when and by whom any of the above medical supplies or drugs may be used.

References

1. Menitove J, ed. Standards for blood banks and transfusion services. 19th ed. Bethesda, MD: American Association of Blood Banks, 1999.
2. Pindyck J, Avorn J, Kuriyan M, et al. Blood donation by the elderly. Clinical and policy considerations. JAMA 1987;257:1186-8.
3. Code of federal regulations, 21 CFR 606.160 (e). Washington, DC: US Government Printing Office, 1998 (revised annually).
4. Beattie KM, Shafer AW. Broadening the base of a rare donor program by targeting minority populations. Transfusion 1986;26:401-4.
5. Vichinsky EP, Earles A, Johnson RA, et al. Alloimmunization in sickle cell anemia and transfusion of racially unmatched blood. N Engl J Med 1990;322:1617-21.
6. Food and Drug Administration. Memorandum: Revised recommendations for the prevention of human immunodeficiency virus (HIV) transmission by blood and blood products. April 23, 1992. Rockville, MD: CBER Office of Communication, Training, and Manufacturers Assistance, 1992.
7. Centers for Disease Control. Update: Universal precautions for prevention of transmission of human immunodeficiency virus, hepatitis B virus, and other bloodborne pathogens in health-care settings. JAMA 1988;260:528-31.
8. Code of federal regulations, 21 CFR 640.3 (a). Washington, DC: US Government Printing Office, 1998 (revised annually).
9. Code of federal regulations, 21 CFR 640.3(f). Washington, DC: US Government Printing Office, 1998 (revised annually).

Suggested Reading

Food and Drug Administration. Memorandum: Exemptions to permit persons with a history of viral hepatitis before the age of eleven years to serve as donors of Whole Blood and Plasma: Alternate procedures. April 23, 1992. Rockville, MD: CBER Office of Communication, Training, and Manufacturers Assistance, 1992.

Food and Drug Administration. Memorandum: Revised recommendations for the prevention of human immunodeficiency virus (HIV) transmission by blood and blood products-section I, parts A & B only. December 5, 1990. Rockville, MD: CBER Office of Communication, Training, and Manufacturers Assistance, 1990.

Holland PV. Why a new standard to prevent Creutzfeldt-Jakob disease? Transfusion 1988;28:293-4.

Infectious disease testing for blood transfusions. NIH Consensus Statement 13:1, January 1995. Bethesda, MD: National Institutes of Health, 1995.

Kasprisin C, Laird-Fryer B, eds. Blood donor collection practices. Bethesda, MD: American Association of Blood Banks, 1993.

Linder J, ed. Practical solutions to practical problems in transfusion medicine and tissue banking. [Supplement 1 to Am J Clin Pathol 1997;107(4).] Chicago, IL: American Society of Clinical Pathologists, 1997.

Smith KJ, Simon TL. Recruitment and evaluation of blood and plasma donors. In: Rossi EC, Simon TL, Moss GS, eds. Principles of transfusion medicine. 2nd ed. Baltimore, MD: Williams & Wilkins, 1995:871-79.

Schmuñis GA. *Trypanosoma cruzi*, the etiologic agent of Chagas' disease: Status in the blood supply in endemic and nonendemic countries. Transfusion 1991;31: 547-57.

Appendix 4-1. Uniform Donor History Questionnaire (May 1998)

Donor History Questions	American Association of Blood Banks (AABB)	Food and Drug Administration (FDA)	Comments
1. Have you ever donated or attempted to donate blood using a different (or another) name here or anywhere else?	No specific requirement.	A record shall be available from which unsuitable donors may be identified so that products from such individuals will not be distributed. [21 CFR 606.160(e) April 1997]	Identifying information should be obtained from the donor.
2. In the past 8 weeks, have you given blood, plasma, or platelets here or anywhere else?	Frequency of blood donation is every 8 weeks. (Standard B2.000)	Frequency of blood donation is every 8 weeks unless otherwise approved by the medical director. (21 CFR 640.3(f) April 1997)	Infrequent plasma donors can donate every 4 weeks. (FDA Memos 3/10/95[1] and 12/14/95[2])
3. Have you for any reason been deferred or refused as a blood donor or told not to donate blood?	No specific requirement.	No specific requirement.	
4. Are you feeling well and healthy today?	The prospective donor shall appear to be in good health. (Standard B2.000)	Donor must be determined to be in general good health. [21 CFR 640.3(b) April 1997]	Requires "yes" answer that tests donor's attention to question content. Initiates sequence of personal health history questions (4-13).
5. In the past 12 months have you been under a doctor's care or had a major illness or surgery?	No specific requirement.	Persons who have received a transfusion of whole blood or a blood component within the past 12 months should not donate blood or blood components. (FDA Memo 4/23/92[1])	
6. Have you ever had chest pain, heart disease, recent or severe respiratory disease?	Prospective donors with diseases of the heart or lungs shall be excluded unless determined to be suitable to donate by a blood bank physician. (Standard B1.700)	Donor must be free of acute respiratory disease. [21 CFR 640.3(b)(4) April 1997]	
7. Have you ever had cancer, a blood disease, or a bleeding problem?	Prospective donors with a history of cancer or abnormal bleeding tendency shall be excluded unless determined to be suitable to donate by a blood bank physician. (Standard B1.700)	Persons with hemophilia or related clotting disorders who have received clotting factor concentrates must not donate blood or blood components. (FDA Memo 4/23/92[3])	
8. Have you ever had yellow jaundice, liver disease, viral hepatitis, or a positive test for hepatitis?	Prospective donors with diseases of the liver shall be excluded unless determined to be suitable to donate by a blood bank physician. (Standard B1.700) Donors with a history of hepatitis after their 11th birthday or a confirmed positive test for HBsAg or a repeatedly reactive test for HBc are indefinitely deferred. (Standard B2.711)	No individual with a history of hepatitis shall be a source of whole blood donation. [21 CFR 640.3(c) April 1997] Exemptions for history of hepatitis before age 11. (FDA Memos 4/23/92[4] and 12/22/93[5])	
9. Have you ever had malaria, Chagas' disease, or babesiosis?	Prospective donors who have had a diagnosis of malaria shall be deferred for 3 years after becoming asymptomatic. (Standard B2.741) A history of babesiosis or Chagas' disease shall be cause for indefinite deferral. (Standard B2.750)	Prospective donors who have had malaria should be deferred for 3 years after becoming asymptomatic. (FDA Memo 7/26/94[6])	

(cont'd)

Appendix 4-1. Uniform Donor History Questionnaire (May 1998) (cont'd)

Donor History Questions	American Association of Blood Banks (AABB)	Food and Drug Administration (FDA)	Comments
10. A. Have you ever taken etretinate (Tegison) for psoriasis?	A. People who have received etretinate (eg, Tegison) shall be indefinitely deferred (B2.530)	A. A donor who has taken or is taking Tegison should be permanently deferred. (FDA Memo 7/28/93[7])	A. Potentially teratogenic. May be present up to 3 years after last use.
B. In the past 3 years, have you taken acitretin (Soriatane)?	B. Donor is to be deferred from date of last use (Proposed for 19th ed. Standards, to be published 1999, B2.520)	B. Donor is to be deferred for 3 years from date of last dose (per manufacturer's insert)	B. Potentially teratogenic. May be present up to 3 years after last use.
C. In the past 3 days have you taken piroxicam (Feldene), aspirin, or anything that has aspirin in it?	C. Ingestion within 3 days of donation of medications known to irreversibly damage platelet function (eg, aspirin-containing medications) or that inhibit platelet function and have a prolonged half-life should preclude the use of a donor as the sole source of platelets for a recipient. (Standard B2.510).	C. No specific requirement for whole blood donation. Donors who have recently taken medication containing aspirin, especially within 36 hours, may not be suitable donors for platelet pheresis. (FDA Guidelines 10/7/88[8])	C. Preferred time varies. May be mandated by state health and safety code.
D. In the past month have you taken isotretinoin (Accutane) or finasteride (Proscar) (Propecia)?	D. For Accutane or Proscar, donor is to be deferred for 1 month after receipt of last dose. (18th ed. Standards B2.520) For Propecia, donor is to be deferred for 1 month after receipt of last dose. (Proposed for 19th ed. Standards, to be published 1999, B2.520)	D. A donor taking Accutane or Proscar should be deferred from donating blood for at least 1 month after receipt of the last dose. (FDA Memo 7/28/93[7]) 1 month deferral. (FDA telephone communication to AABB, January 1998.)	D. Medication questions grouped.
E. In the past 4 weeks have you taken any pills or medications?	E. Drug therapy shall be evaluated by a qualified person to determine suitability to donate blood. (Standards, B1.900)	E. Facility medical director to determine donor acceptability or deferral based on medications. (FDA memo 07-28-93)	E. Medication questions grouped.
11. In the past 4 weeks, have you had any shots or vaccinations?	Donors must be queried about vaccines and immunizations. (Standards B2.610, B2.620, B2.630)	No specific requirement.	
12. In the past 12 months, have you been given rabies shots?	Donor is deferred for 12 months after vaccine treatment for rabies. (Standard B2.640)	No specific requirement.	
13. Female donors: In the past 6 weeks, have you been pregnant or are you pregnant now?	Existing pregnancy or pregnancy in past 6 weeks is cause for deferral. (Standard B1.800)	No specific requirement.	
14. In the past 3 years, have you been outside the United States or Canada?	Residents of countries in which malaria is not considered endemic but who have been in an area in which malaria is considered endemic may be accepted as regular blood donors 1 year after return irrespective of the receipt of antimalarial prophylaxis. (Standard B2.743) Immigrants, refugees, or citizens coming from a country in which malaria is considered endemic may be accepted as blood donors 3 years after departure. (Standard B2.742)	Travelers to an area considered endemic for malaria should not be accepted as donors of whole blood and blood components prior to 1 year after departure. After 1 year, donors free of unexplained symptoms suggestive of malaria may be accepted whether or not they have received antimalarial chemoprophylaxis. Immigrants, refugees, and citizens of endemic countries should not be accepted as donors prior to 3 years after departure. After 3 years, donors free of unexplained symptoms suggestive of malaria may be accepted. (FDA Memo 7/26/94[6])	Initiates sequence of exposure-type questions (14-30)

Appendix 4-1. Uniform Donor History Questionnaire (May 1998) (cont'd)

Donor History Questions	American Association of Blood Banks (AABB)	Food and Drug Administration (FDA)	Comments
15. A. Have you ever received human pituitary-derived growth hormone?	Prospective donors who have a family history of Creutzfeldt-Jakob disease or who have received tissue or tissue derivatives known to be a possible source of the Creutzfeldt-Jakob agent (eg, dura mater, pituitary growth hormone of human origin) shall be deferred indefinitely. (Standard B2.410)	A. The FDA recommends that any donor who has received injections of pit-hGH be permanently deferred. (FDA Memo 7/28/93[7])	
B. Have you received a dura mater (or brain covering) graft?		B. The FDA recommends that persons who have received transplants of dura mater be permanently deferred from donation. (FDA Memo 12/11/96[9])	
C. Have you or any of your blood relatives ever had Creutzfeldt-Jakob disease or have you ever been told that your family is at an increased risk for Creutzfeldt-Jakob disease?		C. The FDA recommends that persons with a family history of Creutzfeldt-Jakob disease (CJD) be permanently deferred from donation unless increased risk is excluded based on specialized testing. (FDA Memo 12/11/96[9])	
16. In the past 12 months, have you had close contact with a person who has yellow jaundice or viral hepatitis, or have you been given Hepatitis B Immune Globulin (HBIG)?	Close contact with a person who has viral hepatitis is a 12-month deferral. (Standard B2.724)	Close contact with person who has viral hepatitis is a 12-month deferral. (FDA Memo 4/23/92[10])	Close contact generally refers to cohabitation or sexual contact. The medical director should establish a policy for these potential donors.
17. In the past 12 months, have you taken (snorted) cocaine through your nose?			
18. In the past 12 months, have you received blood or had an organ or a tissue transplant or graft?	Prospective donors who, during the preceding 12 months, received blood, blood components or derivatives, or other human tissues known to be possible sources of blood-borne pathogens, shall be excluded. (Standard B2.420)	Persons who have received a transfusion of whole blood or a blood component within the past 12 months should not donate blood or blood components. (FDA Memo 4/23/92[3])	Includes immunization with RBCs.
19. In the past 12 months, have you had a tattoo applied, ear or skin piercing, acupuncture, accidental needlestick, or come in contact with someone else's blood?	Prospective donors shall be deferred from donating blood or blood components for transfusion who, within the preceding 12 months, have a history of: 1) A tattoo. 2) Mucous membrane exposure to blood. 3) Nonsterile skin penetration with instruments or equipment contaminated with blood or body fluids. 4) Sexual or household contact with an individual with viral hepatitis. 5) Sexual contact with an individual with HIV or at high risk of HIV infection. (Standards B2.721, B2.722, B2.723, B2.724, B2.275)	Persons who have had any contact with blood and body fluids through percutaneous inoculation (such as injury or accidental needlestick) or through contact with an open wound, nonintact skin, or mucous membrane during the preceding 12 months should be deferred. (FDA Memo 4/23/92[3])	Donors should be questioned about ear piercing, skin piercing, electrolysis, and acupuncture to make sure that single-use equipment, disposals, or properly sterilized needles were used. Health care workers should be carefully evaluated to determine if they have had a needlestick injury or other type of percutaneous or mucasal exposure to patient's blood or an unknown source. Exposure to another person's blood through broken skin or intact mucosal surface is cause for 12-month deferral from the time the exposure occurred.
20. A. In the past 12 months, have you had a positive test for syphilis?	A history of syphilis or gonorrhea, treatment for either, or a confirmed reactive screening test for syphilis shall be cause for deferral for 12 months after completion of therapy. (Standard B2.340)	Persons who have had, or have been treated for, syphilis or gonorrhea during the preceding 12 months should not donate blood or blood components. Persons with a positive (STS) test should be deferred for 12 months. (FDA Memo 12/12/91[11])	
B. In the past 12 months, have you had or been treated for syphilis or gonorrhea?			

(cont'd)

Appendix 4-1. Uniform Donor History Questionnaire (May 1998) (cont'd)

Donor History Questions	American Association of Blood Banks (AABB)	Food and Drug Administration (FDA)	Comments
21. In the past 12 months, have you given money or drugs to anyone to have sex with you?	Donor must be given educational material on AIDS high-risk activity, and such at-risk persons should refrain from donating blood. (Standards B3.100, B2.730)	Men and women who have engaged in sex for money or drugs since 1977 and persons who have engaged in sex with such people during the preceding 12 months should not donate blood or blood components. (FDA Memo 4/23/92[3])	
22. A. At any time since 1977, have you taken money or drugs for sex? B. In the past 12 months, have you had sex, even once, with anyone who has taken money or drugs for sex?	Refer to question #21.	Men and women who have engaged in sex for money or drugs since 1977 and persons who have engaged in sex with such people during the preceding 12 months should not donate blood or blood components. (FDA Memo 4/23/92[3])	
23. A. Have you ever used a needle, even once, to take drugs that were not prescribed for you by a doctor?	A. Stigma of narcotic habituation is permanent deferral. (Standard B2.330)	A. Donor must be free from skin punctures or scars indicative of addiction to self-injected narcotics. [21 CFR 640.3(b)(7) April 1997] Past or present intravenous drug users should not donate blood or blood components. (FDA Memo 4/23/92[3])	
B. In the past 12 months, have you had sex, even once, with anyone who has used a needle to take drugs not prescribed by a doctor?	B. Refer to question #21.	B. Persons who have had sex with any person who is a past or present intravenous drug user should not donate blood or blood components for 12 months. (FDA Memo 4/23/92[3])	
24. Male donors: Have you had sex with another male, even once, since 1977?	Refer to question #21.	Men who have had sex with another man even one time since 1977 should not donate blood or blood components permanently. (FDA Memo 4/23/92[3])	
25. Female donors: In the past 12 months, have you had sex with a male who has had sex, even once, since 1977 with another male?	Refer to question #21.	Persons who have had sex with men who have had sex with another man even one time since 1977 should not donate blood or blood components for 12 months. (FDA Memo 4/23/92[3])	
26. A. Have you ever taken clotting factor concentrates for a bleeding problem such as hemophilia?	No specific requirement.	A. Persons with hemophilia or related clotting disorders who have received clotting factor concentrates should not donate blood or blood components. (FDA Memo 4/23/92[3])	
B. In the past 12 months, have you had sex, even once, with anyone who has taken clotting factor concentrates for a bleeding problem such as hemophilia?		B. Persons who have had sex with any person with hemophilia or related clotting disorders who have received clotting factor concentrates should not donate blood or blood components for 12 months. (FDA Memo 4/23/92[3])	

Appendix 4-1. Uniform Donor History Questionnaire (May 1998) (cont'd)

Donor History Questions	American Association of Blood Banks (AABB)	Food and Drug Administration (FDA)	Comments
27. A. Do you have AIDS or have you had a positive test for the AIDS virus?	Refer to question #21.	A. Persons with clinical or laboratory evidence of HIV infection must not donate blood or blood components. (FDA Memo 4/23/92[3])	
B. In the past 12 months, have you had sex, even once, with anyone who has AIDS or has had a positive test for the AIDS virus?		B. Persons who have had sex with persons with clinical or laboratory evidence of HIV infection should not donate blood or blood components for 12 months. (FDA Memo 4/23/92[3])	
28. Are you giving blood because you want to be tested for HIV or the AIDS virus?	No specific requirement.	No specific requirement.	Direct question to further evaluate donation motive.
29. Do you understand that if you have the AIDS virus, you can give it to someone else even though you may feel well and have a negative AIDS test?	No specific requirement.	Donors should be informed that there is an interval during early infection when the HIV antibody test may be negative although the infection may still be transmitted. (FDA Memo 4/23/92[3])	Queries donor's understanding of "Important Information for Donors." Alternative testing site information should be offered.
30. A. Were you born in, have you lived in, or have you traveled to any African country since 1977?	(Association Bulletin #97-5[11])	(FDA Memo 12/11/96[12])	A. If "no," proceed to the questions about sexual contact. If "yes," the donor should be asked to name the specific country(ies). If the donor identifies an African country *not* listed in the FDA Memo, proceed to question C. If one or more of the countries listed in the FDA Memo is named by the donor, determine if the donor was born in, lived in, or traveled to the country(ies) named by the donor. If the donor was born in or lived in any of the FDA-identified countries, defer him/her indefinitely; questioning stops here. If travel was the donor's risk, ask questions. The Central African Republic was named the Central African Empire in the late 1970s. None of the other countries listed in the FDA Memo has undergone a change in name since 1977. Blood establishments should critically evaluate the potential donor's history and statements, and decide whether the individual could have been in the country long enough to have encountered those local conditions related to risk, such as use of unsterile needles or sexual contact. When donors report demographic HIV-1 Group O risk, no followup actions regarding previously donated blood are necessary.

(cont'd)

Appendix 4-1. Uniform Donor History Questionnaire (May 1998) (cont'd)

Donor History Questions	American Association of Blood Banks (AABB)	Food and Drug Administration (FDA)	Comments
B. When you traveled to <country(ies)> did you receive a blood transfusion or any other medical treatment with a product made from blood?			B. If "no," proceed to question C. If "yes," defer indefinitely.
C. Have you had sexual contact with anyone who was born in or lived in any African country since 1977?			C. If "no," or the donor names a country not identified in the FDA Memo, no deferral. If "yes," ask the donor to specify which country(ies). If donor names a country listed in the FDA Memo, defer him/her indefinitely.
31. In the past 12 months, have you been in jail or prison?	Donors are deferred for 12 months if, in the preceding 12 months, they have been incarcerated in a correctional institution (jail or prison) for more than 72 consecutive hours. (Standard B2.726)	Individuals who have been incarcerated for more than 72 consecutive hours during the previous 12 months should be deferred as donors for 12 months from the last date of incarceration. (FDA Memo 6/8/95[14])	
32. Have you read and understood all the donor information presented to you, and have all your questions been answered?	No specific requirement.	Information should be written in language that ensures that the donor understands the definition of high-risk behavior and the importance of self-exclusion. Donors should not be considered suitable unless information about risks can be communicated in the language appropriate to them and is constructed to be culturally sensitive to promote comprehension. (FDA Memo 4/23/92[4])	

Standards referred to are from the 18th edition of *Standards for Blood Banks and Transfusion Services*, effective January 1, 1998, and for this publication, were reviewed against the 19th edition.

1. FDA Memorandum, March 10, 1995: Revision of FDA Memorandum of August 27, 1982: Requirements for Infrequent Plasma Donors.

2. FDA Memorandum, December 14, 1995: Donor Deferral Due to Red Blood Cell Loss During Collection of Source Plasma.

3. FDA Memorandum, April 23, 1992: Revised Recommendations for the Prevention of HIV Transmission by Blood and Blood Products.

4. FDA Memorandum, April 23, 1992: Exemptions to Permit Persons with a History of Viral Hepatitis Before the Age of Eleven Years to Serve as Donors of Whole Blood and Plasma: Alternative Procedures, 21 CFR 640.120.

5. FDA Memorandum, December 22, 1993: Donor Suitability Related to Laboratory Testing for Viral Hepatitis and a History of Viral Hepatitis.

6. FDA Memorandum, July 26, 1994: Recommendations for Deferral of Donors for Malaria Risk.

7. FDA Memorandum, July 28, 1993: Deferral of Blood and Plasma Donors Based on Medications.

8. FDA Memorandum, October 7, 1988: Revised Guideline for the Collection of Platelets, Pheresis.

9. FDA Memorandum, December 11, 1996: Revised Precautionary Measures to Reduce the Possible Risk of Transfusion of Creutzfeldt-Jakob Disease (CJD) by Blood and Blood Products.

10. FDA Memorandum, April 23, 1992: Revised Recommendations for Testing Whole Blood, Blood Components, Source Plasma and Source Leukocytes for Antibody to Hepatitis C Virus Encoded Antigen (Anti-HCV).

11. FDA Memorandum, December 12, 1991: Clarification of FDA Recommendations for Donor Deferral and Product Distribution Based on the Results of Syphilis Testing.

Appendix 4-1. Uniform Donor History Questionnaire (May 1998) (cont'd)

12. FDA Memorandum, December 11, 1996: Interim Recommendations for Deferral of Donors at Increased Risk for HIV-1 Group O Infection.

13. FDA Accepts AABB Changes to HIV-1 Group O Donor Questions. Association Bulletin #97-5, August 1, 1997.

14. FDA Memorandum, June 8, 1995: Recommendations for the Deferral of Current and Recent Inmates of Correctional institutions as Donors of Whole Blood, Blood Components, Source Leukocytes, and Source Plasma.

15. Donor question of Soriatane. Association Bulletin 99-5. Bethesda, MD: American Association of Blood Banks, 1999.

Note: After the above Uniform Donor History Questionnaire was approved by the FDA in May 1998, information on a new drug came to the attention of the FDA and the AABB. Donors who are taking, or who in the last 3 years have taken, acitretin (Soriatane, Roche Pharmaceuticals, Nutley, NJ) for psoriasis therapy must be deferred. (AABB Association Bulletin 99-5.)

Appendix 4-2. Some Drugs Commonly Accepted in Blood Donors

In many blood centers, blood donation may be allowed by individuals who have taken the following drugs:

- Tetracyclines and other antibiotics taken to treat acne.

- Topical steroid preparations for skin lesions not at the venipuncture site.

- Blood pressure medications, taken chronically and successfully so that pressure is at or below allowable limits. The prospective donor taking antihypertensive drugs should be free from side effects, especially episodes of postural hypotension, and should be free of any cardiovascular symptoms.

- Over-the-counter bronchodilators and decongestants.

- Oral hypoglycemic agents in well-controlled diabetics without any vascular complications of the disease.

- Tranquilizers, under most conditions. A physician should evaluate the donor to distinguish between tranquilizers and antipsychotic medications.

- Hypnotics used at bedtime.

- Marijuana (unless currently under the influence), oral contraceptives, mild analgesics, vitamins, replacement hormones, or weight reduction pills.

Note: Acceptance of donors must always be with the approval of the blood bank's medical director.

5

Autologous Blood Donation and Transfusion

AUTOLOGOUS TRANSFUSION IS AN alternative therapy for many patients anticipating transfusion. Its use has increased considerably with the awareness of infectious diseases transmitted through allogeneic transfusions. The four categories of autologous transfusion are:

1. Preoperative collection (blood is drawn and stored prior to anticipated need).
2. Acute normovolemic hemodilution (blood is collected at the start of surgery and then infused during or at the end of the procedure).
3. Intraoperative collection (shed blood is recovered from the surgical field or circulatory devices and then infused).
4. Postoperative collection (blood is collected from drainage devices and reinfused to the patient).

Each type of autologous transfusion practice offers benefits and risks depending on the type of surgery, condition of the patient, and technology available. Each facility must analyze its own transfusion practices, transfusion practices of other similarly situated institutions, and its own capabilities to determine the appropriate services to be offered.

Whether a facility elects to offer autologous services is an internal decision. Institutions should consider, however, that where feasible for a patient, it is generally accepted that the patient should have the option to use his or her own blood. Also, a US Supreme Court decision probably makes it illegal to offer autologous blood services without offering those services to individuals protected under the Americans with Disabilities Act (ADA)[1], including individuals who have tested positive for the human immunodeficiency virus (HIV). The US Supreme Court has ruled that asymptomatic infection with HIV is a disability protected under the ADA.[1] The case involved a dentist's refusal to fill the cavity of an HIV-positive patient un-

111

less the procedure was performed in a sterile hospital operating room setting. The Court found that the HIV-positive patient was protected under the ADA. As a protected individual, the patient had the right to services offered by the dentist, including in-office cavity filling. If institutions offer autologous services to any patients, they likely will have to offer such services to HIV-positive patients. Long-standing practices that permitted institutions to choose whether to offer autologous services to HIV-positive individuals will have to change.[2]

Patients who are likely to require transfusion therapy and who also meet the donation criteria should be told about the options for autologous transfusion therapies, including the risks and benefits of each, as alternatives to transfusion with allogeneic units. Patients considering autologous transfusion therapy should be informed about the risks and benefits of both the autologous donation process and the autologous transfusion process. Specific issues unique to the use of autologous transfusion in the anticipated surgical procedure should be identified. In addition, patients need information about any special fees for autologous services, the level of infectious disease testing that will be performed, and the possibility that additional, allogeneic, units may be used.

Preoperative Autologous Blood Collection

Frequently cited advantages and disadvantages of preoperative autologous blood donation (PAD) are summarized in Table 5-1. In selected patient subgroups, preoperative collection of autologous blood can significantly reduce exposure to allogeneic blood. Candidates for preoperative collection are stable patients scheduled for surgical procedures in which blood transfusion is likely. For procedures that are unlikely to require transfusion (ie, a maximal surgical blood ordering schedule does not suggest that crossmatched blood be available),[3] the use of preoperative blood collection is not recommended.

Preoperative autologous collections are most beneficial for patients undergoing major orthopedic procedures, vascular surgery, cardiac or thoracic surgery, and radical prostatectomy.[4] Autologous blood should not be collected for procedures that seldom require transfusion, such as cholecystectomy, herniorrhaphy, vaginal hysterectomy, and uncomplicated obstetric delivery.[5]

Special Patient Categories

In special circumstances, preoperative autologous blood collection can be performed

Table 5-1. Autologous Blood Donation

Advantages	Disadvantages
1. Prevents transfusion-transmitted disease	1. Does not affect risk of bacterial contamination
2. Prevents red cell alloimmunization	2. Does not affect risk of ABO incompatibility error
3. Supplements the blood supply	3. Is more costly than allogeneic blood
4. Provides compatible blood for patients with alloantibodies	4. Results in wastage of blood not transfused
5. Prevents some adverse transfusion reactions	5. Increases prevalence of adverse reactions to autologous donation
6. Provides reassurance to patients concerned about blood risks	6. Subjects patient to perioperative anemia and increased likelihood of transfusion

for patients who would not, under any circumstances, be considered for allogeneic donation. Availability of medical support is important in assessing patient suitability. With suitable volume modification, parental cooperation, and attention to preparation and reassurance, pediatric patients can participate in preoperative collection programs.[6] Consultation with programs experienced in pediatric autologous collection may be very helpful. The successful use of autologous blood in a patient with sickle cell disease has been reported,[7] and it may be particularly useful for a patient with multiple alloantibodies; however, the patient may derive greater benefit from allogeneic transfusions that provide hemoglobin A. Red cells containing hemoglobin S require special handling during the cryopreservation process.[8]

Some patients with significant cardiac disease are considered poor risks for autologous blood donation; despite reports of safety in small numbers of patients who underwent autologous blood donation,[9] the risks associated with autologous blood donation[10] in these patients are probably greater than current estimated risks of allogeneic transfusion.[11] Table 5-2 summarizes the contraindications to a patient's participation in an autologous blood donation program.[12]

The collection of autologous blood from pregnant women remains controversial.[13,14] In routine pregnancy and delivery or uncomplicated cesarean section, blood is needed so seldom that autologous collection is considered inappropriate. Many centers give serious consideration to autologous collection for women with alloantibodies to multiple or high-incidence antigens or with placenta previa or other conditions placing them at high risk for ante- or intrapartum hemorrhage.[5] The woman's physician and the blood bank physician should give their approval. A policy should be developed for situations in which autologous blood from the mother is considered for use in the infant.

Voluntary Standards

AABB *Standards for Blood Banks and Transfusion Services* offers uniform standards to be followed in determining patient eligibility; collecting, testing, and labeling the unit; and pretransfusion testing.[15] AABB *Standards* no longer permits allogeneic transfusion of unused autologous units ("crossover") because autologous donors are not, in the strictest sense, volunteer donors and because autologous donors may not meet the strict requirements for allogeneic donors.

Table 5-2. Contraindications to Participation in Autologous Blood Donation Programs

1. Evidence of infection and risk of bacteremia.
2. Scheduled surgery to correct aortic stenosis.
3. Unstable angina.
4. Active seizure disorder.
5. Myocardial infarction or cerebrovascular accident within 6 months of donation.
6. Patients with significant cardiac or pulmonary disease who have not yet been cleared for surgery by their treating physician.
7. High-grade left main coronary artery disease.
8. Cyanotic heart disease.
9. Uncontrolled hypertension.

Regulatory Considerations

Food and Drug Administration (FDA) requirements are somewhat confusing because they evolved over time and vary depending on the test results. The FDA first issued guidance for autologous blood and blood components in March of 1989.[16] This guidance was clarified in a second memorandum issued in February of 1990.[17] Additional requirements may be found in memoranda discussing particular tests.[18-24] Care must be taken to identify the most recent requirements. For example, testing for antibodies to hepatitis B core antigen (anti-HBc) was not required in the 1990 memorandum but is required by a 1991 memorandum on anti-HBc testing.[19] The FDA has indicated that it is working on a guidance document that will consolidate all of the recommendations, but no time frame has been announced for completion.

Testing

The FDA requires testing of autologous donations for syphilis, HIV-1 antigen, anti-HIV-1, anti-HIV-2, antibodies to hepatitis C virus (anti-HCV), hepatitis B surface antigen (HBsAg), and anti-HBc. Testing for human T-cell lymphotropic virus (HTLV-I/II) is not required.

All required tests must be performed if the blood bank is a licensed facility. It is acceptable to perform the required laboratory tests on just the first unit of blood collected from a donor in a 30-day period, provided that no part of the blood is used for any purpose other than autologous transfusion.

If the establishment collects and uses autologous blood only for the autologous donor, the unit is used at the site of the collection, and all products not used by the donor are destroyed, the facility may substitute rigid control procedures and cautionary labeling in place of testing. Both the AABB *Standards*[15(p77)] and the FDA requirements state that the patient's physician must be notified of any abnormal test results.

Labeling

Each autologous unit must be labeled "Autologous Donor" and "Volunteer Donor." In addition, a special label, "For Autologous Use Only," is required. Another special label, "Biohazard," is required for any unit that is confirmed to be positive, or is repeatedly reactive and confirmatory testing is not completed for anti-HIV-1, anti-HIV-2, anti-HCV, HBsAg, anti-HBc, HIV-1 antigen, and syphilis.

Shipping

Conditions permitting use of autologous units with repeatedly reactive or confirmed positive test results vary according to the test. The FDA requires that for syphilis, anti-HBc, and anti-HCV, units may be released but the test results must be made available to the patient's physician. However, for anti-HIV-1 and HBsAg, a written request for use of the unit must be received from the patient's physician before units may be released for use. AABB *Standards*[15(p77)] requires the shipping facility to notify the transfusing facility of any units being shipped that have tested positive for any markers of transfusion-transmitted disease. It is generally accepted that the patient should have the option to use his or her own blood. Thus, the donor center must notify the physician and the transfusing facility of abnormal test results, but they must provide the autologous blood if the patient so desires. If distributed on a common carrier, not under the direct control of the collection facility the product is to meet provisions for shipping an etiologic agent.[25]

Establishing a Preoperative Autologous Blood Collection Program

Each blood center or hospital that decides to conduct an autologous blood collection program must establish its own policies, processes, and procedures. Guidelines exist for establishing a new program or improving an existing one.[12,26-28] Listed below are issues that should be addressed when a program is established.

1. Importance of a comprehensive program of blood conservation.
2. Selection of appropriate patients.
3. Determining the number of units to be collected.
4. Contraindications to use of autologous services.
5. Recommended intervals for preoperative collections.
6. Use of oral iron supplements.
7. Disposition of unused units (impermissibility of crossover).
8. Utilization review criteria for transfusion of autologous units.
9. Management of donor reactions during blood collection.
10. Sources for additional information.

Physician Responsibility

A successful autologous program requires cooperation and communication among all the physicians involved. Responsibility for the health and safety of the patient during the collection process rests with the medical director of the collecting facility; during the transfusion responsibility rests with the patient's physician and the medical director of the transfusion service. The patient's physician initiates the request for autologous services, which must be approved by the transfusion service physician. There should be a transfusion medicine physician available to help assess patients whose medical history suggests a risk for complications if a donor reaction occurs during blood collection.

Supplemental Iron

The patient should be advised about taking supplemental iron. Ideally, supplemental iron is prescribed by the requesting physician before the first blood collection, in time to allow maximum iron intake. Insufficient iron is frequently the limiting factor in collecting multiple units of blood over a short interval. Oral iron is commonly provided, but may be insuffi-

cient to maintain iron stores.[29] The dose and ingestion schedule should be adjusted to minimize gastrointestinal side effects.

Collection

The collection of autologous blood has many elements in common with collection from regular volunteer donors, but numerous special considerations exist.

Requests for autologous blood collection are made in writing by the patient's physician; a request form (which may be a simple prescription or a form designed for the purpose) is kept by the collecting facility. The request should include the patient's name, a unique identification number, the number of units and kind of component requested, the date of scheduled surgery, the nature of the surgical procedure, and the physician's signature.

Collection Schedule

It is important to establish guidelines for the appropriate number of units to be collected. A sufficient number of units should be drawn, whenever possible, so that the patient can avoid exposure to allogeneic blood. A hospital's surgical blood order schedule can provide estimates of transfusion levels for specific procedures. Two-unit collections via an automated red cell apheresis system may also be an option. The collection of units for liquid blood storage should be scheduled as far in advance of surgery as possible, in order to allow compensatory erythropoiesis to prevent anemia.

A schedule for blood collections should be established with the patient. A weekly schedule is often used. The last collection should ordinarily occur no sooner than 72 hours before the scheduled surgery and preferably longer, to allow time for adequate volume repletion. Many programs notify the requesting physician of the total number of units donated when the requested number of units cannot be collected.

Each program should establish a policy regarding rescheduling of surgery beyond the expiration date of autologous units. Options include: 1) discarding the unit; 2) reinfusing it to the patient and then drawing a new autologous unit; and 3) freezing the unit, with or without rejuvenation.

Donor Screening

Because of the special circumstances attending autologous blood transfusion, rigid criteria for donor selection are not required. In situations where requirements for allogeneic donor selection or collection are not applied, alternate requirements must be established by the medical director and recorded in the procedures manual. Individual deviations from the alternate requirements must be approved by the blood bank medical director, usually in consultation with the donor-patient's physician. In any case, however, the hemoglobin concentration of the donor-patient's blood should be no less than 11 g/dL and the packed cell volume, if substituted, should be no less than 33%.

Medical Interview

The medical interview should be structured to the special needs of donor-patients. For example, more attention should be given to questions about medications, associated medical illnesses, and cardiovascular fitness.[10] Questions should elicit any possibility of intermittent bacteremia. Because crossover is not permitted, a substantially shortened set of interview questions can be used for autologous donations; for example, questions related to donor risk for transfusion-transmitted diseases are not necessary.

Volume Collected

For autologous donors weighing >50 kg, the 450-mL collection bag is usually used instead of the 500-mL bag, in case the donor cannot give a full unit. If a low-volume (300-405 mL) unit is collected, the red cells are suitable for storage and subsequent autologous transfusion. The plasma from low-volume units cannot be transfused because of the abnormal anticoagulant/plasma ratio. Undercollected units (<300 mL) may still be suitable for autologous use with approval of the medical director. For patients weighing <50 kg, there should be proportional reduction in the volume of blood collected. Regardless of donor weight, the volume collected should not exceed 10.5 mL/kg of the donor's estimated body weight.

Serologic Testing

The collecting facility must determine ABO and Rh type on all units. Transfusing facilities must retest ABO and Rh type on units drawn at other facilities, unless the collecting facility tests segments from the unit according to AABB standard I3.000 or confirms donor ABO and Rh type using a computer as noted in AABB standard I3.200.

Testing for ABO and Rh type must be performed on a properly labeled blood sample from the patient. Antibody screen and crossmatch are optional if only autologous units are ordered for transfusion.

Labeling

Units should be clearly labeled with the patient's name and some identifying number, the expiration date of the unit, and, if available, the name of the facility where the patient is to be transfused. The unit should be clearly marked "For Autologous Use Only" and carry the classification statement "Autologous Donor." If components have been prepared, the container of each component must be similarly labeled. A biohazard label must be applied when indicated by FDA requirements (see Regulatory Considerations). Labeling requirements for autologous units are detailed in the AABB *Standards*,[15(p77)] which parallel the regulations.

Storage and Shipment

The longest possible shelf life for collected units increases flexibility for the patient and the collecting facility and allows time for the patient to rebuild red cell mass during the interval between blood collection and surgery. Liquid storage is feasible for up to 6 weeks. Some programs store autologous units as Whole Blood for 35 days rather than as Red Blood Cells; Whole Blood is simpler to store, and the risk of volume overload subsequent to transfusion is low. The collection of autologous units more than 6 weeks before scheduled surgery has been described but requires that the red cells be frozen. Although this provides more time for the donor to recover lost red cell mass, freezing and thawing add to the cost of the program, reduce the volume of red cells through processing losses, and complicate blood availability during the perioperative period.

Transfusion of Autologous Units

Some autologous transfusion programs require a system to ensure that if autologous blood is available, it be issued for the recipient and used before allogeneic components are given. A special "autologous" label may be used with numbering to ensure that the oldest units are issued first. Anesthesiologists, surgeons, and physicians should be educated about the importance of selecting autologous components before allogeneic units are given.

Records and Reactions

AABB standards for the proper issue and return of unused autologous units are the same as for allogeneic units.[15(p64-65)] Records must be maintained that identify the unit and all components made from it, from collection and processing through their eventual disposition. The investigation of suspected adverse transfusion events should be the same for autologous and allogeneic units.

Continuous Quality Improvement

Several quality improvement issues have been identified for PAD practices.[5] The most important indicator for autologous blood practice is

how effectively it reduces allogeneic transfusions to participating patients. The "wastage" rate of autologous units for surgical procedures can also be monitored. However, even for procedures such as joint replacement or radical prostatectomy, a well-designed program may result in 50% of collected units being unused.[5] Nevertheless, as much as 25% of autologous blood is collected for procedures that seldom require transfusion, such as vaginal hysterectomies and normal vaginal deliveries. Up to 90% of units collected for these procedures are wasted.[14] The additional costs associated with the collection of autologous units, along with advances in the safety of allogeneic blood, have altered the cost-effectiveness of autologous blood predonation in many situations.[30]

Criteria can be established to monitor the appropriateness of autologous transfusions. These criteria may be the same as, or different from, those established for allogeneic units.[26] As with allogeneic blood, transfusion of preoperatively donated autologous blood carries the same risks associated with administrative error and bacterial contamination. Autologous programs should be monitored for unavailability of autologous blood when needed, the transfusion of allogeneic blood before autologous blood, and identification errors.

Evolving Issues in Preoperative Autologous Services

The Role of Aggressive Phlebotomy and the Use of Erythropoietin

Recent studies of elective orthopedic and coronary artery bypass graft procedures have indicated that blood conservation interventions must generate the equivalent of between three to five blood units in order to avoid allogeneic blood exposure. The efficacy of preoperative autologous donation is dependent on the degree to which the patient's erythropoiesis increases the production of red cells. Studies have shown that the endogenous erythropoietin response is suboptimal at the level of mild anemia produced under "standard" conditions of one blood unit donated weekly. A computer model predicts that if the erythropoietic response to autologous blood phlebotomy is not able to maintain the patient's level of hematocrit during the donation interval, the donation of autologous blood may actually be harmful[31]; this outcome was confirmed in a recent study of patients undergoing hysterectomy,[32] in which the authors demonstrated that preoperative autologous blood donation resulted in perioperative anemia and an increased likelihood of blood transfusion.

In contrast to autologous blood donation under "standard" conditions, studies of "aggressive" autologous blood phlebotomy (twice weekly for 3 weeks, beginning 25-35 days before surgery) have demonstrated that endogenous erythropoietin levels do increase. Studies of exogenous (pharmacologic) erythropoietin therapy to further stimulate erythropoietic re-

covery during autologous phlebotomy or surgical blood loss have been reviewed.[33]

A published mathematical model[31] illustrates the relationship between anticipated surgical blood losses, the level of hematocrit that the physician may want to maintain perioperatively, and the need for autologous blood donation for individual patients (Fig 5-1). Models such as this may be helpful in designing autologous procurement programs or monitoring their value through quality assurance.

Transfusion Trigger

Disagreement exists about the proper hemoglobin/hematocrit level ("transfusion trigger") at which autologous blood should be given.[26] Autologous blood transfusion is not without risks to the recipient; these include misidentification of patients or units, bacterial contamination of stored units, and volume overload. Because researchers and clinicians have not reached agreement about hemoglobin/

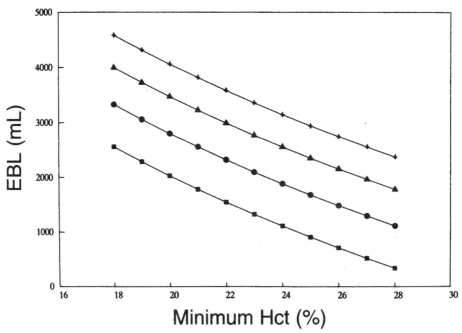

Figure 5-1. Relationship of estimated blood loss and minimum (nadir) hematocrit during hospitalization at various initial hematocrit levels (30%,35%,40%,45%) in a surgical patient with a whole blood volume of 5000 mL. ■ = 30%; ● = 35%; ▲ = 40%; + = 45%. (Reprinted with permission from Cohen and Brecher.[31])

hematocrit levels for optimal oxygen delivery, various aspects of this concern continue to be debated.

Storing Autologous Blood for Speculative Future Needs

Public concern over transfusion-transmitted diseases has stimulated development of facilities that provide long-term storage of autologous frozen blood. Individuals who pay to participate in such a program hope to maintain a supply of autologous blood should it become needed in the future. Arguments against this practice include the lack of availability in emergency situations, and the time required to thaw and wash units along with their subsequently short shelf life. Long-term frozen storage is most suitable for individuals with rare phenotypes and alloantibodies to clinically significant, high-incidence antigens.

Preoperative Collection of Components

Some workers believe that preoperative or intraoperative collection of platelet-rich plasma during cardiopulmonary bypass surgery may improve hemostasis and decrease allogeneic exposures, but others have found no benefit.[26] Preoperative collection of autologous platelets, especially in cardiac surgery, is often impractical because patients may be taking antiplatelet drugs; surgery is often scheduled on an emergency basis; and relatively low numbers of platelets are harvested.

Cost-Effectiveness

While autologous blood collections have become popular, the costs associated with collection are usually higher than those associated with allogeneic blood. The continued need for autologous blood programs has been questioned, because of the reduced risk of allogeneic blood transfusions and pressure to reduce health-care costs.[30] The following suggestions have been made to make autologous blood programs more efficient without sacrificing safety:

1. Standardize the indications for preoperative autologous collections.
2. Utilize only whole blood and discontinue component production.
3. Limit the use of frozen autologous blood.
4. Apply the same transfusion guidelines for autologous and allogeneic blood.
5. Test only the first autologous blood unit for infectious disease markers; subsequent units collected within 30 days need not be tested.

These suggestions related to the potential for improved efficiency must be reviewed against the needs of patients and the ability of the facility to provide comprehensive autologous services for those desiring the alternative.

Acute Normovolemic Hemodilution

Acute normovolemic hemodilution (ANH) is the removal of whole blood from a patient, while restoring the circulating blood volume with an acellular fluid shortly before an anticipated significant surgical blood loss. To minimize the manual labor associated with hemodilution, the blood should be collected in standard blood bags containing anticoagulant on a tilt-rocker with automatic cutoff via volume sensors. The blood is then stored at room temperature and reinfused in the operating room after major blood loss has ceased, or sooner if indicated. Simultaneous infusions of crystalloid (3 mL crystalloids for each 1 mL of blood withdrawn) and colloid (dextrans, starches, gelatin, albumin, 1 mL for each 1 mL of blood withdrawn) have been recommended.[34] Subsequent intraoperative fluid management is based on the usual surgical requirements. Blood units are reinfused in the reverse order of collection. The first unit collected, and therefore the last unit transfused, has the highest hematocrit and concentration of coagulation factors and platelets. While this technique has been primarily developed and utilized in Europe, increasing interest in the United States has led to data[35] that show promise in the use of acute normovolemic hemodilution as an alternative method of autologous blood procurement.

Theoretic Considerations

Conserved Red Cell Mass

The chief benefit of hemodilution is the reduction of red cell losses when whole blood is shed perioperatively at lower hematocrit levels after ANH is completed.[36] Mathematical modeling has suggested that severe hemodilution to preoperative hematocrit levels of less than 20%, accompanied by substantial blood losses, would be required before the red cell volume "saved" by hemodilution became clinically important.[37] The safety and efficacy of more extensive hemodilution is controversial,[38] and may result in little or no additional blood conservation.

Improved Oxygenation

Withdrawal of whole blood and replacement with crystalloid or colloid solution decreases arterial oxygen content, but compensatory hemodynamic mechanisms and the existence of surplus oxygen-delivery capacity make ANH safe. A sudden drop in red cell concentration lowers blood viscosity, thereby decreasing peripheral resistance and increasing cardiac output. If cardiac output can effectively compensate, oxygen delivery to the tissues at a hematocrit of 25-30% is as good as, but no better than, oxygen delivery at a hematocrit of 35-45%.[39]

Preservation of Hemostasis

Because blood collected by ANH is stored at room temperature and is usually returned to the patient within 8 hours of collection, there is little deterioration of platelets or coagulation factors. The hemostatic value of blood collected by ANH is of questionable benefit for orthopedic or urologic surgery because plasma and platelets are rarely indicated in this setting. Its value in protecting plasma and platelets from the acquired coagulopathy of extracorporeal circulation in cardiac surgery (known as "blood pooling") is better established.[40,41]

Clinical Studies

Selected clinical trials of ANH are summarized in Table 5-3. Extensive reviews on the merits of ANH have been published.[49,50] Because ANH and reinfusion are accomplished in the operating room by on-site personnel, procurement and administration costs are minimized. Blood obtained during ANH does not require the commitment of patient time, transportation, and loss of work associated with PAD. The wastage of PAD units (approximately 50% of units collected)[5] also is eliminated with ANH. Additionally, autologous blood units procured by ANH require no inventory or testing costs. ANH eliminates the possibility of an administrative or clerical error that could lead to an ABO-incompatible blood transfusion and death.

Practical Considerations

In each institution, key individuals from the anesthesia, surgery, and transfusion medicine must establish a local database upon which decisions about ANH can be based. ANH is usually employed for procedures with an anticipated blood loss of at least one liter, or more than 20% of the patient's blood volume, provided the preoperative hematocrit is adequate. Suggested criteria for patient selection are listed in Table 5-4.

The following considerations are important in establishing an ANH program:

1. Decisions about ANH should be based on the surgical procedure and on the patient's preoperative blood volume and hematocrit, target hemodilution hematocrit, and other physiologic variables.

Table 5-3. Selected Clinical Trials of Acute Normovolemic Hemodilution (ANH)

Surgery	Estimated Blood Loss (mL)			Postoperative Hematocrit (%)			Allogeneic RBC-Containing Units or Liters ( ) Transfused			Reference
	Control	ANH	p Value	Control	ANH	p Value	Control	ANH	p Value	
Vascular	2250	2458	NS	NR	33.0	NR	6.0	2.6	<0.01	42
Liver resection	1479	1284	NS	37.9	33.8	<0.01	3.8	0.4	<0.001	43
Total hip arthroplasty	1800	2000	NS	38.4	32.4	NS	(2.1)	(0.9)	NR	44
Spinal fusion	5490	1700	<0.005	NR	28.7	NR	8.6	<1	<0.001	45
Colectomy	NR	NR	NR	37.0	35.0	NR	2.4	0	NR	46
Prostate	1246	1106	NS	35.5	31.8	<0.001	0.16	0	NS	47
Prostate	1717	1710	NS	29.5	27.9	<0.05	0.30	0.13	NS	48

Modified from Brecher and Rosenfeld.[37]
NR = not reported; NS = not significant

2. The institution's policy and procedures and the mechanisms for educating staff should be established and periodically reviewed.

3. There should be careful monitoring of the patient's circulating volume and perfusion status during the procedure.

4. Blood must be collected in an aseptic manner, ordinarily into standard blood collection bags with citrate anticoagulant; this may be unnecessary for patients who are systemically heparinized.

5. Units must be properly labeled and stored. The label must contain, at a minimum, the patient's full name, medical record number, date and time of collection, and the statement "For Autologous Use Only." Room temperature storage should not exceed 8 hours. If more time elapses between collection and transfusion, the blood should be stored in a monitored refrigerator. ANH blood collected from an open system (eg, from a central venous line or an arterial catheter) must be transfused within 8 hours if it is stored at room temperature or 24 hours if it is stored in a monitored refrigerator.

Table 5-4. Criteria for Selection of Patients for Acute Normovolemic Hemodilution

1. Likelihood of transfusion exceeds 10% (ie, blood requested for crossmatch according to a maximum surgical blood order schedule).

2. Preoperative hemoglobin level of at least 12 g/dL.

3. Absence of clinically significant coronary, pulmonary, renal, or liver disease.

4. Absence of severe hypertension.

5. Absence of infection and risk of bacteremia.

Intraoperative Blood Collection

The term intraoperative blood collection or recovery describes the technique of collecting and reinfusing blood lost by a patient during surgery. The oxygen-transport properties of recovered red cells are equivalent to stored allogeneic red cells. The survival of recovered blood cells appears to be at least comparable to that of transfused allogeneic red cells.[51] Intraoperative collection is contraindicated when certain procoagulant materials (eg, topical collagen), are applied to the surgical field, as systemic activation of coagulation may result. Microaggregate filters (40 microns) are most often used, as recovered blood may contain tissue debris, small blood clots, or bone fragments.

Cell washing devices can provide the equivalent of 12 units of banked blood per hour to a massively bleeding patient.[52] The incidence of adverse events resulting from reinfusion of recovered blood is not known. Hemolysis of recovered blood can occur during suctioning from the surface instead of from deep pools of shed blood. For this reason, manufacturers' guidelines recommend a maximum vacuum setting of no more than 150 torr. One study found that vacuum settings as high as 300 torr could be used when necessary, without causing excessive hemolysis.[53] The clinical importance of free hemoglobin in the concentrations usually seen has not been established, although excessive free hemoglobin may indicate inadequate washing.[43] Positive bacterial cultures from recovered blood are not unusual, but clinical infection is rare.[54]

Relative contraindications to intraoperative blood collection and recovery include malignant neoplasm, infection, and contaminants in the operative field. Because washing does not remove bacteria from recovered blood, intraoperative recovery should not be used if the operative field has gross bacterial contamination.

Aspiration of other body fluids, such as amniotic or ascitic fluid, should be avoided.

Most programs use machines that collect shed blood, wash it, and concentrate the red cells. This process typically results in 225-mL units of saline-suspended red cells with a hematocrit of 50-60%. Patients exhibit a level of plasma-free hemoglobin that is usually higher than after allogeneic transfusion. Sodium and chloride concentrations are the same as in the saline wash solution, and potassium concentration is low. The infusate contains minimal coagulation factors and platelets.

Clinical Studies

As with preoperative autologous blood donation and acute normovolemic hemodilution, collection and recovery of intraoperative autologous blood should undergo scrutiny with regard to both safety and efficacy. A controlled study in cardiothoracic surgery demonstrated a lack of efficacy when transfusion requirements and clinical outcome were followed.[54] A second study found that only a minority of patients undergoing major orthopedic and cardiac surgery achieved cost equivalence with intraoperative blood recovery using semiautomated instruments compared to banked blood.[55] While the collection of a minimum of one blood unit equivalent is possible for less expensive (with unwashed blood) methods, it is generally agreed that at least two blood unit equivalents need to be recovered using a cell-recovery instrument (with washed blood) in order to achieve cost-effectiveness.[56] The value of intraoperative blood collection has been best defined for vascular surgeries with large blood losses, such as aortic aneurysm repair and liver transplantation.[57]

Medical Controversies

Collection devices that neither concentrate nor wash shed blood before reinfusion increase the risk of adverse effects. Shed blood has undergone varying degrees of coagulation/fibrinolysis and hemolysis, and infusion of large volumes of washed or unwashed blood has been described in association with disseminated intravascular coagulation.[58] Factors that affect the degree of coagulation and clot lysis include:
1. Whether the patient had received systemic anticoagulation.
2. The amount and type of anticoagulant used.
3. The extent of contact between blood and serosal surfaces.
4. The extent of contact between blood and artificial surfaces.
5. The degree of turbulence during collection.

In general, blood collected at low flow rates or during slow bleeding from patients who are not systemically anticoagulated will have undergone coagulation and fibrinolysis and will not contribute to hemostasis upon reinfusion.

The high suction pressure and surface skimming during aspiration and the turbulence or mechanical compression that occurs in roller pumps and plastic tubing make some degree of hemolysis inevitable. High concentrations of free hemoglobin may be nephrotoxic to patients with impaired renal function. Many programs limit the quantity of recovered blood that may be reinfused without processing.

Practical Considerations

Collection and recovery services require the coordinated effort of surgeons, anesthesiologists, transfusion medicine specialists, and specific personnel trained in the use of special equipment. Equipment options may include:
1. Devices that collect recovered blood for direct reinfusion.
2. Devices that collect recovered blood, which is then concentrated and washed in a separate cell washer.
3. High-speed machines that automatically concentrate and wash recovered red cells.

Some hospitals develop their own operations, whereas others contract with outside services. Each hospital's needs should dictate whether blood collection and recovery are used and how they are achieved.

Processing Prior to Reinfusion

Several devices automatically process recovered blood before reinfusion. Vacuum suction and simultaneous anticoagulation are used for collection. To minimize hemolysis, the vacuum level should ordinarily not exceed 150 torr, although higher levels of suction may occasionally be needed during periods of rapid bleeding. Either citrate (ACD) or heparin may be used as an anticoagulant. Blood is held in a reservoir until centrifuged and washed with a volume of saline that varies between 500 and 1500 mL. If not infused immediately, the unit must be labeled with the patient's name and identification number, the date and time collection was initiated, and the statement "For Autologous Use Only."

An alternative approach is to collect blood in a canister system designed for direct reinfusion and then concentrate and wash the recovered red cells in a blood bank cell washer. Intraoperatively collected and recovered blood must be handled in the transfusion service laboratory like any other autologous unit. The unit should be reinfused through a filter.

Direct Reinfusion

Systems are available that collect recovered blood and return it directly. These systems generally consist of a suction catheter attached to a disposable collection bag or rigid plastic canister, to which anticoagulant (citrate or heparin) may have been added. Blood is suctioned into the holding canister before being reinfused through a microaggregate filter. Low-vacuum suction and minimal hemolysis are preferred in nonwashed systems.

Requirements and Recommendations

AABB *Standards*[15(p77)] requires a process that includes patient and storage bag identification and time collected with expiration date. Units collected intraoperatively should be labeled with the patient's first and last name, hospital identification number, the date and time of collection and expiration, and the statement "For Autologous Use Only."[15(p77,79)]

If collected under aseptic conditions with a saline-wash device and if properly labeled, this blood may be stored at room temperature for up to 6 hours or at 1-6 C for up to 24 hours, provided that storage at 1-6 C is begun within 6 hours of initiating the collection.[15(p79)] Note that the allowable interval of room temperature storage is shorter (6 hours) for recovered blood than for ANH blood (8 hours). Storage times are the same for recovered blood whether unwashed or washed. If the blood leaves the patient for washing or storage in a remote location, there must be appropriate procedures to ensure proper labeling of the blood according to AABB *Standards*.[15(p79)]

Hospitals with collection and recovery programs should establish written policies and procedures that are regularly reviewed by a physician who has been assigned responsibility for the program. Transfusion medicine specialists should play an active role in design, implementation, and operation of the program. Written policies must be in place for the proper collection, labeling, and storage of intraoperative autologous blood. Equipment and techniques for collection and infusion must ensure that the blood is aseptic. Periodic testing of recovered blood is recommended, to include measurements of red cell mass and degree of hemolysis in recovered blood. Hemolysis can be monitored by measurement of potassium levels, plasma hemoglobin concentration, or visual inspection. Other possible examples of quality assurance monitoring include demonstration of sterility, the amount of vacuum suction, and the concentration of residual heparin. Quality management should include evaluation of the appropriate use of blood collection and recovery services and adequate training of personnel. Written protocols, procedure logs, machine maintenance, procedures for handling adverse events, and documentation are recommended.[27]

Postoperative Blood Collection

Postoperative blood collection denotes the recovery of blood from surgical drains followed by reinfusion, with or without processing.[27] In some programs, postoperative shed blood is collected into sterile canisters and reinfused, without processing, through a microaggregate filter. Recovered blood is dilute, partially hemolyzed and defibrinated, and may contain high concentrations of cytokines. For these reasons, most programs set an upper limit on the volume (eg, 1400 mL) of unprocessed blood that can be reinfused. If transfusion of blood has not begun within 6 hours of initiating the collection, the blood must be discarded. Hospitals must establish written policies, procedures, labeling requirements, quality assurance, and review consistent with AABB *Standards*.[15]

Clinical Studies

The evolution of cardiac surgery has been accompanied by a broad experience in postoperative conservation of blood. Postoperative autologous blood transfusion is practiced widely, but not uniformly. Prospective and controlled trials have disagreed over the efficacy of postoperative blood recovery in cardiac surgery patients; at least three such studies have demonstrated lack of efficacy,[59-61] while at least two studies have shown benefit.[62,63] The disparity of results in these studies may be explained, in part, by differences in transfusion practices because the reports cited above incorporated criteria for blood transfusion into

their protocols. Additionally, because these were not blind studies, modification of physician transfusion practices may have been an uncredited intervention in these blood conservation studies.

In the postoperative orthopedic surgical setting, a number of reports have similarly described the successful recovery and reinfusion of washed[64] and unwashed[65,66] wound drainage from patients undergoing arthroplasty. The volume of reinfused drainage blood has been reported to be as much as 3000 mL, and averages more than 1100 mL in patients undergoing cementless knee replacement.[66] Because the red cell content of the fluid collected is low (hematocrit levels of 20%) the volume of red cells reinfused is often small.[67]

The safety of reinfused unwashed orthopedic wound drainage has been controversial. Theoretical concerns have been expressed regarding infusion of potentially harmful materials in recovered blood, including free hemoglobin, red cell stroma, marrow fat, toxic irrigants, tissue or methacrylate debris, fibrin degradation products, activated coagulation factors, and complement. Although two small studies have reported complications,[68,69] several larger studies have reported no serious adverse effects when drainage was passed through a standard 40-micron blood filter.[65,66,70]

The potential for decreasing exposure to allogeneic blood among orthopedic patients undergoing postoperative blood collection, whether washed or unwashed, is greatest for cementless bilateral total knee replacement, revision hip or knee replacement, and long segment spinal fusion. As in the case of intraoperative recovery, blood loss must be sufficient to warrant the additional cost of processing technology.[71] As in selection of patients who can benefit from PAD and ANH, prospective identification of patients who can benefit from intra- and postoperative autologous blood recovery is possible if anticipated surgical blood losses and the perioperative "transfusion trigger" are taken into account (Fig 5-1).

References

1. Pub. Law. No. 101-336, 104 Stat. 327 (1990). Codified at 42 U. S. C. §12101-12213.

2. The ADA, HIV, and autologous blood donation. Association Bulletin 98-5. Bethesda, MD: American Association of Blood Banks, 1998.

3. Mintz PD, Nordine RB, Henry JB, Weblu R. Expected hemotherapy in elective surgery. NY State J Med 1976;76:532-7.

4. Kruskall MS, Yomtovian R, Dzik WH, et al. On improving the cost-effectiveness of autologous blood transfusion practices. Transfusion 1994;34:259-64.

5. Renner SW, Howanitz PJ, Bachner P. Preoperative autologous blood donation in 612 hospitals. Arch Pathol Lab Med 1992;116:613-9.

6. Silvergleid AJ. Safety and effectiveness of predeposit autologous transfusions in preteen and adolescent children. JAMA 1987;257:3403-4.

7. Chaplin H, Mischeaux JR, Inkster MD, Sherman LA. Frozen storage of 11 units of sickle cell red cells for autologous transfusion of a single patient. Transfusion 1986;26:341-5.

8. Meryman HT, Hornblower M. Freezing and deglycerolizing sickle trait red blood cells. Transfusion 1976;16:627-32.

9. Mann M, Sacks HJ, Goldfinger D. Safety of autologous blood donation prior to elective surgery for a variety of potentially high risk patients. Transfusion 1983;23:229-32.

10. Popovsky MA, Whitaker B, Arnold NL. Severe outcomes of allogeneic and autologous blood donation: Frequency and characterization. Transfusion 1995;35:734-7.

11. Schreiber GB, Busch MP, Kleinman SH, Korelitz JJ. The risk of transfusion-transmitted viral infections. N Engl J Med 1996;334:1685-90.

12. Thomas MJG, Gillon J, Desmond MJ. Preoperative autologous blood donation. Transfusion 1996;36:633-9.

13. Sayers MH. Controversies in transfusion medicine. Autologous blood donation in pregnancy: Con. Transfusion 1990;30:172-4.

14. Kruskall MS. Controversies in transfusion medicine. The safety and utility of autologous donations by pregnant patients: Pro. Transfusion 1990;30:168-71.

15. Menitove JE, ed. Standards for blood banks and transfusion services. 19th ed. Bethesda, MD: American Association of Blood Banks, 1999.

16. Food and Drug Administration. Memorandum: Guidance for autologous blood and blood components. (March 15, 1989)Rockville, MD: CBER Office of Communication, Training, and Manufacturer's Assistance, 1989.

17. Food and Drug Administration. Memorandum: Autologous blood collection and processing procedures. (February 12, 1990) Rockville, MD: CBER Office of Communication, Training, and Manufacturers Assistance, 1990.

18. Food and Drug Administration. Memorandum: Testing for antibody to hepatitis C virus encoded antigen (anti-HCV). (November 29, 1990) Rockville, MD: CBER Office of Communication, Training, and Manufacturers Assistance, 1990.

19. Food and Drug Administration. Memorandum: FDA recommendations concerning testing for antibody to hepatitis B core antigen (anti-HBc). (September 10, 1991) Rockville, MD: CBER Office of Communication, Training, and Manufacturers Assistance, 1991.

20. Food and Drug Administration. Memorandum: Disposition of blood products intended for autologous use that test repeatedly reactive for anti HCV. (September 11, 1991) Rockville, MD: CBER Office of Communication, Training, and Manufacturers Assistance, 1991.

21. Food and Drug Administration. Memorandum: Clarification of FDA recommendations for donor deferral and product distribution based on the results of syphilis testing. (December 12, 1991) Rockville, MD: CBER Office of Communication, Training, and Manufacturers Assistance, 1991.

22. Food and Drug Administration. Memorandum: Revised recommendations for testing whole blood, blood components, source plasma and source leukocytes for antibody to hepatitis C virus encoded antigen (anti-HCV). (April 23, 1992) Rockville, MD: CBER Office of Communication, Training, and Manufacturers Assistance, 1992.

23. Food and Drug Administration. Memorandum: Recommendations for donor screening with a licensed test for HIV-1 antigen. (August 8, 1995) Rockville, MD: CBER Office of Communication, Training, and Manufacturers Assistance, 1995.

24. Food and Drug Administration. Memorandum: Additional recommendations for donor screening with a licensed test for HIV-1 antigen. (March 14, 1996) Rockville, MD: CBER Office of Communication, Training, and Manufacturers Assistance, 1996.

25. Code of federal regulations. Title 42 CFR Part 72.3. Washington, DC: US Government Printing Office, 1998 (revised annually).

26. National Heart, Lung, and Blood Institute Autologous Transfusion Symposium Working Group. Autologous transfusion: Current trends and research issues. Transfusion 1995;35:525-31.

27. Autologous Transfusion Committee. Guidelines for blood recovery and reinfusion in surgery and trauma. Bethesda, MD: American Association of Blood Banks, 1997.

28. Renner SW, Braley AW, Yomtovian R. Autologous blood transfusion practices. In: AP Q-Probe. Northfield, IL: College of American Pathologists, 1995:95-108.

29. Biesma DH, Kraaijenhagen RJ, Poortman J, et al. The effect of oral iron supplementation on erythropoiesis in autologous blood donors. Transfusion 1992;32:162-5.

30. Etchason J, Petz L, Keeler E, et al. The cost-effectiveness of preoperative autologous blood donations. N Engl J Med 1995;332:719-24.

31. Cohen JA, Brecher ME. Preoperative autologous blood donation: Benefit or detriment? A mathematical analysis. Transfusion 1995;35:640-4.

32. Kanter MH, Van Maanen D, Anders KH, et al. Preoperative autologous blood donation before elective hysterectomy. JAMA 1996;276:798-801.

33. Goodnough LT, Monk TG, Andriole GL. Erythropoietin therapy. N Engl J Med 1997;336:933-8.

34. Goodnough LT, Brecher ME, Monk TG. Acute normovolemic hemodilution in surgery. Hematology 1992;2:413-20.

35. Goodnough LT, Brecher ME, Kanter MH, AuBuchon JP. Transfusion medicine. Second of two parts—blood conservation. N Engl J Med 1999;340(7):525-33.

36. Messmer K, Kreimeier M, Intagliett A. Present state of intentional hemodilution. Eur Surg Res 1986;18:254-63.

37. Brecher ME, Rosenfeld M. Mathematical and computer modeling of acute normovolemic hemodilution. Transfusion 1994;34:176-9.

38. Goodnough LT, Bravo J, Hsueh Y, et al. Red blood cell volume in autologous and homologous units: Implications for risk/benefit assessment for autologous blood "crossover" and directed blood transfusion. Transfusion 1989;29:821-2.

39. Weiskopf RB. Mathematical analysis of isovolemic hemodilution indicates that it can decrease the need for allogeneic blood transfusion. Transfusion 1995;35:37-41.

40. Zetterstrom H, Wiklund L. A new nomogram facilitating adequate heamodilution. Acta Anaesthesiol Scand 1986;30:300-4.

41. Petry AF, Jost T, Sievers H. Reduction of homologous blood requirements by blood pooling at the onset of cardiopulmonary bypass. J Thorac Cardiovasc Surg 1994;1097:1210-4.

42. Davies MJ, Cronin KD, Domainque C. Haemodilution for major vascular surgery-using 3.5% polygeline (Haemaccel). Anaesthesiology Intensive Care 1982;10:265-70.

43. Sejourne P. Poirier A, Meakins JL, et al. Effects of haemodilution on transfusion requirements in liver resection. Lancet 1989;2:1380-2.

44. Rosenberg B, Wulff K. Regional lung function following hip arthroplasty and preoperative normovolemic hemodilution. Acta Anaesthesiol Scand 1979;23:242-7.

45. Kafer ER, Isley MR, Hansen T, et al. Automated acute normovolemic hemodilution reduces blood transfusion requirements for spinal fusion (abstract). Anesth Analg 1986;65(Suppl):S76.

46. Rose D, Coustoftides T. Intraoperative normovolemic hemodilution. J Surg Res 1981;31:375-81.

47. Ness PM, Bourke DL, Walsh PC. A randomized trial of perioperative hemodilution versus transfusion of preoperatively deposited autologous blood in elective surgery. Transfusion 1991;31:226-30.

48. Monk TG, Goodnough LT, Birkmeyer JD, et al. Acute normovolemic hemodilution is a cost-effective alternative to preoperative autologous blood donation by patients undergoing radical retropubic prostatectomy. Transfusion 1995;35:559-65.

49. Goodnough LT, Monk TG, Brecher ME. Acute normovolemic hemodilution should replace preoperative autologous blood donation before elective surgery. Transfusion 1998;38:473-7.

50. Rottman G, Ness PM. Is acute normovolemic hemodilution a legitimate alternative to allogeneic blood transfusions? Transfusion 1998;38:477-80.

51. Williamson KR, Taswell HF. Intraoperative blood salvage: A review. Transfusion 1991;31:662-75.

52. Williamson KR, Taswell HF, Rettke SR, Kromi RAF. Intraoperative transfusion: Its role in orthotopic liver transplantation. Mayo Clin Proc 1989;64:340-5.

53. Gregoretti S. Suction-induced hemolysis at various vacuum pressures: Implications for intraoperative blood salvage. Transfusion 1996;36:57-60.

54. Bell K, Stott K, Sinclair CJ, et al. A controlled trial of intra-operative autologous transfusion in cardiothoracic surgery measuring effect on transfusion requirements and clinical outcome. Transfus Med 1992;2:295-300.

55. Solomon MD, Rutledge ML, Kane LE, Yawn DH. Cost comparison of intraoperative autologous versus homologous transfusion. Transfusion 1988;28:379-82.

56. Bovill DF, Moulton CW, Jackson WS, et al. The efficacy of intraoperative autologous transfusion in major orthopaedic surgery: A regression analysis. Orthopedics 1986;9:1403-07.

57. Goodnough LT, Monk TG, Sicard G, et al. Intraoperative salvage in patients undergoing elective abdominal aortic aneurism repair. An analysis of costs and benefits. J Vasc Surg 1996;24:213-8.

58. de Haan J, Boonstra P, Monnink S, et al. Retransfusion of suctioned blood during cardiopulmonary bypass impairs hemostasis. Ann Thorac Surg 1995;59:901-7.

59. Ward HB, Smith RA, Candis KP, et al. A prospective, randomized trial of autotransfusion after routine cardiac surgery. Ann Thorac Surg 1993;56:137-41.

60. Thurer RL, Lytle BW, Cosgrove DM, Loop FD. Autotransfusion following cardiac operations: A randomized, prospective study. Ann Thorac Surg 1979;27:500-6.

61. Roberts SP, Early GL, Brown B, et al. Autotransfusion of unwashed mediastinal shed blood fails to decrease banked blood requirements in patients undergoing aorta coronary bypass surgery. Am J Surg 1991;162:477-80.

62. Schaff HV, Hauer JM, Bell WR, et al. Autotransfusion of shed mediastinal blood after cardiac surgery. A prospective study. J Thorac Cardiovasc Surg 1978;75:632-41.

63. Eng J, Kay PH, Murday AJ, et al. Post-operative autologous transfusion in cardiac surgery. A prospective, randomized study. Eur J Cardiothorac Surg 1990;4:595-600.

64. Semkiw LB, Schurman OJ, Goodman SB, Woolson ST. Postoperative blood salvage using the cell saver after total joint arthroplasty. J Bone Joint Surg (Am) 1989;71A:823-7.

65. Faris PM, Ritter MA, Keating EM, Valeri CR. Unwashed filtered shed blood collected after knee and hip arthroplasties. J Bone Joint Surg (Am) 1991;73A:1169-77.

66. Martin JW, Whiteside LA, Milliano MT, Reedy ME. Postoperative blood retrieval and transfusion in cementless total knee arthroplasty. J Arthroplasty 1992;7:205-10.

67. Umlas J, Foster RR, Dalal SA, et al. Red cell loss following orthopedic surgery: The case against postoperative blood salvage. Transfusion 1994;34:402-6.

68. Clements DH, Sculco TP, Burke SW, et al. Salvage and reinfusion of postoperative sanguineous

wound drainage. J Bone Joint Surg (Am) 1992;74A:646-51.

69. Woda R, Tetzlaff JE. Upper airway oedema following autologous blood transfusion from a wound drainage system. Can J Anesth 1992;39:290-2.

70. Blevins FT, Shaw B, Valeri RC, et al. Reinfusion of shed blood after orthopaedic procedures in children and adolescents. J Bone Joint Surg (Am) 1993;75A:363-71.

71. Goodnough LT, Verbrugge D, Marcus RE. The relationship between hematocrit, blood lost, and blood transfused in total knee replacement: Implications for postoperative blood salvage and reinfusion. Am J Knee Surg 1995;8:83-7.

6

Apheresis

IN APHERESIS, WHOLE BLOOD IS removed from a donor or patient and separated into components, one or more of which is retained; the remaining elements are then recombined and returned to the donor or patient. Apheresis means "to remove." For consistency, this chapter refers to the removal or collection of components intended for transfusion or to treat a patient's disease by removing a pathologic component as apheresis. The chapter discusses general techniques for separation, the collection of specific components, and several aspects of therapeutic apheresis.

The AABB provides standards[1(pp50-55)] for voluntary compliance for apheresis activities. The Food and Drug Administration (FDA) has established specific requirements that are set forth in the Code of Federal Regulations[2] for apheresis activities. The American Society for Apheresis (ASFA)[3] has published additional guidelines and recommendations. All personnel involved with apheresis activities should be familiar with these sources, and should have documentation that they are qualified by training and experience to perform apheresis. Because apheresis is more complex than ordinary whole blood donation, the apheresis facility must have adequate provisions to care for adverse reactions. These should include equipment, medications, personnel training, and prompt availability of medical care for serious complications.

Separation Techniques

Automated cell-separator devices are used for both component preparation and therapeutic applications of apheresis. Manual apheresis, in which whole blood is collected in multiple bags and centrifuged off-line, involves great care to ensure that the bags are labeled correctly and are returned to the correct donor. With the current available technology this process is seldom used.

Separation by Centrifugation

In most apheresis instruments, centrifugal force separates blood into components based on differences in density. A measured amount of anticoagulant solution is added to the whole blood as it is drawn from the donor or patient. The blood is pumped into a rotating bowl, chamber, or tubular rotor in which layering of components occurs based on density. The desired fraction is diverted and the remaining elements are returned to the donor (or patient) by intermittent or continuous flow.

All systems require prepackaged disposable sets of sterile bags, tubing, and centrifugal devices unique to the instrument. Each has a mechanism to allow the separation device to rotate without twisting the attached tubing. In the intermittent flow method, the centrifuge container is alternately filled and emptied. Most instruments in use today use a continuous flow method that involves the continuous flow of blood through the separator chamber. With either method, single- or dual-vein access techniques are possible. Depending on the procedure and device used, the apheresis procedure time varies from 30 minutes to several hours.

Each manufacturer supplies detailed information and operational protocols. Each facility must have, in a manual readily available to nursing and technical personnel, detailed descriptions of each type of procedure performed, specific for each type of cell separator.[4]

Separation by Membrane Filtration

Filtration of plasma through a membrane allows collection of plasma from healthy donors or therapeutic removal of abnormal plasma constituents, but does not separate specific cellular elements from whole blood.[5] In these instruments, whole blood flows across a membrane containing pores of a defined size. Higher pressure in the blood phase than in the filtrate pushes plasma constituents smaller than the pore size through the membrane into the filtrate. Most instruments have the membranes arranged as hollow fibers, but some have flat plates. Properties of the inner membrane surface repel cellular elements in the laminar flow of blood so that platelets are not activated and red cell survival is not shortened. Plasma permeates the membrane matrix and escapes at right angles to the stream of flow. Varying the pore size allows a degree of selection in the removal of plasma proteins.

Separation by Adsorption

Selective removal of a pathologic material has theoretical advantages over the removal of all plasma constituents. Both membrane and centrifugal devices can be adapted to protocols that selectively remove specific soluble plasma constituents by exploiting the principles of affinity chromatography.[6] Selective removal of low-density lipoproteins (LDLs) in patients with familial hypercholesterolemia has been accomplished using both immunoaffinity (anti-LDL) and chemical affinity (dextran sulfate) columns.[7] Sorbents such as staphylococcal protein A (SPA), monoclonal antibodies, blood group substances, DNA-collodion, and polymers with aggregated IgG attached can extract antibodies, protein antigens, and immune complexes. Returning the depleted plasma along with the cellular components reduces or eliminates the need for replacement fluids. Immunoadsorption may be performed on-line, or the plasma may be separated from the cellular components, passed through an off-line column, and then reinfused.

Component Collection by Apheresis

Whenever components intended for transfusion are collected by apheresis, the donor must give informed consent. The facility must maintain written protocols for all procedures used and must keep records for each cytapheresis procedure as required by AABB *Standards*.[1(p52)]

Platelets, Pheresis

Plateletpheresis is used to obtain platelets from random volunteer donors, from patients' family members, or from donors with matched HLA phenotypes. Because large numbers of platelets can be obtained from a single individual, collection by apheresis reduces the number of donor exposures for patients. Although the correct product name is "Platelets, Pheresis," this component is more commonly called apheresis platelets or single-donor platelets (SDPs). The component must contain at least 3×10^{11} platelets in 75% of units tested[1(p53)] and be equivalent to approximately six units of Platelets (prepared from Whole Blood units). When a very good yield is obtained, the original apheresis unit may be divided into two units, each of which must meet minimum standards independently. Some instruments are programmed to calculate the yield from the donor's hematocrit, platelet count, height, and weight. For alloimmunized patients who are refractory to random allogeneic platelets (see Chapters 16 and 21), platelets from an apheresis donor selected on the basis of a compatible platelet crossmatch or matched for HLA antigens may be the only way to achieve a satisfactory posttransfusion platelet increment.

Donor Selection and Monitoring

Plateletpheresis donors may donate more frequently than whole blood donors, but must meet all other donor criteria. The interval between donations should be at least 48 hours and donors should not undergo plateletpheresis more than twice in a week or more than 24 times in a year.[1(p51)] If the donor donates a unit of Whole Blood or if it becomes impossible to return the donor's red cells during plateletpheresis, at least 8 weeks should elapse before a subsequent plateletpheresis procedure, unless the extracorporeal volume is less than 100 mL.[1(p51-52)] Platelets may be collected from donors who do not meet these requirements if the component is expected to be of particular value to a specific intended recipient, often an HLA-matched donor and if a physician certifies in writing that the donor's health will not be compromised. Donors who have taken aspirin-containing medications within 36 hours of donation are usually deferred because the platelets obtained by apheresis are often the single source of platelets given to a patient. Vasovagal and hypovolemic reactions are rare in apheresis donors, but paresthesias and other reactions to citrate or anticoagulants, are not uncommon (See Complications, later in this chapter). Serious reactions actually occur less often among apheresis donors than among whole blood donors.

Plateletpheresis donors should meet usual donor requirements, including hemoglobin or hematocrit level. A platelet count is not required before the first apheresis collection or if 4 weeks or more have elapsed since the last procedure. If the donation interval is less than 4 weeks, the donor's platelet count should be above 150,000/µL before subsequent plateletpheresis occurs. AABB *Standards* permits documentation of the platelet count from a sample collected immediately before the procedure or from a sample obtained either before or after the previous procedure.[1(p50)] Exceptions to these laboratory criteria should be approved in writing by the apheresis physician. The FDA specifies that the total volume of plasma collected should be no more than 500 mL (or 600 mL for donors weighing more than 175 pounds).[8] The platelet count of each unit should be kept on record, but need not be written on the product label.[8]

Some plateletpheresis programs collect plasma for use as Fresh Frozen Plasma (FFP) in a separate bag during platelet collection. Apheresis can also be used to collect plasma for FFP without platelets, ie, plasmapheresis. In both instances a total serum or plasma protein determination and a quantitative determination of IgG and IgM (or a serum protein electrophoresis) must be determined at 4-month intervals for donors undergoing large-volume plasma collection, if the total annual volume of plasma collected exceeds 12 liters (14.4 L for donors weighing more than 175 pounds).[9,10] The donor's intravascular volume deficit must be less than 10.5 mL per kilogram of body weight at all times.[1(p52)]

Laboratory Testing

Tests for ABO group and Rh type, unexpected alloantibodies, and markers for transfusion-transmitted diseases must be done by the collecting facility in the same manner as for other blood components. Each unit must be tested unless the donor is undergoing repeated procedures to support a single patient, in which case testing for disease markers need be repeated only at 30-day intervals.[1(p53)]

If a unit contains visible red cells, the hematocrit should be determined. FDA guidelines require that, if the component contains more than 2 mL of red cells, a sample of donor blood for compatibility testing be attached to the container.[8] In some instances it may be desirable for the donor plasma to be ABO-compatible with the recipient's red cells, especially if the recipient is a small infant. Quality control of plateletpheresis components is discussed in Chapter 8.

Records

Complete records (see Chapter 1) must be kept for each procedure. All adverse reactions should be documented along with the results of their investigation and follow-up. Records of all laboratory findings and collection data must be periodically reviewed by a knowledgeable physician and found to be within acceptable limits. FDA guidelines require review at least once every 4 months.[8] A cumulative record of red cell losses is required for each donor,[1(p52)] to ensure that red cell loss in a year does not exceed the level of loss permitted for whole blood collection.

Plasma

Apheresis can be used to collect plasma as FFP or for Source Plasma for subsequent manufacturing. FDA requirements for plasma collection are different from those for whole blood or plateletpheresis; personnel who perform serial plasmapheresis must be familiar with both AABB *Standards* and FDA requirements. If plasma is intended for transfusion, testing requirements are the same as those for red cell components. Plasma collected for manufacture of plasma derivatives is subject to different requirements for infectious disease testing.

A distinction is made between "occasional plasmapheresis," in which the donor undergoes plasmapheresis no more often than once in 4 weeks, and "serial plasmapheresis," in which donation is more frequent than every 4 weeks. For donors in an occasional plasmapheresis program, donor selection and monitoring are the same as for whole blood donation. For serial plasmapheresis using either automated instruments or manual techniques, the following principles apply:

1.   Donors must provide informed consent. They must be observed closely during the procedure and emergency medical care must be available.

2.   Red cell losses related to the procedure, including samples collected for testing,

must not exceed 25 mL per week, so that no more than 200 mL of red cells are removed per 8 weeks. If the donor's red cells cannot be returned during an apheresis procedure, hemapheresis or whole blood donation should be deferred for 8 weeks.

3. In manual plasma collection systems, there must be a mechanism to ensure safe reinfusion of the autologous red cells. Before the blood container is separated from the donor for processing, there should be two separate, independent means of identification, so that both the donor and the phlebotomist can ascertain that the contents are those of the donor. Often the donor's signature is one identifier, along with a unique number.

4. In manual procedures on donors weighing 50-80 kg (110-176 lb), no more than 500 mL of whole blood should be removed at one time, or 1000 mL during the session or within a 48-hour period. The limits for donors above 80 kg are 600 mL and 1200 mL, respectively. For automated procedures, the allowable volume has been determined for each instrument by the FDA.[9]

5. At least 48 hours should elapse between successive procedures and donors should not, ordinarily, undergo more than two procedures within a 7-day period. Exceptions are permissible when plasma is expected to have special therapeutic value for a single recipient or if the collection is part of an investigational protocol.

6. At the time of initial plasmapheresis and at 4-month intervals thereafter for donors undergoing plasmapheresis more often than once every 4 weeks, serum or plasma must be tested for total protein and serum protein electrophoresis or quantative immunoglobulins. Results must be within normal limits.[2]

7. A qualified, licensed physician, knowledgeable in all aspects of hemapheresis, must be responsible for the program.

Red Cells

Both AABB *Standards* and FDA-approved protocols address the removal of two allogeneic or autologous red cell units every 16 weeks by an automated apheresis method. Saline infusion is used to minimize volume depletion and the procedure is limited to persons who are larger and have higher hematocrits than current minimum standards for whole blood donors (for males: weight 130 lb, height 5'1"; for females: weight 150 lb, height 5'5"; hematocrit 40% for both sexes).[11]

Granulocytes

The indications for granulocyte transfusion are not well defined. Early studies showed benefit in adults with reversible neutropenia and documented gram-negative infections that did not respond to adequate antibiotic treatment. Experience in marrow transplant patients with fungal infections has been disappointing.[12] A meta-analysis of randomized, controlled trials of granulocyte transfusion indicates that effectiveness depends on an adequate dose ($>1 \times 10^{10}$ granulocytes/day) and crossmatch compatibility (no recipient antibodies to patient antigens).[13] Granulocyte concentrates can induce HLA alloimmunization, may transmit cytomegalovirus infection, and if not irradiated may cause graft-vs-host disease in susceptible recipients. Alloimmunized recipients may sequester HLA-incompatible transfused granulocytes in their lungs and subsequently develop respiratory distress. Prophylactic granulocyte transfusions to adults had been largely abandoned due to pulmonary toxicity and lack of demonstrable efficacy. There is renewed interest in granulocyte transfusion therapy for adults because much larger cell doses can be delivered when cells are collected from donors stimulated with colony-stimulating factors.[14] Some success with granulocyte transfusions has been observed in the treatment of septic infants[15] possibly because the usual dose is relatively larger in these tiny recipients and because HLA alloimmunization is absent.

Drugs Administered for Leukapheresis

A daily dose of at least 1×10^{10} granulocytes is necessary to achieve a therapeutic effect.[16] Collection of this many cells usually requires administration of drugs or other adjuvants to the donor. The donor's consent must include specific permission for any drugs or sedimenting agents to be used.

Hydroxyethyl Starch. A common sedimenting agent, hydroxyethyl starch (HES), causes red cells to aggregate and thereby sediment more completely. Sedimenting agents enhance granulocyte harvest and result in minimal red cell content. Because HES can be detected in donors for as long as a year after infusion, facilities performing granulocyte collections must have a process to control the maximal cumulative dose of any sedimenting agent administered to the donor within a given interval.[1(p52)] Because HES is a colloid, it acts as a volume expander, and donors who have received HES may experience headaches or peripheral edema because of expanded circulatory volume.

Corticosteroids. Corticosteroids can double the number of circulating granulocytes by mobilizing them from the marginal pool. A protocol using 20 mg of oral prednisone at 17, 12, and 2 hours before donation gives superior granulocyte harvests with minimal systemic steroid activity.[17] Before administration of corticosteroids, donors should be questioned about any history of symptoms of hypertension, diabetes, and peptic ulcer.

Growth Factors. Recombinant hematopoietic growth factors, specifically granulocyte colony-stimulating factor, can effectively increase granulocyte yields. Hematopoietic growth factors alone can result in collection of up to 10×10^{10} granulocytes per apheresis procedure. Preliminary evidence suggests that in-vivo recovery and survival of these granulocytes are excellent and that growth factors are well tolerated by donors.[14]

Use of growth factors for stimulation of allogeneic granulocyte donors is not approved by the FDA.

Laboratory Testing

Testing for ABO and Rh, antibody screening, and infectious disease markers on a sample drawn at the time of phlebotomy are required. Red cell content in granulocyte concentrates is inevitable; the red cells should be ABO-compatible with the recipient's plasma and, if more than 2 mL are present, the component should be crossmatched. D-negative recipients should, ideally, receive granulocyte concentrates from D-negative donors.

Storage and Infusion

Because granulocyte function deteriorates during storage, concentrates should be transfused as soon as possible after preparation. AABB *Standards* prescribes a storage temperature of 20-24 C, for no longer than 24 hours.[1(p44)] Agitation during storage is probably undesirable. Irradiation is required before administration to immunodeficient recipients and will probably be indicated for nearly all recipients because of their primary disease. Infusion through a microaggregate filter is contraindicated.

Hematopoietic Progenitor Cells

Cytapheresis for collection of hematopoietic progenitor cells is useful for obtaining progenitor cells for marrow reconstitution in patients with cancer, leukemia in remission, and various lymphomas (see Chapter 25). The AABB has published *Standards for Hematopoietic Progenitor Cells*.[18]

Therapeutic Apheresis

Therapeutic apheresis has been used to treat many different diseases. Cells, plasma, or plasma constituents may be removed from the circulation and replaced by normal plasma, crystalloid, or colloids such as starch, or albumin. The term "therapeutic apheresis" is used for the general procedure and the term "therapeutic plasma exchange" (TPE) is used for procedures in which the goal is removal of plasma, regardless of the solution used as replacement.

The theoretical basis for therapeutic apheresis is to reduce the patient's load of a pathologic substance to levels that will allow improvement. In some conditions, replacement with normal plasma is intended to supply an essential substance that is absent. Other possible outcomes of therapeutic apheresis include alteration of the antigen-to-antibody ratio, modification of mediators of inflammation or immunity, and clearance of immune complexes. Some perceived benefit may be due to a placebo effect. Despite difficulties in documentation, there is general agreement that therapeutic apheresis is effective treatment for some of the conditions listed in Table 6-1 as Category I or Category II.[19-21]

General Considerations

Avoiding overuse or underuse of therapeutic apheresis requires considerable medical knowledge and judgment. The patient should be evaluated for treatment by his or her personal physician and by the apheresis physician. Close consultation between these physicians is important, especially if the patient is small or elderly, has poor vascular access or cardiovascular instability, or has a condition for which apheresis is of uncertain benefit. The apheresis physician should make the final determination about appropriateness of the procedure and suitability of the patient (see Table 6-1).[1(p54),20] When therapeutic apheresis is planned, those involved with the patient's care should establish a treatment plan and the goal of therapy. The end point may be an agreed-upon objective outcome or a predetermined duration for the therapy, whichever is achieved first. It is helpful to document these mutually acceptable goals in the patient's medical record. The nature of the procedure, its expected benefits, its possible risks, and the available alternatives should be explained to the patient by a knowledgeable individual, and the patient's consent should be documented. The procedure should be performed only in a setting where there is ready access to care for untoward reactions, including equipment, medications, and personnel trained in managing serious reactions.

Vascular Access

For most adults needing a limited number of procedures, the antecubital veins are suitable for removal and return of blood. For critically ill adults and for children, indwelling central or peripheral venous catheters are typically used. Especially effective are rigid-wall, large-lumen, double-bore catheters placed in the subclavian, femoral, or internal jugular vein. Catheters of the type used for temporary hemodialysis allow both removal and return of blood at high flow rates. Central catheters can be maintained for weeks if multiple procedures are necessary.

Removal of Pathologic Substances

During TPE, there is continuous removal of plasma that contains the pathologic substance and infusion of replacement fluid. The efficiency with which material is removed can be estimated by calculating the patient's plasma volume and using Fig 6-1. This estimate depends on the following assumptions: 1) the patient's blood volume does not change; 2) mixing occurs immediately; and 3) there is relatively little production or mobilization of the pathologic material during the procedure. As seen in Fig 6-1, removal is greatest early in the procedure and diminishes progressively during the exchange. Exchange is usually limited to 1-1.5 plasma volumes, or approximately 40-60 mL plasma exchanged per kg of body weight in patients with normal hematocrit and average body size. This maximizes the efficacy per procedure but may make it necessary to re-

Table 6-1. Diseases Treated with Apheresis—Treatment Categories in AABB and ASFA Guidelines[21]

Disorder	Procedure	AABB Category	ASFA Category
ABO-incompatible organ or marrow transplant	TPE	III	II
AIDS (symptoms of immunodeficiency)	TPE	IV	NR
Amyotrophic lateral sclerosis	TPE	IV	IV
Aplastic anemia	TPE	IV	III
Bullous pemphigoid	TPE	NR	II
Burn shock, refractory	TPE	III	NR
Cancer (nonhematologic)	TPE/staph protein A	NR	III/III
Chronic inflammatory demyelinating polyneuropathy (CIDP)	TPE	I	I
Coagulation factor inhibitors	TPE	III	II
Cold agglutinin disease	TPE	II	NR
Cryoglobulinemia	TPE	I	I
Cutaneous T-cell lymphoma	Photopheresis/cytapheresis	II/II	I/III
Drug overdose and poisoning (protein bound)	TPE	II	II
Eaton-Lambert syndrome	TPE	II	I
Fabry's disease (glycosphingolipids)	TPE	NR	III
Focal segmental glomerulonephritis	TPE	III	NR
Goodpasture's syndrome	TPE	I	I
Guillian-Barré syndrome	TPE	I	I
Hemolytic transfusion reaction (life-threatening)	Red cell exchange	III	NR
Hemolytic uremic syndrome	TPE	II	II
Hepatic failure (fulminant/acute)	TPE	IV	III
Homozygous familial hypercholesterolemia	TPE/selective removal	I/NR	II/I
Hypereosinophilia	Cytapheresis	IV	NR
Hyperparasitemia (malaria)	Red cell exchange	II	NR
Hyperviscosity	TPE	I	I
Idiopathic thrombocytopenia purpura (ITP)	TPE/staph protein A	IV/III	III/III
Leukemia with hyperleukocytosis syndrome	Cytoreduction	I	I
Leukemia without hyperleukocytosis syndrome	Cytoreduction	IV	NR
Lupus nephritis	TPE	IV	NR
Maternal treatment for hemolytic disease of the newborn (HDN)	TPE	III	III

Table 6-1. Diseases Treated with Apheresis—Treatment Categories in AABB and ASFA Guidelines (cont'd)

Disorder	Procedure	AABB Category	ASFA Category
Multiple sclerosis	TPE/cytapheresis	III	III
Myasthenia gravis	TPE	I	I
Organ transplant rejection	TPE/photopheresis/ cytapheresis	NR/III/III	IV/III/NR
Paraneoplastic syndromes	TPE	NR	III
Paraproteinemic peripheral neuropathy	TPE	NR	II
Pemphigus vulgaris	TPE/photopheresis	II/NR	II/III
Peripherial blood progenitor cells for hematopoietic reconstitution	Cytapheresis	I	NR
Polymyositis/dermatomyositis	TPE/cytapheresis	IV/IV	III-IV*/NR
Posttransfusion purpura	TPE	I	I
Progressive systemic sclerosis	TPE/photopheresis/ lympocytaplasmapheresis	III/III/ NR	III/III/III
Psoriasis	TPE	IV	IV
Quinine/quinidine thrombocytopenia	TPE	II	NR
Rapidly progressive glomerulonephritis	TPE	II	II
Rasmussen's encephalitis	TPE	III	NR
Raynaud's disease	TPE	NR	II
Red cell aplasia	TPE	III	NR
Refsum's disease (phytanic acid)	TPE	I	I
Renal transplant rejection	TPE	IV	IV
Rheumatoid arthritis (RA)	TPE/cytapheresis	IV/III	IV/III
Schizophrenia	TPE	IV	IV
Sickle cell syndromes (prophylactic use in pregnancy)	Red cell exchange	I(III)	I(NR)
Systemic lupus erythematosus (SLE)	TPE	NR	II
Systemic vasculitis (primary or secondary to RA or SLE)	TPE	II	II
Thrombocytosis, symptomatic	Cytoreduction	I	I
Thrombotic thrombocytopenic purpura	TPE	I	I
Thyroid storm	TPE	III	III
Transfusion refractoriness due to alloantibodies	TPE/staph protein A	III/NR	III/III
Warm autoimmune hemolytic anemia	TPE	III	III

*Consensus not reached. NR = disorder not ranked; AABB = American Association of Blood Banks; ASFA = American Society for Apheresis; TPE = therapeutic plasma exchange. Category I = standard acceptable therapy; Category II = sufficient evidence to suggest efficacy usually as adjunctive therapy; Category III = inconclusive evidence of efficacy or uncertain risk/benefit ratio; Category IV = lack of efficacy in controlled trials.

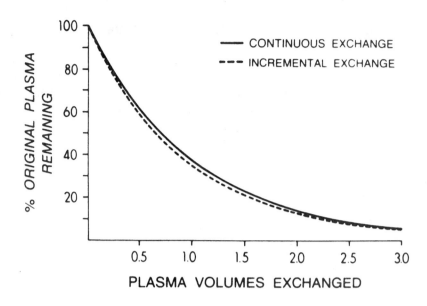

Figure 6-1. The relationship between the volume of plasma exchange and the patient's original plasma remaining.

peat the process. Rarely are two or more plasma volumes exchanged in one procedure. While larger volume exchange causes greater initial diminution of the pathologic substance, overall it is less efficient and requires considerably more time. Larger volume exchanges can increase the risk of coagulopathy, citrate toxicity, or electrolyte imbalance, depending on the replacement fluid.

The rates at which a pathologic substance is synthesized and distributed between intravascular and extravascular compartments affect the outcome of TPE. For example, the abnormal IgM of Waldenstrom's macroglobulinemia is synthesized slowly and remains almost entirely (about 75%) intravascular, making apheresis particularly effective.[22] In contrast, efforts to prevent hydrops fetalis with intensive TPE to lower the mother's level of IgG anti-D have been less successful, in part because about 45% of IgG is in the extravascular fluid and in part because rapid reduction of IgG may cause antibody synthesis to increase rapidly and "rebound" over pretreatment levels.[23] Rebound synthesis may

also complicate TPE treatment of autoimmune diseases. Immunosuppresive agents such as cyclophosphamide, azathioprine, or prednisone may be administered to blunt the IgG rebound response to apheresis.

Plasma removed during TPE should be handled carefully and disposed of properly. Such plasma cannot be used for subsequent manufacture of transfusable plasma derivatives, and must not be shipped interstate without an FDA product license specifically for therapeutic exchange plasma.

Removal of Normal Plasma Constituents

When the quantity of plasma removed during TPE exceeds 1.5 times the plasma volume, different rates of removal and reconstitution are observed for different constituents.[24] For fibrinogen, the third component of complement (C3), and immune complexes, reduction is greater than predicted, with 75-85% of the original substance lost after a one plasma-volume procedure. Normal levels return in 3-4 days. The concentrations of electrolytes, uric acid, Factor VIII, and other proteins, are less affected by a one plasma-volume procedure. A 10% or more decrease in platelet count generally occurs, with 2-4 days needed for a return to preexchange values.[25] Coagulation factors other than fibrinogen generally achieve preapheresis levels within 24 hours. Immunoglobulin removal occurs at about the expected rate of 65% per plasma volume, but recovery patterns vary for different immunoglobulin classes, depending on intravascular distribution and rates of synthesis. (Table 11-3 describes immunoglobulin characteristics.) Plasma IgG levels return to approximately 60% of the pretreatment value within 48 hours because of reequilibration with protein in the extravascular space. These issues are important in planning the frequency of therapeutic procedures. Weekly apheresis permits more complete recovery of normal plasma constituents; daily procedures can be expected to deplete many normal, as well as abnormal, constituents. Also, intensive apheresis reduces the concentration of potentially diagnostic plasma constituents so blood for testing should be drawn before TPE.

Replacement Fluids

The three commonly used replacement solutions are: crystalloids, albumin solutions, and FFP. Table 6-2 presents advantages and disadvantages of each. A combination is often used, the relative proportions being determined by the physician on the basis of the patient's disease and physical condition, the planned frequency of procedures, and cost. Acute treatment of life-threatening conditions usually requires a series of one plasma-volume procedures, often producing significant reduction of coagulation factors. Monitoring the platelet count and fibrinogen level helps determine the need for supplemental platelets or FFP. Because plasma contains citrate, use of FFP does increase the risk of citrate toxicity. Recently, hydroxyethyl starch solutions have been used for partial or full replacement.[26]

Complications

With careful patient selection and attention to technical details, most therapeutic apheresis procedures are completed without complica-

Table 6-2. Comparison of Replacement Fluids

Replacement Solution	Advantages	Disadvantages
Crystalloids	Low cost Hypoallergenic No hepatitis risk	2-3 volumes required Hypo-oncotic No coagulation factors No immunoglobulins
Albumin	Iso-oncotic No contaminating "inflammatory mediators" No hepatitis risk	High cost No coagulation factors No immunoglobulins
Fresh Frozen Plasma	Maintains normal levels of: immunoglobulins complement antithrombin other proteins	Hepatitis, HIV risk Citrate load ABO incompatibility risk Allergic reactions Sensitization

tions. Therapeutic apheresis is often required, however, for patients who are critically ill and at risk for a variety of complications.

Vascular Access. Patients requiring therapeutic apheresis have often been subjected to multiple venipunctures and achieving peripheral vascular access may be difficult. Special venous access, such as surgical placement of an indwelling double-lumen apheresis/dialysis catheter, is often required. Venous access devices may cause further vascular damage, sometimes resulting in thrombosis. Infrequently, they may result in severe complications such as pneumothorax or perforation of the heart or great vessels.[27,28] Other complications include arterial puncture, deep hematomas, and arteriovenous fistula formation. Bacterial colonization often complicates long-term placement and may lead to catheter-associated sepsis, especially in patients receiving steroids or other immunosuppressants. Inadvertent disconnection of catheters may produce hemorrhage or air embolism.

Alteration of Pharmacodynamics. TPE can lower blood levels of drugs, especially those that bind to albumin. Apheresis reduces plasma levels of antibiotics and anticonvulsants, but there is little clinical data suggesting adverse patient outcomes due to apheresis-associated lowering of drug levels. Nevertheless, the pharmacokinetics of all drugs being given to a patient should be considered before starting apheresis, and dosage schedules adjusted if necessary. It is prudent to withhold the administration of drugs scheduled to be given during or up to an hour before apheresis until after the procedure is finished. Removal of plasma cholinesterase may complicate the administration of anesthetic agents such as succinyl choline in the immediate postexchange period.

Hypocalcemia. Most patients and donors with normal parathyroid and liver function maintain calcium homeostasis during apheresis. Symptoms of reduced plasma levels of ionized calcium (perioral paresthesias, tingling, a feeling of vibrations) reflect the rate at which citrate anticoagulant is returned, ionized and bound calcium are removed, and ionized calcium is bound to "calcium-stripped" albumin replacement. Hyperventilation, hypothermia, hypomagnesemia, and the use of FFP as a replacement solution exacerbate citrate toxicity. Hypocalcemia can usually be controlled by reducing the proportion of citrate or slowing the reinfusion rate. If untreated, symptoms may progress to muscle twitching, chills, pressure in the chest, nausea, vomiting, and hypotension. Low ionized calcium concentrations can induce severe cardiac arrhythmias. Asking the patient to report any vibrations or tingling sensations can help determine the appropriate reinfusion rate. Extra precautions must be taken in patients who are unable to communicate or who may metabolize citrate poorly (eg, those with liver failure). Hypocalcemic toxicity can usually be managed by administering oral calcium carbonate or intravenous calcium.[21(p235-238),27]

Circulatory Effects. Hypovolemia and subsequent hypotension may occur during apheresis, especially when the volume of extracorporeal blood exceeds 15% of the total blood volume. Hypotension tends to occur in ill children, the elderly, neurology patients, anemic patients and those treated with intermittent-flow devices that have large extracorporeal volumes. Continuous-flow devices typically do not require large extracorporeal volumes, but can produce hypovolemia if return flow is inadvertently diverted to a waste collection bag, either through operator oversight or mechanical or software failures. Hypovolemia may also be secondary to inadequate volume replacement. During all procedures it is essential to maintain careful and continuous records of the volumes removed and returned. Use of antihypertensive medications, especially angiotensin-converting enzyme (ACE) inhibitors combined with albumin replacement, may also contribute to hypovolemic reactions (see Chapter 27). Patients taking agents that inhibit ACEs have experienced severe hypotensive episodes when treated with SPA columns and with other immunosorbents.[28] Patients should not have received these medications for 72 hours before undergoing immunoabsorption treatment. Because infusion of cold fluids through a central venous catheter may induce arrhythmias, some programs use blood warmers for selected patients.

Infections. Fresh Frozen Plasma is the only commonly used replacement solution with the risk of transmitting infectious viruses. Bacterial colonization and infection related to repeated apheresis usually arise from within the vascular catheter. Intensive apheresis regimens decrease levels of immunoglobulins and the opsonic components of complement. In addition, immunosuppressive drugs to prevent rebound antibody production may further compromise defense mechanisms. Induced immunosuppression superimposed on the patient's underlying condition often results in increased susceptibility to infections.

Mechanical Hemolysis and Equipment Failures. Collapsed or kinked tubing, malfunctioning pinch valves, or improper threading of tubing may damage donor or patient red cells in the extracorporeal circuit. Machine-related hemolysis was observed in 0.07% of over 195,000 apheresis procedures performed in the United Kingdom.[29]

Hemolysis can also occur with incompatible replacement fluids such as D5W (eg, D5W used to dilute 25% albumin) or ABO-discrepant plasma. The operator should carefully observe plasma collection lines for pink discoloration suggestive of hemolysis. Other types of equipment failure, such as problems with the rotating seal, leaks in the plastic, and roller pump failure, are rare.[30]

Allergic Reactions and Respiratory Distress. Respiratory difficulty during or immediately following apheresis can have many causes: pulmonary edema, massive pulmonary embolus, obstruction of the pulmonary microvasculature, anaphylactic reactions, and transfusion-related acute lung injury. Hemothorax or hemopericardium due to vascular erosion by a central venous catheter is typically unsuspected yet may be fatal.[31,32] Pulmonary edema that results from volume overload or cardiac failure is usually associated with dyspnea, an increase in the diastolic blood pressure, and characteristic chest X-ray findings. Acute pulmonary edema can also arise from damage to alveolar capillary membranes secondary to an immune reaction or to vasoactive substances in FFP or colloid solutions prepared from human plasma. Use of FFP as a replacement fluid has been associated with complement activation and with allergic reactions that produce urticaria, swelling of oral mucosa, and bronchospasm; these usually respond to antihistamines and corticosteroids. Predominantly ocular (periorbital edema, chemosis and tearing) reactions have occurred in donors sensitized to the ethylene oxide gas used to sterilize disposable plastic apheresis kits.[33]

Fatalities During Apheresis. Despite the fact that patients undergoing therapeutic apheresis are often critically ill, fatalities during apheresis are comparatively rare. Estimates of case fatality rates range from 3 in 10,000[34] to 1 in 500.[35] Most deaths were due to cardiac arrhythmias or arrest during or shortly after the procedure or to acute pulmonary edema or adult respiratory distress syndrome occurring during a procedure. Rare fatalities resulted from anaphylaxis, vascular perforation, hepatitis, sepsis, thrombosis, and hemorrhage.

Indications for Therapeutic Apheresis

Although therapeutic apheresis has been used in the treatment of many diseases, most published studies are case reports or small uncontrolled series, often providing insufficient evidence of efficacy. Publication bias tends to favor positive results, and physicians should avoid subjecting patients to the high costs and risks of apheresis procedures based on marginal clinical studies. Controlled, randomized, blinded studies of therapeutic apheresis are difficult to conduct, especially because using sham treatments as a control is expensive and carries some risk. However, the complicated apheresis instruments and associated attention from nursing and medical personnel may well create or amplify a placebo effect and bias the evaluation of clinical improvement.

For many of the diseases being treated, the etiology, pathogenesis, and natural history are incompletely understood, and reductions in such measured variables as complement components, rheumatoid factor, or immune complexes cannot reliably be correlated with changes in disease activity. An example is the use of the erythrocyte sedimentation rate (ESR) as an index of rheumatoid activity. The ESR invariably decreases during intensive TPE, but this reflects removal of fibrinogen and not necessarily a decrease in disease activity. For the same reasons, the optimal volume and frequency of exchange are often not established. For severe imminently life-threatening disease, when albumin/saline is the replacement fluid, TPE is initially performed daily. After a few days the fibrinogen or platelet count may be low enough to significantly increase the risk of bleeding. Clinical judgment must then be exercised to decide whether to proceed with TPE using clotting factor/platelet transfusions, or to withhold TPE until the patient rebounds. The conditions discussed below are established indications for therapeutic apheresis.[20,36,37]

Hematologic Conditions

Serum Hyperviscosity Syndrome. Serum hyperviscosity resulting from multiple myeloma or Waldenstrom's macroglobulinemia can cause congestive heart failure; reduced blood flow to the cerebral, cardiac, or pulmonary circulation; or symptoms of headache, vertigo, somnolence, or obtundation. Paraproteins may interfere with hemostasis, leading to hemorrhagic symptoms.

The presence of hyperviscosity correlates only in very general terms with the concentration of paraprotein. Measurement of serum viscosity relative to water is a simple procedure that provides more objective information. For some pathologic proteins serum viscosity is highly temperature dependent, so serum viscosity should be measured at physiologically relevant temperatures. Normal serum viscosity ranges from 1.4 to 1.8 relative to water. Because most patients are not symptomatic until their relative serum viscosity is more than 4.0 or 5.0, patients with mild elevations may not require treatment. For symptomatic hyperviscosity, a single apheresis procedure is usually highly effective.[22]

Hyperleukocytosis. Leukapheresis is often used to treat the dramatically elevated white cell count that can occur in acute leukemia. Several different thresholds have been used: fractional volume of leukocytes (leukocrit) above 20%; total circulating leukocytes above 100,000/μL; and circulating blasts above 50,000/μL.[38] The use of a single laboratory value as an indication for treatment is, however, an oversimplification. Such factors as erythrocyte concentration, leukemic cell type, rate at which the count is rising, potential obstructions to cerebral or pulmonary blood flow, and the patient's coagulation status and general condition must be considered. Most leukemic patients with extreme leukocytosis have significant anemia. Reduced red cell mass reduces blood viscosity, so unless there is an acute need to increase oxygen-carrying capacity, red cells should not be transfused until the leukocytic hyperviscosity crisis is resolved.[38]

In some patients with acute blast crisis or in unusual types of leukemia, both the hematocrit and leukocrit are elevated. If there is evidence of cerebral or pulmonary symptoms, rapid reduction of leukocyte concentration should be considered, although the efficacy of such leukocyte reduction is unproved. More commonly, however, the white cell count rises over weeks or longer, and leukocyte reduction can be effected with chemotherapy, with or without leukapheresis. Leukapheresis is sometimes used to reduce the white cell count to <100,000/μL before the start of chemotherapy, to reduce the likelihood of tumor lysis syndrome. However, there have been no controlled clinical trials to substantiate this approach, and it must be recognized that more malignant cells are present outside the circulation than within the bloodstream.

Thrombocythemia. Therapeutic plateletpheresis is usually undertaken for symptomatic patients with platelet counts above 1,000,000/μL, but the measured count should not, by itself, determine whether platelet reduction is indicated. In patients with evidence of thrombosis or bleeding secondary to thrombocythemia, plateletpheresis can be beneficial. There are no accepted indications for prophylactic plateletpheresis in asymptomatic patients, although the risk of placental infarction and fetal death may justify the procedure in a pregnant woman with severe thrombocythemia.[38]

Thrombotic Thrombocytopenic Purpura/ Hemolytic Uremic Syndrome (TTP/HUS). The conditions described as TTP/HUS are multisystem disorders, in which platelet/fibrin thrombi occlude the microcirculation. They are characterized by varying degrees of thrombocytopenia, microangiopathic hemolytic anemia, renal dysfunction, neurologic abnormalities, and fever. Patients presenting with fulminant TTP usually have platelet counts below 50,000/μL and lactic dehydrogenase (LDH) levels above 1000 IU/mL, resulting from systemic ischemia.[39] The peripheral blood smear characteristically shows increased numbers of schistocytes. Evidence for disseminated intravascular coagulation is generally absent.

TTP usually develops without obvious cause, although episodes may occur after infections, pregnancy, organ transplantation, or following some drug therapies. Recent reports suggest that it is caused by transient antibody to a protease that normally cleaves large von Willebrand factor (vWF) multimers. The unusually large vWF multimers agglutinate circulating platelets, triggering the syndrome.[40,41]

Increasingly, cases of recurrent or relapsing TTP are being recognized. HUS is a similar condition that occurs more commonly in children than adults. HUS may follow diarrheal infections with verotoxin-secreting strains of *Escherichia coli* (strain 0157:H7) or *Shigella*. Compared with patients who have classic TTP, those with HUS have more renal dysfunction and less prominent neurologic and hematologic findings. Most cases do not have antibody to the vWF protease. TTP/HUS can occur after treatment with certain immunosuppressive drugs, including mitomycin C and cyclosporine. Drug-associated TTP/HUS appears to be less responsive to therapy than other variants.

TPE with FFP or Plasma, Cryoprecipitate-Reduced replacement has become the treatment of choice for TTP/HUS.[42] TPE is now thought to remove antibody to the protease and removes substances injurious to endothelial cells and restores a plasma environment that does not promote the development of microthrombi at least in part by removing antibody to protease and large vWF multimers, as well as supplying normal protease. Other largely unproved treatments include prednisone, antiplatelet agents, splenectomy, vincristine, and intravenous immunoglobulin. Because platelet transfusions have anecdotally been associated with disease exacerbation and death, they are contraindicated.

TPE is often performed daily for 1-2 weeks, but the intensity and duration of treatment should be guided by the individual patient's course. Occasionally, prolonged courses of treatment are required. Different forms of plasma may be used as replacement fluid. Many centers replace with FFP, but Plasma, Cryoprecipitate-Removed, solvent/detergent-treated plasma, and stored liquid plasma have also been used.[43]

Therapeutic plasma exchange has impressively improved the survival rate in TTP, from being almost universally fatal before 1964 to 80% survival in a recent series.[42] Signs of response to therapy include a rising platelet count and diminishing elevation of LDH between procedures. As patients recover to near normal LDH and platelet count (100-150,000/μL), TPE is gradually discontinued. Some programs switch from intensive TPE to intermittent plasma exchange or simple plasma infusion, but the efficacy of such a taper has not been established. Despite the success of TPE, TTP/HUS remains a serious condition. Treatment failures continue to occur and to cause major organ damage or death.

Complications of Sickle Cell Disease. Several complications of sickle cell disease are syndromes that can be treated by red cell exchange; these include priapism, stroke or impending stroke, acute chest syndrome, and multiorgan failure. Either manual or automated techniques can be used for red cell exchange, but automated techniques are faster. The goal is to replace red cells containing hemoglobin S with a sufficient number of red cells containing hemoglobin A so that the overall proportion of hemoglobin A in the blood is 60-80%. Many centers select red cells that match the recipient's phenotype for as many antigens as possible, to avoid alloimmunizing these long-term transfusion recipients. At the end of the procedure the patient's hematocrit should be no higher than 30-35% to avoid increased blood viscosity.

Cryoglobulinemia

Significant elevations of cryoglobulins may cause cold-induced vascular occlusion, abnormalities of coagulation, renal insufficiency, or peripheral nerve damage. Removal of cryoglobulins by apheresis can be used to treat acute symptomatic episodes, but definitive therapy depends on identifying and treating the underlying causative condition.

Neurologic Conditions

Myasthenia Gravis. Myasthenia gravis results from autoantibody-mediated blockade of the acetylcholine receptor located on the postsynaptic motor endplate of muscles. Standard treatment includes steroids and acetylcholinesterase inhibitors. TPE is used as adjunctive treatment for patients experiencing exacerbations not controlled by medications and for patients being prepared for thymectomy. A typical treatment protocol is five or six TPE procedures over 1-2 weeks. Concurrent immunosuppression to prevent antibody rebound is recommended. Chronic TPE has been utilized with some success in a small number of patients.

Acute Guillain-Barré Syndrome. Guillain-Barré syndrome is an acute autoimmune demyelinating polyneuropathy that can produce dramatic paralysis in otherwise healthy individuals. The cause is unknown; many cases appear to follow benign viral infections or *Campylobacter jejuni* infection. Most patients recover spontaneously, but as many as one in six may become unable to walk or may develop respiratory failure requiring ventilatory support. Early treatment is beneficial for patients with rapidly progressive disease, and response to therapy is less in patients who remain untreated for several weeks. Recent controlled studies suggest that intravenous immunoglobulin gives results equivalent to five TPE procedures over a 2-week period.[44] Multicenter trials have suggested that TPE, if initiated early, can decrease the period of minimal sensorimotor function.[45] Patients whose illness is not acute in onset or is not characteristic of Guillain-Barré syndrome, or in whom nerve conduction studies show complete axonal block, may have a poorer prognosis and less response to apheresis therapy.

Chronic Inflammatory Demyelinating Polyneuropathy. Chronic inflammatory demyelinating polyneuropathy (CIDP), often seen in HIV patients, is a group of disorders with slow onset and progressive or intermittent course, characterized by elevated spinal fluid protein, marked slowing of nerve conduction velocity, and segmental demyelination of peripheral nerves. A variety of sensorimotor abnormalities result. A variant condition, called the POEMS syndrome, is characterized by polyneuropathy, organomegaly, endocrinopathy, an *M*-protein, and skin changes. CIDP is less responsive to treatment than Guillain-Barré syndrome; it may be idiopathic or associated with benign monoclonal gammopathies. Corticosteroids are the first treatment for CIDP. TPE and intravenous immunoglobulin have equivalent efficacy in patients unresponsive to corticosteroids.[46]

Polyneuropathy Associated with Monoclonal Gammopathy of Undetermined Significance. When polyneuropathy is associated with monoclonal paraproteins of uncertain significance, TPE has been shown to be effective for all variants.[47,48]

Renal Diseases

Rapidly progressive glomerulonephritis (RPGN) associated with antibodies to basement membranes of glomeruli and alveoli, which may result in pulmonary hemorrhage (Goodpasture's disease), usually responds to TPE as an adjunct to immunosuppressive drugs.[36] TPE accelerates the disappearance of antibodies to basement membranes and improves renal function. Therapeutic apheresis has been used in treating the vasculitis associated with RPGN and the presence of antineutrophil cytoplasmic antibody (ANCA-positive RPGN).[49,50] TPE is most effective in the more severe cases.[36]

Myeloma light chains may be toxic to renal tubular epithelium and cause renal failure in up to 10% of cases. TPE is useful as adjunctive therapy in some myeloma cast nephropathy patients but is not associated with improved survival.[36,51]

Other Conditions

TPE has been used as adjunctive treatment for a variety of multisystem diseases. A combination of steroid, cytotoxic agents, and TPE has been used for severely ill patients with polyarteritis nodosa,[52] although most rheumatologic conditions are poorly responsive to TPE. Clinical trials have not shown benefit in the treatment of systemic lupus erythematosus, polymyositis, dermatomyositis, scleroderma, or rheumatoid arthritis.[20]

Homozygous Type II Familial Hypercholesterolemia. Homozygous hypercholesterolemia, a rare disorder of the receptor for low-density lipoproteins, results in severe premature atherosclerosis and early death from coronary artery disease. Prolonged reduction in circulating lipids can be achieved with repeated TPE, often with selective adsorption or filtration techniques.[38] Heterozygous hypercholesterolemia results from several gene defects in the LDL receptor. Some patients with heterozygous hypercholesterolemia also develop high levels of cholesterol and are at increased risk for developing premature atherosclerotic heart disease. Although some of these patients respond to cholesterol-lowering drugs, others may require repeated TPE for control of cholesterol.

Refsum's Disease (Phytanic Acid Disease). Refsum's disease is a rare inborn error of metabolism having toxic levels of phytanic acid, causing neurologic, cardiac, skeletal, and skin abnormalities.[20] TPE is useful in conjunction with a phytanic acid deficient diet and should be started as soon as possible, before permanent damage occurs.

Immune Thrombocytopenia. SPA immunoadsorption is approved by the FDA for treatment of acute and chronic immune thrombocytopenic purpura. Although not FDA-approved, this technique has also been used, with limited success, to treat other auto-immune thrombocytopenias.[53] Many of these protocols are still experimental and random-ized trials have not been done.

Photopheresis

Photopheresis is a technique that separates lymphocytes by apheresis, adds psoralens or other light-activated DNA denaturants, and then subjects the treated cells to ultraviolet ra-diation. This renders the lymphocytes and other nucleated cells incapable of division. The treated cells are then reinfused. This proce-dure, also known as extracorporeal photochemotherapy, has been approved by the FDA for the treatment of cutaneous T-cell lym-phoma and is considered the first line of treat-ment for the erythrodermic phase of this disease.[54]

Periodic Review

A group of responsible physicians (in many in-stitutions, the Hospital Transfusion Commit-tee) should establish and monitor the policies relating to therapeutic apheresis, review the indications for treatment, and maintain sur-veillance of all adverse outcomes.[19] For a re-gional blood center, a Medical Advisory Committee could serve this function.

References

1. Menitove JE, ed. Standards for blood banks and transfusion services. 19th ed. Bethesda, MD: Amer-ican Association of Blood Banks, 1999.
2. Code of federal regulations. Title 21 CFR Part 640. Washington, DC: US Government Printing Office, 1998 (revised annually).
3. American Society for Apheresis. Organizational guidelines for therapeutic apheresis facilities. J Clin Apheresis 1996;11:42-5.
4. Burgstaler EA. Current instrumentation for apheresis. In: McLeod BC, Price TH, Drew MJ, eds. Apheresis: Principles and practice. Bethesda, MD: AABB Press, 1997:85-112.
5. Ciavarella D. Blood processors and cell separators. Transfus Sci 1989;10:165-84.
6. Pineda AA. New apheresis technologies. In: Westphal RG, Kasprisin DO, eds. Current status of hemapheresis: Indications, technology and com-plications. Arlington, VA: American Association of Blood Banks, 1987:71-86.
7. Berger GM, Firth JC, Jacobs P, et al. Three different schedules of low-density lipoprotein apheresis compared with plasmapheresis in patients with ho-mozygous familial hypercholesterolemia. Am J Med 1990;88:94-100.
8. Food and Drug Administration. Memorandum: Re-vised guideline for the collection of Platelets, Pheresis. October 7, 1988. Rockville, MD: CBER Of-fice of Communication, Training, and Manufac-turer's Assistance, 1988.
9. Food and Drug Administration. Memorandum: Volume limits for automated collection of source plasma. November 4, 1992. Rockville, MD: CBER Office of Communication, Training, and Manufac-turer's Assistance, 1992.
10. Food and Drug Administration. Memorandum: Re-quirements for infrequent plasmapheresis donors. March 10, 1995. Rockville, MD: CBER Office of Communication, Training, and Manufacturer's As-sistance, 1995.
11. Food and Drug Administration. Guidance for industry: Recommendations for collecting red blood cells by automated apheresis methods (draft). July 1998. Rockville, MD: CBER Office of Communication, Training, and Manufacturer's As-sistance, 1998.
12. Bhatia S, McCullough J, Perry EH, et al. Granulocyte transfusions: Efficacy in treating fun-gal infections in neutropenic patients following bone marrow transplantation. Transfusion 1994;34:226-32.
13. Vamvakas EC, Pineda AA. Determinants of the effi-cacy of prophylactic granulocyte transfusions: A meta-analysis. J Clin Apheresis 1997;12:74-81.
14. Bandarenko N, Owen HG, Mair DC, Brecher ME. Apheresis: New opportunities. Clin Lab Med 1996;16:907-29.
15. Strauss RG. Granulocyte transfusions. In: Rossi EC, Simon TL, Moss GS, Gould SA, eds. Principles of transfusion medicine. 2nd ed. Baltimore, MD: Williams and Wilkins, 1995:321-8.
16. McCullough J. Granulocyte transfusion. In: Petz LD, Swisher SN, Kleinman S, et al, eds. Clinical practice of transfusion medicine. 2nd ed. New York: Churchill-Livingstone, 1996:413-32.
17. Barnes A, DeRoos A. Increased granulocyte yields obtained with an oral three-dose prednisone premedication schedule (abstract). Am J Clin Pathol 1982;78:267.
18. Menitove JE, ed. Standards for hematopoietic pro-genitor cells. 1st ed. Bethesda, MD: American Asso-ciation of Blood Banks, 1996.
19. AABB Extracorporeal Therapy Committee. Guide-lines for therapeutic hemapheresis. Bethesda, MD: American Association of Blood Banks, 1992.
20. Strauss RG, Ciavarella D, Gilcher RO, et al. An over-view of current management. J Clin Apheresis 1993;8:189-272.
21. Owen HG, Brecher ME. Management of the thera-peutic apheresis patient. In: McLeod BC, Price TH, Drew MJ, eds. Apheresis: Principles and practice. Bethesda, MD: AABB Press, 1997:225-6.
22. Hillyer CD, Berkman EM. Plasma exchange in the dysproteinemias. In: Rossi EC, Simon TL, Moss GS, Gould SA, eds. Principles of transfusion medicine.

2nd ed. Baltimore,MD: Williams and Wilkins, 1995:569-75.

23. Williams WJ, Katz VL, Bowes WA. Plasmapheresis during pregnancy. Obstet Gynecol 1990;76:451-7.

24. Orlin JB, Berkman EM. Partial plasma replacement: Removal and recovery of normal plasma constituents. Blood 1980;56:1055-9.

25. Weinstein R. Basic principles of therapeutic blood exchange. In: McLeod BC, Price TH, Drew MJ, eds. Apheresis: Principles and practice. Bethesda, MD: AABB Press, 1997:279.

26. Brecher ME, Owen HG, Bandarenko N. Alternatives to albumin: Starch replacement for plasma exchange. J Clin Apheresis 1997;12:146-53.

27. Weinstein R. Prevention of citrate reactions during therapeutic plasma exchange by constant infusion of calcium gluconate with the return fluid. J Clin Apheresis 1996;11:204-10.

28. Olbricht CJ, Schaumann D, Fischer D. Anaphylactoid reactions, LDL apheresis with dextran sulphate, and ACE inhibitors. Lancet 1993;341:60-1.

29. Robinson A. Untoward reactions and incidents in machine donor apheresis. Transfusion Today 1990;7:7-8.

30. Westphal RG. Complications of hemapheresis. In: Westphal RG, Kasprisin DO, eds. Current status of hemapheresis: Indications, technology and complications. Arlington, VA: American Association of Blood Banks, 1987:87-104.

31. Duntley P, Siever J, Korwes, ML, et al. Vascular erosion by central venous catheters. Clinical features and outcome. Chest 1992;101:1633-8.

32. Quillen K, Magarace L, Flanagan J, Berkman EM. Vascular erosion caused by a double-lumen central venous catheter during therapeutic plasma exchange. Transfusion 1995;35:510-2.

33. Leitman SF, Boltansky H, Alter HJ, et al. Allergic reactions in healthy plateletpheresis donors caused by sensitization to ethylene oxide gas. N Engl J Med 1986;315:1192-6.

34. Gilcher RO. Apheresis: Principles and practices. In: Rossi EC, Simon TL, Moss GS, Gould SA, eds. Principles of transfusion medicine. 2nd ed. Baltimore, MD: Williams and Wilkins, 1995:537-46.

35. Schmitt E, Kundt G, Klinkmann H. Three years with a national apheresis registry. J Clin Apheresis 1992;7:58-72.

36. Madore F, Lazarus JM, Brady HR. Therapeutic plasma exchange in renal diseases. J Am Soc Nephrol 1996;7:367-86.

37. McLeod BC, Price TH, Drew MJ, eds. Apheresis: Principles and practice. Bethesda, MD: AABB Press, 1997.

38. Klein HG. Principles of apheresis. In: Anderson KC, Ness PM, eds. Scientific basis of transfusion medicine. Philadelphia: WB Saunders, 1994:781-96.

39. Cohen JA, Brecher ME, Bandarenko N. Cellular source of serum lactate dehydrogenase elevation in patients with thrombotic thrombocytopenic purpura. J Clin Apheresis 1998;13:16-9.

40. Furlan M, Robles R, Galbusera M, et al. von Willebrand factor-cleaving protease in thrombotic thrombocytopenic purpura and the hemolytic-uremic syndrome. N Engl J Med 1998;339:1578-84.

41. Tsai H-M, Chun-Yet Lian E. Antibodies to von Willebrand factor-cleaving protease in acute thrombotic thrombocytopenic purpura. N Engl J Med 1998;339:1585-94.

42. George JN, El-Harake M. Thrombocytopenia due to enhanced platelet destruction by nonimmunologic mechanisms. In: Beutler E, Lichtman MA, Coller BS, Kipps TS, eds. Williams' hematology. 5th ed. New York: McGraw-Hill, 1995:1290-1315.

43. Rock G, Shumak KH, Sutton DM, et al. Cryosupernatant as replacement fluid for plasma exchange in thrombotic thrombocytopenic purpura. Br J Haematol 1996;94:383-6.

44. Plasma exchange/Sandoglobulin Guillain-Barré syndrome trial group. Randomised trial of plasma exchange, intravenous immunoglobulin, and combined treatments in Guillain-Barré syndrome. Lancet 1997;349:225-30.

45. Guillain-Barré syndrome study group. Plasmapheresis and acute Guillain-Barré syndrome. Neurology 1985;35:1096-104.

46. vanDoorn PA, Vermeulen M, Brand A. Intravenous immunoglobulin treatment in patients with chronic inflammatory demyelinating polyneuropathy. Arch Neurol 1991;48:217-20.

47. Dyck PJ, Low PA, Windebank AJ, et al. Plasma exchange in polyneuropathy associated with monoclonal gammopathy of undetermined significance. N Engl J Med 1991;325:1482-6.

48. Simovic D, Gorson KC, Popper AH. Comparison of IgM-MGUS and IgG-MGUS polyneuropathy. Acta Neurol Scand 1998;97:194-200.

49. Frasca GM, Zoumparidis NG, Borgnino LC, et al. Plasma exchange treatment in rapidly progressive glomerulonephritis associated with anti-neutrophil cytoplasmic autoantibodies. Int J Artif Organs 1992;3:181-4.

50. Pusey CD, Rees AJ, Evans JJ, et al. A randomized controlled trial of plasma exchange in rapidly progressive glomerulonephritis without anti-GBM antibodies. Kidney Int 1991;40:757-63.

51. Johnson WJ, Kyle RA, Pineda AA, et al. Treatment of renal failure associated with multiple myeloma. Arch Intern Med 1990;150:863-9.

52. Guillevin L, Lhote F, Leon A, et al. Treatment of polyarteritis nodosa related to hepatitis B virus with short-term steroid therapy associated with antiviral agents and plasma exchanges: A prospective trial in 33 patients (abstract). J Clin Apheresis 1993;8:39.

53. Handelsman H. Office of health technology assessment report, No. 7. Protein A columns for the treatment of patients with idiopathic thrombocytopenic purpura and other indications. Rockville, MD: DHHS, PHS, Agency for Health Care Policy and Research, 1991:1-8.

54. Lim HW, Edelson RL. Photopheresis for treatment of cutaneous T-cell lymphoma. Hematol Oncol Clin N Am 1995;9:1117-26.

7

Blood Component Testing and Labeling

EACH DONOR UNIT MUST BE TESTED prior to release for crossmatch and transfusion. Although the scope and characteristics of donor tests have changed over the years, the intent of donor testing, ie, safety of the blood supply, has remained constant. This chapter presents the general principles that apply to testing and labeling of donor blood. Discussion of the infectious complications of blood transfusion is found in Chapter 28. Other aspects of component preparation are covered in Chapter 8.

Testing

General Requirements

Each test on donor blood must be performed strictly in compliance with current instructions provided by the manufacturer of the test materials and equipment in use. If a facility uses reagents or equipment from several different manufacturers, the most current applicable instructions must be followed and the suitability of the equipment or reagent combination must be validated. For tests required by the Food and Drug Administration (FDA) and/or AABB *Standards for Blood Banks and Transfusion Services,*[1] all reagents used must meet or exceed the requirements of the FDA. If controls are supplied by the manufacturer of a licensed test, they must be used for that test. Acceptable sample (specimen) requirements are defined by the manufacturer and considerations usually include the presence and nature of anticoagulant, the age of the sample, and permissible storage intervals and conditions. Tests must be performed on a properly identified sample from the current donation. Each whole blood donation intended for allogeneic use must undergo complete testing. Each test result must be recorded immediately after observation; interpretation is to be recorded only when testing is completed. Testing results must be recorded and records maintained so that any results can be traced for a specific unit and/or component.

Additionally, donors must be notified of any medically significant abnormality detected as a result of laboratory testing. Test results are confidential and must not be released to anyone (other than the donor) without the donor's written consent. At the time of donation, the donor must be told if the policy is to release positive test results to state or local public health agencies, and the donor must agree to those conditions before phlebotomy. In the case of a minor, it is the parent or guardian who gives permission for the phlebotomy and who may receive notification of test results, depending on state or local laws/regulations.

Required Tests

Each donation intended for allogeneic use must be tested for ABO and D. A sample from each donation must be tested for: syphilis; hepatitis B surface antigen (HBsAg); human immunodeficiency virus (HIV) antigen; antibodies to HIV-1, HIV-2, hepatitis B core antigen (HBc), hepatitis C virus (HCV), and human T-cell lymphotropic virus (HTLV I/II).[1(p31)] A combination test for anti-HIV-1/2 may be used. The test for alanine aminotransferase (ALT) is not required.

Equipment Requirements

All equipment used for testing must be properly calibrated and validated upon installation, after repairs, and periodically. There must be a schedule for planned maintenance. All calibra-

tion, maintenance and repair activities must be documented for each instrument. Software used to control the instrument or to interface with the institution's computer system must also be properly validated.

Records Requirements

It must be possible to trace, from its source to its final disposition, any unit of blood and every component from each unit. Records on donor units and recipients must make it possible to investigate adverse consequences to a recipient.

Previous donor records must not be used in place of testing samples from a current donation intended for allogeneic or autologous use. Previous records of a donor's ABO and D typing results must not be used for final labeling of a unit of blood. However, they must be reviewed and compared with the ABO and D test findings on the current donation. If a discrepancy is found between any current or historic test required, the unit must not be used until there is unequivocal resolution of the discrepancy.[1(p35)]

ABO and D Testing

Every unit of blood intended for transfusion must be tested for ABO and D.[2] ABO group must be determined by testing donor red cells with reagent anti-A and anti-B, and donor serum or plasma with A_1 and B red cells. The Rh type must be determined by testing donor red cells with anti-D serum. Red cells nonreactive with anti-D in direct agglutination tests must be tested by a method designed to detect weak D. Red cells reactive with anti-D either by direct agglutination or by the weak D test must be labeled Rh positive. Red cells nonreactive with anti-D by direct agglutination and the weak D test must be labeled Rh negative.

In general, ABO and D testing follows the principle of combining reagent red cells or antisera with donor cells or serum; centrifugation and dispersion of cell suspension; and observation for agglutination. Testing systems most often consist of slides, tubes, microplates (solid phase or liquid), or column agglutination test, eg, gel, etc. See Chapter 13 and Chapter 14 for a more complete discussion of the principles of ABO and D testing.

Antibody Screening

Blood from donors with a history of transfusion or pregnancy should be tested for unexpected antibodies. Because it is usually impractical to segregate blood that should be tested from units that need not be tested, most blood centers test all donor units for unexpected red cell antibodies. Donor serum or plasma may be tested against individual or pooled reagent red cells of known phenotypes. Methods must be those that demonstrate clinically significant red cell antibodies. Several different methods and media can be used to test for donor antibodies. These include incubating donor serum/plasma with reagent red cells in the following types of media: albumin, saline, low-ionic-strength saline (LISS) and polyethylene glycol (PEG). The reagent screening cells should express at least the following antigens: D, C, E, c, e, K, k, Fy^a, Fy^b, Jk^a, Jk^b, Le^a, Le^b, $P1(P_1)$, M, N, S, and s. See Methods Section 3 for antibody detection techniques and Chapter 18 (Pretransfusion Testing) for a discussion of antibody detection.

Most donor centers perform ABO and D typing and antibody screening at the same time because all tests involve red cell antibody-antigen interactions. Automated instruments for typing large numbers of blood samples and detecting red cell antibodies are also available.

Some of the automated techniques have sufficient D sensitivity to obviate the need of a weak D test. These instruments add reagents, incubate reagent and sample appropriately, read the reaction, and provide a result ready for interpretation. In addition, the automated devices incorporate positive sample identification with the use of barcode readers and use anticoagulated blood so that only one tube is needed for both red cell and plasma sampling.

Serologic Test for Syphilis

Syphilis testing has been carried out on donor samples for many years, even though the spirochete, *Treponema pallidum*, is viable for only approximately 96 hours in stored blood.[3]

The most commonly used screening tool detects an antibody sometimes called "reagin," which is directed against cardiolipin, a widely distributed lipoidal antigen. Anticardiolipin characteristically develops in persons who have had untreated syphilitic infection, but these antibodies may also develop, usually transiently, after infection with various bacteria or viruses or after immunization procedures. Persistent anticardiolipin sometimes occurs in patients with autoimmune disorders, especially systemic lupus erythematosus.

The rapid plasma reagin (RPR) test uses cardiolipin-coated carbon particles, which are readily agglutinated upon addition of unheated serum containing the antibody. Unheated serum mixed with the reagent suspension of cardiolipin-coated carbon particles is placed on a plastic-coated white card, which is rotated at room temperature. If the serum contains antibodies, easily visible flocculent black clumps will form against the white background. If antibodies are absent, or below the level of detection, the mixture will remain a homogeneous gray suspension.

Serum that causes agglutination of cardiolipin-coated particles can be tested for the presence of specific antibodies against *T. pallidum* antigens. The simplest procedure is a microhemagglutination assay, in which serum or plasma is tested against lyophilized, formalinized chicken or sheep red cells sensitized with components derived from *T. pallidum*. The specimen is first treated to remove nonspecific reactivity directed against elements present in nonpathogenic treponemes, but heat treatment is not necessary.

Donor units positive for the screening serologic test for syphilis (STS) should not be used for allogeneic transfusion. Before a donor is notified of positive test results, it may be desirable to test for the true treponemal antibodies.

Viral Marker Testing

The screening tests most commonly used to detect viral antigens and antibodies are the enzyme-linked immunosorbent assay (EIA or ELISA). The EIA tests for viral antigens HBsAg and HIV-1 antigen employ a solid support (eg, a bead or microplate) coated with an unlabeled antiserum against the appropriate antigen. The indicator material is the same antibody, labeled with an enzyme whose presence can be detected by color change in the substrate. If the specimen contains antigen, it will bind to the solid-phase antibody and will, in turn, be bound by the enzyme-labeled indicator antibody. To screen for viral antibodies, ie, anti-HIV-1, anti-HIV-2, anti-HBc, anti-HCV, anti-HTLV-I, or anti-HTLV-II, the solid phase (a bead or microtiter well) is coated with antigens prepared from the appropriate viral recombinant proteins or synthetic peptides. Most assays use a capture approach. Serum or plasma is incubated with fixed antigen; if present, antibody binds firmly to the solid phase and remains fixed after excess fluid is washed away. An enzyme-conjugated preparation of antigen is then added; if fixed antibody is present, it binds the labeled antigen, and the antigen-antibody-antigen complex can be quantified by measuring enzyme activity. One assay for anti-HBc uses an indirect capture method (competitive assay), in which an enzyme-antibody conjugate is added to the solid-phase antigen along with the unknown specimen. Any antibody present in the unknown specimen will compete with the enzyme-conjugated antibody and significantly reduce the level of enzyme fixed, compared to results seen when nonreactive material is present. Antigens used in the viral antibody screening tests may be made synthetically or directly from viral particles.

For most of the assays, samples giving nonreactive results on the initial screening test, as defined by the manufacturer's package insert, are considered negative and need not be further tested. Samples reactive on the initial screening test must be repeated in duplicate. Reactivity in one or both of the repeated tests constitutes a positive result and is considered repeatedly reactive. If both the duplicate repeat tests are nonreactive, the test is interpreted as having a negative result.

Before a donor is designated as antigen or antibody positive, a status that may have significant clinical and social consequences and cause permanent exclusion from blood donation, it is important to determine whether the screening result is truly demonstrable for the presence of the antigen or antibody in question. This caution is usually included in the manufacturer's package insert, with recommendations for the handling of initially and repeatedly reactive samples. After the initial test is repeated in duplicate and the specimen is described as repeatedly reactive, the allogeneic unit and all its components must be discarded.

Invalidation of Test Results

In the course of viral marker testing, it may be necessary to invalidate test results if the test performance did not meet the requirements of the manufacturer's package insert (for example, faulty equipment, improper procedure, compromised reagents), or if the control results do not meet the acceptance criteria defined in the package insert. All results, both the reactive and the nonreactive results, obtained in the run must be declared invalid; all specimens involved must be tested in a new run, which becomes the initial test of record. If the batch controls are acceptable and no error is recognized in test performance, the reactive and nonreactive results remain as the initial test of record for the specimens involved. Specimens with reactive results must be retested in duplicate, as required by the manufacturer's instructions.

If defects in test procedure are identified, so that the performance requirements specified by the package insert have not been met, all test results on that run are invalidated. The subsequent assay becomes the initial test of record for all specimens. Failure of performance requirements might involve procedural details, such as incubation times or temperatures; reagent quality, reagents used outside the expiration date, or reagents with evidence of contamination; or equipment problems, such as improper delivery of fluid volumes. Before the test run is invalidated, the problems observed should be reviewed by a supervisor or equivalent, reasons should be analyzed, and corrective action taken, if applicable.

When a test run is invalidated, a record of departure from normal standard operating procedures must be prepared, with a complete description of the reason for invalidation and the nature of corrective actions. New testing must be performed on all samples and controls from the invalidated run, and these results become the initial test of record.[3-5]

Use of External Controls

Other considerations may need to be addressed before the invalidation of test results when external controls are used. Internal controls are the validation materials provided with the licensed assay kit; they are used to demonstrate that the test performs as expected. The controls must consist of at least one positive and one negative sample and cannot be samples used to determine the cutoff value of a test run (those are calibratory, not controls). External controls are surrogate samples, either purchased commercially or developed by the institution, that are not a component of the test kit; they are used for surveillance of test performance. External controls are tested the same as donor samples to augment blood safety efforts and alert the testing facility to the possibility of an increasing risk of error. A facility

may invalidate *nonreactive* test results on the basis of external controls, but if the assay was performed in accordance with manufacturer's specifications and if the internal controls perform as expected, external controls cannot be used to invalidate *reactive* test results. The use of external controls may be more stringent than, but must be consistent with, the package insert's criteria for rejection of test results. These procedures, which should be part of a comprehensive quality program, should be consistent with generally accepted quality control practices.

Before being entered into routine use, external controls must be prequalified, lot by lot, because each control lot may vary with the test kit. One way to prequalify an external control is:

1.   Run the external control for 2 days, four replicates per day, using three different test kit lots. If the external controls do not react as expected, they should not be used.

2.   If the external controls do react as expected, determine the acceptable sample-to-cutoff ratio for the external control (eg, within three standard deviations of the mean).

Perform additional prequalification testing whenever a new lot of test kit or external control is introduced.

1.   Change of test kit lot: Run 20 replicates of the external control with the current kit lot and 20 replicates with the new lot. Apply the paired t test to determine whether there is a significant difference between current kit and new kit in the sample-to-cutoff ratios.

2.   Change of external control lot: Run one sample from the new control lot in parallel with one sample from the current lot, and repeat for 20 runs. Apply paired t test to determine whether differences in mean-absorbance signal-to-cutoff ratio are significant.

The above explanation is a simplified approach to external controls and may warrant the reader pursuing additional chemistry references.

While results of external control reagents may be used to invalidate *nonreactive* results obtained on an assay run, *reactive* results found in a suitably performed assay run may not be invalidated and remain as the initial test of record. Observation of donor population data, such as an unexpectedly increased reactive rate within a test run, may cause *nonreactive* results to be considered invalid. The next assay, performed on a single aliquot from affected specimens, becomes the initial test of record.

Reactive results obtained in a run with an unexpectedly increased reactive rate may not be invalidated unless the entire run fails to meet the performance criteria specified in the package insert. Such reactive results remain the initial test of record. The samples will be tested in duplicate as the repeat test.

External controls may be used to invalidate a duplicate repeat test run when an assay run is valid by test kit acceptance criteria and both the repeated duplicate tests are nonreactive. The duplicate samples may be repeated in duplicate; the second duplicate test becomes the test of record. If either of the original duplicate repeat tests is reactive, the donor(s) must be classified as repeatedly reactive and no further repeat testing should be performed.

Supplemental Tests: Neutralization

In confirmatory neutralization tests, the reactive specimen is incubated with human serum known to contain antibody specific for the antigen in question. If incubation causes the positive reaction to disappear or to diminish by at least 50% and all controls behave as expected, the presence of antigen is confirmed and the original result is considered a true positive. If incubation with known antibody does not affect subsequent reactivity, the original reactivity is considered a false-positive result. Known positive and negative control samples must be tested in parallel with donor or patient samples. Parallel incubations must be performed with a preparation known to contain antibody specific for the antigen in question and with a preparation known to be free of both antigen and antibody. Values for positive and negative controls must fall within stated limits. If neutralization does not meet the specifications stated in the package insert, it may be necessary to repeat the test.

Supplemental Test for EIA-Positive Anti-HIV, -HTLV, and -HCV Tests

The Western Blot test is most often used for the confirmation of repeatedly reactive anti-HIV EIA tests. The technique separates antigenic viral material into bands according to molecular weight. The material is transferred to nitrocellulose membranes. Antibody in the test serum reacts with the individual bands, depending on the specificities. Western Blot results are classified as positive, negative, or indeterminate. Positive results are those with reactivity to at least two of the following HIV proteins: p24, core protein; gp41, transmembrane protein; and gp120/160, external protein and external precursor protein. Indeterminate results are those with other patterns of reactivity.

The immunofluorescence assay (IFA) is used in some blood centers as an alternative to the Western Blot test. Cells infected with virus are fixed on a slide. The sample is incubated with the fixed cells. Antibody in the sample will bind to the antigen sites on the viral particles. The reaction mixture is incubated with fluorescent labeled antihuman IgG. Following incubation and washing, binding of the labeled antihuman IgG is read using a fluorescence microscope with subsequent interpretation of the fluorescence pattern.

While there are FDA-approved Western Blot confirmation tests for anti-HIV, the Western Blot test using recombinant deoxyribonucleic acid (DNA) and viral lysate antigens for anti-HTLV-I/II has not been approved by the FDA. An appropriate supplemental test to confirm a reactive anti-HTLV test is to repeat the test using another manufacturer's EIA test. If that test is repeatedly reactive, the test is considered confirmed. If the test is negative, the anti-HTLV test is considered a false positive.

The FDA has licensed a recombinant immunoblot assay (RIBA) system to further differentiate anti-HCV EIA repeatedly reactive samples. The RIBA system is based on the fusion of HCV antigens to human superoxide dismutase and a recombinant superoxide dismutase to detect nonspecific reactions. A positive result requires reactivity to two HCV antigens and no reactivity to superoxide dismutase. Reactivity to only one HCV antigen or to one HCV antigen and superoxide dismutase is classified as an indeterminate reaction. Results are usually presented as positive, negative, or indeterminate. As with all procedures, it is essential to follow the manufacturer's instructions for classification of test results.

In addition to the previously mentioned confirmatory and supplemental tests, the polymerase chain reaction (PCR) test is also used to better define the presence or absence of viral DNA and ribonucleic acid (RNA). PCR testing on donor samples for infectious disease markers is currently referred to by the more acceptable and specific name of nucleic acid testing (NAT). NAT is among the most sensitive and versatile approaches for the amplification of nucleic acid sequences. RNA is extracted and precipitated from a suspect (repeatedly reactive) sample. RNA is converted to DNA using reverse transcription and PCR; ie, the sample is heated and the double-stranded DNA unwinds to single strands, primers bind to complementary DNA sequences (annealing), and complementary DNA synthesis extends the primers (primer extension). This process is repeated multiple times to yield additional product (amplification). Amplified product may then be detected by hybridization with subsequent electrophoresis of denatured products. Currently NAT testing is used for the detection of

HIV and HCV viral particles. See Chapter 9 for more detailed information on PCR technology.

Supplemental or confirmatory testing may be performed on samples that are repeatedly reactive but, depending on the viral marker, may not be required. When samples are reactive on the *initial* screening test, allogeneic donor units must be quarantined until the results of duplicate repeat testing are available.

Alanine Aminotransferase

Alanine aminotransferase, formerly called serum glutamate pyruvate transaminase or SGPT, is an enzyme present in cells of many tissues but in highest concentration in hepatocytes. Elevated circulating levels of ALT occur when the liver has sustained damage that may have been caused by viral infection, biliary tract disease, drug-associated problems, alcohol toxicity, hemochromatosis, and obesity. Although no longer required by AABB *Standards*,[1] ALT testing is performed in some blood centers.

ALT levels are measured by standard chemistry analyzers, using a variety of procedures and reagents. If ALT is measured in blood intended for allogeneic transfusion, units with a level at or above twice the upper limit of the reference range should not be transfused. An institution may use the range given in the test package insert or may determine it locally, using a community sample of a size sufficient to validate the range.

Additional (Nonrequired) Tests

Optional tests may be performed on units intended for recipients with special needs. For example, cytomegalovirus (CMV) testing is one of the more common optional testing procedures performed in blood centers. CMV can persist in the tissues and leukocytes of asymptomatic individuals for years after initial infection. Blood from persons lacking antibodies to the virus has little risk of transmitting infection and only a small minority of donor units with anti-CMV will actually transmit infection. However, there is presently no way to distinguish infective antibody-positive units from noninfective units containing anti-CMV. Some categories of patients (see Chapter 28) should be protected from possible infection or reinfection with CMV, and one way to achieve this is to select anti-CMV-negative donors when preparing cellular components. Routine testing for anti-CMV is not required by AABB *Standards*,[1] but if it is performed, the usual quality assurance considerations apply. The most common CMV antibody detection methods performed in donor centers are EIA and latex agglutination. However other methods such as indirect hemagglutination, complement fixation, and immunofluorescence are also available.

Latex agglutination for detecting anti-CMV is a method in which latex particles coated with viral antigens are incubated with the unknown specimen. Agglutinates visible to the naked eye will form if antibody is present. Not all latex agglutination test kits are licensed for use in screening blood donors. The package insert will state whether the test detects both IgM and IgG antibodies to the virus; usually an IgG detection method is used.

Summary

Testing of donor blood is only one element in the provision of a safe blood supply and is not a guarantee that blood has zero risk of infectious disease transmission. However, the current testing performed on donor blood ensures that the maximum sensitivity and effectiveness of current technology do their part toward reducing the risk of blood transfusion.

Labeling, Records, and Quarantine

Labeling is a process that includes a final review of records of testing, donation, data on modification of blood components, quality control functions, and any additional informa-

tion obtained after donation. This also includes a review of labels attached to the components and checks to ensure that all labels meet regulatory requirements and are an accurate reflection of the contents of the blood or blood components.[2,6]

All labeling of blood components, products, blood bank specimens, and requests must be performed according to AABB *Standards* and FDA regulations. Blood centers and transfusion services must ensure that labeling is specific and controlled. There should be a mechanism or procedure in place that ensures acceptable label composition, inspection on receipt, secure storage and distribution of labels, archiving of superseded labels, and a master set of labels in use. In addition, procedures should address generation of labels, changes in labels, and modification of labels to reflect label control of altered or new components.

All aspects of labeling (the bag label as well as the *Circular of Information*, including the label size, type size, wording, spacing, and the base label adhesive) are strictly controlled. An international effort, with representation by the FDA and AABB, has established a new labeling guideline. The system, ISBT 128, is an internationally defined system based on barcode symbology called Code 128. It was developed to standardize the labeling of blood so that barcoded labels could be read by blood centers and transfusion services around the world. The system allows for each number assigned to a unit of blood (blood identification number) to be unique. The unique number will allow tracking of a unit of blood from donor to recipient, regardless of where the unit was drawn or transfused. As outlined in the *United States Industry Consensus Standard for the Uniform Labeling of Blood and Blood Components Using ISBT 128*,[6] the information appearing on the label, the location of the label, and the exact wording on the label are standardized. ISBT 128 differs from its predecessor, CODABAR, by including more specific information on the label. One advantage of the standardized system is that additional information on the label allows for better definition of product codes. Other proposed changes include an expanded donation identification number that will include the collection facility identification; barcoded manufacturer's lot number, bag type, etc; barcoded expiration date; and special testing barcode. Use of standardized computer-generated barcode labels (with better differentiation between components, preparation methods, and expiration dates) enhances efficiency, accuracy, and ultimately safety of labeled components. Adherence to the guidelines ensures compliance with AABB *Standards*[1] and FDA regulations. The new guidelines should be implemented by January 1, 2002.[7] Until the new international guidelines are implemented, the 1985 FDA Uniform Labeling Guideline is in effect. More information on ISBT 128 is available from slind@iccbba.com.

Label Requirements

The following information is required[1,2] in clear readable letters on a label firmly attached to the container of all blood and component units:

- The proper name of the component, in a prominent position.
- A unique numeric or alphanumeric identification that relates the original unit to the donor and each component to the original unit.
- The amount of blood collected and the kind and quantity of anticoagulant (not required for cryoprecipitate or for frozen, deglycerolized, rejuvenated, or washed red cells).
- For all blood and blood components, except for a single unit of Cryoprecipitated AHF, all pooled components, and components prepared by apheresis, the volume of the component must appear on the container.
- The expiration dates, including the date and year; if the shelf life is 72 hours or less, the hour of expiration must be stated.

- Recommended storage temperature.
- ABO group and Rh type (Rh type not required for cryoprecipitate).
- Interpretation of unexpected red cell antibody tests when positive (not required for cryoprecipitate or frozen, deglycerolized, rejuvenated, or washed RBCs).
- Results of unusual tests or procedures performed when necessary for safe and effective use. Routine tests done to ensure the safety of the unit need not be on the label if they are listed in the *Circular of Information*.
- Reference to the *Circular of Information*, which must be available for distribution and contains information about dosage, directions for use, route of administration, and contraindications.
- Essential instructions or precautions for use, including the warning that the component may transmit infectious agents, and the two statements: "Caution: Federal law prohibits dispensing without a prescription" and "Properly Identify Intended Recipient."[2]
- The appropriate donor classification statement, "autologous donor," "paid donor," or "volunteer donor" in type no less prominent than that used for the proper name of the component.
- Any additives, sedimenting agents, or cryoprotective agents that might still be present in the component.
- For licensed components, the name, address, and FDA license number of the facility that collected the blood and/or prepared the component. For components, the label must include the name and location of all facilities performing any part of component preparation, but there should not be more than two alphanumeric identifiers on the unit.

Special Labeling

Cellular blood components issued as "Leukocytes Reduced" must be labeled as such. The name and final volume of the component and a unique identifier for the pool must appear on all pooled components. The number of units in the pool and their ABO and Rh type must be on the label or an attached tie tag. Identification numbers of the individual units in the pool should not be on the label but must be in the records of the facility preparing the pool.

Cellular blood components issued as "CMV negative" must be labeled as such. Irradiated blood components must have the appropriate irradiated label and the identification of the facility performing the irradiation.

Records

Current good manufacturing practice regulations, as defined by Title 21 CFR Parts 200 and 600 series,[2,8] state that master production and control records must be a part of the labeling process. These records must be described in the facility's procedures. Before labeling, these records must be reviewed for accuracy and completeness. Appropriate signatures and dates (either electronic or manual) must document the review process. These records would include, but may not be limited to:

- Donation process: that all questions are answered on the donor card, consent is signed, all pre-qualifying tests are acceptable (ie, hemoglobin, blood pressure, etc) and a final review is documented by qualified supervisory personnel.
- Infectious disease testing: if performed at the drawing facility, that tests have acceptable quality control and performance; that daily equipment maintenance was performed and was acceptable; that final results are reviewed to identify date and person performing the review.
- Component preparation: that all blood and blood components were processed and/or modified under controlled conditions of temperature and other physical requirements of each component.
- Transfer of records: if testing is performed at an outside facility, that all records of that facility are up to date, and that the appropriate licensure is indicated. Records, either electronic or manual, must transfer data appropriately. All electronically transferred test records must be transmitted by a previously validated system. Transfer of those results must be performed by a system that properly identifies test results to all appropriate blood and blood components.
- Quarantine: that any nonconforming unit is appropriately isolated.

Components

Master production records must be traceable back to[1,2,7]:

- Dates of all processing or modification
- Identification of the person and equipment used in the process steps
- Identification of batches or in-process materials used
- Weight and measures used in the course of processing
- In-laboratory control results (temperatures, refrigerator, etc)
- Inspection of labeling area before and after use
- Results of component yield when applicable
- Labeling control
- Secondary bag and containers used in processing
- Any sampling performed
- Identification of person performing and checking at each step
- Any investigation made on nonconforming components
- Results of examinations of all review processes

Quarantine

There must be a process to remove nonconforming blood and blood components from the labeling process, until further investigation has occurred. This process must be validated to capture and isolate all blood and blood components that do not conform to requirements in any of the critical areas of collecting, testing, and processing. This must also include a process to capture verbal (phone calls, hearsay) information submitted to the collection facility after the collection process. All nonconforming units must remain in quarantine until they are investigated and all issues are resolved. The units may then be discarded, labeled as nonconforming units (as with autologous units), or labeled appropriately for transfusion if the investigation resolved the problems. If the nonconformance cannot be resolved and the units are from an allogeneic donation, those units must be discarded.

Summary

Once this labeling process has been completed and the appropriate records checked, the blood and blood components are released for distribution. All the requirements in Title 21 CFR 200 and 600 series apply to the final shipment and distribution of the blood and blood components. These components must be shipped in appropriate validated containers to ensure that the correct temperature of the components is maintained during shipping. Invoices must be accurate, and the correct products must be shipped to the correct facility. Records must be kept of all shipments and their final shipping location for purposes of look-back or recall.

References

1. Menitove J, ed. Standards for blood banks and transfusion services, 19th ed. Bethesda, MD: American Association of Blood Banks, 1999.

2. Code of federal regulations. Title 21 CFR Parts 600-799. Washington, DC: US Government Printing Office, 1998 (revised annually).

3. NIH Consensus Development Panel on Infectious Disease Testing for Blood Transfusions. Infectious disease testing for blood transfusion. JAMA 1995;274:1374-9.

4. Food and Drug Administration. Memorandum: Recommendations for the invalidation of test results when using licensed viral marker assays to screen donors, January 3, 1994. Rockville, MD: CBER Office of Communication, Training, and Manufacturers Assistance, 1994.

5. American Association of Blood Banks. Hepatitis history, external controls discussed at BPAC. Blood Bank Week 1992;9:1-4.

6. Food and Drug Administration. Memorandum: United States industry consensus standard for the labeling of blood and blood components using ISBT 128 (draft). November 27, 1998. Rockville, MD: CBER Office of Communication, Training, and Manufacturer's Assistance, 1998.

7. ISBT Code 128 implementation plan. Bethesda, MD: American Association of Blood Banks, 1998.

8. Code of federal regulations. Title 21 CFR Part 200. Washington, DC: US Government Printing Office, 1998 (revised annually).

Suggested Reading

American Association of Blood Banks, American National Red Cross, and America's Blood Centers. Circular of information for the use of human blood and blood components. Bethesda, MD: American Association of Blood Banks, 1998.

Blood Component Preparation, Storage, Shipping, and Transportation

8

DONOR CENTERS AND TRANSFUSION services share a common goal in blood component production: to provide a safe and efficacious component that benefits the intended recipient. To this end and in keeping with current good manufacturing practice regulations of the Food and Drug Administration (FDA), all processes involved in the collection, testing, preparation, storage, and transport of blood and components are monitored for quality, including procedures, personnel, reagents, equipment, and the contents of the components themselves. Processes should ensure the potency and purity of the final product, minimize microbial contamination and proliferation, and prevent or delay the detrimental physical and chemical changes that occur when blood is stored.

Anticoagulants and Preservatives

Whole blood is collected into a bag that contains an approved anticoagulant-preservative solution designed to prevent clotting and to maintain cell viability and function during storage. See Table 8-1 for a comparison of common solutions. Although low storage temperatures slow glycolytic activity, blood cells continue their metabolic activity during storage, consuming nutrients and depleting intracellular energy sources.

Because adenosine triphosphate (ATP) levels in red cells correlate with posttransfusion viability, anticoagulant-preservatives are formulated to promote ATP production. Sufficient dextrose is needed to support ATP generation via the glycolytic pathways. Adenine provides a substrate for the red cell synthesis of ATP, resulting in improved viability when compared to solutions without adenine. Sodium biphosphate acts as a buffer to control the decrease in pH expected from the buildup

161

Table 8-1. Anticoagulant-Preservative Solutions (mg in 63 mL)

	CPD	CP2D	CPDA-1
Ratio (mL solution to blood)	1.4:10	1.4:10	1.4:10
FDA-approved shelf life (days)	21	21	35
Content			
Sodium citrate	1660	1660	1660
Citric acid	188	188	188
Dextrose	1610	3220	2010
Monobasic sodium phosphate	140	140	140
Adenine	0	0	17.3

of lactic acid, an end product of glycolysis. Citrate prevents coagulation by chelating calcium, inhibiting the several calcium-dependent steps of the coagulation cascade.

CPD, CP2D, and CPDA-1

The FDA approves 21-day storage at 1-6 C for red cells from whole blood collected in citrate-phosphate-dextrose (CPD) and citrate-phosphate-dextrose-dextrose (CP2D) and 35 days for red cells collected in citrate-phosphate-dextrose-adenine (CPDA-1).[1] Blood bags intended for a collection volume of 450 mL ± 45 mL of whole blood (ie, 405-495 mL) contain 63 mL of anticoagulant-preservative. With FDA approval, many blood centers collect up to 550 mL whole blood in bags specifically designed for a larger volume. The volume of anticoagulant- preservative in the 500-mL bags is 70 mL. The allowable range of whole blood collected in 500-mL blood bags can vary with manufacturer, but this amount must not exceed 10.5 mL/kg donor weight per donation.

If only 300-404 mL of blood is collected into a blood bag designed for a 450 mL collection, the red cells can be used for transfusion provided the unit is labeled "Low Volume Unit __mL Red Blood Cells."[3(p28)] However, other components should not be prepared from these units. If collection of less than 300 mL is planned, a 450-mL bag should be used and the volume of anticoagulant-preservative solution in that bag should be reduced proportionately. (See Chapter 4 for calculations.) To date, the 500-mL bag has not been approved for low-volume collection.

Additive Systems

Additive red cell preservative solutions consist of a primary collection bag containing an anticoagulant-preservative with at least two satellite bags integrally attached; one is empty and one contains an additive solution, commonly called adenine-saline (AS). AS contains sodium chloride, dextrose, adenine, and other substances that support red cell survival and function up to 42 days.[2] (See Table 8-2.) The volume of AS in a 450-mL collection set is 100 mL; the volume in 500-mL sets may be slightly more (about 110-111 mL), depending on the manufacturer.

AS is added to the red cells remaining in the primary bag after most of the plasma has been removed for further manufacturing. This allows blood centers to use or recover a maximum amount of plasma, yet still prepare a red cell component with a final hematocrit of about 60%, a level that offers excellent flow rates and easy administration. AS must be added to red cells within 72 hours after phlebotomy.

Table 8-2. Content of Additive Solutions (mg/100 mL)

	AS-1 (Adsol®)	AS-3 (Nutricel®)	AS-5 (Optisol®)
Dextrose	2200	1100	900
Adenine	27	30	30
Monobasic sodium phosphate	0	276	0
Mannitol	750	0	525
Sodium chloride	900	410	877
Sodium citrate	0	588	0
Citric acid	0	42	0

Red Cell Changes During Storage

Biochemical changes occur when red cells are stored at 1-6 C; these changes, some of which are reversible, contribute to the "storage lesion" of red cells and to reduction in viability and levels of 2,3-diphosphoglycerate (2,3-DPG). The most striking biochemical changes that affect stored red cells are listed in Table 8-3, but these changes rarely have clinical significance, even in massively transfused recipients.

Oxygen Dissociation

Hemoglobin becomes fully saturated with oxygen in the lungs but characteristically releases only some of its oxygen at the lower oxygen pressure (pO$_2$) of normal tissues. The relationship between pO$_2$ and oxygen saturation of hemoglobin is shown by the oxygen dissociation curve. (See Fig 8-1.) Release of oxygen from hemoglobin at a given pO$_2$ is affected by ambient pH, by intracellular levels of 2,3-DPG, and by other variables.

The oxygen dissociation curve remains constant in shape, but its position relative to the X axis is affected by these variables. The P$_{50}$ is the pO$_2$ level at which hemoglobin is 50% saturated. A high P$_{50}$ means the curve has shifted to the right; at a given tissue pO$_2$, more oxygen will be released. A left shift (lower P$_{50}$) means that less oxygen than normal is released at any given pO$_2$.

The concentration of 2,3-DPG in the red cells affects the release of oxygen to the tissues. High levels cause greater oxygen release at a given pO$_2$. Lower red cell levels of 2,3-DPG increase the affinity of hemoglobin for oxygen, causing less oxygen release at the same pO$_2$. In red cells stored in CPDA-1 or in additive systems, 2,3-DPG levels fall at a linear rate to zero after 2 weeks of storage, and oxygen release is much less than in fresh cells.

Upon entering the recipient's circulation, stored red cells regenerate ATP and 2,3-DPG, resuming normal energy metabolism and hemoglobin function as they circulate in the recipient. It takes approximately 12 hours for severely depleted red cells to regenerate half their 2,3-DPG levels, and about 24 hours for complete restoration of 2,3-DPG and normal hemoglobin function.[5]

Potassium

Red cells lose potassium and gain sodium during the first 2-3 weeks of storage at 1-6 C because sodium/potassium adenosine triphosphatase, which pumps sodium out of red cells and replaces it with potassium, has a very high temperature coefficent and functions poorly in the cold.[1] Supernatant levels of potas-

Table 8-3. Biochemical Changes of Stored Red Blood Cells

Variable	CPD		CPDA-1				AS-1*	AS-3†	AS-5*
	Whole Blood	Whole Blood	Whole Blood	Red Blood Cells	Whole Blood	Red Blood Cells	Red Blood Cells	Red Blood Cells	Red Blood Cells
Days of Storage	0	21	0	0	35	35	42	42	42
% Viable cells (24 hours posttransfusion)	100	80	100	100	79	71	76 (64-85)	84	80
pH (measured at 37 C)	7.20	6.84	7.60	7.55	6.98	6.71	6.6	6.5	6.5
ATP (% of initial value)	100	86	100	100	56 (± 16)	45 (± 12)	60	59	68.5
2,3-DPG (% of initial value)	100	44	100	100	<10	<10	<5	<10	<5
Plasma K+ (mmol/L)	3.9	21	4.20	5.10	27.30	78.50‡	50	46	45.6
Plasma hemoglobin (mg/L)	17	191	82	78	461	658.0‡	N/A	386	N/A
% Hemolysis	N/A	N/A	N/A	N/A	N/A	N/A	0.5	0.9	0.6

* Based on information supplied by the manufacturer.
† From Simon, et al.[4]
‡ Values for plasma hemoglobin and potassium concentrations may appear somewhat high in 35-day stored RBC units; the total plasma in these units is only about 70 mL.

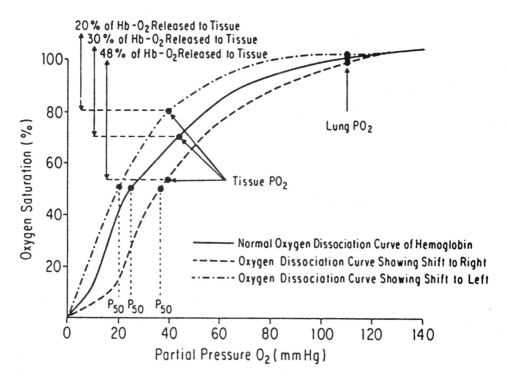

Figure 8-1. Oxygen dissociation curves under different conditions.

sium in a unit of CPDA-1 Red Blood Cells (RBCs) have been reported to increase from 5.1 mmol/L on the day of collection to 23.1 mmol/L on day 7[6] and 78.5 mmol/L on day 35.

Potassium levels in RBC and AS-RBC units seem extraordinarily high when compared to units of Whole Blood of equivalent age. However, their smaller plasma or supernatant fluid volumes (about 70 mL and 150 mL, respectively) must be considered when determining total potassium load.

Coagulation Factors

Blood stored at 1-6 C more than 24 hours has few functional platelets, but stable coagulation Factors II, VII, IX, X, and fibrinogen are well maintained. Heat-labile Factors V and VIII decrease with time and are not considered adequate to correct specific deficiencies in bleeding patients, although levels of 30% for Factor V and 15-20% for Factor VIII have been reported in Whole Blood stored 21 days, and platelets stored at room temperature have been shown to have Factor V levels of 47% (see Appendix 3) and Factor VIII levels of 68% after 72 hours.[7] For better preservation of Factors V and VIII and platelets, Whole Blood is separated into its component parts so that each component can be stored under its optimal conditions.

Platelet Storage Lesion

Metabolic activity in platelets also continues during storage; there is release of granule contents and discharge of cytosolic contents. Morphologic changes occur in the cytoskeleton, surface membrane, and the integrity of antigens and ligands.

Factors that affect the viability and function of stored platelets include:

- Anticoagulant-preservative solution—influences pH, metabolism of glucose, lactate, and HCO_3.
- Storage temperature—influences pH, glucose consumption, and lactate production.
- Composition, size, and surface area of the plastic container—influence oxygenation and metabolism.
- Type of agitation, which affects the release reaction.
- Volume of plasma—influences metabolism, pH, and lactate generation.

Shelf Life

The maximum allowable storage time for a blood component held under acceptable temperatures and conditions is called its "shelf life." For red cells, criteria for determining shelf life for an approved anticoagulant-preservative require that at least 75% of the original red cells (normal allogeneic donor) be in the recipient's circulation 24 hours after transfusion. For other components, shelf life is based on functional considerations. Storage times are listed in Table 8-4.

Blood destined for component production is drawn into a primary bag with integrally attached satellite bags so that the contents are not exposed to air during preparation and separation (ie, a "closed" system). If the airtight system is entered for processing or pooling, it becomes an "open" system; aseptic techniques and pyrogen-free equipment must be used, and allowable storage times change. "Opened" components stored at 1-6 C must be used within 24 hours of preparation, or if stored at 20-24 C, within 4 hours unless otherwise specified.[3(p24)] The new expiration date and time must be noted in the records and on the label.

If an open-system pool or component is to be stored frozen, it must be placed in the freezer within 6 hours after the seal is broken. When these components are thawed, they must be transfused within 24 hours if stored at

Table 8-4. Expiration Dates for Selected Blood Components[3(p41-46)]

Category	Expiration
Whole Blood	ACD/CPD/CP2D—21 days CPDA-1—35 days
Whole Blood Modified	ACD/CPD/CP2D—21 days CPDA-1—35 days
Whole Blood Irradiated	Original outdate (see outdates above per anticoagulant) or 28 days from date of irradiation, whichever is sooner
Red Blood Cells (RBCs)	ACD/CPD/CP2D—21 days CPDA-1—35 days
RBCs, Additive Solutions	42 days
RBCs, Washed	Time approved by FDA
RBCs, Leukocytes Reduced	ACD/CPD/CP2D—21 days CPDA-1—35 days Open system—24 hours Additive solutions—42 days
RBCs, Rejuvenated	24 hours

Table 8-4. Expiration Dates for Selected Blood Components[3(p41-46)] (cont'd)

Category	Expiration
RBCs, Rejuvenated, Washed	24 hours
RBCs, Irradiated	Original outdate above or 28 days from date of irradiation, whichever is sooner
RBCs, Frozen 40% Glycerol	10 years
RBCs, Frozen 20% Glycerol	10 years
RBCs, Deglycerolized	Time approved by FDA
RBCs, Open System	24 hours
RBCs, Open System—Frozen	10 years, 24 hours after thaw
RBCs, Frozen—Liquid Nitrogen	10 years
Platelets	24 hours to 5 days, depending on collection system
Platelets, Pheresis	5 days
Platelets Pooled or in Open System	4 hours, unless otherwise specified
Platelets, Leukocytes Reduced	4 hours open system 5 days closed system
Platelets, Pheresis, Leukocytes Reduced	5 days
Platelets, Irradiated	4 hours open system 5 days closed system
Granulocytes	24 hours
FFP	12 months (−18 C) 7 years (−65 C)
FFP, Thawed	24 hours
FFP, Open System—Thawed	24 hours
Pooled Plasma, Solvent/detergent-treated	12 months
Pooled Plasma, Solvent/detergent-treated Thawed	24 hours
Plasma (frozen within 24 hours)	12 months
Plasma (frozen within 24 hours) Thawed	24 hours
Plasma Thawed	> 24 hours, < 5 days
Plasma Liquid	5 days after expiration of RBCs
FFP—Donor Retested Thawed	24 hours
FFP—Donor Retested	12 months
Plasma, Cryoprecipitate-Reduced, Thawed	24 hours
Cryoprecipitated AHF	12 months
Cryoprecipitated AHF, Thawed	ASAP or within 4 hours if open system or pooled, 6 hours if single unit or pooled

1-6 C.[3(p24)] The AABB requires transfusion within 6 hours for thawed components stored at 20-24 C, but the FDA requires transfusion within 4 hours.

Sterile Connection Devices

Sterile connection devices are used to attach additional bags and compatible tubing to a blood bag without breaking the sterile integrity of the system. The shelf life of components thus prepared is the same as those prepared in a closed system except for Pooled Platelets, which expire 4 hours after pooling.[3(p43)] All sterile connection device welds must be inspected for completeness, integrity, leakage, and air bubbles; procedures must address the action to take if the weld is not satisfactory. Record-keeping should include documentation of the products welded, weld quality control, and lot numbers of software and disposables.[8]

Rejuvenation

It is possible to restore levels of 2,3-DPG and ATP in red cells stored in CPD or CPDA-1 solutions by adding an FDA-licensed solution containing pyruvate, inosine, phosphate, and adenine.[9] (See Method 6.5.) RBCs can be rejuvenated during 1-6 C storage up to 3 days after expiration; then they can be glycerolized and frozen in the same manner as fresh red cells. If rejuvenated red cells are to be transfused within 24 hours, they can be stored at 1-6 C; however, they must be washed before use to remove the inosine, which might be toxic to the recipient. The blood label and component records must indicate the use of rejuvenating solutions.

Component Production

Blood Collection

Blood component quality begins with a healthy donor and a clean venipuncture site to minimize bacterial contamination. To prevent activation of the coagulation system during collection, blood should be collected rapidly and with minimal trauma to tissues. There should be frequent, gentle mixing of the blood with the anticoagulant. Although the target collection time is usually 4-10 minutes, one study has shown Platelets and Fresh Frozen Plasma (FFP) to be satisfactory after collection times of up to 15 minutes.[10]

Immediately after collection, the tubing to the donor arm is stripped and segmented so that it represents the contents of the donor bag. Blood is then cooled toward 1-6 C unless it is to be used for room temperature component production, in which case it should not be cooled below 20 C.[3(p41)]

Whole Blood Fractionation

To simplify the separation or fractionation of whole blood into its component parts, blood is collected into primary bags with one to three satellite bags attached. Set design is based on intended use: RBCs, Platelets, FFP, cryoprecipitate, or neonatal aliquots can be made according to inventory needs. Refer to Method Section 6 for specific component preparation procedures. Whole blood must be separated and prepared components placed into their required storage temperatures within 8 hours of collection.[3(p41)] Records of component preparation should identify each individual performing a significant step in the preparation process.

Centrifugation

Because red cells, platelets and plasma have different specific gravities (1.08-1.09, 1.03-1.04, and 1.023, respectively),[7] they are separated from one another using differential centrifugation. Donor whole blood can also be separated into components during apheresis collection and centrifugation (see Chapter 6).

Rotor size, speed, and duration of spin are critical variables in centrifugation. Method 7.5 describes how to calibrate a centrifuge for platelet separation, but each centrifuge must be calibrated for optimal speeds and spin times for each combination of components prepared in like fashion. Times usually include only the time of acceleration and "at speed," not deceleration time. Once the operating variables are identified for component production, timer accuracy, rpm, and temperature if appropriate, should be monitored periodically to verify equipment performance. Another practical way to assess centrifugation is to monitor quality control data on components prepared in each centrifuge.

If component quality does not meet defined standards, eg, if platelet concentrate yields are inconsistent, the entire process should be evaluated. One might want to reassess the calibration of the centrifuge, the initial platelet counts on the donors, storage time and conditions between blood collection and platelet preparation, sampling technique, and counting methods.

Large centrifuges rotate at high speeds, exerting gravitational forces of thousands of pounds on blood bags, which can have unnoticeable imperfections. Occasionally blood bags rupture or the seals between tubing segments leak during centrifugation. If contamination and clean-up are a concern, blood bags can be overwrapped with plastic bags to contain any leaks. Bags should be positioned so that a broad surface faces the outside wall of the centrifuge; this reduces the centrifugal force on blood bag seams.

Contents in opposing cups of the centrifuge must be equal in weight; uneven weight distribution can impair centrifuge efficiency and damage the rotor. Dry balancing materials are preferable to liquid ones. Weighted rubber discs and large rubber bands are excellent and come in several thicknesses to provide flexibility in balancing. Swinging cups provide better separation between cells and plasma than fixed-angle cups.

Derivative Production

Large pools of plasma harvested from whole blood or obtained by apheresis can be further processed to yield solvent/detergent-treated plasma or derivatives such as albumin, plasma protein fraction, Factor VIII concentrate, immune globulin preparations, and concentrates of Factor IX and Factor IX complex (II, VII, IX, and X).[11]

Testing and Labeling of Donor Units

Refer to Chapter 7 for testing and labeling of blood components.

Blood Component Descriptions

Readers should refer to Chapters 21, 23, and 24 and the current *Circular of Information for the Use of Human Blood and Blood Components* for more detailed indications and contraindications for transfusion.

Red Cell Components

Whole Blood

Fresh Whole Blood contains all blood elements plus the anticoagulant-preservative in the collecting bag. It is used commonly as a source for component production. After 24-hour storage, it essentially becomes red cells suspended in a protein solution equivalent to liquid plasma, with a minimum hematocrit of 38%.

Transfusion of Whole Blood may be appropriate when both red cell mass and total blood volume must be restored, as in massive hemorrhage.

Red Blood Cells

RBCs are units of Whole Blood with most of the plasma removed (see Method 6.4). If prepared from whole blood collected into CPD, CP2D, or CPDA-1, the final hematocrit must be less than 80%.

AS-RBCs contain even less plasma but have a hematocrit between 55 and 65% because of the added AS. RBCs can be prepared at any time during their shelf life, but AS must be added within the first 72 hours of storage. Shelf life at 1-6 C storage depends on the anticoagulant-preservative used and the method of preparation.

RBCs are the component of choice for symptomatic anemia that cannot be treated with pharmaceuticals and for routine blood loss during surgery.

RBCs can be further modified to extend their storage or render them more suitable for specific patient needs, eg, rejuvenated, frozen-deglycerolized, washed, irradiated, leukocyte-reduced, volume-reduced, and split into smaller aliquots. See related sections below and Method Section 6. All modifications must be indicated on the label.

Plasma Components

Fresh Frozen Plasma

FFP is plasma, along with anticoagulant-preservative, placed at −18 C or colder within 8 hours after collection if separated from CPD, CP2D, or CPDA-1 whole blood. If prepared from ACD plasma collected by apheresis, it must be placed into frozen storage within 6 hours.[3(p28)] Stored at −18 C or colder, FFP contains maximum levels of labile and nonlabile clotting factors (about 1 IU per mL) and has a shelf life of 12 months from the date of the whole blood collection. FFP frozen and maintained at −65 C may be stored up to 7 years.[12]

Indications for Use. FFP is used to treat bleeding associated with clotting factor deficiencies when factor concentrates are not available or are not indicated.

Freezing Tips. See Method 6.8 for preparation details. Plasma can be rapidly frozen by placing the bag 1) in a dry ice-ethanol or dry ice-antifreeze bath; 2) between layers of dry ice; 3) in a blast freezer; or 4) in a mechanical freezer maintained at −65 C or colder. Plasma frozen in a liquid bath should be overwrapped with a plastic bag to protect the container from chemical alteration. When a mechanical freezer is used, care must be taken to avoid

slowing the freezing process by introducing too many units at one time.

FFP should be frozen in a manner that makes it easy to detect inadvertent thawing and refreezing. Simple methods to accomplish this are:

- Press a tube into the bag during freezing to leave an indentation that disappears if the unit thaws.
- Freeze the plasma bag in a flat, horizontal position but store it upright. Air bubbles trapped along the bag's uppermost broad surface during freezing will move to the top if thawed in a vertical position.
- Place a rubber band around the liquid plasma bag and remove it after freezing to create an indentation that disappears with thawing.

Thawing FFP for Transfusion. FFP is thawed either at temperatures between 30 and 37 C or in an FDA-approved microwave device.[3(p45)] It is then known as "FFP, Thawed" and should be transfused immediately or stored between 1-6 C for no more than 24 hours. Expiration date and time must be indicated on the label.

FFP thawed in a waterbath must be protected so that entry ports are not contaminated with water. This can be accomplished by wrapping the container in a plastic overwrap, or by positioning the container upright, with entry ports above the water level. Microwave devices should be shown not to exceed temperature limits and not to damage the plasma proteins, and there should be a warning device to indicate if the temperature rises unacceptably. As with any device, there should be a procedure for the quality control of indicated functions.

Thawed Plasma

When FFP prepared in a closed system is thawed but not transfused within 24 hours, the words "fresh frozen" can be crossed out on the label. This product, known as "Thawed Plasma," can be stored at 1-6 C and transfused up to 5 days after thawing. It is similar to FFP except for some reduction in Factor V and a clinically significant reduction in Factor VIII. FFP prepared by apheresis cannot be relabeled or given extended storage because apheresis is an open system.

Indications for Use. Thawed Plasma can be used to treat coagulation factor deficiencies other than Factor VIII.

Plasma, Frozen Within 24 Hours of Collection

Plasma separated and frozen at –18 C between 8 and 24 hours, eg, plasma that cannot meet the stricter time requirements of FFP, can be labeled as "Plasma, Frozen Within 24 Hours of Collection." It contains all the stable proteins found in FFP plus about 150 IU Factor VIII, and can be stored at –18 C up to 12 months from the date of collection.

Indications for Use. This component can be used to treat bleeding associated with stable clotting factor deficiencies.

Thawing for Transfusion. FFP thawing guidelines apply. Once thawed, it should be transfused immediately or stored at 1-6 C up to 5 days after thawing.

Plasma and Liquid Plasma

Plasma in a unit of Whole Blood can be separated at any time during storage, up to 5 days after the expiration date of the Whole Blood. When stored frozen at –18 C or colder, this component is known as Plasma and can be used up to 5 years after the date of collection. If not frozen, it is called Liquid Plasma, which is stored at 1-6 C and transfused up to 5 days after the expiration of the Whole Blood from which it was prepared.

In addition, FFP that is not used within 12 months also can be designated as "Plasma" and, if suitably relabeled and stored frozen, can be used up to an additional 4 years.

Plasma prepared from outdated Whole Blood differs from plasma originally prepared as FFP: high levels of potassium and ammonia build up with prolonged storage on red cells. If cryoprecipitate has been removed from plasma, this must be stated on the label (Plasma, Cryoprecipitate Reduced). When stored at –18 C or colder, this component has a 12-month expiration date from the date of collection.[3(p45)]

Plasma and Liquid Plasma may be useful in treating stable clotting factor deficiencies for which no concentrates are available. Very few other clinical indications exist, although controversy exists over using Plasma, Cryoprecipitate-Reduced to treat thrombotic thrombocytopenic purpura.[13]

Pooled Plasma, Solvent/Detergent-Treated

This recently licensed plasma product, also known as PLAS+®SD, is prepared from pools of no more than 2500 units of ABO type-specific plasma that are frozen to preserve labile coagulation factors. The units are thawed and treated with the solvent tri-n-butyl phosphate, and the detergent, Triton X-100, for 4 hours at 31 C to inactivate lipid-enveloped viruses. The solvent/detergent reagents are then removed by an extraction and column chromatography process and the remaining plasma is sterile-filtered into standardized 200-mL volumes and refrozen.

PLAS+®SD contains labile and stable coagulation factors in amounts similar to FFP (not less than 0.7 IU/mL of Factors V, VII, X, XI, and XIII and 1.8 mL/mL of fibrinogen) but lacks the largest von Willebrand factor multimers.[14]

Indications for Use. Like FFP, PLAS+®SD can be used to treat patients with clotting factor deficiencies when factor concentrates are not available (including congenital deficiencies of Factors I, V, VII, X, and XIII or acquired multiple factor deficiencies), and patients requiring reversal of warfarin therapy, and treatment of thrombotic thrombocytopenic purpura.

Safety Concerns. The use of PLAS+®SD in place of FFP can effectively reduce the already low risk of disease transmission from donors in an infectious seronegative window period for currently tested viral infections: human immunodeficiency virus, types 1 and 2 (HIV-1,2), human T-cell lymphotropic virus, types I and II (HTLV-I/II), hepatitis B virus (HBV), and hepatitis C virus (HCV). It can also reduce the risk from lipid-enveloped viruses not currently recognized. Clinical trials and worldwide experience with PLAS+®SD and solvent/detergent-treated clotting factor concentrate and immunoglobulin preparations have not documented disease transmission from lipid-enveloped viruses.

However, because PLAS+®SD is a pooled product and the solvent/detergent process does not inactivate viruses with nonlipid envelopes, there is still a risk of potential disease transmission from other agents such as parvovirus B19, hepatitis A, and unrecognized pathogens that could contaminate the pool.

Other Approaches to Increase Plasma Transfusion Safety. An alternative product that is also presumed to be safer than FFP is "FFP-Donor Retested." Some facilities store their FFP 90 days or longer, then retest the donor and release the product to stock only if the donor continues to test negative for transfusion-transmitted diseases. This product may prove to be at least as safe as PLAS+®SD because it is not a pooled product and subsequent negative retesting helps verify that the donor was not in an infectious window period.

Transfusion safety is also improved if facilities can link their FFP units to RBC units. Patients who receive both RBCs and "linked FFP" from the same donation have no increased exposure risk from the FFP. Linked FFP or plasma products can be useful for extensive surgical cases that require both RBCs and FFP, but they offer no benefit to those needing only FFP. They require a more complex and innovative inventory management system.

Recovered Plasma and Source Plasma

Blood centers often convert Plasma and Liquid Plasma to an unlicensed component, "Recovered Plasma," which is usually shipped to a fractionator and processed into derivatives such as albumin and/or immune globulins. To ship Recovered Plasma, the collecting facility must have a "short supply agreement" with the manufacturer.[15] Because Recovered Plasma has no expiration date, records for this component must be maintained indefinitely. Plasma collected by plasmapheresis and intended for further manufacturing use is designated "Source Plasma."

Cryoprecipitated AHF

Cryoprecipitated Antihemophilic Factor (AHF) is the cold-insoluble portion of plasma that precipitates when FFP is thawed between 1-6 C. Also known as CRYO, this product is prepared from a single Whole Blood unit collected into CPDA-1, CPD, or ACD, and suspended in less than 15 mL plasma. It contains $\geq$80 IU Factor VIII (AHF), >150 mg of fibrinogen, and some of the Factor XIII originally present in the fresh plasma. CRYO contains both the procoagulant activity (Factor VIII:C) and the von Willebrand factor of the Factor VIII molecule.

Once separated, CRYO is refrozen within 1 hour of preparation and stored at −18 C or colder for up to 1 year after the date of phlebotomy. See Method 6.9 for a preparation procedure.

Cryoprecipitated AHF Pooled

Units of CRYO can be pooled prior to labeling, freezing, and storage. If pooled promptly after preparation using aseptic technique and refrozen immediately, the resulting component is labeled "Cryoprecipitated AHF Pooled," with the number of units pooled stated on the label. The volume of saline, if added to facilitate pooling, must also appear on the label. Instructions to "Use Within 4 Hours After Thawing" must be included on the label unless uniform labeling is used. In this case, the statement should appear in the *Circular of Information* rather than on the container label.

The facility preparing the pool must maintain records of each individual donor traceable to the unique identifier used for the pooled component.[3(p37-38)]

Quality Control

AABB *Standards* requires that all tested individual units of CRYO contain a minimum of 80 IU of Factor VIII and 150 mg of fibrinogen.[3(p29)] Samples from at least 4 donor units should be tested, either individually or in a pool, every month.

For pooled CRYO units, there should be quality control evaluation of at least two containers each month. Each pool must have a Factor VIII content of at least 80 units times the number of donor units in the pool; for fibrinogen, the content should be 150 mg times the number of donor units.[3(p29)]

Indications for Use

CRYO transfusion is used to control bleeding associated with fibrinogen deficiency or Factor XIII deficiency. Although safer plasma products (see PLAS+®SD above) are available for fibrinogen and Factor XIII replacement, some patients may not tolerate their larger volume. CRYO is considered second choice therapy for managing hemophilia A and von Willebrand's disease and should be used only when appropriate virus-inactivated Factor VIII concentrates are not available. CRYO is also used as a source of surgical fibrin sealant. However, a heat-treated fibrin sealant product is also commercially available that offers a disease risk similar to heat-treated Factor VIII concentrates.

Thawing CRYO for Transfusion

CRYO is thawed at temperatures between 30 and 37 C. Bags should remain at that temperature for no more than 15 minutes to minimize the degradation of Factor VIII, although thawing time may need to be extended for frozen pooled CRYO. As with FFP, entry ports should be protected from water contamination if thawed in a waterbath.

Thawed CRYO must be transfused immediately or stored at room temperature (20-24 C) for no more than 6 hours if used as a source of Factor VIII.[16] Products prepared in an open system, either entered or pooled, must be transfused within 4 hours after thawing.

CRYO may be pooled into one bag after thawing to simplify transfusion to a patient requiring multiple units. The pooled product is assigned a unique pool number but records must document the individual units included. See Method 6.10 for guidelines on how to thaw and pool CRYO for transfusion.

Platelets

Platelet concentrates (Platelets) are prepared from units of Whole Blood that have not been allowed to cool below 20 C. Platelet-rich plasma is separated within 8 hours after phlebotomy and the platelets are concentrated by additional centrifugation and removal of most of the supernatant plasma within 24 hours of collection. A procedure for preparation of Platelets from single units of Whole Blood appears in Method 6.11. The final product contains $\geq 5.5 \times 10^{10}$ platelets in 40-60 mL of plasma and normal levels of stable coagulation factors.[3(p30)]

The use of hemapheresis to prepare Platelets, Pheresis is discussed in Chapter 6. These components contain $\geq 3 \times 10^{11}$ platelets in 100-500 mL of plasma. The volume and number of leukocytes vary greatly with the collection equipment and protocol used.

To maintain satisfactory viability and function, platelet products are stored between 20-24 C with gentle continuous agitation for no more than 5 days after phlebotomy.

Drugs That Affect Platelet Function

Many pharmacologic agents can impair platelet function but these altered platelets can, in the presence of normal platelets, provide significant hemostatic effect. Drug intake becomes a consideration only when a donor on such medication is the sole source of transfused platelets for a patient, as happens when adults receive a unit of Platelets, Pheresis or infants are given one platelet concentrate.

Units of Platelets prepared from donors who have ingested aspirin or medications known to irreversibly damage platelet function within 36 hours of blood donation should be labeled so that the transfusing facility will not use the unit as a patient's sole source of platelets. Prospective apheresis donors should be deferred until the drug's effect is over.

Quality Control of Platelet Units

The quality of every method of platelet preparation must be assessed monthly with at least 4 units from each method. Data must show that at least 75% of products tested contain an acceptable number of platelets (3.0×10^{11} for Platelets, Pheresis and 5.5×10^{10} for Platelets) and have a plasma pH of 6.2 or higher at the end of the allowable storage period.

In addition, all platelet products should be inspected prior to release and issue. Units with excessive platelet aggregates should not be used for transfusion. Some facilities assess the "swirling" appearance of platelets by holding platelet bags against a light source and gently squeezing them. This swirl phenomenon correlates well with pH values associated with adequate platelet in vivo viability.[17]

Indications for Use

Platelet transfusions are used to prevent spontaneous bleeding or stop established bleeding in patients with thrombocytopenia or platelet dysfunction. (See Chapters 16 and 21 for dose recommendations.)

Because one plateletpheresis donation can provide the equivalent of a full hemostatic dose of Platelets, Platelets, Pheresis are especially useful when supplying platelets that are seronegative for cytomegalovirus (CMV) or are HLA-matched or crossmatched. The use of HLA-matched donors or serologically cross-matched platelets may improve the response of patients who are refractory to randomly selected platelet units.

Modifications

Platelet components may require further modification to meet special patient needs, much like red cells. They can be irradiated, leukocyte-reduced, volume-reduced, split into smaller aliquots, washed, and even frozen for extended storage. See related sections below and Method Section 6. All modifications must be indicated on the label.

When a patient requires multiple units of Platelets, pooling them into a single bag simplifies issue and transfusion. If Platelets contain a significant number of red cells and ABO groups are mixed, plasma antibodies should be compatible with any red cells present in the pool. Only one unique number is affixed to the final product, but records must reflect the pooling process and all units included in the pool.

Granulocytes

Granulocytes are usually prepared by leukapheresis (see Chapter 6). AABB *Standards* requires that these products contain $\geq 1.0 \times 10^{10}$ granulocytes in at least 75% of units tested.[3(p54)] They also contain other leukocytes, platelets, and as many as 20-25 mL of red cells in 200-300 mL of plasma, depending on the collection procedure. Granulocytes should be transfused as soon as possible after collection but may be stored at 20-24 C without agitation for up to 24 hours.

Buffy coats harvested from fresh Whole Blood units can provide an alternative but significantly smaller ($<1 \times 10^9$) source of granulocytes in urgent neonatal situations but their effectiveness is controversial.[18]

Granulocytes are indicated for severely neutropenic patients who have documented infection unresponsive to aggressive antibiotic therapy.

Meeting Special Patient Needs

Leukocyte-Reduced Blood

Red cell products prepared by a method known to retain at least 85% of the original red cells, but reduce total white cell content to less than 5×10^6 can be labeled as Red Blood Cells, Leukocytes Reduced.[3(p27)] To qualify as leukocyte-reduced, Platelets, Pheresis units should also have fewer than 5×10^6 leukocytes per bag, but Platelets should have the equivalent of fewer than 8.3×10^5 per bag because of their smaller volume.[3(p30,53)]

Preparation Methods

Many methods are known to reduce the number of white cells in a unit of blood with varying efficiency (centrifugation, buffy coat removal, washing, and freezing and deglycerolization), but only special prestorage leukocyte-removing filters reliably provide the $\geq99.9\%$ (log 3) removal needed to meet the 5×10^6 requirement.[7] These filters contain multiple layers of synthetic nonwoven fibers that selectively retain white cells, allowing red cells and/or platelets to flow through.[19]

Leukocyte-removing filters are commercially available in a number of set configurations to facilitate filtration during the separation process before storage or in the laboratory before issue. Filters are also available in plateletpheresis software, so that platelets can be leukocyte-reduced after the collection process.

The timing of leukocyte removal may be significant. Leukocyte removal efficiency increases as the time between collection and depletion is shortened. During storage, leukocytes degranulate, fragment, or die, releasing substances that may promote febrile and allergic transfusion reactions. There were concerns

that early removal of leukocytes would allow bacteria, present at the time of collection, to proliferate. However, studies suggest that early removal may reduce the likelihood of significant bacterial contamination.[20] Bedside filtration is not as effective in preventing reactions in multitransfused patients and should only be used if prestorage components are not available.[21] Nonetheless, cytokines that accumulate during storage (particularly in platelet components) may account for some failures of bedside filtration to prevent febrile reactions.[20] (See Cytokine section below.)

Quality Control Issues

Whatever leukocyte-reduction process is selected, it must be validated in-house before implementation and should be assessed periodically thereafter. Because the residual white cell counts in leukocyte-reduced products are so very low, quality control must be done using a method with sufficient sensitivity; large-volume hemacytometers (see Methods 7.9 and 7.10) and flow cytometry are well suited for this. A representative sampling of leukocyte-reduced components should be tested monthly. This sampling should include a minimum of 1% of the components leukocyte-reduced per month, or 4 units per month per component, whichever is more.[22]

Indications for Use

Leukocyte-reduced components may benefit patients with recurrent febrile nonhemolytic (FNH) transfusion reactions; patients at risk of alloimmunization to HLA antigens, eg, those who require long-term platelet therapy and may become refractory or those who are awaiting organ transplantation; and patients at risk for CMV infection.

Clinical Considerations

The relationship between FNH reactions and the presence of white cells in the transfused component has long been known. Explanations include alloimmunization of the recipient to transfused HLA or granulocyte antigens, adverse effects of transfused microaggregates on the microcirculation, and fragmentation of stored donor granulocytes with release of enzymes and other bioactive compounds. Present thinking attributes most FNH reactions to the actions of cytokines, predominantly those produced by leukocytes in the transfused unit[23] but sometimes produced in the recipient after alloimmune interaction with the donor's leukocytes.[24]

Cytokines. Leukocyte reduction has been used with success to prevent FNH reactions, but in many cases, even near-complete removal of leukocytes at the time of transfusion is ineffective.[25] It is now known that cytokines are generated during storage, at 1-6 C but to a much greater extent at 20-24 C. Levels of interleukin 1 alpha and beta (IL-1α and IL-1β), interleukin 6 (IL-6), and tumor necrosis factor alpha (TNF-α) rise sharply in units stored with resident leukocytes, compared with similar units stored after leukocyte reduction (prestorage leukocyte reduction).[26] Cytokine levels rise in direct proportion to the number of leukocytes.

Platelet Refractoriness. Patients receiving repeated platelet transfusions can become refractory, so that platelet counts do not rise as expected. A platelet refractory state may result from many factors, including splenomegaly, fever, sepsis, drug therapies, platelet consumption in disseminated intravascular coagulation, or development of HLA or platelet-specific antibodies. Administration of leukocyte-reduced platelets may delay or help prevent alloimmunization to HLA antigens as a cause of refractoriness.

Other Effects. Several other adverse effects have been attributed to the presence of leukocytes in components. The simultaneous presence of antigen-presenting cells and cells that express foreign HLA antigens, in the transfused unit, is thought to increase the likelihood of HLA alloimmunization in the recipient.[27] When present in the circulating blood, CMV resides entirely within the cytoplasm of white cells. Removing leukocytes from cellular components, therefore, can reduce the danger of transfusion-transmitted CMV infection or reinfection.[28]

CMV-Negative Blood

To reduce the transmission of CMV infection from cellular blood components to patients at risk, donor units can be tested for CMV antibody. Only those that test negative can be labeled "CMV-negative." Although it has been estimated that less than 2% of healthy donors are able to transmit infection, 40-70% make CMV antibody,[29] so this special product is sometimes in short supply.

Some blood centers offer red cells and platelets that have been leukocyte-reduced, as a "CMV-reduced-risk" alternative. Leukocyte removal with high-efficiency filters can reduce posttransfusion CMV in high-risk neonates and transplant recipients.[28]

Frozen plasma products do not transmit CMV infection and are given without regard to CMV-seroreactivity. However, the passive acquisition of CMV antibody from plasma units can make it falsely appear that a patient has seroconverted.

Indications for Use

CMV-negative blood is indicated for patients who are at risk of significant morbidity or mortality from CMV infections, including fetuses and low birthweight infants, CMV-seronegative pregnant women, CMV-seronegative marrow or solid-organ transplant recipients, or severely immunosuppressed CMV-seronegative transfusion recipients.

Irradiated Blood

Blood components that contain viable lymphocytes (including red cell, platelet, and granulocyte components and nonfrozen plasma) should be irradiated to prevent proliferation of transfused T lymphocytes in recipients at risk, the primary cause of transfusion-associated graft-vs-host disease (GVHD). The AABB and FDA recommend a minimum 25 Gy dose of gamma radiation to the central portion of a blood bag with no less than 15 Gy targeted to the outer portions.[3(p25,30),30]

Irradiation is accomplished using cesium-137 or cobalt-60, in self-contained blood irradiators or hospital radiation therapy machines. Measurement of dose distribution; verification of exposure time, proper mechanical function, and turntable rotation; and adjustment of exposure time as the radioactive source decays should be addressed in the facility's procedures.[31] Records and labels must clearly document the irradiation process and who performed it.

To confirm the irradiation of individual units, radiochromic film labels (available commercially) may be affixed to bags prior to irradiation. When exposed to radiation, the film portion of the label darkens proportionately with exposure, indicating the component received the appropriate dose of irradiation.

Because irradiation damages some red cells and reduces the overall viability (24-hour recovery), red cell components that have been irradiated expire on their originally assigned outdate or 28 days from the date of irradiation, whichever comes first. Platelets sustain minimal damage from irradiation, so their expiration date does not change.

Irradiated blood is essential for patients at risk from transfusion associated GVHD, including fetuses receiving intrauterine transfusion, select immunocompetent or immunocompromised recipients, recipients who are undergoing marrow or progenitor cell transplantation, recipients of platelets selected for HLA or platelet compatibility, and recipients of donor units from blood relatives.

Washed Blood

Red Blood Cells

Washing a unit of RBCs with 1-2 L sterile normal saline removes about 99% of plasma proteins, electrolytes, and antibodies. Overriding the photocell detection system on automated equipment or removing the buffy coat during manual washing also removes some of the leukocytes but not enough to prevent alloimmunization. Up to 20% of the red cell mass may be lost depending on the protocol used. Washed red cells must be used within 24 hours because preparation is usually accomplished in an open system, and removal of the anticoagulant-preservative solution compromises long-term preservation of cell viability and function.

Platelets

Platelets can be washed with normal saline or saline buffered with ACD-A or citrate, using manual or automated methods.[7] Procedures recover about 90% of the platelets and reduce plasma content about 95%; white cell content is not significantly changed. Washed platelets must be used within 4 hours of preparation.

Indications for Use

Washing is indicated to remove plasma antibodies or other constituents that may cause harm or severe side effects in the intended recipient, ie, when potassium content must be reduced for critical patients who cannot tolerate any increase, or when donor plasma is known to contain anti-Pl[A1] or significant leukocyte antibodies. Washing can reduce the incidence of febrile, urticarial, and, possibly, anaphylactic reactions. Patients with clinically significant anti-IgA may require blood from IgA-deficient donors, but RBCs washed with high volumes of saline (3000 mL or more) may be satisfactory.

Frozen Cellular Components

Frozen storage can signficantly extend the shelf life of red cell and platelet components. Unfortunately, the process can also cause cell damage and add considerable expense if not carefully controlled and managed.

Freeze-Thaw Damage

When unprotected cells are frozen, damage may result from cellular dehydration and from mechanical trauma caused by intracellular ice crystals. At rates of freezing slower than 10 C/minute, extracellular water freezes before intracellular water, producing an osmotic gradient that causes water to diffuse from inside the cell to outside the cell. This leads to intracellular dehydration. Moderate to severe dehydration and resulting hypertonicity can cause significant cell injury. When temperature drops at a rapid rate, the osmotic gradient does not develop, minimizing dehydration and volume reduction; however, a spontaneous formation of intracellular ice crystals and accompanying cell damage still occur.

Prevention of freeze-thaw injury requires finding a cooling rate for each tissue or cell suspension that is optimal for minimizing dehydration and ice crystal formation. At the ideal cooling rate, enough water leaves the cell to produce mild intracellular hypertonicity and retard intracellular ice formation, but not so much that there is significant dehydration. Controlling the freezing rate, however, is not sufficient by itself to prevent cellular damage, so cryoprotective agents must be used.

Cryoprotective Agents

Cryoprotective agents are classified as penetrating and nonpenetrating. Penetrating agents such as glycerol and dimethyl sulfoxide (DMSO) are small molecules that freely cross the cell membrane into the cytoplasm. The intracellular cryoprotectant provides an osmotic force that prevents water from migrating outward as extracellular ice is formed. A high concentration prevents formation of ice crystals and consequent membrane damage.[32]

Glycerol, a trihydric alcohol, is a colorless, sweet-tasting, syrup-like fluid that is miscible with water. Pharmacologically, glycerol is rela-

tively inert. If incompletely deglycerolized cells are infused, systemic effects are negligible except for shifts in intracellular fluid volume.

DMSO is a colorless liquid with a sulfur-like smell. It is highly polar and dissolves many water- and lipid-soluble substances. Because DMSO releases heat upon mixture with water, it should be added to the cryoprotectant solution and the mixture should be cooled before it is added to a cell suspension. DMSO, given intravenously, may cause nausea, vomiting, local vasospasm, and an objectionable garlic-like odor and taste.

Nonpenetrating cryoprotective agents (eg, hydroxyethyl starch) are large macromolecules that do not enter the cell. These molecules protect the cells by a process called "vitrification" because they form a noncrystalline "glassy" shell around the cell. This prevents loss of water and dehydration injury, and alters the temperature at which the solution undergoes transition from liquid to solid. Hydroxyethylstarch is a polymeric cryoprotectant initially used for red cells but it has also been used in conjunction with DMSO for the cryopreservation of hematopoietic progenitor cells.

Freezing RBCs

Frozen preservation of RBCs with glycerol is primarily used for storing units with rare blood types and autologous units. Frozen cells can be effectively stockpiled for military mobilization or civilian disasters, but the high cost and the 24-hour shelf life after deglycerolization make them less useful for routine inventory management.

Two concentrations of glycerol have been used to cryopreserve red cells, as shown in Table 8-5. This chapter, and Methods 6.6 and 6.7, discuss only the high-concentration glycerol technique used by most blood banks. Modifications have been developed for glycerolizing, freezing, storing, thawing, and deglycerolizing red cells and are discussed elsewhere.[33] Several instruments are available that partially auto-

Table 8-5. Comparison of Two Methods of Red Blood Cell Cryopreservation

Consideration	High-Concentration Glycerol	Low-Concentration Glycerol
Final glycerol concentration (wt/vol)	Approx. 40%	Approx. 20%
Initial freezing temperature	−80 C	−196 C
Freezing rate	Slow	Rapid
Freezing rate controlled	No	Yes
Type of freezer	Mechanical	Liquid nitrogen
Storage temperature (maximum)	−65 C	−120 C
Change in storage temperature	Can be thawed and refrozen	Critical
Type of storage	Polyvinyl chloride; polyolefin	Polyolefin
Shipping	Dry ice	Liquid nitrogen
Special deglycerolizing equipment required	Yes	No
Deglycerolizing time	20-40 minutes	30 minutes
Hematocrit	55-70%	50-70%
White cells removed	94-99%	95%

mate glycerolization and deglycerolization of red cells. The manufacturer of each instrument provides detailed instructions for use.

Blood intended for freezing can be collected into CPD or CPDA-1 and stored as Whole Blood or RBCs (including AS-RBCs). Ordinarily, red cells are glycerolized and frozen within 6 days of collection or rejuvenated and frozen up to 3 days after they expire,[3(p27)] but RBCs preserved in AS-1, AS-3, and AS-5 can be frozen up to 42 days with adequate recovery.[34]

Some glycerolization procedures require removal of most of the plasma or additive from the RBCs; others do not. The concentration of glycerol used for freezing is hypertonic to blood. Its rapid introduction can cause osmotic damage to red cells, which becomes manifest as hemolysis only after thawing. Therefore, glycerol should be introduced slowly to allow equilibration within the red cells.

The US Department of Defense has adopted a method for high-concentration glycerolization that uses an 800-mL primary collection container suitable for freezing (see Method 6.7).[33] Because the original container is used for both the addition of cryoprotective agent and for freezing, there is less chance of contamination and/or identification error. In addition, the amount of extracellular glycerol is smaller and it is more efficient to store and ship units prepared by this method.

Storage Bags. Storage bag composition can affect the freezing process; less hemolysis may occur in polyolefin than in some polyvinyl chloride (PVC) bags.[35] Contact between red cells and the PVC bag surface may cause an injury that slightly increases hemolysis upon deglycerolization. In addition, polyolefin bags are less brittle at −80 C and less likely to break during shipment and handling than PVC bags.

Freezing Process. Red cells frozen within 6 days of collection with a final glycerol concentration of 40% (wt/vol) must be stored at –65 C or colder. Metal canisters are usually used to protect the plastic bag during freezing, storage, and thawing. Although up to 18 hours at room temperature can elapse between glycerolizing and freezing without increased postthaw hemolysis, an interval no longer than 4 hours is recommended.[36] With current 40% (wt/vol) glycerol methods, controlled rate freezing is unnecessary; freezing is accomplished by placing the RBC container into a –80 C freezer.

Storage. The FDA licenses Red Blood Cells, Frozen for storage up to 10 years when prepared with high glycerol (40% wt/vol) methods. Units stored for up to 21 years have been transfused successfully, and for blood of rare phenotypes, a facility's medical director may wish to extend the storage period. The distinctive nature of such units and the reason for retaining them past the 10-year storage period should be documented.

As units are put into long-term storage, many consider it prudent to freeze samples of serum or plasma for subsequent testing should new donor screening tests be introduced in the future. The type of any specimen saved, date of collection, date of freezing, and specimen location, if necessary, should be included in records of frozen blood.

Not all such specimens may meet the sample requirements of new tests. If stored samples are not available or inappropriate for testing, blood centers will attempt to call the donor back for subsequent testing. Frozen rare RBCs that have not been tested for new disease markers should be transfused only after weighing the risks and benefits to the patient. The label should indicate that the unit has not been completely tested and should identify the missing test(s).

Thawing and Deglycerolizing RBCs

The protective canister and enclosed frozen cells may be placed directly in a 37 C dry warmer or can be overwrapped and immersed in a 37 C waterbath. Units frozen in the primary collection bag system should be thawed at 42 C.[33] The thawing process takes at least 20-25 minutes and should not exceed 40 minutes. Gentle agitation may be used to speed thawing.

Thawed cells contain a high concentration of glycerol that must be gradually reduced to avoid in-vivo or in-vitro hemolysis. Deglycerolization is achieved by washing the red cells with solutions of decreasing osmolarity. In one procedure (see Method 6.6) glycerolized cells are diluted with 150 mL of 12% saline, then washed with 1 L of 1.6% saline, followed by 1 L of 0.9% saline with 0.2% dextrose. The progressive decrease in osmolarity of the washing solutions causes osmotic swelling of the cells, so each solution must be added slowly, with adequate time allowed for mixing and osmotic equilibration.

Any of the commercially available instruments for batch or continuous-flow washing can be used to deglycerolize red cells frozen in a high concentration of glycerol.[33] Because there are many potentially important variations in deglycerolization protocols for each instrument, personnel in each facility should not only follow the manufacturer's instructions, but should also validate their process locally. The process selected must ensure adequate removal of cryoprotectant agents, minimal free hemoglobin, and result in recovery of at least 80% of the original red cell volume following the deglycerolization process.[3(p27)]

When deglycerolization is complete, the integrally connected tubing should be filled with an aliquot of red cells and sealed in such a manner that it can be detached for subsequent compatibility testing. The label must identify both the collecting facility and the facility that prepares the deglycerolized unit.[3(p35)]

When glycerolized frozen red cells from persons with sickle cell trait are suspended in hypertonic wash solutions during deglycerolization and centrifuged, they form a jelly-like mass and hemolyze. Modified wash procedures using only 0.9% saline with 0.2% dextrose after the addition of 12% saline can eliminate this problem.[37] In some cryopreservation programs, donations are screened for the presence of hemoglobin S before being frozen.

Storing Deglycerolized RBCs. When glycerolizing or deglycerolizing involves entering the blood bag, the system is considered "open" and the resulting suspension of deglycerolized cells can be stored for only 24 hours at 1-6 C. A longer postthaw shelf life would make frozen RBCs more useful for inventory management. Sterile connection devices or plastic containers of suitable configuration can be used for preparation and subsequent deglycerolization in a closed system.

When deglycerolized RBCs are stored at 1-6 C for periods up to 14 days, the major observed changes are increased concentrations of potassium and hemoglobin in the supernatant fluid. Red cells that have undergone gamma irradiation and subsequent storage at 1-6 C tolerate freezing with no more detectable damage than unirradiated cells.[38,39]

Refreezing Deglycerolized RBCs. It may occasionally be desirable to refreeze thawed RBC units that have not been used as expected or have been unintentionally thawed. Units that were deglycerolized, stored 20 hours at refrigerator temperature, and then reglycerolized and refrozen showed no loss of ATP, 2,3-DPG, or in-vivo survival,[40] and RBCs subjected three times to glycerolizing, freezing, and thawing exhibited a 27% loss of total hemoglobin.[41] AABB *Standards* does not address refreezing thawed units, because this should not be considered a routine practice. If thawed units are refrozen, the records should document the valuable nature of such units and the reasons for refreezing them.

Clinical Considerations

Deglycerolized RBCs are nearly comparable in volume, hematocrit, and efficacy to standard, liquid-stored RBCs. Virtually all the plasma and anticoagulant and most of the leukocytes and platelets have been removed. Consequently, they are generally safe for IgA-deficient patients with clinically significant IgA antibodies or for patients with severe immune reactions to transfused plasma proteins. Freshly deglycerolized cells have reduced levels of potassium in the supernatant fluid, but potassium levels rise as the cells are stored after deglycerolization.

In-vivo survival and function are comparable to liquid-stored red cells because ATP levels, 2,3-DPG content, and oxygen dissociation curves are unchanged from prefreeze values. Cryopreservation results in some hemolysis, so total red cell mass of a deglycerolized unit is never as large as the original RBC unit. Recurrent FNH reactions, transmission of CMV, and HLA alloimmunization are reduced when deglycerolized RBCs are transfused, but high-performance leukocyte reduction filters are more effective at removing white cells. Some viable lymphocytes remain after freezing and deglycerolization. Deglycerolization cannot substitute for gamma irradiation to prevent GVHD.

Cryopreservation of Platelets

Perhaps because of their greater complexity, platelets appear to sustain greater injury during cryopreservation than red cells, although several protocols have successfully used DMSO as a cryoprotectant.[42,43] Because postthaw platelet recovery and function are significantly reduced when compared to liquid-stored platelets, the clinical use of cryopreserved platelets is not widespread. The primary use of this procedure is to freeze autologous platelets for future use.

Cryopreservation of Hematopoietic Progenitor Cells

See Chapter 25.

Blood Component Storage

Blood Refrigerators

Blood must be stored only in refrigerators that, by design and capacity, maintain the required blood storage temperatures of 1-6 C throughout their interior space. They must have a system to monitor temperatures continuously and record them at least every 4 hours, and an alarm system with an audible signal that activates before blood reaches unacceptable storage temperatures.[3(p39)]

Interiors should be clean, adequately lighted, and well organized. Clearly designated and segregated areas are needed for: 1) unprocessed blood, 2) labeled blood suitable for allogeneic transfusion, 3) rejected, outdated, or quarantined blood, 4) autologous blood, and 5) biohazardous autologous blood. Refrigerators used for the storage of blood and blood components may also be used for blood derivatives, tissues, patient and donor specimens, and blood bank reagents.

Refrigerators for blood storage outside the blood bank, as may be found in surgical suites or emergency rooms, must meet these same standards. Temperature records are required at all times when blood is present. It is usually most practical to make blood bank personnel responsible for monitoring these refrigerators.

Blood Freezers

Blood freezers have the same temperature monitoring and alarm requirements as blood refrigerators and must also be kept clean and well organized. Freezers designated for plasma storage must maintain temperatures colder than –18 C (many function at –30 C or colder); RBC freezers must maintain temperatures colder than –65 C (many maintain temperatures colder than –80 C). Self-defrosting freezers must maintain acceptable temperatures throughout their defrost cycle.

Freezer alarm sensors should be accessible and located near the door, although older units may have sensors located between the inner and outer freezer walls where they are neither apparent nor accessible. In such cases, the location of the sensor can be obtained from the manufacturer and a permanent mark placed on the wall at that location. Clinical engineers may be able to relocate the sensor thermocouple for easier use.

Liquid nitrogen tanks used for blood storage also have alarm system requirements. The level of liquid nitrogen should be measured and the sensor placed somewhere above the minimum height needed.

Room Temperature Storage

Components that require 20-24 C temperatures can be stored on a tabletop in any room with an appropriate ambient temperature, provided the temperature is recorded every 4 hours during storage. Because room temperatures fluctuate, "environmental" or "platelet chambers" have been developed to provide consistent, controlled room temperatures. These chambers are equipped with circulating fans, temperature recorders, and alarm systems, much like blood refrigerators.

In addition, platelets require gentle continuous agitation during storage to facilitate gas exchange within the bag and to reduce the formation of aggregates. Elliptical, circular, and flat-bed agitators are available for table top or chamber use. Elliptical rotators are not recommended for use with storage bags made of polyolefin without plasticizer (PL-732).[44]

Storage Equipment Quality Control

Continuous Temperature Monitoring Systems

Most blood refrigerators, freezers, and chambers have built-in temperature monitoring sensors connected to recording charts and/or digital readout systems for easy surveillance. Digital recording devices measure the difference in potential generated by a thermocouple; this difference is then converted to temperature. Because warm air rises, temperature recording sensors are best placed on a high shelf. They should be immersed in a volume of liquid no greater than the volume of the smallest component stored. Either a glass container or a plastic blood bag may be used. Recording charts and monitoring systems are inspected daily to make sure they function properly.

When recording charts or tapes are changed, they should be dated inclusively (ie, start and stop dates) and labeled to identify the facility, the specific refrigerator or freezer, and the person changing the charts. Any departure from normal temperature should be explained in writing on the chart beside the tracing or on another document. A chart with a perfect circle tracing can indicate that the recorder is not functioning properly or is not sensitive enough to record the expected variations in temperature that occur in any actively used refrigerator.

Blood banks with many refrigerators and freezers may find it easier to use a central monitoring-alarm system that monitors all equipment continuously and simultaneously and prepares a hard-copy tape of temperatures at least once every 4 hours. These systems have an audible alarm that sounds as soon as any connected equipment reaches its predetermined temperature range and indicates the equipment in question. Blood storage equipment so monitored does not require a separate independent recording chart.

Thermometers

Visual thermometers in blood storage equipment provide ongoing verification of temperature accuracy. One should be immersed in the container with the continuous monitoring sensor. The temperature of the thermometer should be compared periodically to the temperature on the recording chart. If the two do not agree within 2 C, both should be checked against a thermometer certified by the National Institute of Standards and Technology (NIST) and suitable corrective action should be

taken. (See Method 7-7.) (A 2-C variation between calibrated thermometers allows for the variation that may occur between thermometers calibrated against the NIST thermometer.)

Thermometers also help verify that temperature is appropriately maintained throughout the storage space. Large refrigerators or freezers may require several thermometers to assess temperature fluctuations. In addition to the one immersed with the continuous monitoring sensor (usually located on a high shelf), at least one other in a similar container is placed on the lowest shelf on which blood is stored. The temperatures in both areas must be within the required range at all times.

Either liquid-in-glass (or analog) thermometers or electronic and thermocouple (or digital) devices can be used for assessing storage temperatures, as long as their accuracy is calibrated against a NIST-certified thermometer or a thermometer with a NIST-traceable calibration certificate (see Method 7.7). Of equal importance is that they be used as intended, according to the manufacturer's recommendations.

Alarm Systems

To ensure that alarm signals will activate at a temperature that allows personnel to take proper action before blood reaches undesirable temperatures, both temperature of activation and power source are tested periodically. The electrical source for the alarm system must be separate from that of the refrigerator or freezer; either a continuously rechargeable battery or an independent electrical circuit served by an emergency generator is acceptable.

Method 7.1 provides a detailed procedure to test the temperatures of activation for refrigerator alarms. Suggestions for freezer alarms are in Method 7.2. Thermocouple devices that function at freezer temperatures are especially useful for determining the temperature of activation with accuracy when sensors are accessible. When they are not, approximate activation temperatures can be determined by checking a freezer's thermometer and recording chart when the alarm sounds after it is shut down for periodic cleaning or maintenance. It can also be assessed by placing a water bottle filled with cold tap water against the inner freezer wall where the sensor is located. When the alarm goes off, usually in a short time, the recording chart can be checked immediately for the temperature of activation.

There must be written instructions for personnel to follow when the alarm sounds. These instructions should include steps to determine the immediate cause of the temperature change and ways to handle temporary malfunctions, as well as steps to take in the event of prolonged failure. It is important to list the names of key people to be notified and what steps should be taken to ensure that proper storage temperature is maintained for all blood, components, and reagents.

Blood Inspections

Stored blood components are inspected immediately before issue for transfusion or shipment to other facilities.[3(p40,65)] These inspections must be documented; records should include the date, donor number, description of any abnormal units, the action taken, and the identity of personnel involved. Visual inspections cannot always detect contamination or other deleterious conditions; nonetheless, blood products that look abnormal must not be shipped or transfused.

Contamination should be suspected if[45]:

- Segments appear much lighter in color than that of the bag.
- The red cell mass looks purple.
- A zone of hemolysis is observed just above the cell mass.
- Clots are visible.
- The plasma or supernatant fluid is murky, purple, brown, or red. Although a green hue from light-induced changes in bilirubin pigments need not cause the unit to be rejected, units with grossly lipemic plasma, identified by its milky appearance, are usually considered unsuitable for transfusion.
- Blood or plasma is observed in the ports or at sealing sites in the tubing. This suggests inadequate sealing or closure, and the unit should, at the very least, be quarantined.

A red cell unit that is questioned for any reason should be quarantined until a responsible person decides its disposition. Evaluation might include inverting it gently a few times to mix the cells with the supernatant fluid because considerable undetected hemolysis, clots, or other alterations may be present in the undisturbed red cell mass. If, after resuspension, resettling and careful examination, the blood no longer appears abnormal, it may be returned to inventory. Appropriate records should be maintained documenting the actions taken, when, and by whom.

In addition, platelets should be inspected for the presence of excessive aggregates. Units of FFP and CRYO should be inspected, when removed from frozen storage, for evidence of thawing and refreezing and for evidence of cracks in the tubing or plastic bag. Unusual turbidity in thawed components may be cause for discard.

Bacteriologic Studies

Bacterial contamination of transfusion components is rare thanks to the use of aseptic technique, the availability of closed systems for collection and preparation, and careful control of storage conditions.

Sterility testing of blood or components plays a role in validating initial production processes. If a transfusion component has an abnormal appearance, or if an adverse clinical reaction appears to be related to contaminated donor blood, culturing may be desirable, and a Gram's-stained smear of supernatant plasma should be examined. Microbiologists can best advise blood center staff on sample requirements and appropriate test methods for detecting potential blood contaminants including cryophilic microorganisms. Making separate cultures from a sealed segment, from the contents of the bag, and from the recipient can provide useful diagnostic information.

Positive cultures should arouse suspicion of donor bacteremia, potentially inadequate donor arm preparation, or improper handling or pooling technique. The donor's health should be reviewed, and other components prepared from that collection should be evaluated.

Transport and Shipping

Blood transported short distances within a facility, eg, to the patient care area for transfusion, requires no special packaging other than that dictated by perceived safety concerns and institutional preferences. However, blood should never unnecessarily be allowed to reach temperatures outside its accepted range. Some transport guidelines may be warranted if transport time is prolonged.

Shipment to areas outside the facility requires additional packaging. Transport containers or coolers and packaging procedures must be validated prior to use to verify that they are able to maintain blood products at required temperatures for the intended time and conditions. Containers must also be able to withstand leakage, pressure, and other conditions incidental to routine handling. Refer to Chapter 2 for more information on shipping regulations and guidelines.

Simple exposure to temperatures outside the acceptable range does not necessarily render blood unsuitable for transfusion. Exceptions may be made under unusual circumstances, such as for autologous units or cells of rare phenotype, but the records must document the reasons for preserving the unit, the evaluation of its continued suitability for transfusion, and the identity of the person responsible for the decision.

Other factors to consider when assessing product acceptability after transport include the length of time in shipment, mode of transportation, magnitude of variance over 10 C, presence of residual ice in the shipping box, the appearance of the unit(s), age of the unit, and its probable subsequent storage before transfusion. The shipping facility should be notified when a receiving facility observes unacceptably high temperatures.

Blood From Mobile Collection Facilities

Whole blood should be transported from the collection site to the component preparation laboratory as soon as possible. Units should be continuously cooled toward 1-6 C unless platelets are to be harvested, in which case, units must not cool below 20 C. The time between collection and the separation of components must not exceed 8 hours.

Whole Blood and RBCs

Liquid red cell components shipped from the collection facility to another facility must be transported in a manner that ensures temperatures between 1-10 C. The upper limit of 10 C can be reached in 30 minutes if a unit of blood, taken from 5 C storage, is left at an ambient temperature of 25 C. Smaller units, as are commonly used in pediatric service, can warm even more quickly.

Wet ice, securely bagged to prevent condensation or water leakage, is the coolant of choice to maintain required temperatures during transport and shipping. An appropriate volume is placed on top of the units within the cardboard box or insulated container.

Platelets and Granulocytes

Every reasonable effort must be made to ensure that platelets and granulocytes are maintained at 20-24 C during shipment. A well-insulated container without added ice, or with a commercial coolant designed to keep the temperature at 20-24 C, is recommended.

Fiber-filled envelopes or newspaper are excellent insulators. For very long distances or travel times in excess of 24 hours, double-insulated containers may be needed.

Frozen Components

Frozen components must be packaged for transport in a manner designed to keep them frozen.[3(p40)] This is achieved by using a suitable quantity of dry ice in well-insulated containers or in standard shipping cartons lined with insulating material, such as plastic air bubble packaging or dry packaging fragments. The dry ice, obtained as sheets, can be layered at the bottom of the container, between each layer of frozen components, and on top.

Shipping facilities should determine optimal conditions for shipping frozen components, which depend on the temperature requirements of the component, the distance to be shipped, the shipping container used, and ambient temperatures encountered. Again, procedures and shipping containers should be validated and periodically monitored. The receiving facility should always observe the shipment temperature and report unacceptable findings to the shipping facility.

Red cells cryopreserved with high-concentration glycerol (40% wt/vol) tolerate fluctuations in temperature between −85 C and −20 C with no significant change in in-vitro recovery or 24-hour posttransfusion survival, so transport with dry ice is quite acceptable. Red cells stored in liquid nitrogen have little tolerance for temperature fluctuations and must be transported in special liquid nitrogen containers.

Blood shipments containing dry ice and liquid nitrogen as a coolant are considered dangerous goods and have special packaging and labeling requirements (see Chapter 2).

Disposition

Both blood centers and transfusion services must maintain records on all blood compo-nents handled that allow units to be tracked from collection to final disposition. Units of blood that cannot be released for transfusion should be returned to the provider or discarded as biohazardous material. The nature of the problem disqualifying the unit should be investigated and the results reported to the blood supplier. Findings may indicate a need to improve donor phlebotomy techniques, donor screening methods, the handling of blood units during processing, or blood storage and transport.

Disposal procedures must conform to the local public health codes for biohazardous waste. Autoclaving and/or incineration is recommended. If disposal is carried out off-site, a contract with the waste disposal firm must be available and should specify that appropriate Environmental Protection Agency, state, and local regulations are followed. (See Chapter 2 for the disposal of biohazardous waste.)

Reissuing Blood Products

Units that have left the control of the transfusion service or donor center and then have been returned must not be reissued for transfusion unless the following conditions have been met:

1. The container closure has not been penetrated or entered in any manner.
2. Red cell components have been maintained continuously between 1 and 10 C, preferably 1-6 C. Blood centers and transfusion services usually do not reissue red cells that have remained out of a monitored refrigerator or been validated cooler for longer than 30 minutes because, beyond that time, the temperature of the component may have risen above 10 C.
3. At least one sealed segment of integral donor tubing remains attached to the container, if the blood has left the premises of the issuing facility.
4. Records indicate that the blood has been reissued and has been inspected prior to reissue.

Blood Component Quality Control

Ensuring safe and efficacious blood components requires applying the principles of quality assurance to all aspects of component collection, preparation, testing, storage, and transport. All procedures and equipment in use must be validated prior to their implementation and periodically monitored thereafter. Staff must be appropriately trained and their competency evaluated. The contents of final products should be periodically assessed to make sure they meet expectations. How much quality assessment is performed is best determined by the institution with input from the compliance officer and with AABB and FDA requirements in mind. Refer to Chapter 1 for general guidelines and Appendix 8-1 for more specific suggestions on quality control summarized from this chapter.

References

1. The code of federal regulations, 21 CFR 610.53(c). Washington, DC: US Government Printing Office, 1998 (revised annually).
2. Beutler E. Preservation of liquid red cells. In: Rossi EC, Simon TL, Moss GS, Gould SA, eds. Principles of transfusion medicine. 2nd ed. Baltimore, MD: Williams and Wilkins, 1995:51-60.
3. Menitove JE, ed. Standards for blood banks and transfusion services. 19th ed. Bethesda, MD: American Association of Blood Banks, 1999.
4. Simon TL, Marcus CS, Myhre BA, Nelson EJ. Effects of AS-3 nutrient-additive solution on 42 and 49 days of storage of red cells. Transfusion 1987;27:178-82.
5. Beutler E, Wood L. The in vivo regeneration of red cell 2,3-diphosphoglyceric acid (DPG) after transfusion of stored blood. J Lab Clin Med 1969;74:300-4.
6. Batton DG, Maisels MJ, Shulman G. Serum potassium changes following packed red cell transfusions in newborn infants. Transfusion 1983;23:163-4.
7. Calhoun L. Blood product preparation and administration. In: Petz LD, Swisher SN, Kleinman S, et al, eds. Clinical practice of transfusion medicine. 3rd ed. New York: Churchill Livingstone, 1996:305-33.
8. Food and Drug Administration. Memorandum: Use of an FDA cleared or approved sterile connecting device (STCD) in blood bank practice. July 29, 1994. Rockville, MD: CBER Office of Communica-

tion, Training, and Manufacturer's Assistance, 1994.
9. Beutler E. Red cell metabolism and storage. In: Anderson KC, Ness PM, eds. Scientific basis of transfusion medicine. Philadelphia: WB Saunders, 1994:188-202.
10. Huh YO, Lichtiger B, Giacco GG, et al. Effect of donation time on platelet concentrates and fresh-frozen plasma. Vox Sang 1989;56:21-4.
11. van Aken WG. Preparation of plasma derivatives. In: Rossi EC, Simon TL, Moss GS, Gould SA, eds. Principles of transfusion medicine. 2nd ed. Baltimore, MD: Williams and Wilkins, 1995:403-13.
12. American Association of Blood Banks, America's Blood Centers, and the American Red Cross. Circular of Information for the Use of Human Blood and Blood Components. July 1997. Bethesda, MD: American Association of Blood Banks, 1997.
13. George JN, El-Harake M. Thrombocytopenia due to enhanced platelet destruction by nonimmunologic mechanisms. In: Beutler E, Lichtman MA, Coller BS, Kipps TJ, eds. Williams' hematology. 5th ed. New York: McGraw-Hill, 1995:1290-315.
14. Product insert: PLAS+®SD, pooled plasma, solvent/detergent-treated. Arlington, VA: American Red Cross, 1998.
15. The code of federal regulations, 21 CFR 601.22. Washington, DC: US Government Printing Office, 1997 (revised annually).
16. The code of federal regulations, 21 CFR 640.54. Washington, DC: US Government Printing Office, 1997 (revised annually).
17. Bertoloni F, Murphy S. A multicenter inspection of the swirling phenomenon in platelet concentrates prepared in routine practice. Transfusion 1996;36:128-32.
18. Rosenthal J, Mitchell SC. Neonatal myelopoiesis and immunomodulation of host defenses. In: Petz LD, Swisher SN, Kleinman S, et al, eds. Clinical practice of transfusion medicine. 3rd ed. New York, NY: Churchill Livingstone, 1996:685-703.
19. Dzik S. Leukodepletion blood filters: Filter design and mechanisms of leukocyte removal. Transfus Med Rev 1993;7:65-77.
20. Buchholz DH, AuBuchon JP, Snyder EL, et al. Effects of white cell reduction on the resistance of blood components to bacterial multiplication. Transfusion 1994;34:852-7.
21. Leukocyte reduction. Association Bulletin 99-7. Bethesda, MD: American Associaton of Blood Banks, 1999.
22. Food and Drug Memorandum: Recommendations and licensure requirements for leuko-reduced blood products. May 29, 1996. Rockville, MD: CBER Office of Communication, Training, and Manufacturer's Assistance, 1996.
23. Brand A. Passenger leukocytes, cytokines and transfusion reactions. N Engl J Med 1994;331:670-1.
24. Dzik WH. Is the febrile response to transfusion due to donor or recipient cytokines? (letter). Transfusion 1992;32:594.
25. Heaton A. Timing of leukodepletion of blood products. Semin Hematol 1991;28:1-2.
26. Heddle NM, Klama L, Singer J, et al. The role of the plasma from platelet concentrates in transfusion reactions. N Engl J Med 1994;331:625-8.

27. Kao KJ. Effects of leukocyte depletion and UVB irradiation on alloantigenicity of major histocompatibility complex antigens in platelet concentrates: A comparative study. Blood 1992;80:2931-7.

28. Regarding leukocyte-reduction for the prevention of transfusion-transmitted cytomegalovirus. Association Bulletin 97-2. Bethesda, MD: American Association of Blood Banks, 1997.

29. Sayers MD. Cytomegalovirus and other herpesviruses. In: Petz LD, Swisher SN, Kleinman S, et al, eds. Clinical practice of transfusion medicine. 3rd ed. New York: Churchill Livingstone, 1996:875-89.

30. Food and Drug Administration. Memorandum: Recommendations regarding license amendments and procedures for gamma irradiation of blood products July 22, 1993. Rockville, MD: CBER Office of Communication, Training, and Manufacturer Assistance, 1993.

31. Tiehen A. Standard operating procedures. In: Butch S, Tiehen A, eds. Blood irradiation: A user's guide. Bethesda, MD: AABB Press, 1996:89-99.

32. Meryman HT. Frozen red cells. Transfus Med Rev 1989;3:121-7.

33. Valeri CR. Frozen red blood cells. In: Rossi EC, Simon TL, Moss GS, Gould SA, eds. Principles of transfusion medicine. 2nd ed. Baltimore, MD: Williams and Wilkins, 1995:61-6.

34. Rathbun EJ, Nelson EJ, Davey RJ. Posttransfusion survival of red cells frozen for 8 weeks after 42-day liquid storage in AS-3. Transfusion 1989;29:213-7.

35. Lovric VA, Klarkowski DB. Donor blood frozen and stored between −20 C and −25 C with 35-day post-thaw shelf life. Lancet 1989;1:71-3.

36. Meryman HT, Hornblower M. A method for freezing and washing RBCs using a high glycerol concentration. Transfusion 1972;12:145-56.

37. Meryman HT, Hornblower M. Freezing and deglycerolizing sickle-trait red blood cells. Transfusion 1976;16:627-32.

38. Suda BA, Leitman SF, Davey RJ. Characteristics of red cells irradiated and subsequently frozen for long term storage. Transfusion 1993;33:389-92.

39. Miraglia CC, Anderson G, Mintz PD. Effect of freezing on the in vivo recovery of irradiated cells. Transfusion 1994;34:775-8.

40. Kahn RA, Auster M, Miller WV. The effect of refreezing previously frozen deglycerolized red blood cells. Transfusion 1978;18:204-5.

41. Myhre BA, Nakasako YUY, Schott R. Studies on 4 C stored frozen reconstituted red blood cells. III. Changes occurring in units which have been repeatedly frozen and thawed. Transfusion 1978;18:199-203.

42. Angelini A, Dragani A, Berardi A, et al. Evaluation of four different methods for platelet freezing: In vitro and in vivo studies. Vox Sang 1992;62:146-51.

43. Borzini P, Assali G, Riva MR, et al. Platelet cryopreservation using dimethylsulfoxide/polyethylene glycol/sugar mixture as cryopreserving solution. Vox Sang 1993;64:248-9.

44. Moroff G, Holme S. Concepts about current conditions for the preparation and storage of platelets. Transfus Med Rev 1991;5:48-59.

45. Kim DM, Brecher ME, Bland LA, et al. Visual identification of bacterially contaminated red cells. Transfusion 1992;32:221-5.

Appendix 8-1. Quality Control (QC) Monitor Suggestions for Component Preparation

Staff	Initial training Annual competency to perform job tasks
Procedures	Initial validation Annual review: Current? Understandable? Complete?
Equipment	Initial validation of performance Periodic review of QC results and actual use practices Adherence to manufacturer's recommendations on use and preventive maintenance
Blood Refrigerators	Daily manual and recorder temperature checks Weekly temperature chart replacement Quarterly alarm activation check Quarterly check of sensor bottle fluid Periodic preventive maintenance and cleaning Periodic check for orderliness
Blood Freezers	Daily manual and recorder temperature checks Weekly temperature chart replacement Quarterly check of sensor bottle fluid, if appropriate Periodic alarm activation check Periodic preventive maintenance and cleaning Periodic check for orderliness
Platelet Chambers	Daily manual and recorder temperature checks Weekly temperature chart replacement Quarterly alarm activation check Quarterly check of sensor bottle fluid (if applicable) Periodic preventive maintenance and cleaning Periodic check for orderliness
Platelet Rotators	Periodic rotation/oscillation check Periodic preventive maintenance and cleaning
Component Centrifuge	Daily temperature check Monthly digital temperature verification Quarterly rpm and timer verification check Function checks—in conjunction with component assessment Periodic preventive maintenance and cleaning
Automated Cell Washers	Record of software/solutions used on what, when, by whom Quarterly rpm and timer verification check Function checks—in conjunction with component assessment Periodic preventive maintenance and cleaning
Waterbaths	Record of what components were thawed, when, by whom Daily temperature check Periodic quadrant check for temperature consistency Periodic preventive maintenance and cleaning
Microwave (for thawing plasma)	Record of what components were thawed, when, by whom Periodic timer and turntable check Periodic temperature check of thawed, control unit Periodic preventive maintenance and cleaning
Thermometers	Monthly check of electronic vs NIST-certified/verified Periodic check of analog for unbroken column and appropriate use Annual check of analog vs NIST-certified standard

(cont'd)

Appendix 8-1. Quality Control (QC) Monitor Suggestions for Component Preparation (cont'd)

Scales	Daily weight check Annual weight check vs NIST-certified weights Periodic preventive maintenance and cleaning
Sterile Connection Device	Inspection record of every weld on what components/disposables, when, by whom Periodic preventive maintenance and cleaning
Leukocyte-Reduction Filters	Periodic white cell pre/postfiltration counts and component volume
Irradiator	Record of irradiated product, exposure time used, turntable rotation Documentation of who performed what and when Periodic timer check Biannual leak test Annual dose delivery verification and calibration Periodic preventive maintenance and cleaning
Coolers/Transport Boxes	Biannual temperature check of products (using extreme transport conditions) Periodic inspection and cleaning
Components	Initial validation of contents and sterility (in conjunction with procedure validation) Use established method "known to produce" whenever possible Periodic monitoring of product content Records of proper storage/transport Additional component-specific checks are listed below
Whole Blood	(no additional checks)
Red Blood Cells	Periodic hematocrit checks (not required for RBC in additive solutions)
Fresh Frozen Plasma	Document times and staff who performed collection, separation, freezing
Cryoprecipitated AHF	Document times and staff who performed thawing, separation, refreezing Monthly Factor VIII/fibrinogen levels and volume on at least 4 units
Platelets	Document times and staff who performed collection, separation Monthly platelet counts, volume and pH on at least 4 units
Platelets, Pheresis	Document software/solutions used Document times and staff who performed collection Monthly platelet counts, volume and pH on at least 4 units per method in use, or 10% of components produced, whichever is more
Granulocytes	White cell count/differential and volume on all units
Frozen-Deglycerolized or Washed Red Blood Cells	Document software/solutions used Document times and staff who performed critical steps Hemolysis check on final wash step Periodic osmolality check on deglycerolized RBCs

Appendix 8-2. Expected Values for Component Quality Control

Component	Expected Value	AABB Standards*	FDA Regulation
Red Blood Cells	≤80%	D3.100	—
Red Blood Cells, Leukocytes Reduced	Retain 85% of original red cells and $\leq 5 \times 10^6$ leukocytes in the final container	D3.400	Ref. 1
Fresh Frozen Plasma	—	—	—
Cryoprecipitated AFH	Factor VIII: ≥80 IU Fibrinogen: ≥150 mg/bag	D4.240 D4.230	21 CFR 640.56(d) —
Platelets	$\geq 5.5 \times 10^{10}$ in 75% of units tested at the maximal storage time or at time of use; pH ≥ 6.2	D5.100 D5.200	21 CFR 640.24(c) pH=6.0 21 CFR 640.24(d); 640.25(b)(2)
Platelets, Leukocytes Reduced	$< 8.3 \times 10^5$ leukocytes in 100% of units tested; $>5.5 \times 10^{10}$ platelets in a least 75% of components tested	D5.300	Ref. 1
Platelets, Pheresis	$\geq 3.0 \times 10^{11}$ platelets in final container in 75% of components tested; pH ≥ 6.2	H3.110	Ref. 2
Platelets, Pheresis (obtained by splitting a plateletpheresis component)	$\geq 3.0 \times 10^{11}$ platelets in final container in 100% of components tested; pH ≥ 6.2	H3.120	—
Platelets, Pheresis, Leukocytes Reduced	$<5.0 \times 10^6$ leukocytes in 100% of components tested *and* $\geq 3.0 \times 10^{11}$ platelets in the final container in at least 75% of components tested; pH ≥ 6.2	H3.200	Ref. 1
Granulocytes, Pheresis	$\geq 1.0 \times 10^{10}$ granulocytes in at least 75% of components tested	H3.400	
Irradiated Components	25 Gy delivered to the midplane of the canister (if a free-standing irradiator is used) or the central midplane if an irradiation field of a radiotherapy instrument is used. Minimum of 15 Gy at any point in the canister.	D1.300	Ref. 3

* Menitove JE, ed. Standards for blood banks and transfusion services, 19th ed. Bethesda, MD: American Association of Blood Banks, 1999.
1. Food and Drug Administration. Memorandum: Recommendations and licensure for leuko-reduced blood products. May 22, 1996. Rockville, MD: CBER Office of Communication, Training, and Manufacturer's Assistance, 1996.
2. Food and Drug Administration. Memorandum: Revised guideline for the collection of Platelets, Pheresis. October 7, 1988. Rockville, MD: CBER Office of Communication, Training, and Manufacturer's Assistance, 1988.
3. Food and Drug Administration. Memorandum: Recommendations regarding license amendments and procedures for gamma irradiation of blood products. July 22, 1993. Rockville, MD: CBER Office of Communication, Training, and Manufacturer's Assistance, 1993.

Molecular Biology in Transfusion Medicine

MODERN MOLECULAR BIOLOGY techniques, including nucleic acid testing, cloning, and sequencing, have revolutionized the study of blood group genetics. This chapter reviews the basic concepts of gene structure, gene expression, and protein synthesis, using as examples our current understanding of the molecular basis of blood group antigens. Technology currently in use for the amplification and identification of genes and gene products is also reviewed. Space does not permit a more detailed discussion of these topics and the interested reader is referred to the suggested reading list at the end of the chapter.

From DNA to mRNA to Protein

Proteins are macromolecules composed of amino acids, the sequences of which are determined by genes. Lipids and carbohydrates are not encoded directly by genes; genetic determination of their assembly and functional structures results from the action of different enzymes. Blood group antigens can be considered gene products, either directly, as polymorphisms of membrane-associated proteins, or indirectly, as carbohydrate configurations catalyzed by glycosyltransferases.

Structure of DNA

Genes consist of specific sequences of deoxyribonucleic acid (DNA) located at specific positions (loci) along a chromosome. Each chromosome consists of a double-stranded molecule of DNA, which is composed of the sugar deoxyribose, a phosphate group, the purine bases adenine (A) and guanine (G), and the pyrimidine bases thymine (T) and cytosine (C). A double strand of DNA consists of two complementary (nonidentical) single strands held together by hydrogen bonds between specific base pairings of A-T and G-C. The two strands form a double helix configuration with the sugar-phosphate backbone on the outside and the paired bases on the inside. (See Fig 9-1.) DNA synthesis is catalyzed by DNA polymerase, which adds a deoxyribonucleotide to the 3′ end of the existing chain. The 3′ and 5′ notation refers to the linkage of the phosphate group to the deoxyribose moieties. Phosphate groups bridge the sugar groups between the fifth carbon atom of one deoxyribose molecule and the third carbon atom of the adjacent deoxyribose molecule and thus create the backbone of the DNA strand. Synthesis always occurs in the direction of 5′ to 3′.

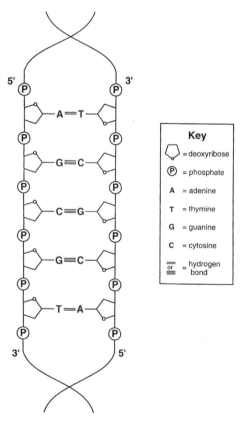

Figure 9-1. Schematic representation of the base pairing of double-stranded DNA.

DNA Transcription

Linear sequences of nucleotides along the DNA strands constitute the genes. Most genes occupy a constant location (locus) in the DNA of a specific chromosome, which may have been determined by mapping of the gene. For protein synthesis to occur (see Fig 9-2), the information encoded in the DNA sequence must be copied (transcription) and transported to the cytoplasmic organelles where protein assembly takes place (translation). Transcription is done by copying one strand of the DNA into messenger ribonucleic acid (mRNA), which is a linear sequence of nucleotides that differs from DNA in the sugar present in its backbone (ribose instead of deoxyribose) and the replacement of thymine by uracil (U), which also pairs with adenine. DNA transcription is catalyzed by the enzyme RNA polymerase. RNA polymerase binds tightly to a specific DNA sequence called the promoter, which contains the site at which RNA synthesis begins (see Fig 9-3). Proteins called transcription factors are required for RNA polymerase to bind to DNA and for transcription to occur. Regulation of transcription can lead to increased, decreased, or absent expression of a gene. For instance, a single base pair mutation in the transcription factor binding site of the Duffy gene promoter impairs the promoter activity and is responsible for the Fy(a–b–) phenotype.[1]

After binding to the promoter, RNA polymerase opens up the double helix of a small local region of DNA, exposing the nucleotides on each strand. The nucleotides of one exposed DNA strand act as a template for complementary base pairing; RNA is synthesized by the addition of ribonucleotides to the elongating chain. As RNA polymerase moves along the template strand of DNA, the double helix is opened before it and closes behind it like a zipper. The process continues until the polymerase encounters a termination (stop) signal, whereupon the enzyme halts synthesis and releases both the DNA template and the new RNA chain.

DNA ⁵' A T G T C T T C G A C G G G A C C T ³' noncoding strand
     ³' T A C A G A A G C T G C C C T G G A ⁵' coding strand

transcription

mRNA   ⁵'A U G | U C U | U C G | A C G | G G A | C C U ³'

translation

protein   Met   Ser   Ser   Thr   Gly   Pro

Figure 9-2. Model of a nucleotide sequence. Sequence is fictitious.

Shortly after the initiation of transcription, the newly formed chain is capped at its 5′ end by the addition of a methylated G nucleotide. The 5′ cap is important for initiating protein synthesis and possibly in protecting the mRNA molecule from degradation during its transport to the cytoplasm. Once the RNA polymerase cleaves the new RNA transcript, another polymerase attaches 100-200 copies of adenylic acid, called the poly-A tail, to the 3′ end of the mRNA. The poly-A tail functions in the export of mature mRNA from the cell nucleus to the cytoplasm, in the stabilization of the mRNA, and as a ribosomal recognition signal required for efficient translation.

mRNA Processing

In eukaryotic cells, the nucleotide sequence of a gene contains regions that are represented in the mRNA and other regions that are not represented. The regions of the gene that are represented in mRNA are called exons, which specify

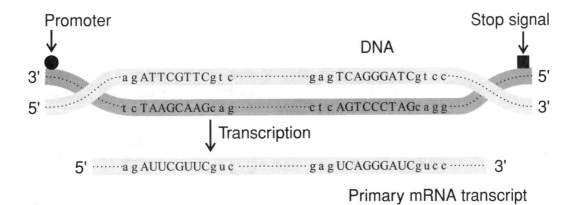

Figure 9-3. The promoter sequence (●) contains the starting site for RNA synthesis. RNA polymerase binds to the promoter and opens up a local region of the DNA sequence. One strand of DNA (lower one in this figure) acts as a template for complementary base pairing. The RNA polymerase copies the DNA in a 5′ to 3′ direction until it encounters a stop signal (■). Lowercase letters represent nucleotides in introns; uppercase letters represent coding bases in exons. The sequence is fictitious.

the protein-coding sequences and the sequences of the untranslated 5′ and 3′ regions. The regions that are not represented in the mRNA are called intervening sequences or introns. In the initial transcription of DNA to RNA, the introns and exons are copied in their entirety, and the resulting product is known as the primary RNA transcript or pre-mRNA. Processing occurs while pre-mRNA is still in the nucleus, and the introns are cut out by a process known as RNA splicing (see Fig 9-4).

RNA splicing depends on the presence of certain highly conserved sequences consisting of GU at the 5′ splice site (donor site) and AG at the 3′ splice site (acceptor site). Additionally, an adenosine residue within a specific sequence in the intron participates in a complex reaction along with a variety of proteins. The reaction results in cleavage and joining of the 5′ and 3′ splice sites, with release of the intervening sequence as a lariat. Substitution of any of these highly conserved sequences can result in inaccurate RNA splicing (see Fig 9-4). Alternative splicing of pre-mRNA may lead to the production of more than one protein from the same gene, such as the production of the Rh blood group C/c and E/e proteins from the *RHCE* gene.[2]

Translation of mRNA

The bases within a linear mRNA sequence are read (or translated) in groups of three, called codons. Each 3-base combination codes for one amino acid. Because there are only 20 amino acids commonly used for protein synthesis, most amino acids can be specified by each of several different codons, a circumstance known as "degeneracy" or "redundancy" in the genetic code. For example, lysine can be specified by either AAA or AAG. Methionine has only the single codon AUG. Three codons (UAA, UGA, and UAG) function as stop signals; when the translation process encounters one of them, peptide synthesis stops.

For the translation of codons into amino acids, cytoplasmic mRNA requires the assistance of transfer RNA (tRNA) molecules. The tRNA molecules interact with the mRNA through specific base pairings and bring with them the amino acid specified by the mRNA codon. The amino acids are thus linked into the growing polypeptide chain. Protein synthesis occurs on ribosomes, which are large complexes of RNA and protein molecules within the rough endoplasmic reticulum. The ribosome binds to the tRNA and to the mRNA, starting at its 5′ end (amino terminus). Protein synthesis

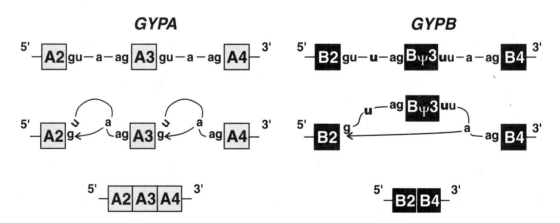

Figure 9-4. Substitution of two nucleotides (boldface) in the intron sequences flanking exon 3 of *GYPB* prevents normal splicing. Instead, all nucleotides between the 5′ donor site of the second intron and the 3′ acceptor site of the third intron are excised. Because exon 3 is not translated, it is called a pseudoexon (Ψ).

therefore occurs from the amino-terminal end toward the carboxyl-terminal end. The protein is produced sequentially until a stop codon is reached, which terminates the translation process and releases the newly synthesized protein.

Many of the steps in the pathway of RNA synthesis to protein production are closely regulated at different levels to control gene expression. Control steps include: initiation of transcription, proofreading of the transcription process, addition of the poly-A tail, transportation of mRNA to the cytosol, initiation of translation, and elongation of the polypeptide chain.

Genetic Mechanisms That Create Polymorphism

Despite the redundancy inherent in degeneracy of the genetic code, molecular events such as substitution, insertion, or deletion of a nucleotide may have far-reaching effects on the protein encoded. Some of the blood group polymorphisms observed at the phenotypic level can be traced to small changes at the nucleotide level. The sequence in Fig 9-2, which is not meant to represent a known sequence, can be used to illustrate the effects of minute changes at the nucleotide level, discussed below.

Nucleotide Substitution

Any of three possible outcomes can follow substitution of a single nucleotide:

1.   Silent mutation. For example, a substitution in the DNA coding strand for serine (UCU) could produce the UCA sequence, which also codes for serine. Thus, there would be no effect on the protein because the codon would still be translated as serine.

2.   Missense response. A substitution of C to T could result in a sequence that changes the product of the codon from serine (UCG) to leucine (UUG). Many blood group polymorphisms reflect a single

amino acid change in an underlying molecule. For example, the K1 antigen has threonine, while K2 has methionine, at amino acid 193. This results from a single C to T substitution in exon 6 of the Kell (*K*) gene.

3.   Nonsense response. A substitution of G to T in the DNA coding strand creates the codon UAG, which is one of the three stop codons. No protein synthesis will occur beyond this point, resulting in a shortened or truncated version of the protein. Depending upon where this nonsense substitution occurs, the synthesized protein may be rapidly degraded, or may retain some function in its abbreviated form. The Cromer blood group antigens reside on the membrane protein decay-accelerating factor (DAF). In the null (Inab) phenotype, a nucleotide substitution of G to A of the *DAF* gene creates a stop codon at position 53, and the cell has no expression of DAF.

Nucleotide substitution outside an exon sequence may also be significant. In *GYPB*, the gene that encodes the red cell membrane protein glycophorin B (GPB), substitutions of two conserved nucleotides required for RNA splicing result in excision of exon 3 as well as introns 2 and 3 (see Fig 9-4). Because exon 3 is a noncoding exon, it is called a pseudoexon.

Nucleotide Insertion and Deletion

Insertion of an entirely new nucleotide results in a frameshift, described as +1, because a nucleotide is being added. Nucleotide deletion causes a −1 frameshift. A peptide may be drastically altered by the insertion or deletion of a single nucleotide. Eventually, this will result in a stop codon.

Gene Rearrangement

Gene rearrangement may occur between misaligned homologous genes located on two copies of the same chromosome. Examples of homologous genes encoding blood group antigens are the *RHD* and *RHCE* genes of the Rh blood group system, and *GYPA* and *GYPB*, which encode the antigens of the MNS blood group system.

Single Crossover

A single crossover is the mutual exchange of nucleotides between two homologous genes. If crossover occurs in a region where paired homologous chromosomes are misaligned, two hybrid genes are formed in reciprocal arrangement (see Fig 9-5). The novel amino acid sequences encoded by the nucleotides at the junction of the hybrid gene may result in epitopes recognized by antibodies in human serum.

Gene Conversion

The process of gene conversion is thought to consist of crossover, a general recombination process, and DNA repair during meiosis. The result is that nucleotides from one homolo-

gous gene are inserted into another without reciprocal exchange. At the site of chromosome crossover during meiosis, a heteroduplex joint can form; this is a staggered joint between nucleotide sequences on two participating DNA strands (see Fig 9-6).

Molecular Techniques

The development of modern molecular techniques has greatly expanded our knowledge of all biological systems. These same techniques are also applicable to the diagnosis of disease, the practice of forensic science, the generation of recombinant proteins, and the production of functional genes for gene therapy. Many of these processes begin with DNA typing and analysis, techniques that are reviewed below.

Isolation of Nucleic Acids

The first step in most molecular biology techniques is the isolation and purification of nucleic acid, either DNA or RNA. For applications of interest to the blood banking community,

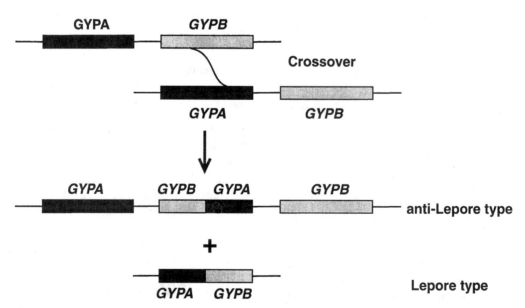

Figure 9-5. Single crossover: exchange of nucleotides between misaligned homologous genes. The products are reciprocal.

the desired nucleic acid is typically human genomic DNA. Genomic DNA is present in all nucleated cells and can be most readily isolated from the nucleated cells of the peripheral blood.

Major manufacturers of products for molecular biology offer kits for the isolation of human genomic DNA from whole blood, cells, and tissues. These kits vary in the quantity and quality of the DNA isolated, in rough proportion to the cost and ease of use of the kit. High quality DNA is of high molecular weight and is relatively free of contamination by protein or RNA. DNA purity is assessed by the ratio of its optical density (OD) at 260 nm to that at 280 nm, with the OD 260/280 ratio for pure DNA being 1.8. Low ratios (<1.6) indicate that the DNA is contaminated with protein or materials used in the isolation procedure, and high ratios (>2.0) indicate that the DNA is contaminated

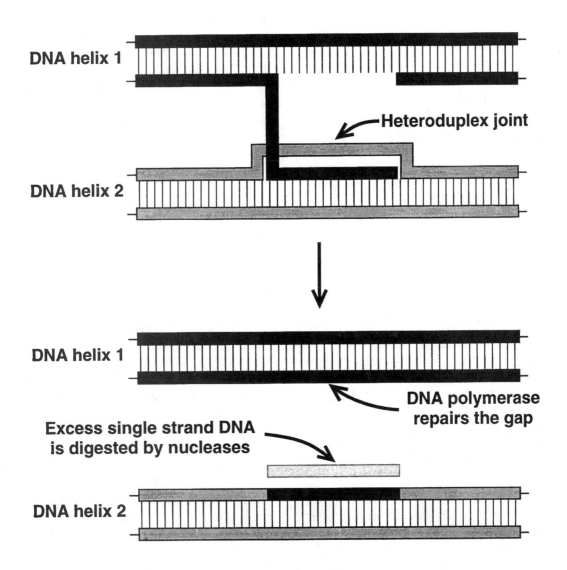

Figure 9-6. Gene conversion: a heteroduplex joint forms between homologous sequences on two genes. DNA polymerase repairs the double strands. Any excess single-stranded DNA is degraded by nucleases, producing a hybrid gene on one chromosome but not the other.

with RNA. If the DNA is pure and of sufficient concentration, it can be quantitated by measurement of the OD at 260 nm. If the DNA is impure or in low concentration, it is best quantitated by electrophoresis in agarose gel along with DNA standards of known concentration, followed by visualization of the DNA with ethidium bromide staining.

For certain molecular biology techniques such as polymerase chain reaction (PCR), the quantity and quality of the genomic DNA used as starting material are not crucial, and good results can be obtained with even nanogram quantities of DNA that has been degraded into small fragments. For other molecular biology techniques such as cloning, larger quantities of high molecular weight DNA are required.

One nucleated cell contains about 6-8 pg of genomic DNA. Based on an average white cell count of 5000/μL, each milliliter of peripheral blood contains about 30 μg of DNA. Commercial DNA isolation kits typically yield in excess of 15 μg of DNA per milliliter of whole blood processed.

Polymerase Chain Reaction

The introduction of the PCR technique has revolutionized the field of molecular genetics.[3] This technique permits specific DNA sequences to be multiplied rapidly and precisely in vitro. PCR can amplify, to a billionfold, a single copy of the DNA sequence under study, provided a part of the nucleotide sequence is known. The investigator must know at least some of the gene sequence in order to synthesize DNA oligonucleotides for use as primers. Two primers are required: a forward primer (5′) and a reverse primer (3′). These are designed so that one is complementary to each strand of DNA and together they flank the region of interest. Primers can be designed that add restriction sites to the PCR product to facilitate its subsequent cloning of the PCR product, or that add a label to facilitate its detection. Labels may incorporate radioactivity, or more frequently, a nonradioactive tag,

such as biotin or a fluorescent dye. The PCR reaction is catalyzed by one of several heat-stable DNA polymerases isolated from bacterial species that are native to hot springs or to thermal vents on the ocean floor. The thermostability of these enzymes allows them to withstand repeated cycles of heating and cooling.

Reaction Procedure

The amplification technique is simple and requires very little DNA (about 100 ng to 1 μg of genomic DNA). The DNA under study is mixed together with a reaction buffer, excess nucleotides, the primers, and polymerase (see Fig 9-7). The reaction cocktail is placed in a thermocycler programmed to produce a series of heating and cooling cycles that result in exponential amplification of the DNA. The target DNA is initially denatured by heating the mixture, which separates the double-stranded DNA into single strands. Subsequent cooling in the presence of excess quantities of single-stranded forward and reverse primers allows them to bind or anneal with complementary sequences on the single-stranded template DNA. The reaction mixture is heated to 70-72 C, the optimal temperature for the thermophil-derived DNA polymerase, which generates a new strand of DNA on the single-strand template, using the nucleotides as building blocks for elongation. The next cycle denatures newly formed double strands, and the DNA copies serve as templates for subsequent synthesis. The number of DNA copies doubles with each cycle, such that after 20 cycles there is a millionfold amplification of the target DNA.

The amplified DNA may be analyzed by agarose gel electrophoresis in the presence of ethidium bromide, which stains DNA and is visible under ultraviolet light. The DNA will be present as a single discrete band equivalent in length to the distance between the 5′ ends of the primers. Alternatively, the DNA sample can be blotted onto a membrane and hybridized to a labeled, allele-specific probe. This is known

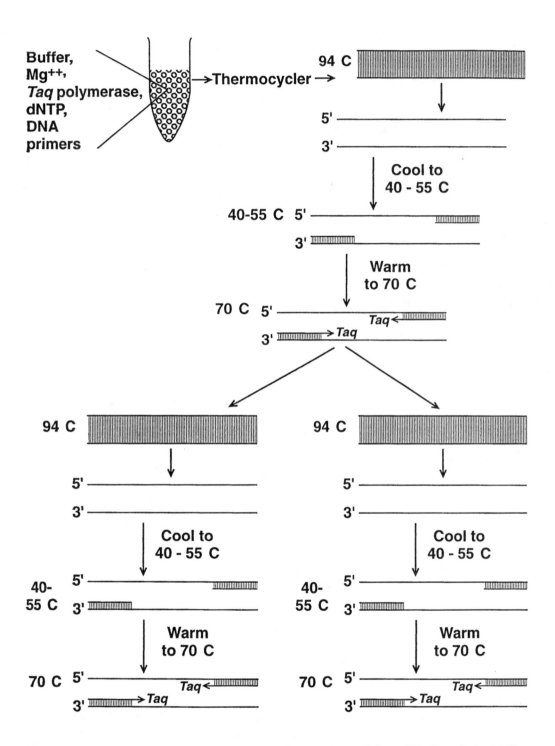

Figure 9-7. The polymerase chain reaction results in the exponential amplification of short DNA sequences such that the target sequence is amplified over a millionfold after 20 cycles. (*Taq* polymerase is used here as an example of a thermostable DNA polymerase.)

as a dot blot and is particularly useful when multiple samples are being analyzed for the same polymorphism.

Variations of the PCR have been developed to meet specific needs. For instance, "long distance" PCR, which has a mixture of thermostable polymerases, can amplify much larger targets (up to 40 kilobases) than those typically amplified by conventional PCR (up to 2 kilobases). It is even possible to perform PCR in situ, in tissue and cells. A related technology, the ligase chain reaction (LCR), uses a thermostable DNA ligase instead of a thermostable DNA polymerase. Rather than amplification of a DNA target segment located between two flanking primers using a DNA polymerase as occurs in PCR, in LCR direct primer ligation occurs with no amplification of an intervening DNA segment. The major advantage of LCR over PCR is its exquisite specificity. Primers for LCR can be designed to detect single nucleotide differences. Other PCR variations include multiplex PCR and kinetic PCR.

Applications of PCR

PCR can be used directly to detect polymorphisms, either by using allele-specific primers in the reaction mixture or by treating the amplified product with restriction enzymes and analyzing the bands that result. In the field of transplantation, PCR using allele-specific oligonucleotides has largely replaced restriction fragment length polymorphism (RFLP) for accurate HLA typing of Class II molecules because it can be done much more rapidly and with greater accuracy and resolution (see Chapter 17).

Amplification of minute quantities of DNA to analyzable levels may significantly affect the practice of transfusion medicine. In screening donor blood for infectious agents, PCR [currently referred to as nucleic acid testing (NAT)] could become the procedure of choice and thus eliminate our reliance on seroconversion, which necessarily occurs well after exposure to viruses or other pathogens (see Chapter 28). PCR is being used for prenatal determination of many inheritable disorders, such as sickle cell disease, in evaluation of hemolytic disease of the newborn (HDN) to type fetal amniocytes,[4] to quantitate residual white cells in filtered blood, and for tracing of donor leukocytes in transfusion recipients. Application of this test system could reduce the need for multiple amniocentesis procedures and improve obstetric management of the fetus at risk of HDN. Long distance PCR is used for cloning, sequencing, and chromosome mapping, and reverse transcriptase PCR for studying gene expression and cDNA cloning. LCR has special applicability in transfusion medicine because of its powerful ability to detect genetic variants.

Restriction Endonucleases

The discovery of bacterial restriction endonucleases provided the key technique for DNA analysis. These enzymes, found in different strains of bacteria, protect a bacterial cell from viral infection by degrading viral DNA after it enters the cytoplasm. Each restriction endonuclease recognizes only a single, specific nucleotide sequence, typically consisting of four to six nucleotides. These enzymes cleave the DNA strand wherever the recognized sequence occurs, generating a number of DNA fragments whose length depends upon the number and location of cleavage sites in the original strand. Many endonucleases have been purified from different species of bacteria; the name of each enzyme reflects its host bacterium, eg, Eco RI is isolated from *Escherichia coli*, Hind III is from *Hemophilus influenzae*, and Hpa I is from *Hemophilus parainfluenzae*.

Restriction Fragment Length Polymorphism Analysis

The unique properties of restriction endonucleases make analysis of RFLP suitable for the detection of a DNA polymorphism. The changes in nucleotide sequence described above (substitution, insertion, deletion) can alter the relative locations of restriction nuclease cutting sites, and thus alter the length of DNA fragments produced. RFLPs are detected using Southern blotting and probe hybridization (see Fig 9-8).

The isolated DNA is cleaved into fragments by digestion with one or more restriction endonucleases. The DNA fragments are separated by electrophoresis through agarose gel and then transferred onto a nylon membrane or nitrocellulose paper. Once fixed to a nylon membrane or nitrocellulose paper, the DNA fragments are examined by application of a probe, which is a small fragment of DNA whose nucleotide sequence is complementary to the DNA sequence under study. A probe may be an artificially manufactured oligonucleotide or may derive from cloned complementary DNA.

The probe is labeled with a radioisotope or some other indicator that permits visualization of the targeted DNA restriction fragments, and is then allowed to hybridize with the Southern blot. Unbound excess probe is washed off, and hybridized DNA is visualized as one or more bands of specific size, dictated by the specific nucleotide sequence. If several individuals are analyzed for a polymorphism, several different banding patterns may be observed.

RFLP analysis has been used in gene mapping and analysis, linkage analysis, characterization of HLA genes in transplantation, paternity testing, and forensic science.

DNA Profiling

Regions of DNA that show great allelic variability ("minisatellites" and "microsatellites") can be studied by the application of RFLP mapping and/or PCR analysis (a process sometimes

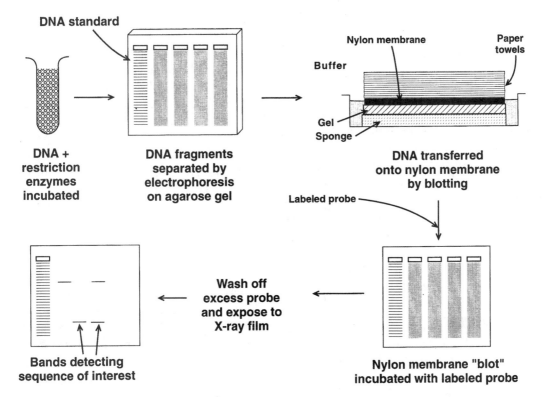

Figure 9-8. Southern blotting: a technique for the detection of polymorphism by gel-transfer hybridization with known probes.

called DNA profiling, DNA typing, or DNA fingerprinting). Minisatellites or VNTR (variable number of tandem repeat) loci consist of tandem repeats of a medium-sized (6-100 base pair) sequence, while microsatellites or STR (short tandem repeat) loci consist of tandem repeats of a short (typically 4 base pair) sequence. Variability stems from differences in the number of repeat units contained within the fragments. There is so much variation between individuals that the chances are very low that the same numbers of repeats will be shared by two individuals, even if related. The VNTR and/or STR patterns observed at four to eight different loci may be unique for an individual and thus constitute a profile or "fingerprint" that identifies his or her DNA.

When DNA profiling was first developed, testing was performed by RFLP analysis. DNA profiling is now increasingly done by amplification of selected, informative VNTR and/or STR loci using locus-specific oligonucleotide primers, followed by measurement of the size of the PCR products produced. PCR products can be separated by size by electrophoresis through polyacrylamide gel and detected by silver staining, or, if the PCR products incorporate a fluorescent tag, by fluorescent detection systems including those designed for automated DNA sequencing. Comparison of the VNTR and STR PCR products with a standard size ladder distinguishes the alleles present in the sample.

DNA profiling is a technique that is extremely powerful for the identification of the source of human DNA; therefore, it has applications in forensic and paternity testing, as well as in the documentation of chimerism, which is of special importance in monitoring allogeneic hematopoietic transplantation.

DNA Cloning

PCR may also be used for analysis of mRNA, which is an especially useful source of genetic material because only the exons of the gene are present. By a modification of PCR called reverse transcriptase PCR, the single-stranded mRNA is converted to double-stranded DNA. The enzyme reverse transcriptase is used to generate a single strand of DNA, which serves as a template for a second strand generated by DNA polymerase. The product is complementary DNA (cDNA) and it is the DNA molecule of choice for cloning and sequencing.

In gene cloning, the DNA containing the gene of interest is inserted into a vector, which is a self-replicating genetic element such as a virus (eg, the bacteriophage lambda gt11) or a plasmid. Plasmids are small circular molecules of double-stranded DNA that occur naturally in bacteria and typically confer antibiotic resistance. After the gene is inserted into the DNA of the vector, the recombinant DNA can be introduced into a bacterial host where it undergoes replication. Because many vectors carry genes for antibiotic resistance, this characteristic can be exploited by growing the host bacteria in the presence of the appropriate antibiotic; only bacteria that have successfully incorporated the recombinant vector will survive to form colonies or clones. Each individual vector potentially contains a different cDNA sequence. The sum of bacterial clones harboring recombinant vectors is called a DNA library. Libraries can be obtained from many commercial sources or can be produced by the individual investigator. The library can be probed through a technique similar to Southern blotting, with an oligonucleotide probe based on part of a known sequence. Positive clones can be selected and a pure culture grown in large quantities. Once purified, the cloned DNA can be recovered for use as a probe or for detailed molecular characterization.

The ability to insert genes into the genomes of virtually any organism including bacteria, plants, invertebrates (such as insects), and vertebrates (such as mammals) permits not only gene characterization, but also genetic engineering, including the production of recombinant proteins (see below) and gene therapy. Although still in the developmental stages, gene therapy promises to have a role in the management of disorders as diverse as inherited genetic diseases, human immunodeficiency virus, and cancer, and in the development of novel vaccines.[5,6]

DNA Sequencing

A major worldwide scientific effort called the Human Genome Project has the aim of obtaining the complete nucleotide sequence of the human genome as well as the genomes of several other key organisms. The initiative is also aimed at improving DNA sequencing technology. Realization of both goals will have a positive impact on transfusion practice. Identification of all human genes will provide a complete blueprint of the proteins that are relevant in transfusion medicine; in turn, this information will have a major impact in the form of recombinant proteins as transfusion components and in-vitro test reagents. It will also have a role in clarifying the disorders that afflict transfusion recipients.

Advances in DNA sequencing have taken the field a long way from the cumbersome manual techniques common in research laboratories until recently.[7] Automated DNA sequencers using laser detection of fluorescently labeled sequencing products detect all four nucleotide bases in a single lane on polyacrylamide gel, and can be optimized for specialty applications such as heterozygote detection and sizing of PCR fragments. Automated DNA sequencers using capillary electrophoresis are especially useful for the rapid sequencing of short DNA templates. DNA sequence can also be obtained using mass spectrometry. Automated sequencers will become increasingly common in clinical laboratories as this technology evolves; if it can be made cost-effective for routine use, then DNA sequencing could become a routine genotyping method.

Recombinant Proteins

The technology to make recombinant proteins includes in-vitro systems in bacteria, yeast, insect cells, and mammalian cells, as well as in-vivo systems involving transgenic plants and animals.[8] A source of DNA corresponding in nucleic acid sequence to the desired protein is first prepared, typically by cloning the cDNA and ligating it into a suitable expression vector. The expression vector containing the DNA of interest is then transfected into the host cell, and the DNA of interest is transcribed under the control of the vector promoter. The resulting mRNA is then translated into protein by the host cell.

Posttranslational modifications such as the addition of carbohydrates to the new protein will be carried out by the host cell. If specific posttranslational modifications required for the new protein's function cannot be carried out by the host cell, then it may be necessary to endow the host cell with additional capabilities, for instance by cotransfection with the cDNA for a specific enzyme. In some instances, posttranslational modification may not be crucial for a recombinant protein to be effective; for instance, granulocyte colony-stimulating factor (G-CSF) is produced in a nonglycosylated form in *E. coli* (Filgrastim) and in a glycosylated form in yeast (Lenograstim).

Recombinant proteins are finding multiple uses in transfusion medicine, as therapeutic agents and vaccine components, in component preparation, in virus diagnosis, and in serologic testing. Recombinant human erythropoietin,[9] G-CSF and granulocyte-macrophage CSF,[10] interferon-alpha, interleukin-2, and Factors VIII,[11] IX,[12] VII, and VIIa[13] are all available and finding clinical acceptance. For instance, recombinant erythropoietin can be used to increase red cell production in anemic patients before surgery, reducing the need for allogeneic blood.[14] It can also be used to increase the amount of autologous red cells that can be withdrawn before surgery from nonanemic patients.[15] Recombinant human thrombopoietin, in clinical trials as of this writing, may reduce the need for platelet transfusion in thrombocytopenia and be of value in augmentation of platelet yields from apheresis donors.[16] In the coagulation arena, several recombinant proteins under evaluation such as protein C, tissue factor pathway inhibitor, Factor XIII, and the hirudins appear promising. Recombinant myeloid growth factors such as G-CSF are used to enhance yields of progenitor cells during apheresis, and to support patients following chemotherapy and hematopoietic transplantation.[17]

Recombinant proteins can be used as transfusion components.[18] Recombinant human hemoglobin has been produced in a number of in-vitro expression systems and in vivo in transgenic swine, and may be useful as a noninfectious blood substitute.[19] Recombinant human serum albumin has been produced in yeast. Alpha-galactosidase, an enzyme that is capable of converting group B cells into group O cells, has been produced in a recombinant form that can modify group B units for transfusion to group A and O recipients.[20] These recombinant proteins and other products under development will undoubtedly affect the variety of transfusion components that will become available in the future.

Recombinant proteins corresponding to proteins from clinically relevant viruses, bacteria, and parasites, some of which may be transmitted by blood transfusion, may be used as vaccine components[21] and as antigens in test kits for the detection of antibodies. Cells transfected with appropriate vectors can be induced to express recombinant proteins at the surface, and as such may become useful as genetically engineered reagent cells for in-vitro testing.

References

1. Tournamille C, Colin Y, Cartron JP, Le Van Kim C. Disruption of a GATA motif in the Duffy gene promoter abolishes erythroid gene expression in Duffy-negative individuals. Nat Genet 1995;10:224-8.
2. Cartron JP. Defining the Rh blood group antigens. Biochemistry and molecular genetics. Blood Rev 1994;8:199-212.
3. Ni H, Blajchman MA. Understanding the polymerase chain reaction. Transfus Med Rev 1994; 8:242-52.
4. Bennett PR, Le Van Kim C, Colin Y, et al. Prenatal determination of fetal RhD type by DNA amplification. N Engl J Med 1993;329:607-10 [comment in N Engl J Med 1993;329:658-60 and 1994;330:795-6].
5. Friedmann T. Overcoming the obstacles to gene therapy. Sci Am 1997;276:80-5.
6. Hillyer CD, Klein HG. Immunotherapy and gene transfer in the treatment of the oncology patient: Role of transfusion medicine. Transfus Med Rev 1996;10:1-14.
7. Griffin HG, Griffin AM. DNA sequencing. Recent innovations and future trends. Appl Biochem Biotechnol 1993;38:147-59.
8. Lubon H, Paleyanda RK, Velander WH, Drohan WN. Blood proteins from transgenic animal bioreactors. Transfus Med Rev 1996;10:131-43.
9. Cazzola M, Mercuriali F, Brugnara C. Use of recombinant human erythropoietin outside the setting of uremia. Blood 1997;89:4248-67.
10. Ganser A, Karthaus M. Clinical use of hematopoietic growth factors. Curr Opin Oncol 1996;8:265-9.
11. VanAken WG. The potential impact of recombinant factor VIII on hemophilia care and the demand for blood and blood products. Transfus Med Rev 1997;11:6-14.
12. White GC II, Beebe A, Nielsen B. Recombinant factor IX. Thromb Haemost 1997;78:261-5.
13. Lusher JM. Recombinant factor VIIa (NovoSeven) in the treatment of internal bleeding in patients with factor VIII and IX inhibitors. Haemostasis 1996;26 Suppl 1:124-30.
14. Braga M, Gianotti L, Gentilini O, et al. Erythropoietic response induced by recombinant human erythropoietin in anemic cancer patients candidate to major abdominal surgery. Hepatogastroenterology 1997;44:685-90.
15. Cazenave JP, Irrmann C, Waller C, et al. Epoetin alfa facilitates presurgical autologous blood donation in non-anaemic patients scheduled for orthopaedic or cardiovascular surgery. Eur J Anaesthesiol 1997;14:432-42.
16. Farese AM, Schiffer CA, MacVittie TJ. The impact of thrombopoietin and related Mpl-ligands on transfusion medicine. Transfus Med Rev 1997; 11:243-55.
17. Ketley NJ, Newland AC. Haemopoietic growth factors. Postgrad Med J 1997;73:215-21.
18. Growe GH. Recombinant blood components: Clinical administration today and tomorrow. World J Surg 1996;20:1194-9.
19. Kumar R. Recombinant hemoglobins as blood substitutes: A biotechnology perspective. Proc Soc Exp Biol Med 1995;208:150-8.
20. Lenny LL, Hurst R, Zhu A, et al. Multiple-unit and second transfusions of red cells enzymatically converted from group B to group O: Report on the end of phase 1 trials. Transfusion 1995;35:899-902.
21. Ellis RW. The new generation of recombinant viral subunit vaccines. Curr Opin Biotechnol 1996;7:646-52.
22. Barbara JA, Garson JA. Polymerase chain reaction and transfusion microbiology. Vox Sang 1993;64:73-81.

23. Power EG. RAPD typing in microbiology—a technical review. J Hosp Infect 1996;34:247-65.

24. Larsen SA, Steiner BM, Rudolph AH, Weiss JB. DNA probes and PCR for diagnosis of parasitic infections. Clin Microbiol Rev 1995;8:1-21.

25. Weiss JB. DNA probes and PCR for diagnosis of parasitic infections. Clin Microbiol Rev 1995;8:113-30.

26. Majolino I, Cavallaro AM, Scime R. Peripheral blood stem cells for allogeneic transplantation. Bone Marrow Transplant 1996;18 Suppl 2:171-4.

27. Gretch DR. Diagnostic tests for hepatitis C. Hepatology 1997;26:43S-7S.

28. Pena SD, Prado VF, Epplen JT. DNA diagnosis of human genetic individuality. J Mol Med 1995; 73:555-64.

29. van Belkum A. DNA fingerprinting of medically important microorganisms by use of PCR. Clin Microbiol Rev 1994;7:174-84.

30. Siegel DL. The human immune response to red blood cell antigens as revealed by repertoire cloning. Immunol Res 1998;17:239-51.

31. Hyland CA, Wolter LC, Saul A. Identification and analysis of Rh genes: Application of PCR and RFLP typing tests. Transfus Med Rev 1995;9:289-301.

Suggested Reading

Garratty G, ed. Applications of molecular biology to blood transfusion medicine. Bethesda, MD: American Association of Blood Banks, 1997.

Sheffield WP. Concepts and techniques in molecular biology—an overview. Transfus Med Rev 1997;11:209-23.

Watson JD, Hopkins NH, Roberts JW, et al. Molecular biology of the gene. Menlo Park, CA: Benjamin/ Cummings, 1987.

Appendix 9-1. Molecular Techniques in Transfusion Practice

Technique	Applications	Examples	References
PCR	Infectious disease testing	Viruses, bacteria, parasites	22 23 24, 25
	Polymorphism detection	HLA, blood group antigens	1, 2, 26
	Prenatal detection	Rh	4
Recombinant proteins/ DNA cloning	Therapy	Erythropoietin, thrombopoietin, G-CSF	9, 10, 16
	Apheresis	G-CSF	26
	Infectious disease testing	Viral testing	27
	Recombinant components	Coagulation factors	11
		Hemoglobin	19
	Component processing	Alpha-galactosidase	20
	Vaccine production	Hepatitis, malaria, HIV	19-21
DNA profiling	Human identification	Chimerism, forensic science	28
	Bacterial identification	Bacterial typing	29
DNA sequencing	Polymorphism detection, heterozygote detection	HLA	7
Phage display/ repertoire cloning	Monoclonal antibody production	Anti-D	30
RFLP	Polymorphism detection	HLA, blood group antigens	31

PCR = polymerase chain reaction; G-CSF = granulocyte colony-stimulating factor; HIV = human immunodeficiency virus; RFLP = restriction fragment length polymorphism.

10

Blood Group Genetics

Basic Principles

LANDSTEINER'S DISCOVERY OF THE ABO blood group system demonstrated that human blood was polymorphic. Red cells provided an easy and accessible means to test for human polymorphisms in individuals of any age, and, as more blood group antigens were discovered, red cell typing provided a wealth of information about human genetics. This chapter presents some of the main concepts of heredity and genetics as applied to the expression and inheritance of blood group antigens. It assumes that the reader has some background in the principles of genetics. Molecular genetics and transfusion medicine are discussed in Chapter 9.

Inheritance of transmissible characteristics or "traits," including blood group antigens, forms the basis of the science of genetics. The genetic material that determines each trait is deoxyribonucleic acid (DNA) (see Chapter 9). Nuclear DNA associates with a variety of proteins to constitute chromosomes. Discrete units of the chromosome, termed genes, encode the information for specific proteins, which in turn determine traits. Humans have 46 chromosomes in each nucleated cell, which exist as 23 pairs (one member of each pair inherited from each parent). This chromosomal makeup constitutes the normal diploid, or 2N, karyotype. Twenty-two of the pairs are alike in both males and females and are called autosomes; the remaining pair are the sex chromosomes, XX in females and XY in males.

Each chromosome consists of two arms joined at a primary constriction, the centromere. The two arms are usually of different lengths: the short, or petite, arm is termed "p", and the long arm is termed "q." When stained, each chromosome displays a unique pattern of bands, which are numbered from the centromere outward (see Fig 10-1). The location of individual genes along the chromosome may be determined and physically "mapped" to specific band locations.

Cells must reproduce their chromosomes as they divide so that each daughter cell receives the full complement of genetic information. Cell division is of two kinds: mitosis and meiosis. Mitosis is the process whereby the body grows or replaces dead or injured somatic cells. In mitosis the chromosomes replicate themselves and lose the relatively homogeneous appearance characteristic of the nucleus in nondividing cells, condensing into tightly coiled structures visible with the light microscope. In the last stage of mitosis, the appropriate 2N number of chromosomes is distributed to each of the two daughter cells (see Fig 10-2), resulting in two cells that are genetically identical to the one original cell.

Meiosis occurs only in primordial cells destined to mature into a reproductive cell or gamete and occurs only once for each such cell. Gametes (sperm and eggs) have 23 chromosomes as a result of meiosis. Unlike somatic cells that are diploid and have a 2N chromosome complement, gametes are haploid, with a 1N chromosome complement.

Genetics and Heredity

Alleles

Alternative forms of genes, any one of which may occupy a single locus on homologous chromosomes, are called alleles. The major alleles of the ABO system are *A*, *B*, and *O*. In the Kell system, two alleles, *K* and *k*, determine the K and k antigens. Individuals who have identical alleles at a given locus on both chromosomes are *homozygous* for the allele (*AA* or *KK* or *kk*). In the *heterozygous* condition, the alleles present at the particular locus on each chromosome are nonidentical (eg, *AO* or *AB* or *Kk*).

In some blood group systems, persons homozygous for an allele have more antigen on their red cells than persons with different alleles. For example, red cells from a person whose genotype is *KK* have a "double dose" of the K antigen, while those from a *Kk* person have a "single dose." The difference in amount

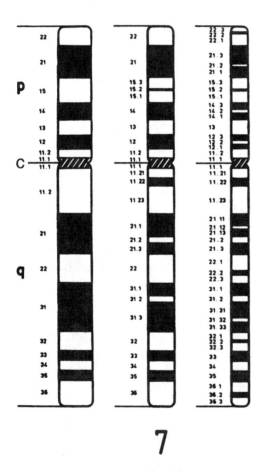

Figure 10-1. Diagram of Giemsa-stained normal human chromosome 7. With increased resolution (left to right), finer degrees of banding are evident. Bands are numbered outward from the centromere (c), which divides the chromosome into p and q arms.[1]

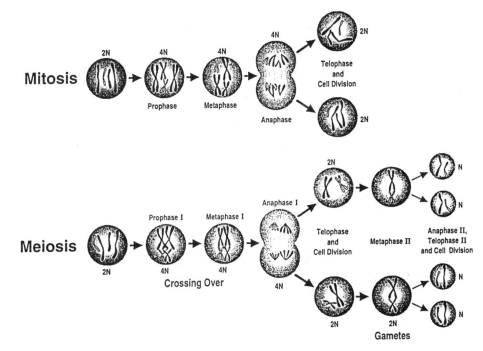

Figure 10-2. The two types of cell division are mitosis and meiosis.

of antigen on red cells between a homozygote and a heterozygote is termed the dosage effect and can often be detected serologically. For example, some anti-K sera may give the following pattern of reactivity:

	Genotype of RBC Donor	
Antibody	**KK**	**Kk**
Anti-K	3+	2+

Dosage effect is not seen with all blood group antigens or even with all antibodies of a given specificity.

Alleles arise by mutation and may result in phenotypic diversity. Mutations may occur at the chromosome, gene or genome (DNA) level (see Chapter 9) and may also result in the creation of new polymorphisms associated with the altered gene. Figure 10-3 illustrates how mutations in the genes that code for the MNS blood group system have resulted in creating various low-incidence MNS system antigens.

Allele (Gene) Frequencies

The frequency of an allele is the proportion it contributes to the total pool of alleles at that locus in a given population; it can be calculated from phenotype frequencies. The sum of allele frequencies at a given locus must equal 1.00. The Kidd blood group system is basically a two-allele system (the silent Jk allele is extremely rare) that can be used to illustrate calculation of frequencies. Calculation, with use of the Hardy-Weinberg equation for a two-allele system, may begin with the observation that 77% of blood samples express the Jk^a antigen.

$$p^2 + 2pq + q^2 = 1$$

In the equation:
p = frequency of Jk^a
q = frequency of Jk^b
p^2 = frequency of Jk^aJk^a
$2pq$ = frequency of $Jk^aJk^b \times 2$
q^2 = frequency of Jk^bJk^b

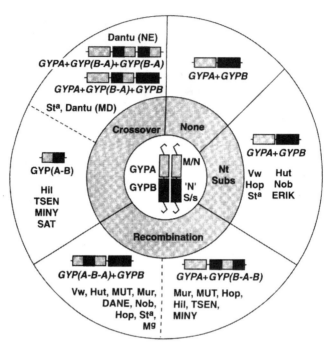

Figure 10-3. How crossover, recombination, and nucleotide substitution (nt subs) result in variations of genes producing glycophorin A and B. The changes are associated with the presence of various low-incidence MNS system antigens. (Reprinted from Reid.[2])

Then

$$p^2 + 2pq = \text{frequency of persons who are Jk(a+) and carry the allele } Jk^a$$

$$= 0.77$$

$$q^2 = 1 - (p^2 + 2pq) = \text{frequency of persons who are Jk(a–) } Jk^b Jk^b \text{ (homozygous for } Jk^b)$$

$$q^2 = 1 - 0.77 = 0.23$$

$$q = \sqrt{0.23}$$

$$q = 0.48 \text{ (allele frequency of } Jk^b)$$

Because the sum of frequencies of both alleles must equal 1.00,

$$p+q = 1$$

$$p = 1 - q$$

$$p = 1 - 0.48$$

$$p = 0.52 \text{ (allele frequency of } Jk^a)$$

Once the allele frequencies have been calculated, the number of Jk(b+) individuals (both homozygous and heterozygous) can be calculated as:

$$2pq + q^2 = \text{frequency of Jk(b+)}$$

$$= 2 (0.52 \times 0.48) + (0.48)^2$$

$$q = 0.73$$

If both anti-Jk[a] and anti-Jk[b] sera are available, allele frequencies can be determined more easily by direct counting. As shown in Table 10-1, the random sample of 100 people tested for Jk[a] and Jk[b] antigens possess a total of 200 alleles at the *JK* locus (each person inherits two alleles, one from each parent, hence 2×100). The frequency of *Jk[a]* is $105 \div 200 = 0.52$ and the frequency of *Jk[b]* is $95 \div 200 = 0.48$.

The Hardy-Weinberg law is generally used to calculate allele and genotype frequencies in a population when the frequency of one genetic

Table 10-1. Gene Frequencies in the Kidd Blood Group System Calculated Using Direct Counting Method*

Phenotype	Individuals	Kidd Genes	Jk^a	Jk^b
Jk(a+b−)	28	56	56	0
Jk(a+b+)	49	98	49	49
Jk(a−b+)	23	46	0	46
Totals	100	200	105	95
Gene Frequency			0.525	0.475

* Assumes absence of silent *Jk* allele.

trait (eg, antigen phenotype) is known. However, it relies on certain basic conditions. These include: no mutation, no migration (in or out) of the population, lack of selective advantage/disadvantage of a particular trait, and a large enough population so that chance alone cannot alter an allele frequency. If all of these conditions are present, the gene pool is in equilibrium and allele frequencies will not change from one generation to the next. In fact, it is not possible to meet all of these conditions in their entirety. The resulting changes in allele frequencies may not be obvious in human populations over a few generations but can accumulate and can explain many of the differences in allele frequencies between populations that are familiar to blood bankers.

Segregation

The realization that many human traits, such as hair or eye color, are passed on from one generation to another goes back to the early days of humanity. Hereditary transmission was not rigorously analyzed until the late 1860s when Gregor Mendel first studied crosses of pea plants exhibiting different morphologies. Mendel's experiments led him to conclude that many pea plant characteristics (phenotypes) were determined by pairs of distinct, separable factors (now termed alleles of genes), one factor coming from each parent. In blood group

genetics this can be illustrated by the inheritance of the ABO antigens (see Fig 10-4). In this example, each member of the parental generation (P₁) is homozygous, for group A or group O. All members of the first filial generation (F₁) will be heterozygous (*AO*) but, having the *A* gene, will express the blood group A anti-

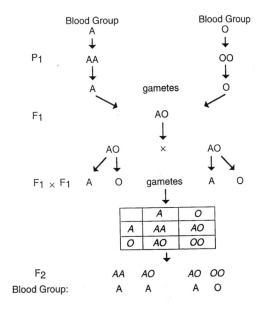

Figure 10-4. Mendel's law of independent segregation, demonstrated by the inheritance of ABO antigens.

gen; *O* is a silent allele. If F_1 individuals mate (in the example, this would be a consanguineous mating), the resulting progeny are termed the second filial generation (F_2). Three genotypes may arise from the mating of F_1 heterozygotes: progeny homozygous for the *A* gene (*AA*); heterozygous for *A* and *O* (*AO*); or homozygous for *O* (*OO*). The ratio of the likelihood of each genotype is 1:2:1, respectively, and is constant for all such $F_1 \times F_1$ matings.

Assortment

Mendel's law of independent assortment states that genes determining various traits are inherited independently from each other. For example, if one parent is group A (homozygous for *A*) and K+k+, and the other parent is group B (homozygous for *B*) and K–k+ (homozygous for *k*), all the F_1 children would be group AB; half would be K+k+ and half K-k+ (see Fig 10-5). A second filial generation could manifest any of the following phenotypes: group A, K+k+; group AB, K+k+; group B, K+k+; group A, K–k+; group AB, K–k+; group B, K–k+. The proportions would be 1:2:1:1:2:1.

Independent assortment applies if the genes are on different chromosomes or on distant portions of the same chromosome. Syntenic genes are those on the same chromosomes.

Linkage

Linkage creates an important exception to the law of independent assortment of genes. During meiosis each pair of homologous chromosomes undergoes a series of recombinations. The resultant reciprocal exchange of segments between the chromatids is termed crossing-over (see Fig 10-6). Genes close together on a chromosome tend to be transmitted together during these recombinations and their alleles therefore do not segregate independently. Sometimes the linkage is very tight so that recombination rarely occurs. For example, the genes encoding the blood group antigens MN and Ss are so close to each other on chromosome 4 that their alleles are inherited as if they were one unit.

The chromosomal location of many genes has been established through linkage to a gene with a previously-established localization. Linkage analysis requires information from families in which at least one parent is heterozygous for two heritable traits. The distribution of alleles from the doubly heterozygous parent to each child is examined to see if the alleles are transmitted in a random assortment or as "linked" pairs. Lod scores (logarithm of the odds) give an estimate of the likelihood of the observed ratio of alleles assuming linkage at various recombination fractions.[1] Lod scores from all informative families can be added together; a combined score greater than +3.0 is considered definitive evidence of linkage.

The demonstration of linkage between the genes controlling ABH secretion (*Se*) and the Lutheran blood group antigens was the first recognized example of autosomal linkage in humans.[3] Analysis of this relationship also provided the first evidence in humans of recombi-

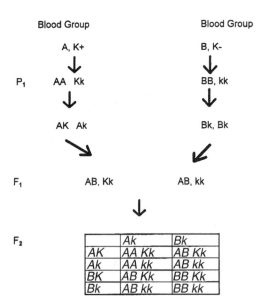

Figure 10-5. Mendel's law of independent assortment, demonstrated by inheritance of ABO and Kell antigens.

(A)   (B)   (C)

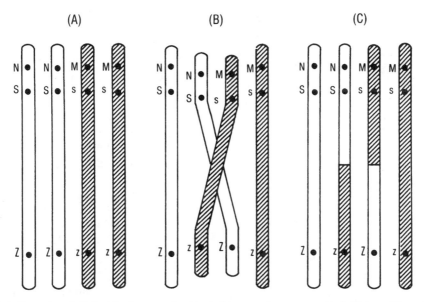

Figure 10-6. Very closely linked loci are rarely affected by crossing-over so that alleles of those loci are inherited together (N and S, M and s in the example shown). Loci on the same chromosome that are not closely linked (the *Ss* locus and the *Zz* locus shown) can demonstrate crossing-over. Crossing-over is one kind of recombination. It occurs between chromatids during meiosis, resulting in segregation of alleles on the same chromosome.

nation due to crossing-over and helped demonstrate that crossing-over occurs more often in females than in males.

Linkage Disequilibrium

When two loci are closely linked, alleles at those loci tend to be inherited together and are said to constitute a haplotype. Again, the close linkage between the loci controlling expression of M and N and of S and s is an example. The approximate frequencies of each of the four alleles are:

$M = 0.53$ $S = 0.33$
$N = 0.47$ $s = 0.67$

If *M, N, S,* and *s* segregated independently, the expected frequency of each haplotype would be the product of the frequencies of the individual alleles. However, the frequencies observed are not those expected:

	Expected Frequency	Observed Frequency
MS =	0.53 × 0.33 = 0.17	0.24
Ms =	0.53 × 0.67 = 0.36	0.28
NS =	0.47 × 0.33 = 0.16	0.08
Ns =	0.47 × 0.67 = 0.31	0.40
	1.00	1.00

This is an example of linkage disequilibrium: alleles of linked loci associate with one another either more or less frequently than would be predicted from allelic frequencies and recombination over many generations.

Another commonly-cited example of linkage disequilibrium occurs in the HLA system (see Chapter 17). The combination of *A1* with *B8* occurs in some populations approximately five times more frequently than would be expected on the basis of frequencies of the individual alleles, an example of *positive* linkage disequilibrium. Linkage disequilibrium may be positive or negative, and it may indicate a selective advantage of one haplotype over another. Over many generations, the alleles of even closely-linked loci may reach equilibrium and associate according to their individual frequencies in the population.

When there is linkage equilibrium, the alleles at two loci associate with frequencies that reflect their individual frequencies. For example, if the alleles are in the population with frequencies:

M	0.53		Z	0.30
N	0.47		z	0.70
	1.00			1.00

then the frequencies of the combination should be the product of the frequency of each allele:

MZ	0.53	$\times$	0.3	$=$	0.16
Mz	0.53	$\times$	0.7	$=$	0.37
NZ	0.47	$\times$	0.3	$=$	0.14
Nz	0.47	$\times$	0.7	$=$	0.33
					1.00

In such a case the alleles are in equilibrium because they are inherited independently.

Patterns of Inheritance

Dominant and Recessive Traits

Traits are the observed expressions of genes. A trait that is observable when the determining allele is present is called *dominant*; when differing alleles on homologous chromosomes each produce an observable trait, the term *codominant* is used. A *recessive* trait is observable only when the allele is not paired with a dominant allele. Describing traits as dominant and recessive depends on the method used to detect gene products. Observable traits are called *phenotypes*. Thus, blood group antigen typing reveals phenotypes. In some cases, *genotypes* may be inferred from the phenotype, especially when family studies are performed, but genotypes are not determined directly by typing red cells.

Autosomal Dominant Trait

An autosomal dominant trait shows a characteristic pattern of inheritance. The trait appears whenever an individual possesses the allele. Figure 10-7(A) presents a pedigree showing the pattern of autosomal dominant inheritance. Typically, each person with the trait has at least one parent with the trait, continuing backward through generations.

Autosomal Recessive Trait

Traits inherited in either autosomal dominant or autosomal recessive fashion typically occur with equal frequency in males and females. People who exhibit a recessive trait are homozygous for the encoding allele. Their parents may or may not express the trait. Parents who lack the trait, however, must necessarily be *carriers*, ie, heterozygotes for an allele whose presence is not phenotypically apparent.

If the frequency of the variant gene is low, the recessive trait will be rare and generally will occur only in members of one generation, not in preceding or successive generations unless consanguineous mating occurs. Blood relatives are more likely to carry the same rare gene than unrelated persons from a random population. When offspring are homozygous for a *rare* allele (frequency: <1:10,000) and display the trait, the parents are often blood relatives (a consanguineous mating). [See Fig 10-7(B).] Recessive traits may remain unexpressed for many generations, so that appearance of a rare recessive trait does not necessarily imply consanguinity, although family ethnicity and geographic origin may be informative. The higher the frequency of the recessive gene, the less likelihood of consanguinity.

Sex-Linked Dominant or Codominant Trait

A male always receives his single X chromosome from his mother. The predominant feature of X-linked inheritance, of either dominant or recessive traits, is absence of male-to-male (father-to-son) transmission of the trait. Because a male passes his X chromosome to all his daughters, all daughters of a man expressing a *dominant* X-linked trait also possess the allele and express the trait. If a woman expresses a dominant trait, but is heterozygous, each child, male or female, has a 50% chance of inheriting that allele and expressing the trait. If the mother possesses the determining allele on both X chromosomes, all her children will express the trait. [See Fig 10-7(C)]. A sex-linked dominant trait of interest in blood group genetics is the Xg[a] blood group. X-linked dominant traits tend to appear in each generation of a kindred, but without male-to-male transmission.

Sex-Linked Recessive Trait

Hemophilia A provides a classic example of X-linked recessive inheritance. [See Fig 10-7(D).] Among the children of an affected male and a female who lacks the determining allele, all sons are normal and all daughters are carriers. Males inherit the trait from carrier

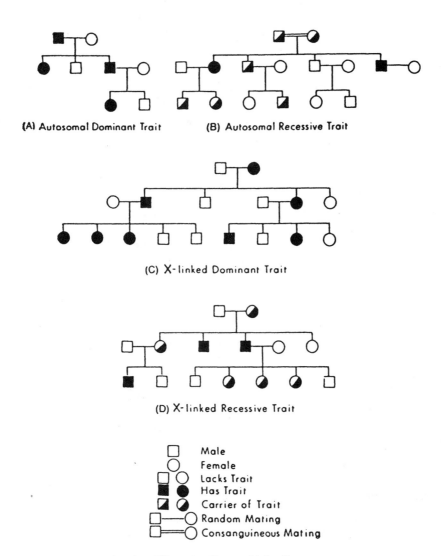

(A) Autosomal Dominant Trait

(B) Autosomal Recessive Trait

(C) X-linked Dominant Trait

(D) X-linked Recessive Trait

□	Male
○	Female
□ ○	Lacks Trait
■ ●	Has Trait
◩ ◑	Carrier of Trait
□—○	Random Mating
□=○	Consanguineous Mating

Figure 10-7. Four pedigrees showing different patterns of inheritance.

mothers or, very rarely, from a mother homozygous for the allele, who therefore expresses the trait. In the mating of a normal male and a carrier female, one half of the male offspring are affected and one half of the females are carriers.

If the recessive X-linked allele is rare, the trait will be exhibited almost exclusively in males. If the X-linked allele occurs more frequently in the population, affected females will be seen because the likelihood increases that an affected male will mate with a carrier female and produce daughters, half of whom will be homozygous for the abnormal allele.

Blood Group Codominant Traits

Blood group antigens, as a rule, are expressed as codominant traits; heterozygotes express the products of both alleles. If an individual's red cells type as both K+ and k+, the Kk genotype may be inferred. Figure 10-8 shows the inheritance patterns of the two active alleles of the Kidd blood group system (Jk^a and Jk^b) and the codominant phenotypic expression of the two antigens Jk^a and Jk^b.

In the ABO system the situation is more complex. The genes of the ABO system control production of glycosyltransferases, not the red cell membrane proteins themselves. In an A^1A^2 heterozygote, the phenotype is A$_1$; the presence of the A^2 allele cannot be inferred. Although the product of the A^1 allele appears dominant to that of the A^2 allele by simple cell typing, techniques that identify the specific transferases reveal that an A^1A^2 heterozygote actually does generate the products of both alleles, ie, both A$_1$ and A$_2$ transferases. Similarly, in an A^2O person, A^2 seems dominant to O. But the O allele determines the appearance of a protein unrelated to A and B transferases. The presence of the genes can be demonstrated by molecular techniques (see Chapter 13).

Chromosomal Assignment

The loci of all major blood group genes have been mapped to one or another of the 22 pairs of autosomes as shown in Table 10-2. The Xg and XK loci are the only blood group systems mapped to the X chromosome.

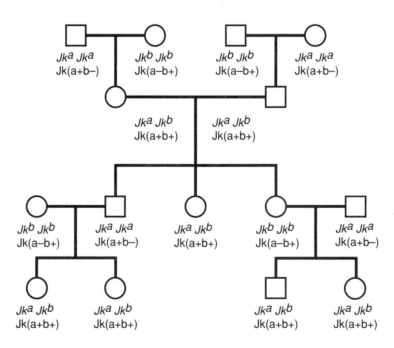

Figure 10-8. Inheritance and codominant expression of Kidd blood group antigens.

Table 10-2. Chromosomal Locations of Human Blood Group System Genes*

System	Gene(s) Designation	Location
ABO	ABO	9q34.1-q34.2
MNS	GYPA, GYPB, GYPE	4q28.2-q31.1
P	P	22q11.2-qter
Rh	RHD, RHCE	1p36.13-p34.3
Lutheran	LU	19q13.2
Kell	KEL	7q33
Lewis	FUT3	19p13.3
Duffy	FY	1q22-q23
Kidd	JK	18q11-q12
Diego	AE1	17q12-q21
Yt	ACHE	7q22
Xg	XG	Xp22.32
Scianna	SC	1p36.2-p22.1
Dombrock	DO	unknown
Colton	AQP1	7p14
Landsteiner-Wiener	LW	19p13.2-cen
Chido/Rodgers	C4A, C4B	6p21.3
Hh	FUT1	19q13.3
Kx	XK	Xp21.1
Gerbich	GYPC	2q14-q21
Cromer	DAF	1q32
Knops	CR1	1q32
Indian	CD44	11p13
OK	CD147	19pter-p13.2
RAPH	unknown	11p15.5

*Modified from Zelinski.[1]

Interaction among alleles or the products of different genes may modify the expression of a trait. The terms "suppressor" and "modifier" are used to describe genes that affect the expression of other genes; however, the mechanism of these postulated gene interactions is not always fully understood. Some phenomena in blood group serology that have been explained by gene interaction are the weakening of the D antigen when the C-determining allele is on the paired chromosome, and the suppression of Lutheran antigenic expression by the dominant modifier gene, *In(Lu)*.

When products of two different genes are important in the sequential development of a biochemical end product, the gene interaction is called epistasis. Failure to express A or B antigens if H substance has not first been produced is an example.

Population Genetics

Some understanding of population genetics is essential for parentage testing and helpful in such clinical situations as predicting the likelihood of finding blood compatible with a serum that contains multiple antibodies. Calculations depend on observation of phenotype frequencies.

Phenotype Frequencies

The frequencies of blood group phenotypes are obtained by testing many randomly selected people of the same race or group and observing the proportion of positive and negative reactions with a given antibody. In a given blood group system, the sum of phenotype frequencies should equal 100% or 1.00. For example, in a Caucasian population, 77% of randomly selected individuals are Jk(a+). The frequency of Jk(a–) individuals should be 23%. If blood is needed for a patient with anti-Jk^a, 23% or approximately one in four ABO-compatible units of blood should be compatible.

Calculations for Combined Phenotypes

If a patient has multiple blood group antibodies, it may be useful to estimate the number of units that will have to be tested in order to find units of blood negative for all the antigens. For example, if a patient has anti-c, anti-K, and anti-Jk^a, how many ABO-compatible units of blood will have to be tested to find 4 units of the appropriate phenotype?

	Phenotype Frequency (%)
c–	20
K–	91
Jk(a–)	23

To calculate the frequency of the combined phenotype, the individual frequencies are multiplied because the phenotypes are independent of one another. Thus, the proportion of persons who are c– is 20%. Of that 20%, 91%

are K– (18%). Of persons both c– and K–, 23% are also Jk(a–)-(4%):

$$0.2 \times 0.91 \times 0.23 = 0.04$$

Approximately 100 units would have to be tested to find four compatible ones. Calculations such as this influence decisions about asking assistance from the local blood supplier or reference laboratory.

Parentage Testing

Blood group antigens, many of which are expressed as codominant traits with simple Mendelian modes of inheritance, are useful in parentage analyses. If one assumes maternity and that test results are accurate, paternity can be excluded in either of two ways:

1. *Direct* exclusion of paternity is established when a genetic marker is present in the child, but is absent from the mother and the alleged father. Example:

Child	Mother	Alleged Father
B	O	O

The child has inherited a *B* gene, which could not be inherited from either the mother or the alleged father, provided that neither the mother nor the alleged father is of the rare O$_h$ phenotype. Based on the phenotypes of mother and child, the *B* gene must have been inherited from the biologic father and is therefore called a paternal *obligatory* gene.

2. Exclusion is *indirect* when the child lacks a genetic marker that the alleged father, given his observed phenotype, must transmit to his offspring. Example:

Child	Mother	Alleged Father
Jk(a+b–)	Jk(a+b–)	Jk(a–b+)

In this case, the alleged father is presumably homozygous for *Jk^b* and should have transmitted *Jk^b* to the child.

Direct exclusion is more convincing than indirect evidence that the alleged father is not the biologic father. Apparent indirect exclusion can sometimes result from the presence of a silent allele. In the example above, the alleged father could have the genotype $Jk^b Jk$ and could have transmitted the silent allele (Jk) to the child. The child's genotype could be $Jk^a Jk$, instead of the far more common $Jk^a Jk^a$. Interpretation of phenotypic data must take into account all biologic and analytic factors known to influence results.

When the alleged father cannot be excluded from paternity, it is possible to calculate the probability of paternity. The probability that the alleged father transmitted the paternal obligatory genes is compared with the probability that any other randomly selected man from the same racial population could have transmitted the genes. The result is expressed as a likelihood ratio (paternity index) or as a percentage (posterior probability of paternity given some prior probability). Methods for parentage analysis include study of many genetic systems other than blood groups. Many parentage testing laboratories currently employ some method of DNA analysis (see Chapter 9) as a means of evaluating cases of disputed parentage. The AABB has developed standards for laboratories that carry out parentage studies.[4]

Chimerism

A chimera is one whose cells are derived from more than one distinct zygotic line. Although rare, this may occur when an anastomosis occurs within the vascular tissues of twin embryos or when two fertilized zygotes fuse to form one individual. This condition, while not hereditary, leads to dual (multiple) phenotypic populations of cells within one individual. Blood types of such rare individuals may demonstrate a mixed-field appearance, with distinct populations of cells of the person's true genetic type, as well as cells of the implanted type. Chimeras also demonstrate immune tolerance: a genetically group O person with im-planted A cells does not produce anti-A. More commonly, chimeras are artificial and arise from transfer of actively dividing cells, eg, through hematopoietic transplantation. (See Chapter 25.)

Blood Group Nomenclature

Until recently, terminology and notations for blood group systems embodied many inconsistencies as blood group serologists failed to follow conventions of classic Mendelian genetics. Listed below are a few examples of the confusion engendered by many decades of uncoordinated scientific publications.

1. An allele that determines a dominant trait often is signified by a capital letter; one that determines a recessive trait is denoted by both lowercase letters. The A and B genes of the ABO system, however, are signified by a capital letter; the traits of these are considered dominant to the O trait, for which the gene is also capitalized. Without prior knowledge, it would be impossible to recognize that these notations represent allelic products in a blood group system.

2. Some codominant traits have been designated with capital letters and allelic relationships with lowercase letters, for example, K and k of the Kell blood group system and C and c of the Rh system.

3. Some codominant traits have identical base symbols but different superscript symbols, such as Fy^a and Fy^b (Duffy system) and Lu^a and Lu^b (Lutheran system).

4. In some allelic pairs, the lower incidence antigen is expressed with an "a" superscript (Wr^a). In others, the "a" superscript denotes the higher incidence antigen (Co^a).

5. Some authors have denoted absence of a serologic specificity with a base symbol devoid of superscripts, and others use a lowercase version of the base symbol.

Thus, in the Lutheran system, the assumed amorphic gene is called *Lu*, not *lu*, while the amorph in the Lewis system is *le*.

Colloquial use of these terminologies, even in some published articles and texts, has compounded their improper use. Early model computers or printers also did not easily accept certain terminologies (eg, superscripts, subscripts, unusual fonts).

In recent years concerted attempts have been made to establish rational, uniform criteria for the notations used to designate phenotype, genotype, and locus information for blood group systems. Issitt and Crookston[5] presented guidelines for the nomenclature and terminology of blood groups. The International Society of Blood Transfusion (ISBT) Working Party on Terminology for Red Cell Surface Antigens has provided a standardized system for classifying blood group antigens.[6] (Similar international committees have established principles for assigning nomenclature of the hemoglobins, immunoglobulin allotypes, histocompatibility antigens, clusters of differentiation and some other serum protein and red cell enzyme systems.) Although many of the older terminologies must be retained to avoid even further confusion, common conventions now exist for correct usage.

Conventional Usage

The following are among the accepted terminologies for expressing red cell antigen phenotypes and genotypes. (See Tables 10-3 and 10-4[7] for examples of correct and incorrect usage.)

1. Genes encoding the expression of blood group antigens are written in italics (or underlined if italics are not available). If the antigen name includes a subscript (A_1), the encoding gene is expressed with a superscript (A^1).

2. Antigen names designated by a superscript or a number (eg, Fy^a, Fy3), are written in normal (Roman) script. Numeric designations are written on the

same line as the letters. Superscript letters are lowercase. (Some exceptions occur, based on historic usage: hr^s, hr^B.)

3. When antigen phenotypes are expressed using single letter designations, results are usually written as + or −, set on the same line as the letter(s) of the antigen: K+ k−.

4. To express phenotypes of antigens designated with a superscript letter, that letter is placed in parentheses on the same line as the symbol defining the antigen: Fy(a+) and Fy(a−).

5. For antigens designated by numbers, the symbol defining the system is notated in capital letters followed by a colon, followed by the number representing the antigen tested. Plus signs do not appear when test results are positive, but a minus sign is placed before negative test results: K:1, K:−1. If tests for several antigens in one blood group have been done, the phenotype is designated by the letter(s) of the locus or blood group system followed by a colon, followed by antigen numbers separated by commas: K:−1,2,−3,4. Only antigens specifically tested are listed; if an antibody defining a specific antigen was not used, the number of the antigen is not listed: K:−1,−3,4.

Although numeric terminology has been devised for various systems and antigens, it should not be assumed that it must replace conventional terminology. Use of conventional antigen names is also acceptable. In some systems, notably Rh, multiple terminologies exist and not all antigens within the system have names in each type.

ISBT Nomenclature

The ISBT Working Party on Terminology for Red Cell Surface Antigens has devised a numeric nomenclature suitable for computerization. A six-digit designation indicates each blood group specificity. The first three numbers identify the blood group system and the

Table 10-3. Examples of Gene, Antigen, and Phenotype Terms[7]

System	Genes	Antigens	Phenotypes
ABO	$A\ A^1\ A^2\ B$	A A$_1$ A$_2$ B	A A$_1$ A$_2$ B
Rh	$D\ C\ E\ c\ e$	D C E c e	D+C+ E−c+e+
MN	$M\ N\ S\ s$	M N S s	M+N+S−s+
P	$P1$	P1	P1+ P1−
Lewis	$Le\ le$	Le^a Le^b	Le(a+) Le(a−b+)
Kell	$K\ k\ Kp^a\ Js^a$	K k Kp^a Js^a	K−k+Kp(a+)Js(a−)
Kell	$K^1\ K^2\ K^3$	K1 K2 K3	K:−1,2,−3
Scianna	$Sc^1\ Sc^2\ Sc$	Sc1 Sc2	Sc:−1,−2,−3
Kidd	$Jk^a\ Jk^b\ Jk^3$	Jk^a Jk^b Jk3	Jk(a+)Jk(a+b+)Jk:3

Table 10-4. Examples of Correct and Incorrect Terminogy[7]

Term Description	Correct Terminology	Incorrect Terminology
Phenotype	Fy(a+)	Fy^{a+}, Fy$^{(a+)}$, Fya$^{(+)}$, Fy^a+, Fya(+), Duffy^a+, Duffy^a-positive
Phenotype	Fy(a+b−)	Fy$^{a+b−}$, Fy$^{(a+b−)}$, Fy^a(+)^b(−), Fy$^{a(+)b(−)}$
Antibody	Anti-Fy^a	Anti Fy^a, Anti-Duffy
Antigen	K	Kell (name of system)
Antibody	Anti-k	Anti-Cellano
Phenotype	K:1, K:−1	K1+, K:1+, K(1), K:(1), K1−, K:1−, K1-negative
Phenotypes	A Rh+, B Rh−	A+ (means positive for A antigen) B− (means negative for B antigen)
Phenotype	M+N−	M(+), MM (implies unproved genotype)
Phenotype	Rh:−1,−2,−3,4,5	Rh:−1,−2,−3,+4,+5 Rh:1−,2−,3−,+4,5+

Note: The examples shown may not represent the only correct terminologies. In the Rh system, for example, use of CDE terminology is also acceptable and is more commonly used. The example demonstrates the correct usage *if* numeric terminology is used.

last three numbers identify the individual specificity. This numerical terminology is designed mainly for computer databases and is not necessarily intended to supplant more common usage.

For ISBT classification, each defined blood group system must be genetically distinct. Assignment of antigens to a specific blood group system is dependent on genetic, serologic, and/or biochemical relationships. Gene cloning has made the task of assignment more definitive and has allowed some designations previously unproved by traditional family studies (ie, the expansion of the Diego system to include a number of low-incidence antigens).

Some recognized antigens, however, have not yet been proved to be part of a recognized system. Collections (termed the 200 series) are apparently related sets of antigens for which definitive genetic information is lacking. Other isolated antigens of high (901 series) or low (700 series) incidence are listed together until genetic information becomes available. In recent years, the number of antigens in these three series has dramatically declined as further genetic and biochemical data allow reassignment.

References

1. Zelinski T. Chromosomal localization of human blood group genes. In: Silberstein LE, ed. Molecular and functional aspects of blood group antigens. Bethesda, MD: American Association of Blood Banks, 1995:41-73.
2. Reid ME. Molecular basis for blood groups and functions of carrier proteins. In: Silberstein LE, ed. Molecular and functional aspects of blood group antigens. Bethesda, MD: American Association of Blood Banks, 1995:75-125.
3. Mohr J. A search for linkage between the Lutheran blood group and other hereditary characters. Acta Path Microbiol Scand 1951;28:207-10.
4. Standards for parentage testing laboratories. 3rd ed. Bethesda, MD: American Association of Blood Banks, 1998.
5. Issitt PD, Crookston MC. Blood group terminology: Current conventions. Transfusion 1984;24:2-7.
6. Daniels GL, Anstee DJ, Cartron J-P, et al. Blood group terminology 1995. ISBT working party on terminology for red cell surface antigens. Vox Sang 1995;69:265-79.
7. Issitt L. Blood group nomenclature. In: Blood groups: Refresher and updates. Bethesda, MD: American Association of Blood Banks, 1995.

Suggested Reading

Alberts B, Bray D, Lewis J, et al. Molecular biology of the cell. 3rd ed. New York: Garland Publishing Inc, 1994.

Daniels G. Human blood groups. Oxford, England: Blackwell Scientific Publications 1995.

Fridey JL, Kasprisin CA, Chambers LA, Rudman SV, eds. Numbers for blood bankers. Bethesda, MD: American Association of Blood Banks, 1995.

Hackel E. Transfusion genetics. In: Anderson KC, Ness PM, eds. Scientific basis of transfusion medicine: Implications for clinical practice. Philadelphia: WB Saunders, 1994:164-76.

Lewis M. Blood groups and genetic concepts: Ruminations. In: Silberstein LE, ed. Molecular and functional aspects of blood group antigens. Bethesda, MD: American Association of Blood Banks, 1995:127-61.

Lewis M, Anstee DJ, Bird GWG, et al. ISBT working party for red cell surface antigens: Los Angeles report. Vox Sang 1991;61:158-60.

Pogo AO, Miller KS, Chaudhuri A, et al. The cloning of blood group genes. In: Edwards-Moulds J, Tregellas WM, eds. Introductory molecular genetics. Arlington, VA: American Association of Blood Banks, 1986:53-76.

Reid ME, McManus K, Zelinski T. Chromosome location of genes encoding human blood groups. Transfus Med Rev 1998;12:151-61.

Rothwell NV. Understanding genetics, a molecular approach. New York: Wiley-Liss Inc, 1993.

Thompson MW, McInnes RR, Willard HF. Thompson & Thompson genetics in medicine. 5th ed. Philadelphia: WB Saunders. 1991.

Walker R. Mathematical genetics. In: Wilson JK, ed. Genetics for blood bankers. Washington, DC: American Association of Blood Banks, 1980:55-100.

11

Immunology

THE SCIENCE OF IMMUNOLOGY IS uniquely intertwined in the field of transfusion medicine. This chapter takes the reader through the elements of the basic cells of the immune system, their relation to each other, their products, and the role they play in the body's defense mechanisms. Immunoglobulin production, variability, and actions are discussed, as well as the functions of each of the immunoglobulin types. The role of complement in the immune system is illustrated by a description of the classical and alternative pathways, including a discussion of the control proteins that are an integral part of those pathways.

Defense Mechanisms

The immune system allows the body to defend itself from externally derived agents and from potentially dangerous altered self constituents. The term immune is derived from Latin for "exempt" or "free from," and the goal of immune activity is to remain free from foreign invasion.

Immune defenses are often classified into two categories, innate and adaptive (also called acquired). Innate defenses are nonspecific; the same mechanisms are deployed against every invasive or harmful stimulus. In adaptive mechanisms, there is recognition of specific features, followed by reactions that vary according to differences in the host organism's previous experiences. Acquired immunity is a late evolutionary development, found only in vertebrates. Innate immunity, on the other hand, results from such near-universal proper-

11

ties and processes as epithelial barriers, proteolytic enzymes, cellular phagocytosis, and inflammatory reactions.

Adaptive responses to foreign or potentially injurious material require an ability to recognize specific agents. Invertebrates react against bodily disturbances but cannot discriminate specific types of injurious agents or distinguish internal from externally derived materials. It is customary to say that the foundations of adaptive immunity are discrimination between "self" and "foreign" and the ability to modify physiologic reactions based on this discrimination. This chapter applies the terms "immunity" and "immune response" to the uniquely vertebrate form of adaptive immunity.

Immune mechanisms reflect the actions of the interrelated cells, tissues, and organs collectively called the immune system. The effector cells of specific immunity are lymphocytes. Of all the body's cells, only lymphocytes have recognition receptors capable of exquisite discrimination among molecular configurations.

Overview of the Immune System

Immune responses can usefully be classified into two main divisions: humoral immunity, which is the generation of antibodies, and cell-mediated immune events. Two main populations of lymphocytes exist: T cells and B cells. It is customary to describe cell-mediated immunity as reflecting the actions of T cells, and humoral immunity as resulting from B-cell actions. It is, however, impossible to discuss the production and the effects of antibodies without discussing all the cells of the immune system, and the complex ways in which they interact. Some widely applicable definitions are given in Appendix 11-1; other terms are defined in the relevant contexts.

The "self" of an individual is the assortment of three-dimensional configurations characteristic of that person's cells and fluid-phase molecules. These are determined by the person's genetic constitution, and for that individual, any and all other molecular configurations are "foreign." During fetal and early-life development, B and T lymphocytes generate receptor molecules that enable each of the millions of lymphocytes to recognize a single specific antigen. When foreign material enters the host, antigen-presenting cells (APCs) isolate molecular configurations and display them as epitopes on the cell surface, in a way that allows exposure to the unique antigen receptors of T and B cells; lymphocytes with a receptor of the appropriate configuration establish intimate cell-to-cell contact.

Contact between the antigen receptor on the lymphocyte membrane and the epitope displayed by the APC initiates the cellular events that generate clones of activated lymphocytes specific for the antigen involved. T cells evince immune activation by secreting an array of cytokines and/or displaying markedly altered behavior toward other cells. Activated B cells differentiate into plasma cells, which secrete antibody [immunoglobulin (or IgG)] molecules into body fluids. Most B-cell responses require participation of simultaneously activated T cells of the same specificity; the T-cell activities of cell-mediated immunity do not involve B-cell participation.

The manifestations of cell-mediated immunity, either in vivo or in vitro, require the presence of viable T cells. Antibody-mediated reactions, on the other hand, are totally independent of B-cell existence, once the proteins have been produced and secreted. Immunoglobulin molecules combine with antigen to form immune complexes under a variety of laboratory and in-vivo conditions that do not involve lymphocytes or plasma cells. The laboratory study of antibodies is called serology.

Cells of the Immune System

All the cells involved in immunity are of hematopoietic origin (ie, they come from the marrow). Blood cells and some immune cells that reside primarily in tissue originate from a pluripotent stem cell. Stem cells, capable of self-renewal and of differentiating into progenitor cells committed to specialized development, constitute less than 0.01% of nucleated marrow cells in immunologically mature individuals.[1]

Cytokines produced by stromal cells of the marrow influence stem cell differentiation into two lines of cells, both capable of limited self-renewal and of evolution into several different cell lines. The lymphoid stem cell, suitably stimulated, gives rise to T and B lymphocytes and to large granular lymphocytes described as natural killer (NK) cells. Descendants of the myeloid stem cell eventually become granulocytes, macrophages, megakaryocytes, and erythrocytes. (See Fig 11-1.)

Lymphocytes

Two of the three lymphocyte cell lines express on their membranes the antigen receptors essential for the immune mechanisms of diversity, recognition, specificity, and memory. NK cells, which lack these receptors, manifest functions that lie outside this discussion. Both B and T lymphocytes exhibit diversity of antigen receptors, meaning that each cell in the overall population possesses membrane molecules of unique configuration, different from the shape of comparable molecules on other cells in the same population. The underlying molecular structure of the antigen receptor differs significantly in B and T lymphocytes, but the process that generates this diversity is the same for both populations.

All cells in the body, whatever their appearance or function, have exactly the same genetic constitution. Cellular differentiation is the process whereby certain genetic capabilities are suppressed and others are enhanced. Embryonic development reflects progressive differentiation into cells and tissues with special capabilities, but in virtually all cell lines except lymphocytes, every member of a given population has the same constitution as every other member. Lymphocytes are unique in that the members of the population differ from one another.

B cells recognize specific antigens present on cell membranes, for which that B cell is capable of producing antibody. The specificity of individual T cells resides in a specialized protein complex, called the T-cell receptor (TCR), present nowhere else in the body other than on the T-cell membrane. (See Fig 11-2.) T lymphocytes do not export immunologically specific molecules; the product of activated T cells is a variety of cytokines.

Generation of Idiotypic Specificity

Antigen receptor molecules of both T cells and B cells consist of two polypeptide chains, synthesized under the direction of two different chromosomal loci. For B cells, the loci are on chromosome 14 and on either chromosome 2 or 22; for T cells they are on chromosome 14 (*not* the same locus as for B cells) and chromosome 7. Before cellular differentiation begins, the deoxyribonucleic acid (DNA) at these loci is in the unmodified germline configuration present in all body cells. During early lymphocyte development, the genetic material at each of these loci undergoes a process of rearrangement unique to each cell.

The germline DNA configuration at these loci exhibits enormous redundancy. For any one polypeptide, synthesis requires the action of a single coding sequence of base pairs. In the germline configuration, these loci contain numerous base-pair sequences, each capable of determining a different sequence of amino acids. Any of these could direct synthesis of a polypeptide but only one can actually exert its effect in any one cell. Rearrangement is the process of selecting a single sequence for each portion of a large protein chain from the as-

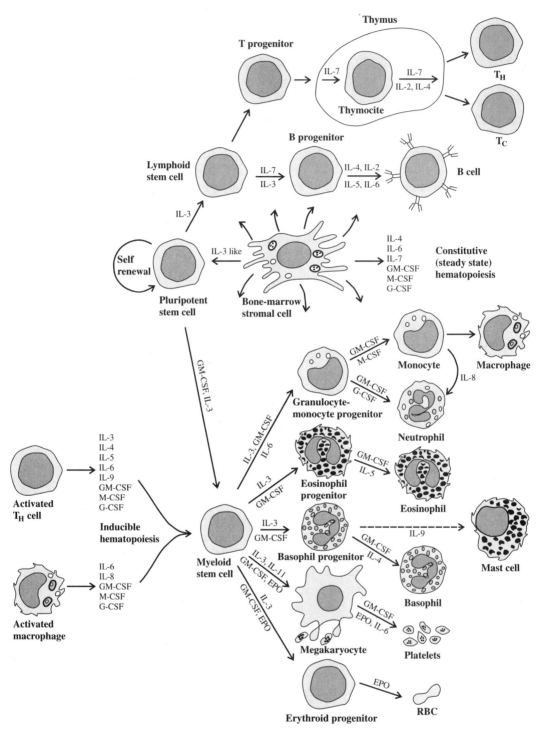

Figure 11-1. The pluripotent stem cell, in the upper middle part of the diagram, gives rise to the lymphoid stem cell and to the myeloid stem cell, from which all other lines of blood cells derive. Cytokines from marrow stromal cells influence the replication and differentiation of stem and later cells. Cytokines from activated members of the highly differentiated T-cell and macrophage lines exert major effects at all stages of myeloid and lymphoid development. (Used with permission from Kuby.[2])

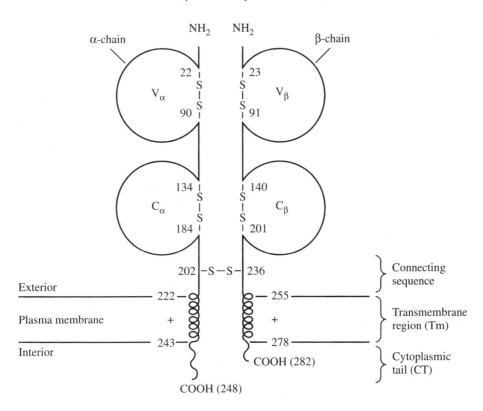

αβ T-cell receptor

Figure 11-2. The T-cell receptor (TCR) molecule allows individual T lymphocytes to recognize individual antigenic configurations. The amino acid sequences in the variable domains of alpha and beta chains (V$_\alpha$ and V$_\beta$) are determined by rearrangement of DNA at loci on chromosome 14 and 7. The TCR is a transmembrane molecule unique to T cells; neither the constituent chains nor the dimer are found anywhere else in the body. (Used with permission from Kuby.[2])

sortment (called the library) available, and of eliminating the unused genetic material.

Each chain in both the B-cell and T-cell receptors consists of a constant portion and a variable portion; the amino acid sequence of the variable portion determines the idiotypic specificity of the molecule. For both receptors, one chain contains selections from three different libraries, called V, D, and J, and the other from two libraries, V and J. An astronomic number of different protein configurations can result from the number of mathematically possible combinations and permutations.

For immunoglobulins, the heavy-chain locus has 250-400 different exons in the V library,

20 in the J library, and six in the D library. The light-chain locus contains a V library of about 300 selections and a J library of four. (See Fig 11-3.) For the TCR, the alpha chain locus has a V library of 50 selections and a J library of 70 selections, while the beta chain locus has 57 choices in the V library, 13 choices in the J library, and two choices in the D library. About 10% of T cells have receptors consisting of a gamma and a delta chain, for which comparable libraries exist at nearby loci on chromosomes 7 and 14. Selection from each library is random; additional sequence variation is introduced through inaccurate splicing or substitution of base pairs where the different exons meet one

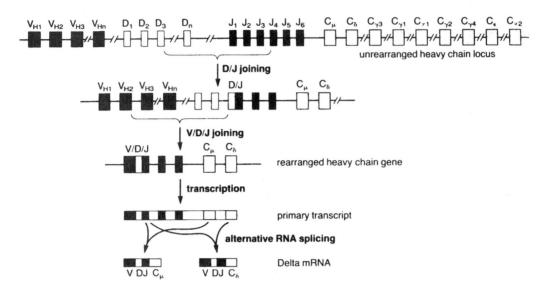

Figure 11-3. Schematic representation of the locus on chromosome 14 for the immunoglobulin heavy chain. The top line shows the germline sequence of DNA; V, D, and J libraries are on the left, sequences for constant-region configurations are on the right. Rearrangement occurs first by selection of one D and one J exon, followed by joining of one V exon to the D/J unit. The V/D/J selection is adjacent to determinants for mu and delta constant regions; alternative splicing allows the primary transcript to generate mRNA for either mu or delta heavy chains with the same variable-region configuration (idiotype). Clonal progeny may, in later generations, attach the V/D/J transcript to exons for other constant-region sequences (isotype switch). (Used with permission from Parslow.[3])

another. The result is generation of more than 10^8 different receptor configurations.

Maturation and Function

From the earliest pro-B form, identified by partial rearrangement of the immunoglobulin heavy-chain locus, to the immunocompetent but unstimulated circulating cell, maturation of B lymphocytes occurs in the marrow. Contact with the marrow stroma is essential for this process. The mature unstimulated B cell circulates continuously until it encounters its antigen. The later events of activation, proliferation, and evolution into an immunoglobulin-secreting plasma cell or persisting memory cell require the immunomodulatory effects of cytokines derived from macrophages and activated T cells.

T lymphocytes mature in the thymus, where contact with thymic stromal cells and their products promotes differentiation of several subpopulations. Developing cells in the thymus are called thymocytes; after thymic processing they enter the circulation as unstimulated T lymphocytes. Besides promoting differentiation, the thymus exerts a selective function, suppressing cells potentially reactive with self configurations. Such suppression is not absolute, as indicated by the existence of pathologic autoreactive immune events.

Membrane Markers

Every cell, of every population and type, has a membrane that displays numerous different molecules that serve numerous different purposes. A molecule that is found only on cells of a certain type or on cells at certain phases of development constitutes a useful marker to identify the cell population. Some membrane molecules serve identifiable physiologic functions, eg, immunoglobulin molecules, which not only mark the underlying cell as a B lymphocyte, but also perform a clearly understood receptor function. For other marker molecules, no function has yet been discovered.

Constitutive and Inducible Molecules. If a certain membrane molecule is always present on a certain cell type, regardless of the cell's functional state, the marker is called a constitutive element of the cell. If molecules are present only after particular stimulation, they are said to be induced by the stimulus.

MHC Products. Membrane molecules produced by the major histocompatibility complex (MHC) on chromosome 6 confer antigenic characteristics classified into the HLA system (see Chapter 17). HLA antigens in the A, B, and C series are called Class I molecules and those of the DP, DQ, and DR series are Class II molecules. Nearly all nucleated human cells constitutively express Class I molecules; Class II molecules are constitutively expressed only on mature B lymphocytes, cells of the monocyte/macrophage lineage (see below), and dendritic cells, which are of somewhat obscure origin. Class II expression is inducible on many other cells following immune stimulation. Unstimulated T lymphocytes do not express Class II molecules, but activated T cells do.

CD Antigens. Many markers characteristic of white cells have been identified with monoclonal antibodies, and have been classified as clusters of differentiation (CD) antigens. Observation of CD antigens is extremely useful in delineating developmental and functional attributes of T and B lymphocytes. Some confusion remains from terms applied when certain markers were first discovered, but most have been included in the CD system. T cells and B cells exhibit numerous CD antigens (see Table 11-1), of which the most important, in terms of identifying functionally significant subpopulations, are CD4 and CD8 (see Subpopulations of T Lymphocytes, below).

Other Membrane Molecules. Receptor molecules, many of which also have CD designations, constitute another category of markers useful in understanding immune activity. Some receptors are constitutively expressed, but others become apparent only with defined activities or at defined maturational stages.

The membranes of lymphocytes and the cells with which they interact express adhesion molecules that promote intimate and productive intercellular contact. Modest levels of these molecules may be present constitutively, but immune activation significantly increases their expression.

Subpopulations of T Lymphocytes

During thymic maturation, T cells acquire one of two membrane molecules, termed CD4 and CD8, that perform several functions. They serve as selective adhesion molecules, restricting the type of APC with which the lymphocyte can interact but enhancing close membrane association with the appropriate APC. They also assist in transmitting messages from the outside environment to the cell interior. CD4 is a transmembrane monomer and CD8 is a dimer of two dissimilar chains, each of which penetrates the membrane.

CD4+ T cells interact only with cells that use Class II molecules to present antigen, while CD8+ cells recognize only antigens presented by Class I molecules. (See Chapter 17, section on biologic function of HLA antigens.) The different MHC configurations present different categories of antigens. Class I molecules present epitopes synthesized within the APC, whereas Class II molecules incorporate and present antigenic material that originated outside the APC and, usually, outside the host. CD4+ cells are preeminent in immune responses to external antigenic stimuli, including those significant in blood group serology.

CD4+ and CD8+ cells differ in their physiologic roles. CD4+ cells, often characterized as helper or T_h cells, secrete cytokines that regulate immune responses in both B cells and T

Table 11-1. Some Major CD Antigens on Cells of the Immune System

CD Designation	Cell Population	Other Cells with Antigen	Comments
CD1	Cortical thymocytes	Some APCs, some B cells	Strength of expression is inverse to expression of TCR/CD3
CD2	Pan-T marker, present on early thymocytes	NK cells	This is a sheep-cell rosette receptor; serves adhesion function
CD3	Mature thymocytes and peripheral T cells	None	This is the invariant portion of the T-cell antigen receptor
CD4	Developing and mature thymocytes, and on 2/3 of peripheral T cells	Possibly some macrophages	Adhesion molecule that mediates MHC restriction; signal transmission; HIV receptor
CD5	Pan-T marker, from late cortical stage	B cells of chronic lymphocytic leukemia; possibly long-lived autoreactive B cells	Function unknown; possibly involved in costimulatory effects of cell-to-cell adhesion
CD8	Developing and mature thymocytes, and on 1/3 of peripheral T cells	None	Adhesion molecule that mediates MHC restriction; signal transmission
CD11a/CD18	Mature T and B cells	All leukocytes; not platelets or red cells	This is the leukocyte function antigen (LFA-1) complex, which interacts with CD54 (ICAM-1)
CD21	Mature B cells	Possibly macrophages	This is receptor for C3d (CR2); also receptor for Epstein-Barr virus
CD25	Activated T and B cells	Macrophages; virally transformed cells	This is IL-2 receptor, earlier called *Tac*
CD28	Mature and activated T cells; plasma cells	None	Receptor for costimulatory effects of B7 on antigen-presenting cells
CD32	Mature B cells	Macrophages, granulocytes, platelets	This is receptor for Fc portion of IgG (Fcγ RII)
CD34	Immature B cells	Hematopoietic cells; endothelial cells	Called "stem cell antigen"; used in laboratory to isolate hematopoietic precursor cells, physiologic function unknown
CD35	Mature and activated B cells	Red cells, macrophages, granulocytes, dendritic cells	This is receptor for C3b (CR1)
CD45	Immature and mature B and T cells	All cells of hematopoietic origin except red cells	Also called leukocyte common antigen (LCA); different leukocytes have different isoforms
CD54	Activated T and B cells	Endothelial cells; various somatic cells after cytokine stimulation	This is the intercellular adhesion molecule (ICAM-1), which interacts with CD11a/CD18 (LFA-1)
CD71	Early thymocytes; activated T and B cells	Activated hematopoietic cells; proliferating cells of other somatic lines	This is the transferrin receptor

CD=clusters of differentiation; APCs=antigen-presenting cells; NK=natural killer; TCR=T-cell receptor; MHC=major histocompatibility complex; HIV=human immunodeficiency virus; IL=interleukin.

cells. Antibody production is either enhanced or suppressed, depending on what type of CD4+ intervention occurs. A separate population of CD4+ cells participates in a form of cell-mediated immunity called delayed hypersensitivity, which is beyond the scope of this discussion. The preeminent function of CD8+ (or T_c) cells is cytotoxicity, also irrelevant to this discussion.

Antigen-Presenting Cells

Immunogenic material from outside the host must undergo significant manipulation before it initiates an immune response. Only small epitopes of larger entities actually combine with antigen receptor molecules. T cells recognize antigens only when they are enclosed in the peptide-binding groove of MHC molecules. Membrane immunoglobulin, the antigen receptor of B lymphocytes, can combine with antigenic material in its native form but, for most antigens, the promoting actions of antigenically stimulated T cells are necessary for a productive B-cell response.

The necessary attributes of the APCs are that it expresses Class II molecules, that it is capable of incorporating (and, usually, of degrading) exogenous antigens, and that it is able to display the MHC-epitope complex on its membrane. Only a few populations meet these requirements: the monocyte-macrophage line, descended from myeloid precursor cells in the marrow; epithelial and other cells in the thymus; a population of obscure lineage but wide distribution called dendritic cells; and, under suitable circumstances, B lymphocytes and endothelial cells that line small venules.[2]

The APCs involved in the majority of immune reactions are dendritic cells and macrophages. Besides processing and presenting antigen, these cells secrete cytokines that enhance the reactivity of B and T cells that have recognized the presented antigen. APCs are nonspecific; the nature of the antigen or its epitopes does not affect either membrane display or production of costimulatory materials. The specificity of acquired immunity resides in the antigen receptors of responding lymphocytes.

The Nature of the Immune Response

The remainder of this chapter describes only the humoral immune response. Many of the concepts also apply, either directly or in modified form, to cellular immunity, but in our current state of understanding, cellular immunity has little direct relevance to transfusion medicine.

Immunoglobulin Chains

The antibody molecule, portrayed schematically in Fig 11-4, consists of four polypeptide chains—two identical chains of 214 amino acids, called light chains, and two identical chains of 440 or more amino acids, called heavy chains. Antigenic specificity resides in the configuration formed by the N-terminal 134 amino acids of the light chain together with the N-terminal 144 amino acids of the heavy chain. Thus, approximately half the light chain and one quarter of the heavy chain are described as variable regions; the remaining portions of both chains are called constant regions. Light chains have a constant region with one of two different amino acid sequences, designated kappa and lambda. The locus for manufacture of kappa light chains is on chromosome 2; that for lambda chains is on chromosome 22. A single cell will synthesize immunoglobulin containing either kappa or lambda chains, never both.

Heavy-Chain Synthesis

The heavy-chain constant region can exhibit any of five major amino acid sequences, called alpha, gamma, delta, epsilon, and mu (α, γ, δ, ε, and μ). Immunoglobulin molecules containing pairs of each chain are designated as classes termed, respectively, IgA, IgG, IgD, IgE, and IgM. The site on chromosome 14 that controls

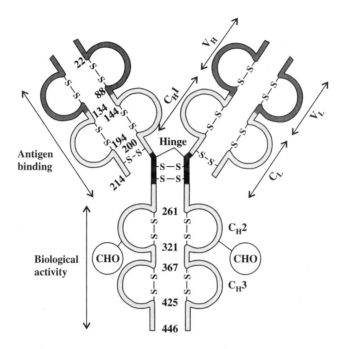

Figure 11-4. The basic four-chain immunoglobulin unit. Idiotypic specificity resides in the variable domains of heavy and light chains (V_H and V_L). Antigen-binding capacity depends on intact linkage between one light chain (V_L and C_L) and the amino-terminal half of one heavy chain (V_H and C_H1), the Fab fragments of the molecule. Disulfide bonds in the hinge region join carboxy-terminal halves of both heavy chains (C_H2 and C_H3, plus C_H4 for mu and epsilon heavy chains), to form the Fc fragment. (Used with permission from Kuby.[2])

heavy-chain manufacture contains DNA sequences for all these peptide sequences, a multiplicity reminiscent of the libraries of V, D, and J sequences available for variable-region structure. A major difference is that selection of one constant-region segment for expression does not automatically eliminate all the others. Rearrangement of variable-region DNA is a one-time event that cannot subsequently be modified. When an unstimulated B cell activates one constant-region segment, this does not prevent its clonal progeny from later synthesizing heavy chains with different constant-region sequences.

Antibody Synthesis

The practical significance of persisting availability of heavy-chain synthesis is that a clone of B cells specific for a single antigenic configuration can, under various conditions of stimulation, synthesize antibody molecules with the same specificity but different heavy chains and, therefore, different functional capacities.

Structural differences within a single overall protein category are called isotypes (see Table 11-2); the five different heavy chains constitute five different isotypes, determining five different classes of antibody molecules. When progeny of a cell that originally produced IgM of a given idiotype begin producing IgG instead, the process is called isotype switch. The antibody that unstimulated B cells synthesize and express on the membrane as antigen receptor is predominantly IgM, with some IgD molecules of the same specificity.

The First Encounter with Antigen

The normal fetus develops in a closed environment, protected from any molecular configurations other than its own. Maturing

Table 11-2. Classification of Immunoglobulins

Type of Variation	Refers to	Examples
Isotypic	Ig classes and subclasses present in *all* members of the species.	IgG, IgA, IgM, etc; IgG1, IgG2, etc
Allotypic	Variations in the amino acid structure of heavy and light chains unrelated to antibody specificity. Present in some but *not all* members of the species.	Gm and Km allotypes
Idiotypic	Idiotypes are the antigen binding sites on the antibody molecule. Present in some but not all antibody molecules within an individual member of the species.	Fab regions of antibody molecules

lymphocytes express antigen receptors but, having had no contact with antigens of corresponding configuration, they circulate as unstimulated cells.

Fixed and Circulating Cells

Once in the outside world, the infant (and subsequently the child and the adult) encounters innumerable foreign configurations. As APCs process these complex materials, membrane-bound MHC molecules display the epitopes. Lymphocytes continuously circulate through the bloodstream, the interstitial fluids, and the lymphatic system, their destinations controlled by homing receptors that interact with endothelial-cell markers in various tissues. Unstimulated T and B cells spend much of their time passing through the spleen, the lymph nodes, and the mucosal surfaces of alimentary and respiratory tracts, locations that are heavily exposed to external elements and are rich in APCs.

Many casual and transient encounters occur between APCs and passing lymphocytes. If, however, an APC displays the antigen complementary to a lymphocyte's receptor, more prolonged contact occurs. Adhesion molecules increase on both the APC and the lymphocyte, generating intimate cell-to-cell contact that

enhances the activation signals produced by initial engagement of the antigen receptor. Engagement of the antigen receptor and presence of suitable costimulatory events cause the unstimulated lymphocyte to undergo intracellular changes preparatory for subsequent proliferation; cells in this phase are called lymphoblasts. Cellular multiplication by geometric proliferation from a single precursor is called clonal expansion.

Immunomodulatory Events

Antibody production requires that B cells and T cells with the same specificity undergo simultaneous activation. Cytokines produced by the APCs and by activated T lymphocytes cause the B cells to multiply and to undergo intracellular changes through which they evolve into immunoglobulin-secreting plasma cells. In turn, the B cells capture and present antigen in ways that influence T cells to secrete cytokines that promote more focused antibody production. Most of the clonal progeny evolve into plasma cells, which lead a short but very active life of antibody production, but some become memory cells. Memory cells, which secrete no immediate product, retain intracellular changes resulting from antigen exposure, and persist in the circulation long after the initial event.

The Primary Immune Response

The time required for the processes to develop is called the lag period. Variables such as the nature and quantity of antigen, route of administration, and protein-synthesizing capacities of the host all determine how long it will be between exposure and the presence of detectable antibody in body fluid.

The antibody class that appears in the bloodstream after first contact with an antigen is always IgM; the lag period can vary from a few days to weeks or even months. Although IgD can be detected on the membrane of unstimulated B lymphocytes, especially in blood of the fetus and infant, secreted antibody has little or no IgD component.

Some days after IgM antibody appears, IgG antibody of the same specificity usually becomes detectable. If there is no further exposure to the eliciting antigen, the level of circulating IgM antibody characteristically peaks and then declines, while IgG antibody of the same specificity persists substantially longer. Cytokines from activated T cells are important for many phases of B-cell response, and are essential for isotype switching and for the generation of memory cells.

T-Independent Immune Responses

B-cell antigen receptors are capable of interacting directly with antigenic material. A variety of polysaccharide configurations, especially those with multiple identical repeats, can initiate B-cell proliferation and antibody secretion without the helper actions of T cells. The resulting antibodies are always IgM; in the absence of T-cell modulatory effects, isotype switch does not occur and no memory cells develop.

Cell-wall polysaccharides of many extracellular bacteria (eg, pneumococcus, many gram-negative bacilli) have this capability. Persons with deficient T-cell function can, through this mechanism, establish and maintain humoral immunity to many common bacterial pathogens. Because there is no memory, continuing antibody production requires continuing exposure to the antigen. Many polysaccharides with this immunogenic property are remarkably resistant to biologic degradation, so that even without the presence of viable or infective bacteria, IgM production may continue for some time. The contact between B cells and these T-independent antigens appears to occur especially in the spleen. Damage to or removal of the spleen impairs the ability to resist many bacterial infections.

Subsequent Contact with Antigen

Initiation of a T-dependent primary response permanently alters the host's immune status. Even if the antigen disappears from the body, circulating T cells and B cells will continue to persist that retain the intracellular alterations caused by antigen exposure. Memory cells respond to renewed antigenic contact far more rapidly than unstimulated cells. No lag period is needed; the required level of cell-to-cell co-stimulation is far less; and the effective dose of antigen can be quite small. Renewed exposure to antigen causes memory B cells to exhibit rapid expansion of IgG-secreting progeny, a process described as an anamnestic (or secondary) immune response.

Anamnestic vs Primary Immune Response

Within a short time after a second or subsequent contact with a T-dependent antigen, the level of circulating IgG antibody rises sharply. This may occur within hours, or a day or so at the most, compared with days or weeks necessary to generate IgG in a primary immune response. Because there has already been significant previous clonal expansion, the number of participating cells will be high and the magnitude of the anamnestic IgG response may be as much as 100 times greater than the primary response.[3] The affinity of antibody molecules for the antigen will also be greater. The repeated dose of antigen also generates an IgM response, but because this occurs without participation of memory cells, the lag period and the magnitude of IgM secretion will be the same as in the primary response.

Other Isotypes

Regulation of IgA and IgE production is less well understood than the mechanisms determining IgM and IgG. Very young children may have measurable IgA or IgE antibodies directed against antigens for which no previous contact can be identified, but these classes have not been seen in known primary immunization. Various regulatory cytokines influence isotype switching in clones of B cells and stimulate or suppress secretion by cells with the capability to produce alpha or epsilon heavy chains. Distinctive stimulatory and regulatory mechanisms presumably exist at body sites where IgA and IgE (see section on individual immunoglobulins, below) exert their effects, but much remains to be explained.

Multiplicity of Response

Immune responses always involve multiple clones because even highly purified antigens express multiple epitopes and because many cells, embodying different structural capacities, respond to antigenic stimulation. Native humoral responses are appropriately described as polyclonal; the immunoglobulin-producing cells have differentiated from numerous cells of origin, which have many features in common but subtle differences in recognition sites. The more complex the initial antigenic stimulus, the more varied will be the clones that respond and the more heterogeneous will be the antibodies that result. This diversity is biologically advantageous. It allows recognition of and attack on variants of the original foreign invader, and calls into action a wider range of defense mechanisms than the effects of a single class or structure of antibody.

Immunoglobulins

The Immunoglobulin Monomer

The basic immunoglobulin unit is a four-chain molecule consisting of two heavy chains and two light chains (see Fig 11-4). Ig molecules for which a corresponding antigen can be identified are called antibodies. All antibodies are immunoglobulins, but Ig molecules for which no complementary material has been recognized are called simply immunoglobulins, not antibodies.

Domains

The amino acids that constitute the heavy and light chains do not exist as a two-dimensional linear sequence similar to beads on a string. The amino acid sequence is the primary structure, on which depend complex intramolecular forces that determine the final three-dimensional shape that the molecule exhibits. Both the heavy and the light chains have loops of amino acids, called domains, that balloon out between disulfide bonds; this brings noncontiguous amino acids into close proximity. Light chains have two domains and heavy chains have either four or five.

The domain nearest the amino terminus of each chain is the site of the tremendous sequence variability described in the earlier section on antibody diversity. In these N-terminal domains, called variable domains (V_L in light chains, V_H in heavy chains), resides the antigenic specificity of the immunoglobulin molecule. The one domain remaining in the light chain and three (or four) in the heavy chain are called constant domains, designated C_L and C_H1, C_H2, C_H3, and C_H4. The five isotypes of heavy chains and two of light chains are identified by the amino acid sequences of the constant domains. The constant domains of heavy chains determine what serologic and biologic behaviors the antibody molecule will express.

Interchain and Intrachain Bonds

Each light chain is joined to one heavy chain by a disulfide bond. One or more disulfide bonds link the two heavy chains at a point between C_H1 and C_H2, in an area of considerable flexibility called the hinge region. These interchain disulfide bonds are highly resistant to cleavage by reducing agents.

Fab and Fc Fragments. Peptide bonds in a polypeptide can be cleaved at predictable sites by proteolytic enzymes. Much information about immunoglobulin structure and function derives from study of cleavage fragments generated by papain digestion of Ig molecules. Papain cleaves the heavy chain at a point just above the hinge, creating three separate fragments. Two are identical, consisting of one light chain linked to the N-terminal half of the heavy chain; the other one consists of the C-terminal halves of the heavy chains, still joined to one another by the hinge-region disulfide bonds. The two identical N-terminal fragments, which retain the specificity of the antibody, are called Fab fragments. The joined C-terminal halves of the heavy chains constitute a nonantibody protein fragment capable of crystallization, called the Fc fragment.

The intact four-chain immunoglobulin monomer interacts with two examples of antigen, each of the Fab segments combining with an antigen molecule. As long as the disulfide bond continues to link light chain with half the heavy chain, a single Fab fragment can combine with a single example of antigen; these monovalent antigen-specific fragments are quite useful in laboratory investigations. Isolated light chains or variable-portion halves of the heavy chain have little or no antigen-combining capacity.

Immunoglobulin Polymers. Disulfide bonds may also join Ig monomers to one another, depending upon the amino acids present in the relevant constant domains. IgG, IgE, and IgD exist only as monomers; there are no polymeric forms of these classes.

The IgM synthesized by unstimulated B cells and expressed on the membrane as the antigen receptor is also a monomer. The mu heavy chain has four constant domains; in the membrane form of IgM, a configuration within the fourth domain allows it to bind to the cell membrane and also to two associated membrane heterodimers through which the message of antigen contact is conveyed to the interior. Following clonal expansion and differentiation to a plasma cell, the activated cell produces mu chains with a slightly different constant-domain configuration. While still in the plasma-cell cytoplasm, five IgM monomers unite through one set of disulfide bonds between C_H3s and another set between C_H4s.[4] The resulting pentamers are secreted to the exterior and constitute the form in which IgM accumulates in body fluids.

Secreted IgA exists in both monomeric and polymeric forms. Monomeric forms predominate in the blood stream, but dimers and trimers, which are secreted by B cells in mucosal surfaces and exocrine tissue, are the biologically active form. Polymeric IgA and pentamers of IgM are translocated from interstitial fluid to surface secretions by interaction with a glycoprotein present on the basolateral surface of epithelial cells, the polymeric immunoglobulin receptor (pIgR).[5]

Other Chains

Pentameric IgM and the dimers and trimers of IgA contain a 15 kD polypeptide called the J chain. Before the polymer leaves the plasma-cell cytoplasm, this chain attaches to the terminal constant domain of two adjacent monomers. No matter how many monomers constitute the polymer, there will be only one J chain; its function is not fully understood, especially because J-chain production has been identified in vertebrate lymphocytes that do not produce immunoglobulin and in superficial and phagocytic cells of invertebrate fauna.[6]

The polymeric Ig molecules present in epithelial secretions also exhibit a subunit called the secretory component. This large polypeptide is a residuum of the pIgR; hence, it is synthesized by epithelial cells and not plasma cells. Epithelial cells ensnare Ig polymers that exhibit a J chain, an interaction that can be blocked by J-chain antibodies.[6] The complex of pIgR and antibody migrates across the epithelial cell to its apical surface, where part of the pIgR is cleaved and destroyed. The remainder persists in the secreted molecule and appears to protect the biologically important surface antibodies from proteolysis in the enzyme-rich secretions of respiratory and alimentary tracts.[5]

Individual Immunoglobulin Classes

IgM

IgM is the first Ig class produced by the maturing B cell. It is the first to appear in the serum of maturing infants, and the first to become detectable in a primary immune response.

Secreted pentameric IgM normally constitutes 5-10% of the immunoglobulin in normal serum; very few of these large molecules diffuse into interstitial fluid. Some IgM is found in epithelial secretions but, as the pIgR (described above) combines preferentially with IgA, most transepithelial movement of polymerized Ig affects IgA and not IgM.

Although the five monomers comprise 10 antigen-combining sites, only five are readily available to combine with most antigens, and IgM antibody is described as pentavalent. Because of their large size and multivalency, IgM molecules readily bind to antigens on particulate surfaces, notably those on red cells or microorganisms. IgM antibodies characteristically bring dispersed antigen- bearing particles together into clumps, the process of agglutination. Although extremely useful as a laboratory endpoint, agglutination probably plays a relatively modest role in biologic events.

Probably the most important biologic effect of IgM is its efficacy in activating the complement cascade, which markedly enhances inflammatory and phagocytic defense mechanisms and may produce lysis of antigen-bearing cells.

IgG

Immunoglobulin G exists only as a monomer; it contributes about 80% of the immunoglobulins in serum and is also present in extravascular fluid. As a relatively small, divalent antibody molecule, it rarely agglutinates saline-suspended particles. It tends to combine with and remain attached to cell-surface antigens, where its presence can be detected in vitro by antiglobulin testing. In vivo, cells or particles coated with IgG undergo markedly enhanced interactions with cells that have receptors for the Fc portion of gamma chains, especially neutrophils and macrophages.

IgG molecules can be classified into four subclasses, designated IgG1, IgG2, IgG3, and IgG4. Structurally, these differ primarily in the characteristics of the hinge region and the number of inter-heavy-chain disulfide bonds; biologically they have significantly different in-vivo properties. IgG3 has the greatest ability to activate complement, followed by IgG1 and, to a much lesser extent, IgG2. IgG4 is incapable of complement activation. IgG1, IgG3, and IgG4 readily cross the placenta, but not IgG2. IgG1, IgG2, and IgG4 have a serum half-life of 23 days, significantly longer than that of other circulating immunoglobulins, but IgG3 survives only slightly longer than IgA and IgM. IgG1 and IgG3 readily interact with the Fc receptors on phagocytic cells, while IgG4 and IgG2 do so far less readily.

IgA

Although there is a large body content of IgA, relatively little is found in the blood, where it contributes only 10-15% of serum immunoglobulin concentration and serves no known physiologic function. Most of the IgA mass and all of its physiologic significance exist in mucosal secretions. The mechanisms whereby secretory IgA protects the host are poorly understood, but the outcome is protection of underlying epithelium from bacterial and viral penetration. Polymeric IgA is thought to combine with environmental antigens to form complexes that are eliminated as surface secretions are excreted, a process that may be important in controlling development of hypersensitivity. The alpha heavy chain has no complement-binding site, but IgA-containing complexes can activate complement through the alternative pathway (see below).

IgE

The concentration of serum IgE is measured in nanograms, compared with milligram levels for other immunoglobulins. Even when patients with severe allergies have markedly elevated serum concentrations, the absolute level is in hundredths of milligrams. Most IgE is present as monomers tightly bound to the membrane of basophilic granulocytes or mast cells when present in the tissues, which have a high-affinity receptor for the C_H4 of the IgE heavy chain. IgE is responsible for immediate hypersensitivity events, such as allergic asthma, hay fever, and systemic anaphylactic reactions. Although this Ig class appears to be involved in reactions to protozoal parasites, no specific protective mechanisms have been identified.

IgD

Serum contains only trace amounts of IgD, which is always a monomer. Most IgD exists as membrane immunoglobulin on unstimulated B cells, where its specific function is obscure.

Table 11-3 summarizes the properties of the five classes of human immunoglobulins.

Antibody Production

Reagent Antibodies

The diversity of the native antibody response is advantageous for the host, but heterogeneous sera are not optimal as in-vitro reagents. The analytic and diagnostic values of antigen-antibody reactions, some of which are described in Chapter 12, depend upon the occurrence of specific and reproducible interactions. Unmodified immune sera vary in the concentration and serologic properties of the antibody molecules they contain, in the epitopes they recognize, and in the presence and characteristics of additional specificities. The ideal serum for reagent purposes is a concentrated suspension of highly specific, well-characterized, uniformly reactive, immunoglobulin molecules. Until the 1970s, the only way to obtain reagent quantities of adequately specific and uniform antibodies was to immunize animals or humans with purified antigens and then perform time-consuming and sometimes unpredictable separation techniques on the resulting sera.

Monoclonal Antibodies

A single stimulated B cell generates clonal offspring that produce antibody specific for a single epitope. Postactivation events can induce differences in heavy-chain isotype, but the idiotypic specificity encoded in heavy- and light-chain variable regions remains the same. When a single B-cell clone is propagated in cell culture, the supernatant fluid contains antibody of a single specificity. Individual cells can be isolated from a polyclonal responding population and their unique products characterized. Screening these cultures allows clones to be selected whose product reacts in the desired way with a desired target. These monoclonal antibodies are highly advantageous for in-vitro testing.

The problem with isolating cells that generate selected antibodies is that, because normal cells reproduce themselves only a limited number of times, the cultured cell lines survive only a short time. In light of the labor required to separate cells and identify monoclonal products, it is frustrating to see the synthesizing cells die off after generating a finite, rather small amount of the desirable protein. Continuous production of a selected antibody requires

Table 11-3. Human Immunoglobulins

Class	IgG	IgA	IgM	IgD	IgE
Structure					
H-chain isotype	γ	α	μ	δ	ε
Number of subclasses	4	2	1	?	?
L-chain, types	κ,λ	κ,λ	κ,λ	κ,λ	κ,λ
Molecular weight (daltons)	150,000	180,000-500,000	900,000	180,000	200,000
Exists as polymer	no	yes	yes	no	no
Electrophoretic mobility	γ	γ	between γ and β	between γ and β	fast γ
Sedimentation constant (in Svedberg units)	6-7S	7-15S	19S	7S	8S
Gm allotypes (H chain)	+	0	0	0	0
Km allotypes (Kappa L chain: formerly Inv)	+	+	+	?	?
Am allotypes	0	+	0	0	0
Serum concentration (mg/dL)	1000-1500	200-350	85-205	3	0.01-0.07
Total immunoglobulin (%)	80	15	5	<0.1	<0.1
Synthetic rate (mg/kg/day)	33	24	6-7	<0.4	<0.02
Serum half-life (days)	23	6	5	2-8	1-5
Distribution (% of total in intravascular space)	45	42	76	75	51
Present in epithelial secretions	no	yes	no	no	no
Antibody activity	yes	yes	yes	probably no	yes
Serologic characteristics	Usually nonagglutinating	Usually nonagglutinating	Usually agglutinating	?	?
Fixes complement	yes	no	yes	no	no
Crosses placenta	yes	no	no	no	no

continuous propagation of the synthesizing cell. Normal antibody-producing cells do not propagate continuously; neoplastic cells do propagate themselves continuously, but they do not synthesize normal protein products.

Hybridomas

In 1976, Köhler and Milstein[7] published their solution to this problem; plasma cells of normal antibody-producing capacity were fused to neoplastic plasma cells of infinite reproductive capacity (ie, myeloma cells). Techniques had previously been developed that cause cell membranes to merge, allowing cytoplasm and nucleus of two different kinds of cells to fuse into a single cell. Plasma cell/myeloma cell hybrids could be maintained in cell culture for prolonged periods, producing large quantities of the selected antibody, and could be stored in a stable fashion.

Köhler and Milstein fused myeloma and plasma cells whose intrinsic properties they exploited ingeniously. The myeloma cells they used were unable to synthesize [hypoxanthine-guanine-phosphoribosyltransferase (HGPRT)], an enzyme needed for nucleic acid production. However, these myeloma cells could renew themselves indefinitely if HGPRT was provided or, alternatively, if a different metabolic pathway was available. The plasma cells were normal plasma cells, able to secrete antibody and to generate HGPRT, but incapable of prolonged replication.

The investigators subjected the fusion products to a growth medium that blocked the alternative pathway for nucleotide production; this caused the HGPRT-deficient myeloma cells to die off and had no effect on normal plasma cells that intrinsically would die after limited replication. The only cells that could metabolize normally and reproduce repeatedly were the fusion products, hybrids in which antibody-producing plasma cells provided the HGPRT and the myeloma cells provided the capacity for infinite reproduction. For this work, Köhler and Milstein were awarded the AABB's Landsteiner award in 1982 and the Nobel prize in 1984.

This starkly simplified explanation of the hybridoma technique leaves out the complications of species origin of the cells and other necessary details. It also ignores the demanding processes of isolating cells, characterizing immunoglobulin specificity, and selecting products with desirable properties.

Applications. The exquisite specificity of monoclonal antibodies is both an advantage and a disadvantage for reagent use. An antibody that gives desirably strong and specific reactions with one epitope of a multivalent antigenic molecule may fail to react with cells whose antigenic expression lacks that particular configuration.

Advantages. Reagent preparations used in blood banking characteristically are blends of several different monoclonal products, thereby increasing the range of variant phenotypes the antiserum can identify. Single or blended monoclonal preparations often react more strongly than immune-serum preparations when tested against cells with weakly expressed antigens. Panels of selected monoclonal specificities permit identification and categorization of a complex antigenic system. Monoclonal antiglobulin specificities are used to identify different immunoglobulin classes or complement proteins on cell membranes; blends of several monoclonals provide, in a single vial, a polyspecific reagent with known target reactivity.

Membrane Markers

Production and selection of monoclonal antibodies have made possible the identification of innumerable cell-membrane markers. The CD antigens, now so important in identifying classes and subsets of white blood cells, were discovered by their reactions with monoclonal antibodies. The term "clusters of differentiation" reflects the fact that different monoclonal sera raised by different investigators could be shown, by cooperative comparisons, to give sufficiently similar results that their target antigens could be provisionally identified. Monoclonal antibodies have greatly expanded the range and the accuracy of diagnosing tumors, of characterizing cells and molecules involved in physiologic events such as inflammation or angiogenesis, and of identifying microorganisms.

Immune Selection

The limitations discussed for monoclonal antibodies have a particularly adverse effect when these antibodies are intended for in-vivo use. Recent advances using phage technology to produce specific antibodies have helped increase opportunities for using these genetically engineered antibodies for a variety of therapeutic treatments.

Phage technology allows for the selection of specific antibodies, produced by cloned phage vectors, to be isolated through specific binding of the antibody to a solid-phase antigen. The resulting structure includes the gene encoding the antibody. This genetically engineered phage mimics the B lymphocyte by expressing an antibody on its surface as well as having an immunoglobulin genotype.[8]

Use of this technology could result in libraries of antibodies with numerous chemically defined specificities from which many different antibodies could be isolated against almost any antigen. Because phage-library-derived antibodies are entirely human, and as such are less immunogenic, they will offer a distinct advantage for in vivo use over monoclonal-hybridoma-derived antibodies. A particularly exciting feature of these libraries could be the ability to fine tune antibodies on demand to react with a specific antigen,[9] thereby offering unique opportunities in the future for clinical and immunologic therapies directed against new viruses or mutated viruses.

Complement

General Concepts

Complement is the term applied to a system of 25-30 serum and membrane proteins that act in a cascading manner—similar to the coagulation, fibrinolytic, and kinin systems—to produce numerous biologic effects. The participating proteins remain inactive until an event initiates the process, whereupon the product of one reaction becomes the catalyst for the next step. (See Fig 11-5.) Each evolving enzyme or complex can act on multiple substrate molecules, creating the potential for tremendous amplification of an initially modest or localized event.

Complement proteins do not recognize specific antigens. Several mechanisms[11] exist for activating the complement cascade, of which only one, the classical pathway, requires the configurational specificity that is the hallmark of acquired immunity. Initiated by interaction between an antibody and its antigen, the classical pathway was first to be discovered and remains the most thoroughly studied. The alternative pathway, also called the properdin system, was discovered decades later, but undoubtedly developed much earlier in evolution. Several other mechanisms are associated with other aspects of the body's innate defense systems.

Biologic Consequences

Complement has three major roles in the intact individual: promotion of acute inflammatory events; alteration of surfaces so that phagocytosis is enhanced; and modification of cell membranes, leading to lysis of the underlying cell. These actions fight off invading bacteria, protect against viral infection, eliminate protein complexes, and enhance development of immune events. They also initiate inflammatory and immune processes that may harm the host, and mediate destruction of cells, especially those in the blood.

Complement Terminology

Complement proteins are designated by numbers (C1, C2, C4 of the classical pathway; C3 and C5 through C9 of the common effector pathway); by uppercase letters (factors D, B, and P of the alternative pathway and some control proteins); and by complex descriptive terms for some of the control proteins. For those activation steps causing protein cleavage, the fragments are given lowercase modifiers (eg, C3a, C3b, C3dg); protein complexes with enzymatic activity are written with a bar on top ($\overline{\text{C1423}}$). Control proteins in serum or on cells usually have descriptive names, eg, C4b-binding protein (C4bBP) and membrane inhibitor of reactive lysis (MIRL), or are identified by letters (factor H).

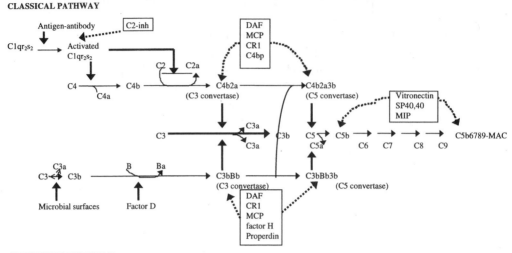

CLASSICAL PATHWAY

ALTERNATIVE PATHWAY

Figure 11-5. Activating steps in the complement cascade. Both classical pathway (top left) and alternative pathway (bottom left) cleave C3 into C3b, which generates continuing activation steps, and C3a, a potent anaphylatoxin. C5a and, to a lesser extent, C4a are also biologically active as anaphylatoxins. Factor P of the alternative pathway acts to stabilize the C3bBb complex, which exerts the critical C3 convertase effect. (Modified from Kirby[2] and McAleer and Sim.[10])

Many cells have receptors on their membranes that interact with one or another complement component or fragment. In their role as complement receptor (CR) proteins, they are numbered CR1 through CR5; as membrane markers distinctive for certain cell types, some have also been given CD numbers.

The Classical Pathway

The Antigen-Antibody Interaction

For the classical pathway of complement activation to occur, an immunoglobulin must react with target antigen. (See Fig 11-5.) Combination with antigen alters the configuration of the immunoglobulin Fc portion, rendering accessible an area in one of the heavy-chain constant domains that interacts with the first component (C1) of complement. C1 can combine only with Ig molecules having an appropriate heavy-chain configuration, which exists in the mu heavy chain and in the gamma chains in IgG subclasses 1, 2, and 3. Of the IgG subclasses, IgG3 most effectively acti-

vates complement, followed by IgG1 and, to a much lesser degree, IgG2.

The C1 component of complement attaches to activation sites on the Fc portion of two or more discrete Ig monomers. The pentameric IgM molecule provides an abundance of closely contiguous Fc monomers. Upon combination with an antigen, a single IgM molecule can initiate the complement cascade. For IgG antibodies to activate the sequence, two separate molecules must attach to antigen sites within 30-40 nm of each other, to provide attachment sites for one C1 molecule.[2] Activation by IgG antibodies depends not only on the concentration and avidity of the antibody but also on the surface distribution of the antigen.

The C1 Complex

Circulating C1 is a macromolecule consisting of three distinct proteins (C1q, C1r, and C1s). C1q is a collagen-like protein comprised of 18 polypeptide chains of three distinct types. The intimate association of C1r and C1s with C1q is stabilized by Ca^{++} ions. In the absence of Ca^{++}, the complex dissociates and the system has no classical-pathway complement activity. Chelating agents such as citrate and oxalate anticoagulants abolish complement capability by removing calcium and other cations needed later in the sequence.

Two or more chains of the C1q portion of C1 attach to the heavy-chain sites uncovered in the antigen-bound Ig molecules, causing a conformational change that allows autocatalytic conversion of inactive C1r to the enzyme activity that cleaves C1s into a serine protease (see Fig 11-6). The substrates for the

C1s serine protease are C4 and C2. Numerous C4 molecules float freely in the fluid surrounding antigen-bound immunoglobulin and its attached C1qrs.

Activation to C3 Convertase

After C1qrs-mediated cleavage, the large residual fragment of C4 (called C4b) binds to the underlying surface. The small cleavage fragment (called C4a) floats free in the surrounding medium, where it has modest anaphylatoxic activity (see section below). C4b on the cell surface attracts the proenzyme mole-

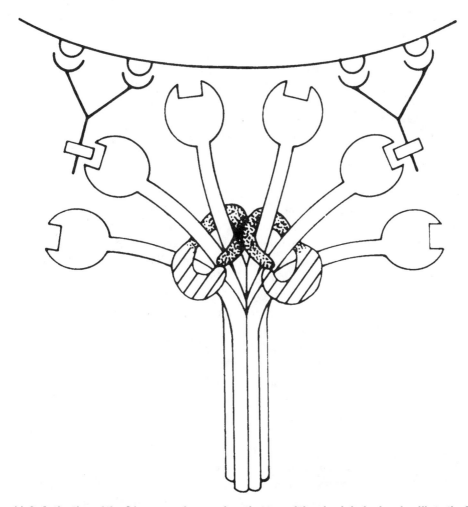

Figure 11-6. Activation of the C1qrs complex requires that two of the six globular heads affix to the Fc portion of an antigen-bound Ig monomer. The consequence of this fixation is that the two C1r subunits (stippled) undergo activation and cleave the two C1s subunits (striped) to uncover a protease whose substrates are C4 and C2. (Used with permission from Widmann.[12])

cule C2, bringing it into range to be cleaved by C1qrs into a small free-floating C2b fragment and a much larger C2a fragment that attaches to the surface. Unlike C4a, C2b has no biologic activity. A single C1qrs can act on numerous molecules of C4 and C2, potentially causing attachment of 100-200 C4b2a molecules to the surface. After this, C1qrs and immunoglobulin are no longer needed; if antibody is dissociated, the process can still continue. C4b2a, now present in large amounts on the membrane or surface, is an active protease whose substrate is the C3 dimer; the C4b2a complex is called C3 convertase, each molecule of which can cleave more than 200 native C3 molecules.

Nearly all the major biologic actions of complement result from the cleavage of C3. The classical pathway and the alternative pathway are both means of generating a C3 convertase. Once C3 is cleaved, the same events occur in the two pathways. Because the initiating events differ, the location and intensity of the consequent reactions may also differ.

The Alternative Pathway

The alternative pathway allows complement activation in the absence of acquired immunity. This constitutes a first-line antimicrobial defense for vertebrates and a mechanism whereby prevertebrates can enhance their inflammatory effectiveness. The alternative pathway is a surface-active phenomenon. It can be triggered by such diverse initiators as dialysis membranes; cell-wall elements of many bacteria, yeasts, and viruses; protein complexes, including those containing antibodies that do not bind complement; anionic polymers such as dextran; and some tumor cells. (See Fig 11-5.)

Four proteins participate in the alternative pathway: factor B, factor D, properdin (factor P), and C3. Fluid-phase C3 undergoes continuous but low-level spontaneous cleavage; the resulting C3b is rapidly inactivated by fluid-phase control proteins. If fluid-phase C3b encounters factor B and the resulting C3bB complex finds a surface sheltered from degradative influences, additional interactions can occur. Factor D acts on bound factor B, generating a C3bBb complex capable of cleaving C3 but susceptible to rapid dissociation. The complex can be stabilized to a half-life of 30 minutes by association with properdin, another event promoted by sequestration on the sheltering surface.

The outcome of alternative-pathway activation is self-perpetuating production of C3 convertase. Of the C3b molecules generated, many attach directly to the surface and render it susceptible to attack by cells that express C3b receptors. Many other C3b molecules associate with the C3bBb complex to form a trimolecular C3bBb3b complex that acts upon C5, the next player in the complement story. The small cleavage fragment, C3a, exerts biologic activity in the fluid phase.

The Common Pathway

Cleavage of C3

C3 is by far the most abundant complement protein; a dimer of 190 kD, its concentration in serum is measured at mg/mL levels. Cleavage of the larger chain yields the small fluid-phase fragment, C3a, a significant promoter of acute inflammatory events (see Anaphylatoxins, below). In the residual large dimer, C3b, there is an uncovered enzymatic site capable of cleaving C5, and also an activated thioester through which C3b can attach to hydroxyl or amino groups on other cell membranes.

The C4b2a3b and C3bBb3b complexes are proteases with C5 convertase activity; cleavage of C5 is their only biologic function. Isolated C3b molecules that are not part of bound complexes often persist on cell membranes and undergo molecular modification by various membrane and fluid-phase regulatory proteins. Some of these modified fragments are called C3d, C3bi, and C3dg; cell-membrane receptors exist for each of these various C3 fragments.

The Completed Cascade Lyses Cells

When C3b engages in C5 convertase activity, the large residual C5b molecule expresses, for a short time, an uncovered binding site that can combine with C6. The intermolecular events that follow C5b generation are associational, not proteolytic. C5b, C6, and C7 unite in a trimolecular complex that has transient ability to unite with the phospholipid bilayer of cell membranes. If the complex forms on a cell and if timing and protein concentrations are right, the C5b67 complex attracts C8 and polymerizes C9 to form the membrane attack complex (MAC) C5b6789, which is capable of forming a pore or large channel that disrupts the membrane and causes leakage of ions and small molecules. The cell, thus lethally damaged, undergoes lysis.

MAC generation can be interrupted at many points. The labile C5b may not associate with C6 in time; the C5b67 complex may not insert firmly into a membrane; a plasma protein called protein S may bind to and inactivate the C5b67; several membrane molecules may prevent polymerization of C9.

Molecules of the C5b67 complex that form on a surface to which it cannot attach will float free into the medium. If there are phospholipid membranes nearby, the C5b67 complex may bind to whatever cell or membrane is in the vicinity; this is the mechanism of so-called innocent-bystander cell lysis.

Regulation of Complement Activation

In any system with such a degree of amplification as the complement system, there is a need to control or regulate the enzyme and activation factors. Control proteins are needed to prevent damage to host tissue and conserve various elements of complement components. Control systems recognized in the complement cascade occur in three stages: a) direct inhibition of serine proteases, b) decay and destruction of convertases, and c) control of membrane attack complexes. The proteins involved in this control are listed in Table 11-4.

Physiologic Effects

Opsonization Enhances Defense

Proteins attached to the surface of cells or microorganisms alter the body's response to the underlying cell or particle. Neutrophils and macrophages phagocytize indiscriminately, engulfing any particle that protrudes their membrane, with no regard to the nature of the material. Engulfment is far more intense, however, if the particle is caused to adhere firmly to the membrane of the phagocytic cell. To achieve this, phagocytic cells have various receptor molecules that bind, as ligands, the Fc configurations of several immunoglobulin heavy chains and several C3 degradation products, especially C3b. This enhancement of phagocytosis resulting from antibody or complement coating of cells or organisms is called opsonization. The opsonic actions of coating (IgG) or complement-activating (IgM, some IgG) antibodies are an important way in which humoral immunity contributes to the body's defenses. Alternative-pathway generation of C3b provides opsonic effect when specific antibodies are absent.

Anaphylatoxins Promote Inflammation

The cleavage fragments C5a and C3a (and to a much lesser extent C4a) have important effects on acute inflammation. The term anaphylatoxin reflects the fact that these molecules bind to receptors on mast cells and basophils, causing them to release histamine and many other mediators that, in certain settings, are associated with anaphylaxis. Their effects on vascular permeability, membrane adhesion properties, and smooth-muscle contraction occur far more generally and constitute a large part of the acute inflammatory response. C5a and C3a also exert a chemotactic effect, causing neutrophils and macrophages to migrate toward the site where complement has been activated and exhibit enhanced activation when they arrive. Both the classical and the alternative pathways generate abundant C5a and C3a; C4a derives only from the classical pathway.

Table 11-4. Control Proteins of the Complement System[12]

Control Function	Control Protein	Discussion
Inhibition of serine protease		
C1r C1s	Serpin—C1 inhibitor (C1-inh)	Of the complement proteases only C1r and C1s are controlled by serpin (C1-inh). Action causes dissociation from C1q-activator complex. Inherited lack of C1-inh responsible for cases of angioedema.
Decay and destruction of convertases		
$\overline{C3}$ and $\overline{C5}$	Enzymatic subcomponents C2a; Bb	C2a, Bb are dissociated from $\overline{C4b}$ and $\overline{C3b}$.
$\overline{C4b2a}$: $\overline{C3bBb}$	Regulatory proteins 1) soluble proteins—factor H and C4bp (C4b-binding protein) 2) Membrane proteins—complement receptor type 1 (CR1); Decay accelerating factor (DAF) 3) Positive control—alternative pathway properdin (factor P) $\overline{C3bBb}$ or $\overline{C3b2Bb}$—stabilizes complex	Regulatory proteins bind to $\overline{C4b2a}$ and $\overline{C3bBb}$ causing dissociation of proteins with decay accelerating activity. CR1-distributed on red cells, white cells, tissue macrophages, and human kidney. DAF-widely distributed on human tissues.
$\overline{C4b}$ or $\overline{C3b}$	Protease factor I—requires cofactors 1) factor H; acts on $\overline{C3b}$ 2) C4bp acts on C4b	C4bp and factor H are found in high concentrations in plasma.
Membrane attack complex (MAC)		
C5b-7	S-protein (vitronectin) SP40,40 MAC-inhibiting protein (MIP)	Inhibits MAC formation. S-protein competes with membrane lipids for binding sites on C5b-7 complex. SP40,40 inhibits assembly of MAC. MIP is also known as HRF (homologous restriction factor).
C5b-7	CD59 (HRF-20 or protectin)	Inhibits lysis by preventing channel formation in their membranes. In paroxysmal nocturnal hemoglobinuria (PNH), individuals lack phosphatidyl-inositol-linked membrane proteins including HRF, CD59, and DAF.

References

1. Quesenberry PJ. Hematopoietic stem cells, progenitor cells, and cytokines. In: Beutler E, Lichtman MA, Coller BS, Kipps TJ, eds. Williams' hematology, 5th ed. New York: McGraw-Hill, 1995:211-28.
2. Kuby J. Immunology, 3rd ed. New York: WH Freeman and Company, 1997.
3. Parslow TG. Immunoglobulins and immunoglobulin genes. In: Stites DP, Terr AI, Parslow TG, eds. Medical immunology, 9th ed. Stamford CT: Appleton & Lange, 1997:95-114.
4. Roitt IM, Brostoff J, Male D. Immunology, 5th ed. London: Mosby, 1998.
5. Raghavan M, Bjorkman PJ. Fc receptors and their interactions with immunoglobulins. Annu Rev Cell Dev Biol 1996;12:181-220.
6. Takahashi T, Iwase T, Takenouchi N, et al. The joining (J) chain is present in invertebrates that do not express immunoglobulins. Proc Natl Acad Sci U S A 1996;93:1886-91.
7. Köhler G, Milstein C. Derivation of specific antibody-producing tissue culture and tumor lines by cell fusion. Eur J Immunol 1976;6:511-9.
8. Marks C, Marks JD. Phage libraries—a new route to clinically useful antibodies. N Engl J Med 1996;335:730-3.
9. Gershoni JM, Stern B, Denisova G. Combinatorial libraries, epitope structure and the prediction of protein conformations. Immunol Today 1997;18:108-10.
10. McAleer MA, Sim RB. The complement system. In: Sim RB, ed. Activators and inhibitors of complement. Dordrecht, The Netherlands: Kluwer Academic Publishers, 1993:1-15.
11. Sakamoto M, Fujisawa Y, Nishioka K. Physiologic role of the complement system in host defense, disease, and malnutrition. Nutrition 1998;14:391-8.
12. Widmann FK, Itatani CA. An introduction to clinical immunology and serology, 2nd ed. Philadelphia: FA Davis, 1998.

Suggested Reading

Abbas AK, Lichtman AH, Pober JS, eds. Cellular and molecular immunology, 3rd ed. Philadelphia: WB Saunders, 1997.

Anderson KC, Ness PM, eds. Scientific basis of transfusion medicine. Philadelphia: WB Saunders, 1994.

Barclay AN, Brown MH, Law SKA, et al. The leukocyte antigen factsbook, 2nd ed. San Diego, CA: Academic Press, 1997.

Bromberg JS, Debruyne LA, Qin L. Interactions between the immune system and gene therapy vectors: Bidirectional regulation of response and expression. Adv Immunol 1998;69:353-409.

Carroll MC. The role of complement and complement receptors in induction and regulation of immunity. Annu Rev Immunol 1998;16:545-68.

Doria G, Frasca D. Genes, immunity and senescence: Looking for a link. Immunologic Rev 1997;160:159-70.

Human Immunology (This journal regularly publishes the most recent deliberations of the international committee on HLA terminology.)

Marchalonis JJ, Schluter SF, Bernstein RM, et al. Phylogenetic emergence and molecular evolution of the immunoglobulin family. Adv Immunol 1998;70:417-506.

Muller D. The molecular biology of autoimmunity. Immunol Allerg Clin N Am 1996;16:659-82.

Stites DP, Terr AI, Passlow TG, eds. Medical immunology, 9th ed. Stamford, CT: Appleton & Lange, 1997.

Vamvakas EC, Blajchman MA, eds. Immunomodulatory effects of blood transfusion. Bethesda, MD: AABB Press, 1999 (in press).

Appendix 11-1. Definitions of Some Essential Terms in Immunology

Adhesion molecule: Any of the many membrane molecules, expressed on white cells and endothelial cells, that allow cells to come into close apposition with each other.

Antigen: Any material capable of specific combination with antibody or with cell-surface receptors of T lymphocytes. Often used as a synonym for "immunogen," although some antigens that react with products of the immune response are not capable of eliciting an immune response.

Antigen-presenting cell (APC): A cell capable of incorporating antigenic epitopes into MHC Class II molecules, and displaying the epitope-MHC complex on its membrane.

Antibody: Immunoglobulin secreted by the plasma-cell progeny of B lymphocytes after stimulation by a specific immunogen. Immunoglobulin molecules on the surface of unstimulated lymphocytes serve as antigen receptors.

Clone: A population of genetically identical cells derived from successive divisions of a single progenitor cell.

Cytokine: A low-molecular-weight protein, secreted from an activated cell, that affects the function or activity of other cells.

Epitope: The small portion of an immunogen, usually 5-15 amino acids or 3-5 glycosides, that combines specifically with the antigen receptor of a T or B lymphocyte.

Idiotype: The molecular configuration unique to the variable portion of an antigen-receptor molecule, reflecting the DNA rearrangement occurring in earliest lymphocyte differentiation and conferring upon the cell its specificity of antigen recognition.

Immune system: A collective term for all the cells and tissues involved in immune activity. Includes, in addition to lymphocytes and cells of monocyte/macrophage lineage, the thymus, lymph nodes, spleen, marrow, portions of the liver, and the mucosa-associated lymphoid tissue.

Immunogen: A material capable of provoking an immune response when introduced into an immunocompetent host to whom it is foreign.

Ligand: A molecule, either free in a fluid milieu or present on a membrane, whose three-dimensional configuration allows it to form a tightly fitting complex with a cell-surface molecule (its receptor) of complementary shape.

Major histocompatibility complex (MHC): A segment of the short arm of chromosome 6, in humans, containing closely linked genes that determine membrane molecules (Class I and Class II) that bear HLA antigens; Class III MHC molecules include several complement components, several enzymes, tumor necrosis factors (TNF α and β), and two heat-shock proteins.

MHC Class I molecules: Heterodimeric membrane proteins determined by genes in the MHC, consisting of a highly polymorphic α chain linked noncovalently with the nonpolymorphic β_2-microglobulin chain; these molecules present antigen to CD8+ T cells, and are the site of HLA antigens of the A, B, and C series.

MHC Class II molecules: Heterodimeric membrane proteins determined by genes in the MHC, consisting of two transmembrane polypeptide chains; these molecules present antigen to CD4+ T cells and exhibit the DP, DQ, and DR series of HLA antigens.

Phagocytosis: The process whereby macrophages and granulocytes ingest particulate material present in the surrounding milieu, and subject it to intracellular alteration.

Receptor: A cell-membrane protein molecule whose three-dimensional configuration allows it to form a tightly fitting complex with another molecule (called its ligand) of complementary shape.

12

Red Cell Antigen-Antibody Reactions and Their Detection

DEMONSTRATION OF RED CELL ANtigen-antibody reactions is key to immunohematology. Agglutination is the endpoint for most tests such as antibody detection and crossmatch. This chapter discusses factors affecting agglutination including methods of inhibiting and enhancing agglutination. When direct agglutination does not occur, the antiglobulin test is frequently used. Several different types of antiglobulin reagents are available, and the test must be performed carefully as there are numerous sources of error. Common alternatives to traditional tube testing and use of antiglobulin reagents are also discussed.

The combination of antibody with antigen may produce a variety of observable results. In blood group serology, the most commonly observed reactions are agglutination, hemolysis, and precipitation.

Agglutination is the antibody-mediated clumping of particles that express antigen on their surface. Clumping of red cells occurs because antibody molecules bind to antigenic determinants on adjacent red cells, bringing them together into a visible aggregate. Agglutination is the endpoint for most tests involving red cells and blood group antibodies and is the primary reaction type discussed in this chapter. In some tests, antibody directly bridges the gap between adjacent cells; in others, antibody molecules attach to, but do not aggregate, the red cells, and an additional step is needed to induce visible agglutination or to otherwise measure the reaction.

12

Hemolysis is the rupture of red cells with release of intracellular hemoglobin. In-vitro antibody-mediated hemolysis depends on activity of the membrane attack unit of complement and does not occur if the antigen and antibody interact in serum that lacks complement or in plasma if the anticoagulant has chelated cations (calcium and magnesium) necessary for complement activation. In tests for antibodies to red cell antigens, hemolysis is a positive result because it demonstrates the union of antibody with antigen that activates the complement cascade. (The actions of complement are described in Chapter 11.) Pink or red supernatant fluid in a test system of antibody and red cells is an important observation and indicates a positive test result. Some antibodies that are lytic in vitro (eg, anti-Vel) may cause intravascular hemolysis in a transfusion recipient. Other antibodies (eg, Lewis and some Kidd antibodies) may lyse cells in vitro but are rarely associated with intravascular hemolysis.

Precipitation is the formation of an insoluble, usually visible, complex when soluble antibody reacts with soluble antigen. Such complexes are seen in test tubes as a sediment or ring and in agar gels as a white line. Precipitation is the endpoint of procedures such as immunodiffusion and immunoelectrophoresis.

Precipitation may not occur, even though soluble antigen and its specific antibody are present. Precipitation of the antigen-antibody complex requires that antigen and antibody be present in optimal proportions. If antibody is present in excess, too few antigen sites exist to crosslink with the molecules and the lattice structure is not formed. Antigen-antibody complexes do form, but do not accumulate sufficiently to form a visible lattice. This phenomenon is called a *prozone*.

The combination of soluble antigen with soluble antibody may also result in a full or partial neutralization of the antibody. Although a visible precipitate is often not produced, such inhibition can be useful in antibody identification procedures by selectively eliminating specific antibodies.

Factors Affecting Agglutination

Agglutination is a reversible chemical reaction and is thought to occur in two stages: 1) sensitization, the attachment of antibody to antigen on the red cell membrane; and 2) formation of bridges between the sensitized red cells to form the lattice that constitutes agglutination. Various factors affect these two stages and can be manipulated to enhance (or decrease) agglutination. The effects of enhancement techniques on the two stages cannot always be clearly delineated.

The First Stage of Agglutination

Before bonding can begin, the antigen and antibody must come together and form a suitable spatial relationship. The chance of association between antibody and antigen can be enhanced in a number of ways, such as agitation or centrifugation, or by varying the concentration of antibody to antigen. As shown in Fig 12-1, antibody and antigen must complement each other with both a structural ("steric") and a chemical fit.

For sensitization to occur, a noncovalent chemical bond must form between antigen and antibody. The forces holding antigens and antibodies together are generally weak (compared with covalent bonds that hold molecules together) and are active only over a very short range. The antigen-antibody combination is reversible and random bonds are constantly made and broken until a state of equilibrium is attained.

Chemical Bonding

Polar bonds are those in which electrons are interchanged between donor and acceptor

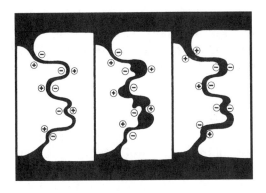

Figure 12-1. Antigen-antibody "goodness of fit." For maximum complementarity, both structural fit and complementary distribution of chemical groups must be achieved. (A) Good structural fit with complementary chemical attraction. (B) Chemical groups are complementary, but structural fit is poor. (C) Good structural fit, but chemical groupings are not attractive and may repel each other. (Reprinted with permission from Moore.[1])

molecules. Reactions taking place in a water-based medium involve polar forces and depend upon water, which is strongly hydrogen-bonded, for their stability. Hydrogen bonds formed between hydrophilic groups (such as -OH, -NH, -COOH) are highly directional and exothermic; that is, they are stronger at lower temperatures. Such hydrogen bonds are usually associated with carbohydrate antigens.

Hydrophobic (or interfacial) bonds are interactions between nonpolar molecules in an aqueous environment. Nonpolar groups mass together, forcing out the water. This action tends to decrease the distance between bonding sites while increasing their attractive forces. Such reactions are endothermic (stronger at higher temperatures) and usually involve protein antigens.

van der Waals bonds result from the mutual attraction between all molecules when brought into very close (and precise) contact with each other. Although there is no transferring or sharing of electrons, the constant motion of electrons within an atom (or molecule) creates a fluctuating dipole. For the brief moment at which one part of the molecule contains more electrons than another, that nonpolar atom becomes temporarily polar and can disrupt an adjacent atom, making it polar also. When atoms or molecules get too close, a strong repulsive force (London's repulsive force) counters the attractive van der Waals force. A temporary bond, termed van der Waals-London or dispersion force, results, which, although weak, may become collectively stronger in larger molecules. van der Waals bonds are responsible for the surface tension formed at the surface of liquids.

Electrostatic or ionic bonds form due to the attraction of ionized or oppositely charged molecules. These are most often associated with COO^- and NH_2^+ groups on amino acid structures of antigens and antibodies. The degree of ionization of molecules is dependent upon the pH of the surrounding medium.

Equilibrium (Affinity) Constant of the Antibody

The equilibrium constant or affinity constant (K_o) of a reaction is determined by the relative rates of association and dissociation. (See Fig 12-2.) For each antigen-antibody reaction the K_o varies. The K_o reflects the degree to which antibody and antigen associate and bind to one another ("goodness of fit") and the speed of the reaction. The higher the K_o value, the better the association, or "fit." When the K_o is large, the reaction occurs more readily and is more difficult to dissociate; such antibodies may have a greater importance clinically. When the K_o is small, a higher ratio of antibody to antigen may be required for detection.

The degree of antigen-antibody "fit" is influenced by the type of bonds predominating. Hydrophobic bonds are usually associated with higher K_o than hydrogen bonds. The K_o is also affected by physical conditions such as the temperature at which the reaction occurs, the pH and ionic strength of the suspending medium, and the relative antigen-to-antibody concentrations. In laboratory tests that use agglutination as an endpoint, altering the physical conditions of the system can increase or decrease the test's sensitivity.

Temperature

Most blood group antibodies react within restricted temperature ranges. Typically these antibodies fall into two broad categories: those reactive at "cold" temperatures (eg, 4-25 C) and those reactive at "warm" temperatures (eg, 30-37 C). Antibodies that react in vitro only at temperatures significantly below 37 C rarely cause destruction of transfused antigen-positive red cells and are generally considered clinically insignificant. (Important exceptions exist.) Many of these "cold-reactive" antibodies have been associated with IgM antibodies, while their "warm-reactive" counterparts have been associated with IgG antibodies. This has led to the mistaken conclusion by many that antibody class determines the temperature of reaction (and clinical significance.) Instead,

All chemical reactions are reversible. Antigen (Ag)-Antibody(Ab) reactions may be expressed as

$$Ag + Ab \underset{\leftarrow}{\rightarrow} AgAb$$

The reaction proceeds until a state of equilibrium is reached. This is controlled by the rate constants of association (k_a) and dissociation (k_d).

$$Ag + Ab \underset{k_d}{\overset{k_a}{\underset{\leftarrow}{\rightarrow}}} AgAb$$

By the law of mass action, the speed of the reaction is proportional to the concentrations of the reactants and their product. The equilibrium constant (K_o) is a function of these intrinsic association constants for the antibody being tested.

$$\frac{[AbAg]}{[Ab][Ag]} = \frac{k_a}{k} = K_o$$

Figure 12-2. The law of mass action and the equilibrium constant.

however, the temperature of antigen-antibody reactivity has more to do with the type of reaction and the chemical nature of the antigen than with the antibody class. Carbohydrate antigens are more commonly associated with "cold-reactive" antibodies and protein antigens with "warm-reactive" antibodies.

Antigen-antibody reactions result in the release of free energy in the form of heat (exothermic reaction) or as a change in entropy or both. (Entropy is an estimate of the degree of randomness of a reaction.) Exothermic reactions are associated primarily with hydrogen bonding to carbohydrate antigens and generally occur best at low temperatures. Entropy-driven reactions are associated with hydrophobic bonding with protein antigens. Rh antibodies, for example, agglutinate better at 37 C due to the protein nature of the antigen (with no attached carbohydrates). Temperature variations have little or no effect upon the K_o of most warm-reactive antibodies. Rather, it is on the speed or rate of the reaction that temperature has its greatest effect. Warm-reactive antibodies may be detected after incubation below 37 C, but much longer incubation times may be required.

Cold-reactive antibodies, on the other hand, are considerably affected by temperature and an increase in temperature results in antigen-antibody dissociation. Thus, the reactivity of anti-P_1, which reacts with glycolipid antigen, can usually be circumvented by testing at 37 C.

pH

Changes in pH can affect noncovalent and electrostatic bonds. For most clinically significant blood group antibodies, optimal pH has not been determined, but is assumed to approximate the physiologic pH range. Occasional antibodies, notably some examples of anti-M, react best at a lowered pH. For most routine testing, a pH around 7.0 should be used. Stored saline often exhibits a pH of 5.0-6.0, causing some workers to use buffered saline in serologic testing.[2]

Incubation Time

The time needed to reach equilibrium differs for different blood group antibodies. Significant variables include temperature requirements, immunoglobulin class, and specific interactions between antigen configuration and the Fab site of the antibody. The addition of enhancement agents to the system can increase the amount of antibody that attaches to antigen in the first 15 minutes and, therefore, can decrease the incubation time needed to reach equilibrium.

For saline systems in which antiglobulin serum is used to demonstrate antibody attachment, 30-60 minutes of incubation at 37 C is adequate to detect most clinically significant antibodies. With some weakly reactive antibodies, association may not reach equilibrium at 30 minutes and extending the incubation time may increase test system sensitivity. Prolonging the incubation time beyond 30 minutes has few disadvantages except for the delay before results are available.

Incubation time at 37 C can usually be reduced to 10-15 minutes in a low ionic strength saline (LISS) solution (including LISS additive solutions). The use of water-soluble polymers [such as polyethylene glycol (PEG)] can also reduce the necessary incubation time, although for different reasons. (See section on Antibody Enhancement Methods.)

Ionic Strength

In normal saline, Na^+ and Cl^- ions cluster around and partially neutralize opposite charges on antigen and antibody molecules. This hinders the association of antibody with antigen. By lowering the ionic strength of the reaction medium, however, this shielding effect can be weakened and the electrostatic attractions enhanced. Reducing the salt concentration of the serum-cell system increases the rate at which antibody and antigen come into proximity and may increase the amount of antibody bound. The use of LISS de-

creases the time required for incubation in routine antibody detection procedures. Extending the incubation time, however, may result in a loss of sensitivity.[3]

Antigen-Antibody Proportions

An excess of antigen to antibody should result in optimal antibody uptake. For inhibition or adsorption tests, such an excess of antigen is desirable. For most red cell tests, however, antigen excess reduces the number of antibody molecules bound per red cell, limiting their ability to agglutinate. Antibody excess is, therefore, desirable in most routine test systems. A commonly used ratio in red cell serology is 2 drops of serum to 1 drop of a 2-5% red cell suspension. If the antibody is weakly reactive (has a low K_o), increasing the quantity of antibody present can increase the test's sensitivity. Very rarely, significant antibody excess may inhibit agglutination, producing a prozone phenomenon comparable to that which occurs with precipitation reactions. Usually, however, increasing antibody concentration enhances the sensitivity of agglutination tests. Reducing the concentration of red cells from 5% to 2-3% doubles the serum-to-cell ratio, as does adding 4 drops of serum to the standard cell suspension. Sometimes it is useful to increase the volume of serum to 10 or even 20 drops, particularly during an investigation of a hemolytic transfusion reaction in which routine testing reveals no antibody. Alterations in the volume of serum significantly affect the ionic strength of test systems in which LISS has reduced the dielectric constant, so procedures must be modified so that the appropriate ratio of serum:LISS is maintained. Chapter 19 gives more details about antibody detection and pretransfusion testing.

The Second Stage of Agglutination

Once antibody molecules attach to antigens on the red cell surface, the sensitized cells must be linked into a lattice. This allows visualization of the reaction. The size and physical properties of the antibody molecules, the concentration of antigen sites on each cell, and the distance between cells all have an effect on the development of agglutinates.

The bridges formed between antibodies interlinked to antigen sites on adjacent red cells usually result from chance collision of the sensitized cells. Under isotonic conditions, red cells cannot approach each other closer than a distance of 50-100 Å. IgG molecules characteristically fail to bridge this distance between red cells and cause sensitization without lattice formation. For larger, multivalent IgM molecules, however, direct agglutination occurs easily. The location and density of antigen sites on the cells may also allow some IgG antibodies to cause direct agglutination; A, B, M, and N antigens, for example, are on the outer edges of red cell glycoproteins and have relatively high densities, allowing IgG antibodies to crosslink. (Although antibodies to the M antigen are often assumed to be IgM because they react best at colder temperatures, many contain an appreciable IgG component.[4])

Red cells suspended in saline have a net negative charge at their surface. Negatively charged molecules on the membrane attract positively charged cations, which reduce but do not neutralize the charge at the surface of shear between the surrounding medium and the cloud of ions attracted to each cell. Zeta potential is a measurement of this net charge. Because like charges repel, the distance between red cells in an ionic medium is proportional to the zeta potential. Once believed to play a major role in antigen-antibody reactions, zeta potential is now considered only a minor factor.

A more important physical property that maintains distance between saline-suspended red cells is the water of hydration. Water molecules tightly bound to hydrophilic macromolecules on the cell surface are thought to act as insulating bubbles, preventing close association between cells. Red cells also have a low interfacial tension (surface tension) induced by van der Waals forces and, therefore, do not self-associate.

Properties of the membrane itself also affect agglutination. Mobility and clustering of antigen-bearing molecules exert an incompletely understood effect.

Various strategies are used to enhance the second stage of agglutination and allow visualization of the reaction. Centrifugation physically forces the cells closer together. The indirect antiglobulin test uses antiglobulin serum to crosslink the reaction. Other methods include reducing the negative charge of surface molecules, reducing the hydration layer around the cell, and introducing positively charged macromolecules that aggregate the cells.

Inhibition of Agglutination

In agglutination inhibition tests, the presence of either antigen or antibody is detected by its ability to inhibit agglutination in a system with known reactants. For example, the saliva from a secretor contains soluble blood group antigens that combine with anti-A, -B, or -H. The indicator system is a standardized dilution of antibody that agglutinates the corresponding cells to a known degree. If the saliva contains blood group substance, incubating saliva with antibody will wholly or partially abolish agglutination of cells added to the incubated mixture. Absence of expected agglutination indicates the presence of soluble antigen in the material under test. Agglutination of the indicator cells is a negative result.

Antibody Enhancement Methods

Albumin Additives

Although used routinely for many years as an enhancement medium, albumin itself probably does little to promote antibody uptake (Stage 1). Much of the enhancement effect attributed to albumin may instead be due to its use in low ionic strength buffer. Albumin may influence the second stage of agglutination by reducing the net negative charge of the red cells or by affecting the interfacial tension between cells, thus predisposing antibody-coated cells to agglutinate. Bovine serum albumin is available as solutions of 22% or 30% concentration, and as a polymerized solution.

Enzymes

The proteolytic enzymes used most often in immunohematology laboratories are bromelin, ficin, papain, and trypsin. While enhancing agglutination by some antibodies, the enzymes denature certain red cell antigens, notably M, N, S, Fy^a, and Fy^b.

Proteolytic enzymes reduce the red cell surface charge by cleaving sialic acid molecules from polysaccharide chains. Sialic acid is a major contributor to the net negative charge at the red cell surface, which helps keep red cells separated from each other in an ionic suspending medium. Enzymes lower the zeta potential of the cell; more important, however, they make the cell less hydrophilic by reducing polar repulsion. The cleaving of proteins also increases the interfacial tension between cells, making them more predisposed to agglutination. Enzyme treatment also causes spicule formation on the red cell. This greatly increases the potential number of contact points.

Any mechanism that reduces the net charge should enhance red cell agglutination, and red cells pretreated with proteolytic enzymes often show enhanced agglutination by IgG molecules. However, red cells pretreated with neuraminidase demonstrate no comparable increase in agglutinability. This difference may be due to the specific activity that each enzyme has on the red cells. Proteases such as papain remove polypeptides, whereas neuraminidase is more specific for sialic acid. This may affect the accessibility of antibody to the antigen site and the ability of certain antigens to cluster within the membrane.

Positively Charged Molecules

In the presence of positively charged polymers such as hexadimethrine bromide (Polybrene®), protamine sulfate, and poly-L-lysine, normal red cells exhibit spontaneous aggregation, which can be dispersed by neutral salts, such as sodium citrate. Any antibody-crosslinked red cells remain agglutinated. The action of these agents may be due to neutralization of the negative charge contributed by the numerous sialic acid residues characteristic of the red cell membrane, a theory supported by the observation that Polybrene® does not affect cells lacking sialic acid (from genetic causes or after treatment with various enzymes). Another explanation for this polycation-induced aggregation is that association of the macromolecules with charged molecules on the cell membrane extrudes the water molecules that form the hydration shell. These positively charged molecules are often used in conjunction with low ionic strength solutions, which also enhance antibody uptake (Stage 1).

Polybrene® generally is added to red cells that have been incubated with antibody at low ionic strength and low pH. If antihuman globulin (AHG) is used in a Polybrene® system, care must be taken to avoid false-positive reactions due to the detection of bound complement components. Polybrene® procedures may be less sensitive in detecting antibodies in the Kell system.

Polyethylene Glycol

PEG is a water-soluble linear polymer used as an additive to increase antibody uptake. Its action is to remove water, taking up more space around the red cell and thereby effectively concentrating antibody,[5] promoting antibody uptake, and, in many cases, enhancing reaction strength. Anti-IgG is usually the AHG reagent of choice with PEG testing, to avoid false-positive reactions with some polyspecific reagents. IgM antibodies, especially those of the ABO and Lewis systems, have diminished reactivity or nonreactivity in PEG procedures. If too high a concentration of PEG is added to a test mixture, proteins may precipitate; fibrinogen in plasma or high levels of IgG may also cause precipitates. These precipitates may be misinterpreted as positive reactions. PEG may be used in conjunction with LISS. PEG can be used in tests with eluates, as well as with serum. PEG can greatly enhance warm-reactive autoantibodies and may, therefore, be disadvantageous when testing patients with autoimmune hemolytic anemias. Centrifugation of PEG with test serum and red cells should be avoided, because the nonspecific aggregates caused by PEG may not disperse; after incubation with PEG, test cells should immediately be washed in saline for the antiglobulin test.

LISS and LISS Additives

LISS (approximately 0.03M) greatly increases Stage 1 uptake of antibody onto red cells, compared with normal saline (approximately 0.17M). To prevent lysis of red cells at such a low ionic strength, a nonionic substance such as glycine is incorporated in the LISS.

Most workers now use a LISS additive reagent rather than LISS itself. These commercially available LISS additives contain macromolecules in addition to ionic salts and buffers. LISS solutions increase the rate of antibody association (Stage 1) when volume proportions are correct. (See Methods 3.2.2 and 3.2.3.) Increasing the volume of serum used in a test will increase the ionic strength of a LISS-additive system, and any alteration in prescribed volumes of serum used requires adjustment of the LISS volume or omission of LISS. For this reason, the use of LISS for routine titration studies and for some other tests is problematic. When LISS is used as an additive reagent, the manufacturer's instructions must be followed.

The Antiglobulin Test

In 1945, Coombs, Mourant, and Race[6] described procedures for detecting attachment of antibodies that did not produce agglutination. This test uses antibody to human globulins and is known as the antihuman globulin test. It was first used to demonstrate antibody in serum, but later the same principle was used to demonstrate in-vivo coating of red cells with antibody or complement components. As used in immunohematology, AHG testing generates visible agglutination of sensitized red cells. The direct antiglobulin test (DAT) is used to demonstrate in-vivo sensitization of red cells. The indirect antiglobulin test (IAT) is used to demonstrate in-vitro reactions between red cells and antibodies that sensitize, but do not agglutinate, cells that express the corresponding antigen.

Principles of the AHG Test

All antibody molecules are globulins. Animals injected with human globulins produce antibody to the foreign protein. After the animal serum is adsorbed to remove unwanted agglutinins, it will react specifically with human globulins and can be called AHG serum. Depending on the material used for immunization and the procedures used to separate the resulting immune products, AHG sera with varying specificities can be produced, notably anti-IgG and antibodies to several complement components. (Hybridoma techniques, now used for the manufacture of most AHG, are described in Chapter 11.)

The antiglobulin antibody combines with the Fc portion of the sensitizing antibody molecules, not with any epitopes native to the red cell (see Fig 12-3). The two Fab sites of the AHG molecule form a bridge between adjacent antibody-coated cells to produce visible agglutination. Cells that have no attached globulin will not be agglutinated. The strength of the observed agglutination is usually proportional to the amount of bound globulin.

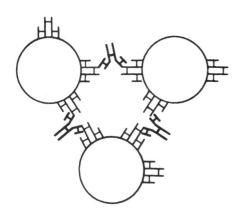

Figure 12-3. The antiglobulin reaction. Rabbit IgG molecules with antihuman globulin specificity are shown reacting with the Fc portion of human IgG molecules coating adjacent red cells (eg, anti-D coating D-positive red cells).

AHG will react with human globulin molecules that are bound to red cells or are present, free in serum. Unbound globulins react preferentially with AHG, and may prevent it from combining with membrane-bound globulin molecules. Unless the red cells are washed free of unbound proteins before addition of AHG serum, the unbound globulins may neutralize AHG and cause a false-negative result.

Direct Antiglobulin Testing

The DAT is used to demonstrate in-vivo coating of red cells with globulins, in particular IgG and C3dg. Washed red cells from a patient or donor are tested directly with AHG reagents. (See Method 3.6.) It is used in investigating autoimmune hemolytic anemia (AIHA), drug-induced hemolysis, hemolytic disease of the newborn (HDN), and alloimmune reactions to recently transfused red cells.

Indirect Antiglobulin Testing

In indirect AHG procedures, serum (or plasma) is incubated with red cells, which are then washed to remove unbound globulins. Agglutination that occurs when AHG is added indi-

cates a reaction between antibody in the serum and antigen present on the red cells. The antibody may be known and the antigen unknown, as in blood grouping tests with AHG-reactive reagents such as anti-Fy^a; the antigenic composition of the red cells may be known and the presence or specificity of antibody unknown, as in antibody detection and identification tests. Both serum and cells are unknown in the AHG crossmatch, and the procedure is used to determine whether any sort of antigen-antibody interaction has occurred.

Methods have been developed that obviate the need to wash coated red cells prior to adding antiglobulin reagent. One method entails purifying specific antibody by adsorption-elution with antigen-positive red cells. Reagent sera processed in this way are not contaminated with unwanted human globulin, so the test system need not be washed before the addition of the AHG reagent. Another technique in which saline washing may not be required is the gel test, described later in this chapter. The gel test uses a microcolumn filled with mixtures of either glass beads or gel, buffer, and sometimes reagents, and can be used for direct or indirect antiglobulin procedures. Density barriers allow separation of test serum from red cells, making a saline washing phase unnecessary.

Antiglobulin Reagents

Monospecific antibodies to human globulins can be prepared by injecting animals with purified IgG, IgA, IgM, C3, or C4. Such sera generally require adsorption to remove unwanted antibodies from the monospecific AHG reagent. These animal-made antisera are themselves polyclonal in nature. Monospecific monoclonal reagents can also effectively be prepared from hybridomas. Monospecific animal or hybridoma-derived antibodies can be combined into reagent preparations containing any desired combination of specificities, or a combination of different clonal products all recognizing the same specificity. Thus, reagents may be polyclonal, monoclonal, blends of monoclonal, or blends of monoclonal and polyclonal antibodies.

The Center for Biologics Evaluation and Research of the Food and Drug Administration (FDA) has established definitions for a variety of AHG reagents[7] as shown in Table 12-1. Antisera specific for other immunoglobulins (IgA, IgM) or subclasses (IgG1, IgG3, etc) exist, but are rarely standardized for routine test tube methods and must be used with rigorous controls.

Polyspecific AHG

Polyspecific AHG reagents are used for direct antiglobulin testing and, in some laboratories, for routine compatibility tests and antibody detection. These reagents contain antibody to human IgG and to the C3d component of human complement. Other anticomplement antibodies may be present, including anti-C3b, -C4b, and -C4d. Currently available, commercially prepared, polyspecific antiglobulin sera contain little, if any, activity against IgA and IgM heavy chains. However, some reagents (although probably not current FDA-licensed antiglobulin sera) may react with IgA or IgM molecules, because the polyspecific mixture may react with lambda and kappa light chains, which are present in immunoglobulins of all classes.

Because most clinically significant antibodies are IgG, the most important function of polyspecific AHG, in most procedures, is detection of IgG. The anticomplement component has limited usefulness in crossmatching and in antibody detection because antibodies detectable only by their ability to bind complement are quite rare. Anti-C3d activity is important, however, for the DAT, especially in the investigation of AIHA. In some patients with AIHA, C3dg may be the only globulin detectable on their red cells.[8]

Table 12-1. Antihuman Globulin Reagents

Reagent	Definition[*]
Polyspecific (Rabbit polyclonal; rabbit/murine monoclonal blend; and murine monoclonal)	Rabbit polyclonal contains anti-IgG and anti-C3d (may contain other anticomplement and other anti-immunoglobulin antibodies); rabbit/murine monoclonal blend contains a blend of rabbit polyclonal antihuman IgG and murine monoclonal anti-C3b and -C3d; murine monoclonal contains murine monoclonal anti-IgG, -C3b, and -C3d.
Anti-IgG (rabbit polyclonal; IgG heavy chains; monoclonal IgG)	Rabbit polyclonal contains anti-IgG with no anticomplement activity (not necessarily gamma chain specific); IgG heavy chains contain only antibodies reactive against human gamma chains; monoclonal IgG contains murine monoclonal anti-IgG.
Anti-C3d and anti-C3b, (rabbit polyclonal) and anti-C3d, -C4b, -C4d (rabbit polyclonal)	Contain only antibodies reactive against the designated complement component(s), with no anti-immunoglobulin activity.
Anti-C3d (murine monoclonal) and anti-C3b, -C3d (murine monoclonal)	Contains only antibodies reactive against the designated complement component, with no anti-immunoglobulin activity.

* As defined by the FDA.[7]

Monospecific AHG Reagents

Licensed monospecific AHG reagents in common use are anti-IgG and anti-C3b,-C3d. The FDA has established labeling requirements for other anticomplement reagents, including anti-C3b, anti-C4b, and anti-C4d, but these products are not generally available. After direct antiglobulin testing with a polyspecific reagent reveals globulins on a red cell specimen, monospecific AHG reagents are used to characterize the coating proteins. Anti-IgG and anti-C3d can also be used in indirect antiglobulin testing to distinguish patterns of reactivity in a single serum that contains both complement-binding and noncomplement-binding antibodies, eg, a mixture of anti-Le^a and anti-E.

Anti-IgG

Reagents labeled "anti-IgG" contain no anticomplement activity. The major component of anti-IgG is antibody to human gamma chains, but unless labeled as "heavy-chain specific," these reagents may exhibit some reactivity with light chains, which are common to all immunoglobulin classes. An anti-IgG reagent not designated "heavy-chain specific" must be considered capable of reacting with light chains of IgA or IgM. A positive DAT with such an anti-IgG does not prove the presence of IgG, although it is rare to have in-vivo coating with IgA or IgM, in the absence of IgG. Many workers prefer anti-IgG over polyspecific AHG in antibody detection and compatibility tests because anti-IgG AHG does not react with complement bound to red cells by cold-reactive antibodies that are not clinically significant.

Anti-C3b, -C3d

Anti-C3b, -C3d reagents prepared by animal immunization contain no activity against human immunoglobulins and are used in situations described for anti-C3d. This type of anti-C3d characteristically reacts with C3b and possibly other epitopes present on C3-coated red cells. Murine monoclonal anti-C3b, -C3d

reagent is a blend of hybridoma-derived antibodies. Monoclonal anti-C3d may be less likely to react with C3b than anti-C3d obtained by animal immunization.

Role of Complement in Antiglobulin Reactions

Complement components may attach to red cells in vivo or in vitro by one of two mechanisms:

1. Complement-binding antibody specific for a red cell antigen may cause attachment of complement to the cell surface as a consequence of specific alloimmune recognition.

2. Immune complexes, of various specificities unrelated to red cell antigens, may be present in plasma and activate complement components that adsorb onto red cells in a nonspecific manner. Attachment of complement to the membrane of cells that are not involved in the specific antigen-antibody reaction is often described as "innocent bystander" complement coating.

Red cells coated with elements of the complement cascade may or may not undergo hemolysis. If the cascade does not go to completion, the presence of bound early components of the cascade can be detected by anticomplement reagents. The component most readily detected is C3 because several hundred C3 molecules may be bound to the red cell by the attachment of only a few antibody molecules. C4 coating also can be detected, but C3 coating has more clinical significance.

Complement as the Only Coating Globulin

Complement alone, without immunoglobulin, may be present on washed red cells in certain situations.

1. IgM antibodies reacting in vitro occasionally attach to red cell antigens without agglutinating the cells. IgM coating is difficult to demonstrate in AHG tests,

partly because IgM molecules tend to dissociate during the washing process and partly because polyspecific AHG contains little if any anti-IgM activity. IgM antibodies may activate complement, and the reaction of antibody with antigen can be demonstrated by identifying the several hundred C3 molecules bound to the cell membrane near the site of antibody attachment.

2.   About 10-20% of patients with warm AIHA have red cells with a positive DAT due to C3 coating alone.[9] No IgG, IgA, or IgM coating is demonstrable with routine procedures, although some specimens may be coated with IgG at levels below the detection threshold for the standard DAT.

3.   In cold hemagglutinin disease, the cold-reactive autoantibody can react with red cell antigens at temperatures up to 32 C, although it does not cause agglutination.[10] Red cells passing through vessels in the skin at this temperature become coated with autoantibody, which activates complement. If the cells escape hemolysis, they return to the central circulation where the temperature is 37 C, and the autoantibody dissociates from the cells, leaving complement components firmly bound to the red cell membrane. The component usually detected by AHG reagents is C3dg.

4.   Immune complexes that form in the plasma and bind weakly and nonspecifically to red cells may cause complement coating. The activated complement remains on the red cell surface after the immune complexes dissociate. C3 remains as the only detectable surface globulin.

Coombs Control or Check Cells

The addition of IgG-coated cells to negative AHG tests (used to detect IgG) is required by AABB *Standards for Blood Banks and Transfu-*sion Services[11] for antibody detection and crossmatching procedures. Added after the antiglobulin test is read, these sensitized cells should react with the antiglobulin sera, giving some verification that the AHG reagent was functional. Reactivity with IgG-sensitized cells demonstrates that AHG was indeed added and that it had not been neutralized.

The use of IgG-sensitized cells does not detect all potential failures of the AHG test. Partial neutralization of the AHG may not be detected at all, particularly if the control cells are heavily coated with IgG. Errors in the original test, such as omission of test serum, improper centrifuge speed, or inappropriate concentrations of test red cells may yield negative test results, but positive results with control cells. Oversensitized control cells may agglutinate when centrifuged.

Complement-coated cells can also be prepared in vitro. These can be used in some cases to control tests with complement-specific reagents.

Some sources of error in antiglobulin tests are given in Tables 12-2 and 12-3.

Other Methods to Detect Antigen-Antibody Reactions

The following methods represent some common alternatives to traditional tube testing and use of antiglobulin serum. Some methods do not allow detection of both IgM and IgG antibodies and may not provide information on the phase and temperature of reactivity of antibodies when classical tube tests are used. Some procedures, reagents, and equipment (as widely used) are available from commercial manufacturers; certain test details may be proprietary.

Solid-Phase Red Cell Adherence Tests

Solid-phase microplate techniques utilize immobilized antigen or antibody. In a direct test, antibody is fixed to a microplate well and red cells are added. If the cells express the corre-

Table 12-2. Sources of Error in Antiglobulin Testing—False-Negative Results

Neutralization of Antihuman Globulin (AHG) Reagent

- Failure to wash cells adequately to remove all serum/plasma. Fill tube at least ¾ full of saline for each wash. Check dispense volume of automated washers.
- If increased serum volumes are used, routine wash may be inadequate. Wash additional times or remove serum prior to washing.
- Contamination of AHG by extraneous protein. Do not use finger or hand to cover tube. Contaminated droppers or wrong reagent dropper can neutralize entire bottle of AHG.
- High concentration of IgG paraproteins in test serum; protein may remain even after multiple washes.[12]

Interruption in Testing

- Bound IgG may dissociate from red cells and either leave too little IgG to detect or may neutralize AHG reagent.
- Agglutination of IgG-coated cells will weaken. Centrifuge and read immediately.

Improper Reagent Storage

- AHG reagent may lose reactivity if frozen. Reagent may become bacterially contaminated.
- Excess heat or repeated freezing/thawing may cause loss of reactivity of test serum.
- Reagent red cells may lose antigen strength on storage. Other subtle cell changes may cause loss of reactivity.

Improper Procedures

- Overcentrifugation may pack cells so tightly that agitation required to resuspend cells breaks up agglutinates. Undercentrifugation may not be optimal for agglutination.
- Failure to add test serum, enhancement medium, or AHG may cause negative test.
- Too heavy a red cell concentration may mask weak agglutination. Too light suspension may be difficult to read.
- Improper/insufficient serum:cell ratios.

Complement

- Rare antibodies, notably some anti-Jk^a, -Jk^b, may only be detected when polyspecific AHG is used and active complement is present.

Saline

- Low pH of saline solution can decrease sensitivity.[2] Optimal saline wash solution for most antibodies is pH 7.0 to 7.2.
- Some antibodies may require saline to be at specific temperature to retain antibody on cell. Use 37 C or 4 C saline.

Table 12-3. Sources of Error in Antiglobulin Testing—False-Positive Results

Cells Agglutinated Prior to Washing

■ If potent agglutinins are present, agglutinates may not disperse during washing. Observe cells prior to addition of antihuman globulin (AHG) or use control tube substituting saline for AHG; reactivity prior to addition of AHG or in saline control invalidates AHG reading.

Particles or Contaminants

■ Dust or dirt in glassware may cause clumping (not agglutination) of red cells. Fibrin or precipitates in test serum may similarly produce cell clumps that mimic agglutination.

Improper Procedures

■ Over-centrifugation may pack cells so tightly that they do not easily disperse and appear positive.

■ Centrifugation of test with polyethylene glycol or positively charged polymers prior to washing may create clumps that do not disperse.

Cells Have Positive Direct Antiglobulin Test (DAT)

■ Cells that are positive by DAT will also be positive in any indirect antiglobulin test. Procedures for removing IgG from DAT-positive cells are given in Methods 2.11, 2.13, and 2.14.

Complement

■ Complement components, primarily C4, may bind to cells from clots or from CPDA-1 donor segments during storage at 4 C and occasionally at higher temperatures. For DATs, use red cells anticoagulated with EDTA, ACD, or CPD.

■ Samples collected in tubes containing silicone gel may have spurious complement attachment.[13]

■ Complement may attach to cells in specimens collected from infusion lines used to administer dextrose-containing solutions. Strongest reactions are seen when large-bore needles are used or when sample volume is less than 0.5 mL.[14]

sponding antigen, they will adhere across the sides of the well; if no antigen-antibody reaction occurs, the red cells settle to the bottom of the well. An indirect test uses red cells of known antigenic composition bound to a well pretreated with a compound such as glutaraldehyde and poly L-lysine or with a potent serum-specific antibody. The test sample is added to the red-cell-coated wells and allowed to react with the cells, after which the plates are washed free of unbound proteins. The indicator for attached antibody is a sus-

pension of anti-IgG-coated red cells. The reaction is positive if the indicator cells adhere across the sides of the well. If they settle to the bottom, it demonstrates that no antigen-antibody reaction has occurred. (See Fig 12-4.) In the indirect test, isolated membrane components (eg, specific proteins), rather than intact cells, can be affixed to the microwell. Solid-phase attachment of antigen or antibody is an integral part of other tests, such as the monoclonal antibody-specific immobilization of erythrocyte antigens (MAIEA) assay, dis-

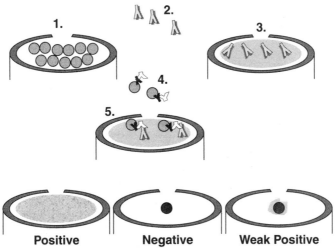

Figure 12-4. Indirect solid phase test. A monolayer of red cells is affixed to a microwell (1). Test serum is added. If antibody (2) is present, it binds to antigens on the affixed red cells (3). Indicator red cells coated with IgG and anti-IgG (4) are then added. The anti-IgG portion binds to any antibody attached to the fixed red cells (5). In a positive test, the indicator red cells are effaced across the microwell. In a negative test, the indicator cells do not bind, but pellet to the center of the well when centrifuged. Weak reactions give intermediate results.

cussed below. Solid-phase systems have also been devised for use in detecting platelet antibodies and in tests for syphilis, cytomegalovirus, and hepatitis B surface antigen.[15-17]

Column Agglutination Technology, Gel Tests, and Affinity Separation

Various methods have been devised in which red cells are filtered through a column containing a medium that separates selected red cell populations. As commercially prepared, the systems usually employ a card or strip of microtubes rather than conventional test tubes. These allow simultaneous performance of several tests. Usually a space or chamber at the top of each column is used for red cells alone or to incubate red cells and serum. As the cells pass through the column (usually on centrifugation), the column medium separates agglutinates from unagglutinated red cells, based on size. Alternatively, in some tests specific antisera or proteins can be included within the column medium itself; cells bearing a specific antigen are selectively captured as

they pass through the medium. When the column contains antiglobulin serum or a protein that specifically binds immunoglobulin, the selected cells will be those sensitized with immunoglobulin. By using a centrifuge time and speed that allow red cells to enter the column but leave serum or plasma above, the need for saline washing for antiglobulin tests can be eliminated.

Typically in column tests, negative test cells pellet to the bottom of the column. In positive tests, the cells are captured at the top of or within the column. An advantage of most such systems is the stability of the final reaction phase, which can be read by several individuals or in some cases documented by photocopying. Column tests generally have sensitivity similar to LISS antiglobulin methods, but some methods have reportedly performed less well in detecting weak antibodies, especially those in the ABO system.[18]

In 1986, Lapierre patented a technology that uses a column of gel particles.[19] As commercially prepared, the gel test uses six microtubes instead of test tubes, contained in

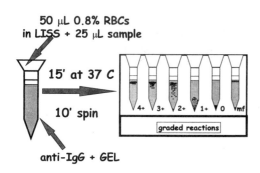

Figure 12-5. Affinity gel.

what is called a card or strip. The gel particles function as filters that trap red cell agglutinates when the cards are centrifuged. Gels containing antiglobulin serum are used to capture sensitized, but unagglutinated cells. Gels with various antisera can be used for typing cells. (See Fig 12-5.)

In another column agglutination technology, a column of glass microbeads in a diluent is used instead of gel. As with the gel test, the beads may either entrap agglutinated cells or antisera, such as anti-IgG, can be added to the diluent.[20]

In affinity column methods, a binding ligand, such as protein A or protein G (which bind the Fc portion of IgG antibody), is bound to a gel medium.[21,22] (See Fig 12-6.) The ligand captures sensitized red cells passing through the column. Alternatively, specific antibody can be attached to the ligand-coated gel. This antibody then specifically binds red cells bearing the appropriate antigen.[23]

Immunofluorescence

Immunofluorescence testing allows identification and localization of antigens inside or on the surface of cells. A fluorochrome such as fluorescein or phycoerythrin can be attached to an antibody molecule, without altering its specificity or its ability to bind antigen. Attachment of fluorescein-labeled antibody to cellu-lar antigen makes the antibody-coated cells appear brightly visible yellow-green or red (depending on the fluorochrome).

Immunofluorescent antibodies can be used in direct or indirect procedures, with the fluorescence analogous to agglutination as an endpoint. In a direct test, the fluorescein-labeled antibody is specific for a single antigen of interest. In an indirect test, fluorescein-labeled antiglobulin serum is added to cells that have been incubated with an unlabeled antibody of known specificity. Immunofluorescent techniques were initially used to detect antigens in or on lymphocytes or in tissue sections. More recently, immunofluorescent antibodies have been used in flow cytometry where, among their many applications, they have been used to quantify fetomaternal hemorrhage, to identify transfused cells and follow their survival in recipients, to measure low levels of cell-bound IgG, and to distinguish homozygous from heterozygous expression of blood group antigens.[24]

Radioimmunoassay

Radioimmunoassay procedures use a suitable radionucleotide as a marker for either antigen or antibody, to be used in either direct or indirect tests. Radiolabeling does not affect anti-

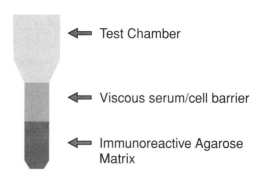

Microcolumn

Figure 12-6. Affinity column test. Test serum and red cells are added to the test chamber of the microcolumn. After centrifugation, the cells pellet at the top (positive) or bottom (negative) of the agarose matrix. (Courtesy Gamma Biologicals, Inc.)

body specificity, and the quantity of antibody bound can be accurately measured. In one indirect technique, the presence and quantity of antigen can be demonstrated by allowing the test material to interact with an unlabeled, known antigen bound to a solid phase. If present, antigen combines with and is immobilized by the solid-phase antibody. Radiolabeled antibody of the same specificity can then attach to the immobilized antigen in a quantitative manner, and be precisely measured with a gamma counter. Radiolabeling is also used in competitive binding procedures in which labeled and unlabeled antibody of the same specificity react with the corresponding antigen. Calculating the proportion of a known dose of labeled material bound in a test system permits calculation of the amount of unlabeled material that must have been present.

Enzyme-Linked Immunosorbent Assay

Enzyme-linked immunosorbent assays (ELISAs) are used to measure either antigen or antibody. Enzymes such as alkaline phosphatase can be bound to antibody molecules without destroying either the antibody specificity or the enzyme activity. The enzyme acts as a quantifiable label, similar to radiolabeling, but enzymes are more stable; are safer, cheaper, and simpler to measure; and, in many cases, provide results that are comparably sensitive. Many tests to detect antibodies to transfusion-transmitted viruses use this principle. ELISA has also been used to detect and measure cell-bound IgG and to demonstrate fetomaternal hemorrhage. When red cells are examined, the test often is called an enzyme-linked antiglobulin test (ELAT).

MAIEA Assay

In the monoclonal antibody-specific immobilization of erythrocyte antigens (MAIEA) assay, red cells are incubated with two antibodies. One contains human alloantibody to a blood group antigen and the other is a nonhuman

(usually mouse monoclonal) antibody that reacts with a different portion of the same membrane protein. The red cells are then lysed and the membrane solubilized, then added to a microwell coated with goat antimouse antibody. This antibody then captures the mouse antibody attached to the membrane protein (with the human antibody also attached). Conjugated antihuman antibody is then added, which reacts with the bound human antibody and gives an ELISA-readable reaction. This method has thus far been used primarily to isolate specific membrane structures for blood group antigens.[25,26]

References

1. Moore BPL. Antibody uptake: The first stage of the hemagglutination reaction. In: Bell CA, ed. A seminar on antigen-antibody reactions revisited. Arlington, VA: American Association of Blood Banks 1982:47-66.

2. Rolih S, Thomas R, Fisher E, Talbot J. Antibody detection errors due to acidic or unbuffered saline. Immunohematology 1993;9:15-18.

3. Jørgensen J, Nielsen M, Nielsen CB, Nøramrk J. The influence of ionic strength, albumin and incubation time on the sensitivity of the indirect Coombs' test. Vox Sang 1980;36:186-91.

4. Smith ML, Beck ML. The immunoglobulin class of antibodies with M specificity (abstract). Transfusion 1971;18:392.

5. deMan AJM, Overbeeke MAM. Evaluation of the polyethylene glycol antiglobulin test for detection of red blood cell antibodies. Vox Sang 1990;58:207-10.

6. Coombs RRA, Mourant AE, Race RR. A new test for the detection of weak and "incomplete" Rh agglutinins. Br J Exp Pathol 1945;26:255-66.

7. Code of federal regulations. 21 CFR 660.55. Washington, DC: US Government Printing Office, 1998 (revised annually).

8. Packman CH, Leddy JP. Acquired hemolytic anemia due to warm-reacting autoantibodies. In: Beutler E, Lichtman MA, Coller BS, Kipps TJ, eds. Williams' hematology. 5th ed. New York: McGraw Hill, 1995:677-685.

9. Sokol RJ, Hewitt S, Stamps BK. Autoimmune haemolysis: An 18-year study of 865 cases referred to a regional transfusion centre. Br Med J 1981;282:2023-7.

10. Packman CH, Leddy JP. Cryopathic hemolytic syndromes. In: Beutler E, Lichtman MA, Coller BS, Kipps TJ, eds. Williams' hematology. 5th ed. New York: McGraw-Hill, 1995:685-91.

11. Menitove JE, ed. Standards for blood banks and transfusion services, 19th ed. Bethesda, MD: American Association of Blood Banks, 1999:59.

12. Ylagen ES, Curtis BR, Wildgen ME, et al. Invalidation of antiglobulin tests by a high thermal amplitude cryoglobulin. Transfusion 1990;30:154-7.

13. Geisland JR, Milam JD. Spuriously positive direct antiglobulin tests caused by silicone gel. Transfusion 1980;20:711-3.

14. Grindon AJ, Wilson MJ. False-positive DAT caused by variables in sample procurement. Transfusion 1981;21:313-4.

15. Plapp FV, Sinor LT, Rachel JM, et al. A solid phase antibody screen. Am J Clin Pathol 1984;82:719-21.

16. Rachel JM, Sinor LT, Beck ML, Plapp FV. A solid-phase antiglobulin test. Transfusion 1985;25:24-6.

17. Sinor L. Advances in solid-phase red cell adherence methods and transfusion serology. Transfus Med Rev 1992;6:26-31.

18. Phillips P, Voak D, Knowles S, et al. An explanation and the clinical significance of the failure of microcolumn tests to detect weak ABO and other antibodies. Transfus Med 1997;7:47-53.

19. Lapierre Y, Rigal D, Adam J, et al. The gel test: A new way to detect red cell antigen-antibody reactions. Transfusion 1990; 30:109-13.

20. Reis KJ, Chachowski R, Cupido A, et al. Column agglutination technology: The antiglobulin test. Transfusion 1993;33:639-43.

21. Bjorck I. Petersson BA, Sjoquist J. Some physiochemical properties of protein A from *Staphylococcus aureus*. Euro J Biochem 1972;29:579-84.

22. Bjorck I, Kronvall G. Purification and some properties of streptococcal protein G. A novel IgG-binding agent. J Immunol 1984;133:969-74.

23. gamma-ReACT™ antibody detection strips. Red cell affinity column test for the detection of IgG antibodies (package insert). Houston, TX: Gamma Biologicals, 1996.

24. Garratty G, Arndt P. Applications of flow cytofluorometry to transfusion science. Transfusion 1994;35:157-78.

25. Petty AC. Monoclonal antibody-specific immobilisation of erythrocyte antigens (MAIEA). A new technique to selectively determine antigenic sites on red cell membranes. J Immunol Methods 1993;161(1):91-5.

26. Petty AC, Green CA, Daniels GL. The monoclonal antibody-specific antigens assay (MAIEA) in the investigation of human red-cell antigens and their associated membrane proteins. Transfus Med 1997;7(3):179-88.

Suggested Reading

Case J. Potentiators of agglutination. In: Bell CA, ed. Seminar on antigen-antibody reactions revisited. Arlington, VA: American Association of Blood Banks, 1982:99-132.

Löw B, Messeter L. Antiglobulin test in low-ionic strength salt solution for rapid antibody screening and cross-matching. Vox Sang 1974;26:53-61.

Malyska H, Weiland D. The gel test. Lab Med 1994;25:81-5.

Mollison PL, Engelfriet FP, Contreras M. Blood transfusion in clinical medicine, 10th ed. Oxford: Blackwell Scientific, 1998.

Rolih SD, Eisinger RW, Moheng MC, et al. Solid phase adherence assays: Alternatives to conventional blood bank tests. Lab Med 1985;16:766-70.

Steane EA. Red blood cell agglutination: A current perspective. In: Bell CA, ed. A seminar on antigen-antibody reactions revisited. Arlington, VA: American Association of Blood Banks, 1982:67-98.

Telen MJ. New and evolving techniques for antibody and antigen identification. In: Nance ST, ed. Alloimmunity: 1993 and beyond. Bethesda, MD: American Association of Blood Banks, 1993:117-39.

Walker P. New technologies in transfusion medicine. Lab Med 1997;28:258-62.

van Oss CJ. Immunological and physiochemical nature of antigen-antibody interactions. In: Garratty G, ed. Immunobiology of transfusion medicine. New York: Marcel Dekker, Inc. 1994:327-64.

13

ABO, H, and Lewis Blood Groups and Structurally Related Antigens

THE ABO BLOOD GROUP SYSTEM was the first to be identified and is the most significant for transfusion practice. Accurate testing of donor and recipient blood for ABO compatibility is essential for the prevention of hemolytic transfusion reactions.

The H antigen serves as a precursor molecule on which A and B antigens are built. Antibodies to the H antigen may be clinically significant.

While some Lewis blood group system phenotypes are rare, Lewis antibodies that cause in-vitro hemolysis have been associated with posttransfusion reactions.

This chapter also discusses the P blood group, the I/i antigens and antibodies, and their significance for transfusion practice.

The ABO, H, P, I, and Lewis blood group antigens reside on structurally related carbohydrate molecules. These carbohydrate molecules carry sugars that may determine several antigens, providing an opportunity for interaction between genetic products in several systems. The antigens arise from the action of specific glycosyltransferases that add individual sugars sequentially to sites on short chains of sugars (oligosaccharides) that often are part of other, much larger molecules. The added sugars are called *immunodominant* because they confer specific antigenic activity on the oligosaccharide chains.

Oligosaccharides are chains of sugars that can be attached to either protein (glycoprotein), sphingolipid (glycosphingolipid), or lipid (glycolipid) carrier molecules. When attached to proteins, oligosaccharides are linked either to the amide nitrogen of asparagine (N-glycan) via an N-acetylglucosamine (GlcNAc) or to the hydroxyl oxygen of serine or threonine (o-glycan) via an N-acetyl-galactosamine (GalNAc). Glycoproteins are associated with the membranes of red cells and other cells. The body's serous and mucous secretions contain soluble glycoproteins with blood group antigen activity. In glycosphingolipids, structurally similar oligosaccharides are attached via glucose (Glc) to ceramide residues. Glycosphingolipids form part of the membranes of red cells, of most endothelial cells, and some epithelial cells. Soluble forms are present in plasma as glycolipids, but are not secreted in body fluids.

The ABO System

A series of tests reported by Karl Landsteiner in 1900 led to the discovery of the ABO blood group system and to the development of routine blood typing procedures.[1] Landsteiner tested blood samples from himself and several colleagues by combining each serum specimen with a suspension of red cells from each person. Noting agglutination in some mixtures but not in others, he was able to classify the blood samples into one of three groups, now named A, B, and O. Landsteiner recognized that the presence or absence of only two antigens, A and B, was sufficient to explain the

three blood groups and he predicted that a fourth group should exist. He also demonstrated that each person's serum contained antibody against the antigen absent from that person's red cells. In 1902 Landsteiner's students von Decastello and Stürli discovered the AB group.

The first blood group system to be discovered, ABO remains the most significant for transfusion practice. It is the only system in which the reciprocal (or antithetical) antibodies (see Table 13-1) are consistently and predictably present in the sera of most people who have had no exposure to human red cells. Because of these antibodies, transfusion of ABO-incompatible blood may cause severe intravascular hemolysis as well as the other manifestations of an acute hemolytic transfusion reaction (see Chapter 27). Testing to detect ABO incompatibility between a recipient and the donor is the foundation on which all pretransfusion testing is based.

Antigens of the ABO System

Biochemical and Genetic Considerations

Glycosphingolipids carrying A or B oligosaccharides are integral parts of the membranes of red cells, epithelial cells, and endothelial cells (Fig 13-1) and are also present in soluble form

Table 13-1. Routine ABO Typing

Reaction of Cells Tested With		Reaction of Serum Tested Against			Interpretation	Incidence (%) in US Population	
Anti-A	Anti-B	A₁ Cells	B Cells	O Cells	ABO Group	Whites	Blacks
0	0	+	+	0	O	45	49
+	0	0	+	0	A	40	27
0	+	+	0	0	B	11	20
+	+	0	0	0	AB	4	4

+ = agglutination; 0 = no agglutination

in plasma. Secreted body fluids such as saliva contain glycoprotein molecules that may, if the person possesses an *Se* gene, carry identical oligosaccharides. A and B oligosaccharides unattached to carrier protein or lipid molecules are also found in milk and urine.

Genes at three separate loci (*ABO*, *Hh*, and *Se*) control the occurrence and the location of the A and B antigens. Three common alleles (*A*, *B*, and *O*) are located at the *ABO* locus on chromosome 9. The *A* and *B* genes encode glycosyltransferases that produce the A and B antigens, respectively.[2] The *O* gene does not encode a functional enzyme. The red cells of group O persons lack A and B antigens, but carry an abundant amount of H antigen, the precursor material on which A and B antigens are built.

Family studies have shown that the genes at the other two loci, *Hh* and *Se* (secretor), are on chromosome 19 and are closely linked.[3] Each locus has two recognized alleles, one of which has no demonstrable product and is considered an amorph. The active allele at the *H* locus, *H*, produces a glycosyltransferase that acts at the cellular level to form the antigen on which A or B is built. The amorph, *h*, is very rare.

The *Se* gene is directly responsible for the expression of H (and indirectly responsible for the expression of A and B) on the glycoproteins in epithelial secretions such as saliva. Eighty percent of the population are secretors. Secretors have inherited the *Se* gene and their secreted glycoproteins express H, which can be converted to A and/or B if they also have the *A* and/or *B* gene. The amorph is called *se*.

The oligosaccharide chains to which the A or B immunodominant sugars are attached may exist as simple repeats of a few sugar molecules linked in linear fashion, or as part of more complex structures, with many sugar residues linked in branching chains. Differences between infants and adults in cellular A, B, and H activity may be related to the number of branched structures present on cellular membranes at different ages. The red cells of infants are thought to carry predominantly linear oligosaccharides, which have only one terminus to which the H (and subsequent A and/or B) sugars can be added. In contrast, the red cells of adults carry a high proportion of branched oligosaccharides. Branching creates additional oligosaccharide chains for potential conversion to H and then to A and B antigens.

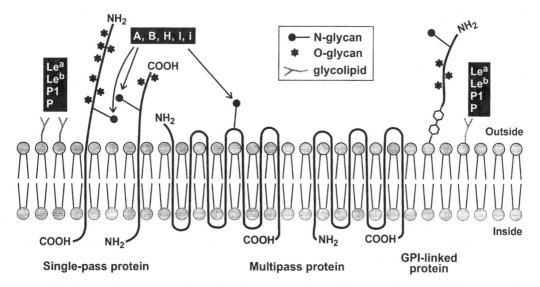

Figure 13-1. Schematic representation of the red cell membrane showing antigen-bearing glycosylation of proteins and lipids. GPI=glycophosphatidylinositol. (Courtesy of ME Reid, New York Blood Center)

A and B glycosyltransferases add specific sugars to oligosaccharide chains that have been converted to H by the fucosyltransferase produced by the *H* gene. A, B, and H antigens are constructed on oligosaccharide chains of four different types (1 to 4) which differ in the linkage of the terminal β-D-galactose (Gal) to N-acetylglucosamine (GlcNAc) and in the characteristics of the carbohydrate chain.[4] The most abundant forms are Type 1 and Type 2 chains. In Type 1 chains, the number 1 carbon of Gal is linked to the number 3 carbon of GlcNAc; in Type 2 chains, the number 4 carbon of GlcNAc is the acceptor for Gal (see Fig 13-2). Type 1 oligosaccharides, carrying A, B, and H activity, are widely distributed in the body. Glycolipids with Type 1 A, B, and H are present in plasma and on endodermally derived tissues such as the epithelial lining of the gut. Glycoproteins with Type 1 chains contribute A, B, and H activity to body fluids and secretions. Unattached Type 1 oligosaccharides can be found in milk and urine. Both Type 1 and Type 2 glycoproteins carrying A, B, and H antigens are found in saliva.

A, B, and H antigens on the red cell surface are formed on Type 2 chains present in highly branched oligosaccharides attached to integral proteins of the red cell membrane, notably bands 3 and 4.5, and on Type 2 oligosaccharides bound to glycolipids. The number of potential A, B, and H sites on red cells is thought to be in excess of two million.[5]

The *H* gene produces a transferase that adds fucose (Fuc) to the number 2 carbon of the terminal galactose of Type 1 and Type 2 chains (see Fig 13-3). The *A* and *B* gene transferases can attach their immunodominant sugars to the number 3 sugar of the same galactose only

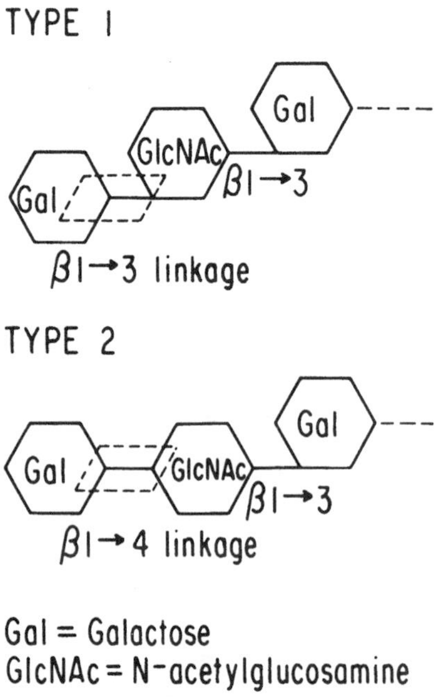

TYPE 1

$\beta1\rightarrow3$ linkage

TYPE 2

$\beta1\rightarrow4$ linkage

Gal = Galactose
GlcNAc = N‾acetylglucosamine

Figure 13-2. Type 1 and 2 oligosaccharide chains differ only in the linkage between the GlcNAc and the terminal Gal.

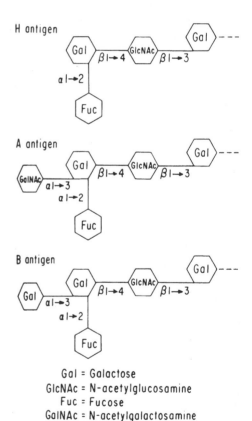

Gal = Galactose
GlcNAc = N-acetylglucosamine
Fuc = Fucose
GalNAc = N-acetylgalactosamine

Figure 13-3. Gal added to the subterminal Gal confers B activity; GalNAc added to the subterminal Gal confers A activity to the sugar. Unless the fucose moiety that determines H activity is attached to the number 2 carbon, galactose does not accept either sugar on the number 3 carbon.

if fucose is already attached, ie, if the core chain has been converted to H. Attachment of the A- or B-defining sugar diminishes the serological detection of H antigen in a reciprocal manner; the expression of A or B and of H are inversely proportional.

Initially, it was believed that the addition of A and B sugars to the terminal galactose halted chain growth, ie, that A or B antigens could not serve as acceptor substrates. The discovery of glycolipids, in which two A structures appeared linked in tandem, altered this dogma (see Fig 13-4).[6]

ABO Genes at the Molecular Level

Yamamoto and Hakomori[7] have shown that *A* and *B* genes differ from one another by seven single-base substitutions. These result in four possible amino acid substitutions (at positions 176, 235, 266, and 268) in the protein sequence of the A and B transferases. Nucleotide substitutions at positions 266 and 268 are most significant in determining sugar specificity, although substitution at position 235 also has some effect. The alleles of *A* and *B* that result in subgroups (phenotypes of A and B that express lower levels of antigen) may have additional mutations that result in enzymes with reduced abilities to convert H antigen. A single nucleotide deletion was found in *A₂* genes close to the carboxyl terminus of the A transferase coding sequence. As a result of frame-shifting, the glycosyltransferase specified by *A₂* possesses an extra domain of 21 amino acids; this domain seems responsible for the low transferase activity and restricted substrate recognition of this enzyme.[8] Subsequently, a number of other substitutions in the *A* gene have been shown to result in the A₂ phenotype in different samples.[9]

The base sequence of the *O* gene appears to be most similar to that of *A*. At least three mechanisms have been shown to account for an inactive product. Substitution of glycine for arginine at amino acid 176 with or without the concomitant substitution of arginine for glycine at position 268 has been observed. In another individual, a base deletion at nucleotide 261 resulted in a truncated inactive protein.[10] All of the variant A and B phenotypes have been shown to be mutations of the *A* or *B* gene, resulting in a less effective transferase.[9]

The *H* and *Se* genes each encode a highly homologous fucosyltransferase. The enzyme produced by *H* acts primarily on Type 2 chains, which predominate on the red cell membranes; the enzyme produced by *Se* prefers (but does not limit its action to) Type 1 chains and acts primarily in the secretory glands. Studies performed on the secretions of individuals with the rare O_h phenotype support the concept that two types of H antigen exist.[11] Persons who lack the *Se* gene have Type 1 and Type 2 chains in their secretions that express no H, A, or B activity. Individuals who lack both *H* and *Se* genes (genotype *hh* and *sese*) have no H and, therefore, no A or B antigens on their red cells or in their secretions. However, H, A, and B antigens are found in the secretions of some *hh* individuals who appear, through family studies, to possess at least one *Se* gene.

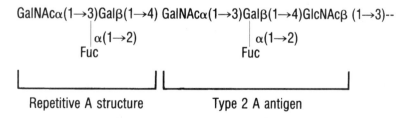

Figure 13-4. Type 3 A antigen structure.

Direct agglutination tests are used to detect A and B antigens on red cells. Reagent antibodies frequently produce weaker reactions with red cells from newborns than with red cells from adults. Although they can be detected on the red cells of 5- to 6-week-old embryos, A and B antigens are not fully developed at birth, presumably because the branching oligosaccharide structures develop gradually. By 2-4 years of age, A and B antigen expression is fully developed and remains fairly constant throughout life.

Subgroups

Subgroups are ABO phenotypes that differ in the amount of antigen carried on red cells and, in secretors, present in the saliva (see Table 13-2) and, as described earlier, are the products of less effective glycosyltransferases. Subgroups of A are more commonly encountered than subgroups of B. The two principal sub-

groups of A are A_1 and A_2. Red cells from A_1 and A_2 persons both react strongly with reagent anti-A in direct agglutination tests. The serologic distinction between A_1 and A_2 cells derives from tests with preparations of the lectin from *Dolichos biflorus* seeds. At appropriate dilution, *Dolichos biflorus* lectin acts as an anti-A_1 and agglutinates A_1 but not A_2 red cells. Approximately 80% of group A or group AB individuals have red cells that are agglutinated by anti-A_1 and thus are classified as A_1 or A_1B. The remaining 20%, whose red cells are agglutinated by anti-A but not by anti-A_1, are called A_2 or A_2B.

Anti-A_1 occurs as an alloantibody in the serum of 1-8% of A_2 persons and 22-35% of A_2B persons.[12] Anti-A_1 can cause discrepancies in ABO testing and incompatibility in crossmatches with A_1 or A_1B red cells. Anti-A_1 usually reacts better or only at temperatures well below 37 C and is considered clinically insignificant unless there is reactivity at 37 C. Rou-

Table 13-2. Serologic Reactions Observed in Persons With A and B Phenotypes[*]

Red Blood Cell Phenotype	Reaction of Cells With Known Antiserum to					Reaction of Serum Against Reagent Red Blood Cells				Saliva of Secretors Contains
	A	B	A,B	H	A_1	A_1	A_2	B	O	
A_1	4+	0	4+	0	4+	0	0	4+	0	A & H
A_{int}	4+	0	4+	3+	2+	0	0	4+	0	A & H
A_2	4+	0	4+	2+	0	†	0	4+	0	A & H
A_3	2+^{mf}	0	2+^{mf}	3+	0	†	0	4+	0	A & H
A_m	0/±	0	0/±	4+	0	0	0	4+	0	A & H
A_x	0/±	0	1+/2+	4+	0	2+/0	1+/0	4+	0	H
A_{el}	0	0	0	4+	0	2+/0	0	4+	0	H
B	0	4+	4+	0		4+	4+	0	0	B & H
B_3	0	1+^{mf}	2+^{mf}	4+		4+	4+	0	0	B & H
B_m	0	0	0/±	4+		4+	4+	0	0	B & H
B_x	0	0/±	0/2+	4+		4+	4+	0	0	H

*Modified from Beattie[12]

†The occurrence of anti-A_1 is variable in these phenotypes. A_2 persons frequently have anti-A_1; A_3 persons usually do not, but a few A_3 individuals with anti-A_1 in the serum have been found.

1+ to 4+, agglutination of increasing strength; ±, weak agglutination; mf, mixed-field pattern of agglutination; 0, no agglutination.

tine testing with anti-A$_1$ is unnecessary for donors or recipients.

Subgroups weaker than A$_2$ occur infrequently and, in general, are characterized by decreasing numbers of A antigen sites on the red cells and a reciprocal increase in H antigen activity. Classification of weak A subgroups is generally based on the:

1. Degree of red cell agglutination by anti-A and anti-A$_1$.
2. Degree of red cell agglutination by anti-A,B.
3. Degree of red cell agglutination by anti-H (*Ulex europaeus*).
4. Presence or absence of anti-A$_1$ in the serum.
5. Presence of A and H substances in the saliva of secretors.

See Table 13-2 for the serologic characteristics of A phenotypes. These classifications are based on tests with polyclonal human antibodies. The red cells may react differently with monoclonal reagents.

Red cells of the A$_{int}$, A$_3$, A$_x$, A$_m$, or A$_{el}$ subgroups are seen only rarely in transfusion practice. A$_{int}$ red cells react more weakly than A$_1$ red cells with anti-A$_1$, yet more strongly with anti-H than A$_2$ red cells; A$_{int}$ phenotype is detected only if anti-A$_1$ testing is performed and quantified. A$_3$ red cells produce a characteristic mixed-field pattern of small agglutinates among many free red cells in tests with anti-A and anti-A,B. A$_x$ red cells are characteristically not agglutinated by human anti-A from group B persons but are agglutinated by anti-A,B from group O persons (see the following section on antibodies). A$_x$ red cells may react with some murine monoclonal anti-A reagents, depending on which monoclonal antibody is selected for the reagent. A$_{el}$ red cells are not agglutinated by anti-A or anti-A,B of any origin, and the presence of A antigen is demonstrable only by adsorption and elution studies. Weak subgroups of A such as A$_x$, A$_m$, and A$_{el}$ cannot reliably be identified on the basis of blood typing tests alone. Saliva studies, adsorp-

tion/elution studies, and family studies provide confirmatory information.

Subgroups of B are even less common than subgroups of A. Criteria for their differentiation resemble those for subgroups of A (see Table 13-2). The widespread use of potent monoclonal anti-A and anti-B reagents has decreased the number of examples of weak A or B subgroups detected because monoclonal antibodies are selected for reagent use based on their ability to agglutinate cells with weak or aberrant antigen expression.

Antibodies to A and B

Ordinarily, individuals possess antibodies directed toward the A or B antigen absent from their own red cells (see Table 13-1). This predictable complementary relationship permits ABO testing of sera as well as of red cells (see Methods 2.2 and 2.3). One hypothesis for the development of these antibodies is based on the fact that the configurations that confer A and B specificities on molecules of the red cell membrane also exist in other biologic entities, notably bacterial cell walls. Bacteria are widespread in the environment, and their presence in intestinal flora, dust, food, and other widely distributed agents ensures a constant exposure of all persons to A-like and B-like antigens. Immunocompetent persons react to the environmental antigens by producing antibodies to those that are absent from their own systems. Thus, anti-A is produced by group O and group B persons and anti-B is produced by group O and group A persons. Group AB people, having both antigens, make neither antibody. This "environmental" explanation for the emergence of anti-A and anti-B remains a hypothesis that has not been proven.

Time of Appearance

Anti-A and anti-B can generally be detected in serum after the first few months of life. Occasionally, infants can be found who already produce these antibodies at the time of birth, but most antibodies present in cord blood are of maternal origin. Antibody production increases, reaching the adult level at 5-10 years of age, and declines later in life. Elderly people usually have lower anti-A and anti-B levels than those seen in young adults. Anti-A and anti-B testing on sera from newborns or infants younger than 4-6 months cannot be considered valid because some or all of the infant's antibodies are acquired by the placental transfer of maternal IgG anti-A and anti-B.

Reactivity of Anti-A and Anti-B

IgM is the predominant immunoglobulin class of anti-A produced by group B individuals and anti-B produced by group A individuals, although small quantities of IgG antibody are also present. IgG is the dominant class of anti-A and anti-B of group O serum. Because IgG readily crosses the placenta and IgM does not, the infants of group O mothers are at higher risk for ABO hemolytic disease of the newborn (HDN) than the infants of group A or B mothers.

The distinguishing features of IgM and IgG anti-A and anti-B are given in Table 13-3. Both immunoglobulin classes preferentially agglutinate red cells at room temperature (20-24 C) or below and efficiently activate complement at 37 C. The complement-mediated lytic capability of these antibodies becomes apparent if serum testing includes an incubation phase at 37 C. Sera from some people will cause hemolysis of ABO-incompatible red cells at temperatures below 37 C. Hemolysis due to ABO antibodies should be suspected when the supernatant fluid of the serum test is pink to red or when the cell button is absent or reduced in size. Hemolysis must be interpreted as a positive result. Because the hemolysis is complement-mediated, it will not occur if reagent red cells are suspended in solutions that contain EDTA or other agents that prevent complement activation, or if plasma is used for testing.

Anti-A,B (Group O Serum)

Serum from a group O individual contains an antibody designated as anti-A,B because it reacts with both A and B red cells, and the anti-A and anti-B specificities cannot be separated by differential adsorption. When group O serum is incubated with group A or group B cells, eluates prepared from each adsorbing cell exhibit reactivity against both A and B test cells. Saliva from a secretor of either A or B substance inhibits the activity of this antibody against both A or B red cells.

Group O serum has been used to prepare potent typing reagents capable of agglutinating either A or B red cells. Reagent preparations containing blended monoclonal antibodies also agglutinate A or B cells. Either form of anti-A,B readily distinguishes group O red cells from the other three groups. Anti-A,B containing blended monoclonal antibodies may react as well as, or better than, polyclonal human anti-A,B with red cells of weak A phenotypes, depending on the monoclonal preparations selected. Some monoclonal reagents are a blend of anti-A and anti-B, designated "anti-A and -B," while others are a blend of anti-A, anti-B, and a third anti-A,B clone, designated "anti-A,B." The manufacturer's directions should be consulted to determine what subgroups will be detected by a given reagent.

Table 13-3. Distinguishing Characteristics of IgM and IgG Anti-A and Anti-B

	IgM	IgG
Reactions enhanced		
—with enzyme-treated rbcs	yes	yes
—by lowering temperatures	yes	no
Readily inhibited by soluble A or B antigens	yes	no
Inactivated by 2-ME or DTT	yes	no
Predominant in non-immunized group A and B donors	yes	no

Anti-A₁

Anti-A₁

In simple adsorption studies, the anti-A of group B serum appears to contain separable anti-A and anti-A₁. Native group B serum agglutinates A₁ and A₂ red cells; after adsorption with A₂ red cells, group B serum reacts only with A₁ red cells. If further tests are performed, however, the differences in A antigen expression between A₁ and A₂ red cells appear to be quantitative rather than qualitative. Anti-A₁ is sometimes found in the sera of persons with A₂ or other subgroup A phenotypes.

A reliable anti-A₁ reagent from the lectin of *Dolichos biflorus* is commercially available or may be prepared (see Method 2.10). The raw plant extract will react with both A₁ and A₂ red cells, but the appropriately diluted reagent preparation will not agglutinate A₂ cells and thus constitutes an anti-A₁.

Anti-B

Anti-B

Anti-B is found in the serum of group A persons. The sera of persons with some subgroups of B may contain anti-B, which can be weakly to strongly reactive. Anti-B may also be present in the sera of persons of the *cis* AB phenotype, a rare occurrence in which both A and B antigens appear to be inherited on the same chromosome. Persons who present with acquired B antigen also have anti-B in their sera because the B antigen on their red cells is the result of transient in-vivo deacetylation of their A antigen.

Routine Testing for ABO

Tests that use anti-A and anti-B to determine the presence or absence of the antigens are often described as direct or red cell tests. The use of reagent A₁ and B red cells to detect anti-A and anti-B in serum is called serum testing. Routine tests on donors and patients must include both red cell and serum tests, each serving as a check on the other.[13,14(p31)] To confirm the ABO type of donor units that have already been labeled or to test blood of infants less than 4 months of age, ABO testing on red cells only is permissible. Procedures for ABO typing by slide, tube, and microplate tests are described in Methods 2.1, 2.2, and 2.3.

In the past, ABO red cell typing reagents were prepared from pools of human sera from persons who had been stimulated with A or B blood group substances to produce antibodies of high titer. Today, ABO typing reagents are manufactured from monoclonal antibodies derived from cultured cell lines. Both types of reagents agglutinate most antigen-positive red cells on direct contact, even without centrifugation. Table 13-4 lists the hybridoma clones in currently available ABO reagents in the United States.

Anti-A and anti-B in the sera of most patients and donors are usually too weak to agglutinate red cells without centrifugation or prolonged incubation. Serum tests should be performed by a method that will adequately detect the antibodies—eg, tube, microplate, column agglutination, or slide techniques (see Methods 2.1, 2.2, and 2.3). Caution should be taken when performing slide testing because of the greater likelihood of spillage and contact with blood.

B(A) Phenotype

B(A) Phenotype

In 1984, Yates et al[15] reported that a 10,000-fold concentrate of purified *B* gene-specified galactosyltransferase, isolated from the sera of group B persons, has the capacity in vitro to attach small amounts of A sugar to human milk fucosyllactose, a blood group H-like structure. High levels of galactosyltransferase associated with the *B* gene can attach the A-determining sugar, GalNAc, to a fucosylated substrate molecule, both in vitro[15] and in vivo.[16] Red cells of some group B individuals were agglutinated by a licensed anti-A reagent that contained a particular murine monoclonal antibody MHO4. These group B individuals had excessively high levels of *B* gene-specified galactosyltransferase, and the designation B(A) was given to this blood group phenotype.[16]

Table 13-4. Monoclonal Antibodies Used in FDA-Approved Monoclonal ABO Antisera in the United States*

	Gamma		Immucor		BCA		Ortho	
Anti-A	BIRMA-1	IgM	BIRMA-1	IgM	BIRMA-1	IgM	MHO4	IgM
			F98 7C6	IgM				
Anti-B	GAMA110	IgM	ES4	IgM	ES4	IgM	NB10.5A5	IgM
			F84 3D6	IgM			NB10.3B4	IgM
			F97 2D6	IgM			NB1.19	IgM
Anti-A,B	BIRMA-1	IgM	BIRMA-1	IgM	BIRMA-1	IgM	MHO4	IgM
	ES4	IgM	ES4	IgM	ES4	IgM	3D3	IgM
	ES15	IgM	ES15	IgM	ES15	IgM	NB10.5A5	IgM
			F98 7C6	IgM			NB1.19	IgM
			F84 3D6	IgM				
			F97 2D6	IgM				
			F125 7B6	IgM				

*The list is not definitive and the manufacturer's directions should be consulted for details.

Recognition of the B(A) phenotype is usually made with the discriminating monoclonal anti-A reagent, with which the B(A) red cells show varying reactivity. The majority of examples react weakly, and the agglutinates are fragile and easily dispersed, although some examples have reacted as strongly as 2+.[16] Sera from these individuals agglutinate both A_1 and A_2 cells. Except for newborns and immunocompromised patients, serum testing should distinguish this phenomenon from the AB phenotype in which a subgroup of A is accompanied by anti-A_1. The transferase for GalNAc should be present in the serum from the $A_{sub}B$ individual and absent in the B(A) sample. Molecular analysis has shown that the transferase determining B(A) exhibits a single amino acid substitution at the second of the four amino acid substitution sites (aa 235) that discriminate between A_1 and B transferases. The amino acid residue it possesses is glycine, which is characteristic of the A_1 transferase.[8]

Nonroutine ABO Testing

Additional reagents may be used for ABO testing, especially anti-A,B for red cell tests and A_2 and O red cells for serum tests. Some workers use anti-A,B in routine tests in the belief that it is more effective than anti-A or anti-B in detecting weakly expressed antigens. This is generally not true of monoclonal reagents. Of the weak subgroups undetected by anti-A or anti-B, only A_x is detected by human anti-A,B, and then only if the serum and cells are incubated at room temperature for 10-60 minutes. Some monoclonal blends labeled anti-A,B react well with red cells of weak subgroups on immediate-spin tests. If the manufacturer's directions recommend using anti-A,B for the detection of weak subgroups, it means that its reactivity against A_x red cells has been demonstrated.[13] AABB *Standards for Blood Banks and Transfusion Services*[14] does not require special techniques to detect weak subgroups because the absence of expected serum antibodies usually distinguishes these specimens from group O specimens (see Table 13-2).

Some commercially marketed sets of serum testing cells contain A_2 red cells in addition to A_1 and B red cells. The A_2 red cells are intended to facilitate the recognition of anti-A_1 in specimens exhibiting a subgroup of A. Because most A specimens do not contain anti-A_1, routine use of this reagent is not necessary unless discrepancies between red cell and serum tests are encountered.

Manufacturers of ABO reagents provide, with each reagent package, detailed instructions for use of the reagent. Testing details may vary from one manufacturer to another, and it is important to follow the directions supplied with the specific reagent in use.

Discrepancies Between Red Cell and Serum Tests

Table 13-1 shows the results and interpretations of routine red cell and serum tests for ABO. A discrepancy exists when the results of red cell tests do not complement serum tests. When a discrepancy is encountered, the discrepant results must be recorded, but interpretation of the ABO group must be delayed until the discrepancy is resolved. If the specimen is from a donor unit, the unit must not be released for transfusion until the discrepancy is resolved. When the blood is from a potential recipient, it may be necessary to administer group O red cells of the appropriate Rh type before the investigation is completed. It is important to obtain sufficient pretransfusion blood samples from the patient to complete any additional studies that may be required.

Red cell and serum test results may be discrepant because of intrinsic problems with red cells or serum, test-related problems, or technical errors (see Table 13-5). Discrepancies

may be signaled either because negative results are obtained when positive results are expected, or positive results are found when tests should have been negative.

Specimen-Related Problems in Testing Red Cells

ABO testing of red cells may give unexpected results for many reasons.

1. A patient who has received red cell transfusions or a marrow transplant may have circulating red cells of more than one ABO group and constitute a transfusion or transplantation chimera.

2. Red cells from individuals with variant *A* or *B* genes may carry poorly expressed antigens. Antigen expression may be weakened on the red cells of some persons with leukemia or other malignancies. Agglutination tests with reagent anti-A and anti-B may fail to give expected reactions.

3. Inherited or acquired abnormalities of the red cell membrane can lead to what is called a polyagglutinable state. The abnormal red cells can be unexpectedly agglutinated by human reagent anti-A, anti-B, or both because human reagents will contain antibodies to the so-called cryptantigens that are exposed in poly-

Table 13-5. Common Causes of False-Negative and False-Positive Results in ABO Testing

False-Negative Results	False-Positive Results
Reagent or test serum not added to a tube	Overcentrifugation of tubes
Hemolysis not identified as a positive reaction	Use of contaminated reagents, red cells, or saline
Inappropriate ratio of serum (or reagent) to red cells	Use of dirty glassware
Tests not centrifuged sufficiently	Incorrect interpretation or recording of test results
Tests incubated at temperatures above 20-24 C	
Incorrect interpretation or recording of test results	

agglutinable states. In general, monoclonal anti-A and anti-B reagents will not detect polyagglutination.

4. Abnormal concentrations of serum proteins, the presence in serum of infused macromolecular solutions or, in cord blood samples, the presence of Wharton's jelly may cause the nonspecific aggregation of serum-suspended cells that simulates agglutination.

5. Exceptionally high concentrations of A or B blood group substances in the serum can combine with and neutralize reagent antibodies to produce an unexpected negative reaction against serum- or plasma-suspended red cells.

6. Serum may contain antibodies to the dyes used to color anti-A and anti-B reagents. These antibodies can cause false-positive agglutination reactions if serum- or plasma-suspended red cells are used in testing.

7. A patient with potent cold-reactive autoagglutinins may have red cells so heavily coated with antibody that the cells agglutinate spontaneously in the presence of diluent, independent of the specificity of the reagent antibody.

8. Serum- or plasma-suspended red cells may give false-positive results with monoclonal reagents if the serum or plasma contains a pH- or diluent-dependent autoantibody.

Specimen-Related Problems in Testing Serum

ABO serum tests are also subject to false results.

1. Small fibrin clots that may be mistaken for agglutinates may be seen in ABO tests if plasma or incompletely clotted serum is used.

2. Abnormal concentrations of proteins, altered serum protein ratios, or the presence of high-molecular-weight plasma expanders can cause nonspecific red cell aggregation that is difficult to distinguish from true agglutination.

3. Antibodies other than anti-A and anti-B in a test sample can agglutinate reagent A_1 or B red cells if they carry the corresponding antigen.

4. Antibodies to constituents of the diluents used to preserve reagent A_1 and B red cells can agglutinate the cells independent of ABO antigens and antibodies.

5. Patients who are immunodeficient due to disease or therapy may have such depressed immunoglobulin levels that there is little or no ABO agglutinin activity. Samples from elderly patients whose antibody levels have declined with age or from patients whose antibodies have been greatly diluted by plasma exchange procedures may also have unexpectedly weak agglutinins.

6. Negative or weak results are seen in serum tests from infants under 4-6 months of age. Serum from newborns is not usually tested because antibodies present are generally passively transferred from the mother.

7. Very high-titer, complement-binding anti-A and anti-B may cause so many C1 molecules to associate with the red cell surface that binding to the membrane antigens is sterically hindered and agglutination does not occur. This phenomenon has been reported in serum typing tests using red cells suspended in diluents that lack EDTA.[17]

8. If the patient has received a marrow transplant of a compatible but dissimilar ABO group, serum antibodies will not agree with red cell antigens. For example, a group A individual who receives group O marrow will have circulating group O red cells but produce only anti-B in the serum.

9. Recent transfusion with plasma components containing ABO agglutinins may cause unexpected reactions.

Resolving ABO Discrepancies

The first step in resolving an apparent problem should be to repeat the tests on the same sample. If initial tests were performed on red cells suspended in serum or plasma, repeat testing should use a saline suspension of washed cells. If the discrepancy persists, the following procedures can be incorporated into the investigation.

1. Obtain a new blood specimen from the donor unit or patient and test the new sample. This should resolve discrepancies due to mislabeled or contaminated specimens.

2. Obtain the patient's history of diagnosis, previous transfusions, marrow transplantation, and medications.

3. Wash the test and reagent red cells several times to remove any serum or chemical constituents that may be causing unexpected positive reactions.

4. Test the red cells with anti-A,B, anti-A$_1$, or anti-H as appropriate for the individual problem.

5. If anti-A$_1$ is suspected, test the serum against several examples of group A$_1$ and A$_2$ red cells.

6. Review the results of the antibody screening test against group O red cells to detect interfering effects from cold-reactive allo- or autoantibodies.

7. Incubate tests and controls for 30 minutes at room temperature to facilitate the detection of weak antigens or antibodies. Tests can be subjected to even lower temperatures, but parallel tests with group O and autologous cells should be observed to rule out interference by broadly reactive agglutinins, such as anti-I or anti-H, that react with the red cells of all adults.

Resolving Discrepancies Due to Absence of Expected Antigens

Red cells of most A or B people are strongly agglutinated (3–4+) by the corresponding re-agent antibody, and the sera of these samples usually strongly agglutinate A$_1$ or B reagent red cells (2–4+). The cause of a discrepancy can sometimes be inferred from the strength of the reactions obtained in red cell or serum tests. For example, serum that strongly agglutinates group B red cells but not A$_1$ cells probably comes from a group A person, even though the red cells are not agglutinated by anti-A or anti-B. A or B antigens may be weakly expressed on cells from individuals who have inherited variant alleles, or with disease-related antigen depression. The following procedures can be used to enhance the detection of weakly expressed antigens.

1. Incubate washed red cells with anti-A and anti-A,B for 30 minutes at room temperature to increase the association of antibody with the scant amount of antigen. Incubating the test system at 4 C may further enhance antibody attachment, but tests performed at 4 C must be controlled with group O red cells to ensure that the reactions observed are due to anti-A and anti-B and not to other cold-reactive agglutinins. The manufacturer's directions for any reagent should be consulted for possible comments or contraindications for such a procedure.

2. Treat the patient's red cells with a proteolytic enzyme such as ficin, papain, or bromelain. Enzyme treatment increases the antigen-antibody reaction with anti-A or anti-B. In some instances, reactions between reagent antibody and red cells expressing antigens will become detectable at room temperature within 30 minutes if enzyme-treated red cells are employed. Enzyme-treated group O red cells must be tested in parallel as a control for the specificity of the ABO reaction. The manufacturer's directions for any reagent should be consulted for possible comments or contraindications for such a procedure.

3. Incubate an aliquot of red cells at room temperature or at 4 C with anti-A or anti-B (as appropriate) to adsorb antibody to the corresponding red cell antigens. Group A, B, and O red cells should be subjected to parallel adsorption and elution with any reagent to serve as a control. Anti-A$_1$ lectin should not be used for adsorption/elution studies. Following incubation, wash the red cells thoroughly and prepare an eluate. (See Method 2.4.) Test the eluate against group A$_1$, B, and O cells. If the red cells carried the A antigen, the eluate will agglutinate A$_1$ but not B or O red cells. Eluates prepared from group B red cells will agglutinate only other B red cells. The eluate prepared from group O cells should be nonreactive. Activity in the control group O eluate invalidates the results obtained with the patient's red cells and can mean either the adsorption/elution procedure was not performed correctly or, rarely, if polyclonal anti-A or anti-B sera are used, other antibodies are present.

4. Test the saliva for the presence of H and A or B substances (see Method 2.5). Saliva tests help resolve ABO discrepancies only if the person is a secretor, but this may not be known until after testing is completed or may be surmised from Lewis typings; see the Lewis discussion.

Resolving Discrepancies Due to Unexpected Reactions with Anti-A and Anti-B

Red cell ABO tests sometimes give unexpected positive reactions. For example, reagent anti-A may weakly agglutinate red cells from a sample in which the serum gives reactions expected of a normal group B or O sample. Variant alleles at the *ABO* locus or problems unrelated to the actions of *ABO* genes may be responsible. The following paragraphs describe some events that can cause unexpected reactions in ABO typing tests and the steps that can be taken to identify them.

Acquired B Phenotype. A serum containing strong anti-B and red cells agglutinated strongly by anti-A and weakly by anti-B suggests the acquired B state. The acquired B phenotype arises when microbial deacetylating enzymes modify the A antigen by altering the A-determining sugar (N-acetylgalactosamine) so that it resembles the B-determining galactose. Only A$_1$ red cells exhibit acquired B activity in vivo. The acquired B antigen develops at the expense of A, so a concomitant decrease in the strength of A may be seen in the acquired B state. If sufficiently numerous, acquired B antigens cause the red cells to be agglutinated by human anti-B. Most red cells with acquired B antigens react weakly with anti-B, but occasional examples are agglutinated quite strongly. Behavior with monoclonal anti-B reagents varies with the particular clone used. Acquired B antigens have been observed with increased frequency in tests with certain FDA-licensed monoclonal anti-B blood grouping reagents containing the ES-4 clone.[18] To confirm that group A$_1$ red cells carry the acquired B structure:

1. Check the patient's diagnosis. Acquired B antigens are usually associated with tissue conditions that allow colonic bacteria to enter the circulation, but acquired B antigens have been found on the red cells of apparently normal blood donors.[18]

2. Test the patient's serum against autologous red cells or known acquired B cells. The individual's anti-B will not agglutinate his or her own red cells that carry the acquired B.

3. Test the red cells with monoclonal anti-B reagents for which the manufacturer's instructions give a detailed description. Unlike most human polyclonal antibodies, some monoclonal antibodies do not react with the acquired B phenotype; this information may be included in the manufacturer's directions.

4. Test the red cells with human anti-B serum that has been acidified to pH 6.0. Acidified human anti-B no longer reacts with the acquired B antigen.

5. If the patient is a secretor, test saliva for the presence of A and B. Secretors whose red cells carry acquired B structures will have A but not B substance in their saliva.

6. Treat the red cells with acetic anhydride, which reacetylates the surface molecules and markedly diminishes the reactivity of acquired B red cells. Reactivity of normal group B antigens is not affected by acetic anhydride.

Acquired A-Like Antigens. ABO discrepancies can be seen in the condition known as Tn polyagglutination, in which defective synthesis of oligosaccharides normally present on sialoglycoprotein molecules leaves abnormal antigenic structures (cryptantigens) exposed on the red cell surface. The residual sugar uncovered is N-acetylgalactosamine, the sugar that confers A specificity. A somatic mutation on hematopoietic progenitor cells results in a permanent population of cells described as Tn-activated. Group O or group B cells that have been Tn-activated behave as if they have acquired an A antigen, which may react with human anti-A reagents. The A-like antigen of Tn-activated red cells can be differentiated from the A produced by the *A*-gene transferase if red cells are treated with proteolytic enzymes before testing. Proteolytic enzymes degrade the molecule that expresses the cryptantigen, abolishing the reactivity with anti-A.

Other forms of polyagglutination may interfere in ABO tests. See Method 2.10 to classify polyagglutinable red cells using lectins.

Mixed-Field Agglutination. Occasional samples are encountered that contain two distinct, separable populations of red cells. Usually this reflects the recent transfusion of group O red cells to a non-group-O recipient or receipt of a marrow transplant of an ABO group different from the patient's own. Red cell mix-

tures also occur in a condition called blood group chimerism, resulting either from intrauterine exchange of erythropoietic tissue by fraternal twins or from mosaicism arising through dispermy. In all such circumstances, ABO red cell tests may give a mixed-field pattern of agglutination. Mixed-field reactions due to transfusion last only for the life of the transfused red cells. After marrow transplantation, the mixed-field reaction usually disappears when the patient's own red cells are no longer produced. Persistent mixed-cell populations do occur in some marrow recipients.[19] Mixed-field reactions that arise through blood group chimerism persist throughout the life of the individual.

Mixed-field agglutination is characteristic of the reaction between A_3 red cells and reagent anti-A. If the agglutinated red cells are removed and the remaining red cells are tested again with anti-A, mixed-field agglutination occurs in the residual, previously nonagglutinated population.

Antibody-Coated Red Cells. Red cells from infants with HDN or from adults suffering from autoimmune or alloimmune conditions may be so heavily coated with IgG antibody molecules that they agglutinate spontaneously in the presence of reagent diluents containing high protein concentrations. Usually this is at the 18-22% range found in some anti-D reagents, but sometimes the sensitized red cells also agglutinate in ABO reagents with protein concentrations of 6-12%. Gentle elution at 45 C or use of EDTA-glycine-acid (EGA) can be used to remove much of this antibody from the red cells so that the cells can be tested reliably with anti-A and anti-B.

Red cells from a specimen containing cold-reactive IgM autoagglutinins may agglutinate spontaneously in saline tests. The antibodies can usually be removed by incubating the cell suspension briefly at 37 C and then washing the cells several times with saline warmed to 37 C. If the IgM-related agglutination is not dispersed by this technique, the red cells can be treated with the sulfhydryl compound dithiothreitol (DTT) (see Method 2.11).

Resolving Discrepancies Due to Unexpected Serum Reactions

The following paragraphs describe some events that can cause unexpected or erroneous serum test results, and the steps that can be taken to resolve them.

1. Immunodeficient patients may not produce detectable levels of anti-A and anti-B. These antibodies are absent from the serum of newborns and may be weak in serum from normal elderly persons. Check the age and diagnosis of the patient.

2. Abnormally high concentrations of anti-A and anti-B have caused prozone reactions that lead to false-negative results. In these instances the ABO group can be inferred by red cell tests, by dilution of the serum, or by the use of EDTA (2.5%)-treated serum.[17]

3. Anti-A_1 in the serum of individuals of A_2, A_2B, or other subgroups agglutinate A_1 reagent red cells. To demonstrate this as the cause of the discrepancy:

   a. Test the serum against several examples of group A_1, A_2, and O red cells, preferably three of each. Only if the antibody agglutinates all A_1 red cells and none of the A_2 or O red cell samples can it be called anti-A_1.

   b. Use appropriately diluted *Dolichos biflorus* lectin to demonstrate that the individual's cells belong to a non-A_1 subgroup.

      Most examples of anti-A_1 react only at temperatures below 30 C and are considered clinically insignificant. Some examples have reactivity at 37 C and should be considered clinically significant; only A_2 or O red cells should be used for transfusion.

4. Strongly reactive cold autoagglutinins, such as anti-I and anti-IH, can agglutinate red cells of all adults, including autologous cells and reagent red cells, at room temperature (20-24 C). With few exceptions, agglutination caused by the cold-reactive autoagglutinin is weaker than that caused by anti-A and anti-B. The following steps can be performed when such reactivity interferes to the point that the interpretation of serum tests is difficult.

   a. Warm the serum and reagent red cells to 37 C before mixing and testing. Read serum tests at 37 C and convert them to the antiglobulin phase, if necessary. Weakly reactive examples of anti-A or anti-B may not be detected by this method because 37 C is above the reactive optimum for these antibodies. In group A and B individuals, ABO antibodies are predominantly of the IgM class and will not be detected in routine antiglobulin tests that employ anti-IgG reagents. Examples of anti-A and anti-B with little or no IgG component can go undetected under these conditions.

   b. Remove the cold-reactive autoagglutinin from the serum using a cold autoadsorption method as described in Method 4.6. The adsorbed serum can then be tested against A_1 and B reagent red cells.

   c. Treat the serum with 0.01M DTT (see Method 3.8) and use the treated serum for serum-typing tests. Because DTT destroys the agglutinating activity of IgM antibodies, tests that use DTT-treated serum must be converted to the antiglobulin phase, in which IgG forms of the antibodies will be detected. Because many group A or B persons do not produce more than minute quantities of IgG anti-A or anti-B, negative tests should be interpreted with caution.

5. Unexpected alloantibodies that react at room temperature, such as anti-P_1 or anti-M, may agglutinate the red cells used in serum tests if the cells carry the corresponding antigen. Ordinarily, one or more of the reagent cells used in the antibody detection test will also be agglutinated at room temperature, but a rare serum may react with an antigen on the serum testing cells that is not present on cells used for antibody detection. Steps to determine the correct ABO type of sera containing other cold-reactive alloantibodies include:

    a. Identify the alloantibody, as described in Chapter 19, and test the reagent A_1 and B cells to determine which, if either, carries the corresponding antigen. Obtain A_1 and B red cells that lack the antigen and use them for serum testing.

    b. Raise the temperature to 30-37 C before mixing the serum and cells. If the thermal amplitude of the alloantibody is below the temperature at which anti-A and anti-B react, this may resolve the discrepancy.

    c. If the antibody detection test is negative, test the serum against several examples of A_1 and B red cells. The serum may contain an antibody directed against an antigen of low incidence, which will be absent from most randomly selected A_1 and B red cells.

6. Sera from patients with abnormal concentrations of serum proteins, or with altered serum protein ratios, or who have received plasma expanders of high molecular weight, can aggregate reagent red cells and mimic agglutination. Some of these samples cause aggregation of the type described as rouleaux. Rouleaux formation is easily recognized on microscopic examination if the red cells assume what has been described as a "stack of coins" formation. More often, the aggregates appear as irregularly shaped clumps that closely resemble antibody-mediated agglutinates. The results of serum tests can often be corrected by diluting the serum 1:3 in saline to abolish its aggregating properties or by using a saline replacement technique (see Method 3.4).

The H System

The H system has two genes, *H* and *h*, and one antigen, H, which serves as the precursor molecule on which A and B antigens are built. On group O red cells, there is no A or B antigen, and the membrane expresses abundant H. The amount of H antigen detected on red cells is, in order of diminishing quantity, $O>A_2>B>A_2B>A_1>A_1B$. As for A and B configurations, H-like antigens are found in nature. Individuals of the rare O_h phenotype, whose red cells lack H, have anti-A and anti-B, and a potent and clinically significant anti-H in their serum. Occasionally, group A_1, A_1B, or (less commonly) B persons have so little unconverted H antigen on their red cells that they produce anti-H. This form of anti-H is relatively weak, virtually always reacts at room temperature or below, and is not considered clinically significant.

O_h Phenotype

The term "Bombay" has been used for the phenotype in which red cells lack H, A, and B because examples of such red cells were first discovered in Bombay, India. The symbol O_h has been selected to denote the phenotype because results of routine ABO typing tests mimic those of group O persons. O_h red cells are not agglutinated by anti-A, anti-B, or anti-A,B reagents, and the serum contains strong anti-A and anti-B. The O_h phenotype becomes apparent when serum from the O_h person is tested against group O red cells, and strong immediate-spin reactions occur. The anti-H of an O_h person reacts over a thermal range of 4-37 C with all red cells except those of other O_h people. O_h persons must be transfused only with O_h blood because their non-red-cell-stimulated antibodies rapidly destroy cells with A, B, or H antigens. The O_h phenotype is demonstrated by the absence of reaction when cells are tested with the anti-H lectin of *Ulex europaeus*. If other examples of O_h red cells are available, further confirmation can be obtained by demonstrating compatibility of the serum with O_h red cells. At the genotypic level, the O_h phenotype arises from the inheritance of *hh* at the *H* locus. The presence or absence of at least one normal *Se* gene will determine whether H, A, and/or B antigens are present in the secretions of these persons.

Para-Bombay Phenotypes A$_h$, B$_h$, and AB$_h$

A$_h$, B$_h$, and AB$_h$ red cells lack serologically detectable H antigen but carry small amounts of A and/or B antigen, depending on the individual's genes at the *ABO* locus. Tests with anti-A or anti-B reagents may or may not give weak reactions, but the cells are nonreactive with anti-H lectin or with anti-H serum from O_h persons. The observed weak A and B antigens are adsorbed onto red cells from the plasma because people of the para-Bombay phenotype have a nonfunctional *H* gene but a normal *Se* gene and will express A, B, and H antigens in their plasma and secretions.[9] The sera of A$_h$ and B$_h$ people contain anti-H in addition to the expected anti-A or anti-B.

The Lewis System

The Lewis system antigens, Le^a and Le^b, are encoded by the *Le* gene and, like the A, B, and H

antigens, result from the action of a glycosyltransferase. The Lewis antigens are not intrinsic to red cells but are expressed on glycosphingolipids adsorbed from plasma onto red cell membranes. The *Le* gene is a fucosyltransferase that adds Fuc in $\alpha(1\rightarrow4)$ linkage to the subterminal GlcNAc of Type 1 oligosaccharides (see Fig 13-2). In Type 2 chains, the number 4 carbon is not available for fucose attachment so Type 2 chains never express Lewis system activity. The oligosaccharides present on molecules intrinsic to the red cell membrane are all Type 2.

Genes and Antigens

The fucosyltransferase encoded by the *Le* gene attaches fucose in $\alpha(1\rightarrow4)$ linkage to the subterminal GlcNAc; this configuration has Le^a activity. The subsequent action of the fucosyltransferase encoded by the *Se* gene attaches a fucose in $\alpha(1\rightarrow2)$ linkage to the terminal Gal. The configuration with two fucose moieties has Le^b activity. Thus, Le^b reflects the presence of both the *Le* and *Se* genes. *Le* without *Se* results in Le^a activity only; *Se* without *Le* has no consequences in terms of Lewis system activity.

Plasma glycosphingolipids are adsorbed to the red cell membrane; if Lewis activity is present, adsorption will confer Lewis reactivity on the circulating cells. Le^b is adsorbed preferentially over Le^a. Individuals possessing both *Le* and *Se* genes will have red cells that express Le^b but not Le^a. Red cells from persons with *Le* but

Table 13-6. Phenotypes in the Lewis System and Their Incidence

Reactions with Anti-			Adult Phenotype Incidence %	
Le^a	Le^b	Phenotype	Whites	Blacks
+	0	Le(a+b−)	22	23
0	+	Le(a−b+)	72	55
0	0	Le(a−b−)	6	22
+	+	Le(a+b+)	rare	rare

not *Se* will express Le^a. The individual who is homozygous for the amorphic allele *le* will have no Lewis reactivity on red cells or on Type 1 oligosaccharides in other tissues. Table 13-6 shows phenotypes of the Lewis system and their frequencies in the population. Red cells that type as Le(a+b+) are only rarely found when human antisera are used in blood typing. Such red cells are seen more frequently when more potent monoclonal anti-Le^a and anti-Le^b reagents are used, and are more common in persons of Asian origin.[20]

Lewis Antibodies

Lewis antibodies occur almost exclusively in the sera of Le(a–b–) individuals, usually without known red cell stimulus. Those people whose red cell phenotype is Le(a–b+) do not make anti-Le^a because small amounts of unconverted Le^a are present in their saliva and plasma. It is most unusual to find anti-Le^b in the sera of Le(a+b–) individuals, but anti-Le^b may exist along with anti-Le^a in the sera of Le(a–b–) individuals. Lewis antibodies are more often found in the sera of pregnant women; however, Lewis antibodies are almost always IgM and do not cross the placenta. Because of this and because Lewis antigens are poorly developed at birth, the antibodies have only rarely been implicated in HDN. Lewis antibodies may bind complement, and fresh serum that contains anti-Le^a (or infrequently anti-Le^b) may hemolyze incompatible red cells in vitro. Hemolysis is more often seen with enzyme-treated red cells than with untreated red cells.

Serologic Characteristics

Most Lewis antibodies agglutinate saline-suspended red cells of the appropriate phenotype. The resulting agglutinates are often fragile and are easily dispersed if red cell buttons are not resuspended gently after centrifugation. Agglutination sometimes is seen after incubation at 37 C, but rarely of the strength seen in tests incubated at room temperature. Some examples of anti-Le^a, and less commonly anti-Le^b, can be detected in the antiglobulin phase of testing. Sometimes this reflects complement bound by the antibody; in other cases, antiglobulin reactivity results from an IgG component of the antibody.

Sera with anti-Le^b activity can be divided into two categories. The more common type reacts best with Le(b+) red cells of group O and A$_2$; these antibodies have been called anti-Le^{bH}. Antibodies that react equally well with the Le^b antigen on red cells of all ABO phenotypes are called anti-Le^{bL}. Anti-Le^{bH}, but not anti-Le^{bL}, can be neutralized by saliva from group O persons who are secretors of H substance but who are Le(a–b–). Table 13-7 lists the serologic behavior of the common Lewis system antibodies.

Table 13-7. Serologic Behavior of the Principal Antibodies of the Lewis and P Blood Groups

| Antibody | In-Vitro Hemolysis | Saline | | Albumin | | Enzyme | | Associated With | |
		4 C	22 C	37 C	AGT	37 C	AGT	HDN	HTR
anti-Le^a	some	most	most	some	many	most	most	no	few
anti-Le^b	rare	most	most	few	some	some	some	no	no
anti-P1	occ	most	some	occ	rare	some	few	no	rare
anti-P	some	most	some	some	some	some	some	no	?
anti-P1+P+P^k	some	most	some	some	some	some	some	rare	?

Recognition of Other Antigens

Two other antibodies (anti-Le[c] and -Le[d]) have been given Lewis designations but the determinants with which they react are glycosphingolipids with Type 1 oligosaccharides from Le(a–b–) persons. Anti-Le[c] reacts with unsubstituted Type 1 chains, on which neither the Gal nor the GlcNAc is linked to fucose. Anti-Le[d] reacts with Type 1 chains from *lele* persons who possess *Se*; the configuration is H antigen expressed on Type 1 chains.

Transfusion Practice

Lewis antigens readily adsorb to and elute from red cell membranes. Transfused red cells shed their Lewis antigens and assume the Lewis phenotype of the recipient within a few days of entering the circulation. Lewis antibodies in a recipient's serum are readily neutralized by Lewis blood group substance in donor plasma. For these reasons, it is exceedingly rare for Lewis antibodies to cause hemolysis of transfused Le(a+) or Le(b+) red cells. However, examples of anti-Le[a] that cause hemolysis in vitro or that give strong reactions in the antiglobulin phase of the crossmatch have been associated with posttransfusion hemolysis.

It is not considered necessary to type donor blood for the presence of Lewis antigens before transfusion or when crossmatching for recipients with Lewis antibodies. Reactions seen on crossmatches with anti-IgG reagents provide a good index of transfusion safety.[21]

Lewis Antigens in Children

Red cells from newborn infants usually react with neither human anti-Le[a] nor anti-Le[b] and are considered to be Le(a–b–). Some can be shown to carry small amounts of Le[a] when tested with potent monoclonal or goat anti-Le[a] reagents. Reliable Lewis typing of young children may not be possible as test reactions may not reflect the correct phenotype until approximately 6 years of age. Among children, the incidence of Le(a+) red cells is high and that of Le(b+) red cells low. The phenotype Le(a+b+) may be transiently observed in children whose phenotypes as adults will be Le(a–b+).

Cord red cells are agglutinated by an antibody called anti-Le[x], which agglutinates adult red cells of Le(a+b–) and Le(a–b+), but not Le(a–b–) phenotypes.[22] In serologic tests, this antibody behaves as if it contains an inseparable combination of anti-Le[a] and -Le[b]. The determinant it defines has been called Le[x], which is present on the majority of cord red cells and on adult red cells that express either Le[a] or Le[b]. Anti-Le[x] is not a more potent or more avid form of anti-Le[a]. The Le[x] determinant is the Type 2 oligosaccharide to which Fuc is attached in $\alpha(1\rightarrow3)$ linkage to GlcNAc; it represents a class of antigens that are developmentally regulated embryonic oligosaccharides.[23] The sialylated form of Le[x] appears to be a ligand for the adhesion receptor called endothelial leukocyte adhesion molecule 1 (ELAM-1) or E-selectin, and thus may play a role in certain metastatic cancers.[24]

The I/i Antigens and Antibodies

The unexpected antibodies most frequently encountered in serologic tests performed at room temperature are anti-H and anti-I. The I antigens reside in the subterminal portions of the oligosaccharides that eventually are converted to H, A, or B antigens and are found on membrane-associated glycoproteins and glycosphingolipids. Both Type 1 and Type 2 oligosaccharide chains of adult red cells include multiple units of $Gal\beta(1\rightarrow4)$ $GlcNAc\beta(1\rightarrow3)$.[25] Two of these disaccharide units linked in a straight chain oligosaccharide constitute the i antigen. On the red cells of adults, many of these linear chains are modified by the addition of branched structures consisting of $Gal\beta(1\rightarrow4)GlcNAc$ linked in $\beta(1\rightarrow6)$ to a galactose residue internal to the repeating sequence. The branching configuration confers I specificity. Different examples of anti-I appear to recognize different portions of the branched oligosaccharide chain.

Fetal red cells carry few branched oligosaccharides and, therefore, are rich in i and poor in I. During the first 2 years of life, I antigen gradually increases at the expense of i. The red cells of most adults are strongly reactive with anti-I and react weakly or not at all with anti-i. Rare adults exist whose red cells are I-negative. Their sera usually contain anti-I, but activity may be so weak as to require enzyme techniques for detection.

Antibodies to I/i

Anti-I characteristically agglutinates red cells from nearly all adults at room temperature and below, but does not react with red cells from cord blood or from I-negative adults. If tests are performed at 4 C, sera from many people whose red cells type I+ can be shown to have autoanti-I. Anti-I is a common autoantibody, but it usually behaves as a cold-reactive agglutinin, acting within a narrow thermal range and, even at 4 C, at a titer no higher than 64. Anti-I assumes pathologic significance in cold agglutinin disease or mixed-type autoimmune hemolytic anemia, in which it behaves as a complement-binding antibody with a high titer and wide thermal range (see Chapter 20). Autoanti-i is less often implicated in symptomatic disease than anti-I. On rare occasions, anti-i may be seen as a relatively weak cold autoagglutinin reacting only at 4-10 C. Patients with infectious mononucleosis often have transient but potent anti-i.

Table 13-8 illustrates the serologic behavior of anti-I and anti-i at 4 C and 22 C. Reaction strengths should be considered relative; clear-cut differences in reactivity between the two are seen only with weaker examples of the antibodies. Titration studies may be needed to differentiate strong examples of the antibodies.

Serum containing anti-I or anti-i is sometimes reactive at the antiglobulin phase of testing. Such reactions rarely indicate antibody activity at 37 C; rather, the reaction is between anticomplement in a polyspecific antiglobulin reagent and complement components bound when serum and cells interact at lower temperatures. The complement remains bound to cell surfaces after the antibody dissociates during 37 C incubation. The problem can usually be avoided either by warming the serum and red cells to 37 C before combining them and then keeping them strictly at 37 C for all phases of testing, including centrifugation and washing. Omitting any potentiator (if used) and using anti-IgG instead of polyspecific antihuman globulin reagent are other ways the reactivity can generally be avoided.

Complex Reactivity

Some antibodies appear to recognize branched oligosaccharides that have been further modified, for example, transferases for H and P1. Anti-IH occurs quite commonly in the serum of A_1 persons; it reacts strongly with red cells that have high levels of H as well as I. Anti-IH reacts very little with group A_1 cells of adults or cord cells of any group, and very strongly with group O cells of adults. Anti-IH should be suspected when serum from a group A patient causes direct agglutination of all cells used for antibody detection but is compatible with all or most group A donor blood.

Table 13-8. Serologic Behavior of the I Blood Group Antibodies with Saline Red Cell Suspensions

		Anti-I	Anti-i
4 C	I_{adult}	4+	0-1+
	i_{cord}	0-2+	3+
	i_{adult}	0-1+	4+
22 C	I_{adult}	2+	0
	i_{cord}	0	2-3+
	i_{adult}	0	3+

The P Blood Group and Related Antigens

The first antigen of the P blood group was discovered by Landsteiner and Levine in 1927, in a series of animal experiments that led also to the discovery of M and N. Originally called P, the name of the antigen was later changed to P1. The designation P has since been reassigned to an antigen present on almost all human red cells. The International Society for Blood Transfusion has made an effort to classify P antigens in a logical manner (see Table 13-9). The P1 antigen is the only antigen of the P blood group system. The P, P^k, and LKE antigens, formerly considered part of the P system, have been assigned to the Globoside collection of antigens. Red cells lacking P1, but shown to possess P, are of the P_2 phenotype.

Biochemistry

The different oligosaccharide determinants of P1 and its related antigens are shown in Fig 13-5. P1 antigen is present on red cells of the P_1 and P_1^k phenotypes. P antigen, also termed globotetrasylceramide or globoside, is present on P1-positive and P1-negative red cells. P^k antigen, also termed globotriaosylceramide or CTH, is present in low amounts on red cells of the P_1 and P_2 phenotypes and is enriched in cells of the rare phenotypes P_1^k and P_2^k. LKE antigen, which has the same structure as the stage-specific embryonic antigen 4, is present in almost all red cells except those of the rare phenotypes p or P^k and in about 2% of P-positive red cells. The p red cells are devoid of P1, P, P^k, and LKE antigens, but enriched in lactosylceramide.

All the antigens described above are exclusively expressed in glycolipids on human red cells, not on glycoproteins.[26] The antigens are built through the addition of sugars to precursor glycosphingolipids, a process thought to be analogous to the development of the A, B, and H antigens. P^k determinants are formed when Gal is added in $\alpha(1\rightarrow4)$ linkage to the terminal Gal residues of lactosylceramide.[27] Subsequently, this structure can be converted to P globoside by the addition of GalNAc in $\beta(1\rightarrow3)$ linkage. Neither P^k nor P serve as substrate for P1. Instead, Gal is added in $\alpha(1\rightarrow4)$ linkage to a different structure called paragloboside to form P1. Paragloboside is the precursor on which cellular A, B, H, I, and i antigens are constructed. The p antigen results from addition of NeuNAc to the terminal galactose in $\alpha(2\rightarrow3)$. The gene specifying the responsible transferase is thought to be independent of the P system.

Rare Phenotypes

Several rare phenotypes are associated with the P blood group. They are shown in Table 13-9. The P^k phenotype occurs when the P^k antigen is not converted to P. Individuals whose red cells have P^k instead of P consistently make a strong

Table 13-9. Phenotypes in the P Blood Group/Globoside Collection

| | Reactions With Anti- | | | | Phenotype Incidence % | |
P_1	P	P^k	P1+P+P^k	Phenotype	Whites	Blacks
+	+	0	+	P_1	79	94
0	+	0	+	P_2	21	6
0	0*	0	0	p		
+	0	+	+	P_1^k	All extremely rare	
0	0	+	+	P_2^k		

*Usually negative, occasionally weakly positive.

alloanti-P that reacts in tests with P+P+(P$_1$ phenotype) and P–P+ (P$_2$ phenotype) red cells. The biphasic hemolysin of paroxysmal cold hemoglobinuria (PCH) is often, but not always, of this specificity. Unlike the IgM anti-P in the sera of P^k persons, the autoreactive anti-P found in people with PCH is IgG.[29(p221)]

Very rare people lack P1, P, and P^k. Red cells from these individuals are said to be of the p phenotype. Characteristically, a potent hemolytic IgM antibody with anti-P1+P+P^k specificity is found in their sera. The antibody, formerly called anti-Tj^a, has caused hemolytic transfusion reactions and, occasionally,

HDN.[29(p139)] There is an association between anti-P1+P+P^k and spontaneous abortions occurring early in pregnancy in p women.[30]

It has been shown that red cells of P$_1^k$ and P$_2^k$ phenotypes can be agglutinated by the meningitis-causing bacterium *Streptococcus suis*[31]; the P antigen has been shown to serve as a receptor for parvovirus B19, which causes erythema infectiosum (Fifth disease).[32] Indeed, persons of p phenotype who lack globoside are naturally resistant to infection with this pathogen. These recent findings implicate the P blood group system in the pathogenesis of these diseases.[32]

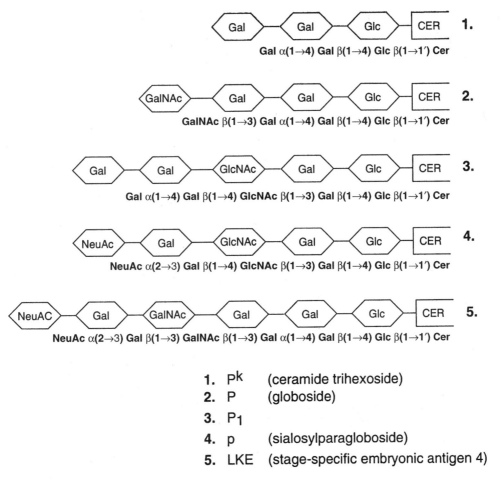

1. P^k (ceramide trihexoside)
2. P   (globoside)
3. P$_1$
4. p   (sialosylparagloboside)
5. LKE   (stage-specific embryonic antigen 4)

Figure 13-5. Biochemical structures of P antigens.[28]

Anti-P1

The sera of P1-negative persons commonly contain anti-P1. If sufficiently sensitive techniques are applied, it is likely that anti-P1 would be detected in the serum of virtually every person of the P_2 phenotype. The antibody reacts optimally at 4 C but may occasionally be detected at 37 C. Because anti-P1 is nearly always IgM, it does not cross the placenta and has not been reported to cause HDN. It has only rarely been reported to cause hemolysis in vivo (Table 13-8).[29(p139),33]

The strength of the P1 antigen varies among different red cell samples, and antigen strength has been reported to diminish when red cells are stored. These characteristics sometimes create difficulties in identifying antibody specificity in serum with a positive antibody screen. An antibody that reacts weakly in room temperature testing can often be shown to have anti-P1 specificity by incubation at lower temperatures or by the use of enzyme-treated red cells. Hydatid cyst fluid or P1 substance derived from pigeon eggs inhibits the activity of anti-P1. Inhibition may be a useful aid to antibody identification, especially if it is present in a serum with antibodies of other specificities.

References

1. Landsteiner K. Zur Kenntnis der anti-fermentativen, lytischen und agglutinierenden Wirkungen des Blutserums und der Lymph. Zbl Balk 1900;27:367.
2. Yamamoto F, Clausen H, White T, et al. Molecular genetic basis of the histo-blood group ABO system. Nature 1990;345:229-32.
3. Larsen RD, Enst LK, Nair RP, Lowe JB. Molecular cloning sequence, and expression of a human GDP-L-fucose: β-D-galactose 2-α-L-fucosyl-transferase cDNA that can form the H blood group antigen. Proc Natl Acad Sci U S A 1990;87:6674-8.
4. Lowe JB. Carbohydrate-associated blood group antigens: The ABO, H/Se and Lewis loci. In: Garratty G. Immunobiology of transfusion medicine. New York: Marcel Dekker, Inc. 1994:3-36.
5. Bermeman Z, van Bockstaele DR, Uyttenbroeck WM, et al. Flow cytometric analysis of erythrocyte blood group A antigen density profiles. Vox Sang 1991;61:265-74.
6. Clausen H, Levery SB, Nudelman E, et al. Repetitive A epitope (type 3 chain A) defined by group A1-specific monoclonal antibody TH-1: Chemical basis of qualitative A1 and A2 distinction. Proc Natl Acad Sci U S A 1985; 82:1199-203.
7. Yamamoto F, Hakomori S. Sugar-nucleotide donor specificity of histo-blood group A and B transferases is based on amino acid substitutions. J Biol Chem 1990;265:19257-62.
8. Yamamoto FI. Review: Recent progress in the molecular genetic study of the histo-blood group ABO system. Immunohematology 1994;10:1-7.
9. Ogasawara K, Yabe R, Uchikawa M, et al. Molecular genetic analysis of variant phenotypes of the ABO blood group system. Blood 1996;88:2732-7.
10. Reid ME, Lomas-Francis C. The blood group antigen factsbook. London: Academic Press, 1997.
11. Mulet C, Cartron JP, Badet J, Salmon C. Activity of α-2-L-fucosyltransferase in human sera and red cell membranes. A study of common ABH blood donors, rare "Bombay" and "Parabombay" individuals. FEBS Lett 1977;84:74.
12. Beattie KM. Discrepancies in ABO grouping. In: A seminar on problems encountered in pretransfusion tests. Washington, DC: American Association of Blood Banks, 1972:129-65.
13. Code of federal regulations. Title 21 CFR, part 660.26. Washington, DC: US Government Printing Office, 1998 (revised annually).
14. Menitove JE, ed. Standards for blood banks and transfusion services. 19th ed. Bethesda, MD: American Association of Blood Banks, 1999.
15. Yates AD, Feeney J, Donald ASR, Watkins WM. Characterisation of a blood group A-active tetrasaccharide synthesized by a blood-group B-gene-specified glycosyltransferase. Carbohydr Res 1984;130:251-60.
16. Beck ML, Yates AD, Hardman J, Kowalski MA. Identification of a subset of group B donors reactive with monoclonal anti-A reagent. Am J Clin Pathol 1989;92:625-9.
17. Judd WJ, Steiner EA, Oberman HJ. Reverse and typing errors due to prozone: How safe is the immediate spin crossmatch? (abstract). Transfusion 1987;27:527.
18. Beck ML, Kowalski MA, Kirkegaard JR, Korth JL. Unexpected activity with monoclonal anti-B reagents. Immunohematology 1992;8:22-3.
19. Branch DR, Gallagher MT, Forman SJ, et al. Endogenous stem cell repopulation resulting in mixed hematopoietic chimerism following total body irradiation and marrow transplantation for acute leukemia. Transplantation 1982;34:226-81.
20. Longworth C, Rolih S, Moheng M, et al. Mouse monoclonal anti-Le[a] and anti-Le[b] as routine grouping reagents (abstract). Transfusion 1985;25:446.
21. Waheed A, Kennedy MS, Gerhan S. Transfusion significance of Lewis system antibodies: Report on a nationwide survey. Transfusion 1981;21:542-5.
22. Arcilla MC, Sturgeon P. Le[x], the spurned antigen of the Lewis blood group system. Vox Sang 1974;26:425-38.
23. Stoolman, LM. Adhesion molecules controlling lymphocyte migration. Cell 1989;56:907-10.
24. Polley MJ, Phillips ML, Wayner E, et al. CD62 and endothelial cell-leukocyte adhesion molecule 1 (ELAM-1) recognize the same carbohydrate ligand, sialyl-Lewis X. Proc Natl Acad Sci U S A 1991;88:6224.

25. Feizi T. The blood group Ii system: A carbohydrate antigen system defined by naturally monoclonal or oligoclonal autoantibodies of man. Immunol Commun 1981;10:127-56.

26. Yang Z, Bergstrom J, Karlsson KA. Glycoproteins with Galalpha4Gal are absent from human erythrocyte membranes, indicating that glycolipids are the sole carriers of blood group P activities. J Biol Chem 1994;269:14620-4.

27. Naiki M, Marcus DM. An immunochemical study of human blood group P_1, P and P_k glycosphingolipid antigens. Biochemistry 1975;14:4837-41.

28. Anstall HB, Blaycock RC. The P blood group system: Biochemistry, genetics and clinical significance. In: Moulds JM, Woods LL, eds. Blood groups: P, I, Sd^a and Pr. Arlington, VA: American Association of Blood Banks, 1991:1-19.

29. Mollison PL, Engelfriet CP, Contreras M. Blood transfusion in clinical medicine. 10th ed. Oxford: Blackwell Scientific Publications, 1997.

30. Cantin G, Lyonnais J. Anti-PP_1P^k and early abortion. Transfusion 1983;33:350-1.

31. Haataja S, Tikkanen K, Liukkonen J, et al. Characterization of a novel bacterial adhesion specificity of *Streptococcus suis* recognizing blood group P receptor oligosaccharides. J Biol Chem 1993;268:4311-7.

32. Brown KE, Hibbs JR, Gallinella G, et al. Resistance to parvovirus B19 infection due to lack of virus receptor (erythrocyte P antigen). N Engl J Med 1994;330:1192-6.

33. Chandeysson PL, Flyte MW, Simpkins SM, Holland PV. Delayed hemolytic transfusion reaction caused by anti-P_1 antibody. Transfusion 1981;21:77-82.

Suggested Reading

Beck ML. Blood group antigens acquired de novo. In: Garratty G, ed. Blood group antigens and disease. Arlington, VA: American Association of Blood Banks, 1983:45-66.

Beck ML. The I blood group collection. In: Moulds JM, Woods LL, eds. Blood groups: P, I, Sd^a and Pr. Arlington, VA: American Association of Blood Banks, 1991:23-52.

Daniels G. Human blood groups. Oxford: Blackwell Science Publications, 1995.

Hakomori SI. Blood group ABH and Ii antigens of human erythrocytes: Chemistry, polymorphism and their developmental change. Semin Hematol 1981;18:39-47.

Hanfland P, Kordowicz M, Peter-Katalinic J, et al. Immunochemistry of the Lewis blood-group system: Isolation and structure of Lewis-c active and related glycosphingolipids from plasma of blood-group O Le(a–b–) nonsecretors. Arch Biochem Biophys 1986;246:655-72.

Issitt PD, Anstee DJ. Applied blood group serology, 4th ed. Durham, NC: Montgomery Scientific Publications, 1998.

Judd WJ. Methods in immunohematology. Miami, FL: Montgomery Scientific Publications, 1988.

Watkins WM. The glycosyltransferase products of the A, B, H and Le genes and their relationship to the structure of the blood group antigens. In: Mohn JF, Plunkett RW, Cunningham RK, Lambert RM, eds. Human blood groups. Basel: Karger, 1977:134-42.

14

The Rh System

THE RH BLOOD GROUP SYSTEM IS extremely complex, and certain aspects of its genetics, nomenclature, and antigenic interactions are not fully understood. After the A and B antigens of the ABO system, the D antigen of the Rh system has the most significant implications for transfusion practice. The D antigen is more immunogenic than virtually all other red cell antigens. The Rh system also contains other clinically significant antigens (C, E, c, and e) and less significant antigens (variant, *cis* product, and G antigens). This chapter concentrates on observations, problems, and solutions commonly encountered in transfusion practice.

The D Antigen and Its Historical Context

Rh Positive and Rh Negative

The unmodified descriptive terms "Rh positive" and "Rh negative" refer to the presence or absence of the red cell antigen D. This chapter uses the DCE nomenclature—a modification of the nomenclature originally proposed by Fisher and Race,[1] which has been able to accommodate our present understanding of the genetics and biochemistry of this complex system. The Rh-Hr terminology of Wiener is presented only in its historical context, as current molecular genetic evidence does not support Wiener's one-locus theory.

Discovery of D

The first human example of the antibody against the D antigen was reported in 1939 by

Levine and Stetson,[2] who found it in the serum of a woman whose fetus had hemolytic disease of the newborn (HDN) and who experienced a hemolytic reaction after transfusion of her husband's blood. In 1940, Landsteiner and Wiener[3] described an antibody obtained by immunizing guinea pigs and rabbits with the red cells of Rhesus monkeys; it agglutinated the red cells of approximately 85% of humans tested, and they called the corresponding determinant the Rh factor. In the same year, Levine and Katzin[4] found similar antibodies in the sera of several recently delivered women, and at least one of these sera gave reactions that paralleled those of the animal anti-Rhesus sera. Also in 1940, Wiener and Peters[5] observed antibodies of the same specificity in the sera of persons whose red cells lacked the determinant and who had received ABO-compatible transfusions in the past. Later evidence established that the antigen detected by animal anti-Rhesus and human anti-D were not identical, but by that time the Rh blood group system had already received its name.

Clinical Significance

After the A and B antigens, D is the most important red cell antigen in transfusion practice. In contrast to A and B, however, persons whose red cells lack the D antigen do not regularly have the corresponding antibody. Formation of anti-D almost always results from exposure, through transfusion or pregnancy, to red cells possessing the D antigen. The D antigen has greater immunogenicity than virtually all other red cell antigens; more than 80% of D-negative persons who receive a D-positive transfusion are expected to develop anti-D. To prevent this, the blood of all recipients and all donors is routinely tested for D to ensure that D-negative recipients are identified and given D-negative blood.

Soon after anti-D was discovered, family studies showed that the D antigen is genetically determined; transmission of the trait follows an autosomal dominant pattern.

Other Important Antigens

By the mid-1940s, four additional antigens, C, E, c, and e, had been recognized as belonging to what is now called the Rh system. Subsequent discoveries have brought the number of Rh-related antigens to 45 (Table 14-1), many of which exhibit both qualitative and quantitative variations. The reader should be aware that these other antigens exist (see the suggested reading list), but in most transfusion medicine settings, the five principal antigens (D, C, E, c, e) and their corresponding antibodies account for more than 99% of clinical issues involving the Rh system.

Genetic and Biochemical Considerations

Attempts to explain the genetic control of Rh antigen expressions have been fraught with controversy. Wiener[8] proposed a single locus with multiple alleles determining surface molecules that embody numerous antigens. Fisher and Race[9] inferred from the existence of antithetical antigens the existence of reciprocal alleles at three individual but closely linked loci. Tippett's prediction[10] that two closely-linked structural loci on chromosome 1 determine production of Rh antigens has been shown to be correct.

Rh Genes

Two highly homologous genes on the short arm of chromosome 1 encode the nonglycosylated polypeptides that express the Rh antigens (Fig 14-1).[11,12] One gene, designated *RHD*, determines the presence of a membrane-spanning protein that confers D activity on the red cell. In Caucasian D-negative persons, the *RHD* gene is deleted and they have no genetic material at this site. However almost all D-negative Blacks of African descent have an inactive, partial or intact *RHD* gene at this locus.[13]

Table 14-1. Antigens of the Rh Blood Group System and Their Incidence

Numerical Designation	Antigen Name	Incidence (%)*			Numerical Designation	Antigen Name	Incidence (%)*		
		White	Black	Overall			White	Black	Overall
Rh1	D	85	92		Rh30	Goᵃ	0	<0.01	
Rh2	C	68	27		Rh31	hrᴮ			98
Rh3	E	29	22		Rh32	Rh32	<0.01	1	
Rh4	c	80	96		Rh33	Har			<0.01
Rh5	e			98	Rh34	Bastiaan			>99.9
Rh6	f	65	92		Rh35	Rh35			<0.01
Rh7	Ce	68	27		Rh36	Beᵃ			<0.1
Rh8	Cᵂ	2	1		Rh37	Evans			<0.01
Rh9	Cˣ			<0.01	Rh39	C-like			>99.9
Rh10	V	1	30		Rh40	Tar			<0.01
Rh11	Eᵂ			<0.01	Rh41	Ce-like	70		
Rh12	G	84	92		Rh42	Ceˢ	<0.1	2	
Rh17	Hr₀			>99.9	Rh43	Crawford			<0.01
Rh18	Hr			>99.9	Rh44	Nou			>99.9
Rh19	hrˢ			98	Rh45	Riv			<0.01
Rh20	VS	<0.01	32		Rh46	Rh46			>99.9
Rh21	Cᴳ			68	Rh47	Dav			>99.9
Rh22	CE			<1	Rh48	JAL			<0.01
Rh23	Dᵂ			<0.01	Rh49	STEM	<0.01	6	
Rh26		80	96		Rh50	FPTT			<0.01
Rh27	cE	28	22		Rh51	MAR			>99.9
Rh28				<0.01	Rh52	BARC			<0.01
Rh29	total Rh			>99.9					

* Incidence in White and Black populations where appropriate.[6,7]

At the locus immediately upstream, the gene *RHCE* determines the C, c, E, and e antigens; its alleles are *RHce*, *RHCE*, *RHcE*, and *RHce*.[14] Much effort has gone into determining if different proteins, resulting from alternative splicing of mRNA, carry C/c and E/e, or if a single polypeptide expresses both sites.[14-16] Evidence derived from transfection studies[17] conclude that both C/c and E/e reside on a single polypeptide product.

Biochemical and Structural Observations

The predicted products of both *RHD* and *RHCE* are proteins of 417 amino acids that, modeling studies suggest, traverse the red cell membrane 12 times and display only short exofacial loops of amino acids on the exterior (Fig 14-1). The polypeptides are fatty-acid acetylated and, unlike most blood group-associated proteins, carry no carbohydrate residues. Within the red cell membrane, the Rh polypeptides form a complex with a glycoprotein, the Rh-associated glycoprotein (RhAG), that has partial homology with the Rh polypeptides but is encoded at a locus on chromosome 6 (Fig 14-1).[18]

Considerable homology exists between the products of *RHD* and *RHCE*; the products of the different alleles of *RHCE* are even more similar.[19] C and c differ from one another in only four amino acids, at positions 16, 60, 68, and 103, of which only the difference between serine and proline at 103 appears to be critical. The presence of proline or alanine at position 226 appears to be the sole characteristic that distinguishes E from e. The D polypeptide, by contrast, possesses 35 amino acids that will be perceived as foreign by D-negative individuals.

The study of Rh_{null} red cells, which lack all Rh antigens, reveals that the Rh proteins are part of a large membrane complex, in which the presence of the Rh proteins appears to be essential for correct expression or presentation of other membrane proteins. The glycoproteins that bear the LW, Duffy, and U antigens all seem to require the presence of Rh proteins for full expression. Rh_{null} cells lack all the LW antigens, are negative for Fy5 of the Duffy system, and have weakened expression of the antigens carried on glycophorin B (S, s, and U).[20] The membrane glycoproteins RhAG and CD47 (which do not bear any blood group antigens) have also been shown to be an integral part of this complex.[19]

Rh Terminology

Three systems of nomenclature were developed before the recent advances in our understanding of the genetics of Rh. Each of these systems of nomenclature has been used to convey genetic and serologic information about the Rh system.

System Notations

The Rh-Hr terminology derives from the work of Wiener,[8] who believed the immediate gene product to be a single entity he called an agglutinogen. Wiener's concept was that each agglutinogen is characterized by numerous individual serologic specificities, called factors, identified by individual specific antibodies. Current biochemical and serologic data do not support this theory.

CDE terminology was introduced by Fisher and Race,[1] who postulated three sets of closely linked genes (C and c, D and d, and E and e). Both gene and gene product have the same letter designation, with italics used for the name of the gene. Although this theory does not fully explain some of the observed Rh antigenic profiles, it does provide the easiest way to communicate research and serologic findings at present. Since the Rh antigens are known to be encoded by the *RHD* and *RHCE* genes, a modified terminology, DCE, is now commonly used. For informal designation of phenotype, particularly in conversation, many workers use a shorthand system based on Wiener's Rh-Hr notation. This does not fit into any system of nomenclature, but these shorthand symbols

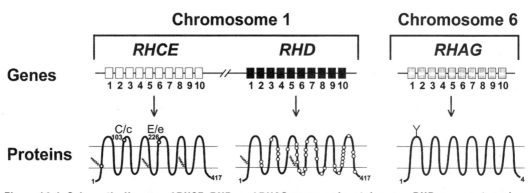

Figure 14-1. Schematic diagram of RHCE, RHD, and RHAG genes and proteins. ○ on RHD represents amino acid differences between RHD and RHCE. ○ On RHCE indicates the critical amino acids involved in C/c and E/e antigen expression. (Courtesy ME Reid, New York Blood Center)

convey information in a convenient and efficient fashion.

Rosenfield and coworkers[21] proposed a system of nomenclature based simply on serologic observations. Symbols were not intended to convey genetic information, merely to facilitate communication of phenotypic data. Each antigen is given a number, generally in order of its discovery or its assignment to the Rh system. The presence of an antigen on a red cell specimen is indicated by the appropriate number placed after the system designation, Rh, followed by a colon; a minus sign before a number indicates that the antigen has been tested for and found to be absent. This system is cumbersome for verbal communication, but well suited for written communication without genetic inference, and for computerized data entry. Table 14-1 lists the antigens currently included in the Rh system. Table 14-2 shows the most common combinations of antigens, expressed as haplotypes. Table 14-3 shows reaction patterns achieved by testing cells with antibodies to the five principal antigens and the descriptive term used for phenotypes in the widely accepted nomenclature based on the Wiener terminology.

Table 14-2. The Principal Rh Gene Complexes and the Antigens Encoded

Haplotype	Genes Present	Antigens Present	Phenotype
R^1	RHD,RHCe	D,C,e	R_1
r	RHce	c,e	r
R^2	RHD,RHcE	D,c,E	R_2
R^0	RHD,RHce	D,c,e	R_0
r'	RHCe	C,e	r'
r''	RHcE	c,E	r''
R^z	RHD.RHCe	D,C,E	R_z
r^y	RHCE	C,E	r^y

Haplotype Notations

The phenotype notations convey haplotypes with the single letters R and r, in roman type, for the haplotypes that produce or do not pro-

Table 14-3. Determination of Likely Rh Phenotypes from the Results of Tests with the Five Principal Rh Blood Typing Reagents

Reagent					Antigens Present	Probable Phenotype
Anti-D	Anti-C	Anti-E	Anti-c	Anti-e		
+	+	0	+	+	D,C,c,e	R_1r
+	+	0	0	+	D,C,e	R_1R_1
+	+	+	+	+	D,C,c,E,e	R_1R_2
+	0	0	+	+	D,c,e	R_0R_0/R_0r
+	0	+	+	+	D,c,E,e	R_2r
+	0	+	+	0	D,c,E	R_2R_2
+	+	+	0	+	D,C,E,e	R_1R_z
+	+	+	+	0	D,C,c,E	R_2R_z
+	+	+	0	0	D,C,E	R_zR_z
0	0	0	+	+	c,e	rr
0	+	0	+	+	C,c,e	r'r
0	0	+	+	+	c,E,e	r''r
0	+	+	+	+	C,c,E,e	r'r''

duce D, respectively. Subscripts or, occasionally, superscripts, indicate the combinations of other antigens present. For example, R_1 indicates D, C, and e together; R_2 indicates D, c, and E; r indicates c and e; R_0 indicates D, c, and e; and so on. Phenotypes appearing to embody homozygous expression of a single haplotype have only one letter; others have two.

Determining Phenotype

In clinical practice, five blood typing reagents are readily available: anti-D, -C, -E, -c, and -e. Table 14-4 shows the incidence of D, C, E, c, and e antigens in White and Black populations. Routine pretransfusion studies include only tests for D. Other reagents are used principally in the resolution of antibody problems or in family studies. The assortment of antigens detected on a person's red cells constitutes that person's Rh phenotype.

Table 14-4. Incidence of the More Common Genotypes in D-Positive Persons

| Antigens Present | Genotype | | Incidence (%) | |
	DCE	Mod. Rh-hr	Whites	Blacks
D,C,c,e	DCe/ce	R^1r	31.1	8.8
	DCe/Dce	R^1R^0	3.4	15.0
	Ce/Dce	$r'R^0$	0.2	1.8
D,C,e	DCe/DCe	R^1R^1	17.6	2.9
	DCe/Ce	R^1r'	1.7	0.7
D,c,E,e	DcE/ce	R^2r	10.4	5.7
	DcE/Dce	R^2R^0	1.1	9.7
D,c,E	DcE/DcE	R^2R^2	2.0	1.3
	DcE/cE	R^2r''	0.3	<0.1
D,C,c,E,e	DCe/DcE	R^1R^2	11.8	3.7
	DCe/cE	R^1r''	0.8	<0.1
	Ce/DcE	$r'R^2$	0.6	0.4
D,c,e	Dce/ce	R^0r	3.0	22.9
	Dce/Dce	R^0R^0	0.2	19.4

Inferring Genotype

Identifying antigens does not always allow confident deduction of genotype. Presumptions regarding the most probable genotype rest on the incidence with which particular antigenic combinations derive from an individual genome complex based on population studies in different ethnic groups. For simplicity, the remainder of this chapter uses DCE terminology to express haplotypes, ie, *DCE* rather than *RHD, RHCE*.

Inferences about genotype are useful in population studies and in the investigation of disputed parentage. Such analyses are also used to predict whether the sexual partner of a woman with Rh antibodies is likely to transmit the genes that will result in offspring negative or positive for the particular antigen.

More recently, molecular techniques involving the polymerase chain reaction (PCR) have been introduced as a reliable method for the determination of fetal genotype from amniocytes.[19] This technique exploits the differences between the *RhD* and *RhCE* genes and may be tailored to target the antigen of choice. However, there are rare occasions when the genotyping results may disagree with the serologic findings.

Serologic Testing for Rh Antigen Expression

To determine whether a person has genes that encode C, c, E, and e, the red cells are tested with antibody to each of these antigens. If the red cells express both C and c or both E and e, it can be assumed that the corresponding genes are present in the individual. If the red cells carry only C *or* c, or only E *or* e, the person is assumed to be homozygous for the particular allele. Titration studies can sometimes document this assumption because the amount or dose of antigen on the red cells from homozygotes often is greater than when the genome includes only a single copy. Tests for the D antigen indicate only its presence or absence; titration results to demonstrate dosage have not given reliable information.

Expression of D

D-negative persons either lack *RHD*, which encodes for the D antigen, or have a nonfunctional RHD gene. Most D-negative persons are homozygous for *RHce*, the gene encoding c and e; less often they may have *RHCe* or *RHcE*, which encode C and e or c and E, respectively. The *RHCE* gene, which produces both C and E, is quite rare.

The genotype of a D-positive person cannot be determined serologically; dosage studies are not effective in showing whether an individual is homozygous or heterozygous for *RHD*. An individual's *RHD* genotype can be assigned only by inference from the antigens associated with the presence of D. PCR amplification and restriction enzyme analysis of the Rh genes may eventually allow highly accurate determination of D genotype.

Interaction between genes results in so-called "position effect." If the interaction is between genes, or the product of genes, on the same chromosome it is called a *cis* effect. If a gene or its product interacts with one on the opposite chromosome, it is called a *trans* effect. Examples of both effects were first reported in 1950 by Lawler and Race,[22] who noted as a *cis* effect that the E antigen produced by *DcE* is quantitatively weaker than E produced by *cE*. They noted as *trans* effects that both C and E are weaker when they result from the genotype *DCe/DcE* than when the genotypes are *DCe/ce* or *DcE/ce*, respectively.

Effect of Ethnic Origin

Ethnic origin influences deductions about genotype because the incidence of Rh genes differs from one geographic group to another. For example, a White person of European descent with the phenotype Dce would probably be *Dce/ce*, but in a Black person of African descent the genotype could as likely be either *Dce/Dce* or *Dce/ce*.

Effect of Gene Frequency

The phenotype DCcEe (line 3 of Table 14-3) can arise from any of several genotypes. In any population, the most probable genotype is *DCe/DcE*. Both these haplotypes encode D; a person with this phenotype will very likely be homozygous for the *D* gene, although heterozygous for the actual combination of genes present on the two chromosomes. Some less likely alternative genotypes could render the person heterozygous at the *D* locus (for example, *DCe/cE*, *DcE/Ce*, or *DCE/ce*), but these are uncommon in all populations. Table 14-4 gives the incidence of the more common genotypes in D-positive persons. The figures given are for Whites and Blacks. In other racial groups, the likelihood of being heterozygous for D is reduced because absence of *RHD* is so uncommon.

Weak Expression of D

Most D-positive red cells show clear-cut macroscopic agglutination after centrifugation with reagent anti-D and can be readily classified as D-positive. Red cells that are not immediately or directly agglutinated cannot as easily be classified. For some D-positive red cells, demonstration of the D antigen requires prolonged incubation with the anti-D reagent or addition of antiglobulin serum after incubation with anti-D. These cells are considered D-positive, even if there has been need for an additional step in testing.

In the past, red cells that required additional steps for demonstration of D were classified as D[u]. The term D[u] is no longer used; red cells that carry weak forms of D are classified as D-positive and may be described as "weak D." Improvement of polyclonal reagents and the more widespread use of monoclonal anti-D reagents have resulted in the routine detection of some D-positive cells that would have been considered weak D when tested with less sensitive polyclonal reagents. Additionally, monoclonal anti-D may react by direct agglutination with epitopes of D that had previously required more sensitive test methods or, occasionally, may fail to react with different epitopes of the D antigen.

Weak D Due to Transmissible Genes

Weak D phenotypes can result from several different genetic circumstances. Some examples of *RHD* encode weak expression of the D antigen. This quantitative characteristic follows a regular pattern of Mendelian dominant inheritance. Weak D expression of this type is fairly common in Blacks, often occurring as part of a *Dce* haplotype. Transmissible genes for weak D expression are considerably less common in Whites, but may be seen as part of an unusual *DCe* or *DcE* haplotype.

Red cell samples with an inherited weak D antigen either fail to react or react very weakly in direct agglutination tests with most anti-D reagents. However, the cells react strongly when antiglobulin serum is added to the system.

Weak D as Position Effect

Perhaps the best-known example of position effect is weakening of the D antigen by a *C* gene in *trans* to the *D* gene. Red cells from some persons of the genotype *Dce/Ce* have weakened expression of D, a suppressive effect exerted by *C* in the *trans* position to an unremarkable *D* on the opposite chromosome. Similar depression of D can be seen with other D-positive haplotypes accompanied by *Ce*. For example, the *DCe/cE* and *DcE/Ce* genotypes encode for the same antigens, but D expression is often perceptibly weaker on cells from the latter individual. Many weak D phenotypes reported in the early literature would, with currently available reagents, appear as normal D. Weak D antigens that have qualitative differences are discussed later in this chapter.

Partial D

The concept that the D antigen consists of multiple, individually-determined constituents arose from observations that some people with D-positive red cells produced alloanti-D that was nonreactive with their own cells. Most D-positive persons who produce alloanti-D have red cells that react strongly when tested with anti-D. Other red cells, especially those of the D^{VI} phenotype, react more weakly than normal D-positive control red cells. Red cells lacking parts of the D antigen complex have been referred to in the past as "D mosaic" or "D variant." Current terminology indicates such red cells, deficient in components of D, are more appropriately described as "partial D."

Categorization of partial D phenotypes was performed originally by cross-testing alloanti-D produced by immunized D-positive persons. The four categories initially described by Wiener have been expanded considerably over the years. Tests of many monoclonal anti-D reagents with red cells of various D categories suggest that the D antigen comprises multiple epitopes. Numbered D categories and other partial-D phenotypes can now be defined in terms of their D epitopes. Tippett et al[23] established at least 10 epitopes, expanding on the seven epitopes demonstrated in 1989,[24] but point out that the D antigen is not large enough to accommodate more than eight distinct epitopes and there must be considerable overlap between them. Following a comprehensive study with many monoclonal anti-D, Jones et al[25] proposed a 30-epitope model. Dogma regarding the existence of many discrete epitopes is giving way to a model that is more topographic in nature. Chang and Siegel liken the fit of antibody to antigen as a "footprint."[26] Given the numerous specificities defined to date, this model seems more appropriate. Molecular studies have elucidated the genetic mechanisms behind many of the partial D phenotypes and have shown that in most cases, the phenotypes arise as the result of nucleotide exchange between the *RhCE* gene and the *RhD* gene.[19]

Not all persons who are D-positive and produce what appear to be anti-D should be assumed to have epitope-deficient red cells. Weakly reactive anti-LW[ab] or anti-LW[a] may react with D-positive cells but not with D-negative cells. A D-positive person whose antibody is a weakly reactive anti-LW[a] may be indistinguishable on initial serologic testing from an individual with a partial-D antigen who has made anti-D to missing epitopes. (See section on LW in Chapter 15.) Anti-LW can easily be differentiated from anti-D by testing the antibody with 0.02M DTT-treated red cells (Method 3.11); the LW antigen is destroyed by sulfhydryl reagents, whereas D is unaffected.

Significance of Weak D in Blood Donors

Transfusion to D-negative recipients of blood with weak expression of the D antigen has long been proscribed, based on the possibility that such red cells could elicit an immune response to D. This possibility may be more apparent than real, as weak forms of the D antigen seem to be substantially less immunogenic than normal D-positive blood. Transfusion of a total of 68 units of blood with weak D to 45 D-negative recipients failed to stimulate production of a single example of anti-D.[27] Although 15 of the 45 recipients were receiving the level of immunosuppression available in the late 1950s, one person in the series made anti-E and a second made anti-K. A report[28] of anti-CD produced in response to D[u]Ce red cells can be better explained as anti-G than as anti-C and an anti-D elicited by the cells described as D[u].

More important than the potential immunogenicity of red cells with weakened expression of D is the possibility of such cells experiencing accelerated destruction if transfused to a recipient with circulating anti-D. Hemolytic transfusion reactions were reported in the early literature, but it is probable that the responsible cells would, with currently available reagents, have been considered straightforwardly D-positive. Hemolytic disease of the newborn has also been reported, but not recently.[29]

Significance of Weak D in Recipients

The transfusion recipient whose red cells test as weak D is sometimes a topic of debate. Most such patients can almost always receive D-positive blood without risk of immunization, but if the weak D expression reflects the absence of one or more D epitopes, the possibility exists that transfusion of D-positive blood could elicit alloanti-D. The same possibility exists, however, for persons whose partial D red cells react strongly with anti-D reagents. AABB *Standards for Blood Banks and Transfusion Services*[30(p31,58)] requires donor blood specimens to be tested for weak expression of D and to be labeled as D-positive if the test is positive, but recipients' specimens need not be tested with anti-D by any procedure other than direct agglutination. Currently available, licensed anti-D reagents are sufficiently potent that most patients with weak D are found to be D-positive. The few patients classified as D-negative, whose D-positive status would have been detected by antiglobulin testing, can receive D-negative blood without problems. Some workers consider this practice wasteful of D-negative blood and prefer to test potential recipients for weak D, and then issue D-positive blood.

If D-positive blood is given to recipients of the weak-D phenotype, it is important to safeguard against careless or incorrect interpretation of tests. D-negative recipients erroneously classified as D-positive, possibly because of a positive direct antiglobulin test (DAT), run the risk of immunization to D if given D-positive blood. Individuals whose weakly expressed D antigen is detectable only in the antiglobulin test will ordinarily be classified as D-negative recipients. If they donate blood subsequently, however, they will be classified as D-positive at the time of blood donation. Personnel in blood centers and transfusion services should be prepared to answer questions from puzzled donors or their physicians. This can present special problems in autologous donations, when the D-negative patient's own blood is labeled as

D-positive. In this case, confirmation of the patient's D status by antiglobulin testing resolves the apparent discrepancy between recipient and donor types.

Other Rh Antigens

Numbers up to 52 have been assigned to Rh red cell antigens (see Table 14-1); some of the numbers have been rescinded or the antigens reassigned but, of the currently included 45, most beyond D, C, c, E, and e (Rh1-5) and their corresponding antibodies are rarely encountered in routine blood transfusion therapy.

Cis Product Antigens

The membrane components that exhibit Rh activity have numerous possible antigenic subdivisions. Each gene or gene complex determines a series of interrelated surface structures, of which some portions are more likely than others to elicit an immune response. The polypeptides determined by the genes in the haplotype *DCe* express determinants additional to those defined as D, C, and e. These include Ce (rhi), a *cis* product that almost always accompanies C and e when they are encoded by the same haplotype. The Ce antigen is absent from red cells on which the C and e were encoded by different haplotypes, for example, in a person of the genotype *DCE/ce*. Similar *cis* product antigens exist for c and e determined by the same haplotype (the antigen called ce or f), for c and E (cE), and for C and E (CE).

Although antibodies directed at *cis* product antigens are encountered infrequently, it would not be correct to consider them rare. Such antibodies may be present, unnoticed in serum containing antibodies of the more obvious Rh specificities; only adsorption with red cells of selected phenotypes would demonstrate their presence. Anti-f (ce) may be present, for example, as a component of some anti-c and anti-e sera, but its presence would have little practical significance. The addi-

tional antibody should not confuse the reaction patterns given by anti-c and anti-e because all red cells that react with anti-f will express both c and e.

Anti-Ce is frequently the true specificity of the apparent anti-C that a *DcE/DcE* person produces after immunization with C-positive blood. This knowledge can be helpful in establishing an individual's Rh genotype. If anti-Ce is the predominant specificity in a reagent anti-C, however, the individual whose C antigen resulted from a *DCE* haplotype may be mistyped unless test methods and control red cells are chosen carefully.[28]

The G Antigen and Cross-Reactions

The G antigen is almost invariably present on red cells possessing either C or D. Antibodies against G appear superficially to be anti-C+D, but the anti-G activity cannot be separated into anti-C and anti-D. The fact that G appears to exist as an entity common to C and D explains the fact that D-negative persons immunized by C–D+ red cells sometimes appear to have made anti-C as well as anti-D. It may also explain why D-negative persons who are exposed to C+D– red cells may develop antibodies appearing to contain an anti-D component. Rare red cells have been described that possess G but lack D. The r^G phenotype is found mostly in Blacks: the G antigen is generally weakly expressed and is associated with the presence of the VS antigen. The r^G phenotype has been described in Whites but is not the same as r^G in Blacks. Red cells also exist that express partial D but lack G entirely; for example, persons of the D^{IIIb} phenotype.[29]

Variant Antigens

Although red cells from most people give straightforward reactions with reagent anti-D, anti-C, anti-E, anti-c, and anti-e sera, some cells give atypical reactions and other seemingly normal red cells stimulate the production of antibodies that do not react with red cells of common Rh phenotypes. It has been convenient to consider C and c, and E and e, as antithetical antigens at specific surface sites. This scheme can be expanded to include variant antigens that seem to occupy the same surface site but have been determined by genes, possibly conversion or misalignment products, that encode proteins that differ from the common Rh determinants. Variant forms of the e antigen have been identified, for example, hr^S or hr^B antigens (Rh19 and Rh31, respectively). Persons who are e-positive and hr^S-negative and/or hr^B-negative are found in some Black populations. The absence of hr^B is associated in most cases with the presence of the VS antigen.[29] Diminished C and markedly diminished e activity characterize the products of the $\overline{R}^N$ gene complex, which also encodes a low-incidence antigen, Rh32. Rh32 is not restricted to this haplotype, however, and is also expressed by red cells of the DBT phenotype. DBT cells also express a partial D antigen. Among Whites, a weakened e antigen is among the products of genes that encode the low-incidence Rh33 and the Rh36 (Be^a) antigens. As our understanding of the molecular genetics of Rh expands, it is clear that gene conversion and crossover events give rise to low incidence antigens in a manner analogous to *GYPA* and *GYPB*, which encode the MNS blood group system antigens (see Chapter 15).[19] Antigens that behave as if they had an antithetical relationship to C/c or E/e have been found, mainly in Whites. The most common is C^w (found in 2% or more of some White populations) and the relationship is phenotypic only, because C^w and C^x are antithetical to the high-incidence antigen, MAR.

Rh$_{null}$ Syndrome and Other Deletion Types

Rh$_{null}$

The literature reports at least 43 persons in 14 families whose red cells appear to have no Rh antigens; others are known but have not been reported. The phenotype, described as Rh$_{null}$, may be produced by at least two different genetic mechanisms. In the more common regulator type of Rh$_{null}$, the absence of a very common unrelated regulator gene ($X'r$) was proposed that prevents expression of the person's normal genes at the Rh locus on chromosome 1. Such persons appear to transmit normal Rh genes to their offspring, in a manner roughly analogous to that in which the A or B transferases are transmitted by people of the Bombay phenotype. These Rh$_{null}$ persons were considered to be homozygous for X^0r, a rare allele of $X'r$, that segregates independently of genes of the Rh system. In some cases, parents or offspring of people with the regulator type of Rh$_{null}$ show overall depression of their Rh antigens, known as Rh$_{mod}$. Recent studies of unrelated individuals of Rh$_{null}$ and Rh$_{mod}$ phenotypes revealed the presence of mutations in the *RhAG* gene, which suggests that *RHAG* is the most likely candidate to be the Rh suppressor gene (X^0r).[31-33]

The other form of Rh$_{null}$ was thought to arise through homozygosity for an amorphic gene at the Rh locus itself, $\overline{r}$, which appears to have no products detectable with Rh testing reagents. Recent studies, however, suggest Rh$_{null}$ gene complexes could direct low levels of Rh polypeptides to be produced.[34] Huang et al[35] have shown that in one family, the amorph Rh$_{null}$ phenotype arises from a double mutation in the *RHCe* gene together with the common deletion of *RHD*. The amorph type of Rh$_{null}$ is considerably rarer than the regulator type. Parents and offspring of this type of Rh$_{null}$ are obligate heterozygotes for the amorph.

Red Cell Abnormalities

Whatever the genetic origin, red cells lacking Rh antigens have membrane abnormalities that shorten their survival. The severity of hemolysis and resulting anemia varies among affected persons, but stomatocytosis, shortened red cell survival, and variably altered activity of other blood group antigens, especially S, s, and U, have been consistent features.

Serologic Observations

A few Rh$_{null}$ probands were recognized because their sera contained Rh antibodies. Some came to light, however, when routine Rh phenotyping of their red cells revealed the absence of any Rh antigens. In three cases, the discovery resulted from deliberate testing for Rh antigens in patients with morphologically abnormal red cells and hemolytic anemia. Immunized Rh$_{null}$ people have produced antibodies varying in specificity from apparently straightforward anti-e or anti-C to several examples that reacted with all red cells tested except those from other Rh$_{null}$ people. This antibody, considered to be "anti-total Rh," has been given the numerical designation anti-Rh29.

Rh$_{mod}$

The Rh$_{mod}$ phenotype represents less complete suppression of Rh gene expression. As for the regulator type of Rh$_{null}$, an unlinked recessive modifier gene is thought to be responsible; it has been named X^Q. Unlike Rh$_{null}$ red cells, those classified as Rh$_{mod}$ do not completely lack Rh and LW antigens. Rh$_{mod}$ red cells show much reduced and sometimes varied activity, depending on the Rh system genes the proband possesses and on the potency and specificity of the antisera used in testing. Sometimes the Rh antigens have sufficiently weakened expression that only adsorption-elution techniques will demonstrate their presence. As in Rh$_{null}$, hemolytic anemia is a feature of the Rh$_{mod}$ condition. It may be appropriate to think of the two abnormalities as being essentially similar, differing only in degree. In one case, at least, mutation in *RHAG* was also shown to result in the Rh$_{mod}$ phenotype. A mutant RhAG protein was demonstrated and this protein is thought to permit expression of some Rh antigens.[31]

D--, D••, and Other Deleted Phenotypes

Rare genes exist that either fail to encode Rh material or encode Rh material lacking activity at the CcEe sites. Some portions of the surface configuration are not detectable, leaving D (or C/c and D) as the only remaining site(s). Red cells that lack C/c and/or E/e antigens may show exceptionally strong D activity, an observation by which such red cells have sometimes been recognized during routine testing with anti-D. The D-- phenotype may be identified in the course of studies to investigate an unexpected antibody. Such persons may have alloantibody of complex specificity because the person's red cells lack all the epitopes expressed on the CcEe polypeptide. A single antibody with anti-Rh17 (anti-Hr$_0$) specificity is often made by persons of this rare phenotype, although some such sera have been reported to contain apparently separable specificities, such as anti-e.

The D•• phenotype is similar in most respects to D--, except that the D antigen is not elevated to the same degree. D•• red cells may be agglutinated weakly by some examples of sera from immunized Rh-deletion persons if the serum sample contains anti-Rh47 in addition to anti-Rh17.[29] Rh47 is a high-incidence antigen encoded by the *RHCE* gene and thus, will be absent from D-- red cells. Another distinguishing characteristic of D•• red cells is that they possess the low-incidence antigen Rh37 (Evans). These rare phenotypes have been shown to arise from the duplication of large portions of *RHD* with the concomitant loss of *RHCE* sequence.[19]

Rh Antibodies in a Patient's Serum

Except for some non-red-cell-stimulated examples of anti-E, anti-C^w, and antibodies to rare low-incidence antigens, most Rh antibodies result from exposure to human red cells through pregnancy or transfusion. D is the most potent immunogen, followed by c and E. Although a few examples of Rh antibodies behave as saline agglutinins, most react best in high-protein, antiglobulin, or enzyme test systems. Even sera containing potent saline-reactive anti-D are usually reactive at higher dilutions in antiglobulin testing. Some workers find enzyme techniques especially useful for detecting weak or developing Rh antibodies.

Detectable antibody usually persists for many years. If serum antibody levels fall below detectable thresholds, subsequent exposure to the antigen characteristically produces a rapid secondary immune response. With exceedingly rare exceptions, Rh antibodies do not bind complement when they combine with their antigens, at least to the extent recognizable by techniques currently used.

Dosage Effect

Anti-D seldom shows any difference in reactivity between red cells from individuals homozygous or heterozygous for *RHD*, but D expression seems to vary somewhat with the accompanying alleles of the genotype. For example, red cells from a *DcE/DcE* individual carry more D antigen sites than red cells from a *DCe/DCe* person and may show higher titration scores with anti-D. Dosage effects can sometimes be demonstrated with some antibodies directed at the E, c, and e antigens and, occasionally, at the C antigen. Quantifying the antigen sites requires specialized techniques such as radioisotope labeling, flow cytometry, immunoferritin localization, or automated procedures.

Concomitant Antibodies

Some Rh antibodies tend to occur in concert. For example, the *DCe/DCe* person manifesting immune anti-E has almost certainly been exposed to c as well as E. Anti-c may be present in addition to anti-E, although substantially weaker and possibly undetectable at the time the anti-E is found, and transfusion of seemingly compatible E–c+ blood may elicit an immediate or somewhat delayed hemolytic reaction. Generally, it is not a sound practice to select donor blood that is negative for all or most of the antigens absent from the recipient's cells when antibody has not been detected, but some practitioners feel that the *DCe/DCe* recipient with detectable anti-E is a case that merits special consideration. Because anti-c occurs frequently with anti-E in immunized people whose red cells are E-negative and c-negative,[36] some practitioners select blood of the patient's own Rh phenotype for transfusion even when the presence of anti-c cannot be demonstrated by test procedures routinely used. Anti-E less consistently accompanies anti-c, as the patient can easily have been exposed to c without being exposed to E. There is little clinical value in pursuing anti-E in serum known to contain anti-c, as the vast majority of c-negative donor blood will be negative for the E antigen.

Rh Typing Tests

Routine Rh typing for donors and patients involves only the D antigen, and techniques to demonstrate weak D are required by AABB *Standards* only for donor blood.[30(p31,58)] Tests for the other Rh antigens are performed only for defined purposes, such as identifying unexpected Rh antibodies, obtaining compatible blood for a patient with an Rh antibody, investigating disputed parentage or other family studies, selecting a panel of phenotyped cells for antibody identification, or evaluating whether a person is likely to be homozygous or heterozygous for *RHD*.

In finding compatible blood for a recipient with a comparatively weak Rh antibody, tests with potent blood typing reagents more reliably confirm the absence of antigen than mere demonstration of a compatible crossmatch. Testing the patient's phenotype may provide confirmation of the antibody specificity and suggest which other Rh antibodies could also be present.

Routine Testing for D

Until recently, high-protein anti-D reagents of human polyclonal origin that were suitable for slide, tube, or microplate tests were used for most routine testing. More recently, monoclonal anti-D reagents have become widely available. Tests may employ red cells suspended in saline, in serum, or in plasma, but permissible test conditions should be confirmed by reading the manufacturer's directions before use. Recommended test procedures may vary somewhat among manufacturers.

Slide tests produce optimal results only when a high concentration of red cells and protein are combined at a temperature of 37 C. Because the slide test must be read within 2 minutes, the red cells and serum on the glass slide must reach 37 C quickly. The viewing surface used to perform slide tests should be kept lighted at all times to maintain a temperature of 45-50 C, permitting rapid warming of the test mixture. The slide test has the serious disadvantage that drying of the reaction mixture can cause the red cells to aggregate, which may be misinterpreted as agglutination. There are also greater biohazard risks associated with increased potential for spillage of the specimen during manipulation. Procedures for microplate tests are similar to those for tube tests, but very light suspensions of red cells are used. Representative procedures for tube, slide, and microplate tests are given in Methods 2.6, 2.7, and 2.8.

If there is an indication to test for weak D, an antiglobulin test should be performed (Method 2.9). A reliable test for weak D expression cannot be performed on a slide. Red cells with weak D, if they are agglutinated at all on a slide test, will invariably exhibit weaker agglutination than that seen with normal D-positive cells. This distinction may not be recognized, however, especially if the reagent has high potency and avidity, unless normal D-positive cells and weak-D cells are tested in parallel and results compared.

High-Protein Reagents

Some anti-D reagents designated for use in slide, rapid tube, or microplate tests contain high concentrations of protein (20-24%) and other macromolecular additives. Such reagents are nearly always prepared from pools of human sera and give rapid reliable results when used in accordance with manufacturers' directions.

Because the macromolecular medium may cause red cells coated with immunoglobulin to aggregate spontaneously, antisera with these additives may produce false-positive reactions. A false-positive result due to spontaneous aggregation could cause a D-negative patient to receive D-positive blood and become immunized. To detect this kind of spurious result when the reagent has high-protein formulation, the red cells must be simultaneously tested with an immunologically inert reagent, identical in formulation to the anti-D in use but lacking the antibody component. If red cells exhibit aggregation in the control test, the results of the anti-D test cannot be considered valid. In most cases the presence or absence of D can be determined with other reagents, as detailed later in this chapter.

The Control for High-Protein Reagents

High-protein reagents may give false-positive results in several other circumstances. Factors in the patient's serum may affect the test if the test is performed on unwashed red cells suspended in the patient's own serum or plasma. Strong autoagglutinins, abnormal serum proteins that promote rouleaux formation, or antibodies directed at an additive in the reagent may cause aggregation that can be mistaken for agglutination by anti-D. The best way to detect possibly invalid reactions is to use, as the immunologically inert control, the diluent used to manufacture the particular anti-D reagent. This material will contain all the additives present in the reagent except for the active antibody. It should, therefore, potentiate spontaneous aggregation to the same degree as the active anti-D.

Manufacturers offer their individual diluent formulations for use as control reagents; if patients' red cells are typed with high-protein reagents, the tests must be controlled with this material. The nature and concentration of additives differ significantly among reagents from different manufacturers. The control reagent from one manufacturer may not produce the same pattern of false-positive reactions as that of another; tests on patients' cells must use a control suitable for the testing procedure. Using 22% or 30% bovine albumin detects even fewer false positives because reagent solutions of bovine albumin lack the other high-molecular-weight potentiators that manufacturers use in high-protein reagents.

Misleading Results with High-Protein Reagents

False Positives. False-positive test results with high-protein reagents include:

1. Cellular aggregation resulting from immunoglobulin coating of the patient's red cells or serum factors that induce rouleaux will give positive results in both the active and the control tubes. Serum factors can be eliminated by thoroughly washing the red cells (with warm saline if cold agglutinins are present or suspected) and retesting the washed red cells. The original high-protein reagent may be used concurrently with a new control tube, if the manufacturer's directions state that the product is suitable for use with saline-suspended cells. If the cells in the control test remain unagglutinated and the anti-D test gives a positive result, the red cells are D-positive. If agglutination still occurs in the control tube, the most likely explanation is immunoglobulin coating of the red cells, which may then be tested with a saline-reactive reagent.

2. Rouleaux, simulating agglutination, may occur if red cells and anti-D are incubated together too long before the test is read. Aggregation may occur rapidly, particularly on a warm slide on which evaporation causes drying, which further increases the protein concentration of the reaction mixture. It is important to follow the manufacturer's recommendation to interpret the test within a limited period, usually no more than 2 minutes.

False Negatives. False-negative test results with high-protein reagents include:

1. Too heavy a red cell suspension in the tube test or too weak a suspension in the slide test may weaken agglutination. To achieve the 40-50% cell suspension required for slide testing, it may be necessary to centrifuge blood from a severely anemic patient and remove some of the plasma before testing the red cells.

2. Saline-suspended red cells may react poorly with some Rh reagents and must not be used for slide testing.

3. Red cells possessing weakly expressed D antigen may not react well within the 2-minute limit of the slide test or upon immediate centrifugation in the tube test.

Low-Protein Reagents

The low-protein, saline-reactive Rh reagents in current use are formulated predominantly with monoclonal antibodies. Immunoglobulin-coated red cells can usually be successfully typed with low-protein Rh reagents that contain saline-agglutinating antibodies and no additives that promote spontaneous cellular aggregation. If such additives are present, the fact should be stated in the "Reagent Description" section of the manufacturer's directions.

Monoclonal Source Anti-D

Monoclonal anti-D reagents are made predominantly from human IgM antibodies, which require no potentiators and agglutinate most D-positive red cells from adults and infants in a saline system. Monoclonal anti-D reagents usually promote reactions stronger than those with polyclonal IgG reagents, but they may fail to agglutinate red cells of some partial-D categories. Adding small amounts of polyclonal anti-D to the monoclonal antibodies provides a reagent that will react with partial-D red cells in antiglobulin tests. Just the right amount of polyclonal material must be added. If the reagent contains too much polyclonal material, IgG molecules may attach to the D sites and block the reactivity of the monoclonal IgM component. If there is too little polyclonal anti-D, the reagent may fail to detect partial D.

Licensed monoclonal/polyclonal blends can be used by all routine typing methods and are as satisfactory as high-protein reagents in antiglobulin tests for weak D. False-negative findings can result, however, if tests using monoclonal reagents are incubated in excess of a manufacturer's product directions. These reagents, prepared in a low-protein medium, can be used to test red cells with a positive DAT, provided those tests are not subjected to antiglobulin testing.

Control for Low-Protein Reagents

Most monoclonal/polyclonal blended reagents have a total protein concentration approximating that of human serum. False-positive reactions due to spontaneous aggregation of immunoglobulin-coated red cells occur no more often with this kind of reagent than with other saline-reactive reagents. False-positive reactions may occur in any saline-reactive test system if the serum contains cold autoagglutinins or a protein imbalance causing rouleaux and the red cells are tested unwashed. It is seldom necessary to perform a separate control test, however. Absence of spontaneous aggregation can usually be demonstrated by observing absence of agglutination by anti-A and/or anti-B in the cell tests for ABO. For red cell specimens that show agglutination in all tubes (ie, give the reactions of group AB, D-positive), a concurrent control must be performed on the patients' cells; this is not required when donors' cells are tested. A

suitable control is to centrifuge a suspension of the patient's red cells with autologous serum or with 6-8% bovine albumin at the same time the anti-D test is centrifuged. If the test is one of several requiring incubation before centrifugation, any negative result on a test performed concurrently serves as an adequate control. A separate control tube would be required only for a red cell specimen that gives positive reactions with all the Rh reagents, ie, is typed as D+C+E+c+e+.

Testing for D in Hemolytic Disease of the Newborn

Because red cells from an infant suffering from HDN are coated with immunoglobulin, a saline-reactive reagent is usually necessary for Rh testing. Occasionally, the infant's red cells may be so heavily coated with antibody that all antigen sites are occupied, leaving none available to react with a saline-reactive antibody of appropriate specificity. This "blocking" phenomenon should be suspected if the infant's cells have a strongly positive DAT and are not agglutinated by a saline-reactive reagent of the same specificity as the maternal antibody.

Anti-D is the specificity responsible for nearly all cases of blocking by maternal antibody. It is usually possible to obtain correct typing results with a saline anti-D after 45 C elution of the maternal antibody from the cord red cells. (See Method 2.12.) Elution liberates enough antigen sites to permit red cell typing, but must be performed cautiously because overexposure to heat may denature or destroy Rh antigens.

Tests for Antigens Other Than D

Reagents are readily available to test for the other principal Rh antigens: C, E, c, and e. These are formulated as either low-protein (usually monoclonal or monoclonal/polyclonal blends) or high-protein reagents. High-protein reagents of any specificity have the same problems with false-positive results as high-protein anti-D and require a comparable control test.

Observation of a negative result in the control test for anti-D does not determine the tests for other Rh antigens because results with anti-D are usually obtained after immediate centrifugation; tests for the other Rh antigens are generally incubated at 37 C before centrifugation. A valid control procedure must be performed concurrently with the test, using the same duration and conditions of incubation, and must be interpreted simultaneously with the actual test.

Rh reagents may give weak or negative reactions with red cells possessing variant antigens. This is especially likely to happen if anti-e is used to test the red cells from Blacks, among whom variants of e are relatively common. It is impossible to obtain anti-e reagents that react strongly and consistently with the various qualitative and quantitative variants of e. Variable reactivity with anti-C reagents may occur if the *DCE* or *CE* haplotypes are responsible for the expression of C on red cells. Variant E and c antigens have been reported but are considerably less common.

Whatever reagents are used, the manufacturer's directions must be carefully followed. The indirect antiglobulin technique must not be used unless the manufacturer's instructions state explicitly that the reagent is suitable for this use. The pools of human sera used to prepare reagents for the other Rh antigens have a significant risk of containing antiglobulin-reactive, "contaminating" specificities. Positive and negative controls should be tested in parallel with the red cells under study. Red cells selected for the positive control should be known to have a single dose of the antigen concerned or be known to show weak reactivity with the reagent. If these reagents are used regularly, they should be included in the routine quality assurance program.

Additional Considerations in Rh Testing

The following limitations are common to all Rh typing procedures, including those performed with high-protein reagents.

False-Positive Reactions

The following circumstances can produce false-positive red cell typing results.

1. The wrong reagent was inadvertently used.
2. An unsuspected antibody of another specificity was present in the reagent. Antibodies for antigens having an incidence of less than 1% in the population may occasionally be present and cause false-positive reactions, even when the manufacturer's directions are followed. Though the antigens occur infrequently, antibodies to them are comparatively common, even in persons with no history of pregnancy or transfusions.

   For crucial determinations, many workers routinely perform replicate tests, using reagents from different sources. This reduces the likelihood of a false classification because discrepant reactions would alert the serologist to the need for further testing. Replicate testing is not an absolute safeguard, however, because reagents from different manufacturers may not necessarily be derived from different sources. The scarcity of donors or of clones producing acceptable titers of such relatively uncommon specificities as anti-C and anti-e, in particular, may cause the same source of raw material to be used by several manufacturers. Different manufacturers' reagents prepared from the same polyclonal source material may, in fact, contain the same "contaminating" antibody.

3. Polyagglutinable red cells may be agglutinated by any reagent containing human serum. Although antibodies that agglutinate these surface-altered red cells are present in most adult human sera, polyagglutinins in reagents very rarely cause problems. Aging, dilution, and various steps in the manufacturing process tend to eliminate these predominantly IgM antibodies.

4. Autoagglutinins and abnormal proteins in the patient's serum may cause false-positive reactions when unwashed red cells are tested.

5. Reagent vials may become contaminated with bacteria, with foreign substances, or with reagent from another vial. This can be prevented by the use of careful technique and the periodic inspection of the vials' contents. Bacterial contamination may not, however, cause recognizable turbidity because the refractive index of bacteria is similar to that of high-protein reagents.

False-Negative Reactions

The following circumstances can produce false-negative red cell typing results.

1. The wrong reagent was inadvertently used.

2. The reagent was not added to the tube, either because of oversight or because the drops of fluid ran down the outside of the tube. It is good practice to add serum to all the tubes before adding the red cells and any enhancement medium.

3. A specific reagent failed to react with a variant form of the antigen.

4. A reagent that contains antibody directed predominantly at a *cis*-product Rh antigen failed to give a reliably detectable reaction with red cells carrying the individual antigens as separate gene products. This occurs most often with anti-C sera.

5. The reagent was used incorrectly because the manufacturer's directions were not followed.

6. The red cell button was shaken so roughly during resuspension that small agglutinates were dispersed.

7. Contamination, improper storage, or outdating cause antibody activity to deteriorate. Chemically modified IgG antibody appears to be particularly susceptible to destruction by proteolytic enzymes produced by certain bacteria.

References

1. Race RR. The Rh genotypes and Fisher's theory. Blood 1948; special issue 2:27-42.
2. Levine P, Stetson RE. An unusual case of intragroup agglutination. JAMA 1939;113:126-7.
3. Landsteiner K, Wiener AS. An agglutinable factor in human blood recognized by immune sera for rhesus blood. Proc Soc Exp Biol NY 1940;43:223.
4. Levine P, Katzin EM. Isoimmunization in pregnancy and the variety of isoagglutinins observed. Proc Soc Exp Biol NY 1940;43:343-6.
5. Wiener AS, Peters HR. Hemolytic reactions following transfusions of blood of the homologous group, with three cases in which the same agglutinogen was responsible. Ann Intern Prn Med 1940;13:2306-22.
6. Daniels GL, Anstee DJ, Cartron JP, et al. Terminology for red cell surface antigens: Makuhari report. Vox Sang 1996;71:246-8.
7. Reid ME, Lomas-Francis C. The blood group antigen factsbook. London: Academic Press, 1997.
8. Wiener AS. Genetic theory of the Rh blood types. Proc Soc Exp Biol Med 1943;54:316-9.
9. Fisher RA, Race RR. Rh gene frequencies in Britain. Nature 1946;157:48-9.
10. Tippett P. A speculative model for the Rh blood groups. Ann Hum Genet 1986;50:241-7.
11. Colin Y, Chérif-Zahar B, Le Van Kim C, et al. Genetic basis of RhD-positive and RhD-negative blood group polymorphisms as determined by southern analysis. Blood 1991;78:2747-52.
12. Aere MA, Thomson ES, Wagner S, et al. Molecular cloning of RhD cDNA derived from a gene present in RhD-positive, but not RhD-negative individuals. Blood 1993;82:651-5.
13. Daniels G, Green C, Smart E. Differences between RhD-negative Africans and RhD-negative Europeans. Lancet 1997;350:862-3.
14. Mouro I, Colin Y, Chérif-Zahar B, et al. Molecular genetic basis of the human Rhesus blood group system. Nat Genet 1993;5:62-5.
15. Anstee DJ, Tanner MJA. Biochemical aspects of the blood group Rh (Rhesus) antigens. Baillieres Clin Haematol 1993;6:401-22.
16. Cartron JP. Defining the Rh blood group antigens. Biochemistry and molecular genetics. Blood Rev 1994;8:199-212.
17. Smythe JS, Avent ND, Judson PA, et al. Expression of *RHD* and *RHCE* gene products using retroviral transduction of K562 cells establishes the molecular basis of Rh blood group antigens. Blood 1996;87:2968-73.
18. Ridgwell K, Spurr NK, Laguda B, et al. Isolation of cDNA clones for a 50 kDa glycoprotein of the human erythrocyte membrane associated with Rh (rhesus) blood-group antigen expression. Biochem J 1992;287:223-8.
19. Huang CH. Molecular insights into the Rh protein family and associated antigens. Curr Opin Hematol 1997;4:94-103.

20. Daniels G, Lomas-Francis C, Wallace M, Tippett P. Epitopes of RhD: Serology and molecular genetics. In: Silberstein LE, ed. Molecular and functional aspects of blood group antigens. Bethesda, MD: American Association of Blood Banks, 1995:193-228.
21. Rosenfield RE, Allen FH Jr, Swisher SN, Kochwa S. A review of Rh serology and presentation of a new terminology. Transfusion 1962;2:287-312.
22. Lawler SD, Race RR. Quantitative aspects of Rh antigens. Proceedings of the International Society of Hematology 1950:168-70.
23. Tippett P, Lomas-Francis C, Wallace M. The Rh antigen D: Partial D antigens and associated low incidence antigens. Vox Sang 1996;70:123-31.
24. Lomas C, Tippett P, Thompson KM, et al. Demonstration of seven epitopes of the Rh antigen D using monoclonal anti-D antibodies and red cells from D categories. Vox Sang 1989;57:261-4.
25. Jones J, Scott ML, Voak D. Monoclonal anti-D specificity and Rh D structure: Criteria for selection of monoclonal anti-D reagents for routine typing of patients and donors. Transfus Med 1995;5:171-84.
26. Chang TY, Siegel DL. Genetic and immunological properties of phage-displayed human anti-Rh(D) antibodies: Implications for Rh(D) epitope topology. Blood 1998;91:3066-78.
27. Schmidt PJ, Morrison EG, Shohl J. The antigenicity of the Rh_0 D^u blood factor. Blood 1962;20:196-202.
28. Van Loghem JJ. Production of Rh agglutinins anti-C and anti-E by artificial immunization of volunteer donors. Br Med J 1947;ii:958-9.
29. Daniels G. Human blood groups. Oxford: Blackwell Scientific Publications, 1995.
30. Menitove JE, ed. Standards for blood banks and transfusion services, 19th ed. Bethesda, MD: American Association of Blood Banks, 1999.
31. Chérif-Zahar B, Raynal V, Gane P, et al. Candidate gene acting as a suppressor of the RH locus in most cases of Rh-deficiency. Nat Genet 1996;12:168-73.
32. Huang C-H. The human Rh50 glycoprotein gene. J Biol Chem 1998;273:2207-13.
33. Hyland CA, Chérif-Zahar B, Cowley N, et al. A novel single missense mutation identified along the RH50 gene in a composite heterozygous Rh_{null} blood donor of the regulator type. Blood 1998;91:1458-63.
34. Connor J, Bar-Eli M, Gillum KD, Schroit AJ. Evidence for a structurally homologous Rh-like polypeptide in Rh_{null} erythrocytes. J Biol Chem 1992;267:26050-55.
35. Huang C-H, Chen Y, Reid ME, Seidl C. Rh_{null} dissease: The amorph type results from a novel double mutation in RhCe gene on D-negative background. Blood 1998;92:664-71.
36. Shirey RS, Edwards RE, Ness PM. The risk of alloimmunization to c (Rh4) in R_1R_1 patients who present with anti-E. Transfusion 1994;34:756-8.

Suggested Reading

Agre P, Cartron JP. Molecular biology of the Rh antigens. Blood 1991;78:551-3.

Cartron JP. Defining the Rh blood group antigens. Blood Rev 1994;8:199-212.

Issitt PD. An invited review: The Rh antigen e, its variants, and some closely related serological observations. Immunohematology 1991;7:29-36.

Issitt PD. The Rh blood group. In: Garratty G, ed. Immunology of transfusion medicine. New York: Marcel Dekker, 1994:111-47.

Issitt PD. The Rh blood group system 1988: Eight new antigens in nine years and some observations on the biochemistry and genetics of the system. Transfus Med Rev 1989;3:1-12.

Issitt PD, Anstee DJ. Applied blood group serology, 4th edition. Durham, NC: Montgomery Scientific Press, 1998.

Moulds JJ. Rh_{nulls}: Amorphs and regulators. In: Walker RH, ed. A seminar on recent advances in immunohematology. Washington, DC: American Association of Blood Banks, 1973:63-82.

Race RR, Sanger R. Blood groups in man. 6th ed. Oxford: Blackwell Scientific Publications, 1968.

Reid ME, Ellisor SS, Frank BA. Another potential source of error in Rh-Hr typing. Transfusion 1975;15:485-8.

Reid ME, Lomas-Francis C. The blood group antigen factsbook. London: Academic Press, 1997.

Sonneborn H-H, Voak D, eds. A review of 50 years of the Rh blood group system. Biotest Bulletin 1997;5(4): 389-528.

Vengelen-Tyler V, Pierce S, eds. Blood group systems: Rh. Arlington, VA: American Association of Blood Banks, 1987.

White WD, Issitt CH, McGuire D. Evaluation of the use of albumin controls in Rh typing. Transfusion 1974;14:67-71.

15

Other Blood Groups

IN ADDITION TO THE ANTIGENS discussed in Chapters 13 and 14, over 200 others are located on red cells, and some are found on other cells or in body fluids. For example, blood group antigens on CD44, CR1 (CD35), and decay accelerating factor or DAF (CD55) molecules are expressed on a broad range of hematopoietic cells.[1] HLA system antigens (see Chapter 17), only occasionally detected on red cells, are present on most other human cells. HPA system antigens are found on the surface of platelets (see Chapter 16). This chapter briefly reviews all the blood group systems. The reader is referred to other texts for more detail on a particular blood group.

Distribution of Antigens

Antigens present in almost all persons are known as high-incidence or public antigens. Others, of very low incidence, are sometimes called private antigens. Antigens that occur as codominant traits, especially pairs such as Jk^a and Jk^b, have more variable incidence and may differ in ethnic groups. For example, the Duffy glycoprotein is known to be a receptor for the parasite *Plasmodium vivax*, one of the causative agents of malaria. In West Africa, where malaria is endemic, the Fy(a–b–) red cell phenotype, very rare in Whites, occurs with an incidence of greater than 80%.

Each of the known antigens described in this chapter was initially identified through the detection of its specific antibody in a serum. Tables listing phenotype frequencies among Whites and Blacks in the US population are given throughout this chapter. Fre-

Table 15-1. Membrane Component and Chromosomal Assignment of the Human RBC Blood Group Systems

ISBT Number	Blood Group	RBC Membrane Component	Chromosome Location
001	ABO	Anion exchanger (AE-1), protein 4.5, lipids	9q34.1-q34.2
002	MNS	M,N: glycophorin A S,s: glycophorin B	4q28-q31
003	P	Glycolipid	22q11.2-qter
004	Rh	Rh proteins	1p36.13-p34.3
005	Lutheran	Lutheran glycoprotein	19q12-q13
006	Kell	Kell protein	7q33
007	Lewis	Type 2 oligosaccharides	19p13.3
008	Duffy	Chemokine receptor	1q22-q23
009	Kidd	Urea transporter	18q11-q12
010	Diego	AE-1	17q12-q21
011	Yt	Acetylcholinesterase	7q22
012	Xg	Xg glycoprotein	Xp22.32
013	Scianna	Scianna protein	1p36.2-p22.1
014	Dombrock	Dombrock glycoprotein	Unknown
015	Colton	CHIP 28 (aquaporin)	7p14
016	LW	LW glycoprotein	19p13.2-cen
017	Chido/Rodgers	C4	6p21.3
018	Hh	AE-1, protein 4.5, lipids	19q13.3
019	Kx	Kx protein	Xp21.1
020	Gerbich	Glycophorin C and D	2q14-q21
021	Cromer	Decay accelerating factor (CD55)	1q32
022	Knops	CR1 (CD35)	1q32
023	Indian	CD44	11p13
024	OK	CD147	19pter-p13.2
025	RAPH	Unknown	11p15.5

quencies among other groups in the population are not given as data are scanty and wide differences between groups of diverse Asian or Native American origins make generalizations about phenotypes inappropriate. Table 15-1 lists the blood group systems, as defined by the International Society of Blood Transfusion (ISBT) working party on blood group terminology, and their gene location.[2-4] Table 15-2 shows the serologic behavior and characteristics of the major blood group antibodies derived from human sources.

The MNS System

M, N, S, s, and U Antigens

The MNS system is a complex system of 40 antigens carried on two glycophorin molecules or hybrid molecules of the two proteins. The M, N,

Table 15-2. Serologic Behavior of the Principal Antibodies of Different Blood Group Systems

Antibody	In-Vitro Hemolysis	Saline 4 C	Saline 22 C	Albumin 37 C	Albumin AGT	Papain/Ficin 37 C	Papain/Ficin AGT	Associated With HDN*	Associated With HTR†
Anti-M	0	Most	Some	Few	Few	0	0	Few	Few
Anti-N	0	Most	Few	Occ.	Occ.	0	0	Rare	No
Anti-S	0	Few	Some	Some	Most	See text		Yes	Yes
Anti-s	0	No	Few	Few	Most	See text		Yes	Yes
Anti-U	0	No	Occ.	Some	Most	Most	Most	Yes	Yes
Anti-Lu^a	0	Some	Most	Few	Few	Few	Few	No	No
Anti-Lu^b	0	Few	Few	Few	Most	Few	Few	Mild	Yes
Anti-K	0		Few	Some	Most	Some	Most	Yes	Yes
Anti-k	0		Few	Few	Most	Some	Most	Yes	Yes
Anti-Kp^a	0		Some	Some	Most	Some	Most	Yes	Yes
Anti-Kp^b	0		Few	Few	Most	Some	Most	Yes	Yes
Anti-Js^a	0		Few	Few	Most	Few	Most	Yes	Yes
Anti-Js^b	0		0	0	Most	Few	Most	Yes	Yes
Anti-Fy^a	0		Rare	Rare	Most	0	0	Yes	Yes
Anti-Fy^b	0		Rare	Rare	Most	0	0	Yes	Yes
Anti-Jk^a	Some		Few	Few	Most	Some	Yes	Mild	Yes
Anti-Jk^b	Some		Few	Few	Most	Some	Most	Mild	Yes
Anti-Xg^a	0		Few	Few	Most	0	0	No report	
Anti-Di^a	0		Some	Some	Most	Some	Some	Yes	Yes
Anti-Di^b	0				Most	Some	Some	Yes	Yes
Anti-Yt^a	0		0	0	Most	0	Some	No	No
Anti-Yt^b	0				All			No report	
Anti-Do^a	0		0	0	Some	Some	Most	No	Yes
Anti-Do^b	0				All		All	No report	
Anti-Co^a	0		0	0	Some	Some	Most	Yes	Yes
Anti-Co^b	0		0	0	Some	Some	Most	No report	
Anti-Sc1	0				All			No report	
Anti-Sc2	0		Some	Some	Most	Most	Most	No report	

*Hemolytic disease of the newborn.
†Hemolytic transfusion reaction.
Occ.=Occasionally
The reactivity shown in the table is based on the tube methods in common use. If tests are carried out by more sensitive test procedures (such as in capillary tubes, in microtiter plates, or by the albumin layering method), direct agglutination (prior to the antiglobulin phase) may be observed more often with some antibodies. Blank spaces indicate a lack of sufficient data for generalization about antibody behavior.

S, s, and U antigens are the most important antigens of the MNS system with regard to transfusion medicine. They have also been important to our understanding of biochemistry and genetics. The M and N antigens are located on glycophorin A (GPA). The S, s, and U antigens are located on glycophorin B (GPB). Table 15-3 shows the frequencies of the common phenotypes of the MNS system. There is considerable linkage disequilibrium between M, N and S, s. The gene complex producing N with s is much more common than that producing N with S. Even though the M and N antigens are encoded by *GYPA* and the S and s antigens are encoded by *GYPB*, the two genes are in very close proximity on chromosome 4.[5]

Red cells that lack S and s may be negative for a high-incidence antigen called U; persons who lack U may make anti-U when exposed to U-positive red cells. Some S–s– red cells have a variant GPB. These red cells may appear to lack U but possess other antigens on glycophorin B, which may be detectable by adsorption-elution studies or in tests using well-characterized anti-U sera and polyethylene glycol (PEG).

Low-Incidence Antigens of the MNS System

The MNS system includes a number of low-incidence antigens. Recent biochemical data attribute the reactivity of various low-incidence determinants to one or more amino acid substitutions; variation in the extent or type of glycosylation; or the existence of a hybrid SGP. Unexpected phenotyping results may occur when variants of the MNS antigens are present. For example, the M^g (MNS11) antigen, product of a rare allele at the *MN* locus, reacts neither with anti-M nor with anti-N reagents. The red cells of a person with the genotype M^gN will give the reactions M–N+, leading to the false conclusion that the genotype is actually *NN*. Similarly, the red cells of a person of the genotype M^gM will give the reactions M+N–. Parentage can be falsely excluded if persons with M^gM or M^gN genotypes are interpreted as being *MM* or *NN*, respectively. Many antibodies to low-incidence antigens occur as a saline agglutinin in sera from persons who have no known exposure to human red cells. The rarity of these antigens makes it unlikely that they will be detected if present.

Biochemistry of the MNS System

Antigens of the MNS system are carried on GPA and GPB, which are single-pass transmembrane glycoproteins. The carboxyl (C) terminus of each glycophorin extends into the cytoplasm of the red cell, while a hydrophobic segment consisting of 23 amino acids is em-

Table 15-3. Phenotypes and Frequencies in the MNS System

| Reactions with Anti- | | | | | | Phenotype Frequency (%) | |
M	N	S	s	U	Phenotype	Whites	Blacks
+	0				M+N–	28	26
+	+				M+N+	50	44
0	+				M–N+	22	30
		+	0	+	S+s–U+	11	3
		+	+	+	S+s+U+	44	28
		0	+	+	S–s+U+	45	69
		0	0	0	S–s–U–	0	Less than 1
		0	0	(+)	S–s–U+w	0	Rare[†]

[†] May not be detected by some antisera and are listed as U–.

bedded within the lipid bilayer. An amino (N) terminal segment extends into the extracellular environment. The molecules are sensitive to cleavage at varying positions by certain proteases. (See Fig 15-1.)

There are approximately 1,000,000 copies of GPA per red cell. M and N blood group antigen activity resides on the extracellular segment, a sequence of 72 amino acids with carbohydrate side chains attached within the first 50 residues of the amino terminus. When GPA carries M antigen activity (GPA^M), the first amino acid residue is serine and the fifth is glycine. When it carries N antigen activity (GPA^N), leucine and glutamic acid replace serine and glycine at positions one and five, respectively. (See Table 15-4.)

Red cells that lack most or all of GPA are described as En(a–). These rare En(a–) individuals may produce antibodies (collectively called anti-En^a) that react with various portions of the extracellular part of the glycoprotein. Some En(a–) persons may produce an antibody against an antigen called Wr^b. Wr^b arises from an interaction between GPA and the anion exchange molecule, AE-1 (also known as band 3). In the absence of GPA (residues 62-76), Wr^b is not expressed and the antibody, anti-Wr^b, is virtually indistinguishable from anti-En^a unless Wr(b–) cells are tested. The gene that encodes Wr^b polymorphism is independent of those of the MNS system. The polymorphism that gives rise to both the Wr^a and Wr^b antigens exists on AE-1.[6] These antigens are part of the Diego system.

GPB is a smaller protein than GPA, and there are fewer copies per red cell. Approximately 200,000 copies of this molecule are present. GPB carries S, s, and probably U antigens. The N-terminal 26 amino acids of GPB

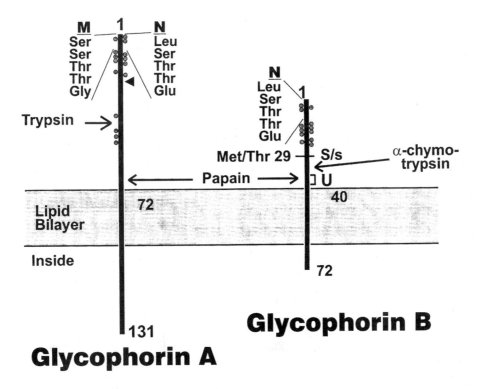

Figure 15-1. Schematic diagram of glycophorin A and glycophorin B. The amino acid sequences that determine M, N, S and s are given. ● indicates an *O*-linked oligosaccharide side chain, ◀ indicates an *N*-linked polysaccharide side chain. Approximate locations of protease cleavage sites are indicated. (Courtesy New York Blood Center)

are identical to the sequence of GPA^N, which accounts for the presence of an N antigen (known as 'N') on all red cells of normal MNS types. Red cells that lack GPB altogether lack not only S, s, and U activity but also 'N'. Immunized individuals of the rare M+N–S–s–U– phenotype can produce anti-N (anti-U/GPB). This antibody will react with all red cells of normal MNS types, whether N-positive or N-negative, and should be considered clinically significant. GPB that expresses S activity has methionine at position 29; GPB with s activity has threonine at that position. (See Fig 15-1.)

The Effect of Proteolytic Enzymes on MNS Antigens

Proteolytic enzymes, such as ficin or papain, cleave red cell membrane sialoglycoproteins (SGPs) at well-defined sites. Reactivity with anti-M and anti-N is abolished by commonly used enzyme techniques. The effect of different enzymes on the expression of MNS system antigens reflects the point at which the particular enzyme cleaves the antigen-bearing SGP and the position of the antigen relative to the cleavage site. (See Fig 15-1 and Table 15-2.) Sensitivity of the antigens to proteases may help in the identification of antibodies to M and N antigens, but the effects of proteases on tests for

the S and s antigens are more variable. In addition, the S antigen is sensitive to trace amounts of chlorine bleach.[7]

Genes Encoding Glycophorins

The genes encoding the MNS system antigens are located on chromosome 4 at 4q28-q31. The gene that encodes GPA is called *GYPA* and the gene that encodes GPB is *GYPB*. The similarities in amino acid sequences of GPA and GPB suggest that both genes derive from a common ancestral gene. *GYPA* and *GYPB* consist of seven and five exons, respectively. The genes share >95% identity. While the genes are highly homologous, *GYPB* results in a shorter protein because a point mutation at the 5' splicing site of the third intron prevents transcription of exon 3, called pseudo exon 3. Following the homologous sequences, *GYPA* and *GYPB* differ significantly in the 3' end sequences.

Hybrid Molecules

Pronounced SGP modifications occur in hybrid molecules that may arise from unequal crossing over or gene conversion between *GYPA* and *GYPB*. Such hybrids have occasionally been noted to carry low-incidence antigens that are due to novel amino acid sequences.

Table 15-4. Partial Structures of Sialoglycoproteins (SGPs) of Common and Variant MNS System Antigens

Antigen		Amino Acid Position								
		1	**2**	**3**	**4**	**5**				
M-active GPA		Ser	Ser*	Thr*	Thr*	Gly	– R			
N-active GPA		Leu	Ser*	Thr*	Thr*	Glu	– R			
'N'-active GPB		Leu	Ser*	Thr*	Thr*	Glu	– R			
		25	**26**	**27**	**28**	**29**	**30**			
S-active GPB	R –	Thr*	Asn	Gly	Glu	Met	Gly	– R		
s-active GPB	R –	Thr*	Asn	Gly	Glu	Thr	Gly	– R		

*=attachment site for *N*-glycan oligosaccharide.
R=rest of protein; Asn=asparagine; Glu=glutamic acid; Gly=glycine; Leu=leucine; Met=methionine; Ser=serine; Thr=threonine.

Hybrid SGPs may carry the amino-terminal portion of GPA and the carboxy-terminal portion of GPB, or vice versa. Other hybrids appear as a GPB molecule with a GPA insert or a GPA molecule with a GPB insert. The low-incidence antigens Hil (MNS20), St^a (MNS15), Dantu (MNS25), and Mur (MNS10), among others, are associated with hybrid SGPs. Some variants are found in specific ethnic groups. For example, the Dantu antigen occurs predominantly in Blacks, although the antigen is of low incidence.

Many of the MNS low-incidence antigens were categorized into a subsystem called the Miltenberger system, based on reactivity with selected sera. As more antigens have been identified and knowledge of the genetic events that give rise to these novel antigens has increased, it is clear that the Miltenberger subsystem is outdated. These antigens should simply be considered glycophorin variants. Many of the corresponding antibodies occur as non-red-cell-stimulated agglutinins, although occasional antiglobulin-reactive examples have been implicated in cases of hemolytic disease of the newborn (HDN).

MNS System Antibodies

The antibodies most commonly encountered are directed at the M, N, S, and s antigens.

Anti-M

Anti-M is detected frequently as a saline agglutinin if testing is done at room temperature. Anti-M is often found in the sera of persons who have had no exposure to human red cells. Although M antibodies are generally thought to be predominantly IgM, many examples that are partly or wholly IgG are frequently found. These antibodies are rarely clinically significant, however. Some examples of anti-M cause stronger agglutination if the pH of the test system is reduced to 6.5 and when testing red cell samples possessing a double dose expression of the M antigen. Examples that react at 37 C or at

the antiglobulin phase of testing and are of high titer should be considered potentially significant. Compatibility testing performed by a strictly prewarmed method (see Method 3.3) should eliminate the reactivity of most examples of anti-M. In a few exceptional cases, anti-M detectable at the antiglobulin phase has caused HDN or hemolysis of transfused cells.

Anti-N

Anti-N is comparatively rare. Examples are usually IgM and typically appear as weakly reactive cold agglutinins. Some powerful and potentially significant IgG examples have been observed in a few persons of the rare phenotypes M+N–S–s–U– and M+N–S–s–U+^{w} because these people lack or possess an altered form of GPB.

Antibodies to S, s, and U

Unlike anti-M and anti-N, antibodies to S, s, and U usually occur following red cell immunization. All are capable of causing hemolytic transfusion reactions (HTRs) and HDN. Although a few saline-reactive examples have been reported, antibodies to S, s, and U are usually detected in the antiglobulin phase of testing. Most investigators have found that papain or ficin destroys the reactivity of S-positive red cells with anti-S. Depending on the enzyme solution employed, the reactivity of anti-s with s-positive red cells is variable with enzymes. At low temperatures, rare examples of anti-S agglutinate ficin- or papain-treated red cells that are U-positive, irrespective of their S antigen status. If enzyme-treated S–U– cells are tested, however, no agglutination occurs. As a consequence, these examples of anti-S could be mistaken for anti-U in enzyme testing.[8] Most examples of anti-U react equally with untreated and ficin- or papain-treated red cells, but there have been examples of broadly reactive anti-U (anti-U/GPB), which detect an enzyme-sensitive determinant.

Anti-U is rare but should be considered when serum from a previously transfused or pregnant Black person contains antibody to a high-incidence antigen.

Kell System

Kell System Antigens

Kell system antigens are expressed on the red cell membrane in low density (K = 3500 sites, k = 2000-5000 sites) and are weakened or destroyed by treatment with reducing agents and with acid. The antigens are carried on one protein and encoded by a single gene. For an in-depth review, see Laird-Fryer, Daniels, and Levitt.[9]

K1 and K2

The K (K1) antigen was first identified in 1946 because of an antibody that caused HDN. The gene responsible (K) is present in 9% of Whites and approximately 2% of Blacks. The existence of the expected allele k (determining the antigen K2) was confirmed when an antithetical relationship was established between K and the antigen detected by anti-k. Anti-k reacts with the red cells of over 99% of all individuals.

Other Kell Blood Group Antigens

Other antithetical antigens of the Kell system include Kp^a (K3), Kp^b (K4), and Kp^c (K21); Js^a (K6) and Js^b (K7); K11 and K17; and K14 and K24. Not all theoretically possible genotype combinations have been recognized in the Kell system. For example, Kp^a and Js^a have never been found to have been produced by the same chromosome. Kp^a is an antigen found predominantly in Whites, and Js^a is found predominantly in Blacks. The haplotype producing K and Kp^a has also not been found. Table 15-5 shows some phenotypes of the Kell system. The table also includes K_o, a null phenotype in which the red cells lack all of the antigens of the Kell system.

Several high-incidence antigens have been assigned to the Kell system because the identifying antibodies were found nonreactive with K_o red cells. For simplicity, various Kell antigens of high and low incidence have not been included in the table.

Phenotypes with Depressed Kell Antigens

K_{mod} is an umbrella term used to describe phenotypes characterized by weak expression of Kell system antigens. Adsorption/elution tests are often necessary for their detection. The K_{mod}

Table 15-5. Some Phenotypes and Frequencies in the Kell System

| Reactions with Anti- | | | | | | | Frequency (%) | |
K	k	Kp^a	Kp^b	Js^a	Js^b	Phenotype	Whites	Blacks
+	0					K+k−	0.2	Rare
+	+					K+k+	8.8	2
0	+					K−k+	91.0	98
		+	0			Kp(a+b−)	Rare	0
		+	+			Kp(a+b+)	2.3	Rare
		0	+			Kp(a−b+)	97.7	100
				+	0	Js(a+b−)	0.0	1
				+	+	Js(a+b+)	Rare	19
				0	+	Js(a−b+)	100.0	80
0	0	0	0	0	0	K_0	Exceedingly rare	

phenotype is thought to arise through the inheritance of two recessive genes. Unlike McLeod red cells, K_{mod} red cells may exhibit elevated Kx antigen activity even greater than that on K_o cells.

Red cells of persons with some Gerbich-negative phenotypes also exhibit depressed Kell phenotypes (see the Gerbich system, later in this chapter). Persons of the Ge:−2,−3 and Ge:−2,−3,−4 (Leach) phenotypes have depression of at least some Kell system antigens.

The *Kp^a* gene weakens the expression of other Kell antigens when in *cis* position. For example, the k antigen of affected red cells reacts more weakly than expected and, with weaker examples of anti-k, may be interpreted as absent. The gene interaction can be recognized only under certain conditions, ie, when *K* is present on the opposite chromosome (*Kp^a* is in *cis* position with *k*) or when there is a K_o gene in *trans* position. If serologic tests are performed carefully, the *cis* modifying effect can also be seen when *Kp^a* is present on both chromosomes.

Biochemistry

The Kell system antigens are carried on a 93-kD single-pass red cell membrane protein. Kell system antigens are easily inactivated by treating red cells with sulfhydryl reagents such as 2-mercaptoethanol (2-ME), dithiothreitol (DTT), or 2-aminoethylisothiouronium bromide (AET). Such treatment is useful in preparing red cells that artificially lack Kell system antigens to aid in the identification of Kell-related antibodies. Treatment with sulfhydryl reagents may impair the reactivity of other antigens (LW^a, Do^a, Do^b, Yt, and others), however, so identification of an antibody as being associated with the Kell system because of reduced reactivity with sulfhydryl-treated red cells should only be tentative. As expected, Kell system antigens are also destroyed by ZZAP, a mixture of DTT and cysteine-activated papain. This susceptibility to

sulfhydryl reagents suggests that disulfide bonds are essential to maintain activity of the Kell system antigens. This hypothesis has been supported by the biochemical characterization of Kell proteins deduced from cloned DNA[10]; these exhibit a number of cysteine residues in the extracellular region. Cysteine readily forms disulfide bonds, which contribute to the folding of a protein. Antigens that reflect protein conformation will be susceptible to any agent that interferes with its tertiary structure. The 2.5-kb gene sequence that has been cloned predicts a 732 amino acid protein.

The function of the Kell protein is unknown, but it has structural similarities to a family of zinc-binding neutral endopeptidases. It has most similarity with the common acute lymphoblastic leukemia antigen (CALLA or CD10), a neutral endopeptidase on leukocytes.

The Kx Antigen, the McLeod Phenotype, and Their Relationship to the Kell System

The Kell protein interacts with the Kx protein.[11] Kx is encoded by *XK*, located on the short arm at Xp21. The normal X-linked allele encodes a 37-kD protein that carries the Kx antigen. Only trace amounts of Kx are found on red cells of normal Kell phenotypes, but elevated levels of Kx are present on K_o red cells. There seems to be a reciprocal relationship between Kx and Kell antigen expression.[11]

The McLeod Phenotype

Red cells that lack Kx exhibit not only markedly depressed expression of Kell system antigens but shortened survival, decreased permeability to water, and acanthocytic morphology. This constellation of red cell abnormalities is called the McLeod phenotype, after the first person in whom these observations were made. Persons with McLeod red cells also have a poorly defined abnormality of the neuromuscular system, characterized by persistently elevated serum levels of the enzyme creatine phosphokinase and, in older people, disordered muscular function. The McLeod phenotype arises through deletion and mutations of the *XK* locus of chromosome X. The biochemical origins of the molecular lesion responsible for the abnormalities of McLeod red cells are still unclear.

In a few instances, the McLeod phenotype has been found in patients with chronic granulomatous disease (CGD), in which granulocytes exhibit normal phagocytosis of microorganisms but inability to kill ingested pathogens. The McLeod phenotype associated with CGD appears to result from deletion of a part of the X chromosome that includes the *XK* locus as well as X-CGD. To date, only CGD McLeod males have produced anti-KL in response to red cell immunization. K_o donor units are not suitable for transfusion to these persons as K_o cells possess Kx, and anti-KL is a combination of anti-Kx and anti-Km. Non-CGD McLeod persons, however, make anti-Km and can be safely transfused with K_o blood.

Kell System Antibodies

Anti-K and Anti-k

Because the K antigen is strongly immunogenic, anti-K is frequently found in sera from transfused patients. Rare examples of anti-K have appeared as a saline agglutinin in sera from subjects never exposed to human red cells. Most examples are of immune origin and are reactive on antiglobulin testing; some bind complement.

Some workers have observed that examples of anti-K react less well in tests that incorporate low ionic strength saline (LISS) solutions (notably the Polybrene® test) than in saline tests or tests that include albumin. Others, however, have not shown differences in antibody reactivity, testing many examples of anti-K in low ionic systems. Anti-K has caused HTRs on numerous occasions, both immediate and delayed.

Because over 90% of donors are K negative, it is not difficult to find compatible blood for patients with anti-K. Anti-k has clinical and serologic characteristics similar to anti-K but occurs much less frequently. Only about one person in 500 lacks the k antigen and finding compatible blood is correspondingly more difficult.

Other Kell System Antibodies

Anti-Kp^a, anti-Kp^b, anti-Js^a, and anti-Js^b are all much less common than anti-K but show similar serologic characteristics and are considered clinically significant. Any of them may occur following transfusion or fetomaternal immunization. Antibody frequency is influenced by the immunogenicity of the particular antigen and by the distribution of the relevant negative phenotypes among transfusion recipients and positive phenotypes among donors. In Black patients frequently transfused with blood from Black donors, anti-Js^a is relatively common in sera that contain multiple antibodies. (The incidence of Js^a in a Black population is approximately 20%. See Table 15-5.) Ordinarily, however, these antibodies are rare. Assistance from a rare donor file is usually needed to find compatible blood for patients immunized to the high-incidence antigens Kp^b and Js^b. Anti-Ku (anti-K5) is the antibody characteristically seen in immunized K_o persons. It appears to be directed at a single determinant because it has not been separable into other Kell specificities. However, antibodies to other Kell system antigens may be present in serum containing anti-Ku. Some people of the K_{mod} phenotype have made an anti-Ku-like anibody.

Duffy System

Duffy System Antigens

The antigens Fy^a and Fy^b are encoded by a pair of codominant alleles at the Duffy (*FY*) locus on chromosome 1. Anti-Fy^a and anti-Fy^b define the four phenotypes observed in this blood group system, namely: Fy(a+b–), Fy(a+b+), Fy(a–b+) and Fy(a–b–) (see Table 15-6). In

Table 15-6. Phenotypes and Frequencies in the Duffy System

Reactions with Anti-			Adult Phenotype Frequency (%)	
Fy^a	Fy^b	Phenotype	Whites	Blacks
+	0	Fy(a+b−)	17	9
+	+	Fy(a+b+)	49	1
0	+	Fy(a−b+)	34	22
0	0	Fy(a−b−)	V. rare	68

Whites, the first three phenotypes are common and Fy(a–b–) individuals are extremely rare. However, the incidence of the Fy(a–b–) phenotype among African-American Blacks is 68% and approaches 100% in some areas of West Africa.[5]

The Duffy gene encodes a glycoprotein that is expressed in other tissues, including brain, kidney, spleen, heart, and lung. In Fy(a–b–) individuals, transcription in the marrow is prevented and Duffy protein is absent from the red cells. However, the Duffy protein is expressed normally in nonerythroid cells of these persons.[12]

A rare inherited form of weak Fy^b called Fy^x has been described and is probably due to a point mutation. The Fy^x antigen may go undetected unless potent anti-Fy^b is used in testing.

Biochemistry

In red cells, the Duffy gene encodes a multipass membrane glycoprotein. The antigens Fy^a, Fy^b, and Fy6 are located on the N-terminal of the Duffy glycoprotein and are sensitive to denaturation by proteases such as ficin, papain, and α-chymotrypsin, unlike Fy3 or Fy5. Fy3 has been located on the last external loop of the Duffy glycoprotein. It is unaffected by protease treatment (reviewed in Pierce and MacPherson[13]). The glycoprotein is the receptor for the malarial parasite *Plasmodium vivax*, and persons whose red cells lack Fy^a and Fy^b are resistant to that form of the disease. In sub-Saharan Africa, notably West Africa, the resistance to *P. vivax* malaria conferred by the Fy(a–b–) phenotype may have favored its natural selection, and most individuals are Fy(a–b–).

The *Fy* locus is located on chromosome 1, near the centromere. The gene has been cloned[13] and the Duffy glycoprotein has been identified as an erythrocyte receptor for a number of chemokines, notably IL-8.[14] Because chemokines are biologically active molecules, it has been postulated that Duffy acts as a sponge for excess chemokines, without ill effect on the red cells.

Duffy System Antibodies

Anti-Fy^a is quite common and may cause HDN and HTRs. Anti-Fy^b is rare and generally is weakly reactive. Although no HDN has been attributed to anti-Fy^b, the antibody has been responsible for mild HTRs. Both antibodies are usually IgG and react best by antiglobulin testing. The glycoprotein that expresses the antigens is cleaved by most proteases used in serologic tests, so anti-Fy^a and anti-Fy^b are usually nonreactive in enzyme test procedures.

Weak examples of anti-Fy^a or anti-Fy^b may give convincing reactions only with red cells that have a double dose of the antigen. In Whites, red cells that express only one of the two antigens are assumed to come from persons homozygous for the gene and to carry a double dose of the antigen. In Blacks, such cells may express the antigen only in single dose, and may not give the expected strong reaction with antibodies that show dosage.

Rarely Encountered Antibodies

Anti-Fy3 was first described in the serum of a White person of the Fy(a–b–) phenotype and is directed at the high-incidence antigen Fy3. The only cells with which it is nonreactive are Fy(a–b–). Unlike Fy^a and Fy^b, the Fy3 antigen is unaffected by protease treatment, and anti-Fy3 reacts well with enzyme-treated cells positive for either Fy^a or Fy^b. Anti-Fy3 is rare but is sometimes made by Black Fy(a–b–) patients lacking Fy3 who have been immunized by multiple transfusions.

Two other rare antibodies have been described, both reactive with papain-treated red cells. One example of anti-Fy4 has been reported. It reacted with red cells of the Fy(a–b–) phenotype and with some Fy(a+b–) and Fy(a–b+) red cells from Blacks but not with Fy(a+b+) red cells, suggesting reactivity with a putative product of the *Fy* gene. However, equivocal results were obtained by different reference laboratories and evidence for the existence of the Fy4 antigen is weak.

Anti-Fy5 is similar to anti-Fy3, except that it fails to react with Rh_{null} red cells that express Fy3 and is nonreactive with cells from Fy(a–b–) Blacks. It does, however, react with the red cells of the White Fy(a–b–) proposita. This provided a hitherto unrecognized distinction between the Fy(a–b–) phenotype so common in Blacks and the one that occurs, but very rarely, in Whites. It has been postulated that Fy5 is formed by the interaction of Rh and Duffy gene products.

Anti-Fy6 is a murine monoclonal antibody that describes a high-incidence antigen in the same region as Fy^a and Fy^b. The antibody reacts with all Fy(a+) and/or Fy(b+) red cells and is nonreactive with Fy(a–b–) red cells.

Kidd System

Jk^a and Jk^b Antigens

The Jk^a and Jk^b antigens are located on the urea transporter, encoded by the *HUT 11* gene on chromosome 18. Jk(a–b–) red cells, which lack the JK protein, are more resistant to lysis by 2M urea.[15] Red cells of normal Jk phenotype swell and lyse rapidly in a solution of 2M urea.

The four phenotypes identified in the Kidd system are shown in Table 15-7. The Jk(a–b–) phenotype is extremely rare, except in some populations of Pacific Island origin. Two mech-

anisms have been shown to produce the Jk(a–b–) phenotype.[16] One is the homozygous presence of the silent *Jk* allele. The other is the action of a dominant inhibitor gene called *In(Jk)*. The dominant suppression of Kidd antigens is similar to the *In(Lu)* suppression of the Lutheran system. (See the next section.)

Kidd System Antibodies

Anti-Jk^a and Anti-Jk^b

Anti-Jk^a was first recognized in 1951 in the serum of a woman who had given birth to a child with HDN. Two years later, anti-Jk^b was found in the serum of a patient who had suffered a transfusion reaction. Both antibodies react best on antiglobulin testing, but saline reactivity is sometimes observed in freshly drawn specimens or when antibodies are newly forming. These antibodies are often weakly reactive, perhaps because they are sometimes detected more readily through the complement they bind to red cells. Some examples may become undetectable on storage. Other examples may react preferentially with red cells from homozygotes.

Some workers report no difficulties in detecting anti-Jk^a and anti-Jk^b antibodies in low ionic tests that incorporate anti-IgG. Others find that an antiglobulin reagent containing an anticomplement component may be important for the reliable detection of these inconsistently reactive antibodies. Stronger reactions may be obtained with the use of PEG or enzyme-treated red cells in antiglobulin testing.

Table 15-7. Phenotypes and Frequencies in the Kidd System

Reactions with Anti-			Phenotype Frequency (%)	
Jk^a	Jk^b	Phenotype	Whites	Blacks
+	0	Jk(a+b–)	28	57
+	+	Jk(a+b+)	49	34
0	+	Jk(a–b+)	23	9
0	0	Jk(a–b–)	Exceedingly rare	

Kidd system antibodies occasionally cause HDN, but the HDN is usually mild. These antibodies are notorious, however, for involvement in severe HTRs, especially delayed hemolytic reactions (DHTRs). DHTRs occur when antibody develops so rapidly in an anamnestic response to antigens on transfused red cells that it destroys the still-circulating red cells. In many cases, retesting the patient's pretransfusion serum confirms that the antibody was, indeed, undetectable in the original tests. This highlights the importance of consulting previous records before selecting blood for transfusion. Patients whose antibody has previously been detected and identified can, by review of past records, be protected against repeated contact with the known immunizing stimulus.

Anti-Jk3

Sera from some rare Jk(a–b–) persons have been found to contain an antibody that reacts with all Jk(a+) and Jk(b+) red cells but not with Jk(a–b–) red cells. Although a minor anti-Jk^a or anti-Jk^b component is sometimes separable, most of the reactivity has been directed at an antigen called Jk3, which is present on both Jk(a+) and Jk(b+) red cells.

Other Blood Group Systems

So far, this chapter has been devoted to systems of red cell antigens. The principal antibodies may be seen fairly frequently in the routine blood typing laboratory. The other blood group systems listed in Table 15-1 will be reviewed here only briefly; the interested reader should refer to other texts and reviews for greater detail.

Lutheran System

Lu^a and Lu^b Antigens

The phenotypes of the Lutheran system as defined by anti-Lu^a (-Lu1) and anti-Lu^b (-Lu2) are shown in Table 15-8. The Lu(a–b–) phenotype is very rare and may arise from one of three distinct genetic circumstances (reviewed in Pierce and MacPherson[13]). In the first, a presumably amorphic Lutheran gene (*Lu*) is inherited from both parents. In the second and most common, the negative phenotype is inherited as a dominant trait attributed to the independently-segregating inhibitor gene, *In(Lu)*, which prevents the normal expression of Lutheran and certain other blood group antigens (notably P$_1$, I, AnWj, In^a, and In^b). The third Lu(a–b–) phenotype is due to an X-borne suppressor, recessive in its effect.

Other Lutheran Blood Group Antigens

A series of high-incidence antigens (LU4, LU5, LU6, LU7, LU8, LU11, LU12, LU13, LU16, LU17, and LU20) has been assigned to the Lutheran system because the corresponding antibodies do not react with Lu(a–b–) red cells of any of the three genetic backgrounds. Two low-incidence antigens, LU9 and LU14, have gained admission to the Lutheran system because of their apparent antithetical relationship to the high-incidence antigens LU6 and LU8, respectively.

Au^a (LU18), an antigen of relatively high incidence [80% of Whites are Au(a+)] and its antithetical partner, Au^b (LU19), present in 50% of Whites, were once considered an independ-

Table 15-8. Phenotypes and Frequencies in the Lutheran System in Whites

Reactions with Anti-		Phenotype	Phenotype Frequency (%)
Lu^a	Lu^b		
+	0	Lu(a+b–)	0.15
+	+	Lu(a+b+)	7.5
0	+	Lu(a–b+)	92.35
0	0	Lu(a–b–)	Very rare

Insufficient data exist for the reliable calculation of frequencies in Blacks.

ent polymorphism but have now been shown to belong to the Lutheran system.[17]

Biochemistry of the Lutheran System

Lutheran antigens are carried on a glycoprotein bearing both *N*-linked and O-linked oligosaccharides. This protein is a member of the Ig superfamily and exists in two forms. They have been shown to have a role in cell adhesion. The antigens are destroyed by trypsin, α-chymotrypsin, and sulfhydryl-reducing agents.[18] These results and results of immunoblotting experiments suggest the existence of interchain or intrachain disulfide bonds. Tests performed with monoclonal anti-Lu^b suggest that the number of Lu^b antigen sites per red cell is low, approximately 600-1600 per Lu(a+b+) red cell and 1400-3800 per Lu(a–b+) red cell.[19]

The *Lu* and *Se* (secretor) loci were shown to be linked in 1951, the first recorded example of autosomal linkage in humans. The two loci have been assigned to chromosome 19. The gene encoding the Lu glycoproteins has been cloned.[20]

Lutheran System Antibodies

The first example of anti-Lu^a (-Lu1) was found in 1945 in a serum that contained several other antibodies. Anti-Lu^a and anti-Lu^b are not often encountered. They are produced in response to pregnancy or transfusion but have occurred in the absence of obvious red cell stimulation. Lutheran antigens are poorly developed at birth. It is not surprising that anti-Lu^a has not been reported to cause HDN; neither has it been associated with HTRs. Anti-Lu^b has been reported to shorten the survival of transfused red cells but causes no, or at most very mild, HDN. Most examples of anti-Lu^a and some anti-Lu^b will agglutinate saline-suspended red cells possessing the relevant antigen, characteristically producing a mixed-field appearance with small to moderately sized, loosely agglutinated clumps of red cells interspersed among many unagglutinated red cells.

Diego System
Diego System Antigens

The Diego system consists of two independent pairs of antigens, called Di^a/Di^b and Wr^a/Wr^b. Each pair contains a low-incidence antigen and an antithetical high-incidence determinant. The system also contains an ever-growing number of low-incidence antigens, such as Bp^a. The antigens are located on AE-1, which is encoded by a gene on chromosome 17. The Di^a/Di^b antigens are useful as anthropological markers, because the Di^a antigen is almost entirely confined to populations of Asian origin, including Native Americans, where the incidence of Di^a can be as high as 36%.

The Wr^a and Wr^b antigens are located on AE-1 in close association with GPA; expression of Wr^b is dependent upon the presence of GPA (see MNS Blood Group System).

Table 15-9. Diego System Antigens

Antigen	ISBT Classification
Di^a	DI1
Di^b	DI2
Wr^a	DI3
Wr^b	DI4
Wd^a	DI5
Rb^a	DI6
WARR	DI7
ELO	DI8
Wu	DI9
Bp^a	DI10
Mo^a	DI11
Hg^a	DI12
Vg^a	DI13
Sw^a	DI14
BOW	DI15
NFLD	DI16
Jn^a	DI17
KREP	DI18

Diego System Antibodies

Anti-Di^a may cause HDN or destruction of transfused Di(a+) red cells. Anti-Di^b is rare but clinically significant when encountered. Anti-Wr^a occurs without red cell immunization. It may be fairly common but passes undetected unless the cells used for antibody screening are Wr(a+). It is a rare cause of HTR or HDN.

Cartwright System

Cartwright Antigens

The Yt blood group system consists of two antigens, Yt^a and Yt^b (see Table 15-10). The antigens are encoded by a gene on chromosome 7. The Yt antigens are located on red cell acetylcholinesterase (AChE),[21] an enzyme important in neural transmission but whose function on red cells is unknown.

Yt Antibodies

Most examples of anti-Yt^a are benign, although in a few cases accelerated destruction of transfused Yt(a+) red cells has been observed. Prediction of the clinical outcome by the monocyte monolayer assay has proved successful.[22] Anti-Yt^a is not known to cause HDN. Anti-Yt^b is rare and has not been implicated in HTR or HDN.

Xg System

Xg Antigen

In 1962, an antibody was discovered that identified an antigen more common among women than among men. This would be expected of an X-borne characteristic because females inherit an X chromosome from each parent, whereas males inherit X only from their mother. The antigen was named Xg^a in recognition of its

Table 15-10. Phenotype Frequencies in Other Blood Group Systems with Codominant Antithetical Antigens

System	Reactions with Anti-		Phenotype	Phenotype Frequency % in Whites*
Yt	Yt^a	Yt^b		
	+	0	Yt(a+b−)	91.9
	+	+	Yt(a+b+)	7.9
	0	+	Yt(a−b+)	0.2
Dombrock	Do^a	Do^b		
	+	0	Do(a+b−)	17.2
	+	+	Do(a+b+)	49.5
	0	+	Do(a−b+)	33.3
Colton	Co^a	Co^b		
	+	0	Co(a+b−)	89.3
	+	+	Co(a+b+)	10.4
	0	+	Co(a−b+)	0.3
	0	0	Co(a−b−)	very rare
Scianna	Sc1	Sc2		
	+	0	Sc:1,−2	99.7
	+	+	Sc:1,2	0.3
	0	+	Sc:−1,2	very rare
	0	0	Sc:−1,−2	very rare
Indian	In^a	In^b		
	+	0	In(a+b−)	very rare
	+	+	In(a+b+)	< 1
	0	+	In(a−b+)	>99

*There are insufficient data for the reliable calculation of frequencies in Blacks.

X-borne manner of inheritance. Table 15-11 gives the phenotype frequencies among White males and females. Enzymes, such as papain and ficin, denature the antigen. The gene encoding Xg^a has been cloned.[23,24]

Xg Antibodies

Anti-Xg^a is an uncommon antibody that usually reacts only on antiglobulin testing, although at least three examples are known that agglutinated saline-suspended red cells. Anti-Xg^a has not been implicated in HDN or HTRs. One example has been reported as an autoantibody. Anti-Xg^a may be useful for tracing the transmission of genetic traits associated with the X chromosome, although linkage with the *Xg* locus has been demonstrated for few traits to date.

Scianna System

Scianna Antigens

Three antigens, Sc1, Sc2, and Sc3, are recognized as belonging to the Scianna blood group system. Sc1 is a high-incidence antigen, whereas Sc2 occurs very infrequently. Sc1 and Sc2 behave as products of allelic genes. (See Table 15-10.) Sc3 is thought to be present on the red cells of any individual who inherits a functional *Sc1* or *Sc2* gene, analogous to Fy3. The antigens are resistant to enzymes routinely used in blood group serology. The gene encoding the Scianna antigens is located on

Table 15-11. Frequencies of the Xg(a+) and Xg(a−) Phenotypes in White Males and Females

Phenotype	Phenotype Frequency (%)	
	Males	Females
Xg(a+)	65.6	88.7
Xg(a−)	34.4	11.3

Frequencies are based on combined results of testing nearly 7000 random blood samples from populations of Northern European origin. There are insufficient data for reliable calculation of frequencies in Blacks.

chromosome 1. The Scianna blood group antigens have been assigned to a glycoprotein of 60-68 kD, but as yet, the function of the protein is unknown.

The low-incidence antigen Rd is encoded by a gene on chromosome 1 at the same locus as *SC*. There is some biochemical evidence that the Rd antigen is part of the Scianna blood group system.

Scianna Antibodies

The antibodies are rare. Anti-Sc1 has not been reported to cause HTR or HDN. Anti-Sc2 has caused mild HDN.

Dombrock Blood Group System

Dombrock Antigens

Initially, this blood group system consisted of Do^a and Do^b, with the phenotype frequency as shown in Table 15-10. The discovery that red cells negative for the high-incidence antigen Gy^a were Do(a−b−)[25] has led to the recent expansion of the Dombrock blood group system. Three high-incidence antigens are: Gy^a, Hy, and Jo^a. The interrelationship of the phenotypes is shown in Table 15-12. Gy(a−) red cells represent the null phenotype. The Gy(a+^{w}), Hy−, and Jo(a−) phenotypes have been found exclusively in Blacks. The Dombrock antigens are located on a glycoprotein of 46-58 kD, the function of which is unknown.

Dombrock Antibodies

Anti-Do^a is an uncommon antibody and is usually found in mixtures of antibodies. It has caused HTRs and HDN.[26] Anti-Do^b is also uncommon and may be found in sera containing multiple specificities. This can make the detection and identification of anti-Do^b difficult. HDN due to anti-Do^b has not been reported, but examples have caused HTR. Antibodies to Gy^a, Hy, and Jo^a may cause shortened survival of transfused antigen-positive red cells or mild HDN. Reactivity of Dombrock antibodies may be enhanced by papain or ficin treatment of red

Table 15-12. Relationship of the Dombrock Blood Group Antigens

Phenotype	Do^a	Do^b	Gy^a	Hy	Jo^a
Normal Do(a+b−)	+	0	+	+	+
Normal Do(a+b+)	+	+	+	+	+
Normal Do(a−b+)	0	+	+	+	+
Gy(a−)	0	0	0	0	0
Hy−	0	(+)	(+)	0	0
Jo(a−)	(+)	0	+	(+)	0

(+)=weak antigen expression

cells but is weakened or destroyed by pronase, trypsin, α-chymotrypsin, and sulfhydryl reagents.

Colton System

Colton Antigens

The Colton system consists of: Co^a, a high-incidence antigen; Co^b, a low-incidence antigen; and Co3, an antigen (like Fy3) considered to be the product of either the *Co^a* or *Co^b* gene. The antigens are products of a gene on chromosome 7. The phenotype frequencies in Whites are shown in Table 15-10. The Colton antigens have been located on membrane protein CHIP 28 (Aquaporin), which functions as the red cell water transporter.[27]

Colton Antibodies

Although rare, anti-Co^a and anti-Co^b have been implicated in HTRs and HDN.[28] Anti-Co^b has caused a HTR[28] but not HDN. Enzyme treatment of red cells enhances reactions with the defining antibodies.

The LW System

LW Antigens

Table 15-13 shows the LW phenotypes and their frequencies. The antigens are denatured by sulfhydryl reagents, such as DTT, and by pronase but are unaffected by papain or ficin.

Association with Rh

The gene encoding the LW antigens is independent of the genes encoding the Rh proteins. Genetic independence was originally established through the study of informative families in which LW has been shown to segregate independently of the *Rh* genes. The *LW* gene has been assigned to chromosome 19 and has been cloned. The glycoprotein it encodes has homology with cell adhesion molecules.[29]

Red cells from persons of the Rh$_{null}$ phenotype are LW(a−b−). It appears that the LW glycoprotein requires an interaction with Rh proteins for expression, although the basis of this interaction is not clear. (For a review of the historic evolution of the LW system, see Storry.[30])

Table 15-13. Phenotypes and Frequencies in the LW System in Whites

Reactions with Anti-		Phenotype	Phenotype Frequency (%)
LW^a	LW^b		
+	0	LW(a+b−)	very rare
+	+	LW(a+b+)	< 1
0	+	LW(a−b+)	>99
0	0	LW(a−b−)	very rare

LW Antibodies

Anti-LW[a] has not been reported to cause HTRs or HDN, and both D-positive and D-negative LW(a+) red cells have been successfully transfused into patients whose sera contained anti-LW[a]. Reduced expression of LW antigens can occur in pregnancy; the antibody may occur as an autoantibody or as an apparent alloantibody in the serum of such a person.

Potent anti-LW[ab] was detected in the serum of a D-positive LW(a–b–) woman whose infant had red cells that had a weakly positive direct antiglobulin test. The antibody had a titer of 32,000 against D-positive red cells and a titer of 400 against D-negative red cells; the proposita's brother typed LW(a–b–). This is the only example of an inherited LW(a–b–). The other reported cases are acquired.

Chido/Rodgers System

Chido/Rodgers Antigens

The Chido (Ch) and Rodgers (Rg) antigens are high-incidence antigens present on the complement component C4. The antigens are not in-trinsic to the red cell. In antigen-positive individuals, the antigens are adsorbed onto red cells from the plasma through an attachment mechanism that remains unclear.[31] Ch has been subdivided into six antigens and Rg, into two antigens. A ninth antigen, WH, requires the interaction of Rg1 and Ch6 for expression. C4 is encoded by two linked genes, *C4A* and *C4B*, on chromosome 6.

Existing sera are poorly classified, but the phenotype frequency may be considered as in Table 15-14.

Chido/Rodgers Antibodies

Antibodies to Ch and Rg are generally benign but may be a great nuisance in serologic investigations. Rapid identification is possible using red cells coated with C4 or by inhibition with pooled plasma from antigen-positive individuals. (See Methods 3.9 and 3.10.)

Gerbich System

Gerbich Antigens

The Gerbich system includes seven antigens, of which three (Ge2, Ge3, and Ge4) are of high inci-

Table 15-14. Some Blood Group Systems of Fairly High Incidence

Antigens	Phenotypes	Approximate Frequency (%) Whites	Blacks
Chido (Ch) and Rodgers (Rg)	Ch+,Rg+	95.0	
	Ch–,Rg+	2.0	
	Ch+,Rg–	3.0	
	Ch–,Rg–	Very rare	
Cost (Cs[a])[†] and York (Yk[a])	Cs(a+),Yk(a+)	82.5	95.6
	Cs(a+),Yk(a–)	13.5	3.2
	Cs(a–),Yk(a+)	2.1	0.6
	Cs(a–),Yk(a–)	1.9	0.6
Knops-Helgeson (Kn[a]) and McCoy (McC[a])	Kn(a+),McC(a+)	97.0	95.0
	Kn(a+),McC(a–)	2.0	4.0
	Kn(a–),McC(a+)	1.0	1.0
	Kn(a–),McC(a–)	Rare	Rare

[†]Although Cs[a] is not part of the Knops blood group system, there is a phenotypic association between Yk[a] and Cs[a].

dence and four (Wb, Ls^a, An^a, and Dh^a) are of low incidence. Several phenotypes that lack one or more of the high-incidence antigens are shown in Table 15-15; all are rare. Red cells with the Gerbich or Leach phenotype have a weakened expression of some Kell system antigens. Ge2, Wb, Ls^a, An^a, and Dh^a are destroyed by papain and ficin, but Ge3 resists protease treatment.

The antigens of the Gerbich blood group system are carried on glycophorin C (GPC) and glycophorin D (GPD). GPC carries Ge3 and Ge4 while GPD carries Ge2 and Ge3. An^a is carried on an altered form of GPD. Dh^a and Wb are located on altered forms of GPC. Ls^a is found on an altered form of GPC and GPD.[32] The proteins are the product of a single gene, *GYPC*, on chromosome 2. GPC is approximately four times more abundant than GPD. The mechanism whereby these two proteins are derived from a single gene involves an alternative initiation site in the gene. GPC and GPD interact directly with protein band 4.1 in the membrane skeleton. It is clear that the interaction is important in maintaining cell shape because deficiencies of either band 4.1 or GPC/D cause elliptocytosis.[32]

Gerbich Antibodies

The antibodies that Ge-negative individuals may produce are shown in Table 15-15; these may be immune or occur with red cell stimulation. Anti-Ge is usually IgG but may have an IgM component. The clinical significance of the antibodies is variable. Antibodies to the low-incidence antigens may be a rare cause of HDN.

Table 15-15. Ge– Phenotypes

Phenotype	Antibody Produced
Ge: −2,3,4 (Yus type)	Anti-Ge2
Ge:−2,−3,4 (Gerbich type)	Anti-Ge2 or anti-Ge3
Ge:−2,−3,−4 (Leach type)	Anti-Ge2, -Ge3, or -Ge4

Cromer System

Cromer Antigens

A total of 10 antigens has been assigned to the Cromer blood group system: seven high-incidence antigens and three low-incidence antigen. (See Table 15-16.) Tc^a is antithetical to the low-incidence antigen Tc^b in Blacks and to Tc^c in Whites. WES^b is the high-incidence antigen antithetical to WES^a. Cr^a, Dr^a, Es^a, and UMC are not associated with low-incidence antigens. IFC is absent only in the null phenotype (INAB). The antigens are sensitive to α-chymotrypsin and pronase treatment.

The antigens are located on the complement regulatory protein called decay accelerating factor (DAF). The protein is encoded by *DAF*, one gene of the regulators of complement activation (RCA) complex, on chromosome 1.

Cromer Antibodies

Antibodies to antigens of the Cromer system are immune-mediated and extremely uncommon. Most examples of anti-Cr^a, -WES^b, and -Tc^a have been found in the sera of Black individuals. The clinical significance of the antibodies is variable, and some examples cause

Table 15-16. Antigens of High and Low Incidence in the Cromer Blood Group System

Antigen	Incidence (%)
Cr^a	>99
Tc^a	>99
Tc^b	< 1
Tc^c	< 1
Dr^a	>99
Es^a	>99
IFC	>99
WES^a	< 1
WES^b	>99
UMC	>99

decreased survival of transfused red cells. The antibodies will not cause HDN possibly because the antigens are present on placental tissue and possibly may adsorb the corresponding maternal antibodies.

Knops System

Knops Antigens

The antigens Kn^a, McC^a, McC^b, Sl^a, and Yk^a have been located on the C3b/C4b receptor (CR1), the primary complement receptor on red cells. CR1 is encoded by a gene on chromosome 1 that, like the gene for DAF, is part of the RCA complex. With the exception of McC^b, all antigens are of high incidence, although some variation is observed between the red cells of Whites and Blacks (see Table 15-14).

Knops Antibodies

The antibodies commonly show variable weak reactivity in the antiglobulin phase of testing but may continue to react even at high dilutions. Moulds et al[33] have shown that the variable reactivity of anti-CR1-related sera is a direct reflection of the number of CR1 sites that exhibit both size and expression polymorphisms and vary widely among individuals in the number per cell. The antibodies are of no clinical significance.

Indian System

Indian Antigens

In^a and In^b are located on CD44, a protein of wide tissue distribution with the characteristics of a cell adhesion molecule.[21] In^a is a low-incidence antigen while In^b is of high incidence (see Table 15-10). In^b shows reduced expression on Lu(a–b–) red cells of the *In(Lu)* type but is normally expressed on Lu(a–b–) red cells from persons homozygous for the *amorph* or possessing the X-borne suppressor gene. The antigens are destroyed by papain and ficin as well as by reducing agents such as 0.2 M DTT. There are few data on the clinical significance of the corresponding antibodies.

OK System

The OK system consists of a single high-incidence antigen, Ok^a. The few rare Ok(a–) individuals to date have been Japanese. Ok^a antigen is carried on a series of glycoproteins that are found on a wide range of human tissues. Proteases do not seem to weaken expression of Ok^a in routine agglutination tests. Anti-Ok^a reacts optimally by an indirect antiglobulin test and appears to be clinically significant in transfusion therapy, causing rapid destruction of Ok(a+) red cells. Monoclonal anti-Ok^a has also been reproduced.

RAPH System

The RAPH system also consists of a single antigen, MER2. It is the first blood group system to be recognized initially by monoclonal antibodies. Human anti-MER2 has subsequently been reported in three Israeli Jews. All three were on renal dialysis, raising the possibility that antibody production may be associated with kidney disease. Since MER2 is detected on the red cells of 92% of those tested, additional examples of the antibody would be expected in the 8% of MER2 individuals. The presence or absence of MER2 on other tissues might also affect antibody production.

The MER2 antigen is sensitive to the actions of trypsin, α-chymotrypsin, pronase, and DTT, but is not affected by treatment with ficin/papine, sialidase or chloroquine. Of the three antibodies studied, all were IgG immunoglobulins and two of the three also bound complement to the red cells. To date there have been no reported transfusion reactions and no information exists on whether these antibodies are capable of causing HDN.

Although the MER2 antigen is not part of the Lutheran system, it is reported that the inhibitor gene *In(Lu)* will slightly depress the MER2 antigen expression.

Blood Group Collections

In addition to the blood group systems, there are collections of antigens that exhibit shared characteristics but do not as yet meet the criteria for blood group status defined by the ISBT.[2] These include Cost (ISBT 205), Ii (ISBT 207, discussed in Chapter 13), and Er (ISBT 208).

Cost

Cs^a and Cs^b are all that remain of this collection after the Knops antigens were identified on CR1. There is, however, an unexplained connection between the Yk^a and Cs^a antigens, such that red cells negative for one antigen are often weak or negative for the other. Anti-Cs^a behaves similarly to antibodies produced to the Knops system antigens and is not considered clinically significant.

Er

The Er collection consists of two antigens, which give rise to four phenotypes: Er(a+b–), Er(a+b+), Er(a–b+), and Er(a–b–). Er^a is a high-incidence antigen present on the red cells of >99% of all individuals, while Er^b has a prevalence of less than 1%. The presence of a silent third allele, *Er*, is thought to account for the Er(a–b–) phenotype as demonstrated by family studies.

High-Incidence Red Cell Antigens Not Assigned to a System or Collection

Table 15-17 lists the antigens of high incidence that are independent of a blood group system or collection. Persons who make alloantibody to a specific blood group antigen necessarily have red cells lacking that antigen. For this reason, antibodies directed at high-incidence antigens are rarely encountered. When these antibodies do occur, however, it may be exceedingly difficult to find compatible blood.

Members of the patient's family, especially siblings, are usually the most promising sources of potential donors.

Absence of a high-incidence antigen generally implies homozygosity for the rare recessive gene that encodes the absence of antigen or the presence of an alternative antigen (usually of low incidence). Both parents of the propositus are ordinarily heterozygous for this gene, so there is one chance in four that each sibling will, like the propositus, be homozygous for the rare gene and lack the high-incidence antigen. In the exceedingly unlikely event that one of the parents is homozygous for the rare gene, the chance that any sibling will be homozygous increases to one in two.

It is often very helpful to know the ethnic group of the patient with an antibody to a high-incidence antigen because the chances of finding a compatible donor may be greatly enhanced if search efforts are targeted. For example, the At(a–) phenotype has been observed only in Blacks. Screening red cells only from Black donors will increase the chances of finding a compatible donor and conserve supplies of a very rare antibody. The antibodies corresponding to these antigens usually react best on antiglobulin testing.

Table 15-17. Some Antigens of High Incidence Not Assigned to a Blood Group System or Collection

Name	Symbol
August	At^a
Vel	Vel
Langeris	Lan
Sid	Sd^a
Duclos	
	JMH
	Jr^a
	Emm
	AnWj
	PEL
	ABTI
	MAM

The Vel Antigen

Vel is a high-incidence antigen that is unaffected by protease and sulfhydryl treatment. It is well developed at birth, but antigen expression is variable.[28] Most examples of anti-Vel react optimally by antiglobulin testing but may agglutinate saline-suspended red cells. Despite its occurrence after known immunizing stimuli, anti-Vel is most commonly IgM and has not been reported to cause HDN. It has, however, been implicated in HTRs. Anti-Vel binds complement, and in-vitro hemolysis of incompatible red cells is often seen when testing freshly-drawn serum containing this antibody. Reactivity of anti-Vel is usually enhanced by enzyme treatment of red cells expressing the antigen.

The Sd^a Antigen

Sd^a is an antigen of fairly high incidence, widely distributed in mammalian tissues and body fluids. The antigen is variably expressed on the red cells of Sd(a+) individuals and may disappear transiently during pregnancy. The strongest expression of Sd^a has been observed on polyagglutinable red cells of the Cad phenotype. Anti-Sd^a is generally reactive by antiglobulin testing. Microscopic examination of positive reactions generally shows mixed-field agglutination, with relatively small, tightly agglutinated clumps of red cells present against a background of free red cells. These agglutinates are refractile and may have a shining appearance.

The frequency of Sd(a–) blood is generally considered to be around 9%, but weakly positive reactions are often difficult to distinguish from negative ones. Sd^a expression may diminish during pregnancy, and the Sd(a–) red cell phenotype is observed in 30-75% of pregnant women.

The immunodominant sugar of Sd^a is N-acetylgalactosamine (GalNAc), also the immunodominant sugar of the A blood group antigen and of the Tamm-Horsfall glyco-protein, found in human and guinea pig urine. Anti-Sd^a activity can be inhibited by incubation with urine from guinea pigs or from Sd(a+) humans. When performing inhibition studies with urine, it is important to ensure the pH is neutral.

Low-Incidence Red Cell Antigens Not Assigned to a Blood Group System or Collection

Many independent low-incidence red cell antigens have been recognized in addition to a growing number that have been assigned to the MNS, Rh, and DI systems. Table 15-18 lists those that have been studied and shown to be inherited in a dominant manner. Antibodies specific for these low-incidence antigens react with so few random blood samples that they virtually never cause difficulties in selecting blood for transfusion. The antibodies are of interest to the serologist, however, because of the unexpectedly high incidence with which they occur, often without an identifiable antigenic stimulus.

Table 15-18. Antigens of Low Incidence Not Assigned to a Blood Group System or Collection

Batty (By)	Jensen (Je^a)
Biles (Bi^a)	Katagiri (Kg)
Box (Bx^a)	Livesay (Li^a)
Christiansen (Chr^a)	Milne
Froese (Fr^a)	Oldeide (Ol^a)
HJK	Os^a
HOFM	Peters (Pt^a)
Hey	Reid (Re^a)
JFV	SW1
JONES	Torkildsen (To^a)

The antigens occur with a frequency of 1 in 500 or less.

Antibodies to Low-Incidence Antigens

Antibodies to low-incidence antigens have sometimes been implicated in transfusion reactions and HDN. These antibodies are usually encountered by chance, when the red cells used for antibody detection or selected for crossmatching happen to carry the corresponding antigen.

Antibodies to low-incidence antigens may also be present as unsuspected contaminants in blood typing reagents prepared from human serum and may cause false-positive test results if the red cells tested carry the antigen. Testing with reagents from different manufacturers may not eliminate this error because it is not uncommon for a single individual with an uncommon antibody to provide the serum used for reagent preparation by different manufacturers.

Some antibodies to low-incidence antigens react as saline agglutinins. They can also occur as IgG antibodies reactive only by antiglobulin testing, even if there has been no exposure to red cell immunization. It is common for several antibodies to occur together in a single serum; multiple specificities are especially likely in sera from patients with autoimmune conditions. A serum that contains autoantibodies often contains a mixture of alloantibodies directed at low-incidence antigens. These are usually separable from the autoantibody and from each other by adsorption with appropriate red cells.

The Bg (Bennett-Goodspeed) Antigens

Antibodies directed at certain leukocyte antigens sometimes cause confusing reactions in serologic tests with red cells. At least three separate specificities have been given names as Bg antigens: Bg^a corresponds to HLA-B7; BgB corresponds to HLA-B17; and Bg^c corresponds to HLA-A28. A fourth antibody in some anti-leukocyte sera reacts with red cells of persons who express HLA-A10. The so-called Bg antigens are expressed to variable degrees on red cells with the result that reactions of differing strength are observed when a single serum containing "anti-Bg" is tested with different Bg+ red cells. Reactivity is most commonly observed in antiglobulin testing, but highly potent anti-Bg sera may directly agglutinate red cells with unusually strong expression of the Bg antigens.

Confident and precise classification of reactivity is made difficult by the weak expression of these antigens on some red cells and by multiple specificities among different examples of the Bg antibodies. These antibodies may also occur as unsuspected contaminants in blood typing sera, where they may cause false-positive reactions with cells having unusually strong expression of the corresponding Bg antigen. Bg-related antigens are denatured by chloroquine diphosphate or by a solution of glycine-HCl/EDTA.

References

1. Anstee DJ, Spring FA. Red cell membrane glycoproteins with a broad tissue distribution. Transfus Med Rev 1989;3:13-23.
2. Lewis M, Anstee DJ, Bird GWG, et al. Blood Group Terminology 1990. From the ISBT working party on terminology for red cell surface antigens. Vox Sang 1990;58:152-69.
3. Lewis M, Anstee DJ, Bird GWG, et al. ISBT working party on terminology for red cell surface antigens: Los Angeles report. Vox Sang 1991;61:158-60.
4. Daniels G, Moulds JJ, Anstee DJ, et al. ISBT working party on terminology for red cell surface antigens: Sao Paolo report. Vox Sang 1993;65:77-80.
5. Race RR, Sanger R. Blood groups in man. 6th ed. Oxford: Blackwell Scientific Publications, 1975.
6. Bruce LJ, Ring SM, Anstee DJ, et al. Changes in the blood group Wright antigens are associated with a mutation at amino acid 658 in human erythrocyte band 3: A site of interaction between band 3 and glycophorin A under certain conditions. Blood 1995;85:299-306.
7. Reid ME, Loomis-Francis C. The blood group antigen factsbook. London: Academic Press 1997.
8. Case J. The behavior of anti-S antibodies with ficin-treated human red cells. In: Abstracts of volunteer papers. 30th Annual Meeting of the American Association of Blood Banks. Washington, DC: American Association of Blood Banks, 1977:36.
9. Laird-Fryer B, Daniels G, Levitt J, eds. Blood group systems: Kell. Arlington, VA: American Association of Blood Banks, 1990.
10. Zelinski T, Coghlan G, Myal Y, et al. Genetic linkage between the Kell blood group system and

prolactin-inducible protein loci: Provisional assignment of KEL to chromosome 7. Ann Hum Genet 1991;55:137-40.

11. Marsh WL. Molecular biology of blood groups: Cloning the Kell gene (editorial). Transfusion 1992;32:98-101.

12. Chaudhuri A, Polyakova J, Zbrezezna V, et al. Cloning of glycoprotein D cDNA which encodes the major subunit of the Duffy blood group system and the receptor for the *Plasmodium vivax* malaria parasite. Proc Natl Acad Sci U S A 1993;90:10793-7.

13. Pierce SP, MacPherson CR, eds. Blood group systems: Duffy, Kidd and Lutheran. Arlington, VA: American Association of Blood Banks, 1988.

14. Horuk R, Chitnis C, Darbonne W, et al. A receptor for the malarial parasite *Plasmodium vivax*: The erythrocyte chemokine receptor. Science 1993;261:1182-4.

15. Heaton DC, McLoughlin K. Jk(a–b–) red blood cells resist urea lysis. Transfusion 1982;22:70-1.

16. Mougey R. The Kidd blood group system. In: Pierce SR, Macpherson CR, eds. Blood group systems: Duffy, Kidd and Lutheran. Arlington, VA: American Association of Blood Banks, 1988:53-71.

17. Zelinski K, Kaita H, Coghlan G, Philipps S. Assignment of the Auberger red cell antigen polymorphism to the Lutheran blood group system: Genetic justification. Vox Sang 1991;61:275-6.

18. Daniels G. Effect of enzymes on and chemical modifications of high-frequency red cell antigens. Immunohematology 1992;8:53-7.

19. Merry AH, Gardner B, Parsons SF, Anstee DJ. Estimation of the number of binding sites for a murine monoclonal anti-Lu^b on human erythrocytes. Vox Sang 1987;53:57-60.

20. Parson SF, Mawby WL, Anstee DJ. Lutheran blood group glycoprotein is a new member of the immunoglobulin superfamily of proteins. Vox Sang 1994;67(suppl):1.

21. Spring FA. Characterization of blood-group-active erythrocyte membrane glycoproteins with human antisera. Transfus Med 1993;3:167-78.

22. Eckrich RJ, Mallory DM. Correlation of monocyte monolayer assays and posttransfusion survival of Yt(a+) red cells in patients with anti-Yt^a (abstract). Transfusion 1993;33(suppl):18S.

23. Ellis NA, Ye T-Z, Patton S, et al. Cloning of *PBDX*, an *MIC2*-related gene that spans the pseudoautosomal boundary on chromosome Xp. Nat Genet 1994;6:394-9.

24. Ellis NA, Tippett P, Petty A, et al. *PBDX* is the *XG* blood group gene. Nat Genet 1994;8:285-90.

25. Banks JA, Parker N, Poole J. Evidence to show that Dombrock antigens reside on the Gy^a/Hy glycoprotein. Transfus Med 1992;Suppl.1:68.

26. Judd WJ, Steiner EA. Multiple hemolytic transfusion reactions caused by anti-Do^a. Transfusion 1991;31:477-8.

27. Smith BL, Preston GM, Spring F, et al. Human red cell aquaporin CHIP. J Clin Invest 1994;94:1043-9.

28. Issitt PD, Anstee DJ. Applied blood group serology. 4th ed. Durham, NC: Montgomery Scientific Publications, 1998.

29. Bailly P, Hermand P, Callebaut I, et al. The LW blood group glycoprotein is homologous to intercellular adhesion molecules. Proc Natl Acad Sci U S A 1994;91:5306-10.

30. Storry JR. Review: The LW blood group system. Immunohematology 1994;8:87-93.

31. Moulds JM, Laird-Fryer B, eds. Blood groups: Chido/Rodgers, Knops/McCoy/York and Cromer. Bethesda, MD: American Association of Blood Banks, 1992.

32. Reid ME, Spring FA. Molecular basis of glycophorin C variants and their associated blood group antigens. Transfus Med 1994;4:139-46.

33. Moulds JM, Moulds JJ, Brown M, Atkinson JP. Antiglobulin testing for CR1-related (Knops/McCoy/Swain-Langley/York) blood group antigens: Negative and weak reactions are caused by variable expression of CR1. Vox Sang 1992;62:230-5.

16

Platelet and Granulocyte Antigens and Antibodies

FOR MOST BLOOD BANKERS, SERO-logic testing has traditionally focused on red cell antibodies and antigens. However, the importance of antibodies to platelets has become increasingly apparent. Although some blood group antigens are shared by red cells, white cells, and platelets, other antigens appear more specific to certain cell types. Detection methods also vary.

This chapter discusses non-HLA or "platelet-specific" antibodies to the antigens found on platelets. Also covered are granulocyte and neutrophil antigens and antibodies. HLA antibodies are discussed in Chapter 17.

Platelet Antigens and Antibodies

The role of platelet antibodies parallel in many ways that of red cell antibodies. Platelet antibodies may be the cause of reduced survival of transfused platelets and are one cause of platelet refractoriness, the lack of adequate platelet count increments following transfusion. In the plasma of a pregnant woman, platelet antibodies may cause neonatal alloimmune thrombocytopenia (NAIT), the platelet equivalent of hemolytic disease of the newborn (HDN). Autoimmune thrombocytopenic purpura (AITP) involves an autoimmune response similar to that in autoimmune hemolytic anemia (AIHA). Some platelet antibodies may be associated with specific drug therapies, resulting in a drug-induced immune thrombocytopenia. Posttransfusion purpura (PTP) is a thrombocytopenia that develops after transfusion when platelet antibody destroys autologous as well as transfused platelets. In many ways it parallels a delayed hemolytic transfusion reaction.

Platelet Antigens

There are several antigens on platelet cell surfaces, some of which are shared with other cell types. The significant antibodies that react with platelets fall into three groups: ABO antibodies, HLA antibodies, and antibodies to "platelet-specific" antigens. Although platelets are often transfused without regard to ABO compatibility, in some cases ABO antibodies (usually IgG antibodies of high titer) in the recipient (usually group O) may react with platelets carrying large amounts of ABO antigen.[1] ABO antigens on platelets are intrinsic parts of the platelet membrane and are also acquired by adsorption from the plasma. The amounts of ABO antigen present are quite variable from individual to individual. ABO antibodies may cause reduced survival of ABO-incompatible platelets and occasional patients may become refractory on this basis. While other antigens usually associated with red cells (Le[a], Le[b], Ii, and P[2] as well as the Cromer antigens associated with decay accelerating factor[3]) are also found on platelets, there is no evidence that antibodies to these antigens significantly reduce platelet survival in vivo.

The largest group of antibodies reactive with platelets are those directed at Class I HLA antigens, shared by platelets and white cells. (See Chapter 17.) These antibodies (usually IgG) are the ones primarily associated with refractoriness to platelet transfusions. Lymphocytotoxicity tests have been used to detect such antibodies. Lymphocytotoxicity tests detect complement-binding antibodies capable of killing lymphocytes. They do not detect those antibodies that do not bind complement. HLA antibodies are often produced by multitransfused individuals or multiparous women. The laboratory detection of lymphocytotoxic antibodies does not necessarily indicate the pa-

tient will experience reduced survival of transfused platelets.

Non-HLA antibodies to antigenic structures on platelets are often termed "platelet specific," although many of these antigens may be found on other body cells as well (especially endothelial cells). Of the dozens of recognized platelet membrane glycoproteins, four (GPIa, Ib, IIb, and IIIa) have been found to be polymorphic and thus capable of inducing production of alloimmune antibodies.[4] A fifth platelet membrane glycoprotein, GPIV or CD36, carries the isoantigen Nak[a].[5] Approximately 3% of Asians and African-Americans lack GPIV on their platelets[6] and can become immunized against Nak[a] by transfusion or by pregnancy. Although antibodies to these various membrane glycoproteins may, in rare instances, be associated with platelet refractoriness, antibodies to platelet-specific antigens more often are associated with autoimmune thrombocytopenia, posttransfusion purpura, and neonatal alloimmune thrombocytopenia.

Several peripheral blood antigen systems on platelets have been recognized and are named human platelet antigens (HPA).[7] (See Table 16-1.[8]) The nomenclature adopted by the International Society of Blood Transfusion classifies the systems numerically according to the date of publication and alphabetically to reflect their frequency in the population.[9,10] As with red cells, different terminologies for platelet antigens often coexist. The first recognized antigen,[11] ZW[a], is now designated HPA-1a of the HPA-1 system. The HPA-1a antigen is often better known as Pl[A1]. HPA-1a (Pl[A1]) is present on the platelets of about 98% of Whites, and anti-HPA-1a (anti-Pl[A1]) is the most frequently encountered clinically significant antibody to a platelet-specific antigen in the White population. Its antithetical antigen, HPA-1b (Pl[A2]) occurs in 27% of Whites.

The HPA-1a and HPA-1b antigens reside on the platelet membrane glycoprotein GPIIIa. Patients with Glanzmann's thrombasthenia Type I, who lack this glycoprotein, do not express HPA-1 antigens. The HPA-1 polymorphism arises by the substitution of a single base pair (leucine in HPA-1a and proline in HPA-1b) in the coding of DNA at position 33. GPIIIa is also the carrier of HPA-4, -6, -7, and -8 antigens. Alleles in each of these systems also arise due to single amino acid substitutions at different positions. The HPA-2 antigen system is situated on GPIb; the HPA-3 system on GPIIb; and the HPA-5 system on GPIa.[12,13]

Table 16-1 summarizes the platelet-specific alloantigen systems described to date. Phenotype frequencies shown are for Whites only. Significant differences in gene frequencies may be found among Black and Asian populations.

On the platelet membrane, the glycoproteins that carry these "platelet-specific" antigens usually occur not singly, but as heterodimeric compounds, ie, each consisting of two different glycoprotein molecules. (See Fig 16-1.[14]) There-

Table 16-1. Human Platelet Antigen Systems

Alloantigen System	Other Published Names	Alleles	Antigen Frequency	Amino Acid Substitution
HPA-1	Pl[A], Zw	HPA-1a (Pl[A1])	98%	GPIIIa
		HPA-1b (Pl[A2])	27%	Leu ↔ Pro$_{33}$
HPA-2	Ko, Sib	HPA-2a (Ko[b])	99%	GPIb
		HPA-2b (Ko[a])	15%	Thr ↔ Met$_{145}$
HPA-3	Bak, Lek	HPA-3a (Bak[a])	85%	GPIIb
		HPA-3b (Bak[b])	63%	Ile ↔ Ser$_{843}$
		Max[b]	99%	GPIIb
		Max[a]	<1%	Val ↔ Met$_{837}$
HPA-4	Pen, Yuk	HPA-4a (Pen[a])	>99%	GPIIIa
		HPA-4b (Pen[b])	<1%	Arg ↔ Gln$_{143}$
HPA-5	Br, Hc, Zav	HPA-5a (Br[b])	99%	GPIa
		HPA-5b (Br[a])	20%	Glu ↔ Lys$_{505}$
HPA-6	Ca, Tu	HPA-6a (Ca[b])	>99%	GPIIIa
		HPA-6b (Ca[a])	<1%	Arg ↔ Gln$_{489}$
HPA-7	Mo	HPA-7a (Mo[b])	>99%	GPIIIa
		HPA-7b (Mo[a])	<1%	Pro ↔ Ala$_{407}$
HPA-8	Sra	HPA-8a (Sr[b])	>99%	GPIIIa
		HPA-8b (Sr[a])	<1%	Arg ↔ Cys$_{636}$
		Gov[a]	81%	
		Gov[b]	74%	
		Va	<1%	
		Gro	<1%	
		Iy[b]	>99%	GPIb
		Iy[a]	<1%	Gly ↔ Glu$_{15}$
HPA-10w		La[a]	<1%	GPIIIa
		La[b]	>99%	Arg ↔ Gln$_{62}$

Modified from McFarland[8]

fore, platelet glycoprotein names are often paired (eg, Ia/IIa, IIb/IIIa or Ib/IX), referring to the alpha and beta chains in each complex. GPIb/IX is a leucine-rich membrane glycoprotein. The Ia/IIa and IIb/IIIa complexes are members of a broadly distributed family of adhesion molecules called integrins. Integrins are essential for platelet adhesion and aggregation because the molecules serve as receptors for ligands such as fibrinogen, von Willebrand factor, collagen, and fibronectin. When present on other cells, the glycoprotein pairings may differ. For example, on platelets, GPIIIa is normally paired with GPIIb. But on endothelial cells, fibroblasts, and smooth muscle, GPIIIa is paired with a different glycoprotein. Thus, these cells share the HPA-1 and HPA-4 antigens of the GPIIIa molecule, but not the HPA-3 antigens of the GPIIb molecule.

Methods of Detecting Platelet Antibodies

Because of their adhesiveness, platelets do not lend themselves to the traditional agglutination tests used for red cells. And, because platelets normally have cell-bound immunoglobulin, attachment of specific platelet antibodies can be difficult to measure. Many initial tests used indirect assays that measured platelet function, such as platelet aggregation or activation assays, particularly assays for serotonin release. Tests that directly detect platelet antibodies were initially technically difficult, time-consuming, and required specialized equipment. Because of their complexity, such methods have also been limited in the number of different platelets that can practically be tested with each sample. Although some methods, including immunofluorescence, flow cytometry, and radio-

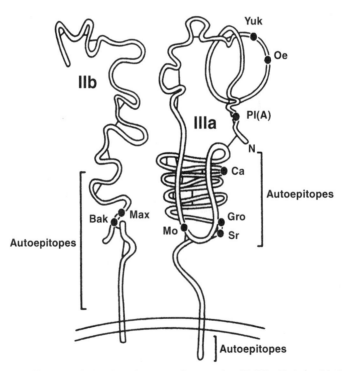

Figure 16-1. Schematic diagram of platelet glycoprotein complex IIb/IIIa. Dots and letters (Yuk, Oe, PI^a, Ca, Gro, Sr, Mo, Bak, Max) designate positions and names of recognized allotypic epitopes. The molecular regions where autoepitopes have been recognized are indicated by brackets.[14]

immunoassay, are utilized as reference methods, the practicality of their use by routine transfusion services or reference laboratories remains limited.

Several newer assays employ solid-phase test systems (see Chapter 12) in which one or more components (eg, whole platelets, isolated proteins, or antibodies) are affixed to a solid medium, usually a microwell; plastic immunobeads may also be used. Antibodies are detected by using red cell indicators or enzyme-linked immunosorbent assay (ELISA) techniques. These methods may vary in their ability to detect antibodies to ABO, HLA, and "platelet-specific" antigens. Some methods more readily allow the identification of antibody specificity. Many tests detect only IgG antibodies; the frequency and clinical significance of IgM and IgA antibodies are not clear.

Some tests are now licensed for use in the United States, and the availability of test kits has made testing more accessible for many laboratories. However, as with red cell antibodies, no single method accurately detects all antibodies and multiple systems must often be used.[15-17] The test methods discussed below are general ones; variations of each test method are also used. Lymphocytotoxicity tests are discussed in Chapter 17.

A solid-phase red cell adherence assay (SPRCA)[18] utilizes microwells coated with either fresh or dried whole platelets. (See Fig 16-2.) After the platelets are affixed to the wells, a patient's plasma is added and any antibody present is allowed to bind directly to the platelets. After a washing phase to remove unbound antibody, indicator red cells coated with antihuman globulin are added and the microwell plate is centrifuged. If the platelets are coated with antibody, the antiglobulin-sensitized red cells will bind to them, leaving a layer of red cells "effaced" across the microwell. If no antibody was present, the red cells form a pellet in the center of the well. Weak reactions give intermediate results. This solid-phase assay can detect HLA, ABO, and

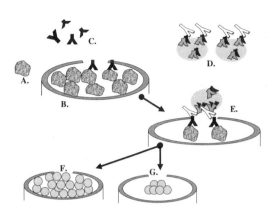

Figure 16-2. SPRCA assay. Platelets (A) are affixed to a microwell (B). Plasma is added and, if present, antibody (C) combines with platelets. After washing, indicator red cells (D) coated with antibody and antihuman globulin are added and combine with the antibody on the platelets (E). If the test is positive, the indicator red cells are effaced across the microwell (F). In a negative test (G), the unbound red cells form a pellet at the bottom of the microwell.

platelet-specific IgG antibodies. Treatment of platelets with chloroquine[19] or acid[20] selectively weakens or destroys HLA antigens, leaving the known platelet-specific antigens intact. Care must be taken in interpreting results because occasionally HLA reactivity may remain with treated platelets, giving potentially misleading results.

Solid-phase methodology can also be used with isolated platelet glycoproteins and isolated HLA antigens. As indicated in Table 16-1, the polymorphic epitopes of several platelet antigens are known, especially to complexes of GPIIb/IIIa and Ia/IIa. Thus, reactivity with selected glycoproteins can indicate specificity. One licensed test kit uses this method coupled with an ELISA as a reaction indicator.[21]

In the modified antigen capture ELISA (MACE) assay, antibody rather than antigen (platelet) is affixed in solid phase. Test platelets and test serum are first incubated to allow any antibody present to combine. The platelets are then lysed and the lysate added to the microwells on which monoclonal antibody to specific glycoproteins has been affixed. This monoclonal antibody then captures the glycoprotein. After washing, an enzyme-labeled antihuman IgG is added. It binds to the human antibody adhering to the glycoprotein. An ELISA method is used to detect this reaction, measuring the color change when substrate is added. (See Fig 16-3.)

In the slightly more complex monoclonal antibody immobilization of platelet antigens (MAIPA) assay,[22,23] monoclonal goat antimouse IgG antibody is affixed to the microplate well. (See Fig 16-4.) Test platelets are first incubated with test serum, washed, and then incubated with a mouse monoclonal antibody specific for platelet glycoprotein. The platelets are then lysed and the diluted lysate added to the microplate well. The bound goat antimouse IgG binds the mouse monoclonal antibody and the attached glycoprotein-human antibody complex. The human antibody is detected by adding an enzyme-labeled goat antihuman IgG. Additional steps may be required to circumvent mouse antibodies in the human test serum, which can cause false-positive results.[24] False-negative results may also occur if the hu-

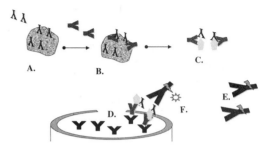

Figure 16-4. MAIPA assay. Antibody (if present) combines with platelets (A) which are then mixed with mouse monoclonal antibody to platelet glycoprotein (B). The cells are lysed to yield a reaction complex (C). This complex is added to microwell on which goat antimouse monoclonal antibody (D) has been immobilized. The reaction complex is captured and conjugated antihuman IgG (E) is then added. In the presence of substrate, a measurable color change occurs (F).

man and mouse monoclonal antibody react with the same or closely similar epitopes, creating a competition for binding sites.

MACE and MAIPA assays have an advantage over the solid-phase assays because reactions between test platelets and test serum occur while the platelets are whole and not immobilized. This avoids the possibility that specific antigenic epitopes are "lost" during either the isolation of glycoprotein or the immobilization stage.

A platelet filtration assay also detects HLA and platelet-specific antigens. The patient's serum or plasma is incubated with one drop of a pooled platelet suspension. After incubation, platelets are washed briefly and applied to an immunofiltration module, which traps them on the surface of a membrane. Platelet-bound antibodies are detected by addition of enzymatically conjugated antihuman IgG and substrate. Positive results are qualitative only. The assay is also used to detect in-vivo platelet-associated IgG. Platelet samples tested in parallel by platelet filtration and SPRCA demonstrated 91% concordance.[25]

Flow cytometry has also been adapted for detection of platelet antibodies using

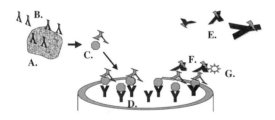

Figure 16-3. MACE assay. Platelets (A) are incubated with serum containing antibody (B). After antigen and antibody have combined, the platelets are washed, then lysed to yield specific glycoprotein (C) attached to antibody. When added to microwell to which monoclonal antibody to the glycoprotein (D) has been affixed, the glycoprotein-antibody complex becomes immobilized. After washing, antihuman IgG (E) is added. This attaches to the platelet antibody (F). If the anti-IgG is conjugated, substrate is added to produce a measurable color change (G).

immunofluorescence methods. (See Chapter 12.) In platelet immunofluorescence tests, fluorescein-labeled antihuman globulin reagent is used to detect antibody bound to intact (whole) platelets. A direct test measures platelet-associated IgG bound in vivo. Indirect tests, in which whole platelets are first incubated with test serum, can be used for platelet crossmatching, although it may be less practical than other methods for testing large numbers of potential donor units. Traditional reading of the test using a fluorescence microscope is subjective; reading by flow cytometry is quantitative and more accurate, but is more expensive.[26,27] Use of these tests is usually limited to specialized laboratories.

Most test methods that utilize fresh whole platelets can also be used to detect platelet-associated IgG. This is important in evaluating suspected cases of immune thrombocytopenic purpura (ITP) and thrombotic thrombocytopenic purpura (TTP). Such methods may also be adapted for direct platelet crossmatching with product in inventory or for typing platelets for specific antigens. Molecular typing by polymerase chain reaction (PCR) is available for many platelet antigens.

Platelet Refractoriness

Failure to obtain an adequate increase in platelet count occurs in about 20-70% of multitransfused thrombocytopenic patients.[28] Patients treated for malignant hematopoietic disorders are particularly likely to become refractory to platelet transfusions. There are, however, no strong consensus criteria for determining refractoriness. A lack of expected response to two platelet transfusions is the most commonly accepted definition. However, some authors use criteria such as poor response to three platelet transfusions within a 2-week period. Response is often determined by calculating either a corrected platelet count increment (CCI) or a percent predicted platelet count increment (PPCI). (See Table 16-2.[29])

Although platelet alloimmunization is one cause of refractoriness, there are many nonimmune reasons that transfused platelets may not yield the expected increase in platelet count. Some of these are listed in Table 16-3. Even when possible immune causes of refractoriness are identified, nonimmune factors are often simultaneously present. No single factor can consistently be cited in many cases.

Immune causes of platelet refractoriness to transfusion include ABO antibodies, HLA antibodies, platelet-specific allo- and autoantibodies, and drug-dependent antibodies. Antibodies to HLA antigens are the most common immune cause and may be detected by lymphocytotoxicity tests or by many of the platelet antibody tests discussed above. Lymphocytotoxicity tests will not detect antibodies that do not bind complement, but these antibodies may be detected by platelet antibody tests. Surprisingly, HLA antibodies may disappear from the patient's plasma despite continued exposure through transfusions.[30]

Several strategies may be considered when selecting platelets for transfusion to refractory patients. Nonimmune causes and ABO incompatibility should be excluded. When antibodies to HLA antigens are demonstrated, one approach is to transfuse single-donor apheresis components matched to the patient's HLA type. This approach is widely used and generally effective.[31] A disadvantage is that a pool of 1000-3000 or more random, HLA-typed potential apheresis donors is generally necessary to find sufficient HLA-compatible matches.[32] Moreover, donor selection on the basis of HLA type can lead to the exclusion of donors of an HLA type different from that of the recipient but potentially effective if the recipient is alloimmunized to other antigenic determinants.[33] Another disadvantage is that posttransfusion determination of HLA-type is difficult if not impossible. In patients likely to require transfusion, HLA-typing should be performed in advance.

Ordering platelets as "HLA-matched," however, does not necessarily lead to receiving HLA-identical or even well-matched platelets. It is important to understand the degree of match that may be provided. (See Table 16-4.) Platelets received following a request for "HLA-matched" are typically the closest match obtainable within the constraints of time and donor availability. In one study,[34] 43% of platelets provided as HLA-matched were relatively poor grade B or C matches. The best increase in CCI is within the subset of grade A and B1U or

B2U HLA matches. According to AABB *Standards for Blood Banks and Transfusion Services*,[35(p68)] HLA-matched platelets should be irradiated to prevent graft-vs-host disease.

A second approach to provide effective platelets is to utilize a pretransfusion platelet crossmatching assay. This approach can be used to predict, and therefore avoid, subsequent platelet transfusion failures.[36] SPRCA is the most widely used method for platelet crossmatch. Good correlation between test results and posttransfusion platelet counts have been

Table 16-2. Determination of Response to Transfused Platelets[29]

A. Calculation of the Corrected Count Increment (CCI)

$$CCI = \frac{PI \times SA \times 10^{11}}{n}$$

PI = platelet count increment

SA = surface area

n = number of platelets transfused

EXAMPLE: If 4×10^{11} platelets are transfused to a patient whose body surface is 1.8 m^2 and the increase in platelet count posttransfusion is 25,000 per µL, then:

$$CCI = \frac{25,000 \times 1.8 \times 10^{11}}{4 \times 10^{11}} = 11,250 \quad \text{platelets per µL per m}^2$$

B. Calculation of Predicted Platelet Count Increment (PPCI) and Percent Predicted Platelet Count Increment (%PPCI)

$$PPCI = \frac{n \times 0.67}{BV \times 1000}$$

n = number of platelets transfused

0.67 = correction factor for splenic uptake

BV = blood volume in mL (weight in kg $\times$ 70 mL/kg)

1000 = conversion factor for mL to µL

$$\%PPCI = \frac{\text{Observed platelet count increment}}{PPCI}$$

EXAMPLE: If 4×10^{11} platelets are transfused to a 70 kg person (blood volume = 70 kg x 70 mL/kg = 4900 mL), then:

$$PPCI = \frac{4 \times 10^{11} \times 0.67}{1000 \times 4900} = 54,700 \text{ platelets / µL}$$

If the observed platelet count increase posttransfusion is 25,000/µL, then:

$$\%PPCI = \frac{27,000}{54,700} = 49\%$$

Table 16-3. Some Nonimmune Causes of Platelet Refractoriness

Active Bleeding

Fever

Sepsis

Splenomegaly (splenic sequestration)

Disseminated Intravascular Coagulation

Marrow Transplantation

Age of the Transfused Platelets

Poor Storage of Platelets Prior to Transfusion

Effects of Drugs (may include immune mechanisms)

Antibiotics

Intravenous Amphotericin B

Thrombotic Thrombocytopenic Purpura

achieved.[18,37,38] Compared with HLA-matching, crossmatching can prove both more convenient and economically advantageous. It avoids exclusion of HLA-mismatched but compatible, donors and has the added advantage of selecting platelets when the antibody(-ies) involved is (are) directed to platelet-specific antigens. Platelet crossmatching, however, will not always be successful. Not all antibodies may be detected. When 70% or more of donors are reactive, finding sufficient compatible units may be problematic and selection of HLA-matched platelets may be more practical. It should be confirmed in such cases that antibodies to platelet-specific antigens are not present; if they are, donors of known platelet antigen phenotype or family members (who may statistically be more likely to share the patient's phenotype) should be tested. Many facilities will use a combination of HLA matching and platelet crossmatching for their refractory patients.

Prevention of Platelet Alloimmunization

HLA and platelet-specific alloantibodies do not occur naturally. They are acquired through exposure to alloantigens through pregnancy and blood transfusion. Studies of HLA alloimmunization in patients transfused with platelets have found the development of antibodies as early as 10 days (but generally 21-28 days) after primary exposure and 4 days after secondary exposure in patients previously transfused or pregnant.[39] The likelihood of HLA alloimmunization related to transfusion in patients not previously sensitized has been found to be variable, ranging from 18%[39] to 50%.[40] The risk of HLA alloimmunization appears to be related to the underlying disease as well as the immunosuppressive effects of treatment regimens. Exposure to leukocytes during

Table 16-4. Classification of Donor/Recipient Pairs on the Basis of HLA Match[33]

A	All four donor antigens are identical to those of recipient
B1U	Only three antigens detected in donor; all present in recipient
B1XC	Three donor antigens identical to recipient; fourth antigen cross-reactive
B2U	Only two antigens detected in donor; both present in recipient
B2UX	Only three antigens detected in donor; two are identical with recipient, third is cross-reactive
BX2	Two donor antigens are identical to those of recipient; third and fourth antigens are cross-reactive
C	One donor antigen is not present in recipient and is not cross-reactive
D	Two donor antigens are not present in recipient and are not cross-reactive

transfusion is probably a greater cause of alloimmunization to HLA antigens than is exposure to HLA antigens on platelets themselves. Platelets carry Class I HLA antigens, but lack Class II antigens necessary for primary sensitization.

Several strategies have evolved to prevent alloimmunization to platelets. These include reduction of concomitant leukocytes, ultraviolet B (UVB) irradiation and limiting exposure to multiple donors (primarily through use of apheresis platelets rather than pooled platelet concentrates). The report of the Trial to Reduce Alloimmunization to Platelets (TRAP) Study Group,[41] indicated that use of either filtered or UVB-irradiated blood components reduced the incidence of HLA antibody generation from 45% to 17-18%. The prevalance of platelet refractoriness was reduced from 18% to 8%. Although a relationship had been reported between alloimmunization and the number of donor exposures,[42] the TRAP study found it was the reduction of leukocytes, not the number of donor exposures, that was significant. Thus, random leukocyte-reduced, pooled platelet concentrates may be clinically equivalent to single-donor apheresis platelets, at least in terms of alloimmunization.[43]

Autoimmune Thrombocytopenic Purpura

Autoantibodies directed against platelet antigens may result in thrombocytopenia. AITP may be secondary to other diseases (eg, malignancy, other autoimmune conditions) or may be idiopathic. Especially in young children, transient acute thrombocytopenia following a viral infection is also autoimmune in nature.

Although analogies to red cell autoimmune hemolytic anemia are evident, there are some differences. As with AIHA, autoantibody may or may not be found free in the plasma. A test to detect cell-bound IgG (analogous to the direct antiglobulin test of red cells) may be helpful. However, a significant amount of platelet-associated IgG is found within the cell, associated with alpha granules, not on the cell surface. This IgG is not an antigen-specific antibody but reflects the overall plasma composition and concentration of IgG. Total platelet IgG (both intracellular and surface-bound) are elevated in AITP and were once considered significant in clinical evaluation of AITP. But it has been shown that total platelet IgG is similarly elevated in patients with nonimmune platelet destruction.[44] Surface-bound IgG is a better indicator of the presence of specific platelet antibodies than total platelet IgG, but surface-bound IgG can also be elevated in some nonimmune thrombocytopenias. (Normal platelets have about 60-200 molecules of surface IgG per cell.)

When eluates are prepared from platelets of patients with AITP, the specificities of most platelet autoantibodies are shown to be directed against structures on glycoprotein complexes IIb/IIIa and/or Ib/IX. The epitopes are heterogeneous; areas of reactivity are indicated in Fig 16-1. (In individuals with human immunodeficiency virus (HIV), platelet autoantibodies and thrombocytopenia may result from structural similarity of GPIIb/IIIa with HIV glycoproteins.[45]) As with red cell autoantibodies, the specificity of platelet autoantibodies may have no clinical utility. Antibodies of specificities similar to those in the eluate may or may not be demonstrable in the plasma.[11] As in AIHA, crossmatching for serologically compatible platelets will likely be unsuccessful for patients with detectable autoantibodies in their plasma because all normal platelets should carry the target complexes.

Posttransfusion Purpura

Posttransfusion purpura is a rare complication of blood transfusion. It is characterized by acute thrombocytopenia occurring approximately 1 week after red cell transfusion. Most patients are multiparous women who have been sensitized to platelets through pregnancies. PTP is also seen in men and women sensitized through previous transfusions. PTP is most often associated with anti-HPA-1a (anti-Pl[A1]), although other specificities have been implicated, almost always associated with antigens on GPIIb/IIIa.[13] PTP differs from transfusion reactions caused by red cell antibodies since the patient's own antigen-negative (usually HPA-1a-negative) platelets as well as any transfused antigen-positive platelets are destroyed. Likewise, transfusion of antigen-negative platelets is usually of no value during the acute phase of PTP, although even transient platelet survival may have short-term benefits.[46] Treatment and/or plasmapheresis with intravenous immunoglobulin (IVIG) are often helpful. The prognosis in PTP is quite good and recurrence after a subsequent transfusion is rare. Following recovery, it is usually recommended that the patient be transfused with washed RBCs or with blood components from antigen-negative (usually HPA-1a-negative) donors.

Neonatal Alloimmune Thrombocytopenia

NAIT (sometimes called neonatal immune thrombocytopenia or NIT) is the platelet equivalent of hemolytic disease of the newborn and occurs with a frequency of 1 in 2000 to 3000 live births. Maternal antibody crosses the placenta to attack the infant's platelets. Unlike HDN, NAIT often (>60%) occurs during the first pregnancy. Affected infants may be severely thrombocytopenic and at high risk, especially for intracranial bleeds. Antibodies to platelet-specific antigens are most often involved. Among Whites, the antibody is most often anti-HPA-1a, although other specificities have been implicated as well. If donor platelets compatible with the mother's plasma are not immediately available, platelets from the mother herself should be considered. When the mother's platelets are used, maternal plasma should be removed or reduced prior to transfusion. Subsequent pregnancies should be carefully monitored because the recurrence rate of NAIT is 90%.[13] When possible, compatible platelets can be maintained on hand at the expected delivery time. Many blood suppliers

attempt to maintain HPA-1a-negative platelets in inventory or have appropriate donors available. Surprisingly, however, provision of random (presumably HPA-1a-positive) platelets may be clinically effective in many cases of NAIT due to anti-HPA-1a alloantibodies and should be considered if HPA-1a-negative product is not readily available.[47]

Maternal plasma antibody is the test sample usually required for the laboratory investigation of possible NAIT. If no antibody is detected (or if the involvement of detected antibody is doubted), testing the maternal plasma with platelets from the father may prove useful. Reactivity with only the father's platelets may indicate the presence of antibody directed to a low-incidence antigen. Because of the frequent association with anti-HPA-1a, typing the mother's platelets for the HPA-1a antigen is helpful. Some workers have proposed typing all pregnant women as a predictive measure. (HPA-1a typing may be performed serologically or by PCR methodology.) However, because antibody production is linked to the HLA-DRw52a phenotype, HPA-1a typing alone will not predict those individuals who will produce antibody. Platelets from the infant can be tested for platelet-bound IgG, but the very low platelet count of affected infants almost always makes this impractical and undesirable. Prenatal detection of maternal antibody to platelet-specific antigens and/or a history of thrombocytopenic infants should be considered potentially important indicators.[48]

Antibodies to HLA antigens can also cause NAIT,[49-51] although the extent of their involvement is controversial. Because HLA antibodies are common in the sera of pregnant women, their presence cannot be considered a good predictor of NAIT. The risk of thrombocytopenia in the fetus may be reduced by adsorption of HLA antibodies by HLA receptors on the placenta. Especially in the absence of antibodies to "platelet-specific" antigens, NAIT due to HLA antibodies should be considered. ABO antibodies may also occasionally be a cause of NAIT.

Drug-Induced Platelet Antibodies

Thrombocytopenia associated with specific drugs is not uncommon. Drugs often implicated include quinidine/quinine, sulfa drugs, heparin, and colloidal gold. Both drug-dependent and drug-independent antibodies may be produced. Drug-independent antibodies, although stimulated by drugs, do not require the continued presence of the drug to react with platelets and are serologically indistinguishable from other platelet autoantibodies. (Unlike typical AITP, these antibodies are transient.) Drug-dependent antibodies apparently combine with platelets in such a way as to create neoantigens to which antibodies are then formed. The drug must be present for the antibody to react. These antibodies can cause a thrombocytopenia of sudden and rapid onset, usually resolving when the drug is discontinued.

Detection Methods

Detection of drug-dependent platelet antibodies remains somewhat problematic. At least in theory, many tests for platelet antibodies can be used to detect drug-dependent antibodies by testing the patient's serum or plasma against platelets (or specific platelet glycoproteins) in the presence of the drug or by testing for platelet-bound IgG after the drug has been administered. Strict controls must be employed. Drug concentration may be critical. In many cases, however, the exact mechanism for drug-induced thrombocytopenia has not been determined, and even when a definitive association has been made, detection of specific antibodies may not be straightforward. SPRCA has been used for detection of a variety of drug-dependent antibodies,[52,53] and solid-phase ELISA tests may be used to detect at least some heparin-dependent antibodies.[54] Flow cytometry has proved to be an effective means of detecting quinine-, quinidine-, and sulfamethoxazole-dependent antibodies, but maintenance of specific drug concentrations during the multiple wash phases is critical.[55,56] Indirect assays, such as serotonin release, platelet aggregation, and platelet factor 4, are also used to detect heparin-dependent antibodies.[57,58] In some cases, determination of the specific glycoprotein to which antibody is directed may provide useful clinical information. For example, drug-dependent antibody to GPIb/IX was associated with a more acute, but reversible quinine-induced thrombocytopenia, whereas antibody to GPIIb/IIIa was associated with a more prolonged course.[59]

Heparin-Induced Thrombocytopenia

Two types of heparin-induced thrombocytopenia (HIT) have been recognized. Type I, of nonimmune origin, presents with mild transient thrombocytopenia within minutes to several days after heparin exposure, but generally resolves despite ongoing heparin therapy and is clinically of little importance. In contrast, immune, or Type II, HIT may lead to life- and limb-threatening thrombotic complications and requires careful evaluation and management of afflicted patients.

The exact incidence rate of HIT is unknown, but it may develop in 3% or more of patients treated with unfractionated heparin. Low-molecular-weight heparin is less likely to be associated with either antibody production or thrombocytopenia.[60] Bovine heparin appears somewhat more likely to cause HIT than porcine heparin. Thrombocytopenia occurs generally within 5-14 days after primary exposure and sooner after secondary exposure to the drug. The platelet count is often less than 100,000/µL and usually recovers within 5-7 days upon discontinuation of heparin.

About 30% of patients with HIT, or approximately 0.9% of patients who receive heparin, develop thrombosis (HITT), which can occur in the arterial, venous, or both systems.[61,62] Patients may develop cardiovascular problems, myocardial infarction, limb ischemia, deep venous thrombosis, or ischemia of other organs. The thrombotic complications may force limb amputation and may prove fatal.

Thrombosis, or a decrease in platelet count to below 100,000-150,000/μL (or 40% of preadministration counts), should raise concern about HIT. *Heparin, including heparin flushes and heparin-coated catheters, should be discontinued* and the patient should be evaluated for laboratory evidence of HIT and signs of thrombosis. In mild-to-moderate thrombocytopenia, monitoring of platelet counts and observation may be sufficient, but due to the high risk of thrombosis, treatment with alternative anticoagulants is frequently recommended. Warfarin should be avoided in the early treatment of HIT because it does not prevent thrombosis in this setting and may provoke limb-threatening venous gangrene. Among suitable anticoagulants are danaparoid, a low-molecular-weight heparinoid, and hirudin, a natural thrombin inhibitor. Selected patients may also benefit from thrombolectomy or thrombolytic therapy. Antiplatelet agents (such as aspirin, dipyridamole, dextran, or prostaglandins), intravenous immune globulin, and plasmapheresis have been used as adjuncts to anticoagulative therapy, particularly for patients who require heparin exposure during cardiopulmonary bypass surgery. Platelet transfusion should be avoided, given that bleeding is a rare complication in HIT and administration of platelets may precipitate thrombosis.[63-65]

Evidence suggests that heparin forms a complex with platelet factor 4, a tetrameric protein released from platelet alpha granules. Antibodies (both IgG and IgM) form against various epitopes on this complex and attach it to activated platelets and receptors. Antibodies to platelet factor 4 alone also may be present. The antibody may also bind to the complexes at other sites, notably on endothelial cells. Thus, HIT might involve activation and damage of not only platelets but also of endothelium, causing increased susceptibility to thrombosis. This new understanding of the mechanism of heparin antibodies is exploited by ELISA tests in which microwells are coated with the complexes rather than with the platelets themselves.[54]

Until recently, laboratory tests for heparin-associated antibodies have relied upon platelet aggregation or activation. The serotonin release assay demonstrated perhaps the best performance characteristics, but platelet aggregation, a simpler test, has been more widely used. Platelets from normal individuals are incubated with the patient's plasma with and without the addition of heparin; increased aggregation is observed with the heparin in a positive test. A two-point method tests using both low-dose and high-dose heparin; an inhibition of aggregation is expected with the higher dose. The heparin-induced platelet activation assay is performed in a microwell and similarly contrasts aggregation with high and low volumes of heparin.

In the serotonin release assay, washed platelets labeled with ^{14}C are incubated with buffer containing calcium ions. The test plasma and heparin are added, and the mixture is agitated at 37 C for 1 hour. The radiation level in the supernatant fluid is then measured to indicate the degree of isotope release. In a positive test, 20% or more of the ^{14}C-serotonin is released. As in the previous tests, when performed with a high quantity of heparin, release should be inhibited. The need for radioactive materials has limited the use of this test. Other methods measure platelet adenosine triphosphate release.

Another approach has been to measure the actual binding of antibody onto platelets. Radioimmunoassays and luminescence (including using flow cytometry) have been utilized. In SPRCA, microwells coated with platelets are incubated with the test serum/plasma and heparin; after washing, indicator red cells are added. Reactivity in tests with heparin but not without indicates heparin antibodies.[52,66] (Similar tests using other drugs may also be performed.[53]) ELISA methods, using whole rather than immobilized platelets, have also been used to detect platelet-bound heparin antibodies.

Granulocyte/Neutrophil Antigens and Antibodies

Granulocyte-specific antibodies have been associated with clinical syndromes similar to those seen with antibodies to red cell and platelet antigens. Autoimmune neutropenia, usually occurring in adults, may be idiopathic or may occur secondary to such diseases as rheumatoid arthritis, systemic lupus erythematosus, or bacterial infections. In autoimmune neutropenia of infancy, usually occurring in children between the ages of 6 months to 2 years, the autoantibody is often self-limiting (with recovery usually in 7-24 months) and the condition is relatively benign and manageable with antibiotics.[67] Drug-dependent antibodies can also cause neutropenia.

Neonatal alloimmune neutropenia (NAN) is caused by maternal antibodies against alloantigens of fetal neutrophils; the most frequent specificities seen are antibodies to the NA1, NA2, and NB1 antigens. (See Table 16-5.) NAN most often occurs in women of the neutrophil alloantigen phenotypes NA1/NA1 and NA2/NA2; it may also occur in women of the rare NA_{null} phenotype who lack the FcRIII protein. Nonhemolytic, febrile transfusion reactions are often associated with granulocyte antibodies, although they are more often due to antibodies to Class I HLA antigens, which also are present on granulocytes. The neutropenia in all these cases can occasionally be life-threatening due to increased susceptibility to infection. In most cases, the patient is managed with antibiotics, intravenous immunoglobulin, granulocyte colony-stimulating growth factor, and plasma exchange.

Transfusion-related acute lung injury (TRALI) has also been reported to be induced by neutrophil antibodies, although some reports suggest that antibodies to HLA antigens are the more common sensitizer. In TRALI, the causative antibodies are found not in the recipient's plasma, but in the plasma of the blood donor (see Chapters 17 and 27). Recent reports have postulated that another etiology for TRALI is possible. This theory suggests that two events must coincide for TRALI to occur: 1) the patient must have a predisposing clinical condition that releases cytokines or other factors that prime neutrophils, causing adherence to endothelium, and 2) the patient must receive a transfusion of biologically active lipids (which also stimulate neutrophils) from stored blood components.[68] (In one study,[68] neutrophil antibodies were detected in only 3 of 10 incidents of TRALI, and none of the donors had HLA antibodies.)

The first granulocyte-specific antigen (NA1) was demonstrated in 1966 by Lalezari and Bernard.[69] NA1 and its antithetical antigen NA2 are present on the glycoprotein FcRIIIb, an IgG Fc receptor molecule. Antibodies to NA1 and NA2 are the most frequently identified. Cells lacking FcRIII have no NA antigens (NA_{null}); this condition may be inherited and is also associated with paroxysmal nocturnal hemoglobinuria, an acquired condition. Depression of granulocyte antigens is also seen in chronic myelogenous leukemia and in premature in-

Table 16-5. Granulocyte Alloantigen Frequencies

Granulocyte-Specific Antigens		Antigens Shared with Other Cells	
NA1	46%	5a	32.6%
NA2	88%	5b	96.4%
NB1	97%	MART	99%
LAN	>99%	Ond	>99%
SAR	>99%	SL	66%
SH	5%		

fants. The FcRIII protein also carries many other granulocyte-specific antigens, including LAN and SH. Other antigens, notably NB1, are not associated with FcRIII. The antigens ND1 and NE1 were originally defined by autoantibodies, rather than by alloantibodies. Antigen typing for NA1, NA2, and SH can be performed on genomic DNA using PCR.[70]

Additional antigens on granulocytes are shared with other cells and are not granulocyte-specific. These include Class I HLA 5a/5b, Mart, Ond, and SL. The group 5 system has two antigens (5a and 5b), which are also present on platelets as well as on lymphocytes. The gene encoding the group 5 system is located on chromosome 4. The antibodies directed at these antigens are usually agglutinins; they occasionally occur in women after pregnancy and may be associated with febrile transfusion reactions. Potent anti-5b agglutinins in transfused plasma have been responsible for TRALI.[71] Mart and Ond, both high-incidence antigens, are also present on monocytes and lymphocytes. SL antigens are shared with T lymphocytes.

Tests for granulocyte antibodies are not widely performed, although the implication of neutrophil antibodies as a cause of TRALI has increased the demand. Agglutination tests, performed in tube, capillary, or microplate formats, use heat-inactivated serum in the presence of EDTA and require fresh granulocytes. Immunofluorescence tests, read with either a fluorescence microscope or a flow cytometer, are also used and are capable of detecting granulocyte-bound antiglobulin. A combination of agglutination and immunofluorescence tests is beneficial.[72] Other methods include chemiluminescence and a monoclonal antibody immobilization of granulocyte antigens (MAIGA) assay, similar to the MAIPA assay. An advantage of the MAIGA assay is its ability to differentiate readily between HLA and granulocyte-specific antibodies. For further information about granulocyte antigens and antibodies, consult the Suggested Reading.

References

1. Ogasawara K, Ueki J, Takenaka M, Furihata K. Study on the expression of ABH antigens on platelets. Blood 1993;82:993-9.
2. Dunstan RA, Simpson MB. Heterogeneous distribution of antigens on human platelets demonstrated by fluorescence flow cytometry. Br J Haematol 1985;61:603-9.
3. Daniels G. Human blood groups. Oxford, England: Blackwell Scientific Publications. 1995:573.
4. Newman PJ, Valetin N. Human platelet alloantigens: Recent findings, new perspectives. Thromb Hemostat 1995;84:234-9.
5. Greenwalt DE, Lipsky RH, Ockenhouse CF, et al. Membrane glycoprotein CD36: A review of its roles in adherence, signal transduction, and transfusion medicine. Blood 1992;80:1105-15.
6. Curtis BR, Aster RH. Incidence of the Nak(a)-negative platelet phenotype in African Americans is similar to that of Asians. Transfusion 1996;36:331-4.
7. McFarland JG. Platelet immunology and alloimmunization. In: Rossi EC, Simon TL, Moss GS, Gould SA, eds. Principles of transfusion medicine. 2nd ed. Baltimore: Williams & Wilkins, 1996:231-44.
8. McFarland J. Nomenclature update: HLA, HPA and RBCs. Platelet specific antigen nomenclature. In: The compendium: A selection of short topic presentations. Bethesda, MD: American Association of Blood Banks, 1997.
9. von dem Borne AEGKr, Décary F. ICSH/ISBT Working Party on Platelet Serology: Nomenclature of platelet-specific antigens. Vox Sang 1990;58:176.
10. von dem Borne AEGKr, Kaplan C, Minchinton R. Nomenclature of human platelet alloantigens. Blood 1995;85:1409-10.
11. van Loghem JJ, Dorfmeijer H, van der Hart M. Serological and genetical studies on a platelet antigen (Zw). Vox Sang 1959;4:161-9.
12. Aster RH. Platelet-specific alloantigen systems: History, clinical significance and molecular biology. In: Nance ST, ed. Alloimmunity: 1993 and beyond. Bethesda, MD: American Association of Blood Banks, 1993:83-116.
13. von dem Borne AEGKr, Sinsek S, van der Schoot, et al. Platelet and neutrophil alloantigens: Their nature and role in immune-mediated cytopenias. In: Garratty G, ed. Immunobiology of transfusion medicine. New York: Marcel Dekker, Inc, 1994:149-71.
14. Müeller-Eckhardt, C. Platelet autoimmunity. In: Silberstein LE, ed. Autoimmune disorders of blood. Bethesda, MD: American Association of Blood Banks, 1996:15-150.
15. Teramura G, Slichter SJ. Report on the Sixth International Society of Blood Transfusion Platelet Serology Workshop. Transfusion 1996;36:75-81.
16. Berchtold P, Muller D, Beardsley D, et al. International study to compare antigen-specific methods used in the measurement of antiplatelet autoantibodies. Br J Haematol 1997;96:477-83.
17. Stockelberg D, Hou M, Jacobsson S, et al. Detection of platelet antibodies in chronic idiopathic thrombocytopenic purpura (ITP). A comparative study using flow cytometry, a whole platelet ELISA, and an antigen capture ELISA. Eur J Haematol 1996;56:72-7.

18. Rachel JM, Sinor LT, Tawfik OW, et al. A solid-phase red cell adherence test for platelet crossmatching. Med Lab Sci 1985;42:194-5.

19. Nordhagen R, Flaathen S. Chloroquine removal of HLA antigens from platelets for the platelet immunofluorescence test. Vox Sang 1985;48:156-9.

20. Kurata Y, Oshida M, Take H, et al. Acid treatment of platelets as a simple procedure for distinguishing platelet-specific antibodies from anti-HLA antibodies: Comparison with chloroquine treatment. Vox Sang 1990;59:106-11.

21. GTI PAKPLUS[TM] Platelet Antibody Screening Kit (package insert). Brookfield, WI: GTI, 1996.

22. Kiefel V, Santoso S, Weisheit M, Müeller-Eckhardt C. Monoclonal antibody-specific immobilization of platelet antigens (MAIPA): A new tool for the identification of platelet-reactive antibodies. Blood 1987;70:1722-6.

23. Kiefel V. The MAIPA assay and its applications in immunohematology. Transfus Med 1992;2:181-8.

24. Morel-Kopp MC, Daviet L, McGregor J, et al. Drawbacks of the MAIPA technique in characterising human anti-platelet antibodies. Blood Coag Fibrinol 1996;7:144-6.

25. Rachel JM, Plapp FV, Hawk SE, et al. A rapid qualitative assay for platelet associated IgG (abstract). Transfusion 1992;32(Suppl):13S.

26. Allen DL, Chapman J, Phillips PK, Ouwehand WE. Sensitivity of the platelet immunofluoresence test (PIFT) and the MAIPA assay for the detection of platelet-reactive alloantibodies: A report on two U.K. National Platelet Workshop exercises. Transfus Med 1994;4:157-64.

27. Kohler M, Dittman J, Legler TJ, et al. Flow cytometric detection of platelet-reactive antibodies and application in platelet crossmatching. Transfusion 1996;36:250-5.

28. Dzik WH. Leukoreduced blood components: Laboratory and clinical aspects. In: Rossi EC, Simon TL, Moss GS, Gould SA, eds. Principles of transfusion medicine. 2nd ed. Baltimore, MD: Williams and Wilkins, 1995:353-73.

29. Petz LD. Diagnosis and management of refractoriness to platelet transfusion. In: Ramsey G, ed. Platelet transfusion: Problems and solutions. Bethesda, MD: American Association of Blood Banks, 1997.

30. Murphy MF, Metcalfe P, Ord J, et al. Disappearance of HLA and platelet-specific antibodies in acute leukemia patients alloimmunized by multiple transfusions. Br J Haematol 1987;67:255-60.

31. Moroff G, Garratty G, Heal JM, et al. Selection of platelets for refractory patients by HLA matching and prospective crossmatching. Transfusion 1992;32:633-40.

32. Bolgiano DC, Larson EB, Slichter SJ. A model to determine required pool size for HLA-typed community donor apheresis programs. Transfusion 1989;29:306-10.

33. Duquesnoy RJ, Filip DJ, Rodey G, et al. Successful transfusion of platelet "mismatched" for HLA antigens to alloimmunized thrombocytopenic patients. Am J Hematol 1997;2:219-26.

34. Dahlke MB, Weiss KL. Platelet transfusions from donors mismatched from crossreactive HLA antigens. Transfusion 1984;24:299-302.

35. Menitove JE, ed. Standards for blood banks and transfusion services, 19th ed. Bethesda, MD: American Association of Blood Banks, 1999.

36. Rachel JM, Summers TC, Sinor LT, et al. Use of a solid phase red blood cell adherence method for pretransfusion platelet compatibility testing. Am J Clin Pathol 1988;90:63-8.

37. O'Connell BA, Schiffer CA. Donor selection for alloimmunized patients by platelet cross matching of random-donor platelet concentrates. Transfusion 1990;20:314-7.

38. Friedberg RC, Donnelly SF, Mintz PD. Independent roles for platelet crossmatching and HLA in the selection of platelets for alloimmunized patients. Transfusion 1994;34:215-20.

39. Howard JA, Perkins HA. The natural history of alloimmunization to platelets. Transfusion 1978;18:496-503.

40. Godeau B, Fromont P, Seror T, et al. Platelet alloimmunization after multiple transfusions: A prospective study of 50 patients. Br J Haematol 1992;81:395-400.

41. The Trial to Reduce Alloimmunization to Platelets Study Group. Leukocyte reduction and ultraviolet B irradiation of platelets to prevent alloimmunization and refractoriness to platelet transfusions. N Engl J Med 1997;337:1861-9.

42. Gmür J, von Felten A, Osterwaider B, et al. Delayed alloimmunization using random single donor platelet transfusions: A prospective study of thrombocytopenic patients with acute leukemia. Blood 1983;62:473-9.

43. Kruskall MS. The perils of platelet transfusions (editorial). N Engl J Med 1997;337:1914-5.

44. George JN. Platelet immunoglobulin G: Its significance for the evaluation of thrombocytopenia and for understanding the origin of α-granule proteins. Blood 1990;76:859-70.

45. Bettaieb A, Fromont P, Louache F, et al. Presence of crossreactive antibody between human immunodeficiency virus (HIV) and platelet glycoproteins in HIV-related immune thrombocytopenic purpura. Blood 1992;80:162-9.

46. Brecher ME, Moore SB, Letendre L. Posttransfusion purpura: The therapeutic value of Pl^A1-negative platelets. Transfusion 1990;30:433-5.

47. Win N. Provision of random-donor platelets (HPA-1a positive) in neonatal alloimmune thrombocytopenia due to anti-HPA-1a alloantibodies. Vox Sang 1996;71:130-1.

48. McFarland JG, Frenzke M, Aster RH. Testing of maternal sera in pregnancies at risk for neonatal alloimmune thrombocytopenia. Transfusion 1989;29:128-33.

49. Koyama N, Ohama Y, Kaneko K, et al. Association of neonatal thrombocytopenia and maternal anti-HLA antibodies. Acta Paediatr Jpn 1991;33:71-6.

50. Lalezari P, Dimitrova A, Diwan A, et al. HLA incompatibility is the most common cause of alloimmune neonatal thrombocytopenia (ANT) (abstract). Blood 1993;82:203a.

51. Lalezari P. HLA incompatibility in neonatal alloimmune thrombocytopenia. Transfus Today 1994;21:6-8.

52. Sinor LT, Stone DL, Plapp FV et al. Detection of heparin-IgG immune complexes on platelets by

solid phase red cell adherence assays. (Immucorrespondence) Norcross, GA: Immucor, Inc, 1990.

53. Leach MF, Cooper LK, AuBuchon JP. Detection of drug-dependent, platelet-reactive antibodies by solid-phase red cell adherence assays. Br J Haematol 1997;97:755-61.

54. GTI-HAT™ for the detection of heparin-associated antibodies (package insert). Brookfield, WI: GTI, 1997.

55. Visentin GP, Wolfmeyer K, Newman PJ, Aster RH. Detection of drug-dependent, platelet-reactive antibodies by antigen-capture ELISA and flow cytometry. Transfusion 1990;30:694-700.

56. Curtis BR, McFarland JG, Wu GG, Visentin GP, Aster RH. Antibodies in sulfonamide-induced immune thrombocytopenia recognize calcium-dependent epitopes on the glycoprotein IIb/IIIa complex. Blood 1994;84:176-83.

57. Amiral J, Bridey F, Dreyfus M, et al. Platelet factor 4 complexed to heparin is the target for antibodies generated in heparin-induced thrombocytopenia. Thromb Haemost 1992;68:95-6.

58. Visentin GP, Ford SE, Scott JP, Aster RH. Antibodies from patients with heparin-induced thrombocytopenia/thrombosis are specific for platelet factor 4 complexed with heparin or bound to endothelial cells. J Clin Invest 1994;93:81-8.

59. Nieminen U, Kekomäki R. Quinidine-induced thrombocytopenia purpura: Clinical presentation in relation to drug-dependent and drug-independent platelet antibodies. Br J Haematol 1992;80:77-82.

60. Warkentin TE, Levine M, Hirsh J, et al. Heparin-induced thrombocytopenia in patients treated with low molecular weight heparin or unfractionated heparin. N Engl J Med 1995; 332:1330-5.

61. Nand S, Wong W, Yuen B, et al. Heparin-induced thrombocytopenia with thrombosis. Am J Hematol 1997;56:12-6.

62. Warkentin TE, Kelton JG. A 14-year study of heparin-induced thrombocytopenia. Am J Med 1996;101:502-7.

63. Warkentin TE, Chong BA, Greinacher A. Heparin-induced thrombocytopenia: Towards consensus. Thromb Haemost 1998;79:1-7.

64. Cancio LC, Cohen DJ. Heparin-induced thrombocytopenia thrombosis. J Am Coll Surg 1998;186:76-91.

65. Gupta AK, Kovacs MJ, Sauder DN. Heparin-induced thrombocytopenia. Ann Pharmacother 1998;32:55-9.

66. Sinor LT, Stone DL. Serological confirmation of heparin induced thrombocytopenia. Clin Hemost Rev 1994;8:9-10.

67. Bux J, Behrens G, Jaeger G, et al. Diagnosis and clinical course of autoimmune neutropenia in infancy: Analysis of 240 cases. Blood 1998;91:181-6.

68. Silliman R, Paterson AJ, Dickey WO, et al. The association of biologically active lipids with the development of transfusion-related acute lung injury: A retrospective study. Transfusion 1997;37:719-26.

69. Lalezari P, Bernard JE. An isologous antigen-antibody reaction with human neutrophils related to neonatal neutropenia. J Clin Invest 1966;45:1741-50.

70. Hessner MJ, Curtis BR, Endean DJ, Aster RH. Determination of neutrophil antigen gene frequencies in five ethnic groups by polymerase chain reaction with sequence specific primers. Transfusion 1996;36:895-9.

71. Nordhagen R, Conradi M, Promtord SM. Pulmonary reaction associated with transfusion of plasma containing anti-5b. Vox Sang 1986;51:102-8.

72. Bux J, Chapman J. Report on the second international granulocyte serology workshop. Transfusion 1997;37:977-83.

Suggested Reading

Platelets

Alving BM. Thrombosis in the antiphospholipid syndrome and in heparin-induced thrombocytopenia. In: Silberstein LE, ed. Autoimmune disorders of blood. Bethesda, MD: American Association of Blood Banks, 1996:171-93.

Blanchette VS, Kühne T, Hume H, et al. Platelet transfusion therapy in newborn infants. Transfus Med Rev 1995;9:215-30.

Bussel JB, Zabusky MR, Berkowitz RL, et al. Fetal alloimmume thrombocytopenia. N Engl J Med 1997;337:22-6.

Freidberg RC. Clinical and laboratory factors underlying refractoriness to platelet transfusions. J Clin Apheresis 1996;11:143-8.

Garratty G. Review: Platelet immunology—similarities and differences with red cell immunology. Immunohematology 1995;11:112-24.

Goldman M, Filion M, Prouix C, et al. Neonatal alloimmune thrombocytopenia. Transfus Med Rev 1994;8:123-31.

Greinacher A, Amiral J, Dummel V, et al. Laboratory diagnosis of heparin-associated thrombocytopenia and comparison of platelet aggregation test, heparin-induced platelet activation test, and platelet factor 4/heparin enzyme-linked immunosorbent assay. Transfusion 1994;34:381-5.

Griffiths E, Dzik WH. Assays for heparin-induced thrombocytopenia. Transfus Med 1997;7:1-11.

Kickler T, Herman JH, eds. Current issues in platelet transfusion therapy and platelet alloimmunity. Bethesda, MD: AABB Press 1999 (in press).

McFarland JG. Laboratory investigation of drug-induced immune thrombocytopenias. Transfus Med Rev 1993;7:275-87.

McPherson RA. Platelet antibody testing for evaluating immune thrombocytopenias. Am J Clin Pathol 1998;109:123-6.

Rolih S. Review: Comparing platelet compatibility to red cell compatibility protocols. Immunohematology 1995;11:133-9.

Rothenberger SS, McCarthy LJ. Neonatal alloimmune thrombocytopenia. From prediction to prevention. Lab Med 1997;28:592-6.

Slichter SJ. Principles of platelet transfusion therapy. In: Hoffman R, Benz EJ Jr, Shattil SJ, et al, eds. Hematology. Basic principles and practice. New York: Churchill Livingstone, 1991:1610-22.

von dem Borne AEGKr, Ouwehand WH, Kuijpers RW. Theoretic and practical aspects of platelet crossmatching. Transfus Med Rev 1990;4:265-78.

Warkentin TE, Smith JW. The alloimmune thrombocytopenic syndromes. Transfus Med Rev 1997;11:296-307.

Granulocytes

Bux J, Stein EL, Bierling P, et al. Characterization of a new alloantigen (SH) on the human neutrophil Fcγ receptor IIIb. Blood 1997;89:1027-34.

Lucas GF. Review: Antibodies and antigens in immune neutropenias. Immunohematology 1995;11:105-11.

McCullough J, Clay M, Stroncek DF. Granulocyte alloantigen systems and their clinical significance. In: Nance ST, ed. Alloimmunity: 1993 and beyond. Bethesda, MD: American Association of Blood Banks, 1993:49-82.

Stroncek DF. Granulocyte immunology: Is there a need to know? Transfusion 1997;37:886-8.

17

The HLA System

THE HLA SYSTEM INCLUDES A complex array of genes and their molecular products. HLA genes contribute to the recognition of self and nonself, to the immune responses to antigenic stimuli, and to coordination of cellular and humoral immunity. These genes determine the antigens of the HLA system.

HLA antigens are highly immunogenic and can be found on several types of cells. Antibodies to HLA antigens are key factors in transfusion-related events such as platelet refractoriness, febrile nonhemolytic transfusion reaction, transfusion-related acute lung injury, and posttransfusion graft-vs-host disease.

Products of the HLA genes, located in the major histocompatibility complex (MHC) on the short arm of chromosome 6, are glycoprotein molecules found on cell surface membranes. Molecules described as Class I are found on the surface of platelets and of most nucleated cells of the body, including lymphocytes, granulocytes, monocytes, and constituents of solid tissues. Mature red cells usually lack HLA antigens demonstrable by conventional methods, but nucleated immature erythroid cells have HLA antigens. Class II molecules have more restricted distribution, being present at all times on B lymphocytes and cells of monocyte/macrophage lineage and on T lymphocytes and other cells after suitable stimulation. Other terms that have been applied to antigens of the HLA system are: major histocompatibility locus antigens, transplantation antigens, and tissue antigens.

17

The molecules that express HLA antigens play a key role in antigen presentation. Immunologic recognition of differences in HLA antigens is probably the first step in the rejection of transplanted tissue. The HLA system is second in importance only to the ABO antigens in influencing the long-term survival of transplanted solid organs and is of paramount importance in marrow transplantation. HLA antigens and antibodies are also important in such complications of transfusion therapy as immune-mediated platelet refractoriness, febrile nonhemolytic (FNH) transfusion reactions, transfusion-related acute lung injury (TRALI), and posttransfusion graft-vs-host disease (GVHD).

Typing for HLA antigens is used to study susceptibility to certain diseases, is of value in parentage testing, and is helpful in forensic investigations. Molecular analysis of the HLA region has enhanced the usefulness of this system for selecting donors for marrow transplantation, for investigation of disease associations, and for anthropologic population studies.

History

Delineation of the first HLA antigen began in the 1950s, when several investigators independently described leukoagglutinating antibodies in the sera of patients immunized by blood transfusion or pregnancy. Further studies revealed that these leukoagglutinins defined a series of polymorphic, genetically determined antigens. By the early 1960s, an association between human leukoagglutinating antibodies and tissue transplantation was inferred from observations of accelerated skin graft rejection in recipients who were preimmunized with peripheral blood leukocytes from the prospective donor. A major technical advance occurred in 1964 with the introduction of the microlymphocytotoxicity test; a modified form of this test is in use today. In the late 1980s, DNA-based techniques became available that permitted detection of the alleles that determine the HLA antigen specificities.

Standardization of HLA nomenclature began in 1967, through a series of international workshops. As increasing numbers of monospecific antisera became available and as understanding of the genetics of the system improved, nomenclature for the HLA antigens was logically expanded and systematized. Nucleic acid sequencing of the genes encoding the HLA molecules has led to a modified nomenclature based on unique allele sequences.[1]

Genetics of the Major Histocompatibility Complex

HLA antigens reside on cell surface glycoproteins that are products of closely linked genes mapped to the p21.3 band on the short arm of chromosome 6 (Fig 17-1). This DNA region is called the MHC and is usually inherited en bloc as a haplotype. Each of the several loci has multiple alleles with codominant expression of the products from each chromosome. The HLA system constitutes one of the most polymorphic genetic systems known in humans.

The *HLA-A*, *HLA-B*, and *HLA-C* genes are responsible for the corresponding A, B, and C antigens, which are characterized as Class I. The *HLA-DR*, *HLA-DQ*, and *HLA-DP* gene cluster codes for the production of correspondingly named antigens characterized as Class II. Located between the Class I and Class II genes is a group of non-MHC genes that code for molecules that include the complement proteins C2, Bf, C4A, C4B; a steroid enzyme (21-hydroxylase); and a cytokine (tumor necrosis factor). This region has sometimes been referred to as Class III.

Organization of Regions

The HLA Class I region contains, in addition to the classical genes *HLA-A*, *HLA-B*, and *HLA-C*,

A.

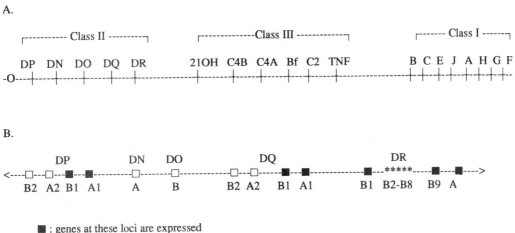

Figure 17-1. (A) The major histocompatibility complex located on the short arm of chromosome 6. The centromere is to the left. The key Class I, II, and III genetic loci are shown. The Class III region contains complement system genes (C2, Bf, C4A, C4B), the 21-hydroxylase gene (21OH), and the gene for tumor necrosis factor (TNF). (B) Greater detail of the Class II region.

other gene loci designated *HLA-E*, *HLA-F*, *HLA-G*, *HLA-H*, *HLA-J*, *HLA-K*, and *HLA-L*. Some Class I genes express nonfunctional proteins or no proteins at all. Genes unable to express a protein product are termed pseudogenes and presumably represent an evolutionary dead end. HLA-G is expressed by the trophoblast and may be involved in the development of maternal immune tolerance of the fetus. Hereditary hemochromatosis (HH), an iron overload disorder with a 10% carrier frequency in Northern Europeans, is associated with two missense mutations in a Class I-like gene.[2] The gene conferring HH was initially called *HLA-H*; however, the *HLA-H* designation had already been assigned to an HLA Class I pseudogene by the World Health Organization (WHO) Nomenclature Committee.[3] The gene conferring HH is now called *HFE*. DNA analysis of the *HLA-C* gene reveals that this locus probably arose from *HLA-B* by gene duplication.

The genetic organization of the MHC Class II region (HLA-D region) is more complex. Class II proteins consist of two dissimilar chains, alpha and beta. There are multiple loci that code for either alpha or beta chains of the Class II MHC proteins. Different haplotypes have different numbers of expressed genes and pseudogenes. The proteins coded by the *DRA* gene and the *DRB1* gene result in HLA-DR1 through HLA-DR18. The products of the *A* gene and the *B3* gene (if present) express HLA-DR52; those of the *A* gene and the *B4* gene (if present) express HLA-DR53; and those of the *A* gene and *B5* gene (if present) express HLA-DR51. The HLA-DQ1 through DQ9 antigens are expressed on the glycoproteins coded by the *DQA1* and *DQB1* genes in the *DQ* gene cluster. Many of the other genes of the *DQ* cluster are probably pseudogenes. A similar organization is found in the *HLA-DP* gene cluster.

The MHC Class III region contains four complement genes, which are generally inherited as a unit termed a complotype. There are more than 10 different complotypes inherited in humans. Two of the Class III genes, *C4A* and *C4B*, code for variants of the C4 molecule. These variants have distinct protein structure and function; the C4A molecule (if present) carries the Rodgers antigen and the C4B molecule (if present) carries the Chido antigen, both of which are adsorbed onto the red cells of individuals who possess the gene.

Patterns of Inheritance

The MHC illustrates a number of genetic principles. Every person has two examples of chromosome 6 and, thus, possesses two HLA haplotypes, one from each parent. A person's pair of haplotypes is referred to as the genotype, which can be determined for that individual by typing multiple individuals within the family and observing which genes are transmitted inseparably. The gene products expressed constitute the phenotype, which is ascertained for each individual by results of typing tests. Because the HLA genes are autosomal and codominant, the phenotype represents the combined expression of both haplotypes. Figure 17-2 illustrates inheritance of haplotypes.

Finding HLA-Identical Siblings

Each child receives one chromosome, hence one haplotype, from each parent. Because each parent has two different number 6 chromosomes, four different combinations of

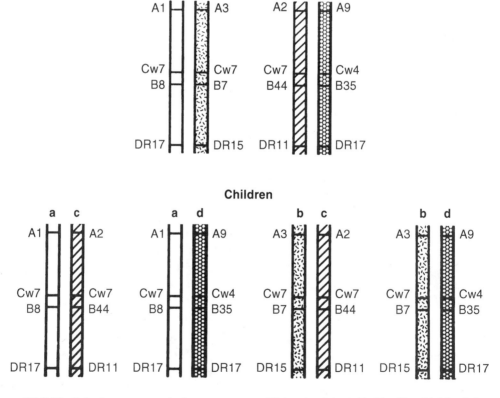

Figure 17-2. The linked genes on each chromosome constitute a haplotype. To identify which haplotypes a person possesses, one must know the antigens present and also the inheritance pattern in the specific kindred. The observed typing results of the father in this family are interpreted into the following phenotype: A1,3;B7,8;Cw7,-;DR15,17. The observed results plus the family study reveal the haplotypes of the father to be: a=A1,Cw7,B8,DR17 and b=A3,Cw7,B7,DR15. Offspring of a single mating pair must have one of only four possible combinations of haplotypes, assuming there has been no crossing over.

haplotypes are possible in the offspring (assuming no recombination). This inheritance pattern is important in predicting whether family members will be compatible donors for transplantation. The chance that two siblings will be HLA-identical is 25%. The chance that any one patient with "n" siblings will have at least one HLA-identical sibling is $1-(3/4)^n$. Having two siblings provides a 44% chance and three siblings a 58% chance that one sibling will be HLA-identical. No matter how many siblings are available for typing (aside from identical twins), the probability will never be 100% for finding an HLA-identical sibling.

Absence of Antigens

Although each chromosome will express its gene products, an individual may test positive for only one antigen at a given locus; the missing antigen is referred to as a "blank." A blank may occur if the individual is homozygous for the detected allele; if the individual expresses an antigen for which appropriate antisera are not available; if there is a technical failure in testing (false-negative); or, very rarely, if there is a null gene. When referring to phenotypes, a blank is often written as "x" (for A locus), "y" (for B locus), or "–" (for any locus) (eg, A1,x;B7,40 orA1,–;B7,40). Family studies must be performed to determine the correct genotype.

Crossing-Over

The genes of the HLA region occasionally demonstrate chromosome crossover, in which segments containing linked genetic material are exchanged between the two chromosomes during meiosis or gametogenesis (see Fig 10-6). These recombinants are then transmitted as new haplotypes to the offspring. Crossover frequency is in part related to the physical distance between genes. For example, the *HLA-A*, *HLA-B*, and *HLA-DR* loci are close together, with 0.8% crossover between the *A* and *B* loci and 0.5% between the *B* and *DR* loci. In family

studies and in parentage testing, the possibility of recombination must be considered.

Linkage Disequilibrium

The MHC system provides many illustrations of linkage disequilibrium, a phenomenon in which certain alleles occur together in the same haplotype more often than would be expected by chance. Expected frequencies for HLA haplotypes are derived by multiplication of the frequencies of each allele. For example, in Whites, the overall frequency of the gene coding for HLA-A1 is 0.15 and for the gene coding for HLA-B8 is 0.10; therefore, 1.5% (0.15 × 0.10) of all HLA haplotypes in Whites would be expected to contain genes coding for both HLA-A1 and HLA-B8 if these were randomly distributed. The actual frequency of the A1 and B8 combination, however, is 7-8% in Whites. Certain allelic combinations occur with increased frequency in different racial groups and constitute common haplotypes in those populations. Linkage disequilibrium in the HLA system is important in studies of parentage because haplotype frequencies in the relevant population make transmission of certain gene combinations more likely than others. Linkage disequilibrium also affects the likelihood of finding suitable unrelated donors for HLA-matched platelet transfusions and for marrow transplantation.

Biochemistry, Tissue Distribution, and Structure

The HLA antigens are cell surface glycoproteins composed of two dissimilar protein chains. They are divided into two classes according to biochemical structure.

Characteristics of Classes

Class I antigens (HLA-A, -B, and -C) have a molecular weight around 56,000 daltons and consist of two chains: a glycoprotein heavy chain (alpha) and, as a light chain, the β_2-microglobulin molecule encoded by a gene on chromosome 15. The alpha chain penetrates the cell membrane. β_2-microglobulin is not attached to the cell membrane; it associates with the alpha chain but is not covalently bound to it. (See Fig 17-3.) The extramembranous portion of the alpha chain consists of three amino acid domains, of which the outer two contain the variable regions conferring the HLA antigen specificity. The amino acid sequence specified for these variable regions varies among the Class I alleles.

Class I molecules are found on platelets and on most nucleated cells in the body, with some exceptions such as neurons, corneal epithelium, trophoblast, and germinal cells. Only vestigial amounts remain on mature red cells, with certain allotypes better expressed than others. These Class I polymorphisms were independently recognized as red cell alloantigens by serologists and were designated as Bennett-Goodspeed (Bg) antigens. The specificities called Bg^a, Bg^b, and Bg^c are now identified as HLA-B7, HLA-B17, and HLA-A28, respectively. Platelets express primarily HLA-A and HLA-B antigens. HLA-C antigens are weakly present and Class II antigens are not expressed on platelets.

Class II antigens (HLA-DR, -DQ, and -DP) have a molecular weight of approximately 63,000 daltons and consist of two dissimilar glycoprotein chains (alpha and beta), both of which traverse the membrane. (See Fig 17-3.) The extramembranous portion of each chain has two amino acid domains, of which the outer one contains the variable regions determined by the Class II alleles. The expression of Class II antigens is more restricted than that of Class I. Class II antigens are expressed constitutively on B lymphocytes, monocytes, and cells derived from monocytes such as macrophages and dendritic cells, intestinal epithelium, and early hematopoietic cells. There is constitutive expression of Class II antigens on some endothelial cells, especially those lin-

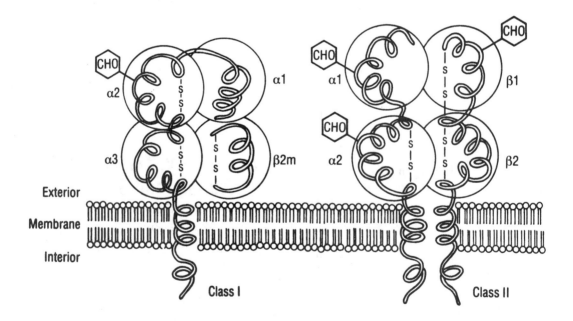

Figure 17-3. Stylized diagram of Class I and Class II MHC molecules showing α and β polypeptide chains, their structural domains, and attached carbohydrate units.

ing the microvasculature. However, in general, endothelium, particularly that of larger blood vessels, is negative for Class II antigen expression, although its expression can be induced (for instance, by interferon-gamma during immune activation). T lymphocytes are negative for Class II antigen expression, but become positive when activated. Class II antigens are expressed abnormally in autoimmune disease and on some tumor cells.

Configuration

A characteristic three-dimensional structure of these molecules can be demonstrated by X-ray crystallographic analysis of purified HLA antigens. (See Fig 17-4.) The outer domains, which contain the regions of amino acid variability and the antigenic epitopes of the molecules, form a structure known as the "peptide-binding groove." Molecules determined by different HLA genes have unique amino acid sequences and, therefore, form unique binding grooves, each able to bind different classes of peptides. The peptide-binding groove is critical for the functional aspects of HLA molecules. See section on Biological Function.

Nomenclature

The extreme polymorphism of the HLA system derives from the existence of multiple alleles at several loci. It is estimated that more than 100 million different phenotypes can result from all combinations of alleles in the HLA system. The extended haplotypes of an individual are nearly unique.

Numerical Assignments

HLA antigens are designated by a number following the letter that denotes the HLA series (eg, HLA-A1 or HLA-B8). Previously, antigenic specificities that were not fully confirmed car-

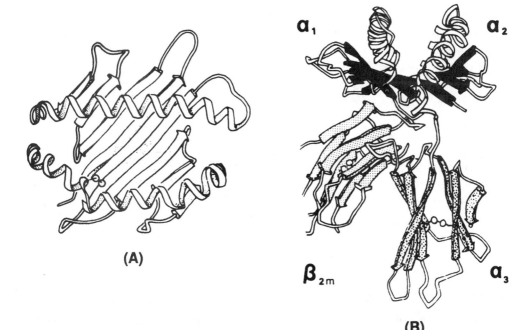

Figure 17-4. Three-dimensional schematic representation of an HLA molecule. (A) The molecule is shown projecting out of the page. The central groove is shown without peptide present. (B) The molecule is shown with the membrane proximal immunoglobulin-like domains (α_3, β_2m) at the bottom and the polymorphic α_1 and α_2 domains at the top. The peptide binding groove is shown on edge at the top center.[4]

ried the prefix "w" (eg, HLA-Aw33) and when identification of the antigen became definitive, the WHO Nomenclature Committee dropped the "w" from the designation. The Committee meets regularly to update nomenclature by recognizing new specificities or genetic loci. The "w" prefix is no longer applied in this manner and is now used only for the following: 1) Bw4 and Bw6, to distinguish these public antigens from other B locus alleles; 2) all C locus specificities, to avoid confusion with components of the complement system; and 3) Dw and DP specificities that were defined by mixed lymphocyte reactions and primed lymphocyte typing. The numeric designations for the HLA-A and HLA-B specificities are not in sequence because numbers were assigned before it was recognized that products thought to reflect one locus actually derived from two genetic loci.

Shared Determinants

As the specificity of HLA typing sera improved, it was found that some epitopes, the part of the antigen that binds antibody, were common to several antigens. Antibodies to these epitopes identified antigens that constituted a group, of which the individual members could be identified by antisera with more restricted activity.

Splits

Antigens originally classified as a single entity can be "split" into individual specificities. The designation for an individual antigen that is a split of an earlier recognized antigen often includes the number of the parent antigen in parentheses, eg, HLA-B44(12).

Cross-Reactive Groups

In addition to "splits," HLA antigens and antigen groups may have other epitopes in common. Antibodies that react with these shared determinants often cause cross-reactions in serologic testing. The collective term for a group of HLA antigens that exhibit such cross-reactivity is cross-reactive group or CREG.

Public Antigens

In addition to splits and CREGs, HLA proteins have reactivity that is common to many different HLA specificities. Called public antigens, these common amino acid sequences appear to represent the less variable portion of the HLA molecule. Two well-characterized public antigens, HLA-Bw4 and HLA-Bw6, are found in the HLA-B series. The Bw4 antigen is also found on some A locus molecules. Public antigens are clinically important because patients exposed to foreign HLA antigens via pregnancy, transfusion, or transplantation can make antibodies to public antigens. A single antibody, when directed against a public antigen, can resemble the sum of multiple discrete alloantibodies.

Nomenclature for Genes

As peptide mapping and nucleotide sequencing are used to investigate the HLA system, increasing numbers of variant HLA alleles are being identified, many of which share a common serologic phenotype. The minimum requirement for designation of a new allele is the sequence of exons two and three for HLA Class I and exon two for HLA Class II (*DRB1*). These exons encode the variable amino acids that confer HLA antigen specificity. A uniform nomenclature has been adopted that takes into account the locus, the protein bearing the antigen, the major serologic specificity, and the variant. For example, several unique variants of HLA-DR4 have been identified by isoelectric focusing, amino acid sequencing, and nucleotide sequencing. The first HLA-DR4 variant is designated DRB1*0401, indicating the locus (DR), the protein (beta 1 chain), an asterisk to represent that an allele name follows, the major serologic specificity (04 for HLA-DR4), and the variant number (variant 01). For Class I variants, in which only one protein chain varies, the protein designation is dropped. Therefore, B*2704 represents the B27 allele, giving rise to the fourth unique variant of the HLA-B27 molecule. Because of the rapid pace with which new alleles are identified, monthly nomenclature updates are published in the journals *Human Immunology*, *Tissue Antigens*, and the *European Journal of Immunogenetics*. Annually, these journals publish an up-to-date listing of the HLA nomenclature.[1]

Biologic Function

The essential function of the HLA system is self/nonself discrimination. Discrimination of self from nonself is accomplished by the interaction of T lymphocytes with peptide antigens. T lymphocytes interact with peptide antigen only when the T-cell receptor for antigen (TCR) engages both an HLA molecule and the antigenic peptide contained with its peptide-binding groove. This limitation is referred to as "MHC restriction."[5]

In the thymus, T lymphocytes whose TCRs bind to a self HLA molecule are selected (positive selection), while those whose TCRs bind a self antigen are deleted (negative selection). Some self-reactive T cells escape negative selection, however. If not functionally inactivated, for instance by the mechanism of anergy, these self-reactive T cells may become involved in an autoimmune process.

Role of Class I

Class I molecules are synthesized, and peptide antigens are inserted into the peptide-binding groove, in the endoplasmic reticulum. Peptide antigens that fit into the Class I peptide-binding groove are typically 8-9 amino acids in length, and are derived from proteins that are made by the cell (endogenous proteins). These endogenous proteins, which may be normal self proteins, altered self proteins such as those found in cancer cells, or viral proteins such as those found in virus-infected cells, are degraded in the cytosol by a large multifunctional protease (LMP) and transported to the endoplasmic reticulum by a transporter associated with antigen processing (TAP). The LMP and TAP genes are both localized to the MHC.

Class I molecules are transported to the cell surface where they are available to interact with CD8-positive T lymphocytes. If the TCR of a T lymphocyte can bind the antigenic peptide in the context of the specific Class I molecule displaying it, then this binding activates the cytotoxic properties of the T cell, which will then attack the cell, characteristically eliciting an inflammatory response. Presentation of antigen by Class I is especially important in a host's defense against viral pathogens and against malignant transformation. Tumor cells that do not express Class I escape this immune surveillance.

Role of Class II

Class II molecules, like Class I molecules, are synthesized in the endoplasmic reticulum, but peptide antigens are not inserted into the peptide-binding groove here. Instead, an invariant chain (Ii) is inserted. The Class II-invariant chain molecule is transported to an endosome where the invariant chain is removed by a specialized Class II molecule called DM (whose locus is also localized to the MHC). A Class II antigenic peptide is then inserted into the peptide-binding groove. Peptide antigens that fit into the Class II peptide-binding groove are typically 12-25 amino acids in length, and are derived from proteins that are taken up by the cell by endocytosis (exogenous proteins). Exogenous proteins, which may be normal self proteins or proteins derived from pathogens such as bacteria, are degraded to peptides by enzymes in the endosomal pathway. Class II molecules are then transported to the cell surface where they are available to interact with CD4-positive T lymphocytes, which secrete immunostimulatory cytokines in response. This mechanism is especially important for the production of antibodies.

Detection of HLA Antigens

Methods for the detection of HLA antigens fall into three groups: serologic assays, cellular assays, and DNA assays. Detailed procedures of commonly used assays are provided in the current edition of the American Society for Histocompatibility and Immunogenetics' *Laboratory Manual*.

Serologic Assays

Lymphocytotoxicity

The microlymphocytotoxicity test can be used to detect HLA-A, -B, -C, -DR, and -DQ antigens. Lymphocytes are used for testing because they are readily obtained from anticoagulated peripheral blood and, unlike granulocytes, give reproducible results. Lymphocytes obtained from lymph nodes or spleen may also be used. HLA typing sera are obtained primarily from multiparous women. Some mouse monoclonal antisera are also available.

HLA sera of known specificities are placed in wells of a microdroplet test plate. A suspension of lymphocytes is added to each well. Rabbit complement is then added and, if sufficient antibody has bound to the lymphocyte membranes, the complement cascade will be activated through the membrane attack complex, leading to lymphocytotoxicity. Damage to the cell membrane can be detected by the addition of dye: cells that have no attached antibody, no activated complement, and no damage to the membrane keep the vital dyes from penetrating; cells with damaged permeable membranes allow the dye to enter. The cells are examined for dye exclusion or uptake under phase contrast microscopy. If a fluorescent microscope is available, fluorescent vital dyes can also be used.

Because HLA-DR and HLA-DQ antigens are expressed on B cells and not on resting T cells, typing for these antigens usually requires that the initial lymphocyte preparation be manipulated before testing to yield an enriched B-cell preparation. This is typically accomplished by use of magnetic beads to which monoclonal antibodies to B cells have been bound.

The interpretation of serologic reactions requires skill and experience. Control wells of known reactivity and careful quality control of reagents are required, especially for the activity of the complement used to induce lymphocytotoxicity. In addition, antigen assignments can be made only on the basis of results obtained with multiple antisera because few reagent antisera have sufficient monospecific reliability to be used alone. The extreme polymorphism of the HLA system, the uneven distribution of antigens among different racial groups, the reliance on biologic antisera and living target cells, and the complexities introduced by splits, CREGs, and public antigens all contribute to difficulties in accurate serologic HLA typing.

Antibodies in Patients

Microlymphocytotoxicity testing can be used to test serum specimens against selected target cells. This is routinely done in HLA crossmatching, which consists of testing serum from a potential recipient against unfractionated lymphocytes (or fractionated T and B lymphocytes) from a potential donor. A variation of the microlymphocytotoxicity test, which uses an antiglobulin reagent, is one of the methods used to increase sensitivity. Flow cytometry is also used as an independent method to increase the sensitivity of the crossmatch.

The extent of HLA alloimmunization can be assessed by testing the patient's serum against a panel of 30-60 or more different target cells. The percent of the panel cells to which the recipient has formed cytotoxic antibodies is referred to as the panel reactive antibody (PRA) level. Determination of PRA can be useful in the investigation of febrile nonhemolytic transfusion reactions, in the workup of platelet refractoriness, and in following patients who are awaiting cadaver solid organ transplants. This "HLA antibody screen" not only detects the presence of HLA antibodies, but may also allow their specificity to be determined. The presence of HLA antibodies can also be demonstrated by using an enzyme-linked immunosorbent assay with solid-phase HLA antigens or by flow cytometric analysis using antigen-coated beads.

Cellular Assays

The mixed lymphocyte culture (MLC) (also called mixed leukocyte culture, mixed lymphocyte reaction, or MLR) primarily detects genetic differences in the Class II region, which includes HLA-DP, HLA-DQ, and HLA-DR. HLA-DR alleles are thought to have the greatest impact in determining MLR reactivity. In the MLR, lymphocytes from different individuals are cultured together, and have the opportunity to recognize foreign HLA-D region antigens and to respond by proliferating. At the end of the co-culture period (usually 5-7 days), the level of DNA synthesis is determined by pulsing the culture with radioactive thymidine. The greater the proliferative response, the greater the uptake of thymidine by the responding cells.

The MLR has provided important information about differences in the HLA-D region, but its interpretation can be difficult. Cells may fail to respond or to stimulate properly. Cells from patients with leukemia may proliferate spontaneously, and cells from patients with abnormal immune systems may not respond. Processing delays can affect results. The National Marrow Donor Program has ceased to require the MLR for unrelated marrow transplants and, instead, requires molecular typing to determine Class II compatibility. High-resolution Class II typing may be needed to establish the extent of Class II antigen compatibility. Modifications of the MLR have been developed for HLA-D typing, using homozygous typing cells, and for HLA-DP typing, using primed lymphocyte typing. These techniques are rarely performed today and have generally been supplanted by DNA assays.

DNA-Based Assays

DNA-based typing has several advantages over serologic and cellular assays: high sensitivity and specificity; small sample volumes; turnaround time, for some methods, as short as a few hours; and absence of the need for cell surface antigen expression or cell viability. While serologic methods can readily distinguish only about 18 different DR antigens, DNA-based methods have identified more than 130 *DRB1* alleles.

PCR Testing

The polymerase chain reaction (PCR) has revolutionized HLA typing.[6] PCR allows generation of large quantities of a particular target segment of DNA. Low-resolution or generic typing detects the HLA serologic equivalents with great accuracy, eg, distinguishes DR15 from DR16, while high-resolution typing distinguishes individual alleles, eg, *DRB1*0101* from *DRB1*0102*. Several PCR-based methods have been developed, of which two general approaches predominate.

Oligonucleotide Probes. The first technique uses sequence-specific oligonucleotide probes (SSOP) and is known as PCR-SSO, PCR-SSOP, or allele-specific oligonucleotide (ASO) hybridization. A PCR product amplified from genomic DNA is applied to a membrane or filter to which the labeled SSOPs are applied. These short DNA segments will hybridize with the complementary sequences and identify groups or individual alleles. Advantages are that all Class II loci can be typed and highly specific information obtained. Disadvantages include potential difficulty in interpretation of results and the need to use multiple filters and perform multiple hybridizations. A variation of this technique, the reverse line or dot blot, eliminates the need for multiple filters and hybridizations by incorporation of a label (such as biotin) into the PCR product during its amplification from genomic DNA. The PCR product is then hybridized to a membrane containing all the relevant SSOPs and its pattern of hybridization with the SSOPs revealed by detection of the incorporated label.

Sequence-Specific Primers. A second major technique uses sequence-specific primers (SSPs) that target a particular DNA sequence. Because SSPs have such specific targets, presence of the amplified material indicates presence of the corresponding allele. Direct visualization of the amplified allele is seen after agarose gel electrophoresis.

Nucleic Acid Sequencing

Nucleic acid sequencing of the HLA genes is used to detect new alleles. With the ever-increasing availability and ease of use of automated sequencers, nucleic acid sequencing may become suitable as a routine HLA typing method.

The HLA System and Transfusion

HLA system antigens and antibodies play an important role in a number of transfusion-related events. These include alloimmunization and platelet refractoriness, FNH transfusion reactions, TRALI, and posttransfusion GVHD. HLA antigens are highly immunogenic. In response to pregnancy, transfusion, or transplantation, immunologically normal individuals are more likely to form antibodies to HLA antigens than to any other antigen system.

Platelet Refractoriness

The incidence of HLA alloimmunization and platelet refractoriness among patients receiving repeated transfusions of cellular components is 20-70%.[7] The refractory state exists when transfusion of suitably preserved platelets fails to increase the recipient's platelet count. Platelet refractoriness may be due to clinical factors such as sepsis, high fever, disseminated intravascular coagulopathy, medications, hypersplenism, complement-

mediated destruction, or a combination of these; or it may have an immune basis.[8] (See Chapter 16 for more information about platelets.)

Antibody Development

Immune-mediated platelet refractoriness is usually caused by antibodies against HLA antigens, but antibodies to platelet-specific antigens may also be involved. HLA alloimmunization can follow pregnancy, transfusion, or organ transplantation because the foreign antigens are the donor MHC antigens themselves. A common example of this is the development of HLA antibodies directed against Class I antigens that occurs with transfusion of platelets, which express only Class I antigens. The presence, in the transfused component, of leukocytes bearing Class I and II antigens elicits alloimmunization. The likelihood of immunization can be lessened with leukocyte-reduced blood components, or by treatment with ultraviolet light, which alters the co-stimulatory molecules or impairs antigen-presenting cell activity. The threshold level of leukocytes required to provoke a primary HLA alloimmune response is unclear and probably varies among different recipients. Some studies have suggested that 5×10^6 leukocytes per transfusion may represent an immunizing dose. In patients who have been previously sensitized by pregnancy or transfusion, exposure to even lower numbers of allogeneic cells is likely to provoke an anamnestic antibody response.

Finding Compatible Donors

The HLA antibody response of transfused individuals may be directed against individual specificities present on donor cells or against public alloantigens. Precise characterization may be difficult. An overall assessment of the degree of alloimmunization can be obtained by measuring the PRA of the recipient's serum. Platelet-refractory patients with a high

PRA are broadly alloimmunized and may be difficult to support with platelet transfusions. HLA-matched platelets, obtained by plateletpheresis, benefit some but not all of these refractory patients. Because donors with a four-antigen match for an immunized recipient are hard to find, strategies for obtaining HLA-matched platelets vary. Selection of partially mismatched donors, based on serologic cross-reactive groups, has been emphasized, but such donors may fail to provide an adequate transfusion response in vivo. An alternative approach to the selection of donors is based on matching for public specificities rather than cross-reactive private antigens. Matching for both HLA and platelet-specific antigens may further improve the success rate in refractory patients. Obtaining an adequate number of readily available HLA-typed donors can prove difficult; it has been estimated that a pool of 1000-3000 or more donors would be needed to provide the transfusion requirements of most HLA-alloimmunized patients.[9]

Patients who may become alloimmunized and refractory should be Class I HLA-typed early in the course of their illness, when enough lymphocytes are present in the peripheral blood to obtain a reliable HLA type. Intensive chemotherapy makes it very difficult to obtain enough cells for HLA typing. HLA-alloimmunized patients often respond to crossmatch-compatible platelets. Crossmatching techniques may assess compatibility for both HLA and platelet-specific antibodies. These histocompatible platelet components are further discussed in Chapter 21.

Febrile Nonhemolytic Transfusion Reactions

HLA antibodies, as well as granulocyte and platelet-specific antibodies, have been implicated in the pathogenesis of FNH transfusion reactions. The recipient's antibodies, reacting with transfused antigens, elicit the release of cytokines (eg, interleukin-1) capable of caus-

ing fever. Serologic investigation, if undertaken, may require multiple techniques and target cells from a number of different donors. (See Chapter 27.)

Transfusion-Related Acute Lung Injury

In TRALI, a transfusion reaction that is being recognized with increasing frequency, acute noncardiogenic pulmonary edema develops in response to transfusion. Pathogenesis appears to reflect the presence of HLA antibodies in donor blood, which react with and fix complement to tissue antigens of the recipient, leading to severe capillary leakage and pulmonary edema. Rarely, HLA antibodies of the recipient react with transfused leukocytes from the donor. (See Chapter 27.)

Posttransfusion Graft-vs-Host Disease

The development of posttransfusion GVHD depends on several factors: the degree to which the recipient is immunocompromised; the number and viability of lymphocytes in the transfused component; and the degree of HLA similarity between donor and recipient. The observation of posttransfusion GVHD with the use of fresh blood components from blood relatives has highlighted the role of the HLA system in GVHD.

Figure 17-5 illustrates the conditions for increased risk of GVHD. The parents have one HLA haplotype in common. Each child, therefore, has a one in four chance of inheriting the same haplotype from each parent, and Child #1 is homozygous for the shared parental HLA haplotype. Transfusion of blood from this person to an unrelated recipient who did not have this haplotype would have no untoward consequences. If, however, Child #1 were a directed donor for the relatives heterozygous for that haplotype (both parents and Child #3), the recipient would not recognize any foreign antigens on the transfused lymphocytes and would not eliminate them. The donor cells, however, would recognize the recipient's foreign HLA antigens, would become activated, proliferate, and attack the host. To avoid this situation, it is recommended that all cellular components known to be from blood relatives be irradiated before transfusion. Other specially chosen donor units, such as HLA-matched platelets, may also present an increased risk of post-transfusion GVHD.

Hemolytic Transfusion Reactions

HLA incompatibility has been implicated as a cause of shortened red cell survival in patients with antibodies to HLA antigens such as Bg^a(B7), Bg^b(B17), and Bg^c(A28) that are expressed, although weakly, on red blood cells. (See Chapter 15.) Such an incompatibility may not be detected with conventional pre-transfusion testing.

HLA Testing and Transplantation

HLA testing is an integral part of organ transplantation. The extent of testing differs for different types of transplants. Organ transplantation is discussed in greater detail in Chapter 26.

Marrow Transplants

It has long been recognized that disparity within the HLA system represents an important barrier to successful marrow transplantation. HLA similarity and compatibility between the donor and the recipient are required for engraftment and to prevent GVHD, but some degree of rejection or GVHD remain common problems for recipients of allogeneic marrow, despite immunosuppressive conditioning.

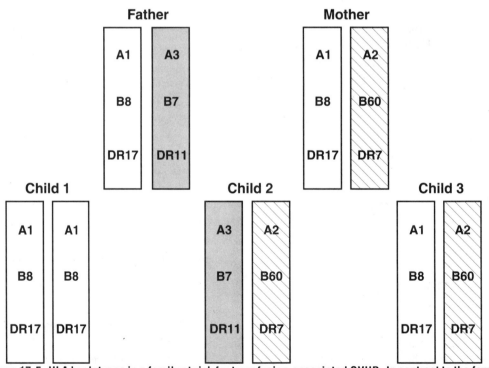

Figure 17-5. HLA haplotypes in a family at risk for transfusion-associated GVHD. In contrast to the family shown in Fig 17-2, each parent shares a common HLA haplotype, HLA-A1,B8,DR17. Child 1 is homozygous for the haplotype shared by the parents and by child 3. The lymphocytes of child 1 are capable of producing posttransfusion GVHD if transfused to either parent or to child 3.

Candidate donors and recipients are tested for HLA-A, -B, -C, -DR, and -DQ antigens.[10] The goal is precise matching of the six HLA-A, -B, and -DR antigens of the recipient and potential donor. DNA typing is performed on samples from both the donor and recipient for optimum assessment of Class I and II region compatibility. Although HLA-identical sibling donors remain the best choice for marrow transplantation, there is increasing use of unrelated donors identified through the National Marrow Donor Program.

Kidney Transplants

ABO compatibility is the most important factor determining the immediate survival of kidney transplants. Because ABH antigens are expressed in varying amounts on all cells of the body, transplanted ABO-incompatible tissue comes into continuous contact with the recipient's ABO antibodies. Of particular importance is the expression of ABH antigens on vascular endothelial cells, because the vascular supply in the transplant is a common site for rejection.

Both the recipient and the donor are ordinarily tested for ABO, HLA-A, -B, and -DR antigens. HLA-C and -DQ testing is also usually performed. Before surgery, a major crossmatch of recipient serum against donor lymphocytes is required. AABB *Standards for Blood Banks and Transfusion Services*[11] requires that the crossmatch be done using a method more sensitive than routine microlymphocytotoxicity testing, such as prolonged incubation, washing, augmentation with antihuman globulin reagents, or flow cytometry. Flow cytometry is the most sensitive method, and is especially useful because it can best predict early acute rejection and delayed graft function, both of which are strong predictors of chronic rejection and long-term allograft survival.[12] Because HLA antibody responses are dynamic, the serum used for the crossmatch is often obtained within 48 hours of surgery and is retained in the frozen state for

any required subsequent testing. An incompatible crossmatch with unfractionated or T lymphocytes is a contraindication to kidney transplantation. The significance of a positive B-cell crossmatch is unclear.

Serum from a patient awaiting cadaver-donor kidney transplant surgery is tested at regular intervals for the degree of alloimmunization by determining the PRA. In addition, many laboratories identify the specificities of HLA alloantibodies formed. If an antibody with a defined HLA specificity is identified in a recipient, it is a common practice to avoid the corresponding antigen when allocating a cadaver-donor allograft. The serum samples used for periodic PRA testing are usually frozen. The samples with the highest PRA are often used, in addition to the preoperative sample, for pretransplant crossmatching.

The approach to kidney transplants using living donors is different. In the past, when several prospective living donors were being considered, MLC testing between the recipient and the donors was sometimes performed, but it is rarely performed today. HLA matching of recipients with kidney donors (both living and cadaveric) contributes to long-term allograft survival by decreasing the likelihood of chronic rejection. Current projected 20-year allograft survival rates are 57% for two-haplotype-matched sibling donors, 30% for one-haplotype-matched parental donors, and 18% for cadaver donors.[13] For cadaver donors with no mismatches with the recipient for HLA-A, -B, and -DR, the projected 20-year allograft survival is 40%. Surprisingly, projected survival for allografts from living, unrelated donors is similar to those from parental donors.[14]

Other Solid Organ Transplants

For liver, pancreas, heart, lung, and heart/lung transplants, ABO compatibility remains the primary immunologic system for donor selection, and determining pretransplant ABO compatibility between donor and recipient is mandatory. HLA-A, -B, and -DR testing is routinely performed on both donor and recipient blood and a major lymphocyte crossmatch is also generally performed. Time constraints, however, often preclude completion of crossmatching and HLA typing before the transplant procedure. Levels of HLA compatibility do correlate with graft survival after heart and lung transplantation. Matching for HLA-DR appears to be beneficial in liver transplantation.

Corneal transplantation is a unique situation in which neither HLA-matching nor immunosuppressive therapy is required. The cornea is a site of "immune privilege" and appears to escape the normal mechanisms of transplant rejection because it lacks HLA antigens and because it expresses CD95 (Fas ligand or FasL), which induces apoptosis in mononuclear cells.

Parentage Testing

HLA typing has proven useful in parentage testing. Advantages of HLA typing in parentage testing include the following: 1) the HLA system is highly polymorphic; 2) the antigens are well developed at birth; and 3) no single haplotype occurs with a high incidence in any population. HLA typing alone can exclude about 90% of falsely accused males. With the addition of red cell antigen typing, the exclusion rate rises to 95% and exceeds 99% when typing for red cell enzymes and serum proteins is included.

HLA typing also provides a rather high level of certainty that a specific person who is not excluded is the parent of a specific child. Haplotype frequencies, rather than gene frequencies, are used in these calculations because linkage disequilibrium is so common in the HLA system. It is important, however, to keep in mind the racial differences that exist in HLA haplotype frequencies, and recombination events must also be considered.

DNA analyses are increasingly used in assessing parentage. A DNA-based assay technique commonly used for paternity testing is restriction fragment length polymorphism, which permits excellent determination of inheritance patterns. (See Fig 17-6.) Other very useful DNA-based assays are detection of alleles with variable numbers of tandem repeats and alleles with variation in the number of short tandem repeats, which assess other polymorphic, non-HLA genetic regions.

HLA and Forensic Pathology

DNA-based assays allow identification of individuals based on extremely small samples of fluid or tissue, such as hairs, epithelial cells, or sperm cells. While a wide range of genetic markers can be used, HLA-DQ allelic typing has become very common, due to the availability of a commercial kit.

HLA and Disease

Many factors determine susceptibility to disease. For some conditions, especially those believed to have an autoimmune etiology, an association exists between HLA phenotype and occurrence of clinical disease.[15] Although the causes for these associations are not yet known, evidence has been accumulating that implicates the HLA molecules themselves in disease susceptibility. For some autoimmune disorders such as celiac disease and rheumatoid arthritis, the peptide-binding grooves of the HLA molecules associated with these disorders appear to bind self peptides that stimulate autoreactive T cells. Another mechanism that could lead to the association of HLA phenotype and disease is for an HLA molecule to select T cells with a particular set of TCRs during thymic selection.

HLA associations with disease may be positive (increased risk of disease for those with a given HLA phenotype) or negative (decreased risk of disease for those with a given HLA phenotype). For example, HLA-DQ8 confers an in-

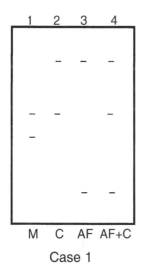

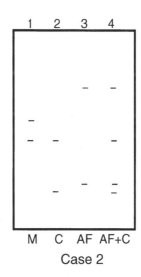

M C AF AF+C	M C AF AF+C
Case 1	Case 2

Figure 17-6. Diagrammatic example of DNA-RFLP analysis for paternity testing. In the two cases, two different sets of trios, mother (M), child (C), and alleged father (AF), are shown. Cut DNA fragments migrate to different positions based on their molecular weight. In lane 4, AF and C are mixed together in order to differentiate between two different bands that migrate to a similar position. In case 1, the alleged father cannot be excluded as the biologic father. Case 2 demonstrates a trio in which the alleged father can be excluded because, while the alleged father and child appear to have a similar band, the two bands are clearly separate in lane 4.

creased risk for type I diabetes, while HLA-DQ6 confers a decreased risk. For some diseases, it appears that more than one HLA locus may be involved in conferring risk.

The use of HLA profiles to identify individuals at risk, however, provides no more than a statistical association, except for a few monogenetic diseases caused by genes directly linked to HLA: 21-hydroxylase deficiency, and C2 or C4 deficiency. For these diseases there is an absolute association in individual families between transmission of these diseases and inheritance of certain HLA genes or haplotypes.

HLA typing has only limited value in most diseases because the association is incomplete, often giving false-negative and false-positive results. The association in Whites of HLA-B27 and ankylosing spondylitis is instructive. The test is highly sensitive; more than 90% of White patients with ankylosing spondylitis possess the HLA-B27 antigen. On the other hand, specificity is low; only 20% of individuals with the B27 antigen will develop ankylosing spondylitis.

Within affected families, expression of the B27 antigen cannot be the only determinant of susceptibility to ankylosing spondylitis, because the association between disease and HLA type is not complete. HLA-B27 typing is most useful in differentiating ankylosing spondylitis from juvenile rheumatoid arthritis.

The degree of association between a given HLA type and a disease is often described in terms of relative risk (RR), which is a measure of how much more frequently a disease occurs in individuals with a specific HLA type when compared to individuals not having that HLA type. Calculation of RR is usually based on the cross-product ratio of a 2×2 contingency table. However, because the HLA system is so highly polymorphic, there is an increased possibility of finding an association between an HLA antigen and a disease by chance alone. Therefore, calculation of RR for HLA disease associations is more complex and is typically done by Haldane's modification of Woolf's formula.[16,17] The RR values for some diseases associated with HLA are shown in Table 17-1.

Table 17-1. HLA-Associated Diseases

Disease	HLA	RR[15]
Celiac disease	DQ2	>250
Ankylosing spondylitis	B27	>150
Narcolepsy	DQ6	>38
Subacute thyroiditis	B35	14
Type I diabetes	DQ8	14
Multiple sclerosis	DR2,DQ6	12
Rheumatoid arthritis	DR4	9
Juvenile rheumatoid arthritis	DR8	8
Grave's disease	DR3	4

RR = relative risk

Future Possibilities

Future research developments in HLA are likely to focus on increased understanding of the molecular biology of the MHC complex and the biologic function of the MHC in the immune response. The use of DNA assays for HLA testing already provides improved clinical testing for transplantation and greater definition in parentage studies.

References

1. Bodmer JG, Marsh SG, Albert ED, et al. Nomenclature for factors of the HLA system, 1996. Tissue Antigens 1997;49:297-321.
2. Feder JN, Gnirke A, Thomas W, et al. A novel MHC class I-like gene is mutated in patients with hereditary haemochromatosis [see comments]. Nat Genet 1996;13(4):399-408.
3. Bodmer JG, Parham P, Albert ED, Marsh SG. Putting a hold on "HLA-H." Nat Genet 1997;15(3):234-5.
4. Bjorkman PJ, Saper MA, Samraovi A, et al. Structure of the human class I histocompatibility antigen, HLA-A2. Nature 1987;329:506-12.
5. Zinkernagel RM, Doherty PC. The discovery of MHC restriction. Immunol Today 1997;18(1):14-7.
6. Begovich AB, Erlich HA. HLA typing for bone marrow transplantation. New polymerase chain reaction-based methods. JAMA 1995;273(7):586-91.
7. Dzik WH. Leukoreduced blood components; Laboratory and clinical aspects. In: Rossi EC, Simon TL, Moss GS, Gould SA, eds. Principles of transfusion medecine. 2nd ed. Baltimore, MD: Williams and Wilkins, 1995:353-73.
8. Friedberg RC. Clinical and laboratory factors underlying refractoriness to platelet transfusions. J Clin Apheresis 1996;11(3):143-8.
9. Bolgiano DC, Larson EB, Slichter SJ. A model to determine required pool size for HLA-typed community donor apheresis programs. Transfusion 1989;29:306-10.
10. Beatty PG. The immunogenetics of bone marrow transplantation. Transfus Med Rev 1994;8(1):45-58.
11. Menitove JE, ed. Standards for blood banks and transfusion services. 19th ed. Bethesda, MD: American Association of Blood Banks, 1999:89.
12. Utzig MJ, Blumke M, Wolff-Vorbeck G, et al. Flow cytometry cross-match: A method for predicting graft rejection. Transplantation 1997;63(4):551-4.
13. Terasaki PI, Cho Y, Takemoto S, et al. Twenty-year follow-up on the effect of HLA matching on kidney transplant survival and prediction of future twenty-year survival. Transplant Proc 1996;28(3):1144-5.
14. Terasaki PI, Cecka JM, Gjertson DW, Takemoto S. High survival rates of kidney transplants from spousal and living unrelated donors. N Engl J Med 1995;333:333-6. [Comment in N Engl J Med 1995;333:379-80.]
15. Thorsby E. Invited anniversary review: HLA associated diseases. Hum Immunol 1997;53:1-11.
16. Haldane JBS. The estimation and significance of the logarithm of a ratio of frequencies. Ann Hum Genet 1955;20:309-11.
17. Woolf B. On estimating the relation between blood groups and disease. Ann Hum Genet 1955;19:251-3.

Suggested Reading

Phelan DL, Mickelson EM, Noreen HS, et al. ASHI laboratory manual. 3rd ed. Lenexa, KS: American Society for Histocompatibility and Immunogenetics, 1994.

Standards for histocompatibility testing. Lenexa, KS: American Society for Histocompatibility and Immunogenetics, 1998.

18

Pretransfusion Testing

THE PURPOSE OF PRETRANSFUSION testing is to select blood components that will not cause harm to the recipient and will have acceptable survival when transfused. If performed properly, pretransfusion tests will confirm ABO compatibility between the component and the recipient and detect most clinically significant unexpected antibodies. This chapter discusses in depth compatibility testing and detection of unexpected antibodies. It also addresses release of blood in routine cases, in urgent cases (including the massive transfusion setting), and in cases where non-group-specific blood has aready been transfused.

The AABB *Standards for Blood Banks and Transfusion Services*[1] requires that the following procedures be performed before blood components are issued for transfusion:

- Positive identification of recipient and recipient's blood sample.
- ABO and Rh typing of recipient's blood.
- Red cell antibody detection tests for clinically significant antibodies using recipient's serum or plasma.
- Comparison of current findings on the recipient's sample with records of previous results.
- Confirmation of ABO type of red cell components.
- Confirmation of the Rh type of Rh-negative units.
- Selection of components of ABO and Rh types appropriate for the recipient.
- Performance of a serologic or computer crossmatch.

18

■ Labeling of products with the recipient's identifying information.

Transfusion Requests

Requests for transfusion may be submitted electronically or on paper and must contain sufficient information for positive recipient identification. *Standards*[1(p56)] requires two independent identifiers to uniquely identify the patient. These identifiers could be the patient's first and last names, an identification number unique to that individual, a birth date, or other identifying system. Other information necessary to process the request includes identification of the component needed, the quantity, any special requests such as irradiation, or leukocyte reduction, and the name of the responsible physician. Gender and age of the recipient, diagnosis, and history of transfusion and pregnancy may be helpful in problem-solving. Each facility should have a written policy defining request acceptance criteria. Blood requests that lack the required information or are illegible should not be accepted. Telephoned requests are acceptable but should be documented in a telephone log or verified by subsequent submission of a properly completed blood requisition before the blood is issued for transfusion.

Patient Identification

Collection of a properly labeled blood sample from the intended recipient is critical to safe blood transfusion. Most hemolytic transfusion reactions result from errors in sample or patient identification.[2] The person drawing the blood sample must identify the intended recipient in a positive manner. Each facility must develop and implement polices and procedures for patient identification and specimen collection.

Most hospitals identify patients with an identification wristband. Ideally, this wristband is placed on the patient prior to specimen collection and remains on the patient until discharge. The same identifying information on the specimen tube submitted for testing will be used to label blood components and this information will be compared against the patient's wristband at the time of transfusion. Some hospitals use an internally generated or commercially available identification band with a substitute or additional "blood bank number" as the unique patient identifier. Commercial systems vary in design. One system uses color coded numbers on wristbands, tubes, and units; another uses a combination lock on the blood component; and yet another system includes a wristband with an embosser for label printing. Another system used by some hospitals, involving barcoded patient identification bands, has been hampered by the cost of hardware needed at the patient bedside.

Hospital policies generally require phlebotomists to collect blood specimens only from patients who have an attached patient identification wristband. However, in some circumstances, it may not be possible for the patient to wear an identification wristband, and an alternative means of positive patient identification may be needed. Circumstances making the use of wristbands difficult include patients with total body burns, extremely premature infants, or inaccessible wristbands during surgery. Some facilities allow identifying information to be placed on a patient's ankle or forehead. Intraoperative patient identification procedures may allow the use of an alternative identification process in lieu of an inaccessible wristband. It is important to remind clinical personnel that transfusions should not be administered to a patient who lacks positive identification.

When the patient's identity is unknown, an emergency identification method may be used. This patient identification must be attached to the patient and affixed or reproduced on blood samples, and this identification must be cross-referenced with the patient's name and hospital identification number or code when they become known. When hospitals allow the use of confidential or alias names, the facility must have policies and procedures that govern their use.

Outpatients may be identified with the use of a patient wristband for the purpose of blood sample collection. Alternative methods of positive patient identification include a driver's license or other photographic identification. Whenever possible, the patient should be asked to state his or her name and to provide confirmation of birth date and address. If a discrepancy is noted, the sample must not be collected until the patient's identity is clarified.

The identification of specimens used for preadmission testing must meet the same requirements as those used for inpatient transfusion—there must be no doubt about the identity of the specimen and the patient. With the advent of patient admission on the same day as surgery, hospitals have devised several mechanisms to identify patients when specimens have been collected several days or weeks prior to surgery. One option is to require that the patient wear an identification wristband. Other facilities use a unique number on specimens and on a patient identification form that the patient must provide on the day of surgery in order for the preadmission specimen to be valid for transfusion.[3] An alternative procedure is to place on the patient's medical record the wristband used to collect the specimen. This wristband would then be attached to the patient upon arrival on the day of surgery.[4]

Regardless of the system used, it must be well known to all those who collect blood specimens and be followed routinely. Ideally, patient identification procedures should be used as a matter of course to identify patients for all treatment methods, not solely transfusions.

Sample Labeling

Before leaving the patient, the phlebotomist must label the blood sample tubes with two unique patient identifiers and the date of collection. Either hand written or imprinted labels may be used as long as the information on the label is identical to that on the wristband and request. There must be a mechanism to identify the phlebotomist[1(p56)]; this certification may go on the label of the tube, on the requisition or be documented in a computer system.

Confirming Sample Identity in the Laboratory

When a sample is received in the laboratory, a trained member of the staff must confirm that the information on the label and on the transfusion request is identical. If there is any doubt about the identity of the patient, a new sample must be obtained.[1(p56)] It is unacceptable for anyone to correct identifying information on an incorrectly labeled sample. Each laboratory should establish policies and procedures that define identifying information and describe how to document receipt of mislabeled specimens.

Blood Sample

Pretransfusion testing may be performed on either serum or plasma.[1(p58)] Plasma may be the preferred specimen for some methods such as tests using gel technology but may sometimes create technical problems in tube tests. Incompletely clotted blood samples may cause small fibrin clots that trap red cells into aggregates that could resemble agglutinates. Serum or plasma collected from patients with high levels of fibrinogen may induce rouleaux formation that could be mistaken for agglutination. Clotting may be incomplete in specimens not intended to be anticoagulated; this usually occurs in patients who have been treated with heparin. Adding thrombin or protamine sulphate to the sample usually corrects the problem or an anticoagulated specimen can be collected.

It is permissible to collect blood from an infusion line. To avoid interference from residual intravenous fluid, the tubing should be flushed with saline and 5 mL or a volume of blood approximately twice the fluid volume in the line should be withdrawn and discarded before collecting the sample.[5]

Appearance of Sample

The appearance of the serum or plasma may create difficulties in detecting antibody-induced hemolysis. Whenever possible, a hemolyzed sample should be replaced with a new specimen. Test results observed with lipemic serum can also be difficult to evaluate. On occasion, it may be necessary to use hemoglobin-tinged or lipemic serum or plasma. Each institution should have a procedure describing the indications for using hemolyzed and lipemic specimens.

Age of Sample

Blood samples intended for use in crossmatching should be collected no more than 3 days before the intended transfusion unless the patient has not been pregnant or transfused within the preceding 3 months. If the patient's transfusion or pregnancy history is uncertain or unavailable, compatibility tests must be performed on blood samples collected within 3 days of RBC transfusions.[1(p58)] This is to ensure that the sample used for testing reflects the recipient's current immunologic status because recent transfusion or pregnancy may stimulate production of unexpected antibodies. Because it is not possible to predict whether or when such antibodies will appear, a 3-day time limit has been selected as an arbitrary interval expected to be both practical and safe. It is short enough to reflect acute changes in immunologic status but long enough to allow the results of preadmission testing completed on Friday (day 0) to be used for surgical cases performed on Monday (day 3). The 3-day requirement applies only to the previously mentioned categories of patients, but many laboratories prefer to standardize their operations by setting a 3-day limit on all specimens used for pretransfusion testing.

Each institution should have a policy that defines the length of time samples may be used. Testing of stored specimens should be performed with reagents approved for use with older specimens. Testing procedures should be based on the specimen storage limitations in the reagent manufacturer's information circulars. Lack of appropriate storage space may also limit the length of time specimens are stored.

Retaining and Storing Blood Samples

The recipient's blood specimen and a sample of the donor's red cells must be sealed or stoppered and kept at refrigerator temperature for at least 7 days after each transfusion.[1(p64)] Donor red cells may be from the remainder of the segment actually used in the crossmatch or a segment removed before issuing the blood. If the opened crossmatch segment is saved, it must be placed in a sealed or stoppered tube labeled with the unit number. Keeping the patient's and donor's samples allows repeat or additional testing if the patient experiences adverse effects.

Serologic Testing

The patient's ABO and Rh type must be determined in order to transfuse ABO- and Rh-compatible components. The *Standards*[1(p58-59)] requires that the red cells of the intended recipient be typed for ABO and Rh and the serum or plasma be tested for expected and unexpected antibodies before components containing red cells are issued for transfusion. There should be written procedures for exceptions during emergencies. When only plasma and platelets or cryoprecipitated antihemophilic globulin are being infused, ABO tests do not need to be repeated. However, some workers will repeat the ABO test if at least two previous types are not on file.

ABO and Rh Typing of the Recipient

To determine the ABO type of the recipient, red cells must be tested with anti-A and anti-B, and the serum or plasma with A_1 and B red cells. The techniques used and interpretation of results are described in Chapter 13. Any discrepant results should be resolved before blood is given. If transfusion is necessary before resolution, the patient should receive type O red cells.

The patient's red cells must also be tested with anti-D, with suitable observations or controls to avoid a false-positive interpretation. Chapter 14 contains a more extensive discussion of Rh typing reagents, appropriate control techniques and weak D forms of the D antigen. If problems in D typing arise, the patient should be given D-negative blood until the problem is resolved. Testing a recipient's red cells for weak D is not necessary because giving D-negative cells causes no harm to recipients of the weak D phenotype. Omitting the test for weak D prevents misinterpretations arising from the presence of a positive direct antiglobulin test (DAT). However, some transfusion services test patient pretransfusion specimens for weak D in order to identify patients who could be given Rh-positive blood components, thus reserving the Rh-negative components for the true Rh-negative patients. Routine testing for other Rh antigens is not required.

Detecting Unexpected Antibodies to Red Cell Antigens

Before deciding upon routine procedures for antibody detection, the blood bank director must decide which antibodies are considered clinically significant. In general, an antibody is considered clinically significant if antibodies of that specificity have been associated with hemolytic disease of the newborn, a hemolytic transfusion reaction, or notable decreased survival of transfused red cells. Antibodies reactive at 37 C and/or in the antiglobulin test are more

likely to be clinically significant than cold-reactive antibodies.[6]

Numerous serologic techniques have been developed that are suitable for detection of blood group antibodies (see Chapter 12 and Chapter 19). Goals in preparing compatible blood for a recipient are to:

- Detect as many clinically significant antibodies as possible.
- Detect as few clinically insignificant antibodies as possible.
- Complete the procedure in a timely manner.

Standards[1(p59)] requires that tests for unexpected antibodies use unpooled reagent red cells in a method that detects clinically significant antibodies and includes an antiglobulin test preceded by incubation at 37 C.

Each negative antiglobulin test must be followed by a control system of IgG-sensitized cells. If alternative procedures are used, there must be documentation of equivalent sensitivity, and the manufacturer's specified controls must be used.

The method chosen should have sufficient sensitivity to detect very low levels of antibody in a recipient's serum. Transfusion of antigen-incompatible red cells to a recipient with a weakly reactive antibody may result in rapid anamnestic production of antibody with subsequent red cell destruction. The same antibody detection procedure may be used for all categories of specimens, including pretransfusion and prenatal tests on patients and screening of donor blood. Once a procedure has been adopted, the method must be described in the facility's standard operating procedures (SOP) manual. Each member of the staff must be trained to perform the procedure and to follow the directions as written.

Reading and Interpreting Reactions

In serologic testing, the hemolysis or agglutination that constitutes the visible endpoint of a red cell antigen-antibody interaction must be observed accurately and consistently. The strength of agglutination or degree of hemolysis observed with each cell sample should be recorded immediately after the test is read. All personnel in a laboratory should use the same interpretations and notations and be consistent in grading reactions. Some laboratories prefer to use a numerical scoring system to indicate reaction strength and others use notations of "Pos" or "Neg." An optical aid such as a convex mirror enhances discrimination in reading tube tests. Microscopic observation is not routinely recommended, but a microscope can be useful in distinguishing rouleaux from true agglutination and detecting specific patterns of agglutination that are characteristic of some antibodies. For example, anti-Sd[a] typically produces small refractile agglutinates in a sea of free red blood cells, giving the appearance of a mixed-field reaction.

Autologous Control

An autologous control or DAT is not required as part of pretransfusion testing. Some workers find that routine observation of an autologous control provides useful information. Others[7] consider it of limited value, even for patients who have recently been transfused, and use it only when antibody identification is required.

Practical Considerations

Antibody detection tests may be performed in advance of, or together with, a crossmatch between the patient's serum and donor red cells. Performing antibody detection tests before crossmatching permits early recognition and identification of clinically significant antibodies and makes the decision about immediate-spin or computer crossmatching easier. Precrossmatch detection of antibodies allows more time to obtain donor units that lack the relevant antigen, facilitating the timely provision of blood for transfusion. The use of a preadmission type and screen has decreased

the urgent processing of transfusion requests on the morning of surgery.

Comparison with Previous Records

Results of tests on a current specimen must be compared with previous transfusion service records if there has been prior testing, and the comparison must be documented.[1(p59)] Concurrence between previous and current ABO and Rh findings gives assurance, but not proof, that no identification errors have occurred and that tests have been correctly performed and interpreted.

Records are reviewed for presence of clinically significant red cell antibodies, for difficulties in testing, for occurrence of significant adverse reactions, and for special blood component needs.[1(p59)] Clinically significant red cell alloantibodies may become undetectable in a recipient's serum over time. Between 30 and 35% of antibodies become undetectable within 1 year and nearly 50% become undetectable after 10 or more years.[8] Even if the current antibody detection test is negative, the antiglobulin phase of the crossmatch is required for patients with a history of any clinically significant alloantibody.[1(p59)]

Crossmatching Tests

Unless there is an urgent need for blood, a crossmatch must be performed. The method used must demonstrate ABO incompatibility and clinically significant antibodies to red cell antigens. When the patient has had a clinically significant antibody identified currently or in the past, blood lacking the relevant antigens should be selected for transfusion even though red cells possessing those antigens are presently compatible in vitro. The crossmatch should include the antiglobulin tests unless no clinically significant antibodies were detected in current screening tests and there is no record of previous detection of such antibodies.[1(p61)] In this situation, only a method to detect ABO incompatibility, such as an immediate-spin or computer crossmatch, is required. It is very rare for the antiglobulin phase of the crossmatch to detect a clinically significant unexpected antibody if the patient's antibody detection test is negative.[9,10]

The potential benefits of omitting a routine antiglobulin crossmatch include decreased turnaround time, decreased workload, reduced reagent costs, and more effective use of blood inventory. The medical director must approve the policy of omitting the antiglobulin phase of the crossmatch for patients who meet the criteria. The methods used for serologic crossmatching may be the same as those used for red cell antibody detection or identification or they may be different. For example, low ionic strength saline (LISS) may be used for both antibody detection and crossmatching, but the antibody identification protocol may be performed using LISS or polyethylene glycol (PEG).

Suggested Procedures for Routine Crossmatching

Red cells used for crossmatching must be obtained from a segment of tubing originally attached to the blood container. For routine tube testing, the cells may be washed and resuspended to a 2-4% concentration in saline. Washing the donor's red cells removes fibrin clots that may interfere with interpretation of results. Because the ratio of serum to cells markedly affects the sensitivity of agglutination tests, it is best to use the weakest cell suspension that can easily be observed for agglutination. If too many red cells are present, weak antibodies may be missed because too few antibody molecules bind to each cell. Many workers find that a 2% concentration yields the best results. For tests using column (gel) or microplate systems, follow the manufacturer's directions.

The simplest serologic crossmatch method is the immediate-spin saline technique, in which serum is mixed with saline-suspended red cells at room temperature and the tube is centrifuged immediately. The immediate-spin crossmatch method is designed to detect ABO incompatibilities between donor red cells and recipient serum. It can be used as the sole crossmatch method only if the patient has no present or previous clinically significant antibodies. Because the testing is performed at room temperature, antibodies such as anti-M, -N, and -P1 may be detected that were not observed if antibody detection tests omitted room-temperature testing. A sample immediate-spin crossmatch technique is illustrated in Method 3.1. An antiglobulin crossmatch procedure that meets the requirements of *Standards*[1] for all routine situations is described in Method 3.2.

Compatibility Testing for Infants

Requirements for compatibility testing for infants are discussed in Chapter 24. An initial pretransfusion specimen must be obtained from the infant to determine ABO and Rh type. For ABO typing, testing only the cells with anti-A and anti-B is required. Serum or plasma from either the infant or the mother may be used to detect unexpected red cell antibodies and for crossmatching; the infant's serum need not be tested for ABO antibodies unless non-group-O cells will be transfused. If no clinically significant unexpected antibodies are present, it is unnecessary to crossmatch donor red cells for the initial or subsequent transfusions. Repeat testing may be omitted for an infant less than 4 months of age during any one hospital admission.

Computer Crossmatch

When no clinically significant antibodies have been detected by antibody screening and history review, it is permissible to omit the antiglobulin phase of the crossmatch and perform only a procedure to detect ABO incompatibility. Computerized matching of blood can be used to fulfill the requirement, provided that the following conditions have been met[1(p57,60)]:

- The computer system has been validated, on site, to ensure that only ABO-compatible whole blood or red cells have been selected for transfusion.
- There is a validated method to detect ABO incompatibility.
- There is a method to identify first-time donors or donors lacking a valid ABO and Rh type on record. For these donors, confirmatory testing shall use a sample obtained from an attached segment. Confirmatory typing should be a validated method.
- The computer system contains the identification number and the product name of the donor unit, the ABO and Rh types of the product, the interpretation of the blood group confirmatory test, and the identification and ABO and Rh type of the recipient.
- If the donor unit ABO and Rh have been confirmed at a facility other than the one performing the computer crossmatch, there must be a method to identify that the confirmation occurred.
- A method exists to verify correct entry of data prior to release of blood components.
- The system contains logic to alert the user to discrepancies between information on the donor unit label and the interpretation of the blood group confirmatory test, and to ABO incompatibilities between recipient and donor unit.

Butch et al[11,12] and Safwenberg et al[13] have described in detail a model computer crossmatch system. Potential advantages of a computer crossmatch include: decreased workload, reduced volume of patients' blood samples, reduced exposure of personnel to blood specimens, and better utilization of blood inventory. Prior to implementation of the computer crossmatch, the Food and Drug Administration (FDA) must approve the request for a variance to regulations on compatibility

testing, found in 21 CFR 606.151.[14] The regulations regarding use of alternative procedures are found in 21 CFR 640.120.[14]

Routine Surgical Blood Orders

Blood ordering levels for common elective procedures can be developed from previous records of blood use. Because surgical requirements vary among institutions, routine blood orders should be based on local transfusion utilization patterns. The surgeons, anesthesiologists, and the medical director of the blood bank should agree on the number of units required for each procedure. See Chapter 3 for a more detailed discussion of blood ordering protocols. Routine blood order schedules are successful only when there is cooperation and confidence among the professionals involved in setting and using the guidelines.

Once a surgical blood ordering schedule has been established, the transfusion service routinely crossmatches the predetermined number of units for each patient undergoing the designated procedures. Routine orders may need to be modified for patients with anemia, bleeding disorders, or other conditions in which increased blood use is anticipated. As with other circumstances that require rapid availability of blood, the transfusion service staff must be prepared to provide additional blood if the need arises.

Type and Screen

Type and screen is a policy in which the patient's blood sample is tested for ABO, Rh, and unexpected antibodies, then stored in the blood bank for immediate crossmatching, should this prove necessary. Crossmatched blood is not labeled and reserved for patients undergoing surgical procedures that rarely require transfusion. The blood bank must have enough donor blood available to meet unexpected needs of patients undergoing operations on a type and screen basis. If transfusion becomes necessary, ABO- and Rh-compatible blood can be safely released after an immediate-spin or electronic crossmatch. However, if the antibody screen is positive, the antibody(ies) must be identified and antigen-negative units for clinically significant antibodies identified for use if needed.

Interpretation of Antibody Screening and Crossmatch Results

Most samples tested have a negative antibody screen and are crossmatch-compatible with units selected. A negative antibody screen does not guarantee that the serum is free of clinically significant red cell antibodies, only that it contains no antibodies that react with the screening cells by the techniques employed. A compatible crossmatch does not guarantee normal red cell survival.

Table 18-1 reviews the possible causes of positive pretransfusion tests. Most of what is known about red cell antigen and antibody reactions comes from work performed in tube testing. This information is not necessarily applicable to antibody detection tests using other technologies such as microtiter plates or column technologies. As these newer methods of antibody screening and identification become more popular, the causes of unexpected reactions, reagent problems, and spurious results will become clearer. Depending on the antigen/antibody reaction strength and the testing conditions, not all of the scenarios will result in positive tests.

The cause of the serologic problems should be identified before transfusion. Chapter 19 reviews techniques for problem resolution. If the patient is found to have clinically significant antibodies, units issued for transfusion should be nonreactive for such antigens when tested with licensed reagents. When licensed reagents are not available (eg, anti-Lan or anti-Jsa), stored patient serum or outdated reagents may be used if controls continue to ensure reagent specificity and sensitivity. When the antibody identified is not reactive at 37 C (anti-M, -N, -P1, -Lea, and/or -Leb)[15] random units may be selected using an antiglobulin crossmatch. Units selected for transfusion are negative by antiglobulin testing although room temperature testing, if performed, may be reactive.

Labeling and Release of Crossmatched Blood at the Time of Issue

Standards[1(p64)] requires that the following activities take place at the time of issue:

■ A tag or label indicating the recipient's two unique identifiers, donor unit number, and compatibility test results, if performed, must be attached securely to the blood container.

■ There must be a mechanism to identify the intended recipient and the requested blood component at the time of issue.

■ Special transfusion requirements must be identified.

Records for each unit of donor blood, component, or pooled component issued must be maintained in the blood bank. The record for each unit should contain:

1. The recipient's two unique identifiers.
2. The product name, including any special processing requirements.
3. The ABO and Rh type (if needed for the component).
4. The donor unit or pool identification number.
5. The donor ABO and Rh type (if needed for the component).
6. The interpretation of the crossmatch tests (if performed). If compatibility testing is not complete at the time of issue, this must be conspicuously indicated.
7. The date and time of issue.
8. The identity of the person issuing the blood.

Table 18-1. Causes of Positive Pretransfusion Tests

Negative Antibody Screen, Incompatible Immediate-Spin Crossmatch

- Donor red cells ABO-incompatible caused by error in selecting donor unit, patient specimen, or labeling of donor unit
- Donor red cells ABO-incompatible caused by failure to detect weak expressions of antigens
- Anti-A_1 in the serum of an A_2 or A_2B individual
- Other alloantibodies reactive at room temperature (ie, anti-M)
- Donor cells polyagglutinable

Negative Antibody Screen, Incompatible Antiglobulin Crossmatch

- Donor red cells have a positive DAT
- Antibody reacts only with cells having strong expression of a particular antigen either because of dosage (eg, Rh, Kidd, Duffy, and MN antigens) or because of intrinsic variation in antigen strength [eg, P1(P_1)]
- Antibody reacts with a low-incidence antigen.
- Passively transferred antibody is present—significant levels of circulating anti-A or -B may be present after infusion of group O platelets to a non-group O recipient

Positive Antibody Screen, Compatible Crossmatches

- Auto-anti-H (-IH)
- Anti-Le^{bH}
- Antibodies dependent on reagent cell diluent

Positive Antibody Screen, Incompatible Crossmatches, Negative Auto Control

- Alloantibody present
- Multiple alloantibodies
- Unexpected interactions with reagents
- Antibody reacting with a high-incidence antigen

Positive Antibody Screen, Incompatible Crossmatches, Positive Auto Control

- Alloantibody present and patient experiencing a delayed serologic or hemolytic transfusion reaction
- Passively transferred alloantibody reactive with the recipient's cells from derivatives
- Cold-reactive autoantibody
- Warm-reactive autoantibody
- Rouleaux formation
- Reagent-related problems

9.   The identity of the person to whom the blood was issued or the destination of the unit.

After the transfusion, a record of the transfusion shall be made a part of the patient's medical record. This information may be part of a computer record or a paper form. Records must contain the identification of the person(s) performing the test and, if blood is issued before resolution of compatibility problems, the final status of the serologic findings.

There should be a system to ensure that the proper blood component is issued for the intended patient. Before issuing a unit of blood, blood bank personnel must inspect the unit to make certain it does not have an abnormal color or appearance and document the inspection. The person issuing the blood should inspect the container to ensure it is not leaking and that the component is not outdated.

Final identification of the recipient and the blood container rests with the transfusionist, who must identify the patient and donor unit and certify that identifying information on forms, tags and labels are in agreement. (See Chapter 22.)

Selection of Units

ABO Compatibility

Whenever possible, patients should receive ABO-identical blood; however, it may be necessary to make alternative selections. If the component to be transfused contains 2 mL or more of red cells, the donor's red cells must be ABO-compatible with the recipient's plasma. Because plasma-containing components can affect the recipient's red cells, the ABO antibodies in transfused plasma should be compat-

ible with the recipient's red cells when feasible. Requirements for components and acceptable alternative choices are summarized in Table 18-2.

Rh Type

Rh-positive blood components should routinely be selected for D-positive recipients. Rh-negative units will be compatible, but should be reserved for D-negative recipients. D-negative patients should receive red-cell-containing components that are D-negative to avoid immunization to the D antigen. Occasionally, ABO-compatible Rh-negative components may not be available for Rh-negative recipients. In this situation, the blood bank physician and the patient's physician should weigh alternative courses of action. The clinician may elect to postpone transfusion, or may decide that the 80% risk of immunization is less significant than the risk of delaying transfusion. Depending on the child-bearing potential of the patient and the volume of red cells transfused, it may be desirable to administer Rh Immune Globulin to a D-negative patient given D-positive blood.[16]

Other Blood Groups

Antigens other than ABO and D are not routinely considered in the selection of units of

Table 18-2. Selection of Components When ABO-Identical Donors Are Not Available

	ABO Requirements
Whole Blood	Must be identical to that of the recipient.[*]
Red Blood Cells	Must be compatible with the recipient's plasma.
Granulocytes, Pheresis	Must be compatible with the recipient's plasma.
Fresh Frozen Plasma	Should be compatible with the recipient's red cells.
Platelets, Pheresis[*]	All ABO groups acceptable; components compatible with the recipient's red cells preferred.
Cryoprecipitated AHF	All ABO groups acceptable.

[*]Because a large volume of plasma is administered, components compatible with the recipient's red cells are preferred.

blood. However, if the recipient has a clinically significant unexpected antibody, antigen-negative blood should be selected for cross-matching. If the antibody is weakly reactive or no longer demonstrable, a licensed reagent should be used to screen donor units before a crossmatch is performed. If there is an adequate quantity of the patient's serum, or if another patient's serum with the same antibody specificity is available, and that antibody reacts well with antigen-positive red cells, that serum may be used to screen for antigen-negative units.

Those units found to be antigen-negative must be confirmed with a licensed reagent. When licensed reagents are not available, stored serum specimens from patients or donors can be used, especially for antibodies to high incidence or uncommon antigens. Antigen-negative units are not usually provided for the patient who has antibodies that are not clinically significant. Problems associated with crossmatching units for patients with these antibodies may sometimes be avoided by altering the serologic technique used for the crossmatch. When crossmatch compatible units cannot be found, the medical director should be involved in the decision to transfuse the patient. (See Chapter 19 and Chapter 20 for additional information on issuing crossmatch incompatible units.)

Blood Administered in Urgent Situations

When blood is urgently needed, the patient's physician must weigh the risk of transfusing uncrossmatched or partially crossmatched blood against the risk of delaying transfusion until compatibility testing is complete. Ideally, a transfusion service physician should provide consultation. The risk that the transfused unit might be incompatible may be judged to be less than the risk of depriving the patient of oxygen-carrying capacity of that transfusion.

Required Procedures

When blood is released before pretransfusion testing is complete, the records must contain a signed statement of the requesting physician indicating that the clinical situation was sufficiently urgent to require release of blood.[1(p66)] Such a statement does not absolve blood bank personnel from their responsibility to issue properly labeled donor blood that is ABO-compatible with the patient. When urgent release is requested, blood bank personnel should:

1. Issue uncrossmatched blood, which should be:

   a. Group O Red Blood Cells if the patient's ABO group is unknown. It is preferable to give Rh-negative blood if the recipient's Rh type is unknown, especially if the patient is female with the potential to bear children.

   b. ABO and Rh compatible, if there has been time to test a current specimen. Previous records must not be used, nor should information be taken from other records such as cards, dog tags, or driver's license.

2. Indicate in a conspicuous fashion on the attached tag or label that compatibility testing was not complete at the time of issue.

3. Begin compatibility tests and complete them promptly. If incompatibility is detected at any stage of testing, the patient's physician and the transfusion service physician should be notified immediately. Standard compatibility tests should be completed promptly for those units issued for initial replacement of the patient's blood volume.

Massive Transfusion

Massive transfusion is defined as infusion, within a 24-hour period, of a volume of blood approximating the recipient's total blood volume. Exchange transfusion of an infant is considered a massive transfusion.

Following massive transfusion, the pretransfusion sample no longer represents the blood currently in the patient's circulation and its use for crossmatching has limited benefit. It is only important to confirm ABO compatibility of units administered subsequently. The blood bank director may implement a more limited pretransfusion testing protocol to be used in these situations. This protocol should be in writing to ensure consistent application by all laboratory personnel.

Blood Administered After Non-Group-Specific Transfusion

Transfusion services sometimes release units for transfusion during emergencies before they receive a sample for blood typing. When it arrives, the sample is a pretransfusion specimen. In most cases, the sample is tested and units of that ABO group are issued for transfusion without concern for anti-A and/or anti-B remaining from the initial emergency-release units. Because most donor units are Red Blood Cells with comparatively little supernatant plasma, or Red Blood Cells (Additive Solution Added) with even less residual plasma, the risks involved in following this practice are minimal. The patient may experience a transient positive DAT.

When patients have been transfused with blood of an ABO group other than their own and additional transfusions are needed, it may be desirable to use units of the patient's own ABO group. The safety of this conversion depends on the status of anti-A and/or anti-B in the intended recipient. Some facilities perform an antiglobulin crossmatch with a freshly drawn specimen and red cells of the patient's original ABO group to assess compatibility.[17]

If the change in blood type involves only the Rh system, return to type-specific blood is simple, because antibodies are unlikely to be present in the plasma of either recipient or donor.

If a patient has received blood of an Rh type other than his or her own before a specimen is collected for testing, it may be difficult to determine the correct Rh type. If there is any question about the recipient's D type, D-negative blood may be transfused. The use of Rh Immune Globulin prophylaxis should be considered when Rh-positive components are transfused to Rh-negative patients. For a more in-depth review of this subject readers are encouraged to consult Garratty.[17]

References

1. Menitove J, ed. Standards for blood banks and transfusion services, 19th ed. Bethesda, MD: American Association of Blood Banks, 1999.
2. Sazama K. Reports of 355 transfusion associated deaths: 1976 through 1985. Transfusion 1990;30:583-90.
3. Butch SH, Stoe M, Judd WJ. Solving the same-day admission identification problem (abstract). Transfusion 1994;34(Suppl):93S.
4. AuBuchon JP. Blood transfusion options: Improving outcomes and reducing costs. Arch Pathol Lab Med 1997;121:40-7.
5. Procedures for the collection of diagnostic blood specimens by venipuncture. 3rd ed. NCCLS document H3-A2, approved standard. Villanova, PA: National Committee for Clinical Laboratory Standards, 1991.
6. Issitt PD, Anstee DJ. Applied blood group serology. Durham, NC: Montgomery Scientific Publications, 1998:873-905.
7. Judd WJ, Barnes BA, Steiner EA, et al. The evaluation of a positive direct antiglobulin test (autocontrol) in pretransfusion testing revisited. Transfusion 1986;26:220-4.
8. Ramsey G, Smietana SJ. Long term follow-up testing of red cell alloantibodies. Transfusion 1994;34:122-4.
9. Oberman HA. The present and future crossmatch. Transfusion 1992;32:794-5.
10. Meyer EA, Shulman IA. The sensitivity and specificity of the immediate-spin crossmatch. Transfusion 1989;29:99-102.
11. Butch SH, Judd WJ, Steiner EA, et al. Electronic verification of donor-recipient compatibility: The computer crossmatch. Transfusion 1994;34:105-9.
12. Butch SH, Judd WJ. Requirements for the computer crossmatch (letter). Transfusion 1994;34:187.
13. Safwenberg J, Hogman CF, Cassemar B. Computerized delivery control—a useful and safe complement to the type and screen compatibility testing. Vox Sang 1997;72:162-8.
14. Code of federal regulations. Title 21 CFR Parts 600-799. Washington, DC: US Government Printing Office, 1998 (revised annually).

15. Shulman IA, Petz LD. Red cell compatibility testing: Clinical significance and laboratory methods. In: Petz LD, Swisher SN, Kleinman S, eds. Clinical practice of transfusion medicine. 3rd ed. New York: Churchill Livingstone, 1996:199-244.

16. Pollack W, Ascari WQ, Crispen JF, et al. Studies on Rh prophylaxis II: Rh immune prophylaxis after transfusion with Rh-positive blood. Transfusion 1971;11:340-4.

17. Garratty G. Problems associated with passively transfused blood group alloantibodies. Am J Clin Pathol 1998;109:169-77.

Suggested Reading

Beck ML, Tilzer LL. Red cell compatibility testing: A perspective for the future. Transfus Med Rev 1996;10:118-30.

Butch SH, Oberman HA. The computer or electronic crossmatch. Transfus Med Rev 1997;11:256-64.

Lumadue JA, Biyd JS, Ness PM. Adherence to a strict specimen-labeling policy decreases the incidence of erroneous blood grouping of blood bank specimens. Transfusion 1997;37:1169-72.

19

Initial Detection and Identification of Alloantibodies to Red Cell Antigens

RED CELL ALLOANTIBODIES OTHER than naturally occurring anti-A or -B are called unexpected red cell alloantibodies, and can be detected by performing an antibody screen. Unexpected alloantibodies can be found in 0.3-38% of the population, depending upon the group of patients or donors studied and the sensitivity of the test methods used.[1,2] In contrast to red cell autoantibodies, which may react with red cells from other individuals, alloantibodies react only with allogeneic red cells. Immunization to red cell antigens may result from pregnancy, transfusion, transplantation, or from injection with immunogenic material. In some instances no specific immunizing event can be identified.

Significance of Alloantibodies

Alloantibodies to red cell antigens may be initially detected in any test that uses serum or plasma [including the ABO test, the antibody detection test (antibody screen), or the crossmatch] or in any eluate prepared from red cells coated with alloantibody. Ordinarily, once an antibody is detected, its specificity should be determined and its clinical significance assessed.

A clinically significant red cell antibody, although difficult to define, could be thought to be one that shortens the survival of transfused red cells or has been associated with hemolytic disease of the newborn (HDN). The degree of clinical significance may even vary with antibodies of the same specificity. Some antibodies cause destruction of incompatible red cells within hours or even minutes, others decrease the survival by only a few days, and some cause no discernible cell destruction. Antibodies of some specificities are known to cause HDN; some may cause a positive direct antiglobulin test (DAT) in the fetus without clinical evidence of HDN; and still others do not cause HDN.

Reported experience with other examples of antibody with the same specificity can be used in assessing clinical significance. Table 15-2 summarizes the expected reactivity and clinical significance of commonly encountered alloantibodies. Marsh et al[3] have published a review of these and other specificities. For some antibodies, few or no data exist, and decisions must be based on the premise that clinically significant antibodies are usually those active at 37 C and/or by the indirect antiglobulin test (IAT). It is not necessarily true, however, that all antibodies active in vitro at 37 C and/or by the IAT are clinically significant.

Antibodies encountered in pretransfusion testing should be identified for assessment of the need to select antigen-negative red cell components for transfusion. Patients with clinically significant antibodies should, whenever practical, receive red cells that have been tested and found to lack the corresponding antigen. In prenatal testing, the specificity and immunoglobulin class of an antibody influence the likelihood of HDN. While identification of unexpected antibodies in donor blood is not required, results of such testing are useful for characterizing the units prior to transfusion and for procuring blood typing reagents or teaching samples. The use of donor units with unexpected antibodies for transfusion should be defined in institutional standard operating procedures.

General Procedures

The techniques employed for antibody detection and antibody identification are similar. The methods employed for antibody detection must be broad enough to detect clinically significant antibodies with differing patterns of reactivity. Antibody identification methods can be more focused and are typically based on the reactivity patterns identified in the antibody detection.

Every facility should establish what techniques for antibody detection and identification will routinely be employed. It is sometimes valuable to develop flowcharts to clearly guide the technologist through the process of selecting additional techniques to identify antibody specificities. This approach is helpful in expediting the identification process and minimizing unnecessary testing.

Specimen Requirements

Either serum or plasma may be used for antibody screening and identification; serum is used more widely, and that is the only term that will be used in this chapter. Plasma is not suitable for detection of complement activation. When autologous red cells are studied, the use of a sample anticoagulated with EDTA avoids problems associated with the in-vitro uptake of complement components by red cells, which may occur with a clotted sample. A 10-mL aliquot of whole blood usually contains enough serum for identifying simple antibody specificities; more may be required for more complex studies.

Medical History

It is useful to know a patient's clinical diagnosis, history of transfusions or pregnancies, and recent drug therapy when performing an antibody identification. In patients who have had recent red cell transfusions, the circulating blood may be so admixed with donor cells that special procedures are needed to separate the autologous red cells for typing (see Method 2.15). Other procedures will be necessary for patients known to have autoantibodies, which may be disease-associated or induced by drugs (see Chapter 20).

Reagents

Screening Cells

Group O red cells suitable for antibody screening of patient serum or plasma are commercially available and are offered as sets of either two or three vials of single-donor red cells. Pooled antibody screening cells are for use in testing serum samples from donors and may not be used for recipients' specimens[4(p59)] because a weak antibody against an antigen present on only one of the cell samples in the pool might not produce a detectable reaction.

The decision to use two or three cells in an antibody screening procedure should be based on circumstances in each individual laboratory. The reagent red cells are selected to express the antigens associated with most clinically relevant antibodies. Reagent cells licensed by the Food and Drug Administration (FDA) for this purpose must express the following antigens: D, C, E, c, e, M, N, S, s, P1, Le^a, Le^b, K, k, Fy^a, Fy^b, Jk^a, and Jk^b.[5] There are no requirements for other antigens, such as Lu^a, V, or C^w. Some weakly reactive antibodies react only with screening red cells from donors who are homozygous for the genes controlling expression of these antigens, a serologic phenomenon called dosage. Antibodies in the Rh, Duffy, and Kidd systems most commonly manifest dosage. Some workers recommend that Jk(a+b−) red cells be used to provide adequate detection of anti-Jk^a.

To prepare the screening cells, reagent red cells are suspended in a preservative solution. Aliquots may be washed and suspended in saline or low ionic strength saline (LISS) solution to their original concentration because test sensitivity diminishes with a cell suspension that is too heavy. Cells should not be stored in these wash solutions more than 24 hours because the solutions may not be sterile and some antigens, Fy^a in particular, deteriorate rapidly in a low-ionic environment.[6] At their expiration date, reagent red cells may be as old as 9 weeks postphlebotomy. They should not be used for required tests beyond their expiration date because the strength of some antigens decreases during storage. Antigen loss may, unpredictably, be more pronounced on the red cells of some donors than on those of others. When not in use, reagent red cells should be refrigerated.

Red Cell Panels

Identification of an antibody to red cell antigens requires testing the serum against a panel of selected red cell specimens with known antigen composition for the major blood groups. They are usually obtained from commercial suppliers, but institutions may assemble their own by using red cells from local sources. Panel cells are (except in special circumstances) group O, allowing serum of any ABO group to be tested.

Each cell of the panel is from a different individual. The cells are selected so that, taking all the cells into account, a distinctive pattern of positive and negative reactions exists for each of many antigens. To be functional, a reagent red cell panel must make it possible to identify with confidence those clinically significant alloantibodies that are most frequently encountered, such as anti-D, -E, -K, and -Fy^a. The phenotypes of the reagent red cells should be distributed such that each of the common alloantibodies, if it is the only one in a serum, can be clearly identified and most others at least tentatively excluded. The pattern of reactivity for most examples of single alloantibodies should not overlap with any other; eg, all of the K+ samples should not be the only ones that are also E+. It may also be valuable to include cells with a double dose of the antigen in question for an antibody that frequently shows dosage preference. To lessen the possibility that chance alone has caused an apparently definitive pattern, there must be a sufficient number of red cell samples that lack, and sufficient red cell samples that carry, most of the antigens listed in Table 19-1.

Commercially prepared panels are generally issued every 2-4 weeks. Each panel contains dif-

Table 19-1. A Reagent Red Cell Panel for Alloantibody Identification

Sample #	Rh Phenotype	Rh C	Cw	c	D	E	e	Kell K	Duffy Fya	Fyb	Kidd Jka	Jkb	P P1	Lewis Lea	Leb	MNS M	N	S	s
1	r'r	+	0	+	0	0	+	0	+	0	+	+	+	0	+	+	+	0	+
2	R_1^w	+	+	0	+	0	+	+	+	+	0	+	+	+	0	+	+	+	+
3	R_1	+	0	0	+	0	+	0	+	+	+	+	0	0	+	+	0	+	0
4	R_2	0	0	+	+	+	0	0	0	+	0	+	+	+	0	0	+	0	+
5	r"r	0	0	+	0	+	+	0	+	+	0	+	0	0	+	+	+	+	0
6	r	0	0	+	0	0	+	0	0	+	+	0	+	0	0	+	+	0	+
7	r	0	0	+	0	0	+	+	0	+	+	0	+	0	+	+	0	+	0
8	r	0	0	+	0	0	+	0	+	0	0	+	+	+	0	0	+	0	+
9	r	0	0	+	0	0	+	0	0	+	+	0	0	0	+	0	+	+	0
10	R_0	0	0	+	+	0	+	0	0	0	+	+	+	0	0	+	+	+	+

+ Denotes presence of antigen; 0 denotes absence of antigen.

ferent cells, with different antigen patterns, so it is essential to use the phenotype listing sheet that comes with the panel in use. Commercial cells usually come as a 2-5% suspension in a preservative medium; they can be used directly from the vial. Washing is generally unnecessary unless the media in which the reagent cells are suspended interfere with alloantibody identification. For solid-phase methods, panels of dried red cell monolayers may be prepared and stored for long periods before use.[7]

Saline-Suspended Red Cells

The simplest serologic method employs saline-suspended red cells that are mixed with the serum to be tested. This system can be incubated at either room temperature or 37 C before centrifugation or centrifuged and read immediately. Antibodies reacting predominantly at temperatures below 37 C, such as anti-M, -N, -P$_1$, -Le^a, and Le^b, are most often detected by this simple technique. Many institutions omit the immediate centrifugation reading and the room temperature incubation phase to avoid finding antibodies that react only at low temperatures and have little clinical significance. Test observation after 37 C incubation may detect some antibodies (eg, potent anti-D, -K, or -E) that can cause direct agglutination of red cells. Also, some antibodies (eg, anti-Le^a, -Jk^a) may be detected by their lysis of antigen-incompatible red cells during this phase.

Most clinically significant antibodies bind to the cells during incubation at 37 C, but do not cause agglutination and are not demonstrable until the antiglobulin test phase. For this reason, many facilities have chosen to eliminate the immediate-spin and room temperature incubation phase reading, but if incubation at both room temperature and 37 C is desired, two sets of tubes may be prepared. One set is incubated at room temperature and the other at 37 C to avoid the positive reaction that polyspecific antihuman globulin serum may elicit if cold-reactive antibodies have bound complement to the cells.

Antiglobulin Reagents

To detect clinically significant antibodies most antibody identification tests include an antiglobulin phase. Either polyspecific or IgG-specific antiglobulin reagents may be used. Polyspecific reagents may detect, or detect more readily, antibodies that bind complement. This may be of concern for the detection of Kidd antibodies.[8] While this may be advantageous in some instances, many workers prefer to use IgG-specific reagents to avoid unwanted reactivity due to in-vitro complement binding by cold-reactive antibodies, which may not be judged to be clinically significant.

Enhancement Media

Although the test system may consist solely of serum and cells, most workers use some kind of enhancement medium. Many different media are available, including LISS, polyethylene glycol (PEG), and albumin. For the initial identification panels, most laboratories use the same enhancement method used in their routine antibody detection and crossmatch tests. Additional enhancement techniques may be employed for more complex identification. Enhancement techniques are discussed later in this chapter.

Autologous Control

It is important to know how a serum under investigation reacts with autologous red cells. This helps determine whether alloantibody, autoantibody, or both are present. Serum that reacts only with the reagent red cells usually contains only alloantibody, whereas reactivity with both reagent and autologous red cells suggests the presence of autoantibody or autoantibody plus alloantibody. A patient with alloantibodies to antigens on recently transfused red cells may have circulating donor red cells coated with alloantibodies that produce a positive autocontrol. The mixed-field pattern that may result may be misinterpreted as being due to autoantibody. A detailed history of recent transfusions should be obtained for all patients with a positive DAT or positive autocontrol.

An autocontrol provides useful information in antibody identification studies by permitting reactions with autologous and reagent red cells to be compared. When test methods used for antibody identification are different from or additional to the initial autocontrol method,

an autologous control is essential. An autocontrol is not required in all circumstances, especially if the serum is not reactive by the method used; therefore, it may not be necessary to prepare enzyme-treated autologous cells when testing the serum against panel cells pretreated with enzyme.

The autologous control, in which serum and autologous cells undergo the same manipulation as serum and reagent cells, is not the same as a DAT. If the autocontrol is positive in the antiglobulin phase, a DAT should be performed. If the DAT is positive, elution studies should be considered if the patient has been recently transfused, if there is evidence of immune hemolysis, and/or if the results of serum studies prove inconclusive. A reactive DAT may also indicate the presence of autoantibody. If autoantibody is detected in the serum, adsorption studies may be necessary to establish that it is not masking coexisting alloantibodies.

Basic Antibody Identification Techniques

Traditional serologic methods in the United States are based on agglutination and performed in test tubes or microplates remain the most commonly used and are the primary techniques discussed in this chapter. Other methods, which modify traditional test endpoints or are not dependent on agglutination, are also available. These include solid-phase, flow cytometry, agglutination test (gel tests) column techniques, as well as some automated systems. Such methods may be used in addition to or instead of the classic techniques discussed below. Interpretation of reaction patterns to identify antibody specificity is the same for all tests.

Initial Observations

Red cell panels are usually employed to investigate a serum already known to contain antibody due to reactivity detected in preliminary tests such as the antibody screening test or crossmatch. These initial tests provide important information about the test phases at which reactivity occurs, and the serum may sometimes be tested only by the technique with which the antibody was originally detected. For initial panels, however, it is common to use the same methods and range of phases used in the initial procedures; typically these include 37 C testing, often with enhancement medium, and IAT. Some workers may choose to include a room temperature incubation. This ensures that the serum has been tested against cells of various phenotypes and antigen strengths, and guards against missing weaker reactions at some phases.

Knowing the phase of initial reactivity may suggest possible specificities. Reactivity only at room temperature, for example, suggests the possibility of anti-M, -P1, -I, -Le^a, or -Le^b. The phenotype of the originally reactive antibody detection cells may also provide clues as to specificity, or help exclude specificities. If multiple panels are available, this information can help in selecting the cells likely to be informative.

If the patient has had antibodies previously identified, this may affect panel selection. For example, if the patient is known to have anti-e, it will not be helpful to test the serum against a panel of 10 cells, nine of which are e-positive. Testing a panel of selected e-negative cells will better reveal any newly formed antibodies.

Sometimes the patient's phenotype influences the selection of reagent cells. For example, if the patient is D-negative and the serum is reactive with D-positive cells in the screening test, an abbreviated panel or select cell panel of D-negative cells may be tested. This can both confirm the presence of anti-D and demonstrate the presence of additional antibodies, but minimizes the amount of testing required to confirm antibody specificity.[9]

Interpreting Results

Antibody screening results are interpreted as positive or negative based on the presence or absence of agglutination. Interpretation of panel results can be a more complex process combining technical knowledge and intuitive skills. Panel results will include a range of positive and negative results at different phases of testing, each of which should be explained by the final conclusion. Determination of the patient's red cell phenotype and the probability of antibody specificity can also play a role in the final interpretation.

Positives and Negatives

Both positive and negative reactions are important in antibody identification. Positive reactions indicate the phase and strength of reactivity, which can suggest specificities expected to react in that manner. Positive reactions also can be compared to the antigen patterns expressed by the panel cells to help assign specificity. Single alloantibodies usually yield definite positive and negative reactions that create a clear-cut antigen pattern with reagent red cell samples. For example, if a serum reacts only with cells 4 and 5 of the reagent red cell panel shown in Table 19-1, anti-E is very likely present. Both reactive samples express E and all nonreactive samples lack E.

Negative reactions are also important in antibody identification because they allow at least tentative exclusion of antibodies to antigens expressed on the nonreactive cells. Exclusion of antibodies is an important step in the interpretation process and must be done to ensure proper identification of all antibodies present.

Exclusion or "Crossing Out"

A widely used first approach to the interpretation of panel results is to exclude specificities based on nonreactivity with the serum tested. Such a system is sometimes referred to as a "cross-out" or "rule-out" method. Once results have been recorded on the worksheet, the antigen profile of the first nonreactive cell is examined. If an antigen is *present* on the cell and the serum *did not react*, the presence of the corresponding antibody may be at least tentatively excluded. Many workers will actually cross out that antigen from the listing on the panel sheet to facilitate the process. After all antigens present on that cell have been crossed off, interpretation proceeds with the other nonreactive cells and additional specificities are excluded. In most cases, this process will leave a group of antigens that still have not been excluded.

Next, the cells reactive with the serum are evaluated. The pattern of reactivity for each nonexcluded specificity is compared to the pattern of reactivity obtained with the test serum. If there is a pattern that matches exactly, that is most likely the specificity of the antibody in the serum. However, if there are remaining specificities that have not been excluded, additional testing may be needed to eliminate remaining possibilities and to confirm the specificity identified. This requires testing the serum against additional cells.

Once tentative identification has been established, testing the serum against cells selected for specific antigenic characteristics gives more information than using an additional, unmodified panel. For example, this approach could be employed if the pattern of positive reactions exactly fits anti-Jk^a, but anti-K and anti-S may still not be excluded. The serum should be tested against selected cells, ideally with the three phenotypes: Jk(a–), K–, S+; Jk(a–), K+, S–; and Jk(a+), K–, S–. The reaction pattern with these cells should both confirm the presence of anti-Jk^a and include or exclude anti-K and anti-S.

While the exclusion (cross-out) approach often identifies simple antibody specificities, it should be considered only a provisional step, particularly if the cross-out was completed based on nonreactivity of cells with heterozygous expression of an antigen. As discussed below, some antibodies may be mistakenly excluded if, for some reason, no reactivity was obtained with a cell positive for the antigen. On occasion, similar patterns may be obtained for different specificities or when multiple antibodies are present.

Computer programs are available that can interpret panel results and assist in the selection of specific panel cells based on a previously identified antibody specificity, thus minimizing the use of cells that do not provide information on newly formed antibodies.[10] Such programs can utilize information read by traditional manual methods and entered by the user, or can be coupled to automated test systems that directly transmit test results.

Probability

Conclusive antibody identification requires serum to be tested against sufficient reagent red cell samples that lack, and that carry, the antigen that appears to correspond to the specificity of the antibody, to ensure that an observed pattern is not due to chance alone.

Calculations

The traditional way to calculate the probability that an antibody has been correctly identified is Fisher's exact method, in which the numbers of positive and negative results are compared with the numbers of cells that express or lack the corresponding antigen.[11] (See Table 19-2.) For this method, a probability (p) value of 0.05 is generally accepted as a minimum value for considering an interpretation statistically valid. (See Table 19-3.) Keeping in mind that the p value is a conditional value, if it is used in antibody identification, the assumption is that the identification is based on unrelated antibodies. This means that chance alone would produce an identical set of results once in 20 similar studies of unrelated antibodies (ie, if identifying anti-D, there is a 1 in 20 chance that identical results could be caused by a non-Rh antibody). Additional factors such as the age or condition of the test cells, inaccurate serum/cell ratio in each test cell, and variation of antigen strength between cells, can also affect the statistical calculations. Most basic red cell panels have limited capacity for conclusive identification of some specificities, especially when multiple antibodies are present. To meet the $p \leq 0.05$ statistical standard, tests with additional cells are often necessary.

Fisher's exact method has been challenged as being too conservative and not addressing population frequencies for antigens for which the cells have *not* been typed. Harris and Hochman[12] have derived an alternative calculation to allow for such antigens. (See Table 19-2.) Comparative p values by their method are also given in Table 19-3. This calculation allows more liberal interpretation of results, and may require less actual testing to confirm specificity.

Interpretation

Most workers rarely use either statistical method in a conscious manner. A standard approach (based on Fisher's exact method) has been to require, for each specificity identified, three antigen-positive cells that do react and three antigen-negative cells that fail to react. This standard is not always possible, but it works well in practice, especially if cells with strong antigen expression are available. A somewhat more liberal approach is derived from calculations by Harris and Hochman,[12] whereby minimum requirements for a p value of 0.05 are met by having two positive and three negative cells, or one positive and seven negative cells (or the reciprocal of either combination). The possibility that the serum fails to react with antigen-positive cells (or of some "false-positive" results) must also be considered in determining specificity.

Additional details on calculating probability may be found in the suggested readings by Race and Sanger, Menitove, and Kanter.

Phenotype of Autologous Red Cells

Once an alloantibody has been identified in a serum, it is often helpful to demonstrate that the autologous red cells are negative for the corresponding antigen. For example, if serum from an untransfused individual appears to contain anti-Fy^a but the autologous red cells have a negative DAT and type as Fy(a+), the

Table 19-2. Calculation of Probability

A.   **Fisher's Exact Method[11]**

The formula for calculating probability (p) is:

$$\frac{(A+B)! \times (C+D)! \times (A+C)! \times (B+D)!}{N! \times A! \times B! \times C! \times D!}$$

B.   **Modification of Harris and Hochman[12]**

$$(A/N)^A (B/N)^B$$

A = number of positive reactions observed with antigen-positive red cell samples
B = number of positive reactions observed with antigen-negative red cell samples
C = number of negative reactions observed with antigen-positive red cell samples
D = number of negative reactions observed with antigen-negative red cell samples
N = number of cells tested
! = factorial, the product of all the whole numbers from 1 to the number involved.

For example, $6! = 6 \times 5 \times 4 \times 3 \times 2 \times 1 = 720$
              $1! = 1$
              $0! = 1$

Consult references and suggested readings for further details on calculations.

data are clearly in conflict and further testing is indicated.

Determination of the patient's phenotype can be difficult if the patient has been transfused recently, generally within 3 months. If a pretransfusion specimen is still available, these red cells should be used to determine the phenotype. Alternatively, the patient's own red cells can be separated from the transfused red cells and then typed. Procedures for this are given in Method 2.15 and Method 2.16. The use of potent blood typing reagents, appropriate controls, and observation for mixed-field reactions often allows an unseparated specimen to be phenotyped. If there is little uncertainty about antibody identification, extensive efforts to separate and type the patient's own red cells are not necessary. The selection of antigen-negative blood for transfusion to patients with clinically significant antibodies, along with the required antiglobulin phase crossmatch[4(p60)] provides additional confirmation of antibody specificity. Definitive testing can be done on the patient's red cells after a period without transfusion. In a chronically transfused patient, definitive testing can be done after an interval during which only antigen-negative blood has been given. However, this assumes that the chronically transfused patient is not aplastic and has not received massive quantities of red cell transfusions because any antigen-positive red cells detected after prolonged transfusion of antigen-negative blood would presumably be the patient's own.

Complex Antibody Problems

Not all antibody identifications are simple. The exclusion procedure does not always lead directly to an answer and additional approaches may be required. Figure 19-1 shows some approaches to identifying antibodies in a variety of situations when the autocontrol is negative.

Table 19-3. Probability Values

No. Tested	No. Positive	No. Negative	p (Fisher[11])	p (Harris and Hochman[12])
5	3	2	0.100	0.035
6	4	2	0.067	0.022
6	3	3	0.050	0.016
7	5	2	0.048	0.015
7	4	3	0.029	0.008
8	7	1	0.125	0.049
8	6	2	0.036	0.011
8	5	3	0.018	0.005
8	4	4	0.014	0.004
9	8	1	0.111	0.043
9	7	2	0.028	0.008
9	6	3	0.012	0.003
10	9	1	0.100	0.039
10	8	2	0.022	0.007
10	7	3	0.008	0.002
10	6	4	0.005	0.001
10	5	5	0.004	0.001

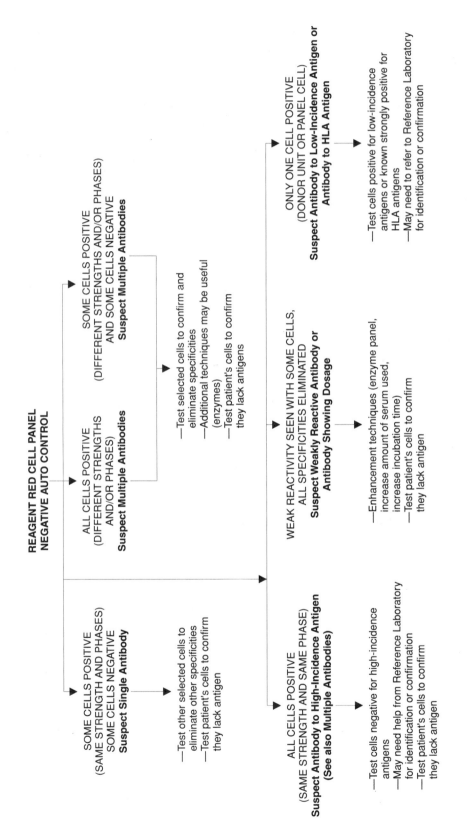

Figure 19-1. Approaches for identifying antibodies (modified from Brendel[13]).

Additional approaches may be needed if the autocontrol is positive; these are discussed later in this chapter.

Variations in Antigen Expression

For a variety of reasons, antibodies do not always react with *all* cells positive for the corresponding antigen. Interpretation by exclusion may cause a given specificity to be crossed out if a cell is antigen-positive and the serum is nonreactive, despite the presence of the antibody. Sometimes, this prevents discernment of any pattern, but in some cases it may, by coincidence, yield a false pattern of specificity. Technical error or weak antibody reactivity are possible causes, and the strength of antigen expression on tested red cells should be kept in mind. Antibody specificities should, when possible, be excluded only on the basis of cells known to bear a strong expression of the antigen.

Zygosity

Reaction strength of some antibodies varies from one red cell sample to another. This may be due to the phenomenon known as dosage, in which antibodies react preferentially with red cells from persons homozygous for the gene that determines the antigen (ie, possessing a "double dose" of the antigen). Red cells from individuals heterozygous for the gene may express less antigen and may react weakly or be nonreactive. Alloantibodies vary in their tendency to recognize dosage. Many antibodies in the Rh, Duffy, MN, and Kidd systems have this trait.

Variation in Adults and Infants

Some antigens (eg, I, P1, Le^a, and Sd^a) are expressed to varying degrees on red cells from different adult donors. This expression is unrelated to zygosity; however, the antigenic differences can be demonstrated serologically. Certain antibodies, including those to I, Le^a, Le^b, Sd^a, Lu^a, Lu^b, Vel, Yt^a, Hy, McC^a, Yk^a, Cs^a, Ch, and Rg antigens, react more weakly with

cord red cells than they do with red cells from adults.

Changes with Storage

Blood group antibodies may react less well with stored red cells than with fresh red cells. The M and P1 antigens deteriorate during storage more rapidly than most others; the rate varies among red cells from different donors. Storage media can affect the rate of antigen deterioration. Fy^a and Fy^b antigens, for example, may be weakened when the cells are stored in a suspending medium of low pH and low ionic strength. The potential loss of antigen reactivity must be considered when using older cells for antibody identification.

Red cells from donor units are often fresher than commercial reagent cells and have been stored in different media. Some antibodies give stronger reactions with suspensions of donor cells than with reagent cells; eg, antibodies in the Knops system and antibodies that react with HLA antigens on red cells often react best with fresh donor cells and may not react at all with stored reagent cells. After frozen storage, reagent cells may give weaker reactions with some antibodies. This can cause misleading patterns, especially when an antibody is interpreted as recognizing a high-incidence antigen on the basis of nonreactivity with one or two thawed specimens. Certain antibodies react more strongly or weakly with cells from different commercial manufacturers, whose suspending media may differ in pH or other characteristics. Enhancement techniques often help resolve problems associated with variations in antigen expression (see Methods 3.2.3, 3.2.4, 3.2.5, and 3.5.5).

The age and nature of the specimen must also be considered when typing red cells. Antigens on cells from clotted samples tend to lose activity faster than cells collected in citrate anticoagulants such as ACD or CPD. Red cells in donor units collected into these anticoagulants generally retain their antigens throughout the standard shelf life of the blood component. If red cells are collected into EDTA they must be tested within 2 days of collection, although some studies have demonstrated significantly longer preservation of most antigens on EDTA-anticoagulated cells.[14]

No Discernible Specificity

Factors other than variation in antigen expression may contribute to difficulty in interpreting results of antibody identification tests. If the reactivity obtained with the serum is very weak and/or if the cross-out process has excluded all likely specificities, alternative approaches to interpretation should be used.

Antigens Present in Common

Instead of excluding antigens on nonreactive cells, one can observe what antigens are common to the reactive cells. For example, if the cells reacting at room temperature are all P1-positive, yet not all the P1-positive cells react, the antibody could be an anti-P1 that does not react with cells having a weaker expression of the antigen. (Such cells are sometimes marked on the panel sheet as "+w".) With this in mind, one could use a method to enhance anti-P1, such as testing at colder temperatures.

If all the reactive cells are Jk(b+), but not all the Jk(b+) cells react, the reactive ones might all be Jk(a–b+), with a double-dose expression of the antigen. Enhancement techniques, such as enzymes, LISS, or PEG, may then help demonstrate reactivity with all the remaining Jk(b+) cells. Typing the patient's cells to confirm they lack the corresponding antigen can also be very helpful.

Inherent Variability

Nebulous reaction patterns that do not appear to fit any particular specificity are characteristic of antibodies (such as anti-Bg[a]) that react with HLA antigens on red cells. These antigens vary markedly in their expression on red cells from different individuals. Rarely, a pattern of

clear-cut reactive and nonreactive tests that cannot be interpreted can result from the incorrect typing of reagent red cells. If the cell is from a commercial source, the manufacturer should immediately be notified of the discrepancy.

Unlisted Antigens

Sometimes a serum reacts with an antigen not routinely listed on the antigen profile supplied by the reagent manufacturer; Yt[b] is one example. Even though serum studies yield clear-cut reactive and nonreactive tests, anti-Yt[b] may not be suspected. In such circumstances it is useful to ask the manufacturer for additional phenotype information. If the appropriate blood typing reagent is available, reactive and nonreactive red cell samples, as well as the autologous red cells, can be tested. However, these problems often have to be referred to an immunohematology reference laboratory.

ABO Type of Red Cells Tested

A serum may react with many or all of the group O reagent red cell samples, but not with red cells of the same ABO phenotype as the autologous red cells. This occurs most frequently with anti-H, -IH, or -Le[bH]. Group O and A_2 red cells have large amounts of H antigen; A_1 and A_1B red cells express very little H (see Chapter 13). Sera containing anti-H or -IH react strongly with group O reagent red cell samples, but autologous A_1 or A_1B red cells or donor cells used for crossmatching may be weakly reactive or nonreactive. Anti-Le[bH] reacts strongly with group O, Le(b+) red cells, but reacts weakly or not at all with Le(b+) red cells from A_1 or A_1B individuals. Such antibodies should be suspected when the antibody screen, which uses group O red cells, is strongly reactive, but serologically compatible A_1 or A_1B donor samples can be found without difficulty.

Multiple Antibodies

When a serum contains two or more alloantibodies, it may be difficult to interpret the results of testing performed on a single panel of reagent red cells. The presence of multiple antibodies may be suggested by a variety of test results.

1. *The observed pattern of reactive and nonreactive tests does not fit that of a single antibody.*

    When the exclusion approach fails to indicate a specific pattern, it is helpful to see if the pattern matches any two combined specificities. For example, if the reactive cells (see Table 19-1) are numbers 2, 4, 5, and 7, none of the specificities remaining after crossing-out exactly fits that pattern, but if both K and E are considered together, a pattern is discerned. Cells 2 and 7 react because of anti-K, cells 4 and 5 because of anti-E. If the typing patterns for no two specificities fit the reaction pattern, the possibility of more than two antibodies must be considered. The more antibodies a serum contains, the more complex the identification and exclusion of specificities will be, but the basic process remains the same.

2. *Reactivity is present at different test phases.*

    When reactivity occurs at several phases, each phase should be evaluated separately. The pattern seen at room temperature may indicate a different specificity from the pattern of antiglobulin results. It is also helpful to look at variability in the strength of reactions seen at each phase of testing. Table 15-2 provides information on the characteristic reactivity phase of several antibodies.

3. *Unexpected reactions are obtained when attempts are made to confirm the specificity of a suspected single antibody.*

    If a serum suspected of containing anti-e reacts with additional samples that are e-negative, another antibody may be present or the suspected antibody may not really be anti-e. Testing a panel of se-lected e-negative cells may help indicate an additional specificity.

4. *No discernible pattern emerges.*

    When uniform or variable reaction strengths may be observed, and dosage or other variation in antigen strength does not provide an explanation, additional approaches and methods of testing are usually indicated. Some helpful steps include:

    a. If strong positive results were obtained, use the exclusion method with nonreactive cells to eliminate some specificities from initial consideration.

    b. If weak or questionable positive results were obtained, test the serum against cells carrying a strong expression of antigens corresponding to any suspected specificities, and combine this with methods to enhance reactivity.

    c. If the patient has not been recently transfused, type the patient's red cells and eliminate from consideration specificities corresponding to antigens present on the autologous cells.

    d. Use methods to inactivate certain antigens on the red cells, eg, enzyme treatment to render cells negative for Fy^a, Fy^b, and S.

    e. Use adsorption/elution methods to separate antibodies. These and other methods that may be helpful are discussed below.

Antibodies to High-Incidence Antigens

If all reagent red cell samples are reactive, but the autocontrol is nonreactive, alloantibody to a high-incidence antigen should be considered, especially if the strength and test phase of reactions are uniform for all cells tested. Antibodies to high-incidence antigens can be identified by testing red cells of selected rare phenotypes, and by testing the patient's autologous red cells with sera known to contain antibodies to high-incidence antigens.

Knowing the race or ethnic origin of the antibody producer can help in selecting additional tests to be performed. Cells that are null for all antigens in a system (eg, Rh_{null} or K_o) or modified red cells (eg, dithiothreitol-treated cells) can help limit possible specificities to a particular blood group.

If cells negative for particular high-incidence antigens are not available, cells positive for lower-incidence alleles can sometimes be helpful. Weaker reactivity with Co(a+b+) cells than with common Co(a+b–) cells, for instance, might suggest anti-Co[a]. Antibodies to high-incidence antigens may be accompanied by other antibodies to common antigens, which can make identification much more difficult. Because the availability of cells negative for high-incidence antigens is limited, it may be necessary to refer specimens suspected of containing antibodies to high-incidence antigens to an immunohematology reference laboratory.

Serologic Clues

Knowledge of the serologic characteristics of particular antibodies to high-incidence antigens can help in identification.

1. Reactivity in tests at room temperature suggests anti-H, -I, -P1, -P, -Tj[a] (-PP_1P^k), some -LW, -Ge, -Sd[a], or -Vel.
2. Lysis of reagent red cells is characteristic of anti-Vel, -P, -Tj[a], and -Jk3. It is also seen with some examples of anti-H and -I.
3. Reduced or absent reactivity in enzyme tests occurs with anti-Ch, -Rg, -In[b], or -JMH and is seen with some examples of anti-Yt[a] and -Ge2 or -Ge3.
4. Weak nebulous reactions in the antiglobulin phase are often associated with anti-Kn[a], -McC[a], -Yk[a], and -Cs[a]. Complement-binding autoantibodies, such as anti-I or anti-IH, give similar results when polyspecific antiglobulin reagents are used.
5. Antibodies such as anti-U, -McC[a], -Sl[a], -Js[b], -Hy, -Jo[a], -Tc[a], -Cr[a], and -At[a] should be considered if the serum is from a Black individual because the antigen-negative phenotypes occur almost exclusively in Blacks. Makers of anti-Kp[b] are almost always White. Anti-Di[b] is usually found among Asians, Hispanics, and Native Americans.

Interpreting a Positive DAT

When a patient produces antibody directed to a high-incidence antigen following transfusion, the posttransfusion red cells may have a positive DAT, and both serum and eluate may react with all cells tested. Because this pattern of reactivity is identical to that produced by many warm reactive autoantibodies that may also appear after transfusion, these two scenarios can be very difficult to differentiate. A posttransfusion alloantibody to a high-incidence antigen would be expected to produce a DAT of mixed-field appearance because only the transfused red cells would be coated with antibody. In practice, however, weak sensitization and mixed-field sensitization can be difficult to differentiate. It may be helpful to use cell separation procedures to isolate autologous cells for testing.

Chapter 15 discusses additional serologic characteristics of antibodies reacting with high-incidence red cell antigens. Problems with these antibodies often have to be referred to an immunohematology reference laboratory.

Antibodies to Low-Incidence Antigens

Reactions between a serum sample and a single donor or reagent red cell sample may be caused by an antibody to a low-incidence antigen, such as anti-Wr[a]. If red cells known to carry low-incidence antigens are available, the serum can be tested against them, or the one reactive red cell sample can be tested with known examples of antibodies to low-incidence antigens. A single serum often contains multiple antibodies to low-incidence antigens, and the expertise and resources of an immunohematology reference laboratory will be required to confirm the suspected specificities.

Serologic Strategies

If antibody to a low-incidence antigen is suspected, transfusion should not be delayed while identification studies are undertaken. If antibody in the serum of a pregnant woman is thought to be directed against a low-incidence antigen, testing the father's red cells can predict the possibility of incompatibility with the fetus, and identifying the antibody is unnecessary. If a newborn has a positive DAT, testing of the mother's serum or an eluate from the infant's cells against the father's red cells (assuming they are ABO-compatible) can implicate an antibody to a low-incidence antigen as the probable cause; identifying the antibody is usually of little importance.

Some reference laboratories do not attempt to identify antibodies to low-incidence antigens, because they are often only of academic interest and resources can better be devoted to problems of greater clinical importance. Identification may be made when time permits and suitable reagents are available. It is often practical to store individual specimens and then perform batch testing, to conserve rare frozen samples of cells or antibodies.

Unexpected Positive Results

When serum reacts with a panel cell designated as positive for a low-incidence antigen, further testing to exclude the antibody is usually unnecessary. For every antigen of low incidence represented on a panel there are many more that are not represented and that are also not excluded by routine testing. Reactivity against low-incidence antigens is not uncommon; although the antigens are rare, antibodies against some of the low-incidence antigens are much less rare. Presumably the testing is being performed because the serum contains some other antibody(-ies) and reactivity with the cell expressing the low-incidence antigen is a coincidental finding. This may complicate interpretation of the panel results, but rarely requires confirmation of antibody specificity or

typing of donor blood to ensure the absence of the antigen. If typing is desired, a negative crossmatch with the patient's serum is sufficient demonstration that the antigen is absent. Many antibodies to low-incidence antigens are reactive only at temperatures below 37 C and are of doubtful clinical significance.

When serum reacts only with red cells from a single donor unit or reagent cell, the other possibilities to consider are that the reactive donor red cells are ABO-incompatible, have a positive DAT, or are polyagglutinable.

Antibodies to Reagent Components and Other Anomalous Serologic Reactions

Antibodies to a variety of drugs and additives can cause positive results in antibody detection and identification tests. The mechanisms are probably similar to those discussed in Chapter 20.

Most of these anomalous reactions are in-vitro phenomena and have no clinical significance in transfusion therapy other than causing laboratory problems that delay provision of a needed transfusion. Very rarely they may cause erroneous interpretations of ABO typing that could endanger the patient. For a more detailed discussion see the suggested reading by Garratty.

Ingredients in the Preservative Solution

Antibodies that react with an ingredient in the solution used to preserve reagent red cells (eg, chloramphenicol, neomycin, tetracycline, hydrocortisone, EDTA, sodium caprylate, or various sugars) may agglutinate cells suspended in that solution. Reactivity may occur with cells from several commercial sources or may be limited to cells from a single manufacturer. The autologous control is often nonreactive, unless the suspension of autologous red cells is prepared with the manufacturer's red cell diluent or a similar preservative. Such reactions can often be circumvented by washing the reagent cells with saline before testing. The role of the preservative can often be confirmed by adding the medium to the autologous control and converting a nonreactive test to a positive test. In some cases, however, washing the reagent cells does not circumvent reactivity and the resolution may be more complex.

Ingredients in Enhancement Media

Antibodies reactive with ingredients in other reagents, such as commercially prepared LISS additives or albumin, can cause agglutination in tests using reagent, donor, and/or autologous red cells. Ingredients that have been implicated include parabens (in some LISS additives), sodium caprylate (in some albumins), and thimerosal (in some saline preparations). LISS and other enhancement media may also dramatically increase the reactivity of some autoantibodies. Antibodies such as anti-I, -IH, or -Pr that ordinarily react only at colder temperatures may even react in the antiglobulin phase when these enhancement media are used. Omitting the enhancement medium, substituting plasma for serum, and/or using anti-IgG rather than polyspecific antiglobulin serum will usually circumvent this reactivity.

In some cases antibodies dependent upon reagent ingredients will also show blood group specificity, eg, paraben-dependent anti-Jk^a, caprylate-dependent anti-c. The autocontrol may be reactive if the patient's own red cells carry the antigen, but the DAT should be negative.

Problems with Red Cells

The age of the red cells can cause anomalous serologic reactions. Antibodies exist that react only with stored red cells; these can cause agglutination of reagent red cells by all techniques and enhanced reactivity in tests with enzyme-treated red cells. Such reactivity is not affected by washing the red cells, and the autocontrol is usually nonreactive. No reactivity will be seen in tests on freshly collected red cells, ie, from freshly drawn donor or autologous blood samples.

The Patient with a Positive Autocontrol

No Recent Transfusions

Reactivity of serum with the patient's own cells may indicate the presence of autoantibody. (See Chapter 20.) If this reactivity occurs at room temperature or below, the cause is often anti-I or other cold autoagglutinin. Reactivity of the autocontrol in the antiglobulin phase usually signifies a reactive DAT and the possibility of autoantibody. If, in addition, the serum reacts with all cells tested, autoadsorption or other special procedures may be necessary to determine whether autoantibody in the serum is masking any significant alloantibodies. If the serum is not reactive or shows only weak reactivity, an eluate may demonstrate more potent autoantibody.

If the DAT is negative, but the autocontrol is positive by IAT, an alternative explanation is required. Such results are unusual and may indicate antibody to a reagent constituent causing in-vitro reactivity with all cells, including the patient's own. It may also indicate that the wrong cells were added to the test.

Cold Autoantibodies. Potent cold autoagglutinins that react with all cells, including the patient's own, can create special problems, especially when reactivity persists at temperatures above room temperature. Cold autoagglutinins may be benign or pathologic. (See Chapter 20 for a more detailed discussion.)

There are two divergent objectives in testing a serum with a potent cold agglutinin. One is to determine if the thermal amplitude is high enough (usually 30 C or above) that the antibody has clinical significance; to do this, in-vitro autoadsorption of the serum must be avoided. Keeping the freshly collected blood warm (37 C) until the serum is separated usually provides an appropriately informative specimen. The second objective, the common one other than cold agglutinin syndrome, is to circumvent the cold-reactive antibody and allow detection of more important antibodies.

Procedures for the detection of alloantibodies in the presence of cold-reactive autoantibodies are discussed in Chapter 20 and include:

1. Prewarmed techniques, in which red cells and serum to be tested, and saline used for washing, are incubated at 37 C before they are combined (see Method 3.3).
2. The use of anti-IgG rather than polyspecific antiglobulin serum.
3. Cold autoadsorption, to remove autoantibodies but not alloantibodies.
4. Heterologous adsorption with rabbit red cells.

Dealing with Warm Autoantibodies. Patients with warm-reactive autoantibody present in their sera create a special problem, because the antibody reacts with virtually all cells tested. If such patients are to be transfused, it is important to detect any clinically significant alloantibodies that the autoantibody may mask. Techniques are discussed in Chapter 20 and Methods 4.9, 4.10, and 4.11.

Reactivity of most warm-reactive autoantibodies is greatly enhanced by such methods as PEG and enzymes, and to lesser extent by LISS and albumin. It may be advantageous to perform antibody detection tests without the enhancement media usually employed. If tests are nonreactive, the same procedure can be used for crossmatching, without the need for adsorptions.

Recent Transfusions

If the autocontrol is positive in the antiglobulin phase, there may be antibody-coated cells in the patient's circulation, causing a positive DAT, which may show mixed-field reactivity. Elution may be helpful, especially when tests on serum are inconclusive. For example, a recently transfused patient may have a positive autocontrol and serum that reacts weakly with most but not all Fy(a+) red cells. It may be possible to confirm anti-Fy[a]

specificity by elution, which concentrates into a small fluid volume the immunoglobulin molecules present in small numbers on each of the red cells in the starting preparation. It is rare for transfused cells to make the autocontrol positive at other test phases, but it can occur, especially with a newly developing or cold-reactive alloantibody.

If the positive DAT does not have a mixed-field appearance and, especially, if the serum is reactive with all cells tested, the possibility of autoantibody should again be considered. Detection of masked alloantibodies may require allogeneic adsorptions.

Accurate phenotyping of red cells may be difficult if the DAT is reactive in any patient, whether or not there has been recent transfusion. A positive DAT will cause the cells to be reactive in any test requiring addition of antiglobulin serum and with some reagent antibodies (notably those in the Rh system) that include an enhancement medium. Many monoclonal reagents can give valid phenotyping results despite a positive DAT.

Immunohematology Reference Laboratories

When antibody problems cannot be resolved (or when specially typed blood is needed) immunohematology reference laboratories can provide consultation and assistance through their access to the American Rare Donor Program. (See Method 3.14.)

Selecting Blood for Transfusion

Once an antibody has been identified, it is also important to decide its clinical significance. Antibodies reactive at 37 C and/or by IAT are potentially clinically significant and those reactive at room temperature and below are not; however, there are many exceptions. For example, anti-Ch, anti-Rg, and many of the Knops and Cost antibodies have little or no clinical effect, despite reactivity by IAT. Anti-Vel, -P, and -Tj^a (-PP$_1$P^k) may react only at cold temperatures yet may cause cell destruction in vivo. Comparison with documented cases in the literature and consultation with immunohematology reference laboratories should provide guidance about previous examples of similar specificities.

Phenotyping Donor Units

Red-cell-containing components selected for transfusion to a patient with a clinically significant antibody should, whenever possible, be tested and found to be negative for the appropriate antigen. Even if the antibody is no longer detectable, the red cells of all subsequent transfusions to that patient should lack the antigen, to prevent a secondary immune response. The transfusion service must maintain records of all patients in whom significant antibodies have been previously identified.[4(p59)] An antiglobulin crossmatch procedure is required if the serum contains, or has previously contained, a significant antibody.

A potent example of the antibody should be used to identify antigen-negative blood. Often, this is a commercial antiserum, but to save expensive or rare reagents, units can first be tested with the patient's serum. The absence of antigen, in nonreactive units, can then be confirmed with the commercial reagent. Sufficiently potent antibodies in patients' specimens that have reactivity as good as, or better than, commercial antibodies, can be stored frozen for future use. If the antibody is of unusual specificity or one for which commercial reagents are not available, a stored sample can be used to select units for transfusion at a later time, especially if the patient's later specimens lose reactivity. If a patient's serum is to serve as a typing reagent, it should be well characterized and retain its reactivity after storage, and appropriate negative and weakly positive controls should be used at the time of testing. The FDA has established the following criteria for licensing some reagents[15]:

1. Anti-K, anti-k, anti-Jk^a, anti-Fy^a, and anti-C^w: dilution of 1:8 to give at least 1+ reaction.
2. Anti-S, anti-s, anti-P1, anti-M, anti-I, anti-c (saline), anti-e (saline), and anti-A$_1$: dilution of 1:4 to give at least 1+ reaction.
3. Most other specificities: undiluted, must give at least a 2+ reaction.

Reagents prepared in-house from sera that meet these dilution criteria can be used.

Source of Antibodies

When selecting units for patients with clinically significant antibodies, some workers recommend typing the chosen units with antibodies from two different sources, but others consider it unnecessary, especially when potent reagents are available. Different lots of antibody from the same manufacturer and even reagents from different manufacturers may not have been prepared from different source material. For some specificities, donors of source plasma or the range of available monoclonal antibodies are limited; if supplies are scarce, manufacturers often share the same resources.

Labeling Units

If a donor unit from a licensed blood establishment is to be labeled with the results of special antigen typing and that unit is shipped from the labeling facility, the FDA requires use of licensed (commercial) reagents.[15] If no licensed reagent is available, the unit may be labeled with appropriate wording (eg, "Typed for Js^b; Js(b–) status not confirmed with licensed reagent"). Except for results of ABO and D typing, there is no requirement that results of antigen typing be on the label of donor units.

When to Test

For certain antibody specificities, special typing of donor units may not be necessary and the patient's serum can be used to select serologically compatible red cells. This is especially true for antibodies that characteristically react below 37 C (eg, anti-M, -P1, -A$_1$) and do not ordinarily exhibit an anamnestic response to the transfusion of antigen-positive red cells. Blood can be selected without antigen typing for transfusion to patients with anti-Le^a or -Le^b, because these antigens are not intrinsic to the red cell and delayed transfusion reactions are not a concern (see Chapter 13).

It is rarely necessary to provide antigen-negative donor units as a prophylactic measure for patients whose cells lack an antigen but who do not have demonstrated antibody. However, special consideration is sometimes given to certain Rh antibodies. When a patient of the R$_1$R$_1$ phenotype has anti-E detected in the serum, some workers suggest that donor blood be negative for both the E and c antigens,[16] based on the assumption that the stimulus to produce the anti-E may also have stimulated an anti-c or anti-cE that remains undetected by routine tests. For an R$_2$R$_2$ patient with demonstrated anti-C, the use of C–e– donor blood may be considered. When an antibody has not been specifically demonstrated, but cannot conclusively be excluded, it may be appropriate to transfuse blood that lacks the antigen.

Tests to Predict Clinical Significance

Certain laboratory procedures have been used to predict the significance of particular antibodies. The monocyte monolayer assay, which quantifies rosetting or phagocytosis of antibody-sensitized red cells, can be used to predict the in-vivo clinical significance of some antibodies. Determination of the IgG subclass of an antibody may help predict the destructive potential of either allo- or autoantibodies. The test for antibody-dependent cellular cytotoxicity (ADCC), which measures lysis of antibody-coated cells, and the chemiluminescence assay, which measures the respiratory release of oxygen radicals after

phagocytosis of antibody-coated cells, have been helpful in predicting in-vivo antibody reactivity, especially for predicting severity of HDN. For cold-reactive antibodies, determination of in-vitro thermal amplitude suggests the likelihood of in-vivo problems.

In-vivo tests may also be used to evaluate significance of a given antibody. The most common technique is infusion of radiolabeled, antigen-positive red cells, usually tagged with ^{51}Cr. It is possible to measure survival of 1 mL or less of infused cells. Flow cytometry can also be used to measure the survival of infused cells, but a larger aliquot of red cells (about 10 mL) is generally required. Small aliquots of incompatible cells may have a faster rate of destruction than an entire unit of red cells.

When Blood of Rare Type Is Needed

Blood of rare type includes not only units negative for high-incidence antigens but also, often, blood negative for a combination of less exotic characteristics. When a patient has multiple antibodies, it can be helpful to determine how rare compatible blood might be, especially when multiple units may be required. To calculate this, the frequency of random donors negative for one antigen must be multiplied by the frequency of donors negative for each of the other antigens. For example, if a serum contains anti-c, -Fy^a, and -S, and among random donors 18% are c-negative, 34% are Fy(a–), and 45% are S-negative, the frequency of compatible units would be: $0.18 \times 0.34 \times 0.45 = 0.028$. If the patient is group O, then, because 45% of random donors are group O, 1.3% (0.028×0.45) of random donors would be compatible with the patient's serum. If any of these three antibodies occurred singly, finding compatible blood would not be too difficult. Clearly, when all three are present, a large number of random donors would be necessary to provide even one unit. The preceding calculation uses frequencies in the Caucasian population. If the donor population is predominantly of a different origin, frequencies for that group would be appropriate. For most blood suppliers the problem might be eased by previous records of donor phenotypes or adequate numbers of units that could be typed.

When units of rare (<1 in 5000) or uncommon (<1 in 1000) type are needed, the American Rare Donor Program can be very helpful. These files, which can be accessed only by personnel of an accredited immunohematology reference laboratory, can identify blood suppliers known either to have units available (usually frozen red cells) or to have the names of suitable donors who may be asked to donate (see Method 3.14).

Family members offer another potential source of rare blood donors. Siblings are often the best source of serologically compatible blood for patients with multiple antibodies or antibodies to high-incidence antigens. The absence of high-incidence antigens usually reflects inheritance, from each parent, of the same rare blood group gene, and offspring of the same parents are far more likely to have the same two rare genes than someone in the random donor population. In most cases, blood from the patient's parents or children (and some siblings) will carry only a single dose of the relevant antigen; if transfusion is essential, and there is no alternative to giving incompatible blood, these heterozygous donors would be considered preferable to random donors. Occasionally, blood from one parent or child also lacks the high-incidence antigen.

In HDN or other alloantibody-associated problems in infants, the mother, if ABO compatible, is often the logical donor. If the mother's red cells are transfused, it is useful to retain the plasma for use as a rare reagent.

If the clinical situation allows, autologous transfusion should be considered for patients for whom compatible blood is difficult to find. For some patients with multiple antibodies for whom autologous transfusion is not an option, it may be necessary to determine whether any of the antibodies is likely to be significantly less destructive than the others and, in a critical situation, give blood incompatible for that antigen alone.

Frequency of Antibody Testing

Once an antibody has been identified in a patient's serum, how frequently should antibody detection and identification tests be performed? A primary antibody response typically will produce detectable antibody over a period of 2 weeks to several months, while a secondary immune response produces detectable antibody in a shorter time, usually within 2-20 days. Shulman[17] found that, in a small number of patients, "new" antibodies could be detected within 1-2 days after transfusion. AABB *Standards*[4(p58)] requires that, for a patient who has been pregnant or received red cells within the preceding 3 months, antibody detection and compatibility tests must be done on a specimen obtained within 3 days of the next scheduled transfusion. The transfusion service may consider testing a fresher specimen when there have been repeated transfusions within the 3-day period, especially if clinical evidence suggests failure of transfused red cells to survive as expected.

It is rarely necessary to repeat identification of known antibodies. The primary concern of subsequent tests is the detection of *other* antibodies. If the known alloantibody is clinically significant, antigen-negative red cells must be selected for all future transfusions, even if the antibody is no longer detectable, and there must be an antiglobulin crossmatch, which serves as one means of detecting additional antibodies. It may be useful, at intervals, to test one or two antigen-positive red cells to confirm whether the known antibody is still present, so as to adopt the most informative procedure for further antibody detection or identification tests.

Depending on the specificity of the known antibody, repeated testing of the patient's serum against routine antibody detection cells is often not informative. It is more useful to test against cells negative for the antigen(s) to which the patient has antibody and positive for other major antigens. This allows detection of most additional antibodies that might develop. Appropriate cells can usually be selected from available red cell panels. If the patient's phenotype is known, selection of appropriate test cells may be simplified. If the patient's cells are known to express a given antigen, the selected cells need not be positive for that antigen because the corresponding antibody would not be anticipated. If appropriate cells are not available to detect additional antibodies, later serum specimens can be tested against cells retained from recently transfused units; these cells presumably carry the antigens that would elicit most newly developing immune response.

Selected Serologic Procedures

Many techniques and methods may be useful in antibody identification. Some of the methods given here are used routinely by many laboratories; others are alternatives that may apply only in special circumstances. It is important to remember that no single method is optimal for detecting *all* antibodies in *all* samples. Any laboratory doing antibody detection or identification should have standard procedures for routine testing, and have access to at least some alternative approaches. Additional procedures are available in a variety of references. See Suggested Reading.

Enhancement Techniques

When a pattern of weak reactions fails to indicate specificity, or when the presence of an antibody is suspected but cannot be demonstrated, use of the following procedures may be helpful. An autologous control should be included with each test performed.

LISS, PEG, Polybrene®

The rationale for these procedures and some technical details are discussed in Chapter 12. Each may be used to enhance reactivity and reduce incubation time. Some antibodies react preferentially by one of these techniques. LISS methods include the use of low ionic strength saline for resuspension of test cells and also, more commonly the use of commercially available low ionic strength additive media. The use of a LISS additive requires no preparatory stages, but care should be taken to closely adhere to the manufacturer's product insert to ensure that the appropriate proportion of serum to LISS is achieved. Commercially prepared LISS additives may include other enhancement components besides low ionic strength saline. Commercially prepared PEG additives are also available and may contain additional enhancing agents. Because LISS, PEG, and Polybrene® enhance autoantibody activity, they may create problems with certain samples. [18]

Enzyme Techniques

Treatment of red cells with proteolytic enzymes enhances their reactivity with antibodies in the Rh, P, I, Kidd, Lewis, and some other blood group systems, and simultaneously destroys or weakens other antigens. (See Table 19-4.) The clinical significance of antibodies that react only with enzyme techniques is questionable. The literature indicates that "enzyme-only" antibodies may have no clinical significance. [20] Procedures for the preparation and use of proteolytic enzyme solutions are given in Methods 3.5 through 3.5.5.

Temperature Reduction

Some alloantibodies (eg, anti-M, -P1) that react at room temperature react better at lower temperatures; specificity may only be apparent below 22 C. An autocontrol is especially important for tests at cold temperatures because

Table 19-4. Alteration of Antigens by Various Agents[*]

Agent	Antigens Usually Denatured or Altered[†]
Proteolytic enzymes[‡]	M, N, S, Fy^a, Fy^b, Yt^a, Ch, Rg, Pr, Tn, Mg, Mi^a/Vw, Cl^a, Je^a, Ny^a, JMH, some Ge, In^b
DTT	Yt^a, JMH, Kn^a, McC^a, Yk^a, LW^a, LW^b, Ge, all Kell, Lutheran, Dombrock, and Cromer blood group antigens
ZZAP (a combination of DTT and proteolytic enzymes)	Alteration of all the antigens listed above

[*]Modified from Wilkinson.[19]
[†]Some antigens listed may be weakened rather than completely denatured. Appropriate controls should be used with modified cells.
[‡]Different proteolytic enzymes may have different effects on certain antigens.

many sera also contain anti-I or other cold-reactive autoantibodies.

Increased Serum-to-Cell Ratio

Increasing the volume of serum incubated with a standard volume of red cells may enhance the reactivity of antibodies present in low concentration. One acceptable procedure is to mix 5-10 volumes of serum with one volume of a 2-5% saline suspension of red cells and incubate for 60 minutes at 37 C; periodic mixing during incubation promotes contact between red cells and antibody molecules. It is helpful to remove the serum before washing the red cells for the antiglobulin test because the standard three or four wash phases may be insufficient to remove all the unbound immunoglobulin present in the additional volume. Additional wash phases are not recommended because bound antibody molecules may dissociate. Increasing the serum-to-red cell ratio is not appropriate in LISS, PEG, or other tests that require specific proportions of serum and additive.

Increased Incubation Time

For most antibodies, a 15-minute incubation period is insufficient to achieve equilibrium and the observed reactions may be weak, particularly in saline or albumin media. Extending incubation to 60 minutes may improve reactivity and help clarify the observed pattern of reactions.

Extended incubation may have a negative effect when LISS or PEG are used. If incubation exceeds the recommended times for these methods, antibody reactivity may be lost. Care must be taken to use all reagents according to the manufacturer's directions as described in the package insert of the reagent. Deviation from the manufacturer's directions may produce erroneous test results.

Alteration of pH

Decreasing the pH of the reaction system to 6.5 enhances the reactivity of certain antibodies, notably some examples of anti-M.[21] If anti-M specificity is suspected because the only cells agglutinated are M+N–, modifying the serum to a pH of 6.5 may reveal a definitive pattern of anti-M reactivity. The addition of one volume of 0.1 N HCl to nine volumes of serum brings the pH to approximately 6.5. The acidified serum should be tested against known M-negative cells as a control for nonspecific agglutination. Some examples of anti-P may similarly benefit from a lower pH.[22]

Low pH, however, significantly decreases reactivity of some antibodies.[23] If unbuffered saline used for cell suspensions and for washing has a pH much below 6.0, antibodies in the Rh, Duffy, Kidd, and MNS systems may lose reactivity. Use of phosphate-buffered saline (see Method 1.6) can control pH and enhance detection of antibodies poorly reactive at a lower pH.[24]

Techniques to Isolate, Remove, or Depress Antibody Reactivity

It is sometimes useful to decrease or eliminate the reactivity of an antibody. This can be done by inhibiting the antibody with specific substances, by physically removing immunoglobulin molecules, or by removing (or weakening) corresponding antigens from the red cells. Such methods can help confirm suspected specificities and promote identification of additional antibodies.

Inhibition Tests

Soluble forms of some blood group antigens exist in such body fluids as saliva, urine, or plasma, or can be prepared from other sources. These substances can be used to inhibit reactivity of the corresponding antibody. If, for example, a suspected anti-P1 does not give a definitive agglutination pattern, loss of reactivity after addition of soluble P_1 substance strongly suggests that this is the specificity. A parallel control with saline is essential.

Inhibition can also be used to neutralize antibodies that mask the concomitant presence of nonneutralizable antibodies. The following soluble blood group substances can be used in antibody identification tests:

1. *Lewis substances.* Le^a and/or Le^b substances are present in the saliva of persons who possess the *Le* gene. Le^a substance is present in the saliva of Le(a+b–) individuals, and Le(a–b+) persons have both Le^a and Le^b substances in their saliva. (See Method 2.5.) Commercially prepared Lewis substance is also available.

2. *P_1 substance.* Soluble P_1 substance is present in hydatid cyst fluid and can also be prepared from pigeon egg whites. Pigeon-derived P_1 substance is available commercially.

3. *Sd^a substance.* Soluble Sd^a blood group substance is present in various body fluids; the most abundant source is urine.[25]

To confirm anti-Sd^a specificity in a serum, urine from a known Sd(a+) individual (or a pool of urine specimens) can be used to inhibit reactivity. Urine known to lack Sd^a substance, or saline, should be used as a negative control. Urine should be dialyzed against phosphate-buffered saline to correct pH and salt concentrations before use. Once dialyzed, Sd(a+) and Sd(a–) urine specimens can be frozen in small aliquots for future use. (See Method 3.12.)

4. *Chido and Rodgers substances.* Ch and Rg antigens are epitopes of the fourth component of human complement (C4).[26,27] Anti-Ch and -Rg react by the IAT with the trace amounts of C4 present on normal red cells; if red cells are coated in vitro with excess C4[28] (see Method 3.9), these antibodies may cause direct agglutination. Anti-Ch and -Rg can be inhibited by plasma from Ch-positive, Rg-positive individuals. (See Method 3.10.) This is a useful test for rapid identification of anti-Ch and -Rg.

5. *Blood group sugars.* Sugars that correspond to the immunodominant configurations of A, B, H, and some other red cell structures can be used to inhibit antibodies. Inhibiting anti-A or -B may allow a serum to be tested against non-group-O cells.

Inactivation of Blood Group Antigens

Certain blood group antigens can be destroyed or weakened by suitable treatment of the cells. (See Table 19-4.) Modified cells can be useful both in confirming the presence of suspected antibodies and in detecting additional antibodies. This can be especially helpful if the antigen is one of high incidence and antigen-negative cells are rare.

Proteolytic enzymes are commonly used to alter red cell antigens. Ficin, papain, trypsin, and bromelin, the enzymes most frequently used, remove M, N, S, Fy^a, Fy^b, Xg^a, JMH, Yt^a,

Ch, Rg, and some Ge antigens. Depending on the specific enzyme and method used, other antigens may also be altered or destroyed. Antigens inactivated by one proteolytic enzyme will not necessarily be inactivated by other enzymes.

Sulfhydryl reagents such as 2-aminoethylisothiouronium bromide (AET) or dithiothreitol (DTT) can be used to weaken or destroy antigens in the Kell system and some other antigens.[29-31] Anti-IgG reagent should be used in tests with DTT- or AET-treated red cells. ZZAP reagent, a mixture of proteolytic enzyme and DTT,[32] denatures antigens in the Kell system, as does treatment with glycine-HCl/EDTA. (See Methods 4.10 and 4.3.) Sulfhydryl treatment alters red cells to induce a state of heightened sensitivity to the actions of complement. With glycine-HCl/EDTA treatment, antigens outside the Kell system that are often destroyed by the sulfhydryl reagents are left intact, although Er[a] antigen may also be denatured.[33]

Chloroquine diphosphate can be used to weaken the expression of Class I HLA antigens (Bg antigens) on red cells.[34] Chloroquine removes the β_2-microglobulin light chain covalently associated with the heavy chain of Class I HLA antigens. This deters reactivity with most HLA-reactive antibodies, although some may still react.[35] Chloroquine treatment also weakens some other antigens, including Rh antigens.

Adsorption

Antibody can be removed from a serum by adsorption to red cells carrying the corresponding antigen. After the antibody attaches to the membrane-bound antigens and the serum and cells are separated, the specific antibody remains attached to the red cells. It may be possible to harvest the bound antibody by elution.

Adsorption techniques are useful in such situations as:

1. Separating multiple antibodies present in a single serum.

2. Removing autoantibody activity to permit detection of coexisting alloantibodies.

3. Removing unwanted antibody (often anti-A and/or anti-B) from a serum that contains an antibody suitable for reagent use.

4. Confirming the presence of specific antigens on red cells through their ability to remove antibody of corresponding specificity from previously characterized serum.

5. Confirming the specificity of an antibody by showing that it can be adsorbed only to red cells of a particular blood group phenotype.

Adsorption serves different purposes in different situations; there is no single procedure that is satisfactory for all purposes. A basic procedure for an antibody adsorption can be found in Method 3.13. The usual serum-to-cell ratio used is one volume of serum to an equal volume of washed, packed red cells. To enhance antibody uptake, the proportion of antigen can be increased by use of a larger volume of cells. The incubation temperature should be that at which the antibody is optimally reactive. Pretreating red cells with a proteolytic enzyme may enhance antibody uptake and reduce the number of adsorptions required for complete removal of antibody. Because some antigens are destroyed by proteases, antibodies directed against these antigens will not be removed by enzyme-treated red cells.

In separating mixtures of antibodies, the selection of red cells of the appropriate phenotype is extremely important, and depends on the object of the separation. If none of the antibodies in the serum has been identified, weakly reactive cells may be used, on the assumption that they are reactive with only a single antibody. The phenotype of the person producing the antibody gives a clue to what specificities might be present, and cells intended to separate those particular antibodies can be chosen. If one or more antibodies have been identified, cells lacking those antigens are usually chosen so that only one antibody is removed. Adsorption requires a substantial volume of red cells. Vials of reagent red cells usually will not suffice, and blood samples from staff members or donor units are the most convenient sources.

Elution

Elution frees antibody molecules from sensitized red cells. Bound antibody may be released by changing the thermodynamics of antigen-antibody reactions, by neutralizing or reversing forces of attraction that hold antigen-antibody complexes together, or by disturbing the structural complementarity between an antigen and its corresponding binding site on an antibody molecule. The usual objective is to recover bound antibody in a usable form.

Various elution methods have been described. Selected procedures are given in Methods 4.1 through 4.5. No single method is best in all situations. Use of heat or freeze-thaw elution is usually restricted to the investigation of HDN due to ABO incompatibility, because these manipulations rarely work well for antibodies outside the ABO system. Acid or organic solvent methods are used for elution of warm-reactive auto- and alloantibodies.

Technical factors that influence the success of elution procedures include:

1. *Incorrect technique.* Such factors as incomplete removal of organic solvents or failure to correct the tonicity or pH of an eluate may cause the red cells used in testing the eluate to hemolyze or to appear "sticky." The presence of stromal debris may interfere with the reading of tests. Careful technique and strict adherence to protocols should eliminate such problems.

2. *Incomplete washing.* The sensitized red cells must be thoroughly washed prior to elution, to prevent contamination of the eluate with residual serum antibody.

If it is *known* that the serum does not contain antibody, saline washing may not be necessary. Six washes with saline are usually adequate, but more may be needed if the serum contains a high-titer antibody. To determine the efficacy of the washing process, supernatant fluid from the final wash phase should be tested for antibody activity and should be inert.

3. *Binding of proteins to glass surfaces.* If the eluate is prepared in the same test tube that was used during the sensitization phase, antibody nonspecifically bound to the test tube surface may dissociate during the elution. Similar binding can also occur from a whole blood sample if the patient has a positive DAT and free antibody in the serum. To avoid such contamination, the washed red cells should be transferred into a clean test tube before the elution procedure is begun.

4. *Dissociation of antibody before elution.* IgM antibodies, such as anti-A or -M, may spontaneously dissociate from the cells during the wash phase. To minimize this loss of bound antibody, cold (4 C) saline can be used for washing. Although this is not a concern with most IgG antibodies, some low-affinity antibodies can also be lost during the wash phase. If such antibodies are suspected, washing with cold LISS instead of normal saline may help maintain antibody association.

5. *Instability of eluates.* Dilute protein solutions, such as those obtained by elution into saline, are unstable. Eluates should be tested as soon after preparation as possible. Alternatively, bovine albumin may be added to a final concentration of 6% wt/vol and the preparation stored frozen. Eluates can also be prepared directly into antibody-free plasma, 6% albumin, or similar protein medium instead of into saline.

Elution techniques are useful for:

1. Investigation of a positive DAT (see Chapter 20).

2. Concentration and purification of antibodies, the detection of weakly expressed antigens, and the identification of multiple antibody specificities. Such studies are used in conjunction with an appropriate adsorption technique, as described above and in Method 2.4.

3. Preparation of antibody-free red cells for use in phenotyping or autologous adsorption studies. Procedures used to remove cold- and warm-reactive autoantibodies from red cells are discussed in Method 4.6 and Method 4.9, and a discussion of autologous adsorption of warm-reactive autoantibodies appears in Chapter 20.

Combined Adsorption-Elution

Combined adsorption-elution tests can be used to help identify weakly reactive antibodies, to separate mixed antibodies from a single serum, or to detect weakly expressed antigens on red cells. The process consists of first incubating serum with selected cells, then eluting antibody from the adsorbing red cells. Both the eluate and treated serum can be used for further testing. Unmodified red cells are generally used for adsorption and subsequent elution. Elution from enzyme- or ZZAP-treated cells may create technical problems.

Adsorption and elution may be used to separate a mixture of antibodies. This test combination is useful in several situations:

1. If the serum contains one or more unidentified antibodies, adsorption-elution can be used to isolate individual antibodies, which are then easier to identify. The serum under investigation should be adsorbed until it no longer reacts with the adsorbing red cells. The adsorbed serum is saved and an eluate prepared from the red cells used from the first adsorption. Cells from subsequent adsorptions can also be used for elution, but the quantity of antibody may be significantly less. Both the adsorbed serum and eluate should be examined for antibody specificity. The goal is that specific antibodies will be apparent in either or both preparations, but this does not always happen. Some antibodies (eg, anti-Kn^a and -McC^a) are difficult to adsorb and elute. The serum may lose all reactivity after adsorption, yet the eluate reacts with all reagent red cell samples; this may indicate the presence of an autoantibody or an antibody to a high-incidence antigen that is variably expressed on different red cells.

2. If the antibodies in a serum have already been presumptively identified, they may be separated by adsorption-elution, either to confirm the specificities or to use one (or more) antibody separately as a reagent. This is especially useful when rare antibodies are detected, because they often occur in serum that contains other antibodies as well.

Adsorption-elution is an effective way to prepare antibodies, especially those to high-incidence antigens, for use with red cells of any ABO type. An eluate prepared from group O red cells known to react with the antibody in question should be devoid of anti-A and -B and contain only the desired specific antibody. Antibodies purified in this manner can be preserved frozen, providing the protein concentration is adjusted, and used as a typing reagent.

This method is also useful with sera containing antibodies to low-incidence antigens. Such sera often contain antibodies to several different low-incidence antigens. Because a cell positive for one low-incidence antigen is usually negative for others, eluates can be obtained that contain only a single specificity.

Weak antigens may also be detected using the adsorption-elution technique. An antibody that does not cause direct agglutination may be adsorbed onto antigen-positive red cells. Occurrence of the antibody-antigen interaction can be demonstrated by loss of antibody reactivity in the adsorbed serum and subsequent recovery of the antibody from red cells used for adsorption would be detected in an eluate prepared from the adsorbing cell.

Antigen detection by adsorption-elution is usually best accomplished using a low serum-to-cell ratio (eg, 2:1 or less). Care should be taken not to dilute the serum, and hence the antibody, with residual saline from inadequately packed red cells. Determining the protein concentrations of the serum by refractometry before or after the adsorption step is an appropriate check for such dilution. A reduction in titration score of 10 or more, using the system described in Method 3.7, is considered evidence for the presence of the relevant antigen on the adsorbing red cells. In critical studies, control adsorptions with red cells known to lack the antigen in question should be undertaken.

A weakly reactive antibody can be demonstrated by showing that it can be adsorbed and eluted by cells known to express a particular antigen. The adsorption-elution process can also be used to concentrate the antibody, making the eluate more reactive than the original serum. A high serum-to-cell ratio (eg, 5:1 or more) should be used to sensitize the red cells. If the volume of eluate is less than the volume of original serum used to coat the red cells, activity should be stronger in the eluate than in the serum. For most methods, the volume of eluate obtained can be controlled by varying the volume of saline or other diluent with which the red cells are incubated. Once prepared, the eluate should be tested against uncoated red cells from the same sample used for adsorption, to establish whether elution occurred.

Use of Sulfhydryl Reagents

Sulfhydryl reagents, such as DTT and 2-mercaptoethanol (2-ME), cleave the disulfide bonds that join the monomeric sub-

units of the IgM pentamer. Intact 19S IgM molecules are cleaved into 7S subunits, which have altered serologic reactivity.[36] The interchain bonds of 7S Ig monomers are relatively resistant to such cleavage. (See Chapter 11 for the structure of immunoglobulin molecules.) Sulfhydryl reagents are used to diminish or destroy IgM antibody reactivity. DTT also destroys certain red cell antigens. The applications of DTT and 2-ME in immunohematology include:

1. Determining the immunoglobulin class of an antibody. (See Method 3.8.)
2. Identifying specificities in a mixture of IgM and IgG antibodies, particularly when an agglutinating IgM antibody masks the presence of IgG antibodies.
3. Determining the relative amounts of IgG and IgM components of a given specificity (eg, anti-A or -B).
4. Dissociating red cell agglutinates caused by IgM antibodies (eg, the spontaneous agglutination of red cells caused by potent cold-reactive autoantibodies). (See Method 2.11.)
5. Dissociating IgG antibodies from red cells using a mixture of DTT and a proteolytic enzyme (ZZAP reagent). (See Method 4.10.)
6. Converting nonagglutinating IgG antibodies into direct agglutinins.[37] Commercially prepared chemically modified blood typing reagents for use in rapid saline tube, slide, or microplate tests have been manufactured in this manner. (See Chapter 12.)
7. Destroying selected red cell antigens (eg, those of the Kell, Dombrock, Cartwright, Gerbich, and LW systems) for use in antibody investigations. (See Method 4.9.)

Titration

The titer of an antibody is usually determined by testing serial twofold dilutions of the serum against selected red cell samples. Results are expressed as the reciprocal of the highest serum dilution that causes macroscopic agglutination. Titration values can provide information about the relative amount of antibody present in a serum, or the relative strength of antigen expression on red cells.

Titration studies are useful in the following situations:

1. *Prenatal studies*. When the antibody is of a specificity known to cause HDN or its clinical significance is unknown, the results of titration studies may contribute to the decision about performing amniocentesis. (See Chapter 23.)

2. *Antibody identification*. Some antibodies that agglutinate virtually all reagent red cell samples may produce an indication of specificity by demonstrating reactivity of different strength with different samples in titration studies. For example, potent autoanti-I may react in the undiluted state with both adult and cord red cells, but titration may reveal reactivity at a higher dilution with adult I+ red cells than with cord red cells.

   Most weakly reactive antibodies lose reactivity when diluted even modestly, but some antibodies that give weak reactions when undiluted continue to react at dilutions as high as 1 in 2048. Such antibodies include anti-Ch, -Rg, -Cs^a, -Yk^a, -Kn^a, -McC^a, -JMH, and other specificities. When weak reactions are observed in indirect antiglobulin tests, titration may be used to indicate specificity within this group. Not all antibodies of the specificities mentioned demonstrate such "high titer, low avidity" characteristics. Thus, while demonstration of these serologic characteristics may help point to certain specificities, failure to do so does not eliminate those possibilities. Antibodies of other specificities may also sometimes react at high titers. Details of titration are given in Method 3.7 and Method 3.10.

3. *Separating multiple antibodies in serum samples containing more than one spec-*

ificity. Titration results may suggest that one antibody reacts at higher dilutions than another. This information can allow the serum to be diluted before testing against a cell panel, effectively removing one antibody and allowing identification of the other.

Other Methods

Methods other than traditional tube techniques may be used for antibody identification. Some are especially useful for identifying individual antibody specificities, for dealing with small volumes of test reagents, for batch testing, or for use with automated systems. Such methods include testing in capillary tubes, microplates, or by solid phase; enzyme-linked immunosorbent assays; column agglutination, eg. gel techniques. Other methods useful in laboratories with specialized equipment include radioimmunoassay, immunofluorescence (including flow cytometric procedures), immunoblotting, and immunoelectrode biosensing. Some of these methods are discussed in Chapter 12.

References

1. Giblett ER. Blood group alloantibodies: An assessment of some laboratory practices. Transfusion 1977;17:299-308.
2. Walker RH, Lin DT, Hatrick MB. Alloimmunization following blood transfusion. Arch Pathol Lab Med 1989;113:254-61.
3. Marsh WL, Reid ME, Kuriyan M, Marsh NJ. A handbook of clinical and laboratory practices in the transfusion of red blood cells. Moneta, VA: Moneta Medical Press, 1993.
4. Menitove JE, ed. Standards for blood banks and transfusion services. 19th ed. Bethesda, MD: American Association of Blood Banks, 1999.
5. Code of federal regulations. Title 21 CFR Part 660.33. Washington, DC: US Government Printing Office, 1998 (revised annually).
6. Lizza C, Myers J, Gindy L. Blood groups. In: Petz LD, Swisher SN, Kleinman S, et al, eds. Clinical practice of transfusion medicine. 3rd ed. New York: Churchill Livingstone, 1996;71:151.
7. Stone DL, Eatz RA, Rolih SD, et al. Red cell antibody identification by solid phase red cell adherence utilizing dried RBC monolayers. Immunohematology 1990;6:12-7.

8.   Howard JE, Winn LC, Gottlieb CE, et al. Clinical significance of anti-complement component of antiglobulin antisera. Transfusion 1982;22:269-72.

9.   Shulman IA, Calderon C, Nelson JM, Nakayama R. The routine use of Rh-negative reagent red cells for the identification of anti-D and the detection of non-D red cell antibodies. Transfusion 1994;34:666-70.

10. Rondeel JMM, vanOpdrop AHB, Dinkelar RB. Application of a computer program to exclude additional unexpected antibodies. Transfusion 1997;37: 298-308.

11. Fisher RA. Statistical methods and scientific inference. 2nd ed. Edinburgh, Scotland: Oliver and Boyd, 1959.

12. Harris RE, Hochman HG. Revised p values in testing blood group antibodies. Transfusion 1986;26:494-9.

13. Brendel WL. Resolving antibody problems. In: Pierce SR, Wilson JK, eds. Approaches to serological problems in the hospital transfusion service. Arlington, VA: American Association of Blood Banks, 1985:51-72.

14. Westhoff CM, Sipherd BD, Toalson LD. Red cell antigen stability in K3EDTA. Immunohematology 1993;9:109-11.

15. Code of federal regulations. Title 21 CFR Part 660.25. Washington, DC: US Government Printing Office, 1998 (revised annually).

16. Shirey RS, Edwards RE, Ness PM. The risk of alloimmunization to c (Rh4) in R1R1 patients who present with anti-E. Transfusion 1994;34:756-8.

17. Shulman IA. Controversies in red blood cell compatibility testing. In: Nance SJ, ed. Immune destruction of red blood cells. Arlington, VA: American Association of Blood Banks, 1989:171-99.

18. Reisner R, Butler G, Bundy K, Moore SB. Comparison of the polyethylene glycol antiglobulin test and the use of enzymes in antibody detection. Transfusion 1996;36:487-9.

19. Wilkinson SL. Serological approaches to transfusion of patients with allo- or autoantibodies. In: Nance SJ, ed. Immune destruction of red blood cells. Arlington, VA: American Association of Blood Banks, 1989:227-61.

20. Issitt PD, Coombs MR, Bredehoeflt SJ, et al. Lack of clinical significance of "enzyme-only" red cell alloantibodies. Transfusion 1993;33:284-93.

21. Beattie KM, Zuelzer WW. The frequency and properties of pH-dependent anti-M. Transfusion 1965;5:322-6.

22. Judd WJ. A pH dependent autoagglutinin with anti-P specificity. Transfusion 1975;15:373-6.

23. Bruce C, Watt AH, Hare V, et al. A serious source of error in antiglobulin testing. Transfusion 1986;26:177-81.

24. Rolih S, Thomas R, Fisher F, Talbot J. Antibody detection errors due to acidic or unbuffered saline. Immunohematology 1993;9:15-8.

25. Morton J, Pickles MM, Terry AM. The Sd^a blood group antigen in tissues and body fluids. Vox Sang 1970;19:472-82.

26. O'Neil GJ, Yang SY, Tegoli J, et al. Chido and Rodgers blood groups are distinct antigenic components of human complement, C4. Nature 1978;273:668-70.

27. Tilley CA, Romans DG, Crookston MC. Localization of Chido and Rodgers to the C4d fragment of human C4 (abstract). Transfusion 1978;18:622.

28. Judd WJ, Kreamer K, Moulds JJ. The rapid identification of Chido and Rodgers antibodies using C4d-coated red blood cells. Transfusion 1981;21:189-92.

29. Advani H, Zamor J, Judd WJ, et al. Inactivation of Kell blood group antigens by 2-amino-ethylisothiouronium bromide. Br J Haematol 1982;51:107-15.

30. Branch DR, Muensch HA, Sy Siok Hian AL, Petz LD. Disulfide bonds are a requirement for Kell and Cartwright (Yt^a) blood group antigen integrity. Br J Haematol 1983;54:573-8.

31. Moulds J, Moulds MM. Inactivation of Kell blood group antigens by 2-amino-ethylisothiouronium bromide. Transfusion 1983;23:274-5.

32. Branch DR, Petz LD. A new reagent (ZZAP) having multiple applications in immunohematology. Am J Clin Pathol 1982;78:161-7.

33. Liew YW, Uchikawa M. Loss of Era antigen in very low pH buffers. Transfusion 1987;27:442-3.

34. Swanson JL, Sastamoinen R. Chloroquine stripping of HLA A,B antigens from red cells (letter). Transfusion 1985;25:439-40.

35. Giles CM. Human leukocyte antigen (HLA) class I (Bg) on red cells studied with monoclonal antibodies. Immunohematology 1990;6:53-8.

36. Freedman J, Masters CA, Newlands M, et al. Optimal conditions for use of sulphydryl compounds in dissociating rbc antibodies. Vox Sang 1976; 30:231-9.

37. Romans DG, Tilley CA, Crookston MC, et al. Conversion of incomplete antibodies to direct agglutinins by mild reduction. Evidence for segmental flexibility within the Fc fragment of immunoglobulin G. Proc Natl Acad Sci U S A 1977;74:2531-5.

Suggested Reading

Boorman KE, Dodd BE, Lincoln PJ. Blood group serology. 6th ed. Edinburgh, Scotland: Churchill Livingstone, 1988.

Crookston MC. Soluble antigens and leukocyte related antibodies. Part A. Blood group antigens in plasma: An aid in the identification of antibodies. In: Dawson RD, ed. Transfusion with "crossmatch incompatible" blood. Washington, DC: American Association of Blood Banks, 1975:20-5.

Daniels G. Human blood groups. 1st ed. Oxford, England: Blackwell Scientific Publications, 1995.

Engelfriet CP, Overbeeke MAM, Dooren MC, et al. Bioassays to determine the clinical significance of red cell antibodies based on Fc receptor-induced destruction of red cells sensitized by IgG. Transfusion 1994;14:617-26.

Garratty G. In-vitro reactions with red blood cells that are not due to blood group antibodies: A review. Immunohematology 1998;14(1):1-11.

Issitt PD, Anstee DJ. Applied blood group serology. 4th ed. Durham, NC: Montgomery Scientific Publications, 1998.

Johnson ST, Rudmann SV, Wilson SM, eds. Serologic problem-solving strategies: A systematic approach. Bethesda, MD: American Association of Blood Banks, 1996.

Judd WJ. Elution of antibody from red cells. In: Bell CA, ed. A seminar on antigen-antibody reactions revisited. Washington, DC: American Association of Blood Banks, 1982:175-221.

Judd WJ. Methods in immunohematology. 2nd ed. Durham, NC: Montgomery Scientific Publications, 1994.

Kanter MH, Poole G, Garratty G. Misinterpretation and misapplication of p values in antibody identification: The lack of value of a p value. Transfusion 1997;37: 816-22.

Kanter MH. Statistical analysis. In: Busch MP, Brecher ME, eds. Research design and analysis. Bethesda, MD: American Association of Blood Banks, 1998:63-104.

Mallory D, ed. Immunohematology methods and procedures. Rockville, MD: American Red Cross, 1993.

Marsh WL, Reid ME, Kuriyan M, et al. A handbook of clinical and laboratory practices in the transfusion of red blood cells. Moneta, VA: Moneta Medical Press, 1993.

Menitove JE. The Hardy-Weinberg principle: Selection of compatible blood based on mathematic principles. In: Fridey JL, Kasprisin CA, Chambers LA, Rudmann SV, eds. Numbers for blood bankers. Bethesda, MD: American Association of Blood Banks, 1995:1-11.

Mollison PL, Engelfriet CP, Contreras M. Blood transfusion in clinical medicine. 10th ed. London: Blackwell Scientific Publications, 1997.

Race RR, Sanger R. Blood groups in man. 6th ed. Oxford, England: Blackwell Scientific Publications, 1975.

Reid ME, Lomas-Francis C. The blood group antigen facts book. New York: Academic Press, 1997.

Rolih S. A review: Antibodies with high-titer, low-avidity characteristics. Immunohematology 1990;6:59-67.

Telen MJ. New and evolving techniques for antibody and antigen identification. In: Nance ST, ed. Alloimmunity: 1993 and beyond. Bethesda, MD: American Association of Blood Banks, 1993:117-39.

20

The Positive Direct Antiglobulin Test and Immune-Mediated Red Cell Destruction

SOME OF THE MOST COMPLEX serologic problems involve the recognition of a positive direct antiglobulin test (DAT) and immune red cell destruction. This chapter addresses the significance of a positive DAT test due to warm or cold autoantibodies or both. Serologic techniques are discussed as well as recommendations for the selection of red cells for transfusion, the mechanisms of drug antibodies, and serologic tools useful in classifying or identifying some of the antibody specificities associated with drugs. The appendix provides a useful index of drugs that have been associated with red cell destruction.

Significance of a Positive Direct Antiglobulin Test

The direct antiglobulin test (DAT) is generally used to determine if red cells have been coated in vivo with immunoglobulin, complement, or both. A positive DAT, with or without shortened red cell survival, may result from:

1. Autoantibodies to intrinsic red cell antigens.

2. Alloantibodies in a recipient's circulation, reacting with antigens on recently transfused donor red cells.

3. Alloantibodies in donor plasma, plasma derivatives, or blood fractions, which react with antigens on the red cells of a transfusion recipient.

4. Alloantibodies in maternal circulation, which cross the placenta and coat fetal red cells.

5. Antibodies directed against certain drugs, which bind to red cell membranes (eg, penicillin).
6. Adsorbed proteins, including immunoglobulins, which attach to abnormal membranes or red cells modified by therapy with certain drugs, notably those of the cephalosporin group.
7. Complement components or, rarely, IgG bound to red cells after the administration of drugs such as quinidine and phenacetin has induced a drug/antidrug interaction.
8. Non-red-cell immunoglobulins associated with red cells in patients with hypergammaglobulinemia or recipients of high-dose intravenous gammaglobulin.[1,2]
9. Antibodies produced by passenger lymphocytes in transplanted organs.[3]

A positive DAT does not necessarily mean that a person's red cells have shortened survival. Small amounts of both IgG and complement appear to be present on all red cells. A range of 5-90 IgG molecules/red cell[4] and 5-97 C3d molecules/red cell[5] (possibly up to 500 or more) appear to be normal on the red cells of healthy individuals.

The DAT can detect a level of 100-500 molecules of IgG/red cell and 400-1100 molecules of C3d/red cell, although newer reagents and more sensitive test methods may detect lower levels of these proteins. As many as 6-8% of hospital patients[6] and between 1 in 1000 and 1 in 14,000 blood donors have a positive DAT without clinical manifestations of immune-mediated red cell destruction.[4]

Most blood donors with positive DATs appear to be perfectly healthy, although some may show signs of increased cell destruction or develop autoimmune hemolytic anemia (AIHA) over time.[7(p222)] Elevated levels of IgG or complement have been noted on the red cells of patients with sickle cell disease, β-thalassemia, renal disease, multiple myeloma, autoimmune disorders (including systemic lupus erythematosus), AIDS, and other diseases with elevated serum globulin or blood urea nitrogen (BUN) levels with no clear correlation between positive DAT and anemia.[2,8] Interpretation of positive DATs must include the patient's history, clinical data, and the results of other laboratory tests.

The Direct Antiglobulin Test

The principles of the DAT are discussed in Chapter 12. Although any red cells may be tested, anticoagulated blood samples are preferred to avoid in-vitro uptake of complement; EDTA is the anticoagulant most frequently recommended. If red cells from a clotted blood sample have a positive DAT, the results should be confirmed on cells from a freshly collected or EDTA-anticoagulated specimen if those results are to be used for diagnostic purposes.

Most DATs are initially performed with a polyspecific antihuman globulin (AHG) reagent capable of detecting both IgG and C3d (see Method 3.6). If positive, tests with more specific anti-IgG and anticomplement reagents may be appropriate. Occasionally, polyspecific AHG reagents react with cell-bound proteins other than IgG or C3d (eg, IgM, IgA, or other complement components); specific reagents to distinguish these proteins are not readily available in most laboratories. If cord blood samples are to be tested, it is appropriate to use anti-IgG AHG only versus a polyspecific AHG reagent.

The Pretransfusion DAT and the Autologous Control

Neither the AABB, in the *Standards for Blood Banks and Transfusion Services*,[9] nor any other accrediting agency requires a DAT or an autologous control (autocontrol) as part of pretransfusion testing. Several studies, however, have shown that eliminating the DAT/autocontrol portion of routine pretransfusion testing carries minimal risk.[6,10]

Evaluation of a Positive DAT

Extent of Testing

Clinical considerations should dictate the extent to which a positive DAT is evaluated. Dialogue with the attending physician is important. Interpretation of the significance of serologic findings requires knowledge of the patient's diagnosis; recent drug, pregnancy, and transfusion history; and information on the presence of acquired or unexplained hemolytic anemia. The results of serologic tests alone are not diagnostic; their significance must be assessed in conjunction with clinical information and such laboratory data as hematocrit, bilirubin, haptoglobin, and reticulocyte count.

Answers to the following questions may help decide what investigations are appropriate:

1. *Is there any evidence of in-vivo red cell destruction?*

   Reticulocytosis, hemoglobinemia, hemoglobinuria, decreased serum haptoglobin, and elevated levels of serum unconjugated bilirubin or lactate dehydrogenase (LD), especially LD1, may be associated with increased red cell destruction. If an anemic patient with a positive DAT does show evidence of hemolysis, testing to evaluate a possible immune etiology is appropriate. IF THERE IS NO EVIDENCE OF INCREASED RED CELL DESTRUCTION, NO FURTHER STUDIES ARE NECESSARY, unless the patient needs transfusion and the serum contains incompletely identified unexpected antibodies to red cell antigens.

2. *Has the patient been recently transfused?*

   Many workers routinely attempt to determine the cause of a positive DAT when the patient has received transfusions within the previous 3 months because the first indication of a developing immune response may be the attachment of antibody to recently transfused red cells. Mixed-field reactivity is the classic observation but may be difficult to observe. Antibody may appear as early as 7-10 days after transfusion in primary immunization and within 2-7 days in a secondary response; these alloantibodies could shorten the survival of red cells already transfused or given in subsequent transfusions.

   Antibodies coating the patient's red cells and/or the transfused red cells may also be present in serum. Elution performed to evaluate a positive DAT often concentrates antibody activity and may facilitate identification of weakly reactive serum antibodies. If the serum contains multiple antibodies, the eluate may contain only one or a few of the serum specificities.

   If a non-group-O patient has received plasma containing anti-A or anti-B (as in transfusion of group O platelets), ABO antibodies may be detected on the recipient's red cells without necessarily implying significantly accelerated red cell destruction. If, however, the recipient of incompatible plasma does appear to have immune hemolysis, the eluate can be tested against A and/or B cells. If the expected ABO antibodies are not detected, other causes of the positive DAT should be sought.

   Intravenous immunoglobulin (IVIG) may contain ABO antibodies, anti-D or, sometimes, other antibodies. Significant red cell destruction due to passive transfer of antibodies from IVIG is rare.

3. *Is the patient receiving any drugs, such as procainamide, α-methyldopa, or intravenous penicillin?*

   Approximately 3% of patients receiving intravenous penicillin, usually at very high doses, and 15-20% of patients receiving α-methyldopa will develop a positive DAT. Fewer than 1% of those patients who develop a positive DAT have hemolytic anemia, however. Procainamide therapy is also associated with positive DATs.[11] Cephalosporins also are associated with positive DATs and second- and third-generation cephalosporins can be associated with immune red cell destruction. Positive DATs associated with other drugs are rare. If a positive DAT is found in a patient receiving such drugs, the attending physician should be alerted so that appropriate surveillance for red cell destruction can be maintained. If red cell survival is not shortened, no further studies are necessary.

4. *Has the patient received a marrow or an organ transplant?*

Passenger lymphocytes of donor origin produce antibodies directed against ABO or other antigens on the recipient's cells, causing a positive DAT.[3]

5. *Is the patient receiving antilymphocyte globulin (ALG), antithymocyte globulin (ATG), or IV RhIG?*

Patients receiving ALG or ATG of animal origin may develop a positive DAT within a few days, apparently related to high-titer heterophile antibodies in these products and the presence of corresponding antibodies in animal-derived AHG sera.[12] Free unbound ALG/ATG in the circulation may cause positive results when the patient's serum is used in indirect antiglobulin testing. Problems due to heterophile antibodies can usually be circumvented by neutralization or by use of the low ionic polycation technique (see Method 3.2.5). Likewise, IV RhIG may cause some patients to develop a positive DAT as a result of passively acquired red cell antibodies in the product.[13]

Serologic Studies

Three investigative approaches are helpful in the evaluation of a positive DAT[13,14]:

1. Test the DAT-positive cells with anti-IgG and anti-C3d AHG reagents to characterize the types of proteins coating the red cells.

2. Test the serum/plasma to detect and identify clinically significant antibodies to red cell antigens.

3. Test an eluate (see Methods 4.1 through 4.5) prepared from the coated red cells with a panel of reagent red cells to define whether the coating protein has alloantibody activity (for investigation of transfusion reactions or HDN). When the only coating protein is complement, eluates are frequently nonreactive. An eluate from the patient's red cells coated only with complement should be tested if there is clinical evidence of antibody-mediated hemolysis, however. Results of these tests combined with the patient's history and clinical data should assist in classification of the problems involved.

Elution

Elution frees antibody from sensitized red cells and recovers antibody in a usable form. Details of eluate preparation are given in Chapter 19 and in Methods 4.1 through 4.5. Table 20-1 lists the advantages and disadvantages of several common elution methods; no single elution method is ideal in all situations. Although many elution methods damage or destroy the red cells, certain techniques (see Methods 2.11, 2.13, and 2.14) remove antibody but leave the cells sufficiently intact to allow testing for various antigens or for use in adsorption procedures. Some antigens may be altered by elution, however, and appropriate controls are essential.

When the cause of the positive DAT is unknown, an eluate may be prepared and tested against a panel of red cells.

In cases of hemolytic disease of the newborn (HDN) or hemolytic transfusion reactions, specific antibody (or antibodies) is usually detected in the eluate. Usually the same specificity can be detected in the patient's (or, in HDN, the mother's) serum, although eluates may help in antibody identification when serum reactions are weak. When the eluate reacts with all cells tested, autoantibody is the most likely explanation, especially if the patient has not been recently transfused. WHEN NO UNEXPECTED ANTIBODIES ARE PRESENT IN THE SERUM, AND IF THE PATIENT HAS NOT BEEN RECENTLY TRANSFUSED, NO FURTHER SEROLOGIC TESTING OF AN ISOLATED AUTOANTIBODY IS NECESSARY.

In eluates prepared from the red cells of random hospital patients, no reactivity is detected in the eluate despite reactivity of the cells with specific anti-IgG. The cause may be that the eluate was not tested against cells positive for the corresponding antigen, notably group A or group B cells. Antigens of low incidence are also absent from most reagent cell panels. It may be appropriate to test the eluate against red cells from recently transfused donor units, which could have caused immunization to a rare antigen, or, in HDN, against cells from the father, from whom the infant may have inherited a rare gene.

Reactivity of eluates can be enhanced by testing against enzyme-treated cells or by the use of enhancement techniques such as polyethylene glycol (PEG). Antibody reactivity can be increased by the use of a concentrated eluate, either by alteration of the fluid-to-cell ratio or by use of commercial concentration devices. Washing the red cells with low ionic strength saline (LISS) instead of normal saline may prevent the loss of antibody while the cells are being prepared for elution.

Certain elution methods give poor results with certain antibodies. When eluates are nonreactive yet clinical signs of red cell destruction are present, elution by a different method may be helpful. If both serum and eluate are nonreactive at all test phases and if the patient has received high-dose intravenous penicillin or other drug therapy, testing to demonstrate drug-related antibodies should be considered. Patients may have a positive DAT and nonreactive eluate with no evidence of hemolysis, and exhaustive pursuit of an explanation is not usually indicated. Toy et al[2] showed that 65-80% of hospital patients with a positive DAT have a negative eluate. It is suggested that these positive DAT results are the result of nonspecific uptake of proteins on the red cells.

Immune-Mediated Hemolysis

Immune-mediated hemolysis (immune hemolysis) is the shortening of red cell survival by the product(s) of an immune response. If marrow compensation is adequate, the re-

Table 20-1. Antibody Elution Techniques

Method	Advantages	Disadvantages
Heat (56 C)	Good for ABO-HDN; quick and easy method	Poor recovery of other blood group allo- and autoantibodies
Freeze-Thaw	Good for ABO-HDN; quick and easy method; requires small volume of cells	Poor recovery of other blood group allo- and autoantibodies
Cold Acid	Quick and easy method; sensitivity comparable to digitonin-acid	Less sensitive for warm auto- and alloantibodies
Digitonin Acid	Nonhazardous; good recovery of most antibodies; available in commercial kit	Time-consuming washing of stroma; less sensitive for Kidd antibodies
Dichloromethane (DCM)	Good for anti-K; nonflammable	Toxic; poor recovery of anti-Fy^b
Glycine-HCl/ EDTA	Good method for preparing eluates, and having red cells rendered DAT negative; sensitivity comparable to digitonin-acid.	Denatures antigens in the Kell system

Modified from Judd[14] and Sigmund.[15]

duced red cell survival may not result in anemia. Immune hemolysis is only one cause of anemia, and many causes of hemolysis are unrelated to immune reactions. The serologic investigations carried out in the blood bank do not determine whether a patient has a "hemolytic" anemia. The diagnosis of hemolytic anemia rests on clinical findings and such laboratory data as hemoglobin or hematocrit values; reticulocyte count; red cell morphology; bilirubin, haptoglobin, and LD levels; and, sometimes, red cell survival studies. The serologic findings help determine whether the hemolysis has an immune basis and, if so, what type of immune hemolytic anemia is present. This is important because the treatment for each type is different.

The terms hemolysis and hemolytic, frequently used to indicate both intravascular and extravascular red cell destruction, may be misleading. As a description of in-vitro antibody reactivity, hemolysis or lysis of the red cells with release of free hemoglobin to the surrounding media, is both obvious and rare. In-vivo lysis of cells and release of free hemoglobin within the intravascular compartment is uncommon and, often, dramatic. Most immune red cell destruction occurs extravascularly, with little or no escaping hemoglobin even in the immune "hemolytic anemias."

Immune hemolytic anemias can be classified in various ways. One classification system is shown in Table 20-2. Autoimmune hemolytic anemias (AIHAs) are subdivided into four

Table 20-2. Classification of Immune Hemolytic Anemias

Autoimmune Hemolytic Anemia
1. Warm Autoimmune Hemolytic Anemia
   a. primary (idiopathic)
   b. secondary (to such conditions as lymphoma, systemic lupus erythematosus (SLE), carcinoma, or to drug therapy)
2. Cold Agglutinin Syndrome
   a. primary (idiopathic)
   b. secondary (to such conditions as lymphoma, mycoplasma pneumonia, infectious mononucleosis)
3. Mixed-Type AIHA
   a. primary (idiopathic)
   b. secondary (to such conditions as SLE, lymphoma)
4. Paroxysmal Cold Hemoglobinuria
   a. primary (idiopathic)
   b. secondary (to such conditions as syphilis, viral infections)
5. DAT-Negative AIHA
   a. primary (idiopathic)
   b. secondary (to such conditions as lymphoma, SLE)

Drug-Induced Hemolytic Anemia

Alloimmune Hemolytic Anemia
1. Hemolytic disease of the newborn
2. Hemolytic transfusion reaction

major types: warm antibody AIHA (WAIHA), cold agglutinin syndrome (CAS), mixed-type AIHA, and paroxysmal cold hemoglobinuria (PCH). Not all cases fit neatly into these categories. Immune hemolysis may also be induced by drugs (discussed in a later section of this chapter). The prevalence of each type can vary depending on the patient population studied.[16-19] (See Table 20-3.)

DATs performed with IgG- and C3-specific AHG reagents as well as the serum and eluate studies described earlier can be used to classify AIHAs. Two additional procedures may be useful: a diagnostic cold agglutinin titer (Method 4.8) and the Donath-Landsteiner test for PCH (Method 4.12). Table 20-4 summarizes the expected serologic results with the major types of AIHA.

The binding of antibody to red cells does not, in itself, damage the cells. It is the phenomena that the bound antibody-antigen complex promotes that may eventually damage

Table 20-3. Serologic Findings in DAT-Positive AIHA

	WAIHA	CAS	Mixed-Type AIHA	PCH	Drug-Induced AIHA
Percent of cases	48%[19] to 70%[20]	16%[20] to 32%[19]	7%[19] to 8%[21]	Rare in adults[20] 32% in children[22]	12%[20] to 18%[19]
DAT	20%[20] to 66%[19] IgG 24%[19] to 63%[20] IgG+C3 7%[19] to 14%[20] C3	91%[19] to 98%[20] C3 only	71%[19] to 100%[20] IgG + C3	94%[19] to 100%[20] C3 only	94%[19] IgG 6%[19] IgG + C3
Immuno-globulin type	IgG (sometimes IgA or IgM, rarely alone)	IgM	IgG, IgM	IgG	IgG
Eluate	IgG antibody	Nonreactive	IgG antibody	Nonreactive	IgG antibody
Serum	57% react by IAT; 13% hemolyze enzyme-treated red cells at 37 C; 90% agglutinate enzyme-treated red cells at 37 C; 30% agglutinate untreated red cells at 20 C; rarely agglutinate untreated red cells at 37 C[20]	IgM hemagglutinating antibody; titer usually >1000 at 4 C; usually react at 30 C in albumin; monoclonal antibody in chronic disease[20,23]	IgG IAT-reactive antibody; IgM hemagglutinating antibody, usually react at 30-37 C in saline; titer at 4 C often <64[19,21,24]	IgG biphasic hemolysin (Donath-Landsteiner antibody)[20,23]	IgG antibody similar to WAIHA[20,23]
Specificity	80% Type I, 20% Type II[25] specificity; Rh specificity; other specificities have been reported*	Usually anti-I but can be anti-i; rarely anti-Pr[26]	Usually specificity unclear[19,21,24,27]; can be anti-I, -i, or other cold agglutinin specificities	Anti-P (nonreactive with p and P^k red cells[20,26]	Specificity often Rh related[2,20]

*See text.

Table 20-4. DAT Results in AIHA Using Anti-IgG and Anti-C3 Reagents[19]

	WAIHA	CAS	Mixed-Type AIHA[*]	PCH	Drug-Induced
No. of patients	355	275	61	17	157
IgG only[†]	67%	1%	18%	0	94%
IgG + C3[†]	24%	1%	71%	0	6%
C3 only[†]	7%	91%	9.8%	94%	0
Polyspecific-positive, monospecific-negative[‡]	1%	0.7%	0	0	0
DAT-negative	1%	6.3%	1.2%	6%	0

*Patients had both cold hemagglutinating autoantibodies reactive to 30 C or higher and warm-reactive autoantibodies.
†With or without IgM and/or IgA.
‡Polyspecific antihuman globulin gives a positive result but monospecific anti-IgG and anti-C3 reagents are negative.

cells. These include complement binding, adherence to Fc receptors on macrophages and monocytes, phagocytosis, and cytotoxic lysis. The IgG subclass of bound antibody may be significant. IgG1 is the subclass most commonly found, sometimes alone but often in combination with other subclasses. The other IgG subclasses occur more often in combination with other subclasses than alone. In general, IgG3 antibodies have the most destructive effects, followed by IgG1. IgG2 antibodies are associated with less destruction and IgG4 with little to no destruction. Some monoclonal antiglobulin reagents may not detect IgG4.

The number of antibody molecules per red cell also plays a role. The number of antibody molecules on the red cells of apparently healthy blood donors with positive DATs (<1000, weakly positive) is far less than that usually seen in patients with AIHA.[4,5] Some patients with apparent immune hemolysis may have negative findings on a routine DAT.

Warm Antibody Autoimmune Hemolytic Anemia

The most common type of AIHA is associated with warm-reactive (37 C) antibodies. Typical serologic findings are described below.

DAT

When IgG-specific and complement-specific AHG reagents are used, three patterns of reactivity may be found: coating with IgG alone, with complement alone, or with both. In approximately 1% of cases the DAT will be positive with a polyspecific AHG reagent but negative with IgG- and complement-specific AHG reagents. Some of these may be due to attachment of IgM or IgA alone.[17,19]

Serum

Autoantibody in the serum typically is IgG and reacts by indirect antiglobulin testing against all cells tested.[20] If the autoantibody has a high binding constant and has been adsorbed by the patient's red cells in vivo, the serum may contain very little free antibody. The serum will contain antibody after all the specific antigen sites on the red cells have been occupied and no more antibody can be bound in vivo. The DAT in such cases is usually strongly positive. Approximately 50% of patients with WAIHA have serum antibodies that react with untreated red cells. When testing with PEG, enzyme-treated red cells, or solid-phase methods, over 90% of these sera can be shown to contain autoantibody. Autoantibodies that hemolyze untreated red cells in vitro at 37 C are rare but, if present, may be associated with significant in-vivo destruction of autologous and transfused cells. Approximately one-third of patients with warm-antibody AIHA have cold-reactive autoagglutinins demonstrable in tests at 20 C, but cold agglutinin titers at 4 C are normal. This does not necessarily mean the patient has CAS in addition to WAIHA.[20] (See mixed-type AIHA below.)

Eluate

The presence of the IgG autoantibody on the red cells should be confirmed by elution at least upon initial diagnosis and/or pretransfusion testing. (See Methods 4.1 through 4.5.) Typically the eluate reacts with virtually all cells tested, with reactivity enhanced in tests against enzyme-treated cells or when PEG is used. Occasionally IgG is present at such low levels that the eluate is nonreactive. The eluate will usually have no serologic activity if the only protein coating the red cells is complement components. Occasionally antibody not detected by the DAT will be detected in the eluate, possibly due to the concentrating effect of eluate preparation.

Specificity of Autoantibody

The specificity of autoantibodies associated with WAIHA appears very complex. In routine tests, all cells tested are usually reactive. Some autoantibodies that have weaker or negative reactivity with cells of rare Rh phenotypes, such as D– –, or Rh$_{null}$, appear to have broad specificity in the Rh system. Apparent specificity for simple Rh antigens (D, C, E, c, e) is occasionally seen, either as the sole autoantibody or as a predominant portion, based on stronger reactivity with cells of certain phenotypes. Such reactivity is often termed a "relative" specificity. Such relative specificity in a serum may be mistaken for alloantibody, but cells negative for the apparent target antigen can adsorb and remove "mimicking" specificity.

Unusual Specificities. Apart from Rh specificity, warm autoantibodies with many other specificities have been reported. When autoantibody specificity is directed to antigens in the Kell system (and perhaps others), the patient's red cells may exhibit depressed expression of the antigen and the DAT may be negative (see below). Dilution and selective adsorption of eluates may uncover specificity or relative specificity of autoantibodies.

Practical Significance. Tests against red cells of rare phenotype and by special techniques have limited clinical application. In rare instances of WAIHA involving IgM agglutinins, determining autoantibody specificity may help differentiate such cases from typical CAS.[28] It is rarely, if ever, necessary to ascertain autoantibody specificity in order to select antigen-negative blood for transfusion. If apparent specificity is directed to a high-incidence antigen (eg, anti-U), or when the autoantibody reacts with all red cells except those of a rare Rh phenotype (eg, D– –, Rh$_{null}$), compatible donor blood is unlikely to be available and there is little point in determining specificity. Such blood, if available, should be reserved for alloimmunized patients of that uncommon phenotype.

Transfusion-Stimulated Autoantibodies. Transfusion itself may lead to the production of autoantibodies that may persist and cause positive DATs for some time after transfusion yet not cause obvious red cell destruction. Such cell-bound autoantibodies sometimes display blood group specificity (eg, E, K, Jk^a). These autoantibodies may persist long after transfused red cells should have disappeared from the circulation, apparently adsorbed to the patient's own antigen-negative red cells.[29]

Transfusion of Patients with Warm-Reactive Autoantibodies

Inherent Risks. Patients with warm-reactive autoantibodies range from those with no apparent decreased red cell survival to those with life-threatening anemia. Patients with little or no evidence of significant in-vivo red cell destruction often tolerate transfusion quite well. In general, however, transfusion of patients with WAIHA carries a greater-than-normal risk; even when autoantibody is not demonstrable in the serum, transfused blood is not truly compatible and effects of the transfusion are likely to be relatively short-lived.

When autoantibody is active in serum, it may be difficult to exclude the presence of alloantibodies, which increases the risk of adverse reaction. Transfusion may stimulate alloantibody production, complicating subsequent transfusions. Transfusion may intensify the autoantibody, inducing or increasing hemolysis and making serologic testing more difficult. Transfusion may depress compensatory erythropoiesis; destruction of transfused cells may increase hemoglobinemia and hemoglobinuria. In patients with active hemolysis, transfused red cells may be destroyed more rapidly than the patient's own red cells. In rare cases, this may promote hypercoagulability and disseminated intravascular coagulation. Transfusion reactions, if they occur, may be difficult to investigate.

Alternatives to Transfusion. Given the inherent risks of transfusion, alternative treatments should be considered. Corticosteroids, which inhibit antibody production and may also inhibit release of lysosomal enzymes, are generally considered a primary therapy. Marked in-vivo hemolysis may require intravenous administration of high doses of steroid. Intravenous immunoglobulin or immunosuppressive drugs such as cyclophosphamide may benefit some patients with autoantibody.[15] Splenectomy is sometimes effective but is usually considered only when other therapies are ineffective or contraindicated. In cases of severe hemolysis, plasma exchange or treatment with complement-inhibiting substances (eg, heparin) have been suggested, although without supportive documentation. Filtration of the plasma through immunoadsorption columns (eg, containing protein A) may temporarily reduce the level of plasma IgG.

Transfusion in WAIHA. Transfusion is especially problematic for patients with rapid in-vivo hemolysis, who may present with a very low hemoglobin level and hypotension. Reticulocytopenia may accompany a rapidly falling hematocrit, and the patient may exhibit coronary insufficiency, congestive heart failure, cardiac decompensation, or neurologic impairment. Under these circumstances transfusion is usually required as a lifesaving measure. The transfused cells may support oxygen-carrying capacity until the acute hemolysis diminishes or other therapies can effect a more lasting benefit. These patients represent a significant challenge because serologic testing may be complex while clinical needs are acute.

Transfusion should not be withheld solely because of serologic incompatibility. The volume transfused should usually be the smallest amount required to maintain adequate oxygen delivery, not necessarily to reach an arbitrary hemoglobin level. Volumes of about 100 mL may be appropriate. The patient should be carefully monitored throughout the transfusion. The dangers of transfusion may be enhanced if the patient has mixed-type AIHA.

Transfusion in Chronic WAIHA. Most patients with WAIHA have a chronic stable anemia, often at relatively low hemoglobin levels. Those with hemoglobin levels above 8 g/dL rarely require transfusion, and many patients with levels of 5 g/dL (or even lower) can be managed with bed rest and no transfusions. Transfusion will be required if the anemia progresses or is accompanied by such symptoms as severe angina, cardiac decompensation, respiratory distress, and cerebral ischemia.

Most patients with chronic anemia due to WAIHA tolerate transfusion without overt reactions, even though the transfused cells may not survive any better than their own. Because transfusion may lead to circulatory overload or to increased red cell destruction, the decision to transfuse should be carefully considered. A few patients without acute hemolysis have had severe hemolytic reactions after transfusion.

This may be due to the sudden availability of large volumes of donor cells and the exponential curve of decay, by which the number of cells hemolyzed is proportional to the number of cells present.[7(pp230,369)] Reports of reactions in patients with HIV suggest that these patients may be more susceptible to transfusion-induced DIC and hypercoagulability.[22,27]

Selecting Blood by Specificity. If the decision is made to transfuse, selection of appropriate donor blood is essential. It is important to determine the patient's ABO type and, if time permits, to detect potentially clinically significant alloantibodies. Adsorption and other special techniques described later in this chapter can greatly reduce the risk of undetected alloantibodies but may be time-consuming. If clinically significant alloantibodies are present, the transfused cells should lack the corresponding antigen(s).

If the autoantibody has apparent and relatively clear-cut specificity for a single antigen (eg, anti-e) and there is active ongoing hemolysis, blood lacking that antigen may be selected. There is evidence that in some patients such red cells survive better than the patient's own red cells.[14,15] In the absence of hemolysis, autoantibody specificity can usually be ignored, although donor units negative for the antigen may be chosen because this is a simple way to circumvent the autoantibody and detect potential alloantibodies. If the autoantibody shows broader reactivity, reacting with all cells but showing some relative specificity (eg, reacts preferentially with e-positive red cells), the use of blood lacking the corresponding antigen is debatable. It may be undesirable to expose the patient to Rh antigens absent from autologous cells, especially D and especially in females who may bear children later, merely to improve serologic compatibility testing with the autoantibody (eg, when a D-negative patient has autoanti-e).

Selecting Blood by Random Testing. In many cases of WAIHA, no autoantibody specificity is apparent. The patient's serum reacts with all red cell samples to the same degree or reacts with red cells from different donors to varying degrees for reasons seemingly unrelated to Rh phenotypes. Even if specificity is identified, the exotic cells used for such identification are not available for transfusion. The most important consideration in such cases is to exclude the presence of clinically important alloantibodies *before* selecting either phenotypically similar or dissimilar, cross-match-incompatible red cells for transfusion. In extremely rare cases in which there is severe and progressive anemia, it may be essential to transfuse blood that does not react with the patient's autoantibody.

Frequency of Testing. According to AABB *Standards,*[9(p58)] a sample of blood must be obtained and tested from a patient within 3 days of a scheduled transfusion. If the patient has not been transfused (or pregnant) within 3 months before the scheduled transfusion, a fresh sample (drawn within 3 days of the transfusion) does not need to be collected or tested. Thus, if an alloantibody investigation was performed on a patient with warm autoantibodies, and no alloantibodies were detected, and there was no history of transfusion or pregnancy within the last 3 months, there is no need to repeat the antibody investigation. Once the patient has been transfused and additional transfusions are ordered, standard I4.000 applies. This poses a problem because it becomes very time-consuming and labor-intensive to repeat the extensive antibody investigation. Although *Standards* requires that a sample be tested every 3 days, some workers contend that in these difficult cases, the continued collection and testing (to include antibody investigation) of patient samples is unnecessary.[30] Disagreeing with that opinion, Leger and Garratty showed that in a large study of patients with AIHA, there was a 40% alloimmunization rate, with many alloantibodies developing after recent transfusions.[31] Branch and Petz,[32] in an editorial, agreed that there is a need to detect newly developed alloantibodies in the multitransfused patient with warm autoantibodies. These two papers offer methods to assist in the detection of alloantibodies in the presence of auto-antibodies.

Cold Agglutinin Syndrome

Cold agglutinin syndrome (also called cold hemagglutinin disease, CHD) is the hemolytic anemia most commonly associated with cold-reactive autoantibodies and accounts for approximately 16-32% of all cases of immune hemolysis.[17,18] (See Table 20-3.) It occurs as an acute or chronic condition. The acute form is often secondary to lymphoproliferative disorders (eg, lymphoma) or *Mycoplasma pneumoniae* infection. The chronic form, which causes mild to moderate hemolysis, is often seen in elderly patients, sometimes associated with lymphoma, chronic lymphocytic leukemia, or Waldenstrom's macroglobulinemia; Raynaud's phenomenon and hemoglobinuria may occur in cold weather. CAS is often characterized by rapid sedimentation at room temperature of red cells in an EDTA specimen. Clumping of red cells may be obvious in such a sample, sometimes so strong that the cells appear to be clotted. Problems with ABO and Rh typing and other tests are not uncommon.

DAT

Complement is the only protein detected on the red cells in almost all cases. The cold-reactive autoagglutinin is usually IgM, which binds to red cells in the comparatively low temperature of the peripheral circulation and causes complement components (C3 and C4 in particular) to attach to the red cells. As the red cells circulate to warmer areas, the IgM dissociates, but the complement remains. Regulatory proteins convert the bound C3 and C4 to C3d and C4d, and it is the anti-C3d (-C4d) component of polyspecific AHG reagents that accounts for the positive DAT. The presence of C3d, per se, does not shorten red cell survival.

In rare cases the cold-reactive autoantibody is IgG, which may or may not bind complement. The presence of this IgG may be missed by the DAT unless all phases of testing are done in the cold, using cold saline and AHG reagents.

Serum

IgM cold-reactive autoagglutinins associated with immune hemolysis usually have a titer above 1000 when tested at 4 C; in vitro, they rarely react with saline-suspended red cells above 32 C. If 30% bovine albumin is included in the reaction medium, 100% and 70% of clinically significant examples will react at 30 C or 37 C, respectively.[33] Hemolytic activity against untreated red cells can sometimes be demonstrated at 20-25 C and, except in rare cases with Pr specificity, enzyme-treated red cells are hemolyzed in the presence of adequate complement.

Determination of the true thermal amplitude or titer of the cold autoagglutinin requires that the specimen be collected and maintained strictly at 37 C until the serum and cells are separated, to avoid in-vitro autoadsorption. Alternatively, plasma can be used from an EDTA-anticoagulated specimen that has been warmed for at least 15 minutes at 37 C (with repeated mixing) and then separated from the cells, ideally at 37 C. This should release autoadsorbed antibody back into the plasma.[24]

In chronic CAS, the IgM autoagglutinin is usually a monoclonal protein with kappa light chains. In the acute form, the autoreactive antibody is polyclonal IgM with normal kappa and lambda light-chain distribution. Rare examples of IgA and IgG cold-reactive auto-agglutinins have also been described.

Eluate

Elution is seldom necessary in obvious cases of CAS. If the red cells have been collected properly and washed at 37 C, there will be no immunoglobulin on the cells and no reactivity will be found in the eluate. Because the serum antibody level is often very high, it is essential to test the last saline wash before elution to ensure that unbound autoagglutinins have been removed.

Specificity of Autoantibody

The autoantibody specificity in CAS is usually of only academic interest. CAS is most often associated with antibodies with I specificity. Less commonly, i specificity is found, usually associated with infectious mononucleosis. On rare occasions, cold-reactive autoagglutinins with Pr or other specificities, are seen (see Method 4.8). Dilution of the serum may be necessary to demonstrate specificity of very high-titer antibodies.

Autoantibody specificity is not diagnostic for CAS. Autoanti-I may be seen in healthy subjects as well as patients with CAS. The nonpathologic forms of autoanti-I, however, rarely react to titers above 64 at 4 C, and are usually nonreactive with I-negative (i_{cord} and i_{adult}) red cells at room temperature. In contrast, the autoanti-I of CAS may react quite strongly with I-negative red cells in tests at room temperature, while equal or even stronger reactions are observed with I-positive red cells. Autoanti-i antibodies react in the opposite manner; they give much stronger reactions with I-negative red cells than with red cells that are I-positive. The cold-reactive autoantibody found in mixed-type AIHA may not show specificity, may react only weakly at 4 C but usually reacts at up to 30 C.[23,24] Procedures to determine the specificities of cold-reactive autoantibodies are given in Method 4.7 and Method 4.8.

Transfusion in CAS

Patients suffering from CAS can often be managed without transfusion. Acute cell destruction may be reduced by keeping the patient in a warm room (about 40 C), to prevent complement binding by the cold agglutinin. Steroid therapy is usually not successful; however, if the antibody is low-titered but reacts at a high thermal range, steroids may be helpful.[16] Plasma exchange has been helpful in some cases, but the effects are usually not lasting. Transient hemolysis associated with infectious diseases requires treatment of the infectious disease.

If transfusion is undertaken, up to 50% of the cells transfused initially may be destroyed until they acquire some resistance to complement destruction by cleavage of C3d.[7(pp326-7)] If transfusion is required, use of a blood warmer is often recommended, but the need for this is controversial.[13]

Pretransfusion Testing. Antibody detection tests should be performed in ways that minimize cold-reactive autoantibody activity yet still permit detection of clinically significant alloantibodies. The use of albumin and other potentiators increases the reactivity of the autoantibodies and should be avoided. To avoid the detection of bound complement, some workers use an IgG-specific reagent, rather than a polyspecific AHG serum.

Adsorption Procedures. When cold-reactive autoantibody reactivity persists, autoadsorption studies (see Method 4.6) can be performed. This should make it possible to detect alloantibodies masked by the cold-reactive autoantibody. If the patient has been recently transfused, rabbit red cells may be used to remove autoanti-I and -IH from sera,[34] but this may remove clinically significant alloantibodies, notably anti-B, -D, -E, and others.[35] A preparation of rabbit red cell stroma is commercially available. Alternatively, allogeneic adsorption studies can be performed as for WAIHA (see below).

Mixed-Type AIHA

Although some patients with WAIHA may also have IgM antibodies that react to high titer at low temperature, a separate mixed-type AIHA accounts for approximately 7-8% of all AIHAs.[19,21,24] These patients have "cold" agglutinins that have low titers at 4 C but high thermal amplitudes, reacting at 30 C or above.

Mixed-type AIHA often presents as an extremely acute condition characterized by very low hemoglobin concentrations and complex serum reactivity present in all phases of testing. Transfusion should be carefully considered, especially because prompt corticosteroid therapy is frequently successful. However, even with steroid therapy, this type of AIHA may be persistent with intermittent periods of hemolysis.

Mixed-type AIHA can be idiopathic or secondary, often associated with systemic lupus erythematosus. Typical serologic findings are described below.

DAT

Both IgG and C3d are usually detectable on patient's red cells.

Serum

Both warm-reactive IgG autoantibodies and cold-reactive, hemagglutinating IgM autoantibodies are present in the serum. These usually result in reactivity at all phases of testing, with virtually all cells tested. The IgM hemagglutinating autoantibody(ies), unlike those in CAS, usually have titers less than 64 at 4 C but react at 30 C or above.[22] If the presence of cold hemagglutinin leads to misclassification as CAS, the option of corticosteroid therapy may be dismissed, but steroids are often effective in mixed-type AIHA. Mixed-type AIHA should also be distinguished from WAIHA in a patient with a strongly reactive but normal cold agglutinin. Care should be taken to avoid loss of antibody reactivity by autoadsorption of the cold agglutinin component.

Albumin and other potentiators of agglutination increase the reactivity of the cold autoagglutinin; anti-IgG, rather than a polyspecific AHG reagent, should be used for the indirect antiglobulin test. If adsorption studies are done to detect alloantibodies, it may be necessary to perform adsorptions at both warm and cold temperatures. The cold (IgM) agglutinin may also be circumvented by treating the serum with sulfhydryl reagents, leaving intact the warm-reactive (IgG) autoagglutinin and most clinically significant alloantibodies.

Eluate

A suitably prepared eluate will contain a warm-reactive IgG autoantibody.

Specificity of Autoantibodies

The unusual cold-reactive IgM hemagglutinating autoantibody can have specificities typical of CAS (ie, I or i) but often has no apparent specificity.[19,21,24] The warm-reactive IgG autoantibody often appears serologically indistinguishable from specificities encountered in typical WAIHA, but may have atypical features.[36]

Transfusion in Mixed-Type AIHA

If blood transfusions are necessary, the considerations in the selection of blood for transfusion are identical to those described for patients with acute hemolysis due to warm antibody-type AIHA (see above). Considerations about blood warmers are the same as for CAS.

Paroxysmal Cold Hemoglobinuria

The rarest form of DAT-positive AIHA is PCH. In the past it was characteristically associated with syphilis, but this association is now unusual. More commonly PCH presents as an acute transient condition secondary to viral infections, particularly in young children. It can also occur as an idiopathic chronic disease in older people. One large study found that none of 531 adults having well-defined immune hemolytic anemias had PCH, while 22 of 68 (32%) children were shown to have PCH.[16]

DAT

The autoantibody in PCH is IgG, but as with IgM cold-reactive autoagglutinins, it reacts with red cells in colder areas of the body (usually the extremities), causes C3 and C4 to bind irreversibly to red cells, and then dissociates from the red cells at warmer temperatures. Red cells washed in a routine manner for the DAT are coated only with complement components, but IgG may be detectable on cells that have been washed with cold saline and tested with cold anti-IgG reagent. Keeping the system nearer its optimal binding temperature allows the cold-reactive IgG autoantibody to remain attached to its antigen.

Serum

The IgG autoantibody in PCH is classically described as a biphasic hemolysin, because binding to red cells occurs at low temperatures but hemolysis does not occur until the coated red cells are warmed to 37 C. This is the basis of the diagnostic test for the disease, the Donath-Landsteiner test (see Method 4.12). The autoantibody may agglutinate normal red cells at 4 C but rarely to titers greater than 64. Because the antibody rarely reacts above 4 C, the serum is usually compatible with random donor cells by routine crossmatch procedures and pretransfusion antibody detection tests are usually nonreactive.

Eluate

Because complement components are usually the only globulins present on circulating red cells, eluates prepared from red cells of patients with PCH are almost invariably nonreactive.

Specificity of Autoantibody

The autoantibody of PCH has most frequently been shown to have P specificity, reacting with all red cells (including the patient's own red cells) except those of the very rare p or P^k phenotypes. Exceptional examples with other specificities have been described.[7(p221)]

Transfusion in PCH

Transfusion is rarely necessary for adult patients with PCH, unless hemolysis is severe. In children, especially under age 6, the thermal amplitude of the antibody tends to be much wider than in adults and hemolysis more brisk, and transfusion may be required as a lifesaving measure. While there is some evidence that p red cells survive better than P-positive (P_1-positive or P_1-negative) red cells,[7(p221)] the prevalence of p blood is approximately 1 in 200,000 and the urgent need for transfusion usually precludes attempts to obtain this rare blood. Transfusion of random donor blood should not be withheld from PCH patients whose need is urgent. Red cells negative for the P antigen should be considered only for those patients who do not respond adequately to random donor blood.

DAT-Negative AIHA

Clinical evidence of hemolytic anemia is present in some patients whose DAT is nonreactive. Frequently autoantibody cannot be detected in either eluate or serum. There may be several reasons the DAT is negative. Antibodies with low binding affinity may dissociate from the red cells during saline washing of the cells for the DAT. Washing with LISS or saline may help retain antibody on the cells. There may be too few antibody molecules on the cell for detection by routine methods but may be demonstrable by methods such as flow cytometry, enzyme-linked antiglobulin tests, solid phase, PEG, or direct Polybrene®.

Nonroutine Reagents

The causative antibody may be IgM or IgA not detected by routine AHG reagents. Anti-IgG, anti-C3d, and the combined anti-C3b,-C3d reagents are the only licensed products available for use with human red cells. AHG reagents that react with IgA, IgM, or C4 are available commercially but have been prepared for use with endpoints other than agglutination. These must be used cautiously and their hemagglutinating reactivity carefully standardized by the user. Quality control must be rigorous. Because agglutination with AHG reagents is more sensitive than precipitation, a serum that appears to be monospecific by precipitation tests may react with several different proteins when used in agglutination tests.

Antigen Depression

The patient with autoantibodies with specificity in the Kell, Rh, LW, Ge, SC, and Lan systems may have depressed red cell expression of the respective antigens. When this occurs, antibody may be detected in the serum and eluate, but the DAT may be negative or very weakly positive. This may provide in-vivo protection of autologous cells. Donor cells of common specific antigen type may be destroyed, but cells lacking the corresponding antigen (usually high-incidence) may survive well. When the autoantibody subsides, autologous cells again express normal amounts of antigen.[7(p228),27]

Serologic Problems with Autoantibodies

In pretransfusion tests on patients with autoantibodies, the following problems may arise:

1. Cold-reactive autoantibodies can cause autoagglutination, resulting in erroneous determinations of ABO and Rh type.
2. Red cells strongly coated with globulins may undergo spontaneous agglutination with high-protein anti-Rh blood-typing reagents, and occasionally even with low-protein reagents.[37]
3. The presence of free autoantibody in the serum may make antibody detection and crossmatching tests difficult to interpret. If time permits, the presence or absence of unexpected, clinically important alloantibody should be determined (see Methods 4.9 through 4.11) before blood is transfused.

Although resolving these serologic problems is important, delaying transfusion in the hope of finding serologically compatible blood

may, in some cases, cause greater danger to the patient. Only clinical judgment can resolve this dilemma. Dialogue with the patient's physician is important.

Resolution of ABO Problems

There are several approaches to the resolution of ABO typing problems associated with cold-reactive autoagglutinins. Often, it is only necessary to maintain the blood sample at 37 C immediately after collection and to wash the red cells with warm (37-45 C) saline before testing. It is helpful to perform a parallel control test, using 6% bovine albumin in saline, to determine if autoagglutination persists. If the control test is nonreactive, the results obtained with anti-A and anti-B are usually valid. If autoagglutination still occurs, interpretation of the results can be difficult, but comparing the strength of the observed reactions may be informative. If the blood sample has been kept at room temperature or if cold-reactive autoagglutinins are particularly potent, it may be necessary to treat the red cells with sulfhydryl reagents.

Dispersing Autoagglutination

Because cold-reactive autoagglutinins are almost always IgM and sulfhydryl reagents denature IgM molecules, reagents such as 2-mercaptoethanol (2-ME) or dithiothreitol (DTT) can be used to abolish autoagglutination (see Method 2.11). Other means of dispersing autoagglutination use the ZZAP reagent[38] or glycine-HCl/EDTA[39] (see Method 4.9 and Method 2.14). Some reagent sera should not be used with chemically modified red cells, eg, monoclonal ABO-typing reagents with enzyme-treated red cells. Appropriate controls are essential for all tests.

An alternative but less effective means of dispersing autoagglutination due to cold-reactive autoantibodies is to incubate the red cells at 37-45 C for 10 minutes and wash the cells several times in saline at that temperature.

Problems with ABO Serum Tests

When the serum agglutinates group O reagent red cells, the results of serum tests may be unreliable. Repeating the tests using prewarmed serum and group A, B, and O red cells at 37 C will often resolve any discrepancy, but anti-A and/or -B in some patients' sera do not react at 37 C. Alternatively, adsorbed serum (either autoadsorbed or adsorbed with allogeneic group O red cells) can be used. Because rabbit red cells express a B-like antigen, sera adsorbed with rabbit red cells or stroma may not contain anti-B, and sera adsorbed in this manner should not be used for ABO serum tests.

Resolution of Rh Problems

Spontaneous agglutination of red cells by cold- or warm-reactive autoantibodies may also cause discrepant Rh typing. The same procedures described for the resolution of ABO problems may be useful. Also, IgG antibody can be dissociated from the cells by treatment with chloroquine diphosphate (Method 2.13), by glycine-HCl/EDTA (Method 2.14), or by other elution methods that leave red cells intact for subsequent typing. IgM-coated cells can be treated with sulfhydryl reagents (such as 2-ME or DTT, Method 2.11) to circumvent spontaneous agglutination.

Detection of Alloantibodies in the Presence of Warm-Reactive Autoantibodies

If the patient who has warm-reactive autoantibodies in the serum needs transfusion, it is important to evaluate the possible simultaneous presence of alloantibodies to red cell antigens. Some alloantibodies may make their presence known by reacting more strongly or at different phases than the autoantibody, but initial studies may not suggest the existence of masked alloantibodies. It is helpful to know which of the common red cell antigens are lacking on the patient's red cells, to predict which clinically significant alloantibodies the patient may have produced or may produce. Antigens absent from autologous cells could well be the target of present or future alloantibodies. When the red cells are coated with IgG, antiglobulin-reactive reagents cannot be used to test IgG-coated cells unless the IgG is first removed (see Method 2.14). Monoclonal reagents or other "saline-reactive" antisera that do not require an antiglobulin test may be helpful in typing the DAT-positive red cells. Cell separation procedures (see Method 2.15 and Method 2.16) may be necessary if the patient has been transfused recently.

Methods to detect alloantibodies in the presence of warm-reactive autoantibodies attempt to remove, reduce, or circumvent the autoantibody. Methods that use PEG, enzymes, gel or solid-phase red cell adherence generally enhance autoantibodies; avoiding these may allow detection of most significant alloantibodies. Other procedures involve adsorption, the principles of which are discussed in Chapter 19. Three widely used approaches are discussed below.

Autologous Adsorption

In a patient who has not been recently transfused, autologous adsorption (see Method 4.9) is the best way to detect alloantibodies in the presence of warm-reactive autoantibodies. The adsorbed serum can be used in the routine antibody detection procedure.

Autoadsorption generally requires some initial preparation of the patient's red cells. At 37 C, in-vivo adsorption will have occurred and all antigen sites on the patient's own red cells may be blocked. It may be necessary, therefore, to remove autoantibody from the red cells to make sites available for adsorption. Treatment of the autologous red cells with proteolytic enzymes increases their capacity to adsorb autoantibody. ZZAP, a mixture of papain or ficin and DTT,[38] is sometimes used to treat the cells (see Method 4.10); the sulfhydryl component makes the IgG molecules more susceptible to the protease and dissociates the antibody molecule from the cell. Multiple sequential autoadsorptions may be necessary if the serum contains high levels of autoantibody. Once autoantibody has been removed, the adsorbed serum is examined for alloantibody activity.

Recent Transfusion. Autologous adsorption is most applicable to patients who have not been recently transfused, so they will not have an admixture of transfused red cells that might adsorb alloantibody. In this context, "recently" usually means within the average life span of transfused red cells (50-60 days). Autologous adsorption studies may be informative even after transfusion as recent as one week, especially if there is evidence of markedly shortened red cell survival of the transfused cells. Failure to detect alloantibody in "autoadsorbed" serum from a recently transfused patient should never be considered conclusive proof that no alloantibody exists.

Sources of Autologous Cells. The patient's own red cells, a portion of which will be younger and less dense than transfused red cells, can sometimes be separated by simple (Method 2.15) or gradient centrifugation for use in autoadsorption experiments. However, these techniques are highly variable and may require expensive equipment and/or considerable expertise in interpretation.

If the patient is to be transfused, it can be advantageous to collect and save additional aliquots of pretransfusion cells, to be used for later adsorptions.

Allogeneic Adsorption

The use of allogeneic red cells for adsorption may be helpful when the patient has been recently transfused or when insufficient autologous red cells are available. The goal is to remove autoantibody and leave the alloantibody in the adsorbed serum. The adsorbing cells must be negative for the antigens against which the alloantibodies react. Because alloantibody specificity is unknown, red cells of different known phenotypes will usually be used to adsorb several aliquots.

Given the number of potential alloantibodies, the task of selecting cells may appear formidable. In actuality, however, the selected cells need only demonstrate those few alloantibodies of clinical significance likely to be present. These include the common Rh antigens (D, C, E, c, and e), K, Fy^a and Fy^b, Jk^a and Jk^b, and S and s. Cell selection is made easier by the fact that cells can be rendered negative for some of these antigens by appropriate treatment prior to adsorption. Antibodies to other antigens are rare, detect low-incidence antigens, or have little clinical significance even if present. Antibodies to high-incidence antigens cannot be excluded by allogeneic adsorptions because the adsorbing cells will almost invariably express the antigen and adsorb the alloantibody along with autoantibody.

Patient's Phenotype Unknown. When the patient's Rh phenotype is not known, group O red cell samples of three different Rh phenotypes (R_1R_1, R_2R_2, and rr) should be selected. One should lack Jk^a and another Jk^b. If treated with ZZAP, these cells would lack all antigens of the Kell system and M, N, S, Fy^a, and Fy^b.

Each aliquot may need to be adsorbed two or three times. The fully adsorbed aliquots are tested against reagent red cells known either to lack or to carry common antigens of the Rh, MNS, Kidd, Kell, and Duffy blood group systems. If an adsorbed aliquot is reactive, that aliquot (or an additional specimen similarly adsorbed) should be tested to identify the antibody. Adsorbing several aliquots with different red cell samples provides a battery of potentially informative specimens. For example, if the aliquot adsorbed with Jk(a–) red cells subsequently reacts only with Jk(a+) red cells, the presence of alloanti-Jk^a can confidently be inferred.

The adsorbed serum can also be used for crossmatching. If the quantity of adsorbed serum is limited, crossmatching may be a more advantageous use than antibody identification; if necessary, adsorbed aliquots may be pooled for compatibility tests.

If ZZAP is not available, cells treated only with proteolytic enzyme can be used, but at least one of the adsorbing cells must be K-negative because Kell system antigens will not be destroyed. Untreated cells may be used, but antibody will be more difficult to remove and the adsorbing cells must, at a minimum, include at least one negative for the S, s, Fy^a, Fy^b, and K antigens in addition to the Rh and Kidd requirements above.

Patient's Phenotype Known. The number of different red cell phenotypes required may be reduced if the patient's phenotype is known or can be determined by separation of autologous from transfused red cells (see Method 2.15). If the patient's Rh and Kidd phenotypes are known or can be determined, adsorption can be performed with a single sample of allogeneic ZZAP-treated red cells of the same Rh and Kidd phenotypes as the patient.

Problems Encountered. Occasionally autoantibody will not be removed by three sequential adsorptions. Further adsorptions can be done, but multiple adsorptions are likely to dilute the serum. If the adsorbing cells do not appear to remove the antibody, the autoantibody may have an unusual specificity that does not react with the cells used for adsorption. For example, autoantibodies with Kell specificity would not be removed by ZZAP-treated cells. Some anti-En^a, -Wr^b, or other antibodies may not react with cells treated with ZZAP or proteolytic enzymes. (See Table 19-4.)

Autoantibodies Mimicking Alloantibodies

Autoantibodies sometimes have patterns of reactivity that are easily mistaken for alloantibody. For example, the serum of a D-negative patient may have apparent anti-C and -e reactivity. The anti-C reactivity may reflect warm-reactive autoantibody even if the patient's cells lack C. The autoantibody nature of the reactivity can be demonstrated by autologous and allogeneic adsorption studies. The apparent alloanti-C would, in this case, be

adsorbed by C-negative red cells, both autologous and allogeneic. This is quite unlike the behavior of a true alloanti-C, which would be adsorbed only by C-positive red cells. In one study, the serum prepared from an initial auto-adsorption would identify alloantibody and autoantibodies mimicking alloantibodies, where serum prepared from an initial allo-adsorption identified most often only alloantibodies. The differences in antibody specificities detected between the auto-adsorbed serum and the alloadsorbed serum probably is a reflection of weaken red cell antigens on autologous adsorbing cells, for which the autoantibody is directed.[40]

Detection of Alloantibodies in the Presence of Cold-Reactive Autoantibodies

Cold-reactive autoagglutinins rarely mask clinically significant alloantibodies if serum tests are conducted at 37 C and if IgG-specific reagents are used for the antiglobulin phase. In rare instances it may be necessary to perform autoadsorption at 4 C (see Method 4.6). Achieving the complete removal of potent cold-reactive autoagglutinins is very time-consuming and may be facilitated by treating the patient's cells with ZZAP or enzymes before adsorption.

If autologous adsorption studies are inappropriate because the patient has been recently transfused or if complete removal of the autoantibody is not possible, tests for alloantibody activity may be carried out *strictly* at 37 C. Both the patient's serum and the reagent red cells should be warmed to 37 C before mixing. The tests should be centrifuged at 37 C. If centrifugation at 37 C is impossible and if time permits, tests can be incubated at 37 C for 1-2 hours to allow the red cells to settle, and they can then be examined for agglutination without centrifugation. Because bovine albumin and other enhancement media increase the reactivity of cold-reactive autoantibodies, their use should be avoided. The red cells should be washed in saline at 37 C and then tested with anti-IgG to avoid the effects of in-vitro complement binding by the cold-reactive autoantibody. EDTA-anticoagulated plasma or serum to which EDTA has been added (2 mL of serum plus 0.25 mL of 4.45% K$_2$EDTA)[41] can also be used to avoid interference by complement-binding autoantibodies.

Drug-Induced Immune Hemolytic Anemias

Drugs sometimes induce the formation of antibodies, either against the drug itself or against intrinsic red cell antigens that may result in a positive DAT, immune red cell destruction, or both. Some of the antibodies produced appear to be dependent on the presence of the drug for their detection or destructive capability while others do not. In some instances, a reactive DAT may result from nonimmunologic effects of the drugs.

The patient's medications may include over-the-counter medications and others not prescribed by a physician. Environmental chemicals can cause similar serologic and clinical effects. These include chlorinated hydrocarbons (found in insecticides) and chemicals used in dyes and manufacturing processes.

Theories of the Immune Response and Drug-Dependent Antibodies

Numerous theories have been suggested to explain how drugs induce immune responses and what relation such responses may have to the positive DAT and immune-mediated cell destruction observed in some patients. For many years, drug-associated positive DATs were classified into four mechanisms: drug adsorption, immune complex formation, nonspecific adsorption, and autoantibody production. Such classification has been useful, but many aspects lacked definitive proof or detailed mechanisms. These theories were further complicated by evidence that some drugs created immune problems involving aspects of more than one mechanism. More recent theories, still unproved, tend toward a more comprehensive approach applicable to all drugs, allowing for differing manifestations.

Most drugs have a molecular weight substantially below the 5-kD level usually considered the threshold for effective immunogenicity. Drugs may act as haptens, eliciting antibody only after they bind firmly to or become part of a protein carrier. Most drugs associated with an immune response react very weakly with cellular proteins, but drug-induced immune responses often show extraordinary specificity to particular cellular targets, such as red cells or platelets. This exquisite specificity renders less plausible the classic explanation of induction by the hapten carrier.

Current theories[42-46] propose that drugs elicit antibodies based on their ability to interact with specific cell membrane components, thus altering the normal components so that they are no longer recognized as self. A new configuration or "neoantigen" is produced, consisting of both drug and cell component. The host's immune system perceives this neoantigen as foreign. The antibody is produced directly against the neoantigen and not against a haptenic constituent.

This theory assumes that drugs bind with variable affinity to particular membrane components present on red cells, granulocytes, or platelets. The degree of association would be expected to reflect such factors as the chemical structure of the drug or its metabolite(s), the concentration of the drug, the structure of cellular membrane proteins, and the capacity of the host proteins to associate with the drug (possibly dependent on pH, temperature, ionic strength and, most probably, host genetic factors). Because conditions must be just right to create a sufficiently high affinity to provoke an immune response, instances of drug-induced immunity are relatively rare.

The polyclonal immune response provoked by such a configuration consists of antibodies that can recognize at least three categories of epitopes. Some react essentially with the drug portion itself, some with combinations of the drug and cellular component, and others with essentially cellular membrane components (see Fig 20-1). In some cases red cells or other specific cell types are the sole or primary targets, while at other times a variety of cell types may be affected. Why certain drugs repeatedly target single or multiple cell lines is not always clear.

Serologic and Clinical Classification

Drug-induced antibodies can be classified into three groups according to their clinical and serologic characteristics. In one group, the drug binds firmly to the cell membrane and antibody is apparently largely directed against the drug itself. This is known as the drug adsorption mechanism. Antibodies to penicillin are the best described of this group.

The second group of drug-dependent antibodies reacts with drugs that do not bind well to the cell membrane. The reactive mechanism of these antibodies was previously described as immune complex formation, but this appears not quite to be the case. Antibodies in this group cause acute intravascular hemolysis but may be difficult to demonstrate serologically.

Antibodies of the third group have serologic reactivity independent of the drug, despite the fact that it was the drug that originally induced the immune response. Serologically, they behave as autoantibodies.

These drugs, especially cephalosporins, are associated with a positive DAT resulting from nonimmune mechanisms. In particular, first-generation cephalosporins alter the red cell membrane in a way that induces nonspecific adsorption of proteins, including but not limited to immunoglobulins. Hemolytic anemia is not usually associated with this mechanism.

Drug-Dependent Antibodies Reactive with Cell-Bound Drug: Penicillin-Type Antibodies

Drugs with a high binding affinity may induce a seemingly drug-specific immune response. The high degree of association with the cellular component(s) may cause the drug to act as a true hapten. These drugs with very high bind-

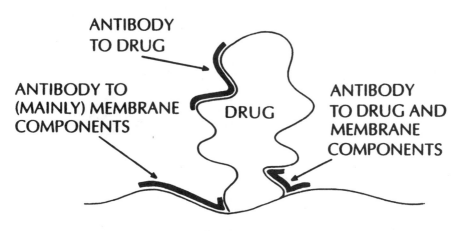

RED CELL MEMBRANE

Figure 20-1. Proposed unifying theory of drug-induced antibody reactions (based on a cartoon by Habibi as cited by Garratty[26]). The thicker darker lines represent antigen-binding sites on the F(ab) region of the drug-induced antibody. Drugs (haptens) bind loosely, or firmly, to cell membranes and antibodies may be made to: a) the drug [producing in-vitro reactions typical of a drug adsorption (penicillin-type) reaction]; b) membrane components, or mainly membrane components (producing in-vitro reactions typical of autoantibody); or c) part-drug, part-membrane components (producing an in-vitro reaction typical of the so-called immune complex mechanism).[26(p55)]

ing affinity may be more immunogenic than drugs that bind to cell membrane components with lower affinity. Because the antibodies produced are directed predominantly to the drug (hapten) itself, they can be expected to be inhibitable by a pure form of the drug (ie, hapten inhibition) and may require that the drug be bound to a solid matrix detection system (ie, red cells) for in-vitro detection.

Such drugs have previously been classified as reacting by the drug adsorption mechanism, with penicillin antibodies the primary example (see Fig 20-2). Hemolytic examples of antipenicillin are not always completely inhib-

ited with pure penicillin. This may reflect the need of these very high titers of antibody for a very high hapten concentration to cause complete inhibition. If this occurs, the in-vitro serologic reactions resemble both the drug adsorption and "immune complex" mechanisms.

General Observations. The clinical and laboratory features of drug-induced immune hemolytic anemia operating through this mechanism are:

1. The DAT is strongly positive due to IgG coating. Complement coating may also be present but weak.

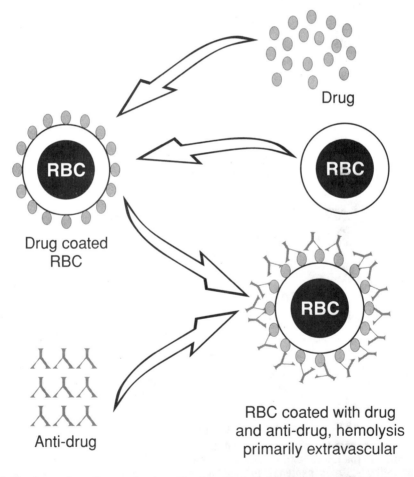

Figure 20-2. The drug-adsorption mechanism. The drug binds tightly to the red cell membrane proteins. If a patient develops a potent anti-drug antibody, it will react with the cell-bound drug. Such rbcs will yield a positive result in the DAT using anti-IgG reagents. Complement is usually not activated and lysis is primarily extravascular in nature. Penicillin-G is the prototype drug.

2. Tests for unexpected serum antibodies are nonreactive unless the patient also has alloantibodies to red cell antigens.
3. Antibody eluted from the red cells reacts with drug-coated red cells but not with uncoated red cells.
4. The serum contains a high-titer IgG antibody, at least when the target is penicillin.
5. Hemolysis occurs only in patients receiving very large intravenous doses of drug; for penicillin, the hemolysis-inducing dose is millions of units daily for a week or more.
6. Hemolysis develops gradually but may be life-threatening if the etiology is unrecognized and drug administration is continued.
7. Discontinuation of the drug is usually followed by increased cell survival, although hemolysis of decreasing severity may persist for several weeks.

Penicillin Antibodies. Approximately 3% of patients receiving large doses of penicillin intravenously (ie, millions of units per day) will develop a positive DAT; only occasionally will these patients develop hemolytic anemia.[7(p231)] Intravascular hemolysis is rare. A possible mechanism for the positive DAT is given in Fig 20-2. The penicillin becomes covalently linked to the red cells in vivo. If the patient has antibodies to penicillin, they bind to the penicillin bound to the red cells. The result is that the penicillin-coated red cells become coated with IgG. Complement is not usually involved. If cell destruction occurs, it takes place extravascularly, probably in the same way that red cells coated with IgG alloantibodies are destroyed.

Drugs such as penicillin have several distinct haptenic groups, of which the most immunogenic is the benzyl-penicilloyl (BPO) group. IgM or IgG antibodies reactive with penicillin-coated red cells have been found in 4% of normal subjects.[7(p231)] The high prevalence of penicillin antibodies in the normal population probably reflects the widespread exposure to this drug. Circulating IgM and IgG antibodies to

penicillin are not involved in allergic reactions to the drug, which are due to IgE antibodies.

Cephalosporins. Cephalosporin drugs, which are related to penicillins, may behave in a similar manner. The drugs bind firmly to red cells, which then interact with the specific cephalosporin antibody. Anticephalosporins may cross-react with penicillin-treated red cells, but cells prepared with the specific cephalosporin may be necessary to demonstrate reactivity.

The cephalosporins are generally classified by "generations," based on their effectiveness against gram-negative organisms (see Table 20-5). Approximately 4% of patients receiving first- or second-generation cephalosporins develop a positive DAT.[47] Some series have reported a higher prevalence, possibly due to drug dosages or the different AHG reagents used. It has been suggested that positive DATs, especially those seen with first-generation cephalosporins, reflect nonimmunologic adsorption of protein (see below), a mechanism not associated with reduced red cell survival. There have been occasional reports of red cell destruction resulting from treatment with first- and second-generation cephalosporins, probably resulting from effects of specific anticephalosporin antibodies. Even more dramatically reduced red cell survival has been associated with newer second- and third-generation cephalosporins, and in some cases a drug-independent autoantibody mechanism may also be involved.[46,48-50] The prevalence and severity of cephalosporin-induced immune red cell destruction appear to be increasing.

Other Drug-Dependent Antibodies: "Immune Complex" Mechanism

This mechanism is the least frequent finding in drug-induced immune-mediated red cell destruction. Quinidine and phenacetin are prototype drugs. The following observations are characteristic:

1. Acute intravascular hemolysis with hemoglobinemia and hemoglobinuria is

Table 20-5. Some Cephalosporins

Generic Name	Trade Name[*]
First Generation	
Cefadroxil	Duricef
Cefazolin	Ancef, Kefzol
Cephalexin	Keflex
Cepalothin	Keflin
Cephapirin	Cefadyl
Cephradine	Anspor
Second Generation	
Cefaclor	Ceclor
Cefamandole	Mandol
Cefmetazole	Zefazone
Cefonicid	Monocid
Cefotetan	Cefotan
Cefoxitin	Mefoxin
Cefprozil	Cefzil
Cefuroxime	Zinacef, Kefurox
Cefuroxime axetil	Ceftin
Intermediate	
Cefixime	Suprax
Third Generation	
Cefoperazone	Cefobid
Cefotaxime	Claforan
Ceftazidime	Fortaz, Ceptaz, Pentacef, Tazicef, Tazidime
Ceftizoxime	Cefizox
Ceftriaxone	Rocephin
Moxalactam	Moxam

[*]Several forms are also marketed under other trade names. This list is intended to be informational, not inclusive.

the usual presentation. Renal failure occurs in approximately 50% of cases.

2. Once antibody has been formed, severe hemolytic episodes may recur after exposure to very small quantities of the drug.
3. The antibody can be either IgM or IgG.
4. Complement may be the only globulin easily detected on the red cells.
5. Drug must be present in vitro for demonstration of the antibody in the patient's serum.

Many drugs have been implicated as causing immune hemolysis, yet most are represented by only one or a few examples. The immune hemolysis was previously attributed to the formation of drug/antidrug immune complexes that interacted loosely and nonspecifically with the red cells, resulting in the binding of complement and red cell lysis.

The neoantigen concept proposes that these drugs do, in fact, associate with the cell membrane, although not with high affinity. The neoantigen, composed partly of drug and partly of membrane components, constitutes the stimulus to antibody formation and the target of antibodies once formed (see Fig 20-1).

The distinction between these "immune complex" drug-dependent reactions and those of the "drug-adsorption" mechanism may be more apparent than real.[51] Classification depends largely on the ability to bind the implicated drug to red cells in vitro for testing.

Drug-Independent Antibodies: Autoantibody Production

Some drugs induce autoantibodies that appear serologically indistinguishable from those of WAIHA. Red cells are coated with IgG, and the eluate as well as the serum react with virtually all cells tested in the absence of the drug. Blood group specificity has been demonstrated at times, similar to that seen in AIHA. The antibody has no in-vitro activity with the drug, directly, or indirectly.

The best studied of such cases are those induced by α-methyldopa. A closely related drug, L-dopa, has also been implicated as have several drugs unrelated to α-methyldopa, including procainamide and nonsteroidal anti-inflammatory drugs (eg, mefenamic acid and sulindac). (See Table 20-6.) In some cases drug-dependent antibodies are also present.

Proof that a drug causes autoantibody production is difficult to obtain. Sufficient evidence would include: demonstration that autoantibody production began after drug administration; resolution of the immune process after withdrawal of the drug; *and* recurrence of hemolytic anemia or autoantibodies if the drug is readministered. The last requirement is crucial and the most difficult to demonstrate.

Possible Mechanisms. Previous theories to explain autoantibody formation include:

1. The drug alters an intrinsic red cell antigen so that it is no longer recognized as self by the immune system.
2. The drug interferes with suppressor T-cell function, allowing overproduction of autoantibody by B cells.[52] Studies attempting to confirm this theory have given mixed results.[46,52]
3. The hemolytic autoantibody is qualitatively different or recognizes a slightly different epitope from the nonhemolytic autoantibody found in the majority of DAT-positive patients receiving α-methyldopa.

Current theories suggest that the drugs bind to the cell membrane and/or subtly alter membrane structures, forming a neoantigen. The autoantibodies produced are those directed against membrane components of the neoantigen, which are crossreactive with the drug and do not require it for subsequent reactivity. Blood group specificity may occur if antigens present on the cell are involved with the neoantigen.[48] With some drugs, drug-dependent antibodies have been shown in addition to drug-independent autoantibodies. Such drug-dependent antibodies have not been demonstrated with α-methyldopa, procainamide, or mefenamic acid, suggesting that at least two different mechanisms may possibly be involved.[46]

α-Methyldopa. The prototype drug responsible for this mechanism, α-methyldopa, is now rarely prescribed, as more effective antihypertensive drugs with fewer side effects have become available. The clinical and laboratory features associated with α-methyldopa-induced autoantibodies are as follows[51,53,54]:

1. Approximately 15% of patients receiving α-methyldopa develop a positive DAT. Only 0.5-1.0% of patients taking α-methyldopa develop hemolytic anemia.
2. The DAT becomes positive only after 3-6 months of α-methyldopa therapy.
3. Red cells are usually coated only with IgG; weak complement coating has been reported occasionally.
4. Development of a positive DAT is dose dependent; approximately 36% of patients taking 3 g of the drug daily develop a positive DAT, compared with 11% of patients receiving 1 g per day.
5. Antibodies in the serum and on the red cells are indistinguishable from those found in WAIHA.

Table 20-6. Some Drugs That May Induce Drug-Independent Antibodies (Autoantibodies)

α-Methyldopa	Cianidanol*	Levodopa
Azapropazone*	Chlorpromazine	Mefenamic acid
Carbimazole*	Cyclofenil	Nomifensine*
Catergen	Diclofenac*	Phenacetin*
Cefotetan*	Fenfluramine	Procainamide
Cefoxitin*	Glafenine*	Streptomycin*
Chaparral	Ibuprofen	Teniposide*
Chlorinated hydrocarbons*	Latamoxef*	Tolmetin*

*These drugs may also induce drug-dependent antibodies.

6. The strength of the positive DAT becomes progressively weaker once α-methyldopa therapy is discontinued. It may take from 1 month to 2 years for the DAT to revert, but in patients with clinical hemolysis, hematologic values usually improve within a week or so after the drug therapy is discontinued.

Nonimmunologic Protein Adsorption

The positive DAT associated with some drugs is due to a mechanism independent of antibody production. Hemolytic anemia associated with this mechanism occurs extremely rarely, if at all.

Cephalosporins (primarily cephalothin) are the drugs with which this was originally associated. Red cells coated with cephalothin (Keflin) and incubated with normal plasma will adsorb albumin, IgA, IgG, IgM, and β, and α (ie, complement) globulins in a nonimmunologic manner. If this occurs, a positive indirect antiglobulin test (IAT) will be seen with AHG reagents to many serum proteins, not only anti-IgG or anti-C3.

It has been suggested that these drugs altered the red cell membrane in some way, making the cells adsorb proteins nonspecifically. A different mechanism has been proposed[55] that suggests cephalothin can bind firmly to red cells in vitro at acid pH by a mechanism unlike that of other β-lactam antibiotics. This alternative binding method leaves exposed a β-lactam moiety of the molecule, to which several proteins can then become bound.

In addition to this nonimmune adsorption of proteins, the cephalosporins can also induce a positive DAT by the drug adsorption mechanism described for penicillin by the so-called immune complex mechanism and by the production of drug-independent autoantibodies (see above). Newer generations of cephalosporins (see Table 20-5) have been associated with severe immune hemolysis.[46,50,51]

Other drugs that may cause nonimmunologic adsorption of proteins and a positive DAT include diglycoaldehyde, suramin, cisplatin, clavulante in Timentin, and sulbactam in Unasyn.[56]

Laboratory Investigation of Drug-Induced Antibodies

The drug-related problems most commonly encountered in the blood bank are those associated with a positive DAT. IgG- and complement-specific AHG reagents are useful in classifying cases of drug-related hemolysis. Typical DAT results are shown in Table 20-3. Drug-dependent antibodies characteristically bind only complement to the cells. Drugs, such as penicillin, that bind firmly to the cells and induce IgG antibodies are usually associated with IgG-only DAT results. Drug-independent antibodies induce serologic phenomena similar to those in AIHA of other etiologies. For investigation of suspected hemolysis due to drug-dependent antibodies, special methods are often required.

Adding Drug to the Test System

The patient's serum should be tested for unexpected antibodies by routine procedures. If the serum does not react with untreated red cells, the tests should be repeated against ABO-compatible red cells in the presence of the drug(s) suspected of causing the problem.

If the drug is one already reported as being immunogenic, testing methods may be available in the case reports. If such information is not available, an initial screening test can be performed with a solution of the drug at a concentration of approximately 1 mg/mL in phosphate-buffered saline at a pH optimal for solubility of the drug. Techniques are given in Method 4.14 and Method 4.15. For some drugs, a solvent other than saline may be required. The physical properties of drugs, such as solubility and stability, may be found in several drug reference books,[57] through consultation with the hospital pharmacist, or by contacting the pharmaceutical company. Detection of some drug-related antibodies can be enhanced if the implicated drug is added to wash solutions. The gel test has also been shown to be very sensitive in detecting drug-dependent antibodies.[58]

If these tests are not informative, attempts can be made to coat normal red cells with the drug, and the patient's serum and an eluate from the patient's red cells tested against the drug-coated red cells. This is the method of choice when penicillin or cephalosporins are thought to be implicated (see Method 4.13). Results definitive for penicillin-induced positive DAT are reactivity of the eluate against penicillin-coated red cells and absence of reactivity between the eluate and uncoated red cells. If the positive DAT is due to complement binding, the eluate is likely to be nonreactive even when the drug is added to the test system.

Other Observations

The actual molecule that induces the immune response may be a metabolite of a drug rather than the drug itself. It may be helpful to test drug metabolites for reactivity by one of the above methods, having obtained the metabolites by collecting serum or urine from other individuals taking the implicated drugs.

Drug-induced immune hemolysis has been associated with apparent blood group specificity. In some reported cases the drug apparently bound to cells in association with specific antigen receptors (eg, Jk^a, e, I).[51] Drugs involved have included chlorpropamide, glafenine, rifampicin, and nomifensine. Most other examples of immune hemolysis associated with these same drugs have not shown blood group specificity.

Drugs that have been reported to cause a positive DAT and hemolytic anemia are listed in Appendix 20-1.

References

1. Heddle N, Kelton JG, Turchyn KL, Ali MAM. Hypergammaglobulinemia can be associated with a positive direct antiglobulin test, a nonreactive eluate, and no evidence of hemolysis. Transfusion 1988;28:29-33.

2. Toy PT, Chin CA, Reid ME, Burns MA. Factors associated with positive direct antiglobulin tests in pretransfusion patients: A case control study. Vox Sang 1985;49:215-20.

3. Ramsey G. Red cell antibodies arising from solid organ transplants. Transfusion 1991;31:76-86.

4. Garratty G. The significance of IgG on the red cell surface. Transfus Med Rev 1987;1:47-57.

5. Freedman J. The significance of complement on the red cell surface. Transfus Med Rev 1987;1:58-70.

6. Judd WJ, Barnes BA, Steiner EA, et al. The evaluation of a positive direct antiglobulin test (autocontrol) in pretransfusion testing revisited. Transfusion 1986;26:220-4.

7. Mollison PL, Engelfriet CP, Contreras M. Blood transfusion in clinical medicine. 10th ed. Oxford, England: Blackwell Scientific Publications, 1997.

8. Clark JA, Tanley PC, Wallas CH. Evaluation of patients with positive direct antiglobulin tests and nonreactive eluates discovered during pretransfusion testing. Immunohematology 1992;8:9-12.

9. Menitove JE, ed. Standards for blood banks and transfusion services. 19th ed. Bethesda, MD: American Association of Blood Banks, 1999.

10. Johnson MFM, Belota MK. Determination of need for elution studies for positive direct antiglobulin tests in pretransfusion testing. Am J Clin Pathol 1988;90:58-62.

11. Kleinman S, Nelson R, Smith L, Goldfinger D. Positive direct antiglobulin tests and immune hemolytic anemia in patients receiving procainamide. N Engl J Med 1984;311:809-12.

12. Shulman IA, Petz LD. Red cell compatibility testing: Clinical significance and laboratory methods. In: Petz LD, Swisher SN, Kleinman S, et al, eds. Clinical practice of transfusion medicine. 3rd ed. New York: Churchill Livingstone, 1996:199-244.

13. Garratty G. Problems associated with passively transfused blood group alloantibodies. Am J Clin Pathol 1998;109:169-77.

14. Judd WJ. Antibody elution from red cells. In: Bell CA, ed. A seminar on antigen-antibody reactions revisited. Arlington, VA: American Association of Blood Banks, 1982:175-221.

15. Sigmund KE. Direct antiglobulin testing. In: Pierce SR, Wilson JK, eds. Approaches to serological problems in the hospital transfusion service. Arlington, VA: American Association of Blood Banks, 1985:101-33.

16. Petz LD. Blood transfusion in acquired hemolytic anemias. In: Petz LD, Swisher SN, Kleinman S, et al, eds. Clinical practice of transfusion medicine. 3rd ed. New York: Churchill Livingstone, 1996:469-99.

17. Packman CH, Leddy JP. Acquired hemolytic anemia due to warm-reacting autoantibodies. In: Beutler E, Lichtman MA, Coller BS, Kipps TJ, eds. Williams' hematology. 5th ed. New York: McGraw-Hill, 1995:677-85.

18. Packman CH, Leddy JP. Cryopathic hemolytic syndromes. In: Beutler E, Lichtman MA, Coller BS, Kipps TJ, eds. Williams' hematology. 5th ed. New York: McGraw-Hill, 1995:685-91.

19. Sokol RJ, Hewitt S, Stamps BK. Autoimmune haemolysis: An 18 year study of 865 cases referred to a regional transfusion centre. Br Med J 1981;282:2023-7.

20. Petz LD, Garratty G. Acquired immune hemolytic anemias. New York: Churchill Livingstone, 1980.

21. Shulman IA, Branch DR, Nelson JM, et al. Autoimmune hemolytic anemia with both cold and warm autoantibodies. JAMA 1985;253:1746-8.

22. Bilgrami S, Cable R, Pisciotto P, et al. Fatal disseminated intravascular coagulation and pulmonary thrombosis following blood transfusion in a patient with severe autoimmune hemolytic anemia and human immunodeficiency virus infection. Transfusion 1994;34:248-52.

23. Petz LD, Branch DR. Serological tests for the diagnosis of immune hemolytic anemias. In: McMillan R, ed. Methods in hematology: Immune cytopenias. New York: Churchill Livingstone, 1983:9-48.

24. Sokol RJ, Hewitt S, Stamps BK. Autoimmune haemolysis. Mixed warm and cold antibody type. Acta Haematol 1983;69:266-74.

25. Branch Dr, Shulman IA, Sy Siok Hian AL, Petz LD. Two district categories of warm autoantibody reactivity with age-fractionated red cells. Blood 1984;63:177-80.

26. Garratty G. Target antigens for red-cell-bound autoantibodies. In: Nance SJ, ed. Clinical and basic science aspects of immunohematology. Arlington, VA: American Association of Blood Banks, 1991:33-72.

27. Telen MJ, Roberts KB, Bartlett JA. HIV-associated autoimmune hemolytic anemia: Report of a case and review of the literature. J Acquir Immune Defic Syndr 1990;3:933-7.

28. Freedman J, Wright J, Lim FC, Garvey MB. Hemolytic warm IgM autoagglutinins in autoimmune hemolytic anemia. Transfusion 1986;26:464-7.

29. Ness PM, Shirey RS, Thomas SK, Buck SA. The differentiation of delayed serologic and delayed hemolytic transfusion reactions: Incidence, long-term serologic findings, and clinical significance. Transfusion 1990;30:688-93.

30. Judd WJ. Investigation and management of immune hemolysis: Autoantibodies and drugs. In: Wallace ME, Levitt JS, eds. Current applications and interpretations of the direct antiglobulin test. Arlington, VA: American Association of Blood Banks, 1988:47-103.

31. Leger RM, Garratty G. Evaluation of methods for detecting alloantibodies underlying warm autoantibodies. Transfusion 1999;39:11-6.

32. Branch DR, Petz LD. Detecting alloantibodies in patients with autoantibodies (editorial). Transfusion 1999;39:6-10.

33. Garratty G, Petz LD, Hoops JK. The correlation of cold agglutinin titrations in saline and albumin with haemolytic anemia. Br J Haematol 1975;35:587-95.

34. Marks MR, Reid ME, Ellisor SS. Adsorption of unwanted cold autoagglutinins by formalde-hyde-treated rabbit erythrocytes (abstract). Transfusion 1980;20:629.

35. Dzik W, Yang R, Blank J. Rabbit erythrocyte stroma treatment of serum interferes with recognition of delayed hemolytic transfusion reactions (letter). Transfusion 1986;26:303-4.

36. Kaji E, Miura Y, Ikemoto S. Characterization of autoantibodies in mixed-type autoimmune hemolytic anemia. Vox Sang 1991;60:45-52.

37. Garratty G, Postoway N, Nance SJ, Brunt DJ. Spontaneous agglutination of red cells with a positive direct antiglobulin test in various media. Transfusion 1984;24:214-7.

38. Branch DR, Petz LD. A new reagent (ZZAP) having multiple applications in immunohematology. Am J Clin Pathol 1982;78:161-7.

39. Byrne PC. Use of a modified acid/EDTA elution technique. Immunohematology 1991;7:46-7.

40. Issitt PD, Coombs MR, Bumgarner DJ, et al. Studies of antibodies in the sera of patients who have made red cell autoantibodies. Transfusion 1996;36:481-6.

41. Issitt PD, Smith TR. Evaluation of antiglobulin reagents. In: Myhre BA, ed. A seminar on performance evaluation. Washington, DC: American Association of Blood Banks, 1976:25-73.

42. Salama A, Müeller-Eckhardt C. Immune-mediated blood cell dyscrasias related to drugs. Semin Hematol 1992;29:54-63.

43. Petz LD, Müeller-Eckhardt C. Drug-induced immune hemolytic anemia. Transfusion 1992;32:202-4.

44. Shulman NR, Reid DM. Mechanisms of drug-induced immunologically mediated cytopenias. Transfus Med Rev 1993;7:215-29.

45. Christie DJ. Specificity of drug-induced immune cytopenias. Transfus Med Rev 1993;7:230-41.

46. Garratty G. Drug-induced immune hemolytic anemia. In: Garratty G, ed. Immunobiology of transfusion medicine. New York: Marcel Dekker, 1994:523-51.

47. Spath P, Garratty G, Petz LD. Studies on the immune response to penicillin and cephalothin in humans: 1. Optimal conditions for titration of hemagglutinating penicillin and cephalothin antibodies. J Immunol 1971;107:845-58.

48. Gallagher NI, Achergen ML, Sokol-Anderson ML, et al. Severe immune-mediated hemolytic anemia secondary to treatment with cefotetan. Transfusion 1992;32:266-8.

49. Garratty G, Nance S, Lloyd M, Domen R. Fatal immune hemolytic anemia due to cefotetan. Transfusion 1992;32:269-71.

50. Garratty G. Immune cytopenias associated with antibiotics. Transfus Med Rev 1993;7:255-67.

51. Packman CH, Leddy JP. Drug-related immune hemolytic anemia. In: Beutler E, Lichtman MA, Coller BS, Kipps TJ, eds. Williams' hematology. 5th ed. New York: McGraw-Hill, 1995:691-7.

52. Kirtland HH III, Mohler DN, Horwitz DA. Methyldopa inhibition of suppressor lymphocyte function. A proposed cause of autoimmune hemolytic anemia. N Engl J Med 1980;302:825-32.

53.   Gilliland BC. Autoimmune hemolytic anemia. In: Rossi EC, Simon TL, Moss GS, Gould SA, eds. Principles of transfusion medicine. 2nd ed. Baltimore, MD: Williams and Wilkins, 1996:101-20.

54.   Klohe EP, Myers TA. Methyldopa inhibits T cell activation and proliferation. Transfusion 1994; 34(Suppl):78S.

55.   Petz LD, Branch DR. Drug-induced immune hemolytic anemia. In: Chaplin H, ed. Methods in hematology: Immune hemolytic anemias. New York: Churchill Livingstone, 1985:47-94.

56.   Garratty G, Arndt PA. Positive direct antoglobulin test and haemolytic anemia following therapy with beta-lactamase inhibitor containing drugs may be associated with nonimmunologic adsorption of protein onto red blood cells. Br J Haematol 1998;100:777-83.

57.   Budvari S, ed. The Merck index. 12th ed. Rahway, NJ: Merck & Co, 1996.

58.   Salama A, Berghöfer H, Müeller-Eckhardt C. Detection of cell-drug (hapten)-antibody complexes by the gel test. Transfusion 1992;32:554-6.

Suggested Reading

Dacie JV. Autoimmune anemia. Arch Intern Med 1975;135:1293-300.

Dacie JV. The haemolytic anemias. Congenital and acquired. II. The auto-immune anemias. 3rd ed. London: J & A Churchill Ltd, 1985.

Engelfriet CP, Overbeeke MAM, von dem Borne AEGKr. Autoimmune hemolytic anemia. Semin Hematol 1992;29:3-12.

Pirofsky B. Autoimmunization and the autoimmune hemolytic anemias. Baltimore: Williams and Wilkins, 1969.

Wallace ME, Levitt JS, eds. Current applications and interpretations of the direct antiglobulin test. Arlington, VA: American Association of Blood Banks, 1988.

Worlledge SM, Blajchman MA. The autoimmune haemolytic anemias. Br J Haematol 1972;23(Suppl): 61-9.

Appendix 20-1. Some Drugs Associated with Immune Hemolysis and/or Positive DATs Due to Drug-Induced Antibodies

Drug	Therapeutic Category	Possible Mechanism
Acetaminophen	Analgesic, antipyretic	DD-IC
Aminopyrine	Analgesic, antipyretic	DD-IC
Amphotericin B	Antifungal, antibiotic	DD-IC
Ampicillin	Antibacterial	DD-IC
Antazoline	Antihistamine	DD-IC
Apazone (azapropazone)	Anti-inflammatory, analgesic	DI, DD-DA
Buthiazide (butizide)	Diuretic, antihypertensive	DD-IC
Carbenicillin	Antibacterial	DD-DA
Carbimazole	Thyroid inhibitor	DD-IC
Carboplatin	Antineoplastic	DD-DA, DD-IC
Carbromal	Sedative; hypnotic	DD-DA
Catergen	Diarrheal astringent, treatment of hepatic disease	DI
Cephalosporins	Antibacterials	
First generation		NIA, DD-DA
Second generation		DD-IC, DD-DA, DI
Third generation		DD-IC, DD-DA, DI
Chaparral		DI
Chlorpropamide	Antidiabetic	DD-IC
Chlorpromazine	Antipsychotic	DI, DD-IC
Cisplatin	Antineoplastic	NIA
Cladribine (chlorodeoxyadenosine)	Antineoplastic	DI
Clavulanate potassium	β-lactamase inhibitor/antibacterial	NIA
Cyanidanol		DI, DD-DA, DD-IC
Cyclofenil	Gonad-stimulating principle	DI
Cyclosporine	Immunosuppressive	DI
Diclofenac	Anti-inflammatory	DI, DD-IC
Diethylstilbestrol	Estrogen	DD-IC
Diglycoaldehyde	Antineoplastic	NIA
Dipyrone	Analgesic, antipyretic	DD-IC, DD-DA
Erythromycin	Antibacterial	DD-DA
Etodolac	Anti-inflammatory, analgesic	IC
Fenfluramine	Anorectic	?
Fenoprofen	Anti-inflammatory, analgesic	DI, DD-IC
Fludarabine	Antineoplastic	DI
Fluorescein	Injectable dye	DD-DA, DD-IC
Fluorouracil	Antineoplastic	DD-IC
Glafenine	Analgesic	DI, DD-IC
Hydralazine	Antihypertensive	DD-IC
Hydrochlorothiazide	Diuretic	DD-IC
Elliptinium acetate	Antineoplastic	DD-IC
Ibuprofen	Anti-inflammatory	DI
Insulin	Antidiabetic	DD-DA?, DD-IC
Interferon	Antineoplastic, antiviral	DI
Isoniazid	Antibacterial, tuberculostatic	DD-DA?, DD-IC
Levodopa	Antiparkinsonian, anticholinergic	DI
Mefenamic acid	Anti-inflammatory	DI
Mefloquine	Antimalarial	DD-IC

Appendix 20-1. Some Drugs Associated with Immune Hemolysis and/or Positive DATs Due to Drug-Induced Antibodies (cont'd)

Drug	Therapeutic Category	Possible Mechanism
Melphalan	Antineoplastic	DD-IC
6-Mercaptopurine	Antineoplastic	DD-DA
Methadone	Narcotic analgesic	?
Methicillin	Antibacterial	DD-DA
Methotrexate	Antineoplastic, antimetabolite	DD-IC
Methyldopa	Antihypertensive	DI
Moxalactam (latamoxef)	Antibacterial	DD-IC, DI
Nafcillin	Antibacterial	DD-DA
Nomifensine	Antidepressant	DI, DD-IC
p-Aminosalicylic acid	Antitubercular	DD-IC
Penicillin G	Antibacterial	DD-DA
Phenacetin	Analgesic, antipyretic	DI, DD-IC
Piperacillin	Antibacterial	DD-DA, DD-IC
Podophyllotoxin	Antineoplastic, cathartic	?
Probenecid	Uricosuric	DD-IC
Procainamide	Cardiac depressant, antiarrhythmic	DI
Propyphenazone	Analgesic, antipyretic, anti-inflammatory	DD-IC
Pyramidon		DD-IC
Quinidine	Cardiac depressant, antiarrhythmic	DD-DA, DD-IC
Quinine	Antimalarial	DD-IC
Ranitidine	Antagonist (to histamine H_2 receptors)	
Rifampin (rifampicin)	Antibacterial, antitubercular	DD-IC
Sodium Pentothal	Anesthetic	DD-IC
Stibophen	Antischistosomal	DD-IC
Streptomycin	Antibacterial, tuberculostatic	DI, DD-DA, DD-IC
Sulbactam sodium	β-lactamase inhibitor/antibacterial	NIA
Sulfonamides	Antibiotics	DD-IC
Sulfonylurea derivatives	Antidiabetic	DD-IC
Sulindac	Anti-inflammatory	DD-DA, DI
Suprofen	Anti-inflammatory, analgesic	DD-IC, DI
Suramin	Antitrypanosomal, antifilarial	NIA
Temafloxacin	Antibacterial	DD-IC
Teniposide	Antineoplastic	DI, DD-IC
Tetracycline	Antibacterial, antirickettsial, antiamebic	DD-DA?, DD-IC
Thiopental	Anesthetic	DD-IC
Tolbutamide	Antidiabetic	DD-DA
Tolmetin	Anti-inflammatory	DI, DD-IC
Triamterene	Diuretic	DD-IC
Trimellitic anhydride	Used in preparation of dyes, resins, etc	?
Zomepirac	Analgesic, anti-inflammatory	DD-DA, DD-IC, DI

Mechanisms listed are based on descriptions in the literature.[39-43,47,50]

DAT = Direct antiglobulin test.

DI = Drug-independent. Associated with autoantibodies similar to those in AIHA. Drug not required for in-vitro demonstration. Mechanisms of autoantibody production may vary.

DD-DA = Drug-dependent. Drug adsorbed onto red cells; antibody reacts with drug on cells.

DD-IC = Drug-dependent. "Immune complex mechanism." Requires drug, serum, and red cells for serologic demonstration. For most of these drugs there are only single or very few case reports.

NIA = Nonimmunologic adsorption of proteins.

? = Mechanism unclear or unknown.

21

Blood Transfusion Practice

21

BLOOD COMPONENT THERAPY administered for appropriate medical indications should result in a therapeutic benefit. Even when therapy is indicated, adverse outcomes may follow hemotherapy. Therefore, transfusion should be undertaken only if the anticipated benefit outweighs the potential risks. This chapter discusses physiologic principles, types of components, indications for use, and contraindications for use for transfusion of red cells, platelets, plasma, granulocytes, and cryoprecipitate. Also addressed are pharmacologic alternatives to transfusion and special transfusion situations.

Where applicable, transfusion services must be in compliance with Food and Drug Administration (FDA) and Health Care Financing Administration (HCFA) rules and regulations. In a hospital, there should be a medical staff committee overseeing transfusion practices; the medical director of the transfusion service should be a member of the committee. This committee should review blood bank activities and statistics and review records of patients transfused with blood or components. The committee should monitor significant developments in transfusion medicine that would affect patients in the health-care institution. The American Association of Blood Banks, the Joint Commission on Accreditation of Healthcare Organizations, and the College of American Pathologists all offer guidelines or standards for voluntary compliance and peer-reviewed educational certification programs to assist transfusion services in providing safe quality service.

Red Blood Cell Transfusion

Physiologic Principles

The primary indication for transfusion of Red Blood Cells (RBCs) is to restore or maintain oxygen-carrying capacity to meet tissue demands. Because demand for oxygen varies greatly among different individuals in different clinical circumstances, a single laboratory measurement (the hematocrit or the hemoglobin) cannot accurately assess the need for transfusion.[1,2]

Normal Oxygen Supply and Demand

Tissues at rest have a constant demand for oxygen. (See Table 21-1.) The oxygen content of blood (mL O_2/mL blood) is determined by the hemoglobin concentration, the binding coefficient of oxygen for normal hemoglobin, the oxygen saturation of hemoglobin (%), and the quantity of oxygen dissolved in the plasma. This is described as:

$$O_2 \text{ content} = (Hb \times 1.39 \times \%\text{sat}) + (pO_2 \times 0.003)$$

Tissue oxygen consumption is calculated as the difference between oxygen delivery in the arterial blood and oxygen return by the venous blood:

$$O_2 \text{ consumption} = \text{Cardiac output} \times Hb \times 1.39 \times (\%\text{sat}_{arterial} - \%\text{sat}_{venous})/100$$

which is expressed as

$$(\text{mL } O_2/\text{minute}) = \text{L/minute} \times g/L \times \text{mL } O_2/g$$

The oxygen saturation of arterial and venous hemoglobin varies with the partial pressure of oxygen dissolved in the plasma. Under normal circumstances, the pO_2 falls from 100 mm Hg in the arteries to 40 mm Hg in the veins as the tissues extract oxygen, and hemoglobin saturation falls from near 100% in the arteries to approximately 75% in the veins. Under normal circumstances, the oxygen extraction ratio is 0.25, ie, the hemoglobin "gives up" only 25% of its oxygen. When tissue demand for oxygen increases or the supply of oxygen decreases, the tissues extract more oxygen from the plasma and from hemoglobin; this results in a lower venous pO_2 and decreased oxygen saturation of the venous blood. Studies in primates suggest that a critical point of limited oxygen delivery is reached when oxygen extraction ratio approaches twice normal or 0.50.[3]

Under normal resting conditions the body has a tremendous reserve of oxygen supply relative to demand. In the average adult, approxi-

Table 21-1. Oxygen Demand by Body Organs

	Blood Flow (mL/min/100 g)	Cardiac Output (%)	Oxygen Consumption (mL/min/100 g)
Brain	55	14	3.00
Heart	80	5	9.00
Kidneys	400	22	5.00
Liver and GI tract	50	23	3.00
Skeletal muscle	9	18	0.15
Skin	10	4	0.20
Remainder	3	14	0.15

mately 1000 mL/minute is available to the tissues and only 250 mL/minute is consumed.

O_2 supply (Calculation will assume a normal hemoglobin of 140 g/L and a pO_2 of 100)

= Cardiac output $\times$ O_2 content$_{arterial}$
= 5 L/minute $\times$ [(140 $\times$ 1.39 $\times$ 100%) + (100 $\times$ 0.003)]
= 5 L/minute $\times$ 200 mL O_2/L
= 1000 mL O_2/minute

O_2 consumption

= Cardiac output $\times$ (O_2 content$_{arterial}$ – O_2 content$_{venous}$)
= 5 L/minute $\times$ (200 mL O_2/L – 150 mL O_2/L)
= 5 L/minute $\times$ 50 mL O_2/L
= 250 mL O_2/minute

Measuring Adequate Oxygen Supply

Because measuring the hemoglobin concentration or hematocrit does not assess the adequacy of oxygen delivery to the tissues, a value for hemoglobin cannot by itself serve as a clinical guide for blood transfusion. Clinical assessment of adequate oxygenation is based on the patient's cardiac performance, hemoglobin concentration, and current oxygen demand. For patients in an intensive care unit or in the operating room, direct measurement of the cardiac output and the systemic oxygen extraction via a pulmonary artery catheter can serve as a useful guide to the overall adequacy of oxygen supply. This approach provides a more physiologic indication for transfusion than measurement of the hematocrit. The mixed venous oxygen saturation and the extraction ratio provide data on total body oxygen consumption that must, like the hematocrit, be interpreted in light of the clinical situation.

Treating Inadequate Oxygen Supply

Tissue oxygen debt results when oxygen demand exceeds supply; tissues convert to anaerobic metabolism and produce increased quantities of lactic acid. Metabolic acidosis, in turn, impairs cardiac performance, further de-

creasing perfusion, and tissue oxygen delivery, resulting in greater tissue hypoxia. Oxygen supply reflects blood flow, gas exchange in the lungs, hemoglobin concentration, oxygen-hemoglobin affinity, and tissue demands for oxygen; all but the oxygen-hemoglobin affinity are subject to substantial variation. RBC transfusion is an excellent means of raising the hemoglobin concentration; in the absence of bleeding or hemolysis, one unit of RBCs raises the average adult's hemoglobin concentration by 1 g/dL. Ways to improve oxygen supply relative to demand independently of transfusion, include increasing tissue perfusion (maximizing cardiac performance), increasing the hemoglobin saturation (supplemental oxygen), and decreasing tissue oxygen demands (bed rest).

The relationship among oxygen delivery, cardiac output, and hemoglobin concentration is shown in Fig 21-1. For example, a patient with a hemoglobin of 6 g/dL and a cardiac index of 5 L/minute/m^2 has an abnormal oxygen delivery. Assuming that the oxygen extraction remains constant, oxygen delivery could be normalized by either a 3 g/dL increase in the hemoglobin concentration to 9 g/dL, or a combination of a smaller increase in hemoglobin coupled with an increase in cardiac index. The most common physiologic response is increased cardiac output as an important compensation for anemia and preventing tissue hypoxia. In addition, anemia results in increased oxygen extraction, which further increases oxygen delivery to tissues.

Whole Blood

Whole Blood provides oxygen-carrying capacity, stable coagulation factors, and blood volume expansion. It may be used for actively bleeding patients who have lost more than 25% of their blood volume acutely, or for patients undergoing exchange transfusions.[1] For actively bleeding patients, the goals of initial treatment should be to stop bleeding and to restore intravascular volume to prevent the de-

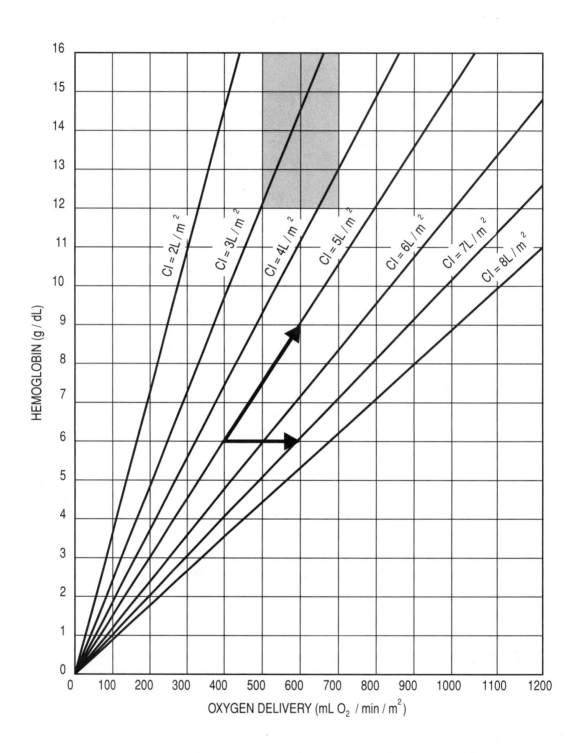

Figure 21-1. Oxygen delivery, cardiac output, and hemoglobin concentration are interrelated. The shaded box represents normal values. An individual with a cardiac index (CI) of 5 L/m^2 and a hemoglobin level of 6 g/dL has inadequate oxygen delivery at 400 mL O$_2$/min/m^2. A rise in either cardiac index or hemoglobin results in increased oxygen delivery to 600 mL/O$_2$/min/m^2.

velopment of hypovolemic shock. Efforts to restore volume by the infusion of crystalloid or colloid solutions should be started immediately. It should be pointed out that Whole Blood is rarely available, and RBCs and Plasma have become the standard for most cases of active bleeding in trauma and surgery.

Red Blood Cells

Red cell components are indicated for the treatment of anemia in normovolemic patients who require an increase in oxygen-carrying capacity and red cell mass.[1] The transfusion of RBCs increases oxygen-carrying capacity with less expansion of blood volume than transfusion of Whole Blood. Patients who have chronic anemia or congestive heart failure, or who are debilitated, may not tolerate the increased volume load provided by Whole Blood. For many adult patients with operative blood loss of only 1000-1200 mL, transfusion may be avoided by the administration of an adequate volume of crystalloid and/or colloid solutions; healthy resting adults can tolerate acute isovolemic hemodilution with hemoglobin concentrations as low as 5 g/dL without demonstrating evidence of inadequate oxygenation.[1,4-6]

The factors determining the oxygen extraction ratio should be considered before transfusions are given to stable patients with a low hematocrit. Patients at bed rest who are not febrile, who do not have congestive heart failure, and who are not hypermetabolic have low oxygen requirements and may tolerate anemia remarkably well. A National Institutes of Health consensus development conference on perioperative blood transfusion emphasized that preoperative transfusions should not be given merely to raise the hemoglobin concentration above 10 g/dL.[7] Transfusion does not improve wound healing, which depends on pO_2 rather than total oxygen content of blood.[4] Patients with chronic anemia tolerate lower hematocrit values better than those with acute anemia because of cardiovascular compensa-

tion and increased oxygen extraction. However, the high oxygen needs of cardiac muscle may precipitate angina in patients with cardiac disease and anemia. A hemoglobin concentration of 8 g/dL adequately meets the oxygen needs of most patients with stable cardiovascular disease. While it is desirable to prevent unnecessary transfusions, anemic patients who are symptomatic should receive appropriate treatment. Anemia may cause symptoms of headache, dizziness, disorientation, breathlessness, pallor (not cyanosis), tachycardia, palpitations, or chest pain.

Platelet Transfusion

Physiologic Principles

Hemostasis occurs in four major phases: the vascular phase, the formation of a platelet plug, the development of fibrin clot on the platelet plug, and the ultimate lysis of the clot. Platelets are essential to the formation of the primary hemostatic plug and provide the hemostatic surface upon which fibrin formation occurs. Deficiencies in platelet number and/or function can have unpredictable effects that range from clinically insignificant prolongation of the bleeding time to major life-threatening defects in hemostasis. Platelet plug formation results from the combined processes of adhesion, activation and release, aggregation, and procoagulant activity. Platelet adhesion to damaged endothelium is mediated largely by the von Willebrand factor, which binds to a glycoprotein (GP) receptor on the platelet surface termed GP Ib. The process of activation and release causes a dramatic change in platelet shape, with extension of long cytoplasmic pseudopod-like structures; a change in the binding properties of membrane activation proteins; the secretion of internal granule contents; and the activation of several metabolic pathways. These changes have many effects, including the recruitment of additional platelets, which aggregate one to another as fibrinogen binds to a platelet surface structure termed GP IIb/IIIa. Platelet membranes have potent procoagulant activity, which serves to localize the formation of fibrin clot.

Assessing Platelet Function

Decreased platelet numbers result from many conditions that decrease platelet production or increase destruction. Platelet function may be adversely affected by such factors as drugs, liver or kidney disease, sepsis, increased fibrin(ogen) degradation, cardiopulmonary bypass, and primary marrow disorders. Platelet hemostasis is best assessed by the medical history and physical examination. Patients with inadequate platelet number or function may demonstrate petechiae, easy bruising, or mucous membrane bleeding.

Laboratory investigation may include the platelet count and bleeding time, which measures both the vascular phase and the platelet phase of hemostasis. While the bleeding time may be a useful diagnostic test in the evaluation of patients with known or suspected abnormalities of platelet function, it is a poor predictor of bleeding,[8] and is not a reliable indicator of the need for platelet transfusion therapy.[9] The measurement of platelet aggregation is useful in investigating abnormal platelet function but, like the bleeding time, is a poor predictor of clinical bleeding.

Platelet Life Span and Kinetics

Platelets normally circulate with a life span of 9.5 days.[10] Conditions that shorten platelet life span include splenomegaly, sepsis, drugs, disseminated intravascular coagulation (DIC), auto- and alloantibodies, endothelial cell activation, and platelet activation. Because the number ($7\text{-}10,000/\mu L/\text{day}$) of platelets consumed by routine plugging of minor endothelial defects is fairly constant, the proportion of the total number of platelets required for maintenance functions increases as the total number of platelets declines. Platelet life span

therefore decreases with progressive thrombocytopenia.[10] Platelets that have been properly collected and stored have a near normal life span when reinfused into the original donor. Platelets transfused to patients, however, frequently have reduced survival. The response to platelet transfusion is best assessed by observing whether bleeding stops, and by measuring the posttransfusion platelet increment. The posttransfusion increment is generally measured between 10 minutes and 1 hour after the completion of the transfusion and is expressed as a corrected count increment (CCI). The CCI corrects for the number of platelets infused and the blood volume of the recipient:

$$\text{CCI at 1 hour} = \frac{(\text{Platelet count}_{post} - \text{Platelet count}_{pre})}{\text{Number of units transfused}} \times \text{BSA (m}^2)$$

or

$$\text{CCI at 1 hour} = \frac{(\text{Platelet count}_{post} - \text{Platelet count}_{pre})}{\substack{\text{Number of platelets transfused} \\ \text{(multiples of } 10^{11})}} \times \text{BSA (m}^2)$$

where BSA is the body surface area in square meters. A CCI above $4000\text{-}5000/\mu L$ (first equation) or above $7000\text{-}10,000/\mu L$ (second equation) suggests an adequate response to allogeneic platelet transfusion. Two consecutive poor CCIs suggest platelet refractoriness.

Platelet Components

Platelets

A single unit of Platelets prepared from an individual unit of Whole Blood may be adequate for transfusion to neonates or infants, but for adults, 4-8 units are ordinarily pooled for transfusion at an approximate dose of 1 unit/10 kg patient body weight. Pooled platelets are probably hemostatically equal to those prepared by apheresis, but the recipient is exposed to a larger number of allogeneic donors.

Platelets, Pheresis

Units of platelets prepared by apheresis technology have a platelet content similar to that of 4-8 units of pooled platelets and, depending on the equipment used, may have a reduced leukocyte content. Platelets, Pheresis are usually transfused without matching for HLA or platelet antigens, and expose the recipient to only one donor per transfusion. For alloimmunized recipients who are refractory to platelet transfusions, the transfusion of a single unit that is HLA-matched or cross-matched may improve the clinical response.

Therapeutic Platelet Transfusion

The proper clinical indications for platelet transfusion are controversial. The decision to transfuse platelets depends on the cause of bleeding, the patient's clinical condition, and the number and function of the circulating platelets.

Bleeding due to thrombocytopenia or abnormal platelet function is an indication for platelet transfusion. Platelet transfusions are most likely to be of benefit when thrombocytopenia is the primary hemostatic defect; other blood components may also be required in patients with multiple defects. Bleeding due to the defects in platelet function that follow cardiopulmonary bypass surgery or ingestion of aspirin-containing compounds often responds to platelet transfusion, but other acquired defects (eg, that found in uremia) respond less well because the transfused platelets tend to acquire the same defect.

Prophylactic Platelet Transfusion

The traditional threshold of 20,000/µL or less for patients with chemotherapy-induced thrombocytopenia has been questioned.[11,12] Platelet transfusion therapy should be tailored to the individual patient; rigid thresholds for transfusion mistakenly assume that all patients carry the same risk of bleeding. Patients with cerebral leukostasis are at high risk for fatal intracranial hemorrhage. In contrast, many stable thrombocytopenic patients can tolerate platelet counts of less than 5000/µL with evidence of minor hemorrhage (eg, petechiae, ecchymoses, or epistaxis) but without serious bleeding.[13,14] Bleeding at any platelet count may be aggravated by fever, infection, or drugs.[10,15]

Despite the widespread use of prophylactic platelet transfusions, few studies have documented their clinical benefit. One study comparing patients given prophylactic transfusions with patients transfused only for clinically significant bleeding found no difference in overall survival or deaths due to bleeding between the groups,[16] even though the prophylactic group received twice as many platelet transfusions. Controlled studies and longitudinal observations have not yielded definitive answers about the benefits of prophylactic transfusions and the risks of inducing alloimmunization.[17-19]

Selection of Platelets

ABO Matching

Because ABO antigens are present on the platelet surface, recovery of group A platelets transfused into group O patients is somewhat decreased.[20] Transfusion of ABO-incompatible plasma present in platelet components may also result in a blunted posttransfusion platelet count increment.[21,22] It may be prudent to use ABO-matched platelets whenever feasible, but it is not usually necessary to delay needed transfusion in order to obtain ABO-compatible platelets.

For infants, it is desirable to avoid administration of plasma that is incompatible with the infant's red cells. If platelet concentrates of an appropriate ABO type are not available, the plasma that contains ABO antibodies incompatible with the recipient's red cells can be removed (see Method 6.12). This is rarely necessary in adults or older children. If transfused ABO antibodies are detected in the recipient's circulation, it may become necessary to use group O red cells for transfusion.

Matching for D

The D antigen is not detectable on platelets and posttransfusion survival of platelets from D-positive donors is normal in recipients with anti-D. However, even with proper preparation, Platelets may contain up to 0.5 mL of red cells and Platelets, Pheresis may contain up to 5 mL; thus, D-negative individuals may become alloimmunized by the residual D-positive red cells in a platelet component. Concomitant immunosuppression may diminish the risk of alloimmunization when platelets are given to patients who are thrombocytopenic because of cytotoxic therapy. The benefit of Rh Immune Globulin (RhIG) in this setting should be weighed against the risk of hematoma formation as a result of the injection.

An intravenous injectable form of RhIG has been approved by the FDA; this is suitable for patients who are at high risk of hematoma formation after intramuscular injection. For immunologically normal D-negative females of childbearing potential, it is especially desirable to avoid administration of platelets from D-positive donors; however, if this is unavoidable, administration of RhIG should be considered. A full dose of RhIG, which is considered immunoprophylactic for up to 15 mL of D-positive red cells, would protect against the red cells in 30 units of D-positive Platelets or 3 units of Platelets, Pheresis.

Refractoriness to Platelet Transfusion

Platelet refractoriness, defined as a poor increment following a dose of platelets, can result from either immune or nonimmune mechanisms. The antibodies that cause immune refractoriness (discussed in Chapter 16) may have either allo- or autoreactivity. The alloantibodies are directed against either platelet alloantigens or Class I HLA antigens. Autoantibodies occur in immune thrombocytopenic purpura (ITP) and in some patients after marrow transplantation. Nonimmune causes of the refractory state include splenomegaly, drugs (eg, amphotericin B), and accelerated platelet consumption. Identifying the cause(s) for an individual patient can be quite difficult, but provision of effective hemostatic support often depends on identifying the dominant cause of refractoriness. See Table 21-2 and the section on HLA-matched platelets. For refractory patients with broadly reactive alloimmunization, the use of leukocyte-reduced platelets may avert a febrile response but may not improve posttransfusion increments.

Table 21-2. Etiology and Management of Platelet Refractoriness

Cause	Management
Immune	
HLA alloantibodies	HLA-matched platelets or crossmatch-compatible platelets
Platelet alloantibodies	Platelet-antigen matched or crossmatch-compatible platelets
Autoantibodies	IVIG, corticosteroids, splenectomy
Drug (eg, heparin)	Stop offending drug
Nonimmune	
Splenomegaly	Treat cause
Drug (eg, amphotericin)	Stop offending drug if possible
Consumption	Treat cause
Sepsis	Treat cause

Table 21-3. Degree of Matching for HLA-Matched Platelets

Match Grade	Description	Examples of Donor Phenotypes for a Recipient Who Is A1,3;B8,27
A	4-antigen match	A1,3;B8,27
B	No mismatched antigens present	
B1U	1 antigen unknown or blank	A1,-;B8,27
B1X	1 cross-reactive group	A1,3;B8,7
B2UX	1 antigen blank and 1 cross-reactive	A1,-;B8,7
C	1 mismatched antigen present	A1,3;B8,35
D	2 or more mismatched antigens present	A1,32;B8,35
R	Random	A2,28;B7,35

HLA Matching

HLA-matched platelets, obtained by apheresis, may give good results in thrombocytopenic bleeding if HLA alloimmunization is causing refractoriness. Platelets manifest Class I HLA antigens, the expression of which results, at least in part, from adsorption of plasma antigens onto the platelet surface. A grading system for HLA-based donor selection is shown in Table 21-3. Note that only with grade A and BU matches is the recipient spared exposure to incompatible antigens. Grade BX donors have antigens that are said to be "cross-reactive" with those of the recipient.

A useful source of HLA-identical or HLA-compatible donors may be the patient's siblings. Siblings who are potential marrow donors, however, are generally not selected because of concern that the recipient may become immunized to other transplantation antigens. Children of the patient are characteristically two-antigen HLA mismatches. Platelets collected from blood relatives of the patient must be irradiated prior to transfusion[23(p68)]; it may also be prudent to irradiate platelets collected from HLA-matched grade A or B donors.[24]

Patients who appear to be broadly alloimmunized to multiple private antigens may,

in fact, be immunized to a limited number of public antigens. The selection of donors based on matching for public antigens may be a more effective strategy than an attempt to coordinate cross-reactive groups. A scheme for donor selection that includes both public and private antigens has been proposed.[25](See Table 21-4.)

Studies of posttransfusion increments indicate that success is most likely with donors who are grade A or BU matches and thus are matched for public antigens, and are also ABO-compatible with the recipient. Mismatching of antigens at the HLA-C locus is usually not important.[8]

Other Problems

Platelet transfusion may fail to produce a satisfactory increment in circulating platelets for many reasons. Alloimmunization to antigens unique to the platelet membrane may contribute in some cases and attempts have been made, with varying success, to characterize antibodies and/or to circumvent their effects by crossmatching techniques. There is also intense interest in, but no consensus about, the importance of leukocyte reduction in the prevention or amelioration of alloimmunization, of febrile reactions, and of adverse immunomodulatory effects of transfusion.

Table 21-4. Strategy for Selection of Platelet Donors Matched for Public and Private HLA Antigens

Public Epitope	Associated Private Epitopes	Approximate Frequency
1C	A1, 36, 10, 11, 19	79%
2C	A2, 28, 9	66%
28C	A28, 33, 34, 26	20%
5C	B5, 15, 18, 35, 53, 70	50%
7C	B7, 22, 27, 42, 40, 13, 47, 48	51%
8C	B8, 14, 18, 39, 51	42%
12C	B12, 21, 13, 40, 41	44%
Bw4/4C	(See Table 15-1)	79%
Bw6/6C	(See Table 15-1)	87%

Example: Recipient phenotype: A1,3;B8,27

Public phenotype (see above): 1C;7C;8C;4C;6C

Potential public mismatches: 2C;5C;12C;28C

Recipient antibody screen: anti-2C (anti-A2,28,9)

If no grade A or BU match is available, select donors lacking potential public mismatches. Failing this, select any donor lacking the 2C public epitope. Otherwise, select donors based on platelet crossmatch.

(Adapted with permission from Rodey.[25])

Contraindications to Platelet Transfusion

There are several conditions for which platelet transfusions may be requested but are contraindicated. Relative contraindications include conditions in which the likelihood of benefit is remote, thus serving only to waste a valuable component. An example would be prophylactic platelet transfusions in a stable patient with platelet refractoriness of known cause.

Platelet transfusion should be avoided, except in life- or organ-threatening hemorrhage, for patients with thrombotic thrombocytopenic purpura (TTP) or heparin-induced thrombocytopenia. These conditions are associated with platelet thrombi and major thrombotic complications may follow platelet transfusions.[26,27] The use of platelet transfusions in immune thrombocytopenia is contro-versial. For a patient with ITP, prophylactic transfusion of platelets prior to splenectomy is usually unnecessary.[28]

Granulocyte Transfusion

The use of granulocyte transfusions for adult recipients is rare. New antibiotics, adverse effects attributable to granulocyte transfusions, and the advent of recombinant growth factors have all contributed to this decline. Nevertheless, in selected patients transfused granulocytes may produce clinical benefits.[29,30] Even if the prevention of cytomegalovirus (CMV) transmission is an issue, granulocytes should not be administered through a leukocyte-reduction filter. The preparation, storage, and pretransfusion testing of granulocytes are discussed in Chapter 8. The use of granulocyte transfusions in neonates is discussed in Chapter 24. Many centers are now using or evaluating hematopoietic stimulation of donors.

Indications and Contraindications

The goals of granulocyte transfusion should be clearly defined before a course of therapy is initiated. In general, the patient should meet the following conditions:

1. Neutropenia (granulocyte count less than 500/μL).
2. Fever for 24-48 hours, unresponsive to appropriate antibiotic therapy, or bacterial sepsis unresponsive to antibiotics or other modes of therapy.
3. Myeloid hypoplasia.
4. A reasonable chance for recovery of marrow function. Patients with documented granulocyte dysfunction, such as those with profound reversible neutropenia or those with chronic granulomatous disease, may also be candidates to receive granulocyte transfusions. Prophylactic granulocyte transfusion is inappropriate.[1]

Other Considerations

Granulocyte transfusions have not been proved effective in patients with localized infections or for the treatment of infections due to agents other than bacteria. It may be prudent to irradiate granulocytes to avoid the risk of graft-vs-host disease (GVHD). CMV transmission can best be prevented by the use of a CMV-seronegative donor.

Special Cellular Blood Components

Leukocyte Reduction

Leukocyte reduction of blood components is a process whereby leukocytes are removed from a blood component. This process has been used for some time for select groups of patients.

Table 21-5. Approximate Leukocyte Content of Blood Components (per Unit)

Whole Blood	10^9
RBCs	10^8
Washed RBCs	10^7
RBCs, Deglycerolized	10^6-10^7
RBCs, leukocyte-reduced by filtration*	$<5 \times 10^6$
Platelets, Pheresis	10^6-10^8
Platelets	10^7
Platelets, Pheresis, leukocyte-reduced*	$<5 \times 10^6$
Platelets, pooled, leukocyte-reduced	$<5 \times 10^6$

*Leukocyte reduction with third-generation leukocyte adsorption filter.

Current FDA guidelines[31,32] and AABB *Standards*[23(p27,53)] define a leukocyte-reduced component as one with $<5 \times 10^6$ residual donor leukocytes per final product (this includes RBCs; Platelets, Pheresis; and pooled Platelets). AABB *Standards*[23(p30)] requires $<8.3 \times 10^5$ leukocytes in Platelets, which are prepared from a single unit of Whole Blood. Therefore, a pool of six Platelet units would have $<5 \times 10^6$ residual donor leukocytes. Quality control must indicate that 100% of units meet these criteria. By comparison, European guidelines define leukocyte-reduced components as those with $<1 \times 10^6$ residual leukocytes per unit and recommend sufficient testing so as to detect a 10% failure rate in the process. The approximate leukocyte content of common blood components is summarized in Table 21-5.

The generally accepted indications for leukocyte reduction for which there are published data include:

1. Reduction of HLA alloimmunization that may lead to patients becoming refractory to platelet transfusions.
2. Reduction of CMV transmission, as the virus is cellularly associated.

3. Reduction of nonhemolytic febrile reactions (due to the removal of the white cells and the prevention of the cytokine buildup that occurs when white cells are stored).

4. Reduction in the risk of *Yersinia enterocolitica* contamination of RBCs.

Controversial and unproven indications for leukocyte reduction include:

1. A possible reduction of immunomodulation that may lead to an increased risk of cancer recurrence or bacterial infections.

2. A possible reduction in the risk of prion disease.

Universal leukocyte reduction has been gaining favor around the world. Several countries have already converted or have announced plans to convert to a leukocyte-reduced blood supply. Similarly, the Blood Product Advisory Committee of the FDA has recommended that the United States implement a leukocyte-reduced cellular blood supply; at the time of this writing, the FDA is considering the possibility. There is a consensus that leukocyte-reduction technology adds value and medical benefit to selected categories of patients and in the absence of considerations of cost, the risk-benefit ratio is highly in favor of universal leukocyte reduction. The decision to convert to a universal leukocyte-reduced blood supply should be made like any other medical decision, taking into account the supply of these components, the risks and benefits, and the contingency plans if these components should not be available when needed.[33]

Irradiation

The only indication for irradiation of a cellular blood component is to prevent GVHD. Although leukocyte-reduced components may be less likely to cause posttransfusion GVHD, irradiation remains the only acceptable method for preventing this adverse effect of transfusion.[23,34] For more details on GVHD, see Chapter 27.

Fresh Frozen Plasma Transfusion

Physiologic Principles

In normal coagulation, the fibrin clot forms on the platelet plug. Coagulation results from a complex but ordered enzyme cascade. See Fig 21-2 and the reviews by Boon[36] and Colman et al.[37] The central procoagulant enzyme is thrombin. The coagulation cascade is often divided into the intrinsic and the extrinsic pathways, the in-vitro activity of which can be measured by the activated partial thromboplastin time (aPTT) and prothrombin time (PT), respectively, but in vivo, the cascades are interdependent. Fresh Frozen Plasma (FFP) contains all the clotting factors, including the labile Factors V and VIII.

Minimal levels of coagulation factors (see Appendix 4) are required for normal formation of fibrin and hemostasis. Normal plasma contains coagulation factors in excess, a reserve that usually allows patients to receive up to a full-volume replacement of red cells and crystalloid/colloid without needing FFP. Patients with liver disease have less physiologic reserve and are more susceptible to dilutional coagulopathy. Rapid replacement of more than one blood volume sometimes results in dilutional coagulopathy, thus requiring monitoring of hemostasis and coagulation tests.

Monitoring Hemostasis

The PT, aPTT, and measurement of fibrinogen level are commonly used to monitor coagulation. Results should be interpreted with three considerations in mind: 1) mild prolongations of the PT or aPTT occur before the residual factor concentration falls below the level normally needed for hemostasis; 2) significant deficiencies of coagulation factors (or the presence of coagulation factor inhibitors) cause clearly prolonged values for the PT or aPTT; and 3) an infusion of FFP that increases the concentration of factors by 20% will have a far

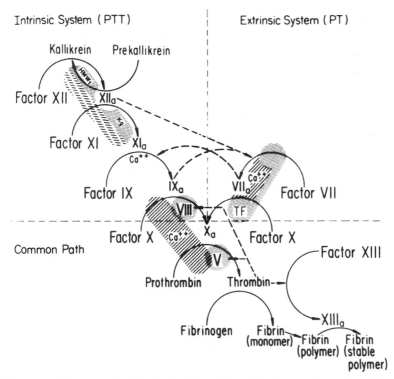

Intrinsic System (PTT)

Extrinsic System (PT)

Figure 21-2. The coagulation cascade. The production of thrombin from prothrombin via the action of activated Factor X (Xa), Factor V, Ca++ and platelet phospholipid is the key step in the formation of a fibrin clot. Activation of Factor X can occur by either the intrinsic or extrinsic systems, but multiple areas of overlap between the two occur. (Adapted with permission from Thompson et al.[35])

greater impact on a greatly prolonged PT or aPTT than on a mildly prolonged PT or aPTT. The infusion of two units of FFP in a patient with a PT of 14.5 seconds (normal 11-13 seconds) is unlikely to provide any clinical benefit and is also unlikely to correct the PT to the normal range.

Indications for FFP

Guidelines exist for the appropriate use of FFP.[14] FFP is a valuable therapeutic component for clinically significant Factor XI deficiency and for other congenital deficiencies for which no suitable clotting factor concentrate is available. FFP is most likely to be of clinical benefit in patients with multiple factor deficiencies, and of limited clinical benefit in patients with inhibitors to any coagulation

factor. Plasma Cryoprecipitate Reduced is the preferred replacement component for plasma exchange treatment of TTP or hemolytic-uremic syndrome (HUS).[26,27]

Vitamin K Deficiency

The most common cause of multiple coagulation abnormalities among hospitalized patients is deficiency of the vitamin K-dependent factors (Factors II, VII, IX, and X). Vitamin K deficiency results in an elevated PT, with or without elevation of aPTT. Before patients are treated with FFP to correct a coagulopathy with an abnormal PT or aPTT, unrecognized vitamin K deficiency should be considered. See later section on Pharmacologic Alternatives to Transfusion.

Although most patients with vitamin K deficiency do not require FFP and are better treated with parenteral vitamin K, transfusion of plasma is occasionally needed to treat active bleeding. Patients with serious hemorrhage should receive FFP or Liquid Plasma, because parenteral vitamin K will require several hours to reverse the deficiency. Because Factors II, VII, IX, and X are stable during storage, plasma provides effective replacement.

One unit of coagulation factor activity is defined as the amount of that factor in 1 mL of normal plasma. Transfusion of 600-1000 mL of FFP into the average-sized adult (3000-mL plasma volume) will generally provide sufficient coagulation factors to achieve hemostatic levels in patients whose vitamin K deficiency results from excess treatment with the antagonist agent coumadin. Concurrent vitamin K supplementation should also be given. Although the PT can provide useful information about response to therapy, the need for additional treatment should be guided by the clinical response and not by the results of laboratory tests. It is rarely necessary to correct the PT or aPTT to normal to achieve adequate hemostasis.

Liver Disease

Patients with liver disease have multiple derangements, each of which contributes to an increased bleeding tendency. Abnormalities include: portal hypertension and engorgement of systemic collateral shunts, splenomegaly with secondary thrombocytopenia, decreased synthesis of all coagulation factors except Factor VIII, dysfibrinogenemia, decreased clearance of fibrin(ogen) degradation products, decreased clearance of fibrinolytic activators, and decreased synthesis of inhibitors of the fibrinolytic system. Because Factor VII has the shortest in-vivo biologic half-life and thus requires the highest synthetic rate, decreased hepatic synthesis prolongs the PT more than the aPTT.

Because the defect in hepatocellular disease is in primary protein synthesis, supplemental vitamin K will not correct the abnormality. FFP is an appropriate replacement therapy for the multiple deficiencies found in severe liver disease, but is often used inappropriately.

The most common error is to attribute all bleeding to coagulopathy and to give systemic treatment when the actual cause is localized bleeding. For example, bleeding esophageal varices usually respond better to local hemostatic measures than to intravenous infusion of FFP. A second common error in treating liver-associated coagulopathy is overdependence on the result of the PT. A normal PT is rarely, if ever, required for cessation of serious bleeding. Active bleeding in a patient with a near-normal PT often reflects an additional problem, such as a mucosal lesion or cut vessel. Because Factor VII has such a short half-life (approximately 5 hours), the posttransfusion concentration of Factor VII will rapidly decline in cirrhotic patients with inadequate endogenous Factor VII synthesis. The goal of FFP therapy in severe liver disease should be to correct or prevent bleeding complications, not to achieve a normal prothrombin time.

Patients with liver disease may also have abnormalities of platelet plug formation and fibrinolysis. Severe splenomegaly may impair the response to platelet transfusions. Platelet function in some patients with liver disease can be enhanced by administration of 1-deamino-8-D-arginine vasopressin (desmopressin, DDAVP).[38] Cryoprecipitate can be given if there is severe hypofibrinogenemia, but FFP contains enough fibrinogen to treat the hypofibrinogenemia of most patients with severe liver disease. Severe hepatic disease results in an increase in systemic fibrinolysis, which may not respond to FFP alone. Antifibrinolytic agents in combination with plasma therapy can be useful in these patients. See section on Pharmacologic Alternatives to Transfusion.

Dilutional Coagulopathy

Massive blood loss and replacement with crystalloid and/or colloid solutions may produce a dilutional coagulopathy,[39] but most patients can tolerate loss and replacement of at least one blood volume without developing impaired hemostasis. Thrombocytopenia generally develops before plasma clotting factors are diluted to the point of causing impaired hemostasis.

FFP is unlikely to be beneficial if the PT is less than 1.5 times the midpoint of the normal range and the aPTT is less than 1.5 times the upper limit of the normal range. If surgical hemostasis has not been achieved and significant continued bleeding is expected, FFP may be indicated.[14] Massive bleeding that requires replacement of more than one blood volume may cause hypotension with tissue ischemia that additionally prolongs the PT or aPTT.

Some patients undergoing intensive daily plasmapheresis may develop significant dilutional coagulopathy; most patients with adequate liver function can tolerate daily one plasma-volume apheresis without requiring supplemental FFP.

Disseminated Intravascular Coagulation

DIC occurs if there is circulating thrombin that induces widespread fibrin formation in the microcirculation and consumption of platelets and coagulation factors, particularly fibrinogen, Factor V, and Factor VIII. Fibrin strands in the microcirculation may cause mechanical damage to red cells, a condition called microangiopathic hemolysis, with deformed red cells (schistocytes) in the circulation.

Widespread microvascular thrombi promote tissue ischemia and release of tissue factor, which further activates thrombin. Fibrinolysis of microvascular fibrin causes increased quantities of fibrin degradation products to enter the bloodstream. A number of clinical conditions can initiate DIC, including shock, tissue ischemia, sepsis, disseminated cancer, and obstetric complications such as abruptio placentae or amniotic fluid embolism. The common precipitating event is a procoagulant signal for thrombin production

that exceeds the normal physiologic defenses against disseminated thrombin activity.

Treatment of DIC depends on correcting the underlying problem and preventing further hypotension and tissue ischemia. If fibrinogen level is below 100 mg/dL, FFP or Cryoprecipitated AHF may be indicated.

Deficiency of Protein C, Protein S, or Antithrombin

Protein C and protein S are vitamin-K-dependent proteins with anticoagulant effects. Protein S converts inactive protein C to an active state, in which it inactivates Factor V and Factor VIII:C and increases vascular release of the fibrinolytic protein, tissue plasminogen activator. Patients with deficiencies of protein C or protein S have a predisposition to thrombotic complications and are often treated with anticoagulants. Coumadin treatment, however, can cause these vitamin-K-dependent proteins to fall to dangerously low levels, leading to skin necrosis and further thrombosis. Transfusion of FFP can serve as an immediate source of supplemental protein C or protein S for patients with severe deficiencies, although a human protein C concentrate is available.

Antithrombin is a circulating protein with anticoagulant properties, is stable in FFP and in refrigerated Liquid Plasma, and is available as a concentrate. Administration of antithrombin is discussed in the section on Plasma Derivatives and Plasma Substitutes.

Other Conditions

Hereditary angioneurotic edema results from a congenital deficiency of C1-esterase inhibitor, an inhibitory protein that regulates complement activation. Patients with this condition may experience life-threatening subglottic edema following complement activation. FFP or Liquid Plasma contains normal levels of C1-esterase inhibitor and can be therapeutic.

Misuse of Fresh Frozen Plasma

Plasma should not be used as a volume expander, as a nutritional source, or to enhance wound healing.[14] Transfusing plasma for volume expansion carries a risk of transmitting disease that can be avoided by using crystalloid or colloid solutions. Plasma is also not a suitable source of immunoglobulins for patients with severe hypogammaglobulinemia. An intravenous preparation of immunoglobulin is available.

FFP is often given prophylactically to patients with mild to moderate prolongation of the PT or aPTT prior to invasive procedures, but there is little or no evidence that this prevents bleeding complications. One study demonstrated that the preprocedure PT or aPTT did not correlate with the likelihood of bleeding following paracentesis or thoracentesis,[40] and two studies have documented that bleeding at the time of liver biopsy could not be predicted by the preprocedure PT, aPTT, or platelet count.[41,42] Because these tests do not accurately predict the risk of bleeding, there is little logic for a transfusion intended to "improve" the results.

Cryoprecipitate Transfusion

Cryoprecipitated AHF (CRYO) is a concentrate of high-molecular-weight plasma proteins that precipitate in the cold, including von Willebrand factor (vWF), Factor VIII, fibrinogen, Factor XIII, and fibronectin. The primary clinical use of CRYO is for intravenous supplementation of Factor XIII and fibrinogen, although it is also used topically as a fibrin sealant. CRYO is seldom used for patients with hemophilia because Factor VIII concentrates (some of which contain vWF activity) are available commercially and have been processed to reduce or eliminate the risk of blood-borne viral infection. Because CRYO contains ABO antibodies, consideration should be given to ABO compatibility when the infused volume will be large relative to the recipient's red cell mass.

von Willebrand Syndromes

von Willebrand syndromes are the most common major inherited coagulation abnormalities.[43] The conditions are usually autosomal dominant and represent a collection of quantitative and qualitative abnormalities of vWF, the major protein mediating platelet adhesion to damaged endothelium. The protein also transports Factor VIII. As a result, patients with von Willebrand syndromes have varying degrees of abnormal platelet plug formation (prolonged bleeding time) and partial deficiency of Factor VIII (prolonged aPTT). vWF exists in the plasma as a family of multimeric molecules with a wide range of molecular weights. The high-molecular-weight species of vWF are the most hemostatically effective. Laboratory evaluation demonstrates a specific deficiency in the level of vWF. vWF is often measured as ristocetin cofactor activity because vWF is required for the platelet-aggregating effect of ristocetin in vitro.

Mild cases of von Willebrand syndrome can often be treated with DDAVP, which causes a release of endogenous stores of Factor VIII and vWF. See section on Pharmacologic Alternatives to Transfusion. However, DDAVP is contraindicated in one type (Type IIb) of the syndrome.

Many Factor VIII concentrates do not contain therapeutic levels of vWF, but at least two with satisfactory levels are commercially available. In the absence of a suitably therapeutic virus-inactivated concentrate, severe von Willebrand syndrome can be treated with FFP or with CRYO. CRYO provides a much higher concentration of high-molecular-weight vWF than FFP. The quantity of CRYO required to treat bleeding episodes or to prepare for major surgery varies greatly among patients with von Willebrand syndromes. In addition to the clinical response of the patient, the template bleeding time, the level of Factor VIII, or the ristocetin cofactor activity may help to guide therapy.

Fibrinogen Abnormalities

Hypofibrinogenemia may occur as a rare isolated congenital deficiency or may be acquired as part of the DIC syndrome. Dysfibrinogenemias may be congenital or acquired and represent conditions in which fibrinogen is immunologically present but functionally defective. Patients with severe liver disease frequently exhibit a dysfibrinogenemia. CRYO is the only concentrated fibrinogen product currently available. On average, one unit of CRYO contains approximately 250 mg of fibrinogen; the minimum required by AABB *Standards* is 150 mg.[23(p29)]

Calculating CRYO Dose for Fibrinogen Content

The amount of transfused CRYO required to raise the fibrinogen level depends upon the nature of the bleeding episode and the severity of the initial deficiency. The amount of CRYO required to raise the fibrinogen level can be calculated as follows:
1. Weight (kg) × 70 mL/kg = blood volume (mL).
2. Blood volume (mL) × (1.0 – hematocrit) = plasma volume (mL).
3. Mg of fibrinogen required = (Desired fibrinogen level in mg/dL – initial fibrinogen level in mg/dL) × plasma volume (mL) × dL/100 mL.
4. Bags of CRYO required = mg of fibrinogen required ÷ 250 mg fibrinogen/bag of CRYO.

Topical Use

The fibrinogen in CRYO has been used during surgery as a topical hemostatic preparation (fibrin sealant or fibrin glue).[44] One to two units of CRYO are thawed and drawn into a syringe. Topical thrombin (usually of bovine origin) is drawn into a second syringe. The contents of the two syringes are simultaneously applied to the bleeding surface, where fibrinogen is converted to fibrin by the action of thrombin. Some patients who have been exposed to fibrin sealant have developed antibodies that inhibit bovine thrombin and human Factor V.[45]

Factor VIII Deficiency

Each unit of CRYO prepared from a single blood donation should contain a minimum of 80 international units (IU) of Factor VIII.[23(p29)] Although no longer the component of choice, CRYO can serve as replacement therapy for patients with hemophilia A if virus-inactivated Factor VIII concentrates are unavailable.[14] If CRYO is used, the amount required to provide a therapeutic dose of Factor VIII is based on calculations similar to those used for AHF (see below).

Plasma Derivatives and Plasma Substitutes

Plasma derivatives are concentrates of specific plasma proteins prepared from pools of plasma. Cohn fractionation, which relies on the precipitation of various plasma proteins in cold ethanol-water mixtures, was developed during World War II and is still used with some modifications.[46] After fractionation, derivatives undergo further processing to purify and concentrate the proteins, and inactivate contaminating viruses. Virus-inactivation procedures include heat treatment, the use of chemical solvents and detergents, or affinity column purification. Some plasma proteins are also produced by recombinant DNA technology. These products appear to be efficacious, well tolerated, and carry little disease risk.

Factor VIII Concentrates

Hemophilia A, a congenital deficiency of Factor VIII, results from an abnormality of a gene on the X chromosome and, therefore, is fully expressed in males and transmitted by female carriers. Factor VIII is critically important in the reactions leading to fibrin formation. The severity of hemophilia A depends upon the patient's level of Factor VIII. Measurement of Factor VIII antigen gives normal results despite deficient Factor VIII coagulant activity, suggesting a functional defect of the Factor VIII molecule. Antigen is typically depressed in von Willebrand's disease. Characteristic laboratory findings include prolonged aPTT, normal PT and template bleeding time, and a severe deficiency of Factor VIII activity.

Clinical Observations

One unit of Factor VIII activity is defined as the Factor VIII content of 1 mL of fresh, citrated, pooled, normal plasma. The measured level of Factor VIII can be expressed as a concentration, a decimal fraction, or as percent activity. For example, a hemophiliac with one-tenth the normal activity of Factor VIII can be said to have a Factor VIII level of 10 units/dL or 0.1 unit/mL or 10% activity. Severe hemophiliacs have Factor VIII levels below 1%, while moderate hemophiliacs typically have 1-5% activity, and mild hemophiliacs have 6-30%. Patients with mild to moderate hemophilia can often be managed without replacement therapy. Careful attention to local hemostasis and the use of topical antifibrinolytics can often prevent the need for transfusions. Systemic levels of Factor VIII can be raised in mild hemophilia with the use of DDAVP,[47] which stimulates the release of endogenous Factor VIII from storage sites. DDAVP is inappropriate therapy for patients with severe hemophilia A, who require Factor VIII replacement.

Product Preparation

Cryoprecipitated AHF (Factor VIII) is prepared from large volumes of pooled normal plasma or cryoprecipitate by various separation methods. Recombinant Factor VIII concentrates are also available. Plasma-derived CRYO is treated for virus inactivation either by heating in solution (pasteurization) or by exposure to a solvent/detergent combination. The specific activity (Factor VIII units/mg protein) of presently available concentrates has been dramatically increased in concentrates prepared with affinity columns or by recombinant technology. As a result, the safety and potency of CRYO have greatly increased and, in hemophiliacs treated exclusively with new preparations, the incidence of posttransfusion viral hepatitis has dramatically declined.[47] The cost of CRYO has also increased, due to the increased complexity of manufacturing and the protein losses resulting from extensive manipulation. CRYO is supplied in lyophilized form and the quantity of Factor VIII activity is stated on the label.

Calculating Dose of Factor VIII

The amount of Factor VIII required depends upon whether therapy is intended as prophylaxis to prevent bleeding or, if bleeding has occurred, the nature of the bleeding episode and the severity of the initial deficiency. For example, treatment for hemarthrosis ordinarily requires more Factor VIII than soft tissue hematomas. When the desired result is determined, the amount of Factor VIII required for transfusion can be calculated as follows:

1. Weight (kg) × 70 mL/kg = blood volume (mL).
2. Blood volume (mL) × (1.0 – hematocrit) = plasma volume (mL).
3. Units of Factor VIII required = (Desired Factor VIII level in units/mL – initial Factor VIII level in units/mL) × plasma volume (mL).

Example: A 70-kg severe hemophiliac with a hematocrit of 40% has an initial Factor VIII level of 2 units/dL (0.02 unit/mL, 2% activity). How many units of Factor VIII concentrate should be given to raise his Factor VIII level to 50 units/dL?

70 kg × 70 mL/kg = 4900 mL
4900 mL × (1.0 – 0.40) = 2940 mL
2940 mL × (0.50 – 0.02) = 1411 units

This dose should produce an expected level of 50 units/dL immediately after transfusion. The therapy of choice for severe hemophilia A is Factor VIII concentrates. CRYO could be used to supply 1411 units of Factor VIII, but at 80 IU per bag, this would require at least 18 bags (and 18 allogeneic donor exposures). The biologic half-life is about 12 hours, but the half-life of initially circulating Factor VIII is about 4 hours because of equilibration with extravascular spaces. It is usually necessary to repeat infusions of CRYO at 8- to 12-hour intervals to maintain hemostatic levels.

The duration of treatment with Factor VIII infusions depends upon the type and location of the hemorrhage (or the reason for prophylaxis) and the clinical response of the patient. After major surgery, the Factor VIII level should be maintained above 40-50 units/dL for at least 10 days. When elective surgery is planned, Factor VIII assays should be made available to serve as a guide to therapy. In emergencies the aPTT can be used as a rough guide to Factor VIII activity.

Treatment of Inhibitors to Factor VIII

About 10-20% of patients with hemophilia A develop a detectable inhibitor to human Factor VIII. These are antibodies that inactivate the portion of the Factor VIII molecule necessary for coagulation activity. Because patients who develop inhibitors may become unresponsive to infusion of human Factor VIII, management can be difficult. Very large doses of human Factor VIII have been given to patients with serious hemorrhages, in an attempt to raise the plasma Factor VIII level to the therapeutic range. Porcine Factor VIII has also been tried because of low cross-reactivity with human Factor VIII antibody.[48]

Factor IX complex (prothrombin complex), which contains Factors II, VII, IX, and X, has been effective in treating bleeding episodes in some patients with Factor VIII inhibitors. However, the clinical response is unpredictable.[49] It is postulated that activated factors in the preparation bypass the step in the coagulation cascade that requires Factor VIII, so that fibrin formation can occur. The exact mechanism of action, however, is uncertain. While Factor IX complex is treated with heat or combinations of solvents and detergents to inactivate viruses, some products may be capable of transmitting hepatitis. They can also induce DIC and have been implicated in thrombotic episodes, including myocardial infarction.[49]

Specially activated Factor IX complex concentrates have been developed for treatment of patients with Factor VIII inhibitors. Controlled trials to demonstrate superiority over standard preparations have been inconclusive, but their use may be justified in selected cases.[50] The risk of thrombotic complications should be kept in mind when these preparations are used.

Although immunosuppressive drugs or intravenous immunoglobulin (IVIG) alone are not successful in eliminating inhibitors in hemophilic patients, cytoxan and IVIG in conjunction with Factor VIII infusions have successfully induced tolerance in some patients.[51] A case report also suggests the recombinant human interferon alpha 2a may be helpful.[51] If hemorrhage is life-threatening, intensive plasmapheresis to remove the inhibiting antibody, coupled with infusions of Factor VIII, can be employed. A recombinant Factor VIIa is currently in clinical trials for treatment of hemophilia A patients with inhibitors.[50]

Factor IX Concentrates

Factor IX deficiency (hemophilia B, Christmas disease) is clinically indistinguishable from Factor VIII deficiency in that both are sex-linked disorders that cause a prolonged aPTT in the presence of a normal PT and bleeding time. The disorder is confirmed by specific measurement of Factor IX activity. Defective synthesis of Factor IX is caused by an abnormal gene on the X chromosome. Factor IX complex concentrate has been used for treatment of hemophilia B for the past 2 decades; Factor IX concentrates containing only trace amounts of Factors II, VII, or X are available and carry much less risk of inducing thrombosis.[52]

Formulas for calculation of Factor VIII dosage (see above) can be used to calculate Factor IX dosage, but the units to be given should be doubled; half of infused Factor IX disappears immediately after infusion for unknown reasons. Factor IX equilibrates with the extracellular fluid with a half-life of about 4 hours. The biologic half-life is about 24 hours. As with hemophilia A, recommended dose and treatment schedules vary with the severity and type of bleeding.

Intravenous Immunoglobulin

IVIG is prepared from modified Cohn fraction II and subjected to virus inactivation. Preparations intended for intramuscular administration contain aggregates that may activate the complement and kinin systems and produce hypotensive and/or anaphylactic reactions if administered intravenously, but the intravenous product contains almost exclusively monomeric IgG molecules.[53]

The indications for the use of intravenous IgG are evolving.[53,54] Some conditions in which intravenous immune globulin is used are listed in Table 21-6. Infusion of IVIG can induce such reactions as headache, vomiting, volume overload, allergic reactions, and pulmonary reactions. Passively transferred ABO antibodies may cause a positive DAT in non-group-O patients, but significant hemolysis is rare.

Antiprotease Concentrates

Antithrombin, also known as heparin cofactor, is synthesized in the liver and circulates in normal plasma at concentrations of 230-400 mg/dL. Combination with heparin causes the antithrombin molecule to expose an arginine site, which neutralizes the serine site on thrombin and on other serine proteases (Factors IX, X, XI, and XII), and thus inactivates these potent enzymes.[55] Patients who are defi-

cient in antithrombin do not effectively inhibit thrombin activity and are prone to thromboembolic diseases.

Congenital antithrombin deficiency can present as unexpected venous thrombosis. Acquired deficiency of antithrombin and venous thrombosis are occasionally seen in patients with severe nutritional deficiency. A low antithrombin level occurs in liver disease as a result of decreased synthesis, but the net result of the hemostatic derangements of cirrhosis is deficient coagulation rather than thrombosis. Heparin forms a complex with antithrombin that results in increased clearance of the heparin antithrombin complex. Some patients on prolonged heparin therapy develop transient antithrombin deficiency and relative heparin resistance. Because of increased formation and clearance of heparin-antithrombin complexes, transfusion of additional antithrombin may overcome heparin resistance in such patients.

A heat-treated concentrate of antithrombin is available, but the risk of virus transmission may not be completely eliminated.[1] The half-life of purified antithrombin is approximately 60-70 hours and the recovery is 1.5 to 2%/IU/kg body weight.[56] Liquid Plasma and FFP are alternative sources of antithrombin. The dosage and endpoint for plasma treatment of patients with antithrombin deficiency are not well defined. Other available concentrates of antiproteases include alpha-1-proteinase inhibitor (alpha-1 antitrypsin) and C1-esterase inhibitor.

Protein C Concentrates

Patients with protein C deficiency are predisposed to thrombotic events, although heterozygotes characteristically have minimal symptoms and rarely need treatment with protein C concentrates. Heterozygotes have plasma levels 40-60% of normal and, if treatment is needed for a thrombotic episode, will be given anticoagulants. Warfarin-induced skin necrosis may occur, however, and protein C infusions can be therapeutic. Homozygous protein C defi-

Table 21-6. Potential Indications and Clinical Uses for Intravenous Immunoglobulin Preparations

Congenital immune deficiencies
  Hypogammaglobulinemia and agammaglobulinemia
  Selective antibody deficiency
  IgG subclass deficiency and recurrent infection
  Premature newborns
Acquired antibody deficiency
  Malignancies with antibody deficiency and recurrent infection: multiple myeloma, chronic lymphocytic leukemia
  Protein-losing enteropathy
  Drug- or radiation-induced humoral immunodeficiency
Prophylaxis or treatment of bacterial and viral diseases
  Pediatric HIV infection for prevention of bacterial and secondary viral infections
  Cytomegalovirus infection in transplant recipients
  Neonatal sepsis
Other
  HIV-related immune thrombocytopenic purpura
  Acute immune thrombocytopenic purpura
  Kawasaki syndrome
  Guillain-Barré syndrome
  Posttransfusion purpura
  Acquired Factor VIII inhibitors
  Thrombotic thrombocytopenic purpura

ciency causes neonatal purpura fulminans, which requires immediate administration of protein C, along with complex regulation of the rest of the coagulation cascade. The half-life of infused protein C is 6-16 hours.[57]

Colloid Solutions

Human albumin (5% and 25%) and plasma protein fraction (PPF) provide volume expansion and colloid replacement without risk of transfusion-transmitted viruses.[58,59] PPF has a greater concentration of nonalbumin plasma proteins than 5% albumin, but is otherwise comparable. Pharmacologic agents such as hydroxyethyl starch or dextran are also commonly used as plasma substitutes for volume expansion.

Physiology of Albumin

The total body albumin mass is about 300 g, of which 40% (120 g) is in the plasma.[60] Daily albumin synthesis in a normal adult approximates 16 g. For each 500 mL of blood lost, only 12 g (4% of body total) of albumin is lost; thus, albumin in a four-unit hemorrhage (2000 mL) will be entirely replaced by normal synthesis in 3 days.

Misuse of Albumin

The use of supplemental albumin to correct hypoalbuminemia due to nutritional deficiency, or to treat ascites and peripheral edema in patients with portal hypertension, is of doubtful clinical benefit.[1] A randomized, controlled clinical trial showed that albumin supplementation in critically ill adults effectively raised the serum albumin concentration, but had no effect on clinical outcome.[61] Hypoalbuminemia secondary to nutritional deficiency is best treated by enteric or parenteral alimentation. Because patients with liver disease and ascites frequently have coexistent hypoalbuminemia, the ascites is frequently misattributed to low serum albumin and low colloid oncotic pressure rather than to portal hypertension. However, patients with cirrhosis who have portal hypertension may exhibit ascites and edema with normal serum oncotic pressure.

Complications of Transfusion with Colloid Plasma Substitutes

Infusions of large quantities of 25% albumin may rapidly increase the intravascular oncotic pressure, drawing a significant volume of water from the extracellular space into the vascular space, and creating the risk of fluid overload. Hypotensive episodes observed with rapid infusion of PPF have been attributed to the presence of vasoactive kinins in the preparation. This complication is rare with present formulations of PPF. Nevertheless, caution should be exercised in the use of PPF for rapid restoration of volume, as in the treatment of hypovolemic shock. IgA-deficient patients with clinically significant class-specific antibodies may react to the IgA present in plasma substitutes. Meta-analysis of randomized studies of human albumin administration in critically ill patients have suggested that its use may actually increase mortality and that the use of albumin be reviewed.[62]

Special Transfusion Situations

Transfusing Patients with Thalassemia and Sickle Cell Disease

Thalassemia and sickle cell disease are inherited syndromes characterized by deficient or abnormal hemoglobin structures and anemia. Thalassemia is caused by a deficiency in alpha or beta chain production and results in a progressive anemia and enlargement of the heart, liver, and spleen. The only current cure for thalassemia is hematopoietic transplantation but, because the anemia can be controlled with red cell transfusions and concurrent iron chelation therapy, the use of this expensive and potentially hazardous therapy is controversial. Patients with thalassemia are transfused to maintain a hemoglobin level of 9-10 g/dL to delay many of the side effects of the disease.[51] Potential complications of such a transfusion regimen are alloimmunization, disease exposure, and iron overload.

Sickle cell disease results from a variant form of hemoglobin A that can irreversibly polymerize and cause red cells to deform (to "sickle") and block circulation or hemolyze. Sickling, which can be triggered by fever, infection, or hypoxia, can lead to pain crises, aplastic crises, leg ulcers, priapism, tissue infarction, and stroke. Most patients with sickle cell disease are asymptomatic most of the time and do not require routine transfusion as do those with thalassemia. Because of the risks from alloimmunization and iron overload, transfusion is not used for uncomplicated pain crises or minor infections. Simple transfusion is indicated for symptomatic anemia, aplastic crises, and blood loss. Patients with a history of stroke or pulmonary or cardiac disease, or who are about to receive general anesthesia are sometimes treated with a hypertransfusion protocol, in which 10 mL/kg are given every 3-4 weeks, to maintain hematocrit at 25-30% and the proportion of hemoglobin at approximately 30%. Red cell exchange is used to manage and/or prevent life- or organ-threatening complications. The clinical management of sickle cell disease has been reviewed.[63]

Patients with thalassemia and sickle cell disease can receive standard red cell components, but some blood banks select as "fresh" a unit as possible and remove leukocytes to avoid febrile, nonhemolytic transfusion reactions. Phenotyping the patient's red cells and providing transfusion units that are as closely antigen-matched as possible help reduce alloimmunization to red cell antigens, although the cost and logistics of such a program may be impractical for many institutions. Patients with sickle cell disease need sickle-cell-negative blood.

Transfusing Known Incompatible Blood

Clinicians must occasionally transfuse a patient for whom no serologically compatible blood is available. The blood bank will make every effort to determine the cause of the incompatibility, which may be due to autoantibody, antibody to a high-incidence antigen, multiple antibody specificities, or a test anomaly (eg, low-ionic-strength-saline-dependent autoantibodies). Test system anomalies, in themselves, do not cause transfusion reactions, but they can mask significant alloantibodies.

If serologic testing fails to resolve the problem or if the problem is identified but compatible units cannot be provided, the physician must weigh the risks and benefits of transfusion and consider what alternative therapies are suitable. If the need is sufficiently urgent, incompatible red cells of the patient's ABO and Rh type may have to be given. Such incompatible transfusion does not always result in immediate hemolysis, and the incompatible cells may remain in the circulation long enough to provide therapeutic benefit.[64]

If time permits and if equipment is available, the survival of a radiolabeled aliquot of the incompatible cells can be determined. Alternatively, a "biologic crossmatch" can be performed by cautiously transfusing 25-50 mL of the incompatible cells, watching the patient's clinical response, and checking a 30-minute posttransfusion specimen for hemoglobin-tinged serum. Such biologic assessment does not guarantee normal survival, but it can indicate whether an acute reaction will occur.

If no adverse symptoms or hemolysis are observed, the remainder of the unit can be transfused slowly, with careful clinical monitoring. If transfusion need is life-threatening, the unit can be given without special testing, but clinical staff should be prepared to treat any reaction that may result.

Transfusing Patients with Autoimmune Hemolytic Anemia

Because of the serologic difficulties that accompany autoimmune hemolytic anemia and the expected short red cell survival, a conservative approach to transfusion is recommended. The presence of underlying alloantibodies should be investigated before beginning transfusions, time permitting. It is very helpful to establish the patient's phenotype before transfusion, to simplify subsequent investigation for the presence of possible alloantibodies. Chapter 20 contains a more complete discussion.

Massive Transfusion

Massive transfusion is defined as replacement approximating or exceeding the patient's blood volume within a 24-hour interval. The etiology of the need for massive transfusion is, by definition, life-threatening and characteristically poses greater risks than those associated with blood transfusion. The most important factor in supporting tissue oxygenation is maintenance of adequate blood flow and blood pressure, by infusing sufficient volume to correct or prevent hypovolemic shock.

Emergency Issue

The transfusion service should establish a standard operating procedure for emergency release of uncrossmatched blood. If the patient requires immediate transfusion, uncrossmatched group O red cells, either D-positive or D-negative, will be given.[22] Once the patient's ABO and Rh types have been determined, uncrossmatched group-specific RBCs can be given; for considerations about Rh, see section below. In institutions whose routine policy requires an antiglobulin crossmatch, the crossmatch is often abbreviated to serologic demonstration of ABO compatibility, if the pretransfusion specimen contains no unexpected antibodies. If unexpected antibodies are present, the decision whether or not to select antigen-negative units for transfusion will depend on the specific alloantibody and the urgency of transfusion. Following large-volume transfusion over a short time, the proportion of the patient's own cells and plasma in the circulation decreases. The pretransfusion specimen ceases to represent the patient's current status and crossmatches using the initial specimen have diminished validity.

Changing Blood Types

The transfusion service should establish guidelines for switching blood types during massive transfusion. The age and gender of the patient are important considerations. When transfusing a young D-negative female, it is usually preferable to switch ABO types before switching Rh; eg, for a group A, D-negative female, switch to group O, D-negative rather than to group A, D-positive. The clinical situation should be evaluated by the transfusion service's physician. If the continuing transfusion requirement is expected to exceed the available supply of D-negative blood, evaluation of the change to D-positive should be made early, to conserve blood for other recipients. Once the patient receives one or more D-positive units, there may be little advantage in returning to D-negative blood.

Coagulation Support During Massive Transfusion

Massive transfusion is often associated with coagulation abnormalities; these have been attributed to dilution of platelets or coagulation factors, but hypoperfusion damage to tissues may play a role.[1] If abnormal bleeding occurs, the results of platelet counts, PT, and aPTT can

guide the need for platelet transfusions, FFP, or CRYO. Additional tests may be indicated to evaluate the possibility of DIC. The preoperative platelet count and fibrinogen will, in theory, decrease by 63% with each blood volume replaced without infusion of platelets or plasma. Platelet counts decrease below 100,000/µL in most adult patients after transfusion of 15-20 RBC units. FFP and platelet transfusions are best administered before generalized bleeding occurs. Although FFP is useful in some massively transfused patients, FFP should not be administered in a fixed ratio to the number of RBC units given. In the absence of significant thrombocytopenia or platelet dysfunction, PT results below 1.5 times the midpoint of normal range are usually associated with adequate hemostasis during surgery. The unpredictable occurrence of generalized bleeding during massive transfusion indicates that simple dilution with platelet-deficient or factor-deficient blood is not the only cause of poor hemostasis.[65]

A principal cause of hemostatic derangement during massive transfusion is hypotension rather than the transfusion itself.[66] Inadequate volume resuscitation and poor tissue perfusion not only promote the release of tissue procoagulant material leading to DIC, but also result in lactic acidosis, acidemia, and poor myocardial performance.

Hypothermia, Tissue Oxygenation, and 2,3-DPG

Hypothermia as a complication of transfusion is discussed in Chapter 27. In hypovolemic shock, the underlying pathophysiologic defect is inadequate tissue oxygenation. Oxygen supply to the tissues is determined by many factors, the most important of which are blood flow (perfusion) and hemoglobin concentration. The level of 2,3-diphosphoglycerate (2,3-DPG) falls in stored RBCs, and this decrease has been suggested as a potential cause of poor tissue oxygenation after massive transfusion. Low 2,3-DPG levels have not been shown to be detrimental to massively transfused patients,[66] although for infants undergoing exchange transfusion, blood with near normal 2,3-DPG levels is frequently requested. Within 3-8 hours after transfusion, previously stored red cells regenerate 50% of normal 2,3-DPG levels.[65]

Pharmacologic Alternatives to Transfusion

Recombinant Growth Factors

Growth factors are low-molecular-weight proteins that regulate hematopoiesis by specific interaction with receptors found on progenitor cells. The use of growth factors to stimulate endogenous blood cell production is an important alternative to the use of blood.[67]

Erythropoietin

Recombinant erythropoietin has been approved for presurgical administration to increase preoperative hemoglobin and hematocrit levels. The clinical use of recombinant erythropoietin has markedly reduced the need for transfusion in patients with end-stage renal disease, and is indicated for treatment of anemia in patients infected with human immunodeficiency virus and for other approved patient groups who are receiving zidovudine. It may also have a role in treating anemia related to chronic disease, to surgery, or to receipt of medications that suppress the marrow.

Other Blood Cell Growth Factors

Granulocyte-macrophage colony-stimulating factor (GM-CSF) and granulocyte colony-stimulating factor (G-CSF) stimulate marrow production of granulocytes. G-CSF has been approved for the treatment of chemotherapy-induced neutropenia for patients undergoing peripheral blood progenitor cell collection and therapy, and for patients with chronic neutropenia.[68,69] The use of these stimulants de-

creases duration of neutropenia, increases tolerance to cytotoxic drugs, and decreases further the need for granulocyte transfusions. GM-CSF has been approved for use in patients undergoing autologous marrow transplantation. Another potential use for GM-CSF and G-CSF is support of patients undergoing allogeneic marrow transplantation or patients receiving antiviral agents that suppress the marrow.[70] Recombinant activators for thrombopoietin receptors are in clinical trials.

Red Cell Substitutes

Stroma-free hemoglobin solution, in which free hemoglobin has been separated from cell membranes, has several characteristics that render it unsuitable as a blood substitute, including a low p50, short circulation time, high oncotic pressure, and vasopressor/nephrotoxic properties. Chemical modifications of hemoglobin solutions may successfully overcome these disadvantages. Hemoglobin produced by recombinant DNA techniques is also being investigated, and fluorocarbon products have shown promise.[71] Fluosol has been approved by the FDA for use during percutaneous transluminal angioplasty. Although this product is no longer available in the United States, it is the only human red cell substitute (better known as oxygen-carrying solution) to gain governmental approval.

DDAVP

DDAVP is a synthetic analogue of vasopressin without significant pressor activity.[72] First used in the treatment of diabetes insipidus, DDAVP is useful in promoting hemostasis. DDAVP appears to cause release of endogenous stores of high-molecular-weight vWF from the vascular subendothelium. Because of its effect on Factor VIII and vWF, DDAVP was initially used as a hemostatic agent in patients with mild to moderate hemophilia A and in patients with von Willebrand syndromes. Because platelet adhesion and the subsequent formation of a platelet plug depend upon vWF, DDAVP has been beneficial in a wide variety of platelet function disorders, including uremia, cirrhosis, drug-induced platelet dysfunction (including aspirin), primary platelet disorders, and myelodysplastic syndromes.[73]

DDAVP can be administered intravenously, subcutaneously, or intranasally. It is usually given as a single injection to treat bleeding or prophylactically before a procedure. Doses are not usually repeated within a 24- to 48-hour period because of tachyphylaxis, the loss of biologic effect with repeated administration of an agent, and the induction of water retention and hyponatremia. Some patients experience facial flushing or mild hypotension, but side effects are rare. Its effect on vWF occurs within 30 minutes and lasts 4-6 hours. DDAVP is contraindicated in the rare Type IIb von Willebrand syndrome, in which platelets have abnormally increased responsiveness to vWF.

Vitamin K

Vitamin K is a fat-soluble vitamin required for hepatocellular synthesis of coagulation proteins. Vitamin-K-dependent enzymes in the liver add a second carboxyl group to glutamyl residues found in Factors II (prothrombin), VII, IX, and X; protein C; and protein S. These additional carboxyl groups provide a second negative charge, allowing Ca^{++}-mediated binding of the factors to cell surfaces.[74] Body stores of vitamin K are limited and last only 2 weeks. As a result, deficiency of vitamin K is one of the most common vitamin defects in nutritionally depleted, hospitalized patients. Absorption of vitamin K from the intestine requires bacterial metabolism of vitamin K precursors in the intestine and the formation of micelles by bile salts. Vitamin K deficiency can occur with antibiotic use as well as in obstructive jaundice and fat malabsorption syndromes. Warfarin-type anticoagulants specifically inhibit the action of vitamin K.

Factor VII has the shortest half-life (5 hours) of the procoagulant factors that are dependent on postsynthetic modification by vitamin-K-dependent enzymes. Vitamin K depletion usually causes a prolongation of the PT that is out of proportion to the aPTT because Factor VII, which has the shortest half-life of the vitamin-K-dependent factors, has little effect on the aPTT. Deficiency of vitamin K is best managed by treatment of the underlying condition and by administration of parenteral vitamin K. If liver function is adequate, coagulation factors will return to effective levels about 12 hours after the intravenous or subcutaneous administration of aqueous vitamin K.

Fibrinolytic Inhibitors

Epsilon aminocaproic acid and tranexamic acid, synthetic analogues of lysine, competitively inhibit fibrinolysis by saturating the lysine binding sites upon which plasminogen and plasmin bind to fibrinogen and fibrin. The drugs can be used locally or systemically.[75] Their use is indicated for the treatment of generalized fibrinolysis, including prostatic surgery and hepatic transplantation, but the dose must be reduced if renal function is impaired. They can be used locally at sites where fibrinolysis contributes to bleeding, eg, mucosal lesions of the mouth and gastrointestinal tract or following cardiopulmonary bypass surgery. Fibrinolytic inhibitors are of benefit in the control of hemorrhage following dental extractions in patients with hemophilia and in the control of upper gastrointestinal bleeding. Fibrinolytic inhibitors may be helpful in controlling bleeding due to severe thrombocytopenia.

Systemic administration of fibrinolytic inhibitors has been associated with serious thrombotic complications, including ureteral obstruction due to clot formation and thrombosis of large arteries and veins. When used in excessive doses, fibrinolytic inhibitors can prolong the bleeding time. These drugs should be employed by physicians with experience in their use.

Aprotinin is a proteinase inhibitor prepared from bovine lung. It inhibits plasmin, kallikrein, trypsin, and, to some extent, urokinase. Aprotinin significantly reduces transfusion requirements when administered during cardiac surgery.[76]

Recombinant Products for Hemostasis

Recombinant gene technology is being used to develop a number of products that may serve as alternatives to plasma products in the treatment of patients with abnormalities of hemostasis. These include recombinant Factor VIIa, albumin, and antithrombin.

References

1. Lane T. Blood transfusion therapy: A physician's handbook. 5th ed. Bethesda, MD: American Association of Blood Banks, 1996.

2. Welch HG, Meehan KR, Goodnough LT. Prudent strategies for elective red blood cell transfusion. Ann Intern Med 1992;116:393-402.

3. Wilkerson DK, Rosen AL, Gould SA, et al. Oxygen extraction ratio: A valid indicator of myocardial metabolism in anemia. J Surg Res 1987;42:629-34.

4. Practice guidelines for blood component therapy: Report by the American Society of Anesthesiologists Task Force on Blood Component Therapy. Anesthesiology 1996;84:732-47.

5. Practice parameter for the use of red blood cell transfusions: Developed by the Red Blood Cell Administration Practice Guidelines Development Task Force of the College of American Pathologists. Arch Pathol Lab Med 1998;122:130-8.

6. Weiskopf RB, Viele MK, Feiner J, et al. Human cardiovascular and metabolic response to acute, severe isovolemic anemia. JAMA 1998;279:217-21.

7. National Institutes of Health Consensus Development Conference. Perioperative red blood cell transfusion. JAMA 1988;260:2700-3.

8. Lind SE. Review: The bleeding time does not predict surgical bleeding. Blood 1991;77:2547-52.

9. Channing Rodgers RP, Levin J. A critical appraisal of the bleeding time. Semin Thromb Hemost 1990; 16:1-20.

10. Slichter SJ. Mechanisms and management of platelet refractoriness. In: Nance SJ, ed. Transfusion medicine in the 1990's. Arlington, VA: American Association of Blood Banks, 1990:95-160.

11. Beutler E. Platelet transfusions: The 20,000/μL trigger. Blood 1993;81:1411-3.

12. Pisciotto PT, Benson K, Hume H, et al. Prophylactic versus therapeutic platelet transfusion practices in hematology and/or oncology patients. Transfusion 1995;35:498-502.

13. Gmur J, Burger J, Schanz U, et al. Safety of stringent prophylactic platelet transfusion policy for patients with acute leukemia. Lancet 1991;338:1224-6.

14. Development Task Force of the College of American Pathologists. Practice parameter for the use of fresh frozen plasma, cryoprecipitate, and platelets. JAMA 1994;271:777-81.

15. Bishop JF, Matthews JP, McGrath K, et al. Factors influencing 20-hour increments after platelet transfusion. Transfusion 1991;31:392-6.

16. Solomon J, Bofenkamp T, Fahey JL, et al. Platelet prophylaxis in acute non-lymphocytic leukemia (letter). Lancet 1978;1:267.

17. Rossi EC, Simon TL. Thrombocytopenia and platelet transfusions. In: Rossi EC, Simon TL, Moss GS, Gould SA, eds. Principles of transfusion medicine, 2nd ed. Baltimore, MD: Williams and Wilkins, 1995:257-62.

18. Petz LD. Platelet transfusions. In: Petz LD, Swisher SN, Kleinman S, et al, eds. Clinical practice of transfusion medicine, 3rd ed. New York: Churchill Livingstone, 1995:359-412.

19. Murphy S. Preservation and clinical use of platelets. In: Beutler E, Lichtman MA, Coller BS, Kipps TL, eds. Williams' hematology, 5th ed. New York: McGraw-Hill, 1995:1643-9.

20. Aster RH. Effect of anticoagulant and ABO incompatibility on recovery of transfused human platelets. Blood 1965;26:732-43.

21. Lee EJ, Schiffer CA. ABO compatibility can influence the results of platelet transfusion. Results of a randomized trial. Transfusion 1989;29:384-9.

22. Heal JM, Masel D, Rowe JM, Blumberg N. Circulating immune complexes involving the ABO system after platelet transfusion. Br J Haematol 1993;85:566-72.

23. Menitove JE, ed. Standards for blood banks and transfusion services, 19th ed. Bethesda, MD: American Association of Blood Banks, 1999.

24. Grishaber JE, Birney SM, Strauss RG. Potential for transfusion-associated graft-versus-host disease due to apheresis platelets matched for class I antigens. Transfusion 1993;33:910-4.

25. Rodey GE. HLA beyond tears. Atlanta, GA: De Novo, Inc, 1991.

26. Rock G, Shumak KH, Sutton DM, et al. Cryosupernatant as replacement fluid for plasma exchange in thrombotic thrombocytopenic purpura. Members of the Canadian Aperesis Group. Br Haematol 1996;94:383-6.

27. Rock GA, Shumak KH, Buskard NA, et al. Comparison of plasma exchange with plasma infusion in the treatment of thrombotic thrombocytopenic purpura. Canadian Apheresis Study Group. N Engl J Med 1991;325:393-7. [Comment in N Engl J Med 1991;325:426-8.]

28. Warkentin TE, Kelton JG. Immune thrombocytopenia and its management. In: Rossi EC, Simon TL, Moss GS, Gould SA, eds. Principles of transfusion medicine, 2nd ed. Baltimore, MD: Williams and Wilkins, 1995:275-95.

29. McCullough J. Granulocyte transfusions. In: Petz LD, Swisher SN, Kleinman S, et al, eds. Clinical practice of transfusion medicine, 3rd ed. New York: Churchill Livingstone, 1995:413-32.

30. Strauss RG. Granulocyte transfusions. In: Rossi EC, Simon TL, Moss GS, Gould SA, eds. Principles

of transfusion medicine, 2nd ed. Baltimore, MD: Williams and Wilkins, 1995:321-8.

31. Food and Drug Administration. Memorandum: Recommendations and license requirements for leukocyte-reduced blood products. (May 29, 1996) Rockville, MD: CBER Office of Communication, Training, and Manufacturers Assistance, 1996.

32. Food and Drug Administration. Draft guidance: For the submission of chemistry, manufacturing and controls, and establishment description information for human blood and blood components intended for transfusion or for further manufacture and for the completion of the FDA form 356h "Application to market a new drug, biologic or antibiotic drug for human use;" part I section III.B-leukocyte reduction. (July 10, 1998) Rockville, MD: CBER Office of Communication, Training, and Manufacturers Assistance, 1998.

33. Leukocyte reduction. Association Bulletin 99-7. Bethesda, MD: American Association of Blood Banks, 1999.

34. Sazama K, Holland P. Transfusion-induced graft-versus-host disease. In: Garratty G, ed. Immunobiology of transfusion medicine. New York: Marcel Dekker, Inc. 1993:631-56.

35. Thompson AR, Harker LA. Manual of hemostasis and thrombosis. 3rd ed. Philadelphia: FA Davis, 1983.

36. Boon GD. An overview of hemostasis. Toxicol Pathol 1993;21:170-7.

37. Colman RW, Marder VJ, Salzman EW, Hirsh J. Overview of hemostasis. In: Colman RW, Hirsh J, Marder VJ, Salzman EW, eds. Hemostasis and thrombosis: Basic principles and clinical practice, 3rd ed. Philadelphia: JB Lippincott, Co. 1993:3-18.

38. Mannucci PM, Vicente V, Vianello L, et al. Controlled trial of desmopressin in liver cirrhosis and other conditions associated with a prolonged bleeding time. Blood 1986;67:1148-53.

39. Murray DJ, Pennell BJ, Weinstein SL, Olson JD. Packed red cells in acute blood loss: Dilutional coagulopathy as a cause of surgical bleeding. Anesth Analg 1995;80:336-42.

40. McVay PA, Toy P. Lack of increased bleeding after paracentesis and thoracentesis in patients with mild coagulopathy. Transfusion 1991;31:164-71.

41. Ewe K. Bleeding after liver biopsy does not correlate with indices of peripheral coagulation. Dig Dis Sci 1981;26:388-93.

42. McVay PA, Toy P. Lack of increased bleeding after liver biopsy in patients with mild hemostatic abnormalities. Am J Clin Pathol 1990;94:747-53.

43. Gralnick HR, Ginsburg D. von Willebrand disease. In: Beutler E, Lichtman MA, Coller BS, Kipps TL, eds. Williams' hematology, 5th ed. New York: McGraw-Hill, 1995:1458-96.

44. Rousou J, Levitsky S, Gonzalez-Lavin L, et al. Randomized clinical trial of fibrin sealant in patients undergoing re-sternotomy or reoperation after cardiac operations: A multicenter study. J Thorac Cardiovasc Surg 1989;97:194-203.

45. Banninger H, Hardegger T, Tobler A, Barth A, et al. Fibrin glue in surgery: Frequent development of inhibitors of bovine thrombin and human factor V. Br J Haematol 1993;85:528-32.

46. van Aken WG. Preparation of plasma derivatives. In: Rossi EC, Simon TL, Moss GS, Gould SA, eds.

Principles of transfusion medicine, 2nd ed. Baltimore, MD: Williams and Wilkins, 1995:403-13.

47. Mannucci PM. Desmopressin: A non-transfusional form of treatment for congenital and acquired bleeding disorders. Blood 1988;72:1449-55.

48. Roberts HR, Hoffman M. Hemophilia and related conditions—inherited deficiencies of prothrombin (factor II), factor V, and factors VII to XII. In: Beutler E, Lichtman MA, Coller BS, Kipps TL, eds. Williams' hematology, 5th ed. New York: McGraw-Hill, 1995:1413-39.

49. Hoyer LW. Acquired anticoagulants. In: Beutler E, Lichtman MA, Coller BS, Kipps TL, eds. Williams' hematology, 5th ed. New York: McGraw-Hill, 1995:1485-96.

50. Lusher JM. Congenital coagulopathies and their management. In: Rossi EC, Simon TL, Moss GS, Gould SA, eds. Principles of transfusion medicine, 2nd ed. Baltimore, MD: Williams and Wilkins, 1995:423-34.

51. Hackel E, Westphal RG, Wilson SM, ed. Transfusion management of some common heritable blood disorders. Bethesda, MD: American Association of Blood Banks, 1992.

52. Smith KJ. Factor IX concentrates: The new products and their properties. Transfus Med Rev 1992;6:124-36.

53. Nydegger UE. Immunoglobulins in clinical medicine. In: Rossi EC, Simon TL, Moss GS, Gould SA, eds. Principles of transfusion medicine, 2nd ed. Baltimore, MD: Williams and Wilkins, 1995:453-64.

54. Kobayashi RH, Stiehm ER. Immunoglobulin therapy. In: Petz LD, Swisher SN, Kleinman S, et al, eds. Clinical practice of transfusion medicine, 3rd ed. New York: Churchill Livingstone, 1995:985-1010.

55. Kurtz SR. Coagulation factor replacement for patients with acquired coagulation inhibitors. In Petz LD, Swisher SN, Kleinman S, et al, eds. Clinical practice of transfusion medicine, 3rd ed. New York: Churchill Livingstone, 1995:433-50.

56. Menitove JE, Gill JC, Montgomery RR. Preparation and clinical use of plasma and plasma fractions. In: Beutler E, Lichtman MA, Coller BS, Kipps TL, eds. Williams' hematology, 5th ed. New York: McGraw-Hill, 1995:1649-63.

57. Bauer KA. The hypercoagulable state. In: Beutler E, Lichtman MA, Coller BS, Kipps TL, eds. Williams' hematology, 5th ed. New York: McGraw-Hill, 1995:1531-50.

58. McClelland DBL. Safety of human albumin as a constituent of biologic therapeutic products. Transfusion 1998;38:690-4.

59. Vermeulen LC Jr, Ratko TA, Erstad BL, et al. A paradigm for consensus. The University Hospital consortium guidelines for the use of albumin, nonprotein colloid, and crystalloid solutions. Arch Intern Med 1995;155:373-9.

60. Doweiko JP, Nompleggi DJ. The role of albumin in human physiology and pathophysiology. Part III: Albumin and disease states. J Parenter Enteral Nutr 1991;15:476-83.

61. Foley E, Borlase B, Dzik WH, et al. Albumin supplementation in the critically ill: A prospective randomized trial. Arch Surg 1990;125:739-42.

62. Cochrane Injuries Group Albumin Reviewers. Human albumin administration in critically ill pa-

tients: Systemic review of randomised controlled trials. Br Med J 1998;317:235-46.

63. Rosse W, Telen M, Ware R. Transfusion support for patients with sickle cell disease. Bethesda, MD: AABB Press, 1998.

64. Mollison PL, Engelfriet CP, Contreras M. Blood transfusion in clinical medicine, 10th ed. Oxford, England: Blackwell Scientific Publications, 1998.

65. Ross S, Jeter E. Emergency surgery—trauma and massive transfusion. In Petz LD, Swisher SN, Kleinman S, et al, eds. Clinical practice of transfusion medicine, 3rd ed. New York: Churchill Livingstone, 1995:563-79.

66. Fakhry SM, Messick WJ, Sheldon GF. Metabolic effects of massive transfusion. In: Rossi EC, Simon TL, Moss GS, Gould SA, eds. Principles of transfusion medicine, 2nd ed. Baltimore, MD: Williams and Wilkins, 1995:615-25.

67. Levegue CM, Yawn DH. Limiting homologous blood exposure. In: Cooper ES, ed. Clinics in laboratory medicine. Selected topics in transfusion medicine. Philadelphia: WB Saunders, 1992;12:771-85.

68. Neupogen® package insert. Thousand Oaks, CA: Amgen, 1998.

69. Leukine® package insert. Seattle, WA: Immunex, 1998.

70. Lieschke GJ, Burgess AW. Drug therapy: Granulocyte colony-stimulating factor and granulocyte-macrophage colony-stimulating factor. N Engl J Med 1992;327:28,35,99-106.

71. Scott MG, Kucik DF, Goodnough LT, Monk TG. Blood substitutes: Evolution and future applications. Clin Chem 1997;43(9):1724-31.

72. Schulman S. DDAVP, the multipotent drug in patients with coagulopathies. Transfus Med Rev 1991;5:132-44.

73. Shattil SJ, Bennett JS. Acquired qualitative platelet disorders due to diseases, drugs, and foods. In: Beutler E, Lichtman MA, Coller BS, Kipps TL, eds. Williams' hematology, 5th ed. New York: McGraw-Hill, 1995:1386-400.

74. Green D. Disorders of the vitamin K-dependent factors. In: Beutler E, Lichtman MA, Coller BS, Kipps TL, eds. Williams' hematology, 5th ed. New York: McGraw-Hill, 1995:1481-5.

75. Marder VJ, Francis CW. Fibrinolysis and therapy with antifibrinolytic agents. In: Beutler E, Lichtman MA, Coller BS, Kipps TL, eds. Williams' hematology, 5th ed. New York: McGraw-Hill, 1995:1517-24.

76. Orchard MA, Goodchild CS, Prentice CRM, et al. Aprotinin reduces cardiopulmonary by-pass-induced blood loss and inhibits fibrinolysis without influencing platelets. Br J Haematol 1993;85:533-41.

Suggested Reading

Herman J, Kickler T, eds. Current issues in platelet transfusion therapy and platelet alloimmunity. Bethesda, MD: AABB Press, 1999.

McCullough J. Transfusion medicine. New York: McGraw-Hill, 1998.

McLeod BC, Price TH, Drew MJ, eds. Apheresis: Principles and practice. Bethesda, MD: AABB Press, 1997.

Mintz PD, ed. Transfusion therapy: Clinical principles and practice. Bethesda, MD: AABB Press, 1998.

Appendix 21-1. Blood Components for Hemostasis

A general clinical algorithm for the use of blood components for hemostasis is shown in Fig 21-3. Decision points in the figure are numbered and discussed below.

1. Blood component therapy is rarely needed for prophylaxis for patients with abnormal laboratory coagulation values, even for patients about to undergo invasive procedures. The risk of bleeding does not correlate well with the results of the PT, aPTT, bleeding time, etc. Another common error is to transfuse blood components to a patient with mildly abnormal coagulation results who is having localized bleeding. Local bleeding is best treated with local measures.

2. The four elements of normal hemostasis are:
   a. Vascular integrity
   b. Platelet plugging
   c. Coagulation and fibrin formation
   d. Fibrinolysis of formed clot

   Severed blood vessels are the most common cause of bleeding. Platelet plugging is essential for the immediate hemostasis seen during surgery and with minor bedside procedures. Abnormalities of platelet function and disorders of fibrin formation are common in hospitalized patients.

3. Platelet hemostasis depends on both function and number.

   Although the bleeding time may be prolonged in patients with known platelet defects, the test has poor sensitivity and specificity and is a poor preoperative predictor of surgical hemostasis. Sick, hospitalized patients often have decreased platelet function, resulting from drugs (especially aspirin-containing compounds and antibiotics), uremia, cardiopulmonary bypass surgery, or liver disease. Cessation of drug administration and treatment of the underlying cause are the first steps to take. Platelet transfusion will not correct the platelet defect in uremia. DDAVP can be an effective adjunct in most syndromes of platelet dysfunction; it improves hemostasis by causing release of endogenous stores of Factor VIII:vWF, thus promoting increased platelet adhesion.

   Decreased platelet numbers result from decreased production, increased destruction, or both. Examination of the marrow helps distinguish these problems. Known platelet destruction syndromes, especially splenomegaly, ITP, TTP, DIC, or drug effects, are often suspected from the history and physical examination. Heparin-associated thrombocytopenia often causes arterial thrombosis rather than bleeding. In the absence of platelet destruction, the platelet count in an average-sized adult should increase by

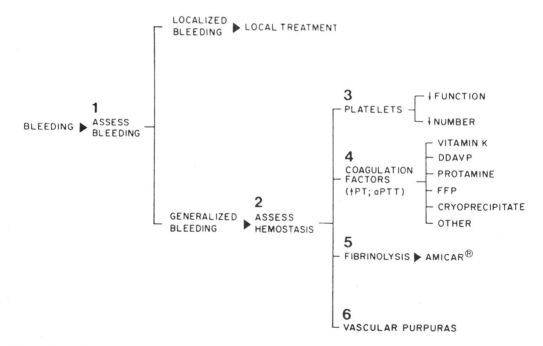

Figure 21-3. Clinical guide to the transfusion of components for hemostasis.

Appendix 21-1. Blood Components for Hemostasis (cont'd)

5000-10,000/μL for each unit of Platelets transfused, or 30,000-50,000/μL for each unit of Platelets, Pheresis.

4. Abnormal PT or aPTT. Mild prolongation of the PT or aPTT (1.5 times midnormal range PT or 1.5 times the upper limit of normal range aPTT) is unlikely to reflect abnormalities that are the cause of bleeding. If prolongation of the PT is out of proportion to the aPTT, suspect vitamin K deficiency or liver disease. Vitamin K deficiency, which is exacerbated by poor nutrition and antibiotics, is the most common coagulation defect among hospitalized patients and should be treated with parenteral vitamin K rather than FFP. Prolongation of the aPTT out of proportion to the PT raises the possibility of von Willebrand's disease, heparin, antiphospholipid antibody (or lupus anticoagulant), or a factor deficiency. This differential can often be resolved by repeating the test on a mixture of equal parts of the patient's plasma and normal plasma. DDAVP is useful in mild von Willebrand's disease and has a rapid onset of action. Protamine will neutralize residual heparin. FFP is most useful in the setting of multifactor deficiency of liver disease, but treatment should be guided chiefly by bleeding, not laboratory values.

Cryoprecipitated AHF is NOT a concentrate of all plasma coagulation factors. Cryoprecipitated AHF is rich in fibrinogen and Factor VIII and its intravenous use should be reserved for patients with bleeding who have severe hypofibrinogenemia (less than 100 mg/dL) or for patients with hemophilia A or severe von Willebrand's disease, when appropriate concentrates are unavailable.

5. Pure fibrinolytic syndromes are rare. Patients with hepatic cirrhosis exhibit chronic low-grade fibrinolysis and have decreased defenses against sudden increases in blood fibrinolytic activity. Inhibitors of fibrinolysis (such as epsilon aminocaproic acid or tranexamic acid) may be a valuable supplement to blood components in such patients.

6. Some conditions result in excessive bleeding in the face of normal blood coagulation. Examples include systemic amyloidosis, angiodysplasia, and the hemorrhagic purpuras such as cryoglobulinemia, myeloma, and vasculitis.

22

Administration of Blood and Components

THE SAFETY AND EFFICACY OF transfusion practice requires that comprehensive policies and procedures for blood administration be designed to prevent or reduce errors. The development of these policies should be a collaborative effort among the medical director of the transfusion service, the directors of the clinical services, and all personnel involved in blood administration. Policies and procedures must be accessible, periodically reviewed for appropriateness, and monitored for compliance. In addition to blood administration policies and procedures, this chapter discusses equipment used in blood administration, compatible IV solutions, and events that should take place just before the actual transfusion.

Before the Transfusion

Informed Consent

The transfusion process begins with the physician's assessment of the patient and the need for transfusion. Coupled with the decision to transfuse, the physician has a responsibility to explain the benefits, risks, and alternatives to transfusion therapy and to ensure that the patient comprehends the material discussed. Other than in emergency situations, the patient should be given an opportunity to ask questions, and his or her informed choice should be documented. State and local laws govern the process of obtaining and documenting informed consent of the patient. Some states have specific requirements for blood transfusion consent. Institutions should be careful to ensure that their individual processes and procedures comply with applicable laws.

Individual institutions have different requirements for obtaining and documenting this interaction, as well as different policies about how often it is necessary.[1] Some facilities require that a consent form, which explains the information in understandable language, be signed by the patient. Others expect the physician to make a note in the medical record stating that the risks of and alternatives to blood transfusion were explained and the patient consented. If a patient is unable to give consent, a responsible family member might be asked. If no family member is available or if emergency need for transfusion leaves no time for consent, it is prudent to note this in the medical record.

Component Selection

There must be a written order by the physician specifying what component is needed, the amount, rate of infusion, and whether there are any special requirements (ie, irradiated, leukocyte-reduced, washed components). While a telephone order may be acceptable during urgent situations, this must be followed by a written request.

The transfusion service personnel determine whether pretransfusion testing is required. Compatibility testing must be performed for transfusion of Whole Blood and all red cell components. For test and specimen requirements refer to Chapter 18. Compatibility testing is not required for platelet and plasma components, but most facilities require that the recipient's ABO and D types be known before components are selected for issue. Whenever possible, plasma-containing components should be compatible with the patient's red cells.

Emergency Release

Blood may be released without completing pretransfusion testing if blood is urgently needed for a patient's survival, provided 1) the records properly document the emergency request and 2) the issued units are of a type unlikely to cause immediate harm to the recipient.

Component Preparation

Some components require special preparation before release for transfusion (see Table 22-1). Because these steps are time-consuming and can significantly shorten the shelf life of the component, preparation should be carefully coordinated with the anticipated time of transfusion. The transfusion service will make every effort to ensure that the component is ready when needed, but not so early that the shelf life expires before administration. Medical and nursing staff need to be aware of special requirements for preparation, and to understand that these times cannot be significantly shortened, even in urgent situations.

Table 22-1. Component Preparation Times

Component	Approximate Time[*]	Shelf Life
RBCs: saline-washed	30 minutes	24 hours
RBCs: thawed-deglycerolized	60 minutes	24 hours
FFP: thawed	30 minutes	24 hours
PLTs: pooled	15 minutes	4 hours
CRYO: thawed	10 minutes	6 hours
CRYO: pooled	15 minutes	4 hours

*Will vary with institutional procedures. RBCs=Red Blood Cells; FFP=Fresh Frozen Plasma; PLTs=Platelets; CRYO=Cryoprecipitated AHF.

Patient Preparation

Patients who are aware of the steps involved in a transfusion experience less anxiety. This is important not only for an adult but also for any child who has the ability to understand what the process is about. In the latter situation it is also essential to educate the parents so that they are better prepared to support their child throughout the transfusion. The transfusionist should explain how the transfusion will be given, how long it will take, what the expected outcome is, what symptoms to report, and that vital signs will be monitored at certain times during the transfusion.

To avoid any delay in transfusion and potential wastage of blood components, venous access should be established before the component is obtained. If a pre-existing line is to be used, it should be checked for patency; signs of infiltration, inflammation, or infection; and for compatibility of the IV solutions with blood. The transfusionist should check the medical record for special instructions and assemble all the necessary transfusion equipment before the blood component is issued. Because it may take several hours for completion of a transfusion, it is important that the recipient be made as comfortable as possible before starting.

Patients with a history of allergic reactions may benefit from premedication with antihistamines. The routine use of antipyretics in patients with a history of simple febrile reactions is controversial because preventing a rise in temperature may mask a significant symptom of hemolytic reactions. Antipyretics typically do not mask other symptoms of hemolysis, such as changes in blood pressure, pulse, or respiration. Premedication orders should be carefully timed with delivery of the unit. Medication ordered intravenously may be given immediately before the start of the transfusion, but orally administered drugs need to be given 30-60 minutes before the start of the transfusion.

Equipment for Transfusion

It is desirable for the medical staff of the transfusion service to participate in the assessment and selection of transfusion equipment and ensure that such items are included in the facility's quality assurance program. Devices such as blood warmers, infusion pumps, or special filters should be evaluated for performance specifications before being used and should be monitored regularly throughout the facility to identify malfunctions and ensure appropriate utilization. This characteristically requires cooperation among personnel of several hospital departments, including transfusion medicine, nursing, quality assurance, and clinical engineering.

Needles and Catheters

Many venous access devices can be used for blood component transfusion. Selection depends on the location, size, and integrity of the patient's veins; the type of medication or solution to be infused; the type of component to be transfused; the volume and timing of the administration; the possibility of interactions among parenteral solutions; and expected duration of intravenous therapy.

Access to Peripheral Veins

Steel needles or plastic catheters are commonly used for short-term transfusion therapy. Catheters are less likely to become dislodged or puncture the vessel wall, but carry risks of infection and thrombophlebitis that increase with time. There should be an institutional policy defining the maximum time a needle or catheter may remain in a vein and providing a surveillance mechanism to confirm that access devices are maintained aseptically and changed as often as specified.

Central Venous Access

Central venous catheters are used for medium- and long-term therapy or for administration of solutions potentially toxic to the peripheral vein, to allow the dilution achieved with high-volume blood flow. Some catheters are placed via special introducing needles and guide-wires; others are surgically implanted. Catheters with a multilumen design have separate infusion ports for each lumen, permitting the simultaneous infusion of fluids without intermixture in the infusion line, thereby avoiding the potential for hemolysis from incompatible fluids.

Size of the Lumen

Needles or catheters used for blood transfusion should be large enough to allow appropriate flow rates, without damaging the vein. There are no strict guidelines limiting the size of the catheter or needle used for transfusion. An 18-gauge needle provides good flow rates for cellular components without excessive discomfort to the patient, but patients with small veins require much smaller needles.

High-pressure flow through needles or catheters with a small lumen may damage red cells,[2,3] unless the transfusion component is sufficiently diluted.[4] Undiluted preparations of red cells flow very slowly through a 23-gauge needle, but dilution with saline to increase the flow rate may cause unwanted volume expansion. If the flow rate will make the infusion process greater than 4 hours per unit, it is desirable to separate the unit into aliquots, and keep part of it under refrigeration in the blood bank while the first portion is transfused. Infusion pumps have also been used to maintain a constant delivery of blood and studies have indicated no significant evidence of hemolysis as the needle size varies[5] (see section on Electromechanical Infusion Devices).

Infusion Sets

Any blood component must be administered through a filter designed to retain blood clots and particles potentially harmful to the recipient.[6(p67)] All filters and infusion devices must be used according to the manufacturer's directions.

Standard Sets

Standard blood infusion sets have in-line filters (pore size: 170-260 microns), drip chambers, and tubing in a variety of configurations. Sets should be primed according to the manufacturer's directions, using either the component itself or a solution compatible with blood (see section on Compatible IV Solutions). For optimal flow rates and performance, filters should be fully wetted and drip chambers filled no more than half full.

Many institutions have a policy of changing sets after every transfusion or of limiting their use to several units or several hours in order to reduce the risks of bacterial contamination. A reasonable time limit is 4 hours. Most standard filters are designed to filter two to four units of blood, but if the first unit required 4 hours for infusion, the filter should not be reused. The filter traps cells, cellular debris, and coagulated protein, resulting in a high protein concentration at the filter surface. The combination of high protein milieu and room temperature conditions promotes growth of any bacteria that might be present. Accumulated material also slows the rate of flow.

Special Sets

High-flow sets for rapid transfusion have large filter surface areas, large-bore tubing, and may have an in-line hand pump. Sets designed for rapid infusion devices also may have "prefilters" to retain particles over 300 microns in diameter and to extend the life of standard blood filters "downstream." Gravity-drip sets for the administration of platelets and cryoprecipitate have small drip chamber/filter areas, shorter tubing, and smaller priming volumes. Syringe-push sets for component administration have the smallest priming volumes and an in-line blood filter that may be inconspicuous.

Microaggregate Filters

Microaggregate filters are designed for transfusion of red cells. Screen- or depth-type filters have an effective pore size of 20-40 microns and trap the microaggregates composed of degenerating platelets, leukocytes, and fibrin strands that form in blood after 5 or more days of refrigerated storage. Microaggregates (smaller than 170 microns in size) pass through standard blood filters.

Microaggregate filters may be used for other components if this use is mentioned in the manufacturer's instructions; however, the large volume required for priming causes a significant portion of these components to be lost if the set is not flushed with saline afterward. Depth-type microaggregate filters, or any filters capable of removing leukocytes, must not be used for transfusion of granulocyte concentrates or hematopoietic cells.[6(p69),7] Hemolysis of red cells has been reported with both microaggregate and leukocyte-reduction filters.[8,9]

Leukocyte-Reduction Filters

Special "third-generation" blood filters can reduce the number of leukocytes in red cell or platelet components to less than 5×10^6, a level that reduces the risk of HLA alloimmunization and transmission of cytomegalovirus as well as the incidence of febrile nonhemolytic transfusion reactions.[10] These filters contain multiple layers of synthetic nonwoven fibers that selectively retain leukocytes but allow red cells and platelets to pass. Selectivity is based on cell size, surface tension characteristics, the differences in surface charge, density among blood cells, and, possibly, cell-to-cell interactions and cell activation/adhesion properties.[11]

Because filters for red cells and filters for platelets do not use the same technology for leukocyte removal and may have strict priming and flow rate requirements, they must be used only with their intended component and only according to the manufacturer's directions.[12]

The use of these filters at the bedside is more complex than the use of standard infusion sets. The filters are expensive and are ineffective if improperly primed or used.[13] Those designed only for gravity-drip infusion should not be used with infusion pumps or applied pressure.

A quality control program that measures the effectiveness of leukocyte reduction is important. Routine methods of automated blood cell counting are not sensitive enough to enumerate the small numbers of leukocytes in leukocyte-reduced components; the use of high-volume manual counting chambers or flow cytometry procedures is preferred.[14,15]

Blood Warmers

Patients who receive blood or plasma at rates faster than 100 mL/minute for 30 minutes have an increased incidence of cardiac arrest as compared with a control group receiving blood warmed to 37 C.[16] Rapid infusion of large volumes of cold blood can lower the temperature of the sinoatrial node to below 30 C, at which point ventricular arrhythmia can occur. Transfusions at such rapid rates generally occur only in the operating room or trauma settings. There is no evidence that patients receiving one to three units of blood over several hours have a comparable risk for arrhythmias; therefore, routine warming of blood is not recommended.[17]

Several types of blood warmers are available: thermostatically controlled waterbaths; dry heat devices with electric warming plates; and high-volume countercurrent heat exchangers with water jackets.[18] Warming devices must not raise the temperature of blood to a level that causes hemolysis.[6(p67)] Devices should have a visible thermometer and, ideally, an audible alarm that sounds before the manufacturer's designated temperature limit is exceeded. The standard operating procedure for warming blood should include guidelines on performing temperature and alarm checks, and instructions on what action to take when warmers are out of range.

Conventional microwave ovens and micro-wave devices for thawing plasma are not de-signed for warming other blood components and can damage red cells.

Electromechanical Infusion Devices

Mechanical pumps that deliver infusions at a controlled rate are useful especially for very slow rates of transfusion used for pediatric, neonatal, and selected adult patients. Some pumps use a mechanical screw drive to ad-vance the plunger of a syringe filled with blood; others use roller pumps or other forms of pres-sure applied to the infusion tubing. Although some can be used with standard blood adminis-tration sets, many require special plastic disposables or tubing supplied by the manufac-turer. Blood filters can be added to the re-quired setups.

The manufacturer should be consulted be-fore blood is administered with an infusion pump designed for crystalloid or colloid solu-tions. Many induce hemolysis, but of a magni-tude that does not adversely affect the patient. Red cells in components with high hematocrit and high viscosity are more likely to be hemolyzed when infused under pressure than red cells in Whole Blood or red cell compo-nents prepared in a manner that reduces vis-cosity.[19] Platelets and granulocytes appear to sustain no adverse effects when infused with a pumping device.[20,21] Proper training of person-nel and appropriate policies for maintenance and quality control should reduce the chances of damage to transfused components.

Pressure Devices

Urgent transfusion situations may require flow rates faster than gravity can provide. The sim-plest method to speed infusion is to use an ad-ministration set with in-line pump that the transfusionist squeezes by hand. Specially de-signed pressure bags or compression devices are also available. These devices operate much like pressure cuffs except that they completely en-case the blood bag and apply pressure more evenly to the bag surface. Such devices should be carefully monitored during use because pres-sures greater than 300 mm Hg may cause the seams of the blood bag to rupture or leak. Large-bore needles are recommended for ve-nous access when the use of external pressure is anticipated. Manually forcing red cells through a small-gauge line may create hemolysis.

Devices for Intraoperative and Postoperative Blood Collection

Several devices are used to recover blood from operative sites, extracorporeal blood circuits, or surgical drains for reinfusion to the patient. Vacuum suction or gravity may be used in the collection process and, depending on the de-vice and application, the blood may be anticoagulated and processed through extra filters and/or washed prior to reinfusion. Autologous blood collection programs must have written policies and procedures that are regularly reviewed for safety and efficacy. Fa-cility records should document the adequate training and competency of personnel operat-ing the equipment. (See Chapter 5.)

Compatible IV Solutions

AABB *Standards for Blood Banks and Transfu-sion Services*[6(p68)] and the *Circular of Information for the Use of Human Blood and Blood Compo-nents*[22] are explicit in stating that medications must not be added to blood or components. If red cells require dilution to reduce their viscosity or if a component needs to be rinsed from the blood bag or tubing, normal saline (0.9% sodium chlo-ride injection, USP) can be used and is the prod-uct of choice. Red cells prepared with an additive solution (AS) ordinarily do not require dilution. These red cell components have a hematocrit of approximately 60%.

Other solutions intended for intravenous use may be added to blood or components or may come into contact with blood in an administration set only if they have been approved for this use by the US Food and Drug Administration (FDA) or if there is documentation to show that their addition to blood is safe and efficacious.[6(p68)] The *Circular of Information* allows the use of ABO-compatible plasma, 5% albumin, or plasma protein fraction, with approval of the patient's physician. Calcium-free, isotonic electrolyte solutions that meet the above requirements also may be used, but they usually are more expensive than saline and offer little benefit in routine transfusion.

Solutions that should not be added to blood components include lactated Ringer's solution, 5% dextrose in water, and hypotonic sodium chloride solutions. Dextrose solution may cause red cells to clump in the tubing and, more important, to swell and hemolyze as dextrose and associated water diffuse from the medium into the cells. Lactated Ringer's solution contains enough ionized calcium (3 mEq/L) to overcome the chelating agents in anticoagulant-preservative or additive solutions, which results in clot development.[23-25]

Blood Administration Policies and Procedures

Delivering Blood to the Patient Area

Institutions should have policies about pick-up and delivery of blood and appropriate training programs for the staff assigned to these functions. Blood is not routinely issued from the controlled environment of the blood bank until all testing is completed, the patient is properly prepared, and the transfusionist is ready to begin the procedure. There must be a mechanism to identify the intended recipient and the requested component at the time of issue.[6(p64)] Transfusion service personnel will review this information, inspect the appearance of the component before releasing it, and ensure there is a system to maintain proper storage temperature during transport. Typically, only one unit is issued at a time unless transfusion need is especially urgent.

Identifying the Recipient and Donor Unit

Accurate identification of the transfusion component and the intended recipient may be the single most important step in ensuring transfusion safety.[26] Most fatal hemolytic transfusion reactions occur because of inadvertent administration of ABO-incompatible red cells.[27] Plasma, platelets, and blood derivatives are also capable of causing serious transfusion reactions. Identification and labeling of donor blood are discussed in Chapter 7; procedures to identify the patient's specimen used for compatibility testing are discussed in Chapter 18. The final steps in safe transfusion practice occur when the transfusion service issues blood for a specific patient and when the blood is administered.

At the Time of Issue

The responsibility for accurately identifying a transfusion component rests with both the transfusion service personnel who issue the blood and the clinical representatives who receive it. Before a unit of blood is issued, transfusion service personnel complete the following steps:

1. The records that identify the intended recipient and the requested component are reviewed.

2. The name and identification number of the intended recipient, the ABO and D type of the recipient, the component unit number, the ABO and D type of the donor unit, and the interpretation of compatibility tests (if performed) are recorded on a transfusion form for each unit. This form or a copy of it becomes a part of the patient's medical record after the transfusion is given. In some institutions the transfusion form is attached to the unit and therefore serves as the tag that is required and described below.

3. A tag or label with the name and identification number of the intended recipient,

the component unit number, and the interpretation of compatibility tests (if performed) must be securely attached to the blood container.

4. The appearance of the unit is checked before issue and a record is made of this inspection.

5. The expiration date (and time if applicable) is checked to ensure that the unit is suitable for transfusion.

6. The name of the person issuing the blood, the name of the person to whom the blood is issued, and the date and time of issue are recorded.

At the Time of Infusion

The transfusionist who administers the blood represents the last point at which identification errors can be detected before the patient receives the component. The transfusionist must check all identifying information immediately before beginning the transfusion and record on the transfusion form that this information has been checked and found to be correct. Any discrepancy must be resolved before the transfusion is started. In most institutions, a second person along with the transfusionist confirms the identity of the blood unit and of the patient. Some institutions also require that the transfusionist check for documentation of informed consent before blood is given.

The following information must be reviewed and found to be correct:

1. Recipient identification. The name and identification number on the patient's identification band must be identical with the name and number on the transfusion form and the tag attached to the unit, if they are not the same. It is desirable to ask the patient to state his or her name, if capable of doing so.

2. Unit identification. The unit identification number on the blood container, the transfusion form, and the tag attached to the unit (if not the same as the latter) must agree.

3. ABO and D. The ABO and D type on the primary label of the donor unit must agree with those recorded on the transfusion form. The recipient's ABO and D type must be recorded on the transfusion form. The patient's type and the type of the component may not be identical, but the information on the transfusion form and that on the container label must be the same.

4. Expiration. The expiration date of the donor unit should be verified as acceptable, before infusion.

5. Compatibility. The interpretation of compatibility testing (if performed) must be recorded on the transfusion form and on the tag attached to the unit (if not the same). If blood was issued before compatibility tests were completed, this must be conspicuously indicated.

6. Physician's order. The nature of the blood or component should be checked against the physician's written order to verify that the correct component and amount are being given.

All identification attached to the container must remain attached until the transfusion has been terminated.

Starting the Transfusion

After checking all the identifying information, the transfusionist must sign the transfusion form to indicate that the identification was correct, to document who started the transfusion, and to record the date and time. A record of the date and time of transfusion, the name and volume of the component, and its identification number may also be required on other parts of the medical record, such as intake/output records, depending on the institution's policy. In addition to informing the patient of the procedure and checking all identification steps, the transfusionist should record the patient's pretransfusion vital signs, ie, temperature, blood pressure, pulse, respiration rate.

Monitoring Performance

The importance of fastidiously following the steps detailed above is underscored by a Belgian study done to assess the safety of blood administration practices in Europe.[28] Baele and colleagues studied the charts and records of 808 patients who received 3485 units of blood over a period of 15 months, to determine if there had been errors in blood administration. They detected 165 errors occurring after blood units had left the blood bank, 15 of which were considered to be major. Seven of the major errors involved patient misidentification that resulted in blood being given to patients for whom it was not intended, constituting 0.74% of patients and 0.2% of units. One error resulted in an ABO-incompatible hemolytic reaction that, surprisingly, was not reported to the blood bank. Eight other major errors occurred in four patients (0.5%), including the administration of five allogeneic units to a patient for whom autologous blood was available, and the transfusion of one anemic patient whose doctor had ordered only a crossmatch. The remaining 150 errors included misrecording (n=61), mislabeling (n=6), and failure to adequately document the transfusion (n=83).

Approaches have included periodic, real-time, and on-site transfusion reviews to improve the practices of transfusionists. Compliance with institutional blood administration policies may require a Quality Assurance/Continuous Improvement program in which continued monitoring and re-education of staff occur when variance with procedures is observed. Such an approach has been initiated in some institutions, resulting in improvement in transfusion practice.[29]

Delay in Starting the Transfusion

Ideally, blood should be requested from the blood bank only at the time it is needed for hemotherapy and administered as soon as possible after issue. If the transfusion cannot be initiated within 30 minutes, the blood should be returned to the blood bank for proper storage. It should not be left at room temperature or stored in an unmonitored refrigerator. Units returned to the blood bank after a period outside of monitored refrigeration will be unsuitable for reissue if the sterility of the container is compromised or if the temperature has reached 10 C or above.

Many blood banks set a time limit past which issued blood will not be accepted back into inventory—often, 30 minutes of exposure to room temperature. If the units have been kept in suitable conditions and the temperature has not exceeded 10 C, longer periods may be acceptable. Units that have been entered after release from the blood bank cannot be accepted into general inventory for later reissue.

Patient Care During Transfusion

The transfusionist should remain with the patient for at least the first 15 minutes of the infusion. The transfusion should be started slowly. Catastrophic reactions from acute hemolysis, anaphylaxis, or bacterial contamination can become apparent after a very small volume enters the patient's circulation. After the first 15 minutes, the patient should be observed and the vital signs recorded; if the patient's condition is satisfactory, the rate of infusion can be increased to that specified in the clinical order. Clinical personnel should continue to observe the patient periodically throughout the transfusion (eg, every 30 minutes) and up to an hour after completion.

Rate of Infusion

The desirable rate of infusion depends upon the patient's blood volume, cardiac status, and hemodynamic condition. No experimental or clinical data exist to support a specific time restriction; however, the *Circular of Information*[22] gives 4 hours as the maximum duration for an infusion. Maximum time should not be confused with recommended time; most transfusions are completed within 2 hours. If rapid transfusion is needed, blood can be infused as rapidly as the patient's circulatory system will tolerate, and the type of vascular access will allow. If it is anticipated that an infusion time of greater than 4 hours may be required, the physician covering the transfusion service should be notified to assess the individual clinical situation.

Except during urgent restoration of blood volume, the first 25-50 mL should be given slowly and the patient should be closely monitored. If an acute reaction does occur, the transfusion can be stopped and exposure minimized; if this "test dose" is well tolerated, the infusion rate can be increased so that infusion is completed within a reasonable time. Administration rates are calculated by counting the drops per minute in the drip chamber and dividing this number by the "drop/mL" rating of the infusion system.

Blood may flow more slowly than desired as a result of obstruction of the filter or needle or excessive viscosity of the component. Steps to investigate and correct the problem include the following:

1. Elevate the blood container to increase hydrostatic pressure.
2. Check the patency of the needle.
3. Examine the filter of the administration set for excessive debris.
4. Consider the addition of 50-100 mL of saline to a preparation of red cells, if there is an order permitting such addition.

Transfusion Follow-up

After each unit of blood has been infused, personnel should record the time, the volume and type of component given, the patient's condition, and the identity of the person who stopped the transfusion and made the observations. Many transfusion services require that a copy of the completed transfusion form be returned to the laboratory. The empty blood bag need not be returned after uncomplicated transfusions, but bags, tubing, and attached

solutions should be returned to the transfusion service if a severe complication occurred. Proper biohazard precautions should be used in the handling of entered containers and used administration sets.

The patient should remain under observation for at least an hour after the transfusion is completed, and posttransfusion vital signs should be recorded according to the protocol established in the institution's procedures manual. Patients who receive transfusions in outpatient or home care settings, or their caretakers, must be given clearly written instructions outlining posttransfusion care, significant symptoms of acute and delayed reactions to watch for, and the appropriate action to take if such symptoms are noted.

Action for Suspected Reactions

Most transfusions proceed without complication, but when adverse reactions do occur, medical and nursing staff must be prepared to deal with them immediately. Different types of reactions, their etiology, symptoms, treatment, and prevention are discussed in Chapter 27. Because severity can vary significantly and symptoms are not specific or decisively characteristic, all transfusions must be carefully monitored and stopped as soon as a reaction is suspected. It may be helpful to summarize common symptoms and the immediate steps to take on the transfusion form that accompanies the unit (see Appendix 22-1). This eliminates the need to search for instructions and helps standardize patient care in an urgent situation.

Quality Management and the Blood Administration Process

The process of blood administration should begin and end with patient safety in mind, starting with the generation of an appropriate order; continuing through collection of the patient specimen, preparation and delivery of the unit, identification of the unit to the recipient, and selection and proper use of equipment; and concluding with patient care during the transfusion and maintenance of appropriate records. Policies, procedures, training, and assessment are all critical to this process and must be monitored as parts of blood usage review.

References

1. Stowell C, ed. Informed consent for blood transfusion. Bethesda, MD: American Association of Blood Banks, 1997.
2. Wilcox GJ, Barnes A, Modanlou H. Does transfusion using a syringe infusion pump and small gauge needle cause hemolysis? Transfusion 1981;21:750-1.
3. Herrera AJ, Corless J. Blood transfusions: Effect of speed of infusion and of needle gauge on hemolysis. J Pediatr 1981;99:757-8.
4. de la Roche MR, Gauthier L. Rapid transfusion of packed red blood cells: Effects of dilution, pressure, and catheter size. Ann Emerg Med 1993;22:1551-5.
5. Ciavarella D, Snyder E. Clinical use of blood transfusion devices. Transfus Med Rev 1988;2:95-111.
6. Menitove JE, ed. Standards for blood banks and transfusion services. 19th ed. Bethesda, MD: American Association of Blood Banks, 1999.
7. Menitove JE, ed. Standards for hematopoietic progenitor cells, 1st ed. Bethesda, MD: American Association of Blood Banks, 1996:25.
8. Schmidt WF, Kim HC, Tomassini N, Schwartz E. Red blood cell destruction caused by a micropore blood filter. JAMA 1982;248:1629-32.
9. Carson TH, Bloom J, Ferguson DB, et al. Delayed hemolysis of white cell-reduced red cells (letter). Transfusion 1994;34:86.
10. Stack G, Judge JV, Snyder EL. Febrile and nonimmune transfusion reactions. In: Rossi EC, Simon TL, Moss GS, Gould SA, eds. Principles of transfusion medicine. 2nd ed. Baltimore, MD: Williams and Wilkins, 1995:733-84.
11. Bruil A, Beugeling T, Feijen J, van Aken WG. The mechanisms of leukocyte removal by filtration. Transfus Med Rev 1995;9:145-66.
12. Dzik WH. Leukoreduced blood components: Laboratory and clinical aspects. In: Rossi EC, Simon TL, Moss GS, Gould SA, eds. Principles of transfusion medicine. 2nd ed. Baltimore, MD: Williams and Wilkins, 1995:353-73.
13. Sprogre-Jakobsen U, Saetre AM, Georgsen J. Preparation of white cell-reduced red cells by filtration: Comparison of a bedside filter and two blood bank filter systems. Transfusion 1995;35:421-6.
14. Lutz P, Dzik WH. Large-volume hemocytometer chamber for accurate counting of white cells (WBCs) in WBC-reduced platelet: Validation and application for quality control of WBC-reduced platelets prepared by apheresis and filtration. Transfusion 1993;33:409-12.
15. Vachula M, Simpson SJ, Martinson JA, et al. A flow cytometric method for counting very low levels of white cells in blood and blood components. Transfusion 1993;33:262-7.
16. Boyan CP, Howland WS. Cardiac arrest and temperature of bank blood. JAMA 1963;183:58-60.
17. Calhoun L. Blood product preparation and administration. In: Petz LD, Swisher SN, Kleinman S, eds. Clinical practice of transfusion medicine. 3rd ed. New York: Churchill Livingstone, 1996:305-33.
18. Iserson KV, Huestis DW. Blood warming: Current applications and techniques. Transfusion 1991;31:558-71.
19. Burch KJ, Phelps SJ, Constance TD. Effect of an infusion device on the integrity of whole blood and packed red cells. Am J Hosp Pharm 1991;48:92-7.
20. Snyder EL, Ferri PM, Smith EO, Ezekowitz MD. Use of electromechanical infusion pump for transfusion of platelets concentrates. Transfusion 1984;24:524-7.
21. Snyder EL, Malech HL, Ferri PM, et al. In vitro function of granulocyte concentrates following passage through an electromechanical infusion pump. Transfusion 1986;26:141-4.
22. American Association of Blood Banks, America's Blood Centers, American Red Cross. Circular of information for the use of human blood and blood components. Bethesda, MD: American Association of Blood Banks, 1998 (revised periodically).
23. Ryden SE, Oberman HA. Compatibility of common intravenous solutions with CDP blood. Transfusion 1975;15:250-5.
24. Dickson DN, Gregory MA. Compatibility of blood with solutions containing calcium. S Afr Med J 1980;57:785-7.
25. Strautz RL, Nelson JM, Meyer EA, Shulman IA. Compatibility of ADSOL-stored red cells with intravenous solutions. Am J Emerg Med 1989;7:162-4.
26. Linden JV, Paul B, Dressler KP. A report of transfusion errors in New York State. Transfusion 1992;32:601-6.
27. Sazama K. Reports of 355 transfusion-associated deaths: 1976-1985. Transfusion 1990;30:583-90.
28. Baele PL, DeBruyere M, Deneys V, et al. Bedside transfusion errors. Vox Sang 1994;66:117-21.
29. Shulman IA, Lohr K, Derdiarian A, Picukaric JM. Monitoring transfusionist practices: A strategy for improving transfusion safety. Transfusion 1994;34:11-5.

Suggested Reading

Kasprisin CA, Rzasa M, eds. Transfusion therapy: A practical approach. Arlington, VA: American Association of Blood Banks, 1991.

Lane T, ed. Blood transfusion therapy: A physician's handbook. 5th ed. Bethesda, MD: American Association of Blood Banks, 1996.

Medication administration and IV therapy manual. 2nd ed. Springhouse, PA: Springhouse Corporation, 1993.

Phillips LD. Manual of IV therapeutics. Philadelphia: FA Davis, 1993.

Nettina SM, ed. The Lippincott manual of nursing practice. 6th ed. Philadelphia: JB Lippincott, 1996.

Weinstein SM. Plumer's principles and practice of intravenous therapy. 5th ed. Philadelphia: JB Lippincott, 1993.

Appendix 22-1. Sample Instructions for Suspected Transfusion Reactions

Common Signs and Symptoms to Watch for:

Abnormal bleeding	Hypotension
Chest/back pain	Itching
Chills	Myalgia
Coughing	Nausea
Cyanosis	Oliguria/anuria
Dyspnea	Pulmonary edema
Facial flushing	Rales
Fever (>1 C)	Rash
Headache	Uneasy feelings
Heat at infusion site	Urticaria (hives)
Hemoglobinuria	Wheezing

Immediate Action to Take:

1. STOP THE TRANSFUSION.
2. Keep the IV open with 0.9% NaCl injection, USP (normal saline).
3. Check all labels, forms, and patient identification to confirm that the unit was intended for the recipient.
4. Notify the patient's physician so that treatment, if necessary, is not delayed.
5. Notify the transfusion service and describe the symptoms. Transfusion service staff can advise what specimens to send per hospital policy.

23

Perinatal Concerns in Transfusion Practice

THE FETOMATERNAL COMPLEX represents special immunohematologic problems for the transfusion service. The mother may exhibit alloimmunization to antigens on fetal cells, and the fetus may be affected by maternal antibodies provoked by previous pregnancies, by previous or present transfusions, or by the ongoing pregnancy. This chapter discusses hemolytic disease of the newborn (HDN) and neonatal alloimmune thrombocytopenia (NAIT)—the two primary immunohematologic concerns during the perinatal period. Also included is a brief discussion of neonatal thrombocytopenia secondary to maternal idiopathic thrombocytopenic purpura.

Hemolytic Disease of the Newborn

In hemolytic disease of the newborn, fetal red cells become coated with IgG alloantibody of maternal origin, directed against an antigen of paternal origin present on the fetal cells and absent from maternal cells. The IgG-coated cells undergo accelerated destruction, both before and after birth, but clinical severity of the disease can vary from intrauterine death to serologic abnormalities detected in an asymptomatic infant.

Physiologic Observations

Accelerated red cell destruction stimulates increased production of red cells, many of which enter the circulation prematurely as nucleated cells, hence the term "erythroblastosis fetalis." Severely affected fetuses may develop

23

generalized edema, called "hydrops fetalis," the pathogenesis of which is not clearly defined. In HDN resulting from anti-D, erythropoiesis in the fetal liver may be so extensive that portal circulation is disrupted and albumin synthesis impaired, thereby reducing plasma colloid osmotic pressure. The severe anemia may cause cardiovascular failure, tissue hypoxia, and death in utero. Intrauterine transfusion may be lifesaving in these circumstances. If live-born, the severely affected infant exhibits profound anemia and heart failure. Less severely affected infants continue to experience accelerated red cell destruction, which generates large quantities of bilirubin. Unlike HDN due to anti-D, anti-K acquired from the maternal circulation suppresses fetal erythropoiesis in addition to peripheral red cell destruction.[1]

Before birth severs the communication between maternal and fetal circulation, fetal bilirubin is processed by the mother's liver. Unconjugated bilirubin is toxic to the developing central nervous system (CNS). At birth, the infant's immature liver is incapable of conjugating the amount of bilirubin that results from destruction of antibody-coated red cells. For the live-born infant with HDN, rising levels of unconjugated bilirubin may pose a greater clinical danger ("kernicterus") than the consequences of anemia. Prematurity, acidosis, hypoxia, and hypoalbuminemia increase the risk of CNS damage. Decisions about undertaking exchange transfusion are based primarily on the bilirubin level, the rate of bilirubin accumulation, and, to a lesser degree, on the severity of the anemia.

Mechanisms of Maternal Immunization

HDN is often classified into three categories, on the basis of the specificity of the causative IgG antibody. In descending order of severity they are:

1.   D hemolytic disease caused by anti-D alone or, less often, in combination with anti-C or anti-E.

2.   "Other" hemolytic disease caused by antibodies against other antigens in the Rh system or against antigens in other systems; anti-c and anti-K are most often implicated.[2]

3.   ABO hemolytic disease possibly caused by anti-A,B in a group O woman or by isolated anti-A or anti-B.

In all but ABO hemolytic disease, maternal antibodies reflect alloimmunization by pregnancy or transfusion. Rising titers of antibody can be documented, at least in the first affected pregnancy, and the infant may be symptomatic at birth. In ABO hemolytic disease, the condition cannot be diagnosed during pregnancy and the infant is rarely symptomatic at birth.

Pregnancy as the Immunizing Stimulus

Pregnancy causes immunization when fetal red cells, possessing a paternal antigen foreign to the mother, enter the maternal circulation, an event described as fetomaternal hemorrhage (FMH). Fetomaternal hemorrhage occurs in up to 75% of pregnancies, usually during the third trimester and immediately after delivery.[3] Delivery is the most common immunizing event but fetal red cells can also enter the mother's circulation after amniocentesis, spontaneous or induced abortion, chorionic villus sampling, cordocentesis, rupture of an ectopic pregnancy, and blunt trauma to the abdomen.

Immunogenic Specificities. The antigen that most frequently induces immunization is D but, in theory, any red cell antigen present on fetal cells and absent from the mother can stimulate antibody production. One retrospective study determined that there was 0.24% prevalence of production, during pregnancy, of clinically significant antibodies other than anti-D. Because other red cell antigens are less immunogenic than D, sensitization is more likely to result from exposure to a large volume of red cells, such as during blood transfusion. Immunization to D, on the other hand, can occur with volumes of fetal blood less than 0.1 mL.[4]

Frequency of Immunization. The probability of immunization to D correlates with the volume of D-positive red cells entering the D-negative mother's circulation.[4] Before the availability of immune prophylaxis against D sensitization, the incidence of anti-D formation following the first pregnancy of D-negative women who had a D-positive, ABO-compatible infant was approximately 8%. An additional 8% developed detectable anti-D during their next D-positive pregnancy,[5] probably reflecting primary immunization during the first D-positive pregnancy and delivery, but without production of detectable levels of antibody. The small numbers of D-positive fetal red cells entering the maternal circulation during the next pregnancy constituted a secondary stimulus sufficient to elicit overt production of IgG anti-D. In susceptible women not immunized after two D-positive pregnancies, later pregnancies may be affected but with diminished frequency.

The overall incidence of D sensitization in untreated multiparous D-negative mothers of D-positive infants is about 18%. Once immunization has occurred, successive D-positive pregnancies often manifest HDN of increasing severity, although some women have a stable or diminishing pattern of clinical disease in subsequent pregnancies.

Effect of ABO Incompatibility. Rh immunization of untreated D-negative women occurs less frequently after delivery of an ABO-incompatible D-positive infant than when the fetal cells are ABO-compatible with the mother. ABO incompatibility between mother and fetus has a substantial but not absolute protective effect against maternal immunization by virtue of the increased rate of red cell destruction by anti-A or anti-B.

Transfusion as the Immunizing Stimulus

It is extremely important to avoid transfusing D-positive Whole Blood or Red Blood Cells to D-negative females of childbearing potential because anti-D stimulated by transfusion characteristically causes severe HDN in subsequent pregnancies with a D-positive fetus. Red cells present in platelet or granulocyte concentrates can constitute an immunizing stimulus; if components from D-positive donors are necessary for young D-negative female recipients, Rh immunoprophylaxis should be considered.

The risk from an allogeneic red cell transfusion of immunization to a red cell antigen other than D has been estimated to be 1-2.5% in the general hospital population.[4] This will endanger the fetus only if the antibody is IgG and directed against an antigen also present on the fetal red cells. For a couple planning to have children, the woman should not be transfused with red cells from her sexual partner or his blood relatives. This form of directed donation increases the risk that the mother will be immunized to paternal red cell antigens or to leukocyte or platelet antigens, which could cause alloimmune cytopenias in future children who share the same paternal antigens.

ABO Antibodies

The IgG antibodies that cause ABO hemolytic disease nearly always occur in the mother's circulation without a history of prior exposure to human red cells. ABO hemolytic disease can occur in any pregnancy, including the first. It is restricted almost entirely to group A or B infants born to group O mothers.

Prenatal Evaluation

Maternal History

Invasive tests, which carry risk to the fetus, should be performed only for pregnancies where the fetus is at risk for HDN. Information about previous pregnancies or blood transfusions is essential in evaluating fetal risk. For a woman with a history of an infant with hydrops fetalis due to anti-D, there is a 90% or more chance of a subsequent fetus being similarly affected.[2] In the first sensitized pregnancy, the risk of a hydropic fetus is 8-10%. Experience with other alloantibodies has not been as extensive as with anti-D; in one series, anti-c and anti-K were by far the most common causes of severe HDN, other than anti-D.[2]

Serologic Studies

Alloantibodies capable of causing HDN can be detected during pregnancy. Initial studies should be performed on all pregnant women as early in pregnancy as possible; these should include tests for ABO and D, and a screen for unexpected red cell antibodies.[5] If the woman's cells are not agglutinated by anti-D, a test for weak D should be done, and the woman should be classified as D-positive if the test for either D or weak D is positive. Very rarely, a D-positive or weak D mother produces anti-D as a result of pregnancy. If a D-negative woman has a negative initial antibody screen, the test should be repeated at 28-30 weeks' gestation before Rh immune globulin (RhIG) is given. It is seldom necessary to repeat the antibody screen on D-positive women unless there is a history of clinically significant red cell antibodies associated with HDN, previous blood transfusion, or trauma to the abdomen.

Antibody Specificity. All positive screens for red cell antibodies require identification of the antibody.[5] The mere presence of an antibody, however, does not indicate that HDN will inevitably occur. Non-red-cell-stimulated IgM antibodies, notably anti-Le[a] and anti-I, are relatively common during pregnancy but do not cross the placenta. IgM antibodies can be distinguished from IgG by treating the serum with 2-mercaptoethanol or dithiothreitol. (See Method 3.8) In addition, the fetal red cells may lack the antigen corresponding to the mother's antibody; the likelihood of fetal involvement can often be predicted by typing the father's red cell antigens.[6] The laboratory report on prenatal antibody studies should include sufficient information to aid the clinician in determining the clinical significance of identified antibody.

Typing the Fetus. It is now possible to establish fetal D type by using the polymerase chain reaction to amplify DNA obtained from amniotic fluid and chorionic villus sampling.[7] At many centers fetal blood is obtained by cordocentesis for Rh typing when the father is heterozygous for the D gene. Fetal typing is also now available for Jk^a/Jk^b,[8] K1/K2,[9] C/c,[10] and E/e[11] antigens.

Maternal Antibody Titer

Antibody titrations can help in decisions about the performance and the timing of invasive procedures, especially if the antibody is anti-D. The antibody titer should be established in the first trimester to serve as a baseline, and the specimen frozen for future comparisons.[5] (See Method 5.3.) Because invasive tests will not be undertaken before 16-18 weeks' gestation, no further titration is indicated until this time. Although the true significance of a rising antibody titer is controversial, it is important that successive titrations be performed with the same methods and with test cells of the same red cell phenotype. Testing previously frozen serum samples in parallel with a current specimen minimizes the possibility that changes in the titer result from differences in technique. Conversely, some institutions have established a critical titer[12] for anti-D below which HDN and hydrops fetalis are considered so unlikely that no further invasive procedures will be undertaken unless the titer is reached. The critical titer for anti-D should be established at each facility and usually is 16 or 32 in antihuman globulin.[12,13] Follow-up testing is recommended for any titer greater than 8.[14] Critical titers for antibodies other than anti-D have not been well defined, although a critical titer similar to that used in cases of anti-D alloimmunization is often utilized. The critical titer for anti-K may be lower than anti-D, typically a value of 8.[15]

Other Measures of HDN Severity

Numerous laboratory procedures have been investigated to improve the accuracy of predicting the severity of hemolysis.[16] The antibody titer discussed above is not always reliable, nor is the serial change in titer. Anti-D quantitation by autoanalyzer and IgG subtype both correlate with severity but do not offer a clear advantage over titration. Many functional assays, including measures of adherence, phagocytosis, antibody-dependent cytotoxicity, and chemiluminescence have been evaluated but not widely adopted. These procedures are usually performed in referral centers and may be useful when additional information is required to manage the most difficult cases.

Amniotic Fluid Analysis

A good index of intrauterine hemolysis and fetal well-being is the level of bile pigment found in amniotic fluid obtained by amniocentesis. Amniocentesis is usually performed in isoimmunized women who have a history of previously affected pregnancies or have an antibody titer at or above the critical titer. Because fetal anemia secondary to K1 alloimmunization has not been associated with elevated levels of bilirubin in amniotic fluid, it

has been recommended that fetal blood sampling be used instead of serial amniocentesis in this disease.[1] Alternatively, a ΔOD_{450} value in the low mid-zone of the Liley curve (see below) indicates the need for fetal blood sampling.[15]

Amniotic fluid is obtained by inserting a long needle through the mother's abdominal wall and uterus into the uterine cavity. The aspirated fluid is scanned spectrophotometrically at wave lengths of 350-700 nm. Peak absorbance of bilirubin is at 450 nm. A rise in optical density from the projected baseline at 450 nm (ΔOD_{450}) is a measure of the concentration of bile pigments.[17] The ΔOD_{450} value is plotted on a graph against the estimated length of gestation, because bile pigment concentration has different clinical significance at different gestational ages. Liley's system[18] (Fig 23-1) of predicting the severity of fetal disease based on the ΔOD_{450} has been used for decades. It delineates three zones to estimate severity of disease: a top zone (zone 3) indicates severe disease, the bottom zone (zone 1) indicates

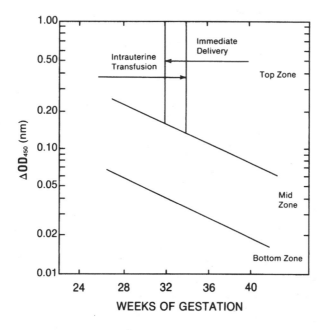

Figure 23-1. Liley graph for collecting data from amniotic fluid studies. Intrauterine transfusion should be done if the ΔOD_{450} value is in the top zone prior to 32 weeks' gestation. After 34 weeks, top zone values indicate immediate delivery. Either intrauterine transfusion or immediate delivery may be indicated for top zone ΔOD_{450} between 32 and 34 weeks, depending on studies of fetal maturity. Modified from Liley.[18]

mild or no disease, and mid-zone (zone 2) values require repeat determination to establish a trend. This method is applicable to pregnancies 27 weeks to term. Queenan et al[19] have proposed a system for managing D-immunized pregnancies, based on the ΔOD_{450} from as early as 14 weeks' gestation. They identified four zones (Fig 23-2), with early invasive intervention recommended if ΔOD_{450} values fall in the highest zone. With both systems, the severity of HDN is more accurately predicted with serial ΔOD_{450} measurements than with a single observation to evaluate whether readings are falling, rising, or stable. In general, the higher the pigment concentration, the more severe the intrauterine hemolysis.

Amniocentesis or cordocentesis may cause FMH, which can boost the titer of existing red cell alloantibody, thereby increasing the severity of HDN, or induce immunization to antigens not already implicated. When amniocentesis/cordocentesis is performed for any reason on a D-negative woman who does not have anti-D, Rh immunoprophylaxis should be given. In most such cases, the D status of the fetus is unknown, but the likelihood is high that if the fetus is D-positive, bleeding caused by the procedure will induce production of anti-D in a woman not previously immunized.

Percutaneous Umbilical Blood Sampling

In the early 1980s, the use of sophisticated ultrasound equipment made it feasible to direct a needle into an umbilical blood vessel, preferably the vein at its insertion into the placenta, and obtain a fetal blood sample. Percutaneous umbilical blood sampling (PUBS, or cordocentesis) allows direct measurement of hematologic and biochemical variables, and accurate assessment of the severity of fetal hemolytic disease.[20] It is important to verify

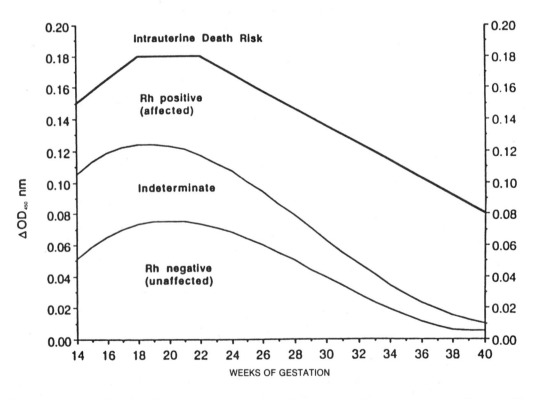

Figure 23-2. Amniotic fluid ΔOD_{450} management zones. (Reproduced with permission from Queenan JT, et al.[19])

that the sample has truly been obtained from the fetus. This is done by evaluating hematologic and serologic findings known to differ between the mother and the fetus, such as red cell size, presence of fetal hemoglobin, and red cell phenotyping.[21]

The fetal mortality rate has been reported to be 1.2%[22] and the procedure carries a high risk of FMH. Its use is recommended only for certain circumstances, such as when serial amniotic fluid determinations indicate severe HDN or when hydrops is present.

Suppression of Maternal Alloimmunization

Several approaches to suppress maternal alloimmunization have been attempted in the last decade, two of which have limited clinical benefit in reducing maternal antibody levels: intensive plasma exchange and the administration of intravenous immunoglobulin (IVIG).[2,20] Plasma exchange can reduce antibody levels by as much as 75%, but rebound usually follows. Plasma exchange has been proposed as a way to delay the need for fetal intervention when there has been hydrops fetalis before 22 weeks' gestation in a previous pregnancy and the father is known to be homozygous for the implicated gene. IVIG infusion has also been shown to stabilize anti-D titers, with best results obtained when started before 28 weeks' gestation and when the fetus is not hydropic.[23] The mechanism of IVIG effect is not clear. It may work by saturating placental Fc receptors and inhibiting the transfer of maternal antibody, by suppressing ingestion of IgG-coated red cells by the fetal reticuloendothelial system, or by introducing anti-idiotype antibodies that modify maternal antibody production. Because these therapies are quite costly and may have only transient benefit, intrauterine transfusion is often necessary.

Intrauterine Transfusion

Intrauterine transfusion carries a 1-3% risk of perinatal loss and should be performed only after careful clinical evaluation.[22] Intrauterine transfusion is seldom feasible before the 20th week of gestation; once initiated, transfusions are usually administered periodically until delivery. The interval between transfusions depends on the presence or absence of hydrops, the gestational age and the amount of blood infused. Intrauterine transfusion can be performed by the intraperitoneal route (IPT) or the direct intravascular approach (IVT) by the umbilical vein. In many instances, IVT is the procedure of choice, but there may be problems of access that make IPT preferable; a combination may also be used to minimize peaks and troughs of fetal hematocrit between procedures. Good outcomes are achieved over 80% of the time and 94% of nonhydropic fetuses survive.[24] Other perinatal conditions that have been treated with intrauterine transfusion include parvovirus infection, large FMH, and alpha thalassemia.[25]

Techniques

IPT is performed through a needle passed, with ultrasonographic monitoring, through the mother's abdominal wall into the abdominal cavity of the fetus. Transfused red cells enter the fetal circulation through lymphatic channels that drain the peritoneal cavity. In IVT, the umbilical vein is penetrated under ultrasound guidance, and a blood sample taken to verify positioning in the fetal vasculature. Blood is infused directly, as either a simple transfusion or as a partial exchange transfusion. IVT can be particularly valuable for very severe cases of HDN associated with hydrops fetalis. In hydropic infants, red cells administered by IPT are not efficiently absorbed.

Selection of Red Cells

The red cells used should be group O, D-negative and negative for the antigen corresponding to the mother's antibody if the specificity is not anti-D. Blood for intrauterine transfusion should be irradiated,[26(p68)] and will often be cytomegalovirus (CMV) seronegative or leukocyte- reduced to decrease the risk of transmitting CMV, especially if the mother is CMV-seronegative or her immune status is unknown. It may also be desirable to transfuse only blood that is known to lack hemoglobin S. For maximal survival of the transfused cells, blood used for intrauterine transfusion should be drawn as recently as possible. Washed or deglycerolized preparations have been used for their normal electrolyte levels, absence of anticoagulant or plasma, low levels of platelets and leukocytes, and low risk of CMV transmission. The hematocrit is usually high to minimize the chance of volume overload in the fetus. Washed, irradiated maternal blood has also been used for intrauterine transfusion.[27] To remove the offending antibody, the red cells are washed and resuspended in saline to a final hematocrit between 75% and 85%.

Volume Administered

The volume transfused may vary with the technique used as well as the fetal size, initial hematocrit, and gestational age. For IPT, a volume calculated by the formula V = (gestation in weeks – 20) × 10 mL appears to be well tolerated by the fetus. The volume of red cells transfused by IVT can be calculated by the following formula[28]:

Fetoplacental volume (mL) =
ultrasound estimated fetal weight (g) × 0.14

Volume to transfuse (mL) =
fetoplacental volume ×

$$\frac{(\text{Hct after IVT} - \text{Hct before IVT})}{\text{Hct of donor cells}}$$

where Hct = hematocrit

Transfusion is repeated on the basis of an estimated decline in fetal hematocrit of approximately 1% per day in an effort to maintain the fetal hematocrit in the range of 27-30%.[29] Blood for intrauterine transfusions and all

blood and cellular components subsequently transfused in the neonatal period should be irradiated to prevent transfusion-associated graft-vs-host disease.[30,31]

Postpartum Evaluation

It is desirable to collect a sample of cord blood, preferably by syringe, from every newborn. This tube should be identified as cord blood and labeled in the delivery suite with the mother's name, the date, the infant's identification, and the hospital's number. Samples should be stored for at least 7 days in the blood bank for testing if the mother is D-negative or if the newborn develops signs and symptoms that suggest HDN.

In cases of suspected HDN, samples of both cord and maternal blood should be tested, as shown in Table 23-1. When the mother is known to have antibodies capable of causing HDN, the hemoglobin or hematocrit and the bilirubin level of cord blood should also be de-

Table 23-1. Serologic Studies Recommended for Maternal and Cord Blood When HDN Is Suspected

Maternal Blood
ABO
Rh
Weak D, if apparently D-negative
Test for FMH, if mother is D-negative and infant is D-positive
Identification of antibody, if present

Cord Blood
ABO
Rh
Weak D, if apparently D-negative
Direct antiglobulin test
Eluate from red cells, if DAT is positive and clinical circumstances warrant
Identification of antibody in eluate

termined. If the mother is D-negative and the infant D-positive, the mother's blood should be tested for FMH (see later section). Tests on the mother's blood present no special problems and can be done with routine techniques. Testing cord blood may present some special problems, which are described below.

ABO Testing

ABO testing on newborns relies entirely on red cell typing. ABO antibodies in cord serum are nearly always of maternal origin and are IgG which, unless present at very high levels, do not agglutinate reagent red cells. In the investigation of possible HDN due to ABO incompatibility, cord serum should be tested for antiglobulin-reactive ABO antibodies. If the infant will be transfused with non-O red cells, antiglobulin-reactive anti-A or -B must be sought.[26(p63)]

D Testing

Newborns who have had successful intrauterine transfusions often type at birth as D-negative or very weakly positive because over 90% of their circulating red cells may be those of the donors. The ABO and direct antiglobulin tests may also give misleading results.

If the infant's red cells are heavily coated with IgG antibodies, tests with anti-D may give either false-positive or false-negative results. (See Chapter 14.)

Antiglobulin Testing

The direct antiglobulin test (DAT) is usually strongly positive in HDN resulting from anti-D or antibodies in other blood groups; reactions are much weaker or even negative in HDN resulting from ABO antibodies. However, the strength of the DAT does not correlate with the severity of hemolysis, especially in ABO HDN. Infants who have received an intrauterine transfusion may have a weak DAT with a mixed-field pattern of agglutination. If the DAT

on cord cells is positive, the antibody can be eluted from the red cells and tested for specificity. It is not necessary to make and test an eluate if the maternal serum has been shown to contain a single red cell antibody. If the mother has multiple antibodies, it is not necessary to identify the hemolyzing antibody because, if transfusion is necessary, all the clinically significant red cell antibodies in the maternal serum must be respected. (See the section on Selection of Blood, later in this chapter.)

If the DAT is positive and the maternal serum has a negative screen for red cell antibodies, suspicion falls on ABO antibodies or on HDN caused by an antibody against a low-incidence antigen not present on reagent red cells. Testing the eluate from the cord cells against A_1 and B red cells should establish the diagnosis of ABO hemolytic disease. In the rare cases of ABO hemolytic disease that require transfusion, only group O red cells should be transfused.

Evaluation of ABO Antibodies. ABO hemolytic disease may be suspected on clinical grounds even though the DAT is negative. Cord blood serum should be tested by the indirect antiglobulin technique against A_1, B, and O red cells. The presence of anti-A, anti-B, or anti-A,B confirms the potential for ABO hemolytic disease. It is often possible to elute anti-A and/or anti-B from the infant's red cells despite a negative DAT, but this step is not necessary for the presumptive diagnosis. If transfusion is required, D-compatible group O blood should be transfused, whether or not the diagnosis has been serologically confirmed.

Antibodies to Low-Incidence Antigens. If ABO hemolytic disease is ruled out, antibody against a low-incidence red cell antigen should be suspected. Testing of the eluate, against the father's red cells with an antiglobulin technique, may provide an answer. The diagnosis can be confirmed by testing the mother's serum against the father's red cells, if they are ABO-compatible. If either or both of these tests are positive, it indicates that the father has transmitted to the child a red cell antigen to which the mother has an IgG antibody. Unless the mother has been exposed to red cells from the father or his blood relations, transfusion would be an unlikely immunizing event for a low-incidence antigen. Because there should be no difficulty in obtaining compatible blood, diagnostic studies can be performed after initial clinical concerns have been resolved.

If the DAT is positive and all attempts to characterize a coating red cell antibody are consistently negative, causes of a false-positive DAT should be considered. (See Chapter 20.)

Exchange Transfusion

Exchange transfusion, the indicated treatment for severe HDN, achieves several desired effects. Removal of the infant's blood reduces 1) the mass of antibody-coated red cells, the destruction of which causes bilirubin levels to rise; 2) a portion of the bilirubin that has accumulated; and 3) the number of unbound antibody molecules available to attach to newly formed antigen-positive cells. The red cells used for replacement are compatible with the antibody and provide increased oxygen-carrying capacity. Fresh frozen plasma, if used, restores not only albumin but also coagulation factors; albumin can be used as a replacement colloid.

Selection of Blood

In most cases the mother's serum is used for crossmatching and the red cells selected for transfusion are compatible with her ABO antibodies as well as the antibody(ies) responsible for the hemolytic process. Group O red cells resuspended in AB plasma are commonly used. In ABO hemolytic disease, the red cells used for exchange must be group O. If the antibody is anti-D, the red cells must be D-negative, but not every exchange transfusion requires group O, D-negative blood. If mother and infant are ABO-identical, group-specific red cells can be used. If the implicated antibody is not anti-D,

D-positive red cells may be given to a D-positive infant.

Maternal serum or plasma is the specimen of choice for crossmatching in exchange transfusion. It is available in large quantity, has the red cell antibody present in high concentration, and can be accurately and completely analyzed before delivery. Confounding factors are that maternal serum may contain antibodies directed against antigens not present on the infant's red cells, or IgM antibodies that have not crossed the placenta.

If maternal blood is not available or is unsuitable for crossmatching, the infant's serum and/or an eluate from the infant's red cells can be used for crossmatching. The eluate provides a concentrated preparation of the antibodies responsible for red cell destruction, but will not contain antibodies that may have crossed the placenta but are directed against antigens absent from the infant's red cells. The concentration of antibody in the infant's serum may be low, especially if most of the molecules are bound to the red cells. Use of the eluate or serum, or of both together, may be indicated if attempts to obtain a maternal specimen would delay therapy.

Subsequent Transfusion

Bilirubin may reaccumulate rapidly after a successful exchange transfusion despite appropriate phototherapy, partly because bilirubin in extravascular fluid will follow the concentration gradient and enter the intravascular space, and partly because residual antibody-coated cells continue to hemolyze. If rising bilirubin levels make a second or third exchange transfusion necessary, the same considerations of red cell selection and crossmatching apply.

Antibody Against a High-Incidence Antigen

Rarely, the mother's antibody reacts with a high-incidence antigen and no compatible blood is available. If this problem is recognized and identified before delivery, the mother's siblings can be evaluated for compatibility and suitability, or compatible donors can be sought through a rare donor file. If this very rare event is not recognized until after delivery, three choices are open:

1. Collect blood from the mother, if the obstetrician agrees. Remove as much plasma as possible, preferably by saline washing, and resuspend the red cells in AB plasma to the desired hematocrit. The unit must be irradiated.

2. If time permits, test the mother's siblings or other close relatives for compatibility and suitability. Blood from blood relations must be irradiated.

3. Use incompatible donor blood for the exchange transfusion if the clinical situation is sufficiently urgent. The exchange will reduce the bilirubin load, the most heavily antibody-coated cells, and the number of unbound antibody molecules. Residual antibody will, however, attach to the transfused cells and one or more additional exchanges will probably be needed as bilirubin accumulates.

Rh Immune Globulin

Rh Immune Globulin is a concentrate of predominantly IgG anti-D derived from pools of human plasma. A full dose of anti-D (approximately 300 µg) is sufficient to counteract the immunizing effects of 15 mL of D-positive red cells; this corresponds to approximately 30 mL of fetal whole blood. RhIG is available in a reduced dose, approximately 50 µg, which is protective for up to 2.5 mL of D-positive fetal red cells. This is used for first-trimester abortion or miscarriage, when the total blood volume of the fetus is less than 2.5 mL. However, it is seldom used at this time due to inaccurate prediction of trimesters and concern about having smaller doses stored and inadvertently given to women who require a full dose. The protective effect of RhIG on D-negative individuals exposed to D-positive cells probably

results from interference with antigen recognition in the induction phase of primary immunization.[32(p95)]

Antepartum Administration

Widespread postpartum use of Rh immunoprophylaxis has reduced pregnancy-associated immunization to the D antigen from approximately 13% to 1-2%. This risk is further decreased to 0.1% if RhIG is also given antepartum at 28 weeks of gestation.[4] The American College of Obstetricians and Gynecologists (ACOG) recommends antepartum RhIG prophylaxis.[33] When the mother receives RhIG during pregnancy, the infant may be born with a positive DAT, but with no evidence of hemolysis. The mother's serum will often exhibit anti-D reactivity. There must be good communication between the patient's physician and the blood bank staff at the institution where delivery takes place, to ensure correct interpretation of laboratory tests made at the time of delivery. The half-life of an injected dose of RhIG, in the absence of significant FMH, is approximately 21 days. Therefore, of 300 µg of anti-D given at 28 weeks, 20-30 µg could remain at the time of delivery 12 weeks later and some anti-D has remained detectable for as long as 6 months.

Antepartum RhIG is given at 28 weeks of gestation, based on the observation that, of women who develop anti-D during pregnancy, 92% do so at or after 28 weeks.[4] Blood obtained before injection of RhIG should be tested for ABO and D, including weak D; and for red cell antibodies, with identification of unexpected antibodies found. A D-negative woman who has antibodies other than anti-D is still a candidate for anti-D immunoprophylaxis.

Postpartum Administration

Cord blood from infants born to D-negative mothers should be tested for the D antigen. A D-negative woman with a D-positive infant should receive one full dose of RhIG within 72 hours of delivery, unless she is known to be alloimmunized to D previously. The presence of residual anti-D from antepartum RhIG does not indicate ongoing protection.

Active vs Passive Antibody. A few laboratory clues that may help distinguish passively administered RhIG from the anti-D of active alloimmunity is that passively acquired anti-D is entirely IgG; if a woman's anti-D is saline-reactive or can be completely or partially inactivated by treating the serum with 2-mercaptoethanol or dithiothreitol, it has an IgM component and probably represents active immunization. Passively acquired anti-D rarely achieves an antiglobulin titer above 4, so a high-titered antibody is likely to indicate active immunization. It is desirable to obtain confirmation from the physician's records, but RhIG should always be given when doubt cannot easily be resolved. It should also be given if there is any problem determining the Rh type.

Postpartum Evaluation. A sample of the mother's blood should be drawn, preferably within 1 hour after delivery, and evaluated for FMH of a quantity greater than that for which 300 µg RhIG is immunosuppressive. If the screening test demonstrates the presence of fetal cells, the extent of FMH must be determined so that an appropriate dose of RhIG can be administered[26(p70),32(pp412,564)] (see below). Postpartum RhIG should be given within 72 hours of delivery; if 72 hours pass without administration of RhIG, it is better to give the treatment late than not at all.

The following women are *not* candidates for RhIG:

1. The D-negative woman whose infant is D-negative.

2. Any D-positive woman. Very rare cases of HDN have been reported in infants whose mothers had a weak D phenotype, but routine RhIG prophylaxis is not recommended for women of the weak D phenotype.[5]

3. A D-negative woman known to be immunized to D.

Other Indications for RhIG

RhIG should be given to a D-negative woman after any obstetric event that might allow fetal cells to enter the mother's circulation: spontaneous or therapeutic abortion, ectopic pregnancy, amniocentesis, chorionic villus sampling, cordocentesis, antepartum hemorrhage, blunt abdominal trauma or fetal death.[34] If pregnancy in a D-negative woman terminates before 13 weeks of gestation, a 50 µg dose of RhIG is adequate to protect against the small fetal blood volume during the first trimester.[35] From 13 weeks' gestation until term, a full dose of RhIG should be given.

Amniocentesis

Amniocentesis can cause FMH and consequent Rh immunization. The D-negative woman who has amniocentesis at 16-18 weeks' gestation for genetic analysis should receive a full dose of RhIG at that time, a second full dose at 28 weeks of gestation, and the usual postpartum dose if the infant is D-positive. If a nonimmunized D-negative woman undergoes amniocentesis for any reason in the second or third trimester, a full dose of RhIG is indicated. If the procedure is repeated more than 21 days later, an additional full dose should be given.[20] If amniocentesis is performed to assess fetal maturity, and if delivery is expected within 48 hours of the procedure, RhIG can be withheld until the infant is born and confirmed to be D-positive. If more than 48 hours will elapse, RhIG should be given following amniocentesis. If delivery occurs within 21 days thereafter and there is no evidence of a massive FMH,[33] additional RhIG may not be essential, but prudent management suggests repeat RhIG administration at delivery.

Screening for Large-Volume FMH

Postpartum administration of RhIG may not prevent immunization if the quantity of D-positive fetal red cells entering the mother's circulation exceeds the immunosuppressive capacity of RhIG. One 300-µg dose protects against 15 mL of D-positive red cells or 30 mL of fetal blood. Only 0.3% of pregnancies are estimated to sustain transplacental hemorrhage greater than 30 mL, but large FMH is an important and preventable cause of failed immunoprophylaxis.[4,35] ACOG recommends postpartum testing for large FMH only for high-risk pregnancies,[33] but Ness and colleagues[36] showed that testing only on the ACOG criteria would miss 50% of mothers actually exposed to large-volume FMH. AABB *Standards* requires examination of a postpartum specimen from all D-negative women at risk of immunization, to detect the presence of FMH that requires more than one dose of RhIG.[26(p70)] In rare cases, a massive FMH can cause fetal death and infuse enough Rh-positive cells into the maternal circulation to simulate a weak D in an Rh-negative patient.[33,37] Unless recognized and treated with an adequate dose of RhIG, this will likely lead to isoimmunization.

"Microscopic Weak D." In the past, some workers looked for D-positive red cells in the mother's D-negative blood by examining microscopically the antiglobulin phase of the test for D ("microscopic weak D test"); mixed-field reactivity indicated a substantial admixture with D-positive cells. This procedure should not be used to identify large FMH, however, because it does not adequately detect the number of cells likely to be involved. When specimens are prepared to simulate a 30-mL D-positive hemorrhage in the circulation of an average-sized D-negative woman, personnel who use this procedure often fail to demonstrate the admixture.[38]

The Rosette Test. The rosette test effectively demonstrates small numbers of D-positive cells in a D-negative suspension. The suspension is incubated with an anti-D reagent of human origin, and antibody molecules attach to sites on D-positive cells in the suspension. Indicator D-positive cells are then added, which react with antibody molecules bound to the surface of the already-present

D-positive cells and form visible agglutinates (rosettes) around them. (See Method 5.1.) This method will detect FMHs of approximately 10 mL,[20,38] a sensitivity that provides a desirable margin of safety for a screening test. Weak D-positive cells do not react as strongly in the rosette procedure as normal D-positive cells. If the newborn is mixed-field positive for weak D, FMH can be evaluated by the Kleihauer-Betke acid-elution test (see below), which identifies fetal hemoglobin, not a surface antigen. The rosette test gives only qualitative results; a positive result must be followed by a quantitative test such as an acid-elution procedure, an enzyme-linked antiglobulin test (ELAT), or flow cytometry.

Quantifying FMH

Historically, quantification of FMH has been achieved by the Kleihauer-Betke acid-elution test, which relies on the differences between fetal and adult hemoglobin in resistance to acid-elution. (See Method 5.2.) Results are reported as percentage of fetal cells, but the precision and accuracy of the procedure may be poor. Because 300 µg of RhIG will protect against FMH of 30 mL of D-positive fetal blood, the number of doses of RhIG required is determined by dividing the estimated volume of fetal blood present by 30.

For example:

1. Kleihauer-Betke reported as 1.3%
2. $(1.3/100) \times 5000$ mL* = 65 mL of fetal blood
3. 65/(30 mL per dose) = 2.2 doses of RhIG required

    * = mother's arbitrarily assigned blood volume

Because quantification by this procedure is inherently imprecise and because the consequences of undertreatment can be serious, it is desirable to provide a safety margin in calculating RhIG dosage. One approach is as follows:

1. When the number to the right of the decimal point is less than 5, round down and add one dose of RhIG (example: If the cal-

culation comes to 2.2 doses, give 3 doses).

2. When the number to the right of the decimal point is 5 or greater, round up to the next number and add one dose of RhIG (example: If the calculation comes to 2.8 doses, give 4 doses).

Not more than five doses of RhIG should be injected intramuscularly at one time. For larger quantities, injections can be spaced over a 72-hour period for patient comfort; an optimal time sequence has not been established. An intravenous preparation of anti-D has been approved by the Food and Drug Administration for use in the suppression of Rh immunization.

Alternative methods used to quantify FMH include ELAT and flow cytometry; both rely on differences between maternal and fetal blood types, unlike the acid-elution procedure that is independent of blood type. Both have sensitivity at least equal to the Kleihauer-Betke technique, and provide a more objective and reproducible endpoint.[39,40] Neither, however, has been routinely adopted by blood banks.

Neonatal Immune Thrombocytopenia

Maternal IgG antibodies to platelets can cross the placenta and cause severe antenatal and neonatal thrombocytopenia. Two categories of immune thrombocytopenia are recognized, and the distinction between them is therapeutically important.

Neonatal Alloimmune Thrombocytopenia

The mechanism of neonatal alloimmune thrombocytopenia (NAIT) is similar to that of HDN. Fetal platelets, expressing a paternal antigen absent from the mother's cells, may enter the mother's circulation during gestation or delivery. If she experiences alloimmunization, the maternal IgG antibody crosses the placenta and causes neonatal thrombocytopenia. The maternal platelet count remains normal. The incidence of NAIT is approximately 1 in 2000 live births.[41]

Unlike HDN, NAIT often affects first-born children, about 60% of cases occurring in a woman's first child. The thrombocytopenia is self-limiting, normally resolving in 2-3 weeks. NAIT varies in severity from mild thrombocytopenia with no clinical signs to overt clinical bleeding; the incidence of intracranial hemorrhage has been reported as 10-30%, with approximately half occurring in utero.[42] Recurrence in subsequent pregnancies is frequent, with equal or increasing severity, so a woman known to be alloimmunized must receive skilled antenatal attention.

Serologic Testing

Serologic diagnosis should be sought in a woman whose infant has had NAIT. Several platelet-specific antigen systems have been associated with NAIT, with HPA-1a antigen (Pl^{A1}) accounting for approximately 90% of cases.[41] Pregnancy, rather than transfusion, is the usual immunizing event. Approximately 2% of the population is HPA-1a negative; approximately 10% of HPA-1a-negative women with HPA-1a-positive infants become immunized.[43] There seems to be an association between developing anti-HPA 1a and possessing the HLA phenotype DRw52a.[43] While antibodies to HLA Class I antigens are frequently encountered in pregnancy, and platelets express Class I antigens, this is a rare cause of NAIT.[44]

Prenatal Considerations

With a knowledge of antibody specificity and gene frequencies, the likelihood of subsequent siblings being affected can be predicted (Table 23-2). The recognized platelet-specific antigens occur in diallelic systems, so typing the father's platelets indicates zygosity. If the father is homozygous for the expression of the antigen, there is no need to determine the fetal antigen status, as all offspring will be affected. If the father is heterozygous for the expression of the antigen, then there is a 50% chance that subsequent offspring will have the offending antigen. In an at-risk pregnancy, the genotype of the fetus (and by inference the platelet phenotype) can be determined by DNA typing on fetal cells obtained by amniocentesis.

When the risk of NAIT is high, a fetal blood sample for platelet count determination can be obtained by cordocentesis as early as 20 weeks' gestation. When the infant is found to be thrombocytopenic, the mother is often given infusions of IVIG in weekly doses of 1 g/kg, with or without steroids, until delivery.[41,42] Alternatively, some authorities would recommend empiric treatment with IVIG in cases of a homozygous paternal genotype for the offending

platelet antigen or in situations where the fetus is found to carry the offending platelet antigen utilizing polymerase chain reaction and amniocentesis.

Sources of Platelets. Maternal platelets are often prepared for use at delivery; when they undergo required testing for infectious disease markers, any previously administered high-dose IVIG will likely cause false-positive immunoassays. It is therefore desirable to test the mother before initiating IVIG therapy and those with confirmed positive results should not be used as a source of platelets. Because cordocentesis carries a risk of serious bleeding in a thrombocytopenic fetus, compatible platelets are often infused if the platelet count is

Table 23-2. Human Platelet Alloantigen System[45]*

Alloantigen System	Allelic Forms	Phenotypic Frequency		Risk of Subsequent Affected Fetus According to Maternal Antibody Specificity[†]	
HPA-1 (P^A)	HPA-1a (Pl^{A1})	72%	HPA-1a/1a	Anti-HPA-1a	86.75%
		26%	HPA-1a/1b		
	HPA-1b (Pl^{A2})	2%	HPA-1b/1b	Anti-HPA-1b	53.60%
HPA-2 (Ko)	HPA-2a (Ko^b)	85%	HPA-2a/2a	Anti-HPA-2a	92.14%
		14%	HPA-2a/2b		
	HPA-2b (Ko^a)	1%	HPA-2b/2b	Anti-HPA-2b	53.35%
HPA-3 (Bak)	HPA-3a (Bak^a)	37%	HPA-3a/3a	Anti-HPA-3a	71.7%
		48%	HPA-3a/3b		
	HPA-3b (Bak^b)	15%	HPA-3b/3b	Anti-HPA-3b	61.9%
HPA-4 (Pen)	HPA-4a (Pen^a)	99%	HPA-4a/4a	Anti-HPA-4a	>99%
		<0.1%	HPA-4a/4b		
	HPA-4b (Pen^b)	<0.1%	HPA-4b/4b	Anti-HPA-4b	~50%
HPA-5 (Br)	HPA-5a (Br^b)	80%	HPA-5a/5a	Anti-HPA-5a	89.7%
		19%	HPA-5a/5b		
	HPA-5b (Br^a)	1%	HPA-5b/5b	Anti-HPA-5b	52.5%

*Phenotypic frequencies for the platelet antigen systems shown are for the Caucasian population only. Significant differences in gene frequencies may be found in African and Asian populations.
[†]Assuming a first-affected pregnancy has been diagnosed with NAIT and there is an incompatibility with the expected antibody and that antibody has been found on parental typing and in the maternal serum. This estimate also assumes the father was not typed for the alternate allele.

low. The platelets can be collected either from the mother or from another donor whose platelets lack the corresponding antigen and whose plasma is compatible with the fetal red cells. If maternal platelets are used, the antibody-containing plasma should be removed and the platelets resuspended in compatible plasma or saline with reduced volume (see Method 6.12). All components for intrauterine transfusion must be irradiated[26(p68)] and should be CMV-negative or leukocyte-reduced.[46]

Scheduling Therapy. Various strategies have been used in the management of fetal thrombocytopenia. Although weekly platelet transfusions have been utilized in the past, the inherent risk of repeated cordocenteses has resulted in the use of IVIG as the preferred treatment. Another approach is administration of a single platelet transfusion just before delivery if cordocentesis reveals severe thrombocytopenia. This approach is usually reserved for pregnancies at extreme risk for intracranial hemorrhage.

Management After Delivery

Platelet counts can continue to decrease after birth and should be monitored. If bleeding appears imminent, compatible platelets should be given. If compatible platelets are not available, the use of high-dose IVIG should be considered, but this treatment has induced variable responses. In patients who do respond, platelet counts usually start increasing within 24-48 hours, although longer periods of time have been seen in some patients.[41] Because response is slow, the neonate with an urgent need for transfusion and no available compatible platelets may have to receive platelets from random donors.

Thrombocytopenia Secondary to Maternal ITP

Infants born to mothers with active idiopathic (autoimmune) thrombocytopenic purpura (ITP) are often not profoundly thrombo-

cytopenic and have a smaller risk of hemorrhage than infants with NAIT.[7,44] The antibody in ITP is usually IgG, which readily crosses the placenta. Occasionally, delivery of a severely thrombocytopenic infant has led to the diagnosis of previously unsuspected ITP in a moderately affected mother (postpartum platelet count 75-100,000/μL). Gestational thrombocytopenia can occur in which a mother with no history of autoimmune disorder has a platelet count less than 150,000/μL.[14] The risk of severe fetal thrombocytopenia (usually defined as platelet count less than 50,000/μL) is 7-10%[47,48] in cases of maternal ITP. The risk of intracranial hemorrhage in infants born to mothers with ITP is low—only six cases have been reported since 1973.[48] Routine fetal platelet assessment is not recommended and cesarean section is reserved for obstetric indications only.[48]

The antibody in ITP has broad reactivity against platelets. If the infant has a high concentration of antibody, there will be uniformly short survival of platelets from random donors, from the mother, or from other family members. Responses do sometimes occur, and in the presence of hemorrhage, platelet transfusions will be used as emergency therapy.[44] Exchange transfusion can be effective in the removal of circulating antibodies and is usually followed by platelet transfusion. Intravenous immunoglobulin therapy may also be effective for severe autoimmune thrombocytopenia.[49]

References

1. Vaughn JI, Manning M, Warwick RM, et al. Inhibition of erythroid progenitor cells by anti-Kell antibodies in fetal alloimmune anemia. N Engl J Med 1998;338:798-803.

2. Bowman JM. Intrauterine transfusion. In: Anderson KC, Ness PM, eds. Scientific basis of transfusion medicine: Implications for clinical practice. Philadelphia: WB Saunders, 1994:403-20.

3. Bowman JM. Treatment options for the fetus with alloimmune hemolytic disease. Transfus Med Rev 1990;4:191-207.

4. Bowman JM. The prevention of Rh immunization. Transfus Med Rev 1988;2:129-50.

5. Judd WJ, Luban NLC, Ness PM, et al. Prenatal and perinatal immunohematology: Recommendations for serologic management of the fetus, newborn infant, and obstetric patient. Transfusion 1990; 30:175-83.

6. Kanter MH. Derivation of new mathematic formulas for determining whether a D-positive father is heterozygous or homozygous for the D antigen. Am J Obstet Gynecol 1992;166:61-3.

7. Bennett PR, Le Van Kim C, Colon Y, et al. Prenatal determination of fetal RhD type by DNA amplification. N Engl J Med 1993;329:607-10.

8. Hessner MJ, Pircon RA, Luhm RA. Development of an allele specific polymerase chain reaction assay of prenatal genotyping of Jk^a and Jk^b of the Kidd blood group system (abstract). Am J Obstet Gynecol 1998;178:52S.

9. Lee S, Bennett PR, Overton T, et al. Prenatal diagnosis of Kell blood group genotypes: KEL1 and KEL2. Am J Obstet Gynecol 1996;175:445-9.

10. Le Van Kim C, Mouro I, Brossard Y, et al. PCR-based determination of the Rhc and RhE status of the fetus at risk for Rhc and RhE hemolytic disease. Br J Haematol 1994;88:193-5.

11. Spence WC, Potter P, Maddalena A, et al. DNA-based prenatal determination of the RhEe genotype. Obstet Gynecol 1995;86:670-2.

12. Management of isoimmunization in pregnancy. ACOG Educational Bulletin Number 227. Washington, DC: American College of Obstetricians and Gynecologists, 1996.

13. Gottvall T, Hilden JO. Concentration of anti-D antibodies in Rh(D) alloimmunized pregnant women as a predictor of anemia and/or hyperbilirubinemia in their newborn infants. Acta Obstet Gynecol Scand 1997;76:733-8.

14. Cohen JA, Brecher ME. Obstetrical and gynecological transfusion practice. In: Speiss BD, Counts RB, Gould SA, eds. Perioperative transfusion medicine. Baltimore, MD: Williams and Wilkins, 1998:507-22.

15. Bowman JM, Pollock JM, Manning FA, et al. Maternal Kell blood group alloimmunization. Obstet Gynecol 1992;79:239-44.

16. Engelfriet CP, Reesink HW, Bowman JM, et al. Laboratory procedures for the prediction of the severity of haemolytic disease of the newborn (international forum). Vox Sang 1995;6961-9.

17. Hume HA. Fetal and neonatal transfusion therapy. In: Pomphilon DH, ed. Modern transfusion medicine. Boca Raton, FL: CRC Press, 1995:193-215.

18. Liley AW. Liquor amnii analysis in the management of the pregnancy complicated by rhesus sensitization. Am J Obstet Gynecol 1961;82:1359-70.

19. Queenan JT, Tomai TP, Ural SH, King JC. Deviation in amniotic fluid optical density at a wavelength of 450 nm in Rh-immunized pregnancies from 14 to 40 weeks' gestation: A proposal for clinical management. Am J Obstet Gynecol 1993;168:1370-6.

20. Moise KJ. Management of red cell alloimmunization in pregnancy. In: Sacher RA, Brecher ME, eds. Obstetric transfusion practice. Bethesda, MD: American Association of Blood Banks, 1993:21-47.

21. Steiner EA, Judd WJ, Oberman HA, et al. Percutaneous umbilical blood sampling and umbilical vein transfusions: Rapid serologic differentiation of fetal blood from maternal blood. Transfusion 1990;30:104-8.

22. Ludomirsky A. Intrauterine fetal blood sampling—a multicenter registry evaluation of 7462 procedures between 1987-1991. Am J Obstet Gynecol 1993;168:318.

23. Margulies M, Voto LS, Mathet E, Margulies M. High dose intravenous IgG for the treatment of severe Rhesus alloimmunization. Vox Sang 1991;61: 181-9.

24. Schumacher B, Moise KJ Jr. Fetal transfusion for red blood cell alloimmunization in pregnancy (review). Obstet Gynecol 1996;88:137-50.

25. Skupski DW, Wolf CF, Bussel JB. Fetal transfusion therapy (review). Obstet Gynecol Surv 1996; 51:181-92.

26. Menitove JE, ed. Standards for blood banks and transfusion services, 19th ed. Bethesda, MD: American Association of Blood Banks, 1999.

27. Gonsoulin WJ, Moise KJ, Milam JD, et al. Serial maternal blood donations for intrauterine transfusion. Obstet Gynecol 1990;75:158-62.

28. Mandelbrot L, Daffos F, Forestier F, et al. Assessment of fetal blood volume for computer-assisted management of in utero transfusion. Fetal Ther 1988;3:60-6.

29. Moise KJ, Carpenter RJ, Kirshon B, et al. Comparison of four types of intrauterine transfusion: Effect on fetal hematocrit. Fetal Ther 1989;4:126-37.

30. Sanders MR, Graeber JE. Posttransfusion graft-versus-host disease in infancy. J Pediatr 1990;117:159-63.

31. Linden JV, Pisciotto PT. Transfusion-associated graft-versus-host disease and blood irradiation. Transfus Med Rev 1992;6:116-23.

32. Mollison PL, Engelfriet CP, Contreras M. Blood transfusion in clinical medicine. 10th ed. Oxford, England: Blackwell Scientific Publications, 1997.

33. Prevention of D isoimmunization. ACOG Technical Bulletin Number 147. Washington, DC: American College of Obstetricians and Gynecologists, 1990.

34. Hartwell EA. Use of Rh immune globulin ASCP Practice Parameter. Am J Clin Pathol 1998; 110:281-92.

35. Depalma L, Luban NLC. Alloimmune hemolytic disease of the newborn. In: Beutler E, Lichtman MA, Coller BS, Kipps TL, eds. Williams' hematology, 5th ed. New York: McGraw-Hill, 1995:697-704.

36. Ness PM, Baldwin ML, Niebyl JR. Clinical high risk designation does not predict excess fetal maternal hemorrhage. Am J Obstet Gynecol 1987;156:154-8.

37. Owen J, Stedman CH, Tucker TL. Comparison of predelivery versus postdelivery Kleihauer-Betke stains in cases of fetal death. Am J Obstet Gynecol 1989;161:663-6.

38. Sebring ES. Fetomaternal hemorrhage-incidence and methods of detection and quantitation. In: Garratty G, ed. Hemolytic disease of the newborn. Arlington, VA: American Association of Blood Banks, 1984:87-117.

39. Riley JZ, Ness PM, Taddie SJ, et al. The detection and quantitation of fetal-maternal hemorrhage using an enzyme-linked antiglobulin test (ELAT). Transfusion 1982;22:472-4.

40. Bayliss KM, Kueck BD, Johnson ST, et al. Detecting fetomaternal hemorrhage: A comparison of five methods. Transfusion 1991;31:303-7.

41. Uhrynowska M, Maslanka K, Zupanska. Neonatal thrombocytopenia: Incidence, serological and clinical observations. Am J Perinatol 1997;14:415-8.

42. Johnson JA, Ryan G, al-Musa A, et al. Prenatal diagnosis and management of neonatal alloimmune thrombocytopenia. Semin Perinatol 1997;21:45-52.

43. Waters AW, Murphy M, Hambley H, Nicolaides K. Management of alloimmune thrombocytopenia in the fetus and neonate. In: Nance SJ, ed. Clinical and basic science aspects of immunohematology. Arlington, VA: American Association of Blood Banks, 1991:155-77.

44. Blanchette VS, Kuhne T, Hume H, Hellman J. Platelet transfusion therapy in newborn infants. Transfus Med Rev 1995;9:215-30.

45. McFarland JG. Prenatal and perinatal management of alloimmune cytopenias. In: Nance ST, ed. Alloimmunity: 1993 and beyond. Bethesda, MD: American Association of Blood Banks, 1993:165-93.

46. Leukocyte reduction for the prevention of transfusion-transmitted cytomegalovirus (TT-CMV). Association Bulletin 97-2. Bethesda, MD: American Association of Blood Banks, 1997.

47. Bussel JB. Immune thrombocytopenia in pregnancy: Autoimmune and alloimmune. J Reprod Immunol 1997;37:35-61.

48. Payne SD, Resnik R, Moore TR, et al. Maternal characteristics and risk of severe neonatal thrombocytopenia and intracranial hemorrhage in pregnancies complicated by autoimmune thrombocytopenia. Am J Obstet Gynecol 1997;177:149-55.

49. Blanchette VS, Kirby MA, Turner C. Role of intravenous immunoglobulin G in autoimmune hematologic disorders. Semin Hematol 1992;29:72-82.

24

Neonatal and Pediatric Transfusion Practice

MANY PHYSIOLOGIC CHANGES accompany the transitions from fetus to neonate, neonate to infant, and throughout childhood. Hematologic values, blood volume, and physiologic responses to stresses such as hypovolemia and hypoxia vary widely. The most dynamic changes occur during early infancy. Consequently, pediatric transfusion concerns are usually divided into two periods: neonates from birth through 4 months, and older infants (>4 months) and children. Some concerns in neonatal transfusion practice overlap those of the perinatal period. Chapter 23 discusses two major perinatal concerns.

Advances in medical care now permit the survival of extremely premature neonates. Blood providers must be capable of furnishing blood components that are tailored to satisfy the specific needs of very low birthweight (VLBW <1500 g) and extremely low birthweight (ELBW <1000 g) patients, whose small blood volumes and impaired organ functions provide little margin for safety. Ill neonates are more likely than hospitalized patients of any other age group to receive red cell transfusions.[1] Advances in critical-care neonatology, such as surfactant therapy, nitric oxide therapy, use of high-frequency ventilators, and adherence to transfusion practice guidelines, have diminished the number of blood transfusions given; most are now given to infants with birth weights less than 1000 g.[1]

Fetal and Neonatal Erythropoiesis

The predominant sites of hematopoiesis in the developing embryo shift from the wall of the yolk sac to the liver to the marrow in the first 24 weeks.[2] Hematopoiesis is regulated by gradually increasing erythropoietin (EPO) levels stimulated by low oxygen tensions during intrauterine life. Fetal red cells, rich in hemoglobin F, are well adapted to low intrauterine oxygen tensions. The high oxygen affinity of fetal hemoglobin enhances transfer of oxygen exchange from maternal erythrocytes to fetal erythrocytes throughout pregnancy.

The "switch" from fetal to adult hemoglobin begins about 32 weeks' gestation; at birth, hemoglobin F constitutes 60-80% of the total hemoglobin. Preterm neonates, therefore, are born with higher levels of fetal hemoglobin than those born at term. The mean cord hemoglobin of healthy term neonates is 16.9 ± 1.6 g/dL, and that of preterm neonates is 15.9 ± 2.4 g/dL.[3] Hemoglobin concentration gradually falls in the first few weeks of life. This has been called "physiologic anemia of infancy" in term newborns and "physiologic anemia of prematurity" in preterm newborns. It is considered physiologic because it is self-limited, is usually well tolerated, and is not associated with any abnormalities in the infant. Erythropoietic activity diminishes secondary to an increase in pulmonary blood flow and rise in arterial pO_2, as well as the increase in red cell content of 2,3-diphosphoglycerate (2,3-DPG) and of hemoglobin A, that enhance the release of oxygen to the tissues. As tissue oxygenation improves, levels of EPO decline and erythropoiesis diminishes. This, along with decreased survival of fetal red cells and expansion of the blood volume due to rapid growth, causes the hemoglobin concentration to decline. The rate of decline is dependent on gestational age at birth; hemoglobin may drop to as low as 8.0 g/dL at 4-8 weeks of age in preterm infants with birthweights of 1000-1500 g and 7.0 g/dL in neonates with birthweights less than 1000 g.[2]

Despite hemoglobin levels that would indicate anemia in older children and adults, the normally developing infant usually maintains adequate tissue oxygenation. Physiologic anemia requires treatment only if the degree or timing of the anemia causes symptoms in the patient.

Unique Aspects of Neonatal Physiology

Infant Size and Blood Volume

Full-term newborns have a blood volume of approximately 85 mL/kg; preterm low birthweight newborns have an average blood volume of 100 mL/kg. As survival rates continue to improve for infants weighing 1000 g or less at birth, blood banks will increasingly be asked to provide blood components for patients whose total blood volume is less than 100 mL. The need for frequent laboratory tests has made replacement of iatrogenic blood loss the most common indication for transfusion of low birthweight preterm neonates. However, the previous practice of replacing blood mL for mL is now giving way to replacement as needed in order to maintain a target hematocrit in certain clinical situations.[1]

Newborns do not compensate for hypovolemia as well as adults. After a 10% volume depletion, a newborn diminishes the left ventricular stroke volume, without increasing the heart rate. To maintain systemic blood pressure, peripheral vascular resistance increases and this, combined with the diminished cardiac output, results in poor tissue perfusion, low tissue oxygenation, and metabolic acidosis.[4]

Erythropoietin Response

Erythropoietin response in newborns differs from that of adults and older children. In older children and adults, oxygen sensors in the kidney recognize diminished oxygen delivery and release EPO into the circulation. In the fetus, the oxygen sensor that stimulates EPO production is believed to be the liver, which appears to be programmed for the hypoxic intrauterine environment.

This hyporesponsiveness to hypoxia protects the fetus from becoming polycythemic. Eventually, EPO production shifts from the liver to the kidneys, a developmental change thought to be regulated by time of conception, not birth, and possibly not beginning until term. After birth, it is the most immature infants who produce the least amount of EPO for any degree of anemia; this may reflect the absence of the developmental shift of erythropoietin production from the liver to the kidneys.[5] Sick preterm neonates who receive many transfusions shortly after birth have reduced circulating levels of fetal hemoglobin. Circulating EPO levels are lower, for a given hematocrit, in preterm neonates with higher proportions of hemoglobin A (which favors release of oxygen to the tissues) relative to hemoglobin F.[5] Erythroid progenitor cells in the hypoproliferative marrow of these preterm infants show normal intrinsic sensitivity to EPO. Clinical trials of recombinant human erythropoietin (r-HuEPO) in premature neonates show that the number of transfusions and severity of anemia can be lessened.[6] However, in view of the changing patterns of transfusion practice in VLBW infants and strategies to decrease donor exposure in this group of patients, the ultimate role of r-HuEPO in the management of "anemia of prematurity" is not clearly delineated.[1,7]

Cold Stress

Hypothermia in the newborn causes exaggerated effects, including increased metabolic rate, hypoglycemia, metabolic acidosis, and a tendency toward apneic episodes that may lead to hypoxia, hypotension, and cardiac arrest. Because exchange transfusion with blood at room temperature may decrease a newborn's rectal temperature by 0.7-2.5 C, blood for exchange transfusion should be warmed. The usual method is to use an in-line warmer. Blood should not be warmed under a radiant heater (either large or small volumes). When transfusions are given to infants in the phototherapy unit, the tubing should be introduced through the side port because red cells in the tubing that enters the top port may be hemolyzed.[8]

Immunologic Status

Infants have an immature and inexperienced cellular and humoral immune system. Antibodies present derive almost entirely from the maternal circulation. Transplacental transfer of immunoglobulin and other proteins is independent of molecular size; IgG (150 kD) is transferred much more readily than albumin (64 kD). In humans, maternal IgM does not reach the fetus and IgA is not readily transferred, although low levels have been found in the newborn.

All four subclasses of IgG are transported across the placenta, but the rate varies between individual mother-fetus pairs. Early in pregnancy (approximately 12 weeks), IgG probably passes from mother to fetus by diffusion, and concentration in fetal serum is low for all subgroups. Between 20 and 33 weeks of gestation, fetal IgG levels rise markedly, apparently due to maturation of a selective transport system that involves, in part, specific protein receptors on the membrane of placental cells.[9] IgG1, the predominant subclass in maternal blood, crosses the placenta first and is transported in greatest quantity. Cord blood has higher antibody concentrations than maternal blood. Catabolism of IgG occurs more slowly in the fetus than in the mother,[10] so that transplacental maternal antibody is conserved during the neonatal period.

A fetus exposed to an infectious process in utero or an infant exposed shortly after birth may produce small amounts of IgM detectable by sensitive techniques, but unexpected red cell alloantibodies of either IgG or IgM class are rarely formed during the neonatal period.[11] The mechanism responsible for the lack of alloantibody production is not clearly understood and is most probably multifactorial including deficient T helper function, enhanced T suppresser activity, and poor antigen-presenting cell (APC) function.[11]

The cellular immune response is critical to the occurrence of transfusion-associated graft-vs-host disease (TA-GVHD). In the newborn, TA-GVHD has been reported most often in the clinical setting of confirmed or suspected congenital immunodeficiency. It has been recommended that infants with suspected and/or documented T-cell immunodeficiency receive irradiated blood components. The majority of cases being reported outside this setting have occurred in infants who received intrauterine transfusion followed by postnatal exchange transfusion.[12] A proposed explanation is that lymphocytes given during intrauterine transfusion could induce host tolerance, impairing rejection of lymphocytes given in the subsequent exchange transfusions. There have also been rare cases of TA-GVHD reported in association with extreme prematurity, neonatal alloimmune thrombocytopenia, and the use of extracorporeal membrane oxygenation (ECMO).[12,13] Obviously, there are several risk factors other than the immune status that predispose recipients to TA-GVHD, such as the number and viability of lymphocytes in the transfused component as well as the likelihood of a one-way HLA match. The true incidence of TA-GVHD in the neonatal setting is not known. However, on the basis of data from Japan, it appears that the incidence of reported TA-GVHD is far less than would be expected.[13] The transfusion recipient's immune response is critical to the occurrence of TA-GVHD; the postulated mechanism for this apparent decreased susceptibility of newborns to TA-GVHD is thought to be extrathymic and/or thymic semitolerance of allogeneic donor T lymphocytes. As for all

patients, directed-donor units from biologic relatives should be irradiated.[13]

Metabolic Problems

Acidosis or hypocalcemia may occur after large-volume whole blood or plasma transfusion because the immature liver of the newborn metabolizes citrate inefficiently. Immature kidneys have reduced glomerular filtration rate and concentrating ability, and newborns may have difficulty excreting excess potassium, acid, and/or calcium.

Potassium

Although potassium levels increase rapidly in the plasma of stored red cells, small-volume, simple transfusions administered slowly have little effect on serum potassium concentration in newborns. It has been calculated that transfusion of 10 mL/kg of red cells (hematocrit 80%) obtained from a unit of blood stored for 42 days in extended storage medium would deliver 0.1 mEq of potassium.[14] This is much less than the daily potassium requirement of 2-3 mEq/kg for a 1-kg patient. Serum potassium may, however, rise rapidly after infusion of large volumes of red cells in such circumstances as surgery, exchange transfusion, or extracorporeal circulation, depending upon the plasma potassium levels in the blood and manipulation of the blood component.

In stored irradiated blood, the problem of potassium leak is potentiated; it may be desirable, for selected patients, to wash irradiated cells if they have subsequently been stored.[15] It is preferable to perform irradiation as close to the time of administration as possible.

2,3-Diphosphoglycerate

Neonates with respiratory distress syndrome or septic shock have decreased levels of 2,3-DPG. Alkalosis and hypothermia may further increase the oxygen affinity of hemoglobin, shifting the dissociation curve to the left and making oxygen even less available to the tissues. Arterial oxygenation may be further compromised by respiratory distress syndrome or other pulmonary disease. Mechanisms that compensate for hypoxia in adults, such as increased heart rate, are limited in newborns. If a large proportion of an infant's blood volume has come from transfusion of 2,3-DPG-depleted blood, this may cause problems that would not affect older children or adults. Because 2,3-DPG levels decrease in stored blood, exchange transfusion in newborns should use the freshest blood conveniently available. For small-volume transfusions, the medical necessity for fresh blood has never been demonstrated and arguments have been raised to suggest it is unnecessary.[1]

Cytomegalovirus Infection

Perinatal infection by cytomegalovirus (CMV) may occur, acquired either in utero or during the birth process, and neonates can be infected during breast feeding or by close contact with mothers or nursery personnel. CMV can also be transmitted by transfusion, although the risk from the current blood supply is small.[16]

Infection in newborns has extremely variable manifestations, ranging from asymptomatic seroconversion to death. Studies of CMV in neonatal transfusion recipients reveal the following observations:

1. The overall risk of symptomatic posttransfusion CMV infection seems to be inversely related to the seropositivity rate in the community. Where many adults are positive for CMV antibodies, the rate of symptomatic CMV infection in newborns is low.
2. Symptomatic CMV infection during the neonatal period is uncommon in children born to seropositive mothers.
3. The risk of symptomatic posttransfusion infection is high in multitransfused preterm infants weighing less than 1200 g who are born to seronegative mothers.[14]

4. The risk of acquiring CMV infection is directly proportional to the cumulative number of donor exposures incurred during transfusion.
5. Cytomegalovirus in blood is associated with leukocytes. The risk of virus transmission can be reduced by transfusion of blood from seronegative donors or of components that contain very small numbers of CMV-containing leukocytes. Deglycerolized red cells, both seronegative and seropositive, have been used successfully.[17] The use of washed red cells may have some effect, but the use of washed cells for this indication remains controversial.[18] Leukocyte reduction with highly efficient leukocyte-reduction filters also appears to be an effective way of reducing CMV infection.[19,20]

Red Cell Transfusions in Infants Less Than 4 Months of Age

Red Blood Cells (RBCs) are the component most often transfused during the neonatal period. Many of the physiologic considerations mentioned affect decisions about indications for transfusion selection and administration of red cell components, and the requirements for compatibility testing.

Compatibility Testing

Because the neonate and young infant are immunologically immature, alloimmunization to red cell antigens is rare during the neonatal period. A study of 90 neonates who received 1269 transfusions from different donors found no instances of antibody production even with use of very sensitive detection techniques.[21] Other investigators confirm the relative infrequency of alloantibodies directed against red cell, as well as HLA, antigens.[11,18]

Because alloimmunization is extremely rare and repeated testing increases iatrogenic blood loss, AABB *Standards for Blood Banks and Transfusion Services*[22(p62-63)] requires only limited pretransfusion serologic testing for infants under 4 months old. Initial testing must include ABO and D typing of red cells and a screen for red cell antibodies; the antibody detection test may be done on either serum or plasma, from either the mother, or, if not available, the infant.

During any one hospitalization, compatibility testing and repeat ABO and D typing may be omitted, provided that the screen for red cell antibodies is negative; that all red cells transfused are group O or ABO-identical or ABO-compatible; and that red cells are either D-negative or the same D type as the patient. Before giving non-group-O red cells, the neonate's serum should be checked for passively acquired maternal anti-A or anti-B. If the antibody is present, ABO-compatible red cells lacking the corresponding A or B antigen should be used until the antibody is no longer detected. If an unexpected non-ABO red cell antibody is detected in the infant's specimen or the mother's serum contains a clinically significant red cell antibody, the infant should be given either red cell units tested and found to lack the corresponding antigen(s) or units compatible by antiglobulin crossmatch; this should continue for as long as maternal antibody persists in the infant's blood. The institution's policy will determine how frequently to recheck the screen for red cell antibodies; once a negative result is obtained, subsequent crossmatches and/or provision of blood lacking the target antigen are unnecessary. It is important to avoid transfusion of any component that may transfer unexpected antibody or ABO-incompatible antibodies to the infant.

It is unnecessary to test the infant's serum for anti-A and/or anti-B as a component of blood typing. If there will be non-group-O transfusion, testing for passively acquired maternal anti-A and/or anti-B must include the antiglobulin phase. If antibody is detected and for as long as it remains present, transfused cells must lack the corresponding antigen, but still need not be crossmatched.

Indications for Red Cell Transfusion

Certain events in the perinatal period cause anemia for which the benefits of red cell transfusion are unquestioned. These include spontaneous fetomaternal or fetoplacental hemorrhage, twin-twin transfusion, obstetric accidents, and internal hemorrhage. A venous hemoglobin of less than 13 g/dL in the first 24 hours of life indicates severe anemia.[23] For severely anemic neonates with congestive heart failure, it may be necessary to remove aliquots of their dilute blood and transfuse concentrated red cells, a "partial exchange" transfusion, to avoid intravascular volume overload. Most red cell transfusions in the neonatal period, however, are given either to replace iatrogenic blood loss or to treat the physiologic decline in hemoglobin (anemia of prematurity) when it complicates clinical problems.

Because tissue need for oxygen cannot be measured directly and because so many variables determine oxygen availability, no universally accepted criteria exist for transfusion of preterm or term neonates. Despite the widespread use of micromethods for laboratory tests and beginning use of in-situ monitoring devices, infants sustain significant cumulative blood loss from laboratory sampling. In a sick neonate, red cell replacement is usually considered when approximately 10% of the blood volume has been removed. The decision to transfuse a newborn for anemia should include evaluation of the hemoglobin levels expected for age and of the patient's clinical status and amount of blood loss over time. Transfusion may be more aggressive in the infant in respiratory distress who is hypoxic and more vulnerable to cerebral hemorrhage.

Considerable controversy surrounds the correlation of the "signs of anemia" in the preterm infant (tachycardia, tachypnea, recurrent apnea, decreased vigor, and poor weight gain of unexplained origin) with response to RBC transfusions.[1] When red cells are transfused, they are usually given in small volumes of 5-15 mL/kg. The hematocrit of the red cell component transfused will depend on the anticoagulant/preservative used and how the original unit is processed to provide small component transfusions for neonates. A transfusion of 10 mL/kg of red cells adjusted to a hematocrit greater than 80% just prior to release for transfusion should raise the hemoglobin concentration by approximately 3 g/dL. A transfusion of 10 mL/kg of red cells in additive solution, which have a hematocrit of approximately 65%, will result in a posttransfusion hemoglobin increment of less than 3 g/dL.

Red Cell Components Used for Neonatal Transfusion

The small-volume requirements of transfusion to neonatal recipients make it possible to prepare several aliquots from a single donor unit, thus limiting donor exposure and decreasing donor-related risks. Several technical approaches are available to realize this advantage and to minimize wastage.

Aliquoting for Small-Volume Transfusion

A multiple-pack system is a common technique for providing small-volume red cell transfusions.[24] If a single unit of Whole Blood is apportioned into four integrally attached containers ("quad packs"), the original seal remains intact and, until entered, each container has the expiration date of the original unit. Aliquots from an individual quad pack can be transferred to even smaller containers, each with a 24-hour shelf life if stored refrigerated.

Each aliquot must be fully labeled as it is prepared, including the time it outdates, and the origin and disposition of each aliquot must be recorded. Sterile connecting devices have made it much easier to prepare aliquots without decreasing shelf life of the original unit. With this technique, a recipient can receive multiple small-volume transfusions from a single donation until the expiration of the original unit, thereby reducing donor exposure.[25]

A multiportion system is useful in settings where syringe pumps are used for small-volume transfusions for large numbers of patients. Blood is collected into either single or multiple packs. If multiple bag sets are used, the hematocrit can be adjusted to any desired level by removal of plasma during manufacture. Alternatively, the red cells in Whole Blood can be concentrated by gravity sedimentation for 12 hours, which results in a hematocrit of approximately 65%.[26] Bags are hung in an inverted position in the refrigerator and sedimented cells are drawn through one of the access ports.

A resealable sampling or injection site coupler inserted into the access port permits repeated entry. Once the coupler is inserted, the contents of a bag stored at 1-6 C have a 24-hour shelf life. The precise volume of blood requested can be aspirated into a syringe through a large-bore needle inserted through the sampling site coupler. Aseptic technique should be used and the sampling site coupler protected from contamination.

The filled syringe should be closed with a sterile cap, and must be appropriately labeled for the recipient. The distribution of syringe aliquots must be recorded in the same fashion as for full units of blood. Use of syringes for multiportion distribution allows precise measurement of components and efficient use of donor resources, but enlarges the dissemination of any transmissible organisms that the unit might contain.

Red Cells with Additive Solution

Red cells used for pediatric transfusions were traditionally stored in CPDA-1.[24] Additive solutions (AS) used as anticoagulant-preservatives contain additional adenine and dextrose and some contain mannitol. There is concern about the potential side effects of these additives, particularly when units are fresh or transfusion volumes are high. The metabolites of adenine in large volume are known to be nephrotoxic in animals and humans, but there is little information about the effects in preterm infants. With mannitol infusion, there is concern about renal toxicity and about the diuretic effect, which may cause unacceptable fluctuations in cerebral blood flow. Table 24-1 lists differences between CPDA-1 and one of the additive solutions (AS-1), in total quantities and in the small-volume transfusion usual for VLBW infants. When the dose of transfused red cells is small (10-15 mL/kg), the recipient is exposed to relatively small amounts of constituents. Clinical comparisons of red cells stored in these two preservatives show transfusions of cells prepared in the extended-storage additive solution to have no apparent detrimental effects and, after adjustment for the lower hematocrit of the component, to be as effective as CPDA-1 cells in increasing hemoglobin.[27] There have been no clinical trials specifically addressing the use of AS-3 or AS-5 red cells in this setting. The constituents of these additive solution red cells are described in Chapter 8.

A review based on theoretical calculations also suggests that red cells preserved in extended-storage media present no substantive risks when used for small-volume transfusions.[28] For preterm infants with severe hepatic or renal insufficiency, however, removing the additive-containing plasma may be beneficial, particularly if there will be multiple transfusions that could have a cumulative effect. The safety of red cells stored with additives for massive transfusions, such as cardiac surgery or exchange transfusion, has not been confirmed.[28]

Transfusion Administration

Vascular access is often difficult in the tiny newborn and in any infant requiring long-term or repeated intravenous infusions. Within a short time after birth, the umbilical artery may be cannulated. Transfusion through a 23- or 25-gauge needle or a 22- or 24-gauge vascular catheter has been shown to cause little hemolysis and to be safe. Transfusions through smaller gauge catheters have been less well evaluated.

It is not usually necessary to warm small-volume transfusions that are given

Table 24-1. Constituents of CPDA-1 and AS-1

CPDA-1	AS-1
Anticoagulant solution per 100 mL	Anticoagulant solution per 100 mL
Dextrose, 3.2 g	Dextrose, 2.2 g
Trisodium citrate, 2.6 g	Sodium chloride, 900 mg
Citric acid, 327 mg	Mannitol, 750 mg
Monobasic sodium phosphate, 222 mg	Adenine, 27 mg
Adenine, 27.5 mg	
Transfused products (hematocrit = 75%)	Transfused products (hematocrit = 60%)
Dextrose, 17 mg	Dextrose, 76 mg
Trisodium citrate, 14 mg	Sodium chloride, 33 mg
Citric acid, 1.8 mg	Citrate, 8.5 mg
Phosphate, 1.2 mg	Phosphate, 3.2 mg
Adenine, 0.1 mg	Adenine, 0.9 mg
	Mannitol, 25 mg

Transfused products have been calculated for a 1 kg neonate receiving a transfusion of 10 mL/kg. All calculations are based on the volume of plasma constituents and the red cell mass. (Reproduced with permission from Goodstein,[27] data adapted from Luban.[28])

slowly, but it is important to be able to control the volume and rate of infusion. Constant-rate electromechanical syringe delivery pumps provide this control and cause minimal hemolysis, even when used with in-line third-generation filters.[29,30]

The length of the plastic tubing used can add significantly to the volume required for a transfusion. Infusion sets identified as suitable for platelets or components have less dead space than standard sets because they have short tubing and a small 170-micron filter. Pediatric microaggregate filters (20- or 40-micron) are useful for their small priming volume, not for the removal of microaggregates. Hemolysis occurs when stored blood is given by negative pressure filtration through these filters.[31] However, leukocyte reduction by filtration appears to be effective in reducing the risk of transfusion-transmitted CMV.[19,20]

Exchange Transfusion for Hyperbilirubinemia

The fetal liver has limited capacity to conjugate bilirubin. When the fetus is in utero, unconjugated bilirubin crosses the placenta for excretion through the mother's hepatobiliary system. After birth, transient mild hyperbilirubinemia normally occurs during the first week of life and is referred to as "physiologic jaundice." Liver function is less mature, and jaundice worsens in premature neonates. When the level of unconjugated bilirubin is excessive, bilirubin may cross the blood-brain barrier and concentrate in the basal ganglia and cerebellum; the resulting damage to the CNS is called kernicterus. Phototherapy with fluorescent blue lights is the most common treatment for hyperbilirubinemia; exchange transfusion is reserved for phototherapy failures. The most common reason, however, for an exchange to be performed in a neonate is to correct hyperbilirubinemia.

Pathologic processes that may result in excessively high unconjugated bilirubin levels in neonates include immune-mediated hemolysis, nonimmune hemolysis, bile excretion defects and impaired albumin binding. Exchange transfusion removes unconjugated bilirubin and provides additional albumin to bind residual bilirubin. If hyperbilirubinemia is due to antibody-mediated hemolysis, exchange transfusion is additionally beneficial in removing free antibody and antibody-coated red cells and providing antigen-negative red cells that will survive normally.

Exchange transfusion should be performed before bilirubin rises to levels at which CNS damage occurs. Several factors affect the threshold for toxicity. CNS damage occurs at lower levels if there is prematurity, decreased albumin binding capacity, or the presence of such complicating conditions as sepsis, hypoxia, acidosis, hypothermia, or hypoglycemia. In full-term infants, kernicterus usually does not develop at bilirubin levels less than 20 mg/dL but in sick, VLBW infants, kernicterus has occurred at bilirubin levels as low as 10 mg/dL.[32]

The rate at which bilirubin rises is more predictive of imminent need for exchange transfusion than the absolute level. Neonates in whom bilirubin is rising faster than 1 mg/dL/hour and/or who have significant anemia may require exchange transfusion.[32] A two-volume exchange transfusion decreases the serum bilirubin. However, the observed efficiency of bilirubin removal is less than the theoretical predicted efficiency as a result of reequilibration between bilirubin in plasma and in extravascular tissues while the exchange is taking place. Also, in the subsequent few hours, more extravascular bilirubin enters the circulation to equilibrate with lowered serum levels. Although phototherapy is usually instituted after the initial exchange, the rebound rise in bilirubin, combined with continued bilirubin production, may so elevate the serum level that a repeat exchange is needed. Indications for repeat exchange are similar to those for the initial exchange.

Exchange Transfusion for Other Causes

In the neonatal period, disseminated intravascular coagulation (DIC) occurs secondary to many conditions, including shock, sepsis, asphyxia, and necrotizing enterocolitis. The diagnosis is based on the clinical features as well as on the age-corrected results of coagulation screening tests, low levels of platelets and fibrinogen, and presence of fibrin degradation products. Transfusion of plasma and platelet components may improve hemostasis, but the most important therapy for neonatal DIC is to treat the underlying disease. Exchange transfusion has given variable results, perhaps because only the sickest infants have been selected to receive this therapy.

Exchange transfusion is also occasionally used to remove other toxins, such as drugs or chemicals given to the mother near the time of delivery, drugs given in toxic doses to the neonate/infant, or substances such as ammonia that accumulate in the newborn because of prematurity or inherited metabolic diseases.

Technique of Exchange Transfusion

Choice of Components

Many different combinations of blood components have provided safe and effective exchange transfusion; no single component or combination is unequivocally best. Most frequently used are red cells reconstituted with 5% albumin, or with FFP if coagulation factors are required simultaneously. If AS red cells are used, depending on the clinical situation, it may be beneficial to remove the additive-containing plasma. The red cells used for exchange transfusion should lack hemoglobin S, to avoid any possibility of intravascular sickling once the patient is switched from autologous red cells to a donor red cell population.[22(p62)]

Historically, if the blood was anticoagulated with citrate, calcium was administered to the patient to offset its calcium-binding effects. This practice does not appear to have any significant effects on ionized calcium levels and, despite low serum levels of ionized calcium, clinical tetany is rarely seen during exchange transfusion.[32] Calcium should never be infused through the same infusion line as transfused blood because it can precipitate clotting.

The glucose load administered during exchange transfusion can be extremely high. This stimulates the infant to secrete insulin, which leads to rebound hypoglycemia. It is important to monitor blood glucose levels for the first few hours after the procedure.

Unconjugated bilirubin binds to albumin. Increased intravascular binding is thought to enhance diffusion of extravascular bilirubin into the circulation, thereby increasing the total quantity of bilirubin removed during the exchange. There have been conflicting results, however, as to the efficacy of administering albumin either before or during exchange to enhance bilirubin removal. A study that compared 15 hyperbilirubinemic neonates given albumin with 27 who received none found similar efficiency of bilirubin removal in both groups.[33] Because infusing albumin raises the colloid osmotic pressure and increases intravascular volume, it should be given cautiously, if at all, to neonates or infants who are severely anemic, have increased central venous pressure, or are in renal or congestive heart failure.

Exchange transfusion may cause dilutional thrombocytopenia and/or coagulopathy that requires transfusion of platelets or Fresh Frozen Plasma (FFP). As with glucose for rebound hypoglycemia, platelet counts and coagulation tests should be monitored following exchange transfusion.

Volume and Hematocrit

An exchange transfusion equal to twice the patient's blood volume is typically recommended for newborns and rarely is more than one full unit of donor blood required. In practice, the calculated volume for exchange is an estimate. The final hematocrit of transfused material should be approximately 40-50%, with sufficient plasma to provide clotting factors (if needed) and albumin to bind bilirubin. In the unusual event that the infant's condition demands a high postexchange hematocrit, a small-volume transfusion of red cells can be given following the exchange, or units with a higher hematocrit used for exchange. It is important to keep the blood mixed during the exchange; if it settles in the container, the final aliquots will not have the intended hematocrit. The infant's hematocrit and bilirubin level should be measured on the last aliquot removed in the exchange.

Vascular Access

Exchange transfusions in the newborn period are usually accomplished via catheters in the umbilical vessels. Catheterization is easiest within hours of birth, but it may be possible to achieve vascular access at this site for several days. The catheters should be radiopaque to facilitate radiographic monitoring during and after placement. If umbilical catheters are not available for exchange transfusion, small central venous or saphenous catheters may be used.

Methods Used

Two methods of exchange transfusion are in common use. In the isovolumetric method, there is vascular access through two catheters of identical size. Withdrawal and infusion occur simultaneously, regulated by a single peristaltic pump. The umbilical artery is usually used for withdrawal, and the umbilical vein for infusion.

The push-pull technique can be accomplished through a single vascular access. A three-way stopcock joins the unit of blood, the patient, and an extension tube that leads to the graduated discard container. An in-line blood warmer and a standard blood filter should be incorporated in the administration set. The maximum volume of each withdrawal and infusion will depend on the infant's size and

hemodynamic status, and the rate at which exchange transfusion occurs may alter the infant's hemodynamic status. The procedure should take place over 1 to 1.5 hours.

Transfusion of Other Components

While approximately 80% of VLBW infants can be expected to receive multiple red cell transfusions, only 15-20% will also receive other components.[1,34]

Platelet Transfusion

The normal platelet count in newborns is similar to that in adults. A platelet count less than 150,000/μL in a full-term or premature infant is abnormal. Approximately 20% of infants in neonatal intensive care units have mild to moderate thrombocytopenia, which is the most common hemostatic abnormality in the sick infant.[35] Neonatal thrombocytopenia may result from impaired production or increased destruction of platelets, abnormal distribution, or a dilutional effect secondary to massive transfusion such as exchange transfusion. Increased destruction is the most usual cause; it may be associated with a multitude of conditions and is usually transient.[34] Neonatal alloimmune thrombocytopenia is discussed in Chapter 23.

Indications

Platelet transfusion is indicated in neonates and young infants with platelet counts below 50,000/μL who are experiencing bleeding.[35] The use of prophylactic platelet transfusions in the newborn remains controversial. Bleeding is rare in adults with thrombocytopenia unless the platelet count is less than 10,000/μL,[36] but preterm neonates and infants with other complicating illnesses may bleed at higher platelet counts. Factors that may contribute to bleeding at higher platelet counts include: quantitatively lower concentration of plasma coagulation factors; circulation of an anticoagulant that enhances inhibition of thrombin; intrinsic or extrinsic platelet dysfunction; and increased vascular fragility.[37] Of major concern is intraventricular hemorrhage, which occurs in up to 40% of preterm neonates in the first 72 hours. While prophylactic platelet transfusions increase platelet counts and shorten the bleeding time in these infants, the incidence or extent of intraventricular hemorrhage is not reduced.[37] After a platelet transfusion, a posttransfusion platelet count soon after transfusion can evaluate survival in the circulation, but may not predict hemostatic efficacy. Repeated platelet transfusions, without an appropriate rise, may not be beneficial.

Platelet Components

A platelet dose of 5-10 mL/kg body weight should raise the platelet count of an average full-term newborn by 50,000-100,000/μL, depending on the platelet concentration in the component used.[13,36] The platelet component should be group-specific, if possible, and should not contain clinically significant unexpected red cell antibodies. Transfusion of incompatible plasma is more dangerous in infants, with their very small blood volume, than in adults. If it is necessary to give a platelet unit that contains incompatible plasma (due to antibodies in the ABO or other blood groups), plasma can be removed (see Method 6.12) and the platelets resuspended in saline or albumin. FFP can be substituted as the resuspending medium if the patient also requires clotting factors. Routine centrifugation of platelets to reduce the volume of transfusion is not necessary.[34,35] If platelets have been volume-reduced and placed in a syringe, the pH declines rapidly, a potential problem for an already ill, acidotic patient.[38] Therefore, if there is a need to reduce the volume of platelets, it should be done just before transfusion and the component should be infused within 4 hours.

Granulocyte Transfusion

Neonates are more susceptible than older children to severe bacterial infection due to both quantitative and qualitative defects of neutrophil function and, in the absence of pathogen-specific maternal antibody, to deficiency of humoral immunity. Group B streptococcus is the most frequent cause of early-onset neonatal sepsis and, despite improvement in antimicrobial therapy and intensive care, it is still associated with a high mortality rate. Controversy surrounds several issues in granulocyte transfusions for neonates, including dose, neutrophil level at which to transfuse, type of component to use, and efficacy as compared to other forms of therapy.[39] There have been encouraging observations on the use of intravenous immunoglobulin (IVIG) in the treatment of early neonatal sepsis as well as preliminary studies of hematopoietic growth factors (eg, granulocyte colony-stimulating factor) in the treatment of overwhelming bacterial infection in the newborn.[39,40]

Indications

While the precise role of granulocyte transfusion for neonatal sepsis is unclear, certain clinical situations exist in which granulocyte transfusion may be considered as supplemental treatment to antibiotic therapy. Candidates for possible granulocyte transfusion are infants with strong evidence of bacterial septicemia, an absolute neutrophil count below 3000/μL, and a diminished marrow storage pool, such that less than 7% of nucleated cells in the marrow are granulocytes at the stage of metamyelocytes or more mature forms.[14,23]

Granulocyte Components

The component of choice is a granulocyte concentrate harvested by standard apheresis techniques. Smaller quantities of granulocytes can be harvested, by gravity sedimentation or by an automated method, from the buffy coat of units of freshly donated whole blood. However, the efficacy of buffy coat transfusions has not been proved.[41,42] The dose currently recommended is 1×10^9 neutrophils/kg body weight, in a volume of 15 mL/kg.[14,23] This should be continued until an adequate white cell mass is achieved or the patient has clinically improved. Based on the fact that granulocyte concentrates contain large numbers of lymphocytes, there is general consensus that all granulocyte transfusions should be irradiated to prevent GVHD. Some institutions may irradiate all blood components being transfused to neonates as it may be difficult for the blood bank to identify which neonates are at risk for GVHD. For granulocyte transfusions to neonates, donors are usually selected who are CMV seronegative and ABO- and D-compatible with the infant.

Transfusion to Enhance Hemostasis

Elements of the hemostatic system of the newborn are similar to those of older children and adults, but the concentration of many proteins is decreased. Coagulation factors do not cross the placenta, but are independently synthesized by the fetus, progressively increasing with gestational age. At birth, the infant's prothrombin time and partial thromboplastin time are prolonged, compared to older children and adults, due primarily to physiologically low levels of the vitamin-K-dependent factors (II, VII, IX, and X), and contact factors (XI, XII, prekallikrein, and high-molecular-weight kininogen).[43] Proteins C and S and antithrombin inhibitors of coagulation are also at low levels.[43] These two systems usually balance each other, so that spontaneous bleeding and thrombosis in the healthy newborn are rare, but very little reserve capacity exists for responding to pathologic insults. Therefore, serious bleeding may occur in the first week of life in the sick premature infant, as a result of hemostatic immaturity coupled with an acquired disorder of hemostasis.

Neonates not only have physiologically low levels of the vitamin-K-dependent factors; they

also may become vitamin-K-deficient during the first 2-5 days of life, placing them at risk of bleeding. This "hemorrhagic disease of the newborn" is now rare in developed countries because intramuscular vitamin K is routinely given at birth. If vitamin K therapy is omitted and especially if the neonate is breast fed, life-threatening hemorrhage may occur, which should be treated with FFP.[44]

Although hereditary deficiencies of coagulation factors may be apparent in the newborn, significant bleeding is rare. Coagulopathy more often results from an acquired defect such as liver disease or DIC.[44] While component therapy replacement may temporarily correct the hemostatic problem, treatment of the underlying disease will ultimately reduce the need to treat the acquired defect.

Newborns who are heterozygous for deficiencies of inhibitory proteins rarely experience complications in the absence of another pathologic insult. The homozygous form of protein C deficiency has, however, caused life-threatening thrombotic complications in the newborn period; initial treatment has included plasma infusions.[44]

Fresh Frozen Plasma

Fresh frozen plasma may be used to replace coagulation factors in newborns, particularly if multiple factors are involved, such as in vitamin K deficiency. The usual dose is 10-15 mL/kg, which should increase factor activity by 10-20% unless there is marked consumptive coagulopathy.[44] As with red cell transfusions, there are several methods to provide small-volume FFP infusion while limiting donor exposure and wastage of components. Collection of blood into a multiple pack allows three or four aliquots to be prepared for freezing. Once thawed, these aliquots can be further divided and used for several patients within a 24-hour period. As for all patients, FFP must be ABO-compatible and free of clinically significant unexpected antibodies.[22(p62)] Group AB FFP is often used because a single unit provides compatible small aliquots for several neonates requiring FFP simultaneously.

Cryoprecipitate

Cryoprecipitate is rich in fibrinogen and coagulation Factors VIII and XIII. This component is often used in conjunction with platelet transfusions to treat DIC in the newborn. In DIC, fibrinogen and platelets are the elements most often severely depleted. The plasma in which the platelets are suspended is a source of stable coagulation factors. Cryoprecipitate provides concentrated levels of additional fibrinogen and storage-labile Factor VIII. In an infant, one bag is sufficient to achieve hemostatic levels. As with FFP and platelets, the cryoprecipitate should be ABO-compatible with the neonatal recipient. Random donor cryoprecipitate is not recommended in the newborn with hemophilia A. Recombinant Factor VIII products or virus-inactivated, monoclonal-antibody-purified, plasma-derived products are the usual treatment.[45]

Neonatal Polycythemia

A venous hematocrit greater than 65% or hemoglobin in excess of 22 g/dL any time in the first week of life defines polycythemia, a condition that occurs in approximately 5% of all newborns; groups at special risk are small-for-gestational-age infants and infants of diabetic mothers. As the hematocrit rises above 50% the viscosity of blood increases exponentially and oxygen transport decreases.[32] The infant has limited ability to compensate for hyperviscosity by increasing cardiac output and may develop congestive heart failure. Impairment of blood flow can cause CNS abnormalities, pulmonary and renal failure, and necrotizing enterocolitis. Phlebotomy can be used to normalize the hematocrit to 55-60% and improve tissue perfusion, while maintaining the blood volume.

Whole blood is removed and the volume replaced with 5% albumin or crystalloid (such as normal saline), the choice being based on the quantity needed and on the infant's clinical condition. Plasma is not recommended because, if coagulation problems are present, the volume given is insufficient to correct them and because necrotizing enterocolitis has been reported with its use in this procedure.[46] A formula to approximate the volume of colloid replacement required for the exchange is:

Volume of replacement fluid =

$$\frac{\text{blood volume} \times (\text{observed hemoglobin} - \text{desired hemoglobin})}{\text{observed hemoglobin}}$$

Extracorporeal Membrane Oxygenation

ECMO is a modified cardiopulmonary bypass technique that has been used for short-term support for cardiac or respiratory failure. It is performed in specialized centers and only for patients in whom conventional medical therapy has failed and anticipated survival with such therapy is limited. The use of ECMO in patients other than neonates is not widespread. It is more successful in infants, whose small blood volume allows for total cardiorespiratory support, and whose primary respiratory problem often resolves after 1-2 weeks of support. ECMO provides gas exchange independent of the patient's lungs, allowing them time to improve or heal without exposure to aggressive ventilator support and the secondary lung damage this may cause.

Individual ECMO centers establish their own specific criteria for transfusion and blood component selection. Because systemic heparinization is necessary, bleeding complications are frequent. The ECMO team should be in close communication with the blood bank or transfusion service staff and there should be mutual agreement on protocols to ensure consistency of care. Many infants requiring ECMO have been transferred from other hospitals, where they may already have received numerous transfusions. The amount of red cell, platelet, and FFP support required to maintain hematologic and hemodynamic equilibrium will vary depending on the clinical situation.[47]

Transfusion Practices in Older Infants and Children

The indications for transfusion of red cells and other components in older infants (>4 months) and children are similar to those for adults, after correction for differences in blood volume, ability to tolerate blood loss, and age-appropriate hemoglobin and hematocrit levels. The most common indication for red cell transfusion in children is to reverse or prevent tissue hypoxia resulting from decreased red cell mass associated with surgical procedures or in response to anemia of chronic diseases or hematologic malignancies. It is important to remember that normal hemoglobin and hematocrit levels are lower in children than adults. Pediatric patients may remain asymptomatic despite extremely low levels of hemoglobin, particularly if the anemia has developed slowly.

The decision to transfuse should be based not only on the hemoglobin level but also on the presence or absence of symptoms, the functional capacity of the child, the etiology of the anemia, the possibility of using alternative therapies, and the presence or absence of additional clinical conditions that increase the risk for developing hypoxia. If small-volume transfusions are required, many of the methods described to provide small-volume transfusions to neonates can be applied. All pediatric patients over 4 months of age, however, must be tested for ABO and D type as well as for the presence of clinically significant antibodies before red cell transfusions. If the child has been exposed to allogeneic red cells during the 3

months prior to transfusion, an antibody screen must be performed within 3 days of the scheduled transfusion. If the antibody screen is negative a crossmatch limited to the immediate-spin reaction may be performed. If the antibody screen is positive the crossmatch must include an antiglobulin phase and red cells that lack the antigen against which the clinically significant antibody is directed must be selected.

Red Cell Support for Children with Hemoglobinopathies

In certain childhood conditions, chronic red cell transfusions are given not only to treat tissue hypoxia but also to suppress endogenous hemoglobin production. Approximately 6-10% of children with sickle cell disease suffer a stroke; two-thirds of these children experience recurrent stroke.[48] One goal of transfusion for such patients is to reduce the percentage of circulating red cells capable of sickling, while avoiding an increase in blood viscosity, in order to reduce the risk of stroke. It is important to remember that raising the hematocrit, without significantly reducing the percent of sickle cells, could increase viscosity and negate any beneficial effects of the transfusion.[49] The rate of recurrent stroke can be reduced to 0-10% by maintaining a hemoglobin level of 8-9 g/dL with a hemoglobin S level less than 30%, in children who have had a cerebrovascular accident. This can usually be achieved with a simple or partial exchange transfusion every 3-4 weeks. There are no definite criteria for when it is safe to discontinue transfusion therapy; therefore, it is often continued indefinitely.[48] Because of concern about iron overload, some workers follow several uneventful years of transfusions to keep hemoglobin S below 30% with a less aggressive protocol that maintains hemoglobin S between 40% and 50%.[50] Erythrocytapheresis has also been used in this setting in a small cohort of patients with evidence of improvement in iron balance.[51] A recent study showed that transfusion to maintain a hemoglobin S level less than 30% in children who have abnormal results on transcranial Doppler ultrasound reduced the risk of a first stroke.[52] The benefits of this transfusion therapy, however, must be weighed against the complications of transfusion, such as iron overload and alloimmunization. Blood for transfusion to a patient with sickle cell disease should be screened for hemoglobin S.

Red cell transfusions are also used to treat acute complications associated with sickle cell disease, such as splenic sequestration, aplastic crisis, overwhelming pneumonia, or pulmonary infarction. A study evaluating preoperative transfusion protocols found that a conservative protocol, in which the hemoglobin was raised to 10 g/dL, was as effective in preventing perioperative complications as an aggressive approach to decrease hemoglobin S levels to below 30%.[53]

Transfusions are given to children with severe anemia due to thalassemia, not only to improve tissue oxygenation but also to suppress erythropoiesis, because the characteristically brisk, ineffective erythropoiesis causes many of the complications associated with the disease. So-called hypertransfusion in which the pretransfusion hemoglobin is kept between 8 and 9 g/dL, allows normal growth and development, as well as normal levels of activity for the child's age. Supertransfusion programs aim to maintain a pretransfusion hemoglobin concentration between 11 and 12 g/dL, in order to decrease iron absorption from the gastrointestinal tract. The results of maintaining near-normal hemoglobin levels are still controversial. Iron overload is a complication in these patients, requiring chelation therapy beginning early in childhood.[54]

Antibody Production in Sickle Cell and Thalassemia Patients

The frequency of red cell alloimmunization in chronically transfused children varies with the disease, the number of transfusions given, and the ethnic background of donors and recipi-ents.[55-57] Antibodies to the common antigens of the Rh, Kell, Duffy, and Kidd systems are often identified. It may be desirable, therefore, to phenotype the patient's red cell antigens as completely as possible before beginning transfusion therapy, and to maintain a permanent record of the results. This can be helpful in selecting compatible blood if alloimmunization occurs. The practice of transfusing only phenotypically matched units is controversial.[48,58] In patients who have already become immunized and are at high risk of developing additional antibodies, use of phenotypically matched units may be a reasonable approach. Leukocyte-reduced blood components may be considered for these chronically transfused patients, to diminish development of alloimmunization to HLA antigens, particularly if subsequent marrow transplantation is possible, and to prevent febrile transfusion reactions.[59]

Platelets and Plasma

The indications for FFP and platelet transfusions in older infants and children parallel those for adults. Platelet transfusions are most often given as prophylaxis to children receiving chemotherapy. Prophylactic platelet transfusions are seldom given when platelet counts are above 10,000-20,000/μL, but as with red cell transfusion and hemoglobin, the indication for platelet transfusion should not be the platelet count only. When additive risk factors such as fever, sepsis, DIC, or clotting abnormalities are present, the platelet count may need to be higher to prevent spontaneous hemorrhage. In the absence of such factors a much lower level may be safe.[34]

References

1. Hume H, Bard H. Small volume red blood cell transfusions for neonatal patients. Transfus Med Rev 1995;9:187-99.
2. Bregnara C, Platt OS. The neonatal erythrocyte and its disorders. In: Nathan DG, Orkin SH, eds. Nathan

and Oski's hematology of infancy and childhood. 5th ed. Philadelphia: WB Saunders 1998:19-52.

3. Blanchette V, Doyle J, Schmidt B, Zipursky A. Hematology. In: Avery GB, Fletcher MA, MacDonald MG, eds. Neonatology: Pathophysiology and management of the newborn. 4th ed. Philadelphia: JB Lippincott, 1994:952-99.

4. Wallgren G, Hanson JS, Lind J. Quantitative studies of the human neonatal circulation. Acta Paediatr Scand 1967;179(suppl):43-54.

5. Shannon KM. Anemia of prematurity: Progress and prospects. Am J Pediatr Hematol Oncol 1990;12:14-20.

6. Ohls RK, Harcum J, Schibler KR, Christensen D. The effect of erythropoietin on the transfusion requirements of preterm infants weighing 750 grams or less: A randomized, double-blind, placebo-controlled study. J Pediatr 1997;131:661-5.

7. Widness JA, Seward VJ, Kromer IJ, et al. Changing patterns of red cell transfusion in very low birth weight infants. J Pediatr 1996;129:680-7.

8. Luban NLC, Mikesell G, Sacher RA. Techniques for warming red blood cells packaged in different containers for neonatal use. Clin Pediatr 1985;24:642-5.

9. Pridjian G. Fetomaternal interractions: Placental physiology and its role as a go-between. In: Avery GB, Fletcher MA, MacDonald MG, eds. Neonatology: Pathophysiology and management of the newborn. 4th ed. Philadelphia: JB Lippincott, 1994:126-43.

10. Pollock JM, Bowman JM. Placental transfer of Rh antibody (anti-D IgG) during pregnancy. Vox Sang 1982;43:327-34.

11. DePalma L. Review: Red cell alloantibody formation in the neonate and infant: Considerations for current immunohematologic practice. Immunohematology 1992;8:33-7.

12. Sanders MR, Graeber JE. Posttransfusion graft-versus-host disease in infancy. J Pediatr 1990;117:159-63.

13. Ohto H, Anderson KC. Posttransfusion graft-versus-host disease in Japanese newborns. Transfusion 1996;36:117-23.

14. Strauss RG. Neonatal transfusion. In: Anderson KC, Ness PM, eds. Scientific basis of transfusion medicine. Implications for clinical practice. Philadelphia: WB Saunders, 1994:421-42.

15. Strauss RG. Routinely washing irradiated red cells before transfusion seems unwarranted. Transfusion 1990;30:675-7.

16. Delage G. Transfusion-transmitted infections in the newborn. Transfus Med Rev 1995;9:271-6.

17. Brady MT, Milam JD, Anderson DC. Use of deglycerolized red blood cells to prevent post-transfusion infection with cytomegalovirus in neonates. J Infect Dis 1984;150:334-9.

18. Strauss RG. Selection of white cell-reduced blood components for transfusions during infancy. Transfusion 1993;33:352-7.

19. Bowden RA, Slichter SJ, Sayers M, et al. A comparison of filtered leukocyte-reduced and cytomegalovirus (CMV) seronegative blood products for the prevention of transfusion-associated CMV infection after marrow transplant. Blood 1995;86:3598-603.

20. Gilbert GL, Hayes K, Hudson H, et al. Prevention of transfusion-asssociated cytomegalovirus infection in infants by blood filtration to remove leukocytes. Lancet 1989;1:1228-31.

21. Ludvigsen C, Swanson JL, Thompson TR, McCullough J. The failure of neonates to form red cell alloantibodies in response to multiple transfusions. Am J Clin Pathol 1987;87:250-1.

22. Menitove JE, ed. Standards for blood banks and transfusion services. 19th ed. Bethesda, MD: American Association of Blood Banks, 1999.

23. Blanchette VS, Hume HA, Levy GJ, et al. Guidelines for auditing pediatric blood transfusion practices. Am J Dis Child 1991;145:787-96.

24. Levy GJ, Strauss RG, Hume H, et al. National survey of neonatal transfusion practices, I: Red blood cell therapy. Pediatrics 1993;91:523-9.

25. Cook S, Gunter J, Wissel M. Effective use of a strategy using assigned red cell units to limit donor exposure for neonatal patients. Transfusion 1993;33:379-83.

26. White KJ, Wilson JK, Barnes A. Sedimented red cells (letter). Transfusion 1980;20:476.

27. Goodstein MH, Locke RG, Wlodarczyk D, et al. Comparison of two preservation solutions for erythrocyte transfusions in newborn infants. J Pediatr 1993;123:783-8.

28. Luban NLC, Strauss RG, Hume HA. Commentary on the safety of red cells preserved in extended-storage media for neonatal transfusions. Transfusion 1991;31:229-35.

29. Burch KJ, Phelps SJ, Constance TD. Effect of an infusion device on the integrity of whole blood and packed red blood cells. Am J Hosp Pharm 1991;48:92-7.

30. Criss VR, De Palma L, Luban NLC. Analysis of a linear peristaltic infusion device for the transfusion of red cells to pediatric patients. Transfusion 1993;33:842-4.

31. Longhurst DM, Gooch W, Castillo RA. In vitro evaluation of a pediatric microaggregate blood filter. Transfusion 1983;23:170-2.

32. Maisels JF. Jaundice. In: Avery GB, Fletcher MA, MacDonald MG, eds. Neonatology: Pathophysiology and management of the newborn. 4th ed. Philadelphia: JB Lippincott, 1994:630-725.

33. Chan G, Schoff D. Variance in albumin loading in exchange transfusions. J Pediatr 1976;88:609-13.

34. Strauss RG, Levy GJ, Sotelo-Avila C, et al. National survey of neonatal transfusion practices: II. Blood component therapy. Pediatrics 1993;91:530-6.

35. Blanchette VS, Kuhne T, Hume H, Hellman J. Platelet transfusion therapy in newborn infants. Transfus Med Rev 1995;9:215-30.

36. Beutler E. Platelet transfusions: The 20,000/μL trigger. Blood 1993;81:1411-3.

37. Andrew M, Vegh P, Caco C, et al. A randomized, controlled trial of platelet transfusions in thrombocytopenic premature infants. J Pediatr 1993;123:285-91.

38. Pisciotto P, Snyder EL, Snyder JA, et al. In vitro characteristics of leukocyte-reduced single unit platelet concentrates stored in syringes. Transfusion 1994;34:407-11.

39. Sweetman RW, Cairo MS. Blood component and immunotherapy in neonatal sepsis. Transfus Med Rev 1995;9:251-8.

40. Rosenthal J, Cairo MS. Neonatal myelopoiesis and immunomodulation of host defenses. In: Petz LD, Swisher SN, Kleinman S, et al, eds. Clinical practice of transfusion medicine, 3rd ed. New York: Churchill Livingstone, 1996:685-703.

41. Baley JE, Stork EK, Warkentin PI, Shurin SB. Buffy coat transfusion in neutropenic neonates with presumed sepsis: A prospective randomized trial. Pediatrics 1987;80:712-20.

42. Wheeler JC, Chauvenet AR, Johnson CA, et al. Buffy coat transfusion in neonates with sepsis and neutrophil storage pool depletion. Pediatrics 1987;79:422-5.

43. Andrew M, Paes B, Johnston M. Development of the hemostatic system in the neonate and young infant. Am J Pediatr Hematol Oncol 1990;12:95-104.

44. Andrew M. Transfusion in the newborn: Plasma products. In: Kennedy M, Wilson S, Kelton J, eds. Perinatal transfusion medicine. Arlington, VA: American Association of Blood Banks, 1990:145-77.

45. DiMichele D. Hemophilia 1996: New approach to an old disease. Pediatr Clin N Am 1996;43:709-36.

46. Black VD, Rumack CM, Lubchenco LD, Koops BL. Gastrointestinal injury in polycythemic term infants. Pediatrics 1985;76:225-31.

47. Kevy SV. Extracorporeal therapy for infants and children. In: Petz LD, Swisher SN, Kleinman S, et al, eds. Clinical practice of transfusion medicine, 3rd ed. New York: Churchill Livingstone, 1996:733-55.

48. Sharon BI, Honig GR. Management of congenital hemolytic anemias. In: Rossi EC, Simon TL, Moss GS, Gould SA, eds. Principles of transfusion medicine, 2nd ed. Baltimore, MD: Williams and Wilkins, 1995:141-59.

49. Schmalzer EA, Lee JO, Brown AK, et al. Viscosity of mixtures of sickle and normal red cells at varying hematocrit levels: Implications for transfusion. Transfusion 1987;27:228-33.

50. Cohen AR, Martin MB, Silber JH, et al. A modified transfusion program for prevention of stroke in sickle cell disease. Blood 1992;79:1657-61.

51. Adams DM, Schultz WH, Ware RF, Kinney TR. Erythrocytapheresis can reduce iron overload and prevent the need for chelation therapy in chronically transfused pediatric patients. J Pediatr Hematol Oncol 1996;18:3-7.

52. Adams RJ, McKie VC, Hsu L, et al. Prevention of a first stroke by transfusions in children with sickle cell anemia and abnormal results on transcranial doppler ultrasonography. N Engl J Med 1998;339:5-11.

53. Vichinsky EP, Heberkern CM, Neumayr L, et al. A comparison of conservative and aggressive transfusion regimens in the perioperative management of sickle cell disease. N Engl J Med 1995;333:206-13.

54. Hoffbrand AV, Al-Refaie F, Davis B, et al. Long-term trial of deferiprone in 51 transfusion-dependent iron overload patients. Blood 1998;91:295-300.

55. Rosse WF, Gallagher D, Kinney TR, et al. Transfusion and alloimmunization in sickle cell disease. Blood 1990;76:1431-7.

56. Spanos T, Karageorge M, Ladis V, et al. Red cell alloantibodies in patients with thalassemia. Vox Sang 1990;58:50-5.

57. Rosse WF, Telen M, Ware RE. Transfusion support for patients with sickle cell disease. Bethesda, MD: AABB Press, 1998.

58. Tahhan HR, Holbrook CT, Braddy LR, et al. Antigen-matched donor blood in the transfusion management of patients with sickle cell disease. Transfusion 1994;34:562-9.

59. Lane TA, Anderson KC, Goodnough LT, et al. Leukocyte reduction in blood component therapy. Ann Intern Med 1992;117:151-62.

25

Hematopoietic Transplantation

HEMATOPOIETIC STEM CELLS ARE cells capable of self-renewal, differentiation into all blood-cell lineages, and, in sufficient numbers, giving rise to complete sustained hematopoietic engraftment. In contrast, hematopoietic progenitor cells are committed to a blood-cell lineage and do not have the capacity for sustained self-renewal. Both cell populations are referred to as hematopoietic progenitor cells (HPCs) in this chapter. Similarly, circulating cell collections are sometimes referred to as peripheral blood progenitor cells (PBPCs), peripheral blood stem cells (PBSCs), or blood stem cells (BSCs). The context in which such terms are used should be sufficient to explain the intended meaning.

Brecher and Cronkite's[1] 1951 cross-circulation experiments in lethally irradiated parabiotic rats first established that circulating HPCs could be successfully "transplanted." In less than five decades, HPC transplantation has advanced from a research procedure performed in a few centers to a common medical procedure performed in many tertiary care centers.

HPC transplantation can be classified as autologous, allogeneic, syngeneic, and xenogeneic. Autologous HPC transplantation is technically not a transplant, but rather the "rescue" of a patient with the patient's own HPCs following an otherwise lethal or near-lethal dose of radiation or chemotherapy given to treat malignancies of the marrow and metastatic or recurrent solid tumors. The patient's own HPCs are removed and cryopreserved for protection from the lethal effects of therapeutic or ablative irradiation or chemotherapy.

Allogeneic HPC transplantation involves the infusion of HPCs from another human in order to rescue the patient following a similar lethal dose of radiation or chemotherapy. Such transplants are preferred when patients have severe immunodeficiency, aplastic anemia, marrow involvement with their malignancy, or are incapable of supplying their own autologous "normal" HPCs, as with hemoglobinopathies (thalassemias or sickle cell disease). Allogeneic cells may be derived from an HLA-matched related donor or from an HLA-matched unrelated donor. In the special case of an identical twin donor and recipient, such transplants are referred to as syngeneic.

Xenogeneic HPC transplantation would involve HPC transplants derived from a nonhuman species. However, due to currently insurmountable immunologic barriers and disease concerns, these transplants are not now clinically feasible.

Sources of progenitor cells include marrow, peripheral blood, umbilical cord blood, and fetal liver (although this source is not in routine clinical use). Once collected, the HPCs may be subjected to ex-vivo manipulation, eg, removal of incompatible red cells or plasma and/or cell selection (purging) prior to the transplant. In some cases certain cell populations are "positively" selected (selectively isolated) such as CD34-positive cells in an autologous marrow with known or potential malignant cell contamination. Alternatively, some cell populations may be "negatively selected" (culled out or destroyed) such as by antibody-mediated lysis of malignant cells, or, in the allogeneic setting, by depletion of T cells that cause graft-vs-host disease (GVHD).

Diseases Treated with Hematopoietic Transplantation

Several diseases have been treated with HPC transplantation. Table 25-1 lists categories of conditions for which hematopoietic transplantation has shown promising or curative results.[2,3]

The success rate of HPC transplantation depends on the disease of the patient being treated, stage of the disease, age and condition of the patient, and degree of HLA match between the donor and the patient. Overall survival rates are generally 30-60% for otherwise fatal diseases.

Sources of Hematopoietic Progenitor Cells

Historically, marrow was the primary source of hematopoietic cells for transplantation. Currently, in autologous transplants, PBPCs may be used in conjunction with marrow, but are more commonly used as the sole source of hematopoietic reconstitution. Initially, the majority of adult allogeneic transplants utilized marrow. However, PBPC transplants are becoming more common for both adult and pediatric allogeneic transplants. Umbilical cord blood transplants have provided promising results in pediatric patients for whom a matched unrelated allogeneic marrow or PBPC donor were unavailable. Clinical studies are in progress to determine the safety and efficacy of this approach, whether adults can be effectively transplanted, and the extent of HLA mismatch that can safely and effectively provide durable engraftment.

Autologous Marrow

Whether marrow is an option for autologous rescue after high-dose chemo/radiotherapy depends on the overall "health" of the marrow. Fibrosis renders marrow inaspirable and thus impossible to harvest. Metastatic or necrotic infiltrates eliminate marrow as a transplant source as well.[4] Prior pelvic irradiation may deplete the HPC population in the marrow to the extent that an adequate dose for transplantation is unobtainable.[5] Other factors such as poor anesthesia risk, obesity, or refusal of marrow collection can limit marrow as an option.[6] Mobilized PBPCs result in earlier engraftment and are commonly utilized in the above situations and in heavily treated patients.

Allogeneic Marrow

Allogeneic transplants address many of the problems associated with an autologous transplant for a patient with malignant disease. For other patients, such as those with marrow failure, immunodeficiency, inborn errors of metabolism, or hemoglobinopathy, an allogeneic transplant is the only relevant type of graft. However, because it is difficult to identify a good HLA match, allogeneic transplantation is associated with a major risk that immunocompetent donor T cells reacting against recipient tissues will cause GVHD. Even in HLA-identical (six-antigen match) do-

Table 25-1. Possible Indications for Hematopoietic Transplantation

Congenital immune deficiencies
    severe combined immunodeficiency disease
    Wiskott-Aldrich syndrome
Marrow failure syndromes
    severe aplastic anemia
    Fanconi's anemia
    Diamond-Blackfan anemia (congenital hypoplastic anemia)
Inborn disorders
    mucopolysaccharidoses
    adrenoleukodystrophy
    osteopetrosis
Hemoglobinopathies
    thalassemia
    sickle cell disease
Malignant or premalignant diseases of marrow
    acute leukemia
    chronic myelogenous leukemia
    Hodgkin's and non-Hodgkin's lymphoma
    myelodysplastic/myeloproliferative disorders
    multiple myeloma
Solid tumors
    neuroblastoma
    Wilm's tumor
    breast cancer
    ovarian cancer
    testicular cancer
Other
    paroxysmal nocturnal hemoglobinuria
    acquired aplastic anemia
    autoimmune disorders

nor/recipient pairs, up to 6% of the grafts will fail and GVHD will occur in 20-60% of cases as a result of nucleated cells exhibiting minor histocompatibility antigens that are not linked to the major histocompatibility complex antigens.[6,7] This occurs despite immuno-suppressive therapy administered for several months after the procedure.[8]

Graft-vs-Host Disease

GVHD occurs in two forms—acute and chronic. Acute GVHD cases present anywhere from a few days to 100 days after transplanta-tion. The skin, the gastrointestinal tract, and the liver are most commonly involved, al-though usually not concurrently.[9] The site and severity determine the clinical grade of acute GVHD (Table 25-2). The risk of GVHD is greater in unrelated and related mismatched transplants than in HLA-identical transplants and in transplants of opposite gender.[9]

In a multicenter data analysis, 5809 adult patients received non-T-cell-depleted marrow transplants from HLA-identical siblings. The frequency of Grade 0 GVHD in this group was 20-49%; Grade I was 12-36%; Grade II was 12-25%; Grade III was 10-24%; and Grade IV was 5-16%.[10] In HLA-identical sibling trans-plants for chronic myelogenous leukemia 30-40% will develop Grade II acute GVHD of which as many as 15% will progress to Grade III or IV. Of patients receiving matched unre-lated marrow transplants for the same diagno-sis, 60-80% acquire Grade II GVHD, with 50% progressing to Grades III and IV.[7]

Chronic GVHD characteristically occurs spontaneously months after transplantation or

Table 25-2. Recommended Staging and Grading of Acute GVHD—Extent of Organ Involvement[10]

	Skin	Liver	Gut
Stage			
1	Rash on <25% of skin[*]	Bilirubin 2-3 mg/dL[†]	Diarrhea >500 mL/day[‡] or persistent nausea[§]
2	Rash on 25-50% of skin	Bilirubin 3-6 mg/dL	Diarrhea >1000 mL/day
3	Rash on >50% of skin	Bilirubin 6-15 mg/dL	Diarrhea >1500 mL/day
4	Generalized erythroderma with bullous formation	Bilirubin >15 mg/dL	Severe abdominal pain with or without ileus
Grade[¶]			
I	Stage 1-2	None	None
II	Stage 3 or	Stage 1 or	Stage 1
III	–	Stage 2-3 or	Stage 2-4
IV[‡‡]	Stage 4 or	Stage 4	–

[*]Use "Rule of Nines" or burn chart to determine extent of rash.
[†]Range given as total bilirubin. Downgrade one stage if an additional cause of elevated bilirubin has been documented.
[‡]Volume of diarrhea applies to adults. For pediatric patients, the volume of diarrhea should be based on body surface area. Gut staging criteria for pediatric patients not addressed. Downgrade one stage if an additional cause of diarrhea has been documented.
[§]Persistent nausea with histologic evidence of GVHD in the stomach or duodenum.
[¶]Criteria for grading given as minimum degree of organ involvement required to confer that grade.
[‡‡]Grade IV may also include lesser organ involvement but with extreme decrease in performance status.

following acute GVHD, (generally after posttransplant day 50) and may severely affect the patient's quality of life. In addition to the symptoms found in the acute form, chronic autoimmune type disorders such as biliary cirrhosis, Sjogren's syndrome, and systemic sclerosis may develop. Chronic GVHD is common in allogeneic transplant patients who survive beyond day 100, and can be found in 30-40% of patients. Both forms of GVHD predispose the patient to infections. To decrease or eliminate GVHD in these transplants, marrow can be T-cell-reduced (depleted) and the patient can be treated prophylactically with a variety of immunosuppressive drug therapies.

GVHD has been associated with both a decreased disease relapse and (with chronic GVHD) improved overall survival in leukemia patients. Such an effect is believed to be secondary to the graft rejecting residual malignant cells and has been termed the graft-vs-leukemia (GVL) effect.[3,8] A major clinical challenge has been in attempting to maximize the GVL effect while minimizing the adverse sequelae of GVHD.

Related Transplantation

For adult allogeneic transplants the best chance of finding a six-antigen HLA match is among the patient's genetic sisters and brothers with parents and children at least a haplotype match. There is a 25% chance of a sibling being a complete match, a 50% chance of a haplotype match, and a 25% chance of a complete mismatch. Pediatric patients are more tolerant of partially mismatched grafts and, therefore, have a larger available donor pool.[4] In the rare instance a recipient has an identical twin, a syngeneic transplant may be optimal because the donor and recipient cells are genotypically identical and the risk of GVHD is reduced.[5] However, syngeneic grafts do not provide the graft-vs-tumor effect found in allogeneic transplants. Even if a match is found within the family, possible donation may

be limited by the donor's health or willingness to donate.

Matched Unrelated Donor Transplantation

Matched unrelated donor searches can be initiated for the 60-70% of candidates without an HLA-identical sibling donor. There are multiple marrow donor databases available worldwide. The largest is the National Marrow Donor Program (NMDP, Minneapolis, MN).[11] Pilot studies determined that marrow transplantation between HLA-matched but unrelated individuals could be accomplished successfully. As of 1999 the NMDP had over 3.2 million persons registered as potential donors and had facilitated over 7000 transplant procedures. Upon initial search 80% of transplantation candidates usually find an HLA phenotypic match. However, patients from racial or ethnic minorities have a lower chance of success in such a donor search (Caucasian, 85%; Hispanic, 76%; Asian/Pacific Islander, 62%; African American, 59%; and American Indian/Alaska Native, 50%). The median time from initiating a search to receiving a transplant is 120 days. The most common diagnosis in patients undergoing transplantation is chronic myelogenous leukemia (CML).[11]

The NMDP has traditionally relied on serologic HLA matching. However, HLA typing disparities have been a persistent problem. In a study of 57,158 new donors, of 2308 randomly selected individuals who were routinely typed and also typed by a quality control HLA laboratory, 48% had one or more discrepancies.[11] The discrepancies were at the A locus (35%), the B locus (53%), and the DR locus (12%). Most discrepancies involved cross-reactive groups.

Recently, it has also been recognized that in addition to serologic matching for HLA-A, -B, and -DR loci, the HLA-DRB1 alleles also affect survival. Typing of the HLA-DRB1 allele requires the use of DNA techniques.[12] Because of the HLA typing discrepancies and the prognostic importance of DNA-defined alleles, DNA typing is emerging as the typing technique of choice.

A directory of transplant centers, outcome results, and charges is available from the NMDP. A preliminary search can be initiated by an individual hematologist or oncologist by contacting the NMDP at 1-800-654-1247.

In 462 unrelated transplants (multicenter) 40% of the low risk patients were disease-free at 2 years while 20% of the high risk patients were disease-free at 2 years. However, with improved control of GVHD and increased application of DNA-based HLA typing, some single centers have reported more recent 2-year disease-free survival rates of 55-74% in CML patients.[11,12] These results, in some cases, now approach those of HLA-identical sibling transplants.

Peripheral Blood Progenitor Cells

Peripheral blood progenitor cell collection involves mobilizing the hematopoietic cells from the marrow compartment into the peripheral blood by subcutaneous injection of hematopoietic growth factors and/or by treatment with chemotherapy prior to collection (autologous only). Once in the circulation, the PBPCs are collected by leukapheresis. Up to five leukapheresis procedures may be necessary depending on the number of HPCs available from the marrow, the mobilization efficiency, the timing of the PBPC collection to correspond with maximal circulation of the cells, and the length of PBPC collections. PBPC collection is less invasive than a marrow harvest and carries no anesthesia risk, but this is balanced against the frequent need for central venous catheters in autologous donors and the known and unknown risks of administering hematopoietic growth factors to normal individuals (allogeneic donors). If the required cell dose can be obtained in one to three collections, PBPC transplants are also less expensive with the same hematopoietic reconstitution as marrow.[6] While used routinely for adults, PBPC collections are frequently not the best approach for small children (particularly infants) as there are many technical problems as-

sociated with such collections.[4] The decision to employ marrow or PBPCs to procure an allogeneic graft should be indvidualized and based on both the patient and donor characteristics.

Umbilical Cord Blood

Despite the fact that over 3 million individuals are registered with the NMDP, patients in need of an allogeneic HPC transplant have less than an 85% chance of finding a matched donor. Because of the unavailability of donors and the prolonged time involved in obtaining HPCs from a donor (time that a recipient may not have), attention has turned to alternative sources of HLA-typed HPCs. Umbilical cord blood (UCB), which in clinical practice are routinely discarded, are emerging as one such source, especially for children, on whom most of the following data are based.

Wagner and colleagues found that recipients of sibling cord blood matched for at least five of six antigens had a 72% survival, at a median follow-up of 1.6 years.[13] Kurtzberg and others have reported UCB transplants that differed by as many as three HLA antigens from the recipient that have successfully engrafted, without causing clinically significant GVHD.[14,15] Days to a neutrophil count of ≥500/µL in unrelated transplants have been reported to range from 14 to 37 (median 22) with platelet counts of 50,000 and 100,000/µL by a median of 82 and 115 days, respectively. Similarly, the placental blood program at the New York Blood Center reported that by acturial analysis of 562 recipients, neutrophil engraftment was 81% by day 42 (median-28 days) and 85% by day 180 for platelets (median-day 90). Overall, relatively little GVHD has been noted in recipients of cord blood transplants.[13-16] This may reflect either the "immature" nature of cord cells or possibly the decreased susceptibility of pediatric recipients to GVHD. Of concern is whether the relatively small number of progenitor cells collected from placentas would be sufficient to produce long-term engraftment of an adult-sized recipient. In-vitro data have suggested that placental blood has an increased capacity for proliferation and self-renewal compared to marrow and thus might be capable of engrafting an adult-sized recipient.[17] Recently, 22 cases of successful engraftment of placental blood from unrelated donors in recipients who weighed more than 45 kg have been reported.[14,15,18] This early success bodes well for the future of umbilical cord blood transplantation.

Related

To date, sibling-derived umbilical cord blood has been used as a source of hematopoietic engraftment in more than 100 allogeneic transplants in Europe and North America.[13]

Unrelated

In order for UCB to be a feasible alternative to marrow or PBPC in allogeneic transplants, it is essential to have a frozen inventory of ready-to-use HLA-typed products. The first large-scale program of its kind was the Placental Blood Program at the New York Blood Center, which began collecting placental products in 1992 and has stored in excess of 7705 UCB units and has provided cells for 562 transplants in 98 marrow transplant centers.[16,19,20] In Europe, 65 unrelated UCB transplants have been reported.[15] Most recently, the National Heart, Lung, and Blood Institute of the National Institutes of Health has funded multiple cord banks that plan to bank 15,000 placental products.

Autologous

Companies have begun to market to parents the freezing and long-term storage of their child's UCB cells against the day when the child might need them.[21,22] The chance of an individual needing a cord blood transplant by age 18 is estimated to be 1 in 200,000.[22] To date, there has been only one case of an autologous cord cell transplant. However, this involved a case of anticipated adenosine deaminase defi-

ciency in a patient who received a transplant of genetically modified cord cells; the outcome of the transplant has yet to be reported.[23]

Fetal Liver

Rarely, liver tissue from 12- to 16-week-old aborted fetuses has been used successfully to transplant children with congenital immunodeficiencies.[4,5] Hematopoiesis occurs in the fetal liver for several months, but at the time of birth occurs solely in the marrow cavity. While fetal liver is a source of HPCs, UCB is more readily available and has fewer ethical issues associated with it.

Donor Suitability

Donor Evaluation

Autologous Setting

In the autologous setting, the major concern regarding suitability for transplantation arises from the sensitivity of the malignancy to the myeloablative regimen. A second area of concern is the mobilization of sufficient cells from the patient to reconstitute the marrow after myeloablation. Before collection, the patient's marrow should be assayed for residual malignancy and marrow cellularity. Patients scheduled for an autologous transplant should undergo an extensive history and physical examination to identify any risks from the marrow harvest and/or apheresis procedures.

Allogeneic Setting

In the allogeneic setting, there are many issues involved in selecting a donor. Initially donor selection is based on HLA compatibility between the donor and the recipient. Ideally, a full six-antigen match should be found; however, transplant procedures have been sucessfully performed using one-antigen mismatched and haploidentical donors.

If more than one HLA-identical donor is found, there are secondary issues that can affect the eventual donor choice. Given the high morbidity and mortality rate associated with cytomegalovirus (CMV) infection, the CMV status of the donor is often the deciding factor in the selection process. The use of parous females or sex-mismatched individuals as donors is associated with an increased risk of GVHD, as is a history of prior transfusion of the donor.[24-27] Therefore, when more than one HLA-identical donor is available, the selected donor would ideally be CMV negative (in the case of CMV negative recipients); of the same gender as the recipient; if female, nonparous; and untransfused.

Infectious Disease Testing

Regardless of the hematopoietic cell source, infectious disease testing is critical. The donor must be screened in order to minimize the risk of disease transmission to an already immunocompromised recipient. All donors, autologous or allogeneic, should be tested for hepatitis B surface antigen (HBsAg), antibody to hepatitis B core antigen (anti-HBc), antibody to human T-cell lymphotropic virus (anti-HTLV), antibody to human immunodeficiency virus, type 1 (anti-HIV-1), antibody to human immunodeficiency virus, type 2 (anti-HIV-2), HIV-1 (p24) antigen, antibody to hepatitis C virus (anti-HCV), serologic test for syphillis, and CMV within 30 days of the scheduled collection. Donors who are positive for anti-HIV-1, anti-HIV-2 or HIV-1 antigen should not be used as a source for the transplant. Other positive disease markers do not necessarily prohibit use of collections from a particular donor. Components from such donors may be used with the informed consent of both the recipient and the attending physician and will require alternative methods of storage.[28,29]

In cases of allogeneic placental blood transplant, a sample for infectious disease studies should be collected from the mother within 48 hours of delivery and tested within 7 days. All the studies listed above should be performed; any positive results should be reported to the mother and the mother's physician; and the donation should not be used unless specific approval is granted by an approved Investigational Review Board or applicable regulatory agency.[11,29]

CMV infection is one of the leading causes of posttransplant mortality in the allogeneic setting. It is important to ascertain the CMV status of the donor and the recipient in cases of allogeneic transplant. A recipient may develop primary CMV infection if he or she is CMV negative and receives a CMV-positive graft.[27] Recipients who are CMV positive may experience reinfection or reactivation during the myeloablative regimen.[30]

Collection of Products

When applicable, HPCs must be collected and processed under Institutional Review Board approved protocols in accordance with written guidelines.[29] Institutions should have documentation from the Food and Drug Administration of Investigational New Drug (IND) approval or Investigational Device Exemption (IDE) when appropriate for the manipulation of products.

Marrow Harvest

A marrow harvest is the same for an allogeneic donor as for an autologous patient. The procedure is performed under sterile conditions in the operating room. A general, epidural, or spinal anesthetic is employed. Routine harvest sites include the posterior and anterior iliac crests and, rarely, sternum (in the adult). The posterior iliac crest provides the richest site of marrow. The sternum yields a generous nucleated cell count per milliliter of marrow; however, the overall aspirable volume is limited. The anterior iliac crest provides the poorest yields in terms of nucleated cell count and available volume. In the autologous patient, prior radiation therapy to an aspiration site may result in hypocellular yields. In general, these sites are unsuitable for harvest and should be avoided.

The volume of marrow aspirated at each puncture site is usually 2-5 mL and should not exceed 10 mL.[31] Therefore, several hundred aspirations must be performed. Repeated large volume aspirations from the same site results in lowered nucleated cell counts due to hemodilution. Several bony sites may be aspirated through a single skin puncture, thereby minimizing external trauma, scar formation, and postharvest pain. For most harvests, the target dose is equivalent to 10-15 mL of marrow per kilogram of recipient body weight.[31] The NMDP limits the volume harvested from its donors to a maximum of 1500 mL. Many centers use the cell number requested for transplant and the cell count on the product during collection to determine the final collection volume.

Once aspirated, the marrow should be mixed and diluted with an anticoagulant (usually preservative-free heparin and/or ACD). Although marrow had historically been harvested with culture media, such as TC 199 (Life Technologies, Grand Island, NY), many centers are now using buffered electrolyte solutions such as Plasmalyte (Baxter Healthcare Corporation, Deerfield, IL).[32,33] Because of reports that the presence of preservative in aspirated marrow may inhibit or delay engraftment by impairing HPC proliferation and maturation, preservative-free heparin is preferred for marrow harvest.[33] In some institutions, the donor may be given a bolus of preservative-free heparin prior to the harvest, to protect against lipid embolism.[31,34] In addition, many choose to heparinize the collection syringes prior to use, reducing the risk of clotting. The marrow aliquots are pooled into a sterile vessel or a harvest collection bag equipped with filters of graduated size. While many collecting centers filter the marrow, there is no evidence that filtration is essential. The marrow is then transferred to a sterile blood bag and transported to the processing laboratory, where samples are removed for graft evaluation, quality assurance testing, and possible manipulation of the product and/or cryopreservation.

Collection Targets

The recipient's body weight and type of manipulation of the collection, if any, will determine the volume of marrow to be collected. The generally accepted minimum target (after processing), for an allogeneic transplant is 2.0×10^8 nucleated cells per kilogram of recipient body weight. In the autologous setting 1.0×10^8 cells/kg (after processing) is recommended. Marrow harvests in autologous patients who have received alkylating agents as therapy may yield fewer progenitor cells relative to the total nucleated cells collected. In these cases, extra marrow should be obtained if possible.[34] Different treatment protocols will have specific collection targets. If the harvested product is to be manipulated (ie, T-cell depletion, ex-vivo tumor purging), additional marrow (up to double the reinfusion target) should be collected. Donors harvested for the NMDP will have specific marrow prescriptions (target nucleated dose) based on the recipient's body weight and type of processing required.

Clinical Considerations

The age of the donor and, in the autologous setting, the previous treatment regimen influence the HPC yield (Table 25-3).[5] Due to the volume of marrow removed, red cell transfusions may be required in both autologous and allogeneic donors. Frequently, allogeneic donors will have an autologous red cell unit collected 2-3 weeks before the harvest. Most red cell transfusions occur after the harvest to avoid marrow dilution. Allogeneic blood should be irradiated before transfusion, if given during the procedure. In transplants that require marrow manipulation, the recovered red cells may be returned to the donor. Similar

Table 25-3. Factors Reported to Affect the Mobilization of Hematopoietic Cells

1. Mobilization technique
    a. Chemotherapy–degree of transient myelosuppression
    b. Growth factors–type, schedule, dose
    c. Use of combined chemotherapy and growth factors
2. Extent of prior chemotherapy/radiation
3. Age of patient
4. Presence of marrow metastases

Adapted with permission from Lane.[6]

red cell recovery may be performed in the autologous setting.

Peripheral Blood Progenitor Cells

Alternative sources for HPCs include the peripheral blood. Historically, patients undergoing autologous HPC rescue in conjunction with their marrow harvest would have PBPCs collected in the unmobilized or steady state.[35] While reinfusion of these peripheral collections often facilitated cell recovery after myeloablative therapy, engraftments were slow.[5] With the development and use of recombinant colony-stimulating factors to mobilize large numbers of CD34-positive cells for collection, the time to hematopoietic recovery was further reduced.[36,37] Platelet reconstitution was most striking and decreased patient hospital stays by 7-10 days.[5] HPCs are now routinely mobilized from the marrow into the peripheral blood by hematopoietic growth factors (with or without chemotherapy), which include granuloctye colony-stimulating factor (G-CSF) and granulocyte-macrophage colony-stimulating factor (GM-CSF) or a combination of the two.[6] (See section on colony-forming cell assays for additional information on growth factors.) Lane[6] summarized

the increase in colony-forming units–granulocyte-macrophage (CFU-GM) observed in PBPCs after mobilization (see Table 25-4). In general, a 20- to 50-fold increase was observed with chemotherapy alone, G-CSF alone, or both GM-CSF and G-CSF; GM-CSF alone showed an approximate 10-fold increase. The combined use of chemotherapy and growth factors produced an approximately 70-fold increase. Beyer and colleagues[38] demonstrated that median time to an unsupported platelet count of $\geq 20,000/\mu L$ was 10 days in the chemotherapy plus G-CSF mobilized PBPC transplant group vs 17 days in the autologous marrow transplant group. Currently, the focus is to use harvested PBPCs as the sole source of hematopoietic reconstitution.[39] Effective mobilization in the autologous patient is influenced by previous chemotherapy/radiation.[5] Allogeneic donors are mobilized with hematopoietic growth factors alone.

The optimal timing of a PBPC collection, the time when the greatest number of cells capable of sustaining colony formation[35] are in the circulation, is controversial. Clonogenic assays have traditionally been used to monitor

Table 25-4. Techniques of PBPC Mobilization

Method	Increase in Blood CFU-GM
Chemotherapy alone	20- to 50-fold
Hematopoietic growth factors alone	
G-CSF	20- to 50-fold
GM-CSF	~10-fold
GM-CSF and G-CSF	20- to 50-fold
Chemotherapy and growth factors	~70-fold (range, 25- to 250-fold)

Reproduced with permission from Lane.[6]
CFU-GM=colony-forming units–granulocyte-macrophage; G-CSF=granulocyte colony-stimulating factor; GM-CSF=granulocyte-macrophage colony-stimulating factor.

the hematopoietic potential of the autologous marrow graft. However, the prolonged culture time (2 weeks) prevents this assay from being a real-time indicator for the collection of PBPCs. The most common practice, which is simple but indirect, is to base the time of collection on changes in blood counts.[35,36] Early studies suggested that collections should begin when the leukocyte count exceeded 1.0×10^9/L. It is now clear that the optimal time to begin PBPC collection is when the leukocyte count first exceeds 5×10^9/L.[35,36] However, the leukocyte concentration does not always correlate with the number of HPCs in the peripheral blood. Primitive and committed progenitor cells express CD34 antigens on their surface.[40] Phenotypic analysis of CD34-positive cells by flow cytometry provides a more real-time measurement of CD34+ content in a PBPC collection or hematopoietic graft and can be used to determine when to initiate PBPC collection. Numerous investigators have studied the relationship between CFU-GM numbers and CD34+ values.[41-43] Many variables are thought to influence this relationship. Differences in culture techniques and CD34 flow cytometric analysis methods also play a role in this variability.[44-46]

In most autologous patients, venous access is obtained through a dual- or triple-lumen central venous apheresis catheter. Good peripheral access of the allogeneic donor is critical. Blood cell separators generally process two to three blood volumes per procedure. In the pediatric setting, it may be necessary to prime the cell separator with compatible red cells. The donor, autologous or allogeneic, will undergo daily procedures for approximately 2-5 hours each. Large-volume leukapheresis procedures (processing at least three blood volumes or 15-20 liters) are performed at many centers to reduce the overall number of collections. Investigational studies have demonstrated the recruitment of noncirculating PBPCs into the peripheral circulation with large-volume collections.[47-50] Hillyer[50] reported

a 2.5-fold increase in CFU-GM when >15 liters of blood were processed.

Collection Targets

The adequacy of a PBPC collection is gauged by the CD34+ dose, which is the number of CD34+ cells per kilogram of recipient body weight. The reported minimum threshold of CD34+ cells necessary for neutrophil and platelet engraftment in the autologous patient has ranged from 2 to 5×10^6/kg.[5] This minimum target is a broad guideline and even higher doses have been associated with accelerated platelet engraftment.[51] As with the marrow harvest, the type of processing will also influence the volume of PBPCs necessary for collection. Some institutions have made a distinction between an optimal cell dose for autologous vs allogeneic PBPC grafts and recommend that the latter contain at least threefold more progenitor cells, although clinical necessity for this has not been proved.[36] Clinical trials are under way to determine a more defined minimum dose in the allogeneic setting.

Clinical Considerations

PBPC collections are not associated with the minimal morbidity that may accompany marrow harvests. However, the frequency and length of collections may cause donors discomfort and side effects. Complete blood counts are performed before and after each apheresis procedure to monitor the hematocrit and platelet values. Red cell and/or platelet transfusions are often required for the autologous patient. Reports[52,53] have described thrombocytopenia in allogeneic donors, which may complicate the collection process. Stroncek and others[53,54] have discussed the symptoms associated with cytokine therapy for mobilization. Ninety percent of donors experience side effects. The most common complaint is bone pain followed by headaches, body aches, fatigue, nausea, and/or vomiting.

Umbilical Cord Blood

Umbilical cord blood can be collected from either a delivered or undelivered placenta.[19,20,55] If the cord collection will interfere with obstetric care of the mother, the cord blood should be collected after delivery of the placenta. Collection of the cord blood is preferably initiated within 15 minutes of parturition. To minimize the risk of bacterial contamination, the surface of the cord should be disinfected similar to the preparation of skin for a blood donation. A large-bore needle connected to a blood collection bag containing CPDA, CPD, or ACD anticoagulant is inserted into the umbilical vein so that the placental blood drains by gravity into the bag. A delivered placenta can be suspended in a plastic-lined, absorbent cotton pad above the collection bag. CPDA is a preferred anticoagulant as it is isotonic and has a neutral pH. However, other closed system arrangements using ACD or heparin are in use in some centers. In 5-10 minutes 64 mL ± 27.2 (SD) are typically collected.

Informed consent from the biologic mother must be obtained. The informed consent can be obtained either before the delivery (anytime during the pregnancy) or after the delivery.[29]

A personal and family medical history of the biologic mother and father, if available, of the prospective cord blood cell donor must be obtained and documented before, or within 48 hours of, the collection.[29] Cord blood collections are not acceptable for allogeneic use if there is a family history (biologic mother, father, or sibling) of genetic disorders that may affect graft effectiveness in the recipient or otherwise expose the recipient to a genetic disorder through the transplant.[29]

Red cells from the cord blood collection or from the infant donor must be typed for ABO/Rh and a screen for unexpected red cell antibodies must be performed using either the mother's serum or plasma or a sample from either the infant donor or the cord blood collection.[29] White cells from the cord blood must be typed for HLA (HLA-A and -B antigen testing, and DNA-based Class II typing) by an American Society of Histocompatibility and Immunogenetics (ASHI)-accredited laboratory.[29] Samples should be frozen for pretransplant confirmation of HLA type by the transplant facility.

Many centers freeze a sample of the mother's serum until the time the cord blood is used for transplantation. Such samples may be useful in clarifying difficulties in HLA typing, particularly if there is a large amount of maternal contamination. If new tests for infectious disease markers are introduced during the time of storage, this sample is also available for such testing.

Processing of Hematopoietic Progenitor Cells

Buffy Coat Separation of Marrow

A marrow harvest may result in a product volume of up to 2000 mL containing plasma, red cells, white cells, progenitor cells, platelets, and fatty substance. In the case of an autologous marrow harvest where the product will be stored for use after the patient undergoes myeloablative therapy, it is necessary to process the harvest to facilitate cryopreservation. Decreasing the marrow volume by plasma and harvest media removal helps to minimize the volume to be cryopreserved. The reduced product volume requires less dimethylsulfoxide (DMSO) for cryopreservation, resulting in fewer DMSO-related toxicities at infusion. Concentrating a product may also reduce the amount of costly reagents required for a tumor cell purge.[56] In the case of allogeneic marrow cells, it may be necessary to remove incompatible red cells or plasma, before infusion, to prevent hemolytic reactions.

Red cells and granulocytes are not effectively preserved with the currently accepted cryopreservation techniques; therefore, their removal prior to freezing is desirable.[57] Lysed red cells may result in renal or other hemolysis-related toxicities.[58] The by-products of granulocyte breakdown as well as the presence of platelets can result in clumping of the thawed product and decreased progenitor cell viability.[59]

The end point of basic marrow processing is a buffy coat with a modest depletion of red cells and a significant volume reduction. This is generally achieved through the differential centrifugation of marrow by any number of manual or automated techniques.

Manual Buffy Coat Preparations

Manual buffy coat preparation involves the centrifugation of marrow in conical tubes or transfer bags. Once centrifuged, the marrow supernatant is removed, followed by the collection of the buffy coat. The remaining red cells may be pooled and washed for reinfusion to the donor. Buffy coats collected in this fashion should recover >75% of the original nucleated cell count.[60]

The disadvantage in using manual methods for buffy coat collection is the risk of bacterial contamination inherent in open system processing.[29] In addition, the resulting buffy coat contains a large number of red cells and granulocytes, both of which can result in problems at the time of infusion.

Red cell and granulocyte content is virtually eliminated when density gradient separation is employed in conjunction with the buffy coat preparation by either manual or automated methods. Although mononuclear cell recoveries may be adequate (>50%), the introduction of a chemical (eg, ficoll-hypaque) that is not currently approved for human use decreases its desirability as a widely accepted method of marrow processing.[61-63]

Automated Buffy Coat Preparations

Several cell washers and apheresis instruments have been adapted for the semiautomated and automated processing of marrow. The recoveries using automated or semiautomated methods vary according to instrument and operator. The COBE 2991 (COBE BCT, Inc, Lakewood, CO) has been used for the collection of buffy coats with a recovery of >80% of the initial nucleated cell count and a decrease in volume of up to 80%.[64] A double buffy coat method with this instrument has been reported with a 77% recovery of the initial nucleated count, 104% recovery of the CFU-GM and a red cell volume of less than 9 mL.[65] Although these methods allow for separation of a buffy coat while maintaining the nucleated cell and CFU-GM counts, they still contain a large number of granulocytes and red cells.

A more purified mononuclear product has been reported with a number of apheresis devices. The CS-3000 (Fenwal Division, Baxter Healthcare Corporation, Deerfield, IL) has been used with reported recoveries of 87% of the original mononuclear count with a 98% depletion of red cells.[66] The COBE Spectra™ has also been used with recoveries reported at 94% of the initial mononuclear count and 132% recovery of the CFU-GM with a 99% reduction in red cells.[63]

Employment of such apheresis machines in buffy coat processing provides a highly purified product with better than average recovery of mononuclear and CFU-GM fractions and a depletion of red cells comparable to manual density gradient separation.

Techniques for Cell Selection and/or Purging of Hematopoietic Progenitor Cells

Selection of the CD34+ HPCs

CD34 is a cell surface antigen present on uncommitted and some committed HPCs. As a cell undergoes differentiation and maturation, this antigen level decreases. This property, coupled with the use of monoclonal antibodies specific for the different epitopes of the CD34 molecule, permits physical separation procedures. There are several methods of immunoselection available, such as fluorescent-activated cell sorting (FACS), immunomagnetic beads, and avidin-biotin immuno-adsorption columns.[67] Selection of CD34+ HPCs may be associated with a reduction of tumor cells (autologous) or T cells (allogeneic). The clinical utility of CD34 selection for tumor or T-cell reduction is under investigation.

Fluorescent-Activated Cell Sorting

A fluorescent-activated cell sorter combines a flow cytometer with a physical separation methodology (such as droplet or fluid switch sorting) that segregates individual cells based on the expression of molecules with predefined properties.[68] While this technique is sensitive, it is not commonly employed for large-scale purification of a graft.

Immunoadsorption Systems

Immunomagnetic Separation. Various immunomagnetic separation techniques, direct or indirect, are available. Some are primarily useful in selecting stem cells for ex-vivo culturing studies and others are being evaluated in clinical trials for patient therapy. Typically, a CD34 antibody is coupled to a magnetic bead. This complex is incubated with mononuclear cells and the cells expressing the CD34 antigen bind to the antibody-coated beads, forming rosettes. A magnet is applied to separate the rosetting CD34+ cells from the nonrosetting cells. Bead detachment, which varies among methods, may be accomplished through anti-Fab fragments or enzymatic treatment ie, chymopapain.[69] The Isolex® 300 system (Baxter Healthcare Immunotherapy Division, Irvine, CA), a magnetic cell separator, is a semi-automated instrument for clinical scale CD34+ selection applications. This method uses antibody-coated Dynal paramagnetic beads to rosette the CD34+ cells. The CD34+ cells are removed from the beads by chymopapain, specifically ChymoCell-T (Baxter Healthcare Immunotherapy Division, Irvine, CA).[70] The use of a fully automated device (Isolex® 300I) and a peptide release agent to replace the

chymopapain is currently under investigation.[71]

Other techniques of magnetic cell separation employ superparamagnetic microbeads that remain attached to the HPC surface.[72] One such method, magnetic cell sorting (MACS®) was first introduced on a small scale (Miltenyi Biotec GmbH, Bergisch Gladbach, Germany) by Miltenyi.[73] The CliniMACS (Miltenyi Biotec GmbH) is a clinical-scale version of the MACS® system that is available in Europe.[74] This system employs antibody-conjugated iron-dextran microbeads. The magnetically stained cells are separated over a high gradient magnetic column and a microprocessor controls the elution of the CD34+ cells.

Avidin-Biotin Selection. The avidin-biotin immunoadsorption columns exploit the high-affinity interaction between the protein avidin and the vitamin biotin. Cells are incubated with biotin-labeled antibody to the CD34 antigen and processed over a column containing avidin-conjugated beads. The labeled CD34+ cells bind to the beads and the unlabeled cells wash through. The CD34+ cells are then eluted by gentle agitation. This system is available for both research and clinical applications. The CEPRATE® SC Stem Cell Concentrator (originally CellPro Inc, Bothell, WA; now Baxter Healthcare Corporation) is a fully automated closed system clinical-scale instrument.[75] This system was the first CD34 selection technique to be used for human autologous transplant.[76] The CEPRATE® SC Stem Cell Concentrator has been widely used for clinical trials both in Europe and the United States. The CEPRATE® SC Stem Cell Concentrator is approved for use in the United States for CD34 selection in autologous marrow and PBPC processing for the purposes of diminishing toxicity of DMSO and reduction of tumor cell load.

Physical Parameter Separation

Low density (1.055-1.065 g/mL) hematopoietic progenitors can be separated from higher density mature cells by centrifugation on a density gradient or counterflow centrifugal elutriation.[77]

Density Gradient Centrifugation. A CD34+ enrichment kit (Activated Cell Therapy, ACT Mountain View, CA) uses silan-coated colloidal silica to separate HPCs based on their buoyancy during centrifugation. This technique for CD34 selection is undergoing clinical trials involving autologous transplantation.[78]

Counterflow Centrifugal Elutriation. Counterflow centrifugal elutriation (CCE) is a method of separating cells based on their size and density. A continuous-flow centrifuge (Beckman Instruments Inc., Palo Alto, CA) and unique chamber design allow for the basic separation principle: two opposing forces (centrifugal force and counter media flow) acting upon cells at the same time. As cells are pumped into the chamber (centripetal direction) they align according to their sedimentation properties. With adjustment of the counter flow rate, the centrifugal and counterflow forces are balanced and a gradient of flow rates exists across the chamber. By gradually increasing the flow rate of the media or decreasing the speed of the rotor, cells can be eluted out of the chamber and collected. Smaller, slower sedimenting cells elute first.[79] Although this technique is used primarily for T-cell depletion, CCE has been applied to CD34+ cell selection. CD34+ cells are heterogenous and will elute in subset fractions that are useful for repopulation experiments and ex-vivo expansion trials.[80]

Autologous Tumor Purging

Purging or negative selection refers to the removal of tumor cells that may contaminate the autologous graft. In patients with hematopoietic disease or malignancies that frequently involve the marrow (lymphoma, breast cancer), minimal residual disease contributes to relapse.[81] While autologous PBPCs have a lower probability than marrow of tumor contamination and fewer tumor cells/mL, they still may contain large numbers of viable tu-

mor cells. Studies have demonstrated that tumor cells may be mobilized from the marrow into the peripheral circulation.[82,83] Whether tumor purging effectively decreases the likelihood of relapse is controversial. Because some purging methods may damage hematopoietic progenitor cells, the probability of residual disease or relapse should be carefully balanced against the higher graft failure rate or increased mortality from prolonged aplasia that may be associated with tumor purging.[84] Numerous techniques for autologous purging (marrow and PBPC) are available. The goal of all purging methods—whether physical, immunologic, or pharmacologic—is the destruction or removal of the malignant clone while maintaining the efficacy of the HPCs necessary for engraftment.[85]

Pharmacologic Techniques. In-vivo antineoplastic therapy produces greater tumor cell kill due to the differential sensitivity of malignant cells over normal cells. In-vitro pharmacologic purging is an effort to expand this therapeutic ratio. In-vitro purging allows for dose and exposure intensification without concern for organ toxicity as higher drug concentrations can be used on isolated hematopoietic grafts ex vivo, which then can be administered in vivo. However, the drug concentration must be at nontoxic levels before reinfusion. Activated oxazaphosphorines (4-Hydroperoxycyclophosphamide, mafosfamide) were the most frequently used compounds but are generally no longer in use in the United States. Cisplatin, methylprednisolone, etoposide (VP-16), daunomycin, vincristine, and others have been investigated in preclinical models or used in clinical trials. Results from purged autologous transplants for acute myelogenous leukemia with either of these drugs showed prolonged aplasia with less than 1% CFU-GM survival. Median times for granulocyte and platelet recoveries were 45 and 86 days, respectively. In the non-Hodgkin's lymphoma setting, CFU-GM survival averaged 4% and median granulocyte and platelet recoveries decreased to 23 and 29 days, respectively. Diagnosis and previous cytotoxic therapy are thought to influence the engraftment kinetics.[84]

Photosensitizing Dyes. The basic principle of this technology is that light can injure or kill cells in the presence of photosensitizers. Photosensitizers are naturally occurring molecules that absorb light. Despite concerns over dependable light sources and light delivery systems, Phase I and Phase II studies are progressing. Four dyes (merocyanine 540, sulfonated chloroaluminum phthalocyanine, 1-pyrinedodecanoic acid, and Photofrin II) have been evaluated in preclinical studies for marrow purging. Leukemia and lymphoma cells show higher sensitivity to photoirradiation in contrast to normal HPCs.[86,87]

Physical Techniques. Separation methods based on cell size and density through gradient-generating reagents or CCE do not achieve adequate tumor cell depletion.[84] However, the combined use of physical and immunologic techniques will require further study.

Immunologic Techniques. The development of monoclonal antibodies coupled with the discovery of tumor-associated antigens opened the field for immunologic purging.[88] Monoclonal antibodies may be directed at tumor-specific antigens or cell-differentiation antigens.[84] The immunologic techniques differ primarily by the method of target cell removal. Monoclonal antibodies are used in conjunction with complement, bound to toxins, or coupled to magnetic beads. The choice of monoclonal antibody and the heterogeneity of antigen expression on the target cell affect the success of the purge or the level of depletion. Many investigators employ a cocktail of monoclonal antibodies in an effort to enhance the purging efficiency.[88-90]

Complement mediated cytotoxicity is frequently used if the antibody is of IgM isotype or if the expected level of antigen density is high.[84] A predetermined volume of complement is incubated with the target cells to achieve the desired concentration. The incubation time (usually 1 hour) may be repeated with fresh reagents. With multiple treatments, a 4-6 log reduction can be achieved.[88] Complement-dependent methods frequently rely upon animal sources (typically rabbit). The use of non-human-derived reagents is an area of concern, especially in the immunocompromised patient. Such products may lead to cross-species disease transmission.

Immunomagnetic cell separation, either by direct or indirect method, employs an antibody-coated magnetic bead to target the antigen or antigens of interest. A recent study described a 5-log tumor cell depletion with two cycles using the indirect method for B-cell lymphoma. Colony assays showed only a 20% reduction in CFU-GM and multipotential CFU (CFU-GEMM).[89] In a cell line model experiment, Kvalheim et al[89] showed a 4-log depletion using a cocktail of monoclonal antibody coupled to magnetic beads compared to a 1- to 2-log depletion using complement mediated cytotoxicity.

Immunotoxins (monoclonal antibody conjugated to a toxic molecule) bind to the target cell surface with concomitant ingestion resulting in cell death. A combination of two immunotoxins directed against three breast cancer cell lines resulted in a 5-log kill in experiments reported by Kvalheim.[89] Several toxins are available to target specific cell types.[84]

T-Cell Depletion

In allogeneic HPC transplantation, GVHD is a significant complication. Because the disease process is mediated by host reactive T cells, depletion strategies are utilized to target and remove these cells in an effort to decrease the incidence or at least lessen the severity of GVHD. Many of the techniques outlined for positive selection and tumor purging are applicable to T-cell depletion (Table 25-5).[8,91]

In T-cell-depleted grafts, two major areas of concern are graft failure and recurrent leukemia. Most instances of graft failure (initial or

Table 25-5. Methods of T-Cell Depletion

Nonimmunologic

    Counterflow centrifugal elutriation

    Soybean agglutinin and sheep RBC rosetting

    Pharmacologic/cytotoxic drugs

Immunologic

    Monoclonal antibodies with or without complement

    Immunotoxins

    Immunomagnetic beads

---

late) are due to immunologic rejection. Early transplants involving depleted grafts in patients with CML showed a 50% or greater relapse rate. In contrast, patients who developed GVHD had a lower relapse rate. Subsequent clinical and investigational data provided evidence of an immune-mediated GVL effect.[8]

Current research and developmental efforts are focused on determining the optimal level of T-cell depletion. Dreger et al[92] reported a comparison of T-cell depletion methods (CAMPATH-1 plus complement, immunomagnetic CD34+ selection, and biotin-avidin-mediated CD34+ selection). The immunomagnetic method provided a 4-log reduction in T cells vs a 3.1-log reduction with the biotin-avidin method. Monoclonal antibody treatment with autologous complement yielded a 2.1-log reduction. The challenge of minimizing the severity of GVHD and maintaining the GVL effect is ongoing. Additional studies are examining the role of subpopulations of T cells and/or cytokines in potentiating the GVL effect.[8,93]

ABO Incompatibilities

While HLA compatibility is crucial in the successful engraftment of myelosuppressed or ablated patients, ABO compatibility is not. Pluripotent and very early committed HPCs do not possess ABH antigens, allowing engraftment to successfully occur regardless of the ABO compatibility between the recipient and donor. ABO incompatibility does not appear to result in any increase in the incidence of delayed neutrophil or platelet engraftment, graft failure, or rejection. However, delayed red cell engraftment or hemolysis may occur (Table 25-6).

Major ABO Incompatibility

If the donor has red cells that are incompatible with the recipient (eg, a group AB donor and a non-group-AB recipient), red cells present in the aspirated marrow may be rapidly hemolyzed at the time of infusion. Fortunately, the HPC preparation can be processed to remove mature red cells. The group O recipient who receives a group A graft may continue to produce anti-A and anti-B for 3-4 months or longer in rare instances, and the presence of anti-A may delay erythropoiesis by the group A marrow; group A red cells appear in the circulation when the recipient's anti-A disappears. Granulocyte and platelet production are not affected.[94] During the period of red cell aplasia, the patient can be supported with irradiated group O red cells.[95] Circulating donor white cells are usually found about 2½ weeks after transplantation and platelets follow at about 4 weeks after transplantation.[96] In all cases, red cells used for transfusion of the recipient must be compatible with both the donor and the recipient. In some centers, group O red cells are frequently given to all major ABO-incompatible transplant recipients in order to avoid confusion.

Minor ABO Incompatibility

Before infusion of a graft from a plasma incompatible donor (such as a group-O donor to a non-group O recipient), the plasma is removed to avoid infusion of preformed anti-A and/or anti-B. Approximately 10-15% of such transplants are characterized by rather abrupt onset

Table 25-6. Potential Problems in ABO- and Rh-Incompatible Marrow Transplantation

| | Example | | |
Incompatibility	Donor	Patient	Potential Problems
ABO			
Major incompatibility	Group A	Group O	Hemolysis of red cells in donor marrow, failure or delay of red cell engraftment
Minor incompatibility	Group O	Group A	Hemolysis of patient's red cells by antibody in marrow or produced after engraftment; graft-vs-host disease due to anti-A
Rh	Negative	Positive	Hemolysis of patient's red cells by (donor) antibody produced after engraftment
	Positive	Negative with anti-D	Hemolysis of red cells from newly engrafted marrow stem cells

of immune hemolysis, which begins about 7-10 days after transplantation and may last for 2 weeks. The direct antiglobulin test (DAT) is positive; anti-A and/or anti-B can be recovered in the eluate and hemoglobinemia and/or hemoglobinuria may occur. An additional 30% of such transplant recipients develop a positive DAT without experiencing gross hemolysis. This phenomenon is due to alloantibodies produced by passenger B lymphocytes in the marrow.[95] Although transient, the hemolysis may persist for up to 2 weeks and may require transfusion with group O red cells (Fig 25-1). In all cases, plasma used for transfusion should be compatible with both the donor and the recipient. In some centers, group AB plasma products may be given to all minor ABO-incompatible transplant recipients in order to avoid confusion.

Chimerism

In spite of the intensive pretransplant chemotherapy and irradiation, some of the host's hematopoietic cells may survive and subsequently coexist with cells produced by the transplanted marrow. This dual cell population, called hematopoietic chimerism, may have an effect on immunologic tolerance.[97]

Processing in the Presence of ABO Incompatibilities

Major ABO Incompatibility. Two approaches have been employed with major ABO incompatibilities: 1) removal of or decrease in the isoagglutinin level in the recipient or 2) the removal of the red cells in the donor marrow.

Attempts to remove or decrease the isoagglutinin titer in recipients involve the use of large-volume plasma exchange with or without the subsequent infusion of donor type red cells as a secondary effort to absorb any additional isoagglutinins.[98,99]

Other approaches to ABO-incompatible products include red cell depletion. The most prevalent method in use is red cell sedimentation. This procedure is relatively quick and inexpensive, and can be performed in a closed system. The most common sedimenting agent is 6% hydroxyethyl starch (HES), although dextran can be used. HES is combined with

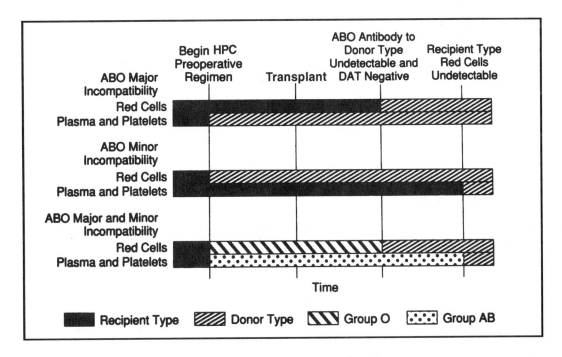

Figure 25-1. Recommended ABO group of blood components for use in patients receiving ABO-incompatible HPC transplant. DAT=direct antiglobulin test. HPC=hematopoietic progenitor cell. (Modified with permission from McCullough et al.[95])

marrow in a ratio of 1:8 or 1:7. Once combined, the marrow/HES mixture is allowed to sediment for 45-90 minutes. HES promotes rouleaux formation, causing the red cells to settle and leaving the nucleated cells in the plasma. After the red cells have sedimented they are drained off in a secondary bag. Sedimenting in this fashion allows for the retention of 76-90% of the initial nucleated cells and 60-99% of the CFU-GM. Residual red cell content should be less than 1% of the total postsedimentation volume.[100-102]

Other methods of red cell depletion are less commonly employed. Some institutions promote red cell depletion using density gradient separation, others use continuous flow apheresis machines such as the COBE Spectra™ and the Fenwal CS-3000 with mononuclear cell recoveries of 94% and 87% and red cell depletion of 99% and 98%, respectively.[63,66]

Minor ABO Incompatibility. Circulating isoagglutinins in the donor marrow are not al-ways predictive of posttransplant hemolysis. The level of hemolysis is theoretically dependent on the volume of marrow infused relative to the recipient's plasma volume and the IgM titer of the donor. Incompatible plasma can be easily removed by centrifugation. Plasma removal using this method removes approximately 75% of the plasma volume while recovering >70% of the initial nucleated cell count.[102]

Umbilical Cord Blood Processing

Although initial work with the processing of umbilical cord cells found unacceptably high progenitor cell losses with manipulation,[103] these obstacles have been overcome. Unlike cryopreservation laboratories that store relatively few autologous or allogeneic marrow or PBPC products (typically less than a few hundred products at any one time), a successful cord bank would be expected to store thousands of products for prolonged periods.

Therefore, attempts to reduce umbilical cord blood bulk (and therefore storage space, liquid nitrogen requirements, and cost) have been actively pursued. Currently, many centers are following the approach used by the New York Blood Center, which involves sedimentation and volume reduction prior to cryopreservation.[19,20,55]

Freezing and Storage

Conditions for the short-term or long-term storage of HPCs vary due to the length of time between collection and infusion and the type of processing the product will undergo.

Allogeneic Products

The collection of allogeneic marrow is generally timed to coincide with the completion of the recipient's preparative regimen. Because of the brief storage period required, the product is maintained in the liquid state. Unseparated marrow can be stored in the liquid state for up to 3 days at either 4 C or 22 C without any significant loss in viability of either uncommitted or committed progenitors.[104] The ability to store unmanipulated marrow under these conditions is vital in the context of the NMDP or other transplant registries where unrelated marrow samples are collected and then transported great distances for transplant.

PBPCs may also be stored in the liquid state under the same conditions as marrow. The nucleated cell concentration in the product should be monitored to ensure cell viability over a 24-hour period at 4 C.[105]

Autologous Products

Due to the length of time required for treatment and/or product collection in the case of PBPCs, autologous products are cryopreserved and stored until the time of infusion. Cryopreservation also allows marrow or PBPCs to be collected while the patient is in remission and stored should a relapse occur (speculative storage). At present, no expiration date has been defined for these products; however, marrow stored for 11 years has been used for transplant with sustained engraftment.[106]

Controlled-Rate Freezing

The purpose of cryopreservation is to freeze cells in such a way as to allow for their long-term storage with a minimal loss of cell viability or reconstitutive ability. The main obstacle to maintaining viability during cryopreservation and storage is the formation of intracellular ice crystals along with an increase in external osmolarity, both resulting in cell lysis. In addition to solution effects, thermal shock, the time required for phase change (liquid state to solid state), and the posttransition freezing rate all present problems for cryopreservation.[107]

The adverse effects caused by the formation of intracellular ice crystals or by cell dehydration can be minimized by a slow cooling rate and the addition of a cryoprotective agent such as DMSO. DMSO facilitates the flow of liquid across cell membranes, helping to adjust the external osmotic balance. Cryoprotectants such as DMSO have colligative properties that prevent the formation of ice crystals within the cells by binding with water molecules.[108] The most widely used cryoprotectant today consists of 20% DMSO and 20% plasma or albumin prepared in an electrolyte solution or tissue culture media. The plasma or albumin provides a protein source, which aids in preventing cell damage during freezing and thawing. The cryoprotectant is then combined with an equal volume of product immediately prior to freezing, resulting in a final cell suspension containing 10% DMSO and 10% plasma.

The effects of thermal shock, phase transition time, and posttransition freezing rate can all be minimized by a slow controlled rate of freezing.[107] This method of freezing requires the use of a computer-controlled programmable freezing chamber. The freezer is designed to cryopreserve cells at an optimal rate of

1-3 C/minute until a temperature of –90 to –100 C is reached.[109-111] With the combination of a cryoprotectant and a programmed rate of freezing, cryopreservation and long-term storage of HPCs are possible with minimal damage to the cells.

Non-Controlled-Rate Freezing

Mechanical, methanol bath immersion or "uncontrolled rate" freezing is advocated by some investigators as a viable and cost-effective alternative to controlled-rate freezing.[112-114] The principle is that products once mixed with a DMSO/HES combination or DMSO solution alone can be frozen and stored without the aid of a programmable freezer or liquid nitrogen. The products are stored in a –80 C mechanical freezer. HPCs stored in this fashion have successfully engrafted after as long as 2 years of storage.[114] In some cases, the combination of the metal canisters the bags are placed in, the bag itself, and the volume of product frozen produce a freezing rate of approximately 3 C/minute, which falls within the optimal range previously discussed.[115] The major deterrent to the widespread use of mechanical freezing centers around safety issues regarding mechanical failure of the freezer and the lack of long-term storage and engraftment data.

Liquid Nitrogen Storage

While products frozen in a mechanical freezer are frequently stored at –80 C, products cryopreserved using a programmable freezer generally are stored in a liquid nitrogen freezer. A continual debate regarding liquid nitrogen storage arises from the question of whether products should be stored in the liquid or vapor phase of liquid nitrogen. In liquid phase storage temperatures are easily maintained at –180 C and colder. Products are completely immersed in liquid nitrogen; therefore, temperature fluctuations within the freezer and within the products themselves are minimal. Should an electrical or liquid nitrogen

supply crisis occur, enough liquid nitrogen is present in the freezer to sustain adequate storage conditions for several days.

The storage temperature achieved with vapor phase, while not as cold as liquid phase, averages –140 C, a temperature that has been shown to allow for viable long-term marrow storage.[106] The major drawbacks to vapor phase storage include the large fluctuation in temperature when the freezer is entered as well as the variation in storage temperature throughout the freezer itself. The reaction time in cases of electrical or liquid nitrogen supply emergencies is significantly shorter than with liquid phase. The advantage of vapor phase storage is the possibly decreased risk of cross-contamination that has become an issue with liquid phase storage.[116] A 1995 report by Tedder and colleagues showed the ability of the hepatitis B virus to withstand cryopreservation and utimately contaminate other products stored within the same liquid nitrogen freezer.[116]

Storage of Untested or Infectious Products

Infectious disease testing of HPC donors should be completed within 30 days of collection.[28,29] Current regulations call for alternative storage for products that are untested or have a positive disease marker. Some institutions comply by storing all products in vapor phase, while other institutions use an overwrap, placing the component in an outer plastic bag that is sealed before storage.

Transportation and Shipping

In some cases, a hematopoietic component must be transported from one center to another. In all cases, precautions should be taken to protect the component from rough handling, extremes of temperature and pressure, x-ray examination, breakage, and spillage. In the case of cryopreserved components, the use of a liquid nitrogen "dry shipper" is desirable. Such "dry shippers" have liquid nitrogen absorbent material between the walls of the container that allow the inside of the container to maintain temperatures in the range of −180 C for up to 10-14 days.

Thawing and Infusion

For all components, final identification is done by the nurse or physician performing the infusion. Flow through the central venous catheter is confirmed and the cells are infused by gravity drip, calibrated pump, or manual push with or without an in-line filter (a standard 170-micron red cell infusion filter is acceptable). Prolonged exposure to DMSO ex vivo at 22-37 C may be harmful to HPCs. Although DMSO was thought to be toxic to HPCs, it is now known to be nontoxic after short-term exposure (up to 1 hour) at the concentration used for cryopreservation of HPCs.[117] To minimize the thawed cells' exposure to DMSO, many centers rapidly thaw one bag at a time near the bedside.[31] Some centers place product bags in secondary containment bags before thawing; others immerse the bag, all but the access ports, directly into sterile water or saline at 37-40 C.[107] The bag is kneaded gently until all solid clumps have thawed. The cells are then infused (usually 10-15 mL per minute). Products frozen in both DMSO and HES may also be washed and resuspended in the laboratory before infusion to prevent cell aggregation.[107]

Side effects associated with infusions include nausea, diarrhea, flushing, bradycardia, hypertension, and abdominal pain. In general, such side effects may justify slowing, but not halting, the infusion until the symptoms pass.[28,118] Sudden and severe hypotension can result in the absence of adequate antihistamine premedication.[59] The patient is hydrated and the urine "alkalinized." This facilitates the clearance of hemoglobin caused by red cell lysis, which occurs during freezing and reduces the risk of renal complications.[31,59] If the

total infusion volume exceeds 10 mL/kg of recipient body weight, many centers divide the volume over a morning and afternoon infusion or over two consecutive days.

Postthaw laboratory samples are best collected directly from the patient's infusion bags instead of freezing separate individual specimens as these samples are identical to the infused product.[118]

One possible set of guidelines for the infusion of cryopreserved cells is listed in Table 25-7.

Evaluation and Quality Control of Hematopoietic Products

Cell Counts

Each hematopoietic product is analyzed to determine the total cell concentration and the mononuclear cell concentration, which are used to calculate the number of cells per kilogram (of the recipient) or cell dose for each product. These doses, in combination with other assays, determine the number of collections necessary to achieve engraftment.[119] In addition, they are used to calculate the percent recovery providing a quality control measure for processing procedures and equipment.[120]

In general, automated cell counts provide the most rapid and accurate value. However, platelet/cellular aggregates in PBPCs or fat globules in marrow specimens can falsely decrease or increase cell counts.[119,121] In such cases, manual cell counts may be preferable. It is important that cell counts are not overestimated, as this may result in prolonged time to engraftment or graft failure.

Bacterial and Fungal Cultures

Sterility is essential when dealing with blood products for infusion to immunosuppressed patients. This is particularly important with marrow, which is frequently collected in an open system, and with products that require

Table 25-7. One Possible Set of Guidelines for Infusion of Cryopreserved Cells[59]

1. 12 hours before marrow infusion, start hydration with D5W1/4NS with 50 mEq/L NaHCO$_3$ and 20 mEq/L KCl with a goal of achieving a urine output of 2-3 mL/kg/hr and a urine pH of ≥7.
2. Immediately before marrow infusion, medicate with:

   a. Mannitol 0.2 g/kg (maximum 12.5 g)

   b. Diphenhydramine 1 mg/kg (maximum 50 mg)

   c. Hydrocortisone 4 mg/kg (maximum 250 mg)

   d. Antiemetics as needed

   Repeat medications if additional cells are to be infused after a break of more than 3 hours.
3. Infuse thawed marrow aliquots rapidly (50 mL over 5-10 minutes) to minimize clumping.
4. Do not infuse volumes of over 10 mL/kg recipient weight or containing more than 1 g/kg recipient weight of dimethylsulfoxide without medical approval.

multiple manipulations (Table 25-8).[122] Culture growth can result from contamination during the collection or product processing, or as a result of an infected catheter or the patient's sepsis. Skin commensals are the predominant isolates from these cultures. In all cases it is important to identify the source, the degree of contamination, and the causative organism—given the fact that this product is intended for transplantation in an immunocompromised recipient. Each product must be tested for aerobic, anaerobic, and fungal contamination at least once during the course of processing, usually just before freezing or infusion with allogeneic transplants.[29] A positive culture does not necessitate immediate discard of the product, as these are frequently irreplaceable cells.[119] Thus, positive

Table 25-8. Percent Contamination of Hematopoietic Cellular Products

	No. of Products Tested	% Contaminated	Reference
Marrow	291	0	122
	227	1.3	123
	317	6.0	124
	194	<0.1	125
Peripheral blood progenitor cells	1380	0.65	122
	560	0.7	123
	576	0.5	124
	1040	0.2	126
Cord blood			
vaginal delivery	Not available	8.0	17
surgical delivery	Not available	3.0	17

results need to be reviewed by the appropriate physician on a case-by-case basis and sensitivities ordered if the organism is a potential pathogen present in clinically significant numbers.

CD34 Analysis/Enumeration

CD34 is the cluster designation given to a transmembrane glycoprotein present on immature hematopoietic cells, some mature endothelial cells, and stromal cells. The antigen has an approximate molecular weight of 110 kD and carries a negative charge. Cells expressing the CD34 antigen encompass the lineage-committed cells as well as the most pluripotent cells, which will reconstitute trilineage hematopoiesis[128]; 1-3% of normal marrow cells express this antigen. In normal peripheral circulation, CD34 expression is rare (0.01-0.1%).[46]

CD34 enumeration is a technique in evolution. The rapid growth in the development of antibodies directed to the antigen is one contributing factor. In 1989, the IV International Leukocyte Differentiation Antigens Workshop identified seven CD34 antibodies. By the 1995 workshop, several new antibodies were classified.[46] In 1996, Höffkes et al[129] reported the development of a new monoclonal antibody specific for the CD34 antigen. CD34 antibodies are directed to different epitopes of the antigen. These epitopes are divided into three classes based on their sensitivities to neuraminidase and the O-sialoglycoprotease from *Pasturella haemolytica*.[46] Class I antibodies, antibodies directed at a Class I sialic-acid-dependent epitope, fail to detect some CD34 antigens. Class II and Class III antibodies are directed at different sialic-acid-independent epitopes. Class II and Class III antibodies also differ in their binding affinities to fluorochrome conjugates.[46]

As a cell differentiates and acquires other surface markers, CD34 expression diminishes. Stages of differentiation may be studied by the expression or coexpression of other antigens.

This principle (loss of CD34 expression) has been applied to evaluate the quality of HPC grafts. The current approach is to use a method based on multiparameter flow cytometry to determine the number of CD34+ cells and to calculate a subsequent CD34+ dose based on the recipient's weight (the number of CD34+ cells in a product per kilogram of recipient body weight). Various mobilization strategies may be employed to increase the number of CD34+ cells available for collection. Marrow, peripheral blood, and cord blood, including their manipulated forms, may be measured for CD34 content by flow cytometry.

Numerous flow cytometric analysis methods for CD34 enumeration exist.[46,130,131] Because these methods differ, correlation of CD34 dose values from site to site is often unreliable. Recent studies have documented the variability of CD34 analysis methods and results as well as examined possible causes of the variability.[45,46,132,133] Due to the "rare event" nature of CD34 enumeration, several procedural components play a critical role in the assay. Selection of the CD34 antibody clone, fluorescent conjugate, lysing solution, lyse-wash format, gating strategy, and the number of events analyzed are some of the factors that influence the end result.[134]

Growing awareness of and concern about the need for a standardized approach to CD34 analysis have prompted several collaborative groups such as the International Society of Hematotherapy and Graft Engineering (ISHAGE) to propose guidelines for CD34+ cell determination by flow cytometry.[46,135] Alternate approaches are available and will continue to be developed and investigated as more is discovered about the CD34 antigen and other markers for the pluripotent HPC.[136]

Colony-Forming Cell Assays

Culture systems are available that can demonstrate in-vitro proliferative capacity of a hematopoietic sample. It is thought that short-term (generally within 2 weeks) repopulating potential is produced from the committed HPCs. Long-term repopulating ability is thought to be a result of the pluripotential HPCs that are principally necessary for a complete and sustained engraftment.

Reconstitutive potential of committed HPCs can be quantitated in semisolid media such as methylcellulose. The semisolid medium can be prepared or purchased in different formulations of nutrients and growth factors.[137] Cultures are incubated in a 5% carbon dioxide humid environment at 37 C for 10-14 days.

Three types of colonies originate from HPCs in short-term culture. Erythropoietic precursors form burst-forming unit–erythroid (BFU-E) colonies, which are characterized by one or more tightly formed clusters of hemoglobinized (dusky red) erythroblasts.[137] The CFU-GM has been found by some investigators to be most predictive of engraftment. CFU-GM colonies form a "star burst" or "fried egg" appearance of white cells emanating from a central point and thinning out at the periphery of a circle. These colonies may be composed of only macrophages, only granulocytes, or a mixture of both. Colony-forming unit-granulocyte, erythrocyte, monocyte, megakaryocyte (CFU-GEMM or multipotential CFU) is a rare colony type thought to originate from a more immature HPC. Morphologically it resembles a mixture of a BFU-E and a CFU-GM.

Cultures may be useful to assess engraftment potential; however, because media, culture techniques, and colony identification are quite variable, interinstitutional comparisons are difficult. Reported CFU-GM doses below which engraftment may be delayed range from 1.5×10^5 to 5.0×10^5/kg.[120]

Long-term cultures require a liquid medium in which growth factors are provided by an adherent stromal layer of cells (feeder layer) instead of recombinant forms added directly to a semisolid medium. In normal marrow long-term culture-initiating cells (LTC-ICs) occur in one out of 2×10^4 cells, and at 5 weeks one LTC-IC can produce a total of 4 CFU-GM, BFU-E, or CFU-GEMM.[137] Long-term cultures are not routinely used clinically because of the 5- to 8-week incubation requirements. However, they may be useful in evaluating developmental procedures involving product manipulation.[119] In addition, these culture techniques are used in ex-vivo expansion systems using culture flasks or perfusion bioreactors.[138]

Tumor Cell Detection

Tumor cell detection techniques have been developed to screen products suspected of tumor cell contamination and to evaluate purged products. The majority of these assays use monoclonal antibodies that specifically bind tumor antigens. Detection and quantitation can then be done by flow cytometry, immunofluorescence, or immunohistochemical staining. Sensitivity varies with technique from 0.1% down to 0.0004% of cells examined. In some cases, neoplastic culture assays may be used; however, they are not as sensitive as immunologic methods.[139] Preliminary studies indicate that the presence of tumor cells may be associated with a reduced disease-free survival.[140,141]

Residual T-Cell Detection

The method of T-cell detection and quantitation depends on the procedure used to reduce the number of T cells. Physical separation techniques such as elutriation or antibody-mediated CD34 selection methods maintain the antigenic structure of the cells. Thus, immunofluorescent studies or flow cytometry can be used to evaluate products.[139] Other methods use inactivation or complement-mediated lysis to reduce T-cells, which require limiting dilution assays to enumerate residual viable cells.

Regulations

In 1997, the FDA published a proposed approach to the regulation of cellular and tissue-based products.[142] HPCs from placental/umbilical cord blood and peripheral blood are covered by this proposal. As part of this initiative, the FDA has indicated that it may consider using voluntary standards in lieu of promulgating more comprehensive regulations. Although the proposed approach has not been fully implemented, many of the policies, regulations, and guidance documents needed to implement this approach have been published.[143-146] The FDA has established a Tissue Action Plan and readers should refer to this subject on the CBER web site for the most complete up-to-date information.

Standards

In 1996 the AABB and the Foundation for the Accreditation of Hematopoietic Cell Therapy (FAHCT) published separate, but substantially similar, standards for HPCs.[28,29] In 1999, the AABB revised its *Standards for Hematopoietic Progenitor Cells*, first edition, to incorporate quality system concepts.[147] Further revisions found in the second edition[148] are intended to expand the quality systems approach and to meet the FDA's needs with regard to adopting voluntary standards. The AABB *Standards for Hematopoietic Progenitor Cells* addresses services in the collection, processing, storage, and distribution of HPCs. Other agencies such as the National Marrow Donor Program also publish voluntary standards. FAHCT standards address services provided by HPC clinical transplant programs as well as services in the collection, processing, storage, and distribution of HPCs.

References

1. Brecher G, Cronkite EP. Post-irradiation parabiosis and survival in rats. Proc Soc Exp Biol Med 1951;77:292-4.
2. Warkentin PI. Clinical background for marrow and progenitor cell processing. In: Lasky LC, Warkentin PI, eds. Marrow and progenitor cell processing for transplantation. Bethesda, MD: American Association of Blood Banks, 1995:1-20.
3. Armitage JO. Bone marrow transplantation. N Engl J Med 1994;330:827-38.
4. Chan KW, Wadsworth LD. Pediatric bone marrow transplantation and processing. In: Areman EM, Deeg HJ, Sacher RA, eds. Bone marrow and stem cell processing: A manual of current techniques. Philadelphia: FA Davis, 1992:363-85.
5. Deeg HJ. Bone marrow and stem cell transplantation: Sorting the chaff from the grain. In: Areman EM, Deeg HJ, Sacher RA, eds. Bone marrow and stem cell processing: A manual of current techniques. Philadelphia: FA Davis, 1992:17-29.
6. Lane TA. Mobilization of hematopoietic progenitor cells. In: Brecher ME, Lasky LC, Sacher RA, Issitt LA, eds. Hematopoietic progenitor cells: Processing, standards and practice. Bethesda, MD: American Association of Blood Banks, 1995:59-108.
7. Champlin R. Bone marrow transplantation from HLA-matched unrelated donors as treatment for leukemia. J Hematother 1993;2:323-27.
8. Champlin R, Kyoung L. T-cell depletion to prevent graft-versus-host disease following allogeneic bone marrow transplantation. In: Areman EM, Deeg HJ, Sacher RA, eds. Bone marrow and stem cell processing: A manual of current techniques. Philadelphia: FA Davis, 1992:163-217.
9. Kanfer E. Graft-versus-host disease. In: Treleaven J, Wiernik P, eds. Color atlas and text of bone marrow transplantation. London: Mosby-Wolfe, 1995:185-8.
10. Przepiorka D, Weisdorf D, Martin P, et al. Meeting report: Consensus conference on acute GVHD grading. Bone Marrow Transplant 1995;15:825-8.
11. Beatty PG, Kollman C, Howe CW. Unrelated-donor marrow transplants: The experience of the National Marrow Donor Program. Clin Transpl 1995:271-7.
12. Hansen JA, Gooley TA, Martin PJ, et al. Bone marrow transplants from unrelated donors for patients with chronic myeloid leukemia. N Engl J Med 1998;338:962-8.
13. Wagner JE, Kernan NA, Steinbuch M, et al. Allogeneic sibling umbilical-cord-blood transplantation in children with malignant and non-malignant disease. Lancet 1995;346:214-9.
14. Kurtzberg J, Laughlin M, Graham ML, et al. Placental blood as a source of hematopoietic stem cells for transplantation into unrelated recipients. N Engl J Med 1996;335:157-66.
15. Gluckman E, Rocha V, Boyer-Chammard A, et al. Outcome of cord-blood transplantation from related and unrelated donors. N Engl J Med 1997;337:373-81.
16. Rubenstein R, Carrier C, Scaradavou A, et al. Otcomes among 562 recipients of placental-blood transplants from unrelated donors. N Engl J Med 1998;339:1565-77.
17. Lu L, Xiao M, Shen RN, et al. Enrichment, characterization, and responsiveness of single primitive CD34+ human umbilical cord blood hematopoietic progenitors with high proliferative and replating potential. Blood 1993;81:1679-90.
18. Laporte JP, Gorin NC, Rubinstein P, et al. Cord-blood transplantation from an unrelated do-

nor in an adult with chronic myelogenous leukemia. N Engl J Med 1996;335:167-70.

19. Rubinstein P, Taylor PE, Scaradavou A, et al. Unrelated placental blood for bone marrow reconstitution: Organization of the placental blood program. Blood Cells 1994;20:587-600.

20. Rubinstein P, Dobrila L, Rosenfield RE, et al. Processing and cryopreservation of placental/umbilical cord blood for unrelated bone marrow reconstitution. Proc Natl Acad Sci U S A 1995;92:10119-22.

21. Mehta SN. Umbilical-blood storage: Uncertain benefits, high price. The Wall Street Journal 1995 Nov 14;Sect B:1-2.

22. Rubin R. A hard sell to bank your baby's blood. U.S. News & World Report 1996 July 29:60-1.

23. Fishman RHB. Frozen cord blood used for human gene therapy. Lancet 1997;349:705.

24. Flowers MED, Pepe MS, Longton G, et al. Previous donor pregnancy as a risk factor for acute graft-versus-host disease in patients with aplastic anemia treated by allogeneic marrow transplantation. Br J Haematol 1990;74:492-6.

25. Bross DS, Tutschka PJ, Farmer ER, et al. Predictive factors for acute graft-versus-host disease in patients transplanted with HLA identical bone marrow. Blood 1984;63:1265-70.

26. Gale RP, Bortin MM, Van Bekkum DW, et al. Risk factors for acute graft-versus-host disease. Br J Haematol 1987;67:397-406.

27. Bensinger WI, Deeg JH. Transfusion support and donor considerations in marrow transplantation. In: Sacher RA, AuBuchon JP, eds. Marrow transplantation: Practical and technical aspects of stem cell reconstitution. Bethesda, MD: American Association of Blood Banks, 1992:157-84.

28. Warkentin PI, ed. Standards for hematopoietic progenitor cell collection, processing and transplantation. 1st ed. Omaha, NE: Foundation for the Accreditation of Hematopoietic Cell Therapy, 1996.

29. Menitove JE, ed. Standards for hematopoietic progenitor cells. 1st ed. Bethesda, MD: American Association of Blood Banks, 1996.

30. Height S, Shields M. Problems following bone marrow transplantation-pulmonary complications. In: Treleaven J, Wiernik P, eds. Color atlas and text of bone marrow transplantation. London: Mosby-Wolfe, 1995:169-80.

31. Patterson K. Bone marrow harvesting. In: Treleaven J, Wiernik P, eds. Color atlas and text of bone marrow transplantation. London: Mosby-Wolfe, 1995:101-7.

32. Areman EM, Dickerson SA, Kotula PL, et al. Use of a licensed electrolyte solution as an alternative to tissue culture medium for bone marrow collection. Transfusion 1993;33:562-6.

33. Killian D, Wright P, Bentley SA, et al. A cost-effective and Food and Drug Administration-approved alternative to tissue culture media in cryopreservation (letter). Transfusion 1996;36:476.

34. Treleaven JG. Bone marrow harvesting and reinfusion. In: Gee AP, ed. Bone marrow processing and purging. Boca Raton, FL: CRC Press, 1991:32-4.

35. Juttner CA, To LB. Collection and processing of peripheral blood stem cells. In: Aremen EM, Deeg HJ, Sacher RA, eds. Bone marrow and stem cell processing: A manual of current techniques. Philadelphia: FA Davis, 1992:68-90.

36. Leitman SF, Read SJ. Hematopoietic progenitor cells. Semin Hematol 1996;33:341-58.

37. Peters WP, Drago SS, Tepperberg M, et al. Collection, cryopreservation and use of peripheral blood progenitor cells primed with colony-stimulating factor. In: Sacher RA, AuBuchon JP, eds. Marrow transplantation: Practical and technical aspects of stem cell reconstitution. Bethesda, MD: American Association of Blood Banks, 1992:51-60.

38. Beyer J, Schwella N, Zingsem J, et al. Hematopoietic rescue after high-dose chemotherapy using autologous peripheral-blood progenitor cells or bone marrow: A randomized comparison. J Clin Oncol 1995;13:1328-35.

39. Bandarenko N, Owen HG, Mair DC, et al. Apheresis new opportunities. In: Polesky HF, Perry EH, Ilstrup SJ, eds. Clinics in laboratory medicine. Philadelphia: WB Saunders, 1996:907-14.

40. Civin CL, Strauss LC, Brovall C, et al. Antigenic analysis of hematopoiesis. III. A hematopoietic progenitor cell surface antigen defined by a monoclonal antibody raised against KG-1a cells. J Immunol 1984;133:157-65.

41. Bensinger WI, Longin K, Appelbaum F, et al. Peripheral blood stem cells (PBPCs) collected after recombinant granulocyte colony stimulating factor (rhG-CSF): An analysis of factors correlating with the tempo of engraftment after transplantation. Br J Haematol 1994;87:825-31.

42. Bender JG, Lum L, Unverzagt KL, et al. Correlation of colony-forming cells, long-term culture initiating cells and CD34+ cells in apheresis products from patients mobilized from peripheral blood progenitors with different regimens. Bone Marrow Transplant 1994;13:479-85.

43. Chabannon C, Le Coroller AG, Faucher C, et al. Patient condition affects the collection of peripheral blood progenitors after priming with recombinant granulocyte colony-stimulating factor. J Hematother 1995;4:171-9.

44. Sovalat H, Wunder E, Zimmerman R, et al. Multicentric determination of CD34+ cells. In: Wunder E, Sovalat H, Henon P, Serke S, eds. Hematopoietic stem cells: The mulhouse manual. Dayton, OH: AlphaMed Press, 1995:61-6.

45. Brecher ME, Sims L, Schmitz J, et al. North American multicenter study on flow cytometric enumeration of CD34+ hematopoietic stem cells. J Hematother 1996;5:227-36.

46. Sutherland DR, Anderson L, Keeney M, et al. The ISHAGE guidelines for CD34+ cell determination by flow cytometry. J Hematother 1996;5:213-26.

47. Malachawski ME, Comenzo RL, Hillyer CD, et al. Large-volume leukapheresis for peripheral blood stem cell collection in patients with hematologic malignancies. Transfusion 1992;32:732-5.

48. Passos-Coelho JL, Braine HG, Davis JM, et al. Predictive factors for peripheral-blood progenitor-cell collections using a single large-volume leukapheresis after cyclophosphamide and

granulocyte-macrophage colony-stimulating factor mobilization. J Clin Oncol 1995;13:705-14.

49. Hillyer CD, Lackey DA, Hart KK, et al. CD34+ progenitors and colony-forming units-granulocyte macrophage are recruited during large-volume leukapheresis and concentrated by counterflow centrifugal elutriation. Transfusion 1993;33:316-21.

50. Hillyer CD. Large volume leukapheresis to maximize peripheral blood stem cell collection. J Hematother 1993;2:529-32.

51. Glaspy JA, Shpall EJ, LeMaistre et al. Peripheral blood progenitor cell mobilization using stem cell factor in combination with Filgrastim in breast cancer patients. Blood 1997;90:2939-51.

52. Stroncek DF, Clay ME, Smith J, et al. Changes in blood counts after the administration of granulocyte-colony-stimulating factor and the collection of peripheral blood stem cells from healthy donors. Transfusion 1996;36:596-600.

53. Bandarenko N, Brecher ME, Owen H, et al. Thrombocytopenia in allogeneic peripheral blood stem cell collections (letter). Transfusion 1996;36:668.

54. Stroncek DF, Clay ME, Petzoldt ML, et al. Treatment of normal individuals with granulocyte-colony-stimulating factor: Donor experiences and the effects on peripheral blood CD34+ cell counts and on the collection of peripheral blood stem cells. Transfusion 1996;36:601-10.

55. Rubinstein P, Carrier C, Taylor P, Stevens CE. Placental and umbilical cord blood banking for unrelated marrow reconstitution. In: Brecher ME, Lasky LC, Sacher RA, Issitt LA, eds. Hematopoietic progenitor cells: Processing, standards and practice. Bethesda, MD: American Association of Blood Banks, 1995:1-17.

56. Spitzer TR. Bone marrow component processing. In: Areman EM, Deeg JH, Sacher RA, eds. Bone marrow and stem cell processing: A manual of current techniques. Philadelphia: FA Davis, 1992:95-9.

57. Areman EM. Mononuclear cell concentration and processing techniques. In: Sacher RA, AuBuchon JP, eds. Marrow transplantation practical and technical aspects of stem cell reconstitution. Bethesda, MD: American Association of Blood Banks, 1992:31-50.

58. Smith DM, Weisenburger DD, Bireman P, et al. Acute renal failure associated with autologous bone marrow transplantation. Bone Marrow Transplant 1987;2:196-201.

59. Rowley SD. Storage of hematopoietic cells. In: Sacher RA, AuBuchon JP, eds. Marrow transplantation practical and technical aspects of stem cell reconstitution. Bethesda, MD: American Association of Blood Banks, 1992:105-27.

60. Dickson LG, Hill MG. Buffy coat concentration/buffy coat preparation. In: Areman EM, Deeg JH, Sacher RA, eds. Bone marrow and stem cell processing: A manual of current techniques. Philadelphia: FA Davis, 1992:101-3.

61. Rowley SD, Davis JM, Piantadosi S, et al. Density-gradient separation of autologous bone marrow grafts before ex vivo purging with 4-hydroxycylophosphamide. Bone Marrow Transplant 1990;6:321-7.

62. Graves VL, McCarthy LJ, Jansen J, et al. Automated ficoll-hypaque marrow processing using the COBE 2991. In: Areman EM, Deeg JH, Sacher RA, eds. Bone marrow and stem cell processing: A manual of current techniques. Philadelphia: FA Davis, 1992:138-41.

63. Davis JM, Schepers KG, Eby LL, et al. Comparison of progenitor cell concentration techniques: Continuous flow separation versus density-gradient isolation. J Hematother 1993;2:314-20.

64. Gilmore MJ, Prentice HG, Corringham RE, et al. A technique for the concentration of nucleated bone marrow cells for in vitro manipulation or cryopreservation using IBM 2991 cell processor. Vox Sang 1983;45:294-302.

65. Rosenfeld CS, Tedrow H, Bogel F, et al. A double buffy coat method for red cell removal from ABO-incompatible marrow. Transfusion 1989;29:415-8.

66. Rodriguez JM, Carmona M, Noguerol P, et al. A fully automated method for mononuclear bone marrow cell collection. J Clin Apheresis 1992;7:101-9.

67. Silvestri F. CD34+ cell purification by immunomagnetic beads/chymopapain system from normal and myeloid leukemias bone marrow and peripheral blood for research use. In: Wunder E, Sovalat H, Henon P, Serke S, eds. Hematopoietic stem cells: The mulhouse manual. Dayton, OH: AlphaMed Press, 1995:161-9.

68. Larsen JK. Principles, capacity and limitations of immunofluorescent flow sorting of rare cell species. In: Wunder E, Sovalat H, Henon P, Serke S, eds. Hematopoietic stem cells: The mulhouse manual. Dayton, OH: AlphaMed Press, 1995:133-40.

69. Wunder E, deWynter E. Purification of CD34+ cells. In: Wunder E, Sovalat H, Henon P, Serke S, eds. Hematopoietic stem cells: The mulhouse manual. Dayton, OH: AlphaMed Press, 1995:125-82.

70. Zimmerman TM, Bender JG, Lee WJ, et al. Large-scale selection of CD34+ peripheral blood progenitors and expansion of neutrophil precursors for clinical applications. J Hematother 1996;5:247-53.

71. Marolleau JP, Brice P, Cortivo LD, et al. CD34+ Selection by immunomagnetic selection (Isolex® 300) for patients with malignancies (abstract). Blood 1996;88(Suppl 1):110a.

72. Devernardi N, Camilla C, Traore Y, et al. Antibody-coated magnetic particles for CD34+ cell separation. In: Wunder E, Sovalat H, Henon P, Serke S, eds. Hematopoietic stem cells: The mulhouse manual. Dayton, OH: AlphaMed Press, 1995:183-200.

73. Miltenyi S, Guth S, Radbruch A, et al. Isolation of CD34+ hematopoietic progenitor cells by high-gradient magnetic cell sorting (MACS). In: Wunder E, Sovalat H, Henon P, Serke S, eds. Hematopoietic stem cells: The mulhouse manual. Dayton, OH: AlphaMed Press, 1995:201-13.

74. McNiece I, Briddell R, Stoney G, et al. Large-scale isolation of CD34+ cells using the Amgen cell selection device results in high levels of purity and recovery. J Hematother 1997;6:5-11.

75. Heimfield S, Berenson RJ. Clinical transplantation of CD34+ hematopoietic progenitor cells: Positive selection using a closed, automated avidin-biotin immunoadsorption system. In: Wunder E, Sovalat H, Henon P, Serke S, eds. Hematopoietic stem cells: The mulhouse manual. Dayton, OH: AlphaMed Press, 1995:231-9.

76. Berenson RJ, Bensinger WI, Hill RS, et al. Engraftment after infusion of CD34+ marrow cells in patients with breast cancer or neuroblastoma. Blood 1991;77:1717-22.

77. Lanza F, Castoldi G. Large scale enrichment of CD34+ cells by percoll density gradients: A CML-based study design. In: Wunder E, Sovalat H, Henon P, Serke S, eds. Hematopoietic stem cells: The mulhouse manual. Dayton, OH: AlphaMed Press, 1995:255-70.

78. Laport GF, Zimmerman TM, Grinblatt DL, et al. A phase I/II trial of the ACT CD34+ enrichment kit to enrich mobilized peripheral blood stem cells (PBPC) for breast cancer patients receiving myeloablative chemotherapy (MC) (abstract). Blood 1996;88(Suppl 1):110a.

79. Gao IK, Noga SJ, Wagner JE, et al. Implementation of a semiclosed large scale counterflow centrifugal elutriation system. J Clin Apheresis 1987;3:154-60.

80. Wunder E, Herbein G, Sovalat H, et al. Separation of hematopoietic cells of different maturity in mononuclear cell subsets generated by elutriation. In: Wunder E, Sovalat H, Henon P, Serke S, eds. Hematopoietic stem cells: The mulhouse manual. Dayton, OH: AlphaMed Press, 1995:271-9.

81. Brenner MK, Rill DR, Moen RC, et al. Gene-marking to trace origin of relapse after autologous bone-marrow transplantation. Lancet 1993;341:85-6.

82. Ross AA, Cooper BW, Lazarus HM, et al. Detection and viability of tumor cells in peripheral blood stem cell collections from breast cancer patients using immunocytochemical and clonogenic assay techniques. Blood 1993;82:2605-10.

83. Brugger W, Bross KJ, Glatt M, et al. Mobilization of tumor cells and hematopoietic progenitor cells into peripheral blood of patients with solid tumors. Blood 1994;83:636-40.

84. Rowley SD, Davis JM. Purging techniques in autologous transplantation. In: Armen EM, Deeg HJ, Sacher RA, eds. Bone marrow and stem cell processing: A manual of current techniques. Philadelphia: FA Davis, 1992:218-35.

85. Rowley SD, Davis JM. The use of 4-HC in autologous purging. In: Gee AP, ed. Bone marrow processing and purging. Boca Raton, FL: CRC Press, 1991:248-62.

86. Sieber F. Extracorporeal purging of bone marrow grafts by dye-sensitized photoirradiation. In: Gee AP, ed. Bone marrow processing and purging. Boca Raton, FL: CRC Press, 1991:263-80.

87. Yamazaki T, Sieber F. Effect of hypothermia on the merocyanine 540-mediated purging of hematopoietic cells. J Hematother 1997;6:31-9.

88. Ball ED. Monoclonal antibodies and complement for autologous marrow purging. In: Gee AP, ed.

Bone marrow processing and purging. Boca Raton, FL: CRC Press, 1991:281-8.

89. Kvalheim G, Wang MY, Pharo A, et al. Purging of tumor cells from leukapheresis products: Experimental and clinical aspects. J Hematother 1996;5:427-36.

90. Nimgaonkar M, Kemp A, Lancia J, et al. A combination of CD34 selection and complement mediated immunopurging (anti-CD15 monoclonal antibody) eliminates tumor cells while sparing normal progenitor cells. J Hematother 1996;5:39-48.

91. Fujimori Y, Kanamaru A, Hashimoto N, et al. Second transplantation with CD34+ bone marrow cells selected from a two-loci HLA-mismatched sibling for a patient with chronic myeloid leukemia. Br J Haematol 1996:94:123-5.

92. Dreger P, Viehmann K, Steinmann J, et al. G-CSF mobilized peripheral blood progenitor cells for allogeneic transplantation: Comparison of T cell depletion strategies using different CD34+ selection systems or CAMPATH-1. Exp Hematol 1995;23:147-54.

93. Krenger W, Ferrara J. Dysregulation of cytokines during graft-versus-host disease. J Hematother 1996;5:3-14.

94. Long GD, Blume KG. Allogeneic and autologous bone marrow transplantation. In: Beutler E, Lichtman MA, Coller BS, Kipps TL, eds. Williams' hematology. 5th ed. New York: McGraw-Hill, 1995:172-94.

95. McCullough J. Collection and use of stem cells; role of transfusion centers in bone marrow transplantation. Vox Sang 1994;67(S3):35-42.

96. Mathey B, Storb R. Allogeneic bone marrow transplantation: Current problems and possible solutions. In: Rossi EC, Simon TL, Moss GS, Gould SA, eds. Principles of transfusion medicine. 2nd ed. Baltimore, MD: Williams and Wilkins, 1995:493-508.

97. Good R. Mixed chimerism and immunological tolerance. N Engl J Med 1993;328:801-2.

98. Buckner CD, Clift RA, Sanders JE, et al. ABO incompatible marrow transplants. Transplantation 1978;26:233-8.

99. Hershko C, Gale RP, Ho W, Fitchen J. ABH antigens and bone marrow transplantation. Br J Haematol 1980;44:65-73.

100. Dinsmore RE, Reich LM, Kapoor N, et al. ABH incompatible bone marrow transplantation: Removal of erythrocytes by starch sedimentation. Br J Haematol 1983;54:441.

101. Warkentin PI, Hilden JM, Kersey JH, et al. Transplantation of major ABO-incompatible bone marrow depleted of red cells by hydroxyethyl starch. Vox Sang 1985;48:89-104.

102. Lasky LC, Warkentin PI, Kersey JH, et al. Hemotherapy in patients undergoing blood group incompatible bone marrow transplantation. Transfusion 1983;23:277-85.

103. Broxmeyer HE, Douglas GW, Hangoc G, et al. Human umbilical cord blood as a potential source of transplantable hematopoietic stem/progenitor cells. Proc Natl Acad Sci U S A 1989;86:3828-32.

104. Lasky LC, McCullough J, Zajani ED. Liquid storage of hematopoietic progenitors by clonal assay. Transfusion 1986;26:331-4.

105. Lane TA, Peterson S, Young D, et al. Effect of storage on engraftment of mobilized peripheral blood progenitor cells (abstract). Blood 1996;88(Suppl): 68a.

106. Aird W, Laborpin M, Gorin NC, Anten JH. Long term cryopreservation of human stem cells. Bone Marrow Transplant 1992;9:487-90.

107. Gorin NC. Cryopreservation and storage of stem cells. In: Areman EM, Deeg JH, Sacher RA, eds. Bone marrow and stem cell processing: A manual of current techniques. Philadelphia: FA Davis, 1992:138-41.

108. Meryman HT. Cryoprotective agents. Cryobiology 1971;8:173-83.

109. Leibo SP, Farrant J, Mazur P, et al. Effects of freezing on marrow stem cell suspensions: Interactions of cooling and warming rates in the presence of PVP, sucrose or glycerol. Cryobiology 1970;6:315-32.

110. Mazur P. Theoretical and experimental effects of cooling and warming velocity in the survival of frozen and thawed cells. Cryobiology 1966;2:181-92.

111. Lewis JP, Passovoy M, Trobaugh FE. The effect of cooling regimens on the transplantation potential of marrow. Transfusion 1967;7:17-32.

112. Hernandez-Navarro F, Ojeda E, Arrieta R, et al. Hematopoietic cell transplantation using plasma and DMSO without HES, with non-programmed freezing by immersion in a methanol bath: Results in 213 cases. Bone Marrow Transplant 1998;21:511-7.

113. Galmes A, Besalduch J, Bargay J, et al. Cryopreservation of hematopoietic progenitor cells with 5-percent dimethyl sulfoxide at –80 degrees C without rate-controlled freezing. Transfusion 1996;36:794-7.

114. Stiff PJ, Murgo AJ, Zaroules CG, et al. A simplified bone marrow cryopreservation method. Blood 1988;71:1102-3.

115. Stiff PJ, Murgo AJ, Zaroules CG, et al. Unfractionated marrow cell cryopreservation using dimethylsulfoxide and hydroxyethyl starch. Cryobiology 1983;21:17-21.

116. Tedder RS, Zuckerman MA, Goldstone AH, et al. Hepatitis B transmission from contaminated cryopreservation tank. Lancet 1995;346:137-40.

117. Rowley SD, Anderson GL. Effect of DMSO exposure without cryopreservation on hematopoietic progenitor cells. Bone Marrow Transplant 1993;11:389-93.

118. Gee AP. Quality control in bone marrow processing. In: Gee AP, ed. Bone marrow processing and purging: A practical guide. Boca Raton, FL: CRC Press, 1991:19-27.

119. Davis JM, Schepers KG. Quality control of hematopoietic progenitor cell products. In: Brecher ME, Lasky LC, Sacher RA, Issitt LA, eds. Hematopoietic progenitor cells: Processing, standards and practice. Bethesda, MD: American Association of Blood Banks, 1995:159-81.

120. Lasky LC, Johnson NL. Quality assurance in marrow processing. In: Areman EM, Deeg HJ, Sacher RA, eds. Bone marrow and stem cell processing: A manual of current techniques. Philadelphia: FA Davis, 1992:386-443.

121. Bentley SA, Taylor MA, Killian DE, et al. Correction of bone marrow nucleated cell counts for the presence of fat particles. Am J Clin Pathol 1995;140:60-4.

122. Sacher RA, Areman EM. Bone marrow processing for transplantation. In: Areman EM, Deeg HJ, Sacher RA. Bone marrow and stem cell processing: A manual of current techniques. Philadelphia: FA Davis, 1992:1-16.

123. Webb IJ, Coral FS, Andersen JW, et al. Sources and sequelae of bacterial contamination of hematopoietic stem cell components: Implications for the safety of hematotherapy and graft engineering. Transfusion 1996;36:782-8.

124. Cohen A, Tepperberg M, Waters-Pick B, et al. The significance of microbial cultures of the hematopoietic support for patients receiving high-dose chemotherapy. J Hematother 1996;5:289-94.

125. Padley D, Koontz F, Trigg ME, et al. Bacterial contamination rates following processing of bone marrow and peripheral blood progenitor cell preparations. Transfusion 1996;36:53-6.

126. Lazarus HM, Magalhaes-Silverman M, Fox RM, et al. Contamination during in vitro processing of bone marrow for transplantation: Clinical significance. Bone Marrow Transplant 1991;7:241-6.

127. Espinosa MT, Fox R, Creger RJ, Lazarus HM. Microbiologic contamination of peripheral blood progenitor cells collected for hematopoietic cell transplantation. Transfusion 1996;36:789-93.

128. Wunder I, Sovalat H, Fritsch G, et al. Report on the European workshop on peripheral blood stem cell determination and standardization, Mulhouse, France. J Hematother 1992;1:131-42.

129. Höffkes HG, Lowe JA, Pedersen RO, et al. BIRMA-K3, a new monoclonal antibody for CD34 immunophenotyping and stem and progenitor cell assay. J Hematother 1996;5:261-70.

130. Siena S, Bregni M, Brando B, et al. Flow cytometry for clinical estimation of circulating hematopoietic progenitors for autologous transplantation in cancer patients. Blood 1991;2:400-9.

131. Roscoe RA, Rybka WB, Winkelstein A, et al. Enumeration of CD34+ hematopoietic stem cells for reconstitution following myeloablative therapy. Cytometry 1994;16:74-9.

132. Johnsen HE. Report from a Nordic Workshop on CD34+ cell analysis: Technical recommendations for progenitor cell enumeration in leukapheresis from multiple myeloma patients. J Hematother 1995;4:21-8.

133. Chang A, Ma DDF. The influence of flow cytometric gating strategy on the standardization of CD34+ cell quantitation: An Australian multicenter study. J Hematother 1996;5:605-16.

134. Säberlich S, Kirsch A, Serke S. Determination of CD34+ hematopoietic cells by multiparameter flow cytometry: Technical remarks. In: Wunder E, Sovalat H, Hénon P, Serke S eds. Hematopoietic stem cells: The mulhouse manual. Dayton, OH: AlphaMed Press, 1994:45-60.

135. Johnsen HE. Toward a worldwide standard for CD34+ enumeration? (letter) J Hematother 1997; 6:83-4.

136. Sims LC, Brecher ME, Gertis K, et al. Enumeration of CD34 positive stem cells: Evaluation and comparison of three methods. J Hematother 1997;6:213-26.

137. Sutherland HJ, Eaves AC, Eaves CJ. Quantitative assays for human hemopoietic progenitor cells. In: Gee AP, ed. Bone marrow processing and purging: A practical guide. Boca Raton, FL: CRC Press, 1991:155-71.

138. Donahue RE, Carter CS. Ex-vivo expansion of hematopoietic progenitor and stem cells. In: Brecher ME, Lasky LC, Sacher RA, Issitt LA, eds. Hematopoietic progenitor cells: Processing, standards and practice. Bethesda, MD: American Association of Blood Banks, 1995:41-57.

139. Moss TJ. Detection of metastatic tumor cells in bone marrow. In: Gee AP, ed. Bone marrow processing and purging: A practical guide. Boca Raton, FL: CRC Press, 1991:121-35.

140. Pecora AL, Lazarus EM, Cooper B et al. Breast cancer contamination in peripheral blood cell (PBPC) collections association with bone marrow disease and type of mobilization (abstract). Blood 1997;89(Suppl):99a.

141. deMagalhaes-Silverman M, Hammert L, Lembersky B, et al. High dose chemotherapy and autologous stem cell support followed by posttransplant doxorubicin and taxol as initial therapy for metastatic breast cancer: Hematopoietic tolerance and efficacy (abstract). Blood 1997;89(Suppl):383a.

142. Food and Drug Administration. A proposed approach to the regulation of cellular and tissue-based products. Fed Regist 1997;62:9721-2.

143. Food and Drug Administration. Human tissue intended for transplantation; Final rule, 21 CFR 16 and 1270. Fed Regist 1997;62:40429-47.

144. Food and Drug Administration. Guidance for Industry: Guidance for screening and testing of donors of human tissue intended for transplantation. July 1997. Rockville, MD: CBER Office of Communications, Training, and Manufacturers Assistance, 1997.

145. Food and Drug Administration. Establishment registration and listing for manufacturers of human cellular and tissue-based products; Proposed rule, 21 CFR 207, 807, 1271. Fed Regist 1998;63: 26744-55.

146. Food and Drug Administration. Request for proposed standards for unrelated allogeneic peripheral and placental/umbilical cord blood hematopoietic stem/progenitor cell products; Request for comments. Fed Regist 1998;63:2985-88.

147. Interim standards for Standards for Hematopoietic Progenitor Cells. Association Bulletin 99-4. Bethesda, MD: American Association of Blood Banks, 1999.

148. Menitove JE, ed. Standards for hematopoietic progenitor cell services, second edition. Bethesda, MD; American Association of Blood Banks, 1999 (in press).

26

Tissue Banking and Solid Organ Transplantation

TRANSPLANTATION OF ORGANS, tissues, and cells is a rapidly developing field that holds great promise for ameliorating or curing many diseases, maladies, disorders, or conditions. This chapter address some of the aspects of tissue and organ transplantation that are important to transfusion medicine professionals. Briefly discussed are prevention of transmissible diseases, bone banking, skin banking, other allografts, and the key role of transfusion in supporting solid organ transplantation.

In recent years, the number of cornea, bone, skin, heart valve, and other cadaveric tissue donations[1,2] has exceeded donation of solid organs[3] (Tables 26-1 and 26-2). The hospital blood bank, transfusion service, community blood center, and regional blood center are uniquely qualified to provide essential support for organ and tissue transplantation and

Table 26-1. Organ and Tissue Donation in the United States

Type of Cadaver Donor	Annual Donations
Cornea	46,045
Bone	5,202
Tendon	2,985
Skin	1,814
Hearts (for heart valves)	1,598
Dura mater	113
Organ	4,994

Table 26-2. Allografts Transplanted Annually in the United States

Tissue	Transplants (Estimated)
Cadaver tissue	
bone	302,548
tendon	5,724
fascia	3,191
cardiovascular tissue allografts	2,341*
skin (sq ft)	3,330
dura	435
cornea	46,300
Cadaver organ	
kidney[†]	7,833
heart	2,138
liver	3,677
pancreas[†]	909
lung	727
heart-lung	38
Living donor organ	
kidney[†]	2,966
liver[‡]	38
heart[‡]	2
lung[‡]	7
pancreas[†‡]	9

*Includes 749 aortic valves, 431 pulmonic valves, and 635 saphenous veins.
[†]Includes 850 combined kidney and pancreas transplants. Simultaneous kidney-pancreas transplants are counted twice, both in kidney transplants and in pancreas transplants.
[‡]Includes living heart donors who donate their healthy heart when they become heart-lung recipients (a "domino" transplant), liver segmental donations, lung lobar donations, and partial pancreatic donations.

Table 26-3. Skills and Experience Appropriate for Institutions Undertaking Tissue Banking

Community support

Public accountability

Public education with a broad-based public information system

Donor recruitment

Counseling

Medical overview

Donor selection

Donor testing including automated virology testing to avoid transcription errors

Cellular cryopreservation

Temperature-controlled and monitored storage

Regulatory compliance

Transportation infrastructure

Financial relations with hospitals

Computerized inventory control

Record-keeping

Logistics management

Investigation of adverse reactions

Peer review of medical, scientific, and operational practice

Recipient matching

Concern over the balance of the adequacy and safety of supply

Reputation for dependable service

Commitment to research and development

24-hours-per-day, 7-days-per-week operation

Reproduced with permission.[4]

to serve as tissue banks (Table 26-3).[4] It is common for hospital blood banks to provide transfusion support for organ and tissue recipients and, in some cases, to store, keep records of, and dispose of tissue for allografts. AABB *Standards for Blood Banks and Transfusion Services*[5] addresses the receipt, storage, transportation, and records of tissue allografts. Additional guidance for the collection and provision of tissue and organ allografts is available from federal regulations, Public Health Service Guidelines, and the standards, guidelines, and technical manuals of other national or local organizations.[6-13]

Transplant-Transmitted Diseases and Preventive Measures

The widened availability of tissue and organ grafts has encouraged new clinical uses and highlighted not only their effectiveness and advantages but also their drawbacks, side effects, and complications. Both organs and tissues can transmit bacterial, fungal, and viral diseases from the donor to the recipient (Table 26-4), but careful donor screening and testing, along with disinfection and sterilization steps for specific tissues, can markedly reduce the risk.

Risk Reduction for Cadaveric Tissues

Crucial to the safety of cadaveric transplants is an evaluation of the potential donor's suitability. Listed below are the questions, examinations, and tests undertaken to ensure that material from the potential donor poses the least possible threat of disease transmission.

1. Review of health history, through interviews with next of kin, significant other, and health-care provider, and review of medical records.
    a. No history of infection, malignant disease,* or neurodegenerative disease
    b. No history of autoimmune processes*
    c. No history of exposure to hormone derived from human pituitary gland
2. Review for evidence of high-risk behavior (exclusion for any of the donor-deferral items included in sections B2.300, B2.400, and B2.700 of *Standards for Blood Banks and Transfusion Services*).[5]
3. Serologic tests on suitable blood specimens[9] (see below for more detail).
    a. Hepatitis B surface antigen (HBsAg)
    b. Antibodies to human immunodeficiency viruses 1 and 2 (anti-HIV-1, -2)
    c. Antibody to hepatitis C virus (anti-HCV)
    d. Antibody to human T-cell lymphotropic virus (anti-HTLV-I and -II)
    e. Serologic test for syphilis
4. Physical examination.
    a. No evidence of intravenous drug use
    b. No jaundice
    c. No external signs of infection
5. Autopsy examination, if performed.

Consent and Donor Suitability

Written consent for transplantation use of any tissue or organ must be obtained from a living donor or from the next of kin for a cadaveric donor, except when corneas are procured under legislative consent. Even if the deceased carried a signed and witnessed donor card, consent should be obtained to ensure that next of kin have no objections and that the deceased had not decided to revoke the card. State and federal "required request" statutes exist, mandating that the next of kin or responsible party be given the option for tissue or organ donation whenever a medically suitable donor dies. All applicable federal, state, and local laws concerning the consent of next of kin must be obeyed. When the next of kin signs consent for tissue donation, he or she should specify which tissues may be donated and whether the permission includes tissue to be used for research.

Living donors and the families of deceased donors are not responsible for expenses involved in recovery and processing of donated tissues and organs. They do not receive compensation for the donation. However, donors of reproductive tissue in some instances are compensated for their time, risk, and inconvenience. Tissues can be recovered up to 24 hours after death if the body is refrigerated, whereas organs must be recovered from a

---

* Acceptance of such a donation may be at the discretion of the tissue bank's medical director.[9]

Table 26-4. Infectious Diseases Reported to Have Been Transmitted by Organ and Tissue Allografts[14,15]

Allograft	Infectious Disease/Disease Agent
Bone	HIV-1
	Hepatitis C
	Hepatitis, unspecified type
	Bacteria
	Tuberculosis
Cornea	Hepatitis B
	Creutzfeldt-Jakob disease
	Rabies
	Cytomegalovirus (?)
	Bacteria
	Fungus
Dura	Creutzfeldt-Jakob disease
Heart valve	Hepatitis B
	Tuberculosis
Skin	Bacteria
	Cytomegalovirus (?)
	HIV-1 (?)
Pericardium	Creutzfeldt-Jakob disease
	Bacteria
Solid organ (eg, kidney, liver, heart)	HIV-1
	Hepatitis B
	Hepatitis C
	Cytomegalovirus
	Epstein-Barr virus
	Parvovirus
	Toxoplasmosis
	Chagas' disease
	Malaria
	Bacteria
	Tuberculosis
	Strongyloidiasis
	Sarcoidosis
Pancreatic islet	Bacteria
Semen	Hepatitis B
	Hepatitis C (?)
	Gonorrhea
	Syphilis (?)
	HIV-1
	HTLV-I (?)
	Human papilloma virus (?)
	Trichomonas vaginalis
	Chlamydia trachomatia
	Cytomegalovirus (?)
	Ureaplasma urealyticum
	HSV-2
	Mycoplasma hominis
	Group B streptococcus

brain-dead donor whose circulation has been maintained. (See Table 26-5.) Eyes as a source of corneal allografts should be removed within 12 hours of death to ensure viability of endothelial cells.

Each prospective cadaveric donor must be evaluated against suitable criteria for the specific tissue(s) and organ(s) to be collected; eg, deceased newborns are not suitable for bone donation because of their cartilaginous skeletal structure, but may be candidates for heart valve donation. Although exceptions may be made in specific cases, the medical suitability of a donor is based on absence of infection and malignancy as determined by the medical history, physical examination, laboratory tests, and autopsy, if performed. Donation of organs and tissues does not ordinarily cause delays in funerals or prevent family viewing of the body.

Serologic Testing

Federal regulations require that donors of tissues and organs be tested for HBsAg, anti-HIV-1 and -2, and anti-HCV with tests licensed by the Food and Drug Administration (FDA) and performed by a laboratory certified under the provisions of the Clinical Laboratory Improvement Amendments of 1988.[6,7] National standard-setting organizations, such as the American Association of Tissue Banks (AATB),[9,10] Eye Bank Association of America (EBAA),[12] the American Society for Reproductive Medicine, and the United Network for Organ Sharing (UNOS),[13] may require additional tests for infectious disease markers. For living donors of semen or bone, tests for anti-HIV-1/2 and anti-HCV must be repeated on a sample obtained 6 months after donation and the results found negative before these tissues can be released for use.[9,10] ABO typing is required for organ grafts. HLA typing is essential for kidney grafts but for only a small percent of corneal grafts and not for bone grafts.[16] The role of HLA typing in cardiovascular, lung, and liver transplantation remains uncertain. Other tests, such as antibody to cytomegalovirus (anti-CMV) are also generally performed on organ donors. For cadaveric donors, tests may be performed on a blood sample obtained before administration of transfusions or fluids; these

Table 26-5. Kinds of Donors Providing Organs and Tissue for Transplantation

Living Donor	Cadaveric Donor (Neurologic Death)	Cadaveric Donor (Cardiorespiratory and Neurologic Death)
Blood	Kidney	Cornea
Semen	Heart	Bone
Oocyte	Liver	Skin
Bone	Pancreas	Tendon
Marrow	Lung	Fascia lata
Peripheral blood progenitor cells		Heart valve
Amnion		Saphenous vein
Umbilical vein		Fetal tissue
Kidney		Dura mater
Pancreas		Cartilage
Liver		
Lung		
Fetal tissues (the mother is the donor)		

patients may have received large volumes of replacement fluids shortly before death, and the consequent hemodilution may cause false-negative results.[14] If donor serum collected before blood transfusion or intravenous fluid administration is not available from other sources, a pretransfusion sample is often available from the blood bank, as blood banks hold specimens collected for compatibility for at least 7 days. Algorithms for determining the suitability of a donor sample are available.[6,7] For example, the sample is not suitable for infectious disease marker testing if the total volume of colloid (plasma, dextran, platelets, or hetastarch) transfused in 48 hours plus the total volume of crystalloid infused in the hour prior to obtaining the sample exceed the patient's plasma volume *or* the sum of the volume of blood transfused (RBCs, whole blood, reconstituted blood) and colloid transfused in 48 hours plus the total volume of crystalloid infused in the hour prior to obtaining the sample exceed the patient's blood volume. Testing of cadaveric blood specimens can also be complicated by postmortem hemolysis, which can cause misleading test results (eg, false-positive HBsAg).[17,18]

Bone Banking

Except for blood cells and semen, bone is the most commonly transplanted tissue or organ (Table 26-2). When bone grafting is needed, fresh autologous bone, usually removed from the iliac crest during surgery, is generally considered the most effective graft material. As with blood, the use of autologous bone for graft material is not risk free and there may be morbidity and infectious complications. The quantity of bone graft needed for some surgical procedures may make the use of autologous bone impractical. Allografts are used for these patients and for patients in whom the prolongation of surgery, extra bleeding, and potential complications of autograft collection are considered undesirable. Bone allografts have achieved widespread clinical application for acetabular and proximal femur support in revisions of failed hip prostheses; packing of benign bone cysts; spinal fusion to treat disc disease or scoliosis; reconstruction of maxillo-facial defects; and correction of healed fractures. Demineralized bone powder is commonly used by periodontal surgeons to restore alveolar bone in periodontal pockets.

Selection

Because bone transplantation is a nonurgent surgical procedure, selection of a cadaveric donor can be a careful process that includes interviewing the next of kin concerning the medical history, including HIV and hepatitis risk behaviors; testing the blood for infectious disease markers; and examining the body and evaluating the results of an autopsy, if performed. The safety of this widely used graft material rests upon careful donor selection and subsequent steps for processing and sterilization.

Processing

The surgeon today has access to a wide choice of processed bone allografts: freeze-dried or frozen, cancellous or cortical, with or without treatment with sterilants. Common formats include frozen or freeze-dried cancellous cubes or chips, cortical struts, and cortical-cancellous blocks and dowels. Bone can be stored frozen or, if freeze-dried to a low residual moisture content (6% or less by gravimetric analysis or 8% by nuclear magnetic resonance spectrometry), at room temperature for 5 years (Table 26-6). Unlike frozen bone, freeze-dried tissue has undergone extensive processing to remove blood and marrow and has been exposed to alcohol—conditions that reduce the risk of disease transmission. Most bone allografts used in the United States are freeze-dried to simplify storage, and treated with gamma irradiation or ethylene oxide to

Table 26-6. Recommended Preservation Conditions and Dating Periods for Human Tissue and Organs

Tissue or Organ	Storage Condition	Dating Period
Bone	−40 C	5 years
	−20 C	6 months
	1-10 C	
	Liquid nitrogen	Not defined
	Lyophilized, room temperature	5 years
Tendon	−40 C	5 years
Fascia lata	Lyophilized, room temperature	5 years
	−40 C	5 years
Articular cartilage	−40 C	5 years
	Liquid nitrogen, immersed	Not defined
Skin	0-10 C	7-14 days
	−50 C	6 months to 1 year
Cornea	2-6 C	10 days
Hematopoietic cells	0-4 C	24 hours
	Liquid nitrogen, immersed	Not defined
	Liquid nitrogen, vapor phase	Not defined
Heart valve, vein, artery	−100 C	Not defined
Dura	Lyophilized, room temperature	Not defined
Kidney	Refrigerated	48-72 hours
Liver	Refrigerated	8-24 hours
Heart	Refrigerated	3-5 hours
Heart-lung	Refrigerated	3-5 hours
Pancreas	Refrigerated	12-24 hours
Semen	Liquid nitrogen, immersed	Not defined
	Liquid nitrogen, vapor phase	Not defined

reduce the risk of infectious disease transmission. Demineralization of bone is believed to make its proteins and growth factors more readily available, thereby enhancing its capacity to promote healing and bone formation.

Skin Banking

A human skin allograft is the dressing of choice for deep burn wounds if sufficient amounts of skin for autografting are unavailable. A skin allograft provides temporary coverage; speeds reepithelialization; acts as a metabolic barrier against loss of water, electrolytes, protein, and heat; and provides a physical barrier to bacterial infection. Skin allografts are replaced periodically until sufficient autograft skin can be obtained. A skin allograft may also be used for donor sites for pedicle flaps and skin autografts, and for traumatically denuded areas or unhealed areas of chronic injury, such as decubitus ulcers.

Skin donation involves removing a layer of skin 0.015 inch thick. After collection, refrigerated skin can be stored at 1-10 C for up to 14 days. For refrigerated storage, standard tissue-culture nutrient media are used, with added antibiotics. Skin can also be frozen soon after collection, usually with 10-15% glycerol. Skin is often cryopreserved as 3×8-inch strips on fine-mesh gauze in flat cryopreservation bags. Cryogenic damage is minimized by controlled-rate freezing at about 1 C per minute, followed by storage in liquid nitrogen. Alternatively, skin placed in aluminum plates inside insulated boxes can be placed directly into a −50 C mechanical freezer. This simple process also provides a slow, predictable freezing rate and maintains cellular viability. The optimal freezing procedure and the maximal storage period that maintain viability and structural integrity in the frozen state have not been determined. Skin should be transported to the operating room on ice if stored at 4 C, or on dry ice if cryopreserved. Thawing and application of the skin graft are described in detail elsewhere.[10]

Heart Valves

Human heart valve allografts provide long-term function for aortic valve replacement—superior to that of mechanical or porcine valves. Recipients of human heart valve allografts do not require anticoagulation; the incidence of thromboembolism is low. These allografts seem resistant to infection. They are the graft of choice for children, to avoid long-term anticoagulation; for pregnant women, to avoid teratogenic risks of anticoagulants; and for patients with infection at the aortic root. The widespread use of human valve allografts has been slow because implantation is technically difficult, and appropriately sized valve allografts are not always readily available.

To obtain valve allografts, hearts are aseptically collected in the operating room or in the autopsy room. Subsequently, in the tissue bank, the pulmonic and aortic valves are dis-

sected out, cryopreserved with dimethyl-sulfoxide (DMSO), and stored in liquid nitrogen. Compared with valves stored at 5 C in antibiotics and culture medium, cryopreserved heart valves are associated with increased cell viability; reduced incidence of valve degeneration, rupture, and leaflet perforation; and reduced occurrence of valve-related death.[19]

Records of Stored Tissue Allografts

In two cases when HIV and HCV were transmitted through unprocessed frozen bone or organs and tendon allografts respectively from two cadaveric donors to multiple recipients,[20,21] investigations revealed several hospitals with insufficient records to identify recipients of other tissue from the same infected donors. Voluntary standards of national professional associations and government regulations require hospitals and tissue banks to have a record-keeping system that identifies the donor and allows tracking of any tissue from the donor (or supplier source) to the recipient.[5,9] Records must show the source facility, the identification number of the donor or lot, storage temperatures, and all recipients or other final disposition of each tissue. These records must be retained indefinitely. Hospitals should have procedures in place to recognize adverse outcomes of tissue use and to report them to the institution supplying the tissue.

The Role of Transfusion in Kidney Transplants

Historically, blood transfusions were avoided in patients awaiting kidney transplants because of the belief that they would immunize the recipient to transplantation antigens found on the transfused leukocytes and thereby preclude transplantation. Kissmeyer-Nielsen et al[22] demonstrated that hyperacute rejection of renal allografts was associated with pre-formed cytotoxic antibodies directed against white blood cells. In many patients, however, transfusions were unavoidable, either because of intractable anemia or because early dialysis equipment required priming with blood. If transfusion was unavoidable, efforts were made to provide Red Blood Cells Leukocytes Reduced (freezing and deglycerolizing the red cells was the technique most often applied). In 1973, Opelz et al[23] noted decreasing kidney allograft survival when hemodialysis staff attempted to avoid the blood prime and limit pretransplant blood transfusions. The association between fewer transfusions and declining renal allograft survival led transplant centers to initiate deliberate pretransplant transfusion protocols in the mid-1970s. Subsequent studies have supported the theory that pretransplant blood transfusions enhance renal allograft survival through mechanisms of inducing tolerance that remain imperfectly understood.[24,25] In the 1980s, following the introduction of cyclosporine, the association between pretransplant transfusions and improved graft survival diminished.[26] This caused many centers to return to the practice of transfusion avoidance or the use of Red Blood Cells Leukocytes Reduced (by filtration) in order to prevent HLA alloimmunization that might preclude successful engraftment. However, in recipients of a one or two DR loci mismatched graft, transfusions have continued to improve the 1-year graft survival by 8-10%. Therefore, once again transfusion supports the practice of pretransplant transfusions.[27] The introduction of erythropoietin has reduced the need for red cell transfusions in patients awaiting a renal transplant.

Liver Transplants

A liver transplant program presents one of the greatest challenges to the donor center and hospital transfusion service, demanding maximal support in terms of preparedness, supply, and responsiveness. Massive blood loss and hypocoagulability due both to preexisting liver disease and to the anhepatic interval during the procedure create complex problems for the transfusion service. The liver is the major site for synthesis of clotting factors and other essential proteins and is a prime regulator of acid-base, electrolyte, and glucose homeostasis. The three surgical phases of the procedure—recipient hepatectomy, anhepatic interval, and biliary reconstruction—seriously derange these functions.

Support Required

Institutions that begin a liver transplant program must make a major commitment to this support. Cooperation and communication are required among the hospital administration; staff of the operating room and intensive care unit; personnel of the respiratory therapy, radiology, gastroenterology, and anesthesiology services; the coagulation and transfusion laboratories; and the regional donor center. The institutional commitment must extend 24 hours a day, 365 days a year, because there may be no more than a few hours' advance notice of a liver transplant. Additional staff for the hospital blood bank must be consistently available on an on-call basis in order to meet the transfusion requirements. The surgical procedure frequently takes place at night or on weekends because of the availability of the donor organ and in order to avoid disrupting the operating room schedule. The surgical procedure takes an average of 6-8 hours but may take up to 24 hours and involve massive blood use and several surgical teams.

The blood bank should be notified as soon as the donor organ becomes available and the decision for transplantation is made. The blood bank obtains a generous blood sample from the recipient for crossmatching, but there may be more than one patient waiting for a liver and the surgeons may be undecided about the specific recipient. Therefore, the blood bank may have to perform numerous crossmatches for patients who may have different ABO and Rh types. Liver transplant programs initially used hundreds of units of blood and components per patient. Although blood use has steadily declined over the years, liver transplant procedures frequently use a volume of blood components equal to one whole-body blood volume and sometimes several blood volumes. Intraoperative blood recovery, frequently plays a major role in the conservation of red cells in such cases.

Considerations of ABO and Rh

Except in emergencies, donor livers should be ABO-compatible with the recipient. ABO-identical Red Blood Cells (RBCs) and Fresh Frozen Plasma (FFP) are generally used for transfusion support of group O and group A recipients. Group B recipients who need large quantities of red cells can be switched to group O RBCs. Group AB recipients needing massive transfusion are often switched to group A RBCs to conserve group O RBCs for other patients. If the supply of AB FFP is insufficient, early use of group A RBCs followed by a switch to group A FFP is appropriate. A general rule for massive transfusions is to switch red cells first, then switch plasma, and reverse the order when returning to the patient's original blood type.[25]

Special considerations apply to the recipient of an out-of-group but ABO-compatible liver transplant. In a group A patient receiving a group O liver, lymphocytes of donor origin may produce ABO antibodies that cause hemolysis that begins several days after the procedure and may continue for 2 weeks or longer.[28] Although passenger lymphocytes may produce antibodies in any out-of-group but compatible combination, significant hemolysis is seen most often in the recipient of a group O liver.

Transfusion support of Rh-negative patients not immunized to the D antigen is not standardized.[25] Because successful pregnancy has occurred after liver transplantation, most programs consider it preferable to provide D-negative units to D-negative premenopausal females, if needs are expected to be moderate. Should massive blood loss occur, the patient could then be switched intraoperatively to D-positive blood, if necessary. For premenopausal females without anti-D, several programs reserve 10 units of D-negative RBCs; if more than 10 units are required, they switch to D-positive blood.[25] Production of anti-D occurs less frequently in D-negative liver transplant patients exposed to the D antigen than in other D-negative patients. In some programs, D-negative males and postmenopausal D-negative females without anti-D are transfused exclusively with D-positive blood.

Red Cell Alloantibodies

Liver transplant patients with clinically significant red cell alloantibodies represent a special challenge to blood banks. Sometimes, a sufficient quantity of antigen-negative blood can be secured before surgery. Some programs reserve a limited number of antigen-negative units for use at the beginning of surgery, when alloantibody is present, and at the end of massive blood loss, when transfused cells are expected to remain in circulation. Antibody screening during the interval of massive blood loss can help guide use of antigen-positive units during surgery.

Coagulation Considerations

During surgery, hemodilution, platelet consumption, disordered thrombin regulation, and fibrinolysis derange the hemostatic process. The coagulopathy is especially severe during the anhepatic and early reperfusion stage. The following tests are useful: the hematocrit guides the use of red cells, colloids, and crystalloids; the platelet count guides transfusion of platelets; the prothrombin time and activated partial thromboplastin time guide FFP use; and fibrinogen determinations guide use of Cryoprecipitated AHF and antifibrinolytic agents.[25,29,30]

Other Organ Transplants

Blood bank support for cardiac transplantation is very similar to that routinely used for other surgical procedures in which cardiopulmonary bypass is employed. The blood bank may also provide ABO testing and assist in release of ABO-compatible organs to prevent ABO-mismatched organ transplantation. Pancreatic transplants have comparatively low transfusion requirements, but a specimen from the recipient should routinely be examined for clinically significant unexpected red cell antibodies; in some institutions the protocol calls for crossmatching several units.

Transfusion Service Support for Organ Transplantation

The blood bank provides vital support for a clinical transplantation program. Close communication with the surgeons and other professionals involved in the program is essential. Transfusion practices in the peritransplant period have a major effect on morbidity, mortality, and graft survival rates.

Potential recipients of solid organ transplants are generally available well before the procedure, so there is ample time to obtain a history and perform laboratory tests. It is important for the transfusion service to know if there have been previous pregnancies, transplants, or transfusions.

Laboratory tests routinely performed include: ABO and Rh type, direct antiglobulin test (DAT), a screen for unexpected red cell antibodies, and determination of CMV serostatus. HLA typing and HLA antibody studies are routine for organ recipients.

Passenger lymphocyte hemolysis (typically "ABO" incompatible hemolysis) as discussed previously in regard to liver transplantation can also occur with other solid organ transplants such as lung, heart, and kidney. In the case of a recipient receiving an ABO compatible but non-group-identical organ, prophylactic use of mutually ABO-compatible erythrocytes (compatible for the donor and the recipient) has been suggested for intraoperative and postoperative infusions, during the first postoperative month, or at the appearance of an antibody. At present, there is no consensus on this issue. It is important to remember that if immediate-spin or computer crossmatching is routinely performed following an ABO-unmatched transplant, ABO incompatibility due to these IgG antibodies may be missed. In such cases, the routine use of a crossmatch with an antihuman globulin phase or the use of a DAT (which may detect such cases earlier than a crossmatch) are recommended.[31] If ABO hemolysis is present, the patient should be transfused with group O RBCs.

Cytomegalovirus Status

CMV infection, a serious and often fatal complication in transplant recipients, is related to the presence of CMV in the donor and recipient and the degree to which the recipient is immunosuppressed. The primary test used to determine CMV status is the demonstration of circulating antibody. CMV-seronegative recipients of CMV-seronegative transplants characteristically receive transfusion components processed to reduce risk of CMV transmission, either by preparation from seronegative donors or by leukocyte reduction to 5×10^6 or below.

ABO Types

The ABO antigens are important in transplantation practice because they constitute very strong histocompatibility antigens that are expressed on vascular endothelium. Major ABO mismatching can cause rapid graft rejection due to endothelial damage by ABO antibodies and subsequent widespread thrombosis within the graft. ABO matching is important to the success of vascularized grafts (ie, kidney, heart, liver, and pancreas), but ABO matching is not important in tissue grafts (ie, fascia, bone, heart valves, skin, and cornea).

The definition of an ABO-compatible graft is the same as that for a red cell transfusion. A group O donor of tissue or organ is a universal donor whose graft can be transplanted into recipients of all blood groups. Case reports document rare successful organ transplants with major ABO incompatibility but these are biological curiosities.[32] A_2 donor kidneys can be successfully transplanted into group O recipients with survival comparable to that of group O donor kidneys.[33] ABO-incompatible transplants have occurred, often with fatal results, due to errors of record-keeping or labeling. It has been estimated that inadvertent ABO-incompatible heart or kidney transplants occur with a frequency of 1 per 1000![34] This underscores the importance of a final ABO check of donor and recipient blood at the transplant facility to reduce this risk.

FDA Regulation of Tissue

The FDA currently regulates human tissue collected for transplantation.[6,7] The FDA plans to regulate both human cellular and tissue-based products.[35] As proposed the FDA would require all facilities that recover, process, store, or distribute human cellular and tissue-based products to register with the agency and list their products via an electronic system. Products not covered by this proposed approach include xenogeneic tissue, vascularized organs, minimally manipulated marrow, transfusable blood products, products used in the propagation of cells or tissues, and products that are secreted or extracted from cells or tissues. Infectious disease testing would be required for allogeneic tissues, except reproductive tissue from sexually intimate partners. Good tissue banking practice involving record-keeping, labeling, product tracking, recalls, and notification of infectious disease transmission would be required for certain tissues. The level of reg-

ulation would be determined by several factors including degree of manipulation, whether the product is a combination product (combined with a drug or device), and whether it is used for a systemic function. Some products will not require premarket approval. Other products, such as biologic products, would require a Biological License Application (BLA) submission with a Chemical and Manufacturing Control (CMC) section. Clinical safety and effectiveness data would be gathered under an investigational new drug (IND) exemption and premarket approval of a license would be required. Still other products, such as medical device products, would be regulated under medical devices requirements.

References

1. Strong M, Eastlund T, Mowe J. Tissue bank activity in the United States: 1992 survey of AATB-inspected tissue banks. Tissue Cell Rep 1996;3:15-8.
2. 1996 EBAA statistical report. Washington, DC: Eye Bank Association of America, 1996.
3. UNOS scientific registry (as of April 8, 1997). Richmond, VA: United Network for Organ Sharing, 1997. (http://204.127.237.11/sta_tran.htm)
4. Warwick RM, Eastlund T, Fehily D. Role of the blood transfusion service in tissue banking. Vox Sang 1996;71:71-7.
5. Menitove JE, ed. Standards for blood banks and transfusion services. 19th ed. Bethesda, MD: American Association of Blood Banks, 1999.
6. Food and Drug Administration. Human tissue intended for transplantation. Fed Regist 1997;62: 40429-47.
7. Food and Drug Administration. Guidance for Industry: Screening and testing of donors of human tissue intended for transplantation. July 1997. Rockville, MD: CBER Office of Communication, Training, and Manufacturer's Assistance, 1997.
8. Centers for Disease Control and Prevention. Guidelines for preventing HIV transmission through organ and tissue transplantation. MMWR 1994;43(RR-8):1-17.
9. Kagan RJ, ed. Standards for tissue banking. McLean, VA: American Association of Tissue Banks, 1998.
10. Technical manual for tissue banking. McLean, VA: American Association of Tissue Banks, 1992.
11. Campagnari KD, O'Malley J. Standards of the American Red Cross Tissue Services, 6th ed. Washington, DC: American Red Cross Tissue Services, 1994.
12. Medical standards of EBAA. Washington, DC: Eye Bank Association of America, 1997.

13. Articles of incorporation, by-laws, and policies of UNOS. Richmond, VA: United Network for Organ Sharing, 1995 (revised at least annually).

14. Human immunodeficiency virus transmitted from an organ donor screened for HIV antibody—North Carolina. MMWR 1987;36:306-8.

15. Linden JV, Critser JK. Therapeutic insemination by donor II: A review of the known risks. Reprod Med Rev 1995;4:19-29.

16. Choo SY, Eastlund T. Tissue transplantation and HLA typing. Tissue Cell Rep 1995;2:3-4.

17. Eastlund T. Infectious disease transmission through cell, tissue and organ transplantation. Reducing the risk through donor selection. Cell Transplant 1995;4:455-77.

18. LeFor WM, McGonigle AF, Wright CE, Shires DL. The frequency of false positive HBsAg screening test results with cadaver tissue donors is dependent upon the assay procedure used. Tissue Cell Rep 1996;3:6-170.

19. O'Brien MF, Stafford EG, Gardner MAH, et al. Cryopreserved viable allograft aortic valves. In: Yankoh AC, Hetzer R, Miller DC, et al, eds. Cardiac valve allografts 1972-1987. New York: Springer-Verlag, 1988:311-21.

20. Simonds RJ, Holmberg SD, Hurwitz RL, et al. Transmission of human immunodeficiency virus type 1 from a seronegative organ and tissue donor. N Engl J Med 1992;326:726-32.

21. Conrad EU, Gretch D, Obermeyer K, et al. The transmission of hepatitis C virus by tissue transplantation. J Bone Joint Surg 1995;77A:214-23.

22. Kissmeyer-Nielsen F, Olsen S, Petersen VP, et al. Hyperacute rejection of kidney allografts, associated with preexisting humoral antibodies against donor cells. Lancet 1966;2:662.

23. Opelz G, Sengar DPS, Mickey MR, Terasaki P. Effect of blood transfusion on subsequent kidney transplants. Transplant Proc 1973;5:253-9.

24. Blumberg N, Heal JM. Transfusion-associated immunomodulation. In: Anderson KC, Ness PM, eds. Scientific basis of transfusion medicine. Philadelphia: WB Saunders, 1994:580-96.

25. Dzik WH. Solid organ transplantation. In: Petz LD, Swisher SN, Kleinman S, et al, eds. Clinical practice of transfusion medicine, 3rd ed. New York: Churchill Livingstone, 1996:783-806.

26. Lundgren G, et al. HLA matching and pretransplant blood transfusions in cadaveric renal transplantation—a changing picture with cyclosporin. Lancet 1986;2:66-9.

27. Iwaki y, Cecka JM, Terasaki PI. The transfusion effect in cadaver kidney transplants, yes or no. Transplantation 1990;49:56-9.

28. Triulzi DJ, Shirey RS, Ness PM, Klein AS. Immunohematologic complications of ABO-unmatched liver transplants. Transfusion 1992;32: 829-33.

29. Triulzi DJ, Bontempo FA, Kiss JE, Winkelstein A. Transfusion support in liver transplantation. Transfus Sci 1993;14:345-52.

30. Motschman TL, Taswell HF, Brecher ME, et al. Blood bank support of a liver transplantation program. Mayo Clin Proc 1989;64:103-11.

31. Brecher ME. Hemolytic transfusion reactions. In: Rossi E, Simon T, Moss G, Gould S. Principles of transfusion medicine, 2nd ed. Baltimore, MD: Williams and Wilkins, 1995:747-63.

32. Alexandre GPJ, Squifflet JP, DeBruyere M, et al. ABO-incompatible related and unrelated living donor renal allografts. Transplant Proc 1986;18: 1090-2.

33. Breimer ME, Brynger H, Rydberg L, et al. Transplantation of blood group A2 kidneys to O recipients. Biochemical and immunological studies of group A antigens in human kidneys. Transplant Proc 1985;17:2640-3.

34. Terasaki PI. Red-cell crossmatching for heart transplants (letter). N Engl J Med 1991;325:1748-9.

35. Food and Drug Administration. A proposed approach to the regulation of cellular and tissue-based products. Fed Regist 1997;62:9721-2.

Noninfectious Complications of Blood Transfusion

Classification

Transfusion reactions may be divided into four broad categories as shown in Table 27-1. This chapter deals with preventive measures of noninfectious transfusion reactions in the clinical setting, as well as recognition and treatment of reactions that do occur. Infectious risks of transfusion are discussed in Chapter 28.

All personnel involved in ordering and administering transfusions must be able to recognize a transfusion reaction so that appropriate actions can be taken promptly. Listed below are signs and symptoms that may be associated with acute transfusion reactions and can aid in their recognition.

MOST TRANSFUSIONS PROVIDE safe and effective temporary replacement of blood components. As with other medical interventions, however, transfusions are associated with certain risks, and only when the expected benefits outweigh the potential risks should transfusion therapy be initiated.

This chapter addresses the four broad categories of transfusion reactions: 1) acute immunologic, 2) acute nonimmunologic, 3) delayed immunologic, and 4) delayed nonimmunologic. For each individual type of reaction, the pathophysiology, treatment, and prevention are discussed. More detailed coverage is available elsewhere.[1]

- Fever with or without chills, defined as 1 C (2 F) increase in body temperature associated with the transfusion.
- Shaking chills (rigors) with or without fever.

Table 27-1. Categories and Management of Adverse Transfusion Reactions*

Acute (<24 hours) Transfusion Reactions–Immunologic

Type	Incidence	Etiology	Signs and Symptoms	Laboratory Testing	Therapeutic/Prophylactic Approach
Hemolytic (symptomatic)	1:33,000- 1:12,000	Red cell incompatibility	Chills, fever, hemoglobinuria, renal failure, hypotension, DIC, oliguria, oozing from IV site, back pain, pain along infusion vein	■ Direct antiglobulin test ■ Plasma-free hemoglobin (visual inspection) ■ Further tests as clinically indicated	■ Keep renal output >100 mL/hr with fluid replacement and IV diuretic (furosemide) ■ Support blood pressure with dopamine (renal-sparing dose) ■ DIC therapy with coagulation factor support vs heparin
Fever/chill, nonhemolytic	1:200-1:100 (0.5-1%)†	■ Antibody to donor leukocytes ■ Accumulated cytokines in bag	Rigors, rise in temperature (1 C), headache, malaise, vomiting	■ Leukocyte antibodies ■ Cytokines (research only)	■ Premedication with aspirin-free antipyretic (acetaminophen) ■ Leukocyte-reduced blood
Allergic	1:100-1:33 (1-3%)	Antibody to donor plasma proteins	Pruritis, rash, urticaria, flushing	Usually none	■ Antihistamine (PO or IM) ■ Temporarily stop unit; restart slowly after resolution of symptoms ■ Consider antihistamines before next transfusion
Anaphylactic	1:170,000- 1:18,000	Antibody to donor plasma proteins (most commonly anti-IgA)	Urticaria, erythema, anxiety, respiratory distress, hypotension, laryngeal/pharyngeal edema, bronchospasm	■ Anti-IgA ■ IgA, quantitative (optional screening test)	■ Epinephrine (adult dose: 0.3-0.5 mL of 1:1000 solution SC or IM; in severe cases 1:10,000 IV)

Acute (<24 hours) Transfusion Reactions—Nonimmunologic

Reaction	Frequency	Etiology	Signs and Symptoms	Laboratory	Management
					■ Antihistamines, corticosteroids, beta-2 agonists ■ IgA-deficient blood components
Atypical reaction associated with ACE inhibition	Variable	Inhibited metabolism of bradykinin with infusion of bradykinin or activators of prekallikrein	Flushing, hypotension	Bradykinin, kininogens, ACE (research only)	■ Withdrawal of ACE inhibition ■ Use of nonalbumin plasma replacement for plasmapheresis ■ Use of positively charged filters or differential centrifugation for leukocyte reduction
Circulatory overload	1:10,000–1:100	Volume overload	Dyspnea, orthopnea, productive cough with pink, frothy sputum, tachycardia, hypertension, headache	N/A	■ Upright posture ■ Oxygen ■ IV diuretic (furosemide), morphine ■ Rotating tourniquets ■ Phlebotomy (250-mL increments)
Hemolytic (without symptoms or "pseudo hemolytic")	Unknown	Physical or chemical destruction of blood, freezing, heating, hemolytic drug or solution added to blood	Hemoglobinuria	■ Plasma-free hemoglobin ■ Direct antiglobulin test (should be negative)	■ Identify and eliminate cause
Air embolus	Unknown	Air infusion via line	Sudden shortness of breath, acute cyanosis, pain, cough, hypotension, cardiac arrythmia	N/A	■ Lay patient on left side with legs elevated above chest and head

(continued)

Table 27-1. Categories and Management of Adverse Transfusion Reactions (cont'd)*

Type	Incidence	Etiology	Signs and Symptoms	Laboratory Testing	Therapeutic/Prophylactic Approach
Hypocalcemia	Unknown	■ Massive transfusion of citrated blood and/or delayed metabolism of citrate ■ Apheresis procedures	Paresthesia, tetany, arrhythmia	■ Ionized calcium ■ Prolonged Q-T interval on EKG	■ Slow calcium infusion while monitoring ionized calcium levels in severe cases ■ PO calcium supplement for mild symptoms during apheresis procedures
Hypothermia	Unknown	■ Rapid infusion of cold blood	Cardiac arrhythmia	N/A	■ Employ blood warmers

Delayed (> 24 hours) Transfusion Reactions—Immunologic

Type	Incidence	Etiology	Signs and Symptoms	Laboratory Testing	Therapeutic/Prophylactic Approach
Alloimmuniza-tion, RBC antigens	1:100 (1%)	Immune response to foreign antigens on RBC, or WBC and platelets (HLA)	Usually none—but may result in platelet refractoriness, difficulty finding compatible blood for subsequent transfusions, delayed hemolytic reactions and hemolytic disease of the newborn	■ Direct and indirect antiglobulin test ■ Lymphocytotoxicity test	■ Avoid unnecessary transfusions ■ Leukocyte-reduced blood
HLA	1:10 (10%)				
Hemolytic (often asymptom-atic)	1:11,000-1:5000	Anamnestic immune response to RBC antigens	Weakness, unexplained fall in posttransfusion hemoglobin, elevated serum bilirubin	■ Urine hemosiderin ■ Antiglobulin test ■ Plasma-free hemoglobin (other markers of RBC lysis as clinically indicated)	■ Identify antibody ■ Transfuse with antigen-negative blood as needed

Graft-vs-host disease	Rare	Functioning lymphocytes transfused to immunosuppressed patient; may occur in immunocompetent patient receiving HLA-matched lymphocytes	Erythroderma, maculopapular rash, anorexia, nausea, vomiting, diarrhea, hepatitis, pancytopenia, fever	■ Skin biopsy	■ Methotrexate, corticosteroids ■ Irradiation of blood components for patients at risk (including blood related donors and HLA-selected components)
Posttransfusion purpura	Rare[3]	Platelet antibodies (usually against Pl^{A1})	Purpura, bleeding, fall in platelet count 8-10 days following transfusion	Anti-Pl^{A1}	■ IVIG ■ Pl^{A1}-negative platelets ■ Plasmapheresis
Immuno-modulation	Unknown	Incompletely understood interaction of donor WBC or plasma factors with recipient immune system	■ Tolerance induction ■ Postsurgical wound infection ■ Possibly other transfusion effects	■ Lymphocyte immunophenotyping ■ Cytokine profiles (research only)	

Delayed (>24 hours) Transfusion Reactions–Nonimmunologic

Iron overload	Unknown	Multiple transfusions in transfusion-dependent patients (congenital anemias, aplastic anemias, etc)	Cardiomyopathy, arrhythmias, hepatic and pancreatic failure	Iron studies	Deferoxamine (iron chelation)‡

* For platelet refractoriness see Chapter 16; for septic transfusion reactions see Table 28-1; for recent summaries of transfusion reactions see also DeChristopher[2] and US GAO Report.[3]

† Quoted rate refers to RBC transfusion in the general hospital population; considerably higher rates were observed in multitransfused hematology patients and following platelet transfusions (see Heddle et al[4]).

‡ Additional or alternative approaches in the prevention of iron overload are transfusion of neocytes (Spanos et al[5]) and RBC exchange by apheresis (Adams et al[6]).

ACE=angiotensin-converting enzyme; ARDS=acute respiratory distress syndrome; DIC=disseminated intravascular coagulation; EKG=electrocardiogram; IM=intramuscular; IV=intravenous; IVIG=intravenous immunoglobulin; N/A=not applicable; PO=by mouth; RBC=red blood cell; SC=subcutaneous; WBC=white blood cell.

- Pain at infusion site or in chest, abdomen, or flanks.
- Blood pressure changes, usually acute, either hypertension or hypotension.
- Respiratory distress, including dyspnea, tachypnea, or hypoxemia.
- Skin changes, including flushing, itching, urticaria, or localized or generalized edema.
- Nausea with or without vomiting.
- Circulatory shock in combination with fever, severe chills, hypotension, and high-output cardiac failure. This is suggestive of acute sepsis, but may also accompany an acute hemolytic transfusion reaction. Circulatory collapse without fever and chills may be the most prominent finding in anaphylaxis.
- Urine color changes. This may be the earliest indication of an acute hemolytic reaction in anesthetized patients.

Acute Transfusion Reactions

Immune-Mediated Hemolysis

Pathophysiology

The most severe hemolytic reactions occur when transfused red cells interact with preformed antibodies in the recipient; interaction of transfused antibodies with the recipient's red cells rarely causes symptoms, although there may be accelerated red cell destruction. The interaction of antibody with antigen on the red cell membrane can initiate a sequence of neuroendocrine responses, complement activation, coagulation effects, and cytokine effects that result in the clinical manifestations of an acute hemolytic transfusion reaction (HTR). Most severe acute HTRs result from transfusion of ABO-incompatible red cells[7]; although antibodies other than ABO isoagglutinins can and do cause HTRs, the results are seldom catastrophic. Symptoms of an acute HTR, sometimes misleadingly mild, may begin

after the infusion of as little as 10-15 mL of incompatible blood. In anesthetized patients who cannot report symptoms, the manifestations of an acute HTR may be limited to diffuse bleeding at the surgical site, hypotension, or hemoglobinuria.

Neuroendocrine Response. The combination of antibody with membrane antigen forms immune complexes capable of activating Hageman factor (Factor XIIa), which, in turn, acts on the kinin system to generate bradykinin. Bradykinin increases capillary permeability and arteriolar dilatation, causing a fall in systemic arterial pressure. Vasoactive amines induced by complement and platelet activation may also contribute to hypotension. Development of hypotension provokes a sympathetic nervous system response, characterized by rising levels of norepinephrine and other catecholamines that produce vasoconstriction in organs with a vascular bed rich in alpha-adrenergic receptors, notably the renal, splanchnic, pulmonary, and cutaneous capillaries. Coronary and cerebral vessels, which have few alpha-adrenergic receptors, participate minimally in the reaction. Histamine and serotonin, vasoactive amines that mediate many clinical concomitants of the HTR, are released from granules of mast cells and platelets as immune complexes activate the complement system and platelet responses.

Complement Activation. Immune complex formation on the red cell membranes activates complement. If the enzymatic cascade proceeds to completion, intravascular hemolysis results. If complement activation terminates with C3 activation and release of anaphylatoxins (see Chapter 11), red cells coated with C3b circulate and are removed by interaction with phagocytes that have receptors for C3b. Complement activation is characteristically rapid and complete in ABO-associated reactions, and intravascular red cell destruction releases both free hemoglobin and red cell stroma into the plasma. Although free hemoglobin was, historically, considered the cause of renal failure, current thought attributes acute tubular necrosis and renal failure largely to alpha-adrenergic-mediated vasoconstriction and the presence of antibody-coated cell stroma and fibrin thrombi in the renal vasculature. With most non-ABO blood group antibodies, complement activation is usually incomplete; hemoglobinemia and circulation of stromal fragments do not occur, but consequences of complement activation, most notably release of anaphylatoxins and opsonization of red cells, may have adverse effects.

Coagulation Activation. The antigen-antibody interaction may activate the intrinsic clotting cascade through Hageman factor activation, through circulation of incompatible red cell stroma, and/or by release of thromboplastic materials from white cells and platelets. If disseminated intravascular coagulopathy (DIC) occurs, it may cause some or all of the following: 1) formation of thrombi within the microvasculature and ischemic damage to tissues and organs; 2) consumption of fibrinogen, platelets, and Factors V and VIII; 3) activation of the fibrinolytic system; and 4) generation of fibrin degradation products. The outcome can be a systemic hemorrhagic state characterized by oozing or uncontrolled bleeding.

Cytokines. Leukocytes exposed to antigen-antibody complexes secrete a variety of cytokines whose combined effects include the induction of fever, hypotension, mobilization of neutrophils from marrow, activation of endothelial cells to express adhesion molecules and procoagulant activity, activation of T and B lymphocytes, and priming of neutrophils. Prominent among the implicated cytokines are tumor necrosis factor (TNF), interleukin-1b (IL-1b), interleukin-6 (IL-6), and interleukin-8 (IL-8).[8,9] The complete role of cytokines in the consequences of immune hemolysis remains to be defined.

Renal Failure. Renal failure is the most prominent sequela of an untreated acute HTR. The combination of systemic hypotension, re-active vasoconstriction, and formation of intravascular thrombi compromises renal cortical blood supply. The resulting ischemia may be transient or may progress to acute tubular necrosis and renal failure.

Treatment

The treatment of an acute HTR depends on the amount of incompatible blood transfused, the specificity of the offending antibody, and the clinical severity of the reaction.[10]

Vigorous treatment of hypotension and promotion of adequate renal blood flow are the primary concerns; if shock can be prevented or adequately treated, renal failure may be avoided. Adequacy of renal perfusion can be monitored by measurement of urine output, with a goal of maintaining urine flow rates above 100 mL/hour in adults for at least 18-24 hours. The usual first support is intravenous normal saline, but underlying cardiac and/or renal disease may complicate therapy, and it is important to avoid overhydration. Invasive monitoring of pulmonary capillary wedge pressure is recommended in guiding fluid therapy in the face of hemodynamic instability. Diuretics help to improve blood flow to the kidneys and increase urine output. Intravenous furosemide at a dose of 40-80 mg for an adult or 1-2 mg/kg for a child not only has a diuretic effect but also improves blood flow to the renal cortex. This dose may be repeated once, and the patient should be adequately hydrated. Mannitol has been used in the past; an osmotic diuretic, it increases blood volume and thereby may also increase renal blood flow. If no diuretic response occurs within a few hours of instituting fluid and diuretic therapy, there is a strong likelihood that acute tubular necrosis has occurred and further fluid administration and diuretic therapy may be harmful.

Treatment of hypotension with pressor agents that decrease renal blood flow, such as dopamine in higher doses, is contraindicated. However, in low doses (less than 5 μg/kg/minute), dopamine increases cardiac output, dilates the renal vasculature, and has been recommended in the management of acute HTRs.[10]

DIC with resultant bleeding or generalized oozing may be a predominant clinical finding in some HTRs and may be the initial presentation in an anesthetized patient. Heparin has been recommended by some, both to forestall DIC when an ABO incompatibility is first discovered and to treat the established coagulopathy. Others believe the dangers outweigh potential benefits, especially because the immune event that provoked the DIC is self-limited. Administration of Platelets, Fresh Frozen Plasma (FFP), and Cryoprecipitated AHF (as a source of fibrinogen) may be necessary if bleeding due to DIC is organ- or life-threatening.

Acute hemolytic reactions are very rare and few clinicians have first-hand experience with them. Because medical management of an acute HTR is often complicated and may require aggressive interventions such as hemodialysis, consultation with a physician experienced in the organ systems most damaged or in critical care medicine may be prudent when treating a patient with a severe acute HTR.

Frequency

Clerical and other human errors leading to mistaken identity are the most common causes of ABO-incompatible transfusion, either by administration of blood to the wrong person, or by administration of the wrong unit of blood or red cells to the intended recipient. A study of transfusion errors in New York State in the early 1990s estimated the incidence rate of ABO-incompatible red cell transfusions at 1:33,000 to 1:12,000.[11] A survey of 3601 institutions by the College of American Pathologists found 843 acute HTRs reported over a 5-year period, of which 50 (6%) were fatal.[12] Estimates of mortality rates from acute HTR generally range from about 1 in 600,000 to 1 in 100,000 transfusions. The lower rate is based on the

15-16 fatal acute HTRs reported per year to the Food and Drug Administration (FDA) and may represent underreporting.[7]

Prevention

Because misidentification causes the majority of acute immune-mediated HTRs, the best hope for prevention lies in preventing or detecting errors in every phase of the transfusion process. In each institution there should be systems designed to prevent or detect errors in patient and unit identification at the time of phlebotomy (sample acquisition), at all steps in laboratory testing, at the time of issue, and when the transfusions are given. Quality system models are available to provide a framework for instituting and assessing such systems.[13] Active participation by physicians and management, as well as by nursing, technical, and clinical personnel, is essential.

Crucial in the prevention of transfusion mishaps are training and assessment of personnel performing transfusions.[14] Ensuring that all clinical staff recognize signs of acute reactions and stop the transfusion before a critical volume of blood is administered is essential to preventing harm to the patient.

Non-Immune-Mediated Hemolysis

Causes

Red cells may undergo in-vitro hemolysis if the unit is exposed to improper temperatures during shipping or storage, or is mishandled at the time of administration. Malfunctioning blood warmers, use of microwave ovens or hot waterbaths, or inadvertent freezing may all cause temperature-related damage. Mechanical hemolysis may be caused by the use of roller pumps (such as those used in cardiac bypass surgery), pressure infusion pumps, pressure cuffs, or small-bore needles.[15] Osmotic hemolysis in the blood bag or infusion set may result from the addition of drugs or hypotonic solutions such as distilled water or 5% dextrose solutions, and inadequate deglycerolization of frozen red cells may cause the cells to hemolyze after infusion. Finally, hemolysis may be a sign of bacterial growth in blood units. In a patient with transfusion-associated hemolysis for which both immune and nonimmune causes have been eliminated, the possibility might be considered that the patient or donor has an intrinsic red cell defect such as glucose-6-phosphatase dehydrogenase deficiency.

Treatment

Treatment depends on the cause of nonimmune hemolysis. If the patient develops a severe reaction with hypotension, shock, and renal dysfunction, intensive clinical management is required even before the cause of the mishap is investigated. If the patient exhibits only hemoglobinemia and hemoglobinuria, supportive therapy may be sufficient.

Prevention

There should be written procedures for all aspects of procuring, processing, and issuing blood, and administering transfusions. All staff should be trained in the proper use of equipment, intravenous solutions, and drugs used during the administration of blood and blood components. Equipment must be properly maintained and records kept of how and when items are used. Intravenous medications must never be injected into blood bags,[16(p68)] and care must be exercised in selection and use of intravenous access devices. Chapter 22 discusses details of administering transfusions.

Transfusion-Associated Sepsis

Bacterial contamination of transfused blood should be considered if the patient experiences severe rigors, especially if they are accompanied by cardiovascular collapse and/or fever over 40 C.[17] For a more detailed discussion of this potentially life-threatening transfusion complication see Chapter 28.

Febrile Nonhemolytic Reactions

Pathophysiology

A febrile nonhemolytic (FNH) reaction is often defined as a temperature increase of >1 C associated with transfusion and without any other explanation. The 1 C definition is arbitrary; the same events might cause temperature increments of 0.5 C or 2 C without altering the physiologic significance. Febrile reactions complicate 0.5-1.5% of red cell transfusions,[4] and are often accompanied by chills and/or rigors. Multitransfused patients and those who receive platelets may experience such reactions at a much higher rate. Most are benign, although some may cause significant discomfort or hemodynamic changes. The temperature rise may begin early in the transfusion or be delayed in onset for up to several hours after completion of the transfusion. Previous opportunities for alloimmunization, especially pregnancies and multiple transfusions, increase the frequency of FNH reactions.

Some FNH reactions are thought to result from an interaction between antibodies in the recipient's plasma and antigens present on transfused lymphocytes, granulocytes, or platelets. Infusion of bioactive substances, including cytokines and so-called biologic response modifiers that accumulate in the blood bag during storage, and provocation of cytokine release in the recipient, probably account for many others.[4,18-20] Because fever may be an initial manifestation of an acute HTR or a septic reaction to transfusion, any observation of an unexplained transfusion-associated rise in temperature warrants prompt attention. The diagnosis of an FNH reaction is made after excluding other possible explanations for the fever.

Evaluation of Transfusion-Associated Fever

An acute rise in body temperature may be the sole or primary symptom of a hemolytic or septic transfusion reaction. These possibilities should therefore be considered before a diagnosis of an FNH transfusion reaction is made. Guidelines for evaluation of a suspected acute transfusion reaction are presented later in this chapter.

Treatment

Traditionally, occurrence of an FNH reaction has caused the transfusion to be discontinued.[21] However, some workers believe that an FNH reaction should not routinely cause discontinuation of a transfusion,[22] depending on whether the patient has symptoms or signs that suggest hemolysis or bacterial contamination. The fever of an FNH reaction usually responds to antipyretics. Meperidine injection may be useful in patients with severe shaking chills. Acetaminophen (650 mg for an adult) is preferred to the use of salicylates because the former drug does not affect platelet function. Antihistamines are not indicated because most FNH reactions do not involve histamine release.

Prevention

Febrile reactions in an alloimmunized individual can often be prevented by the transfusion of blood components with a residual leukocyte content of less than 5×10^8 leukocytes per unit.[23] Transfusion of red cells or platelets that are leukocyte-reduced to this extent frequently prevents FNH reactions, but not always.[24] Antibodies to platelet antigens or infusion of cytokines accumulated in the stored component may still cause the recipient to experience a temperature rise.[4] Preliminary studies suggest that FNH reactions to platelet transfusions are more effectively prevented by using prestorage leukocyte-reduced platelet components, which would preclude the accumulation of cytokines.[4]

Urticaria (Hives)

Pathophysiology

The typical urticarial reaction is a form of cutaneous hypersensitivity, triggered by exposure to a soluble substance in donor plasma to which the recipient has been sensitized. The reaction is characterized by rash and/or hives and itching, and is usually not accompanied by fever or other adverse findings. Urticaria may complicate approximately 1-3% of transfusions.[25]

Treatment

If urticaria is the only adverse event noted, the transfusion may be temporarily interrupted while an antihistamine (eg, diphenhydramine, 25-50 mg) is administered orally or parenterally. If symptoms are mild and promptly relieved, the transfusion may be resumed, provided the interrupted infusion can be completed within the duration that institutional policy mandates for transfusion. If the patient develops extensive urticaria or a confluent total body rash during transfusion, it would be prudent to discontinue administration of the unit even if symptoms have responded to treatment.

Prevention

Recipients who have frequent transfusion-associated urticarial reactions may respond well to administration of antihistamine one-half hour before transfusion. If reactions are recurrent and especially severe, transfusion of washed red cell or platelet components, or red cells that have been frozen, thawed, and deglycerolized may prove helpful.

Anaphylactic Reactions

The incidence of these most severe transfusion reactions fortunately is low, estimated from approximately 1 in 170,000 to 1 in 18,000 with an FDA reported mortality rate of about 1 per year.[25]

Pathophysiology

Anaphylactic transfusion reactions, sometimes called immediate generalized reactions, may begin after infusion of only a few milliliters, with systemic symptoms that often are mild at first but can progress to loss of consciousness, shock, and, in rare cases, death. Symptoms may involve one or several systems, notably the respiratory tract (cough, bronchospasm, dyspnea), the gastrointestinal tract (cramps, nausea, vomiting, diarrhea), the circulatory system (arrhythmias, hypotension, syncope), or the skin (generalized flushing, urticaria). These manifestations appear to reflect generalized activity of IgE antibodies, although they may not be demonstrable in the serum of most patients. Routinely detectable IgA antibodies are of IgG or IgM class; however, IgE anti-IgA has been demonstrated in common variable immunodeficiency.[26]

IgA Deficiency. The classic explanation for these reactions is the presence of class-specific antibodies to IgA in persons congenitally deficient in this immunoglobulin class. IgA deficiency is the most common congenital immune deficiency, affecting 1 in 700-800 persons of European descent, of whom as many as 30%[27] have circulating IgA antibodies. Anaphylactic transfusion reactions, however, are quite rare (1:170,000 to 1:18,000) and only a fraction of such patients (17.5%) have an immediate generalized reaction that is associated with IgA antibody.[28]

Other Conditions. Transfusion-related events that can mimic generalized IgE-mediated reactions include anaphylactoid/atypical reactions associated with angiotensin-converting enzyme (ACE) inhibition and transfusion-related acute lung injury (TRALI), discussed below. Coincidental occurrence of myocardial infarction, pulmonary embolism, or other medical catastrophes could present with similar symptoms and should not be overlooked. Besides IgA/anti-IgA reactions, the differential diagnosis for anaphylaxis induced by transfusion must include reactions to other constituents, such as preexisting antibodies to other serum proteins, complement-derived anaphylatoxins, or drugs or other soluble allergens in the transfusion component.[26] Finally, preformed histamine, serotonin, and platelet-activating factor in stored platelets may be capable of producing bronchospasm, hypotension, or both, mimicking an immediate hypersensitivity reaction.[26]

Treatment

Generalized reactions may not begin immediately; some develop as long as an hour after transfusion is completed. Good transfusion practice calls for close observation during the first quarter hour of infusion and less intensive but nonetheless continuing surveillance throughout and after the transfusion. The immediate treatment of an anaphylactic transfusion reaction should be to stop the transfusion; keep the access line open with normal saline; and treat hypotension, beginning with administration of epinephrine and continuing with the administration of plasma volume expander solutions (isotonic crystalloid or colloid solutions).

In mild to moderate cases, epinephrine (1:1000) should be delivered subcutaneously or intramuscularly in a starting dose of 0.3-0.5 mL in adults, or 0.01 mL in children. This dose may be repeated a second and third time at 5- to 15-minute intervals. In severe reactions (eg, systolic blood pressure below 80 mm Hg, laryngeal edema with upper airway compromise, or respiratory failure), the drug should be given intravenously (1:10,000), because time is important and drug absorption is unreliable in hypotensive patients. Aerosolized or intravenous beta-2 agonists, histamine antagonists, theophylline, and glucagon may be required in selected patients in whom bronchospasm is unresponsive to epinephrine treatment, or in whom epinephrine is ineffective because of preexisting beta-blocker therapy. Intravenous corticosteroids are not helpful for acute therapy, but have a role in reducing the risk of recurring or protracted anaphylaxis. Oxygen therapy should be administered, as required clinically, with endotracheal intubation if there is significant upper airway obstruction.

Continued hemodynamic instability may require invasive hemodynamic monitoring. Under no circumstances should the transfusion be restarted. Treatment will be initiated on clinical grounds; diagnosis is made retrospectively.

Prevention

IgA-deficient patients who have had a prior life-threatening anaphylactic reaction should receive blood components that lack IgA. Components prepared from IgA-deficient blood donors may be obtained from regional blood suppliers. An immediate need for red cells may be met by the use of units that have been frozen, thawed, and deglycerolized or by repeated automated washing of standard units.[25] Platelets, if needed, should also be thoroughly washed.[29] If plasma components must be given, IgA-deficient donors will be needed. It may be possible to collect and store autologous blood components from patients known to have experienced anaphylactic reactions.

Anaphylactoid or Atypical Reactions Associated with Angiotensin-Converting Enzyme Inhibition

Therapeutic plasma exchange with albumin replacement has resulted in flushing and hypotension in patients on concurrent ACE inhibitor therapy.[30] The latter is widely used in the management of hypertension or heart failure. It has been suggested that the reported symptoms are caused by rapid infusion of low levels of prekallikrein activator (a metabolite of clotting Factor XII) found in the albumin product, which activates prekallikrein to bradykinin, a naturally occurring vasoactive peptide. Metabolism of bradykinin is inhibited by the ACE inhibitor, leading to an accumulation of bradykinin.[30] Similar reactions have also been observed in association with the contact of plasma with negatively charged dialysis membranes, leukocyte reduction filters, low density lipoprotein adsorption columns, and

Staph protein A immunoadsorption columns. Similar to the postulated mechanism for the interaction of albumin and ACE inhibition, activation of clotting Factor XII by surface contact (typically with an anionic surface) together with blockage of ACE activity by an ACE inhibitor can result in an anaphylactoid reaction.[31] Some of the hypotensive reactions observed following platelet transfusion may be caused by a similar mechanism.[32]

Transfusion-Related Acute Lung Injury

Pathophysiology

TRALI should be considered whenever a transfusion recipient experiences acute respiratory insufficiency and/or X-ray findings are consistent with pulmonary edema, but without evidence of cardiac failure. The current incidence rate of TRALI is not known, but data from one institution in the 1980s suggest that this complication may occur as frequently as 1 in 5000 transfusions.[33] The severity of the respiratory distress is usually disproportional to the volume of blood infused, which is usually too small to produce hypervolemia. The reaction may include chills, fever, cyanosis, and hypotension. TRALI may result from multiple mechanisms. Transfused antibodies to HLA or neutrophil antigens may react with the recipient's leukocytes, causing a sequence of events that increase the permeability of the pulmonary microcirculation, so that fluid enters the alveolar air spaces.[33] Rarely, antibodies in the recipient's circulation may interact with transfused granulocytes and initiate the same events.[34] Severe pulmonary reactions, often of uncertain etiology, may occur after granulocyte transfusions, particularly in patients with known or inapparent lung infections or with conditions likely to allow prompt complement activation.[35]

Because specific antibodies may be absent, some cases of TRALI appear to result from other mechanisms; alternative causes may include complement activation to generate the anaphylatoxins C3a and C5a; direct aggregation of granulocytes into leukoemboli that lodge in the pulmonary microvasculature; or transfusion of cytokines that have accumulated in stored blood components. Recently, reactive lipid products from donor blood cell membranes have been implicated in the pathogenesis of TRALI.[36] These substances accumulate during blood bank storage and are capable of neutrophil priming with subsequent damage of pulmonary capillary endothelium in the recipient, particularly in the setting of sepsis. If any kind of acute pulmonary reaction is suspected, the transfusion should be stopped immediately and not resumed even if symptoms abate.

Treatment

Clinical management focuses on reversing progressive hypoxemia with oxygen therapy and ventilatory assistance, if necessary. Treatment often includes intravenous steroids, whose role is unproved. Most patients recover adequate pulmonary function within 2-4 days.[33,37]

Prevention

If antibody in donor plasma can be shown to have caused an acute pulmonary reaction, blood from that donor should not be used for plasma-containing components. No special precautions are needed for the patient if the problem was donor-specific and components from other donors are available.

Circulatory Overload

Pathophysiology

Transfusion therapy may cause acute pulmonary edema due to volume overload. Few data are available on the incidence rate of transfusion-induced circulatory overload in the general population, but young children and the elderly are considered most at risk, and incidence rates of up to 1% have been observed in a study of elderly orthopedic patients.[38] Rapid increases in blood volume are especially poorly tolerated by patients with compromised cardiac or pulmonary status and/or chronic anemia with expanded plasma volume. Infusion of 25% albumin, which shifts large volumes of interstitial fluid into the vascular space, may also cause circulatory overload. Hypervolemia must be considered if dyspnea, cyanosis, orthopnea, severe headache, hypertension, or congestive heart failure occur during or soon after transfusion.

Treatment

Symptoms usually improve when the infusion is stopped and the patient is placed in a sitting position. Diuretics and oxygen are often indicated and, if symptoms are not relieved, multiple medical interventions may be required, including phlebotomy.

Prevention

Except in conditions of ongoing, rapid blood loss, anemic patients should receive blood transfusions slowly. Administration of diuretics before and during the transfusion may be helpful. For very susceptible patients, the transfusion component can be divided, allowing part to be stored in the blood bank or transfusion service while the remainder is administered at a suitably slow rate.

Metabolic Reactions

Among the numerous complications that may accompany massive transfusion, metabolic abnormalities and coagulopathy are particularly important. Patients who are losing blood rapidly may have preexisting or coexisting coagulopathies or develop coagulopathies during resuscitation. Left ventricular function can be depressed by some or all of the following metabolic derangements: hypothermia from refrigerated blood; citrate toxicity; lactic acidosis from systemic underperfusion; and tissue ischemia, often complicated by hyperkalemia. Hemostatic abnormalities may include dilutional coagulopathy, DIC, shock, and liver and platelet dysfunction.

Citrate Toxicity

Pathophysiology. When large volumes of FFP, Whole Blood, or Platelets are transfused at rates exceeding 100 mL/minute, or at lower rates in the presence of liver disease, plasma citrate levels may rise with resultant symptomatic hypocalcemia through citrate binding of calcium. Hypocalcemia is more likely to cause clinical manifestations in patients who are in shock or are hypothermic. Prolonged apheresis procedures put patients and occasionally blood donors at some risk. Exchange transfusion, especially in tiny infants who are already ill, requires careful attention to all electrolytes.

Treatment and Prevention. Intravenous administration of calcium solutions to patients with hypocalcemia could cause iatrogenic hypercalcemia and ventricular arrhythmias. Unless a patient has a predisposing condition that hinders citrate metabolism, hypocalcemia due merely to citrate overload requires no treatment other than the slowing or discontinuation of the transfusion. Massively transfused patients or those with severe liver disease may benefit from measurement of ionized calcium levels as a guide to replacement therapy. Calcium should not be administered through the access line used for transfusion, and must never be added directly to the blood container, as the blood will clot.

Hypothermia

Pathophysiology. Ventricular arrhythmias may occur in patients who receive rapid infusions of large volumes of cold blood, especially if administered via central catheters positioned close to the cardiac conduction system.[39] Hypothermia increases the cardiac toxicity of hypocalcemia or hyperkalemia and can result in serious ventricular arrhythmias and poor left ventricular performance. Other complications of hypothermia include impaired hemostasis with development of a bleeding tendency and higher susceptibility to wound infections.[40] The use of high-volume blood warmers prevents the undesired hypothermic effects of rapid and massive transfusion of cold blood.

Treatment and Prevention. Hypothermia-induced arrhythmias may be avoided by pulling the catheter back from the cardiac atrium. Generalized effects of hypothermia can be prevented by reducing the rate of infusion, or by using blood warmers. AABB *Standards for Blood Banks and Transfusion Services* mandates that warming not cause hemolysis and that warming be done only by an FDA-approved device.[16(p67)] Attention to proper protocol is critical during the use of blood-warming devices, as overheating of blood can cause hemolysis which has resulted in fatalities.[7]

Hyperkalemia and Hypokalemia

Pathophysiology. When red cells are stored at 1-6 C, the potassium level in the supernatant plasma or additive solution increases. Rarely, this causes hyperkalemic problems in the recipient because of rapid dilution, redistribution into cells, and excretion after infusion. Hypokalemia is more of a threat,[41] as potassium-depleted red cells may extract potassium from the recipient's plasma and the bicarbonate metabolized from infused citrate may cause alkalosis, which in turn causes serum potassium to drop. Hyperkalemia is most likely to occur in massively transfused patients who are persistently hypotensive, who are poorly perfused, or who have lactic acidosis. Hyperkalemia may be a problem in premature infants and newborns receiving relatively large transfusions, such as in cardiac surgery or exchange transfusion.

Treatment and Prevention. No treatment or preventive strategy is usually necessary, provided the patient is adequately resuscitated from whatever condition required the massive transfusion. For large-volume transfusion to sick infants, many workers prefer red cells that are no more than 7-10 days old, but for small-volume transfusions, units may be safely used until their expiration date.[42]

Air Embolism

Air embolism can occur if blood in an open system is infused under pressure or if air enters the system while containers or blood administration sets are being changed. Symptoms include cough, dyspnea, chest pain, and shock.

If air embolism is suspected, the patient should be placed on the left side with the head down, to displace the air bubble from the pulmonic valve.[37] Aspiration of the air is sometimes attempted.

Air embolism was more of a threat when blood came in glass bottles than it is with plastic collection and administration systems. Proper use of infusion pumps, equipment for blood recovery or apheresis, and tubing couplers is, however, still essential to prevent this transfusion complication.

Evaluation of a Suspected Acute Transfusion Reaction

The Role of Clinical Personnel Attending the Patient

Medical personnel attending the patient are generally the first to suspect that a transfusion reaction has occurred and the first to take action.

1. If a transfusion reaction is suspected, the transfusion should be stopped to limit the volume of blood infused. All labels, forms, and patient identification should be checked to determine whether the transfused component was intended for the recipient. The transfusion service and the patient's physician should be notified immediately.

2. An intravenous line should be maintained with normal saline (0.9% sodium chloride) or other solution approved by the FDA for administration with blood, at least until a medical evaluation of the patient has been completed.

3. A responsible physician should evaluate the patient to determine whether a transfusion reaction has occurred, what kind it is, and what actions should be undertaken. The physician should evaluate the clinical findings with the possibilities in mind of acute hemolytic reaction, anaphylaxis, transfusion-induced sepsis, and TRALI, because these are conditions that require aggressive medical management and must be reported promptly to the laboratory.

4. If the observed events are limited to urticaria or circulatory overload, the transfusion service need not evaluate post-reaction blood or urine samples. If there are signs and symptoms other than urticaria or circulatory overload, and if there is even a possibility of acute HTR, anaphylaxis, TRALI, transfusion-induced sepsis, or other serious problems, a postreaction blood sample(s) should be sent to the laboratory for evaluation, as stipulated by institutional policy. The specimen(s) must be carefully drawn, to avoid mechanical hemolysis, and be properly labeled. In addition, the transfusion container (with whatever contents remain), the administration set (without the needle), the attached intravenous solutions, and all related forms and labels should be sent to the laboratory, following standard precautions. In some cases, a postreaction urine sample will be useful.

The Role of the Laboratory

The laboratory should perform three steps as soon as possible after receiving notification and the clinical material, regardless of what kind of component is thought to be implicated:

check for clerical errors, check for hemolysis, and check for evidence of blood group incompatibility by performing a direct antiglobulin test (DAT).

Check for Identification Errors. The identification of each patient's sample and donor's blood component must be checked for errors. If an error is discovered, the patient's physician or other responsible health-care professional must be notified immediately, and a search of appropriate records should be initiated to determine whether misidentification or incorrect issue of other specimens or components has put other patients at risk. Once the acute crisis has passed, each step of the transfusion process should be reviewed to find the source of error.

Visual Check for Hemolysis. The serum or plasma in a postreaction blood specimen must be inspected for evidence of hemolysis and compared against a prereaction sample, if available. Pink or red discoloration after, but not before, the reaction suggests destruction of red cells and release of free hemoglobin. Intravascular hemolysis of as little as 5-10 mL of red cells may produce visible hemoglobinemia.[43] Hemolysis due to poor collection technique or other medical interventions can cause hemoglobinemia; if faulty sampling is suspected, examination of a second specimen should resolve the question. Myoglobin, released from injured muscle, may also cause pink or red plasma and might be suspected if a patient has suffered severe trauma or muscle injury.[44] If the sample is not drawn until 5-7 hours after an episode of acute hemolysis, hemoglobin degradation products, especially bilirubin, may be in the bloodstream and cause yellow or brown discoloration. Rising bilirubin may begin as early as 1 hour postreaction, peak at 5-7 hours, and disappear within 24 hours, if liver function is normal.

In examining a postreaction urine specimen, it is important to differentiate among hematuria (intact red cells in the urine), hemoglobinuria (free hemoglobin in the urine), and myoglobinuria (free myoglobin in the urine). In acute HTRs, free hemoglobin released from damaged cells can cross the renal glomeruli and enter the urine, but hematuria and myoglobinuria would not be expected. Urine examination should be done on the supernatant fluid after centrifugation of a freshly collected specimen; misleading free hemoglobin may be present if previously intact red cells in a specimen undergo in-vitro hemolysis during transportation or storage.

Serologic Check for Incompatibility. A DAT must be performed on a postreaction specimen, preferably one anticoagulated with a chelating agent (such as EDTA), to avoid coating of red cells by complement proteins. If the postreaction DAT is positive, a DAT should be performed on red cells from the pretransfusion specimen (unless this had already been done as part of pretransfusion testing) and used for comparison. If transfused incompatible cells have been coated with antibody but not immediately destroyed, the postreaction specimen DAT is likely to be positive, often with a mixed-field agglutination pattern. If the transfused cells have been rapidly destroyed, the postreaction DAT may be negative if the specimen is drawn several hours later. Nonimmune hemolysis, eg, from thermal damage or mechanical trauma, causes hemogobinemia but not a positive DAT.

Additional Laboratory Evaluation

If any of the three initial checks and tests (error check, visual inspection for plasma-free hemoglobin, DAT) gives positive or suspicious results, the diagnosis of acute HTR should be vigorously pursued. Even if no error or apparent incompatibility is found, the possibility of acute HTR should still be considered if the patient's clinical presentation is strongly suggestive. The tests listed below help characterize the cause of the HTR, if one has occurred, or clarify the immunologic and serologic status of patients in whom the diagnosis is unclear. Some or all may be performed, following a written institutional protocol, at the discretion of the physician in charge of the transfusion service.

1. Perform ABO and Rh testing on the patient's prereaction and postreaction samples and on blood from the unit or an attached segment. If ABO and Rh typing on the prereaction and postreaction samples do not agree, there has been an error in patient or sample identification, or in testing. If sample mix-up or mislabeling has occurred, another patient's specimen may also have been incorrectly labeled; it is important to check records of all specimens received at approximately the same time. If blood in the bag is not of the ABO type noted on the bag label, there has been an error in unit labeling.

2. Perform antibody detection tests on prereaction and postreaction samples and on the donor blood. If a previously undetected antibody is discovered, it should be identified (see Chapter 19). Once the antibody is identified, retained samples from transfused donor units should be tested for the corresponding antigen. If a previously undiscovered antibody is present in a postreaction specimen but not in a prereaction sample, the reason may be anamnestic antibody production following a recent transfusion or, less likely, passive transfer of antibody in a recently transfused component. It may be desirable to use enhancement techniques, such as increased serum-to-cell ratio, low ionic strength saline, Polybrene®, polyethylene glycol, or enzyme techniques, when retesting the prereaction specimen.

3. Repeat crossmatch tests, with prereaction and postreaction samples in parallel. Even if the routine procedure is an immediate-spin or computer crossmatch, the antiglobulin technique should be applied to the investigative crossmatches.

4. Perform DAT and antibody detection tests on additional specimens obtained at intervals after the transfusion reaction. A first postreaction sample may have serologically undetectable levels of a significant alloantibody, especially if all the antibody molecules have attached to the incompatible transfused cells. In this event, antibody levels would rise rapidly, and antibody detection and identification would become possible within a few days.

5. Perform frequent checks of the patient's hematocrit or hemoglobin values, to see whether the transfused cells produce the expected therapeutic rise, or whether a decline occurs after an initial increase. In patients with sickle cell anemia, survival of transfused red cells can be followed by evaluation of the levels of hemoglobin A. In any patient with phenotypic differences between autologous and transfused cells, flow cytometry, if available, can be used to follow survival.[45]

6. Perform in-vivo red cell survival studies, if indicated, to demonstrate the rare occurrence of acute HTR in the absence of detectable alloantibody.[46] When the patient is phenotyped in preparation for such studies, it is important that the sample be one that contains only the patient's red cells. This may be difficult if the patient has received transfusions within the previous several weeks. Method 2.15 gives a technique for obtaining autologous red cells from a patient who has been transfused. If an antigen is present on the donor's red cells and absent from those of the patient, its presence or absence in postreaction samples indicates whether the transfused cells have survived and remained in the circulation.

7. Measure haptoglobin level if results can be obtained promptly enough to help in the diagnosis. It is important to compare prereaction and postreaction levels, and

to consider whether hemoglobin leakage from stored donor cells may have depressed posttransfusion haptoglobin levels.

8. Examine the blood remaining in the unit and the administration tubing for evidence of hemolysis, especially if a nonimmune HTR is suspected. Depending on how the blood was damaged, hemolysis may be present in the container and the administration tubing, or only in the administration tubing. For example, if a hypotonic solution had been added to the container, both the blood in the container and in the administration tubing would be hemolyzed. If a faulty infusion device had been used during blood administration, hemolysis might be present in the administration tubing, but not in the container.

9. Test the patient's serum for presence of anti-IgA if the presentation suggests an anaphylactic reaction.[25] Preliminary information can be obtained by quantitation of IgA, given that normal IgA levels generally preclude formation of class-specific anti-IgA.[27] However, the value of screening for IgA levels has been questioned. Subclass- or allotype-specific antibodies may develop in patients with normal IgA levels, and these have occasionally caused anaphylactic reactions.[25] Therefore, it has been recommended that IgA-deficient blood components be provided until the results of the test for anti-IgA are available.[25]

10. Examine the returned unit for any abnormal appearance, including clots or any brownish, opaque, muddy, or purple discoloration. If the clinical presentation suggests bacterial sepsis, a Gram's stain and aerobic and anaerobic bacterial cultures of the contents should be performed, even if the unit looks normal.[47] A segment from the donor unit (if available) may also be examined by smear and culture. Treatment for suspected bacterial contamination should be based on clinical considerations, as a delay in therapy may result in severe morbidity or death. Treatment includes prompt intravenous administration of antibiotics after blood and other appropriate cultures are obtained, combined with therapy for shock.

11. Examine the patient's pretransfusion sample and a sample of the donor's plasma for antibodies to HLA and/or neutrophil antigens, if the clinical presentation suggests TRALI. Crossmatching recipient lymphocytes or granulocytes with implicated donor sera can provide supportive evidence for TRALI.

Delayed Consequences of Transfusion

Alloimmunization to Red Cell Antigens

Pathophysiology

Primary alloimmunization, evidenced by appearance of newly formed antibodies to red cell antigens, becomes apparent weeks or months after transfusion. It has been estimated that alloimmunization occurs in unselected immunocompetent recipients with a risk of 1-1.6% per donor unit provided that D-negative recipients receive D-negative cellular components.[48] In a recent prospective study, overall 2.6% of transfused recipients became alloimmunized.[49] Hemolysis is generally not observed in this situation, because the cells that constitute the primary immune stimulus have usually disappeared before circulating antibody achieves a clinically significant level.

Serologic Observations. Once alloimmunization has occurred, antibodies may diminish to undetectable levels,[50] especially antibodies in the Kidd system (anti-Jk^a and anti-Jk^b). If red cells that express the antigen are subsequently transfused, however, an anamnestic response may cause the appearance, within hours or days, of IgG antibodies that react with the transfused red cells. If antibody attaches to the circulating donor cells, the patient's DAT may become positive even though serum antibody has not yet become detectable. In such a case, elution and identification of the antibody become important, as it may be several hours or longer before sufficient levels of the emerging antibody allow the detection and identification of the alloantibody in the serum. Once serum antibody becomes detectable, crossmatches are likely to be incompatible, but before that point, antigen-positive cells will appear to be suitable for transfusion. If an anamnestic response is discovered by the clinical laboratory, both the transfusion service director and the patient's clinician should be notified and the possibility of a delayed HTR (DHTR) should be investigated.

Delayed Reactions. In most cases, anamnestic antibody production causes only a delayed serologic reaction, but in some patients hemolysis will result from the combination of high antibody levels and large numbers of transfused red cells in the circulation. The reported frequency of clinically detectable hemolysis ranged from 1 in 11,000 to 1 in 5,000 transfusions,[49,51,52] or 0.05 to 0.07% of transfused recipients.[49,52] The most common presenting signs of a DHTR are fever, declining hemoglobin, and mild jaundice. Some DHTRs present as the absence of anticipated hemoglobin or hematocrit elevation after transfusion, or as a fever of unknown origin. Other clinical problems are infrequent; there may be unexplained jaundice, and hemoglobinuria is occasionally noted, but acute renal failure is uncommon.[53] If a DHTR is suspected, a freshly obtained blood sample may be tested for unexpected alloantibodies, both in the serum and, by DAT, on red cells. The results, if positive, should be compared with the patient's prior test results. Discovery of a previously unde-tected red cell antibody in a patient manifesting hemolysis strongly suggests a DHTR.

Treatment

Specific treatment is rarely necessary, although it may be prudent to monitor the patient's urine output and renal function and observe for changes in coagulation functions. If transfusions are still needed, donor units should be selected that lack the antigen corresponding to the newly discovered antibody. If such units are unavailable and transfusion is necessary, the risk of a possible overt, acute HTR should be weighed against the risk of delaying transfusion. Passenger lymphocyte hemolysis, a variant of DHTR, is covered in Chapter 26.

Prevention

Future transfusions for the patient should lack the antigen(s) responsible for the anamnestic response, even if the antibody again becomes undetectable. Some facilities issue a medical alert card with this information for the patient to carry and present at the time of hospitalization or transfusion in a different facility. It is to prevent these problems that *Standards* mandates permanent preservation of records of clinically significant antibodies, and review of previous records before red cells are issued for transfusion.[16(p57,83)]

Posttransfusion Autoantibody

Occasionally, transfusion of allogeneic platelets stimulates production of autoantibodies; in some of these patients, hemolytic anemia or thrombocytopenia may occur.[54] See Chapter 20 for more details.

Alloimmunization to Leukocyte Antigens and Refractoriness to Platelet Transfusions

See Chapter 16 and Chapter 17.

Transfusion-Associated Graft-vs-Host Disease

Transfusion-associated graft-vs-host disease (TA-GVHD) is a usually fatal immunologic transfusion complication associated with engraftment and clonal expansion of donor lymphocytes in a susceptible host.[55,56] The engrafted lymphocytes mount an immunologic attack against recipient tissues, including hematopoietic cells, leading to refractory pancytopenia with bleeding and infectious complications, which are primarily responsible for the 90-100% mortality rate in afflicted patients. TA-GVHD is rare in US transfusion recipients and has been observed almost exclusively in immunocompromised patients. In contrast, over 200 cases of TA-GVHD have been described in Japan alone,[57] with incidence rates reaching 1:660 patients undergoing cardiovascular surgery. Greater genetic homogeneity of the Japanese population and frequent use of fresh Whole Blood from related donors are thought to be the primary reasons for the surprisingly frequent occurrence of TA-GVHD in that country.

Pathophysiology

The pathophysiology of TA-GVHD is complex and incompletely understood. Key mechanisms include escape of donor T lymphocytes present in cellular blood components from immune clearance in the recipient and subsequent clonal expansion of these cells with immune destruction of host tissues. This results in some or all of the following clinical findings: fever; dermatitis or erythroderma, often starting on palms, soles, earlobes, and face, ranging from edema to full blistering; hepatitis, with elevations in alanine and aspartate aminotransferases, alkaline phosphatase, and bilirubin; enterocolitis, with 3-4 liters per day of secretory diarrhea; pancytopenia, with hypocellular marrow and a reduction in all marrow elements; and immunodeficiency. Cytokine dysfunction, recruitment of recipient cells into the immune reaction and release of biologic mediators, in particular nitric oxide, all play a role in the pathogenesis.[58] Clinical symptoms typically appear within 10-12 days of the transfusion.

Factors that determine an individual patient's risk for TA-GVHD include whether and to what degree the recipient is immunodeficient; the degree of HLA similarity between donor and recipient; and the number of transfused T lymphocytes capable of multiplication.[55] GVHD may occur in an immunologically normal recipient if the donor is homozygous for an HLA haplotype for which the recipient is heterozygous, and the component contains large numbers of viable T cells.

Treatment and Prevention

At present, there is no effective treatment for TA-GVHD, which emphasizes the need for prevention.

Gamma irradiation of cellular blood components is the accepted standard method to prevent TA-GVHD. The dose mandated by AABB *Standards* is a minimum of 2500 cGy targeted to the midplane of the container and a minimum dose of 1500 cGy delivered to all other parts of the component.[16(p25)] This renders T lymphocytes incapable of replication without affecting the function of red cells, platelets, and granulocytes.

AABB *Standards* recommends irradiation of cellular components in the following situations[16(p68-69)]: 1) cellular components intrauterine transfusions, 2) for patients identified at risk for TA-GVHD, 3) transfusions of cellular components between blood relatives, and 4) transfusion of HLA-selected products. Transfusion to transplant recipients of allogeneic marrow or peripheral blood progenitor cells is considered good practice. Published guidelines[59] specifically recommend component irradiation for patients who will be undergoing allogeneic hematopoietic transplantation imminently, neonates undergoing exchange transfusion or use of extracorporeal membrane oxygenation, and patients with Hodgkin's disease. Possible indications may include patients with marrow suppression and an absolute lymphocyte count less than 500/μL, low-birth-weight neonates, patients with opportunistic infections, and patients receiving ablative therapy in preparation for an autologous marrow transplant.

Posttransfusion Purpura

Posttransfusion purpura (PTP) is an uncommon event, although over 200 cases have now been published. It is characterized by abrupt onset of severe thrombocytopenia (platelet count <10,000/μL) 5-10 days following blood transfusion in a previously pregnant or transfused patient.[60] Patients are typically perimenopausal and postmenopausal women and rarely men. Most cases involve patients whose platelets lack the HPA-1a (Pl[A1]) antigen, which occurs in <2% of the population, and who form an antibody directed against this antigen. PTP is usually self-limited with full recovery, ie, a platelet count >100,000/μL, within 21 days. Historically, 10-15% of patients have been reported to die from PTP, typically from intracranial bleeding, and thus treatment is desirable.

Pathophysiology

The antibody destroys not only the transfused HPA-1a-positive platelets, but also the patient's own HPA-1a-negative platelets. The mechanism for the destruction of autologous platelets remains the subject of investigation. At least four possible mechanisms have been described and include 1) a "recycled" or solubilized antigen, 2) destruction mediated by antigen-antibody complex, 3) a cross-reacting antibody, and 4) an autoantibody.

Treatment

The role of steroids remains controversial. Plasma exchange typically achieves platelet counts of 20,000/μL in 1-2 days,[61] but the use of high-dose intravenous immunoglobulin (IVIG) is now supplanting this therapy.[61,62] With the use of IVIG, recovery to platelet counts of 100,000/μL is typically achieved within 4-5 days. The mechanism of action is thought to be due to either reticuloendothelial blockade or possibly nonspecific binding of immunoglobulin to platelet surfaces, thereby blocking the binding of the circulating antigen. As patients are completely refractory to random platelet transfusions, they are contraindicated. Antigen-negative platelets can be of benefit in PTP, and, in conjunction with IVIG, reversal of this disorder in 1 day is now possible.[63,64] Unfortunately, the time necessary to procure such platelets often limits their usefulness, as the patients are frequently no longer in danger of bleeding by the time such a platelet product becomes available.

Immunomodulatory Effects of Transfusion

Transfusion has been known to modulate immune responses at least since observations of improved renal allograft survival in transfused patients in the 1970s. This beneficial tolerance-inducing effect of transfusion raised concerns that transfusion may have other, adverse, effects in different clinical settings, including solid tumor recurrence and increased rates of postoperative bacterial infection.[65] Despite numerous retrospective, and several large prospective studies, the clinical significance of transfusion-associated immunomodulation and the usefulness of preventive strategies such as leukocyte reduction of transfused components remain controversial.[66] At a minimum the available data suggest that the relationship between transfusion and the immune system is more complex than previously considered.[67-69]

Iron Overload

Every red cell unit contains approximately 200 mg of iron. Chronically transfused patients, especially those with hemoglobinopathies, have progressive and continuous accumulation of iron and no physiologic means of excreting it. Storage occurs initially in reticuloendothelial sites, but when these are saturated, there is deposition in parenchymal cells. The threshold for clinical damage is lifetime exposure to greater than 50-100 units of red cells in a nonbleeding person.[70] Iron deposition interferes with function of the heart, liver, and endocrine glands; hepatic failure and cardiac toxicity cause most of the morbidity and mortality.

Treatment is directed at removing iron without reducing the patient's circulating hemoglobin. Metered subcutaneous infusion of deferoxamine, an iron-chelating agent, is valuable for reducing body iron stores in such patients, but the regimen of nightly infusion by subcutaneous pumping is both arduous and expensive, and often compromises compliance. In chronic red cell transfusion-dependent patients with hemoglobinopathies, prophylactic use of neocytes to prolong the intertransfusion interval[5] or red cell exchange to minimize additional iron loads[6] have been used.

Records of Transfusion Complications

Each transfusion service must maintain indefinitely the records of patients who have had transfusion complications or evidence of alloimmunization. Possible cases of blood contamination and transmission of disease must also be reported to the institution where the blood was drawn.

Records must be kept, and consulted, to prevent patients who have had a transfusion reaction from being exposed to known offending agents in subsequent transfusions. For example, patients with a history of IgA-related anaphylactic reactions should be transfused with plasma products that lack IgA. A history of repeated or severe FNH reactions might prompt the use of leukocyte-reduced cellular blood components. Patients with red cell alloantibodies sometimes test negative in an

antibody detection test, if sufficient time has passed between the stimulating event and testing.[50] Routine checking of records for evidence of past alloimmunization can prevent some DHTRs. Routine checking of previous results of ABO and Rh testing may disclose an error in testing or in the identification of a current sample.

Records of Patients with Special Needs

In addition to records of transfusion reactions, transfusion services should maintain records of patients who need specially prepared or manipulated components. This is especially important in institutions where physicians rotate frequently, and the need for irradiated, leukocyte-reduced, or IgA-deficient components may not be known to a particular physician writing an individual order.

Reporting Transfusion Fatalities

Fatalities resulting directly from the effects of transfusion must be reported to the Director, Office of Compliance, Center for Biologics Evaluation and Research, FDA, within 24 hours and by written report within 7 days (21 CFR 606.170). Patients who are critically ill and near death often receive transfusions in close temporal proximity to death, and clinical suspicion of cause and effect may occasionally be raised. The overwhelming majority of deaths are unrelated to transfusion, but if there is a suggestion that a transfusion might have contributed to death, it may be prudent to pursue an investigation.

In the absence of such errors as administration of ABO-incompatible blood or of physiologic events clearly attributable to acute hemolysis, anaphylaxis, TRALI, or sepsis, transfusion is highly unlikely to be acutely responsible for death. The review should include all available medical and laboratory records and results of an autopsy, if performed.

On the other hand, if an investigation does reveal evidence or possibility of hemolysis, anaphylactic or pulmonary events, unexplained sepsis, or ambiguous identification records, the case may warrant more extensive inquiry.

References

1.   Popovsky MA, ed. Transfusion reactions. Bethesda, MD: AABB Press, 1996.
2.   DeChristopher PJ, Anderson RR. Risks of transfusion and organ and tissue transplantation: Practical concerns that drive practical policies. Am J Clin Pathol 1997;107(Suppl 1):S2-S11.
3.   US General Accounting Office. Blood supply: Transfusion-associated risks. GAO/PEMD-97-2. Washington, DC: US Government Printing Office, 1997.
4.   Heddle NM, Kelton JG. Febrile nonhemolytic transfusion reactions. In: Popovsky MA, ed. Transfusion reactions. Bethesda, MD: AABB Press, 1996:45-80.
5.   Spanos T, Ladis V, Palamidou F, et al. The impact of neocyte transfusion in the management of thalassemia. Vox Sang 1996;70(4):217-23.
6.   Adams DM, Schultz WH, Ware RE, Kinney TR. Erythrocytapheresis can reduce iron overload and prevent the need for chelation therapy in chronically transfused pediatric patients. J Pediatr Hematol Oncol 1996;18(1):46-50.
7.   Sazama K. Report of 355 transfusion-associated deaths: 1976-1985. Transfusion 1990; 30:583-90.
8.   Davenport RD, Kunkel SL. Cytokine roles in hemolytic and non-hemolytic transfusion reactions. Transfus Med Rev 1994;8:157-68,85-97.
9.   Davenport RD. Inflammatory cytokines in hemolytic transfusion reactions. In: Davenport RD, Snyder EL, eds. Cytokines in transfusion medicine: A primer. Bethesda, MD: AABB Press, 1996.
10. Capon SM, Goldfinger D. Acute hemolytic transfusion reaction, a paradigm of the systemic inflammatory response: New insights into pathophysiology and treatment. Transfusion 1995;35:513-20 (Erratum in Transfusion 1995;35:794.)
11. Linden JV, Paul B, Dressler KP. A report of 104 transfusion errors in New York State. Transfusion 1992;32:601-6.
12. Simon T. Proficiency testing program. CAP Survey 1991 J-C. Northfield, IL: College of American Pathologists, 1991.
13. Berte LM, ed. A model quality system for the transfusion service. Bethesda, MD: American Association of Blood Banks, 1997.
14. Shulman IA, Lohr K, Derdiarian A, Picukaric JM. Monitoring transfusionist practices: A strategy for improving transfusion safety. Transfusion 1994;34:11-5.
15. Beauregard P, Blajchman MA. Hemolytic and pseudo-hemolytic transfusion reactions: An overview of the hemolytic transfusion reactions and the clinical conditions that mimic them. Transfus Med Rev 1994;8:184-99.
16. Menitove J, ed. Standards for blood banks and transfusion services. 19th ed. Bethesda, MD: American Association of Blood Banks, 1999.
17. Blajchman MA. Transfusion-associated bacterial sepsis: The phoenix rises yet again. Transfusion 1994;34:940-2.
18. Ferrara JLM. The febrile platelet transfusion reaction: A cytokine shower. Transfusion 1995;35: 89-90.
19. Davenport RD, Burdick M, Moore SA, Kunkel SL. Cytokine production in IgG-mediated red cell incompatibility. Transfusion 1993;33:19-24.
20. Brand A. Passenger leukocytes, cytokines, and transfusion reactions. N Engl J Med 1994;331: 670-1.
21. Widmann FK. Controversies in transfusion medicine: Should a febrile transfusion response occasion the return of the blood component to the blood bank? Pro. Transfusion 1994;34:356-8.
22. Oberman HA. Controversies in transfusion medicine: Should a febrile transfusion response occasion the return of the blood component to the blood bank? Con. Transfusion 1994;34:353-5.
23. Lane TA, ed. Blood transfusion therapy: A physician's handbook. 5th ed. Bethesda, MD: American Association of Blood Banks, 1996.
24. Dzieczkowski JS, Barrett BB, Nester D, et al. Characterization of reactions after exclusive transfusion of white cell-reduced cellular blood components. Transfusion 1995;35:20-5.
25. Vamvakas EC, Pineda AA. Allergic and anaphylactic reactions. In: Popovsky MA, ed. Transfusion reactions. Bethesda, MD: AABB Press, 1996:81-123.
26. Greenberger PA. Plasma anaphylaxis and immediate type reactions. In: Rossi EC, Simon TL, Moss GS, Gould SA, eds. Principles of transfusion medicine. 2nd ed. Baltimore, MD: Williams and Wilkins, 1995:765-71.
27. Sandler SG, Eckrich R, Malamut D, et al. Hemagglutination assays for the diagnosis and prevention of IgA anaphylactic transfusion reactions. Blood 1994;84:2031-5.
28. Sandler SG, Mallory D, Malamut D, Eckrich R. IgA anaphylactic transfusion reactions. Transfus Med Rev 1995;9:1-8.
29. Pineda AA, Zylstra VW, Clare DE, et al. Viability and functional integrity of washed platelets. Transfusion 1989;29:524-7.
30. Owen HG, Brecher ME. Atypical reactions associated with use of angiotensin-converting enzyme inhibitors and apheresis. Transfusion 1994;34:891-4.
31. Shiba M, Tadokoro K, Sawanobori M, et al. Activation of the contact system by filtration of platelet concentrates with a negatively charged white cell-removal filter and measurement of venous blood bradykinin level in patients who received filtered platelets. Transfusion 1997;37:457-62.
32. Hume HA, Popovsky MA, Benson K, et al. Hypotensive reactions: A previously uncharacterized complication of platelet transfusion? Transfusion 1996;36:904-9.
33. Popovsky MA, Moore SB. Diagnostic and pathogenetic considerations in transfusion-related acute lung injury. Transfusion 1985;25:573-7.
34. Clay ME, Stroncek DF. Granulocyte immunology. In: Anderson KC, Ness PM, eds. Scientific basis of transfusion medicine. Philadelphia: WB Saunders, 1994:244-79.
35. McCullough J. Granulocyte transfusion. In: Petz LD, Swisher SN, Kleinman S, et al, eds. Clinical

practice of transfusion medicine, 3rd ed. New York: Churchill Livingstone, 1996:413-32.

36. Silliman CC, Paterson AJ, Dickey WO, et al. The association of biologically active lipids with the development of transfusion-related acute lung injury: A retrospective study. Transfusion 1997;37:719-26.

37. Jenner PW, Holland PV. Diagnosis and management of transfusion reactions. In: Petz LD, Swisher SN, Kleinman S, et al, eds. Clinical practice of transfusion medicine, 3rd ed. New York: Churchill Livingstone, 1996:905-29.

38. Audet AM, Popovsky MA, Andrzejewski C. Transfusion-associated circulatory overload in orthopedic surgery patients: A multi-institutional study. Immunohematology 1996;12(2):87-9.

39. Iserson KV, Huestis DW. Blood warming: Current applications and techniques. Transfusion 1991;31:558-71.

40. Sessler DI. Current concepts: Mild perioperative hypothermia. N Engl J Med 1997;336:1730-7.

41. Stack G, Judge JV, Snyder EL. Febrile and nonimmune transfusion reactions. In: Rossi EC, Simon TL, Moss GS, Gould SA, eds. Principles of transfusion medicine. 2nd ed. Baltimore, MD: Williams and Wilkins, 1996:773-84.

42. Liu EA, Manino FL, Lane TA. Prospective, randomized trial of the safety and efficacy of a limited donor exposure transfusion program for premature neonates. J Pediatr 1994;125:92-6.

43. Domen RE. Proficiency testing program. CAP Survey 1994 J-A. Northfield, IL: College of American Pathologists, 1994.

44. Henry JB. Clinical diagnosis and management by laboratory methods. 19th ed. Philadelphia: WB Saunders, 1996.

45. Nance ST. Flow cytometry in transfusion medicine. In: Anderson KC, Ness PM, eds. Scientific basis of transfusion medicine. Philadelphia: WB Saunders, 1994:707-25.

46. Baldwin ML, Barrasso C, Ness PM, Garratty G. A clinically significant erythrocyte antibody detectable only by ^{51}Cr survival studies. Transfusion 1983;23:40-4.

47. Sazama K. Bacteria in blood for transfusion: A review. Arch Pathol Lab Med 1994;118:350-65.

48. Lostumbo MM, Holland PV, Schmidt PJ. Isoimmunization after multiple transfusions. N Engl J Med 1966;275:141-4.

49. Heddle NM, Soutar RL, O'Hoski PL, et al. A prospective study to determine the frequency and clinical significance of alloimmunization post-transfusion. Br J Hematol 1995;91:1000-5.

50. Ramsey G, Smietana SJ. Long-term follow-up testing of red cell alloantibodies. Transfusion 1994;34:122-4.

51. Ness PM, Shirey RS, Thoman SK, Buck SA. The differentiation of delayed serologic and delayed hemolytic transfusion reactions: Incidence, long-term serologic findings, and clinical significance. Transfusion 1990;30:688-93.

52. Vamvakas EC, Pineda AA, Reisner R, et al. The differentiation of delayed hemolytic and serologic transfusion reactions: Incidence and predictors of hemolysis. Transfusion 1995;35:26-32.

53. Brecher ME. Hemolytic transfusion reactions. In: Rossi EC, Simon TL, Moss GS, Gould SA, eds. Principles of transfusion medicine. 2nd ed. Baltimore, MD: Williams and Wilkins, 1996:747-63.

54. Garratty G. Autoimmune hemolytic anemia. In: Garratty G, ed. Immunobiology of transfusion medicine. New York: Marcel Dekker, 1994:493-521.

55. Sazama K, Holland P. Transfusion-induced graft-versus-host disease. In: Garratty G, ed. Immunobiology of transfusion medicine. New York: Marcel Dekker, 1994:631-56.

56. Shivdasani RA, Anderson KC. Graft-versus-host disease. In: Petz LD, Swisher SN, Kleinman S, et al, eds. Clinical practice of transfusion medicine. 3rd ed. New York: Churchill Livingstone, 1996:931-46.

57. Ohto H, Anderson KC. Survey of transfusion-associated graft-versus-host disease in immunocompetent recipients. Transfus Med Rev 1996;10:31-43.

58. Ferrara JLM. Cytokine dysregulation as a mechanism of graft versus host disease. Curr Opin Immunol 1993;5:794-9.

59. Przepiorka D, LeParc GF, Stovall MA, et al. Use of irradiated blood components. Practice Parameter. Am J Clin Pathol 1996;106:6-11.

60. McFarland JG. Alloimmune thrombocytopenias. In: Rossi EC, Simon TL, Moss GS, Gould SA, eds. Principles of transfusion medicine. 2nd ed. Baltimore, MD: Williams and Wilkins, 1995:297-307.

61. McLeod BC, Strauss RG, Ciavarella D, et al. Management of hematological disorders and cancers. J Clin Apheresis 1996:211-30.

62. Mueller-Eckhardt C, Kiefel V. High-dose IgG for post-transfusion purpura-revisited. Blut 1988;57:163-7.

63. Brecher ME, Moore SB, Letendre L. Posttransfusion purpura: The therapeutic value of PL^{A1}-negative platelets. Transfusion 1990;30:433-5.

64. Win N, Matthey F, Slater NGP. Blood components—Transfusion support in post-transfusion purpura due to HPA-1a immunization. Vox Sang 1996;71:191-3.

65. Blumberg N, Heal JM. Effects of transfusion on immune function: Cancer recurrence and infection. Arch Pathol Lab Med 1994;118:371-9.

66. Blajchman MA. Allogeneic blood transfusions, immunomodulation, and postoperative bacterial infection: Do we have the answers yet? Transfusion 1997;37:121-5.

67. Vamvakas EC. Perioperative blood transfusion and cancer recurrence: Meta-analysis for explanation. Transfusion 1995;35:760-8.

68. Tietze M, Kluter H, Troch M, Kirchner H. Immune responsiveness in orthopedic surgery patients after transfusion of autologous or allogeneic blood. Transfusion 1995;35:378-83.

69. Vamvakas EC, Blajchman MA, eds. Immunomodulatory effects of blood transfusion. Bethesda, MD: AABB Press, 1999.

70. Sharon BI, Honig GR. Management of congenital hemolytic anemias. In: Rossi EC, Simon TL, Moss GS, Gould SA, eds. Principles of transfusion medicine. 2nd ed. Baltimore, MD: Williams and Wilkins, 1996:141-59.

28

Infectious Complications of Blood Transfusion

Hepatitis

AS A RESULT OF THE ACCELERATED introduction of new tests and procedures to enhance safety, the risk of acquiring an infectious disease from a transfusion in the United States is lower today than ever before (see Table 28-1).[1-4] However, viral, bacterial, and parasitic diseases are still rarely transmitted by transfusions, and there is also the potential for novel infectious agents entering the blood supply. This chapter summarizes the major infectious risks of transfusion; the interested reader is referred to recent textbooks[5,6] and reports[2,7] that review these and other potential infectious complications in greater detail.

Hepatitis is inflammation of the liver that can be caused by many different toxic and infectious agents, including hepatitis A-E, and G viruses (HAV, HBV, HCV, HDV, HEV, HGV), as well as cytomegalovirus (CMV) and Epstein-Barr virus (EBV). Infectious agents pose a serious threat to transfusion recipients if they persist in the circulation of asymptomatic blood donors and can cause clinically significant acute or chronic disease manifestations in recipients.

The vast majority of posttransfusion hepatitis in the past was attributable to HBV and HCV, both of which can establish prolonged carrier states in donors characterized by high-titer viremia in the absence of symptoms. HBV and HCV also cause significant long-term liver-related morbidity and mortality.[7] These viruses will be considered in detail (see below).

Table 28-1. Infectious Risks of Blood Transfusion in the United States

Infectious Agent or Outcome	Estimated Risk/Unit Transfused	Estimated Transmission Rate of At-Risk Units (%)*	Reference
Virus			
Human immunodeficiency virus, types 1 and 2[†]	1:493,000 (1:2,778,000-1:202,000)	90	1
Human T cell lymphotropic virus, types I and II[†]	1:641,000 (1:2,000,000-1:256,000)	30	1
Hepatitis A virus	1:1 million	90	2
Hepatitis B virus[†]	1:63,000 (1:147,000-1:31,000)	70	1, 2
Hepatitis C virus[†]	1:103,000 (1:288,000-1:28,000)	90	1
Parvovirus	1:40,000-1:3,300	Low?	3, 4
Bacteria[‡]			
Red Blood Cells	1:500,000	N/A	2
Platelets	1:10,200		
Platelets, Pheresis	1:19,500		
Parasites			
Trypanosoma cruzi	1:42,000	<10	2
Malaria, babesia	Rare (<1:1 million)	Not reported	2

* Defined as units that are either screening test confirmed positive (HIV, HTLV, HBV, HCV, *T. cruzi*), viremic (HAV, parvovirus), or parasitemic (malaria, babesia).
[†] Risk projections are based on window period transmissions (95% confidence interval). Estimates for HIV risk do not consider the impact of HIV-1 antigen testing.
[‡] Septic reaction caused by bacterial toxins, rather than infection.

HAV and HEV, which are enterically transmitted viruses, circulate only transiently during the acute phase of infection. Because the viremic individual is usually clinically ill and not a candidate for donation, HAV and HEV are not a serious threat to transfusion recipients. However, HAV viremia may be present for up to 28 days before symptoms develop, and isolated cases have been reported associated with transfusion of cellular components[8] and Factor VIII concentrate.[9] Because HAV lacks a lipid envelope, it is not inactivated by solvent/detergent treatment; additional inactivation methods are under development to prevent recurrence of such outbreaks. HEV is exceedingly rare in the United States, and there have been no documented cases of transfusion transmission.

HDV, formerly called the delta agent, can cause infection and serious hepatitis after transfusion or other parenteral exposure. However, as HDV is a defective virus only found in HBV carriers, screening donors for HBV infection simultaneously eliminates the risk of HDV.[5] HGV (also called GBV-C) is a recently discovered virus, distantly related to HCV, which has a high prevalence rate (>1%) among asymptomatic donors. Although HGV is unequivocally transfusion-transmissible,[10] a causal relationship has not been established (despite intensive study) between HGV infection and hepatitis or any other disease manifestation. Although HGV infection has been detected in a small fraction of patients with transfusion- and community-acquired hepatitis, these cases are very mild, and it is unclear if HGV is causative or coincidental.[11] Another recently identified agent, TTV, appears similar to HGV with respect to prevalence and transmissibility but there is a lack of clinical disease significance. Thus, screening blood donors for HGV and TTV is not currently recommended. Hepatitis associated with CMV and EBV is also very mild in the absence of severe immunodepression; therefore, screening for this purpose is not recommended, except in unusual situations.[12]

Clinical Manifestations of Hepatitis

Most individuals who acquire HBV or HCV infection have a subclinical primary infection without obvious symptoms or physical evidence of disease. Some develop overt hepatitis with jaundice, nausea, vomiting, abdominal discomfort, fatigue, dark urine, and elevation of liver enzymes. Signs and symptoms usually resolve spontaneously. Acute hepatitis C tends to be milder than hepatitis B. Rarely, the clinical course of HBV and HCV infections may be complicated by fulminant hepatitis. Of greater concern is a propensity of these infections to evolve to chronic hepatitis, with a significant proportion demonstrating long-term progression to cirrhosis, liver failure, or hepatocellular carcinoma. Hepatitis A and E tend to be clinically mild in otherwise healthy hosts and virtually never progress to chronic hepatitis or a chronic carrier state.[13] A clinical disease association for hepatitis G has yet to be documented.

Chronic Carriers of HBV

After initial HBV infection, a proportion of patients fail to clear infectious material from the bloodstream and become chronic carriers for years or even for life. HBV carriers produce, in addition to the infectious viral particle, large amounts of noninfectious envelope protein detected by the assay for hepatitis B surface antigen (HBsAg). The risk of becoming an HBsAg carrier is strongly age-dependent; about 5% of those infected with HBV as adults become chronic HBsAg carriers, while 95% recover completely and develop protective antibody against HBsAg (anti-HBs). In contrast, 90% or more of infants infected perinatally become carriers, and many progress to cirrhosis and cancer. According to World Health Organization estimates the number of HBsAg carriers is expected to reach 400 million worldwide[14] with a prevalence of up to 10% in some Asian countries, 0.1-0.5% in the general US population, and 0.02-0.04% in US blood donors. A small proportion (<10%) of HBsAg carriers develop clinical manifestations such as hepatic insufficiency, cirrhosis, or hepatocellular carcinoma.

Chronic Carriers of HCV

Most people who are initially infected with HCV become chronic HCV carriers, with approximately 85% having persistent HCV RNA in the serum and liver for years to decades. At least 50% of such HCV carriers have biochemical and histologic evidence of chronic liver disease.[15] Despite this chronic inflammatory process, most HCV-infected individuals remain asymptomatic. However, at least 20% of patients develop cirrhosis within 20 years of chronic HCV infection, and 1-5% may develop hepatocellular carcinoma if chronic infection persists for more than 20 years. Recommendations for clinical management of persons with chronic HCV infection were developed by a National Institutes of Health consensus conference.[7,16]

Markers of Viral Infection

Laboratory tests can identify markers of previous exposure and probable current infectivity for HBV and HCV, which are useful for screening and diagnostic applications. Table 28-2

..

Table 28-2. Molecular and Serologic Tests in the Diagnosis of Viral Hepatitis

Virus			Test Reactivity					Interpretation
HBV	DNA	HBsAg	Anti-HBc		Anti-HBs	HBeAg	Anti-HBe	
			Total	IgM				
	+	+	+/–	+/–	–	+/–	–	Early acute HBV infection/chronic carrier
	+	+	+	+	–	+	–	Acute infection
	+/–	–	+	+	–	+/–	+/–	Early convalescent infection/possible early chronic carrier
	+/–	+	+	–	–	+/–	+/–	Chronic carrier*
	–	–	+	–	+	–	+/–	Recovered infection
	–	–	–	–	+	–	–	Vaccinated or recovered infection
	–	–	+	–	–	–	–	Recovered infection? False positive?
	+	–	–	–	–	–	–	Window period

Virus	RNA	HBsAg	Anti-HBc	Anti-HBs	Anti-Delta	Interpretation
HDV	+	+	+	–	+	Acute or chronic HDV infection
	–	–	+	+	+	Recovered infection

Virus	RNA	Anti-HCV (Screening EIA)	Recombinant Antigens (RIBA)				Interpretation
			5-1-1	c100-3	c33c	c22-3	
HCV	+/–	+	Not available				Possible acute or chronic HCV infection
	–	+	–	–	–	–	False positive

						Interpretation
+/–	+	+	+	–	–	Probable false positive (if RNA is negative); possible acute infection (if RNA is positive)†
+/–	+	–	+	+	+	Early acute, or chronic infection (if RNA is positive); false positive or late recovery (if RNA is negative)†
+	+	+/–	+	+	+	Acute or chronic infection
–	+/–	+	+	+	+	Recovered HCV†

HAV	RNA	Anti-HAV		Interpretation
		Total	IgM	
	+	+	+	Acute HAV
	–	+	–	Recovered HAV/vaccinated

HEV	RNA	Anti-HEV		Interpretation
		Total	IgM	
	+	+	+	Acute HAV
	+	+	–	Recovered HEV

HBsAg = hepatitis B surface antigen; anti-HBc = antibody to hepatitis B core antigen; anti-HBs = antibody to HBsAg; HBeAg = hepatitis B e antigen; anti-delta = antibody to delta antigen; anti-HAV = antibody to hepatitis A virus; anti-HCV = antibody to hepatitis C virus; anti-HEV = antibody to hepatitis E virus; SC = seroconversion.

* Those with HBeAg are more infectious and likely to transmit vertically.

† Anti-5-1-1 and anti-c100-3 generally appear later than anti-c22-3 and anti-c33c during seroconversion and may disappear spontaneously, during immunosuppression or after successful antiviral therapy.[11]

lists the molecular and serologic markers commonly used in the diagnosis of hepatitis. Figure 28-1 illustrates the sequence of test results typical of individuals with acute HBV infection that completely resolves. The period between exposure to HBV and emergence of circulating markers of infection (HBV DNA or HBsAg) is usually about 2-6 weeks.[8,13] HBV DNA (detectable by nucleic acid amplification techniques) is the first marker to appear, followed by detectable HBsAg 5-10 days later. Antibody to the HBV core protein (anti-HBc) usually appears several weeks later, first as IgM and then as IgG. The clearance of HBsAg and appearance of anti-HBs signal resolution of infection. Two additional HBV markers, HBeAg or its antibody (anti-HBe), are useful diagnostic and prognostic markers but are not employed in donor screening. An asymptomatic HBsAg-positive individual may either be in the early phase of acute HBV infection (without anti-HBc or with IgM anti-HBc) or a chronic HBV carrier (with IgG anti-HBc). HBsAg particles are produced in excess during acute and chronic infection;

blood from individuals with circulating HBsAg can infect others. Current screening immunoassays detect approximately 0.1 to 0.2 ng/mL HBsAg or approximately 3×10^7 particles.[8] The number of HBsAg particles in most acute and chronic infections exceeds this level, but transmission of HBV from HBsAg seronegative donors has been described. Polymerase chain reaction allows detection of as few as 10 genomic copies of HBV DNA,[8] but not all detected viral DNA appears to be infectious.[13] The value of adding genomic amplification testing to blood donor screening is under investigation.[17] HBV vaccines contain noninfectious HBsAg protein, which may result in false-positive HBsAg screening test results for a few days following the inoculation. Resulting protective antibodies are directed against HBsAg; vaccination does not produce anti-HBc.

Figure 28-2 shows the proposed structure of the genome of HCV and the specific gene products incorporated in test kits for anti-HCV. Tests for antibodies to HCV are enzyme

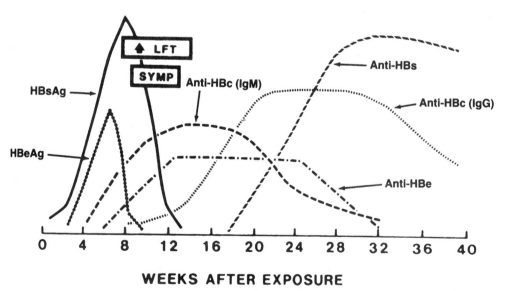

WEEKS AFTER EXPOSURE

Figure 28-1. Serologic markers in hepatitis B virus infection that resolved without complications. In the acute phase, markers often appear before onset of liver function (LFT) abnormalities and symptoms (SYMP). Anti-HBs and anti-HBc persist after recovery and indicate immunity. In chronic carriers (not shown) HbsAg persists and anti-HBc is usually present, while anti-HBs is absent (HBeAg and anti-HBe may be present, see Table 28-2). HBV DNA (not shown) may be detected approximately 1-2 weeks before HBsAg.

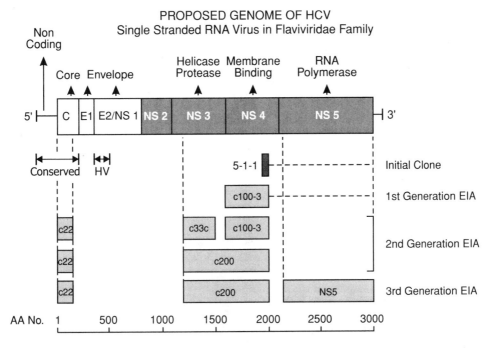

Figure 28-2. Proposed HCV genome and recombinant proteins used in testing for anti-HCV. The second-generation test for anti-HCV detects antibody to c200 (including c33c and c100-3) and c22-3. Capability for antibody detection to a nonspecific protein (NS-5) was added in the third-generation test (reprinted with permission from Alter[15]).

immunoassays (EIAs) using recombinant antigens of HCV coated on a solid phase as the capture reagent. Anti-HCV is detectable by third-generation EIAs approximately 10 weeks after infection. HCV RNA is present at high concentrations in plasma during most of the period from exposure to antibody seroconversion. Anti-HCV is detected in 40-50% of samples from patients at initial diagnosis of acute hepatitis, either transfusion- or community-acquired.[18]

The clinical significance of a positive screening test for anti-HCV in healthy blood donors is unclear without supplemental testing. Between 0.5 and 1.4% of US blood donors have repeatedly reactive EIA results.[8] Approximately 0.3% have asymptomatic chronic HCV infection,[19] and their blood is potentially infective; others have false-positive results. A recombinant immunoblot assay (RIBA) has been licensed by the Food and Drug Administration

(FDA) for further differentiation of repeatedly reactive EIA results. An individual who is positive by RIBA is considered to have true anti-HCV antibody; in 70-90% of these cases, HCV nucleic acid is detectable by polymerase chain reaction (PCR). The infectivity of units that are positive for HCV RNA approaches 100%.[20,21] In contrast, EIA-reactive donors with negative or indeterminate RIBA results are rarely infected or infectious. Regardless of RIBA results, a donation with a repeatedly reactive EIA result cannot be used for transfusion. Donors with negative RIBA results may be considered for reentry (Table 28-3).

Surrogate Markers

Before HCV was identified and anti-HCV testing feasible, several tests on donor blood were introduced to reduce the risk of non-A,non-B (NANB) hepatitis following transfusion. In 1987, the AABB mandated testing whole blood

Table 28-3. Reentry of Donors with Repeatedly Reactive Screening Tests

	Repeatedly Reactive for					Reentry Status
Anti-HIV-1 or -1/2	Anti-HIV-2	HIV-1-Ag	HBsAg	Anti-HCV		
Initial sample						
Licensed Western blot positive or indeterminate or IFA reactive	Different HIV-2 EIA RR	Confirmed by neutralization	Confirmed by neutralization or anti-HBc RR	RIBA indeterminate or positive		Not eligible for reentry
Licensed Western blot or IFA NR	Different HIV-2 EIA NR and licensed Western blot or IFA NR	Not confirmed by neutralization	HBsAg specificity not confirmed by neutralization and anti-HBc NR	RIBA negative		Evaluate for reentry
Follow-up sample						
(drawn 6 months later)	(drawn 6 months later)	(drawn 8 weeks later)	(drawn 8 weeks later)	(drawn 6 months later)		
EIA RR or Western blot positive or indeterminate or IFA reactive	RR HIV-1 or different HIV-2 EIA RR or a licensed Western blot or IFA reactive or indeterminate	HIV-1-Ag RR, neutralization confirmed or not confirmed	HBsAg RR or anti-HBc RR	EIA RR or RIBA indeterminate or positive		Not eligible for reentry
Original EIA method NR and whole virus lysate anti-HIV-1 EIA NR and licensed Western blot or IFA NR	Screening test and a different HIV-2 EIA NR and licensed Western blot or IFA NR	HIV-1-Ag and anti-HIV-2 EIA NR or HIV-1-Ag RR, not confirmed (temporary deferral for additional 8 weeks)	HBsAg NR and anti-HBc NR	Licensed multiantigen EIA method NR and RIBA negative		Eligible for reentry

NR=nonreactive; RR=repeatedly reactive; RIBA=recombinant immunoblot assay; IFA=immunofluorescence assay; EIA=enzyme immunoassay; anti-HIV-1=antibody to human immunodeficiency virus, type 1; anti-HIV-2=antibody to human immunodeficiency virus, type 2; HIV-1-Ag=HIV-1 antigen; HBsAg=hepatitis B surface antigen; anti-HCV=antibody to hepatitis C virus; anti-HBc=antibody to hepatitis B core.

donations for alanine aminotransferase (ALT) and anti-HBc as surrogates for the direct detection of the NANB agent. Current very sensitive tests for anti-HCV have essentially eliminated the value of surrogate tests in preventing hepatitis.[23] AABB *Standards for Blood Banks and Transfusion Services* no longer requires ALT testing and allows reentry of otherwise suitable donors who had previously been excluded solely because of elevated ALT.[24] Anti-HBc testing is continued, pending further study of its value in the prevention of HBV transmission.

Current Risk of Posttransfusion Hepatitis

The risk of posttransfusion HBV or HCV infection has decreased dramatically, from an estimated 1% per unit risk only a decade ago to an estimated 1 in 60,000-100,000 risk today (see Table 28-1 and Fig 28-3).[19] The development of progressively improved HCV antibody tests, combined with stringent selection measures for donors, has contributed to this remarkable decline.[25] The anticipated introduction of nu-

cleic acid screening assays for HCV offers the promise of virtual eradication of this transfusion complication.[26]

Quarantine and Recipient Tracing (Look-Back)

Donations with repeatedly reactive screening test results (HBsAg, anti-HBc, anti-HCV) cannot be used for transfusion. In addition, in-date units from collections preceding the current unsuitable donation may need to be quarantined as follows:

- Extending back 10 years or 12 months from the most recent negative test result for anti-HCV repeatedly reactive confirmed or not tested units.

- Extending back 5 years or 12 months from the most recent negative test result for anti-HBs and anti HBc repeatedly reactive confirmed or not tested units.

Depending on the results of licensed supplemental tests and prior screening tests, the quarantined units may be released for transfu-

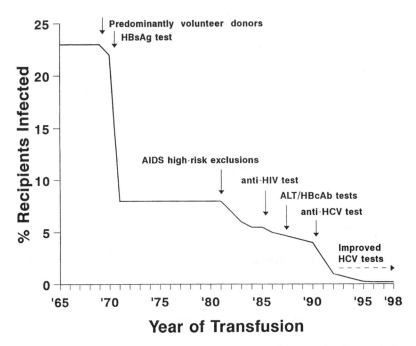

Figure 28-3. The decline in posttransfusion hepatitis and presumed causative factors (adapted with permission from Alter[22]).

sion or further manufacture, or will have to be destroyed.[27] In September 1998, the FDA issued a guidance document recommending tracing of transfusion recipients who may have been infected with HCV from blood donors who were later identified as seropositive for the virus (HCV look-back).[28] Notified recipients should be counseled and offered testing. If they test positive, life-style changes (including avoidance of alcohol) and antiviral treatment may be warranted to reduce the likelihood of disease progression. Unfortunately, earlier experiences from Canada and several European countries indicate that the number of transfusion recipients who ultimately benefit from look-back may be small.[29]

Human Immunodeficiency Viruses

The human immunodeficiency viruses, type 1 (HIV-1) and type 2 (HIV-2) are the etiologic agents of AIDS. The AIDS syndrome was recognized in 1981, well before the discovery of the causative virus in 1984. Wider implications of the immune disorder were noted when, in 1982, AIDS was reported in three hemophiliacs,[30] and in a 17-month-old infant whose multiple transfusions at birth included a unit of platelets from a donor who subsequently developed AIDS.[31] Within a few years, studies established that well over 50% of hemophiliacs who received clotting factor concentrates in the early 1980s developed HIV-1 infection.[32] In some regions of the United States up to 1% of single-donor unit transfusions were infected with HIV in the early 1980s.[33]

Clinical Manifestations of HIV Infection

HIV is a cytopathic retrovirus that preferentially infects CD4-positive T lymphocytes (helper T cells) in lymph nodes and other lymphoid tissue.[34] Following primary infection, HIV replicates and disseminates initially as cell-free virions, and 10 days to 3 weeks after infection, viremia is first detectable in the plasma. During this time, about 60% of acutely infected persons develop an acute retroviral syndrome, characterized by a flu-like illness with fever, enlarged lymph nodes, sore throat, rash, joint and muscle pain—with or without headache, diarrhea, and vomiting. As HIV-1 antibodies appear, the disease enters a clinically latent stage; however, viral replication and dissemination continue unabated. The virus can be transmitted by blood or genital secretions during this phase. Tissue monocytes may serve as a latently infected reservoir in nonlymphoid tissues.

Persistent infection with an asymptomatic clinical status has been estimated to last a median of 10-12 years in the absence of treatment.[35] After years of asymptomatic standoff, both plasma viremia and the percentage of infected T lymphocytes increase. Loss of the immune functions served by helper T cells impairs immune reactivity, and there may be inappropriate immune activation and cytokine secretion. Eventually there is a sharp decline in the number of CD4+ T lymphocytes and the vast majority of infected individuals succumb to opportunistic illnesses fostered by profound immunosuppression.

Enumeration of viral load and CD4+ cells is used to guide clinical and therapeutic management of HIV-infected persons. The AIDS classification system devised by the Centers for Disease Control and Prevention (CDC) is based on the number of CD4+ T cells ($\leq 200/\mu L$ defines AIDS), the presence or absence of systemic symptoms, and existence of any of the 26 clinical conditions considered to be AIDS-defining illnesses.[36] Among these conditions are otherwise unusual malignancies, such as Kaposi's sarcoma, central nervous system lymphoma, and a wide array of devastating, potentially lethal opportunistic infections with fungi and parasites, the most common being *Pneumocystis carinii* pneumonia.

Recent advances in treatment of HIV and opportunistic infections, coupled with new tools for measuring HIV replication, have dramatically enhanced the survival of infected persons.[37] Unfortunately, worldwide the disease is still spreading rapidly, and for the majority of HIV-infected individuals in developing countries, effective therapy is either not available or not affordable.

Risk Factors for HIV Infection

Infected individuals are at risk of infecting others through sexual contact, childbirth, breast-feeding, and parenteral exposure to blood. Those identified early as being at highest risk were men who had sex with other men; prostitutes and their contacts; needle-sharing drug users; hemophiliacs who received clotting factor concentrates; and, to a lesser extent, recipients of blood transfusions. By 1989 the rate of infection within each group was no longer increasing exponentially and appeared to have reached a plateau in the populations most at risk.[38] HIV seroprevalence had stabilized in most US cities. Although heterosexual transmission, especially male-to-female, and mother-to-child transmission have attracted increasing concern,[34] these modes of transmission are also stable in the United States.

HIV-2 and HIV-1, Group O

First discovered in 1985, HIV-2 causes endemic infection in many countries in West Africa but is seldom seen elsewhere.[39] The first case of HIV-2 infection in the United States was reported in March 1988 in a young West African who had recently immigrated to the United States. The spectrum of disease attributable to HIV-2 is similar to that caused by HIV-1; however, there appears to be a longer incubation period and lower incidence of progression to AIDS.[40] HIV-2 is spread both sexually and from mother to child but transmission is less efficient than for HIV-1.

Tests in the United States on parenteral drug users, persons with sexually transmitted diseases, newborn infants, and homosexual men confirm the very limited prevalence and transmission of the agent.[40] HIV-1/HIV-2 combination tests were implemented in this country in 1991. Since then, several HIV-2-infected donors have been identified; none appeared to have been infected in the United States.

On the basis of genetic variation, at least five HIV-1 subtypes have been identified. Viral strains with the greatest genetic difference from the other isolates were classified as group O (outlier group). In Cameroon and surrounding West African countries, an estimated 1-2% of HIV infections are caused by group O viral strains.[41] As with HIV-2, group O isolates have rarely been seen outside this geographic area. Concern arose when studies demonstrated that some group O viral isolates were not reliably detected by several EIA tests used for blood donor screening.[42] In response, the FDA is requiring manufacturers to modify their screening tests to ensure sensitivity to a panel of group O strains. As an interim measure, until reliable detection of group O infections is established, the FDA also recommended permanent deferral of blood and plasma donors who were born, resided, or traveled in West Africa since 1977, or had sexual contact with someone identified by these criteria.[43] The current risk of group O infection in the United States is very low. As of 1997, only two such infections had been reported; both involved immigrants from West Africa who had never donated blood or plasma. Furthermore, surveillance testing for HIV-1 divergent strains did not detect any group O viral isolates among 1072 serum samples from high- and low-risk population groups in the United States and Puerto Rico.[44]

Transfusion Considerations

Transfusion-Transmitted HIV-1

All blood components can transmit HIV-1. By the mid-1990s over 7500 cases of AIDS had been reported in which transfusion or a tissue transplant was the only identifiable risk. In addition, approximately 4200 cases occurred in hemophiliacs who received clotting factor concentrates. Transfusion-associated AIDS, including cases in hemophiliacs, constituted about 2.3% of all AIDS cases.[45] All but about 30 involved transfusions given before routine anti-HIV testing began in 1985.

Most but not all recipients of HIV-infected blood transfusions become infected. In one large study, HIV infection developed in 89.5% of recipients who received blood from anti-HIV-positive donors.[39] Transmission rates correlated with component type and viral load in the donation.[39] With the exception of coagulation factor concentrates, plasma derivatives such as albumin and immune globulins have not been reported to transmit HIV infection. No transmission of HIV attributable to coagulation factors has been documented in the United States since introduction of donor screening and virus inactivation techniques in the mid-1980s.

Transfusion-Transmitted HIV-2 and HIV-1, Group O

There have been two reports of possible HIV-2 transmission through blood component use, both in Europe. Two women were infected by Whole Blood obtained from a donor who developed AIDS at least 16 years after becoming infected with HIV-2; both women were asymptomatic 14 years after transfusion.[46] Two hemophilia patients who received clotting factors were also infected. Due to their extremely low prevalence, no HIV-2 or HIV-1 group O transmissions have been reported in the United States by blood transfusion or any other transmission route.

Current Risk of Posttransfusion HIV

Figure 28-4 presents a summary of HIV risk from transfusion over the past 2 decades. Since 1985, only rare cases of HIV transmission by

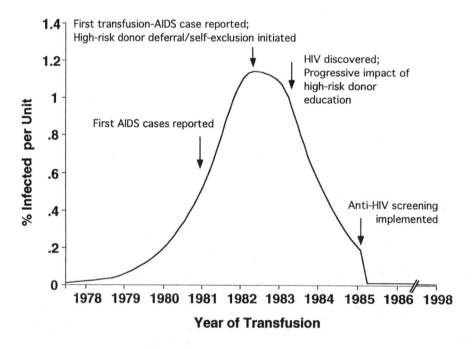

Figure 28-4. Projected risk of HIV-1 infection per unit of blood transfused in the San Francisco bay area from 1978 to 1998. Main events that shaped the course of the epidemic in transfusion recipients are indicated. The risk in the United States as a whole probably trailed that in San Francisco by approximately one year and the peak risk was lower (adapted with permission from Busch et al[33]).

transfusion have been reported, virtually all resulting from donations by a recently infected individual not yet reactive on an anti-HIV screening test. With screening tests available before 1992, the seronegative interval ("window period") averaged 45 days. Presently available, more sensitive screening tests have closed the antibody-negative window to approximately 22-25 days.[39] Introduced in 1996, p24 antigen screening has further reduced the potentially infectious window by an estimated 6 days,[47] although it appears that fewer HIV-infected units were intercepted by the introduction of this test than had been expected based on the calculated reduction of the infectious window period (see Screening and Confirmation for HIV Antigen below). Risk from seronegative donations will vary in proportion to the incidence of HIV infection in the donor community. Recent overall estimates of posttransfusion HIV risk in the United States range from approximately 1 in 450,000 to 1 in 660,000 transfusions.[1,48] These figures do not reflect the (presumably modest) impact of p24 antigen screening.

HIV Testing of Blood Donors

AABB *Standards*[24(p31)] and FDA regulations[49,50] require that all units of blood and components be nonreactive for anti-HIV-1, anti-HIV-2, and HIV-1 antigen(s) (HIV-1-Ag) before they are issued for transfusion. Figure 28-5 shows the sequence of screening and confirmatory testing for anti-HIV-1/2. EIA is the test of choice of most donor centers for donor screening.

Because the consequence of missing even one true positive is great, screening tests are designed to have high sensitivity both to

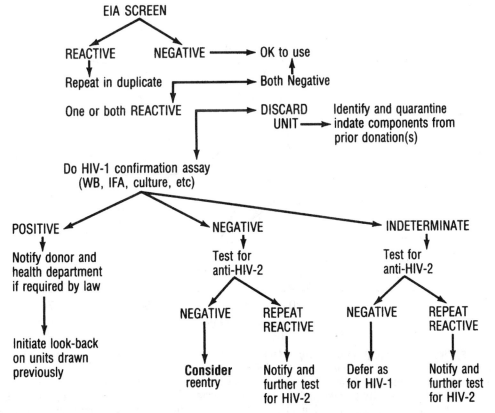

Figure 28-5. Decision tree for anti-HIV-1/HIV-2 testing of blood donors. IFA=immunofluorescence assay; WB=Western blot.

immunovariant viruses and to low-titer antibody during seroconversion. EIA-detectable antibody develops 2-4 weeks after exposure,[39] days to a week after the onset of symptoms,[51] and about 6 days after the onset of HIV p24 antigenemia.[47] A few days later, HIV-1 antibodies become detectable by the HIV-1 Western immunoblot. With very rare exceptions, all persons infected with HIV develop anti-HIV reactivity detectable by EIA and Western blot that persists for life.

More sensitive tests using PCR or other nucleic acid amplification (NAT) technologies may detect additional potentially infectious donors (Fig 28-6). In an effort to further improve the safety margin of blood components, several major blood collecting organizations have begun implementing NAT on an investigational basis. Available data suggest that implementation of HCV NAT will result in a reduction in the risk of HCV from 1:100,000 to 1:500,000-

1:1,000,000 per unit and reduce the window period for HCV from 70-80 days to 10-30 days. Similarly, it has been estimated that such HIV NAT could reduce the window period for HIV from 16 days to 10 days, although this would not measurably effect the current risk of HIV transmission of 1:1,000,000 per unit.[53]

Confirmatory Testing for Antibodies to HIV-1/2

If the disease has low prevalence in the test population, the likelihood is high that most positive screening test results will be false positive. Additional, more specific supplemental tests are helpful to confirm the screening test results. The most commonly used of these tests for antibodies to HIV-1/2 is the Western blot. With this technique, protein components (in this instance, antigenic viral material) are separated into bands according to molecular weight and transferred to a nitrocellulose

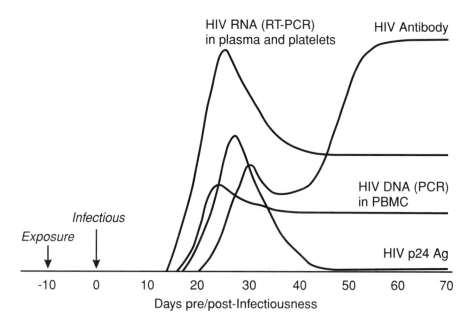

Figure 28-6. Virologic events during primary HIV infection. After initial infection and propagation of HIV in lymph nodes, a blood donor becomes infectious (defined as day 0) with HIV RNA being detectable in plasma on days 14-15, HIV DNA detectable in leukocytes at days 17-20, and HIV antibodies detectable between days 20 and 25. Anti-HIV persists indefinitely, but may be lost in the preterminal stage of the disease, in parallel with a surge in viral burden, indicating collapse of the immune system (adapted with permission from Busch[52]). HIV=human immunodeficiency virus; RT-PCR=reverse transcriptase polymerase chain reaction; PBMC=peripheral blood mononuclear cells.

membrane. Antibody(ies) in the test serum reacts with individual bands, depending on the specificity(ies) present. Most persons infected with HIV, whether asymptomatic or exhibiting AIDS, show multiple bands, representing antibodies to essentially all of the various gene products. A fully reactive test serum should react with the p17, p24, p26, and p55 *gag* proteins; the p31, p56, and p66 *pol* proteins; and the gp41, gp120, and gp160 *env* glycoproteins.

According to current FDA and CDC criteria, a sample is defined as anti-HIV-positive if at least two of the following bands are present: p24, gp41, or gp120/160.[54] Negative Western blot results have no bands present. Western blot results classified as indeterminate have some bands present but do not have the pattern defining HIV positivity. Individuals infected with HIV may have indeterminate patterns when initially tested, but develop additional bands within 6 weeks. Healthy individuals with initial indeterminate patterns continue to have negative or indeterminate results on repeat samples, and are negative on clinical examination and additional tests, including viral cultures and PCR.[55,56] Healthy donors who continue to show the same indeterminate pattern for more than 6 months can be reassured that they are unlikely to have HIV infection, but they are not currently eligible to donate blood. Recently, several groups have identified in blood donors Western blot patterns that were identified as false-positive results; for these, testing (using RNA PCR) is recommended to resolve the infectious status of the donor.[57]

The FDA has approved reentry protocols to qualify donors with negative confirmatory test results as suitable for subsequent donations (see Table 28-3).[50] Reentry requires retesting at least 6 months later, to detect delayed seroconversion; the use of EIA tests based on whole-virus lysate; and use of either a licensed Western blot to ensure appropriate sensitivity of the methods or an FDA-licensed immunofluorescence assay.[49,58] The later sample must also be nonreactive in an EIA test for anti-HIV-2, if standard testing does not include HIV-2, and a test for HIV-1-Ag.

Screening and Confirmation for HIV Antigen

Since March 1996, AABB *Standards*[24(p31)] and FDA regulations[59] have required that all units of blood and blood components be nonreactive for an FDA-licensed test for HIV-1-Ag, (in practice, p24 antigen). This decision was based on studies showing that HIV-1-Ag appears in blood early in the course of infection, approximately 1 week before antibody is detectable. Transmission of HIV has been reported from transfusion of seronegative blood later shown to contain p24 antigen; the donors subsequently seroconverted.[35] Mathematic models, constructed with findings from geographic areas with very high incidence of new HIV infections, suggest that routine antigen testing would detect one antigen-positive/antibody-negative donation in every 1.6 million tested.[47] In fact, only two infected window phase (p24 antigen-positive/anti-HIV-negative) volunteer donors were identified in the first 1.5 years of screening,[60] and a third used confidential unit exclusion, for an observed rate of 1 in 6 million donations.

When the EIA screening test for HIV-1-Ag is repeatedly reactive, a confirmatory neutralization test should be performed to aid in counseling the donor and to determine the need for product quarantine, look-back, and deferral.[59] Although donors whose sera show neutralization with this test are classified as confirmed positive for HIV-1-Ag and must be permanently deferred, studies involving reverse transcriptase polymerase chain reaction (RT-PCR) and follow-up of such donors have established that only a small proportion are infected with HIV, ie, most are false-positive neutralizations.[60] Donors whose sera show no neutralization with this test are currently considered not confirmed, but must be reported as HIV-1-Ag indeterminate; they should be temporarily deferred from donation for a minimum of 8 weeks.

Donors can be reentered if they have been retested after this period, and are found to be nonreactive for the HIV-1-Ag screening test and for the HIV antibody test. Unfortunately, approximately 70% of donors with indeterminate results remain p24 antigen-indeterminate on follow-up and must be indefinitely deferred. As with antibody-reactive units, units from HIV-1-Ag repeatedly reactive donations cannot be used for transfusion or for further manufacturing into injectable products and must be quarantined and destroyed.

Positive Tests in Autologous Donors

Whether HIV EIA repeatedly reactive autologous donations should be withheld from transfusion is controversial.[61] These units may be supplied for autologous use if the following conditions are met: 1) there is a written, signed, and dated request from the patient's physician authorizing this shipment, 2) there is a written statement from the transfusion service indicating willingness to receive this product, and 3) the transfusion service takes responsibility for ensuring that there is documented verification of the accurate identity of the transfusion recipient. These units must be labeled "BIOHAZARD" and "FOR AUTOLOGOUS USE ONLY."

Whether a facility elects to offer autologous services is an internal decision. Institutions should consider, however, that where feasible for a patient, it is generally accepted that the patient should have the option to use his or her blood. Also, a US Supreme Court decision probably makes it illegal to offer autologous blood services without offering those services to individuals protected under the Americans with Disabilities Act, including individuals who have tested positive for HIV.[62]

Recipient Tracing (Look-Back)

Identification of persons who have received seronegative or untested blood from a donor later found to be infected by HIV is referred to as "look-back." Because the interval between receipt of an infected transfusion and onset of AIDS can be very long, recipients are usually unaware of their infection and may be infectious to others. To identify these individuals, blood centers must have procedures to notify recipients of previous donations from any donor later found to have a confirmed positive test for anti-HIV[24(p74)] or a confirmed positive test for HIV-1-Ag. If a patient with AIDS is known to have donated previously, recipients of blood or blood products from these donations should be traced and notified. Recipient tracing and testing are usually done through the patient's physician, not through direct contact with the patient. In a companion rule, the FDA and Health Care Financing Administration (HCFA) have established timelines and standards defining look-back.[63-66] If recipients of units that were donated at least 12 months before the last known negative test are tested and found negative, earlier recipients are probably not at risk, as infectivity earlier than 12 months before a negative screening test is extremely unlikely.

Human T-Cell Lymphotropic Viruses

HTLV, Type I

Human T-cell lymphotropic virus, type I (HTLV-I) was the first human retrovirus isolated and the first to be causally associated with a malignant disease of humans, adult T-cell lymphoma-leukemia (ATL).[67] HTLV-I is also associated with the neurologic condition HTLV-associated myelopathy (HAM), often called tropical spastic paraparesis (TSP). HAM was described before TSP. Both these conditions occur in a small minority (no more than 2-4%) of persons harboring the virus. Infection during childhood is an important aspect of, and possibly a requirement for, developing ATL many years later, whereas childhood or adult infection can cause HAM, with a variable latent period.

Prevalence of HTLV-I infection shows striking geographic clustering, with pockets of high endemicity in parts of southern Japan and certain Pacific Islands; sub-Saharan Africa; and the Caribbean basin, Central America, and South America. Transmission is by mother to child through breast milk, by sexual contact (predominantly male-to-female), and by exposure to blood.

HTLV, Type II

Human T-cell lymphotropic virus, type II (HTLV-II) was described several years after HTLV-I. There is at least 60% similarity of genetic sequences to HTLV-I[67]; antibodies to either show strong cross-reactivity in tests with viral lysates. HTLV-II also shows clustering, but in different populations. High prevalence has been noted among some Native American populations and in intravenous drug users in the United States, in whom seroprevalence is 1-20%. The only disease associated with HTLV-II has been HAM; its occurrence seems to be somewhat less frequent than with HTLV-I.[68]

Clinical Observations

For both HTLV-I and -II, infection persists lifelong, as does the presence of antibody. Studies of prevalence and transmission use seroconversion as the endpoint for diagnosis. Infection does not cause any recognizable acute events, and with the exception of those developing ATL or HAM, infected individuals experience few, if any, health consequences. Most carriers are asymptomatic and completely unaware of the infection.

Transmission

Both viruses are very strongly cell-associated. Contact with infected viable lymphocytes can cause infection, but plasma appears to be not, or much less, infective. Cellular components from infected donors cause seroconversion in 40-60% of recipients in Japan, but apparently in a much smaller proportion of US recipients.[67] After refrigerated storage for 10 days or more, red cells transfused from an infected donor are far less likely to result in seroconversion, presumably due to degradation of lymphocytes that transmit the virus.[69,70] Transfusion-transmitted HTLV-I infection has been associated with HAM of rather rapid onset and at least one case of ATL.

Donor Tests

Donor screening for anti-HTLV-I began in the United States in late 1988; at that time the rate of confirmed positive tests was approximately 0.02%, or 1 in 5000 units collected, a figure that has since declined at least 10-fold as seropositive persons have been removed from the donor pool.[1,48] The current combined risk of transfusion-transmitted HTLV-I/II infection has been estimated as about 1 in 500,000 units (see Table 28-1). Further risk reduction can be expected from the implementation of combination HTLV-I/II EIA tests in blood donor screening. The first such test was licensed in 1997 in the United States. By utilizing viral lysates from both HTLV-I and HTLV-II viruses, the test offers sensitive detection of anti-HTLV-I as well as anti-HTLV-II. The originally licensed anti-HTLV-I EIA screening tests might have missed up to 50% of HTLV-II infections.[71,72]

Further testing of serum that is repeatedly reactive for anti-HTLV-I/II against antigen preparations specific for the two agents (HTLV-I or HTLV-II), or by PCR on material from peripheral blood mononuclear cells, can characterize the infecting agent. Half or more of blood donors reactive on EIA screening prove to have HTLV-II infections. A donation that is repeatedly reactive on EIA may not be used for transfusion. Although there is no FDA requirement to perform additional testing (no confirmatory test for HTLV is licensed), most centers do so, and if supplemental tests are positive, the donor is notified and permanently deferred (see Table 28-4). Another recom-

Table 28-4. Recommended Actions for HTLV-I/II Testing

First Donation to Be Tested for HTLV-I/II Antibodies				Subsequent Donation(s)			
EIA	WB/RIPA	Donation	Donor	Second Manufacturer EIA	WB/RIPA	Donation	Donor
Repeatedly reactive	Positive	Destroy all components*	Defer and counsel	Not applicable/Donor deferred			
Repeatedly reactive	Negative or indeterm.	Destroy all components*	No action	Repeatedly reactive	Any result	Destroy all components*	Defer and counsel
				Nonreactive†	Not done	All components acceptable	No action

HTLV-I=human T-cell lymphotropic virus, type I; HTLV-II=human T-cell lymphotropic virus, type II; EIA=enzyme immunoassay; WB=Western blot; RIPA=recombinant immunoprecipitation assay.

* Destroyed unless appropriately labeled as positive for HTLV-I/II antibodies, and labeled for laboratory research use or further manufacture into in-vitro diagnostic reagents.

† Assuming that separate prior donations have been repeatedly reactive for HTLV-I/II antibody no more than once. If separate prior donations had been repeatedly reactive for HTLV-I/II antibodies on *two or more* occasions, the donor should have been indefinitely deferred.

mended approach is to test donor serum with a second manufacturer's EIA test kit. If that test is positive, the donor is indefinitely deferred. If a donor tests repeatedly reactive by the EIA screening assay on two or more occasions, he or she must be notified and indefinitely deferred, regardless of the results of supplemental tests.[71]

Quarantine and Look-Back

In-date prior collections of blood or components from donors who subsequently are found repeatedly reactive for anti-HTLV-I/II need to be quarantined. Because recipients of units from seropositive donors do not consistently seroconvert, and because many seropositive donors have lifelong infection, the time frame for look-back is not self-evident. Five years or 12 months from the last test-negative donation was adopted as a reasonable approach.[71] A definite separation between infective and noninfective donations is more likely to occur with donors who acquired infection as adults (usually through intravenous drug use or through sexual contact with intravenous drug users) or with individuals from geographic areas of high prevalence. The screening requirement in place since 1988 has probably removed from the active donor pool most donors with lifelong infection.

Cytomegalovirus

Cytomegalovirus (CMV), a member of the human herpes virus family, is a ubiquitous DNA virus that causes widespread infection; transmission can occur through infectious body secretions, including urine, oropharyngeal secretions, breast milk, blood, semen, and cervical secretions. About 1% of newborns are infected, transplacentally or through exposure to infected cervical secretions at delivery or by breast milk. In early childhood, CMV is often acquired through close contact, especially day-care settings; in adulthood, through sexual

intercourse. The prevalence of anti-CMV ranges from 40-90% among healthy blood donors.[73] The rate increases with age and is generally higher in lower socioeconomic groups and in developing countries.

Clinical Observations

In persons with an intact immune system, CMV infection may be asymptomatic and remain latent in tissues and leukocytes for many years. Infection, either primary or reactivation of latent infection, can be associated with a mononucleosis-like syndrome of sore throat, enlarged lymph nodes, lymphocytosis, fever, viremia, viruria, and hepatitis. Intrauterine infection may cause jaundice, thrombocytopenia, cerebral calcifications, and motor disabilities; the syndrome of congenital infection causes mental retardation and deafness, and may be fatal.

CMV causes serious morbidity and mortality in premature infants and in recipients of organ, marrow, or peripheral blood progenitor cell transplants.[73] Pneumonitis, hepatitis, retinitis, and multisystem organ failure are manifestations of infection, which can result from blood transfusions. Other causes, however, such as organ transplants from CMV-positive donors or reactivation of latent virus, may be as much or more of a risk than transfusion.

Transfusion-Transmitted CMV

Infection with CMV varies greatly according to socioeconomic status and geographic region. Although approximately 50% of blood donors can be expected to be CMV-seropositive, it has been estimated that currently less than 1% of seropositive cellular blood components are able to transmit the virus.[12] Posttransfusion hepatitis may, rarely, be due to CMV. The postperfusion mononucleosis syndrome that first focused attention on CMV in transfused components in the early 1960s is now rarely seen. Posttransfusion CMV infection is generally of no clinical consequence in immuno-competent recipients and intentional selection of CMV-reduced-risk blood (see below) is not warranted.

In light of the potential for severe disease in immunocompromised patients, however, several recipient categories have been identified, which should be protected from the risk of CMV transmission.[12] These include low-birthweight premature infants born to seronegative mothers; seronegative recipients of marrow from CMV-negative donors; seronegative pregnant women, because the fetus is at risk of transplacental infection; and recipients of intrauterine transfusions. Often included in this category are seronegative recipients of any organ transplant from a seronegative donor; seronegative individuals who are candidates for autologous or allogeneic marrow transplants; and those few patients with AIDS who are free of CMV infection.

Preventive Measures

Blood from donors who test negative for CMV antibody has virtually no risk of transmitting CMV,[12,73] but the supply of seronegative blood is limited. Another approach is to remove leukocytes from donated blood. Although the precise leukocyte population that harbors the virus has not been defined, leukocyte removal with high-efficiency filters, to 5×10^6 leukocytes per component or less, can significantly reduce, if not prevent, posttransfusion CMV in high-risk neonates and transplant recipients.[74,75] Prophylactic therapy with CMV immune globulin and prophylactic use of antiviral agents are being investigated as an option for high-risk immunosuppressed organ transplant recipients.[12]

Other Viruses and Infectious Proteins (Prions)

The transmissibility and clinical significance of several other members of the human herpes virus family (Epstein-Barr virus, human herpes viruses 6 and 8), parvovirus, and others are being studied.[12,73,76] Actively investigated is also the possibility that infectious proteins, so-called prions, may be transmitted by transfusion. Prions have been implicated in causing Creutzfeldt-Jakob disease (CJD) and related neurologic illnesses.

Epstein-Barr Virus

Epstein-Barr virus (EBV) causes most cases of infectious mononucleosis and is closely associated with the endemic form of Burkitt's lymphoma in the Far East, and with nasopharyngeal carcinoma. Most persons have been infected by the time they reach adulthood; although usually asymptomatic, infection persists, mainly in B lymphocytes and oropharyngeal epithelium.[73] Infection is spread by contact with infected saliva. Primary infection in children is either asymptomatic or is characterized by a sore throat and enlarged lymph nodes. Primary infection in older, immunologically mature persons usually causes a systemic syndrome, infectious mononucleosis, with fever; tonsillar infection, sometimes with necrotic ulcers; enlarged lymph nodes; hematologic and immunologic abnormalities; and sometimes hepatitis or other organ involvement. EBV infection targets B lymphocytes, which undergo polyclonal proliferation and then induce a T-lymphocyte response, seen as "atypical lymphocytes."

Transfusion-transmitted EBV infection is usually asymptomatic, but has been a rare cause of the postperfusion syndrome that followed massive transfusion of freshly drawn blood during cardiac surgery and is a rare cause of posttransfusion hepatitis.[77] EBV plays a role in the development of nasopharyngeal carcinoma and at least one form of Burkitt's lymphoma, and has the in-vitro capacity to immortalize B lymphocytes. Although it contributes to the development of lymphoproliferative disorders in immunosuppressed recipients of hematopoietic and organ transplants, there is no evidence that transfusion-transmitted EBV infection contributes to the development of malignancies in transfusion recipients. Given a 90% seropositivity rate for EBV among blood donors and essentially no risk for clinical disease from transfusion-transmitted EBV in immunocompetent recipients, serologic screening for this virus has not been considered helpful. As for CMV, leukocyte reduction of cellular blood components could prevent EBV infection in severely immunosuppressed seronegative patients who may be at risk for clinical disease.

Human Herpesviruses 6 and 8

As with CMV and EBV, human herpesvirus 6 (HHV-6) is a cell-associated virus that integrates in the genome of B and T lymphocytes, causing lifelong infection with the possibility of reactivation and significant clinical disease in immunocompromised transplant patients. Most healthy adults have evidence of prior infection and no specific recommendations have been made to protect seronegative recipients from primary infection.

Human herpesvirus 8 (HHV-8), also known as Kaposi's sarcoma virus in recognition of its apparent causal role in the pathogenesis of this rare vascular tumor,[78] has recently been detected in a healthy individual during blood donation.[79] Epidemiologic studies, however, suggest that the virus is primarily propagated by sexual transmission; the prevalence of seropositivity appears to be low in the general population. Blood-borne transmission of HHV-8 seems to be rare.[80]

Parvovirus

Parvovirus B19 is the cause of erythema infectiosum or "fifth disease," a contagious febrile illness of early childhood. Infections in adults may be associated with arthritis, but are generally benign. More ominously, parvovirus can infect and lyse red cell precursors in the marrow.[3] This may result in sudden and severe anemia in patients with underlying chronic hemolytic disorders who depend on active erythropoiesis to compensate for shortened red cell survival. Patients with cellular immunodeficiency, including those infected with HIV, are at risk for chronic viremia and associated hypoplastic anemia. Infection during pregnancy predisposes to spontaneous abortion, fetal malformation, and hydrops from severe anemia and circulatory failure.[4]

The red cell P antigen is the cellular receptor for parvovirus B19, and people who do not have the P antigen are naturally resistant to infection.[81] About 30-60% of normal blood donors have antibodies to parvovirus, which indicate immunity rather than chronic persistent infection.[3] Viremia occurs only in the early phases of infection and there is no evidence for a carrier state; the incidence of viremia in blood donors has been estimated to range from 1 in 3,300 to 1 in 40,000.[4] Parvovirus lacks a lipid envelope and is therefore not inactivated by solvent/detergent treatment or heat inactivation utilizing temperatures below 100 C.[3] The virus has been found regularly in clotting factor concentrates and has been transmitted to hemophiliacs. Rare transmission through cellular blood components and plasma, but not intravenous immunoglobulin and albumin, has been reported.[4]

Colorado Tick Fever

Caused by an identically named virus, Colorado tick fever presents as an acute illness acquired from tick bites in the mountainous regions of the western United States. The virus can persist in peripheral blood up to 90 days after symptoms disappear, but no chronic asymptomatic carrier state has been reported. The virus has been transmitted by blood transfusion.[82] In the only reported case, the blood donor developed the febrile illness 4 days after removing an attached tick and 18 hours after donating blood. The virus was isolated from a segment of the donated unit of blood after 2 weeks of storage and from peripheral blood of the recipient who had colon carcinoma and developed a prolonged febrile illness.

Tick-Borne Encephalitis Virus

Tick-borne encephalitis virus is a flavivirus transmitted by the bite of ticks from various parts of the world. One variety (Kumlinge disease) is restricted to southwestern Finland and nearby islands where 126 patients had serologic evidence of infection. Of these, three were laboratory acquired and two were acquired by transfusion.[83] The blood donors became ill with Kumlinge disease only hours after donating but they neglected to inform the blood bank.

Creutzfeldt-Jakob Disease

CJD is a degenerative brain disorder that is rapidly fatal once symptoms of progressive dementia and motor disturbances develop. Approximately 85% of cases are sporadic, presumably caused by infection with a proteinaceous particle smaller than a virus, now usually termed a prion. Symptoms do not develop until many years to several decades after the initial infection. Ten to fifteen percent of cases are familial, caused by inheritance of one of at least 20 described mutations in the prion gene that, in its nonmutated form, encodes for a normal cellular protein. In the United States and worldwide, there is about one case of CJD per million people, nearly all in older individuals. In the vast majority of cases, the mode of acquisition is unknown. The agent causing CJD is resistant to commonly used disinfectants and sterilants. Fatal CJD has been transmitted through administration of growth hormone derived from human pituitary, allografting of dura mater, and insertion of contaminated intracerebral electrodes.[84]

Early experimental studies in animals and humans raised the possibility that dementing illnesses such as Alzheimer's disease and CJD could be transmitted by blood transfusion. This was based on the demonstration of the agent in human leukocytes and the development of degenerative changes at the intracerebral sites where human cells were introduced into hamsters or mice.[85] Subsequent studies have failed to confirm transmissibility of Alzheimer's disease through blood leukocytes,[86] and population-based, case-control studies have shown no evidence that blood transfusion is a risk factor for the development of CJD.[87,88]

More recent studies confirmed that a CJD-like illness can be transferred between hamsters by intracerebral injection of blood from infected animals. Moreover, fractionated blood remained infectious when injected into the brain, suggesting that the agent could spread to plasma products.[88] However, so far transmission of CJD through blood transfusion has never been reported and remains a mere theoretical possibility. Nevertheless, individuals at increased risk for CJD are excluded from donating blood[89]; this group includes persons who have received tissue or tissue derivatives known to be a source of the CJD agent (eg, dura mater, pituitary growth hormone of human origin) and persons with a family history of CJD.[24(p13)] For the purposes of donor exclusion, unit quarantine, and unit destruction, family history has been defined as having one blood relative who has had this diagnosis.[90] Look-back and recipient notification are only recommended when there are at least two genetically related family members with CJD, suggesting that the donor would be at increased risk for developing the familial form of the disease.[90]

In 1996 the first cases of an unusual outbreak or cluster of CJD was recognized in the United Kingdom (UK). These cases were later termed nvCJD, and appeared to be caused by the same prion responsible for bovine spongiform encephalopathy. This prion is distinct from the prion found in classical CJD, and its etiology is still being discussed. As a result of more recent studies and the link of nvCJD to B cells, the transmission of nvCJD through blood transfusions is continuing to be investigated.[91,92] In the absence of absolute data, the UK has instituted a universal leukocyte reduction requirement for cellular blood components and has discontinued sending plasma from donors drawn in the UK for further fractionation into injectable products.

Nonviral Infectious Complications of Blood Transfusion

Bacterial Contamination

Bacterial contamination, one of the earliest recognized complications of stored blood, remains an important cause of transfusion morbidity and mortality. It accounted for 29 (16%) of transfusion fatalities reported to the FDA between 1986 and 1991.[93] A single organism, *Yersinia enterocolitica*, was implicated in 21 reported cases of transfusion-associated sepsis from 1985-1996.[94] The rate of adverse reactions due to bacterial contamination of blood components has recently been estimated as 1 in 1700 pooled platelet units and 1 in 500,000 red cell components[2] (see Table 28-1). More precise data on the frequency of bacterial contamination of blood products in the United States are expected from a year-long collaborative study by the CDC, AABB, Department of Defense, and American Red Cross.[95]

No matter how carefully blood is drawn, processed, and stored, complete elimination of microbial agents is impossible. Bacteria are believed to originate with the donor, either from the venipuncture site or from unsuspected bacteremia.[93] Bacterial multiplication is more likely in components stored at room temperature than in refrigerated components, especially when room-temperature storage is in gas-permeable containers.[96] Organisms that multiply in refrigerated blood and components are often gram-negative; gram-positive organisms are more often seen at room temperature. Strict adherence to phlebotomy protocols and scrupulous attention to sterile techniques during component preparation and storage should minimize contamination arising from sources outside the donor.

Infusion of bacterially contaminated components can cause a devastating septic reaction, with mortality rates up to 26%.[93] In red cell components, the reactions may reflect the effects of endotoxin produced by such gram-negative organisms as *Pseudomonas* species, *Citrobacter freundii*, *Escherichia coli*, and *Yersinia enterocolitica*. *Bartonella* and *Brucella* species have also caused septic transfusion reactions.

Clinical Considerations

Severe reactions are characterized by fever, shock and disseminated intravascular coagulation (DIC). If bacterial contamination is suspected, the transfusion should be stopped immediately and a Gram's stain and blood culture should be obtained from the unit and recipient as promptly as possible after the reaction is observed. Color change to dark purple or black, clots in the bag, or hemolysis suggest contamination, but the appearance of the blood in the bag is often unremarkable. Bacterial multiplication may cause the oxygen in a red cell unit to be consumed, resulting in hemoglobin desaturation and erythrocyte lysis, both of which contribute to a darkening of the unit compared to the color of the blood in the attached sealed segments.[97] The presence of bacteria in a Gram's stain of the component is confirmatory, but absence of visible organisms does not exclude the possibility, especially if blood contained in attached segments was used for the Gram's stain. The patient's blood, the suspect component, and intravenous solutions in all the administration tubing used should be cultured for aerobic and anaerobic organisms at various temperatures.

Treatment should not await the results of these investigations, and should include immediate intravenous administration of antibiotics combined with therapy for shock, renal failure, or DIC, if present.

Preventive Measures

Prevention of septic reactions depends upon reducing or preventing bacterial contamination of components. Careful selection of blood donors by medical history and physical examination is the first and most important step.

The donor's present appearance and recent medical history should indicate good health; additional questioning may be needed if there is present or recent history of antibiotic use, of medical or surgical interventions, or of any constitutional symptoms. Questions to elicit the possibility of bacteremia are especially important for autologous donors, who may have undergone recent hospitalization, antibiotic therapy, or invasive diagnostic or therapeutic procedures; there have been several reports of *Yersinia* sepsis complications following infusion of stored autologous blood.[98] At the time of donation, the donor's temperature and pulse should be within normal limits.

There must be scrupulous attention to selecting and cleansing the donor's phlebotomy site. Skin preparation reduces but does not prevent the contamination of components by bacteria. Scarred or dimpled areas associated with previous dermatitis or repeated phlebotomy can harbor bacteria and should be avoided.

Care in the preparation of components and handling of materials used in administration is essential. If a waterbath is used, components should be protected by overwrapping, outlet ports should be inspected for absence of trapped fluid, and the waterbath should be frequently emptied and disinfected.

The color and character of the component should be checked before its release for transfusion. In some cases comparing the color of blood in the container with that of the sealed segments (the bag should not be darker than the attached segments) can be helpful.[97] The extent of bacterial growth in platelet components correlates with the duration of storage. In 1983, in recognition of technically improved storage conditions, the FDA increased storage limits of platelets at room temperature from 3 to 7 days, but again reduced the limits to a maximum of 5 days in 1986, responding to reports of bacterial contamination after more than 5 days of storage.[99]

Eventually, the use of detection systems may allow units to be monitored for contamination at the time of issue. Approaches under consideration include Gram's stain, chemiluminescent probe systems, automated cultures, and demonstration of glucose consumption.[100,101] Strategies aimed at eliminating or inactivating contaminating bacteria are also under investigation. These include prestorage leukocyte reduction, use of antibiotics in the storage media, and photochemical treatment of collected units. Of the latter, psoralen activated by ultraviolet A light is entering clinical trials; the method appears to have the potential for reliable inactivation of bacteria, viruses, and parasites, including intracellular forms.[102]

Syphilis

Syphilis is caused by the spirochete *Treponema pallidum* and is characteristically spread by sexual contact. The phase of spirochetemia is brief and the organisms survive only a few days at 4 C, so although transmission by transfusion is possible, its occurrence is exceedingly rare (three reported cases in the literature in 27 years[103]). Syphilis transmission by transfusion is not prevented by subjecting the donor blood to standard serologic tests for syphilis (STS) because seroconversion occurs well after the phase of spirochetemia. Most positive STS results on donors reflect either immunologic abnormalities unrelated to syphilis (biologic false-positives) or inadequately treated syphilis that is more of a threat to the individual being tested than to a potential recipient. Performance of the STS is still required.[24(p31)]

Malaria

Malaria is caused by several species of the intraerythrocytic protozoan genus *Plasmodium*. Transmission usually results from the bite of an anopheles mosquito, but infection can follow transfusion of parasitemic blood. In the United States, malaria is probably the most commonly recognized parasitic complication of transfusion; the risk in the United States is estimated at 0.25 case per million transfusions.[104] The species involved in transfusion-transmitted malaria in the United States are *P. malariae* (40%), *P. falciparum* (25%), *P. vivax* (20%), and *P. ovale* (15%).[104] Fever, chills, headache, and hemolysis occur a week to several months after the infected transfusion; morbidity varies but can be severe, and deaths have occurred, especially from *P. falciparum*. Adding to the risk of a fatal outcome may be a delay in the diagnosis because of lack of suspicion and unfamiliarity with the disease in nonendemic areas.

Malaria parasites survive for at least a week in components stored at room temperature or at 4 C. The parasites can also survive cryopreservation with glycerol and subsequent thawing. Any component that contains red cells can transmit infection, via the asexual form of the intraerythrocytic parasite.

Asymptomatic carriers are the source of transfusion-transmitted malaria, although the parasite density is very low. Asymptomatic infections rarely persist more than 3 years, but asymptomatic *P. falciparum* and *P. vivax* infections may persist for 5 years, *P. ovale* for 7 years, and *P. malariae* can remain transmissible for the lifetime of the asymptomatic individual. There are no practical serologic tests to detect transmissible malaria in asymptomatic donors. Malaria transmission is prevented by deferral of prospective donors with increased risk of infectivity, based on their medical and travel history. AABB *Standards*[24(p18)] defers, from donation of red cells, persons who have had malaria in the preceding 3 years. Casual travelers to areas in which malaria is endemic are deferred for a year, but because early or prolonged exposure may reduce the incidence or severity of symptoms, immigrants, refugees, or citizens of areas in which the disease is endemic are deferred for 3 years after leaving the area. Updated information on malaria risks worldwide is available,[105] including an on-line resource (http://www.cdc.gov/travel/yellowbk/hom.htm).

Babesia

Clinical Events

Human babesiosis, caused by the intra-erythrocytic parasite *Babesia microti* and at least one other *Babesia* species is the second most commonly reported transfusion-transmitted parasitic infection.[104] Babesiosis is usually transmitted by the bite of an infected deer tick, from the coastal lands and islands of northeastern United States including Martha's Vineyard, Cape Cod, and Long Island. Geographic areas of the hosts and the vectors appear to be expanding.[106] Cases of transfusion-transmitted babesiosis have also been reported from both Minnesota and Washington state.[107]

The parasite can survive for up to 35 days at 4 C liquid storage, and has been transmitted by platelet components, presumably through residual red cells. In an area in which babesiosis is endemic, the risk of posttransfusion babesiosis was found to be 0.17% for red cells; no cases were associated with platelets.[108] Symptoms of transfusion-transmitted babesiosis are often so mild that the true nature of the infection may go undiagnosed; this may explain the small number of cases documented in the United States. In symptomatic cases, fever develops 1-4 weeks after infection, sometimes associated with chills, headaches, hemolysis, and hemoglobinuria. Rarely, the infection is life-threatening, due to rapidly progressive hemolytic anemia, renal failure, and DIC. Asplenic or immunocompromised transfusion recipients are at greatest risk.[104]

Preventive Measures

As with malaria, the *Babesia* carrier state may be asymptomatic. Persons with a history of babesiosis are indefinitely deferred, because lifelong parasitemia can follow recovery from symptomatic illness. More restrictive policies, such as not collecting blood in areas in which the disease carriers are endemic in spring and summer months when tick bites are more common, would probably have only limited value. No test is currently available for mass screening to detect asymptomatic carriers of *Babesia* species.

Chagas' Disease

American trypanosomiasis, or Chagas' disease, is endemic in South and Central America and is caused by the protozoan parasite *Trypanosoma cruzi*. The human host sustains infection after the bite of reduviid bugs (called cone-nosed or "kissing" bugs), which usually exist in hollow trees, palm trees, and in thatched-roofed mud or wooden dwellings.

Clinical Events

T. cruzi infects humans whose skin or mucosa comes in contact with feces of infected reduviid bugs, usually as the result of a bite. Recent infections are usually either asymptomatic, or the very mild signs and symptoms go undetected. Rarely, the site of entry evolves into an erythematous nodule called a chagoma, which may be accompanied by lymphadenopathy. Fever and enlargement of the spleen and liver may follow. Recently infected young children may experience acute myocarditis or meningoencephalitis. Acute infection usually resolves without treatment, but persisting low-level parasitemia is usual and up to 20-40% of chronically infected people develop cardiac or gastrointestinal symptoms years or decades later.[109]

Transfusion Considerations

Blood transfusion is the major source of infection with *T. cruzi* in South American urban centers that receive large numbers of immigrants from endemic rural areas. Three cases of transfusion-transmitted Chagas' disease have been reported in the United States.[110] They occurred in New York, Los Angeles, and Texas, all in immunocompromised recipients.

Reasonably sensitive and specific EIA screening tests for antibodies to *T. cruzi*, as well as confirmatory Western blot and radioimmunoprecipitation assays have been developed.[111,112] When used in several US blood centers located in geographic areas with a large immigrant population from Central or South America, the seroprevalence was 0.1-0.2% among at-risk donors, who were identified by questionnaire.[113,114] However, look-back studies identified no infected recipients; it is also likely that not all at-risk donors can be identified by questionnaire.[113] As a consequence, if blood donor screening were to be implemented, testing of all donors may be necessary. Currently, there is no evidence suggesting that the introduction of routine blood donor screening for antibodies to *T. cruzi* would significantly improve the safety of the US blood supply.

Toxoplasmosis

Toxoplasmosis is caused by the ubiquitous parasite *Toxoplasma gondii* and infection has been reported as an unusual transfusion complication in immunocompromised patients.[104] The disease has not been considered a problem in routine transfusion practice.

Lyme Disease

Lyme disease is the most common tick-borne disease in the United States. *Borrelia burgdorferi*, the causative spirochete, is transmitted through bites of the deer tick. No tranfusion-related cases have been reported, but chronic subclinical infections do occur and experimentally inoculated organisms can survive conditions of frozen, refrigerated, or room temperature storage.[101] On the other hand, the phase of spirochetemia seems to be associated with symptoms that would render a potential donor ineligible, and in two reported cases where the donor became ill shortly after donation, the recipient did not develop infection.[101] Potential donors who give a history of Lyme disease should be completely asymptomatic and should have completed a full course of antibiotic therapy before they are permitted to donate.[115]

Parasitic Worms

There have been occasional reports of parasitic worm infections transmitted by transfusion in countries other than the United States.[104] Microfilariasis is a potential transfusion risk in tropical zones, acquired by donors through bites by insects carrying *Wuchereria bancrofti* or *Leishmania* species.

Reducing the Risk of Infectious Disease Transmission

Inactivation/Destruction of Agents in Derivatives or Plasma Products

The first intervention specifically added to reduce the risk of hepatitis transmission was pasteurization (ie, heating to 60 C for 10 hours), used for albumin products since 1948.[116] In those rare instances when infections have occurred with albumin or plasma protein fractions prepared with this step, the processing had been compromised.

Immunoglobulins

The plasma fractionation process used for most immunoglobulin products employs cold ethanol precipitation, which concentrates HCV in the Factor VIII-rich cryoprecipitate and other fractions, and leaves little in the immunoglobulin fraction. The immunoglobulin fraction also has a high concentration of virus-neutralizing antibodies, and the resulting product for intramuscular application has a remarkably low risk of virus transmission.[117] Preparations of immunoglobulin intended for intravenous administration (IVIG) were expected to be similarly free of disease transmission. However, NANB hepatitis transmission did occur in the 1980s during initial clinical trials of IVIG products in the United States and with routinely manufactured IVIG products in Europe.[118] In late 1993 and early 1994, a worldwide outbreak with approxi-

mately 200 reported HCV infections[119] was traced to a single IVIG preparation licensed in the United States.[120] In this case transmission may have occurred because of lack of virus inactivation steps in the specific manufacturing process for this product[121] and absence of neutralizing anti-HCV with resultant accumulation of virus particles in the immunoglobulin fraction.[119] Anti-HCV-positive source plasma has been excluded from the manufacture of IVIG since 1992. The importance of the manufacturing method is underscored by outbreaks of HCV infection from intravenous anti-D immunoglobulin in Germany in the late 1970s[122] and in Ireland from the late 1970s to the early 1990s.[123] Both products were prepared by anion exchange chromatography rather than the standard cold-ethanol (Cohn) fractionation.[124] To prevent further HCV outbreaks, the FDA has required since 1994 virus clearance steps in the manufacturing process of immunoglobulin, or proof of absence of HCV from the final product by nucleic acid amplification testing. In the near future, NAT technology will likely be applied to screening of source plasma as an additional layer of safety.

Coagulation Factors

Until the early 1980s, clotting factor concentrates frequently transmitted viral infections. As the significance of HIV transmission became recognized, virus inactivation steps were applied more rigorously to concentrates of Factor VIII and other clotting factors. Unfortunately, a large proportion of the hemophiliac population receiving concentrates before processing was improved became infected with HIV. Chronic hepatitis was an additional complication in almost all hemophiliacs receiving older clotting factor products.[125]

The thermal instability of Factor VIII made it difficult to develop an effective heat treatment, until a practical approach was adopted in 1985. Since then, many disinfection steps have been introduced and factor concentrates are now, in general, very safe products. Each process has its own set of advantages and disadvantages. Application of organic solvents and detergents inactivates viruses with a lipid- containing envelope (eg, HIV, HBV, HCV, HTLV, EBV, CMV, HHV-6, HHV-8), but is ineffective against nonenveloped agents such as HAV, parvovirus B19, and the Colorado tick fever virus. Virus inactivation steps have the potential drawback of reducing the potency and biologic effectiveness of the product. Another concern is whether virus inactivation steps affect immunogenicity, especially the induction of Factor VIII inhibitors in hemophiliac patients.

Unavoidable Risks of Human Plasma. Many methods are highly effective against enveloped virus, but sporadic reports of viral transmission continue to occur, possibly due to accident or error during the manufacturing process. The current combination of heat treatment, solvent/detergent treatment, and purification steps with monoclonal antibodies provides clotting factor concentrates with a risk of transmitting hepatitis and HIV that is lower than the risk associated with use of Cryoprecipitated Factor VIII derived from individual voluntary whole blood donations. Absolute safety of products derived from human plasma may be unattainable; starting with the safest possible donated plasma is of primary importance.[126]

Avoiding Human Plasma. Factor VIII concentrates have been produced by recombinant DNA technology, are licensed for use and have become the preparation of choice for previously untreated hemophiliacs.[127] Batches are produced by culture of mammalian cells engineered to secrete Factor VIII into the supernatant medium, which is purified by ion-exchange chromatography and immunoaffinity chromatography using a mouse monoclonal antibody against human Factor VIII. Except for the addition of human albumin to stabilize Factor VIII, the product is free of human proteins, HIV, hepatitis viruses, and other unwanted agents and therefore avoids many of the risks associated with using human plasma. On the other hand, recombinant prod-

ucts have a relatively short history of use, and there is no guarantee that they are risk-free.

Frozen Plasma

Virus inactivation steps, originally developed for plasma fractionation, are being considered for transfusions of frozen plasma. The options under study include organic solvents and detergents, pasteurization, and use of photochemicals.[128] Solvent/detergent treatment, effective against lipid-enveloped viruses, involves addition of 1% Triton X-100 and 1% tri-n-butyl phosphate (TNBP) to pooled plasma, followed by oil extraction of the TNBP and chromatographic adsorption of the Triton X-100. To protect Factor VIII during pasteurization, stabilizers are added and subsequently removed by ultrafiltration. Photochemicals such as methylene blue and psoralens can be added to individual plasma units, which are then exposed to ultraviolet A light. Of these three approaches, solvent/detergent treatment of plasma has been the most studied and validated. After several years of experience with this method in Europe, solvent/detergent-treated plasma is being introduced into transfusion practice in the United States.

Processing Cellular Components

The use of chemicals to inactivate viruses in red cell and platelet components is actively being studied and photochemical treatment with light-activated psoralen is being investigated in clinical trials.[102] Most inactivation protocols evaluated to date have employed photochemicals. These photoreactive compounds are added to the blood component, which is then exposed to light of a specific wavelength. Of these, methylene blue acts by generating reactive oxygen species that inactivate pathogenic organisms. In contrast, psoralen, exposed to ultraviolet A light, crosslinks and blocks nucleic acid and thereby prevents nucleic-acid-based organisms from transcription of their message and proliferation.

Reporting Transfusion-Associated Infections

Unexplained infectious disease reported in a transfusion recipient must be investigated for the possibility of transfusion-transmitted illness.[24(p74)] Hepatitis is expected to become apparent within 2 weeks to 6 months if it resulted from transfusion, but even within this interval the cause need not necessarily have been blood-borne infection. Blood centers and transfusion services must have a mechanism to encourage recognition and reporting of possible transfusion-associated infections. HIV infection thought to be a result of transfusion should also be reported to the blood supplier, although the interval between transfusion and the recognition of infection or symptoms may be years.

Infection in a recipient should be reported to the collecting agency so that donors shown or suspected to be infective can be evaluated and recipients of other components from the implicated or other donations can be contacted and, if necessary, tested. A donor who proves to have positive results on tests during the investigation must be placed on an appropriate deferral list.

The *Code of Federal Regulations* (21 CFR 606.170b) requires that fatalities attributed to transfusion complications (eg, hepatitis, AIDS, and hemolytic reactions) be reported to the Director, Center for Biologics Evaluation and Research (CBER), Office of Compliance, Division of Inspections and Surveillance, 1401 Rockville Pike, Suite 200N, HFM-650, Rockville, MD 20852-1448. A report should be made by telephone (301-594-1191) within one working day and a written report should be submitted within 7 days.

Management of Posttransfusion Infections

Implicated Donors

If documented transfusion-associated hepatitis, HIV, or HTLV-I/II occurs in a patient who received only a single unit, that donor must be permanently excluded from future donations, and the name placed in a file of permanently deferred individuals. If posttransfusion viral infection occurs after exposure to blood from several donors, it is not necessary to exclude all of the potentially implicated donors. If only a few donors are involved, it may be desirable to recall them to obtain an interim medical history and to perform additional tests. Donors found to have been implicated in more than one case of transfusion-associated viral infection should be appropriately investigated and possibly deferred permanently according to procedures established by the collecting agency.

Notification

A donor who will be permanently excluded as a future blood donor, because of a positive test implication in posttransfusion viral infection, must be notified of this fact. Follow-up testing should, ideally, be done by the donor's own physician, and the collecting agency should obtain the donor's consent to release available information to a designated health-care provider. If the donor does not have a physician, a blood bank physician or other trained staff member should provide initial counseling and appropriate medical referral. The notification process and counseling must be done with tact and understanding, and the fears and concerns of the donor should be addressed. The donor should be told clearly why he or she is deferred and, when appropriate, about the possibility of being infectious to others. Notification should occur promptly because a delay in notification can delay initiation of treatment or institution of measures to prevent spread to others.

Use of Immunoglobulins

It is not recommended practice to give intramuscular or intravenous immune serum globulin or hepatitis B immune globulin prophylactically to prevent posttransfusion hepatitis[129]; these agents have not been shown to prevent posttransfusion hepatitis B, and the available evidence is conflicting about their effect on posttransfusion hepatitis C.[130,131] If there has been inadvertent transfusion of known marker-positive blood, or needlestick exposure to infectious material, HBIG may prevent or attenuate HBV infection.[132] Prophylaxis with immunoglobulin is ineffective in preventing HCV transmission following occupational exposures and is not recommended for this indication.[133]

References

1. Schreiber GB, Busch MP, Kleinman SH, Korelitz JJ. The risk of transfusion-transmitted viral infections. The Retrovirus Epidemiology Donor Study. N Engl J Med 1996;334:1685-90.
2. US General Accounting Office. Blood supply: Transfusion-associated risks. GAO/PEMD-97-1. Washington, DC: US Government Printing Office, 1997.
3. Luban NL. Human parvoviruses: Implications for transfusion medicine. Transfusion 1994;34:821-7.
4. Prowse C, Ludlam CA, Yap PL. Human parvovirus B19 and blood products. Vox Sang 1997;72:1-10.
5. Rossi EC, Simon TL, Moss GS, Gould S, eds. Principles of transfusion medicine. 2nd ed. Baltimore, MD: Williams and Wilkins, 1996.
6. Petz LD, Swisher SN, Kleinman S, et al, eds. Clinical practice of transfusion medicine. 3rd ed. New York: Churchill Livingstone, 1996.
7. Centers for Disease Control and Prevention. Recommendations for prevention and control of hepatitis C virus (HCV) infection and HCV-related chronic disease (RR-19). MMWR Morb Mortal Wkly Rep 1998;47:1-39.
8. Menitove J. Hepatitis. In: Anderson K, Ness P, eds. Scientific basis of transfusion medicine. Implications for clinical practice. Philadelphia: WB Saunders, 1994:620-36.
9. Dodd R. Hepatitis. In: Petz LD, Swisher SN, Kleinman S, et al, eds. Clinical practice of transfusion medicine. 3rd ed. New York: Churchill Livingstone, 1996:847-73.
10. Alter HJ, Nakatsuji Y, Melpolder J, et al. The incidence of transfusion-associated hepatitis G virus infection and its relation to liver disease. N Engl J Med 1997;336:747-54.
11. Alter MJ, Gallagher M, Morris TT, et al. Acute non-A-E hepatitis in the United States and the role of hepatitis G virus infection. Sentinel Counties Viral Hepatitis Study Team. N Engl J Med 1997;336:741-6.
12. Sayers M. Cytomegalovirus and other herpesviruses. In: Petz LD, Swisher SN, Kleinman S, et al, eds. Clinical practice of transfusion medicine. 3rd ed. New York: Churchill Livingstone, 1996:875-89.
13. Koff R, Seef L, Dienstag J. Transfusion-transmitted hepatitis. In: Rossi EC, Simon TL, Moss GL, Gould S, eds. Principles of transfusion medicine. 2nd ed. Baltimore, MD: Williams and Wilkins, 1996:675-86.
14. Lee WM. Hepatitis B virus infection. N Engl J Med 1997;337:1733-45.
15. Alter HJ. To C or not to C: These are the questions. Blood 1995;85:1681-95.
16. National Institutes of Health. National Institutes of Health consensus development conference panel statement: Management of hepatitis C. Hepatology 1997;26:2S-10S.
17. Busch MP, Stramer S, Kleinman S. Evolving applications of nucleic acid amplification assays for prevention of virus transmission by blood components and derivatives. In: Garratty G, ed. Applications of molecular biology to blood transfusion medicine. Bethesda, MD: American Association of Blood Banks, 1997:123-76.
18. Alter HJ, Purcell RH, Shih JW, et al. Detection of antibody to hepatitis C virus in prospectively followed transfusion recipients with acute and chronic non-A, non-B hepatitis. N Engl J Med 1989;321:1494-500.
19. Alter H. Transfusion-transmitted non-A, non-B and hepatitis C infections. In: Rossi EC, Simon TL, Moss GL, Gould S, eds. Principles of transfusion medicine. 2nd ed. Baltimore, MD: Williams and Wilkins, 1996:687-98.
20. Ebeling F, Naukkarinen R, Leikola J. Recombinant immunoblot assay for hepatitis C virus antibody as predictor of infectivity (letter). Lancet 1990;335:982-3.
21. Van der Poel CL, Cuypers HT, Reesink HW, et al. Confirmation of hepatitis C virus infection by new four-antigen recombinant immunoblot assay. Lancet 1991;337:317-9.
22. Alter H. You'll wonder where the yellow went: A 15-year retrospective of posttransfusion hepatitis. In: Moore SB, ed. Transfusion-transmitted viral diseases. Bethesda, MD: American Association of Blood Banks, 1987:53-86.
23. Busch MP, Korelitz JJ, Kleinman SH, Lee SR, et al. Declining value of alanine aminotransferase in screening of blood donors to prevent posttransfusion hepatitis B and C virus infection. The Retrovirus Epidemiology Donor Study. Transfusion 1995;35:903-10.
24. Menitove J, ed. Standards for blood banks and transfusion services. 19th ed. Bethesda, MD: American Association of Blood Banks, 1999.
25. Tobler LH, Busch MP. History of posttransfusion hepatitis. Clin Chem 1997;43:1487-93.
26. NAT implementation. Association Bulletin 99-3. Bethesda, MD: American Association of Blood Banks, 1999.
27. Food and Drug Administration. Memorandum: Recommendations for the quarantine and disposition of units froom prior collections from donors with repeatedly reactive screening tests for hepatitis B virus (HBV), hepatitis C virus (HCV), and human T-lymphotropic virus type I (HTLV-I). Rockville, MD: CBER Office of Communication, Training, and Manufacturer's Assistance, 1996.

28. Food and Drug Administration. Guidance for industry: Current good manufacturing practice for blood and blood components: (1) quarantine and disposition of units from prior collections from donors with repeatedly reactive screening tests for antibody to hepatitis C virus (anti-HCV); (2) supplemental testing and the notification of consignees and blood recipients of donor test results for anti-HCV. Rockville, MD: CBER Office of Communication, Training, and Manufacturer's Assistance, 1998.

29. Goldman M, Juodvalkis S, Gill P, Spurli G. Hepatitis C lookback. Transfus Med Rev 1998;12:84-93.

30. Centers for Disease Control. *Pneumocystis carinii* pneumonia among persons with hemophilia A. MMWR 1982;31:365-7.

31. Centers for Disease Control. Possible transfusion-associated acquired immune deficiency syndrome (AIDS)—California. MMWR 1982;31:652-4.

32. Ragni MV, Winkelstein A, Kingsley L, et al. 1986 update of HIV seroprevalence, seroconversion, AIDS incidence, and immunologic correlates of HIV infection in patients with hemophilia A and B. Blood 1987;70:786-90.

33. Busch MP, Young MJ, Samson SM, et al. Risk of human immunodeficiency virus (HIV) transmission by blood transfusions before the implementation of HIV-1 antibody screening. The Transfusion Safety Study Group. Transfusion 1991;31:4-11.

34. Levine A, Liebman H. The acquired immunodeficiency syndrome (AIDS). In: Beutler E, Lichtman M, Coller B, Kipps T, eds. Williams' hematology. New York: McGraw-Hill, 1995:975-97.

35. Mayer A, Busch M. Transfusion-transmitted HIV infection. In: Anderson K, Ness P, eds. Scientific basis of transfusion medicine. Implications for clinical practice. Philadelphia: WB Saunders, 1994:659-68.

36. Centers for Disease Control. 1993 revised classification system for HIV infection and expanded surveillance case definition for AIDS among adolescents and adults. MMWR 1992;41:1-19.

37. Centers for Disease Control. Update: Trends in AIDS incidence—United States, 1996. MMWR 1997;46:861-7.

38. Brookmeyer R. Reconstruction and future trends of the AIDS epidemic in the United States. Science 1991;253:37-42.

39. Busch M. Transfusion-associated AIDS. In: Rossi EC, Simon TL, Moss GL, Gould SA, eds. Principles of transfusion medicine. 2nd ed. Baltimore, MD: Williams and Wilkins, 1996:699-708.

40. O'Brien T, George JR, Holmberg SD. Human immunodeficiency virus type 2 infection in the United States. Epidemiology, diagnosis, and public health implications. JAMA 1992;267:2775-9.

41. Peeters M, Gueye A, Mboup S, et al. Geographical distribution of HIV-1 group O viruses in Africa. AIDS 1997;11:493-8.

42. Schable C, Zekeng L, Pau CP, et al. Sensitivity of United States HIV antibody tests for detection of HIV-1 group O infections. Lancet 1994;344:1333-4.

43. Food and Drug Administration. Memorandum: Interim recommendations for deferral of donors at increased risk for HIV-1 group O infection. Rockville, MD: CBER Office of Communication, Training, and Manufacturer's Assistance, 1996.

44. Pau CP, Hu HDJ, Spruill C, et al. Surveillance for human immunodeficiency virus type 1 group O infections in the United States. Transfusion 1996;36:398-400.

45. Centers for Disease Control. First 500,000 AIDS cases—United States, 1995. MMWR 1995;44:849-53.

46. Dufoort G, Courouce AM, Ancelle-Park R, Bletry O. No clinical signs 14 years after HIV-2 transmission via blood transfusion (letter). Lancet 1988;2:510.

47. Kleinman S, Busch MP, Korelitz JJ, Schreiber GB. The incidence/window period model and its use to assess the risk of transfusion-transmitted human immunodeficiency virus and hepatitis C virus infection. Transfus Med Rev 1997;11:155-72.

48. Lackritz EM, Satten GA, Aberle-Grasse J, et al. Estimated risk of transmission of the human immunodeficiency virus by screened blood in the United States. N Engl J Med 1995;333:1721-5.

49. Food and Drug Administration. Memorandum: Revised recommendations for the prevention of human immunodeficiency virus (HIV) transmission by blood and blood products. April 23, 1992. Rockville, MD: CBER Office of Communication, Training, and Manufacturer's Assistance, 1992.

50. Code of federal regulations. Title 21 CFR Part 610.45. Washington, DC: US Government Printing Office, 1998 (revised annually).

51. Busch MP. HIV and blood transfusions: Focus on seroconversion. Vox Sang 1994;67(Suppl 3):13-8.

52. Busch M. Retroviruses and blood transfusion: The lessons learned and the challenge yet ahead. In: Nance S, ed. Blood safety: Current challenges. Bethesda, MD: American Association of Blood Banks, 1992:1-44.

53. NAT implementation. Association Bulletin #99-3. Bethesda, MD: American Association of Blood Banks, 1999.

54. Centers for Disease Control. Interpretive criteria used to report western blot results for HIV-1-antibody testing—United States. MMWR 1991;40:692-5.

55. Henrard DR, Phillips J, Windsor I, et al. Detection of human immunodeficiency virus type 1 p24 antigen and plasma RNA: Relevance to indeterminate serologic tests. Transfusion 1994;34:376-80.

56. Celum CL, Coombs RW, Jones M, et al. Risk factors for repeatedly reactive HIV-1 EIA and indeterminate western blots. A population-based case-control study. Arch Intern Med 1994;154:1129-37.

57. Kleinman S, Busch MP, Hall L, et al. False-positive HIV-1 test results in a low-risk screening setting of voluntary blood donation. Retrovirus Epidemiology Donor Study. JAMA 1998;280:1080-5.

58. Food and Drug Administration. Memorandum: Use of fluorognost HIV-1 immunofluorescent assay (IFA). April 23, 1992. Rockville, MD: CBER Office of Communication, Training, and Manufacturer's Assistance, 1992.

59. Food and Drug Administration. Memorandum: Recommendation for donor screening with a li-

censed test for HIV-1 antigen. August 8, 1995. Rockville, MD: CBER Office of Communication, Training, and Manufacturer's Assistance, 1995.

60. Stramer S, Aberle-Grasse J, Brodsky J, et al. United States blood donor screening with p24 antigen; one year experience (abstract). Transfusion 1997;37(Suppl):1S.

61. Mintz P. Participation of HIV-infected patients in autologous blood programs. JAMA 1993;269: 2892-4.

62. Pub. Law. 101-336, 104 Stat. 327 (1990). Codified at 42 U.S.C. §12101-12213.

63. Food and Drug Administration. Current good manufacturing practice for blood and blood components: Notification of consignees receiving blood and blood components at increased risk for transmitting HIV infection. Fed Regist 1996;61: 47413-23.

64. Health Care Financing Administration. Medicare and Medicaid programs; hospital standard for potentially HIV infectious blood and blood products. Fed Regist 1996;61:47423-34.

65. Code of federal regulations. Title 21 CFR Part 610.46-47. Washington, DC: US Government Printing Office, 1998 (revised annually).

66. Code of federal regulations. Title 21 CFR Part 482.27(c). Washington, DC: US Government Printing Office, 1998 (revised annually).

67. Hjelle B. Transfusion-transmitted HTLV-I and HTLV-II. In: Rossi EC, Simon TL, Moss GL, Gould SA, eds. Principles of transfusion medicine. 2nd ed. Baltimore, MD: Williams and Wilkins, 1996:709-16.

68. Murphy EL, Fridey J, Smith JW, et al. HTLV-associated myelopathy in a cohort of HTLV-I and HTLV-II-infected blood donors. The REDS investigators. Neurology 1997;48:315-20.

69. Sullivan MT, Williams AE, Fang CT, et al. Transmission of human T-lymphotropic virus types I and II by blood transfusion. A retrospective study of recipients of blood components (1983 through 1988). The American Red Cross HTLV-I/II Collaborative Study Group. Arch Intern Med 1991;151:2043-8.

70. Kleinman S, Swanson P, Allain JP, Lee H. Transfusion transmission of human T-lymphotropic virus types I and II: Serologic and polymerase chain reaction results in recipients identified through look-back investigations. Transfusion 1993;33:14-8 [comment in Transfusion 1993; 33:4-6].

71. Food and Drug Administration. Guidance for industry: Donor screening for antibodies to HTLV-II. Rockville, MD: CBER Office of Communication, Training, and Manufacturer's Assistance, 1997.

72. Rios M, Khabbaz RF, Kaplan JE, et al. Transmission of human T cell lymphotropic virus (HTLV) type II by transfusion of HTLV-I-screened blood products. J Infect Dis 1994;170:206-10.

73. Gunter K, Luban N. Transfusion-transmitted cytomegalovirus and Epstein-Barr virus diseases. In: Rossi EC, Simon TL, Moss GL, Gould SA, eds. Principles of transfusion medicine. 2nd ed. Baltimore: Williams & Wilkins, 1996:717-32.

74. Leukocyte reduction for the prevention of transfusion-transmittd cytomegalovirus. Association Bulletin #97-2. Bethesda, MD: American Association of Blood Banks, 1997.

75. Bowden RA, Slichter SJ, Sayers M, et al. A comparison of filtered leukocyte-reduced and cytomegalovirus (CMV) seronegative blood products for the prevention of transfusion-associated CMV infection after marrow transplant. Blood 1995;86:3598-603.

76. Dodd R. Epidemiology of transfusion-transmitted diseases. In: Anderson K, Ness P, eds. Scientific basis of transfusion medicine. Implications for clinical practice. Philadelphia: WB Saunders, 1994:599-619.

77. Giusti G, Galanti B, Gaeta GB, Gallo C. Etiological, clinical and laboratory data of post-transfusion hepatitis: A retrospective study of 379 cases from 53 Italian hospitals. Infection 1987;15:111-4.

78. Offermann MK. HHV-8: A new herpesvirus associated with Kaposi's sarcoma. Trends Microbiol 1996;4:383-6.

79. Blackbourn DJ, Ambroziak J, Lennette E, et al. Infectious human herpesvirus 8 in a healthy North American blood donor. Lancet 1997;349:609-11.

80. Operskalski EA, Busch MP, Mosley JW, Kedes DH. Blood donations and viruses (letter). Lancet 1997;349:1327.

81. Brown KE, Hibbs JR, Gallinella G, et al. Resistance to parvovirus B19 infection due to lack of virus receptor (erythrocyte P antigen). N Engl J Med 1994;330:1192-6.

82. Centers for Disease Control. Transmission of Colorado tick fever by blood transfusion—Montana. MMWR 1975;24:422,427.

83. Wahlberg P, Saikku P, Brummer-Korvenkontio M. Tick-borne viral encephalitis in Finland. The clinical features of Kumlinge disease during 1959-1987. J Intern Med 1989;225:173-7.

84. Manuelidis L. The dimensions of Creutzfeldt-Jakob disease. Transfusion 1994;34:915-28.

85. Manuelidis EE, de Figueiredo JM, Kim JH, et al. Transmission studies from blood of Alzheimer disease patients and healthy relatives. Proc Natl Acad Sci U S A 1988;85:4898-901.

86. Godec MS, Asher DM, Kozachuk WE, et al. Blood buffy coat from Alzheimer's disease patients and their relatives does not transmit spongiform encephalopathy to hamsters. Neurology 1994;44:1111-5.

87. Esmonde TF, Will RG, Slattery JM, et al. Creutzfeldt-Jakob disease and blood transfusion. Lancet 1993;341:205-7.

88. Ricketts MN, Cashman NR, Stratton EE, ElSaadany S. Is Creutzfeldt-Jakob disease transmitted in blood? Emerg Infect Dis 1997;3:155-63.

89. Food and Drug Administration. Memorandum: Revised precautionary measures to reduce the possible risk of transmission of Creutzfeldt-Jakob disease (CJD) by blood and blood products. August 5, 1995. Rockville, MD: CBER Office of Communication, Training, and Manufacturer's Assistance, 1995.

90. Food and Drug Administration. Memorandum: Revised precautionary measures to reduce the possible risk of transmission of Creutzfeldt-Jakob Disease (CJD) by blood and blood products. December 11, 1996. Rockville, MD: CBER Office of Communi-

cation, Training, and Manufacturer's Assistance, 1996.

91. Kein MA, Frigg R, Flechsig E, et al. A crucial role for B cells in neuroinvasive scrapie. Nature 1997;390:687-90.

92. Turner NL, Ironside JW. New-variant Creutzfeldt-Jakob disease: The risk of transmission by blood transfusion. Blood Rev 1998;12:225-68.

93. Sazama K. Bacteria in blood for transfusion. A review. Arch Pathol Lab Med 1994;118:350-65.

94. Centers for Disease Control. Red blood cell transfusions contaminated with Yersinia enterocolitica—United States, 1991-1996, and initiation of a national study to detect bacteria-associated transfusion reactions. MMWR 1997;46:553-5.

95. Bacterial contamination of blood components. Association Bulletin 96-6. Bethesda, MD: American Association of Blood Banks, 1996.

96. Morrow JF, Braine HG, Kickler TS, et al. Septic reactions to platelet transfusions. A persistent problem. JAMA 1991;266:555-8.

97. Kim DM, Brecher ME, Bland LA, et al. Visual identification of bacterially contaminated red cells. Transfusion 1992;32:221-5.

98. Haditsch M, Binder L, Gabriel C, et al. *Yersinia enterocolitica* septicemia in autologous blood transfusion. Transfusion 1994;34:907-9.

99. Anderson KC, Lew MA, Gorgone BC, et al. Transfusion-related sepsis after prolonged platelet storage. Am J Med 1986;81:405-11.

100. Burstain J, Workman K, Brecher M. Inexpensive and rapid detection of bacterially contaminated platelets using urine dipsticks (abstract). Transfusion 1995;35(Suppl):64S.

101. Benson K. Bacterial and parasitic infections. In: Petz LD, Swisher SN, Kleinman S, et al, eds. Clinical practice of transfusion medicine. 3rd ed. New York: Churchill Livingstone, 1996:891-903.

102. Ben-Hur E, Moor AC, Margolis-Nunno H, et al. The photodecontamination of cellular blood components: Mechanisms and use of photosensitization in transfusion medicine. Transfus Med Rev 1996;10:15-22.

103. Cooper L, Brecher M. Bacterial contamination. In: Linden J, Bianco C, eds. Blood safety and surveillance. New York: Marcel Dekker, 1999 (in press).

104. Shulman I. Transmission of parasitic infections by blood transfusion. In: Rossi EC, Simon TL, Moss GL, Gould SA, eds. Principles of transfusion medicine. 2nd ed. Baltimore, MD: Williams and Wilkins, 1996:733-8.

105. United States Department of Human Health Services. CDC health information for international travel. Atlanta, GA: Centers for Disease Control and Prevention, 1998 (revised annually).

106. Herwaldt BL, Springs FE, Roberts PP, et al. Babesiosis in Wisconsin: A potentially fatal disease. Am J Trop Med Hyg 1995;53:146-51.

107. Herwaldt BL, Kjemtrup AM, Conrad PA, et al. Transfusion-transmitted babesiosis in Washington State: First reported case caused by a WA1-type parasite. J Infect Dis 1997;175:1259-62.

108. Gerber MA, Shapiro ED, Krause PJ, et al. The risk of acquiring Lyme disease or babesiosis from a blood transfusion. J Infect Dis 1994;170:231-4.

109. Schmunis GA. *Trypanosoma cruzi*, the etiologic agent of Chagas' disease: Status in the blood supply in endemic and nonendemic countries. Transfusion 1991;31:547-57.

110. Appleman MD, Shulman IA, Saxena S, Kirchhoff LV. Use of a questionnaire to identify potential blood donors at risk for infection with *Trypanosoma cruzi*. Transfusion 1993;33:61-4.

111. Winkler MA, Brashear RJ, Hall HJ, et al. Detection of antibodies to *Trypanosoma cruzi* among blood donors in the southwestern and western United States. II. Evaluation of a supplemental enzyme immunoassay and radioimmunoprecipitation assay for confirmation of seroreactivity. Transfusion 1995;35:219-25.

112. Winkler MA, Brashear RJ, Hall HJ, et al. Detection of antibodies to *Trypanosoma cruzi* among blood donors in the southwestern and western United States. I. Evaluation of the sensitivity and specificity of an enzyme immunoassay for detecting antibodies to *T. cruzi*. Transfusion 1995;35:213-8 [comment in Transfusion 1995;35:186-8].

113. Leiby DA, Read EJ, Lenes BA, et al. Seroepidemiology of *Trypanosoma cruzi*, etiologic agent of Chagas' disease, in US blood donors. J Infect Dis 1997;176:1047-52.

114. Shulman IA, Appleman MD, Saxena S, et al. Specific antibodies to *Trypanosoma cruzi* among blood donors in Los Angeles, California. Transfusion 1997;37:727-31.

115. Aoki SK, Holland PV. Lyme disease—another transfusion risk? Transfusion 1989;29:646-5.

116. Suomela H. Inactivation of viruses in blood and plasma products. Transfus Med Rev 1993;7:42-57.

117. Centers for Disease Control. Safety of therapeutic immune globulin preparations with respect to transmission of human T-lymphotropic virus type III/lymphadenopathy-associated virus infection. MMWR 1986;35:231-3. (Erratum in MMWR 1986;35:607.)

118. Williams PE, Yap PL, Gillon J, et al. Non-A, non-B hepatitis transmission by intravenous immunoglobulin (letter). Lancet 1988;2:501. (Erratum in Lancet 1988;2:584.)

119. Yu MW, Mason BL, Guo ZP, et al. Hepatitis C transmission associated with intravenous immunoglobulins (letter). Lancet 1995;345:1173-4.

120. Centers for Disease Control. Outbreak of hepatitis C associated with intravenous immunoglobulin administration—United States, October 1993-June 1994. MMWR 1994;43:505-9.

121. Farrugia A, Walker E. Hepatitis C virus transmission by intravenous immunoglobulin (letter). Lancet 1995;346:373-5.

122. Meisel H, Reip A, Faltus B, et al. Transmission of hepatitis C virus to children and husbands by women infected with contaminated anti-D immunoglobulin. Lancet 1995;345:1209-11.

123. Power JP, Lawlor E, Davidson F, et al. Hepatitis C viraemia in recipients of Irish intravenous anti-D immunoglobulin (letter). Lancet 1994;344:1166-7.

124. Foster PR, McIntosh RV, Welch AG. Hepatitis C infection from anti-D immunoglobulin (letter). Lancet 1995;346:372.

125. Makris M, Preston FE. Chronic hepatitis in haemophilia. Blood Rev 1993;7:243-50.

126. Prowse C. Kill and cure. The hope and reality of virus inactivation. Vox Sang 1994;67(Suppl 3): 191-6.

127. Lusher JM, Arkin S, Abildgaard CF, Schwartz RS. Recombinant factor VIII for the treatment of previously untreated patients with hemophilia A. Safety, efficacy, and development of inhibitors. Kogenate Previously Untreated Patient Study Group. N Engl J Med 1993;328:453-9.

128. Horowitz B, Prince AM, Hamman J, Watklevicz C. Viral safety of solvent/detergent-treated blood products. Blood Coagul Fibrinolysis 1994;5 (Suppl 3):S21-8; discussion S29-S30.

129. Seeff L. The efficacy of and place for HBIG in the prevention of type B hepatitis. In: Szmuness W, Alter H, Maynard J, eds. Viral hepatitis: 1981 International Symposium. Philadelphia: The Franklin Institute Press, 1982:585-95.

130. Sanchez-Quijano A, Pineda JA, Lissen E, et al. Prevention of post-transfusion non-A, non-B hepatitis by non-specific immunoglobulin in heart surgery patients. Lancet 1988;1:1245-9.

131. Conrad ME. Prevention of post-transfusion hepatitis (letter). Lancet 1988;2:217.

132. Kobayashi R, Stiehm E. Immunoglobulin therapy. In: Petz LD, Swisher SN, Kleinman S, et al, eds. Clinical practice of transfusion medicine. 3rd ed. New York: Churchill Livingstone, 1996:985-1010.

133. Centers for Disease Control. Recommendations for follow-up of health-care workers after occupational exposure to hepatitis C virus. MMWR 1997;46:603-6.

Methods

The methods that follow are in a format based on a modification of the *Guidelines for Clinical Laboratory Procedure Manuals*, 2nd edition, (NCCLS Document GP2-A2, Vol. 12, No. 10, July 1992) of the National Committee for Clinical Laboratory Standards. Their inclusion in this edition of the *Technical Manual* is a subjective decision of the Technical Manual Committee.

Readers are encouraged to refer to previous editions of the manual for methods not appearing in this edition, as exclusion from the current edition does not necessarily indicate that their use is prohibited. However, some procedures, such as xylene and chloroform elution techniques, were removed because the chemicals used in the procedures could present a safety risk. Thus, readers are cautioned when referring to procedures in previous editions, as they have not been reviewed by the Committee for content and safety.

There are often many different ways to perform the same test procedure. Although some workers may prefer other methods, those given here are reliable, straightforward, and of proven value. Although the investigation of unusual serologic problems often requires flexibility in thought and methodology, adoption of uniform methods for routine procedures in the laboratory is imperative. In order for laboratory personnel to have reproducible and comparable results in a test procedure, it is essential that everyone in the laboratory perform the same test in the same manner.

General Laboratory Methods

Introduction

The methods outlined in the following sections are examples of acceptable procedures. Other acceptable procedures may be used by facilities if desired. To the greatest extent possible, the written procedures conform to the *Guidelines for Clinical Laboratory Procedure Manuals* developed by the National Committee for Clinical Laboratory Standards. As indicated in Title 21 CFR Part 606.65, the manufacturer's instructions (eg, product insert) for reagents and supplies licensed by the Food and Drug Administration (FDA) should be followed. Any deviation should be approved by the medical director and must be incorporated in a standard operating procedure. (Note: Deviations may also require concurrence from FDA.) It is important to remember the use of personal protective equipment and Universal Precautions when appropriate. Chapter 2 contains more specific details pertaining to safety.

Reagent Preparation

Many procedures include formulas for reagent preparation. Labels for reagents prepared in-house must contain the following:
- Name of solution.
- Date of preparation.
- Expiration date (if known).
- Storage temperature.
- Initials of person preparing solution.

Temperatures

Whenever specific incubation or storage temperatures are given, the following ranges are considered satisfactory:

Stated Temperature	Acceptable Range
4 C	2-8 C
Room temperature	20-24 C
37 C	36-38 C
56 C	54-58 C

Serologic Incubation Times

It is not acceptable to shorten incubation intervals below the specific times indicated. Extension of incubation times up to twice those stated for serologic tests usually does not impair the detection of antigen-antibody reactions, unless specifically prohibited in the package insert. Extended incubation may increase the number of false-positive results, and stated incubation times should not be exceeded when treating red cells with proteolytic enzymes.

Stated Incubation Time	Maximum Acceptable Range
Immediate-spin	Without undue delay
1-5 minutes	10 minutes
5-30 minutes	60 minutes
30-120 minutes	180 minutes

Centrifugation Variables

Centrifugation speeds (relative centrifugal force) and times should be standardized for each piece of equipment. (See Methods Section 7.)

Reference

Guidelines for clinical laboratory procedure manuals. 2nd ed. (NCCLS Document GP2-A3, Vol. 12, No. 10.) Wayne, PA: National Committee for Clinical Laboratory Standards, 1997.

Method 1.1. Shipment of Blood Specimens

Principle

The US Postal Service regulations for mailing blood samples, sharps, and other medical devices are frequently updated. The Centers for Disease Control and Prevention (CDC) of the Department of Health and Human Services (DHHS) and the Department of Transportation (DOT) revise 42 CFR 72 and 49 CFR 173, respectively. The shipping specifications described here are consistent with current CDC revisions to 42 CFR 72, "Interstate Shipment of Etiologic Agents." Most commercial airlines enforce the requirements of the International Air Transport Association (IATA).

Specimens

A clinical or diagnostic specimen is any human or animal material including, but not limited to, blood and its components. If there is reasonable belief that no etiologic agents are present, clinical specimens may be shipped with less stringent packaging and labeling requirements. An etiologic agent is defined as a microbiologic agent or its toxin that causes, or may cause, human disease.

Materials

1. Dry Ice (solid carbon dioxide): If dry ice is used, place it outside the secondary container. Steps must be taken to avoid both pressure buildup and loosening of secondary containers as the dry ice vaporizes.

   The weight of dry ice should not exceed 5 pounds for air shipments. Consult the Domestic Mail Manual (section C023),[1] 49 CFR 173.217 and 175.10(a)(13),[2] and IATA Dangerous Goods Regulations.[3]

   Dry Ice Labels: The outside package must be labeled with a diamond-shaped Class 9 symbol for miscellaneous hazardous materials; the words "carbon dioxide, solid" or "dry ice"; "UN 1845," the United Nations hazardous material category for dry ice; the name of the contents being cooled, eg, frozen medical specimens; and the weight of dry ice. (See Fig 1.1-1.)

2. Clinical/Diagnostic Specimens
   a. Packaging:
      1) Securely sealed primary container(s) (eg, test tube), with total volume not larger than 1 L or 1 kg.
      2) A leakproof secondary container such as a sealable plastic

PACKAGING FOR A CLINICAL SPECIMEN
(VOLUME >50 mL AND <4000 mL)

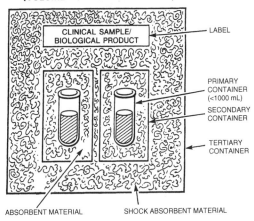

Figure 1.1-1. Appropriate packaging of clinical specimen material.

bag or container with screw cap.

3) Sufficient nonparticulate absorbent material (paper toweling, gauze, disposable diaper) to absorb all liquid contents in case of leakage.

4) For total shipment volumes exceeding 50 mL, a tertiary container of fiberboard or equivalent DOT-approved material (200-lb burst strength). (See Fig 1.1-1.) Each package is limited to a total volume of 4000 mL or 4 kg.

b. Labels: The package must identify the contents: Clinical Specimens.

3. Etiologic Specimens

a. Packaging:

1) Primary, watertight secondary containers and absorbent material as described for clinical specimens.

2) A tertiary (or outer) container constructed of 200-lb burst-strength corrugated cardboard, wood, or other material of equivalent strength.

Shipments of etiologic agents may contain multiple secondary containers, but the total volume of the shipment may not exceed 4 L or 4 kg. The label shown in Fig 1.1-2 must be on the outer shipping container.

b. Labels: The label for Etiologic Agents/Biohazard conforming to 42 CFR 72.3 as shown in Fig 1.1-2 except:

1) The color of material on which the label is printed must be white, with the symbol in red and the printing in red or white.

2) The label must be a rectangle measuring 2 inches high by 4 inches long.

3) The red symbol, measuring 1.5 inches in diameter, must be centered on a white square measuring 2 inches on each side.

4) The size of the letters on the label must be:

Etiologic agents   -10 pt. rev.

Biomedical materials   -14 pt.

In case of damage or
   leakage   -10 pt. rev.

Notify Director CDC   - 8 pt. rev.

Note: The agency prefers to receive calls on 800-232-0124, but (404) 633-5313 may still be used.

The secondary container(s) and the outer shipping container must also bear a label with the name, address, and telephone number of the shipper.[4]

Standard Form 420 A-1 [8-89]
Prescribed by Dept. HHS [42 CFR 72]
420-301

CLINICAL SPECIMENS
BIOLOGICAL PRODUCTS

BIOHAZARD

Packaged in Compliance with 42 CFR Part 72

IN CASE OF DAMAGE
OR LEAKAGE, *NOTIFY*
CENTERS FOR DISEASE CONTROL
(404) 633-5313

Figure 1.1-2. Label for etiologic agents/biomedical material.

Procedure

1. Place the sealed primary container in the secondary container.

2. Add sufficient nonparticulate absorbent material to cover all sides of the primary container and to absorb the entire contents in case of breakage.

3. Seal the secondary container securely.

4. For clinical specimens of more than 50 mL and all etiologic agents, place the secondary container in a tertiary or outer shipping container.

5. For volumes of 50 mL or more, place shock absorbent materials (at least equal in volume to the absorbent material) at the top, bottom, and sides between the secondary container and the outer shipping container.

6. Apply appropriate etiologic agent and dry ice labels.

7. For ground shipping by the US Postal Service, use only First Class Mail, Priority Mail, or Express Mail. Etiologic agents must be given to air carriers as "outsides," which means that they are not to be enclosed in mailbags.

8. For air transportation of etiologic agents more than 50 mL, attach the Infectious Substances label (135.4, International Mail Manual), the proper shipping name, and UN number. Complete a "Shipper's Declaration for Dangerous Goods" and attach labeling for "Cargo Aircraft Only."

9. Attach a return address label that includes the sender's telephone number for notification in case of damage. It is recommended that the consignee's telephone number be included as well as the address.

10. Notify the consignee at the time of shipment of etiologic agents, so that if the shipment is not received within 5 days of the expected arrival date, the CDC can be notified and tracing can be initiated.

Cautions

Unsuspecting transportation or postal workers must not be exposed to infectious materials because packaging was inadequate. Sufficient absorbent material calculated to absorb all potentially infectious material in the event of breakage or spillage must be used. Integrity of packaging should be ensured by using only tested, approved materials.

The recipient of inadequately packaged samples should document the incident and follow up appropriately to ensure correction of unsafe practices. Packages should only be opened by trained staff wearing latex gloves.

Notes

1. The carrier, the receiver, or anyone handling packages that are damaged or leaking must, upon discovery of damage or leakage, isolate the package; notify the CDC by telephone at (800) 232-0124 or (404) 633-5313 within 24 hours; and provide a description of the condition of the package, the name and address of the shipper, and other pertinent information.

2. If breakage occurs during shipment, the package should be handled with extreme caution and the entire package (including containers, contents, and packaging materials) should be autoclaved before discard. Supervisory personnel should be notified if the contents are lost in transit or if the damage appears related to inadequate packaging by the sender.

3. Etiologic agents cannot be imported unless they are in conformance with 42 CFR 71 (Foreign Quarantine Regulations) and accompanied by a permit issued by the Director, CDC. Contact the CDC at (800) 232-0124 or (404) 639-3883.

4. 42 CFR supersedes postal regulations for shipment of etiologic agents.

5. Consult 29 CFR 1910.1030 (g)(1), *Communications of hazards to employees, Labels and signs*.

References

1. Domestic mail manual, Issue 51, January 1, 1999.
2. Code of federal regulations. Title 49, Parts 173 and 175. Washington, DC: US Government Printing Office, 1998 (revised annually).
3. Dangerous goods regulations. 37th ed. Montreal: International Air Transport Association, 1996.
4. Code of federal regulations. Title 42, Part 72. Washington, DC: US Government Printing Office, 1998 (revised annually).

Method 1.2. Treatment of Incompletely Clotted Specimens

Principle

Fibrin generation may continue in serum separated from incompletely clotted blood, especially during incubation at 37 C. This produces strands of protein that entrap red cells and make it difficult to evaluate agglutination. Blood from patients who have recently received heparin may not clot at all, and blood from patients with excessive fibrinolytic activity may reliquefy or may contain protein fragments that interfere with examination for agglutination.

Materials

1. Thrombin: dry human/bovine thrombin or thrombin solution (50 units/mL in saline).
2. Glass beads.
3. 1% Protamine sulfate: 10 mg/mL in saline.
4. Epsilon aminocaproic acid (EACA): 0.25 g/mL in saline.

Procedure

1. *To accelerate clotting*: Either of the following techniques may be used:

   a. Add to whole blood or the separated serum either the amount of dry thrombin that adheres to the tip of an applicator stick or 1 drop of thrombin solution per mL of blood.

   b. Gently agitate separated serum with small glass beads, at 37 C, for several minutes. Then centrifuge and use the supernatant serum.

2. *To neutralize heparin:* Add 1 or more drops of protamine sulfate solution to 4 mL of whole blood. Protamine sulfate may work more rapidly when briefly incubated (5-10 min) at 37 C.

3. *To inhibit fibrinolytic activity:* Add 0.1 mL of EACA to 4 mL of whole blood.

Notes

1. The use of ACD collection tubes may help to eliminate the problem of incompletely clotted specimens.

2. Because preparations of human thrombin may contain anti-A and anti-B, carefully observe tests on treated serum for misleading results.

3. Use protamine sparingly. Excess protamine promotes rouleaux formation and, in great excess, will inhibit clotting.

Method 1.3. Solution Preparation—Instructions

Principle

The basic definitions, calculations, and instructions given below serve as a review of simple principles necessary for solution preparation.

1. Mole, gram-molecular weight: Weight, expressed in grams equal to the atomic or molecular weight of the substance.

2. Molar solution: A one molar (1 M) solution contains one mole of solute in a liter of solution. The solvent is assumed to be

distilled or deionized water unless otherwise indicated.

3. Gram-equivalent weight: Weight, in grams, of a substance that will produce or react with 1 mole of hydrogen ion.

4. Normal solution: A one normal (1 N) solution contains one gram-equivalent weight of solute in a liter of solution.

5. Percentage solutions: The percent designation of a solution gives the weight or volume of solute present in 100 units of total solution. Percent can be expressed as:
    a. Weight/weight (w/w), indicating grams of solute in 100 g of solution.
    b. Volume/volume (v/v), indicating milliliters of solute present in 100 mL of solution.
    c. Weight/volume (w/v), indicating grams of solute in 100 mL of solution. Unless otherwise specified, a solution expressed in percentage can be assumed to be w/v.

6. Water of crystallization, water of hydration: Molecules of water that form an integral part of the crystalline structure of a substance. A given substance may have several crystalline forms, with different numbers of water molecules intrinsic to the entire molecule. The weight of this water must be included in calculating molecular weight of the hydrated substance.

7. Anhydrous: The salt form of a substance with no water of crystallization.

8. Atomic weights (rounded to whole numbers):
    H, 1; O, 16; Na, 23; P, 31; S, 32; Cl, 35; K, 39

9. Molecular weights:
    HCl: $1 + 35 = 36$; NaCl: $23 + 35 = 58$
    KCl: $39 + 35 = 74$
    H_2O: $(2 \times 1) + 16 = 18$
    NaH_2PO_4: $23 + (2 \times 1) + 31 + (4 \times 16) = 120$
    $NaH_2PO_4 \cdot H_2O$: $23 + (2 \times 1) + 31 (4 \times 16) + (2 \times 1) + 16 = 138$
    KH_2PO_4: $39 + (2 \times 1) + 31 + (4 \times 16) = 136$
    H_2SO_4: $(2 \times 1) + 32 + (4 \times 16) = 98$

Examples

1. Molar solutions:
    1 M KH_2PO_4 = 136 g of solute made up to 1 L
    0.15 M KH_2PO_4 = $(136 \times 0.15) = 20.4$ g of solute made up to 1 L
    0.5 M NaH_2PO_4 = $(120 \times 0.5) = 60$ g of solute made up to 1 L

2. Molar solution with hydrated salt:
    0.5 M $NaH_2PO_4 \cdot H_2O$ = $(138 \times 0.5) = 69$ g of the monohydrate crystals made up to 1 L

3. Normal solutions:
    1 N HCl = 36 g of solute made up to 1 L. One mole HCL dissociates into one mole H^+, so gram-equivalent weight and gram-molecular weight are the same.
    12 N HCl = $(36 \times 12) = 432$ g of solute made up to 1 L
    1 N H_2SO_4 = $(98 \div 2) = 49$ g of solute made up to 1 L. One mole H_2SO_4 dissociates to give two moles of H^+, so the gram-molecular weight is double the gram-equivalent weight.

4. Percent solution:
    0.9% NaCl (w/v) = 0.9 g of solute made up to 100 mL of solution

Notes

Accurate results require accurate preparation of reagents. It is important to carefully read and follow all instructions and labels.

1. Weigh only quantities appropriate for the accuracy of the equipment. The operator's manual should give these specifications.

2. Prepare the largest volume that is practical. There is greater accuracy in measuring larger volumes than smaller volumes. If a reagent balance is accurate to ±0.01 g, the potential error in weighing 0.05 g (50 mg) will be 20%, whereas the potential error in weighing 0.25 g (250 mg) will be only 4%. If the solution retains its activity when stored appropri-

ately, it is usually preferable to prepare a large volume. If the solution deteriorates rapidly, smaller volumes may be preferred to reduce waste.

3. Note whether a substance is in the hydrated or anhydrous form. If the instructions give solute weight for one form, and the available reagent is in another form, be sure to adjust the measurements appropriately. For example, if instructions for 0.5 M NaH_2PO_4 call for 60 g, and the reagent is $NaH_2PO_4 \cdot H_2O$, find the ratio between the weights of the two forms:

$$\left(\frac{NaH_2PO_4 \cdot H_2O}{NaH_2PO_4} = \frac{138}{120} = 1.15 \right)$$

and multiply the designated weight by that figure (60 g × 1.15 = 69 g).

4. Dissolve the solute completely before making the solution to the final volume. This is especially important for substances, such as phosphates, that dissolve slowly. For example, to make 500 mL of 0.15 M KH_2PO_4:

   a. Weigh 10.2 g of solute in a weighing boat or glass [(0.15 × 136) ÷ 2], as only 500 mL will be made.

   b. Place 350 mL of water in a 500-mL volumetric flask on a magnetic stirrer. Add the stirring bar and adjust it to a slow, steady stirring speed.

   c. Add 10.2 g of salt, then rinse the boat with several aliquots of water until no salt remains. Numerous small-volume rinses remove adherent material more effectively than a few larger volumes. Add the rinse water to the material in the flask and stir until the salt is completely dissolved.

   d. If pH measurement is unnecessary, add water to the 500-mL mark, adjusting the volume for the stirring bar, and mix thoroughly. For solutions needing pH adjustment, see next step.

5. Adjust the pH of the solution before bringing it to final volume so that addition of water (or other solvent) does not markedly change the adjusted pH. For example, to bring 500 mL of 0.1 M glycine to pH 3:

   a. Add 3.75 g of glycine (H_2NCH_2COOH: molecular weight, 75) to 400-475 mL of water in a beaker. Dissolve completely, using a magnetic stirrer.

   b. Add a few drops of concentrated (12 N) HCl and measure pH after acid is thoroughly mixed. Continue adding HCl until pH is 3.0.

   c. Transfer the solution to a 500-mL volumetric flask. Rinse beaker and stirring bar with aliquots of water, adding the rinse water to the flask. Use the rinses to contribute to the total 500 mL volume.

   d. Measure the pH of the solution at final volume.

References

1. Remson ST, Ackerman PG. Calculations for the medical laboratory. Boston, MA: Little, Brown & Co., 1977.
2. Henry JB, ed. Clinical diagnosis and management by laboratory methods. 18th ed. Philadelphia: WB Saunders, 1991.

Method 1.4. Serum Dilution

Principle

Serum is sometimes diluted in saline or other diluent to determine its relative antibody concentration. It is customary to express the volume of diluted serum in terms of the unit 1, which means 1 part of serum *contained* in the total number of parts of the dilution. For example, to test the serum at one-tenth its original concentration, a dilution of 1 part in 10 may be made by mixing 1 mL of serum with 9 mL of saline. The *final volume is 10*, ie, 1 *in* 10, not 1 *plus* 10. Each tenth of the diluted material contains one-tenth (1/10 or 0.1) of the unmodified serum.

Procedure

1. Diluting an Existing Dilution
    a. A new higher dilution can be prepared from diluted material by adding more diluent. The formula for calculating either the new higher final dilution or the amount of diluent to add to obtain a new higher final dilution is:

    $$\frac{\text{reciprocal of present serum dilution}}{\text{volume of serum dilution used}} = \frac{\text{reciprocal of new final dilution}}{\text{total final volume}}$$

    b. *Example*: Serum dilution is one in two and volume of serum dilution is 1.0 mL. If 4.0 mL of saline is added, what will be the new final dilution?

    $$\frac{2}{1} = \frac{X}{5}$$

    X = 10 or 1 in 10 dilution

2. Diluting a Dilution to a Specified Volume
    a. The formula for calculating the volume of diluent to add to a dilution to achieve a certain quantity of a new higher final dilution is:

    $$\frac{\text{reciprocal of present dilution}}{\text{volume of present dilution needed}} = \frac{\text{reciprocal of final dilution}}{\text{total final volume required}}$$

    b. *Example*: Present serum dilution is one in two, total final volume is 100 mL, and new final serum dilution is 1 in 10. How much serum (diluted one in two) will have to be added to make up a final volume of 100 mL of a 1 in 10 dilution?

    $$\frac{2}{X} = \frac{10}{100}$$

X = 20 or 20 mL of serum (dilution of one in two) must be added to 80 mL of diluent to obtain 100 mL of a 1 in 10 dilution.

Method 1.5. Dilution of % Solutions

Procedure

1. Dilutions can be prepared from more concentrated solutions by the use of the following formula:

    $(\text{Volume}_1 \times \text{Concentration}_1) = (\text{Volume}_2 \times \text{Concentration}_2)$

    $$V_1 \times C_1 = V_2 \times C_2$$

    where V_1 and C_1 represent original volume and concentration, and V_2 and C_2 represent final desired volume and concentration.

2. *Example:* 30% albumin is available, but 2 mL of 6% albumin is needed. How should the albumin be diluted?

    $$V_1 \times 30 = 2 \times 6$$
    $$30V_1 = 12$$
    $$V_1 = 12 \div 30 = 0.4$$

    Therefore, mix 0.4 mL of 30% albumin with 1.6 mL saline to obtain 2.0 mL of 6% albumin, or for small-volume use, mix 4 drops 30% albumin with 16 drops saline to obtain 20 drops of 6% albumin.

Method 1.6. Preparation and Use of Phosphate Buffer

Principle

Mixtures of acids and bases can be prepared at specific pH values and used to buffer (render) other solutions to that pH. The following procedure includes a method for preparing phosphate-buffered saline (PBS) at a neutral pH, which can then be used as a diluent in serologic tests.

Reagents

1. Prepare acidic stock solution (solution A) by dissolving 22.16 g of $Na_2HPO_4 \cdot H_2O$ in 1 L of distilled water. This 0.16 M solution of the monobasic phosphate salt (monohydrate) has a pH of 5.0.

2. Prepare alkaline stock solution (solution B) by dissolving 22.7 g of Na_2HPO_4 in 1 L of distilled water. This 0.16 M solution of the dibasic phosphate salt (anhydrous) has a pH of 9.0.

Procedure

1. Prepare working buffer solutions of the desired pH by mixing appropriate volumes of the two solutions. A few examples are:

pH	Solution A	Solution B
5.5	94 mL	6 mL
7.3	16 mL	84 mL
7.7	7 mL	93 mL

2. Check the pH of the working solution before using it. Add small volumes of acid solution A or alkaline solution B to achieve the desired pH.

3. To prepare PBS of a desired pH, add one volume of phosphate buffer at that pH to nine volumes of normal saline.

References

1. Hendry EB. Osmolarity of human serum and of chemical solutions of biologic importance. Clin Chem 1961;7:156-64.
2. Dacie JV, Lewis SM. Practical haematology. 4th ed. London, England: J and A Churchill, Ltd, 1968:540-1.

Method 1.7. Preparation of EDTA-Saline for Use in the Immediate-Spin Crossmatch

Principle

Anti-A and anti-B cause direct agglutination and/or lysis of red cells. Direct agglutination is usually readily observed, but with high-titered, complement-fixing IgG anti-A and/or anti-B, the first component of human complement (C1) may sterically hinder agglutination when tests are performed by immediate-spin technique. This complement fixation can be prevented by using saline that contains the chelating agent EDTA, which sequesters the Ca^{++} ions needed for the integrity of the C1 molecule.

Reagents

1. Ethylenediaminetetraacetic acid, dipotassium salt dihydrate ($K_2EDTA \cdot 2H_2O$), 500 g (eg, Aldrich Chemical Co, Milwaukee, WI).
2. Sodium hydroxide (NaOH) pellets, 40 g.
3. Normal saline: 0.85% or 0.9% (w/v) sodium chloride, 20 L.

Procedure

1. Add 500 g K_2EDTA to 20 L saline; mix well.
2. Pour a little of the solution into a 1 L container and add 40 g NaOH.
3. Place the container on a magnetic stirrer and allow NaOH pellets to dissolve completely. Return NaOH-containing solution to the 20-L container.
4. Mix well and allow to stand overnight, to ensure that all chemicals are completely dissolved.
5. Mix again and perform the quality control tests described below. Record the data for each batch.

Notes

1. Each batch of EDTA-saline should be shown either to inhibit lysis of sheep red cells (available in most immunology laboratories) by human serum, or to inhibit lysis of A or B human red cells by hemolytic anti-A or anti-B.
2. The osmolarity of the EDTA saline should be 450 mOsm/kg and the pH should be 6.7 ± 0.2.

Reference

Judd WJ, Steiner EA, O'Donnell DB, Oberman HA. Discrepancies in ABO typing due to prozone: How safe is the immediate-spin crossmatch? Transfusion 1988; 28:334-8.

Method 1.8. Grading Test Results

Principle

The purpose of grading reactions is to allow comparison of reaction strengths. This is beneficial in detecting multiple antibody specificities or antibodies exhibiting dosage. The grading of agglutination reactions should be standardized among all members of the laboratory staff, in the interest of uniformity and reproducibility of test results. Most laboratories define their own version of a grading system, which is described in a written procedure available to all staff. Many systems use assigned numeric values (scores) for the observed reactions, as described by Marsh.

Materials

1. Centrifuged serologic tests for agglutination.
2. Agglutination viewer.

Procedure

1. Gently shake or tilt the tube and disrupt the red cell button in the tube.
2. Observe the way that cells are dispersed from the red cell button.
3. Record reactivity by comparing the agglutinates to the descriptions in Table 1.8-1. The reactivity should be assessed when the red cells have been completely resuspended from the button.

Interpretation

Refer to Table 1.8-1.

Notes

1. Serum overlying the centrifuged cell button must be inspected for hemolysis,

Table 1.8-1. Interpretation of Agglutination Reactions

Strength of Reaction	Grade	Score Value	Appearance
4+	"Complete"	12	A single agglutinate. No free red cells detected.
3½+	4+^{w} or 3+^{s}	11	
3+	3+	10	Strong reaction. A number of large agglutinates.
2½+	3+^{w} or 2+^{s}	9	Many large agglutinates with a few smaller clumps, no free cells.
2+	2+	8	Large agglutinates in a sea of smaller clumps, no free red cells.
2+^{w}	2+^{w}	7	Many agglutinates—medium and small, no free red cells.
1½+	1+^{s}	6	Many medium and small agglutinates, and free red cells in the background.
1+	1+	5	Many small agglutinates and a background of free red cells.
1+^{w}	1+^{w}	4	Many very small agglutinates with a lot of free red cells.
½ or −	± Macro	3	Weak granularity in the rbc suspension. A few macroscopic agglutinates but numerous agglutinates microscopically.
Trace or micro	(+) Micro	2	Appears negative macroscopically. A few agglutinates of 6-8 red cells in most fields.
Questionable	(0^R) Rough	1	Rare agglutinates observed microscopically.
0	0	0	An even red cell suspension. No agglutinates detected.

*Micro = microscopic; macro = macroscopic.

which is a positive sign of an antigen-antibody reaction, provided the pretest serum was *not* hemolyzed and no hemolytic agent was added to the test.

2. The character of the agglutination should be noted and recorded. Loose, "stringy," mixed-field, or refractile agglutinates should be noted, as they provide valuable clues in the investigation of unexpected findings, eg, mixed populations (posttransfusion red cell samples)

or certain antibody specificities (some anti-Lu or anti-Sd^a).

3. Mixed-field agglutination is generally the norm when using pooled cells for antibody detection and adding check cells to negative antiglobulin tests.

Reference

Marsh WL. Scoring of hemagglutination reactions. Transfusion 1972;12:352-3.

Red Cell Typing Methods

Method 2.1. Slide Test for Determination of ABO Type of Red Cells

Principle

See Chapter 13 for a discussion of the principles of testing for ABO types.

Specimen

The reagent manufacturer's instructions must be consulted before performing slide tests; some manufacturers recommend performing slide tests with whole blood, while others specify the use of red cell suspensions of lighter concentrations prepared in saline, serum or plasma.

Reagents

1. Monoclonal or polyclonal anti-A.
2. Monoclonal or polyclonal anti-B.
3. Anti-A,B (optional).

All reagents must be used in accordance with the manufacturer's instructions.

Procedure

1. Place 1 drop of anti-A on a clean, labeled glass slide.
2. Place 1 drop of anti-B on a separate clean, labeled glass slide.
3. Place 1 drop of anti-A,B on a third slide, if parallel tests are to be performed with this reagent, or on a single clean, labeled slide if this is the only test performed.
4. Add to each drop of reagent on the slides 1 drop of well-mixed suspension (in saline, serum, or plasma) of the red cells to be tested. (Consult reagent manufacturer's instructions to determine the correct cell concentration to be used.)
5. Mix the reagents and red cells thoroughly, using a clean applicator stick for each reagent, and spread the mixture

over an area approximately 20 mm × 40 mm.

6. Gently tilt the slide continuously for up to 2 minutes. Do not place the slide over a heated surface, such as an Rh viewbox.

7. Read, interpret, and record the results of the reactions on all slides.

Interpretation

1. Strong agglutination of red cells in the presence of any ABO typing reagent constitutes a positive result.

2. A smooth suspension of red cells at the end of 2 minutes is a negative result.

3. Samples that give weak or doubtful reactions should be retested using Method 2.2.

Notes

1. Slide testing imposes much greater risk of contact between specimen and technologist than occurs with tube testing. Personnel should follow safety measures detailed in the facility's procedures manual.

2. Slide testing is not suitable for detection of ABO antibodies in serum from patients or donors.

Method 2.2. Tube Tests for Determination of ABO Type of Red Cells and Serum

Principle

See Chapter 13 for a discussion of the principles of testing for ABO types. The following procedure is an acceptable representative method but the manufacturer's instructions for the specific reagents must be consulted.

Specimen

The reagent manufacturer's package insert must be consulted to determine specific speci-men requirements. Generally, clotted or anti-coagulated blood samples may be used for ABO testing. The red cells may be suspended in native serum, plasma, or saline, or may be washed and resuspended in saline.

Reagents

1. Monoclonal or polyclonal anti-A.

2. Monoclonal or polyclonal anti-B.

3. Anti-A,B. Note: Use of this reagent is optional.

4. A_1, A_2, and B red cells. These can be obtained commercially or the testing laboratory can prepare a 2-5% suspension on each day of use. (Note: The use of A_2 cells is optional.)

All reagents must be used in accordance with the manufacturer's instructions.

Procedures

Testing Red Cells

1. Place 1 drop of anti-A in a clean, labeled test tube.

2. Place 1 drop of anti-B in a clean, labeled tube.

3. Place 1 drop of anti-A,B in a clean, labeled tube, if tests are to be performed with this reagent.

4. Add to each tube 1 drop of a 2-5% suspension (in saline, serum, or plasma) of the red cells to be tested. Alternatively, the equivalent amount of red cells can be transferred to each tube with clean applicator sticks.

5. Mix the contents of the tubes gently and centrifuge them according to reagent manufacturer's directions. Typically, this is 15-30 seconds at approximately 900-1000 × g.

6. Gently resuspend the cell buttons and examine for agglutination.

7. Read, interpret, and record test results. Compare test results on red cells with those obtained in testing serum (see below).

Testing Serum

1. Label two clean test tubes as A_1 and B. (Note: Label additional tube if optional test with A_2 red cells is to be performed.)
2. Add 2 or 3 drops of serum to each tube.
3. Add 1 drop of A_1 reagent cells to the tube labeled A_1.
4. Add 1 drop of B reagent cells to the tube labeled B.
5. Add A_2 cells to the appropriate tube, if this optional test is being performed.
6. Mix the contents of the tubes gently and centrifuge them according to reagent manufacturer's directions. Typically, this is 15-30 seconds at approximately 900-$1000 \times g$.
7. Examine the serum overlying the cell buttons for evidence of hemolysis. Gently resuspend the cell buttons and examine for agglutination.
8. Read, interpret, and record test results. Compare test results on serum with those obtained in testing red cells (see above).

Interpretation

1. Agglutination of tested red cells and either hemolysis or agglutination in tests on serum constitute positive test results.
2. A smooth cell suspension after resuspension of the cell button is a negative test result.
3. Interpretation of serum and cell tests for ABO is given in Table 13-1 of Chapter 13.
4. Any discrepancy between results of tests on serum and cells should be resolved before an interpretation is recorded for the patient's or donor's ABO type. See Chapter 13.

Note

Positive reactions characteristically show 3+ to 4+ agglutination by reagent ABO antibodies; reactions between test serum and reagent red cells are often weaker. The serum tests may be incubated at room temperature for 5-15 minutes. See Chapter 13 for discussion of weakly reactive samples.

Method 2.3. Microplate Test for Determination of ABO Type of Red Cells and Serum

Principle

See Chapter 13 for discussion of the principles of testing for ABO. Microplate techniques can be used to test for antigens on red cells and for antibodies in serum.

A microplate can be considered as a matrix of 96 "short" test tubes; the principles that apply to hemagglutination in tube tests also apply to tests in microplates.

Microplates may be rigid or flexible, with either U-shaped or V-shaped bottoms. U-bottom plates are more widely used because results can be read either after centrifuging the plate and observing the characteristics of resuspended red cells or by observing the streaming pattern of the cells when the plate is placed at an angle. Either reading technique permits estimation of the strength of agglutination.

Specimen

Refer to Method 2.2.

Equipment

1. Dispensers: Semiautomated devices are available for dispensing equal volumes to a row of wells. Special plate carriers can be purchased to fit common table-top centrifuges.
2. Washers: Semiautomated washers are normally used to wash cells before adding antiglobulin serum. U-bottom plates are preferred for washing red cells because the cell samples resuspend more easily.

3. Microplate readers: Automated photometric devices are available that read microplate results by the light absorbance in U-bottom wells to differentiate between positive and negative tests. Ninety-six absorbance values can be processed in less than 1 minute and the results interfaced with a microprocessor. The automated reader passes light beams through the bottoms of the microplate wells. Negative results produce high optical density readings because the red cells dispersed over the well bottom absorb more light than the concentrated button of cells obtained in a positive result. The microprocessor component of the reader interprets the reactions and prints the blood testing results. The manufacturer's instructions for collection and preparation of serum and cell specimens must be followed.

4. Centrifuges: Appropriate conditions must be established for each centrifuge. The following times and relative centrifugal forces, expressed as g, are suggested. Consult the manufacturer's directions for specific information.
    For flexible U-bottom (U) microplate:
    a. $700 \times g$ for 5 seconds for red cell testing, serum testing, and immediate-spin phase of antibody screening.
    b. $700 \times g$ for 20 seconds for washing red cells for the antihuman globulin (AHG) test.
    c. $700 \times g$ for 5 seconds after addition of AHG serum.
    For rigid U microplate:
    a. $400 \times g$ for 30 seconds for red cell testing, serum testing, and immediate-spin phase of antibody screening.
    b. $400 \times g$ for 3 minutes for washing red cells for the AHG test.
    c. $400 \times g$ for 30 seconds after addition of AHG serum.

Reagents

Food and Drug Administration (FDA) requirements for microplate use: Many manufacturers supply ABO or Rh typing reagents that are licensed for use as undiluted reagents in microplate tests. Most reagent red cells licensed for use in tube tests can be used in U-bottom plates without additional preparation other than dilution to a 2-5% concentration. If an FDA-licensed laboratory wishes to employ reagents in a manner not specified by the manufacturer (eg, diluting an antiserum before use), the laboratory must submit a description of its procedure to the Center for Biologics Evaluation and Research (CBER). The user who changes the test conditions assumes responsibility for appropriate reagent evaluation. Unlicensed blood banks and transfusion services do not need FDA approval for microplate use but must have documentation supporting the use of any procedure that differs from the manufacturer's instructions.

1. Monoclonal or polyclonal anti-A.
2. Monoclonal or polyclonal anti-B.
3. Anti-A,B. Note: Use of this reagent is optional.
4. Group A_1, A_2, and B red cells. These can be obtained commercially or the testing laboratory can prepare a 2-5% suspension on each day of use. (Note: The use of A_2 cells is optional.)

Procedures

Testing Red Cells

1. Place 1 drop of anti-A and anti-B in separate clean wells of a U-bottom microplate. If tests with anti-A,B are to be performed, add this reagent to a third well.
2. Add 1 drop of a 2-5% saline suspension of red cells to each well containing blood typing reagent.
3. Mix the contents of the wells by gently tapping the sides of the plate.
4. Centrifuge the plate at the appropriate conditions established for the centrifuge.

5. Resuspend the cell buttons by manually tapping the plate or with aid of a mechanical shaker.

6. Read, interpret, and record results. Compare test results on red cells with those obtained in testing serum.

Testing Serum

1. Add 1 drop of a 2-5% suspension of reagent A_1 and B red cells to separate clean wells of a U-bottom microplate. (Note: If optional test on A_2 cells will be performed, add A_2 cells to a third well.)

2. Add 1 drop of serum or plasma under test to each well.

3. Mix the contents of the wells by gently tapping the sides of the plate.

4. Centrifuge the plate at the appropriate conditions established for the centrifuge.

5. Resuspend the cell buttons by manually tapping the plate or with the aid of a mechanical shaker.

6. Read, interpret, and record results. Compare test results on serum with those obtained in testing red cells.

Note

To enhance weak serum reactions, the plates may be incubated at room temperature for 5-10 minutes, and then the centrifugation, reading, and recording steps may be repeated.

Interpretation

1. Agglutination in any well of red cell tests and hemolysis or agglutination in any well of a serum test constitute positive results.

2. A smooth suspension of red cells after resuspension of the cell button is a negative test.

3. The interpretation of ABO tests is given in Table 13-1 of Chapter 13.

4. Any discrepancy between results on cell and serum tests should be resolved before an interpretation is recorded for the patient's or donor's ABO group. See Chapter 13.

Method 2.4. Confirmation of Weak A or B Subgroup by Adsorption and Elution

Principle

See Chapter 13 for discussion of the principle of testing for ABO types.

Specimen

Refer to Method 2.2.

Reagents

1. Human anti-A and/or anti-B. Because some monoclonal ABO typing reagents are sensitive to changes in pH and osmolarity, they may not be suitable for use in adsorption/elution tests.

2. Eluting agent: See Methods Section 4.

Procedure

1. Wash 1 mL of the red cells to be tested at least three times with saline. Remove and discard the supernatant saline after the last wash.

2. Add 1 mL of reagent anti-A (if a weak variant of A is suspected) or 1 mL of anti-B (if a weak variant of B is suspected) to the washed cells.

3. Mix the red cells with the reagent antibody and incubate them at 4 C for 1 hour, mixing occasionally.

4. Centrifuge the mixture to pack the red cells. Remove all supernatant reagent.

5. Transfer the red cells to a clean test tube.

6. Wash the cells at least eight times with large volumes (10 mL or more) of cold (4 C) saline. Save an aliquot of the final wash supernatant fluid and test it in parallel with the eluate.

7.   Use an elution method suitable for recovery of ABO antibodies, eg, heat or Lui freeze thaw elution techniques can be used to remove antibody from the cells. See Methods Section 4.

8.   Centrifuge to pack the cells and transfer the supernatant eluate to a clean test tube.

9.   Test the eluate and the final wash solution (from step 6), in parallel, against three examples of group O cells and three examples of cells expressing the relevant antigen (A_1 cells for suspected anti-A, B cells for anti-B). Add 2 drops of eluate or wash to 1 drop of cells, and examine for agglutination after immediate centrifugation, after 15 minutes' incubation at 37 C, and in an indirect antiglobulin test.

Interpretation

1.   The presence of anti-A or anti-B in the eluate, hence the presence of A or B antigen on the test cells, is confirmed if: a) the eluate reacts with all three antigen-positive cells, at any phase; b) the eluate is nonreactive at all phases with all three group O cells; and c) the final wash solution is nonreactive with all six cells.

  If the eluate does not react with the A or B cells, it may indicate that the test cells do not express the antigen and cannot adsorb the relevant antibody; alternatively, it could reflect failure to prepare the eluate correctly.

  If the eluate reacts with some or all of the A or B cells and also with some or all of the O cells, it indicates recovery of some other or additional antibody in the adsorption/elution process.

2.   If the wash solution reacts with the A or B cells, tests on the eluate cannot be considered valid. This can occur if unbound reagent antibody was not adequately removed before beginning elution, if the cells were not adequately washed, or if

there was dissociation of bound antibody during the wash process.

3.   A and B cells can be used as positive/negative controls and tested in parallel.

Reference

Beattie KM. Identifying the causes of weak or "missing" antigens in ABO grouping tests. In: The investigation of typing and compatibility problems caused by red blood cells. Washington, DC: American Association of Blood Banks, 1975:15-37.

Method 2.5. Saliva Testing for A, B, H, Le^a, and Le^b

Principle

Approximately 78% of individuals possess the *Se* gene that governs the secretion of water-soluble ABH antigens into all body fluids with the exception of cerebrospinal fluid. These secreted antigens can be demonstrated in saliva by inhibition tests with ABH and Lewis antisera. See Chapter 13.

Specimen

1.   Collect 5-10 mL of saliva in a small beaker or wide-mouthed test tube. Most people can accumulate this much in several minutes. To encourage salivation, the subject may be asked to chew wax, paraffin, or a clean rubber band, but not gum or anything else that contains sugar or protein.

2.   Centrifuge saliva at $900\text{-}1000 \times g$ for 8-10 minutes.

3.   Transfer supernatant to a clean test tube and place in boiling waterbath for 8-10 minutes to inactivate salivary enzymes.

4.   Recentrifuge at $900\text{-}1000 \times g$ for 8-10 minutes, remove clear or slightly opalescent supernatant fluid, and discard the opaque or semisolid material. Dilute the supernatant fluid with an equal volume of saline.

5. Refrigerate, if testing is to be done within several hours. If testing will not be done on the day of collection, freeze the sample and store at –20 C. Frozen samples retain activity for several years.

Reagents

1. Human (polyclonal) anti-A and anti-B. Note: Some monoclonal reagents may not be appropriate for use, therefore, appropriate controls are essential.
2. Anti-H lectin from *Ulex europaeus*: Obtained commercially or prepared by saline extraction of *Ulex europaeus* seeds.
3. Polyclonal (rabbit/goat/human) anti-Le^a. There are no published data on the suitability of monoclonal Lewis antibodies.
4. A$_1$ and B red cells, as used in Method 2.2.
5. Group O, Le(a+b–) red cells, as used for antibody detection or identification. See Chapter 19.
6. Specimens, frozen or fresh, saliva from persons known to be secretors or nonsecretors, to use as positive and negative controls.

Procedures

Selection of Blood Grouping Reagent Dilution

1. Prepare doubling dilutions of the appropriate blood typing reagent.
2. To 1 drop of each reagent dilution add 1 drop of 2-5% saline suspension of red cells. Use A$_1$, B, or O cells to determine, respectively, A, B, or H secretor status. Use Le(a+b–) red cells to determine Lewis secretor status.
3. Centrifuge each tube and examine macroscopically for agglutination.
4. Select the highest reagent dilution that gives 2+ agglutination.

Inhibition Test for Secretor Status

1. Add 1 drop of appropriately diluted blood grouping reagent to each of four tubes.

For ABH studies, the tubes should be labeled "Secretor," "Nonsecretor," "Saline," and "Unknown." For Lewis studies, they will be "Lewis-positive," "Lewis-negative," "Saline," and "Unknown."

2. Add 1 drop of the appropriate saliva to the "Secretor," "Nonsecretor," and "Unknown" tubes, and 1 drop of saline to the tube marked "Saline."
3. Mix the contents of the tubes. Incubate them for 8-10 minutes at room temperature.
4. Add 1 drop of 2-5% saline suspension of washed indicator cells to each tube, group A, B, or O for ABH secretor status, as appropriate, or Le(a+) for Lewis testing.
5. Mix the contents of the tubes. Incubate them for 30-60 minutes at room temperature.
6. Centrifuge each tube, and inspect each cell button macroscopically for agglutination.

Interpretation

1. Agglutination of indicator cells by antibody in tubes containing saliva indicates that the saliva does not contain the corresponding antigen.
2. Failure of known antibody to agglutinate indicator cells after incubation with saliva indicates that the saliva contains the corresponding antigen.
3. Failure of antibody in the saline control tube to agglutinate indicator cells invalidates the results of saliva tests; this usually reflects use of reagents that are too dilute. Redetermine the appropriate reagent dilution, as described above, and repeat the testing.
4. For further interpretation see Table 2.5-1.

Notes

1. Include as controls saliva from a known secretor and nonsecretor. For ABH sta-

tus, use saliva from previously tested *Se* and *sese* persons. For Lewis testing, use saliva from a person whose red cells are Le(a+b−) or Le(a−b+) as the positive control; use saliva from a Le(a−b−) person as the negative control. Aliquots of saliva from persons of known secretor status may be frozen for later use.

2. This screening procedure can be adapted for the semiquantitation of blood group activity by testing serial saline dilutions of saliva. The higher the dilution needed to remove inhibitory activity, the more blood group substance is present in the saliva. Saliva should be diluted before its incubation with antibody. To detect or to measure salivary A or B substance in addition to H substance, the same procedure can be used with diluted anti-A and anti-B reagents. The appropriate dilution of anti-A or anti-B is obtained by titrating the reagent against A_1 or B red cells, respectively.

3. A Lewis-positive person shown to be a secretor of A, B, and H can be assumed to have Le^b as well as Le^a in the saliva. A

Le(a+) person who does not secrete A, B, or H substances lacks the *Se* gene and will have only Le^a in the saliva.

4. Specimens with a high concentration of soluble antigen may give a false negative result. This type of specimen requires dilution prior to testing.

Method 2.6. Slide Test for Rh Testing

Principle

See Chapter 14 for a discussion of the principles of Rh typing.

Specimen

Refer to Method 2.2.

Reagents

1. Reagent anti-D: Suitable reagents include polyclonal high-protein, chemically modified low-protein, or blended IgM/IgG monoclonal/polyclonal low-protein reagents. Follow the instructions

Table 2.5.-1. Interpretation of Saliva Testing

	Testing with Anti-H			
Unknown Saliva	Se Saliva (H Substance Present)	Non-Se Saliva (H Substance Not Present)	Saline (Dilution Control)	Interpretation
2+	0	2+	2+	Nonsecretor of H
0	0	2+	2+	Secretor of H

	Testing With Anti-Le^a			
Unknown Saliva	Le-positive Saliva	Le-negative Saliva	Saline (Dilution Control)	Interpretation
2+	0	2+	2+	Lewis-negative
0	0	2+	2+	Lewis-positive[*]

*A Lewis-positive person shown to be a secretor of ABH can be assumed to have Le^b as well as Le^a in saliva. A Le(a+) person who is *sese* and does not secrete ABH substance will have only Le^a in saliva.

from the manufacturer of the anti-D in use before performing slide tests; the method presented here is a representative procedure.

2. Rh control reagent: The manufacturer's instructions will indicate the type of reagent to use, if needed.

Procedure

1. Place 1 drop of anti-D serum onto a clean, labeled slide.
2. Place 1 drop of the appropriate control reagent onto a second labeled slide. (The manufacturer's instructions will indicate type of control, if needed.)
3. To each slide add 2 drops of a well-mixed 40-50% suspension (in autologous or group-compatible serum or plasma) of the red cells to be tested.
4. Thoroughly mix the cell suspension and reagent, using a clean applicator stick for each test, spreading the reaction mixture over an area approximately 20 mm × 40 mm.
5. Place both the slides on the viewbox and tilt them gently and continuously to observe them for agglutination (see note 1). Most manufacturers stipulate that the test must be read within 2 minutes because drying of the reaction mixture may cause formation of rouleaux, which may be mistaken for agglutination.
6. Interpret and record the results of the reactions on both slides.

Interpretation

1. Agglutination with anti-D and a smooth suspension on the control slide constitute a positive test result and indicate that the cells being tested are D-positive.
2. No agglutination with either anti-D or the Rh control suggests that the cells are D-negative. Testing by the antiglobulin procedure (see Method 2.9) will show if

there is weak expression of D on cells that are not agglutinated on slide testing.

3. If there is agglutination on the control slide, results of the anti-D test must not be interpreted as positive without further testing.
4. Drying around the edges of the reaction mixture must not be confused with agglutination.

Notes

1. Slide testing imposes much greater risk of contact between specimen and technologist than occurs with tube testing. Personnel should follow safety measures detailed in the facility's procedures manual.
2. For slide tests using low-protein anti-D, a negative result on slide testing with either anti-A or anti-B serves as the control reaction.

Method 2.7. Tube Test for Rh Testing

Principle

See Chapter 14 for a discussion of the principles of Rh typing.

Specimen

Refer to Method 2.2.

Reagents

1. Reagent anti-D: Suitable reagents include polyclonal high-protein, chemically modified low-protein, or blended IgM/IgG monoclonal/polyclonal low-protein reagents. Follow the instructions from the manufacturer of the anti-D in use before performing slide tests. The method presented here is a representative procedure.

2. Rh control reagent: The manufacturer's instructions will indicate the type of control to use, if needed.

Procedure

1. Place 1 drop of anti-D serum in a clean, labeled test tube.
2. Place 1 drop of the appropriate control reagent in a second labeled tube.
3. Add to each tube 1 drop of a 2-5% suspension (in saline, serum or plasma) of the red cells to be tested; alternatively, the equivalent amount of red cells can be transferred to each tube with clean applicator sticks.
4. Mix gently and centrifuge for the time and speed specified by the manufacturer. Typically this is 30-45 seconds at 900-1000 $\times g$.
5. Gently resuspend the cell button and examine for agglutination. If a stick was used to transfer the red cells, adding 1 drop of saline to each tube will make it easier to resuspend the cell button.
6. Grade reactions and record test and control results.

Interpretation

1. Agglutination in the anti-D tube, combined with a smooth suspension in the control tube, indicates that the red cells under investigation are D-positive.
2. A smooth suspension of red cells in both the anti-D and the control tubes is a negative test result. Although specimens from most patients may be designated as D-negative at this point, all females undergoing delivery, abortion, or invasive obstetric procedures as well as donor blood must be further tested for the presence of weakly expressed D antigen. The serum-and-cell mixture used in steps 1-5, above, may be used to test for weak D, providing the manufacturer's directions state that the reagent is suitable for the test for weak D.

Notes

1. Most commercially prepared antisera provide a 2+ or greater agglutination with D-positive cells. A facility may choose to do additional testing on results with agglutination of <2+. Required testing must be defined in the facility's procedures manual.
2. A negative tube test with anti-A and/or anti-B serves as a valid control when a low-protein anti-D reagent has been used.

Method 2.8. Microplate Test for Determination of Rh Type

Principle

See Chapter 14 for a discussion of the principles of Rh typing and Method 2.3 for a discussion of microplate testing.

Specimen

Refer to Method 2.2. Clotted or anticoagulated samples may be used for Rh testing. Follow the manufacturer's instructions for specimen preparation when using semiautomated microplate readers.

Reagents

Use only anti-D approved for use in microplate tests. See discussion in Method 2.3.

Procedure

The following is a representative method; the manufacturer's instructions should be followed for specific reagents and equipment.

1. Place 1 drop of the Rh reagent in a clean well of the microplate. If the reagent requires the use of an Rh control, add 1 drop of the control to a second well.
2. Add 1 drop of a 2-5% saline suspension of red cells to each well.

3. Mix the contents of the wells by gently tapping the sides of the plate.
4. Centrifuge the plate at appropriate conditions established for the centrifuge.
5. Resuspend the cell buttons manually by tapping the plate or with the aid of a mechanical shaker.
6. Read, interpret, and record results.
7. Incubate negative tests at 37 C for 15 minutes.
8. Centrifuge the plate at appropriate conditions established for the centrifuge.
9. Resuspend the cell buttons manually by tapping the plate or with the aid of a mechanical shaker.
10. Read, interpret, and record results.

Interpretation

Agglutination with Rh reagent after the immediate-spin or 37 C incubation phase indicates a positive test, provided there is no agglutination with the control reagent. See Table 14-3 of Chapter 14 for determining Rh phenotypes from reactions obtained with Rh blood typing reagents.

Method 2.9. Test for Weak D

Principle

Some red cells express the D antigen so weakly that the cells are not directly agglutinated by most anti-D reagents. Weak D expression can be recognized most reliably by an indirect antiglobulin procedure after incubation of the test red cells with anti-D.

Specimen

Refer to Method 2.2.

Reagents

1. Reagent anti-D: Suitable reagents include polyclonal high-protein, chemically modified low-protein, or blended IgM/IgG monoclonal/polyclonal low-

protein reagents, but the manufacturer's package insert should be consulted before any anti-D reagent is used for this purpose. Not every anti-D reagent is suitable for the weak D test, either because testing by the manufacturer has not shown reliable reactions with red cells that express weak D, or because the reagent contains other antibodies that react when antiglobulin serum is added.
2. Antihuman globulin reagent, either polyspecific or anti-IgG.
3. IgG-coated red cells.

Procedure

Note: If the original, direct test with anti-D was performed by tube testing, the same tube may be used for the weak D test, providing the manufacturer's directions so state. In this case, proceed directly to step 4, after recording the original anti-D tube test as negative.

1. Place 1 drop of anti-D serum in a clean, labeled test tube.
2. Place 1 drop of the appropriate control reagent in a second labeled test tube.
3. To each tube add 1 drop of a 2-5% suspension in saline of the red cells to be tested. It is permissible to use a direct antiglobulin test on the test cells as a control, but the indirect antiglobulin procedure with Rh control reagent is preferable, as this ensures that all reagent components that might cause a false-positive result are represented.
4. Mix and incubate both tubes according to reagent manufacturer's directions. Typically this is 15-30 minutes at 37 C.
5. If a reading is desired after the 37 C incubation phase, centrifuge according to the reagent manufacturer's directions. Typically this is 15-45 seconds at 900-1000 $\times g$.
6. Gently resuspend the cell buttons and examine them for agglutination. If the test red cells are strongly agglutinated in the anti-D tube but not in the control tube,

record the test sample as D-positive and do not proceed with the antiglobulin phase of the test.

7. If the test cells are not agglutinated or results are doubtful, wash the cells three or four times with large volumes of saline.

8. After the final wash, decant the saline completely, blot the rims of the tubes dry, and add 1 or 2 drops of antiglobulin reagent, according to the manufacturer's directions.

9. Mix gently and centrifuge according to manufacturer's directions. Typically this is 15-30 seconds at 900-1000 $\times g$.

10. Gently resuspend each cell button, examine them for agglutination, and grade and record the test result.

11. If the test result is negative, add known IgG-sensitized red cells, and repeat centrifugation and examination for agglutination. Agglutination at this point confirms the presence of active antiglobulin reagent in the test mixture.

Interpretation

1. Either a diluent control or direct antiglobulin test must accompany the test for weak D. Agglutination in the anti-D tube and none in the control tube constitutes a positive test result. The blood must be classified as D-positive. It is incorrect to report such red cells as being "D-negative, weak D-positive" or "D-negative, D^u."

2. Absence of agglutination in the tube with anti-D is a negative result, indicating that the cells do not express D and should be classified as D-negative.

3. If there is agglutination at any phase in the control tube, no valid interpretation of the weak D test can be made. If the specimen is from a potential transfusion recipient, Rh-negative blood should be given until the D type can be resolved. If the specimen is from a donor, the unit should not be used for transfusion.

4. The causes of false-positive and false-negative antiglobulin tests are discussed in Chapter 20.

Note

Some facilities may elect to do an additional reading after the 37 C incubation before completing the antiglobulin phase of testing. If this optional reading is performed, the facility's procedures manual should indicate its policy on interpretation of this result and on additional testing requirements.

Method 2.10. Preparation and Use of Lectin

Principle

Saline extracts of seeds react with specific carbohydrates on cell membranes and make useful typing reagents that are highly specific at appropriate dilutions. Diluted extract of *Dolichos biflorus* agglutinates A$_1$ red cells but not A$_2$. *Ulex europaeus* extract reacts with the H determinant; it agglutinates in a manner proportional to the amount of H present (O>A$_2$>B>A$_2$B>A$_1$>A$_1$B red cells). Other lectins useful for special purposes include *Arachis hypogaea* (anti-T), *Glycine max* (anti-T, -Tn), *Vicia graminea* (anti-N) and the *Salvia* lectins (*S. horminum*, anti-Tn/Cad; *S. sclarea*, anti-Tn). To investigate red cell polyagglutination, prepare and test the cells with *Arachis*, *Glycine*, *Salvia*, and *Dolichos* lectins. The anticipated reactions with various types of polyagglutinable red cells are shown in Table 2.10-1.

Reagents

Seeds: *Arachis hypogaea* (peanuts) and *Glycine max* (soy beans) may be obtained from health-food stores, pharmacies or commercial seed companies. The seeds should be raw.

Table 2.10-1. Reactions Between Lectins and Polyagglutinable Red Cells

	T	Th	Tk	Tn	Cad
*Arachis hypogaea**	+	+	+	0	0
Dolichos biflorus†	0	0	0	+	+
Glycine max (soja)	+	0	0	+	+
Salvia sclarea	0	0	0	+	0
Salvia horminum	0	0	0	+	+

*T and Th cells give weaker reactions with *Arachis* after protease treatment; Tk reactivity is enhanced after protease treatment.
†A and AB cells may react due to anti-A reactivity of *Dolichos* lectin.

Procedure

1. Grind seeds in a food processor or blender until the particles look like coarse sand. Mortar and pestle may be used, or seeds can be used whole.
2. In a large test tube or small beaker, place ground seeds and three to four times their volume of saline. (Seeds vary in the quantity of saline they absorb.)
3. Incubate at room temperature for 4-12 hours, stirring or inverting occasionally.
4. Transfer supernatant fluid to a centrifuge tube and centrifuge for 5 minutes, to obtain clear supernatant. Collect, then filter the supernatant fluid and discard seed residue.
5. Determine activity of extract with appropriate red cells, as below.
   For *Dolichos biflorus*:
   a. Add 1 drop of 2-5% saline suspension of known A_1, A_2, A_1B, A_2B, B, and O red cells to appropriately labeled tubes.
   b. Add 1 drop of extract to each tube.
   c. Centrifuge 15 seconds.
   d. Inspect for agglutination and record results.
   e. Lectin should agglutinate A_1 and A_1B cells but not A_2, A_2B, B, or O cells. The native extract often ag-

glutinates all cells tested. To make the product useful for reagent purposes, add enough saline to the extract so there is 3+ or 4+ agglutination of A_1 and A_1B cells, but not of A_2, A_2B, B, or O cells.

For *Ulex europaeus*:
a. Add 1 drop of 2-5% saline suspension of known A_1, A_2, A_1B, B, and O cells to appropriately labeled tubes.
b. Add 1 drop of extract to each tube.
c. Centrifuge 15 seconds.
d. Inspect for agglutination and record results.
e. Strength of agglutination should be in the order of $O > A_2 > B > A_1 > A_1B$.
f. Dilute extract with saline, if necessary, to a point that O cells show 3+ or 4+ agglutination, A_2 and B cells show 1+ to 2+ agglutination, and A_1 or A_1B cells are not agglutinated.

Notes

1. To facilitate grinding hard seeds, the seeds can be covered with saline and soaked for several hours before grinding. The container used for soaking should not be tightly closed because some beans release gas during the soaking process, which could cause the container to explode.
2. The saline extracts may be stored in the refrigerator for several days; they may be stored indefinitely if frozen.
3. Tests should include a positive and negative control.

Method 2.11. Use of Sulfhydryl Reagents to Disperse Autoagglutination

Principle

See Chapter 20 for a discussion of autoagglutination dispersion.

Specimen

Red cells to be evaluated.

Reagents

1. 0.01 M dithiothreitol (DTT): 0.154 g of DTT dissolved in 100 mL of phosphate-buffered saline (PBS) at pH 7.3; or 0.1 M 2-mercaptoethanol (2-ME), 0.7 mL of stock solution of 14 M 2-ME diluted in 100 mL of PBS at pH 7.3.
2. Phosphate-buffered saline at pH 7.3.

Procedure

1. Dilute red cells to a 50% concentration in PBS.
2. Add an equal quantity of 0.01 M DTT in PBS, or 0.1 M 2-ME in PBS, to the cells.
3. Incubate at 37 C for 10 minutes (2-ME) or 15 minutes (DTT).
4. Wash cells three times in normal saline and resuspend them.
5. Dilute the treated red cells to a 2-5% concentration in saline for use in blood grouping tests.

Reference

Reid ME. Autoagglutination dispersal utilizing sulfydryl compounds. Transfusion 1978;18:353-5.

Method 2.12. Gentle Heat Elution for Testing DAT-Positive Red Cells

Principle

When red cells are heavily coated with IgG, testing with antiglobulin-reactive sera is difficult and testing with high-protein agglutinating reagents is impractical. To perform red cell antigen typing, it may be necessary to dissociate antibody from the cells by elution without damaging membrane integrity or altering antigen expression. The gentle heat elution procedure employed to prepare immunoglobulin-free red cells differs from procedures intended to recover active antibody. To demonstrate that elution has not damaged antigen reactivity of the test red cells, it is important to treat in parallel an aliquot of uncoated, normal red cells known to express the antigen for which the individual's cells will be tested.

Reagent

Antihuman globulin.

Specimen

Test cells with a positive DAT.

Procedure

1. Place one volume of washed, packed antibody-coated red cells and three volumes of normal saline in a test tube of appropriate size. In another tube, place the same volumes of saline and washed, packed red cells positive for the antigen under test. This will provide a check that the elution technique does not destroy the antigen reactivity.
2. Incubate the contents of both tubes at approximately 45 C for 10-30 minutes. The tubes should be agitated frequently. The time of incubation should be roughly proportional to the degree of antibody coating, as indicated by strength of antiglobulin reactivity.
3. Centrifuge the tubes and discard the supernatant saline.
4. Test the person's cells for degree of antibody removal by comparing a direct antiglobulin test on the treated cells with the antiglobulin results on untreated red cells. If the antibody coating is reduced but still present, steps 1 through 3 can be repeated; the control cells should similarly be subjected to a second treatment.
5. Test the treated cells for the desired antigen.

Notes

1. This procedure becomes unnecessary if IgM monoclonal reagents are available; these reagents cause direct agglutination and are not affected by bound immunoglobulin.
2. As with nontreated patient cells, results of antigen typings in recently transfused patients should be interpreted with caution because of the potential presence of donor cells.

Method 2.13. Dissociation of IgG by Chloroquine for Red Cell Antigen Testing of Red Cells with a Positive DAT

Principle

Red cells with a positive direct antiglobulin test (DAT) cannot accurately be tested with blood typing reagents that require an indirect antiglobulin technique. Under controlled conditions, chloroquine diphosphate dissociates IgG from the red cell membrane with little or no damage to its integrity. Use of this procedure permits complete phenotyping of red cells coated with warm-reactive autoantibody, including tests with reagents solely reactive by indirect antiglobulin techniques.

Specimen

Red cells with a positive DAT due to IgG coating.

Reagents

1. Chloroquine diphosphate solution prepared by dissolving 20 g of chloroquine diphosphate in 100 mL of saline. Adjust to pH 5.1 with 1 N NaOH, and store at 2-6 C.
2. Control red cells, carrying a single-dose expression of antigens for which the test samples are to be phenotyped.
3. Anti-IgG antiglobulin reagent.

Procedure

1. To 0.2 mL of washed, packed IgG-coated cells add 0.8 mL of chloroquine diphosphate solution. Similarly treat the control sample.
2. Mix and incubate at room temperature for 30 minutes.
3. Remove a small aliquot (eg, 1 drop) of the treated test cells and wash them four times with saline.
4. Test the washed cells with anti-IgG.
5. If this treatment has rendered the cells nonreactive with anti-IgG, wash the total volumes of treated test cells and control cells three times in saline and make a 2-5% suspension in solution to use in subsequent blood typing tests.
6. If the treated red cells still react with anti-IgG after 30 minutes of incubation with chloroquine diphosphate, steps 3 and 4 should be repeated at 30-minute intervals (for a maximum incubation period of 2 hours), until the sample tested is nonreactive with anti-IgG. Then proceed as described in step 5.

Notes

1. Chloroquine diphosphate does not dissociate complement proteins from the cell membrane. If red cells are coated with both IgG and C3, only anti-IgG should be used in tests performed after chloroquine treatment.
2. Incubation with chloroquine diphosphate should not be extended beyond 2 hours. Prolonged incubation at room temperature or incubation at 37 C may cause hemolysis and loss of red cell antigens.
3. Some denaturation of Rh antigens may occur. This is most often noted when red cells have hemolyzed after incubation with chloroquine diphosphate, or when saline-reactive or chemically modified anti-Rh reagents are used. Only high-

protein reagents and controls should be used for testing chloroquine-treated red cells.

4. When chloroquine-treated red cells are typed for antigens other than those in the Rh system, a parallel tube containing an immunologically inert reagent such as 6% bovine albumin should also be tested.

5. Chloroquine diphosphate may not completely remove antibody from sensitized red cells. DAT results on red cells from some persons, particularly those with a strongly positive initial test, may only be diminished in strength.

6. In addition to its use for removal of autoantibodies, this method can be used for removal of Bg (HLA)-related antigens from red cells. Appropriate Bg controls should be used.

References

1. Edwards JM, Moulds JJ, Judd WJ. Chloroquine diphosphate dissociation of antigen-antibody complexes: A new technique for phenotyping rbcs with a positive direct antiglobulin test. Transfusion 1982;22:59-61.
2. Swanson JL, Sastamoinen R. Chloroquine stripping of the HLA-A,B antigens from red cells (letter). Transfusion 1985;25:439-40.

Method 2.14. Acid Glycine/ EDTA Method to Remove Antibodies from Red Cells

Principle

Acid glycine/EDTA can be used to dissociate antibody molecules from red cell membranes. The procedure has been used with some success to prepare eluates, but is more frequently employed to dissociate IgG from cells for use in blood typing tests or adsorption procedures. All common red cell antigens can be detected after treatment with acid glycine/EDTA except antigens of the Kell system. Thus, cells treated in this manner cannot be used to determine Kell system phenotypes. Autoantibody-coated cells

can be wholly or partially freed from coating immunoglobulins by acid glycine/EDTA treatment and can then be used for autoadsorption; further treatment with a dilute solution of enzyme may enhance antibody uptake.

Specimen

Red cells to be evaluated.

Reagents

1. 10% EDTA prepared by dissolving 2 g of disodium ethylenediamine tetraacetic acid (Na_2EDTA) in 20 mL of distilled or deionized water.

2. 0.1 M glycine-HCl buffer (pH 1.5) prepared by diluting 0.75 g of glycine to 100 mL with isotonic (unbuffered) saline. Adjust the pH to 1.5 using concentrated HCl.

3. 1.0 M TRIS-NaCl prepared by dissolving 12.1 g of tris(hydroxymethyl)aminomethane (TRIS) and 5.25 g of sodium chloride (NaCl) to 100 mL with distilled or deionized water.

Procedure

1. Wash the red cells to be treated six times with isotonic saline.

2. In a test tube, mix together 20 volumes of 0.1 M acid glycine-HCl (pH 1.5) with five volumes of 10% EDTA. This is the acid glycine/EDTA reagent.

3. Place 10 volumes of washed packed red cells in a clean tube.

4. Add 20 volumes of acid glycine/EDTA.

5. Mix the contents of the tube thoroughly.

6. Incubate the mixture at room temperature for no more than 2-3 minutes.

7. Add one volume of 1.0 M TRIS-NaCl and mix the contents of the tube.

8. Centrifuge at 900-1000 $\times g$ for 1-2 minutes, then aspirate, and discard the supernatant fluid.

9. Wash the red cells four times with saline.

10. Test the washed cells with anti-IgG; if nonreactive with anti-IgG, the cells are

ready for use in blood typing or adsorption procedures.

Notes

1. Overincubation of red cells with acid glycine/EDTA causes irreversible damage to cell membranes.
2. Include a parallel control reagent, such as 6% bovine albumin, when typing treated red cells.
3. Use anti-IgG, not a polyspecific antiglobulin reagent, in step 10.

References

1. Louie JE, Jiang AF, Zaroulis CG. Preparation of intact antibody-free red cells in autoimmune hemolytic anemia (abstract). Transfusion 1986;26:550.
2. Byrne PC. Use of a modified acid/EDTA elution technique. Immunohematology 1991;7:46-7.
3. Champagne K, Spruell P, Chen J, et al. EDTA/glycine-acid vs. chloroquine diphosphate treatment for stripping Bg antigens from red blood cells (abstract). Transfusion 1996;36:21S.

Method 2.15. Separation of Transfused from Autologous Red Cells by Simple Centrifugation

Principle

Newly formed autologous red cells generally have a lower specific gravity than transfused red cells and may be separated from the transfused population by simple centrifugation. Newly formed autologous cells concentrate at the top of the column of red cells when blood is centrifuged in a microhematocrit tube, providing a simple method for recovering autologous cells in a blood sample from recently transfused patients. Note: Red cells from patients with hemoglobin S or spherocytic disorders are not effectively separated by this method. See Method 2.16 for an alternative procedure.

Specimen

Red cells from whole blood collected into EDTA.

Materials

1. Microhematocrit equipment: centrifuge, plain (not heparinized) glass hematocrit tubes, and sealant such as Seal-ease®.
2. 2-mL syringe and 23-gauge needle.

Procedure

1. Wash the red cells three times in saline. For the last wash, centrifuge them at $900\text{-}1000 \times g$ for 5-15 minutes. Remove as much of the supernatant fluid as possible without disturbing the buffy coat. Mix thoroughly.
2. Fill 10 microhematocrit tubes to the 60-mm mark with well-mixed, washed red cells.
3. Seal the ends of the tubes by heat, or with sealant.
4. Centrifuge all tubes in a microhematocrit centrifuge for 15 minutes.
5. Cut the microhematocrit tubes 5 mm below the top of the column of red cells. This 5-mm segment contains the least dense, hence youngest, circulating red cells.
6. Flush the red cells from the 5-mm column in the cut hematocrit tubes into a clean test tube, using a saline-filled syringe and 23-gauge needle. Alternatively, place the cut microhematocrit tubes into larger test tubes (10 or 12×75 mm) and centrifuge them at $1000 \times g$ for 1 minute. Remove the empty glass hematocrit tubes.
7. Wash the separated red cells three times in saline before resuspending them to 2-5% in saline for testing.

Notes

1. Separation is better if 3 or more days have elapsed than if the sample is obtained shortly after transfusion.

2. The packed red cells should be mixed continuously while the microhematocrit tubes are being filled.
3. Separation techniques are only effective if the patient is producing normal or above-normal numbers of reticulocytes. This method will be ineffective in patients with inadequate reticulocyte production, notably patients transfused for aplastic anemia.
4. Some red cell antigens may not be as strongly expressed on reticulocytes as on older cells. Particular attention should be given to determinations of the E, e, c, Fy^a, Jk^a, and Ge antigens.

References

1. Reid ME, Toy P. Simplified method for recovery of autologous red blood cells from transfused patients. Am J Clin Pathol 1983;79:364-6.
2. Vengelen-Tyler V, Gonzales B. Reticulocyte rich RBCs will give weak reactions with many blood typing antisera (abstract). Transfusion 1985;25:476.

Method 2.16. Separation of Transfused from Autologous Red Cells in Patients with Hemoglobin S Disease

Principle

Red cells from patients with sickle cell disease, either hemoglobin SS or SC, are resistant to lysis by hypotonic saline, in contrast to red cells from normal persons and those with hemoglobin S trait. This procedure permits isolation of autologous red cells from patients with hemoglobin SS or SC disease who have recently been transfused.

Specimen

Red cells to be evaluated.

Reagents

1. Hypotonic saline (0.3% w/v NaCl): NaCl, 3 g; distilled water to 1 L.
2. Normal saline (0.9% w/v NaCl): NaCl, 9 g; distilled water to 1 L.

Procedure

1. Place 4 or 5 drops of red cells into a 10 or 12×75-mm test tube.
2. Wash the cells six times with 0.3% NaCl, or until the supernatant fluid no longer contains grossly visible hemoglobin. For each wash, centrifuge at $1000 \times g$ for 1 minute.
3. Wash the cells twice with 0.9% NaCl to restore tonicity. For each wash, centrifuge at $200 \times g$ for 2 minutes to facilitate removal of residual stroma.
4. Resuspend the remaining intact red cells to a 2-5% concentration for phenotyping.

Note

Larger volumes, for use in adsorption studies, can be processed in a 16×100-mm test tube.

Reference

Brown D. A rapid method for harvesting autologous red cells from patients with hemoglobin S disease. Transfusion 1988;28:21-3.

3

Antibody Detection, Antibody Identification, and Serologic Compatibility Testing Methods

Method 3.1. Immediate-Spin Compatibility Testing to Demonstrate ABO Incompatibility

Principle

See Chapter 18 for a discussion of the principles of compatibility testing.

Specimen

Some workers prefer to suspend the donor red cells in EDTA saline because high-titered anti-A or -B can initiate complement coating, which can cause steric hindrance of agglutination.[1] EDTA prevents complement activation by chelating Ca^{2+} needed for classical-pathway activation of complement (see Chapter 11).

Reagents

1. Normal saline: 0.85% or 0.9% (w/v) sodium chloride.
2. Donor red cells, 2-5% suspension in normal saline or EDTA saline. (See Method 1.7 for preparation of EDTA saline.)
3. Patient's serum (which must be drawn within 3 days of the expected transfusion if the patient is within the 3-month window of serologic instability, as required by Section I4.000 of *Standards for Blood Banks and Transfusion Services*[2]).

Procedure

1. Label a glass test tube for each donor red cell suspension being tested with the patient's serum.
2. Add 2 drops of the patient's serum to each tube.

3. Add 1 drop of the suspension of donor red cells to the appropriate test tube.

4. Mix the contents of the tube(s) and centrifuge them for 15-20 seconds at approximately 900-1000 $\times g$.

5. Examine the tube(s) for hemolysis, gently resuspend the red cell button(s), and examine them for agglutination. Microscopic readings are generally not necessary.

6. Read, interpret, and record test results.

Interpretation

1. Agglutination or hemolysis constitutes a positive (incompatible) test result.

2. A smooth suspension of red cells after resuspension of the red cell button constitutes a negative result and indicates a compatible immediate-spin crossmatch.

References

1. Judd WJ, Steiner EA, O'Donnell DB, Oberman HA. Discrepancies in ABO typing due to prozone; how safe is the immediate-spin crossmatch? Transfusion 1988;28:334-8.
2. Menitove JE, ed. Standards for blood banks and transfusion services, 19th ed. Bethesda, MD: American Association of Blood Banks, 1999:58

Method 3.2. Indirect Antiglobulin Test (IAT) for the Detection of Red Cell Antibodies

Principle

For a discussion of the principles of saline, albumin, low ionic strength saline (LISS), enzyme and polyethylene glycol (PEG) indirect antiglobulin testing, see Chapters 12, 18, and 19. Low ionic Polybrene® (LIP); a highly cationic quaternary ammonium polymer, brings normal red cells together in aggregates that are dispersed on addition of citrate. Red cells sensitized with antibody are irreversibly aggregated by Polybrene®. In the LIP procedure, red cells are incubated with serum in a low-ionic-strength medium, which facilitates attachment of antibody to red cells, and Polybrene® is then added. After centrifugation, sodium citrate is added to reverse the aggregating effect of Polybrene®. Antibody-mediated agglutination persists after addition of citrate, but uncoated cells will be dispersed. If antiglobulin serum is to be added after reversal of Polybrene® effect, additional citrate is used to wash the cells.

Saline, albumin, LISS, PEG, and LIP techniques are suitable for use in pretransfusion testing. Enzyme techniques are more appropriately used for antibody identification.

Specimen

Serum or plasma may be used. Specimen age must comply with pretransfusion specimen requirements in AABB *Standards for Blood Banks and Transfusion Services*.

Reagents

1. Normal saline.
2. Bovine albumin (22% or 30%).
3. LISS additive obtained commercially or made as follows:
   a. Add 1.75 g of NaCl and 18 g of glycine to a 1 liter volumetric flask.
   b. Add 20 mL of phosphate buffer prepared by combining 11.3 mL of 0.15 M KH_2PO_4 and 8.7 mL of 0.15 M Na_2HPO_4.
   c. Add distilled water to the 1 liter mark.
   d. Adjust pH to 6.7 with NaOH.
   e. Add 0.5 g of sodium azide as a preservative.

   Note: Adding sodium azide at this concentration raises the ionic strength from 0.0355 to 0.043. This does not affect serologic reactivity.

4. PEG, 20% w/v: to 20 g of 3350 MW PEG (SIGMA Chemicals, St. Louis, MO), add

phosphate-buffered saline (PBS) pH 7.3 (see Method 1.6) to 100 mL.

5.   LIP Reagents

a.   Low ionic medium (LIM): To a 500-mL volumetric flask, add 25 g of dextrose and 1 g of $Na_2EDTA \cdot 2H_2O$. Fill flask to 500-mL mark with distilled water.

b.   Polybrene®: *Stock solution* (10% w/v): Add 5g of Polybrene® (Aldrich Chemical Co, Milwaukee, WI) to 50 mL of normal saline. Store in plastic container at 1-6 C. *Working solution* (0.05% w/v): Mix 0.1 mL of stock solution with 19.9 mL of normal saline. Store in plastic container at 1-6 C.

c.   Resuspending solution: 0.2 M trisodium citrate made by adding 5.88 g of $Na_3C_6H_5O$ to a 100-mL volumetric flask and filling to the 100-mL mark with distilled water; *5% dextrose* made by adding 5 g of dextrose to 100 mL of distilled water; *working solution* made by mixing 60 mL of 0.2 M trisodium citrate with 40 mL of 5% dextrose.

d.   Washing solution (for antiglobulin testing): 0.01 M of sodium citrate made by diluting 0.2 M of trisodium citrate (see above) to 1 in 20 with normal saline (eg, add 50 mL of 0.2 M trisodium citrate to 950 mL of saline).

6.   Antihuman globulin (AHG) reagent. Polyspecific or anti-IgG may be used unless otherwise indicated. Anti-IgG need not be heavy-chain specific.

7.   Commercially available unpooled group O antibody screening cells. Pooled group O screening cells may be used only for donor testing. Patient testing must be done with unpooled cells.

8.   IgG-coated red cells, for addition to negative AHG tests.

Method 3.2.1. Saline Indirect Antiglobulin Test

Procedure

1.   Add 2 drops of serum to properly labeled tubes.

2.   Add 1 drop of reagent O cells or donor red cells as a 2-5% saline suspension to each tube and mix.

3.   Centrifuge and observe for hemolysis and agglutination. Grade and record the results.

4.   Incubate at 37 C for 30-60 minutes.

5.   Centrifuge and observe for hemolysis and agglutination. Grade and record the results.

6.   Wash the cells three or four times with saline and completely decant the final wash.

7.   Add AHG to the dry cell button according to the manufacturer's directions. Mix well.

8.   Centrifuge and observe for reaction. Grade and record the results.

9.   Confirm the validity of negative tests by adding IgG-coated red cells.

Method 3.2.2. Albumin (or LISS-Additive) Indirect Antiglobulin Test

Procedure

1.   Add 2 drops of serum to properly labeled tubes.

2.   Add an equivalent volume of 22% or 30% bovine albumin or LISS additive (unless manufacturer's directions state otherwise.)

3.   Add 1 drop of a 2-5% saline-suspended reagent or donor red cells to each tube and mix.

4.   Incubate at 37 C for 15-30 minutes. For LISS, incubate for 10-15 minutes or follow the manufacturer's directions.

5.   Centrifuge and observe for hemolysis and agglutination. Grade and record the results.

6.   Perform the test described in Method 3.2.1, steps 6-9.

Method 3.2.3. LISS Indirect Antiglobulin Test

Procedure

1.   Wash reagent or donor red cells three times in normal saline and completely decant saline.
2.   Resuspend the cells to a 2-5% suspension in LISS.
3.   Add 2 drops of serum to properly labeled tube.
4.   Add 2 drops of LISS-suspended red cells, mix, and incubate according to manufacturer's directions. Typically this is 10-15 minutes at 37 C.
5.   Centrifuge according to manufacturer's directions. Typically this is 15-30 seconds at 900-1000 $\times g$ and observe for hemolysis and agglutination by gently resuspending the cell button. Grade and record results.
6.   Perform the test described in Method 3.2.1, steps 6-9.
     Note: Commercial LISS additive solutions are available. The manufacturer's instructions should be followed for the proper use of these preparations.

Method 3.2.4. PEG Indirect Antiglobulin Test

Procedure

1.   For each cell sample to be tested, mix 2 drops of test serum, 4 drops of 20% PEG in PBS, and 1 drop of a 2-5% suspension of red cells.
2.   Incubate according to manufacturer's directions. Typically this is 37 C for 15 minutes.
3.   DO NOT CENTRIFUGE.
4.   Wash the cells four times with saline and completely decant the final wash.
5.   Perform the AHG test, using anti-IgG, described in Method 3.2.1, steps 7-9.

Note: Commercial PEG additive solutions are available. The manufacturer's instructions should be followed for the proper use of these preparations.

Method 3.2.5. LIM Indirect Antiglobulin Test[3]

Procedure

1.   Prepare a 1% suspension of donor or reagent red cells in the serum used for testing. This can be done as follows: Wash 1 drop of 2-5% saline suspension, decant the supernatant saline, shake the cell button lightly to resuspend it, and decant it forcefully. Add 0.1 mL of serum to the cells that remain in the tube.
2.   Add 1.0 mL of LIM solution. Mix and incubate for 1 minute at room temperature.
3.   Add 0.1 mL of 0.05% Polybrene® to each tube and mix.
4.   Centrifuge according to manufacturer's directions. Typically this is 10 seconds at 900-1000 $\times g$ and decant supernatant fluid. DO NOT RESUSPEND BUTTON.
5.   Add 0.1 mL of resuspending solution. Shake tube gently and observe it for persistence of agglutination. Note: If strength of agglutination is weak, examine the test and a known negative control microscopically. DO NOT RECENTRIFUGE.
6.   If desired, the antiglobulin test may be performed as follows:
     a.   Add 0.05 mL (50 mL) of resuspending solution to each tube and mix.
     b.   Wash the cells three times with 10 mM of sodium citrate solution.
     c.   Add 2 drops of anti-IgG to the dry button and mix.
     d.   Centrifuge for 15 seconds at 900-1000 $\times g$. Read and record results.
     e.   Add IgG-coated red cells to each negative tube.

Interpretation (for Antiglobulin Tests, Methods 3.2.1-3.2.5)

1. The presence of agglutination/hemolysis after incubation at 37 C constitutes a positive test.
2. The presence of agglutination after addition of AHG constitutes a positive test.
3. Antiglobulin tests are negative when no agglutination is observed after initial centrifugation and the IgG-coated cells added afterward are agglutinated. If they are not agglutinated, the negative result is invalid and the test must be repeated.
4. For the LIP procedure, agglutination that persists after addition of resuspending solution constitutes a positive test.

Controls

1. The procedure used for the detection of unexpected antibodies in pretransfusion testing should be checked daily with weak examples of antibody. Control sera can be prepared from reagent grade typing sera diluted with 6% bovine albumin to give 2+ reactions by IAT. Human sources of IgG antibodies are also acceptable.
2. When the LIP technique is used to test an unknown serum against reagent red cells, an inert serum should be tested against a random red cell sample for comparative purposes.
3. When a blood typing reagent is used to test an unknown red cell sample, the positive control should be a reagent red cell with single-dose expression of the antigen (ie, from a heterozygote) and the negative control should be a reagent cell known to lack the antigen.

Notes

1. The incubation times and the volume and concentration of red cells indicated are those given in the literature. Individual laboratories may choose to standard-ize techniques with somewhat different values. See Chapter 12 for other limitations when modifying procedures. In all cases, the manufacturer's package insert should be consulted before modifying a procedure.
2. For the PEG procedure:
   a. Omit centrifugation after 37 C incubation, as red cells will not resuspend readily.
   b. Use anti-IgG rather than polyspecific AHG to avoid unwanted positive reactions due to C3-binding autoantibodies.
3. LISS additive and PEG solutions are available from various commercial sources. Manufacturers' instructions should be followed when using these reagents.

Reference

Menitove JE, ed. Standards for blood banks and transfusion services, 19th ed. Bethesda, MD: American Association of Blood Banks, 1999:58.

Method 3.3. Prewarming Technique

Principle

Prewarming may be useful in the detection and identification of red cell antibodies that bind to antigen only at 37 C, especially in testing sera of patients with cold-reactive autoantibody activity that may mask the simultaneous presence of clinically significant antibodies.

The technique should be used with some caution, as it may reduce the sensitivity of detection for some potentially significant antibodies.[1,2]

Specimen

Serum or plasma may be used. Specimen age must comply with pretransfusion specimen requirements in AABB *Standards for Blood Banks and Transfusion Services*.[3]

Reagents

1. Normal saline.
2. Bovine albumin (22% or 30%).
3. LISS additive obtained commercially or made as follows:
   a. Add 1.75 g of NaCl and 18 g of glycine to a 1 liter volumetric flask.
   b. Add 20 mL of phosphate buffer prepared by combining 11.3 mL of 0.15 M KH_2PO_4 and 8.7 mL of 0.15 M Na_2HPO_4.
   c. Add distilled water to the 1 liter mark.
   d. Adjust pH to 6.7 with NaOH.
   e. Add 0.5 g of sodium azide as a preservative.

   Note: Adding sodium azide at this concentration raises the ionic strength from 0.0355 to 0.043. This does not affect serologic reactivity.
4. PEG, 20% w/v: to 20 g of 3350 MW PEG (SIGMA Chemicals, St. Louis, MO), add phosphate-buffered saline (PBS) pH 7.3 (see Method 1.6) to 100 mL.
5. LIP Reagents
   a. Low ionic medium (LIM): To a 500-mL volumetric flask, add 25 g of dextrose and 1 g of $Na_2EDTA \cdot 2H_2O$. Fill flask to 500-mL mark with distilled water.
   b. Polybrene®: *Stock solution* (10% w/v): Add 5g of Polybrene® (Aldrich Chemical Co, Milwaukee, WI) to 50 mL of normal saline. Store in plastic container at 1-6 C. *Working solution* (0.05% w/v): Mix 0.1 mL of stock solution with 19.9 mL of normal saline. Store in plastic container at 1-6 C.
   c. Resuspending solution: 0.2 M trisodium citrate made by adding 5.88 g of $Na_3C_6H_5O$ to a 100-mL volumetric flask and filling to the 100-mL mark with distilled water; *5% dextrose* made by adding 5 g of dextrose to 100 mL of distilled water; *working solution* made by mixing 60 mL of 0.2 M trisodium citrate with 40 mL of 5% dextrose.
   d. Washing solution (for antiglobulin testing): 0.01 M of sodium citrate made by diluting 0.2 M of trisodium citrate (see above) to 1 in 20 with normal saline (eg, add 50 mL of 0.2 M trisodium citrate to 950 mL of saline).
6. Antihuman globulin (AHG) reagent. Polyspecific or anti-IgG may be used unless otherwise indicated. Anti-IgG need not be heavy-chain specific.
7. Commercially available unpooled group O antibody screening cells. Pooled group O screening cells may be used only for donor testing. Patient testing must be done with unpooled cells.
8. IgG-coated red cells, for addition to negative AHG tests.

Procedure

1. Prewarm a bottle of saline to 37 C.
2. Label one tube for each reagent or donor sample to be tested.
3. Add 1 drop of 2-5% saline-suspended red cells to each tube.
4. Place the tubes containing red cells and a tube containing a small volume of the patient's serum at 37 C; incubate for 5-10 minutes.
5. Using a prewarmed pipette, transfer 2 drops of prewarmed serum to each tube containing prewarmed red cells. Mix without removing tubes from the incubator.
6. Incubate at 37 C for 30-60 minutes.
7. Without removing the tubes from the incubator, fill each tube with prewarmed (37 C) saline. Centrifuge and wash three or four times with 37 C saline.
8. Add anti-IgG, according to the manufacturer's directions.

9. Centrifuge and observe for reaction. Grade and record the results.
10. Confirm the validity of negative tests by adding IgG-coated red cells.

Note

The prewarming procedure described above will not detect alloantibodies that agglutinate at 37 C or lower and are not reactive in the antiglobulin phase. To demonstrate these antibodies, testing (including centrifugation) may have to be done at 37 C. If time permits, a tube containing a prewarmed mixture of serum and cells can be incubated at 37 C for 60-120 minutes, and the settled red cells examined for agglutination by resuspending the button without centrifugation.

References

1. Judd WJ. Controversies in transfusion medicine. Prewarmed tests: Con. Transfusion 1995;35:271-7.
2. Mallory D. Controversies in transfusion medicine. Prewarmed tests: Pro—why, when, and how—not if. Transfusion 1995;35:268-70.
3. Menitove JE, ed. Standards for blood banks and transfusion services, 19th ed. Bethesda, MD: American Association of Blood Banks, 1999:58.

Method 3.4. Saline Replacement to Demonstrate Alloantibody in the Presence of Rouleaux

Principle

Rouleaux are aggregates of red cells that, characteristically, adhere to one another on their flat surface, giving a "stack of coins" appearance when viewed microscopically. Rouleaux formation is an in-vitro phenomenon resulting from abnormalities of serum protein concentrations, and the patient is often found to have liver disease, multiple myeloma, or some other condition associated with abnormal globulin levels. It may be difficult to detect antibody-associated agglutination in a test system containing rouleaux-promoting serum. In the saline replacement technique, serum and cells are incubated to allow antibody attachment, but the serum is removed and saline is added as the resuspending medium.

Specimen

Red cells to be evaluated.

Reagents

Saline.

Procedure

After routine incubation and resuspension, proceed with the following steps if the appearance of the resuspended cells suggests rouleaux formation:
1. Recentrifuge the serum/cell mixture.
2. Remove the serum, leaving the cell button undisturbed.
3. Replace the serum with an equal volume of saline (2 drops).
4. Resuspend the cell button gently and observe for agglutination. Rouleaux will disperse when suspended in saline, whereas true agglutination will remain.

Reference

Issitt PD, Anstee DJ. Applied blood group serology. 4th ed. Durham, NC: Montgomery Scientific Publications, 1985:605.

Method 3.5. Enzyme Techniques

Method 3.5.1. Preparation of Ficin Enzyme Stock

Principle

The enzyme preparations used in blood banking differ from lot to lot, so each time a stock enzyme solution is prepared, its reactivity should be tested and incubation periods standardized for optimal effectiveness. See Method 3.5.3. For a discussion of the principles of enzyme testing see Chapter 19.

Reagents

1. Dry enzyme powder, 1% w/v 1 g.
2. Phosphate-buffered saline (PBS), pH 7.3: see Method 1.6.

Procedure

1. Place 1 g of powdered ficin in a 100-mL volumetric flask. Handle ficin carefully because it is harmful if it gets in the eyes or is inhaled. It is desirable to wear gloves, mask, and apron, or to work under a hood.
2. Add PBS, pH 7.3 to 100 mL, to dissolve ficin. Agitate vigorously by inversion, rotate for 15 minutes, or mix with a magnetic stirrer until mostly dissolved. The powder will not dissolve completely.
3. Collect clear fluid, either by filtration or centrifugation, and prepare small aliquots. Store aliquots at –20 C or colder. Do not refreeze thawed solution.

Method 3.5.2. Preparation of Papain Enzyme Stock

Principle

The enzyme preparations used in blood banking differ from lot to lot, so each time a stock enzyme solution is prepared, its reactivity should be tested and incubation periods standardized for optimal effectiveness. See Method 3.5.3. For a discussion of the principles of enzyme testing see Chapter 19.

Reagents

1. L-cystine hydrochloride 0.5M, 0.88 gram in 10 mL distilled water.
2. Dry enzyme powder, 1% w/v 2 g.
3. PBS 0.067 M at pH 5.4, prepared by combining 3.5 mL of Na_2HPO_4 and 96.5 mL of KH_2PO_4.

Procedure

1. Add 2 g of powdered papain to 100 mL of PBS. Handle papain carefully because it

is harmful to mucous membranes. Use appropriate protective equipment.
2. Agitate enzyme solution for 15 minutes at room temperature.
3. Collect clear fluid by filtration or centrifugation.
4. Add L-cystine hydrochloride and incubate solution at 37 C for 1 hour.
5. Add PBS at pH 5.4 to final volume of 200 mL. Store aliquots at –20 C or colder. Do not refreeze aliquots.

Method 3.5.3. Standardization of Enzyme Procedures

Principle

For a two-stage enzyme procedure, the optimal dilution and incubation conditions must be determined for each new lot of stock solution. The technique given below for ficin can be modified for use with other enzymes.

Reagents

1. Stock solution of ficin in PBS, pH 7.3.
2. Several sera known to contain no unexpected antibodies.
3. Anti-D that agglutinates only enzyme-treated Rh-positive red cells and does not agglutinate untreated Rh-positive cells.
4. Anti-Fy[a] of moderate or strong reactivity.
5. Red cells positive for both D and Fy[a].

Procedure

1. Dilute one volume of stock ficin solution with nine volumes of PBS, pH 7.3.
2. Label three tubes: 5 minutes, 10 minutes, and 15 minutes.
3. Add equal volumes of washed red cells and 0.1% ficin to each tube.
4. Mix and incubate at 37 C for the time designated. Incubation times are easily controlled if the 15-minute tube is prepared first, followed by the 10- and 5-minute tubes at 5-minute intervals. Incubation will be complete for all three tubes at the same time.

5. Immediately wash the red cells three times with large volumes of saline.

6. Resuspend treated cells to 2-5% in saline.

7. Label four tubes for each serum to be tested: untreated, 5 minutes, 10 minutes, 15 minutes.

8. Add 2 drops of the appropriate serum to each of the four tubes.

9. Add 1 drop of the red cell suspension to each of the labeled tubes.

10. Mix and incubate at 37 C for 15 minutes.

11. Centrifuge, and examine for agglutination by gently resuspending button.

12. Wash cells three or four times with saline and test them by the indirect antiglobulin test.

Interpretation

Table 3.5.3-1 shows possible results with D-positive Fy(a+) cells and the sera indicated. In this case, the optimal incubation time would be 10 minutes. Incubation for only 5 minutes does not completely abolish Fy^a activity or maximally enhance anti-D reactivity. Incubation for 15 minutes causes false-positive antiglobulin reactivity with inert serum.

If incubation for 5 minutes proves to overtreat the cells, it is preferable to use a more dilute working solution of enzyme than to reduce incubation time because it is difficult to achieve accurate determination and monitoring of very short incubation times. Additional tests can evaluate a single dilution at different incubation times, or a single incubation time can be used for different enzyme dilutions.

Method 3.5.4. Evaluating Treated Red Cells

Principle

After optimal incubation conditions have been determined for a lot of enzyme solution, treated red cells should be evaluated before use to demonstrate that they are adequately, but not excessively, modified. Satisfactory treatment produces cells that are agglutinated by an antibody that causes only indirect antiglobulin test reactivity of unmodified cells, but are not agglutinated or aggregated by inert serum.

Specimen

Enzyme treated red cells.

Reagents

1. Sera known to contain an antibody to agglutinate enzyme treated cells.

2. Sera free of any unexpected antibodies.

Procedure

1. Select an antibody that agglutinates enzyme-treated red cells positive for the antigen but gives only AHG reactions with unmodified cells. Many examples of

Table 3.5.3-1. Hypothetical Results with D-Positive, Fy(a+) Cells

Cells and Enzyme		Inert Serum	Anti-D	Anti-Fy^a
Untreated	37 C incubation	0	0	0
	antihuman globulin test	0	1+	3+
5 minutes	37 C incubation	0	1+	0
	antihuman globulin test	0	2+	1+
10 minutes	37 C incubation	0	2+	0
	antihuman globulin test	0	2+	0
15 minutes	37 C incubation	0	2+	0
	antihuman globulin test	w+	2+	w+

anti-D in sera from patients behave in this way.

2. Add 2 drops of the selected antibody-containing serum to a tube labeled "positive."
3. Add 2 drops of a serum free of unexpected antibodies to a tube labeled "negative."
4. Add 1 drop of 2-5% suspension of enzyme-treated red cells to each tube.
5. Mix and incubate 15 minutes at 37 C.
6. Centrifuge and resuspend the cells by gentle shaking.
7. Examine macroscopically for the presence of agglutination.

Interpretation

There should be agglutination in the "positive" tube and no agglutination in the "negative" tube. If agglutination occurs in the "negative" tube, the cells have been overtreated; if agglutination does not occur in the "positive" tube, treatment has been inadequate.

Method 3.5.5. One-Stage Enzyme Technique

Specimen

Serum to be tested.

Reagent

Reagent red cells.

Procedure

1. Add 2 drops of serum to an appropriately labeled tube.
2. Add 2 drops of a 2-5% saline suspension of reagent red cells.
3. Add 2 drops of papain solution and mix well.
4. Incubate at 37 C for 30 minutes.
5. Centrifuge; gently resuspend the cells and observe them for agglutination. Grade and record the results.
6. Proceed with the antiglobulin procedure described in Method 3.2.1, steps 6-9.

Method 3.5.6. Two-Stage Enzyme Technique

Specimen

Serum to be tested.

Reagent

Reagent red cells.

Procedure

1. Prepare a diluted enzyme solution (papain or ficin) by adding 9 mL of PBS, pH 7.3 to 1 mL of stock enzyme.
2. Add one volume of diluted enzyme to one volume of packed, washed reagent red cells.
3. Incubate at 37 C for the time determined to be optimal for that enzyme solution.
4. Wash treated cells at least three times with large volumes of saline and resuspend them to 2-5% concentration in saline.
5. Add 2 drops of serum to be tested to an appropriately labeled tube.
6. Add 1 drop of 2-5% suspension of enzyme-treated cells.
7. Mix and incubate for 30 minutes at 37 C.
8. Centrifuge; gently resuspend the cells and observe them for agglutination. Grade and record the results.
9. Proceed with the antiglobulin procedure described in Method 3.2.1, steps 6-9.

Notes

1. An alternative Method for steps 4 and 5 (Method 3.5.5) or steps 7 and 8 (Method 3.5.6) is to incubate the serum and enzyme-treated cells at 37 C for 60 minutes and then to examine the settled cells for agglutination without centrifugation. This can be useful for serum with strong cold-reactive agglutinins and can sometimes prevent the occurrence of false-positive results.

2. Microscopic examination is not recommended for routine use and is particularly inappropriate with enzyme-enhanced tests because false-positive reactions will often be detected.

3. Either papain or ficin may be used in a two-stage procedure.

References

1. Issitt PD, Anstee DJ. Applied blood group serology. 4th ed. Durham, NC: Montgomery Scientific, 1998.
2. Ellisor S. Action and application of enzymes in immunohematology. In: Bell CA, ed. A seminar on antigen-antibody reactions revisited. Arlington, VA: American Association of Blood Banks, 1982:133-74.
3. Judd WJ. Methods in immunohematology. 2nd ed. Durham, NC: Montgomery Scientific, 1994.

Method 3.6. Direct Antiglobulin Test (DAT)

Principle

See Chapter 20 for a discussion of the principles of direct antiglobulin testing.

Specimen

Red cells from an anticoagulated blood sample.

Reagents

1. Antihuman globulin (AHG) reagent: polyspecific antiglobulin reagent, anti-IgG, anticomplement antisera.

2. Bovine albumin, 6% suspension, prepared by diluting 22% or 30% reagent albumin with saline for a control if necessary. A control is required when all antisera tested give a positive result.

Procedure

1. Dispense 1 drop of a 2-5% suspension of red cells into each tube.

2. Wash each tube 3-4 times with saline. Completely decant the final wash.

3. Immediately add antisera and mix. For the amount of antisera required refer to the manufacturer's directions.

4. Centrifuge according to the manufacturer's directions. Typically this is 15-30 seconds at 900-1000 $\times g$.

5. Examine the cells for agglutination. Grade and record the reaction.

6. If using polyspecific AHG or anti-C3d, incubate nonreactive tests at room temperature for 5 minutes, then centrifuge, and read again.

7. Add 1 drop of IgG-coated red cells to nonreactive tests that contain either polyspecific AHG or anti-IgG.

8. Centrifuge according to the manufacturer's directions.

9. Examine the cells for agglutination and record the reaction.

Interpretation

1. The DAT is positive when agglutination is observed either after immediate centrifugation or after the centrifugation that followed room temperature incubation. IgG-coated red cells usually give immediate reactions, whereas complement coating may be more easily demonstrable after incubation.[1,2] Although suggestive, this distinction cannot reliably demonstrate the nature of the coating globulin. Monospecific AHG reagents are needed to confirm which globulins are present.

2. The DAT is negative when no agglutination is observed at either test phase, providing the IgG-coated cells added in step 7 have been agglutinated. If the globulin-coated cells are not agglutinated, the negative DAT result is considered invalid and the test must be repeated. A negative DAT does not necessarily mean that the red cells have no attached globulin molecules. Polyspecific and anti-IgG reagents detect as few as 200-500 molecules of IgG per cell,[1] but patients may experience au-

toimmune hemolytic anemia when IgG coating is below this level.[2]

3. No interpretation can be made if the results with all antisera used to perform a DAT and the 6% bovine albumin control are reactive. This indicates spontaneous agglutination, which must be resolved before further testing is performed.

References

1. Mollison PL, Engelfriet CP, Contreras M, eds. Blood transfusion in clinical medicine. 10th ed. Oxford, England: Blackwell Scientific Publications, 1997.
2. Petz LD, Garratty G. Acquired immune hemolytic anemia. New York. Churchill-Livingstone, 1980.

Method 3.7. Antibody Titration

Principle

Titration is a semiquantitative method used to determine the concentration of antibody in a serum sample, or to compare the strength of antigen expression on different red cell samples. The usual applications of titration studies are: 1) estimating antibody activity in alloimmunized pregnant women, to determine whether and when to perform more complex invasive investigation of fetal condition (see Chapter 23); 2) elucidating autoantibody specificity (see Chapter 20); 3) characterizing antibodies as high-titer, low-avidity, traits common in antibodies to antigens of the Knops and Chido/Rodgers systems, Cs[a], and JMH (see Chapter 15); and 4) observing the effect of sulfhydryl reagents on antibody behavior, to determine immunoglobulin class (IgG or IgM). See Method 5.3 for titration studies specifically to assist in monitoring clinically significant antibodies in the pregnant woman.

Specimen

Serum (antibody) to be titrated.

Reagents

1. Red cells that express the antigen(s) corresponding to the antibody specificity (ies), in a 2-5% saline suspension. Uniformity of cell suspensions is very important to ensure comparability of results.
2. Saline. (Note: Dilutions may be made with albumin if desired.)

Procedure

The master dilution technique for titration studies is as follows:

1. Label 10 test tubes according to the serum dilution (eg, 1 in 1, 1 in 2, etc). A 1 in 1 dilution means one volume of serum undiluted; a 1 in 2 dilution means one volume of serum in a final volume of two, or a 50% solution of serum in the diluent. See Methods 1.4 and 1.5.
2. Deliver one volume of saline to all test tubes except the first (undiluted 1 in 1) tube.
3. Add an equal volume of serum to each of the first two tubes (undiluted and 1 in 2).
4. Using a clean pipet, mix the contents of the 1 in 2 dilution several times, and transfer one volume into the next tube (the 1 in 4 dilution).
5. Continue the same process for all dilutions, using a clean pipet to mix and transfer each dilution. Remove one volume of diluted serum from the final tube and save it for use if further dilutions are required.
6. Label 10 10 × 75 mm or 12 × 75 mm tubes for the appropriate dilutions.
7. Using separate pipets for each dilution, transfer 2 drops of each diluted serum into the appropriately labeled tubes, and add 1 drop of the red cell suspension.
8. Mix well, and test by a serologic technique appropriate to the antibody (see Chapter 19).
9. Examine test results macroscopically; grade and record the reactions. The

prozone phenomenon (see Chapter 12) may cause reactions to be weaker in the more concentrated serum preparations than in higher dilutions; to avoid misinterpretation of results, it may be preferable to examine first the tube containing the most dilute serum and proceed through the more concentrated samples to the undiluted specimen.

Interpretation

1. Observe the highest dilution that produces 1+ macroscopic agglutination. The titer is the reciprocal of the dilution level and is reported as, for example, 32—*not* 1 in 32 or 1:32 (see Table 3.7-1). If there is agglutination in the tube containing the most dilute serum, the endpoint has not been reached, and additional dilutions should be prepared and tested.

2. In comparative studies, a significant difference in titer is three or more dilutions. Variations in technique and inherent biologic variability can cause duplicate tests to give results that differ by one dilution in either direction. Serum containing antibody at a true titer of 32 may, on replicate tests, show reactivity ceasing in the 1:32 tube, the 1:64 tube, or the 1:16 tube.

3. Titer values alone can be misleading, without additional evaluation of strength of agglutination. The observed strength of agglutination can be assigned a number and the sum of these numbers for all tubes in a titration study represents the score, another semiquantitative measurement of antibody reactivity. The arbitrarily assigned threshold for significance in comparing scores is a difference of 10 or more between different test samples.

Table 3.7-1 shows the results obtained with three sera, each of which shows no more agglutination after 1:256. The differences in score, however, indicate considerable variation in strength of reactivity. The results with sample 3 are characteristic of antibodies with high-titer, low-avidity characteristics (eg, endpoint as high as 256, score only 33).

Table 3.7-1. Examples of Antibody Titers, Endpoints, and Scores

| | | Reciprocal of Serum Dilution | | | | | | | | | | |
		1	2	4	8	16	32	64	128	256	512	Titer*	Score
Sample 1	Strength:	3+	3+	3+	2+	2+	2+	1+	±	±	0	64(256)	
	Score:	10	10	10	8	8	8	5	3	2	0		64
Sample 2	Strength:	4+	4+	4+	3+	3+	2+	2+	1+	±	0	128(256)	
	Score:	12	12	12	10	10	8	8	5	3	0		80
Sample 3	Strength:	1+	1+	1+	1+	±	±	±	±	±	0	8(256)	
	Score:	5	5	5	5	3	3	3	2	2	0		33

*In prenatal testing, or for reagent evaluation, the titer is usually determined from the highest dilution of serum that gives a reaction ≥ 1+ (score 5). This may differ significantly from the titration endpoint (shown in parentheses), as with the reactions of an antibody with high-titer, low-avidity characteristics, manifested by Sample 3.

Notes

Titration is a semiquantitative technique. Technical variables greatly affect the results and care should be taken to achieve the most uniform possible practices.

1. Careful pipetting is essential. Pipettes with disposable tips that can be changed after each dilution are recommended.
2. Optimal time and temperature of incubation and time and force of centrifugation must be used consistently.
3. The age, phenotype, and concentration of the test cells will influence the results. When the titers of several antibody-containing sera are to be compared, all should be tested against red cells (preferably freshly collected) from the same donor. If this is not possible, the tests should use a pool of reagent red cells from donors of the same phenotype. When a single serum is to be tested against different red cell samples, all samples should be collected and preserved in the same manner, and diluted to the same concentration before use.
4. Completely reproducible results are virtually impossible to achieve. Comparisons are valid only when specimens are tested concurrently. In prenatal testing of sequential serum samples to detect changing antibody activity, samples should be frozen for comparison with subsequent specimens. Each new sample should be tested in parallel with the immediately preceding sample. In tests with a single serum against different red cell samples, material from the master dilution must be used for all tests.
5. Measurements are more accurate with large volumes than with small volumes; a master dilution technique (see above) gives more reliable results than individual dilutions for a single set of tests. The volume needed for all planned tests should be calculated and an adequate quantity of each dilution prepared.

Method 3.8. Use of Sulfhydryl Reagents to Distinguish IgM from IgG Antibodies

Principle

Treating IgM antibodies with sulfhydryl reagents abolishes both agglutinating and complement-binding activities. Observations of antibody activity before and after sulfhydryl treatment are useful in determining immunoglobulin class. Sulfhydryl treatment can also be used to abolish IgM antibody activity to permit detection of coexisting IgG antibodies. For a discussion of IgM and IgG structures see Chapter 11.

Specimen

2 mL of serum to be treated.

Reagents

1. Phosphate-buffered saline (PBS) at pH 7.3.
2. 0.01 M dithiothreitol (DTT), prepared by dissolving 0.154 g of DTT in 100 mL of pH 7.3 PBS. Store at 2-6 C.

Procedure

1. Dispense 1 mL of serum into each of two test tubes.
2. To one tube, labeled control, add 1 mL of pH 7.3 PBS.
3. To the other tube, labeled test, add 1 mL of 0.01 M DTT.
4. Mix and incubate at 37 C for 30-60 minutes.
5. Test the antibody activity in each sample by titration against red cells of appropriate phenotype.

Interpretation

See Table 3.8-1.

Table 3.8-1. Effect of Dithiothreitol on Blood Group Antibodies

Test Sample	Dilution					Interpretation
	1/2	1/4	1/8	1/16	1/32	
Serum + DTT	3+	2+	2+	1+	0	IgG
Serum + PBS	3+	2+	2+	1+	0	
Serum + DTT	0	0	0	0	0	IgM
Serum + PBS	3+	2+	2+	1+	0	
Serum + DTT	2+	1+	0	0	0	IgG + IgM*
Serum + PBS	3+	2+	2+	1+	0	

*May also indicate only partial inactivation of IgM.

Notes

1. 2-mercaptoethanol can also be used for this purpose. See Method 2.11 for preparation.

2. Sulfhydryl reagents used at low concentration may weaken antigens of the Kell system. For investigation of antibodies in the Kell system, it may be necessary to use alkylation with iodoacetic acid, followed by dialysis.

3. Gelling of a serum or plasma sample may be observed during treatment with DTT. This can occur if the DTT has been prepared incorrectly, and has a concentration above 0.01 M. Gelling may also occur if serum and DTT are incubated too long. An aliquot of the sample undergoing treatment can be tested after 30 minutes of incubation; if the activity thought to be due to IgM has disappeared, there is no need to incubate further. Gelled samples cannot be tested for antibody activity because overtreatment with DTT causes the denaturation of all serum proteins.

Reference

Mollison PL, Engelfriet CP, Contreras M, eds. Blood transfusion in clinical medicine. 10th ed. Oxford, England: Blackwell Scientific Publications, 1997.

Method 3.9. Rapid Identification of Anti-Ch and -Rg

Principle

For a discussion of the principles of rapid identification of anti-Ch and anti-Rg see Chapter 19.

Method 3.9.1. Preparation of C4d-Coated Red Cells

Specimen

Whole blood: group O, from a known Ch+ or Rg+ individual; collected within the previous 7 days and anticoagulated with ACD, CPD or CPDA-1.

Reagents

1. Anti-IgG: need not be heavy-chain-specific.

2. Phosphate buffer: 0.1 M at pH 7.7 (see Method 1.6); KH_2PO_4 (13.6 g/L), 10 mL; Na_2HPO_4 (14.2 g/L), 90 mL.

3. Trypsin (1% w/v): trypsin, 1:250 (Difco Laboratories, Detroit, MI), 1 g; 0.05 N HCl, 100 mL; agitate at room temperature for 15 minutes; leave overnight at 4 C; store at 4 C. Centrifuge to remove insoluble materials before use.

4. Sucrose/EDTA: sucrose, 10 g; K$_3$EDTA, 0.15 g; distilled water to 100 mL.

Procedure

1. Mix 1 mL of whole blood with 10 mL of sucrose/EDTA.
2. Incubate at 37 C for 15 minutes.
3. Wash the red cells three times with saline; the cells are now coated with C4b.
4. Dilute one part of trypsin with nine parts of pH 7.7 phosphate buffer.
5. Mix 0.1 mL of C4b-coated red cells with 0.1 mL of diluted trypsin, for conversion of the C4b to C4d.
6. Prepare uncoated control cells by mixing 0.1 mL of washed red cells from the whole blood sample with 0.1 mL of the diluted trypsin.
7. Incubate test and control cells at 37 C for 30 minutes.
8. Wash cells three times with saline.
9. Resuspend to a 5% concentration with phosphate-buffered saline; store at 4 C for up to 1 week.

Method 3.9.2. Testing for Anti-Ch/Anti-Rg

Specimen

Serum to be tested.

Reagents

1. C4d coated red cells. Refer to Method 3.9.1.
2. Anti-IgG.

Procedure

1. Label two tubes for test and control. Add 1 drop of C4d-coated red cells to the test tube and 1 drop of control cells to the control tube.
2. Add 2 drops of the serum to be tested to each tube, and incubate at room temperature for 5 minutes.
3. Centrifuge at 1000 $\times g$ for 15 seconds.

4. Examine the cells macroscopically; grade and record the results.
5. Wash the cells four times with saline and completely decant the final wash supernatant.
6. To the dry cell buttons, add anti-IgG according to the manufacturer's directions.
7. Centrifuge according to manufacturer's directions. Typically this is 15-30 seconds at 900-1000 $\times g$.
8. Resuspend the cell buttons and examine them macroscopically; grade and record the results.

Interpretation

1. Strong agglutination of C4d-coated red cells, but not of trypsin-treated control red cells indicates presence of either anti-Ch or anti-Rg.
2. Equal agglutination of C4d-coated cells and of control cells indicates the presence of either trypsin-dependent panagglutinins or of an alloantibody unrelated to anti-Ch or -Rg. No conclusion can be drawn about anti-Ch or -Rg in the test serum.
3. There may be a weak reaction between anti-IgG and with the trypsin-treated control cells. If the C4d-coated cells are strongly reactive and the control cells only weakly reactive, the presence of anti-Ch or anti-Rg is strongly suggested.

Notes

1. There is no need to incubate tests at 37 C before testing with anti-IgG.
2. The exact amount of K$_3$EDTA required for preparing 10 mL of sucrose-EDTA can be obtained from a 16 $\times$ 100-mm (10 mL) Vacutainer® tube (B2991-54, from American Scientific Products, McGaw Park, IL).

Reference

Judd WJ, Kraemer K, Moulds JJ. Rapid identification of Chido and Rodgers antibodies using C4d-coated red cells. Transfusion 1981;21:189-92.

Method 3.10. Plasma Inhibition to Distinguish Anti-Ch and -Rg from Other Antibodies with HTLA Characteristics

Principle

For a discussion of the principles of plasma inhibition of anti-Ch and -Rg see Chapter 19.

Specimen

Serum to be tested.

Reagents

1. Reactive red cell samples.
2. A pool of six or more normal plasma samples.
3. 6% bovine albumin, prepared from stock 22% or 30% bovine albumin by dilution with saline.
4. Anti-IgG.

Procedure

1. Prepare serial twofold dilutions of test serum in saline. The dilution range should be from 1 in 2 to 1 in 512, or to one tube beyond the known titer as determined above (Method 3.7). The volume prepared should be not less than 0.3 mL for each red cell sample to be tested.
2. For each red cell sample to be tested, place 2 drops of each serum dilution into each of two appropriately labeled 10 or 12 × 75-mm test tubes.
3. To one tube add 2 drops of pooled plasma.
4. To the other tube add 2 drops of 6% albumin.
5. Gently agitate the contents of each tube and incubate them at room temperature for at least 30 minutes.
6. Add 1 drop of a 2-5% suspension of red cells to each tube.
7. Gently agitate the contents of each tube and incubate them at 37 C for 1 hour.
8. Wash the cells four times in saline, add anti-IgG, and centrifuge them according to manufacturer's directions. Typically this is 15-30 seconds at 900-1000 × g.
9. Resuspend the cell buttons and examine them for agglutination; confirm all nonreactive tests microscopically. Grade and record the results.

Interpretation

Inhibition of antibody activity in the tubes to which plasma has been added suggests anti-Ch or anti-Rg specificity. This inhibition is often complete; the presence of partial inhibition suggests the possibility of additional alloantibodies. This possibility can be tested by preparing a large volume of inhibited serum and testing it against a reagent red cell panel to see if the nonneutralizable activity displays antigenic specificity.

Notes

1. Diluted bovine albumin is used as the negative control because it provides a protein concentration in the incubated serum.
2. Antibodies to Bg antigens (HLA-active material inconsistently present on red cells) may also be partially inhibited by plasma.
3. An alternative procedure for identifying anti-Ch or anti-Rg is adsorption, described in the reference below.

Reference

Ellisor SS, Shoemaker MM, Reid ME. Adsorption of anti-Chido from serum using autologous red blood cells coated with homologous C4. Transfusion 1982;22:243-5.

Method 3.11. Dithiothreitol (DTT) Treatment of Red Cells

Principle

DTT is an efficient reducing agent that can disrupt the tertiary structure of proteins by irreversibly reducing disulfide bonds to free sulfhydryl groups. Without tertiary structure, protein-containing antigens can no longer bind antibodies that are specific for them, abolishing serologic reactivity previously established as present. Red cells treated with DTT will not react with antibodies in the Kell blood group system, most antibodies in the Knops system, or with most examples of anti-LW^a, -Yt^a, -Yt^b, -Do^a, -Do^b, -Gy^a, -Hy, and -Jo^a.[1] This inhibition technique may be helpful in identifying some of these antibodies, or in determining if a serum contains additional underlying alloantibodies.

Specimen

Red cells to be tested.

Reagents

1. Prepare 0.2 M DTT by dissolving 1 g of DTT powder in 32 mL of phosphate-buffered saline (PBS), pH 8.0. Divide into 1 mL volumes and freeze aliquots at –18 C or colder.
2. PBS at pH 7.3, see Method 1.6.
3. Red cells known to be positive for the antigen in question and, as a control, red cells known to be positive for K, which is consistently disrupted by DTT.
4. Anti-K, either in reagent form or strongly expressed in a serum specimen.

Procedure

1. Wash one volume of the test cells and the control cells with PBS. After decanting, add four volumes of 0.2 M DTT, pH 8.0.
2. Incubate at 37 C for 30-45 minutes.
3. Wash four times with PBS. Slight hemolysis may occur; if hemolysis is excessive, repeat the procedure using fresh red cells and a smaller volume of DTT, eg, two or three volumes.
4. Resuspend the cells to a 2-5% suspension in PBS.

5. Test DTT-treated cells with serum containing the antibody in question. Test K-positive red cells with anti-K.

Interpretation

1. The control K-positive red cells should give negative reactions when tested with anti-K; if they do not, the DTT treatment has been inadequate. Other antigens in the Kell system can also serve as the control.
2. If reactivity of the test serum is eliminated, the suspected antibody specificity may be confirmed. Enough red cells should be tested to exclude most other clinically significant alloantibodies.

Note

Treatment of red cells with 0.2 M DTT, pH 8.0 is optimal for denaturation of all antigens of the Kell, Cartwright, LW, and Dombrock systems, and most antigens of the Knops system. Lower concentrations of DTT may selectively denature particular blood group antigens (ie, 0.002 M DTT will denature only Js^a and Js^b antigens). This property may aid in certain antibody investigations.

Reference

Branch DR, Muensch HA, Sy Siok Hian S, Petz LD. Disulfide bonds are a requirement for Kell and Cartwright (Yt^a) blood group antigen integrity. Br J Haematol 1983;54:573-8.

Method 3.12. Urine Neutralization of Anti-Sd^a

Principle

For a discussion of anti-Sd^a neutralization by urine see Chapter 15.

Specimen

Serum containing antibody thought to be Sd^a.

Reagents

1. Urine from a known Sd(a+) individual, or from a pool of at least six individuals of unknown Sd^a type prepared as follows: Collect urine and immediately boil for 10 minutes. Dialyze against phosphate-buffered saline (PBS), pH 7.3 at 4 C for 48 hours. Change PBS several times. Centrifuge. Dispense supernatant into aliquots, which can be stored at –20 C until thawed for use.
2. PBS, pH 7.3. See Method 1.6.
3. Polyspecific antihuman globulin (AHG) reagent.

Procedure

1. Mix equal volumes of thawed urine and test serum (0.2 mL is the volume required to test three red cell samples).
2. Prepare dilution control tube containing equal volumes of serum and PBS.
3. Prepare a urine control tube by mixing equal volumes of thawed urine and PBS.
4. Incubate all tubes at room temperature for 30 minutes.
5. Mix 1 drop of each test red cell sample with 2 or 3 drops from each of the tubes: neutralized serum, serum with PBS, and urine with PBS.
6. Incubate all tubes for 20-30 minutes at room temperature.
7. Wash cells three times with saline, and add polyspecific AHG.
8. Centrifuge, read, and record results. It may be helpful to examine them microscopically.

Interpretation

1. Persistent agglutination in the test samples means either that partial or no neutralization was achieved or that underlying antibodies are present. Microscopic examination may be helpful in distinguishing these outcomes; agglutination due to anti-Sd^a has a refractile,

mixed-field appearance on microscopic examination.
2. No agglutination in the neutralized tube with persistent agglutination in the dilution control tube and absence of hemolysis and agglutination in the urine control tube means that the antibody has been neutralized and is quite probably anti-Sd^a.
3. Absence of agglutination in the dilution control tube means that the dilution in the neutralization step was too great for the antibody present and the results of the test are invalid. The urine control tube provides assurance that no substances in the urine are agglutinating or damaging the red cells.

Note

Urine may also contain ABO and Lewis blood group substances, depending upon the ABO, Lewis and secretor status of the donor.

Reference

Judd WJ. Methods in immunohematology. 2nd ed. Durham, NC: Montgomery Scientific Publications, 1994.

Method 3.13. Adsorption Procedure

Principle

See Chapter 19.

Specimen

Serum containing antibody to be adsorbed.

Reagents

Red cells that carry the antigen corresponding to the antibody specificity to be adsorbed (may be autologous cells).

Procedure

1. Wash the selected red cells at least three times with saline.

2. After the last wash, centrifuge the red cells at 800-1000 $\times g$ for at least 5 minutes, and remove as much of the supernatant saline as possible. Additional saline may be removed by touching the red cell mass with a narrow piece of filter paper.

3. Mix appropriate volumes of the packed red cells and serum, and incubate them at the desired temperature for 30-60 minutes.

4. Mix the serum/cell mixture periodically throughout the incubation phase.

5. Centrifuge the red cells at 800-1000 $\times g$ for 5 minutes to pack cells tightly. Centrifuge at the incubation temperature, if possible, to avoid dissociation of antibody from the red cell membranes.

6. Transfer the supernatant fluid, which is the adsorbed serum, to a clean test tube. If an eluate is to be prepared, save the red cells.

7. Test an aliquot of the adsorbed serum, preferably against an additional aliquot of the cells used for adsorption, to see if all antibody has been removed.

Interpretation

If reactivity remains, the antibody has not been completely removed. No reactivity signifies that antibody has been completely adsorbed.

Notes

1. Adsorption is more effective if the area of contact between the red cells and serum is large; use of a large-bore test tube (13 mm or larger) is recommended.

2. Multiple adsorptions may be necessary to completely remove an antibody, but each successive adsorption increases the likelihood that the serum will be diluted and unadsorbed antibodies weakened.

3. Repeat adsorptions should use a fresh aliquot of cells and not the cells from the prior adsorption.

4. Enzyme pretreatment of the adsorbing cells can be performed to increase antibody uptake for enzyme resistant antigen.

Reference

Judd WJ. Methods in immunohematology. 2nd ed. Durham, NC: Montgomery Scientific Publications, 1994.

Method 3.14. Using the American Rare Donor Program

Principle

The American Rare Donor Program (ARDP) helps to locate blood products for patients requiring rare or unusual blood. The ARDP maintains a database of rare donors submitted by immunohematology reference laboratories that are accredited by the AABB or the American Red Cross (ARC). Donors are considered rare due to the absence of a high-incidence antigen, absence of multiple common antigens, or IgA deficiency.

All requests to the ARDP must originate from an AABB- or ARC-accredited immunohematology reference laboratory to ensure that the patient in question has been accurately evaluated and reported. User fees have not been established for services provided by the ARDP; all shipping and rare unit fees are established by the institution that ships the units.

Procedure

1. A hospital blood bank, transfusion service or blood center encounters a patient identified as needing rare blood.

2. The institution contacts the nearest AABB- or ARC-accredited immunohematology reference laboratory to supply the needed blood.

3. If the laboratory cannot supply the blood, it contacts the ARDP. *All* requests to the

ARDP *must* come from an AABB- or ARC-accredited laboratory (or another rare donor program). Requests received directly from a nonaccredited facility will be referred to the nearest accredited institution.

4. The institution contacting the ARDP (requesting institution) *must* confirm the identity of the antibody(ies) by serologic investigation or by examining the serologic work performed by another institution.

5. ARDP personnel search the computer database for centers that have submitted donors matching the needed phenotype. These centers are then contacted by ARDP personnel regarding availability of units. After the required number of units are located, ARDP personnel communicate to the requesting institution the name(s) of the shipping center(s).

6. The requesting and shipping institutions should discuss and agree on charges and testing requirements before units are shipped.

7. If an initial search obtains insufficient number of units, the following mechanisms can be used by ARDP staff to obtain needed units: 1) communication to all ARDP participating centers alerting them to search their inventories and/or recruit donors matching the needed phenotype, 2) contacting other rare donor files such as those administered by the World Health Organization, Japanese Red Cross, etc.

Investigation of a Positive Direct Antiglobulin Test Methods

Elution Techniques

The objective of all elution techniques is to interfere with the noncovalent binding forces that hold antibody-antigen complexes together on the red cell surface. The cell membrane can be physically disrupted by heat, ultrasound, freeze-thawing, detergents, or organic solvents. The binding forces of antigen-antibody complexes can be interrupted by alterations in pH or salt concentration. The reader should refer to Chapter 2 for the proper handling of hazardous chemicals that are sometimes used in these techniques. For a comparison of the advantages and disadvantages of various elution methodologies see Chapter 20.

Method 4.1. Citric Acid Elution

Principle

Citric acid elution is suitable for the investigation of a positive direct antiglobulin test (DAT)

associated with warm-reactive (IgG) auto- or alloantibodies. In conjunction with adsorption techniques, it can be used to separate mixtures of IgG antibodies against red cell antigens.

Specimen

Packed DAT-positive red cells washed six times with saline.

Reagents

1. Eluting solution: citric acid (monohydrate), 1.3 g; KH_2PO_4, 0.65 g; saline to 100 mL; store at 4 C.
2. Neutralizing solution: Na_3PO_4, 13.0 g; distilled water to 100 mL; store at 4 C.
3. Supernatant saline from final wash of the red cells to be tested.

Procedure

1. Chill all reagents to 4 C before use.
2. Place 1 mL of packed red cells in a 13 × 100-mm test tube.

3. Add 1 mL of eluting solution and note the time.

4. Stopper the tube and mix by inversion for 90 seconds.

5. Remove the stopper and promptly centrifuge the tube at 900-1000 $\times g$ for 45 seconds.

6. Transfer supernatant fluid to a clean test tube and add 5-6 drops of neutralizing solution; save red cells for use in adsorption studies if needed.

7. Check pH; adjust it, if necessary, to pH 7.0 by adding more neutralizing solution.

8. Centrifuge at 900-1000 $\times g$ for 2-3 minutes to remove precipitate that forms after neutralization. Harvest the supernatant eluate and test it in parallel with the supernatant saline from the final wash.

Notes

1. Once the red cells have been rendered DAT-negative, they may be tested for the presence of blood group antigens, except those of the Kell blood group system. Expression of antigens in the Kell system is markedly weakened after citric acid treatment.

2. Citric-acid-modified red cells may also be treated with a protease and used in autologous adsorption studies.

Reference

Burich MA, AuBuchon JP, Anderson HJ. Antibody elution using citric acid (letter). Transfusion 1986;26:116-7.

Method 4.2. Cold-Acid Elution

Principle

See Method 4.1.

Specimen

Packed DAT-positive red cells washed six times with saline.

Reagents

1. Glycine-HCl (0.1 M, pH 3.0), prepared by dissolving 3.75 g of glycine and 2.922 g of sodium chloride in 500 mL of distilled water. Adjust pH to 3.0 with 12 N HCl. Store at 4 C.

2. Phosphate buffer (0.8 M, pH 8.2), prepared by dissolving 109.6 g of Na_2HPO_4 and 3.8 g of KH_2PO_4 in approximately 600 mL of distilled water. Adjust pH, if necessary, with either 1 N NaOH or 1 N HCl. Dilute to a final volume of 1 L with distilled water. Store at 4 C (see note 2).

3. Normal saline, at 4 C.

4. Supernatant saline from final wash of red cells to be tested.

Procedure

1. Place the red cells in a 13 × 100-mm test tube and chill them in an ice bath for 5 minutes before adding the glycine-HCl.

2. Add 1 mL of chilled saline and 2 mL of chilled glycine-HCl to 1 mL of washed red cells.

3. Mix and incubate the tube in an ice bath for 1 minute.

4. Quickly centrifuge the tube at 900-1000 $\times g$ for 2-3 minutes.

5. Transfer the supernatant eluate into a clean test tube, and add 0.1 mL of pH 8.2 phosphate buffer for each 1 mL of eluate (see note 3).

6. Mix and centrifuge at 900-1000 $\times g$ for 2-3 minutes.

7. Transfer the supernatant eluate into a clean test tube, and test in parallel with the supernatant saline from the final wash.

Notes

1. Keep glycine in an ice bath during use, to maintain correct pH.

2. Phosphate buffer will crystallize during storage at 4 C. Redissolve it at 37 C before use.

3. Addition of phosphate buffer restores neutrality to the acidic eluate. Unneutralized acidity may cause hemolysis of the reagent red cells used in testing the eluate. The addition of 22% bovine albumin (one part to four parts of eluate) may reduce such hemolysis.

References

Rekvig OP, Hannestad K. Acid elution of blood group antibodies from intact erythrocytes. Vox Sang 1977;33:280-5.

Judd WJ. Methods in immunohematology, 2nd ed. Durham, NC: Montgomery Scientific Publications, 1994.

Method 4.3. Glycine-HCl/EDTA Elution

Principle

See Method 4.1.

Specimen

Packed DAT-positive red cells washed six times with saline.

Reagents

1. Disodium EDTA (10% w/v): $Na_2EDTA \cdot 2 H_2O$, 10 g; distilled water to 100 mL.

2. Glycine-HCl (0.1 M at pH 1.5): glycine 3.754 g; NaCl, 2.922 g; distilled water to 500 mL; adjust to pH 1.5 with 12 N HCl; store at 4 C.

3. TRIS base (1 M): TRIZMA® BASE (SIGMA Chemicals, St. Louis, MO), 12.1 g; distilled water to 100 mL.

4. Supernatant saline from final wash of the red cells to be tested.

Procedure

1. Mix 4 mL of glycine-HCl and 1 mL of EDTA in a 16 × 100-mm test tube.

2. Immediately add 1 mL of washed red cells and mix well.

3. Incubate at room temperature for 1-2 minutes.

4. Centrifuge the tube at 900-1000 × g for 2-3 minutes.

5. Transfer the supernatant eluate into a clean test tube, and adjust to pH 7.5 with 1 M TRIS base.

6. Mix and centrifuge at 900-1000 × g for 2-3 minutes.

7. Transfer the supernatant eluate into a clean test tube, and test it in parallel with the supernatant saline from the final wash.

Notes

1. Once the red cells have been rendered DAT-negative, they may be tested for the presence of blood group antigens, except those in the Kell system. Treatment with glycine-HCl/EDTA denatures Kell system antigens.

2. Red cells modified with glycine-HCl/EDTA may be treated with a protease and used in autologous adsorption studies.

Reference

Byrne PC. Use of a modified acid/EDTA elution technique. Immunohematology 1991;7:46-7.

Method 4.4. Heat Elution

Principle

Heat elution is best suited for the investigation of ABO hemolytic disease of the newborn, and for elution of IgM antibodies from red cells. It should not routinely be used for the investigation of abnormalities caused by IgG auto- or alloantibodies.

Specimen

Packed DAT-positive red cells washed six times with saline.

Reagents

1. 6% bovine albumin, prepared by diluting 22% or 30% bovine albumin with saline.
2. Supernatant saline from final wash of the red cells to be tested.

Procedure

1. Mix equal volumes of washed packed cells and 6% bovine albumin in a 13 × 100-mm test tube.
2. Place the tube at 56 C for 10 minutes. Agitate the tube periodically during this time.
3. Centrifuge the tube at 900-1000 × g for 2-3 minutes, preferably in a heated centrifuge.
4. Immediately transfer the supernatant eluate into a clean test tube, and test in parallel with the supernatant saline from the final wash.

Reference

Issitt PD, Anstee DJ. Applied blood group serology, 4th ed. Durham, NC: Montgomery Scientific Publications, 1998.

Method 4.5. Lui Freeze Thaw Elution

Principle

See Method 4.1.

Specimen

Packed red blood cells washed six times with saline.

Procedure

1. Mix 0.5 mL of the red cells to be tested with 3 drops of saline in a test tube.
2. Cap the tube, then rotate the tube to coat the tube wall with cells.
3. Place the tube in a freezer at –20 C to –70 C for 10 minutes.

4. Remove the tube from the freezer and thaw quickly with warm tap water.
5. Centrifuge for 2 minutes at 900-1000 × g.
6. Transfer supernatant to a clean test tube and test in parallel with the supernatant saline from the last wash.

Reference

Feng CS, Kirkley KC, Eicher CA, et al. The Lui elution technique: A simple and efficient method for eluting ABO antibodies. Transfusion 1985;25:433-4.

Method 4.6. Cold Autoadsorption

Principle

Although most cold autoantibodies do not cause a problem in serologic tests, some potent cold-reactive autoantibodies may mask the concomitant presence of clinically significant alloantibodies. In these cases, adsorbing the serum in the cold with autologous red cells can remove autoantibody, permitting detection of underlying alloantibodies. In the case of most nonpathologic cold autoantibodies, a simple quick adsorption of the patient serum with enzyme-treated cells will remove most cold antibody. See Method 3.5-5. A more efficient method of removing immunoglobulins is the use of ZZAP reagent, a combination of proteolytic enzyme and powerful reducing agent. ZZAP treatment removes IgM and complement from autologous cells and uncovers antigen sites that can be used to bind free autoantibody in the serum.

Specimen

2 mL of serum or plasma to be adsorbed.

Reagents

1. 1% cysteine-activated papain or 1% ficin (see Method 3.5.1).
2. Phosphate-buffered saline (PBS) at pH 6.5 and pH 8.0 (see Method 1.6).

3. 0.2 M of dithiothreitol (DTT) prepared by dissolving 1 g of DTT in 32.4 mL of pH 8.0 PBS. Dispense into 3 mL aliquots and store at –20 C or colder.

4. 2 mL of packed autologous red cells.

Procedure

1. Prepare ZZAP reagent by mixing 0.5 mL of 1% cysteine-activated papain with 2.5 mL of 0.2 M DTT and 2 mL of pH 6.5 PBS. Alternatively, use 1 mL of 1% ficin, 2.5 mL of 0.2 M DTT, and 1.5 mL of pH 6.5 PBS. Adjust the pH to 6.5.

2. Add 2 mL of ZZAP reagent to 2 mL of packed autologous red cells. Mix and incubate at 37 C for 20-30 minutes.

3. Wash the cells three times in saline. Centrifuge the last wash for 3-5 minutes at 900-1000 $\times g$, and remove as much of the supernatant saline as possible (see note below).

4. To the tube of ZZAP-treated red cells add 2 mL of the autologous serum. Mix, and incubate at 4 C for 30-40 minutes.

5. Centrifuge at 900-1000 $\times g$ for 4-5 minutes, and transfer the serum into a clean tube.

6. Steps 2 through 5 may be repeated if the first autoadsorption does not satisfactorily remove the autoantibody activity.

7. After the final adsorption, test the serum with reagent red cells for alloantibody activity.

Notes

1. To avoid dilution of the serum and possible loss of weak alloantibody activity, it is important in step 3 to remove as much of the residual saline as possible. Placing a narrow strip of filter paper into the packed cells helps blot up saline that surrounds the red cells.

2. If the reactivity of the autoantibody is not diminished, a possible explanation is that the target autoantigen has been de-

stroyed by either papain or DTT. The adsorption should be repeated against untreated autologous red cells washed several times in warm saline.

Reference

Branch DR. Blood transfusion in autoimmune hemolytic anemias. Lab Med 1984;15:402-8.

Method 4.7. Determining the Specificity of Cold-Reactive Autoagglutinins

Principle

For a discussion of specificity of cold-reacting autoantibodies see Chapter 22.

Specimen

Serum, separated at 37 C from a blood sample allowed to clot at 37 C; or plasma, separated from an anticoagulated sample after periodic inversion at 37 C for approximately 15 minutes.

Reagents

Test red cells of the following phenotypes:

1. Two examples of adult group O, I-positive cells; they can be the reagent cells routinely used for alloantibody detection.

2. The patient's own (autologous) red cells.

3. Red cells of the same ABO group as the patient, if the patient is not group O. If the patient is group A or AB, use both A_1 and A_2 cells.

4. Group O, I-positive cells treated with ficin or papain.

5. Group O, I-negative cord blood or cells from an i_{adult} individual, if available, or both.

Procedure

1. Prepare serial twofold dilutions of the serum or plasma in saline. The dilution

range should be from 1 in 2 to 1 in 4096 (12 tubes), and the volumes prepared should not be less than 1 mL.

2. Mix 3 drops of each dilution with 1 drop of a 2-5% saline suspension of each red cell sample.

3. Incubate at room temperature for 15 minutes.

4. Centrifuge for 15-30 seconds at 900-1000 $\times g$. Examine macroscopically for agglutination. Grade and record the results.

5. Transfer the tubes to 4 C, and incubate them at this temperature for 1 hour.

6. Centrifuge according to manufacturer's directions. Typically this is 15-30 seconds at 900-1000 $\times g$. Examine macroscopically for agglutination. Grade and record the results.

Interpretation

Table 4.7-1 summarizes the reactions of the commonly encountered cold-reactive autoantibodies. In cold agglutinin syndrome, anti-I is seen most frequently but anti-i and anti-Pr specificities may also be encountered. Some examples of anti-I react more strongly with red cells that have a strong expression of H antigen (eg, O and A_2 cells); such antibodies are called anti-IH. All autoantibodies with specificity related to the I system exhibit enhanced reactivity against protease-treated red cells, whereas anti-Pr antibodies react weakly (if at all) with enzyme-treated cells. Anti-Pr reacts equally with untreated red cells of I or i phenotypes.

Notes

1. Potent examples of cold-reactive autoantibodies may not show apparent specificity when titration studies are performed at room temperature or 4 C. In such circumstances, tests can be incubated at 30-37 C (see reference). Differential reactivity may be more apparent if incubation times are prolonged and agglutination is evaluated after settling, without centrifugation.

2. Some workers use this procedure for determining both titer and specificity. If multiple readings are taken after incubation at different temperatures, the specificity, titer, and thermal amplitude of the autoantibody can be determined with a single set of serum dilutions.

Table 4.7-1. Comparative Reactions to Demonstrate Specificity of Cold-Reactive Autoantibodies

Red Cells	Antibody Specificity				
	Anti-I	Anti-i	Anti-H[*]	Anti-IH[*]	Anti-Pr
Oi (adult)	NR/↓	↑	≡	↓	≡
Oi (cord)	NR/↓	↑	<	↓	≡
A_1I	≡	≡	↓	↓	≡
OI (enzyme-treated)	↑	↑	↑	↑	NR/↓
Autologous	≡	≡	↓	↓	≡

NR = nonreactive   ≡ = equal to OI red cells
↑ = stronger than OI red cells   < = equal to or weaker than OI red cells
↓ = weaker than OI red cells
*Anti-H and anti-IH antibodies are seen predominantly in A_1 and A_1B individuals.

Reference

Petz LD, Branch DR. Serological tests for the diagnosis of immune hemolytic anemias. In: McMillan R, ed. Methods in hematology: Immune cytopenias. New York: Churchill-Livingstone, 1983:2-48.

Method 4.8. Titration of High-Titer Cold-Reactive Autoagglutinins

Principle

Cold-reactive autoantibodies, if present at very high titers, may suggest a pathologic cold agglutinin disease. This may result in overt hemolysis and systemic symptoms, and may indicate underlying immunohematologic neoplasia.

Specimen

Serum, separated at 37 C from a sample allowed to clot at 37 C; or plasma, separated from an anticoagulated sample after periodic inversion at 37 C for approximately 15 minutes.

Reagents

1. 2-5% saline suspension of washed group O, I-positive red cells. They can be prepared from a segment taken from a donor unit drawn within the preceding 7 days or from a specimen drawn into EDTA within the preceding 2-3 days.
2. Phosphate-buffered saline (PBS) at pH 7.3 (see Method 1.6).

Procedure

1. Make a master dilution of the patient's serum (see Method 3.7).
2. Add to each tube 2 drops of a 2-5% cell suspension of washed group O, I-positive red cells.
3. Mix, and incubate at 4 C for 1 hour.
4. Do not centrifuge the test mixtures. Examine the settled red cells macroscopically for agglutination. Grade and record the results.

Interpretation

The titer is the reciprocal of the highest serum dilution at which agglutination is observed. Titers above 40 are considered elevated, but hemolytic anemia due to cold-reactive autoagglutinins rarely occurs unless the titer is above 640. Titers below 640 may be obtained when the autoantibody has anti-i specificity. To titrate anti-i, use I-negative cells, either cord cells (i_{cord}) or cells from an i_{adult} individual.

Notes

1. It is important to use separate pipettes for each tube when preparing serum dilutions because the serum carried from one tube to the next when a single pipette is used throughout may cause falsely high titration endpoints. The difference can convert a true titer of 4000 to an apparent titer of 100,000, when use of separate pipettes is compared with use of a single pipette.
2. Serum dilutions can be prepared more accurately with large volumes (eg, 0.5 mL) than with small volumes.

Reference

Henry JB, ed. Clinical diagnosis and management by laboratory methods. 18th ed. Philadelphia: WB Saunders, 1991:667.

Method 4.9. Autologous Adsorption of Warm-Reactive Autoantibodies

Principle

Warm-reactive autoantibodies in serum may mask the concomitant presence of clinically significant alloantibodies. Adsorption of the serum with autologous red cells can remove autoantibody from the serum, permitting detection of underlying alloantibodies. However, autologous red cells in the circulation are coated with autoantibody. Autologous adsorption of warm-reactive autoantibodies can be achieved by dissociating autoantibody from the red cell membrane, thereby uncovering antigen sites that can bind free autoantibody to remove it from the serum. Treatment of the cells with enzymes enhances the adsorption process by removing membrane structures that otherwise hinder the association between antigen and antibody.

The most effective procedure involves the use of ZZAP reagent, a mixture of a proteolytic enzyme and a sulfhydryl reagent. Treatment of IgG molecules with a sulfhydryl reagent increases their susceptibility to digestion by proteases. When IgG-coated red cells are treated with ZZAP reagent, the immunoglobulin molecules lose their integrity and dissociate from the cell surface and the action of the proteolytic enzyme increases the adsorbing capacity of the treated cells. An alternative method that does not require pretreatment of the cells has been described using PEG.[2]

Red cells from recently transfused patients should not be used for autoadsorption because transfused red cells present in the circulation are likely to adsorb the alloantibodies that are being sought.

Specimen

2 mL of serum or plasma to be adsorbed.

Reagents

1. 1% cysteine-activated papain or 1% ficin (see Method 3.5.1).
2. Phosphate-buffered saline (PBS) at pH 6.5 and pH 8.0 (see Method 1.6).
3. 0.2 M of DTT prepared by dissolving 1 g of DTT in 32.4 mL of pH 8.0 PBS. Dispense into 3 mL aliquots and store at −18 C or colder.
4. 2 mL of packed autologous red cells.

Procedure

1. Prepare ZZAP reagent by mixing 0.5 mL of 1% cysteine-activated papain with 2.5 mL of 0.2 M DTT and 2 mL of pH 6.5 PBS. Alternatively, use 1 mL of 1% ficin, 2.5 mL of 0.2 M DTT, and 1.5 mL of pH 6.5 PBS. Check pH and adjust it to 6.5 if necessary.
2. To each of two tubes containing 1 mL of packed red cells add 2 mL of ZZAP reagent. Mix, and incubate at 37 C for 20-30 minutes with periodic mixing.
3. Wash the red cells three times in saline. Centrifuge the last wash for at least 5 minutes at 900-1000 ×g. Use suction or a Pasteur pipette to remove as much of the supernatant as practical.
4. Add serum to an equal volume of ZZAP-treated red cells, mix, and incubate at 37 C for approximately 20-45 minutes.
5. Centrifuge and carefully remove serum.
6. Steps 4 and 5 should be repeated once more using the once-adsorbed patient's serum and the second aliquot of ZZAP-treated cells.
7. After the second adsorption, test the serum against a specimen of group O reagent cells. If reactivity persists repeat steps 4 and 5.

Interpretation

Two adsorptions ordinarily remove sufficient autoantibody so that alloantibody reactivity, if present, is readily apparent. If the twice-autoadsorbed serum reacts with determined specificity, as shown by testing against a small antibody identification panel, then the defined specificity of the antibody is probably an alloantibody. If the serum reacts with all cells on the panel, either additional autoadsorptions are necessary, or the serum contains an antibody (eg, anti-Ge) that does not react with ZZAP-treated cells and thus will not be adsorbed by this procedure. To confirm this possibility, test the reactive autoadsorbed serum against reagent cells that have been pretreated with the ZZAP reagent.

Notes

1. ZZAP treatment destroys all Kell system antigens and all other antigens that are destroyed by proteases, including M, N, Fy[a], Fy[b], and S. ZZAP reagent also denatures the s antigen and antigens of the LW, Gerbich, Cartwright, Dombrock, and Knops systems. If the autoantibody is suspected to have specificity in any of these blood groups, an alternative procedure is to perform autoadsorption with autologous cells treated only with 1% ficin or 1% cysteine-activated papain.

2. There is no need to wash red cells before treatment with ZZAP.

References

1. Branch DR, Petz LD. A new reagent (ZZAP) having multiple applications in immunohematology. Am J Clin Pathol 1982;78:161-7.
2. Leger RM, Garratty G. Evaluation of methods for detecting alloantibodies underlying warm autoantibodies. Transfusion 1999;39:11-6.

Method 4.10. Differential Warm Adsorption or Autologous Adsorption Using ZZAP-Treated Allogeneic Red Cells

Principle

Red cells treated with ZZAP lack all Kell, MNSs, Duffy, and Gerbich antigens; most LW, Cartwright, Dombrock, and Knops antigens; and any other antigens destroyed by enzymes. Adsorption of serum with selected red cells of known phenotypes will remove autoantibody and leave antibodies to most blood group systems. Specificity of the antibodies that remain after adsorption can be confirmed by testing against a panel of reagent red cells. This procedure can be used to detect underlying alloantibodies if the patient has been recently transfused, or if insufficient autologous red cells are available and the patient's phenotype is unknown.

Specimen

Serum containing warm-reactive auto-antibodies, or eluate from DAT-positive cells.

Reagents

1. 1% cysteine-activated papain or 1% ficin (see Method 3.5.1).

2. Phosphate-buffered saline (PBS) at pH 6.5 and pH 8.0 (see Method 1.6).

3. 0.2 M of DTT prepared by dissolving 1 g of DTT in 32.4 mL of pH 8.0 PBS. Dispense into 3 mL aliquots and store at −18 C or colder.

4. Group O red cells of the phenotypes R_1R_1, R_2R_2, and rr. They can be reagent cells or from any blood specimen that will yield a sufficient volume of packed red cells.

Procedure

1. Prepare ZZAP reagent by mixing 0.5 mL of 1% cysteine-activated papain with 2.5 mL of 0.2 M DTT and 2 mL of pH 6.5 PBS. Alternatively, use 1 mL of 1% ficin, 2.5 mL of 0.2 M DTT, and 1.5 mL of pH 6.5 PBS. Check pH and adjust it to 6.5 if necessary.

2. Wash 1 mL of each red cell specimen once in a large volume of saline, centrifuge to pack, and remove the supernatant saline.

3. To each volume of washed packed cells, add two volumes of working ZZAP reagent. Invert several times to mix.

4. Incubate at 37 C for 20-30 minutes. Mix periodically throughout incubation.

5. Wash the red cells three times with large volumes of saline. Remove last wash as completely as possible to prevent dilution of the serum.

6. For each of the red cell specimens, mix one volume of ZZAP-treated cells with an equal volume of patient's serum, mix, and incubate at 37 C for 30-60 minutes, mixing occasionally.

7. Centrifuge at 900-1000 $\times g$ for approximately 5 minutes and harvest supernatant serum.

8. Test adsorbed serum from each of the three tubes against a new aliquot of the cells used for adsorption. If reactivity is present, repeat steps 6 and 7 with a fresh aliquot of ZZAP-treated red cells until no reactivity remains. The three samples of adsorbed serum can then be tested against an antibody identification panel and the results compared for demonstration of persisting and removed alloantibody activity. See section on allogeneic adsorption in Chapter 20.

Notes

1. If the autoantibody is very strong, three or more aliquots of adsorbing cells should be prepared. If the first adsorption is unsuccessful, the use of a higher proportion of cells to serum/eluate may enhance effectiveness.

2. The adsorbing red cells should be tightly packed to remove residual saline that might dilute the antibodies remaining in the serum/eluate.

3. Agitate the serum/cell mixture during incubation to provide maximum surface contact.

4. If adsorption has no effect on the autoantibody, adsorption with untreated red cells may be tried.

References

Branch DR, Petz LD. A new reagent (ZZAP) having multiple applications in immunohematology. Am J Clin Pathol 1982;78:161-7.

Judd WJ. Methods in immunohematology, 2nd ed. Durham, NC: Montgomery Scientific Publications, 1994.

Method 4.11. One-Cell Sample ZZAP Allogeneic Adsorption

Principle

If the Rh and Kidd phenotypes of a recently transfused patient are known or can be determined, autoantibody activity can be adsorbed from the serum onto a single allogeneic red cell sample, leaving serum that can be evaluated for the presence of alloantibodies. The red cells used should have the same Rh and Kidd phenotypes as the patient; they can be treated with ZZAP to denature Kell, Duffy, and MNS antigens. This method is a simplified version of the previous adsorption procedure, but it should be used only if the patient's Rh and Kidd phenotypes are known.

Specimen

Serum to be tested.

Reagents

1. ZZAP reagent (see Method 4.10).
2. ABO compatible red cells of the patient's Rh and Kidd phenotypes; they can be reagent cells or cells from any blood specimen that will yield sufficient packed cells.

Procedure

1. Wash the selected allogeneic red cells once in a large volume of saline, and centrifuge to pack them.

2. Add two volumes of ZZAP reagent to one volume of these packed cells, mix, and incubate at 37 C for 20-30 minutes, with periodic mixing.

3. Wash the cells three times with saline and remove the last wash as completely as possible to prevent dilution of the serum.

4. To one volume of ZZAP-treated cells add an equal volume of the patient's serum, mix, and incubate at 37 C for 30-60 minutes, mixing occasionally.

5. Centrifuge at 900-1000 × g for approximately 5 minutes and harvest the supernatant serum.
6. Test the adsorbed serum against a fresh aliquot of the cells used for adsorption. If reactivity persists, repeat steps 4 and 5 with a fresh aliquot of ZZAP-treated cells until the serum is no longer reactive.

Method 4.12. The Donath-Landsteiner Test

Principle

The primary application of this test is the differential diagnosis of immune hemolysis and specific diagnosis of paroxysmal cold hemoglobinuria (PCH). The patient for whom this procedure should be considered is one with a positive direct antiglobulin test (DAT) due to C3 alone; demonstrable hemoglobinemia, hemoglobinuria, or both; and no evidence of autoantibody activity in serum or the eluate made from the DAT-positive cells. For a discussion of PCH see Chapter 22.

Specimen

Serum separated from a freshly collected blood sample maintained at 37 C.

Reagents

1. Freshly collected normal serum, to use as a source of complement.
2. 50% suspension of washed group O red cells that express the P antigen.

Procedure

1. Label three sets of three 10 × 75-mm test tubes as follows: A1-A2-A3; B1-B2-B3; C1-C2-C3.
2. To tubes 1 and 2 of each set, add 10 volumes of the patient's serum.
3. To tubes 2 and 3 of each set, add 10 volumes of fresh normal serum.

4. To all tubes, add one volume of the 50% suspension of washed P-positive red cells and mix well.
5. Place the three "A" tubes in a bath of melting ice for 30 minutes, and then at 37 C for 1 hour.
6. Place the three "B" tubes in a bath of melting ice, and keep them in melting ice for 90 minutes.
7. Place the three "C" tubes at 37 C, and keep them at 37 C for 90 minutes.
8. Centrifuge all tubes, and examine the supernatant fluid for hemolysis.

Interpretation

The Donath-Landsteiner test is considered positive when the patient's serum, with or without added complement, causes hemolysis in the tubes that were incubated first in melting ice and then at 37 C (ie, tubes A1 and A2), and there is no hemolysis in any of the tubes maintained throughout at 37 C or in melting ice. The A3, B3, and C3 tubes serve as a control for complement activity and should not manifest hemolysis.

Notes

1. The biphasic nature of the hemolysin associated with PCH requires that serum be incubated with cells at cold temperature first and then at 37 C.
2. Active complement is essential for demonstration of the antibody. Because patients with PCH may have low levels of serum complement, fresh normal serum should be included in the reaction medium as a source of complement.
3. To avoid loss of antibody by cold autoadsorption before testing, the patient's blood should be allowed to clot at 37 C, and the serum separated from the clot at this temperature.

Reference

Dacie JV, Lewis SM. Practical hematology, 4th ed. London: Churchill, 1968.

Method 4.13. Detection of Antibodies to Penicillin or Cephalothin (Most Cephlosporins)

Principle

See Chapter 22 for discussion of the mechanisms by which drugs cause a positive direct antiglobulin test (DAT). The preparations of drugs used should, to the extent possible, be the same as those given to the patient.

Specimen

Serum or eluate to be studied.

Reagents

1. Barbital-buffered saline (BBS) at pH 9.6, prepared by dissolving 20.6 g of sodium barbital in 1 L of saline. Adjust to pH 9.6 with 0.1 N HCl. Store at 4 C.
2. Phosphate-buffered saline (PBS), pH 6.0 (see Method 1.6). 0.1 M of TRIS-buffered saline may be used as an alternative.
3. Penicillin (approximately 1×10^6 units per 600 mg).
4. Cephalothin sodium.
5. Washed, packed group O red cells.

Procedure

1. Prepare penicillin-coated cells by incubating 1 mL of red cells with 600 mg of penicillin in 15 mL of BBS for 1 hour at room temperature. Wash three times in saline and store in PBS at 4 C for up to 1 week.
2. Prepare cephalothin-coated cells by incubating 1 mL of red cells with 300 mg of cephalothin sodium in 10 mL of PBS, pH 6.0 for 1 hour at 37 C with frequent mixing. Wash three times in saline and store in PBS for up to 1 week at 4 C. Cephalosporins other than cephalothin can also be coated onto red cells using this method.

3. Mix 2 or 3 drops of serum or eluate with 1 drop of 5% saline suspension of drug-coated red cells.
4. Test, in parallel, uncoated red cells from the same donor.
5. Incubate the tests at 37 C for 30-60 minutes. Centrifuge, and examine macroscopically for agglutination. Grade and record the results.
6. Wash the cells four times in saline, and test by an indirect antiglobulin technique using polyspecific or anti-IgG reagents.

Interpretation

Antibodies to penicillins or cephalosporins will react with the drug-coated red cells but not with uncoated cells. Antibodies to either drug may cross-react with cells coated with the other drug (ie, antipenicillin antibodies may attach to cephalothin-coated cells and vice versa). Antibodies to most of the cephalosporins will react with cephalothin-coated cells. In some cases, it may be necessary to coat cells with the actual drug under investigation.

Notes

1. Reactivity of serum or eluate with cephalothin-coated cells but not untreated cells indicates antibody to cephalosporins, which may also cross-react with penicillin-coated cells.
2. The process of coating cells with cephalothin may cause them to adsorb all proteins nonimmunologically, and reactions may occur with normal serum. Such reactivity is rare if a low-pH method is used to couple cephalothin to the cells (see reference).
3. If there is grossly visible hemolysis of cephalothin-coated red cells of pH 6.0, recheck the pH and make sure it is not below 6.0.
4. Drug-coated red cells may be kept in PBS at 4 C for up to 1 week.

5. When available, a serum/plasma specimen known to contain antibody with the drug specificity being evaluated should be included as a control specimen.

    Note: Red cells coated with other drugs, such as cefatetan, can be prepared in a similar manner. (See Chapter 20.)

Reference

Petz LD, Branch DR. Drug-induced immune hemolytic anemia. In: Chaplin H, ed. Methods in hematology: Immune hemolytic anemias. New York: Churchill-Livingstone, 1985:47-94.

Method 4.14. Demonstration of Immune-Complex Formation Involving Drugs

Principle

For a discussion of the mechanism of drug-induced formation see Chapter 20.

Specimen

Patient's serum.

Reagents

1. Drug under investigation, in the same form (tablet, solution, capsules) that the patient is receiving.
2. Phosphate-buffered saline (PBS) at pH 7.0-7.4 (see Method 1.6).
3. Fresh, normal serum known to lack unexpected antibodies, as a source of complement.
4. Group O reagent red cells, one aliquot treated with a proteolytic enzyme (see Method 3.5.5) and one untreated.

Procedure

1. Prepare a 1 mg/mL suspension solution of the drug in PBS. Centrifuge, and adjust the pH of the supernatant fluid to 7.0 with either 1 N NaOH or 1 N HCl, as required.

2. Using 0.2 mL of each reactant, prepare the following test mixtures:
    a. Patient's serum + drug
    b. Patient's serum + complement (normal serum) + drug
    c. Patient's serum + complement (normal serum) + PBS
    d. Normal serum + drug
    e. Normal serum + PBS

3. To 3 drops of each test mixture, add 1 drop of a 2-5% saline suspension of group O reagent red cells. To another 3 drops of each test mixture add 1 drop of a 5% saline suspension of enzyme-treated group O reagent red cells.

4. Mix, and incubate at 37 C for 1-2 hours, with periodic gentle mixing.

5. Wash the cells four times in saline, and test with a polyspecific antiglobulin reagent.

6. Centrifuge and examine for agglutination and/or hemolysis.

Interpretation

Hemolysis, agglutination, or coating can occur. Reactivity in any of the tests containing patient's serum to which the drug was added, and absence of reactivity in the corresponding control tests containing PBS instead of the drug, indicates a drug/anti-drug interaction.

Notes

1. The drug may be more easily dissolved by incubation at 37 C and vigorous shaking of the solution. If the drug is in tablet form, crush it with a mortar and pestle before adding PBS.

2. Many drugs will not dissolve completely, but enough may enter solution to react in serologic tests. Other methods, obtained from the manufacturer or other publications, may be needed to dissolve adequate quantities of some drugs.

3. When available, a serum/plasma specimen known to contain antibody with the

drug specificity being evaluated should be included as a control specimen.

References

Garratty G. Laboratory investigation of drug-induced immune hemolytic anemia. Supplement to: Bell CA, ed. A seminar on laboratory management of hemolysis. Washington, DC: American Association of Blood Banks, 1979.

Petz LD, Branch DR. Drug-induced immune hemolytic anemia. In: Chaplin H, ed. Methods in hematology: Immune hemolytic anemias. New York: Churchill Livingstone, 1985:47-94.

Method 4.15. Ex-vivo Demonstration of Drug/Anti-Drug Complexes

Principle

Immune drug/anti-drug complexes can activate complement and cause hemolysis in vivo. These immune complexes may be demonstrable by serologic testing in the presence of the drug, but with some drugs (notably nomifensine), antibodies are directed against metabolites of the drug rather than the native drug. Serum and/or urine from volunteers who have ingested therapeutic levels of the drug can be used as a source of these metabolites.

This procedure is used to investigate drug-associated immune hemolysis, particularly when the use of the preceding methods has been uninformative.

Specimen

Test serum, separated at 37 C from blood clotted at 37 C.

Reagents

1. Polyspecific antihuman globulin (AHG) reagent.
2. Drug metabolites from volunteer drug recipients.
   a. Serum separated at 37 C from blood clotted at 37 C. Obtain samples immediately before (VS$_0$), at 1 hour (VS$_1$) and 6 hours (VS$_6$) after drug administration. Divide serum into 1-mL aliquots and store them at 1-6 C for a few hours or at –20 C or colder until use.
   b. Urine obtained immediately before (VU$_0$), at 1 hour (VU$_1$), 3.5 hours (VU$_{3.5}$), 7 hours (VU$_7$), and 16 hours (VU$_{16}$) after drug administration. Divide it into 1-mL aliquots and store them at 1-6 C for a few hours or at –20 C or colder until use.
3. Freshly collected normal human serum, known to lack unexpected antibodies as a source of complement.
4. Phosphate-buffered saline (PBS) at pH 7.3 (see Method 1.6).
5. Pooled group O reagent red cells washed three times with saline and resuspended to a 2-5% concentration with PBS.
6. Pooled ficin-treated group O red cells, 2-5% suspension in PBS.

Procedure

1. For each serum (VS) and/or urine (VU) sample collected from volunteer drug recipients, prepare two sets of the following test mixtures, using 0.1-mL volumes of each reactant:
   a. Test serum + VS (or VU)
   b. Test serum + VS (or VU) + complement
   c. Complement + VS (or VU)
2. Using 0.1-mL volumes, prepare duplicate control tubes of:
   a. Test serum + PBS
   b. Test serum + complement + PBS
   c. Complement + PBS
3. To one set of test mixtures and control tubes, add 1 drop of the untreated red cells.
4. To the other set of test mixtures and control tubes, add 1 drop of ficin-treated red cells.

5. Agitate the contents of each tube and incubate at 37 C for 1 or 2 hours, with periodic agitation.

6. Centrifuge at 900-1000 $\times g$ for 10-20 seconds, examine macroscopically for agglutination, and/or hemolysis and grade and record the results.

7. Wash the cells four times with saline and completely decant the final supernatant fluid.

8. Add polyspecific AHG according to the manufacturer's directions.

9. Centrifuge at 900-1000 $\times g$ for 10-20 seconds, examine the cells macroscopically, and grade and record the results.

Interpretation

Hemolysis, direct agglutination, or reactivity with AHG indicates reactivity. Reactivity in any of the tubes containing test serum and VS or VU, and absence of reactivity in all the control tubes indicates antibody against a metabolite of the drug in question.

Notes

1. Complement may be omitted from step 1b, above, if the VS samples have been kept on ice and are used for testing within 8 hours of collection.

2. The sample collection times given are those optimal for antibodies to nomifensine metabolites; different collection times may be required for other drugs.

3. Approval of the institutional ethics committee should be obtained for the use of volunteers for obtaining drug metabolites.

Reference

Salama A, Mueller-Eckhardt C. The role of metabolite-specific antibodies in nomifensine-dependent immune hemolytic anemia. N Engl J Med 1985;313:469-74.

Hemolytic Disease of the Newborn Methods

Method 5.1. Indicator Cell Rosette Test for Fetomaternal Hemorrhage

Principle

This test detects D-positive red cells in the blood of a D-negative woman whose fetus or recently delivered infant is D-positive. When anti-D is added to the mother's blood, the small number of D-positive fetal cells do not undergo direct agglutination; if the mixed cell population is incubated with reagent antibody, the D-positive cells become coated with anti-D and exhibit mixed-field agglutination when antiglobulin serum is added. Because the mixed-field agglutination may be difficult to detect, the rosette procedure uses D-positive red cells as the indicator to demonstrate antibody coating. When D-positive cells are added to a cell mixture in which some cells are coated with anti-D, they form easily visible rosettes of several cells clustered around each antibody-coated D-positive cell.

Although the number of rosettes is roughly proportional to the number of D-positive red cells present in the original mixture, this test provides only qualitative information about fetal-maternal admixture. Specimens giving a positive result should be subjected to further testing to quantify the number of fetal cells. The acid-elution procedure given below, flow cytometry, or the enzyme-linked antiglobulin test (ELAT) are acceptable choices.

Specimen

A 2-5% saline suspension of washed red cells from the mother's postdelivery blood sample.

Reagents

Prepared reagents are commercially available. The steps below can be used for in-house preparation.

1. Negative control: 2-5% saline suspension of washed red cells known to be D-negative.

2. Positive control: 2-5% saline suspension of a mixture containing approximately 0.6% D-positive red cells and 99.4% D-negative red cells. The positive control can be prepared by adding 1 drop of a 3% suspension of washed D-positive red cells to 15 drops of a 3% suspension of washed D-negative red cells. Mix well, then add 1 drop of this cell suspension to 9 drops of the 3% suspension of D-negative red cells. Mix well.

3. Indicator red cells: 0.2-0.5% saline suspension of group O, R_2R_2 red cells. Either enzyme-treated or untreated cells in an enhancing medium can be used.

4. Chemically modified or high-protein reagent anti-D serum. Some monoclonal/polyclonal blended reagents are unsuitable for use in this method. The antisera selected for use should be evaluated for suitability before incorporation into the test procedure.

Procedure

1. To each of three 12×75 mm test tubes, add 1 drop (or volume specified in manufacturer's instructions) of reagent anti-D.

2. Add 1 drop of maternal cells, negative control cells, and positive control cells to the appropriately labeled tubes.

3. Incubate at 37 C for 15-30 minutes, or as specified by manufacturer's instructions.

4. Wash cell suspensions at least four times with large volumes of saline, to remove all unbound reagent anti-D. Decant saline completely after last wash.

5. To the dry cell button, add 1 drop of indicator cells and mix thoroughly to resuspend them. Add enhancing medium if appropriate.

6. Centrifuge tubes for 15 seconds at approximately $1000 \times g$.

7. Resuspend cell button and examine the red cell suspension microscopically at 100-150× magnification.

8. Examine at least 10 fields and count the number of red cell rosettes in each field.

Interpretation

Absence of rosettes is a negative result. With enzyme-treated indicator cells, up to one rosette per three fields may occur in a negative specimen. With untreated indicator cells and an enhancing medium, there may be up to six rosettes per five fields in a negative test. The presence of more rosettes than these allowable maximums constitutes a positive result and the specimen should be examined with a test that quantifies the amount of fetal blood present.

The presence of rosettes or agglutination in the negative control tube indicates inadequate washing after incubation, allowing residual anti-D to agglutinate the D-positive indicator cells. A strongly positive result is seen with red cells from a woman whose Rh phenotype is weak D rather than D-negative; massive fetomaternal hemorrhage may produce an appearance difficult to distinguish from those caused by a weak D phenotype, and a quantitative test for fetal cells should be performed. If the infant's cells are shown to be weak D, a negative result on the mother's specimen should be interpreted with caution.

Reference

Sebring ES, Polesky HF. Detection of fetal maternal hemorrhage in Rh immune globulin candidates. Transfusion 1982;22:468-71.

Method 5.2. Acid-Elution Stain (Modified Kleihauer-Betke)

Principle

Fetal hemoglobin resists elution under acid conditions but adult hemoglobin is affected.

When a thin blood smear is exposed to an acid buffer, hemoglobin from adult red cells is leached into the buffer so that only the stroma remains; fetal cells retain their hemoglobin. The approximate volume of fetomaternal hemorrhage can be calculated from the percentage of fetal red cells in the maternal blood film.

Specimen

Mother's postdelivery blood sample.

Reagents

Prepared reagents are commercially available in kit form. The steps below can be used for in-house preparations.

1. Stock solution A (0.1 M of citric acid). $C_6H_8O_7 \bullet H_2O$, 21.0 g, diluted to 1 liter with distilled water. Keep in refrigerator.
2. Stock solution B (0.2 M of sodium phosphate). $Na_2HPO_4 \bullet 7H_2O$, 53.6 g, diluted to 1 liter with distilled water. Keep in refrigerator.
3. McIlvaine's buffer, pH 3.2. Add 75 mL of stock solution A to 21 mL of stock solution B. Prepare fresh mixture for each test. This buffer mixture should be brought to room temperature or used at 37 C.
4. Erythrosin B 0.5% in water.
5. Harris hematoxylin (filtered).
6. 80% ethyl alcohol.
7. Positive control specimen. 10 parts of anticoagulated adult blood, mixed with one part of anticoagulated ABO-compatible cord blood.
8. Negative control specimen. Anticoagulated adult blood.

Procedure

1. Prepare very thin blood smears, diluting blood with an equal volume of saline. Air dry.
2. Fix smears in 80% ethyl alcohol for 5 minutes.
3. Wash smears with distilled water.
4. Immerse smears in McIlvaine's buffer, pH 3.2, for 11 minutes at room temperature or 5 minutes at 37 C. This reaction is temperature-sensitive.
5. Wash smears in distilled water.
6. Immerse smears in erythrosin B for 5 minutes.
7. Wash smears completely in distilled water.
8. Immerse smears in Harris hematoxylin for 5 minutes.
9. Wash smears in running tap water for 1 minute.
10. Examine dry using 40× magnification, count a total of 2000 red cells, and record the number of fetal cells observed.
11. Calculate percent of fetal red cells in the total counted.

Interpretation

1. Normal adult red cells appear as very pale ghosts, while fetal cells are bright pink and refractile.
2. The conversion factor used to indicate the volume (as mL of whole blood) of fetomaternal hemorrhage is: percent of fetal red cells observed × 50.

Note

The accuracy and precision of this procedure are poor and allowance should be made in determining the needed dose of RhIG in massive fetomaternal hemorrhage. If there is doubt about giving additional RhIG, it is preferable to give too much than too little.

Reference

Sebring ES. Fetomaternal hemorrhage—incidence and methods of detection and quantitation. In: Garratty G, ed. Hemolytic disease of the newborn. Arlington, VA: American Association of Blood Banks, 1984:87-118.

Method 5.3. Antibody Titration Studies to Assist in Early Detection of Hemolytic Disease of the Newborn

Principle

Antibody titration is a semiquantitative method of determining antibody concentration. Serial, twofold dilutions of serum are prepared and tested for antibody activity. The reciprocal of the highest dilution of plasma or serum that gives a 1+ reaction is referred to as the titer (ie, 1 in 128 dilution; titer = 128).

In pregnancy, antibody titration is performed to identify women with significant levels of antibodies that may lead to hemolytic disease of the newborn (HDN) and, for low-titer antibodies, to establish a baseline for comparison with titers found later in pregnancy. Titration of non-Rh antibodies should be undertaken only after discussion with the obstetrician as to how the data will be used in the clinical management of the pregnancy.

Specimen

Serum for titration (containing potentially significant unexpected antibodies to red cell antigens, 1 mL). If possible, test the current sample in parallel with the most recent previously submitted (preceding) sample from the current pregnancy.

Materials

1. Antihuman IgG: need not be heavy-chain specific.
2. Dilute bovine albumin (approx. 6% w/v), optional: 22% (w/v) bovine albumin, 1 mL; isotonic saline, 3 mL.
3. Eppendorf® pipettes, or equivalent: 0.1-0.5 mL delivery, with disposable tips.
4. Red Blood Cells (RBCs): group O reagent RBCs with double-dose expression of antigen to which the serum contains antibody (use R_2R_2 RBCs when titrating anti-D); wash three times and dilute to a 2% suspension with isotonic saline. NOTE: Avoid using Bg+ RBCs, because this may result in falsely high values, especially with sera from multiparous women.

Quality Control

1. Test the preceding sample in parallel with the current sample.
2. Prepare dilutions using a separate pipette for each tube. Failure to do so will result in falsely high titers due to carry-over.
3. Confirm all negative reactions with IgG-coated RBCs (see Step 9 below).

Procedure

1. Using 0.5-mL volumes, prepare serial twofold dilutions of serum in saline or 6% albumin. The initial tube should contain undiluted serum and the doubling dilution range should be from 1 in 2 to 1 in 2048 (total of 12 tubes).
2. Place 0.1 mL of each dilution into appropriately labeled 10 or 12 × 75-mm test tubes.
3. Add 0.1 mL of RBCs to each dilution.
4. Gently agitate the contents of each tube; incubate at 37 C for 1 hour.
5. Wash the RBCs four times with saline; completely decant the final wash supernatant.
6. To the dry RBC buttons thus obtained, add anti-IgG according to the manufacturer's directions.
7. Centrifuge as for hemagglutination tests.
8. Examine the RBCs macroscopically; grade and record the reactions.
9. Add IgG-coated RBCs to all negative tests; recentrifuge and examine the tests macroscopically for mixed-field agglutination; repeat antibody detection tests when tests with IgG-coated RBCs are nonreactive.

Results

The titer is reported as the reciprocal of the highest dilution of serum at which 1+ agglutination is observed. A titer ≥16 is considered significant and may warrant monitoring for HDN by cordocentesis, high-resolution ultrasound, or examination of the amniotic fluid for bilirubin pigmentation.

Notes

1. Titration studies should be performed upon initial detection of the antibody; save an aliquot of the serum (frozen at –20 C or colder) for comparative studies with the next submitted sample.

2. When the titer is <16 and the antibody specificity has been associated with HDN, it is recommended that repeat titration studies be performed every 2-4 weeks, beginning at 18 weeks' gestation; save an aliquot of the serum (frozen at –20 C or colder) for comparative studies with the next submitted sample.

3. When the decision has been made to monitor the pregnancy by an invasive procedure such as amniocentesis, no further titrations are warranted.

4. Each institution should develop a policy to ensure some degree of uniformity in reporting and interpreting antibody titers.

5. For antibodies to low-incidence antigens, consider using paternal RBCs.

6. Do not use enhancement techniques [albumin, polyethylene glycol, low ionic strength saline (LISS)] or enzyme-treated RBCs, because elevated titers may be obtained.

7. LISS should not be used as a diluent in titration studies; nonspecific uptake of globulins may occur in serum-LISS dilutions.

8. Failure to obtain the correct results may be caused by 1) incorrect technique, notably, failure to use separate pipette tips for each dilution or 2) failure to mix thawed frozen serum.

References

Judd WJ, Luban NLC, Ness PM, et al. Prenatal and perinatal immunohematology: Recommendations for serologic management of the fetus, newborn infant, and obstetric patient. Transfusion 1990;30:175-83.

Judd WJ. Methods in immunohematology, 2nd ed. Durham, NC: Montgomery Scientific Publications, 1994.

Blood Collection, Storage, and Component Preparation Methods

Method 6.1. Copper Sulfate Method for Screening Donors for Anemia

Principle

This method estimates the hemoglobin content of blood from its specific gravity. A drop of blood in contact with copper sulfate solution of specific gravity 1.053 becomes encased in a sac of copper proteinate, which prevents dispersion of the fluid or any change in specific gravity for about 15 seconds. If the specific gravity of the blood is higher than that of the solution, the drop will sink within 15 seconds; if not, the drop will hesitate, remain suspended, or rise to the top of the solution. A specific gravity of 1.053 corresponds to a hemoglobin concentration of 12.5 g/dL.

This is not a quantitative test; it shows only whether the prospective donor's hemoglobin is below or above the acceptable level of 12.5 g/dL. False-positive reactions are rare; donors whose drop of blood sinks nearly always have an acceptable hemoglobin level. False-negative reactions occur fairly commonly and can cause inappropriate deferral.[1,2] Measuring hemoglobin by another method or determining hematocrit sometimes reveals that the prospective donor is, after all, acceptable.

Reagents and Materials

1. Copper sulfate solution at specific gravity 1.053, available commercially. Store in tightly capped containers to prevent evaporation. The solution should be kept at room temperature or brought to room temperature before it is used.

2. Sterile gauze, antiseptic wipes, and sterile lancets.

3. Containers for disposal of sharps and other biohazardous materials.

4. Capillary tubes coated with anticoagulant and dropper bulbs, or device to collect capillary blood without contact.

Procedure

1. Into a labeled, clean, dry tube or bottle, dispense a sufficient amount (at least 30 mL) of copper sulfate solution to allow the drop to fall approximately 3 inches. Change solution daily or after 25 tests. Be sure the solution is adequately mixed before beginning each day's determinations.
2. Clean the site of skin puncture thoroughly with antiseptic solution and wipe dry with sterile gauze.
3. Puncture the finger firmly, near the end but slightly to the side, with a sterile, disposable lancet or springloaded, disposable needle system. If earlobe is used, puncture the fleshy, dependent portion. A good free flow of blood is important. Do not squeeze the puncture site repeatedly, as this may dilute the drop of blood with tissue fluid and lower the specific gravity.
4. Collect blood in an anticoagulated capillary tube without allowing air to enter the tube.
5. Let one drop of blood fall gently from the tube at a height about 1 cm above the surface of the copper sulfate solution.
6. Observe for 15 seconds.
7. Dispose of lancets, capillary tubes, and blood-contaminated gauze in appropriate biohazard containers.

Interpretation

1. If the drop of blood sinks, the donor's hemoglobin is at an acceptable level for blood donation.
2. If the drop of blood does not sink, the donor's hemoglobin may not be at an acceptable level for blood donation. If time and equipment permit, it is desirable to perform a quantitative measurement of hemoglobin or hematocrit.

Notes

1. A certificate of analysis from the manufacturer should be obtained with each new lot of copper sulfate solution.
2. Used solution should be disposed of as biohazardous material because of the blood in the container.
3. Use care to prevent blood from contaminating work surfaces, the donor's clothing, or other persons or equipment.

References

1. Lloyd H, Collins A, Walker W, et al. Volunteer blood donors who fail the copper sulfate screening test: What does failure mean, and what should be done? Transfusion 1988;28:4679.
2. Nelson DA, Morris MW. Basic examination of blood. In: Henry JB, ed. Clinical diagnosis and management by laboratory methods. 18th ed. Philadelphia: WB Saunders, 1991:553-603.

Method 6.1.1. Quality Control for Copper Sulfate Solution

Either of the two methods presented below is acceptable for quality control of copper sulfate solution.

Functional Validation of Copper Sulfate Solution

Principle

Copper sulfate solution can be checked for suitability in donor screening by observing the behavior (sinking or floating) of drops of blood of known hemoglobin concentration.

Procedure

1. Obtain several (3-6, if possible) blood samples with hemoglobin levels known to be in a range around 12.5 g/dL.

2. Gently place a drop of each blood sample into a vial of copper sulfate solution of stated specific gravity of 1.053.

3. Drops of all blood samples with hemoglobin at or above 12.5 g/dL must sink and those with hemoglobin levels below 12.5 g/dL must float.

4. Record the date of testing, the name of the manufacturer, the lot number, the expiration date, the results, and the initials of the person performing the test. Document corrective action if the desired results are not achieved.

Measurement of Specific Gravity of Copper Sulfate Solution

Principle

The specific gravity of the copper sulfate solution can be measured directly and the result compared to the value stated by the manufacturer.

Procedure

1. When measured with a calibrated hydrometer, a specific gravity of 1.053 ± 0.0003 g/mL renders the copper sulfate solution acceptable for use in donor screening.

2. Record the date of testing, the name of the manufacturer, the lot number, the expiration date, the initials of the person performing the test, and the identification of the instrument used for measurement. Document corrective action if the desired results are not achieved.

Method 6.2. Arm Preparation for Blood Collection

Detailed instructions are specific to each manufacturer and should be followed as indicated. The following procedure is written in general terms as an example.

Principle

Iodophor compounds, or other sterilizing compounds, are used to sterilize the venipuncture site prior to blood collection.

Materials

1. Scrub solution: 0.7% aqueous solution of iodophor compound (eg, PVP-iodine or polymeriodine complex); available in prepackaged single-use form.

2. Prep solution: 10% PVP-iodine; available in prepackaged single-use form.

3. Sterile gauze.

Procedure

1. Apply tourniquet or blood pressure cuff; identify venipuncture site and release tourniquet/cuff.

2. Scrub area at least 4 cm (1.5 inches) in all directions from the intended site of venipuncture (ie, 8 cm or 3 inches in diameter) for a minimum of 30 seconds with 0.7% aqueous solution of iodophor compound. Excess foam may be removed, but the arm need not be dry before the next step.

3. Starting at the intended site of venipuncture and moving outward in a concentric spiral, apply "prep" solution; let stand for 30 seconds or as indicated by manufacturer.

4. Cover the area with dry, sterile gauze until the time of venipuncture. After the skin has been prepared, it must not be touched again. Do not repalpate the vein at the intended venipuncture site.

Note

For donors sensitive to iodine (tincture or PVP), another method (eg, Exidine[7] scrub; available commercially) should be designated by the blood bank physician. Green soap is acceptable and widely used for iodine-sensitive donors.

Reference

Smith LG. Blood collection. In: Green TS, Steckler D, eds. Donor room policies and procedures. Arlington, VA: American Association of Blood Banks, 1985:2545.

Method 6.3. Phlebotomy and Collection of Samples for Processing and Compatibility Tests

Principle

Blood for transfusion and accompanying samples is obtained from prominent veins on the donor's arm, usually in the area of the antecubital fossa.

Materials

1. Sterile collection bag containing anticoagulant, with integrally attached tubing and needle.
2. Metal clips and hand sealers.
3. Balance system to monitor volume of blood drawn.
4. Sterile gauze and clean instruments (scissors, hemostats, forceps).
5. Test tubes for sample collection.
6. Device for stripping blood in tubing.
7. Dielectric sealer (optional).

Procedure

1. Prepare donor arm as described in Method 6.2.
2. Inspect bag for any defects and discoloration. Apply pressure to check for leaks. The anticoagulant and additive solutions should be inspected for appropriate volume, color, and particulate contaminants.
3. Position bag below the level of the donor's arm.
    a. If balance system is used, be sure counterbalance is level and adjusted for the amount of blood to be drawn. Unless metal clips and a hand sealer are used, make a very loose overhand knot in tubing. Hang the bag and route tubing through the pinch clamp. A hemostat should be applied to the tubing before the needle is uncapped to prevent air from entering the line.
    b. If balance system is not used, be sure to monitor the volume of blood drawn.
4. Reapply tourniquet or inflate blood pressure cuff. Have donor open and close hand until previously selected vein is again prominent.
5. Uncover sterile needle and do venipuncture immediately. A clean, skillful venipuncture is essential for collection of a full, clot-free unit. Once the bevel has penetrated the skin, palpation of the skin above the needle stem may be performed with a gloved finger, provided the needle is not touched. When needle position is acceptable, tape the tubing to the donor's arm to hold needle in place and cover site with sterile gauze.
6. Release the hemostat. Open the temporary closure between the interior of the bag and the tubing.
7. Have donor open and close hand slowly every 10-12 seconds during collection.
8. Keep the donor under observation throughout the donation process. The donor should never be left unattended during or immediately after donation.
9. Mix blood and anticoagulant gently and periodically (approximately every 45 seconds) during collection. Mixing may be done by hand or by continuous mechanical mixing.
10. Be sure blood flow remains fairly brisk, so that coagulation activity is not triggered. If there is continuous, adequate blood flow and constant agitation, rigid time limits are not necessary. However, units requiring more than 15 minutes to draw may not be suitable for preparation

of Platelets, Fresh Frozen Plasma, or Cryoprecipitated AHF. The time required for collection can be monitored by indicating the time of phlebotomy or the maximal allowable time (start time plus 15 minutes) on the bag label.

11. Monitor volume of blood being drawn. If a balance is used, the device will interrupt blood flow after the proper amount has been collected. One mL of blood weighs at least 1.053 g, indicated by the minimum allowable specific gravity for donors. A convenient figure to use is 1.06 g/mL; a unit containing 405-495 mL should weigh 429-525 g plus the weight of the container and anticoagulant.

12. Clamp tubing near venipuncture using a hemostat, metal clip, or other temporary clamp. Release blood pressure cuff/tourniquet to 20 mm Hg or less and fill the tube(s) for blood processing sample(s) by a method that prevents contamination of the contents of the bag. This can be done in several ways.

    a. If the blood collection bag contains an inline needle, make an additional seal with a hemostat, metal clip, hand sealer, or a tight knot made from previously prepared loose knot just distal to the inline needle. Open the connector by separating the needles. Insert the proximal needle into a processing test tube, remove the hemostat, allow the tube to fill and reclamp tubing. Donor needle is now ready for removal.

    b. If the blood collection bag contains an inline processing tube, be certain that the processing tube, or pouch, is full when the collection is complete and the original clamp is placed near the donor needle. The entire assembly may now be removed from the donor.

    c. If a straight-tubing assembly set is used, the following procedure

should be used. Place a hemostat on the tubing, allowing about four segments between the hemostat and the needle. Pull tight the loose overhand knot made in step 3. Release the hemostat and strip a segment of the tubing free of blood between the knot and the needle (about 1 inch in length). Reapply the hemostat and cut the tubing in the stripped area between the knot and the hemostat. Fill the required tube(s) by releasing the hemostat and then reclamp the tubing with the hemostat. Since this system is open, biosafety level 2 precautions should be followed.

13. Deflate cuff and remove tourniquet. Remove needle from arm, if not already removed. Apply pressure over gauze and have donor raise arm (elbow straight) and hold gauze firmly over phlebotomy site with the other hand.

14. Discard needle assembly into biohazard container designed to prevent accidental injury to and contamination of personnel.

15. Strip donor tubing as completely as possible into the bag, starting at seal. Work quickly, to prevent the blood from clotting in the tubing. Invert bag several times to mix thoroughly; then allow tubing to refill with anticoagulated blood from the bag. Repeat this procedure a second time.

16. Seal the tubing attached to the collection bag into segments, leaving a segment number clearly and completely readable. Attach a unit identification number to one segment to be stored as a retention segment. Knots, metal clips, or a dielectric sealer may be used to make segments suitable for compatibility testing. It must be possible to separate segments from the unit without breaking sterility of the bag. If a dielectric sealer is used, the knot or clip should be removed from the distal

end of the tubing after creating a hermetic seal.

17. Reinspect the container for defects.
18. Recheck numbers on the container, processing tubes, donation record, and retention segment.
19. Place blood at appropriate temperature. Unless platelets are to be removed, whole blood should be placed at 1-6 C immediately after collection. If platelets are to be harvested, blood should not be chilled, but should be stored in a manner intended to reach a temperature of 20-24 C until platelets are separated.[1] Platelets must be separated within 8 hours after collection of the unit of whole blood.

Notes

If the needle is withdrawn and venipuncture is attempted again, preparation of the site must be repeated as in Method 6.2.

In addition to routine blood donor phlebotomy, this procedure may be adapted for use in therapeutic phlebotomy.

References

1. Menitove J, ed. Standards for blood banks and transfusion services, 19th ed. Bethesda, MD: American Association of Blood Banks, 1999:22.
2. Smith LG. Blood collection. In: Green TS, Steckler D, eds. Donor room policies and procedures. Arlington, VA: American Association of Blood Banks, 1985:25-45.
3. Huh YO, Lightiger B, Giacco GG, et al. Effect of donation time on platelet concentrates and fresh frozen plasma. Vox Sang 1989;56:214.
4. Sataro P. Blood collection. In: Kasprisin CA, Laird-Fryer B, eds. Blood donor collection practices. Bethesda, MD: American Association of Blood Banks, 1993:89-103.

Method 6.4. Preparation of Red Blood Cells

Principle

Red Blood Cells are obtained by removal of supernatant plasma from centrifuged Whole Blood. The volume of plasma removed determines the hematocrit of the component. When Red Blood Cells are preserved in CPDA-1, maximal viability during storage requires an appropriate ratio of cells to preservative. A hematocrit of 80% or less ensures presence of adequate glucose for red cell metabolism and citrate to maintain acceptable pH levels for up to 35 days of storage.

Materials

1. Freshly collected Whole Blood, obtained by phlebotomy as described in Method 6.3. Collect blood in a collection unit with integrally attached transfer container(s).
2. Plasma extractor.
3. Metal clips and hand sealer.
4. Clean instruments (scissors, hemostats).
5. Dielectric sealer (optional).
6. Refrigerated centrifuge.

Procedure

1. Centrifuge whole blood using a "heavy" spin (see Method 7.5), with a temperature setting of 4 C. If the blood has separated by sedimentation, centrifugation is not necessary.
2. Place the primary bag containing centrifuged or sedimented blood on a plasma expressor, and release the spring, allowing the plate of the expressor to contact the bag.
3. Clamp the tubing between the primary and satellite bags with a hemostat or, if a mechanical sealer will not be used, make a loose overhand knot in the tubing.
4. If two or more satellite bags are attached, apply the hemostat to allow plasma to flow into only one of the satellite bags. Penetrate the closure of the primary bag. A scale, such as a dietary scale, may be used to measure the expressed plasma. Remove the appropriate amount of plasma to obtain the desired hematocrit.

5. Reapply the hemostat when the desired amount of supernatant plasma has entered the satellite bag. Seal the tubing between the primary bag and the satellite bag in two places.

6. Check that the satellite bag has the same donor number as that on the primary bag and cut the tubing between the two seals.

Notes

1. If blood was collected in a single bag, modify the above directions as follows: after placing the bag on the expressor, apply a hemostat to the tubing of a sterile transfer bag, aseptically insert the cannula of the transfer bag into the outlet port of the bag of blood, release the hemostat and continue as outlined above.

2. Collection of blood in an additive system allows a removal of a greater volume of plasma in step 4. After the plasma is removed, the additive is allowed to flow from the attached satellite bag into the

Table 6.4-1. Removing Plasma from Units of Whole Blood (To Prepare RBCs with Known Hematocrit)

Hematocrit of Segment from Whole Blood Unit	Volume of Plasma to Be Removed	Final Hematocrit of Red Blood Cell Unit
40%	150 mL	56%
39%	150 mL	55%
38%	160 mL	55%
37%	165 mL	54%
36%	170 mL	54%
35%	180 mL	54%
34%	195 mL	55%
33%	200 mL	55%

red cells. Be sure that an appropriate label and dating period are used.

3. The removal of 230-256 g (225-250 mL) of plasma will generally result in a red cell component with a hematocrit between 70 and 80%.

4. See Table 6.4-1 to prepare Red Blood Cells of a specific (desired) hematocrit.

Method 6.5. Rejuvenation of Red Blood Cells

Principle

Rejuvenation is a process to restore depleted metabolites and improve the function and posttransfusion survival of stored red cells. The rejuvenating solution is not intended for intravenous administration; after warm incubation with the solution, the red cells are washed and either glycerolized for frozen storage or kept at 1-6 C for transfusion within 24 hours. The rejuvenating solution approved by the Food and Drug Administration contains pyruvate, inosine, phosphate, and adenine. It may be used only with Red Blood Cells (RBCs) prepared from Whole Blood collected into CPD or CPDA-1, and may be added at any time between 3 days after collection and 3 days after the expiration of the unit. However, use of the rejuvenation solution on red cells before 14 days of storage is not routinely done because the treated cells may develop supranormal levels of 2,3-diphosphoglycerate, which impairs oxygen uptake.

Reagents and Materials

1. Red Blood Cells stored at 1-6 C and prepared from Whole Blood collected in CPD or CPDA-1. Post collection Red Blood Cells suspended in CPD from day 3 to day 24 or in CPDA-1 from day 3 to day 38 may be used. The solution is not approved for use with cells stored in additive solutions.

2. Red Blood Cell rejuvenation solution, in 50-mL sterile vial (Rejuvesol™, Cytosol Laboratories, Braintree, MA); also called rejuvenating solution.
3. Waterproof plastic bag.
4. Metal clips and hand sealer.
5. Sterile airway.

Procedure

1. Connect the container of rejuvenating solution to the RBCs, using a transfer set and aseptic technique.
2. Allow 50 mL of rejuvenating solution to flow by gravity into the container of red cells. Gently agitate the cell/solution mixture during this addition. Note: A sterile airway is required if the solution is in a bottle.
3. Seal the tubing near the blood bag, and incubate the mixture for 1 hour at 37 C. Either a dry incubator or circulating waterbath can be used. If placed in a waterbath, the container should be completely immersed; use of a waterproof overwrap is essential to prevent contamination.
4. For use within 24 hours, wash the rejuvenated cells with saline (2 L unbuffered 0.9% NaCl) by an approved protocol. Storage of the washed cells should be at 1-6 C for no longer than 24 hours.
5. If the rejuvenated cells are to be cryopreserved, the standard glycerolization protocol adequately removes the rejuvenation solution from the processed cells.
6. Be sure that units are appropriately labeled and that all applicable records are complete.

References

1. Valeri CR, Zaroules CG. Rejuvenation and freezing of outdated stored human red cells. N Engl J Med 1972;287:1307-13.
2. Brecher ME, ZylstraHalling VW, Pineda AA. Rejuvenation of erythrocytes preserved with AS-1 and AS-3. Am J Clin Pathol 1991;96:76-79.

Method 6.6. Red Cell Cryopreservation Using High-Concentration Glycerol —Meryman Method

Principle

Cryoprotective agents make possible the longterm (10 or more years) preservation of red cells in the frozen state. High-concentration glycerol is particularly suitable for this purpose. A practical method for Red Blood Cells (RBCs) in a 450-mL bag is described below.

Materials

(See Chapter 8 for additional information on frozen cellular components).

1. Donor blood, collected into CPD or CPDA-1.
    a. Complete all blood processing on units intended for freezing.
    b. RBCs preserved in CPD or CPDA-1 may be stored at 1-6 C for up to 6 days before freezing.
    c. RBCs preserved in AS-1 and AS-3 may be stored at 1-6 C for up to 42 days before freezing.
    d. RBCs that have undergone rejuvenation (see Method 6.5) may be processed for freezing up to 3 days after their original expiration.
    e. RBCs in any preservative solution that have been entered for processing must be frozen within 24 hours of puncturing the seal.
2. Storage containers, either polyvinyl chloride or polyolefin bags.
3. 6.2 M glycerol lactate solution (400 mL).
4. Cardboard or metal canisters for freezing.
5. Hypertonic (12%) sodium chloride solution.
6. 16% NaCl, 1 liter for batch wash.

7. Isotonic (0.9%) NaCl with 0.2% dextrose solution.

8. 37 C waterbath or 37 C dry warmer.

9. Equipment for batch or continuous-flow washing, to deglycerolize cells frozen in high-concentration glycerol.

10. Freezing tape.

11. Freezer (–65 C or colder).

Procedure

Preparing RBCs for Glycerolization

1. Prepare RBCs from Whole Blood units. Weigh the RBC unit to be frozen. The combined weight of the cells and the collection bag should be between 260 g and 400 g.

2. Underweight units can be adjusted to approximately 300 g either by the addition of 0.9% NaCl or by the removal of less plasma than usual. Record the weight and, if applicable, document the amount of NaCl added.

3. Record the Whole Blood number, ABO and Rh type, anticoagulant, date of collection, date frozen, expiration time, and the identification of the person performing the procedure. If applicable, document the lot number of the transfer bag.

4. Warm the red cells and the glycerol to at least 25 C by placing them in a dry warming chamber for 10-15 minutes or by allowing them to remain at room temperature for 1 to 12 hours. The temperature must not exceed 42 C.

5. Apply a "Red Blood Cells, Frozen" label to the freezing bag in which the unit will be frozen. The label must also include: name of the facility freezing the unit; Whole Blood number; ABO and Rh type; date collected; date frozen; the cryoprotective agent used; and the expiration date.

Glycerolization

1. Document the lot numbers of the glycerol, the freezing bags, and, if used, the 0.9% NaCl.

2. Place the container of red cells on a shaker and add approximately 100 mL of glycerol as the red cells are gently agitated.

3. Turn off the shaker and allow the cells to equilibrate, without agitation, for 5-30 minutes.

4. Allow the partially glycerolized cells to flow by gravity into the freezing bag.

5. Add the remaining 300 mL of glycerol slowly in a stepwise fashion, with gentle mixing. Add smaller volumes of glycerol for smaller volumes of red cells. The final glycerol concentration is 40% w/v.

6. Allow some glycerolized cells to flow back into the tubing so that segments can be prepared.

7. Maintain the glycerolized cells at temperatures between 25 and 32 C until freezing. The recommended interval between removing the RBC unit from refrigeration and placing the glycerolized cells in the freezer should not exceed 4 hours.

Freezing and Storage

1. Place glycerolized unit in a cardboard or metal canister and place in a freezer at –65 C or colder.

2. Label the top edge of the canister with freezing tape marked with the Whole Blood number, ABO and Rh type, the date frozen, and the expiration date.

3. Do not bump or handle the frozen cells roughly.

4. The freezing rate should be less than 10 C/min.

5. Store the frozen RBCs at –65 C or colder for up to 10 years. For blood of rare phenotypes, a facility's medical director may wish to extend the storage period. The unusual nature of such units and the reason for retaining them past the routine 10-year storage period must be documented.

Thawing and Deglycerolizing

1. Place the protective canister containing the frozen cells in either a 37 C waterbath or 37 C dry warmer.
2. Agitate gently to speed thawing. The thawing process takes at least 10 minutes. Thawed cells should be at 37 C.
3. After the cells are thawed, use a commercial instrument for batch or continuous-flow washing to deglycerolize cells. Follow the manufacturer's instructions.
4. Record the lot numbers and manufacturer of all solutions and software used. Apply a "Red Blood Cells, Deglycerolized" label to the transfer pack, and be sure that the label includes identification of the collecting facility, the facility preparing the deglycerolized cells, the ABO and Rh type of the cells, the Whole Blood number, and the expiration date and time.
5. Dilute the unit with a quantity of hypertonic (12%) NaCl solution appropriate for the size of the unit. Allow to equilibrate for approximately 5 minutes.
6. Wash with 1.6% NaCl until deglycerolization is complete. Approximately 2 liters of wash solution are required. To check for residual glycerol, see Method 6.7.1.
7. Suspend the deglycerolized cells in isotonic (0.9%) saline with 0.2% dextrose.
8. Fill the integrally attached tubing with an aliquot of cells sealed in such a manner that it will be available for subsequent compatibility testing.
9. Deglycerolized RBCs must be stored at 1-6 C for no longer than 24 hours.

Notes

1. An aliquot of the donor's serum or plasma should be frozen and stored at −65 C or colder for possible future use if new diagnostic tests are mandated.
2. When new diagnostic tests have been mandated and stored units do not have aliquots available for testing, the units may have to be issued with a label stating that the test has not been performed. The reason for distributing an untested component should be documented. If a specimen from the donor is obtained and tested after the unit was stored, the date of testing should be noted on the unit when it is issued.

Reference

Meryman HT, Hornblower M. A method for freezing and washing RBCs using a high glycerol concentration. Transfusion 1972;12:145-56.

Method 6.7. Red Cell Cryopreservation Using High-Concentration Glycerol —Valeri Method

Principle

Red Blood Cells (RBCs) collected in an 800-mL primary collection bag in CPDA-1 and stored at 1-6 C for 3-38 days can be biochemically rejuvenated and frozen with 40% w/v glycerol in the 800-mL primary container. See Method 6.5 for additional information.

Materials

1. Quadruple plastic bag collection system with 800-mL primary bag.
2. Hand sealer clips.
3. Empty 600-mL polyethylene cryogenic vials (Corning 25702 or Fisher 033746).
4. Sterile connection device with wafers.
5. Freezing tape.
6. 600-mL transfer bag.
7. 50 mL of Red Blood Cell Processing Solution (Rejuvesol™, Cytosol Laboratories, Braintree, MA).
8. Heat-sealable 8″ × 12″ plastic bags.
9. Rejuvenation harness (Fenwal 4C1921 or Cutter 98052).

10. Sterile filtered airway needle (BD 5200), for Fenwal rejuvenation harness only.

11. 500 mL of glycerolyte 57 solution (Fenwal 4A7833) or 500 mL of 6.2 M glycerolization solution (Cytosol PN5500).

12. Labels—Red Blood Cells, Frozen, Rejuvenated.

13. Corrugated cardboard storage box (7" × 5.5" × 2" outside dimensions).

14. Heat sealing device.

15. Plastic bag for overwrapping.

Procedure

Preparing RBCs for Glycerolization

1. Collect 450 mL of Whole Blood in the primary bag. Invert the bag, fold it about 2 inches from the base, secure the fold with tape, and place the bag upright in a centrifuge. Centrifuge and remove all visible supernatant plasma. The hematocrit of the RBC unit must be 75 ± 5%.

2. Store RBCs at 1-6 C in the 800-mL primary bag, along with the adapter port on the tubing that connects the primary bag and transfer pack.

3. Centrifuge the stored cells to remove all visible plasma before undertaking rejuvenation. The gross and net weights of the RBCs should not exceed 352 and 280 g, respectively.

4. Transfer the plasma to the integrally connected transfer pack, fold the integral tubing and replace the hand sealer clip (not crimped).

5. Attach an empty 600-mL transfer pack to the integral tubing of the primary collection bag, using a sterile connection device.

6. Transfer 1 mL of plasma to each of three cryogenic vials to be used for future testing.

Biochemical Modification of the Cells

1. Using Fenwal Rejuvenation Harness: Aseptically insert the needle of the Y-type Fenwal Harness into the rubber stopper of a 50-mL Red Blood Cell Processing Solution bottle and the coupler of the set into the adapter port of the primary collection bag. Insert the filtered airway needle into the rubber stopper of the Red Blood Cell Processing Solution bottle.

2. Using Cutter Rejuvenation Harness: Aseptically insert the *vented white spike with the drip chamber* into the rubber stopper of the Red Blood Cell Processing Solution bottle and the *nonvented spike* into the special adapter port on the primary collection bag.

3. With gentle manual agitation, allow 50 mL of Red Blood Cell Processing Solution to flow directly into the red cells.

4. Heatseal the tubing of the harness set that connects the Red Blood Cell Processing Solution to the adapter port. The second tubing of the harness Y-set is used to add glycerol (see below).

5. Completely overwrap the 800-mL primary bag, the integrally connected empty transfer pack, and the coupler of the Y-type harness and incubate in a 37 C waterbath for 1 hour.

Glycerolization

1. Remove the numbered crossmatch segments, leaving the initial segment and number attached to the collection bag. Weigh the unit.

2. Determine the amount of glycerol to be added based on the gross or net weight of the unit from the values shown in Table 6.7.1-1. Mark the volume of glycerol to be added on the glycerol bottle for each of the three steps, using the factory graduations on the bottle.

3. Aseptically insert the coupler of the rejuvenation harness into the outlet port of the rubber stopper on the glycerol solution bottle. For Fenwal harness only, insert a filtered airway needle into the vent portion of the glycerol bottle stopper.

Table 6.7.1-1. Amount of Glycerol Needed for Different Weights of Red Cell Units

Gross Weight of Unit (grams)*	Net Weight of Unit (grams)	Initial Addition of Glycerol (mL)	Second Addition of Glycerol (mL)	Third Addition of Glycerol (mL)	Total Glycerol Added (mL)
222-272	150-200	50	50	250	350
273-312	201-240	50	50	350	450
313-402	241-330	50	50	400	500

*Weight of the empty 800-mL primary bag with the integrally attached transfer pack and the adapter port is 72 grams (average).

4. Place the bag on a shaker. Add the amount of glycerol shown in Table 6.7.1-1 for the first volume while the bag is shaking at low speed (180 oscillations/minute).

5. Equilibrate the mixture for 5 minutes without shaking and add the second volume. Equilibrate for 2 minutes. Add the third volume of glycerol, using vigorous manual shaking.

6. Heat-seal the tubing between the empty bottle of glycerol and the tubing proximal to the adapter port. Ensure that the transfer pack remains integrally attached to the primary collection bag.

7. Centrifuge the mixture of red cells and glycerol, transfer all visible supernatant glycerol to the transfer pack, resuspend, and mix.

8. Seal the tubing 4 inches from the primary collection bag, detach the transfer pack containing the supernatant fluid, and discard.

9. Affix an overlay blood component label, the facility label, and an ABO/Rh label. Record the expiration date on the label.

10. Weigh the unit just before freezing and record the weight.

11. Fold over the top portion of the primary bag (approximately 2 inches). Place the primary bag into a plastic bag overwrap and heatseal the outer bag across the top so that there is as little air as possible.

12. Place one vial of plasma and the plastic bag containing the glycerolized red cells in the cardboard box. Store the other two vials, suitably identified, at –65 C or colder for future testing, if needed.

13. Affix a "Red Blood Cells, Frozen, Rejuvenated" label, an ABO/Rh label, a facility label, and the original unit number on the outside of the box. Record separately or affix on the cardboard box the collection, freezing, and expiration dates.

14. Freeze the unit in a –80 C freezer. No more than 4 hours should be allowed to elapse between the time the unit was removed from the 4 C refrigerator and the time the cells are placed in the –80 C freezer.

Thawing and Deglycerolization

See Method 6.6.

References

1. Package insert. Rejuvesol™, Cytosol Laboratories, Braintree, MA.
2. Valeri CR. SOP red blood cell collected in the CPDA-1 800-mL primary PVC Plastic Bag Collection System and stored for 3-35 days (indated rejuvenated red cells) or for 36-38 days (outdated rejuvenated red cells). Biochemically modified with PIPA solution prior to glycerolization in the primary 800-mL bag with the special adapter port using 40% w/v glycerol and storage at –80 C, washed in the Haemonetics Blood Processor 115, and stored at 4 C for 24 hours prior to transfusion. Boston, MA: Naval Blood Research Laboratory, Boston University School of Medicine.

Method 6.7.1. Checking the Adequacy of Deglycerolization of Red Blood Cells

Principle

Glycerolization of red cells for frozen storage creates a hyperosmolar intracellular fluid, which must be restored to physiologically compatible levels before the cells are transfused. Inadequately deglycerolized red cells will be hemolyzed by contact with normal saline, or with serum or plasma if subjected to crossmatching. During deglycerolization, the last solution in contact with the cells is normal saline; the easiest way to determine adequacy of glycerol removal is to determine the level of free hemoglobin in the final wash. An adequate estimate of hemolysis can be achieved by comparing the color of the wash fluid with the blocks in a commercially available color comparator. Alternatively, normal saline can be added to an aliquot of deglycerolized cells and the color of the supernatant fluid evaluated against the color comparator.

Materials and Equipment

1. Semiautomated instrument for deglycerolizing cryopreserved Red Blood Cells.
2. Transparent tubing, as part of disposable material used to deglycerolize individual unit.
3. Color comparator, available commercially.

Procedure

1. Interrupt the last wash cycle at a point when wash fluid is visible in the tubing leading to the disposal bag.
2. Hold the comparator block next to an accessible segment of tubing, against a well-lighted white ground.
3. Note coloration of the wash fluid which should be no stronger than the block, indicating 3% hemolysis.

4. If level of hemolysis is excessive, continue wash process until color is within acceptable limits.
5. Record observation for the individual unit and for quality assurance program.
6. If unacceptable hemolysis occurs repeatedly, document corrective action.

Method 6.8. Preparation of Fresh Frozen Plasma from Whole Blood

Principle

Plasma is separated from cellular blood elements and frozen to preserve the activity of labile coagulation factors. Plasma must be prepared for freezing within 8 hours of phlebotomy.

Materials

1. Freshly collected Whole Blood, obtained by phlebotomy as described in Method 6.3, in a collection unit with integrally attached transfer container(s).
2. Metal clips and hand sealer.
3. Clean instruments (scissors, hemostats).
4. Dielectric sealer (optional).
5. Plasma extractor.
6. Freezing apparatus.

Procedure

1. Centrifuge blood soon after collection, using a "heavy" spin (see Method 7.5). Use a refrigerated centrifuge at 1-6 C unless also preparing platelets (see Method 6.11).
2. Place primary bag containing centrifuged blood on a plasma extractor and place the attached satellite bag on a scale adjusted to zero. Express the plasma into the satellite bag and weigh the plasma.
3. Seal the transfer tubing with a dielectric sealer or metal clips, but do not obliterate

the segment numbers of the tubing. Place another seal nearer the transfer bag.

4. Label the transfer bag with the unit number before it is separated from the original container. Record the volume of plasma on the label.

5. Cut the tubing between the two seals. The tubing may be coiled and taped against the plasma container, leaving the segments available for any testing desired.

6. Place plasma at −18 C or colder within 8 hours of collection from the donor.

Method 6.9. Preparation of Cryoprecipitated AHF from Whole Blood

Principle

Coagulation Factor VIII (antihemophilic factor, AHF) can be concentrated from freshly collected plasma by cryoprecipitation. Cryoprecipitation is accomplished by slow thawing, at 1-6 C, plasma that has been prepared for freezing within 8 hours of phlebotomy.

Materials

1. Freshly collected Whole Blood, obtained by phlebotomy as described in Method 6.3, in a collection unit with at least two integrally attached transfer containers.

2. Metal clips and hand sealer.

3. Clean instruments (scissors, hemostats).

4. Dielectric sealer (optional).

5. Plasma extractor.

6. Refrigerated centrifuge.

7. Freezing apparatus: suitable freezing devices include blast freezers or mechanical freezers capable of maintaining temperatures of −18 C or colder; dry ice; or an ethanol dry ice bath. In a bath of 95% ethanol and chipped dry ice, freezing will be complete in about 15 minutes.

Procedure

1. Collect blood in a collection unit with two integrally attached transfer containers.

2. Centrifuge blood shortly after collection at 1-6 C, using a "heavy" spin (see Method 7.5). Collect at least 200 mL (205 g) of cell-free plasma for processing into cryoprecipitate.

3. Promptly place plasma in a freezing device so that freezing is started within 8 hours of phlebotomy. Plasma containers immersed in liquid must be protected with a plastic overwrap.

4. Allow the plasma to thaw at 1-6 C by placing the bag in a 1-6 C circulating waterbath or in a refrigerator. If thawed in a waterbath, use a plastic overwrap (or other means) to keep container ports dry.

5. When the plasma has a slushy consistency, separate liquid plasma from the cryoprecipitate by one of the procedures below:

    a. Centrifuge the plasma at 1-6 C using a "heavy" spin. Hang the bag in an inverted position and allow the separated plasma to flow rapidly into the transfer bag, leaving the cryoprecipitate adhering to the sides of the primary bag. Separate the cryoprecipitate from the plasma promptly, to prevent the cryoprecipitate from dissolving and flowing out of the bag. Ten to 15 mL of supernatant plasma may be left in the bag for resuspension of the cryoprecipitate after thawing. Refreeze the cryoprecipitate immediately.

    b. Place the thawing plasma in a plasma expressor when approximately one tenth of the contents is still frozen. With the bag in an upright position, allow the supernatant plasma to flow slowly into the transfer bag, using the ice crystals at the top as a filter. The cryoprecipitate paste will adhere to the sides of the bag or to the ice. Seal the bag when about 90% of the cryoprecipitate-poor plasma has been removed and refreeze the cryoprecipitate immediately.

6. Store at –18 C or colder, preferably –30 C or colder, for up to 12 months from the date of blood collection.

Note

Cryoprecipitated AHF may be prepared from Fresh Frozen Plasma at any time within 12 months of collection. The expiration date of cryoprecipitated AHF is 12 months from the date of phlebotomy, not from the date it was prepared.

Method 6.10. Thawing and Pooling Cryoprecipitated AHF

Principle

Cryoprecipitated AHF should be rapidly thawed at 30-37 C, but should not remain at this temperature once thawing is complete. The following method permits rapid thawing and pooling of this product.

Materials

1. Circulating waterbath at 37 C (waterbaths designed for thawing plasma are available commercially, as are specially designed dry heat devices).
2. Medication injection ports.
3. Sterile 0.9% sodium chloride for injection.
4. Syringes and needles.

Procedure

1. Cover the container with a plastic overwrap to prevent contamination of the ports with unsterile water, or use a device to keep the containers upright with the ports above water.
2. Resuspend the thawed precipitate carefully and completely, either by kneading it into the residual 10-15 mL of plasma or by adding approximately 10 mL of 0.9% sodium chloride and gently resuspending.
3. Pool by inserting a medication injection site into a port of each bag. Aspirate contents of one bag into a syringe and inject into the next bag. Use the ever-increasing volume to flush each subsequent bag of as much dissolved cryoprecipitate as possible, until all contents are in final bag.
4. Thawed Cryoprecipitated AHF must be stored at room temperature. If pooled, it must be administered within 4 hours of first entry. Thawed units, if not entered, must be administered within 6 hours of thawing if intended for replacement of Factor VIII. Pools of thawed individual units may not be refrozen.

Method 6.11. Preparation of Platelets from Whole Blood

Principle

Platelet-rich plasma is separated from Whole Blood by "light-spin" centrifugation and the platelets are concentrated by "heavy-spin" centrifugation with subsequent removal of supernatant plasma (see Method 7.5).

Materials

1. Freshly collected Whole Blood, obtained by phlebotomy as described in Method 6.3, in a collection unit with two integrally attached transfer containers. The

final container must be a plastic approved for platelet storage. Keep blood at room temperature (20-24 C) before separating platelet-rich plasma from the red cells. This separation must take place within 8 hours of phlebotomy.

2. Metal clips and hand sealer.

3. Scissors, hemostats.

4. Plasma extractor.

5. Dielectric sealer (optional).

6. Centrifuge, calibrated as in Method 7.5.

Procedure

1. Do not chill the blood at any time before or during platelet separation. If the temperature of the centrifuge is 1-6 C, set the temperature control of the refrigerated centrifuge at 20 C and allow the temperature to rise to approximately 20 C. Centrifuge the blood using a "light" spin (see Method 7.5).

2. Express the platelet-rich plasma into the transfer bag intended for platelet storage. Seal the tubing twice between the primary bag and Y connector of the two satellite bags and cut between the two seals. Place the red cells at 1-6 C.

3. Centrifuge the platelet-rich plasma at 20 C using a "heavy" spin (see Method 7.5).

4. Express the platelet-poor plasma into the second transfer bag and seal the tubing. Some plasma should remain on the platelet button for storage, but no exact volume can be designated. AABB *Standards* requires that sufficient plasma remain with the platelet concentrate to maintain the pH at 6.2 or higher for the entire storage period. This usually requires a minimum of 35 mL of plasma when storage is at 20-24 C, but 50-70 mL is preferable.

5. The platelet concentrate container should be left stationary, with the label side down, at room temperature for approximately 1 hour.

6. Resuspend the platelets in either of the following ways:
   a. Manipulate the platelet container gently by hand to achieve uniform resuspension.
   b. Place the container on a rotator at room temperature. The slow, gentle agitation should achieve uniform resuspension within 2 hours.

7. Maintain the platelet suspensions at 20-24 C with continuous gentle agitation.

8. Platelets should be inspected before issue to ensure that no platelet aggregates are visible.

Notes

The platelet-poor plasma may be frozen promptly and stored as Fresh Frozen Plasma (FFP), if the separation and freezing are completed within 8 hours of phlebotomy. The volume of FFP prepared after platelet preparation will be substantially less than that prepared directly from Whole Blood.

Reference

Menitove J, ed. Standards for blood banks and transfusion services, 19th ed. Bethesda, MD: American Association of Blood Banks, 1999:30.

Method 6.12. Removing Plasma from Platelet Concentrates

Principle

While optimal storage of platelets requires an adequate volume of plasma, a few patients requiring platelet therapy may not tolerate large-volume intravenous infusion. Stored platelets may be centrifuged and much of the plasma removed shortly before transfusion, but appropriate resuspension is essential. After centrifugation and plasma removal, the platelets must remain at room temperature, without agitation, for 20-60 minutes, before resuspension into the remaining plasma. Transfusion must take place within 4 hours of the time the platelet bag was entered. Volume reduction can be performed on individual concentrates or on a pool of several units.

No consensus exists regarding the optimal centrifugation rate. One study[1] found 35-55% platelet loss in several units centrifuged at $500 \times g$ for 6 minutes, compared with 5-20% loss in units centrifuged at $5000 \times g$ for 6 minutes or $2000 \times g$ for 10 minutes. The authors recommend $2000 \times g$ for 10 minutes, to avoid any risk that higher centrifugal force might inflict on the plastic container. A study by Moroff et al[2] found mean platelet loss to be less than 15% in 42 units centrifuged at $580 \times g$ for 20 minutes.

Materials

1. Platelet concentrate(s), prepared as described in Method 6.11.
2. Metal clips and hand sealer.
3. Scissors, hemostats.
4. Dielectric sealer (optional).
5. Centrifuge, calibrated as in Method 7.5.
6. Plasma extractor.

Procedure

1. Pool platelets, if desired, into a transfer pack, using standard technique. Single platelet concentrates may need volume reduction for pediatric recipients. Hemapheresis components can be processed directly.
2. Centrifuge at 20-24 C, using one of the following protocols:
   a. $580 \times g$ for 20 minutes.
   b. $2000 \times g$ for 10 minutes.
   c. $5000 \times g$ for 6 minutes.
3. Without disturbing the contents, transfer the bag to a plasma extractor. Remove all but 10-15 mL plasma from single units, or somewhat more volume, proportionately, from a pool or from a component prepared by hemapheresis.

4. Mark expiration time on bag as 4 hours after the time the unit was entered.
5. Leave bag at 20-24 C without agitation for 20 minutes if centrifuged at $580 \times g$, or for 1 hour if centrifuged at 2000 or $5000 \times g$.
6. Resuspend platelets as described in Method 6.11.

Notes

1. If a sterile connection device is used for removing plasma from a hemapheresis component or individual platelet concentrate, the unit can be considered sterile and it is not necessary to impose the 4-hour expiration interval required for entered Platelets. There are, however, no data to support storage of reduced-volume platelet concentrates.
2. Reduced-volume platelet concentrates may not be distributed as a licensed product.
3. Platelets that have been pooled must be used within 4 hours of entering the units, whether or not they have been volume-reduced. Pooled platelets may not be distributed as a licensed product.

References

1. Simon TL, Sierra ER. Concentration of platelet units into small volumes. Transfusion 1984;24:173-5.
2. Moroff G, Friedman A, RobkinKline L, et al. Reduction of the volume of stored platelet concentrates for use in neonatal patients. Transfusion 1984;24:144-6.

Method 6.13. Surgical Bone Donor Selection

Principle

Bone for allogeneic transplantation can be collected from living donors undergoing orthopedic surgery (eg, total hip replacement), and stored frozen at −65 C or colder for use as needed. If these activities are performed in a transfusion service, they must be under the supervision of the medical director.

Bone can also be collected from cadavers, but the collection, preparation, and processing are usually conducted in multipurpose tissue banks.

Materials

1. Medical history and consent form for collection of bone.
2. Bone donation information pamphlet.
3. Documentation of physical examination.

Procedure

1. Identify patients scheduled for total hip and knee replacement as they are candidates for femoral head and tibial wedge donations, respectively. This can be done at the time of autologous blood donation or when the surgery is scheduled.
2. Provide each suitable donor with the facility's bone donation information pamphlet and request their consideration.
3. Complete a health history assessment, using the medical history form for collection of surgical bone.
4. Apply to bone donors the same criteria for recipient safety that are used for allogeneic blood donation. Exclude from bone donation patients with severe bone disease or severe rheumatoid arthritis.
5. Inform the donor that infectious disease testing for various forms of hepatitis, HIV, HTLV-I and syphilis are required at the time of donation.
6. Inform the donor that infectious disease retesting for antibodies to human immunodeficiency virus and hepatitis C virus will be required 6 or more months after donation.
7. Informed consent for surgical bone donors shall specify the type of tissue to be donated and the general purpose for which it will be used (eg, transplant or research). Consent shall also include a statement that the blood samples from the donor will be tested for certain transmissible diseases and that confirmed positive test results will be reported to the appropriate health officials (if required by law). If this statement is not specifically written on the consent document, the individual obtaining the informed consent shall document that this was discussed.
8. Have the donor sign the health history and consent for bone collection.
9. When bone is collected, record the date of donation (ie, date of surgery) in the department's surgical bone schedule.
10. All applicable medical records should be reviewed prior to tissue distribution.

References

1. Standards for tissue banking. McLean, VA: American Association of Tissue Banks, 1998.
2. Code of federal regulations. Title 21 CFR Part 16.1 and 21 CFR Part 1270. Washington, DC: US Government Printing Office, 1997 (revised annually).
3. Technical manual for tissue banking. McLean, VA: American Association of Tissue Banks, 1992.
4. Technical manual for surgical bone banking. McLean, VA: American Association of Tissue Banks, 1987.
5. Kakaiya RM, Jackson B. Regional programs for surgical bone banking. Clin Orthop 1990;251:290-4.

Method 6.14. Surgical Bone Collection

Principle

Advance preparation and a standard protocol are required to collect surgical bone from candidate donors.

Materials

1. Single or double (smaller container inside a larger one) collection containers, either plastic or glass.
2. Impermeable wrapping material.
3. Marking pen.
4. Sterilization facility.

5. Thioglycollate and trypticase soy broth culture tubes.
6. Collection record form.
7. Disposition record form.

Procedure

1. Prepare glass containers for sterilization.
2. Wrap the glass containers in two to three layers of impermeable wrapping material. Include a sterilization indicator on one of the internal wraps. Tape wrapping to keep it shut.
3. Sterilize with a validated sterilization technique for the applicable equipment.
4. Examine the sterilized containers for appropriate color change of the sterilization indicator strip, and ensure that the wrapping material is not damaged and that each container package is labeled with an expiration date, generally 6-60 months, unless event-related sterilization is used.
5. Before bone is collected, obtain a specimen of the prospective donor's blood for ABO/Rh and disease marker testing. Tests routinely performed on blood donors (HBsAg, HIV-1-Ag, anti-HIV-1/2, anti-HCV, serologic test for syphilis, anti-HBc, anti-HTLV, HTLV-I, ABO and Rh typing) are acceptable as the tests of record for bone donation if done within 14 days of collection, or a sample can be obtained and tested at the time of bone donation.
6. Surgical bone is collected by the surgeon who will decide, after visual examination, whether it is suitable for transplantation use. Aerobic and anaerobic cultures must be obtained, either by swab or by placing small pieces of bone into the culture vessels.
7. An aliquot of specimens retained as suitable for transplantation can be submitted for routine histologic examination. The remaining bone is made available for storage and eventual use.

8. Bone should be placed in the container soon after its collection and the lid closed securely.
9. The container should be labeled in the operating room with the patient's name, hospital number, birth date, and the date and time of collection. The hospital name may be included if the bone is to be stored in a regional program. Culture tubes should be similarly labeled. The bone container, the culture tubes, and the completed history and consent forms are forwarded to the blood bank.
10. The collection record form should include the following information: expiration dates and lot numbers of collection container and culture tubes; the patient's name, birth date, social security number, and hospital number; the name of the surgeon; and the date and time of collection.
11. If the collected bone is held in the operating room before transport to the blood bank, the container should be placed on ice. Bone can be stored at 1-6 C for up to 48 hours before it is frozen at −65 C or colder.

Method 6.15. Surgical Bone Preparation and Packaging

Principle

Preparation of surgical bone requires inspection of the collected bone, completion of necessary blood tests, proper labeling and quarantine of the collected bone until satisfactory results are reported for cultures and for the precollection and 6-month postcollection tests for disease markers. The expiration date of bone stored at −40 C or colder is 5 years; if storage is at −20 C to −39 C, bone can only be used for 6 months.

Materials

1. Scale to weigh the bone.
2. Plastic adhesive tape.
3. Bone container base label.
4. Unique identification numbers.
5. Test requisition forms.
6. Freezer.
7. Plastic bags.
8. Heat sealer for plastic bags.
9. Autoclave or incinerator.
10. ABO/Rh label.
11. Transplant record form
12. Disposition record form.

Procedure

1. Visually inspect the bone received from the operating room to determine that the bone graft is not fragmented. Do not open the container.
2. Verify that the information recorded on the container label, culture tubes, collection record form, and on the surgical bone medical history form is correct.
3. Check to ensure that the lid of the container is closed tightly.
4. Weigh the container and deduct the weight of the empty container to obtain the weight of the bone. Record this weight on collection record form.
5. Apply plastic adhesive tape to the lid to ensure further security.
6. When all of the above information is verified, remove the temporary label that was applied in the operating room and apply a bone container base label.
7. Record the following information on the base label: the descriptive name of the bone (eg, femoral head, tibial wedge, femoral head fragmented, ilium block), the unique donor number, weight or dimensions of the deposit, collection date (optional), and expiration date. The base label should contain the name of the facility responsible for the determination of donor suitability and for preparation,

packaging, labeling, and distribution of the bone (if different), the recommended storage conditions, and the preservative or antibiotic, if any.

8. Apply the unique identification number to the medical history form, collection record, blood sample tubes, culture tubes and test requisition forms.
9. Place the container in the quarantine section of the freezer at –40 C or colder and record the time of placement on the collection record form.
10. Prepare a test requisition form for routine donor screening and for aerobic and anaerobic cultures. Apply the unique donor number to each requisition form.
11. Submit the blood samples for ABO/Rh, anti-HIV-1 and -2, HBsAg, HIV-1-Ag, anti-HBc, anti-HTLV, HTLV-I, anti-HCV, a serologic test for syphilis, and HIV-1 antigen testing, if performed. Detection of red cell antibodies is not necessary.
12. Submit the thioglycollate and trypticase soy broth culture tubes for culture for 7-14 days.
13. Keep the bone specimen in quarantine until the results of repeat testing for anti-HIV-1 and anti-HCV after 180 days are received and are nonreactive.
14. Record the results of donor blood tests and the cultures on the collection record form. If the test results indicate that the bone should not be released for transplantation, discard the bone and arrange for autoclaving or incineration for final disposition. Record the discard on the disposition record.
15. If results of the initial blood tests, the cultures, and the 6-month tests show that the bone is suitable for release, review the surgical bone medical history form and the collection record form. If all reviews confirm suitability for release, label the container as described below.
16. Remove the bone from quarantine section of the freezer and remove the outer

plastic bag. Record the expiration date on the base label.

17. The container may become frosted with ice. If so, apply warmth with the palm of the hand to defrost the area where the label is to be applied. Apply appropriate ABO/Rh label.

18. Place the container into a plastic bag and seal it with heat. Staple the transplant record form to the outer plastic bag. The transplant record form should be enclosed in a small plastic bag to prevent damage from moisture.

19. Immediately place the container into the section of the freezer designated for bones that are ready for release.

20. The expiration date is 5 years for storage at –40 C or colder. If stored between –20 C and –39 C, the expiration date should be 6 months.

21. A serum or plasma sample from the initial test specimen and the 180-day specimen shall be frozen and archived.

Notes

Bone Inventory

1. Store bones from donors awaiting 6-month testing in the quarantine section of the freezer. This section should be physically distinct from the section containing bones ready for distribution.

2. A large inventory of ready-to-use bones is possible if a –40 C freezer is available because of the outdating period of several years.

3. Some transfusion services have –20 C (or colder) freezers for Fresh Frozen Plasma; these can be used to store surgical bone for 6 months.

4. A minimal effective inventory may be two to four surgical bones. Institutions with busy orthopedic services will usually have larger inventories.

5. ABO matching between recipient and bone donor is not necessary, but

Rh-negative recipients are often given bone from Rh-negative donors. If Rh-positive bone is used in an Rh-negative recipient, RhIG prophylaxis may be indicated. In the absence of surgical bones, other cadaveric bone products can be used. See "Cadaveric Bone" section below.

6. Each bone in quarantine or ready inventory must be recorded in the inventory log. A record of distribution should also be made in the log.

7. A package insert should be included with the bone when it is distributed.

Cadaveric Bone

1. Numerous products, frozen or freeze-dried, prepared from cadaveric donor bones are available.

2. Frozen cadaveric bone specimens can be quite large and are stored at –40 C or colder. Large grafts, such as proximal and distal femur, proximal tibia, hemipelvis, and others, may be obtained from tissue banks.

3. Freeze-dried bone is supplied in vacuum-packed glass containers or packs and is stored at room ambient (monitoring not required) temperature or colder for 2-5 years or longer. Storage conditions for serum albumin preparations are suitable for freeze-dried bone. Freeze-dried small preparations include cancellous cubes, tricortical ilium blocks, matchsticks, cancellous or cortical powder, and many other products.

4. Thaw or reconstitute bone according to the instructions in the package insert.

5. In general, frozen bone specimens are thawed in the operating room in a sterile basin containing sterile saline at room temperature; massive specimens may require several hours to thaw.

6. Massive specimens of freeze-dried bone should be reconstituted by aseptic introduction of saline into the vac-

uum-packed glass container or in a sterile basin and placement in the refrigerator. Reconstitution may require 4-18 hours, depending upon the size and thickness of the graft. Small freeze-dried bones are reconstituted in the operating room with saline within 15-30 minutes.

7. At the direction of the surgeon, antibiotics may be added to the reconstitution medium.

8. Records for inventory, storage, distribution, discard, and transplant of cadaveric bone are similar to those for surgical bone.

Method 6.16. Surgical Bone Transportation

Principle

Surgical bone should be transported from the operating room on wet ice. Frozen bone should be removed from inventory and transported on dry ice to the operating room for transplantation.

Materials

1. Blood transport boxes.
2. Plastic bags.
3. Crushed or cubed ice.
4. Dry ice.

Procedure

At the Time of Collection

1. Fill the plastic bag with sufficient wet ice and tie knots to prevent ice spillage.
2. Place the bag into a suitably sized transport box.
3. Place the bone container on the top of the ice and pack the empty space with newspaper or other packing to keep the container from moving inside the box. If glass containers are used, sufficient

packing to prevent jarring helps avoid cracking of the containers.

At the Time of Bone Transplantation

Transport frozen surgical bone using dry ice. The procedure is similar to that for transporting Fresh Frozen Plasma between facilities.

Method 6.17. Surgical Bone Utilization

Principle

Before bone is issued, it is necessary to document release and recipient data.

Materials

1. Requisition for bone.
2. Order record form.
3. Blood transport boxes.
4. Dry ice.
5. Transplant record.

Procedure

1. Requests are made by the patient's physician.
2. Record the date of order; the recipient's name and hospital number; the name of the individual placing the order; the surgeon's name; the type and quantity of bone ordered; and the date of transplant surgery. Record the name of the person filling the order.
3. Transport the bone on dry ice to the operating room. Bone is thawed before use by allowing the unopened container to remain at room temperature for 15-30 minutes in the operating room.
4. Bone must be removed aseptically from the container. Thawing cannot be assessed until the bone is cut. The surgeon generally removes soft tissues before bone is used. Shaping and cutting is also performed by the surgeon as needed. Surgical bones are generally used for re-

construction of acetabular and proximal femoral defects. They may also be used to fill a variety of other small bone defects.

5. When bone is used, a transplant record should be completed and returned to the facility providing the graft. The following information should be recorded: date of transplant, recipient's name and hospital number, surgeon's name, the type of bone, unique identification number of the graft, and any complications.

Method 6.18
Cryopreservation of Hematopoietic Progenitor Cells Using a Controlled-Rate Freeze

Principle

Cryopreservation by controlled-rate freezing allows for the long-term storage of hematopoietic progenitor cells. Freezing at a rate of 1 C/min in the presence of a cryopreservative such as dimethyl sulfoxide (DMSO) prevents the formation of intracellular ice crystals and prevents cell damage from high concentration of extracellular solutes.

Specimen

Marrow is collected in the operating room using standard procedures. The anticoagulated marrow is then processed to reduce the product volume as well as the red cell and granulocyte content.

Peripheral blood progenitor cells (PBPCs) are harvested using a continuous-flow cell separator. PBPCs are processed only to decrease product volume prior to cryopreservation. The manufacturer's instructions for use and quality control on specific instruments should be followed.

Materials

1. 60 cc syringes
2. 3 cc syringes
3. Sample site couplers
4. 300-mL transfer bag
5. 250-mL bag
6. 10-mL sample bag
7. Dimethyl sulfoxide (DMSO)
8. Plasma-Lyte 148 (PL-148)[1] or other buffered crystalloid solution approved for in-vivo use.
9. Laminar flow hood
10. Controlled-rate freezer—eg, Cryomed Model 1010
11. Liquid nitrogen storage canisters
12. Hematron sealer
13. Hand-held sealer
14. Product labels[2]

Controls

An aliquot containing a minimum of 1.0×10^8 nucleated cells is placed in a 10-mL Stericon bag, labeled so as to identify the component from which it was taken, and frozen under the same conditions as the component. The aliquot will be thawed, prior to infusion, for additional testing if problems arise during processing, freezing, or storage. The aliquot should also be tested if the product has been frozen for longer than one year.

Procedure

Product Preparation

Note: All manipulations when possible should be performed within a laminar flow hood.

1. Use a cryomarker to label the freezing bags with the patient's name, medical record number, product number, aliquot designation, product type and date of collection or follow the manufacturer's recommended methods of labeling the bags.
2. Complete a product label for each freezing bag. Attach a label to the bottom of the freezing bag with an elastic band or piece of string.[1]

3. Mix the product bag. Draw 1.0×10^8 cells from the bag and transfer them into the 10-mL Stericon freezing bag.

4. Draw the remaining product into 60-cc syringes. Draw no more than 30 mL of product into each syringe. Transfer each syringe's contents to a labeled freezing bag.

5. Refrigerate all freezing bags at 2-6 C while the cryoprotectant is being made.

Cryoprotectant

Note: The cryoprotectant volume should equal the postprocessing product volume.

1. Seal and remove the transfer tubing from a 300-mL transfer bag. Label the bag with the patient's name, medical record number, product number, and "CRYO." Insert a sample site coupler into the center port of the bag.

2. Calculate the amount of each of the cryoprotectant as follows:

    % of component/100 × total
    volume of cryoprotectant

    For example: 20% DMSO/100 × 25 mL total volume = 5.0 mL of DMSO

3. Draw the required volume of PL-148 into a 60-cc syringe. Add the PL-148 to the "CRYO" bag.

4. Draw the required volume of DMSO into the appropriate size syringe. Add the DMSO to the "CRYO" bag. Allow the PL-148/DMSO mixture to cool. The bag may be refrigerated or placed on wet ice to facilitate cooling.

5. Draw the required volume of donor plasma into the appropriate size syringe. In cases where the recipient red cells carry an antigen to donor antibody, 5% albumin should be substituted for donor plasma.

6. Add the donor plasma/5% albumin to the "CRYO" bag once the PL-148/DMSO mixture has cooled. Mix the cryoprotectant thoroughly.

7. Use 60-cc syringes to aliquot cryoprotectant in volumes equal to the volume of product in each freezing bag.

Cryopreservation

1. Place the required number of freezing presses in the freezing chamber. Place the sample thermocouple between the plates of the press.

2. Turn on the microcomputer and chart drive. Remove the cap from the chart drive pen and check the pen calibration.

3. Select the desired user-defined freezing program. An example is given in Table 6.18-1.

4. Once the sample temperature is −5 C ± 2 C add the cryoprotectant to the freezing bag. Attach the cryoprotectant syringe to the previously used line on the corresponding freezing bag.

5. Slowly add the cryoprotectant while mixing the product. Without detaching the syringe draw the air out of the freezing bag. Air pockets may result in unusual freezing curves or bag ruptures during thawing. Close the tubing clamp and remove the syringe.

6. Seal the tubing three times below the level of the yellow bag ports. Cut the tubing at the center seal.

7. Place the bags in the freezing presses, placing the sample thermocouple under the bag containing the largest volume.

8. Return the presses to the freezing chamber and allow the sample temperature to reach −5 C ± 2 C. When the target temperature is reached press RUN. The microprocessor will automatically cycle through the chosen program.

9. When the freeze is complete, place the freezing bags into a canister labeled with the patient's name, medical record number, product number, and aliquot designation. Place canisters in the previously assigned locations in the liquid nitrogen storage freezer.

Table 6.18-1. A Sample User-Defined Freezing Program

Prog. No./ Sect No.	Function	Temp./Time	Target Temp.	Probe Mode	Add Key
1.1	Wait	0 C	–5 C	Chamber	
1.2	Ramp	2 C/min	+4 C	Chamber	
1.3	Ramp	1 C/min	–10 C	Sample	
1.4	Ramp	17 C/min	–45 C	Chamber	COOL+
1.5	Ramp	10 C/min	–18 C	Chamber	
1.6	Ramp	1 C/min	–60 C	Chamber	COOL+
1.7	Ramp	3 C/min	–100 C	Chamber	COOL+
1.8	END				

10. Review the freezing curve to ensure phase changes occurred within documented limits.

References

1. Killian D, Wright P, Bentley SA, Brecher ME. A cost-effective and Food and Drug Administration approved alternative to tissue culture media in cryopreservation (letter). Transfusion 1996;36:476.
2. Menitove J, ed. Standards for hematopoietic progenitor cells. First edition. Bethesda, MD: American Association of Blood Banks 1996:17.

Method 6.19. Removal of Red Cells in Marrow Using Hydroxyethyl Starch

Principle

The removal of red cells from allogeneic marrow is essential in cases where the recipient plasma contains antibodies against antigens on the donor red cells. The addition of hydroxyethyl starch aids the formation of rouleaux, thereby increasing the rate at which the red cells sediment. Once sedimented, the red cells can be removed.

Specimen

Marrow is harvested in the operating room under standard conditions. The marrow is anticoagulated with heparin and media (eg, Plasma-lyte 148).[1] The media-heparin is added to the marrow in a ratio of 1:5. The volume of marrow harvested is generally 400-1500 mL. The volume collected, however, is dependent on the nucleated cell concentration of the marrow.

Materials

1. Laminar flow hood
2. 1000-mL transfer bags
3. 600-mL transfer bags
4. Platelet pooling set
5. Sample site couplers
6. 3-way stopcock
7. Plasma-lyte 148 (PL-148) or other tissue culture media approved for in-vivo use.
8. Hetastarch (average molecular weight 450,000) 6% in 0.9% sodium chloride (HES)

Procedure

Note: All manipulations whenever possible should be done within a laminar flow hood.

1. Determine the total marrow volume. Insert a sample site coupler into the marrow bag. Attach a 3-way stopcock to the sample site coupler. Remove samples for nucleated cell count, hematocrit, and blood type.

2. Calculate the volume of PL-148 needed to reduce the marrow hematocrit to 25 ± 2%. Calculate the volume of HES required for sedimentation. Add one part HES to every seven parts marrow/media. Add the media and HES through the stopcock. Mix well.

3. Divide the marrow/media/HES mixture prior to sedimentation. Use 600-mL or 1000-mL bags; the sedimentation bags should be 3/4 full. Clamp the transfer tubing on the sedimentation bags with hemostats. Seal and remove all but three extensions on a platelet pooling set. Attach the extensions to the marrow bag and the sedimentation bags. Divide the marrow evenly.

4. Invert the sedimentation bags and hang them in the laminar flow hood. Allow the red cells to sediment until a plasma-cell interface is evident, approximately 45-75 minutes.

5. Attach 600-mL transfer bags to the transfer tubing on the sedimentation bags. Release the hemostats on the tubing and allow the red cells to drain. Discard the red cell bags.

6. Pool the nucleated rich plasma. Remove samples for nucleated cell count, red cell count, bacterial cultures, and colony assays.

7. Label the product for infusion.[2]

Note: The red cell content after sedimentation should be <1% by volume.

References

1. Areman EM, Dickerson SA, Kotula PL, et al. Use of a licensed electrolyte solution as an alternative to tissue culture medium for bone marrow collection. Transfusion 1993;33:562-6.

2. Menitove J, ed. Standards for hemotopoietic progenitor cells. First edition. Bethesda, MD: American Association of Blood Banks, 1996: 17.

3. Warkentin PI, Hilden JM, Kersey JH, et al. Transplantation of major ABO-incompatible bone marrow depleted of red cells by hydroxyethyl starch. Vox Sang 1985;48:89-104.

Method 6.20. Processing of Marrow for Plasma Removal

Principle

Harvested allogeneic marrow is centrifuged and the majority of the plasma is removed. In addition to reducing the volume of the product, plasma removal reduces the presence of alloantibodies present in the marrow. This is significant in cases where the donor marrow contains antibodies to antigens on recipient red cells.

Specimen

Marrow is harvested in the operating room under standard conditions. The marrow is anticoagulated with heparin and media (Plasma-lyte 148 or tissue culture media).[1] The media/heparin is added to the marrow in a ratio of 1:5. The volume of marrow harvested is generally 400-1500 mL. The volume collected, however, is dependent on the nucleated cell concentration of the marrow.

Materials

1. 600-mL transfer bags
2. Sample site couplers
3. 60-cc syringes
4. 15-gauge needles
5. Centrifuge
6. Laminar flow hood
7. Heat sealer
8. Plasma expressor

Procedure

Note: All manipulations when possible should be performed within a laminar flow hood.

1. Determine the total marrow volume. Insert a sample site coupler into the marrow bag. Remove sample for nucleated cell counts, type and crossmatch.

2. Divide the marrow into the appropriate number of 600-mL transfer bags. Centri-

fuge the marrow bags at $4100 \times g$ for 10 minutes at 22 C.

3. Place each centrifuged bag on a plasma expressor. Attach a 600-mL transfer bag to a port on the spun marrow bag.

4. Release the plasma expressor and remove the plasma to within 2 inches of the cell line. Remove and discard the plasma bags.

5. Thoroughly mix the marrow. Insert sample site couplers into the bags. Use 60-cc syringes with 15-gauge needles to determine the volume of marrow in each bag.

Once the volume is determined, pool the marrow into one of the processing bags.

6. Thoroughly mix the pooled marrow. Remove samples for nucleated cells count, bacterial cultures, and colony assays.

7. Label the product for infusion.[2]

References

1. Areman EM, Dickerson SA, Kotula PL, et al. Use of a licensed electrolyte solution as an alternative to tissue culture medium for bone marrow collection. Transfusion 1993;33:562-6.

2. Menitove J, ed. Standards for hematopoietic progenitor cells. First edition. Bethesda, MD: American Association of Blood Banks, 1996:17.

7

Quality Control for Equipment Methods

Method 7.1. Testing Refrigerator Alarms

Principle

The alarm on each blood storage refrigerator should be checked periodically for proper functioning. Monthly checks are appropriate until consistent behavior has been demonstrated; quarterly checks are appropriate thereafter. The high and low temperatures of activation must be checked and the results recorded. AABB *Standards for Blood Banks and Transfusion Services*[1] requires the alarm setting to activate at a temperature that will allow intervention before blood or components reach an undesirable temperature. Some alarm systems have a push button for checking the electrical circuits and alarm; these checks should be performed regularly.

Refrigerators and freezers must be equipped with a system for continuous temperature monitoring and an audible alarm. The alarm should sound at a temperature that allows appropriate action to be taken before stored components reach undesirable temperatures. It is essential to have a functioning alarm and to have, in a conspicuous place, directions for corrective measures to take if the refrigerator temperature cannot be corrected rapidly. The diversity of equipment available makes it impossible to give specific instructions applicable to all units. The procedures manual for each facility must include a detailed description of the method(s) in local use. If the instruction manual for the alarm system does not provide suitable directions for testing the alarm, the manufacturer or a refrigeration expert should be consulted. (See Chapter 1, Appendix 1-1 for quality control testing intervals.)

Procedure

1. Be sure that the alarm circuits are operating, the alarm is switched on, and the

starting temperature is 1-6 C. Immerse an easy-to-read mercury thermometer in the container with the alarm thermocouple.

2. For low activation: Place the container with the thermocouple and thermometer in a pan containing an ice and water slush at a temperature of –4 C or colder. To achieve this temperature, add several spoonfuls of table salt to the ice.

3. Close the refrigerator door, to avoid changing the temperature of the storage compartment.

4. Keep the container in the pan of cold slush, and gently agitate it periodically until the alarm sounds. Record this temperature as the low-activation temperature.

5. Remove the container from the slush bath. Allow the fluid to return to normal temperature, and record the temperature at which the audible or visible alarm signal stops.

6. For high activation: Place the container with thermocouple and thermometer in a pan containing water at 12-15 C. Keep refrigerator door closed. Allow the fluid in the container to warm slowly, with occasional agitation. Record temperature at which alarm sounds as high-activation temperature.

7. Remove container from warm pan, and record temperature at which audible or visible alarm signal stops.

8. Record the date, the identity of the refrigerator, the low temperature of activation, the high temperature of activation, and the name or initials of the person performing the test.

9. If temperatures of activation are too low or too high, take appropriate corrective actions, record the nature of the corrections, and repeat the alarm check to document that the corrections were effective.

Notes

1. The thermocouple for the alarm should be easily accessible and equipped with a cord long enough so that it can be easily manipulated.

2. The thermocouple for the recording thermometer need not be in the same container as that of the alarm.

3. When the temperatures of activation are checked, the temperature change should occur slowly enough that measurements and recording are accurate. Too rapid a change in temperature may give the false impression that the alarm does not sound until an inappropriate temperature is registered.

4. The low temperature of activation should be no lower than 1 C; the high temperature of activation should be no higher than 6 C. Low activation at or above 1 C and high activation at or below 6 C are acceptable.

5. The amount of fluid in which the thermocouple is immersed must be no larger than the volume of the smallest component stored in that refrigerator. The thermocouple may be immersed in a smaller volume, but this means that the alarm will go off with smaller temperature changes than those registered in a larger volume of fluid. Excessive sensitivity may create a nuisance.

6. With the one-time assistance of a qualified electrician, the required refrigerator and freezer alarm checks of units with virtually inaccessible temperature probes can be performed with an electrical modification cited by Wenz and Owens.[2]

7. Alarms should sound simultaneously at the site of the refrigerator and at the location of the remote alarms, if remote alarms are employed.

References

1. Menitove J, ed. Standards for blood banks and transfusion services. 19th ed. Bethesda, MD: American Association of Blood Banks, 1999:39.

2. Wenz B, Owens RT. A simplified method for monitoring and calibrating refrigerator alarm systems. Transfusion 1980;20:75-8.

Method 7.2. Testing Freezer Alarms

Principle

Freezer temperatures may rise to unacceptable levels for a variety of reasons, some fairly common. It is essential to have a functioning alarm and to have, in a conspicuous place, directions for corrective measures to take if the freezer temperature cannot be corrected rapidly. Common causes of rising temperature include:
1. Improperly closed freezer door or lid.
2. Low level of refrigerant.
3. Compressor failure.
4. Dirty heat exchanger.
5. Loss of electrical power.

Refrigerators and freezers must be equipped with a system for continuous temperature monitoring and an audible alarm. The alarm should sound at a temperature that allows appropriate action to be taken before stored components reach undesired temperatures. The diversity of equipment available makes it impossible to give specific instructions applicable to all units. The procedures manual for each facility must include a detailed description of the method(s) in local use. If the instruction manual for the alarm system does not provide suitable directions for testing the alarm, the manufacturer or a refrigeration expert should be consulted.

Procedure

1. Test alarms at regular intervals, frequently enough to achieve and maintain personnel competency and to detect malfunctions. For equipment in good condition, quarterly checks are usually sufficient.
2. Protect frozen components from exposure to elevated temperatures during the test.
3. Use a thermometer or thermocouple, independent from that built into the system, that will accurately indicate the temperature of alarm activation. Compare these readings with the temperatures registered on the recorder.
4. Warm the alarm probe and thermometer slowly. The specific temperature of activation cannot accurately be determined during rapid warming, and the apparent temperature of activation will be too high.
5. Record the temperature at which the alarm sounds, the date of the test, the identity of the person testing and any observations that might suggest impaired activity.
6. Return the freezer and the alarm system to their normal conditions.
7. If the alarm sounds at too high a temperature, take appropriate corrective actions, record the nature of the correction, and repeat the alarm check to document that the corrections were effective.

Notes

1. Test battery function, electrical circuits, and power-off alarms more frequently than the test of activation temperature. Record function, date, and identity of person performing the testing.
2. For units with the sensor installed in the wall or in air, apply local warmth to the site or allow the temperature of the entire compartment to rise to the point at which the alarm sounds. Remove frozen contents or protect frozen contents with insulation while the temperature rises.
3. For units with the thermocouple located in antifreeze solution, pull the container and the cables outside the freezer chest for testing, leaving the door shut and the contents protected.
4. For units with a tracking alarm that sounds whenever the temperature reaches a constant interval above the setting on the temperature controller, set the controller to a warmer setting and

note the temperature interval at which the alarm sounds.

5. Liquid nitrogen freezers must have alarm systems that activate at an unsafe level of contained liquid nitrogen.

Method 7.3. Monitoring Temperature During Shipment

Principle

Some form of temperature indicator or monitoring is desirable when shipping blood over a regular route. The temperature of the contents of a shipping box used for Whole Blood or liquid-stored red cell components can be ascertained when the shipment is received, as follows.

Procedure

1. Remove two bags of blood or components.
2. Promptly place the sensing end of a liquid-in-glass or electronic thermometer between the bags (labels facing out) and secure the "sandwich" with two rubber bands.
3. After a few minutes, read the temperature.
4. If the temperature of red-cell-containing components exceeds 10 C, quarantine the units until appropriate disposition of them is determined.

Notes

Other suitable methods for monitoring shipments are:

1. Use time/temperature tags, one tag per shipping carton. This will record if the temperature has exceeded 10 C.
2. Place a "high-low" mercury thermometer (Taylor Instruments, Rochester, NY) in the shipping box. This simple, reus-

able thermometer measures and records the highest and lowest temperatures during any period.

3. Place an R&D temperature indicator (Chek Lab Inc, Aurora, IL) in the shipping carton. This reusable device consists of a wax-like material enclosed in a small glass ampule. Small black beads are embedded in the wax. If the temperature exceeds 10 C, the wax will melt, permitting the beads to settle to the bottom.

Method 7.4. Calibrating a Serologic Centrifuge

Principle

Each centrifuge is to be calibrated upon receipt and after adjustments or repairs. Calibration evaluates the behavior of red cells in solutions of different viscosities, not the reactivity of different antibodies.

For Immediate Agglutination

Materials

1. Serum containing an antibody that produces 1+ macroscopic agglutination.
2. One sample of red cells positive for the corresponding antigen and one negative sample. Prepare a fresh suspension of cells in the concentration routinely used in the laboratory (eg, 2-5%).
   a. For saline-active antibodies: Serum from a group A person (anti-B) diluted with 6% albumin to give 1+ macroscopic agglutination (3 mL of 22% bovine albumin + 8 mL of normal saline = 6% bovine albumin).
   Positive control: Group B red cells in a 2-5% saline suspension.
   Negative control: Group A red cells in a 2-5% saline suspension.
   b. For high-protein antibodies: 1 part anti-D diluted with 25-30 parts of

22% or 30% albumin to give 1+ macroscopic agglutination.
Positive control: D-positive red cells in a 2-5% saline suspension.
Negative control: D-negative red cells in a 2-5% saline suspension.

Procedure

1. For each set of tests (saline and high-protein antibodies), prepare five 10 × 75-mm or 12 × 75-mm tubes for positive reactions and five tubes for negative reactions. Add serum and cell suspensions to each tube just before centrifugation.
2. In pairs, one positive and one negative, centrifuge the tubes for different times (eg, 10 seconds, 20 seconds, 30 seconds). Observe each tube for agglutination and record observations. (See the example in Table 7.4-1.)

Interpretation

The optimal time of centrifugation is the shortest time required to fulfill these criteria:
1. Agglutination in the positive tubes is as strong as determined in preparing reagents.
2. There is no agglutination or ambiguity in the negative tubes.
3. The cell button is clearly delineated and the periphery is sharply defined, not fuzzy.

4. The supernatant fluid is clear.
5. The cell button is easily resuspended.
In the example shown in the table, these criteria are met by the 30-second and the 45-second spins; the optimal time for these tests in this centrifuge is 30 seconds.

For Washing and Antiglobulin Testing

Tests in which antihuman globulin (AHG) serum is added to red cells may require centrifugation conditions different from those for immediate agglutination. Centrifugation conditions appropriate for both washing and AHG reactions can be determined in one procedure. Note that this procedure does not monitor the completeness of washing; use of globulin-coated cells to control negative AHG reactions provides this check. The following procedure addresses only the mechanics of centrifugation.

Materials

1. AHG reagent, unmodified.
2. *Positive control:* a 2-5% saline suspension of D-positive red cells incubated for 15 minutes at 37 C with anti-D diluted to give 1+ macroscopic agglutination after addition of AHG.
3. *Negative control:* a 2-5% suspension of D-negative red cells, incubated for 15 minutes at 37 C with 6% albumin.
4. Saline, large volumes.

Table 7.4-1. Serologic Centrifuge Test Results

Criteria	Time in Seconds				
	10	**15**	**20**	**30**	**45**
Supernatant fluid clear	No	No	Yes	Yes	Yes
Cell button clearly delineated	No	No	No	Yes	Yes
Cells easily resuspended	Yes	Yes	Yes	Yes	Yes
Agglutination	±	±	1+	1+	1+
Negative tube is negative	Yes	Yes	Yes	Yes	Resuspends roughly

Procedure

1. Prepare five tubes containing 1 drop of positive cells and five tubes containing 1 drop of negative control cells.
2. Fill tubes with saline and centrifuge them in pairs, one positive and one negative, for different times (eg, 30, 45, 60, 90 and 120 seconds). The red cells should form a clearly delineated button, with no cells trailing up the side of the tube. After the saline has been decanted, the cell button should be easily resuspended in the residual fluid. The shortest time that accomplishes these goals is the optimal time for washing.
3. Repeat washing process on all pairs two more times, using time determined to be optimal.
4. Decant supernatant saline thoroughly.
5. Add AHG to each of the pairs and centrifuge for different times (eg, 10, 15, 20, 30 and 45 seconds).

Interpretation

Select optimal time as in previous procedure.

Method 7.5. Calibrating Centrifuges for Platelet Separation

Principle

Successful preparation of platelet concentrates requires adequate but not excessive centrifugation; the equipment used must perform in a consistent and dependable manner. Each centrifuge used to prepare platelets should be calibrated upon receipt and after adjustment or repair.

Materials

1. Freshly collected Whole Blood (WB), obtained by phlebotomy, in a bag with two integrally attached transfer containers.
2. A specimen of blood from the donor, anticoagulated with EDTA, in addition to the specimens drawn for routine processing.
3. Metal clips and hand sealer.
4. Clean instruments (scissors, hemostats).
5. Plasma extractor.
6. Dielectric sealer (optional).
7. Centrifuge suitable for preparation of platelet concentrates.

Procedure

Preparation of Platelet-Rich Plasma

1. Perform a platelet count on the anticoagulated specimen. If the platelet count is below 133,000/μL, this donor's blood should not be used for calibration.
2. Calculate the number of platelets in the unit of WB: platelets/μL $\times$ 1000 $\times$ mL of WB = number of platelets in WB.
3. Prepare platelet-rich plasma (PRP) at a selected speed and time (see "light spin," Table 7.5-1).
4. Place a temporary clamp on the tubing so that one satellite bag is closed off. Express the PRP into the other satellite bag. Seal the tubing close to the primary bag and disconnect the two satellite bags. Do not remove the temporary clamp between the satellite bags until the next step.
5. Strip the tubing several times so that the tubing contains a representative sample of PRP.
6. Seal off a segment of the tubing and disconnect it, so that the bag of PRP remains sterile.
7. Perform a platelet count on the sample of PRP in the segment. Calculate the number of platelets in the bag of PRP: platelets/μL $\times$ 1000 $\times$ mL of PRP = number of platelets in PRP.
8. Calculate percent yield:

$$\frac{\text{number of platelets in PRP} \times 100}{\text{number of platelets in WB}} = \% \text{ yield}$$

Table 7.5-1. Centrifugation for Component Preparation

Heavy Spin

Packed red cells ⎱
Platelet concentrates ⎰ 5000 x *g*, 5 minutes

Cell-free plasma ⎱
Cryoprecipitate ⎰ 5000 x *g*, 7 minutes

Light Spin

Platelet-rich plasma   2000 x g, 3 minutes

To calculate relative centrifugal force in g:

$$rcf \text{ (in g)} = 28.38 \text{ R*} \left(\frac{rpm}{1000} \right)^2$$

*R=radius of centrifuge rotor in inches

Times include acceleration but not deceleration times. Times given are approximations only. Each individual centrifuge must be evaluated for the preparation of the various components.

9. Repeat the above process three or four times with different donors, using different speeds and times of centrifugation, and compare the yields achieved under each set of test conditions.
10. Select the shortest time and lowest speed that result in the highest percent of platelet yield without unacceptable levels of red cell content.

Preparation of Platelet Concentrate

1. Centrifuge the PRP at a selected time and speed to prepare platelet concentrate (PC). (See "heavy spin," Table 7.5-1.)
2. Express the platelet-poor plasma into the second attached satellite bag and seal the tubing, leaving a long section of tubing attached to the platelet bag.
3. Place the platelets on an agitator and leave them for at least 1 hour to ensure that they are evenly resuspended. Platelet counts performed immediately after centrifugation will not be accurate.
4. Strip the tubing several times, mixing its contents well with the contents of the

platelet bag. Let the concentrate flow back into the tubing. Seal off a segment of the tubing so that the platelet bag remains sterile.

5. Perform a platelet count on the contents of the segment.
6. Calculate the number of platelets in the concentrate: platelets/μL × 1000 × mL of PC = number of platelets in platelet concentrate.
7. Calculate percent yield:

$$\frac{\text{number of platelets in PC} \times 100}{\text{number of platelets in PRP}} = \% \text{ yield}$$

8. Repeat steps 1 through 7 on PRP from different donors, using different speeds and times of centrifugation, and compare the yields achieved under each set of test conditions.
9. Select the shortest time and lowest speed that result in the highest percent of platelet yield in the platelet concentrate.

Notes

1. It is not necessary to recalibrate a centrifuge unless the instrument has undergone adjustment or repairs, or levels of platelet recovery fall below acceptable levels.
2. Each centrifuge used for preparing platelets must be calibrated individually. Use the conditions determined to be optimal for each instrument.

Method 7.6. Performance Testing of Automatic Cell Washers

Principle

Antihuman globulin (AHG) is inactivated readily by unbound immunoglobulin. The red cells to which AHG will be added must be washed free of all proteins and suspended in a protein-free medium. A properly functioning cell washer must add large volumes of saline to each tube, resuspend the cells, centrifuge them adequately, and decant the saline to leave a dry cell button.

Materials

1. Test tubes (10 × 75 mm or 12 × 75 mm).
2. Bovine albumin, or an additive routinely used to potentiate antigen-antibody reactions.
3. IgG-coated red cells, known to give 1-2+ reaction in antiglobulin testing.
4. Normal saline.
5. Antihuman globulin: anti-IgG or polyspecific reagent.

Procedure

1. To each of 12 tubes add 2 drops of bovine albumin, 2 or 3 drops of donor or patient serum, and 1 drop of IgG-coated red cells.
2. Place the tubes in a centrifuge carrier, seat the carrier in the cell washer, and start the wash cycle.
3. After addition of saline in the second cycle, stop the cell washer. Inspect the contents of all tubes. There should be an equal volume of saline in all tubes. (The correct volume will be indicated in the manufacturer's directions.) Tubes should not be more than 80% full, to avoid splashing and cross-contamination.
4. Observe all tubes to see that the red cells have been completely resuspended. Red cells should not stream up the sides of the test tubes.
5. Continue the washing cycle.
6. After the third wash and decant cycle, stop the cell washer and inspect all tubes to see that saline has been completely decanted and that each tube contains a dry cell button. The size of the cell button should be the same size as at the start of the wash cycle and should be the same in all tubes.

7. Complete the wash cycle. Add AHG according to the manufacturer's directions, centrifuge, and examine all tubes for agglutination. If the cell washer is functioning properly, all tubes should show the same degree of agglutination.

Notes

1. Further investigation is needed if:
   a. The amount of saline varies from tube to tube or cycle to cycle.
   b. The cell button is not resuspended completely.
   c. Any tube has weak or absent agglutination in the antiglobulin phase.
   d. Any tube has significant decrease in the size of the cell button.
2. Cell washers that automatically add AHG should be additionally checked for uniform addition of AHG. In step 7 above, AHG would be added automatically, and failure of addition would be apparent by absence of agglutination. The volume of AHG should be inspected and found to be equal in all tubes. The volume of AHG delivered automatically by cell washers should be checked monthly to ensure that it is as specified in the manufacturer's directions and that delivery is uniform in all tubes.
3. Many manufacturers market AHG colored with green dye for use in automated cell washers so that it will be immediately obvious if no reagent has been added.

Method 7.7. Standardization and Calibration of Thermometers

Principle

Thermometers used during collection, processing, and storage of blood and blood components should be calibrated and standardized to prevent inaccurate indication of temperatures. Each thermometer should be calibrated before initial use, and any time thereafter if there is reason to suspect change or damage.

Method 7.7.1. Liquid-in-Glass Laboratory Thermometers

Principle

Liquid-in-glass thermometers used to monitor the operating temperature of blood bank equipment should be calibrated and standardized at a temperature close to that required by the instrument for which they will be used.

Materials

1. National Institute of Standards and Technology (NIST)-certified thermometer or thermometer with NIST-traceable calibration certificate.
2. Liquid-in-glass (often referred to as equipment) thermometer.
3. Suitable water container(s).
4. Crushed ice.
5. Record form.

Procedure

1. Before choosing a thermometer for a particular application, consider all the governing factors; be sure that the thermometer will be used for its proper immersion; and follow the manufacturer's instructions. When using a certified thermometer, read and follow the applicable notes.
2. Categorize the thermometers and test them in groups, comparing similar thermometers. Do not attempt to compare dissimilar thermometers in a single procedure.
3. Place a numbered piece of tape around the top of each thermometer being tested.
4. Fill a suitable container with water of a temperature close to that which the thermometer will monitor. To calibrate at 37

C, place the NIST thermometer and thermometers to be tested at a uniform depth in a standard incubation waterbath. To calibrate for the 1-6 C range, fill a suitable container with an appropriate mixture of water and crushed ice. Make sure that the tips of all devices are at the same level, and are in the liquid, not the upper ice.

5. Stir constantly in a random motion until the desired temperature is reached. Allow the thermometers to equilibrate for 5 minutes.
6. Observe and record the temperature of each thermometer. A result is acceptable if the reading on a thermometer agrees with the NIST thermometer within 1 C. If the expected result is not achieved, the thermometer should be returned to the distributor (if newly purchased), or labeled with the correction factor and used in noncritical work, or discarded. It is desirable to label a thermometer with the directions from the NIST thermometer. This is especially helpful if the calibrated thermometers are compared with each other, and their variations from the NIST thermometer could give a false reading.
7. Observe the thermometers for any split in the column, which will cause inaccurate readings. The methods for reuniting the separated mercury are given by Ween.[1] Document corrective action.
8. Record the date of testing, the thermometer identification numbers, the temperature readings and the initials of the person who performed the test.

Reference

1. Ween S. Care and use of liquid-in-glass laboratory thermometers. ISA Transactions 1968;7:93-100.

Method 7.7.2. Electronic Oral Thermometers

Principle

Calibration must be verified for all electronic thermometers, even those described as "self-calibrating." Calibration must be performed before initial use and periodically thereafter.

Procedure

1. Use any of the following methods to verify calibration:
    a. Follow the manufacturer's instructions for verifying calibration.
    b. Use a commercially available calibration device by following the instructions provided by the device's manufacturer.
    c. Calibrate the thermometer by inserting the probe in a waterbath that has been standardized with a NIST-certified thermometer. A result is acceptable if the reading on the thermometer agrees with the NIST thermometer within 0.1 C.
2. If expected results are not achieved, unsatisfactory thermometers should be returned to the distributor. Document corrective actions.
3. Record the date of testing, thermometer identification numbers, temperature readings, and the initials of the person performing the test.

Method 7.8. Monitoring Cell Counts of Apheresis Components

Principle

When cellular components are prepared by apheresis, it is essential to ascertain cell yields without compromising the sterility of the component.

Materials

1. Component collected by apheresis.
2. Metal clips and hand sealer.
3. Clean instruments (scissors, hemostats).

4. Dielectric sealer (optional).
5. Cell counting equipment.

Procedure

1. Strip tubing attached to the well-mixed component bag four times to ensure that contents of tubing accurately represent the entire contents of the bag.
2. Seal a 5-8 cm (2-3 inch) segment distal to the collection bag. There should be approximately 2 mL of fluid in the segment. Double-seal the end of the tubing next to the component bag and detach the segment.
3. Empty the contents of the segment into a suitably labeled tube.
4. Determine cell counts; for results reported as cells/μL, change values to cells/mL by multiplying by 1000 (or 10^3).
5. Multiply cells/mL by the volume of the component, in mL, to obtain total cell count in the component.

Method 7.9. Counting Residual White Cells in Leukocyte-Reduced Red Cell Concentrates

Principle

The residual white cell content of leukocyte-reduced Red Blood Cells or Whole Blood can be determined using a large-volume hemocytometer. First, the red cells in the aliquot to be counted are lysed, and then the leukocyte nuclei are stained with a crystal violet stain. The Nageotte counting chamber has a volume 56 times that of the standard hemocytometer.[1] Accuracy of counting is improved by examining a larger volume of minimally diluted specimen, as compared with standard counting techniques.

Materials

1. Hemocytometer chamber with 50 μL counting volume (eg, Nageotte Brite Line Chamber®, Hausser Scientific, Horsham, PA).
2. Crystal violet stain: 0.01% w/v crystal violet in 1% v/v acetic acid (eg, Turks solution, Columbia Diagnostics, Springfield, VA).
3. Red cell lysing agent (eg, Zapoglobin®, Coulter Diagnostics, Miami, FL).
4. Pipetter with disposable tips accurate to 40 μL.
5. Talc-free gloves, clean plastic test tubes, plastic petri dish, filter paper.
6. Light microscope with 10× ocular lens and 20× objective.

Procedure

1. Pipet 40 μL of lysing agent into a clean test tube.
2. Place a representative sample of the component to be tested in a clean test tube. The hematocrit of the sample to be tested should not exceed 60%.
3. Pipet 100 μL of the sample into the tube containing 40 μL of lysing agent. Pipet up and down several times, to mix the two fluids, until the pipette tip is no longer coated with intact red cells.
4. Pipet 360 μL of crystal violet stain into the mixture and mix fluids by pipetting them up and down. The final volume is now 500 μL.
5. Fit the hemocytometer with a coverslip and, using a pipette, load the mixture until the counting area is completely covered but not overflowing.
6. Cover the hemocytometer with a moist lid to prevent evaporation (a plastic petri dish into which a piece of damp filter paper has been placed works well) and let it rest undisturbed for 10-15 minutes, allowing the white cells to settle in the counting area of the chamber.
7. Remove the moist lid, place the hemocytometer on the microscope and, using a 20× objective, count the white cells present in the entire 50-μL counting volume.
8. Calculations:
   a. The white cell concentration in the original sample, expressed in cells/μL equals the number of observed cells divided by 10. (The correction factor of 10 is needed because the 50-μL sample was diluted 5-fold by lysing agent and stain.)
   b. The white cell content of the leukocyte-reduced component is determined as: total white cells present = white cells/μL × 10^3 (to give white cells/mL) × the volume of the component in mL.

Notes

1. Use talc-free gloves because talc particles that contaminate the counting chamber can be misread as white cells.
2. Experience identifying crystal-violet stained white cells can be obtained by examining samples from components that have not been leukocyte-reduced.
3. White cells deteriorate during refrigerated storage; counts on stored blood may give inaccurate results.
4. The accuracy of the counting method can be validated from a reference sample with a high white cell content that has been quantified by another means. This reference sample can be used for serial dilutions in blood that has been rendered extremely leukocyte-reduced by two passages through a leukocyte reduction filter. Counts obtained on the serially diluted samples can be compared to the expected concentration derived by calculation.
5. This counting technique is not known to be accurate at concentrations lower than 1 white cell/μL.

References

1. Lutz P, Dzik WH. Large-volume hemocytometer chamber for accurate counting of white cells (WBCs) in WBC-reduced platelets; validation and application for quality control of WBC-reduced platelets prepared by apheresis and filtration. Transfusion 1993;33:409-12.
2. Dzik WH, Szuflad P. Method for counting white cells in white cell-reduced red cell concentrates (letter). Transfusion 1993;33:272.

Method 7.10. Counting Residual White Cells in Leukocyte-Reduced Platelets

Principle

The residual white cell content of leukocyte-reduced platelet concentrates can be determined using a large-volume hemocytometer. Crystal violet is used to stain the leukocyte nuclei. The Nageotte counting chamber has a volume 56 times that of a standard hemocytometer.[1] The sample can be counted with only minimal dilution, which increases accuracy at very low cell concentrations.

Materials

1. Hemocytometer chamber with 50-μL counting volume (eg, Nageotte Brite Line Chamber®, Hausser Scientific, Horsham, PA).
2. Crystal violet stain: 0.01% w/v crystal violet in 1% v/v acetic acid (eg, Turks solution, Columbia Diagnostics, Springfield, VA).
3. Pipetter with disposable tips accurate to 40 μL.
4. Talc-free gloves, clean plastic test tubes, plastic petri dish, filter paper.
5. Light microscope with 10× ocular lens and 20× objective.

Procedure

1. Place a representative sample of the platelet concentrate in a clean test tube.
2. Pipet 100 μL of the platelet sample into a clean test tube.
3. Pipet 400 μL of crystal violet stain into the 100 μL of platelets and pipet up and down to mix the fluids. The final volume is 500 μL.
4. Fit the hemocytometer with a coverslip and, using a pipette, load the stained mixture until the counting area is completely covered but not overflowing.
5. Cover the hemocytometer with a moist lid to prevent evaporation (a plastic petri dish into which a piece of damp filter paper has been placed works well) and let it rest undisturbed for 10-15 minutes, to allow the white cells to settle in the counting area of the chamber.
6. Remove the moist lid, place the hemocytometer on the microscope, and, using a 20× objective, count the white cells present in the entire 50-μL volume of the counting chamber.
7. Calculations:
   a. The white cell concentration in the original sample, expressed in cells/μL, equals the number of observed white cells divided by 10. (The correction factor of 10 is needed because the 50-μL sample was diluted 5-fold by stain.)
   b. The white cell content of the leukocyte-reduced platelet concentrate is determined as: total white cells present = white cells/μL × 10^3 (to give white cells/mL) × volume of the component, in mL.

Notes

1. Talc-free gloves are recommended because talc particles that contaminate the counting chamber can be misread as white cells.
2. Experience identifying crystal-violet stained white cells can be obtained by examining samples from platelets that have not been leukocyte-reduced.

3. The accuracy of the counting method can be validated from a reference sample with a high white cell content that has been quantified by another means. This reference sample can be used for serial dilutions in a platelet concentrate that has been rendered extremely leukocyte-reduced by two passages through a leukocyte reduction filter. Counts obtained on serially diluted samples can be compared to the expected concentration derived by calculation.

4. This counting technique is not known to be accurate at concentrations lower than 1 white cell/μL of leukocyte-reduced platelet concentrate.

Reference

Lutz P, Dzik WH. Large-volume hemocytometer chamber for accurate counting of white cells (WBCs) in WBC-reduced platelets: Validation and application for quality control of WBC-reduced platelets prepared by apheresis and filtration. Transfusion 1993;33:409-12.

Appendices

Appendix 1. Normal Values in Adults

Determination	SI Units	Conventional Units
Alanine aminotransferase (ALT)	4-36 U/L at 37 C	4-36 U/L at 37 C
Bilirubin, total	2-21 μmol/L	0.1-1.2 mg/dL
Haptoglobin	0.6-2.7 g/L	60-270 mg/dL
Hematocrit		
Males	0.40-0.54	40-54%
Females	0.38-0.47	38-47%
Hemoglobin		
Males	135-180 g/L	13.5-18.0 g/dL
Females	120-160 g/L	12.0-16.0 g/dL
Hemoglobin A_2	0.015-0.035 total Hb	1.5-3.5% total Hb
Hemoglobin F	0-0.01 total Hb	<1% total Hb
Hemoglobin (plasma)	5-50 mg/L	0.5-5.0 mg/dL
Immunoglobulins		
IgG	8.0-18.0 g/L	800-1801 mg/dL
IgA	1.1-5.6 g/L	113-563 mg/dL
IgM	0.5-2.2 g/L	54-222 mg/dL
IgD	5.0-30 mg/L	0.5-3.0 mg/dL
IgE	0.1-0.4 mg/L	0.01-0.04 mg/dL
Methemoglobin	<0.01 total Hb	<1% total Hb
Platelet count	$150\text{-}450 \times 10^9$/L	$150\text{-}450 \times 10^3$/mm^3
Red cells		
Males	$4.6\text{-}6.2 \times 10^{12}$/L	$4.6\text{-}6.2 \times 10^6$/mm^3
Females	$4.2\text{-}5.4 \times 10^{12}$/L	$4.2\text{-}5.4 \times 10^6$/mm^3
Reticulocyte count	$25\text{-}75 \times 10^9$/L	$25\text{-}75 \times 10^3$/mm^3
Viscosity, relative	1.4-1.8 × water	1.4-1.8 × water
White cells	$4.5\text{-}11.0 \times 10^9$/L	$4.5\text{-}11.0 \times 10^3$/mm^3

(Reprinted with permission from Henry JB. Clinical diagnosis and management by laboratory methods. 18th ed. Philadelphia: WB Saunders, 1991.)

Appendix 2. Selected Normal Values in Children

		SI Units	Conventional Units
Bilirubin (total)			
Cord	Preterm	<30 mmol/L	<1.8 mg/dL
	Term	<30 mmol/L	<1.8 mg/dL
0-1 day	Preterm	<137 mmol/L	<8 mg/dL
	Term	<103 mmol/L	<6 mg/dL
1-2 days	Preterm	<205 mmol/L	<12 mg/dL
	Term	<137 mmol/L	<8 mg/dL
3-7 days	Preterm	<274 mmol/L	<16 mg/dL
	Term	<205 mmol/L	<12 mg/dL
7-30 days	Preterm	<205 mmol/L	<12 mg/dL
	Term	<120 mmol/L	<7 mg/dL
Thereafter	Preterm	<34 mmol/L	<2 mg/dL
	Term	<17 mmol/L	<1 mg/dL

	Hemoglobin	WBC	Platelets
26-30 weeks' gestation	11.0-15.8 g/dL	$1.7\text{-}7.1 \times 10^9/L$	$180\text{-}327 \times 10^9/L$
Term	13.5-19.5 g/dL	$9\text{-}30 \times 10^9/L$	$192 \times 10^9/L$ (mean)
1-3 days	14.5-22.5 g/dL	$9.4\text{-}34 \times 10^9/L$	$252 \times 10^9/L$ (mean)
2 weeks	13.4-19.8 g/dL	$5\text{-}20 \times 10^9/L$	
1 month	10.7-17.1 g/dL	$4\text{-}19.5 \times 10^9/L$	
2 months	9.4-13.0 g/dL		
6 months	11.1-14.1 g/dL	$6\text{-}17.5 \times 10^9/L$	
6 months-2 years	10.5-13.5 g/dL	$6\text{-}17 \times 10^9/L$	$150\text{-}350 \times 10^9/L$
2-6 years	11.5-13.5 g/dL	$5\text{-}15.5 \times 10^9/L$	$150\text{-}350 \times 10^9/L$
6-12 years	11.5-15.5 g/dL	$4.5\text{-}13.5 \times 10^9/L$	$150\text{-}350 \times 10^9/L$
12-18 years			
Male	13.0-16.9 g/dL	$4.5\text{-}13.5 \times 10^9/L$	$150\text{-}350 \times 10^9/L$
Female	12.0-16.0 g/dL	$4.5\text{-}13.5 \times 10^9/L$	$150\text{-}350 \times 10^9/L$

Appendix 2. Selected Normal Values in Children (cont'd)

	IgG	IgM	IgA
Newborn	831-1231 mg/dL	6-16 mg/dL	<3 mg/dL
1-3 months	312-549 mg/dL	19-41 mg/dL	8-34 mg/dL
4-6 months	241-613 mg/dL	26-60 mg/dL	10-46 mg/dL
7-12 months	442-880 mg/dL	31-77 mg/dL	19-55 mg/dL
13-24 months	553-971 mg/dL	35-81 mg/dL	26-74 mg/dL
25-36 months	709-1075 mg/dL	42-80 mg/dL	34-108 mg/dL
3-5 years	701-1157 mg/dL	38-74 mg/dL	66-120 mg/dL
6-8 years	667-1179 mg/dL	40-80 mg/dL	79-169 mg/dL
9-11 years	889-1359 mg/dL	46-112 mg/dL	71-191 mg/dL
12-16 years	822-1070 mg/dL	39-79 mg/dL	85-211 mg/dL

Activated Partial Thromboplastin Time

Preterm	70 seconds
Full-term	45-65 seconds

Prothrombin Time

Preterm	12-21 seconds
Full-term	13-20 seconds

(Reprinted with permission from The Harriet Lane Handbook. 13th ed, St. Louis, MO: Mosby, 1993.)

Appendix 3. Typical Normal Values in Tests of Hemostasis and Coagulation (Adults)

Test	Normal Value
Activated partial thromboplastin time	25-35 seconds
Bleeding time	2-8 minutes
Coagulation factors	500-1500 U/L
Fibrin degradation products	<10 mg/L
Fibrinogen	2.0-4.0 g/L
Plasma D-dimers	<200 mg/L
Protein C	70-1400 U/L
Protein S (total)	70-1400 U/L
Prothrombin time	10-13 seconds
Thrombin time	17-25 seconds

(Reprinted with permission from Henry JB. Clinical diagnosis and management by laboratory methods. 18th ed. Philadelphia: WB Saunders, 1991.)

Appendix 4. Coagulation Factors

Factor	Name	In-vivo Half-life	In vitro, 4 C Half-life	% of Normal Needed for Hemostasis	% In Vivo Recovery	Initial Therapeutic Dose
I	Fibrinogen	3-6 days	Years	12-50	50-70	1 bag cryoprecipitate/7 kg body weight
II	Prothrombin	2-5 days	>21 days	10-25	50	10-20 units/kg body weight
V	Labile factor, Proaccelerin	4.5-36 hours	10-14 days	10-30	~80	10-20 mL plasma/kg body weight
VII	Stable factor, Proconvertin	2-5 hours	>21 days	>10	100	10-20 units/kg body weight
VIII	Antihemophilic factor	8-12 hours	7 days	30-40	60-70	15-50 units/kg body weight
IX	Plasma thromboplastin component, Christmas factor	18-24 hours	>21 days	15-40	20	30-80 units/kg body weight
X	Stuart-Prower factor	20-42 hours	>21 days	10-40	50-95	10-20 units/kg body weight
XI	Plasma thromboplastin antecedent (PTA)	40-80 hours	3-4 days	20-30	90	10-20 mL/kg body weight
XIII	Fibrin stabilizing factor	12 days	>21 days	<5	50-100	500 mL plasma every 3 weeks
AT	Antithrombin	60-90 hours	>42 days	80-120%	50-100	40-50 IU/kg body weight

Notes:
1. All dosings are provided as a general guideline for initial therapy, the exact loading dose and maintenance intervals should be individualized for each patient.
2. One unit of coagulation factor is present in each mL of fresh frozen plasma.
3. DDAVP is the treatment of choise for patients with hemophilia A who are responders.
4. Composite data from the following references:
   a. Beutler E, Lichtman MA, Coller BS, Kipps TL, eds. Williams' hematology, 5th ed. New York: McGraw-Hill, 1995:1413-58, 1657.
   b. Mollison PL, Engelfreit CP, Contreras M. Blood transfusion in clinical medicine. 9th ed. Oxford: Blackwell Scientific Publications, 1993:657-69.
   c. Huestis DW, Bove JR, Case J, eds. Practical blood transfusion. 4th ed. Boston, MA: Little Brown and Co, 1988:319.
   d. Counts RB, Haisch C, Simon TL, et al. Hemostasis in massively transfused trauma patients. Ann Surg 1979;190:91-9.
   e. Package inserts.

Appendix 5. Approximate Normal Values for Red Cell, Plasma, and Blood Volumes

	Infant[1]		Adult[2]	
	Premature	Term Birth at 72 hours	Male	Female
Red Cell Volume mL/kg	50	40	26	24
Plasma Volume mL/kg	58	47	40	36
Blood Volume mL/kg	108	87	66	60

The adult values should be modified to correct for:
1. Below age 18: Increase values by 10%.
2. Weight loss:
   a. Marked loss within 6 months—calculations made at original weight.
   b. Gradual loss over a longer time—calculations made at present weight and raised 10-15%.
3. Obese and short: values are reduced by 10%.
4. Elderly: values are reduced by 10%.
5. Pregnancy[3]:

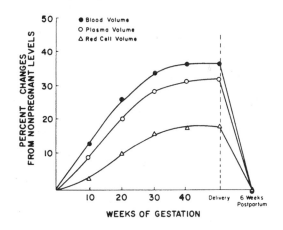

WEEKS OF GESTATION

Estimation of Body Surface Area[4]:

$$BSA(m^2) = \frac{\sqrt{Ht(cm) \times Wt(kg)}}{3600} \text{ or } \frac{\sqrt{Ht(in) \times Wt(lb)}}{3131}$$

Blood Volume (BV)[5]:
   BV = 2740 mL/m^2—males
   BV = 2370 mL/m^2—females
Hematocrit[6]:
   Venous hematocrit = H_v (blood obtained by vein or finger puncture)
   Whole-body hematocrit = H_B
   $H_B = (Hv) \times (0.91)$

References

1. Miller D. Normal values and examination of the blood: perinatal period, infancy, childhood and adolescence. In: Miller DR, Baehner RL, McMillan CW, Miller LP, eds. Blood diseases of infancy and childhood. St. Louis: C.V. Mosby, 1984:21,22.
2. Albert SN. Blood volume. Springfield: Charles C. Thomas, 1963:26.
3. Peck TM, Arias F. Hematologic changes associated with pregnancy. Clin Obstet Gynecol 1979;22:788.
4. Mosteller RD. Simplfied calculation of body-surface area. N Engl J Med 1987;317:1098.
5. Shoemaker WC. Fluids and electrolytes in the acutely ill adult. In: Shoemaker WC, Ayres S, Grenvik A, et al, eds. Textbook of critical care. 2nd ed. Philadelphia: WB Saunders Co., 1989:1130.
6. Mollison PL, Englefreit CP, Contreras M. Blood transfusion in clinical medicine. 9th edition. Oxford: Blackwell Scientific Publications, 1993.

Appendix 6. Directory of Organizations

American Association of Blood Banks (AABB)
8101 Glenbrook Road
Bethesda, MD 20814-2749
(301) 907-6977
FAX: (301) 907-6895
www.aabb.org

American Association of Tissue Banks (AATB)
1350 Beverly Road, Suite 220A
McLean, VA 22101
(703) 827-9582
FAX: (703) 356-2198
www.aatb.org

American Blood Resources Association (ABRA)
P.O. Box 669
Annapolis, MD 21404-0669
(410) 263-8296
FAX: (410) 263-2298

American Medical Association (AMA)
515 N. State Street
Chicago, IL 60610
(312) 464-5000 (call for specific dept.)
FAX: (312) 464-4184
www.ama-assn.org

American National Red Cross
1616 North Ft. Myer Drive
Arlington, VA 22209-3100
(703) 312-5600
FAX: (703) 312-8481
www.crossnet.org

American Society of Anesthesiologists (ASA)
520 N. Northwest Highway
Park Ridge, IL 60068-2573
(847) 825-5586
FAX: (847) 825-1692
www.asahq.org

American Society of Clinical Pathologists (ASCP)
2100 West Harrison Street
Chicago, IL 60612-3798
(312) 738-1336
FAX: (312) 738-1619
www.ascp.org

American Society for Apheresis (ASFA)
3900 East Timrod St.
Tucson, AZ 85711
(520) 327-8584
FAX: (520) 322-6778

American Society of Hematology
1200 19th Street NW, Suite 300
Washington, DC 20036-2422
(202) 857-1118
FAX: (202) 857-1164
www.hematology.org

American Society for Histocompatibility
   and Immunogenetics (ASHI)
P.O. Box 15804
Lenexa, KS 66285-5804
(913) 541-0009
FAX: (913) 541-0156
www.swmed.edu/home_pages/ASHI/ashi.htm

America's Blood Centers (ABC)
725 15th Street, NW
Suite 700, The Folger Building
Washington, DC 20005
(202) 393-5725
FAX: (202) 393-1282
www.americasblood.org

Armed Services Blood Program Office (ASBPO)
5109 Leesburg Pike
Falls Church, VA 22041-3258
(703) 681-8024
FAX: (703) 681-7541
www.tricare.osd.mil/asbpo

Centers for Disease Control and Prevention (CDC)
1600 Clifton Road, NE
Atlanta, GA 30333
(404) 639-3311
FAX: (404) 639-3296
www.cdc.gov

College of American Pathologists (CAP)
325 Waukegan Road
Northfield, IL 60093-2750
(800) 323-4040
FAX: (847) 832-8000
www.cap.org

Food and Drug Administration
Center for Biologics Evaluation and Research
   (CBER)
1401 Rockville Pike, HFB1
Bethesda, MD 20852-1448
(301) 827-1800
or phone (800) 835-4709
FAX: (301) 827-0440
www.fda.gov/cber/

Appendix 6. Directory of Organizations (cont'd)

International Society of Blood Transfusion (ISBT)
National Blood Service/Lancaster
PO Box 111
Royal Lancaster Infirmary
Ashton Road
Lancaster LA1 4GT
tel: (1524) 306272
FAX: (1524) 306273

Joint Commission on Accreditation of Healthcare
    Organizations (JCAHO)
1 Renaissance Boulevard
Oakbrook Terrace, IL 60181
(630) 792-5000
FAX: (630) 792-5005
www.jcaho.org

National Bone Marrow Donor Registry (NBMDR)
3433 Broadway Street NE, Suite 500
Minneapolis, MN 55413
(800) 627-7692
FAX: (612) 627-5899
www.marrow.org

National Committee for Clinical Laboratory
    Standards (NCCLS)
940 West Valley Rd
Suite 1400
Wayne, PA 19087
(610) 688-0100
FAX: (610) 688-0700
www.nccls.org

National Hemophilia Foundation (NHF)
116 West 32nd Street, 11th Floor
New York, NY 10001
(212) 328-3700
FAX: (212) 328-3777
www.infonhf.org

United Network for Organ Sharing (UNOS)
1100 Boulders Parkway, Suite 500
P.O. Box 13770
Richmond, VA 23225-8770
(804) 330-8500
FAX: (804) 330-8507
www.unos.org

Appendix 7. AABB-Accredited Immunohematology Reference Laboratories

ARIZONA

Blood Systems Laboratories
6220 East Oak Street
Scottsdale, AZ 85257
Phone: (602) 675-5490
Fax: (602) 675-5491

CALIFORNIA

.American Red Cross Blood Services
Southern California Region
1130 South Vermont Avenue
Los Angeles, CA 90006
Phone: (213) 739-5600
Fax: (213) 739-5455

Blood Bank of San Bernardino and Riverside
    Counties
384 Orange Show Road
P.O. Box 5729
San Bernardino, CA 92408
Phone: (909) 386-6858
Fax: (909) 381-2036

Blood Centers of the Pacific - Irwin Center
270 Masonic Avenue
San Francisco, CA 94118-0318
Phone: (415) 749-6680
Fax: (415) 749-6688

Sacramento Medical Foundation Blood Center
1625 Stockton Blvd.
Sacramento, CA 95816-7089
Phone: (916) 456-1500 Ext. 432
Fax: (916) 457-7541

UCSF Stanford Health Care:
Stanford Hospital & Clinics
Transfusion Services, Room H-1404
300 Pasteur Drive
Stanford, CA 94305-5626
Phone: (650) 723-6444
Fax: (650) 723-9178

COLORADO

Bonfils Blood Center
717 Yosemite Circle
Denver, CO 80220
Phone: (303) 363-2245
Fax: (303) 363-2279

CONNECTICUT

American Red Cross Blood Services
Connecticut Region
209 Farmington Avenue
Farmington, CT 06032
Phone: (860) 678-2764
Fax: (860) 674-8115

DISTRICT OF COLUMBIA

Walter Reed Army Medical Center
6825 16th Street, NW
Building 2, Rm. 4E01
Blood Bank, DPALS
Washington, DC 20307-5001
Phone: (202) 782-6989
Fax: (202) 782-4985

FLORIDA

Central Florida Blood Bank (CFBB)
32 West Gore Street
Orlando, FL 32806
Phone: (407) 849-6100 Ext. 319
Fax: (407) 649-8517

Community Blood Centers of S. Florida, Inc.
1700 North State Road 7
Lauderhill, FL 33313
Phone: (954) 777-2677
Fax: (954) 485-2823

Florida Blood Services
St. Petersburg Main
445 31st Street, North
St. Petersburg, FL 33713
Phone: (813) 322-2126
Fax: (813) 322-5421

GEORGIA

American Red Cross Blood Services
Southern Region, Georgia Division
1925 Monroe Drive, NE
Atlanta, GA 30324
Phone: (404) 253-5580
Fax: (404) 876-6984

ILLINOIS

LifeSource Blood Services
1205 North Milwaukee Avenue
Glenview, IL 60025
Phone: (847) 803-7900
Fax: (847) 803-7940

Appendix 7. AABB-Accredited Immunohematology Reference Laboratories (cont'd)

Michael Reese Hospital & Medical Center
Transfusion/Lab 2-Blum
2929 S. Ellis Avenue
Chicago, IL 60616
Phone: (312) 791-5794
Fax: (312) 791-2725

INDIANA

Central Indiana Regional Blood Center, Inc.
3450 North Meridian Street
Indianapolis, IN 46208
Phone: (317) 916-5188
Fax: (317) 927-1724

LOUISIANA

The Blood Center
2017 Tulane Avenue
New Orleans, LA 70112
Phone: (504) 592-1569
Fax: (504) 592-1581

Medical Center of Louisiana - Charity Hospital
Blood Bank
1532 Tulane Avenue
New Orleans, LA 70112
Phone: (504) 568-3502
Fax: (504) 568-2635

Memorial Medical Center
Division of Transfusion Medicine
2700 Napoleon Avenue
New Orleans, LA 70115
Phone: (504) 897-5946
Fax: (504) 896-5674

MARYLAND

The Johns Hopkins Hospital
600 North Wolfe Street
Transfusion Medicine Div., Carnegie Rm. 667
Baltimore, MD 21287-6667
Phone: (410) 955-6580
Fax: (410) 955-0618

The National Institutes of Health
Clinical Center/Dept. of Transfusion Medicine
Bldg. 10, Room 1C711
10 Center Drive, MSC 1184
Bethesda, MD 20892-1184
Phone: (301) 496-8335
Fax: (301) 496-9990

MASSACHUSETTS

Brigham and Womens Hospital
Blood Transfusion Service
75 Francis Street
Boston, MA 02115
Phone: (617) 732-7290
Fax: (617) 277-9013

Massachusetts General Hospital
Blood Tansfusion Services - Gray J240
32 Fruit Street
Boston, MA 02114-2690
Phone: (617) 726-3619
Fax: (617) 726-6832

MICHIGAN

American Red Cross Blood Services
Great Lakes Region
1800 East Grand River Avenue
Lansing, MI 48912
Phone: (517) 484-2224
Fax: (517) 484-9618

American Red Cross Blood Services
Southeastern Michigan Region
P.O. Box 33351
Detroit, MI 48232-5351
Phone: (313) 494-2712 & 2713
Fax: (313) 833-2799

University of Michigan Hospitals
Univ. Hospitals/Dept. of Pathology, UH-2G-332
1500 East Medical Center Dr.
Ann Arbor, MI 48109-0054
Phone: (734) 936-6870
Fax: (734) 763-4095

MINNESOTA

Mayo Medical Center
Transfusion Medicine/Ref. Lab.
200 First Street, SW
Rochester, MN 55905
Phone: (507) 284-4208
Fax: (507) 266-4180

Memorial Blood Center of Minneapolis
2304 Park Avenue, South
Minneapolis, MN 55404
Phone: (612) 871-3300 Ext. 2233
Fax: (612) 871-1359

(continued)

Appendix 7. AABB-Accredited Immunohematology Reference Laboratories (cont'd)

MISSOURI

American Red Cross Blood Services
Missouri-Illinois Region
Blood Bank Services
4050 Lindell Boulevard
St. Louis, MO 63108
Phone: (314) 658-2084
Fax: (314) 658-2075

Community Blood Center of Greater Kansas City
4040 Main Street
Kansas City, MO 64111
Phone: (816) 968-4057 & 4053
Fax: (816) 968-4430

NEW YORK

Univ. of Rochester Med. Center/
Strong Memorial Hospital
601 Elmwood Avenue
Blood Bank, Box 608
Rochester, NY 14642
Phone: (716) 275-2251
Fax: (716) 473-6886

NORTH CAROLINA

Duke University Medical Center
Transfusion Service
Duke North
Box 2928, Rm. 7500
Durham, NC 27710
Phone: (919) 681-2644
Fax: (919) 681-8969

OHIO

American Red Cross Blood Services
Central Ohio Region
995 E. Broad Street
Columbus, OH 43205
Phone: (614) 253-2740 Ext. 270
Fax: (614) 253-2487

American Red Cross Blood Services
Northern Ohio Region
3747 Euclid Avenue
Cleveland, OH 44115-2501
Phone: (216) 431-3019
Fax: (216) 431-3246

American Red Cross Blood Services
Western Lake Erie Region
2275 Collingwood Blvd.
Toledo, OH 43620
Phone: (419) 248-3330 Ext. 315, 316
Fax: (419) 321-1754

Community Blood Center
349 S. Main Street
Dayton, OH 45402-2715
Phone: (937) 461-4248 Ext. 3264
Fax: (937) 461-2738

Hoxworth Blood Center/
University of Cincinnati Medical Center
3130 Highland Avenue
P.O. Box 670055
Cincinnati, OH 45267-0055
Phone: (513) 558-1547
Fax: (513) 558-1533

OKLAHOMA

Sylvan N. Goldman Center
Oklahoma Blood Institute
1001 N. Lincoln Blvd.
Oklahoma City, OK 73104
Phone: (405) 297-5654
Fax: (405) 297-5759

OREGON

American Red Cross Blood Services
Pacific Northwest Region
3131 North Vancouver Avenue
P.O. Box 3200
Portland, OR 97208
Phone: (503) 284-0209
Fax: (503) 284-9899

PENNSYLVANIA

American Red Cross Blood Services
National Reference Laboratory
 for Blood Group Serology
700 Spring Garden Street
Philadelphia, PA 19123-3594
Phone: (215) 451-4176
Fax: (215) 451-2538

Hosp. of the Univ. of Pennsylvania (HUP)
Blood Bank - 6th Founders Bldg.
3400 Spruce Street
Philadelphia, PA 19104
Phone: (215) 662-6890
Fax: (215) 662-6891

Appendix 7. AABB-Accredited Immunohematology Reference Laboratories (cont'd)

The Institute for Transfusion Medicine
3636 Boulevard of the Allies
Pittsburgh, PA 15213
Phone: (412) 209-7470
Fax: (412) 209-7482

Miller Memorial Blood Center
1465 Valley Center Parkway
Bethlehem, PA 18017
Phone: (610) 691-5850 Ext. 240
Fax: (610) 691-5748

RHODE ISLAND

Rhode Island Blood Center
405 Promenade Street
Providence, RI 02908
Phone: (401) 453-8365, 8324 & 8363
Fax: (401) 453-8557

TENNESSEE

Baptist Memorial Hospital
Blood Bank
899 Madison Avenue
Memphis, TN 38146
Phone: (901) 227-5043
Fax: (901) 227-5042

TEXAS

Gamma Biologicals, Inc.
3700 Mangum Road
Houston, TX 77092
Phone: (713) 681-8481 Ext. 3062
Fax: (713) 956-3333

Gulf Coast Regional Blood Center
1400 La Concha Lane
Houston, TX 77054-1802
Phone: (713) 791-6286
Fax: (713) 791-6242

University of Texas Medical Branch
Blood Bank
301 University Boulevard
Galveston, TX 77555-0717
Phone: (409) 772-8329
Fax: (409) 772-3193

UTAH

Associated Regional and
University Pathologists, Inc. (ARUP)
500 Chipeta Way
Salt Lake City, UT 84108-9975
Phone: (801) 583-2787 Ext. 22
Fax: (801) 583-2712

VIRGINIA

American Red Cross Blood Services
Mid-Atlantic Region
611 W. Brambleton Avenue
Norfolk, VA 23510
Phone: (757) 446-7713
Fax: (757) 640-1101

WISCONSIN

The Blood Center of SE Wisconsin, Inc.
638 North 18th Street
Milwaukee, WI 53233-2121
Phone: (414) 937-6205
Fax: (414) 937-6461

Appendix 8. AABB-Accredited Parentage Testing Laboratories

ALABAMA

Immunogenetics/DNA Diagnostic Laboratory
University of Alabama Health Sciences Center
223 Professional Arts Building
1025 18th Street, South
Birmingham, AL 35294-4400
(205)-934-7107

ARIZONA

Blood Systems, Inc.
2424 W. Erie Dr.
Tempe, AZ 85282
(602)-675-7000

CALIFORNIA

Genescreen (FDL)
Parentage Testing
7237 East Southgate Dr. Suite E
Sacramento, CA 95823
(916)-421-4225

Genetic Profiles
6122 Nancy Ridge Dr.
San Diego, CA 92121
(619)-623-0840

Children's Hospital and Health Center
Genetic Services
3020 Children's Way
San Diego, CA 92123
(619)-495-4911

Long Beach Genetics
2384 E. Pacifica Place
Rancho Dominguez, CA 90220
(310)-632-8900

COLORADO

Immunological Associates of Denver
Parentage Testing Lab.
717 Yosemite Circle, 2nd floor
Denver, CO 80220
(303)-365-9000

Analytical Genetic Testing Center, Inc.
7808 Cherry Creek South Dr., #201
Denver, CO 80231
(303)-750-2023

CONNECTICUT

Lifecodes Corporation
550 West Ave.
Stamford, CT 06902

(203)-328-9504

HAWAII

St. Francis Medical Center
Parentage Testing
2230 Liliha Street
Honolulu, HI 96817
(808)-547-6536

LOUISIANA

ReliaGene Technologies, Inc.
5525 Mounes St., Suite 101
New Orleans, LA 70123
(800)-256-4106

MARYLAND

Cellmark Diagnostics
National Legal Laboratories, Inc.
Germantown, MD 20876
(301)-428-4980

Baltimore Rh Typing Laboratory Inc.
400 West Franklin Street
Baltimore, MD 21201
(410)-225-9595

MASSACHUSETTS

CBR Laboratories, Inc.
Parentage Testing
800 Huntington Ave.
Boston, MA 02115-6399
(617)-731-6470

Univ. of Massachusetts Medical Center
Tissue Typing Laboratory
55 Lake Ave., North
Worcester, MA 01655
(508)-856-2428

MICHIGAN

Parentage Testing
2248 E. Mount Hope Suite 103
Okemos, MI 48864
(517)-349-3890

MINNESOTA

Memorial Blood Centers of Minnesota
Paternity Laboratory
2304 Park Ave. South
Minneapolis, MN 55404
(612)-871-3300

Appendix 8. AABB-Accredited Parentage Testing Laboratories (cont'd)

MISSISSIPPI

Medical Genetics Consultants
Legal Genetics
910 Washington Ave.
Ocean Springs, MS 39564
(601)-872-3680

Scales Biological Laboratory, Inc.
220 Woodgate Drive, S.
Brandon, MS 39042
(601)-825-3211

MISSOURI

Cross Clinical Laboratories
527 W. 39th St.
Kansas City, MO 64111-2907
(816)-960-1930

Paternity Testing Corporation
3501 Berrywood Dr.
Columbia, MO 65201
(573)-442-9948

NEVADA

University of Nevada School of Medicine
Department of Microbiology
Howard Medical Sciences Building
Reno, NV 89557-0046
(702)-784-4494

NEW JERSEY

Clinical Testing and Research, Inc.
20 Wilsey Square
Ridgewood, NJ 07450
(201)-652-2088

NEW YORK

SUNY Health Science Center at Syracuse
Parentage Testing Laboratory
750 E. Adams Street
Syracuse, NY 13210
(315)-464-4775

NORTH CAROLINA

Laboratory Corporation of America Holdings
1447 York Court/P.O. BOX 2230
Burlington, NC 27215
(800)-334-5161 03538

OHIO

GeneScreen
5698 Springboro Pike
Dayton, OH 45449
(937)-294-0973

DNA Diagnostics Center
205-C Corporate Ct.
Fairfield, OH 45014
(800)-362-2368

Medical College of Ohio Dept. of Pathology
DNA Profiling Laboratory
3355 Glendale Ave.
Toledo, OH 43614
(419)-381-5636

Genetica DNA Laboratories, Inc.
8740 Montgomery Road
Cincinnati, OH 45236
(800)-433-6848

OKLAHOMA

Chapman Institute of Medical Genetics
Children's Medical Center
5300 E. Skelly Drive
Tulsa, OK 74135
(918)-628-6363

OREGON

ARC Blood Services—Pacific-NW Region
3131 North Vancouver Ave.
PO Box 3200
Portland, OR 97208
(503)-280-1449

RHODE ISLAND

Rhode Island Blood Center
Parentage Testing Laboratory
405 Promenade Street
Providence, RI 02908
(401)-453-8363

SOUTH DAKOTA

Identity Genetics, Inc.
2308 6th St., East
P.O. Box 877
Brookings, SD 57006
(605)-697-5300

(continued)

Appendix 8. AABB-Accredited Parentage Testing Laboratories (cont'd)

TENNESSEE

Micro Diagnostics, Inc.
1400 Donaldson Pike, Suite A15
Nashville, TN 37217
(615)-360-5000

Molecular Pathology Laboratory
907 E. Lamar Alexander Parkway
Maryville, TN 37804
(423)-981-2332

Gene Proof Technologies
301 Summit View Dr., Suite 100
Brentwood, TN 37027
(615)-889-0444

TEXAS

Univ. of North Texas Health Services Center
DNA Identity Laboratory
3500 Camp Bowie Blvd.
Fort Worth, TX 76107
(817)-735-5014

Genescreen
2600 Stemmons FWY
Suite 133
Dallas, TX 75207
(800)-752-2774

South Texas Blood and Tissue Center
6211 IH Center
San Antonio, TX 78201
(210)-731-5558

Identigene
7400 Fannin, Suite 1212
Houston, TX 77054
(800)-362-8973

The Methodist Hospital Histocompatibility
Clinical Immunology Laboratory
6565 Fannin MS F501
Houston, TX 77030
(713)-790-3127

UTAH

DNA Diagnostic Lab, University of Utah
Eccles Genetics Institute
10 North 2030 East, Rm 7400
Salt Lake City, UT 84112
(801)-581-8334

VIRGINIA

Fairfax Identity Laboratories
Genetics and IVF Institute
3025 Hamaker Court, Suite 203
Fairfax, VA 22031
(703)-698-3919

WASHINGTON

Genelex Corporation
2203 Airport Way South
Suite 350
Seattle, WA 98134
(206)-382-9591

WISCONSIN

ARC Blood Services—Badger Region
4860 Sheboygan Ave.
PO BOX 5905
Madison, WI 53705-0905
(608)-233-9300

The Blood Center of SE Wisconsin, Inc
Parentage Testing Lab.
PO Box 2178
Milwaukee, WI 53201-2178
(414)-937-6198

INDEX

Page numbers in italics represent tables or figures

C